California
Law Manual
for the
Administration of Justice

*

West's
Criminal Justice Series

WEST PUBLISHING COMPANY
St. Paul, Minnesota 55102
March, 1979

CONSTITUTIONAL LAW

Cases and Comments on Constitutional Law 2nd Edition by James L. Maddex, Professor of Criminal Justice, Georgia State University, 486 pages, 1979.

CORRECTIONS

Corrections—Organization and Administration by Henry Burns, Jr., Professor of Criminal Justice, University of Missouri–St. Louis, 578 pages, 1975.

Legal Rights of the Convicted by Hazel B. Kerper, Late Professor of Sociology and Criminal Law, Sam Houston State University and Janeen Kerper, Attorney, San Diego, Calif., 677 pages, 1974.

Selected Readings on Corrections in the Community 2nd Edition by George G. Killinger, Member, Board of Pardons and Paroles, Texas and Paul F. Cromwell, Jr. Director of Juvenile Services, Tarrant County, Texas, 357 pages, 1978.

Readings on Penology—The Evolution of Corrections in America 2nd Edition by George G. Killinger, Paul F. Cromwell, Jr., and Jerry M. Wood, about 350 pages, 1979.

Selected Readings on Introduction to Corrections by George G. Killinger and Paul F. Cromwell, Jr., 417 pages, 1978.

Selected Readings on Issues in Corrections and Administration by George G. Killinger, Paul F. Cromwell, Jr. and Bonnie J. Cromwell, San Antonio College, 644 pages, 1976.

Probation and Parole in the Criminal Justice System by George G. Killinger, Hazel B. Kerper and Paul F. Cromwell, Jr., 374 pages, 1976.

Introduction to Probation and Parole 2nd Edition by Alexander B. Smith, Professor of Sociology, John Jay College of Criminal Justice and Louis Berlin, Formerly Chief of Training Branch, New York City Dept. of Probation, 270 pages, 1979.

CRIMINAL JUSTICE SYSTEM

Introduction to the Criminal Justice System 2nd Edition by Hazel B. Kerper as revised by Jerold H. Israel, 520 pages, 1979.

Introduction to Criminal Justice by Joseph J. Senna and Larry J. Siegel, both Professors of Criminal Justice, Northeastern University, 540 pages, 1978.

Study Guide to accompany Senna and Siegel's Introduction to Criminal Justice by Roy R. Roberg, Professor of Criminal Justice, University of Nebraska–Lincoln, 187 pages, 1978.

Introduction to Law Enforcement and Criminal Justice by Henry M. Wrobleski and Karen M. Hess, both Professors at Normandale Community College, Bloomington, Minnesota, 525 pages, 1979.

CRIMINAL LAW

California Law Manual for the Administration of Justice by Joel Greenfield, Sacramento City College and Rodney Blonien, Executive Director, California State Peace Officer's Association, about 700 pages, 1979.

Cases and Materials on Basic Criminal Law by George E. Dix, Professor of Law, University of Texas, and M. Michael Sharlot, Professor of Law, University of Texas, 649 pages, 1974.

West's Criminal Justice Series

CRIMINAL LAW—Continued

Readings, on Concepts of Criminal Law by Robert W. Ferguson, Administration of Justice Dept. Director, Saddleback College, 560 pages, 1975.

Principles, Cases and Readings on Criminal Law by Thomas J. Gardner, Professor of Criminal Justice, Milwaukee Area Technical College and Victor Manian, Milwaukee County Judge, 782 pages, 1975.

Principles of Criminal Law by Wayne R. LaFave, Professor of Law, University of Illinois, about 600 pages, 1978.

CRIMINAL PROCEDURE

Teaching Materials on Criminal Procedure by Jerry L. Dowling, Professor of Criminal Justice, Sam Houston State University, 544 pages, 1976.

Criminal Procedure for the Law Enforcement Officer 2nd Edition by John N. Ferdico, Assistant Attorney General, State of Maine, 409 pages, 1979.

Cases, Materials and Text on the Elements of Criminal Due Process by Phillip E. Johnson, Professor of Law, University of California, Berkeley, 324 pages, 1975.

Cases, Comments and Questions on Basic Criminal Procedure 4th Edition by Yale Kamisar, Professor of Law, University of Michigan, Wayne R. LaFave, Professor of Law, University of Illinois and Jerold H. Israel, Professor of Law, University of Michigan, 790 pages, 1974. Supplement Annually.

EVIDENCE

Criminal Evidence by Thomas J. Gardner, Professor of Criminal Justice, Milwaukee Area Technical College, 694 pages, 1978.

Criminal Evidence by Edward J. Imwinkelried, Professor of Law, University of San Diego; Paul C. Giannelli, Associate Professor, Case Western Reserve University; Francis A. Gilligan, Adjunct Professor, Jacksonville State University; Fredric I. Lederer, Associate Professor, Judge Advocate General's School, U.S. Army, 425 pages, 1979.

Law of Evidence for Police 2nd Edition by Irving J. Klein, Professor of Law and Police Science, John Jay College of Criminal Justice, 632 pages, 1978.

Criminal Investigation and Presentation of Evidence by Arnold Markle, The State's Attorney, New Haven County, Connecticut, 344 pages, 1976.

INTRODUCTION TO LAW ENFORCEMENT

The American Police—Text and Readings by Harry W. More, Jr., Professor of Administration of Justice, California State University of San Jose, 278 pages, 1976.

Police Tactics in Hazardous Situations by the San Diego, California Police Department, 228 pages, 1976.

Law Enforcement Handbook for Police by Louis B. Schwartz, Professor of Law, University of Pennsylvania and Stephen R. Goldstein, Professor of Law, University of Pennsylvania, 333 pages, 1970

Police Operations—Tactical Approaches to Crimes in Progress by Inspector Andrew Sutor, Philadelphia, Pennsylvania Police Department, 329 pages, 1976.

Introduction to Law Enforcement and Criminal Justice by Henry Wrobleski and Karen M. Hess, both Professors at Normandale Community College, Bloomington, Minnesota, 525 pages, 1979.

JUVENILE JUSTICE

Text and Selected Readings on Introduction to Juvenile Delinquency by Paul F. Cromwell, Jr., George G. Killinger, Rosemary C. Sarri, Professor, School of Social Work, The University of Michigan and H. N. Solomon, Professor of Criminal Justice, Nova University, 502 pages, 1978.

Juvenile Justice Philosophy: Readings, Cases and Comments 2nd Edition by Frederic L. Faust, Professor of Criminology, Florida State University and Paul J. Brantingham, Department of Criminology, Simon Fraser University, 467 pages, 1979.

Introduction to the Juvenile Justice System by Thomas A. Johnson, Professor of Criminal Justice, Washington State University, 492 pages, 1975.

West's Criminal Justice Series

JUVENILE JUSTICE—Continued

Cases and Comments on Juvenile Law by Joseph J. Senna, Professor of Criminal Justice, Northeastern, University and Larry J. Siegel, Professor of Criminal Justice, Northeastern University, 543 pages, 1976.

MANAGEMENT AND SUPERVISION

Selected Readings on Managing the Police Organization by Larry K. Gaines and Truett A. Ricks, both Professors of Criminal Justice, Eastern Kentucky University, 527 pages, 1978.

Criminal Justice Management: Text and Readings by Harry W. More, Jr., 377 pages, 1977.

Effective Police Administration: A Behavioral Approach 2nd Edition by Harry W. More, Jr., Professor, San Jose State University, about 350 pages, 1979.

Police Management and Organizational Behavior: A Contingency Approach by Roy R. Roberg, Professor of Criminal Justice, University of Nebraska at Omaha, 350 pages, 1979.

Police Administration and Management by Sam S. Souryal, Professor of Criminal Justice, Sam Houston State University, 462 pages, 1977.

Law Enforcement Supervision—A Case Study Approach by Robert C. Wadman, Rio Hondo Community College, Monroe J. Paxman, Brigham Young University and Marion T. Bentley, Utah State University, 224 pages, 1975.

POLICE—COMMUNITY RELATIONS

Readings on Police—Community Relations 2nd Edition by Paul F. Cromwell, Jr., and George Keefer, Professor of Criminal Justice, Southwest Texas State University, 506 pages, 1978.

PSYCHOLOGY

Interpersonal Psychology for Law Enforcement and Corrections by L. Craig Parker, Jr., Criminal Justice Dept. Director, University of New Haven and Robert D. Meier, Professor of Criminal Justice, University of New Haven, 290 pages, 1975.

VICE CONTROL

The Nature of Vice Control in the Administration of Justice by Robert W. Ferguson, 509 pages, 1974.

Cases, Text and Materials on Drug Abuse Law by Gerald F. Uelman, Professor of Law, Loyola University, Los Angeles and Victor G. Haddox, Professor of Criminology, California State University at Long Beach and Clinical Professor of Psychiatry, Law and Behavioral Sciences, University of Southern California School of Medicine, 564 pages, 1974.

*

California
Law Manual
for the
Administration of Justice

Rodney J. Blonien
Assistant Attorney General
Office of the Attorney General
Sacramento, California

Joel I. Greenfield
Associate Dean of Occupational Education
Sacramento City College
Sacramento, California

West Publishing Company
St. Paul • New York • Los Angeles • San Francisco

Acknowledgment

The editors wish to acknowledge the patient assistance of Dicy Salmon in the preparation of this manuscript.

COPYRIGHT © 1979 By WEST PUBLISHING CO.
50 West Kellogg Boulevard
P.O. Box 3526
St. Paul, Minnesota 55165

All rights reserved
Printed in the United States of America

Library of Congress Cataloging in Publication Data

Blonien, Rodney.
    California law manual for the administration of justice.

    (Criminal justice series)
    1. Criminal justice, Administration of—California. I. Greenfield, Joel I., joint author. II. California. Laws, statutes, etc. III. Title. IV. Series.
KFC1102.B56   345'.794'052   78-31963

ISBN 0-8299-0252-X

To my wife Noreen and
my children Ryan, Jessica, and Molly.

Rod Blonien

To Aaron, Bret and the administration of
justice professionals in the State of California.

Joel Greenfield

Rodney Blonien is currently an assistant Attorney General for the State of California. He has served as Executive Director of the California Peace Officers Association, Assistant Legal Affairs Secretary to former Governor Reagan, and as a Deputy Attorney General for California. He is a graduate of the University of San Francisco and holds a J.D. from the University of Santa Clara.

Joel Greenfield is currently the Associate Dean of Occupational Education at Sacramento City College. His criminal justice background includes service as a full time administration of justice instructor, Director of the Sacramento Center—Northern California Criminal Justice Training and Education System, Police Officer/Lieutenant—Sacramento Police Department. Mr. Greenfield is a member of the Academy of Criminal Justice Sciences and the past President of the California Association of Administration of Justice Educators. He is a graduate of California State University—Sacramento and holds an M.P.A. degree from the University of Southern California.

Summary of Contents

	Page
Foreword	xvii
Introduction	xix
Information about the Complete California Codes and this Volume of Selected Statutes	xix
Additional Features of the Volume	xx
Explanation	xxii
Selected Sections of West's Annotated California Codes	xxiii
Penal Code	1
Vehicle Code	270
Health and Safety Code	378
Business and Professions Code	417
Welfare and Institutions Code	424
Evidence Code	471
Annotated Table of Cases	531
Major Case Law Opinions	534
How to Do Legal Research	667
Glossary	674
Index	687

*

Table of Contents

	Page
Foreword	xvii
Introduction	xix
Selected Sections of West's Annotated California Codes	xxiii

Penal Code

		Page
Part 1.	Of Crimes and Punishments	5
	Crimes By and Against Public Officials	7
	Crimes Against Public Justice	9
	Crimes Against the Person	17
	Crimes Against Religion and Morals	46
	Crimes Against Public Health and Safety	56
	Crimes Against the Public Peace	56
	Terrorist Threats	58
	Crimes Against Property	59
	Malicious Mischief	79
	Miscellaneous Crimes	83
	General Provisions	93
Part 2.	Of Criminal Procedure	96
	Prevention of Public Offenses	97
	Mode of Prosecution	98
	Arrest and Peace Officer Status	102
	Grand Jury	140
	Pleading's	144
	Sentencing	162
	Compelling Attendance of Witnesses	189
	Criminal Insanity	191
	Miscellaneous Criminal Procedure	199
	Search Warrants	210
	Fugitives From Justice	222
Part 3.	Of Imprisonment and the Death Penalty	229
	Prisoners Maintenance and Rights	229
	County Jails	232
	Offenses by Prisoners	237
	Unauthorized Communications with Prisoners	238
	Powers and Duties of Governor	240
Part 4.	Prevention of Crimes and Apprehension of Criminals	246
	General Provisions	270

TABLE OF CONTENTS

Vehicle Code

Division		Page
1.	Words and Phrases Defined	271
2.	Administration	273
3.	Registration of Vehicles and Certificates of Title	274
3.5	Registration and Transfer of Vessels	277
3.6	Vehicle Sales	277
4.	Special Antitheft Laws	277
5.	Occupational Licensing and Business Regulations	278
6.	Drivers' Licenses	278
6.5	Motor Vehicle Transactions with Minors	292
7.	Financial Responsibility Laws	292
9.	Civil Liability	293
10.	Accidents and Accident Reports	293
11.	Rules of the Road	296
12.	Equipment of Vehicles	336
13.	Towing and Loading Equipment	353
14.	Transportation of Explosives	354
14.5	Transportation of Radioactive Materials	354
14.7	Flammable Liquids	354
14.8	Safety Regulations	354
14.9	Motor Vehicle Damage Control	354
15.	Size, Weight, and Load	355
16.	Implements of Husbandry	356
16.5	Off-Highway Vehicles	356
16.7	Registration and Licensing of Bicycles	358
17.	Offenses and Prosecution	358
18.	Penalties and Disposition of Fees, Fines, and Forfeitures	376

Health and Safety Code

Division		
10.	Uniform Controlled Substances Act	378
11.	Explosives	414

Business and Professions Code

Division		
1.	Department of Consumer Affairs	418
1.5	Denial, Suspension and Revocation of Licenses	419
2.	Healing Arts	419
3.	Professions and Vocations Generally	420
4.	Real Estate	420
5.	Weights and Measures	420
6.	Business Rights	421

TABLE OF CONTENTS

Division		Page
7.	General Business Regulations	421
8.	Special Business Regulations	421
9.	Alcoholic Beverages	421
30.	Repeals	423

Welfare and Institutions Code

Division		
	General Provisions	424
1.	Administration of Welfare and Institutions	424
2.	Children	424
2.5	Youths	458
3.	Narcotic Addicts	461
4.	State Department of Health	462
5.	Community Mental Health Services	462
6.	Admissions and Judicial Commitments	465
7.	Mental Institutions	467
8.	Miscellaneous	467
8.5	Aging	469
9.	Public Social Services	469
10.	State Department of Rehabilitation	470
11.	Office of Alcoholism	470
20.	Repeals	470

Evidence Code

Division		
1.	Preliminary Provisions and Construction	472
2.	Words and Phrases Defined	472
3.	General Provisions	474
4.	Judicial Notice	478
5.	Burden of Proof; Burden of Producing Evidence; Presumptions and Inferences	483
6.	Witnesses	489
7.	Opinion Testimony and Scientific Evidence	495
8.	Privileges	496
9.	Evidence Affected or Excluded By Extrinsic Policies	513
10.	Hearsay Evidence	514
11.	Writings	526

Annotated Table of Cases	531
Major Case Law Opinions	534
How to Do Legal Research	667
Glossary	674
Index	687

Foreword

It has been said that when men are pure, laws are useless; when men are corrupt, laws are broken. Not surprisingly then, the administration of justice, conceived in the interest of controlling corruption and preserving a sense of order, has been the cornerstone of modern day civilizations. Criminal law emerged early to safeguard the personal and property rights of individuals. Other statutes have evolved in response to the manifold self governing needs of an increasingly complex society.

For law enforcement, criminal law as reflected in the various state codes and interpreted by our judicial system is undeniably the basis for all law enforcement in a free society. It is imperative, therefore, that professional law enforcement be well versed in those laws and procedures which are often complex, ambiguous, and difficult; if not frustrating to translate into action on the street. As past president of the California Peace Officers Association, I have observed that law enforcement agencies throughout the state employ diverse police practices. These variations, coupled with an absence of clarity in some criminal law and rapidly changing court interpretations, dictate that an authoritative compendium of California law be available and consulted on a regular basis.

This text, capable of being updated periodically, fulfills a critical need for a comprehensive, easily referenced handbook which contains the most current and frequently impacting legal statutes of California. Having been a Deputy Sheriff and currently a Police Chief, I am acutely aware of the legal issues which confront police personnel in the course of performing their daily enforcement duties. This helpful volume, incorporating such benefits as a glossary and introduction to legal research will predictably become indispensable to law enforcement personnel, attorneys, students, and other criminal justice agents. Armed with the confidence and competence that familiarity with the law breeds, we can look forward to the attainment of peace, security, justice and progress.

Jay R. Stroh
Police Chief
City of Inglewood

*

Introduction

This text is intended to serve as an instructional supplement for administration of justice students and criminal justice professionals in agency training programs, academies, regional training centers, community colleges, state colleges and universities in the State of California. The text may also serve as an operational aid and reference to libraries, offices and field units.

The content of this volume includes selected sections of the major statutory codes impacting the administration of criminal justice. In addition to the content of the statute, selected sections contain annotations in the form of case citations, statute cross references, case notes and, where appropriate, entire cases. Entire cases included are considered to be highly illustrative of a particular legal issue or significant as "landmark" cases affecting a major change in interpretation and/or application of the law. Selections from the Business and Professions, Evidence, Health and Safety, Penal, Vehicle and Welfare and Institutions Codes are included in the text.

Administration of justice students and criminal justice professionals will find this volume to be a useful companion in providing the more important and most frequently encountered aspects of law relating to the general administration of justice, principles and procedures of the justice system, criminal law, legal aspects of evidence, fundamentals of investigation, traffic control, juvenile justice and narcotics/drug control. This volume will supplement all classes in the administration of justice education curriculum and may be used during several semesters.

As you will discover, much of the statutory law deals with definitions and rules which are refined and interpreted by court decisions. As you participate in administration of justice study, whether as a student or professional practitioner, you will find that concepts presented in class or field experiences can be better understood by reference to the specific definitions, statutes and interpretative cases applicable to California law.

Information About the Complete California Codes and this Volume of Selected Statutes

The present system of Codes in California was anticipated by the enactment in 1872 of the Civil Code, the Code of Civil Procedure, the Penal Code, and the Political Code. The first three of these Codes are still in existence, but the subject matter of the Political Code is now largely covered by the Government Code.

INTRODUCTION

The intensive codification program which produced the current set of Codes was launched in 1929 with the enactment of Stats.1929, c. 750, and was completed in 1953 with the enactment of the Unemployment Insurance Code. The set then consisted of twenty-five Codes including the three enacted in 1872. The total was increased to twenty-seven with the adoption of the Commercial Code in 1963, and of the Evidence Code in 1965.

Stats.1929, c. 750, which launched the codification program, created the California Code Commission, and charged it with the duty of revising all laws of the state. The work of revision was to comprehend the preparation of a statutory record showing the status and disposition of acts theretofore adopted, the codification, consolidation, compilation or revision of all statutes in force; and the express repeal of all statutes theretofore repealed by implication, held unconstitutional, or rendered obsolete by the revision. The final report of the Code Commission was submitted September 1, 1953.

An essential preliminary part of the Code Commission's work was the preparation of a statutory record showing origin, amendments, and repeals of state laws enacted since 1850. The first volume of Statutory Record was published in 1933. Thereafter a supplementary volume was published for the period 1933–1948, another for the period 1949–1958, and another for the period 1959–1968. The Record is supplemented and brought to date in each volume of the session laws.

The California Law Revision Commission was created in 1953 (Government Code § 10300) and charged with the duty of recommending changes deemed necessary to eliminate defects and anachronisms, to modify or eliminate antiquated and inequitable rules of law, and to bring the law into harmony with modern conditions (Government Code § 10330). The recommendations of the Commission have resulted in the enactment of numerous revisions of, as well as additions to, the law.

Additional Features of the Volume

Notes. In addition to featuring the text of selected statutes, this volume includes a variety of special notations to assist the reader in understanding the history, impact, relationship or significance of certain legal provisions. The following types of notes may be found supplementing featured sections:

Notes—These are comments by the text authors to highlight, explain or summarize particular points of interest related to the practical application of selected statutes. Notes also refer readers to related cases contained in the table of cases section of this volume. See section 16000 B & P for an example of a note.

INTRODUCTION

Notes of Decisions—These are brief descriptive summaries of facts, issues and decisions by courts of record. The note illustrates the interpretation and application of the selected statute to a factual situation. Subject subheadings are used to highlight specific topics when several notes of decisions are featured. The case citation is included to allow the reader to research the full case if desired. See section 844 PC for an example of notes of decisions.

Comment—Assembly or Senate Committee on Judiciary—These notes give insight to the legislative history and reasoning leading to the enactment of a particular statute. See section 451 EvC for an example of comments.

Comment—Law Revision Commission—These notes explain the reasoning behind legislative changes which have been made from recommendations developed by the State Law Revision Commission. See section 453 EvC for an example.

Study Cases. This volume contains a major section of edited cases covering significant principles of law. Particular attention is given to California cases which have resulted in administration of justice procedures unique to this state. The table of cases provides a review of the selected cases and a hint of the court decision.

Legal Research. Recognizing that searching for legal information in a law library may be a confusing, intimidating and frustrating experience, the volume contains a brief section on legal research. A sample research problem is included to help the reader "walk through" the process of finding the law.

Glossary. A glossary is included to provide definitions of special legal terms or phrases.

A complete listing of the codes includes:

BUSINESS AND PROFESSIONS	INSURANCE
CIVIL	LABOR
CIVIL PROCEDURE	MILITARY AND VETERANS
COMMERCIAL	PENAL
CORPORATIONS	PROBATE
EDUCATION	PUBLIC RESOURCES
ELECTIONS	PUBLIC UTILITIES
EVIDENCE	REVENUE AND TAXATION
FINANCIAL	STREETS AND HIGHWAYS
FISH AND GAME	UNEMPLOYMENT INSURANCE
FOOD AND AGRICULTURAL	VEHICLE
GOVERNMENT	WATER
HARBORS AND NAVIGATION	WELFARE AND INSTITUTIONS
HEALTH AND SAFETY	

INTRODUCTION

Explanation

The complete California Codes are organized into major subject divisions which are further divided into chapters, articles and sections. The California law making it unlawful to drive a motor vehicle unless licensed is Vehicle Code, Division 6—Drivers' Licenses; Chapter 1—Issuance of Licenses, Expiration and Renewal; Article 1—Persons required to be licensed, exemptions and age limits; Section 12500—Unlawful to drive unless licensed. This volume of selected law most frequently utilized or encountered by criminal justice students and practitioners has eliminated chapter and article headings to conserve space and to minimize confusion where sections were omitted. All division headings have been included, even when no sections from that division were selected for inclusion.

Selected Sections of West's Annotated California Codes

Codes Included

Penal Code	1
Vehicle Code	270
Health and Safety Code	378
Business and Professions Code	417
Welfare and Institutions Code	424
Evidence Code	471

†

PENAL CODE

The Penal Code was one of the four original codes first enacted in 1872.

The Penal Code provides for the essential elements of the tri-partite system we have come to call the Criminal Justice System.

Law Enforcement

The Penal Code authorizes and empowers peace officers to make arrests, conduct lawful searches and to enforce the laws enacted by the legislature. The vast majority of criminal conduct is defined and contained in this Code. The definitions of many crimes have not changed since this code was first enacted in 1872.

The Court System

The Penal Code sets forth the framework for the prosecution of criminal cases from the filing of the complaint to sentencing following a conviction. The function of the District Attorneys, criminal procedure, and the grand jury are all provided for in this Code.

Corrections

The enforcement of the penal sanction, or the sentence is also part of this Code. Accordingly, it makes provision for a state department of corrections, county jails, probation, and parole. This code also details the rights of inmates of state prisons, and the procedures which the Community Release Board and the Department of Corrections must follow in their dealings with prisoners.

The primary focus of this text is law enforcement and the court system.

The Penal Code underwent a significant and substantial change on July 1, 1977, when the Determinate Sentencing Law became effective and the prior Indeterminate Law was repealed. The chief impact of this change places the responsibility for determining the length of sentences with the court, rather than the Adult Authority. The Community Release Board (the successor to the Adult Authority) however, still determines lengths of sentences for those convicted of murder in the first degree, kidnapping for purposes of ransom, and a few other selected crimes which are punishable by life in prison.

Part		Section
	TITLE OF ACT	1
	PRELIMINARY PROVISIONS	2
1.	OF CRIMES AND PUNISHMENTS	26
2.	OF CRIMINAL PROCEDURE	681
3.	OF IMPRISONMENT AND THE DEATH PENALTY	1999
4.	PREVENTION OF CRIMES AND APPREHENSION OF CRIMINALS	11000

PRELIMINARY PROVISIONS

§ 7. Words and phrases

Words used in this code in the present tense include the future as well as the present; words used in the masculine gender include the feminine and neuter; the singular number includes the plural, and the plural the singular; the word "person" includes a corporation as well as a natural person; the word "county" includes "city and county"; writing includes printing and typewriting; oath includes affirmation or declaration; and every mode of oral statement, under oath or affirmation, is embraced by the term "testify," and every written one in the term "depose"; signature or subscription includes mark, when the person cannot write, his name being written near it, by a person who writes his own name as a witness; provided, that when a signature is made by mark it must, in order that the same may be acknowledged or serve as the signature to any sworn statement, be witnessed by two persons who must subscribe their own names as witnesses thereto.

The following words have in this code the signification attached to them in this section, unless otherwise apparent from the context:

1. The word "willfully," when applied to the intent with which an act is done or omitted, implies simply a purpose or willingness to commit the act, or make the omission referred to. It does not require any intent to violate law, or to injure another, or to acquire any advantage;

2. The words "neglect," "negligence," "negligent," and "negligently" import a want of such attention to the nature or probable consequences of the act or omission as a prudent man ordinarily bestows in acting in his own concerns;

3. The word "corruptly" imports a wrongful design to acquire or cause some pecuniary or other advantage to the person guilty of the act or omission referred to, or to some other person;

4. The words "malice" and "maliciously" import a wish to vex, annoy, or injure another person, or an intent to do a wrongful act, established either by proof or presumption of law;

5. The word "knowingly" imports only a knowledge that the facts exist which bring the act or omission within the provisions of this code. It does not require any knowledge of the unlawfulness of such act or omission;

6. The word "bribe" signifies anything of value or advantage, present or prospective, or any promise or undertaking to give any, asked, given, or accepted, with a corrupt intent to influence, unlawfully, the person to whom it is given, in his action, vote, or opinion, in any public or official capacity;

7. The word "vessel," when used with reference to shipping, includes ships of all kinds, steamboats, canalboats, barges, and every structure adapted to be navigated from place to place for the transportation of merchandise or persons;

8. The words "peace officer" signify any one of the officers mentioned in Chapter 4.5 (commencing with Section 830) of Title 3 of Part 2;

9. The word "magistrate" signifies any one of the officers mentioned in Section 808;

10. The word "property" includes both real and personal property;

11. The words "real property" are coextensive with lands, tenements, and hereditaments;[1]

12. The words "personal property" include money, goods, chattels, things in action, and evidences of debt;

13. The word "month" means a calendar month, unless otherwise expressed; the word "daytime" means the period between sunrise and sunset, and the word "nighttime" means the period between sunset and sunrise;

14. The word "will" includes codicil;[2]

15. The word "writ" signifies an order or precept in writing, issued in the name of the people, or of a court or judicial officer, and the word "process" a writ or summons issued in the course of judicial proceedings;

---

1. **Hereditaments.** Things capable of being inherited regardless of whether they are real or personal property.

2. **Codicil.** A supplement or an addition to a will; it may explain, modify, add to, or alter the provisions of a will.

16. Words and phrases must be construed according to the context and the approved usage of the language; but technical words and phrases, and such others as may have acquired a peculiar and appropriate meaning in law, must be construed according to such peculiar and appropriate meaning;

17. Words giving a joint authority to three or more public officers or other persons, are construed as giving such authority to a majority of them, unless it is otherwise expressed in the act giving the authority;

18. When the seal of a court or public officer is required by law to be affixed to any paper, the word "seal" includes an impression of such seal upon the paper alone, or upon any substance attached to the paper capable of receiving a visible impression. The seal of a private person may be made in like manner, or by the scroll of a pen, or by writing the word "seal" against his name;

19. The word "state," when applied to the different parts of the United States, includes the District of Columbia and the territories, and the words "United States" may include the district and territories;

20. The word "section," whenever hereinafter employed, refers to a section of this code, unless some other code or statute is expressly mentioned;

21. To "book" signifies the recordation of an arrest in official police records, and the taking by the police of fingerprints and photographs of the person arrested, or any of these acts following an arrest.
(Amended by Stats.1968, c. 1222, p. 2316, § 51.)

§ 8. Intent to defraud; sufficiency

What intent to defraud is sufficient. Whenever, by any of the provisions of this Code, an intent to defraud is required in order to constitute any offense, it is sufficient if an intent appears to defraud any person, association, or body politic or corporate, whatever.
(Enacted 1872.)

§ 17. Felony; misdemeanor; classification of offenses

(a) A felony is a crime which is punishable with death or by imprisonment in the state prison. Every other crime or public offense is a misdemeanor except those offenses that are classified as infractions.

(b) When a crime is punishable, in the discretion of the court, by imprisonment in the state prison or by fine or imprisonment in the county jail, it is a misdemeanor for all purposes under the following circumstances:

(1) After a judgment imposing a punishment other than imprisonment in the state prison.

(2) When the court, upon committing the defendant to the Youth Authority, designates the offense to be a misdemeanor.

(3) When the court grants probation to a defendant without imposition of sentence and at the time of granting probation, or on application of the defendant or probation officer thereafter, the court declares the offense to be a misdemeanor.

(4) When the prosecuting attorney files in a court having jurisdiction over misdemeanor offenses a complaint specifying that the offense is a misdemeanor, unless the defendant at the time of his arraignment or plea objects to the offense being made a misdemeanor, in which event the complaint shall be amended to charge the felony and the case shall proceed on the felony complaint.

(5) When, at or before the preliminary examination or prior to filing an order pursuant to Section 872, the magistrate determines that the offense is a misdemeanor, in which event the case shall proceed as if the defendant had been arraigned on a misdemeanor complaint.

(c) When a defendant is committed to the Youth Authority for a crime punishable in the discretion of the court, by imprisonment in the state prison or by fine or imprisonment in the county jail, the offense shall, upon the discharge of the defendant from the Youth Authority, thereafter be deemed a misdemeanor for all purposes.
(Amended by Stats.1976, c. 1070, p. ——, § 1.)

§ 18. Punishment for felony not otherwise prescribed; alternate sentence to county jail

Except in cases where a different punishment is prescribed by any law of this state, every offense declared to be a felony, or to be punishable by imprisonment in a state prison, is punishable by imprisonment in any of the state prisons for 16 months, or two or three years; provided, however, every offense which is prescribed by any law of the state to be a felony punishable by imprisonment in any of the state prisons or by a fine, but without an alternate sentence to the county jail, may be punishable by imprisonment in the county jail not exceeding one year or by a fine, or by both.
(Amended by Stats.1976, c. 1139, p. ——, § 98, operative July 1, 1977.)

§ 19. Punishment for misdemeanor; punishment not otherwise prescribed

Except in cases where a different punishment is prescribed by any law of this State, every offense declared to be a misdemeanor is punishable by imprisonment in the county jail not exceeding six months, or by fine not exceeding five hundred dollars, or by both.
(Amended by Stats.1933, c. 848, p. 2216, § 1.)

§ 19a. Punishment for misdemeanor; maximum confinement

In no case shall any person sentenced to confinement in a county or city jail, or in a county or joint county penal farm, road camp, work camp, or other county adult detention facility, or committed to the sheriff for placement in any such county adult detention facility, on conviction of a misdemeanor, or as a condition of probation upon conviction of either a felony or a misdemeanor, or upon commitment for civil contempt, or upon default in the payment of a fine upon conviction of either a felony or a misdemeanor, or for any reason except upon conviction of more than one offense when consecutive sentences have been imposed, be committed for a period in excess of one year; provided, however, that the time allowed on parole shall not be considered as a part of the period of confinement.
(Amended by Stats.1957, c. 139, p. 734, § 2.)

§ 19d. Applicability of provisions of law relating to misdemeanors as applicable to infractions

Except as otherwise provided by law, all provisions of law relating to misdemeanors shall apply to infractions, including but not limited to powers of peace officers, jurisdiction of courts, periods for commencing action and for bringing a case to trial and burden of proof.
(Added by Stats.1968, c. 1192, p. 2255, § 4, operative Jan. 1, 1969.)

§ 20. Crime; unity of act and intent, or criminal negligence

To constitute crime there must be unity of act and intent. In every crime or public offense there must exist a union, or joint operation of act and intent, or criminal negligence.
(Enacted 1872.)

Notes of Decisions

Intent to commit a particular crime is generally manifested by circumstances connected with the offense, and specific intent to rob may be inferred from circumstances connected with the robbery. People v. Johnson (1972) 104 Cal.Rptr. 807, 28 C.A.3d 653.

Evidence, including evidence that defendant's activities in soliciting on amusement ground parking lot required diversion of off loading of trams and that defendant knew that his conduct was substantially certain to result in such interference, sustained conviction for trespass under provision of § 602 prohibiting entering lands with intention of interfering with lawful business. In re Ball (1972) 100 Cal.Rptr. 189, 23 C.A.3d 380.

From standpoint of lawfulness of assembly, intent of people is usually determined from surrounding circumstances. People v. Uptgraft (1970) 87 Cal.Rptr. 459, 8 C.A.3d Supp. 1, certiorari denied 91 S.Ct. 152, 400 U.S. 911, 27 L.Ed.2d 151.

An instruction: "The word 'willfully,' when applied to the intent with which an act is done or omitted, implies simply a purpose or willingness to commit the act or make the omission referred to, and it does not require any intent to violate law or to injure another or to acquire any advantage"—if error, could not have prejudiced defendant in prosecution for sale of liquor where all that there was necessary for the jury to find was that defendant sold the liquor. People v. Tomasovich (1922) 206 P. 119, 56 C.A. 520.

"Mens rea" means that there must be a joint operation and intent to constitute the commission of a criminal offense. People v. Hernandez (1964) 39 Cal.Rptr. 361, 393 P.2d 673, 61 C.2d 529, 8 A.L.R.3d 1092.

To be an "unlawful act", within meaning of involuntary manslaughter statute (§ 192), act must be dangerous to human life or safety and meet conditions of this section, requiring that in every crime there must exist union or joint operation of act and intent, or criminal negligence. People v. Villalobos (1962) 25 Cal.Rptr. 111, 208 C.A.2d 321.

Union of act and intent, or criminal negligence, is an invariable element of every crime unless it is excluded expressly or by necessary implication. People v. Stuart (1956) 302 P.2d 5, 47 C.2d 167, 55 A.L.R.2d 705.

§ 21. Intent; manifestation; persons of sound mind defined

Intent, how manifested, and who considered of sound mind. The intent or intention is manifested by the circumstances connected with the offense, and the sound mind and discretion of the accused. All persons are of sound mind who are neither idiots nor lunatics, nor affected with insanity.
(Enacted 1872.)

Notes of Decisions

The intent with which an act is done may be gathered from all circumstances shown in evidence. People v. Schrader (1939) 90 P.2d 331, 32 C.A.2d 543; People v. De Soto (1939) 92 P.2d 466, 33 C.A.2d 478; People v. Turley (1953) 259 P.2d 724, 119 C.A.2d 632.

Before a person may be found guilty of a crime it is not essential that the proof should show that such person entertained any intent to violate the law since it is sufficient that he intentionally committed forbidden act. People v. Bateman (1959) 345 P.2d 334, 175 C.A.2d 69.

§ 22. Voluntary intoxication; no excuse for crime; consideration on questions of purpose, motive or intent

Drunkenness no excuse for crime. When it may be considered. No act committed by a person while in a state of voluntary intoxication is less criminal by reason of his having been in such condition. But whenever the actual existence of any particular purpose, motive, or intent is a necessary element to constitute any particular species or degree of crime, the jury may take into consideration the fact that the accused was intoxicated at the time, in determining the purpose, motive, or intent with which he committed the act.
(Enacted 1872.)

Notes of Decisions

Voluntary intoxication may not be considered when crime charged is a "general intent" crime, that is, one requiring nothing more than intent to do the proscribed act, but it may be considered in determining whether particular purpose, motive or intent actuated the accused so that where specific intent is necessary element of crime, jury may consider fact of defendant's voluntary intoxication. People v. Foster (1971) 97 Cal.Rptr. 94, 19 C.A.3d 649.

Part 1
OF CRIMES AND PUNISHMENTS

§ 26. Persons capable of committing crime; exceptions

All persons are capable of committing crimes except those belonging to the following classes:

One—Children under the age of 14, in the absence of clear proof that at the time of committing the act charged against them, they knew its wrongfulness.

Two—Idiots.

Three—Lunatics and insane persons.

Four—Persons who committed the act or made the omission charged under an ignorance or mistake of fact, which disproves any criminal intent.

Five—Persons who committed the act charged without being conscious thereof.

Six—Persons who committed the act or made the omission charged through misfortune or by accident, when it appears that there was no evil design, intention, or culpable negligence.

Seven—Persons (unless the crime be punishable with death) who committed the act or made the omission charged under threats or menaces sufficient to show that they had reasonable cause to and did believe their lives would be endangered if they refused.
(Amended by Stats.1976, c. 1181, p. —, § 1.)

Notes of Decisions

If defendant at time of offense was insane under the California M'Naghten test, it makes no difference whether the period of insanity lasted several months or merely a period of hours. People v. Kelly (1973) 111 Cal.Rptr. 171, 516 P.2d 875, 10 C.3d 565.

Unconsciousness is ordinarily complete defense to charge of criminal homicide, but if state of unconsciousness results from intoxication voluntarily induced, it is not a complete defense even though the defendant is unable to achieve specific state of mind; requisite element of criminal negligence is deemed to exist irrespective of unconsciousness and defendant stands guilty of involuntary manslaughter. People v. Graham (1969) 78 Cal.Rptr. 217, 455 P.2d 153, 71 A.C. 320.

This section providing that persons who commit acts or make omissions charged under threats or menaces sufficient to show they had reasonable cause to and did believe their lives would be in danger if they refused are not capable of committing crimes contemplates that threat or menace be accompanied by direct or implied demand or request that actor commit the criminal act. People v. Richards (1969) 75 Cal.Rptr. 597, 269 C.A.2d 768.

Evidence established that 16-year-old boy who defendant threatened with commitment to mental institution, physical beatings, and other threats to his general wellbeing was not an accomplice of defendant even though he slept in same bed with defendant and knew acts were wrong. People v. Anderson (1968) 70 Cal.Rptr. 231, 264 C.A.2d 271.

On motion of defendant, who was convicted of first degree murder on a plea of guilty when he was 13 years of age, for leave to withdraw plea of guilty and to enter plea of not guilty, evidence justified trial court's conclusion that at the time of the commission of the crime charged defendant knew its wrongfulness and that at time he entered his plea of guilty he knew its import. People v. Thompson (1949) 211 P.2d 1, 94 C.A.2d 578.

§ 27. Persons liable to punishment

The following persons are liable to punishment under the laws of this state:

1. All persons who commit, in whole or in part, any crime within this state;

2. All who commit any offense without this state which, if committed within this state, would be larceny, robbery, or embezzlement under the laws of this state, and bring the property stolen or embezzled, or any part of it, or are found with it, or any part of it, within this state;

3. All who, being without this state, cause or aid, advise or encourage, another person to commit a crime within this state, and are afterwards found therein.
(Amended by Stats.1905, c. 478, p. 638, § 1.)

Notes of Decisions

Section 778a and this section providing that all persons who commit, in whole or in part, any crime within state are liable to

§ 27

punishment under laws of state and that, whenever a person, with attempt to commit a crime, does any act within state in execution or part execution of such intent, culminating in commission of a crime, either within or without state, such person is punishable for such crime in state in same manner as if crime had been committed entirely within state require the doing of an act within state amounting to an "attempt" to commit offense charged, within definition of attempt in criminal cases generally, that is, an act beyond mere preparation. People v. Utter (1972) 101 Cal.Rptr. 214, 24 C.A.3d 535, appeal after remand 108 Cal.Rptr. 909, 34 C.A.3d 366.

§ 30. Classification

Classification of parties to crime. The parties to crimes are classified as:

1. Principals; and,
2. Accessories.

(Enacted 1872.)

§ 31. Principals defined

Who are principals. All persons concerned in the commission of a crime, whether it be felony or misdemeanor, and whether they directly commit the act constituting the offense, or aid and abet in its commission, or, not being present, have advised and encouraged its commission, and all persons counseling, advising, or encouraging children under the age of fourteen years, lunatics or idiots, to commit any crime, or who, by fraud, contrivance, or force, occasion the drunkenness of another for the purpose of causing him to commit any crime, or who, by threats, menaces, command, or coercion, compel another to commit any crime, are principals in any crime so committed.

(Enacted 1872.)

Notes of Decision

An aider and abettor's fundamental purpose, motive and intent is to aid and assist perpetrator in latter's commission of crime and may so aid and assist with knowledge or awareness of wrongful purpose of perpetrator or may so act because he has same evil intent as perpetrator. People v. Vasquez (1972) 105 Cal.Rptr. 181, 29 C.A.3d 81.

Test of aiding and abetting is whether accused directly or indirectly aided perpetrator; the extent of such knowledge is question of fact provable by circumstantial evidence. People v. Long (1970) 86 Cal.Rptr. 590, 7 C.A.3d 586.

A person who is present when a crime is committed and who engages in conduct aiding and assisting perpetrator with knowledge of latter's criminal intent aids and abets in its commission. People v. Herrera (1970) 86 Cal.Rptr. 165, 6 C.A.3d 846.

If female defendant aided and abetted male defendant in robbery out of which murders arose she was a principal and equally guilty of felony murder. People v. Terry (1970) 85 Cal.Rptr. 409, 466 P.2d 961, 2 C.3d 362, certiorari dismissed 92 S.Ct. 1619, 406 U.S. 912, 32 L.Ed.2d 112.

It is not necessary that one be physically present when crime is committed to abet or encourage its commission. People v. Bohmer (1975) 120 Cal.Rptr. 136, 46 C.A.3d 185, certiorari denied 96 S.Ct. 402, 423 U.S. 990, 46 L.Ed.2d 308.

To "aid" does not imply guilty knowledge or felonious intent, but means to assist and supplement the efforts of another, while to "abet" includes knowledge of the wrongful purpose of the perpetrator, and counsel and encouragement of the crime. People v. Bond (1910) 109 P. 150, 13 C.A. 175; People v. Lewis (1908) 98 P. 1078, 9 C.A. 279.

"Accomplice" is one who knowingly, voluntarily and with common intent with principal offender, unites in commission of crime. People v. Horton (1963) 28 Cal.Rptr. 666, 213 C.A.2d 185.

To be an accomplice one must knowingly, voluntarily, and with common intent unite with the principal offender in the commission of the crime. People v. Platnick (1958) 326 P.2d 585, 161 C.A.2d 313.

§ 32. Accessories defined

Every person who, after a felony has been committed, harbors, conceals or aids a principal in such felony, with the intent that said principal may avoid or escape from arrest, trial, conviction or punishment, having knowledge that said principal has committed such felony or has been charged with such felony or conviction thereof, is an accessory to such felony. (Amended by Stats.1935, c. 436, p. 1484, § 1.)

Notes of Decisions

An affirmative falsehood to a public investigator, made with intent to shield perpetrator of crime, may form the aid or concealment denounced by this section. People v. Duty (1969) 74 Cal.Rptr. 606, 269 C.A.2d 97.

Factors which finder of fact may consider in determining whether one has aided and abetted commission of crime include presence at crime, companionship and conduct of accused before and after offense, possession of stolen property and flight with companion committing burglary. People v. Morga (1969) 78 Cal.Rptr. 120, 273 A.C.A. 215.

One who stays in an automobile and enables or assists those who are doing the actual robbing to make a successful getaway is as much a principal, and aids and abets the crime completely as though he were present and assisted in the actual taking of the property. People v. Dills (1959) 340 P.2d 273, 171 C.A.2d 256.

The consent to participate in crime, which constitutes one an "accessory to crime," must be knowingly, willingly, and voluntarily given, with full appreciation of nature of act. People v. Battilana (1942) 126 P.2d 923, 52 C.A.2d 685.

§ 33. Accessories; punishment

Except in cases where a different punishment is prescribed, an accessory is punishable by a fine not exceeding five thousand dollars ($5,000), or by imprisonment in the state prison, or in a county jail not exceeding one year, or by both such fine and imprisonment.

(Amended by Stats.1976, c. 1139, p. —, § 101, operative July 1, 1977.)

CRIME BY AND AGAINST PUBLIC OFFICIALS

§ 67. Bribes; giving or offering to executive officers; punishment

Every person who gives or offers any bribe to any executive officer in this state, with intent to influence him in respect to any act, decision, vote, opinion, or other proceeding as such officer, is punishable by imprisonment in the state prison for two, three or four years, and is disqualified from holding any office in this state.
(Amended by Stats.1976, c. 1139, p. —, § 103, operative July 1, 1977.)

Notes of Decisions

County deputy sheriff was an "executive officer" for purposes of this section. People v. Strohl (1976) 129 Cal.Rptr. 224, 57 C.A.3d 347.

Evidence was sufficient to sustain finding of existence of conspiracy to bribe state and city officers, to engage in bookmaking, and to obstruct justice. People v. Canard (1967) 65 Cal.Rptr. 15, 257 C.A.2d 444, certiorari denied 89 S.Ct. 231, 393 U.S. 912, 21 L.Ed.2d 198.

Giver and receiver of a bribe are not guilty of a conspiracy, since the two crimes required different motives or purposes. People v. Wolden (1967) 63 Cal.Rptr. 467, 255 C.A.2d 798, certiorari denied, 88 S.Ct. 2032, 391 U.S. 965, 20 L.Ed.2d 877, certiorari denied 88 S.Ct. 2032, 391 U.S. 965, 20 L.Ed.2d 877.

§ 67½. Bribes; giving or offering to ministerial officers, employees, or appointees

Every person who gives or offers as a bribe to any ministerial officer, employee, or appointee of the State of California, county or city therein or political subdivision thereof, any thing the theft of which would be petty theft is guilty of a misdemeanor; if the theft of the thing so given or offered would be grand theft the offense is a felony.
(Amended by Stats.1939, c. 603, p. 2019, § 1.)

Notes of Decisions

It was not an essential of the crime of bribery that bribe was offered to official with actual authority as long as official's act falls within general scope of duties, and he purported to act in official capacity. People v. Longo (1953) 259 P.2d 53, 119 C.A.2d 416.

Bribery or attempted bribery or any attempt corruptly to influence official action of police officers constitutes the criminal offense of bribery. Oppenheimer v. Clifton's Brookdale (1950) 220 P.2d 422, 98 C.A.2d 403.

Offer

The offer or solicitation of a bribe need not be stated in express language as such, it being sufficient that words used carry import of bribe and were evidently intended to bear that meaning. People v. Vollmann (1946) 167 P.2d 545, 73 C.A.2d 769.

Under this section and § 67, relating to the giving of bribe to executive or ministerial officers to influence their actions as such, it is necessary to prove only that the bribe was given with the intent to influence actions of such officers, without showing an understanding or agreement, such as is necessary under § 137, relating to falsifying testimony, understanding or agreement. Ex parte Jang (1938) 78 P.2d 250, 25 C.A.2d 529.

§ 68. Bribes; executive or ministerial officers, employees, or appointees; asking or receiving; punishment

Every executive or ministerial officer, employee or appointee of the State of California, county or city therein or political subdivision thereof, who asks, receives, or agrees to receive, any bribe, upon any agreement or understanding that his vote, opinion, or action upon any matter then pending, or which may be brought before him in his official capacity, shall be influenced thereby, is punishable by imprisonment in the state prison for two, three or four years; and, in addition thereto, forfeits his office, and is forever disqualified from holding any office in this state.
(Amended by Stats.1976, c. 1139, p. —, § 104, operative July 1, 1977.)

Notes of Decisions

The crime described in this section, penalizing receiving a bribe is complete when officer or employee "asks, receives, or agrees to receive, any bribe", and no action on part of victim is necessary to complete the offense. People v. Brigham (1946) 163 P.2d 891, 72 C.A.2d 1.

Officer convicted of receiving bribe could not hold public office after serving sentence less period allowed for good behavior and after being restored to citizenship by governor's order, since not receiving a "pardon." Donham v. Gross (1930) 290 P. 884, 210 C. 190.

A police officer of a city charged with bribery, in violation of this section, in promising, for consideration, not to arrest another if such other should engage in the sale of intoxicating liquor in violation of the National Prohibition Law, commonly known as the Volstead Act, may be prosecuted in the state courts for his violation of this code; his prosecution not being limited to the courts of the United States. Harris v. Superior Court of Sacramento County (1921) 196 P. 895, 51 C.A. 15.

§ 69. Obstructing or resisting executive officers in performance of their duties; attempts; threats; violence; punishment

Every person who attempts, by means of any threat or violence, to deter or prevent an executive officer from performing any duty imposed upon such officer by law, or who knowingly resists, by the use of force or violence, such officer, in the performance of his duty, is punishable by a fine not exceeding five thousand dollars ($5,000) or by imprisonment in the state prison * * *, or in a county jail not exceeding one year, or by both such fine and imprisonment.
(Amended by Stats.1976, c. 1139, p. —, § 105, operative July 1, 1977.)

§ 69

Notes of Decisions

This section is designed to protect a police officer (who is an executive officer) against violent interference with the performance of his duties, rather than interference with court process which is covered by § 166. People v. Buice (1964) 40 Cal.Rptr. 877, 230 C.A.2d 324.

This section is not confined to interference with officer serving process of court. Id.

Term "executive officer" as used in this section includes police officers. Id.

This section prescribing punishment for an attempt to prevent an executive officer from performing his duty and § 148, prescribing punishment for persons who wilfully resist any public officer in discharge of his duty are distinguishable in that latter section is more general in terms and applies to interference with or obstruction of any public officer in the discharge of his duties while former section is limited solely to executive officers. People v. Buice (1964) 40 Cal.Rptr. 877, 230 C.A.2d 324.

§ 70. Emolument gratuities or reward; executive or ministerial officers; employees or appointees; asking or receiving; exception

Every executive or ministerial officer, employee or appointee of the State of California, county or city therein or political subdivision thereof, who knowingly asks, receives or agrees to receive any emolument, gratuity or reward, or any promise thereof excepting such as may be authorized by law for doing an official act, is guilty of a misdemeanor.

This section shall not be construed to prohibit deputy registrars of voters from receiving compensation when authorized by local ordinance from any candidate, political committee, or statewide political organization for securing the registration of voters. (Amended by Stats.1975, c. 1164, p. ——, § 1.)

§ 71. Threatening public officers and employees and school officials

Every person who, with intent to cause, attempts to cause, or causes, any officer or employee of any public or private educational institution or any public officer or employee to do, or refrain from doing, any act in the performance of his duties, by means of a threat, directly communicated to such person, to inflict an unlawful injury upon any person or property, and it reasonably appears to the recipient of the threat that such threat could be carried out, is guilty of a public offense punishable as follows:

(1) Upon a first conviction, such person is punishable by a fine not exceeding five thousand dollars ($5,000), or by imprisonment in the state prison, or in a county jail not exceeding one year, or by both such fine and imprisonment.

(2) If such person has been previously convicted of a violation of this section, such previous conviction shall be charged in the accusatory pleading, and if such previous conviction is found to be true by the jury, upon a jury trial, or by the court, upon a court trial, or is admitted by the defendant, he is punishable by imprisonment in the state prison.

As used in this section, "directly communicated" includes, but is not limited to, a communication to the recipient of the threat by telephone, telegraph, or letter.
(Amended by Stats.1976, c. 1139, p. ——, § 106, operative July 1, 1977.)

Editors' Note

For threats against public officials and all others, also see Penal Code Section 422, which was added in 1977. Section 422 provides that any person who willfully threatens to commit a crime which will result in death or great bodily injury, with the intent to terrorize another or with reckless disregard for the risk of terrorizing another, is guilty of a felony.

The elements of Penal Code Section 422 may be easier to prove. Additionally, 422 applies to all people, and there is no requirement of direct communication.

§ 72. Fraudulent claims; presentation; intent; punishment

Every person who, with intent to defraud, presents for allowance or for payment to any state board or officer, or to any county, city, or district board or officer, authorized to allow or pay the same if genuine, any false or fraudulent claim, bill, account, voucher, or writing, is punishable either by imprisonment in the county jail for a period of not more than one year, by a fine of not exceeding one thousand dollars ($1,000), or by both such imprisonment and fine, or by imprisonment in the state prison, by a fine of not exceeding ten thousand dollars ($10,000), or by both such imprisonment and fine.

As used in this section "officer" includes a "carrier," as defined in Section 14057 or 14555 of the Welfare and Institutions Code, authorized to act as an agent for a state board or officer or a county, city, or district board or officer, as the case may be.
(Amended by Stats.1976, c. 1139, p. ——, § 107, operative July 1, 1977.)

§ 77. Application of chapter to administrative and ministerial officers

Preceding sections to apply to administrative and ministerial officers. The various provisions of this

OF CRIMES AND PUNISHMENTS

§ 118a

Chapter apply to administrative and ministerial officers, in the same manner as if they were mentioned therein.
(Enacted 1872.)

CRIMES AGAINST PUBLIC JUSTICE

§ 95. Corrupt influencing of jurors, arbitrators, umpires, or referees; attempts; punishment

Every person who corruptly attempts to influence a juror, or any person summoned or drawn as a juror, or chosen as an arbitrator, or umpire, or appointed a referee, in respect to his verdict in, or decision of any cause, or proceeding, pending, or about to be brought before him, either:

One—By means of any communication, oral or written, had with him except in the regular course of proceedings;

Two—By means of any book, paper, or instrument exhibited, otherwise than in the regular course of proceedings;

Three—By means of any threat, intimidation, persuasion, or entreaty; or,

Four—By means of any promise, or assurance of any pecuniary or other advantage;

—is punishable by fine not exceeding five thousand dollars ($5,000), or by imprisonment in the state prison.
(Amended by Stats.1976, c. 1139, p. —, § 112, operative July 1, 1977.)

§ 102. Injuring, destroying or taking personal property from custody of officer

Retaking goods from custody of officer. Every person who willfully injures or destroys, or takes or attempts to take, or assists any person in taking or attempting to take, from the custody of any officer or person, any personal property which such officer or person has in charge under any process of law, is guilty of a misdemeanor.
(Enacted 1872.)

§ 115. Procuring or offering false or forged instrument for record

Offering false or forged instruments to be filed of record. Every person who knowingly procures or offers any false or forged instrument to be filed, registered, or recorded in any public office within this State, which instrument, if genuine, might be filed, or registered, or recorded under any law of this State or of the United States, is guilty of felony.
(Enacted 1872.)

Notes of Decisions

A falsehood must be material in order to sustain charge of perjury. People v. Pierce (1967) 56 Cal.Rptr. 817, 423 P.2d 969, 66 C.2d 53.

Perjury is a specific intent crime. People v. Walker (1967) 55 Cal.Rptr. 726, 247 C.A.2d 554, certiorari denied 88 S.Ct. 60, 389 U.S. 824, 19 L.Ed.2d 77.

This section, making offering of forged instruments for filing a felony, when instrument, if genuine, might be filed or registered, was applicable to a deed properly acknowledged in form, expressing valuable consideration, regardless of defective form or certification. People v. Baender (1924) 228 P. 536, 68 C.A. 49.

A will is an "instrument" within meaning of this section, making it a felony to knowingly procure or offer any false or forged instrument to be filed in any public office. Ex parte Horowitz (1949) 203 P.2d 513, 33 C.2d 534.

§ 118. Perjury defined

Every person who, having taken an oath that he will testify, declare, depose, or certify truly before any competent tribunal, officer, or person, in any of the cases in which such an oath may by law be administered, wilfully and contrary to such oath, states as true any material matter which he knows to be false, and every person who testifies, declares, deposes, or certifies under penalty of perjury in any of the cases in which such testimony, declarations, depositions, or certification is permitted by law under penalty of perjury and wilfully states as true any material matter which he knows to be false, is guilty of perjury.
(Amended by Stats.1957, c. 1612, p. 2959, § 2.)

Editors' Note

Penal Code section 1103(a) provides that no person shall be convicted of perjury where the proof of falsity rests solely upon the contradicted testimony of a single person.

Thus to sustain a conviction for perjury the contradicted facts must be able to be testified to by more than one witness.

§ 118a. False affidavit as to testimony as perjury; subsequent contrary testimony

Any person who, in any affidavit taken before any person authorized to administer oaths, swears, affirms, declares, deposes, or certifies that he will testify, declare, depose, or certify before any competent tribunal, officer, or person, in any case then pending or thereafter to be instituted, in any particular manner, or to any particular fact, and in such affidavit willfully and contrary to such oath states as true any material matter which he knows to be false,

§ 118a

is guilty of perjury. In any prosecution under this section, the subsequent testimony of such person, in any action involving the matters in such affidavit contained, which is contrary to any of the matters in such affidavit contained, shall be prima facie evidence that the matters in such affidavit were false.
(Added by Stats.1905, c. 485, p. 648, § 1.)

§ 119. Oath defined

The term "oath," as used in the last two sections, includes an affirmation and every other mode authorized by law of attesting the truth of that which is stated.
(Amended by Stats.1905, c. 485, p. 648, § 2.)

§ 123. Materiality and effect of testimony; knowledge of witness

Witnesses' knowledge of materiality of his testimony not necessary. It is no defense to a prosecution for perjury that the accused did not know the materiality of the false statement made by him; or that it did not, in fact, affect the proceeding in or for which it was made. It is sufficient that it was material, and might have been used to affect such proceeding.
(Enacted 1872.)

Notes of Decisions

Test of materiality of false statement made under oath is, for purposes of perjury, one of tendency to influence, and, therefore, false statement having such tendency may be perjury even though it did not in fact affect the proceeding in or for which it was made if it might have been used to affect such proceeding. People v. Poe (1968) 71 Cal.Rptr. 161, 265 C.A.2d 385.

§ 125. Unqualified statement of that not known to be true

Statement of that which one does not know to be true. An unqualified statement of that which one does not know to be true is equivalent to a statement of that which one knows to be false.
(Enacted 1872.)

Notes of Decisions

This section, providing that an unqualified statement of that which one does not know to be true is equivalent to a statement of that which one knows to be false must be read in conjunction with § 118 defining perjury. People v. Bass (1959) 346 P.2d 216, 175 C.A.2d 383; People v. Nelson (1940) 97 P.2d 1043, 36 C.A.2d 515.

A reckless statement in a judicial proceeding which is not known to be true is "perjury" if in truth such averment is false. People v. Agnew (1947) 176 P.2d 724, 77 C.A.2d 748.

§ 126. Punishment

Perjury is punishable by imprisonment in the state prison for two, three or four years.
(Amended by Stats.1976, c. 1139, p. —, § 118, operative July 1, 1977.)

§ 127. Subornation of perjury; definition; punishment

Subornation of perjury. Every person who willfully procures another person to commit perjury is guilty of subornation of perjury, and is punishable in the same manner as he would be if personally guilty of the perjury so procured.
(Enacted 1872.)

Notes of Decisions

Elements of crime of subornation of perjury consist of: corrupt agreement to testify falsely; proof that perjury has in fact been committed; statements of perjurer were material; and evidence that such statements were willfully made with knowledge as to falsity thereof. People v. Jones (1967) 62 Cal.Rptr. 304, 254 C.A.2d 200, certiorari denied 88 S.Ct. 1101, 390 U.S. 980, 19 L.Ed.2d 1278.

§ 128. Procuring execution of innocent person; punishment

Every person who, by willful perjury or subornation of perjury procures the conviction and execution of any innocent person, is punishable by death or life imprisonment without possibility of parole. The penalty shall be determined pursuant to Penal Code Sections 190.3 and 190.4.
(Amended by Stats.1977, c. 316, p. —, § 3, urgency, eff. Aug. 11, 1977.)

§ 129. False return required to be under oath

Every person who, being required by law to make any return, statement, or report, under oath, willfully makes and delivers any such return, statement, or report, purporting to be under oath, knowing the same to be false in any particular, is guilty of perjury, whether such oath was in fact taken or not.
(Added by Stats.1905, c. 485, p. 648, § 5.)

§ 132. Offering forged, altered, or ante-dated book, document, or record

Offering false evidence. Every person who upon any trial, proceeding, inquiry, or investigation whatever, authorized or permitted by law, offers in evidence, as genuine or true, any book, paper, document, record, or other instrument in writing, knowing the same to have been forged or fraudulently altered or ante-dated, is guilty of felony.
(Enacted 1872.)

§ 134. Preparing false documentary evidence

Preparing false evidence. Every person guilty of preparing any false or ante-dated book, paper, record, instrument in writing, or other matter or thing, with intent to produce it, or allow it to be produced for any fraudulent or deceitful purpose, as genuine or true, upon any trial, proceeding, or inquiry whatever, authorized by law, is guilty of felony.
(Enacted 1872.)

§ 135. Destroying or concealing documentary evidence

Destroying evidence. Every person who, knowing that any book, paper, record, instrument in writing, or other matter or thing, is about to be produced in evidence upon any trial, inquiry, or investigation whatever, authorized by law, willfully destroys or conceals the same, with intent thereby to prevent it from being produced, is guilty of a misdemeanor.
(Enacted 1872.)

§ 136. Preventing or dissuading witness from attending

(a) Every person who willfully and unlawfully prevents or dissuades any person who is or may become a witness, from attending upon any trial, proceeding, or inquiry, authorized by law, is guilty of a misdemeanor.

(b) Every person who willfully and unlawfully prevents or dissuades by means of force or threats of unlawful injury to person or property, any person who is or may become a witness, from attending upon any trial, proceeding, or inquiry, authorized by law, is punishable by fine not exceeding one thousand dollars ($1,000), or by imprisonment in the county jail not exceeding one year, or by imprisonment in the state prison or by both such fine and imprisonment in the county jail or in the state prison.
(Amended by Stats.1976, c. 1125, p. —, § 13.7; Stats.1976, c. 1139, p. —, § 119, operative July 1, 1977.)

§ 136½. Dissuading witness from attending; bribe

Every person who gives or offers or promises to give to any witness or person about to be called as a witness, any bribe upon any understanding or agreement that such person shall not attend upon any trial or other judicial proceeding, or every person who attempts by means of any offer of a bribe to dissuade any such person from attending upon any trial or other judicial proceeding, is guilty of a felony.
(Amended by Stats.1963, c. 1939, p. 3993, § 1.)

§ 137. Influencing testimony; Inducing false testimony or the withholding of true testimony

(a) Every person who gives or offers, or promises to give, to any witness, or person about to be called as a witness, any bribe, upon any understanding or agreement that the testimony of such witness shall be thereby influenced is guilty of a felony.

(b) Every person who attempts by force or threat of force or by the use of fraud to induce any person to give false testimony or withhold true testimony is guilty of a felony.

As used in this subdivision, "threat of force" means a credible threat of unlawful injury to any person or property which is communicated to a person for the purpose of inducing him to give false testimony or withhold true testimony.

(c) Every person who knowingly induces another person to give false testimony or withhold true testimony is guilty of a misdemeanor.
(Amended by Stats.1977, c. 67, p. —, § 1.)

§ 138. Witness asking or receiving bribe

Every person who is a witness, or is about to be called as such, who receives, or offers to receive, any bribe, upon any understanding that his testimony shall be influenced thereby, or that he will absent himself from the trial or proceeding upon which his testimony is required, is guilty of a felony.
(Amended by Code Am.1873–74, c. 614, p. 425, § 11.)

§ 142. Officer refusing to receive or arrest person charged with offense; punishment

Any peace officer who has the authority to receive or arrest a person charged with a criminal offense and willfully refuses to receive or arrest such person shall be punished by a fine not exceeding five thousand dollars ($5,000), or by imprisonment in the state prison, or in a county jail not exceeding one year, or by both such fine and imprisonment.
(Amended by Stats.1976, c. 1139, p. —, § 120, operative July 1, 1977.)

Notes of Decisions

A peace officer may release from custody a person who has been arrested by a citizen's arrest and delivered into the officer's custody without violating this section. 52 Ops.Atty.Gen. 65, 4–18–69.

That officer who accepted custody of plaintiff from third person who had made citizen's arrest first conducted independent investigation did not render him civilly liable, where there was no evidence of knowledge, or presumption of knowledge, of illegality of arrest. Kinney v. Contra Costa County (1970) 87 Cal.Rptr. 638, 8 C.A.3d 761.

§ 142   PENAL CODE

There was neither false arrest nor false imprisonment chargeable either to county or its police officer where officer accepted custody of plaintiff from third person who had made citizen's arrest; county and officers had immunity from civil liability. Kinney v. Contra Costa County (1970) 87 Cal.Rptr. 638, 8 C.A.3d 761.

Detention of an accused beyond the forty-eight hour statutory maximum without accused being taken before a magistrate is illegal. Rogers v. Superior Court of Alameda County (1956) 291 P.2d 929, 46 C.2d 3.

§ 145. Officer delaying to take arrested person before magistrate

Delaying to take person arrested before a magistrate. Every public officer or other person, having arrested any person upon a criminal charge, who willfully delays to take such person before a magistrate having jurisdiction, to take his examination, is guilty of a misdemeanor.
(Enacted 1872.)

Notes of Decisions

When arrest is made without warrant by public peace officer or private person, the potential defendant must, without unnecessary delay, be taken before nearest or most accessible magistrate in county in which offense is triable and complaint stating charge against arrested person must be laid before such magistrate. People v. Hiser (1968) 72 Cal.Rptr. 906, 267 C.A.2d 47.

Where defendant was arrested in Los Angeles by an officer from Ventura County, fact that after his arrest defendant was taken before a magistrate in Ventura County was not improper on the ground that defendant was not taken before the nearest magistrate in the county in which the arrest was made. People v. McCarty (1958) 330 P.2d 484, 164 C.A.2d 322.

§ 146. Arrests, seizures, levies, or dispositions without process or authority

Making arrests, etc., without lawful authority. Every public officer, or person pretending to be a public officer, who, under the pretense or color of any process or other legal authority, arrests any person or detains him against his will, or seizes or levies upon any property, or dispossesses any one of any lands or tenements, without a regular process or other lawful authority therefor, is guilty of a misdemeanor.
(Enacted 1872.)

Notes of Decisions

Good faith alone is not sufficient to justify an arrest without a warrant, but probable cause for arrest exists if facts and circumstances known to officer warrants a prudent man in believing that offense has been committed, and the law looks only at facts and circumstances presented to officer at time he is required to act, though it does examine all those facts in determining probable cause. People v. Ingle (1960) 2 Cal.Rptr. 14, 348 P.2d 577, 53 C.2d 407, certiorari denied 81 S.Ct. 79, 364 U.S. 841, 5 L.Ed.2d 65.

A search is not illegal if a man of ordinary care and prudence, knowing what an officer knows, would be led to believe, or conscientiously entertain a strong suspicion, that a bag in plain sight of the officer contained marijuana. People v. One 1955 Ford Victoria (1961) 13 Cal.Rptr. 910, 193 C.A.2d 213.

§ 146a. Impersonating an officer; punishment

Any person who falsely represents himself to be a public officer, or investigator, inspector, deputy or clerk in any state department and in such assumed character arrests or detains or threatens to arrest or detain, or otherwise intimidates any person or searches the person, building, or other property of any person, or obtains money, or property, or other thing of value, shall be deemed guilty of a misdemeanor and upon conviction thereof shall be punished by imprisonment in the county jail not exceeding six months, or by a fine not exceeding two thousand five hundred dollars ($2,500), or by both.
(Amended by Stats.1976, c. 1125, p. —, § 13.8.)

§ 146b. Simulating official inquiries

Every person who, with intent to lead another to believe that a request or demand for information is being made by the State, a county, city, or other governmental entity, when such is not the case, sends to such other person a written or printed form or other communication which reasonably appears to be such request or demand by such governmental entity, is guilty of a misdemeanor.
(Added by Stats.1959, c. 2135, p. 5048, § 1.)

§ 146c. Use of terms "peace officer," "police" or "law enforcement" in name of nongovernmental organization; soliciting members; misdemeanor

Every person who designates any nongovernmental organization by any name, including, but not limited to any name which incorporates the term "peace officer," "police," or "law enforcement," which would reasonably be understood to imply that the organization is composed of peace officers, when, in fact, less than 90 percent of the voting members of the organization are peace officers or firemen, active or retired, is guilty of a misdemeanor.

Every person who solicits another to become a member of any such organization so named, of which less than 90 percent of the voting members are peace officers or firemen, or to make a contribution thereto or subscribe to or advertise in a publication of such organization, or who sells or gives to another any badge, pin, membership card, or other article indicating membership in such organization, knowing that less than 90 percent of the voting members are peace officers or firemen, active or retired, is guilty of a misdemeanor.

As used in this section, "peace officer" includes those mentioned in Chapter 4.5 (commencing with Section 830) of Title 3 of Part 2, plus any other officers in any segment of law enforcement who are employed by the state or any of its political subdivisions.
(Amended by Stats.1973), c. 167, p. 470, § 14.)

§ 146d. Sale or gift of membership card, badge or device implying less rigorous law enforcement as to recipient

Every person who sells or gives to another a membership card, badge, or other device, where it can be reasonably inferred by the recipient that display of the device will have the result that the law will be enforced less rigorously as to such person than would otherwise be the case is guilty of a misdemeanor.
(Added by Stats.1963, c. 1180, p. 2680, § 2.)

§ 146e. Peace officers; unauthorized publication of addresses or telephone numbers

Every person who maliciously, and with the intent to obstruct justice or the due administration of the laws, publishes, disseminates, or otherwise discloses the residence address or telephone number of any peace officer while designating the peace officer as such, without the authorization of the agency which employs such peace officer, is guilty of a misdemeanor.
(Added by Stats.1970, c. 1143, p. 2026, § 1.)

Editors' Note

The provisions of this section are reinforced by Vehicle Code Sections 1808, and 1808.4. These sections provide that at the request of the peace officer, his home address will become confidential should someone so request this information from the Department of Motor Vehicles.

§ 147. Officer inhumanely or oppressively treating prisoners; punishment

Inhumanity to prisoners. Every officer who is guilty of willful inhumanity or oppression toward any prisoner under his care or in his custody, is punishable by fine not exceeding two thousand dollars, and by removal from office.
(Enacted 1872.)

§ 148. Resisting, delaying, or obstructing officer; punishment

Every person who wilfully resists, delays, or obstructs any public officer, in the discharge or attempt to discharge any duty of his office, when no other punishment is prescribed, is punishable by a fine not exceeding one thousand dollars, or by imprisonment in a county jail not exceeding one year, or by both such fine and imprisonment.
(Amended by Stats.1957, c. 139, p. 742, § 30.)

Notes of Decisions

Defendant who stood in doorway of apartment and who refused to give consent to officers who requested permission to enter to search for juvenile suspected of breaking window did not thereby obstruct officer in performance of his duties. People v. Wetzel (1974) 113 Cal.Rptr. 32, 520 P.2d 416, 11 C.3d 104.

A public officer's attempt to make unlawful arrest may be reasonably resisted either by person whom officer attempts to arrest or by others coming to such person's aid. Jackson v. Superior Court in and for Merced County (1950) 219 P.2d 879, 98 C.A.2d 183.

When an officer is armed with a writ of possession lawful on its face, a person who resists the officer seeking to execute it is guilty of a crime. People v. Vargas (1960) 3 Cal.Rptr. 925, 179 C.A.2d Supp. 863, certiorari denied 81 S.Ct. 71, 364 U.S. 830, 5 L.Ed.2d 58.

§ 148.1. False report of secretion of explosive or facsimile bomb; penalty

(a) Any person who reports to any police officer, sheriff, employee of a fire department or fire service, district attorney, newspaper, radio station, television station, deputy sheriff, deputy district attorney, member of the California Highway Patrol, employees of the Department of Justice, employees of an airline, employees of an airport, employees of a railroad or busline, an employee of a telephone company, occupants of a building or a news reporter in the employ of a newspaper or radio or television station, that a bomb or other explosive has been or will be placed or secreted in any public or private place knowing that such report is false, is guilty of a crime punishable by imprisonment in the state prison, or imprisonment in the county jail not to exceed one year.

(b) Any person who maliciously informs any other person that a bomb or other explosive has been or will be placed or secreted in any public or private place, knowing that such information is false, is guilty of a crime punishable by imprisonment in the state prison, or imprisonment in the county jail not to exceed one year.

(c) Any person who maliciously gives, mails, sends, or causes to be sent any false or facsimile bomb to another person or places or causes to be placed any false or facsimile bomb, with the intent that any

§ 148.1

other person thinks it is a real bomb and with knowledge that it is a false or facsimile bomb, is guilty of a crime punishable by imprisonment in the state prison, or imprisonment in the county jail not to exceed one year.
(Amended by Stats.1977, c. 165, p. ——, § 4, urgency, eff. June 29, 1977, operative July 1, 1977.)

Editors' Note

Also see Penal Code Sections 71, 148.3, and 422.

§ 148.2. Illegal conduct at burning of building; misdemeanor

Every person who willfully commits any of the following acts at the burning of a building or at any other time and place where any fireman or firemen or emergency rescue personnel are discharging or attempting to discharge an official duty, is guilty of a misdemeanor:

1. Resists or interferes with the lawful efforts of any fireman or firemen or emergency rescue personnel in the discharge or attempt to discharge an official duty.

2. Disobeys the lawful orders of any fireman or public officer.

3. Engages in any disorderly conduct which delays or prevents a fire from being timely extinguished.

4. Forbids or prevents others from assisting in extinguishing a fire or exhorts another person, as to whom he has no legal right or obligation to protect or control, from assisting in extinguishing a fire.
(Amended by Stats.1973, c. 471, p. 946, § 1.)

§ 148.3. False report of emergency; punishment

(a) Any individual who reports, or causes any report to be made, to any city, county, city and county, or state department, district, agency, division, commission, or board, that an "emergency" exists, knowing that such report is false, is guilty of a misdemeanor and, upon conviction thereof, shall be punishable by imprisonment in the county jail, not exceeding one year, or by a fine, not exceeding one thousand dollars ($1,000), or by both such fine and imprisonment.

(b) Any individual who reports, or causes any report to be made, to any city, county, city and county, or state department, district, agency, division, commission, or board, that an "emergency" exists, knowing that such report is false, and great bodily injury or death is sustained by any person as a result of such false report, is guilty of a felony and upon conviction thereof shall be punishable by imprisonment in the state prison, or by a fine of not more than five thousand dollars ($5,000), or by both such fine and imprisonment.

(c) "Emergency" as used in this section means any condition which results in, or which could result in, the response of a public official in an authorized emergency vehicle, or any condition which jeopardizes or could jeopardize public safety and results in, or could result in, the evacuation of any area, building, structure, vehicle or of any other place which any individual may enter.
(Amended by Stats.1976, c. 1139, p. ——, § 122, operative July 1, 1977.)

§ 148.4. Fire alarms; tampering with system; false alarms; punishment

(a) Any person who willfully and maliciously tampers with, molests, injures, or breaks any fire protection equipment, fire protection installation, fire alarm apparatus, wire, or signal, or willfully and maliciously sends, gives, transmits, or sounds any false alarm of fire, by means of any fire alarm system or signal or by any other means or methods, is guilty of a misdemeanor and upon conviction thereof shall be punishable by imprisonment in the county jail, not exceeding one year, or by a fine, not exceeding one thousand dollars ($1,000), or by both such fine and imprisonment.

(b) Any person who willfully and maliciously sends, gives, transmits, or sounds any false alarm of fire, by means of any fire alarm system or signal, or by any other means or methods, and great bodily injury or death is sustained by any person as a result thereof, is guilty of a felony and upon conviction thereof shall be punishable by imprisonment in the state prison or by a fine of not less than five hundred dollars ($500) nor more than five thousand dollars ($5,000), or by both such fine and imprisonment.
(Amended by Stats.1978, c. 456, p. ——, § 1.)

§ 148.5. False report of criminal offense; misdemeanor

Every person who reports to any police officer, sheriff, district attorney, deputy sheriff, deputy district attorney, or member of the California Highway Patrol that a felony or misdemeanor has been committed, knowing such report to be false, is guilty of a misdemeanor.
(Added by Stats.1957, c. 813, p. 2028, § 1.)

§ 149. Officer unnecessarily assaulting or beating any person; punishment

Every public officer who, under color of authority, without lawful necessity, assaults or beats any person, is punishable by a fine not exceeding five thousand dollars ($5,000), or by imprisonment in the state prison, or in a county jail not exceeding one year, or by both such fine and imprisonment.
(Amended by Stats.1976, c. 1139, p. —, § 124, operative July 1, 1977.)

Notes of Decisions

Provocation by words and acts in protest against being taken into custody upon inability to immediately post bail on charge of minor traffic violation did not justify police officer's use of force upon protesting prisoner who was at the time in his custody. People v. Giles (1945) 161 P.2d 623, 70 C.A.2d Supp. 872.

Narcotic inspector or officer who commits unprovoked assault and battery on individual without cause in apprehending individual without warrant on suspicion or upon mere information that individual may be guilty of misdemeanor becomes a "trespasser" and is liable as such for injuries inflicted. Boyes v. Evans (1936) 58 P.2d 922, 14 C.A.2d 472.

§ 151. Advocacy to kill or injure peace officer; punishment

(a) Any person who advocates the willful and unlawful killing or injuring of a peace officer, with the specific intent to cause the willful and unlawful killing or injuring of a peace officer, and such advocacy is done at a time, place, and under circumstances in which the advocacy is likely to cause the imminent willful and unlawful killing or injuring of a peace officer is guilty of (1) a misdemeanor if such advocacy does not cause the unlawful and willful killing or injuring of a peace officer, or (2) a felony if such advocacy causes the unlawful and willful killing of injuring of a peace officer.

(b) As used in this section, "advocacy" means the direct incitement of others to cause the imminent willful and unlawful killing or injuring of a peace officer, and not the mere abstract teaching of a doctrine.
(Added by Stats.1971, c. 1248, p. 2455, § 1.)

§ 153. Compounding or concealing crimes; punishment

Every person who, having knowledge of the actual commission of a crime, takes money or property of another, or any gratuity or reward, or any engagement, or promise thereof, upon any agreement or understanding to compound or conceal such crime, or to abstain from any prosecution thereof, or to withhold any evidence thereof, except in the cases provided for by law, in which crimes may be compromised by leave of court, is punishable as follows:

1. By imprisonment in the state prison, or in a county jail not exceeding one year, where the crime was punishable by death or imprisonment in the state prison for life;

2. By imprisonment in the state prison, or in the county jail not exceeding six months, where the crime was punishable by imprisonment in the state prison for any other term than for life;

3. By imprisonment in the county jail not exceeding six months, or by fine not exceeding five hundred dollars ($500), where the crime was a misdemeanor.
(Amended by Stats.1976, c. 1139, p. —, § 125, operative July 1, 1977.)

§ 166. Criminal contempts; conduct constituting

Criminal contempts. Every person guilty of any contempt of Court, of either of the following kinds, is guilty of a misdemeanor:

1. Disorderly, contemptuous, or insolent behavior committed during the sitting of any Court of justice, in immediate view and presence of the Court, and directly tending to interrupt its proceedings or to impair the respect due to its authority;

2. Behavior of the like character committed in the presence of any referee, while actually engaged in any trial or hearing, pursuant to the order of any Court, or in the presence of any jury while actually sitting for the trial of a cause, or upon any inquest or other proceedings authorized by law;

3. Any breach of the peace, noise, or other disturbance directly tending to interrupt the proceedings of any Court;

4. Willful disobedience of any process or order lawfully issued by any Court;

5. Resistance willfully offered by any person to the lawful order or process of any Court;

6. The contumacious and unlawful refusal of any person to be sworn as a witness; or, when so sworn, the like refusal to answer any material question;

7. The publication of a false or grossly inaccurate report of the proceedings of any Court;

8. Presenting to any Court having power to pass sentence upon any prisoner under conviction, or to any member of such Court, any affidavit or testimony or representation of any kind, verbal or written, in aggravation or mitigation of the punishment to be

§ 166

imposed upon such prisoner, except as provided in this Code.
(Enacted 1872.)

§ 170. Search warrant or warrant of arrest; malicious procuring

Maliciously procuring search warrant. Every person who maliciously and without probable cause procures a search warrant or warrant of arrest to be issued and executed, is guilty of a misdemeanor.
(Enacted 1872.)

§ 182. Definition; punishment; venue

If two or more persons conspire:

1. To commit any crime.

2. Falsely and maliciously to indict another for any crime, or to procure another to be charged or arrested for any crime.

3. Falsely to move or maintain any suit, action or proceeding.

4. To cheat and defraud any person of any property, by any means which are in themselves criminal, or to obtain money or property by false pretenses or by false promises with fraudulent intent not to perform such promises.

5. To commit any act injurious to the public health, to public morals, or to pervert or obstruct justice, or the due administration of the laws.

6. To commit any crime against the person of the President or Vice President of the United States, the Governor of any state or territory, any United States justice or judge, or the secretary of any of the executive departments of the United States.

They are punishable as follows:

When they conspire to commit any crime against the person of any official specified in subdivision 6, they are guilty of a felony and are punishable by imprisonment in the state prison for five, seven, or nine years.

When they conspire to commit any other felony, they shall be punishable in the same manner and to the same extent as is provided for the punishment of the said felony. If the felony is one for which different punishments are prescribed for different degrees, the jury or court which finds the defendant guilty thereof shall determine the degree of the felony defendant conspired to commit. If the degree is not so determined, the punishment for conspiracy to commit such felony shall be that prescribed for the lesser degree, except in the case of conspiracy to commit murder, in which case the punishment shall be that prescribed for murder in the first degree.

If the felony is conspiracy to commit two or more felonies which have different punishments and the commission of such felonies constitute but one offense of conspiracy, the penalty shall be that prescribed for the felony which has the greater maximum term.

When they conspire to do an act described in subdivision 4 of this section, they shall be punishable by imprisonment in the state prison, or by imprisonment in the county jail for not more than one year, or by a fine not exceeding five thousand dollars ($5,000), or both.

When they conspire to do any of the other acts described in this section they shall be punishable by imprisonment in the county jail for not more than one year, or in the state prison, or by a fine not exceeding five thousand dollars ($5,000), or both.

All cases of conspiracy may be prosecuted and tried in the superior court of any county in which any overt act tending to effect such conspiracy shall be done.
(Amended by Stats.1978, c. 579, p. ——, § 1.)

Notes of Decisions

"Criminal conspiracy" is an agreement between two or more persons that they will commit an unlawful object, or achieve a lawful object by unlawful means, and in furtherance of the agreement, have committed one overt act toward the achievement of their objective. People v. Fujita (1974) 117 Cal.Rptr. 757, 43 C.A.3d 454, certiorari denied 95 S.Ct. 1952, 421 U.S. 964, 44 L.Ed.2d 451.

Rule that agreement by two persons to commit a particular crime cannot be prosecuted as a conspiracy when the crime is of such a nature to necessarily require the participation of two persons for its commission is inapplicable where completion of the substantive offense necessarily involves a third person. Hutchins v. Municipal Court of Santa Monica Judicial Dist., Los Angeles County (1976) 132 Cal.Rptr. 158, 61 C.A.3d 77.

To establish a conspiracy, it is not necessary to establish that the parties entered into a formal written or oral agreement; it is sufficient that the people show a mutual understanding, which may be established by circumstantial evidence. People v. Lockett (1972) 102 Cal.Rptr. 41, 25 C.A.3d 433.

To prove a conspiracy, it is not necessary to show that purpose or object of conspiracy was accomplished. People v. Witt (1975) 125 Cal.Rptr. 653, 53 C.A.3d 154, certiorari denied 96 S.Ct. 1518.

A conspiracy exists from the time of forming the criminal agreement until it terminates by abandonment, frustration or the achieving of conspiracy's objective; an original conspirator who does not withdraw from conspiracy before its termination is guilty of the crime of conspiracy during the whole period of its duration; if he should at sometime during the period be armed with a dangerous or deadly weapon, though the conspiracy never reaches the point of an overt attempt to commit the conspired crime, a question arises whether the minimum sentence to which he might be subject if convicted of conspiracy is to be enlarged because of that possession of a weapon. People v. Mares (1975) 124 Cal.Rptr. 718, 51 C.A.3d 1013.

Conspirator, aider, or abettor in murder plot was culpable for all homicides regardless of who actually killed the victims. People v. Manson (1976) 132 Cal.Rptr. 265, 61 C.A.3d 102.

Where an accomplice in a conspiracy to commit arson for purpose of defrauding an insurer accidently burned himself to death, his coconspirator could not be charged with murder under theory of vicarious responsibility rule. People v. Earnest (1975) 120 Cal.Rptr. 485, 46 C.A.3d 792.

One who becomes party to conspiracy after formation thereof does not become liable for every criminal act done before he joined. People v. Donahue (1975) 120 Cal.Rptr. 489, 46 C.A.3d 832.

Where allegedly obscene film was completed by one defendant two years before other two defendants became users of such film, the two defendants who exhibited film, absent some proof of agreement, did not become conspirators with producing defendant to produce, direct and distribute film in question. Id.

§ 184. Overt act; venue

No agreement amounts to a conspiracy, unless some act, beside such agreement, be done within this state to effect the object thereof, by one or more of the parties to such agreement and the trial of cases of conspiracy may be had in any county in which any such act be done.
(Amended by Stats.1919, c. 125, p. 171, § 2.)

CRIMES AGAINST THE PERSON

§ 187. Murder defined; death of fetus

(a) Murder is the unlawful killing of a human being, or a fetus, with malice aforethought.

(b) This section shall not apply to any person who commits an act which results in the death of a fetus if any of the following apply:

(1) The act complied with the Therapeutic Abortion Act, Chapter 11 (commencing with Section 25950) of Division 20 of the Health and Safety Code.

(2) The act was committed by a holder of a physician's and surgeon's certificate, as defined in the Business and Professions Code, in a case where, to a medical certainty, the result of childbirth would be death of the mother of the fetus or where her death from childbirth, although not medically certain, would be substantially certain or more likely than not.

(3) The act was solicited, aided, abetted, or consented to by the mother of the fetus.

(c) Subdivision (b) shall not be construed to prohibit the prosecution of any person under any other provision of law.
(Amended by Stats.1970, c. 1311, p. 2440, § 1.)

Notes of Decisions

Evidence in prosecution for murder was sufficient to support finding that blows administered by defendant were proximate cause of victim's death even though immediate cause of demise was pneumonia. People v. Matta (1976) 129 Cal.Rptr. 205, 57 C.A.3d 472.

Failure, in prosecution for murder, burglary, and arson of dwelling house, to instruct that to hold defendant responsible for murder finding was required that deaths were proximately caused by fire and were not result of alleged intervening negligence of adults in failing to get children out of house safely was not error. People v. Nichols (1970) 89 Cal.Rptr. 721, 474 P.2d 673, 3 C.3d 150, certiorari denied 91 S.Ct. 1388, 402 U.S. 910, 28 L.Ed.2d 652.

Exact time of viability may differ for each fetus. People v. Smith (1976) 129 Cal.Rptr. 498, 59 C.A.3d 751.

Under this section proscribing murder of a fetus as construed to apply only to intentional killing of viable human fetus, "viability" would be defined as having attained such form and development of organs as to be normally capable of living outside uterus. Id.

This section proscribing murder of human fetus only applies to murder of a viable human fetus. Id.

Legally, a fetus is not a person. Id.

Viable fetus in process of being born is "human being" within meaning of homicide statutes (§ 187 et seq.) Keeler v. Superior Court of Amador County (1970) 87 Cal.Rptr. 481, 470 P.2d 617, 2 C.3d 619, 40 A.L.R.3d 420.

In adopting language of 1850 legislature defining murder, legislature intended to exclude from its reach the act of killing an unborn fetus. Id.

Elements of offense—In general

"Murder" is the unlawful killing of a human being with malice aforethought, malice being implied where no considerable provocation appears or when the circumstances attending the killing show an abandoned and malignant heart. People v. Endner (1946) 165 P.2d 712, 73 C.A.2d 20; People v. Weeks (1930) 286 P. 514, 104 C.A. 708.

Any unlawful killing of a human being with malice aforethought, express or implied, "when no considerable provocation appears," is murder, under the express provisions of this section, and § 188, regardless of the degree. People v. Ford (1914) 143 P. 1075, 25 C.A. 388; People v. Suhr (1914) 143 P. 1088, 25 C.A. 805.

Motel owners, who conspired to set fire to premises to collect insurance, could not be charged with murder for death of accomplice, who died from burns sustained when he negligently set the fire. People v. Jennings (1966) 52 Cal.Rptr. 329, 243 C.A.2d 324.

Deliberation and premeditation, elements of offense

Evidence which is sufficient to sustain a finding of "premeditation" and "deliberation" falls into three basic categories: (1) "planning" activity; (2) "motive" to kill victim, and (3) manner of killing. People v. Anderson (1968) 73 Cal.Rptr. 550, 447 P.2d 942, 70 C.2d 15.

Finding of premeditation and deliberation could not be sustained in prosecution for first-degree murder in the absence of any evidence of defendant's actions prior to the killing, in the lack of motive or reason from which jury could reasonably infer that defendant intended to kill his victim and where there was not a manner of killing employed from which jury could reasonably infer that the wounds were deliberately calculated to result in death. Id.

§ 187

Malice, elements of offense

Malice aforethought is an essential element of crime of murder whether it be of first degree or of second degree. People v. Cayer (1951) 228 P.2d 70, 102 C.A.2d 643; People v. Wells (1949) 202 P.2d 53, 33 C.2d 330, certiorari denied 70 S.Ct. 43, 338 U.S. 836, 94 L.Ed. 510; People v. Bender (1945) 163 P.2d 8, 27 C.2d 164.

Malice may be established when defendant initiates a gun battle and, under such circumstances, he may be convicted of murder for a killing committed by another during such battle. People v. Reed (1969) 75 Cal.Rptr. 430, 270 C.A.2d 37.

Under this section defining murder, malice is expressed when there is manifested a deliberate intention unlawfully to take away the life of a fellow creature, and it is implied when no considerable provocation appears, or when circumstances attending the killing show an abandoned and malignant heart. People v. Johnson (1968) 67 Cal.Rptr. 122, 260 C.A.2d 343.

Mental state in general, defenses

Defense of mental illness not amounting to legal insanity is a significant issue in any case in which it is raised by substantial evidence, and its purpose and effect are to ameliorate the law governing criminal responsibility, prescribed by the McNaughton rule. People v. Nicolaus (1967) 56 Cal.Rptr. 635, 423 P.2d 787, 65 C.2d 866; People v. Goedecke (1967) 56 Cal.Rptr. 625, 423 P.2d 777, 65 C.2d 850, 22 A.L.R.3d 1213.

In prosecution for robbery, assault by means of force likely to produce great bodily harm, burglary and murder, wherein defense counsel did not attempt to show that because of mental abnormality, not amounting to legal insanity, defendant did not possess required mental state at time he committed acts and counsel failed to do so because he did not know that evidence of mental abnormality was admissible in guilt phase of trial, defendant was deprived of effective representation, a crucial defense was withdrawn from case, thereby reducing trial to farce and sham, and trial was fundamentally unfair and constituted denial of due process of law. People v. McDowell (1968) 73 Cal.Rptr. 1, 447 P.2d 97, 69 C.2d 737.

Intoxication may be basis of diminished capacity as defense to murder either as concomitant of mental illness or intoxication, where existence of any other mental illness is not demonstrated. People v. Juarez (1968) 65 Cal.Rptr. 630, 258 C.A.2d 349.

Jury was properly permitted to consider evidence of defendant's alleged intoxication in deciding his mental state at time of killings, and was justified in view of weakness of evidence, in rejecting theory that defendant had acted in drunken stupor and that he had committed only manslaughter or second-degree murder. People v. Modesto (1967) 59 Cal.Rptr. 124, 427 P.2d 788, 66 C.2d 695, certiorari denied 88 S.Ct. 574, 389 U.S. 1009, 19 L.Ed.2d 608.

Notes of Decisions

Malice aforethought is found where one acts with wanton disregard for human life by doing an act that involves high probability that act will result in death. People v. Matta (1976) 129 Cal.Rptr. 205, 57 C.A.3d 472.

Malice may be implied from felonious assault without justification or mitigating circumstances. People v. Roberts (1975) 123 Cal.Rptr. 893, 51 C.A.3d 125.

To predicate defendant's guilt of homicide on theory of vicarious liability, it is necessary to prove that coconspirator committed murder, i. e., that he caused death of another human being and that he acted with malice. People v. Antick (1975) 123 Cal.Rptr. 475, 539 P.2d 43, 15 C.3d 79.

Person may deliberate, premeditate and intend to kill his victim, yet not act with malice aforethought, so that maximum offense on which he could be found guilty would be voluntary manslaughter. People v. Fusselman (App.1975) 120 Cal.Rptr. 282.

If defendant commits an act that is likely to cause serious injury or death to another in spite of an awareness of his obligation to act within the general body of laws regulating society, he exhibits that wanton disregard for human life or antisocial motivation that constitutes malice aforethought. Id.

Mental state constituting "malice aforethought" does not necessarily require any ill will or hatred of the person killed, but it does require of the defendant an awareness of the obligation to act within the general body of laws regulating society. People v. Eckstrom (1974) 118 Cal.Rptr. 391, 43 C.A.3d 996.

Proof of malice aforethought, which is required to convict of murder in any degree, can be rebutted by a showing that defendant's mental capacity was reduced by mental illness, mental defect or intoxication. People v. Horn (1974) 115 Cal.Rptr. 516, 524 P.2d 1300, 12 C.3d 290.

Ill will toward or hatred of victim are not requisites of malice as that term is used in defining murder. People v. Sedeno (1974) 112 Cal.Rptr. 1, 518 P.2d 913, 10 C.3d 703.

For malice aforethought to be established, with regard to a killing resulting from an act involving high degree of probability of death, such act must have been done for a base, antisocial purpose, accused must have been aware of duty imposed on him not to commit acts involving risk of great injury or death and he must have acted despite such awareness, and with respect to each of such three issues, evidence of a diminished capacity must be weighed in the balance. People v. Poddar (1974) 111 Cal.Rptr. 910, 518 P.2d 342, 10 C.3d 750.

The three categories of evidence bearing on premeditation and deliberation are (1) defendant's "planning" activity before the killing, (2) his prior relationship with the victim as reflecting upon his motive, and (3) the manner of the killing as it bears upon preexisting reflection to take the victim's life in a particular way. People v. Smith (1973) 108 Cal.Rptr. 698, 33 C.A.3d 51.

§ 188. Malice, express malice, and implied malice defined

Malice defined. Such malice may be express or implied. It is express when there is manifested a deliberate intention unlawfully to take away the life of a fellow creature. It is implied, when no considerable provocation appears, or when the circumstances attending the killing show an abandoned and malignant heart.
(Enacted 1872.)

§ 189. Murder; degrees

All murder which is perpetrated by means of a destructive device or explosive, poison, lying in wait, torture, or by any other kind of willful, deliberate, and premeditated killing, or which is committed in the perpetration of, or attempt to perpetrate, arson, rape, robbery, burglary, mayhem, or any act punishable under Section 288, is murder of the first degree; and all other kinds of murders are of the second degree.

As used in this section, "destructive device" shall mean any destructive device as defined in Section 12301, and "explosive" shall mean any explosive as defined in Section 12000 of the Health and Safety Code.
(Amended by Stats.1970, c. 771, p. 1456, § 3, eff. Aug. 19, 1970.)

Notes of Decisions

Felony-murder rule—In general

Felony-murder rule allows the implication of malice as an element of murder from the committing of an inherently dangerous felony. People v. Poddar (1974) 111 Cal.Rptr. 910, 518 P.2d 342, 10 C.3d 750.

The unlawful killing of human being as a result of commission or attempt to commit crime of robbery by defendant with specific intent to commit robbery was murder of the first degree despite defense contention that prosecution must establish that there was a murder, not merely a killing, under "felony-murder" rule. People v. Obie (1974) 116 Cal.Rptr. 283, 41 C.A.3d 744.

Where defendant killed victim during commission or attempt to commit robbery, defendant was guilty of first-degree murder whether the killing was done intentionally or accidentally. Id.

Perimeter of connection between underlying felony and death of victim is, for purpose of application of felony-murder doctrine, that the homicide must be the direct causal result of the commission of a felony. People v. Taylor (1970) 89 Cal.Rptr. 697, 11 C.A.3d 57.

Under the felony-murder doctrine, the intent required for the conviction of murder is imputed from specific intent to commit concomitant felony. People v. Stines (1969) 82 Cal.Rptr. 850, 2 C.A.3d 970.

Homicide is committed in perpetration of felony if killing and felony are parts of one continuous plan or transaction. People v. Subia (1966) 48 Cal.Rptr. 584, 239 C.A.2d 245; People v. Cartier (1960) 5 Cal.Rptr. 573, 353 P.2d 53, 54 C.2d 300.

Felony-murder rule is a rule of substantive law and withdraws from jury the requirement that they find either express malice or implied malice which is manifested in an intent with conscious disregard for life to commit acts likely to kill, and instruction thus relieves jury of necessity of finding one of the elements of murder. People v. Lilliock (1968) 71 Cal.Rptr. 434, 265 C.A.2d 419.

Intent, deliberation and premeditation

Verdict of murder in the first degree on a theory of a wilful, deliberate and premeditated killing, is proper only if the slayer killed as result of careful thought and weighing of considerations; as a deliberate judgment or plan; carried on cooly and steadily, according to a preconceived design. People v. Anderson (1968) 73 Cal.Rptr. 550, 447 P.2d 942, 70 C.2d 15.

Statutory requirement for first-degree murder that it be found to have been willful, deliberate, and premeditated indicates intention to require substantially more reflection than may be involved in mere formation of specific intent to kill. People v. Risenhoover (1968) 73 Cal.Rptr. 533, 447 P.2d 925, 70 C.2d 39, certiorari denied 90 S.Ct. 123, 396 U.S. 857, 24 L.Ed.2d 108.

Second-degree murder—In general

"Second-degree murder" is the unlawful killing of a human being with malice aforethought, which is not perpetrated by poison, lying in wait, or torture, is not willful, deliberate and premeditated, and is not committed in perpetration of, or attempt to perpetrate arson, rape, robbery, burglary, or mayhem. People v. Thomas (1945) 156 P.2d 7, 25 C.2d 880. See, also, People v. Ward (1949) 208 P.2d 448, 93 C.A.2d 4.

Where defendant is not a fully normal or mature, mentally well person and the extent of his understanding, reflection upon and comprehension of the homicide and its consequences, with realization of enormity of the evil involved, appears to have been materially vague and detached, he can be guilty of no more than second-degree murder. People v. Caylor (1968) 66 Cal.Rptr. 448, 259 C.A.2d 191.

Where trial court failed to determine degree of murder for which defendant was convicted, defendant would be deemed to have been found guilty of murder of the second degree. In re Harris (1967) 64 Cal.Rptr. 319, 434 P.2d 615, 67 C.2d 876.

Whether defendants who had been seen to enter victim's automobile shortly before the killing had as purpose of abduction of victim the felonious taking of the automobile which was subsequently found some two miles from murder scene, mired and abandoned, were jury questions. People v. Lara (1967) 62 Cal.Rptr. 586, 432 P.2d 202, 67 C.2d 365, certiorari denied 88 S.Ct. 2303, 392 U.S. 945, 20 L.Ed.2d 1407.

All murders not of the first degree are "murder in the second degree," or the unlawful killing with malice but without deliberation or premeditation. People v. Nerida (1938) 83 P.2d 964, 29 C.A.2d 11.

Deliberation and premeditation, second-degree murder

Proof of malice without further proof that homicide was willful, deliberate and premeditated would establish second-degree murder rather than first-degree murder. People v. Stansbury (1968) 69 Cal.Rptr. 827, 263 C.A.2d 499.

Second-degree murder is unpremeditated murder with malice aforethought. People v. Landrum (1968) 67 Cal.Rptr. 911, 261 C.A.2d 372.

§ 190. Murder; degrees; punishment

Every person guilty of murder in the first degree shall suffer death, confinement in state prison for life without possibility of parole, or confinement in state prison for life. The penalty to be applied shall be determined as provided in Sections 190.1, 190.2, 190.3, 190.4, and 190.5. Every person guilty of murder in the second degree is punishable by imprisonment in the state prison for five, * * * seven, or 11 years.
(Amended by Stats.1978, c. 579, p. ——, § 2.)

§ 190.1. Death penalty; determination of guilt; special circumstances; further proceedings

A case in which the death penalty may be imposed pursuant to this chapter shall be tried in separate phases as follows:

(a) The defendant's guilt shall first be determined. If the trier of fact finds the defendant guilty of first degree murder, it shall at the same time determine the truth of all special circumstances charged as enumerated in Section 190.2, except for a special circumstance charged pursuant to paragraph (5) of subdivision (c) of Section 190.2 where it is alleged that the defendant had been convicted in a prior proceeding of the offense of murder of the first or second degree.

§ 190.1

(b) If the defendant is found guilty of first degree murder and one of the special circumstances is charged pursuant to paragraph (5) of subdivision (c) of Section 190.2 which charges that the defendant had been convicted in a prior proceeding of the offense of murder of the first or second degree, there shall thereupon be further proceedings on the question of the truth of such special circumstance.

(c) If the defendant is found guilty of first degree murder and one or more special circumstances as enumerated in Section 190.2 has been charged and found to be true, his sanity on any plea of not guilty by reason of insanity under Section 1026 shall be determined as provided in Section 190.4. If he is found to be sane, there shall thereupon be further proceedings on the question of the penalty to be imposed. Such proceedings shall be conducted in accordance with the provisions of Sections 190.3 and 190.4.
(Added by Stats.1977, c. 316, p. —, § 7, urgency, eff. Aug. 11, 1977.)

§ 190.2. Death penalty or life imprisonment without parole; special circumstances

The penalty for a defendant found guilty of murder in the first degree shall be death or confinement in the state prison for life without possibility of parole in any case in which one or more of the following special circumstances has been charged and specially found, in a proceeding under Section 190.4, to be true:

(a) The murder was intentional and was carried out pursuant to agreement by the person who committed the murder to accept a valuable consideration for the act of murder from any person other than the victim;

(b) The defendant, with the intent to cause death, physically aided or committed such act or acts causing death, and the murder was willful, deliberate, and premeditated, and was perpetrated by means of a destructive device or explosive;

(c) The defendant was personally present during the commission of the act or acts causing death, and with intent to cause death physically aided or committed such act or acts causing death and any of the following additional circumstances exists:

(1) The victim is a peace officer as defined in Section 830.1, subdivision (a) or (b) of Section 830.2, subdivision (a) of Section 830.3, or subdivision (b) of Section 830.5, who, while engaged in the performance of his duty was intentionally killed, and the defendant knew or reasonably should have known that such victim was a peace officer engaged in the performance of his duties.

(2) The murder was willful, deliberate, and premeditated; the victim was a witness to a crime who was intentionally killed for the purpose of preventing his testimony in any criminal proceeding; and the killing was not committed during the commission or attempted commission of the crime to which he was a witness.

(3) The murder was willful, deliberate, and premeditated and was committed during the commission or attempted commission of any of the following crimes:

(i) Robbery in violation of Section 211;

(ii) Kidnapping in violation of Section 207 or 209. Brief movements of a victim which are merely incidental to the commission of another offense and which do not substantially increase the victim's risk of harm over that necessarily inherent in the other offense do not constitute a violation of Section 209 within the meaning of this paragraph.

(iii) Rape by force or violence in violation of subdivision (2) of Section 261; or by threat of great and immediate bodily harm in violation of subdivision (3) of Section 261;

(iv) The performance of a lewd or lascivious act upon the person of a child under the age of 14 years in violation of Section 288;

(v) Burglary in violation of subdivision (1) of Section 460 of an inhabited dwelling house with an intent to commit grand or petit larceny or rape.

(4) The murder was willful, deliberate, and premeditated, and involved the infliction of torture. For purposes of this section, torture requires proof of an intent to inflict extreme and prolonged pain.

(5) The defendant has in this proceeding been convicted of more than one offense of murder of the first or second degree, or has been convicted in a prior proceeding of the offense of murder of the first or second degree. For the purpose of this paragraph an offense committed in another jurisdiction which if committed in California would be punishable as first or second degree murder shall be deemed to be murder in the first or second degree.

(d) For the purposes of subdivision (c), the defendant shall be deemed to have physically aided in the act or acts causing death only if it is proved beyond a reasonable doubt that his conduct constitutes an assault or a battery upon the victim or if by word or conduct he orders, initiates, or coerces the actual killing of the victim.

(Added by Stats.1977, c. 316, p. —, § 9, urgency, eff. Aug. 11, 1977.)

Editors' Note

In 1976, the California Supreme Court, in the case of Rockwell v. Superior Court, 134 Cal.Rptr. 650 (1976), declared the predecessor of this Section to be unconstitutional. This section and sections 190.3 and 190.6 which became effective on August 11, 1977, were re-written to meet the objections of the Supreme Court. The mitigation phase of the trial as provided for in Sections 190.3 and 190.4 is the most significant change. However, you will also note that the list of special circumstances has also been expanded and changed.

Subdivision (d) of 190.2, allows for a vicarious application of the death penalty where the defendant did not personally and directly cause the death, but where he ordered, initiated, or coerced the actual killing; or if he physically aided the killing by perpetrating an assault or battery on the victim.

If A and B enter a bank and rob the bank and B shoots and kills a teller, the death penalty would be possible for B, but not for A in this case.

If A had ordered the killing, the death penalty would apply to A, likewise if A holds the victim or commits an assault or battery on the victim.

Read Rockwell v. Superior Court, 134 Cal.Rptr. 650 (1976), in table of cases, included in this text.

---

§ 190.3. Death penalty or life imprisonment; determination by trier; evidence of aggravating and mitigating circumstances; factors

If the defendant has been found guilty of murder in the first degree and a special circumstance has been charged and found to be true, or if the defendant may be subject to the death penalty after having been found guilty of violating subdivision (a) of Section 1672 of the Military and Veterans Code, or Section 37, 128, 219 or 4500 of this code, the trier of fact shall determine whether the penalty shall be death or life imprisonment without possibility of parole. In the proceedings on the question of penalty, evidence may be presented by both the people and the defendant as to any matter relevant to aggravation, mitigation, and sentence, including, but not limited to, the nature and circumstances of the present offense, the presence or absence of other criminal activity by the defendant which involved the use or attempted use of force or violence or which involved the expressed or implied threat to use force or violence, and the defendant's character, background, history, mental condition and physical condition.

However, no evidence shall be admitted regarding other criminal activity by the defendant which did not involve the use or attempted use of force or violence or which did not involve the expressed or implied threat to use force or violence. As used in this section, criminal activity does not require a conviction.

However, in no event shall evidence of prior criminal activity be admitted for an offense for which the defendant was prosecuted and was acquitted. The restriction on the use of this evidence is intended to apply only to proceedings conducted pursuant to this section and is not intended to affect statutory or decisional law allowing such evidence to be used in other proceedings.

Except for evidence in proof of the offense or special circumstances which subject a defendant to the death penalty, no evidence may be presented by the prosecution in aggravation unless notice of the evidence to be introduced has been given to the defendant within a reasonable period of time, as determined by the court, prior to the trial. Evidence may be introduced without such notice in rebuttal to evidence introduced by the defendant in mitigation.

In determining the penalty the trier of fact shall take into account any of the following factors if relevant:

(a) The circumstances of the crime of which the defendant was convicted in the present proceeding and the existence of any special circumstances found to be true pursuant to Section 190.1.

(b) The presence or absence of criminal activity by the defendant which involved the use or attempted use of force or violence or the expressed or implied threat to use force or violence.

(c) Whether or not the offense was committed while the defendant was under the influence of extreme mental or emotional disturbance.

(d) Whether or not the victim was a participant in the defendant's homicidal conduct or consented to the homicidal act.

(e) Whether or not the offense was committed under circumstances which the defendant reasonably believed to be a moral justification or extenuation for his conduct.

(f) Whether or not the defendant acted under extreme duress or under the substantial domination of another person.

§ 190.3

(g) Whether or not at the time of the offense the capacity of the defendant to appreciate the criminality of his conduct or to conform his conduct to the requirements of law was impaired as a result of mental disease or the affects of intoxication.

(h) The age of the defendant at the time of the crime.

(i) Whether or not the defendant was an accomplice to the offense and his participation in the commission of the offense was relatively minor.

(j) Any other circumstance which extenuates the gravity of the crime even though it is not a legal excuse for the crime.

After having heard and received all of the evidence, the trier of fact shall consider, take into account and be guided by the aggravating and mitigating circumstances referred to in this section, and shall determine whether the penalty shall be death or life imprisonment without the possibility of parole.

(Added by Stats.1977, c. 316, p. —, § 11, urgency, eff. Aug. 11, 1977.)

§ 190.4. Special circumstances; special findings; penalty hearing; application for modification

(a) Whenever special circumstances as enumerated in Section 190.2 are alleged and the trier of fact finds the defendant guilty of first degree murder, the trier of fact shall also make a special finding on the truth of each alleged special circumstance. The determination of the truth of any or all of the special circumstances shall be made by the trier of fact on the evidence presented at the trial or at the hearing held pursuant to subdivision (b) of Section 190.1.

In case of a reasonable doubt as to whether a special circumstance is true, the defendant is entitled to a finding that it is not true. The trier of fact shall make a special finding that each special circumstance charged is either true or not true. Wherever a special circumstance requires proof of the commission or attempted commission of a crime, such crime shall be charged and proved pursuant to the general law applying to the trial and conviction of the crime.

If the defendant was convicted by the court sitting without a jury, the trier of fact shall be a jury unless a jury is waived by the defendant and by the people, in which case the trier of fact shall be the court. If the defendant was convicted by a plea of guilty the trier of fact shall be a jury unless a jury is waived by the defendant and by the people.

If the trier of fact finds that any one or more of the special circumstances enumerated in Section 190.2 as charged is true, there shall be a separate penalty hearing, and neither the finding that any of the remaining special circumstances charged is not true, nor if the trier of fact is a jury, the inability of the jury to agree on the issue of the truth or untruth of any of the remaining special circumstances charged, shall prevent the holding of the separate penalty hearing.

In any case in which the defendant has been found guilty by a jury, and the jury has been unable to reach a unanimous verdict that one or more of the special circumstances charged are true, and does not reach a unanimous verdict that all the special circumstances charged are not true, the court shall dismiss the jury and shall order a new jury impaneled to try the issues, but the issue of guilt shall not be tried by such jury, nor shall such jury retry the issue of the truth of any of the special circumstances which were found by a unanimous verdict of the previous jury to be untrue. If such new jury is unable to reach the unanimous verdict that one or more of the special circumstances it is trying are true, the court shall dismiss the jury and impose a punishment of confinement in state prison for life.

(b) If defendant was convicted by the court sitting without a jury, the trier of fact at the penalty hearing shall be a jury unless a jury is waived by the defendant and the people, in which case the trier of fact shall be the court. If the defendant was convicted by a plea of guilty, the trier of fact shall be a jury unless a jury is waived by the defendant and the people.

If the trier of fact is a jury and has been unable to reach a unanimous verdict as to what the penalty shall be, the court shall dismiss the jury and impose a punishment of confinement in state prison for life without possibility of parole.

(c) If the trier of fact which convicted the defendant of a crime for which he may be subjected to the death penalty was a jury, the same jury shall consider any plea of not guilty by reason of insanity pursuant to Section 1026, the truth of any special circumstances which may be alleged, and the penalty to be applied, unless for good cause shown the court discharges that jury in which case a new jury shall be drawn. The court shall state facts in support of the finding of good cause upon the record and cause them to be entered into the minutes.

(d) In any case in which the defendant may be subjected to the death penalty, evidence presented at any prior phase of the trial, including any proceeding upon a plea of not guilty by reason of insanity pursuant to Section 1026, shall be considered at any subsequent phase of the trial, if the trier of fact of the prior phase is the same trier of fact at the subsequent phase.

(e) In every case in which the trier of fact has returned a verdict or finding imposing the death penalty, the defendant shall be deemed to have made an application for modification of such verdict or finding pursuant to subdivision (7) of Section 1181. In ruling on the application the judge shall review the evidence, consider, take into account, and be guided by the aggravating and mitigating circumstances referred to in Section 190.3, and shall make an independent determination as to whether the weight of the evidence supports the jury's findings and verdicts. He shall state on the record the reason for his findings.

The judge shall set forth the reasons for his ruling on the application and direct that they be entered on the Clerk's minutes.

The denial of the modification of a death penalty verdict pursuant to subdivision (7) of Section 1181 shall be reviewed on the defendant's automatic appeal pursuant to subdivision (b) of Section 1239. The granting of the application shall be reviewed on the people's appeal pursuant to paragraph (6) of subdivision (a) of Section 1238.

The proceedings provided for in this subdivision are in addition to any other proceedings on a defendant's application for a new trial.
(Added by Stats.1977, c. 316, p. ——, § 12, urgency, eff. Aug. 11, 1977.)

§ 190.5. Death penalty; exclusions; persons under 18; person not personally present at nor physically aiding in commission of act causing death; proof

(a) Notwithstanding any other provision of law, the death penalty shall not be imposed upon any person who is under the age of 18 years at the time of commission of the crime. The burden of proof as to the age of such person shall be upon the defendant.

(b) Except when the trier of fact finds that a murder was committed pursuant to an agreement as defined in subdivision (a) of Section 190.2, or when a person is convicted of a violation of subdivision (a) of Section 1672 of the Military and Veterans Code, or Section 37, 128, 4500, or subdivision (b) of Section 190.2 of this code, the death penalty shall not be imposed upon any person who was a principal in the commission of a capital offense unless he was personally present during the commission of the act or acts causing death, and intentionally physically aided or committed such act or acts causing death.

(c) For the purposes of subdivision (b), the defendant shall be deemed to have physically aided in the act or acts causing death only if it is proved beyond a reasonable doubt that his conduct constitutes an assault or a battery upon the victim or if by word or conduct he orders, initiates, or coerces the actual killing of the victim.
(Added by Stats.1977, c. 316, p. ——, § 13, urgency, eff. Aug. 11, 1977.)

§ 190.6. Legislative finding; limitations

The Legislature finds that the imposition of sentence in all capital cases should be expeditiously carried out.

Therefore, in all cases in which a sentence of death has been imposed, the appeal to the State Supreme Court must be decided and an opinion reaching the merits must be filed within 150 days of certification of the entire record by the sentencing court. In any case in which this time requirement is not met, the Chief Justice of the Supreme Court shall state on the record the extraordinary and compelling circumstances causing the delay and the facts supporting these circumstances. A failure to comply with the time requirements of this section shall not be grounds for precluding the ultimate imposition of the death penalty.
(Added by Stats.1977, c. 316, p. ——, § 14, urgency, eff. Aug. 11, 1977.)

§ 192. Manslaughter; voluntary, involuntary, and in driving a vehicle defined; construction of section

Manslaughter is the unlawful killing of a human being, without malice. It is of three kinds:

1. Voluntary—upon a sudden quarrel or heat of passion.

2. Involuntary—in the commission of an unlawful act, not amounting to felony; or in the commission of a lawful act which might produce death, in an unlawful manner, or without due caution and circumspection; provided that this subdivision shall not apply to acts committed in the driving of a vehicle.

3. In the driving of a vehicle—

§ 192 PENAL CODE

(a) In the commission of an unlawful act, not amounting to felony, with gross negligence; or in the commission of a lawful act which might produce death, in an unlawful manner, and with gross negligence.

(b) In the commission of an unlawful act, not amounting to felony, without gross negligence; or in the commission of a lawful act which might produce death, in an unlawful manner, but without gross negligence.

This section shall not be construed as making any homicide in the driving of a vehicle punishable which is not a proximate result of the commission of an unlawful act, not amounting to felony, or of the commission of a lawful act which might produce death, in an unlawful manner.
(Amended by Stats.1945, c. 1006, p. 1942, § 1.)

Editors' Note
Read People v. Hawkins in table of cases included in this text.

Notes of Decisions

"Manslaughter" is unlawful killing of human being. People v. Villalobos (1962) 25 Cal.Rptr. 111, 208 C.A.2d 321.

"Manslaughter" is a killing in an unlawful manner. People v. Jackson (1962) 20 Cal.Rptr. 592, 202 C.A.2d 179.

Voluntary manslaughter, in general

"Voluntary manslaughter" is a wilful act which is characterized by presence of an intent to kill engendered by sufficient provocation and by absence of premeditation, deliberation and, by presumption of law, malice aforethought. People v. Wynn (1968) 65 Cal.Rptr. 210, 257 C.A.2d 664. People v. Alfreds (1967) 59 Cal.Rptr. 647, 251 C.A.2d 666; People v. Miller (1966) 53 Cal.Rptr. 720, 245 C.A.2d 112, certiorari denied 88 S.Ct. 640, 389 U.S. 968, 19 L.Ed.2d 459, certiorari dismissed 88 S.Ct. 2258, 392 U.S. 616, 20 L.Ed.2d 1332; People v. Taylor (1962) 17 Cal.Rptr. 233, 197 C.A.2d 372; People v. Brubaker (1959) 346 P.2d 8, 53 C.2d 37, certiorari denied 81 S.Ct. 703, 365 U.S. 824, 5 L.Ed.2d 702; People v. Doyle (1958) 328 P.2d 7, 162 C.A.2d 158; People v. Bridgehouse (1957) 303 P.2d 1018, 47 C.2d 406; People v. Bender (1945) 163 P.2d 8, 27 C.2d 164.

Voluntary killing without malice falls within class of unlawful homicides known as manslaughter, and two types of voluntary manslaughter are referred to in statute, that is deliberate killings upon sudden quarrel or heat of passion, do not exhaust categories of offense since there is at least the further type which occurs during a period of diminished capacity. People v. Stephanson (1968) 66 Cal.Rptr. 155, 259 C.A.2d 181.

If evidence that defendant did not have specific mental state which is an element of crime with which he is charged raises a reasonable doubt in mind of trier of fact, defendant cannot be convicted. People v. Moore (1968) 65 Cal.Rptr. 450, 257 C.A.2d 740.

The specific intent required to convict of voluntary manslaughter is almost invariably an inference to be drawn by the jury from circumstantial evidence and the character of weapon and consequence of its use are relevant to trier of fact on issue of intent. People v. Welborn (1966) 51 Cal.Rptr. 644, 242 C.A.2d 668.

Nonstatutory voluntary manslaughter

"Nonstatutory voluntary manslaughter" is the intentional killing of a human being in which the defendant did not attain the mental state constituting malice because of mental illness, mental defect, or intoxication and it may be intentional, voluntary, deliberate, premeditated and unprovoked. People v. Stines (1969) 82 Cal.Rptr. 850, 2 C.A.3d 970.

Nonstatutory voluntary manslaughter differs from murder in that the element of malice is negated by showing that defendant's mental capacity has been reduced by mental illness, mental defect, or intoxication. Id.

An explicit instruction on nonstatutory manslaughter must be given when defense of diminished capacity has been asserted. People v. Welborn (1969) 82 Cal.Rptr. 845, 2 C.A.3d 715.

Involuntary manslaughter, in general

Testimony that defendant entered dwelling in state of intoxication only intending to frighten one of two girls sleeping in house and that, when he struck blows which resulted in girls' deaths, he did so without conscious intent either to strike or injure them would have permitted jury to have found defendant guilty of involuntary manslaughter. People v. Modesto (1963) 31 Cal.Rptr. 225, 382 P.2d 33, 59 C.2d 722, appeal after remand 42 Cal.Rptr. 417, 398 P.2d 753, 62 C.2d 436, appeal after remand 59 Cal.Rptr. 124, 427 P.2d 788, 66 C.2d 695, certiorari denied 88 S.Ct. 574, 389 U.S. 1009, 19 L.Ed.2d 608.

If person commits unlawful act that does not amount to a felony there must be showing that unlawful act was committed with criminal intent or criminal negligence in order for person to be guilty of crime of "involuntary manslaughter." People v. Villalobos (1962) 25 Cal.Rptr. 111, 208 C.A.2d 321.

Battery was not necessarily included in offense of involuntary manslaughter. People v. Williams (1961) 11 Cal.Rptr. 142, 189 C.A.2d 254.

"Manslaughter" is the unlawful killing of a human being without malice, and to be involuntary it must have been done in commission of an unlawful act not amounting to a felony, or in commission of a lawful act which might produce death, in an unlawful manner or without due caution or circumspection. People v. Tophia (1959) 334 P.2d 133, 167 C.A.2d 39.

Where deadly force is threatened and deadly force is used by way of self-defense, requirement of involuntary manslaughter statute that killing be in commission of lawful act which might produce death is met. Id.

Heat of passion, elements and nature of offense

In order to determine whether element of provocation had displaced element of malice aforethought and effectuated reduction of offense to manslaughter, fundamental of inquiry is whether or not defendant's reason was, at time of his act, so disturbed or obscured by some passion to such extent as would render ordinary men of average disposition liable to act rashly or without due deliberation and reflection, and from this passion rather than from judgment. People v. Morse (1969) 76 Cal.Rptr. 391, 452 P.2d 607, 70 C.2d 711.

To be sufficient to reduce a homicide to "manslaughter" the heat of passion must be such as would naturally be aroused in the mind of an ordinary, reasonable person, under the given facts and circumstances, or in the mind of a person of ordinary self-control. People v. Brunk (1968) 65 Cal.Rptr. 727, 258 C.A.2d 453.

To be sufficient to reduce homicide to manslaughter, heat of passion must be such as would naturally be aroused in minds of ordinary, reasonable person under given facts and circumstances, or in mind of person of ordinary self-control. People v. Lopez (1962) 23 Cal.Rptr. 532, 205 C.A.2d 807.

§ 193. Manslaughter; punishment

(a) Voluntary manslaughter is punishable by imprisonment in the state prison for two, four, or six years.

(b) Involuntary manslaughter is punishable by imprisonment in the state prison for two, three or four years.

(c) A violation of subsection 3 of Section 192 of this code is punishable as follows: In the case of a violation of subdivision (a) of said subsection 3 the punishment shall be either by imprisonment in the county jail for not more than one year or in the state prison, and in such case the jury may recommend by their verdict that the punishment shall be by imprisonment in the county jail; in the case of a violation of subdivision (b) of said subsection 3, the punishment shall be by imprisonment in the county jail for not more than one year. In cases where, as authorized in this section, the jury recommends by their verdict that the punishment shall be by imprisonment in the county jail, the court shall not have authority to sentence the defendant to imprisonment in the state prison, but may nevertheless place the defendant on probation as provided in this code.
(Amended by Stats.1978, c. 579, p. —, § 3.)

§ 194. Murder and manslaughter; time of death; computation

To make the killing either murder or manslaughter, it is requisite that the party die within three years and a day after the stroke received or the cause of death administered. In the computation of such time, the whole of the day on which the act was done shall be reckoned the first.
(Amended by Stats.1969, c. 593, p. 1225, § 1.)

§ 195. Excusable homicide

Excusable homicide. Homicide is excusable in the following cases:

1. When committed by accident and misfortune, in lawfully correcting a child or servant, or in doing any other lawful act by lawful means, with usual and ordinary caution, and without any unlawful intent.

2. When committed by accident and misfortune, in the heat of passion, upon any sudden and sufficient provocation, or upon a sudden combat, when no undue advantage is taken, nor any dangerous weapon used, and when the killing is not done in a cruel or unusual manner.
(Enacted 1872.)

§ 196. Justifiable homicide; public officers

Justifiable homicide by public officers. Homicide is justifiable when committed by public officers and those acting by their command in their aid and assistance, either—

1. In obedience to any judgment of a competent Court; or,

2. When necessarily committed in overcoming actual resistance to the execution of some legal process, or in the discharge of any other legal duty; or,

3. When necessarily committed in retaking felons who have been rescued or have escaped, or when necessarily committed in arresting persons charged with felony, and who are fleeing from justice or resisting such arrest.
(Enacted 1872.)

Editors' Note

The California Courts of Appeal in 1977, in two different opinions, *Kortum* and *Peterson*, changed the judicial interpretation of Penal Code § 196. In these cases, which are currently under review by the California Supreme Court, the court held that a police officer may only use deadly force when in pursuit, if the officer is pursuing someone who has perpetrated a violent felony. The court, however, did not define the term violent felony.

§ 197. Justifiable homicide; any person

Homicide is also justifiable when committed by any person in any of the following cases:

1. When resisting any attempt to murder any person, or to commit a felony, or to do some great bodily injury upon any person; or,

2. When committed in defense of habitation, property, or person, against one who manifestly intends or endeavors, by violence or surprise, to commit a felony, or against one who manifestly intends and endeavors, in a violent, riotous or tumultuous manner, to enter the habitation of another for the purpose of offering violence to any person therein; or,

3. When committed in the lawful defense of such person, or of a wife or husband, parent, child, master, mistress, or servant of such person, when there is reasonable ground to apprehend a design to commit a felony or to do some great bodily injury, and immi-

§ 197 PENAL CODE

nent danger of such design being accomplished; but such person, or the person in whose behalf the defense was made, if he was the assailant or engaged in mutual combat, must really and in good faith have endeavored to decline any further struggle before the homicide was committed; or,

4. When necessarily committed in attempting, by lawful ways and means, to apprehend any person for any felony committed, or in lawfully suppressing any riot, or in lawfully keeping and preserving the peace. (Amended by Stats.1963, c. 372, p. 1159, § 2.)

Notes of Decisions

"Justifiable homicide" connotes only the use of force which is necessary, or which reasonably appears to be necessary, to resist other party's misconduct; and use of excessive force destroys the justification. People v. Young (1963) 29 Cal.Rptr. 595, 214 C.A.2d 641.

Defendant is not without justification in killing because he might have resorted to other means to secure his safety, where peril was swift and imminent and necessity for action immediate. People v. Collins (1961) 11 Cal.Rptr. 504, 189 C.A.2d 575.

Defense of person—In general

The acts which a defendant may do and justify under plea of self-defense depend primarily upon his own conduct and secondly upon conduct of deceased. People v. Cox (1944) 153 P.2d 362, 67 C.A.2d 166; People v. Brown (1911) 114 P. 1004, 15 C.A. 393; People v. Rilarcosa (1937) 65 P.2d 1325, 19 C.A.2d 537.

One who as reasonable man is justified in believing that assailant intends to commit felony on him has right in defense of his person to use all force necessary to repel assault even to taking life of assailant, and is not bound to retreat. People v. Collins (1961) 11 Cal.Rptr. 504, 189 C.A.2d 575.

Threats alone, unaccompanied by some act which induces in defendant a reasonable belief that bodily injury is about to be inflicted, does not justify a homicide. People v. Lucas (1958) 324 P.2d 933, 160 C.A.2d 305.

The right of necessary self-defense, which will render a homicide justifiable, deals with an emergency situation in which a certain degree of elasticity is essential if defense is to be of any practical value to person assaulted. People v. Toledo (1948) 193 P.2d 953, 85 C.A.2d 570.

Duty to retreat, defense of person

Where a person seeks or induces a quarrel which leads to the necessity in his own defense of using force against his adversary, the right to stand his ground and defend himself is not immediately available to him, but instead he must first decline to carry on the affray, must honestly endeavor to escape from it, and must clearly and fairly inform his adversary of his desire for peace and of his abandonment of contest, and only then will the law justify him in thereafter standing his ground and using force upon his antagonist. People v. Moore (1954) 275 P.2d 485, 43 C.2d 517; People v. McDonnel (1949) 211 P.2d 910, 94 C.A.2d 885.

One who has sought a combat may endeavor to decline a further encounter, and, if he does so in good faith, he may justify the killing of his adversary. People v. Hecker (1895) 42 P. 307, 109 C. 451, 30 L.R.A. 403; People v. Wong Ah Teak (1883) 63 C. 544; People v. Bush (1884) 3 P. 590, 65 C. 129.

Defense of property

Trial judge's dismissal sua sponte of felony manslaughter prosecution brought against one who fatally shot person he apprehended stripping his automobile was an abuse of discretion in absence of evidence showing that shooting was either justifiable or excusable homicide and mandate issued directing setting aside of dismissal and proceeding with trial. People v. Superior Court In and For San Francisco County (1967) 57 Cal.Rptr. 892, 249 C.A.2d 714.

If defendant, a private citizen, willfully shot the person he had arrested when found trespassing upon his land, he was guilty of an offense, but if he had no intention of shooting him, but fired merely to frighten him into submission, the question of his guilt of an assault depended on the question whether he acted with criminal negligence, or according to the standard prescribed for reasonable men under such circumstances. People v. Lathrop (1920) 192 P. 722, 49 C.A. 63.

Homicide in defense of one's property is justifiable, when necessary to defeat or prevent a felonious aggression thereon. People v. Flanagan (1881) 60 C. 2, 44 Am.R. 52, 7 P.C.L.J. 675.

Assault, particular justifiable homicides

Defendant, who had been attacked with a knife and club by one partially intoxicated and quarrelsome, was not required to retreat, since no duty to retreat is imposed on one who is without fault exposed to a sudden, felonious attack, and though the killing, to be excusable, must be under absolute necessity, actual or apparent, such a condition exists as a matter of law when an innocent person is placed in sudden jeopardy. People v. Estrada (1923) 213 P. 67, 60 C.A. 477.

Where defendant, assaulted and beaten in own home by deceased, whom he ordered to leave, and told he would kill if he attempted to return, was entitled to stand his ground and slay deceased, who seized deadly weapon and turned with manner and language indicating intention to slay or seriously injure defendant. People v. McDonnell (1917) 163 P. 1046, 32 C.A. 694.

§ 198. Justifiable homicide; sufficiency of fear

Bare fear not to justify killing. A bare fear of the commission of any of the offenses mentioned in Subdivisions 2 and 3 of the preceding section, to prevent which homicide may be lawfully committed, is not sufficient to justify it. But the circumstances must be sufficient to excite the fears of a reasonable person, and the party killing must have acted under the influence of such fears alone.
(Enacted 1872.)

Notes of Decisions

Grounds and cause of belief

If appearances are such as to justify a reasonable man in believing that it is necessary to instantly kill another in order to save himself from death or great bodily harm, and he does so believe, he is not required to exercise any due care or circumspection as to the manner of killing. People v. Hatchett (1944) 146 P.2d 469, 63 C.A.2d 144; People v. Thomson (1905) 79 P. 435, 145 C. 717.

In homicide prosecution, wherein defendant claimed that killing was justified, defendant was entitled to corroborate his testimony that he was in fear for his life by proving reasonableness of such fear. People v. Davis (1965) 47 Cal.Rptr. 801, 408 P.2d 129, 63 C.2d 648.

If the person who is attacked knows there is no intent to do great bodily harm, then the killing of the one attacking is not justified. People v. Armstrong (1951) 235 P.2d 242, 106 C.A.2d 490.

Necessity for taking life

One who as reasonable man is justified in believing that assailant intends to commit felony on him has right in defense of his person to use all force necessary to repel assault even to taking life of assailant, and is not bound to retreat. People v. Collins (1961) 11 Cal.Rptr. 504, 189 C.A.2d 575.

Defendant is not without justification in killing because he might have resorted to other means to secure his safety, where peril was swift and imminent and necessity for action immediate. Id.

To justify killing in self-defense it must not only appear to accused as reasonable man that he had reason to believe and did believe that he was in danger of his life or of receiving great bodily harm, but it must also appear to his comprehension, as reasonable man, that to avoid such danger it was absolutely necessary to take life of deceased. People v. Orosco (1925) 239 P. 82, 73 C.A. 580.

§ 199. Justifiable and excusable homicide; discharge of defendant

Justifiable and excusable homicide not punishable. The homicide appearing to be justifiable or excusable, the person indicted must, upon his trial, be fully acquitted and discharged.

(Enacted 1872.)

§ 203. Definition

Every person who unlawfully and maliciously deprives a human being of a member of his body, or disables, disfigures, or renders it useless, or cuts or disables the tongue, or puts out an eye, or slits the nose, ear, or lip, is guilty of mayhem.

(Amended by Code Am.1873–74, c. 614, p. 427, § 17.)

§ 204. Punishment

Mayhem is punishable by imprisonment in the state prison for two, four, or six years.

(Amended by Stats.1978, c. 579, p. —, § 4.)

§ 207. Definition

Every person who forcibly steals, takes, or arrests any person in this state, and carries him into another country, state, or county, or into another part of the same county, or who forcibly takes or arrests any person, with a design to take him out of this state, without having established a claim, according to the laws of the United States, or of this state, or who hires, persuades, entices, decoys, or seduces by false promises, misrepresentations, or the like, any person to go out of this state, or to be taken or removed therefrom, for the purpose and with the intent to sell such person into slavery or involuntary servitude, or otherwise to employ him for his own use, or to the use of another, without the free will and consent of such persuaded person; and every person who, being out of this state, abducts or takes by force or fraud any person contrary to the law of the place where such act is committed, and brings, sends, or conveys such person within the limits of this state, and is afterwards found within the limits thereof, is guilty of kidnaping.

(Amended by Stats.1905, c. 493, p. 653, § 1.)

Editors' Note

Read People v. Lauresen, 8 Cal.3d 192, 104 Cal.Rptr. 425 (1972); in Table of Cases included in this text.

Notes of Decisions

Violation of this section defining kidnapping can occur in absence of an "associated crime." In re Earley (1975) 120 Cal.Rptr. 881, 534 P.2d 721, 14 C.3d 122.

Where the movements of victim are slight or insubstantial they cannot constitute kidnapping. People v. Brown (1974) 114 Cal.Rptr. 426, 523 P.2d 226, 11 C.3d 784.

The determining factor in the crime of kidnapping is the actual distance of the victim's movements; the minimum movements necessary for the commission of the crime are present where the victim is forcibly taken into another part of the same county. People v. Stanworth (1974) 114 Cal.Rptr. 250, 522 P.2d 1058, 11 C.3d 588.

An aggravated kidnapping conviction is improper where movement of victim is merely incidental to commission of offense otherwise involved and where movement of victim does not substantially increase risk of harm to him over and above that necessarily present in underlying crime itself. People v. Stephenson (1974) 111 Cal.Rptr. 556, 517 P.2d 820, 10 C.3d 652.

Movement of victim from house where victim's mother was sleeping to a point 200 feet away on beach underneath pier was substantial in character rather than trivial, and thus supported simple kidnapping conviction, notwithstanding contention that movement was merely incidental to sex acts for which defendant was also charged. People v. Stender (1975) 121 Cal.Rptr. 334, 47 C.A.3d 413.

Where defendant forced victims at gunpoint to walk for distance of one-quarter of a mile, such a distance was not "slight" or "insubstantial" and defendant was guilty of kidnapping the victims although his intent from the start was to rape and murder the victims. People v. Stanworth (1974) 114 Cal.Rptr. 250, 522 P.2d 1058, 11 C.3d 588.

Where defendant forcibly took victim through Richmond, onto a freeway and then to a parking lot in Berkeley, the movements of the victim in her vehicle were more than "trivial" and the forcible movements constituted "kidnapping" although accomplished for the purpose of commission of offense of rape. Id.

Movement is forcible within this section where it is accomplished through giving of orders which victim feels compelled to obey because he or she fears harm or injury from accused and such apprehension is not unreasonable under circumstances. People v. Stephenson (1974) 111 Cal.Rptr. 556, 517 P.2d 820, 10 C.3d 652.

There need not be an underlying crime before violation of kidnapping statute can be found to occur; although an underlying crime may preclude a conviction of either aggravated or simple kidnapping, forcible movement against will of person capable of giving consent constitutes simple kidnapping. People v. Apo (1972) 102 Cal.Rptr. 242, 25 C.A.3d 790.

Asportation of victim a distance of miles not only subjected her to greater risk of harm than that normally incident to crimes of rape and robbery but subjected her to the actuality of greater harm in form of five hours of confinement during which she suffered bestial attacks perpetrated by defendant and others with attendant mental and physical trauma, and thus constituted kidnapping. People v. Hunter (1971) 97 Cal.Rptr. 29, 19 C.A.3d 336.

§ 208. Punishment

Kidnapping is punishable by imprisonment in the state prison for three, five or seven years.
(Amended by Stats.1978, c. 579, p. ——, § 5.)

§ 209. Punishment; kidnapping for ransom, or to commit extortion or robbery

(a) Any person who seizes, confines, inveigles, entices, decoys, abducts, conceals, kidnaps or carries away any individual by any means whatsoever with intent to hold or detain, or who holds or detains, such individual for ransom, reward or to commit extortion or to exact from relatives or friends of such person any money or valuable thing, or any person who aids or abets any such act, is guilty of a felony and upon conviction thereof shall be punished by imprisonment in the state prison for life without possibility of parole in cases in which any person subjected to any such act suffers death or bodily harm, or shall be punished by imprisonment in the state prison for life with the possibility of parole in cases where no such person suffers death or bodily harm.

(b) Any person who kidnaps or carries away any individual to commit robbery shall be punished by imprisonment in the state prison for life with possibility of parole.
(Amended by Stats.1977, c. 316, p. ——, § 15.)

Editors' Note

Read People v. Laursen in table of cases included in this text.

Notes of Decisions

Bodily harm sufficient to sustain conviction of kidnapping for robbery with bodily harm must either be directly inflicted by kidnapper, or must be proximate result, the reasonably foreseeable consequence, of kidnapper's intentional acts. People v. Isitt (1976) 127 Cal.Rptr. 279, 55 C.A.3d 23.

Under this section establishing life imprisonment, without possibility of parole, as punishment for kidnapping for purpose of ransom or robbery, if victim suffers bodily harm, trivial or insubstantial bodily harm incidental to all forcible kidnapping does not evoke aggravated penalty of parole deprivation; only a substantial injury does so. In re Maston (1973) 109 Cal.Rptr. 164, 33 C.A.3d 559.

Cuts on arm and toe, superficial abrasions, facial bruises, and a four-inch knee laceration requiring stitches to close suffered by kidnapping victim in automobile collision which occurred while kidnapper was attempting to avoid apprehension constituted "bodily harm" within this section. People v. Dacy (1970) 85 Cal.Rptr. 57, 5 C.A.3d 216.

Purpose of this section proscribing kidnapping to commit robbery is to impose harsher criminal sanctions than are generally included for robbery to deter the carrying away of persons during the commission of a robbery in a manner which substantially increases the risk that someone will suffer grave bodily or psychic injury, or death. People v. Laursen (1972) 104 Cal.Rptr. 425, 501 P.2d 1145, 8 C.3d 192, appeal dismissed, certiorari denied 93 S.Ct. 2738, 412 U.S. 915, 37 L.Ed.2d 142.

True test in each case, in determining whether defendant's movement of victim, in connection with another offense, constitutes kidnapping is not mere mileage but whether movements substantially increase risk of harm beyond that inherent in crime itself. People v. Timmons (1971) 93 Cal.Rptr. 736, 482 P.2d 648, 4 C.3d 411.

Decision giving new interpretation to amendment of this section applied in favor of defendants convicted under this section after amendment but before decision, since what they did was not proscribed by this section. People v. Mutch (1971) 93 Cal.Rptr. 721, 482 P.2d 633, 4 C.3d 389.

Forcing service station attendant to lie down behind a truck parked on station premises 20 to 30 feet away did not substantially increase risk of harm to attendant over and above that normally present in crimes of robbery and assault, and did not constitute "kidnapping" for purpose of robbery. In re Crumpton (1973) 106 Cal.Rptr. 770, 507 P.2d 74, 9 C.3d 463.

Although movements of victims present in store during robbery and who were taken upstairs and tied were purely incidental to crime of robbery and would not support kidnapping convictions, movements of victim who was removed from store, forced into automobile and compelled to drive two to three miles before being cast out of his automobile, accompanied by prisoner's threats to kill victim if police were called, would support kidnapping conviction. Bryant v. Craven (1971) 97 Cal.Rptr. 40, 19 C.A.3d 933.

Defendant, who forced two separate motorists to drive him in their automobiles following his automobile accident, and who stole first motorist's wallet and wanted second motorist's purse, could not be convicted of kidnapping for purpose of robbery or simple kidnapping, as lesser offense included within charge of kidnapping for purpose of robbery, absent showing that defendant's asportation of motorists was not merely incidental to commission of robbery or that it substantially increased risk of harm over and above that necessarily present in crime of robbery itself. People v. Lobaugh (1971) 95 Cal.Rptr. 547, 18 C.A.3d 75.

§ 210. Extortion by posing as kidnapper or by claiming ability to obtain release of victim; punishment; exception

Every person who for the purpose of obtaining any ransom or reward, or to extort or exact from any person any money or thing of value, poses as, or in any manner represents himself to be a person who has seized, confined, inveigled, enticed, decoyed, abducted, concealed, kidnapped or carried away any person, or who poses as, or in any manner represents himself to be a person who holds or detains such person, or who poses as, or in any manner represents himself to be a person who has aided or abetted any such act, or who poses as or in any manner represents himself to be a person who has the influence, power, or ability, to obtain the release of such person so seized, confined, inveigled, enticed, decoyed, abducted, concealed, kidnapped or carried away, is guilty of a felony and upon conviction thereof shall be punished by imprisonment for two, three or four years.

Nothing in this section prohibits any person who, in good faith believes that he can rescue any person who has been seized, confined, inveigled, enticed, decoyed, abducted, concealed, kidnapped or carried away, and who has had no part in, or connection with, such confinement, inveigling, decoying, abducting, concealing, kidnapping, or carrying away, from offering to rescue or obtain the release of such person for a monetary consideration or other thing of value. (Amended by Stats.1976, c. 1139, p. —, § 137, operative July 1, 1977.)

§ 211. Definition

Robbery defined. Robbery is the felonious taking of personal property in the possession of another, from his person or immediate presence, and against his will, accomplished by means of force or fear. (Enacted 1872.)

Editors' Note

Read People v. Laursen in table of cases included in this text.

Notes of Decisions

Prosecution was required to prove specific intent to commit robbery in order to obtain conviction for first-degree robbery. People v. Crawford (1967) 61 Cal.Rptr. 472, 253 C.A.2d 524, certiorari denied 88 S.Ct. 1254, 390 U.S. 1006, 20 L.Ed.2d 108.

A necessary criminal element in the crime of robbery is the existence in the mind of the perpetrator of the specific intent to permanently deprive an owner of his property, and unless such intent exists that crime is not committed. People v. Deatherage (1967) 57 Cal.Rptr. 501, 249 C.A.2d 363.

Felonious intent requisite to robbery is same intent common to offenses constituting theft. People v. Butler (1967) 55 Cal.Rptr. 511, 421 P.2d 703, 65 C.2d 569.

Prosecution does not have to prove that gun was loaded or was real to obtain first-degree robbery conviction; any pistol, even a short one, may be "dangerous" within this section in view of possibility of using the pistol as a bludgeon. People v. Aranda (1965) 47 Cal.Rptr. 353, 407 P.2d 265, 63 C.2d 518.

Defendant, who had kidnapped and raped victim and, after she asked for her purse, picked it up and removed money from it, had taken the money from her "immediate presence" within second-degree robbery statute and had accomplished the taking by means of force or fear, in view of her testimony that she was "scared". People v. Fields (1961) 12 Cal.Rptr. 249, 190 C.A.2d 515.

In robbery prosecution, the amount and value of an item of personal property is immaterial, since robbery does not depend upon the value of the property taken, and, the other elements being present, the crime is made out even though the property taken be of slight value. People v. Simmons (1946) 172 P.2d 18, 28 C.2d 699; People v. Thomas (1941) 113 P.2d 706, 45 C.A.2d 128.

Evidence established that defendant who was positively identified by off-duty policeman was lookout during course of robbery and was principal in robbery. People v. Johns (1967) 64 Cal.Rptr. 899, 257 C.A.2d 429.

The crime of robbery is not confined to act of taking property from victims; nature of crime is such that robber's escape with his loot is just as important to execution of crime as obtaining possession of loot in the first place; thus the crime of robbery is not complete until robber has won his way to place of temporary safety. People v. Carroll (1970) 83 Cal.Rptr. 176, 463 P.2d 400, 1 C.3d 581.

There is robbery if defendant, by means of force or fear, takes man's wallet and, after finding it to be empty, casts it aside. People v. Graham (1969) 78 Cal.Rptr. 217, 455 P.2d 53, 71 C.2d 303.

Since it was necessary for defendant, after disarming victim, to take victim's loaded gun in order to make good his escape, defendant's getaway from scene with victim's gun was a continuation of victim's holdup, and defendant was armed with a loaded gun at time of commission of robbery within meaning of section 211a even if defendant had used his own allegedly unloaded gun in commission of the crime. People v. Rostamo (1967) 58 Cal.Rptr. 74, 249 C.A.2d 983.

In prosecution for robbery, no motive need be shown. People v. Ottenstror (1954) 273 P.2d 289, 127 C.A.2d 104.

A straight razor is a "dangerous or deadly weapon" within meaning of this section, defining first degree robbery. People v. Jones (1963) 27 Cal.Rptr. 429, 211 C.A.2d 63, certiorari denied 84 S.Ct. 100, 375 U.S. 847, 11 L.Ed.2d 74.

Brick, which defendant used to strike robbery victim on head, was "dangerous and deadly weapon. People v. Walker (1962) 17 Cal. Rptr. 896, 198 C.A.2d 387.

A revolver, even if unloaded and not operable, is a "dangerous or deadly weapon" within this section proscribing robbery perpetrated while armed with a dangerous or deadly weapon. People v. Torres (1971) 97 Cal.Rptr. 139, 19 C.A.3d 724.

§ 211a. Robbery of operator of motor vehicle, streetcar, or trackless trolley; punishment

The robbery of any person who is performing his duties as operator of any motor vehicle, streetcar, or trackless trolley used for the transportation of persons for hire, is punishable by imprisonment in the state prison for three, four, or six years. (Amended by Stats.1978, c. 579, p. —, § 6.)

§ 212. Fear defined

The fear mentioned in Section 211 may be either:

1. The fear of an unlawful injury to the person or property of the person robbed, or of any relative of his or member of his family; or,

§ 212

2. The fear of an immediate and unlawful injury to the person or property of anyone in the company of the person robbed at the time of the robbery.
(Amended by Stats.1963, c. 372, p. 1160, § 3.)

Notes of Decisions

In robbery prosecution, the people were not "bound" by store clerk's testimony that he was not in fear, where there was other evidence to support conclusion that he acted in fear and would not have disgorged proceeds of his employer's till except in fear of harm which might come to him or his employer if he failed to comply with defendant's demands. People v. Renteria (1964) 39 Cal.Rptr. 213, 393 P.2d 413, 61 C.2d 479.

In robbery prosecution, evidence of victim's fear for her own safety or that of companions was sufficient to sustain conviction. People v. De Georgio (1960) 8 Cal.Rptr. 295, 185 C.A.2d 413.

§ 213. Punishment

Except as provided in Section 211a, robbery is punishable by imprisonment in the state prison for two, three, or five years.

Notwithstanding Section 664, attempted robbery is punishable by imprisonment in the state prison.
(Amended by Stats.1978, c. 579, p. ——, § 7.)

§ 214. Train robbery; acts with intention of committing

Every person who goes upon or boards any railroad train, car or engine, with the intention of robbing any passenger or other person on such train, car or engine, of any personal property thereon in the possession or care or under the control of any such passenger or other person, or who interferes in any manner with any switch, rail, sleeper, viaduct, culvert, embankment, structure or appliance pertaining to or connected with any railroad, or places any dynamite or other explosive substance or material upon or near the track of any railroad, or who sets fire to any railroad bridge or trestle, or who shows, masks, extinguishes or alters any light or other signal, or exhibits or compels any other person to exhibit any false light or signal, or who stops any such train, car or engine, or slackens the speed thereof, or who compels or attempts to compel any person in charge or control thereof to stop any such train, car or engine, or slacken the speed thereof, with the intention of robbing any passenger or other person on such train, car or engine, of any personal property thereon in the possession or charge or under the control of any such passenger or other person, is guilty of a felony.
(Added by Stats.1905, c. 494, p. 653, § 1.)

§ 216. Administering poison; intent; punishment

Every person who, with intent to kill, administers, or causes or procures to be administered, to another, any poison or other noxious or destructive substance or liquid, but by which death is not caused, is punishable by imprisonment in the state prison for two, four, or six years.
(Amended by Stats.1978, c. 579, p. ——, § 8.)

§ 217. Assault with intent to murder; punishment

Every person who assaults another with intent to commit murder, is punishable by imprisonment in the state prison for two, four, or six years.
(Amended by Stats.1978, c. 579, p. ——, § 9.)

§ 217.1. Executive and judicial officers

Every person who attempts to kill, or who commits any assault upon the President or Vice President of the United States, the Governor of any state or territory, any United States justice or judge, or the secretary of any of the executive departments of the United States, is guilty of a felony and is punishable by imprisonment in the state prison for three, five, or seven years.
(Amended by Stats.1978, c. 579, p. ——, § 10.)

Notes of Decisions

Nature of the assault, especially the nature and use of the weapon, seriousness and location of the wound, and the likely consequences are among the circumstances that may support a finding that an assault was made with intent to murder. People v. Dorsey (1969) 75 Cal.Rptr. 658; People v. Dick (1968) 66 Cal.Rptr. 891, 260 C.A.2d 369; People v. Williams (1967) 59 Cal.Rptr. 905, 252 C.A.2d 147.

Where attack is made on person of another with deadly weapon in such manner, coupled with threat to kill, that it leaves no reasonable doubt that perpetrator intended to murder his victim, perpetrator has committed crime of assault with intent to commit murder and has also committed crime of attempt to murder. People v. Meriweather (1968) 69 Cal.Rptr. 880, 263 C.A.2d 559.

Although assault with a deadly weapon with intent to commit murder requires a specific intent to kill, the murder which defendant must intend need not show premeditation. People v. Sartain (1968) 73 Cal.Rptr. 799, 268 C.A.2d 486.

Intent

The specific intent to kill is an essential ingredient of the offense of assault with intent to murder. People v. Stephens (1916) 157 P. 572, 29 C.A. 616; People v. Mendenhall (1902) 67 P. 325, 135 C. 344; People v. Kafoury (1911) 117 P. 938, 16 C.A. 718.

That defendant charged with assault with intent to murder did not follow up assault to make certain that the victim would die did not conclusively disprove an earlier intent to kill. People v. Dorsey (1969) 75 Cal.Rptr. 658, 270 C.A.2d 423.

Although assault with a deadly weapon with intent to commit murder requires a specific intent to kill, the murder which defendant must intend need not show premeditation. People v. Sartain (1968) 73 Cal.Rptr. 799, 268 C.A.2d 486.

Court's finding that defendant did not have specific intent to commit attempted murder was not inconsistent with court's findings that he did conceive specific intent to commit two armed robberies. People v. Wilson (1968) 67 Cal.Rptr. 678, 261 C.A.2d 12.

Overt acts, elements of offense

Unprovoked assault accompanying an attempt to collect a debt constitutes crime of assault, or if deadly weapon is used, assault with deadly weapon. People v. Butler (1967) 55 Cal.Rptr. 511, 421 P.2d 703, 65 C.2d 569.

After preparation for commission of crime of murder, if defendant performs acts which amount to commencement of accomplishment of intended offense, such acts constitute overt acts sufficient to meet requirement that a direct ineffectual act be done toward commission of murder to constitute crime of attempted murder. People v. Parrish (1948) 197 P.2d 804, 87 C.A.2d 853.

To establish an assault with intent to murder, it is not essential that the person assaulted should have been desperately or even seriously wounded to show murderous intent, and such intent is shown by proof of an assault with a large knife and the infliction of wounds, indicating that the knife used was of a deadly character, and that a more dangerous injury did not result because of the struggles of the person assaulted. People v. Martinez (1911) 120 P. 786, 17 C.A. 579.

For conviction for assault with intent to commit rape, prosecution must prove the assault and an intent on part of defendant to use whatever force is required to complete the sexual act against the will of the victim. People v. Puckett (1975) 118 Cal.Rptr. 884, 44 C.A.3d 607.

Striking of customer who entered pharmacy while robbery was in progress was within legislative purpose effected by this section providing for punishment of person who assaults another with intent to commit robbery. People v. Green (1969) 83 Cal.Rptr. 491, 3 C.A.3d 240.

Proof that defendant committed acts constituting an assault and, in committing such acts, was motivated by intent to commit rape is essential to conviction for assault with intent to commit rape. People v. Green (1960) 4 Cal.Rptr. 304, 180 C.A.2d 537.

The crime of assault with intent to commit rape is committed if defendant intended to have sexual intercourse with his victim and to use force to overcome her resistance, and crime is complete if, at any moment during assault, the accused intends to have carnal knowledge of his victim and to use, for that purpose, whatever force may be required. People v. House (1958) 320 P.2d 542, 157 C.A.2d 151.

If defendant intends to have sexual intercourse with his victim, and to use force to overcome her resistance, assault with intent to commit rape is committed. People v. Frye (1953) 255 P.2d 105, 117 C.A.2d 101; People v. Nye (1951) 237 P.2d 1, 38 C.2d 34.

Evidence in prosecution for assault with intent to commit rape justified jury in finding that defendant was the person who committed the offense. People v. Clifton (1967) 56 Cal.Rptr. 74, 248 C.A.2d 126, appeal after remand 76 Cal.Rptr. 193, 270 C.A.2d 860.

Crime of assault with intent to commit rape is complete if at any moment during assault defendant intends to have carnal knowledge of victim and to use for that purpose whatever force may be required, and hence fact that defendant desisted is immaterial. People v. Lutes (1947) 179 P.2d 815, 79 C.A.2d 233; People v. Harshaw (1946) 161 P.2d 978, 71 C.A.2d 146.

Assault with intent to rape is established by proof that defendant intended to have sexual intercourse with his victim and to use force to overcome her resistance. People v. Peckham (1967) 57 Cal.Rptr. 922, 249 C.A.2d 941.

To support conviction for crime of assault with intent to commit rape, prosecution must prove the assault and an intent on part of defendant to use whatever force is required to complete the sexual act against the will of the victim; it is the state of mind of the defendant, not of the victim, which is in issue. People v. Roth (1964) 39 Cal.Rptr. 582, 228 C.A.2d 522.

§ 218. Train wrecking; attempt; punishment

Every person who unlawfully throws out a switch, removes a rail, or places any obstruction on any railroad with the intention of derailing any passenger, freight or other train, car or engine, or who unlawfully places any dynamite or other explosive material or any other obstruction upon or near the track of any railroad with the intention of blowing up or derailing any such train, car or engine, or who unlawfully sets fire to any railroad bridge or trestle, over which any such train, car or engine must pass with the intention of wrecking such train, car or engine, is guilty of a felony, and shall be punished by imprisonment in the state prison for life without possibility of parole.
(Amended by Stats.1976, c. 1139, p. —, § 141.5, operative July 1, 1977.)

§ 219. Train derailing or wrecking; punishment

Every person who unlawfully throws out a switch, removes a rail, or places any obstruction on any railroad with the intention of derailing any passenger, freight or other train, car or engine and thus derails the same, or who unlawfully places any dynamite or other explosive material or any other obstruction upon or near the track of any railroad with the intention of blowing up or derailing any such train, car or engine and thus blows up or derails the same, or who unlawfully sets fire to any railroad bridge or trestle over which any such train, car or engine must pass with the intention of wrecking such train, car or engine, and thus wrecks the same, is guilty of a felony and punishable with death or imprisonment in the state prison for life without possibility of parole in cases where any person suffers death as a proximate result thereof, or imprisonment in the state prison for life with the possibility of parole, in cases where no person suffers death as a proximate result thereof. The penalty shall be determined pursuant to Sections 190.3 and 190.4.
(Amended by Stats.1977, c. 316, p. —, § 16.)

§ 219.1. Throwing missiles at common carrier vehicles with intent to wreck or do bodily harm; punishment

Every person who unlawfully throws, hurls or projects at a vehicle operated by a common carrier,

§ 219.1

while such vehicle is either in motion or stationary, any rock, stone, brick, bottle, piece of wood or metal or any other missile of any kind or character, or does any unlawful act, with the intention of wrecking such vehicle and doing bodily harm, and thus wrecks the same and causes bodily harm, is guilty of a felony and punishable by imprisonment in the state prison for two, four, or six years.
(Amended by Stats.1978, c. 579, p. ——, § 11.)

§ 220. Assault with intent to commit rape, sodomy, mayhem or robbery; punishment

Every person who assaults another with intent to commit rape, sodomy, or mayhem is punishable by imprisonment in the state prison for two, four, or six years.
(Amended by Stats.1978, c. 579, p. ——, § 12.)

§ 221. Assault to commit other felony; punishment

Every person who is guilty of an assault, with intent to commit any felony, except an assault with intent to commit murder, the punishment for which assault is not prescribed by the preceding section, is punishable by imprisonment in the state prison, or in a county jail not exceeding one year, or by fine not exceeding one thousand dollars ($1,000), or by both.
(Amended by Stats.1976, c. 1125, p. ——, § 15; Stats.1976, c. 1139, p. ——, § 145.5, operative July 1, 1977.)

§ 222. Administering stupefying drugs to assist in commission of felony

Administering stupefying drugs. Every person guilty of administering to another any chloroform, ether, laudanum, or other narcotic, anaesthetic, or intoxicating agent, with intent thereby to enable or assist himself or any other person to commit a felony, is guilty of felony.
(Enacted 1872.)

§ 236. Definition

False imprisonment defined. False imprisonment is the unlawful violation of the personal liberty of another.
(Enacted 1872.)

§ 237. Punishment

False imprisonment is punishable by fine not exceeding five hundred dollars ($500), or by imprisonment in the county jail not more than one year, or by both. If such false imprisonment be effected by violence, menace, fraud, or deceit, it shall be punishable by imprisonment in the state prison.
(Amended by Stats.1976, c. 1139, p. ——, § 148, operative July 1, 1977.)

§ 240. Assault defined

Assault defined. An assault is an unlawful attempt, coupled with a present ability, to commit a violent injury on the person of another.
(Enacted 1872.)

Notes of Decisions

Though pointing unloaded shotgun does not constitute "present ability" to commit violent injury on person of another, nor does threatening to shoot someone with toy gun or candy pistol, automatic rifle does present such "present ability" when there are loaded cartridges in magazine of rifle even though firing chamber is empty; only instantaneous transfer is necessary. People v. Ranson (1974) 114 Cal.Rptr. 874, 40 C.A.3d 317.

To constitute assault, there must be physical means to accomplish an injury. People v. Pena (1972) 101 Cal.Rptr. 804, 25 C.A.3d 414.

"Assault" within section 220 providing for punishment of every person who assaults another with intent to rape does not mean that defendant must have the ability to commit the crime attempted, in view of statutory definition of assault under this section as an unlawful attempt, coupled with present ability, to commit violent injury on the person of another. People v. Peckham (1967) 57 Cal.Rptr. 922, 249 C.A.2d 941.

An "assault" is an unlawful attempt coupled with a present ability to commit a violent injury on the person of another, and the intent may be inferred from the doing of the wrongful act. People v. Roshid (1961) 12 Cal.Rptr. 794, 191 C.A.2d 692.

Threatening to shoot another with toy gun does not constitute assault because there is no ability to commit violence or any injury with it on person of another. People v. Vaiza (1966) 52 Cal.Rptr. 733, 244 C.A.2d 121.

Under this section, defining assault, word "violent" is not synonymous with "bodily harm", but includes any wrongful act committed by means of physical force against person of another, and is synonymous with "physical force", the kind of physical force being immaterial. People v. Whalen (1954) 269 P.2d 181, 124 C.A.2d 713; People v. McCoy (1944) 153 P.2d 315, 25 C.2d 177; People v. Bumbaugh (1941) 120 P.2d 703, 48 C.A.2d 791.

Assault and battery are not synonymous terms, and an "assault" is an attempt to strike, while a "battery" is the successful attempt. People v. McCaffrey (1953) 258 P.2d 557, 118 C.A.2d 611.

§ 241. Assault; punishment

An assault is punishable by fine not exceeding five hundred dollars ($500), or by imprisonment in the county jail not exceeding six months, or by both. When it is committed against the person of a peace officer or fireman, and the person committing the offense knows or reasonably should know that such victim is a peace officer or fireman engaged in the performance of his duties, and such peace officer or fireman is engaged in the performance of his duties, the offense shall be punished by imprisonment in the county jail not exceeding one year or by imprisonment in the state prison.

As used in this section, "peace officer" refers to any person designated as a peace officer by Section 830.1, by subdivisions (a) to (e), inclusive, of Section 830.2, Section 830.5, or by subdivision (a) of Section 830.6, as well as any policeman of the San Francisco Port Commission and each deputized law enforcement member of the Wildlife Protection Branch of the Department of Fish and Game.
(Amended by Stats.1976, c. 420, p. —, § 1; Stats.1976, c. 1126, p. —, § 1; Stats.1976, c. 1138, p. —, § 1; Stats.1976, c. 1139, p. —, § 149.2, operative July 1, 1977.)

§ 242. Battery defined

Battery defined. A battery is any willful and unlawful use of force or violence upon the person of another.
(Enacted 1872.)

Notes of Decisions

Municipal police officer who was at fairgrounds during political rally pursuant to mutual assistance agreement with sheriff's department and who was assigned to a sheriff's marked unit patrolling grounds when he arrived was authorized under office of sheriff's department to perform peace officer's duties on fairgrounds at time he was struck by a rock thrown by defendant and corpus delicti of charged battery on a police officer was therefore proved. People v. Blake (1971) 98 Cal.Rptr. 409, 21 C.A.3d 211.

Barefooted defendant's kicking of police officer in shins constituted a battery upon a peace officer even though the officer was not harmed and his shins were protected by motorcycle boots. People v. Martinez (1970) 83 Cal.Rptr. 914, 3 C.A.3d 886.

Evidence sustained simple battery conviction of defendant who, when police officer verbally identified himself and told her she was under arrest for shoplifting and that he was going to handcuff her, kicked police officer and scratched him. People v. Madison (1970) 84 Cal.Rptr. 71, 3 C.A.3d 984.

A "battery" is simply a consummated assault. People v. Glover (1967) 65 Cal.Rptr. 219, 257 C.A.2d 502.

Assault and battery are not synonymous terms, and an "assault" is an attempt to strike, while a "battery" is the successful attempt. People v. McCaffrey (1953) 258 P.2d 557, 118 C.A.2d 611.

A battery cannot be committed without assaulting the victim but an assault can occur without committing a battery. Id.

"Battery" includes and implies an assault, and there can be no battery without an "assault". People v. Mendoza (1943) 131 P.2d 622, 55 C.A.2d 625.

The only legal justification of battery is self defense. People v. Mayes (1968) 68 Cal.Rptr. 476, 262 C.A.2d 195.

Acts constituting battery

Where defendant, in order to protect himself from person advancing upon him, pulled out loaded gun which he used as a club, defendant upon pulling out gun had the "present ability" to commit a violent injury on person within § 240 and when defendant used butt of gun to strike advancing person, a wrongful act committed by means of physical force against person of another occurred within this section. People v. Tophia (1959) 334 P.2d 133, 167 C.A.2d 39.

If a nine year old boy throws a rock at an eight year old girl and inadvertently strikes another eight year old girl, he is liable under doctrine of transferred intent for the battery on the second girl. Singer v. Marx (1956) 301 P.2d 440, 144 C.A.2d 637.

One making unprovoked assault on another by knocking him unconscious with blow of fist to jaw, causing him to fall and strike his head on rail of railway track, was guilty of battery, though victim did not sustain great bodily injury, as required to warrant conviction of assault by means of force likely to produce such injury. People v. Fuentes (1946) 169 P.2d 391, 74 C.A.2d 737.

§ 243. Battery; punishment

A battery is punishable by fine of not exceeding one thousand dollars ($1,000), or by imprisonment in the county jail not exceeding six months, or by both. When it is committed against the person of a peace officer or fireman, and the person committing the offense knows or reasonably should know that such victim is a peace officer or fireman engaged in the performance of his duties, and such peace officer or fireman is engaged in the performance of his duties, the offense shall be punished by imprisonment in the county jail not exceeding one year or by imprisonment in the state prison. When it is committed against a person and serious bodily injury is inflicted on such person, the offense shall be punished by imprisonment in the county jail for a period of not more than one year or imprisonment in the state prison for two, three, or four years.

As used in this section, "peace officer" refers to any person designated as a peace officer by Section 830.1, by subdivisions (a) to (e), inclusive, of Section 830.2, Section 830.5, or by subdivision (a) of Section 830.6, as well as any policeman of the San Francisco Port Commission and each deputized law enforcement member of the Wildlife Protection Branch of the Department of Fish and Game.

As used in this section, "serious bodily injury" means a serious impairment of physical condition, including, but not limited to, the following: loss of consciousness; concussion; bone fracture; protracted loss or impairment of function of any bodily member or organ; a wound requiring extensive suturing; and serious disfigurement.
(Amended by Stats.1976, c. 420, p. —, § 2; Stats.1976, c. 1126, p. —, § 3; Stats.1976, c. 1138, p. —, § 3; Stats.1976, c. 1139, p. —, § 150.5, operative July 1, 1977.)

Notes of Decisions

Resistance to an unlawful arrest constitutes the misdemeanor offense of a battery since the victim officer is not engaged in the performance of his duties; however, if the officer is making a lawful arrest, resistance becomes a felony; however, one may properly resist the use of excessive force regardless of whether the arrest is

§ 243 PENAL CODE

technically lawful or unlawful. People v. Henderson (1976) 129 Cal.Rptr. 844, 58 C.A.3d 349.

Where police officer, who was moonlighting as security guard at school dance, was in act of retrieving his baton which he intended to use to restore order and to prevent further damage to public property when he was struck by defendant with crutch, and such officer earlier was assisting school official in charge of the dance in enforcing § 626.8 proscribing the remaining upon or reentering of school premises after having been asked to leave, such officer was "engaged in the performance of his duties" within this section, and §§ 242, 415 establishing punishment for battery committed upon a peace officer when person committing the offense knows victim is police officer engaged in performance of his duties. People v. Townsend (1971) 98 Cal.Rptr. 25, 20 C.A.3d 688.

To constitute felonious conduct proscribed by this section governing punishment for battery committed against peace officer, assault must be on peace officer who is actually engaged in performance of his duties. People v. Soto (1969) 80 Cal.Rptr. 627, 276 C.A.2d 81.

Crime of battery upon peace officer does require by statute the particular mental state that defendant knows or reasonably should know that victim is peace officer engaged in performance of his duties. People v. Glover (1967) 65 Cal.Rptr. 219, 257 C.A.2d 502.

§ 243.1. Battery against custodial officer in performance of duties

When a battery is committed against the person of a custodial officer as defined in Section 831 of the Penal Code, and the person committing the offense knows or reasonably should know that such victim is a custodial officer engaged in the performance of his duties, and such custodial officer is engaged in the performance of his duties, the offense shall be punished by imprisonment in the state prison.
(Added by Stats.1976, c. 1139, p. —, § 150.1, operative July 1, 1977.)

§ 243.2. Battery against state department of justice peace officers; punishment; definition

A battery is punishable by fine of not exceeding one thousand dollars ($1,000), or by imprisonment in the county jail not exceeding six months, or by both. When it is committed against the person of a peace officer, and the person committing the offense knows or reasonably should know that such victim is a peace officer engaged in the performance of his duties, and such peace officer is engaged in the performance of his duties, the offense shall be punished by imprisonment in the county jail not exceeding one year or by imprisonment in the state prison.

As used in this section, "peace officer" refers to any person designated as a peace officer by subdivision (a) of Section 830.3.

This section shall be operative July 1, 1977.
(Added by Stats.1976, c. 1390, p. —, § 2.)

§ 243.4. Battery against certain federal peace officers; punishment; definition

A battery is punishable by fine of not exceeding one thousand dollars ($1,000), or by imprisonment in the county jail not exceeding six months, or by both. When it is committed against the person of a peace officer engaged in the performance of his duties as a member of a security department of a school district pursuant to Section 39670 of the Education Code, and the person committing the offense knows or reasonably should know that such victim is such a peace officer engaged in the performance of his duties, the offense shall be punished by imprisonment in the county jail not exceeding one year or by imprisonment in the state prison.
(Amended by Stats.1978, c. 703, p. —, § 3.)

§ 244. Assault with caustic chemicals; punishment

Every person who willfully and maliciously places or throws, or causes to be placed or thrown, upon the person of another, any vitriol, corrosive acid, or caustic chemical of any nature, with the intent to injure the flesh or disfigure the body of such person, is punishable by imprisonment in the state prison for two, three or four years.
(Amended by Stats.1976, c. 1139, p. —, § 151, operative July 1, 1977.)

§ 245. Assault with deadly weapon or force likely to produce great bodily injury; punishment

(a) Every person who commits an assault upon the person of another with a deadly weapon or instrument or by any means of force likely to produce great bodily injury is punishable by imprisonment in the state prison for two, three or four years, or in a county jail not exceeding one year, or by fine not exceeding five thousand dollars ($5,000), or by both such fine and imprisonment. When a person is convicted of a violation of this section, in a case involving use of a deadly weapon or instrument, and such weapon or instrument is owned by such person, the court may, in its discretion, order that the weapon or instrument be deemed a nuisance and shall be confiscated and destroyed in the manner provided by Section 12028.

(b) Every person who commits an assault with a deadly weapon or instrument or by any means likely to produce great bodily injury upon the person of a peace officer or fireman, and who knows or reasonably should know that such victim is a peace officer or fireman engaged in the performance of his duties, when such peace officer or fireman is engaged in the performance of his duties shall be punished by imprisonment in the state prison for three, four, or five years.

As used in this section, "peace officer" refers to any person designated as a peace officer by Section 830.1, by subdivisions (a) to (e), inclusive, of Section 830.2, Section 830.5, or by subdivision (a) of Section 830.6, as well as any policeman of the San Francisco Port Commission and each deputized law enforcement member of the Wildlife Protection Branch of the Department of Fish and Game.
(Amended by Stats.1976, c. 420, p. —, § 2; Stats.1976, c. 1126, p. —, § 3; Stats.1976, c. 1138, p. —, § 3; Stats.1976, c. 1139, p. —, § 150.5, operative July 1, 1977.)

Notes of Decisions

Use of hands or fists alone is sufficient to support a conviction of assault by means of force likely to produce great bodily injury. People v. Wingo (1975) 121 Cal.Rptr. 97, 534 P.2d 1001, 14 C.3d 169.

Crime of assault by means of force likely to produce great bodily injury may be committed by means of hand or fist alone. People v. Rupert (1971) 98 Cal.Rptr. 203, 20 C.A.3d 961.

All that is required to sustain a conviction of assault with a deadly weapon is proof that there was an assault, that it was with a deadly weapon, and that the defendant intended to commit a violent injury on another. People v. Birch (1969) 83 Cal.Rptr. 98, 3 C.A.3d 167.

Intent required to be shown in prosecution for assault with a deadly weapon may be inferred from doing of the wrongful act. People v. Dinkins (1966) 52 Cal.Rptr. 134, 242 C.A.2d 892.

Specific intent is not necessary for crime of assault with a deadly weapon. Newman v. Larsen (1964) 36 Cal.Rptr. 883, 225 C.A.2d 22.

Offense prescribed by this section calling for punishment of every person who commits assault with deadly weapon or instrument or by any means likely to produce great bodily injury upon peace officer known to be performing his duties is one created for public benefit, and any protection of the officers, involved in any particular case is incidental. People v. Baca (1966) 55 Cal.Rptr. 681, 247 C.A.2d 487.

The offense of assault with a deadly weapon is a nonfatal offense, and is an attempt coupled by present ability which includes such acts as firing a gun without intent to hit. People v. Welborn (1966) 51 Cal.Rptr. 644, 242 C.A.2d 668.

Offense of assault with deadly weapon upon police officer requires defendant's reasonable awareness of his victim's identity as police officer engaged in performance of his duties. In re Cline (1967) 63 Cal.Rptr. 233, 255 C.A.2d 115, certiorari denied, 88 S.Ct. 2311, 392 U.S. 938, 20 L.Ed.2d 1397.

The pointing of an unloaded gun at the prosecuting witness, accompanied by a threat, without any attempt to use it otherwise, is not an "assault with a deadly weapon," and cannot sustain a conviction for assault, for want of present ability to commit a violent injury on the person threatened in the manner attempted. People v. Bennett (1918) 173 P. 1004, 37 C.A. 324.

Aggravated assault, like any other assault, may be committed without infliction of any physical injury. People v. Samuels (1967) 58 Cal.Rptr. 439, 250 C.A.2d 501, certiorari denied 88 S.Ct. 1404, 390 U.S. 1024, 20 L.Ed.2d 281.

A "deadly weapon" is one likely to produce death or great bodily injury, but deadly character of weapon may depend upon manner in which it is used and in that case the determination of a weapon's character as deadly or not is one for the jury under proper instructions. People v. Tophia (1959) 334 P.2d 133, 167 C.A.2d 39.

Intent

Intent required to be shown in prosecution for assault with a deadly weapon may be inferred from doing of the wrongful act. People v. Dinkins (1966) 52 Cal.Rptr. 134, 242 C.A.2d 892.

Specific intent is not necessary for crime of assault with a deadly weapon. Newman v. Larsen (1964) 36 Cal.Rptr. 883, 225 C.A.2d 22.

Specific intent is not an element of the crime of assault with a deadly weapon, and the requisite intent may be inferred from the doing of the wrongful act. People v. Herd (1963) 34 Cal.Rptr. 141, 220 A.C.A. 859.

Specific intent is not essential to assault by means of force likely to produce great bodily injury and use of described force is what counts, not the intent with which it is employed. People v. Finley (1963) 33 Cal.Rptr. 31, 219 C.A.2d 330, certiorari denied 84 S.Ct. 1174, 377 U.S. 912, 12 L.Ed.2d 181.

§ 245.2. Assault upon police officer with deadly weapon or force likely to produce great bodily injury; punishment

Every person who commits an assault with a deadly weapon or instrument or by any means likely to produce great bodily injury upon the person of a peace officer, and who knows or reasonably should know that such victim is a peace officer engaged in the performance of his duties, when such peace officer or fireman is engaged in the performance of his duties shall be punished by imprisonment in the state prison for three, four, or five years. When a person is convicted of a violation of this section, in a case involving use of a deadly weapon or instrument, and such weapon or instrument is owned by such person, the court may, in its discretion, order that the weapon or instrument be deemed a nuisance and shall be confiscated and destroyed in the manner provided by Section 12028.

As used in this section, "peace officer" refers to any person designated as a peace officer by subdivision (a) of Section 830.3.

This section shall become operative July 1, 1977.
(Added by Stats.1976, c. 1133, p. —, § 2.)

§ 245.4. Assault with deadly weapon upon peace officer; punishment; ownership of weapon deemed nuisance; definition

Every person who commits an assault with a deadly weapon or instrument or by any means likely to produce great bodily injury upon the person of a peace officer engaged in the performance of his duties as a member of a security department of a

§ 245.4

school district pursuant to Section 39670 of the Education Code, and who knows or reasonably should know that such victim is such a peace officer engaged in the performance of his duties, shall be punished by imprisonment in the state prison for three, four, or five years.

When a person is convicted of a violation of this section, in a case involving use of a deadly weapon or instrument, and such weapon or instrument is owned by such person, the court may, in its discretion, order that the weapon or instrument be deemed a nuisance and shall be confiscated and destroyed in the manner provided by Section 12028.
(Amended by Stats.1978, c. 703, p. —, § 4.)

§ 246. Shooting at inhabited dwelling or occupied building or occupied motor vehicle; punishment

Any person who shall maliciously and willfully discharge a firearm at an inhabited dwelling house, occupied building, occupied motor vehicle, inhabited house car, as defined in Section 362 of the Vehicle Code, or inhabited camper, as defined in Section 243 of the Vehicle Code, is guilty of a felony, and upon conviction shall be punished by imprisonment in the state prison for two, three or four years, or by imprisonment in the county jail not exceeding one year. As used in this section, "inhabited" means currently being used for dwelling purposes, whether occupied or not.
(Amended by Stats.1978, c. 579, p. —, § 13.)

§ 247. Shooting at aircraft

Any person who willfully and maliciously discharges a firearm at an aircraft, whether parked, in motion, or in flight, and whether occupied or unoccupied, is guilty of a felony.

As used in this section "aircraft" means any contrivance intended for and capable of transporting persons through the airspace.
(Added by Stats.1968, c. 1052, p. 2039, § 1.)

§ 261. Rape defined

Rape is an act of sexual intercourse, accomplished with a female not the wife of the perpetrator, under either of the following circumstances:

1. Where she is incapable, through lunacy or other unsoundness of mind, whether temporary or permanent, of giving legal consent;

2. Where she resists, but her resistance is overcome by force or violence;

3. Where she is prevented from resisting by threats of great and immediate bodily harm, accompanied by apparent power of execution, or by any intoxicating narcotic, or anaesthetic substance, administered by or with the privity of the accused;

4. Where she is at the time unconscious of the nature of the act, and this is known to the accused;

5. Where she submits under the belief that the person committing the act is her husband, and this belief is induced by any artifice, pretense, or concealment practiced by the accused, with intent to induce such belief.
(Amended by Stats.1970, c. 1301, p. 2405, § 1.)

Notes of Decisions

In order for defendant to be guilty of forcible rape, there must be some showing of resistance on the part of prosecutrix, although extent to which she must resist defendant's advances is for victim only to determine, and she is required to go no further than is necessary to make manifest her unwillingness to yield to attack. People v. Peckham (1965) 42 Cal.Rptr. 673, 232 C.A.2d 163; People v. Austin (1962) 18 Cal.Rptr. 209, 198 C.A.2d 669; People v. Newlan (1959) 343 P.2d 618, 173 C.A.2d 579.

Although victim must resist in fact, and extraordinary resistance is not required and the amount thereof need be only such as to manifest her refusal to consent to act. People v. Nash (1968) 67 Cal.Rptr. 621, 261 C.A.2d 216, certiorari denied 89 S.Ct. 315, 393 U.S. 944, 21 L.Ed.2d 281.

In determining degree of resistance required to establish the offense of rape, relative strength of parties and uselessness of victim's resistance are among the factors to be considered. People v. Nash (1968) 67 Cal.Rptr. 621, 261 C.A.2d 216, certiorari denied 89 S.Ct. 315, 393 U.S. 944, 21 L.Ed.2d 281.

Requisite specific intent of offense of rape is to have sexual intercourse with victim and to use force to overcome her resistance. People v. Tidmore (1963) 32 Cal.Rptr. 444, 218 C.A.2d 716.

"Rape" consists of an act of sexual intercourse accomplished with a female not the wife of the perpetrator where the victim is prevented from resisting by the threat of great and immediate bodily harm accompanied by apparent power of execution. People v. Burroughs (1962) 19 Cal.Rptr. 344, 200 C.A.2d 629.

Consent—In general

Offer of proof of defendant's reasonable belief that prosecutrix had reached age of consent could demonstrate a sufficient basis upon which, when fully developed, trier of fact could find in defendant's favor in prosecution for statutory rape; overruling People v. Ratz, 115 Cal. 132, 46 P. 915 and People v. Griffin, 117 Cal. 583, 49 P. 711 and disapproving People v. Sheffield, 9 Cal.App. 130, 98 P. 67. People v. Hernandez (1964) 39 Cal.Rptr. 361, 393 P.2d 673, 61 C.2d 529, 8 A.L.R.3d 1092.

Lack of female's consent is not, in one sense, an element of offense of statutory rape, but in broader sense, lack of consent remains an element but law makes a conclusive presumption of lack thereof because female is presumed too innocent and naive to understand implications and nature of her act. Id.

Adult female's understanding of nature and consequences of sexual act must be intelligent understanding to constitute "consent." People v. Boggs (1930) 290 P. 618, 107 C.A. 492.

Violation of § 288 prohibiting lewd and lascivious conduct on child under 14 years does not involve consent of any sort, thereby placing public policies underlying it and statutory rape on different footings. People v. Toliver (1969) 75 Cal.Rptr. 819, 270 C.A.2d 492, certiorari denied 90 S.Ct. 193, 396 U.S. 895, 24 L.Ed.2d 172.

Force or fear overcoming resistance

Consent to intercourse induced by fear is no consent at all and when a woman reasonably determines that she cannot resist without peril to her life or safety, no further resistance is demanded by the law and the necessity of resistance is to be measured by all of the circumstances of the case. People v. Hinton (1959) 333 P.2d 822, 166 C.A.2d 743.

Where defendant held open blade of knife at woman's throat area, talked of having killed a man in army and of killing her, and stated he would stick knife into her neck if she did not submit, it was not unreasonable for woman to believe that means of effecting great and immediate bodily harm were within defendant's reach and to be afraid to resist or scream for help and defendant was guilty of rape. People v. Adkins (1958) 331 P.2d 195, 165 C.A.2d 29.

If female is prevented from resisting by threats of great and immediate bodily harm, accompanied by apparent power of execution, rape is committed. People v. Frye (1953) 255 P.2d 105, 117 C.A.2d 101.

Threats, force and violence

It is the threat of violence which puts the victim in fear that is one of the important elements of the crime of attempted rape by threats of violence. People v. Flores (1968) 73 Cal.Rptr. 118, 267 C.A.2d 452.

Threats of great and immediate bodily harm used to overcome resistance of woman constitutes sufficient force for crime of rape, and such threats need not be expressed in words, but acts and conduct or exhibition of weapon may be used to convey the threat. People v. Benavidez (1967) 63 Cal.Rptr. 357, 255 C.A.2d 563.

A threat may be expressed by acts or conduct as well as by words. People v. Winters (1958) 329 P.2d 743, 163 C.A.2d 619.

If female is prevented from resisting by threats of great and immediate bodily harm, accompanied by apparent power of execution, rape is committed under conditions prescribed by statute. People v. Tollack (1951) 233 P.2d 121, 105 C.A.2d 169.

Attempts

Attempted rape requires intent and attempt to make penetration. People v. Ray (1961) 9 Cal.Rptr. 678, 187 C.A.2d 182.

Crime of attempted rape is complete if there is a concurrence of the intent to commit such crime with a direct, although ineffectual, act towards its commission. People v. Thomas (1958) 331 P.2d 82, 164 C.A.2d 571.

To constitute an attempt to commit rape, it is not necessary that the act done should be the last proximate one for the completion of the offense or that there be any penetration whatever. Id.

§ 261.5. Unlawful sexual intercourse with female under age 18

Unlawful sexual intercourse is an act of sexual intercourse accomplished with a female not the wife of the perpetrator, where the female is under the age of 18 years.
(Added by Stats.1970, c. 1301, p. 2406, § 2.)

§ 263. Rape; essentials; sufficiency of penetration

Penetration sufficient. The essential guilt of rape consists of the outrage to the person and feelings of the female. Any sexual penetration, however slight, is sufficient to complete the crime.
(Enacted 1872.)

Notes of Decisions

Rape requires penetration, however slight. People v. Ray (1961) 9 Cal.Rptr. 678, 187 C.A.2d 182.

To constitute "rape" it is not necessary that there be complete penetration, in view of statutory provision that any sexual penetration, however slight, is sufficient to complete the crime of rape. People v. George (1949) 205 P.2d 464, 91 C.A.2d 537.

In prosecution for rape, sexual penetration may be shown by circumstantial as well as direct evidence. People v. Swanson (1962) 22 Cal.Rptr. 178, 204 C.A.2d 169, certiorari denied 83 S.Ct. 516, 371 U.S. 958, 9 L.Ed.2d 505; People v. Haywood (1955) 280 P.2d 180, 131 C.A.2d 259; People v. Vicencio (1945) 162 P.2d 650, 71 C.A. 361.

Sexual penetration which is essential ingredient of offense of rape of female unconscious of nature of act may be proved by circumstantial evidence. People v. Minkowski (1962) 23 Cal.Rptr. 92, 204 C.A.2d 832.

§ 264. Rape; unlawful intercourse; recommendation of jury; discretion of court

Rape, as defined in Section 261, is punishable by imprisonment in the state prison for three, six or eight years. Unlawful sexual intercourse, as defined in Section 261.5, is punishable either by imprisonment in the county jail for not more than one year or in the state prison, and in such case the jury shall recommend by their verdict whether the punishment shall be by imprisonment in the county jail or in the state prison; provided, that when the defendant pleads guilty to an offense under Section 261.5 the punishment shall be in the discretion of the trial court, either by imprisonment in the county jail for not more than one year or in the state prison.
(Amended by Stats.1978, c. 579, p. ——, § 14.)

§ 264.1. Rape; acting in concert by force or violence; punishment

The provisions of Section 264 notwithstanding, in any case in which defendant, voluntarily acting in concert with another person, by force or violence and against the will of the victim, committed the rape, either personally or by aiding and abetting such other person, such fact shall be charged in the indictment or information and if found to be true by the jury, upon a jury trial, or if found to be true by the court, upon a court trial, or if admitted by the defendant, defendant shall suffer confinement in the state prison for five, seven, or nine years.
(Amended by Stats.1978, c. 579, p. ——, § 15.)

§ 264.2. Denial of probation

Probation shall not be granted to, nor shall the execution or imposition of sentence be suspended for, any person convicted of violating subdivision (2) or (3) of Section 261, or Section 264.1.

This section does not prohibit the adjournment of criminal proceedings pursuant to Division 3 (commencing with Section 3000) or Division 6 (commencing with Section 6000) of the Welfare and Institutions Code.
(Added by Stats.1978, c. 1308, p. —, § 1.)

§ 266. Inveiglement or enticement of unmarried female under 18 for purposes of prostitution, etc.; aiding and abetting; procuring female for illicit intercourse by false pretenses; punishment

Every person who inveigles or entices any unmarried female, of previous chaste character, under the age of 18 years, into any house of ill fame, or of assignation, or elsewhere, for the purpose of prostitution, or to have illicit carnal connection with any man; and every person who aids or assists in such inveiglement or enticement; and every person who, by any false pretenses, false representation, or other fraudulent means, procures any female to have illicit carnal connection with any man, is punishable by imprisonment in the state prison, or by imprisonment in a county jail not exceeding one year, or by a fine not exceeding one thousand dollars ($1,000), or by both such fine and imprisonment.
(Amended by Stats.1976, c. 1139, p. —, § 157, operative July 1, 1977.)

§ 266a. Abduction or procurement by fraudulent inducement for prostitution; punishment

Every person who, within this state, takes any person against his or her will and without his or her consent, or with his or her consent procured by fraudulent inducement or misrepresentation, for the purpose of prostitution, as defined in subdivision (b) of Section 647, is punishable by imprisonment in the state prison, and a fine not exceeding one thousand dollars ($1,000).
(Amended by Stats.1976, c. 1139, p. —, § 158, operative July 1, 1977.)

§ 266b. Abduction to live in illicit relation; punishment

Every person who takes any other person unlawfully, and against his or her will, and by force, menace, or duress, compels him or her to live with such person in an illicit relation, against his or her consent, or to so live with any other person, is punishable by imprisonment in the state prison.
(Amended by Stats.1976, c. 1139, p. —, § 159, operative July 1, 1977.)

§ 266d. Receiving money for placing person for purposes of cohabitation

Any person who receives any money or other valuable thing for or on account of placing in custody any other person for the purpose of causing the other person to cohabit with any person to whom the other person is not married, is guilty of a felony.
(Amended by Stats.1975, c. 996, p. —, § 2.5.)

§ 266e. Purchasing person for purposes of prostitution or placing person for immoral purposes

Every person who purchases, or pays any money or other valuable thing for, any person for the purpose of prostitution as defined in subdivision (b) of Section 647, or for the purpose of placing such person, for immoral purposes, in any house or place against his or her will, is guilty of a felony.
(Amended by Stats.1975, c. 996, p. —, § 3.)

§ 266f. Sale of person for immoral purposes

Every person who sells any person or receives any money or other valuable thing for or on account of his or her placing in custody, for immoral purposes, any person, whether with or without his or her consent, is guilty of a felony.
(Amended by Stats.1975, c. 996, p. —, § 4.)

§ 266g. Placing or permitting placement of wife in house of prostitution; punishment

Every man who, by force, intimidation, threats, persuasion, promises, or any other means, places or leaves, or procures any other person or persons to place or leave, his wife in a house of prostitution, or connives at or consents to, or permits, the placing or leaving of his wife in a house of prostitution, or allows or permits her to remain therein, is guilty of a felony and punishable by imprisonment in the state prison for two, three or four years; and in all prosecutions under this section a wife is a competent witness against her husband.
(Amended by Stats.1976, c. 1139, p. —, § 160, operative July 1, 1977.)

Notes of Decisions

Under this section, providing that every man who places or leaves his wife in a house of prostitution, or connives at or consents to, or permits, the placing or leaving of his wife in a house of prostitution, or allows or permits her to remain therein, is guilty of a felony, proof of commission of any one or more of the disjunctively stated acts warrants conviction. People v. Coronado (1943) 135 P.2d 647, 57 C.A.2d 805.

§ 266h. Pimping; punishment

Any person who, knowing another person is a prostitute, lives or derives support or maintenance in whole or in part from the earnings or proceeds of such person's prostitution, or from money loaned or advanced to or charged against such person by any keeper or manager or inmate of a house or other place where prostitution is practiced or allowed, or who solicits or receives compensation for soliciting for such person, is guilty of pimping, a felony, and is punishable by imprisonment in the state prison for two, three or four years.

(Amended by Stats.1976, c. 1139, p. —, § 161, operative July 1, 1977.)

§ 266i. Pandering; punishment

Any person who: (a) procures another person for the purpose of prostitution; or (b) by promises, threats, violence, or by any device or scheme, causes, induces, persuades or encourages another person to become a prostitute; or (c) procures for another person a place as inmate in a house of prostitution or as an inmate of any place in which prostitution is encouraged or allowed within this state; or (d) by promises, threats, violence or by any device or scheme, causes, induces, persuades or encourages an inmate of a house of prostitution, or any other place in which prostitution is encouraged or allowed, to remain therein as an inmate; or (e) by fraud or artifice, or by duress of person or goods, or by abuse of any position of confidence or authority, procures another person for the purpose of prostitution, or to enter any place in which prostitution is encouraged or allowed within this state, or to come into this state or leave this state for the purpose of prostitution; or (f) receives or gives, or agrees to receive or give, any money or thing of value for procuring, or attempting to procure, another person for the purpose of prostitution, or to come into this state or leave this state for the purpose of prostitution, is guilty of pandering, a felony, and is punishable by imprisonment in the state prison for two, three, or four years.

(Amended by Stats.1976, c. 1139, p. —, § 162, operative July 1, 1977.)

Notes of Decisions

Pandering and pimping statutes (this section and § 266h) are both designed to discourage prostitution by discouraging persons other than prostitute from augmenting and expanding prostitute's operation or increasing supply of available prostitutes. People v. Hashimoto (1976) 126 Cal.Rptr. 848, 54 C.A.3d 862.

The purpose of this section is to cover all the various ramifications of the social evil of pandering and include them all in the definition of the crime, with a view of effectively combating the evil sought to be condemned. People v. Fixler (1976) 128 Cal.Rptr. 363, 56 C.A.3d 321.

Defendants, photographer and "photo editor" for publisher of various magazines devoted to the depiction of sexual activity procured, caused, and induced 14-year-old girl to engage in lewd acts and sexual intercourse for money within meaning of this section by providing her money to "model" for various photographs and by directing her performances. People v. Fixler (1976) 128 Cal.Rptr. 363, 56 C.A.3d 321.

§ 267. Abduction; person under 18 for purposes of prostitution; punishment

Every person who takes away any other person under the age of 18 years from the father, mother, guardian, or other person having the legal charge of the other person, without their consent, for the purpose of prostitution, is punishable by imprisonment in the state prison, and a fine not exceeding one thousand dollars ($1,000).

(Amended by Stats.1976, c. 1139, p. —, § 163, operative July 1, 1977.)

§ 270. Failure to provide; parent; punishment; effect of custody; evidence; applicability of section; artificial insemination; treatment by spiritual means

If a parent of a minor child willfully omits, without lawful excuse, to furnish necessary clothing, food, shelter or medical attendance, or other remedial care for his or her child, he or she is guilty of a misdemeanor punishable by a fine not exceeding one thousand dollars ($1,000), or by imprisonment in the county jail not exceeding one year, or by both such fine and imprisonment. If a court of competent jurisdiction has made a final adjudication in either a civil or a criminal action that a person is the parent of a minor child and the person has notice of such adjudication and he or she then willfully omits, without lawful excuse, to furnish necessary clothing, food, shelter, medical attendance or other remedial care for his or her child, this conduct is punishable by imprisonment in the county jail not exceeding one year or in a state prison not exceeding one year and one day, or by a fine not exceeding one thousand dollars ($1,000), or by both such fine and imprisonment. This statute shall not be construed so as to relieve such parent from the criminal liability defined herein for such omission merely because the other

§ 270

parent of such child is legally entitled to the custody of such child nor because the other parent of such child or any other person or organization voluntarily or involuntarily furnishes such necessary food, clothing, shelter or medical attendance or other remedial care for such child or undertakes to do so.

Proof of abandonment or desertion of a child by such parent, or the omission by such parent to furnish necessary food, clothing, shelter or medical attendance or other remedial care for his or her child is prima facie evidence that such abandonment or desertion or omission to furnish necessary food, clothing, shelter or medical attendance or other remedial care is willful and without lawful excuse.

The court, in determining the ability of the parent to support his or her child, shall consider all income, including social insurance benefits and gifts.

The provisions of this section are applicable whether the parents of such child are or were ever married or divorced, and regardless of any decree made in any divorce action relative to alimony or to the support of the child. A child conceived but not yet born is to be deemed an existing person insofar as this section is concerned.

The husband of a woman who bears a child as a result of artificial insemination shall be considered the father of that child for the purpose of this section, if he consented in writing to the artificial insemination.

If a parent provides a minor with treatment by spiritual means through prayer alone in accordance with the tenets and practices of a recognized church or religious denomination, by a duly accredited practitioner thereof, such treatment shall constitute "other remedial care", as used in this section.
(Amended by Stats.1976, c. 673, p. —, § 1.)

Notes of Decisions

Principal statutory objectives of statutes relating to nonsupport are to secure the support of the child and to protect the public from burden of supporting a child who has a parent able to support him. People v. Sorensen (1968) 66 Cal.Rptr. 7, 437 P.2d 495, 68 C.2d 280, 25 A.L.R.3d 1093.

Demonstration of defendant's financial inability to pay for child's medical care is lawful excuse for failure to provide care. People v. Arnold (1967) 58 Cal.Rptr. 115, 426 P.2d 515, 66 C.2d 438.

§ 270a. Failure to provide support for spouse; punishment

Every individual who has sufficient ability to provide for his or her spouse's support, or who is able to earn the means of such spouse's support, who willfully abandons and leaves his or her spouse in a destitute condition, or who refuses or neglects to provide such spouse with necessary food, clothing, shelter, or medical attendance, unless by such spouse's conduct the individual was justified in abandoning such spouse, is guilty of a misdemeanor.
(Amended by Stats.1976, c. 1170, p. —, § 1.)

§ 270d. Fine; disposition

In any case where there is a conviction and sentence under the provisions of either Section 270 or Section 270a, should a fine be imposed, such fine shall be directed by the court to be paid in whole or in part to the spouse of the defendant or guardian or custodian of the child or children of such defendant, except as follows:

If the children are receiving public assistance, all fines, penalties or forfeitures imposed and all funds collected from the defendant shall be paid to the county department. Money so paid shall be applied first to support for the calendar month following its receipt by the county department and any balance remaining shall be applied to future needs, or be treated as reimbursement for past support furnished from public assistance funds.
(Amended by Stats.1974, c. 893, p. 1893, § 2.)

§ 271. Desertion of child under 14 with intent to abandon; punishment

Every parent of any child under the age of 14 years, and every person to whom any such child has been confided for nurture, or education, who deserts such child in any place whatever with intent to abandon it, is punishable by imprisonment in the State prison or in the county jail not exceeding one year or by fine not exceeding five hundred dollars ($500) or by both.
(Amended by Stats.1945, c. 250, p. 713, § 1.)

§ 271a. Abandonment or failure to maintain child under 14; false representation that child is orphan; punishment

Every person who knowingly and willfully abandons, or who, having ability so to do, fails or refuses to maintain his or her minor child under the age of fourteen years, or who falsely, knowing the same to be false, represents to any manager, officer or agent of any orphan asylum or charitable institution for the care of orphans, that any child for whose admission into such asylum or institution application has been made is an orphan, is punishable by imprisonment in

the state prison, or in the county jail not exceeding one year, or by fine not exceeding five hundred dollars, or by both.
(Amended by Stats.1909, c. 190, p. 297, § 2.)

§ 272. Causing, encouraging or contributing to delinquency of persons under 18 years; inducing disobedience to court order; punishment

Every person who commits any act or omits the performance of any duty, which act or omission causes or tends to cause or encourage any person under the age of 18 years to come within the provisions of Sections 600, 601, or 602 of the Welfare and Institutions Code or which act or omission contributes thereto, or any person who, by any act or omission, or by threats, commands, or persuasion, induces or endeavors to induce any person under the age of 18 years or any ward or dependent child of the juvenile court to fail or refuse to conform to a lawful order of the juvenile court, or to do or to perform any act or to follow any course of conduct or to so live as would cause or manifestly tend to cause any such person to become or to remain a person within the provisions of Sections 600, 601, or 602 of the Welfare and Institutions Code, is guilty of a misdemeanor and upon conviction thereof shall be punished by a fine not exceeding two thousand five hundred dollars ($2,500), or by imprisonment in the county jail for not more than one year, or by both such fine and imprisonment in a county jail, or may be released on probation for a period not exceeding five years. The district attorney shall prosecute all violations charged under this section.
(Amended by Stats.1976, c. 1068, p. —, § 1; Stats.1976, c. 1125, p. —, § 16.)

Notes of Decisions

Intercourse with 16-year-old girl who told defendants that she was 19 years old was the kind of act which would tend to cause girl to become or remain delinquent, and it was not necessary that prosecution show that act actually had that result. People v. Norris (1967) 62 Cal.Rptr. 66, 254 C.A.2d 296.

Mere fact that defendant was walking on street with 20 year old friend, who had bottle of liquor, did not constitute reasonable cause to believe that defendant was committing or attempting to commit an offense in arresting officer's presence either by aiding or abetting his friend in committing a crime or contributing to the delinquency of a minor. People v. Simon (1956) 290 P.2d 531, 45 C.2d 641.

The use of a minor to transport narcotics necessarily contributes to delinquency of that minor. People v. De Paula (1954) 276 P.2d 600, 43 C.2d 643.

§ 273.5. Corporal injury; infliction by spouse upon his or her spouse or by person cohabiting with person of opposite sex

(a) Any person who willfully inflicts upon his or her spouse, or any person who willfully inflicts upon any person of the opposite sex with whom he or she is cohabiting, corporal injury resulting in a traumatic condition, is guilty of a felony, and upon conviction thereof, shall be punished by imprisonment in the state prison or the county jail for not more than one year.

(b) Holding oneself out to be the husband or wife of the person with whom one is cohabiting is not necessary to constitute cohabitation as the term is used in this section.
(Added by Stats.1977, c. 912, p. —, § 3.)

§ 273a. Willful cruelty or unjustifiable punishment of child; endangering life or health

(1) Any person who, under circumstances or conditions likely to produce great bodily harm or death, willfully causes or permits any child to suffer, or inflicts thereon unjustifiable physical pain or mental suffering, or having the care or custody of any child, willfully causes or permits the person or health of such child to be injured, or willfully causes or permits such child to be placed in such situation that its person or health is endangered, is punishable by imprisonment in the county jail not exceeding one year, or in the state prison.

(2) Any person who, under circumstances or conditions other than those likely to produce great bodily harm or death, willfully causes or permits any child to suffer, or inflicts thereon unjustifiable physical pain or mental suffering, or having the care or custody of any child, willfully causes or permits the person or health of such child to be injured, or willfully causes or permits such child to be placed in such situation that its person or health may be endangered, is guilty of a misdemeanor.
(Amended by Stats.1976, c. 1139, p. —, § 165, operative July 1, 1977.)

Notes of Decisions

This section proscribing a person from wilfully causing or permitting a child to be placed in a situation likely to produce great bodily harm or death requires proof of criminal negligence which means that the defendant's conduct must amount to a reckless, gross or culpable departure from the ordinary standard of due care; it must be such a departure from what would be the conduct of an ordinary prudent person under the same circumstances as to be incompatible with a proper regard for human life. People v. Peabody (1975) 119 Cal.Rptr. 780, 46 C.A.3d 43.

§ 273a

Where evidence in prosecution of mother for endangering the person and health of a child pointed strongly to direct infliction of physical pain and mental suffering on the child by the defendant herself, an instruction requiring a finding of "criminal negligence" was not required, sua sponte. People v. Atkins (1975) 125 Cal.Rptr. 855, 53 C.A.3d 348.

§ 273b. Confinement of minor under 16 with adult prisoners; restriction

No child under the age of 16 years must be placed in any place of confinement, or in any courtroom, or in any vehicle for transportation to any place, in company with adults charged with or convicted of crime, except in the presence of a proper official.
(Amended by Stats.1941, c. 106, p. 1081, § 8.)

§ 273d. Corporal punishment or injury; infliction upon child; felony; punishment

Any person who willfully inflicts upon any child any cruel or inhuman corporal punishment or injury resulting in a traumatic condition is guilty of a felony, and upon conviction thereof shall be punished by imprisonment in the state prison, or in the county jail for not more than one year.
(Amended by Stats.1977, c. 912, p. ——, § 2.)

Notes of Decisions

The word "willfully" in this section making it a felony to willfully inflict cruel punishment or injury on a child resulting in traumatic condition does not require a specific intent to inflict cruel or inhuman punishment or traumatic injury but requires only the more general intent to inflict upon a child any cruel or inhuman corporal punishment or injury. People v. Atkins (1975) 125 Cal.Rptr. 855, 53 C.A.3d 348.

The statutory term a "traumatic condition" is not, as a matter of law, a term the meaning of which is within knowledge of jurors, but is a technical term within meaning of rule that court should define legal and technical terms used in instructions but need not define commonplace words, especially in absence of a request therefor. People v. Burns (1949) 200 P.2d 134, 88 C.A.2d 867.

§ 278. Definition, punishment; return; expenses

(a) Every person, not having a right of custody, who maliciously takes, entices away, detains or conceals any minor child with intent to detain or conceal such child from a parent, or guardian, or other person having the lawful charge of such child shall be punished by imprisonment in the state prison for two, three or four years, a fine of not more than ten thousand dollars ($10,000), or both, or imprisonment in a county jail for a period of not more than one year, a fine of not more than one thousand dollars ($1,000), or both.

(b) A child who has been detained or concealed in violation of subdivision (a) shall be returned to the person having lawful charge of the child. Any expenses incurred in returning the child shall be reimbursed as provided in Section 4605 of the Civil Code. Such costs shall be assessed against any defendant convicted of a violation of this section.
(Added by Stats.1976, c. 1399, p. ——, § 10; Amended by Stats.1976, c. 1399, p. ——, § 10.5.)

Notes of Decisions

In this section, penalizing "maliciously, forcibly or fraudulently" taking or enticing away minor child, "forcibly" does not necessarily imply the use of physical force, and "maliciously" imports a wish to vex, annoy or injure another person, or intent to do a wrongful act established either by proof or presumption of law, and "fraudulently" is very broad in its meaning, and no definite and invariable rule can be laid down as a general proposition defining "fraud", which includes all surprise, trick, cunning, dissembling and other unfair ways by which another is deceived. People v. Casagranda (1941) 111 P.2d 672, 43 C.A.2d 818.

§ 280. Concealment of child or removal from county pending adoption proceeding

Every person who willfully causes or permits the removal or concealment of any child in violation of Section 226.10 of the Civil Code is punishable as follows:

(a) By imprisonment in the county jail for not more than one year if the child is concealed within the county in which the adoption proceeding is pending or in which the child has been placed for adoption, or is removed from such county to a place within this state; or

(b) By imprisonment in the state prison, or by imprisonment in the county jail for not more than one year if the child is removed from such county to a place outside of this state.
(Amended by Stats.1976, c. 1139, p. ——, § 171, operative July 1, 1977.)

§ 281. Bigamy defined

Bigamy defined. Every person having a husband or wife living, who marries any other person, except in the cases specified in the next section, is guilty of bigamy.
(Enacted 1872.)

§ 282. Bigamy; exceptions

Exceptions. The last section does not extend—

1. To any person by reason of any former marriage, whose husband or wife by such marriage has been absent for five successive years without being known to such person within that time to be living; nor,

2. To any person by reason of any former marriage which has been pronounced void, annulled, or dissolved by the judgment of a competent Court. (Enacted 1872.)

§ 283. Bigamy; punishment

Bigamy is punishable by a fine not exceeding five thousand dollars ($5,000) or by imprisonment in a county jail not exceeding one year or in the state prison.
(Amended by Stats.1976, c. 1139, p. ——, § 172, operative July 1, 1977.)

§ 285. Incest

Persons being within the degrees of consanguinity within which marriages are declared by law to be incestuous and void, who intermarry with each other, or who commit fornication or adultery with each other, are punishable by imprisonment in the state prison.
(Amended by Stats.1976, c. 1139, p. ——, § 174, operative July 1, 1977.)

§ 286. Sodomy; punishment

(a) Sodomy is sexual conduct consisting of contact between the penis of one person and the anus of another person.

(b)(1) Any person who participates in an act of sodomy with another person who is under 18 years of age shall be punished by imprisonment in the state prison, or in a county jail for a period of not more than one year.

(2) Any person over the age of 21 years who participates in an act of sodomy with another person who is under 16 years of age shall be guilty of a felony.

(c) Any person who participates in an act of sodomy with another person who is under 14 years of age and more than 10 years younger than he, or who has compelled the participation of another person in an act of sodomy by force, violence, duress, menace, or threat of great bodily harm, shall be punished by imprisonment in the state prison for three, six, or eight years.

(d) Any person who, while voluntarily acting in concert with another person, either personally or by aiding and abetting such other person, commits an act of sodomy by force or violence and against the will of the victim shall be punished by imprisonment in the state prison for five, seven, or nine years.

(e) Any person who participates in an act of sodomy with any person of any age while confined in any state prison, as defined in Section 4504, or in any local detention facility as defined in Section 6031.4, shall be punished by imprisonment in the state prison, or in a county jail for a period of not more than one year.

(f) Any person who commits an act of sodomy, and the victim is at the time unconscious of the nature of the act and this is known to the person committing the act, shall be punished by imprisonment in the state prison, or in a county jail for a period of not more than one year.
(Amended by Stats.1978, c. 579, p. ——, § 16.)

§ 286.5. Sexually assaulting animal; misdemeanor

Any person who sexually assaults any animal protected by Section 597f for the purpose of arousing or gratifying the sexual desire of the person is guilty of a misdemeanor.
(Added by Stats.1975, c. 71, p. ——, § 8.5.)

§ 287. Sodomy; sufficiency of penetration

Any sexual penetration, however slight, is sufficient to complete the crime of sodomy.
(Amended by Stats.1975, c. 71, p. ——, § 9.)

§ 288. Lewd or lascivious acts upon the body of a child under 14; intent; punishment

Any person who shall willfully and lewdly commit any lewd or lascivious act including any of the acts constituting other crimes provided for in Part 1 of this code upon or with the body, or any part or member thereof, of a child under the age of 14 years, with the intent of arousing, appealing to, or gratifying the lust or passions or sexual desires of such person or of such child, shall be guilty of a felony and shall be imprisoned in the state prison for a term of three, five, or seven years.
(Amended by Stats.1978, c. 579, p. ——, § 17.)

Notes of Decisions

Unless police officer has probable cause to search, he has no right to retreat to clandestine position to peer into restroom, and knowledge gained by or attributable to such clandestine observations suffers from constitutional infirmities which require its exclusion as evidence; People v. Crafts, 13 Cal.App.3d 457, 91 Cal.Rptr. 563; People v. Heath, 266 Cal.App.2d 754, 72 Cal.Rptr. 457; People v. Roberts, 256 Cal.App.2d 488, 64 Cal.Rptr. 70; People v. Maldonado, 240 Cal.App.2d 812, 50 Cal.Rptr. 45; People v. Hensel, 233 Cal.App.2d 834, 43 Cal.Rptr. 865; People v. Young, 214 Cal.App.2d 131, 29 Cal.Rptr. 492; People v. Norton, 209 Cal.App.2d 173, 25 Cal.Rptr. 676, disapproved to extent of any conflict. People v. Triggs (1973) 106 Cal.Rptr. 408, 506 P.2d 232, 8 C.3d 884.

While a specific intent to commit a violation of this section must be shown beyond a reasonable doubt and the jury was so instructed, such intent may be shown by circumstantial evidence. People v. Worthington (1974) 113 Cal.Rptr. 322, 38 C.A.3d 359.

§ 288a. Oral copulation; punishment

(a) Oral copulation is the act of copulating the mouth of one person with the sexual organ of another person.

(b)(1) Any person who participates in an act of oral copulation with another person who is under 18 years of age shall be punished by imprisonment in the state prison, or in a county jail for a period of not more than one year.

(2) Any person over the age of 21 years who participates in an act of oral copulation with another person who is under 16 years of age shall be guilty of a felony.

(c) Any person who participates in an act of oral copulation with another person who is under 14 years of age and more than 10 years younger than he, or who has compelled the participation of another person in an act of oral copulation by force, violence, duress, menace, or threat of great bodily harm, shall be punished by imprisonment in the state prison for three, six, or eight years.

(d) Any person who, while voluntarily acting in concert with another person, either personally or by aiding and abetting such other person, commits an act of oral copulation by force or violence and against the will of the victim shall be punished by imprisonment in the state prison for five, seven, or nine years.

(e) Any person who participates in an act of oral copulation while confined in any state prison, as defined in Section 4504 or in any local detention facility as defined in Section 6031.4, shall be punished by imprisonment in the state prison, or in a county jail for a period of not more than one year.

(f) Any person who commits an act of oral copulation, and the victim is at the time unconscious of the nature of the act and this is known to the person committing the act, shall be punished by imprisonment in the state prison, or in a county jail for a period of not more than one year.
(Amended by Stats.1978, c. 579, p. ——, § 18.)

§ 289. Sexual battery

(a) Every person who causes the penetration, however slight, of the genital or anal openings of another person, by any foreign object, substance, instrument, or device, by use of force, violence, duress, menace, or threat of great bodily harm, and against the will of the victim, for the purpose of sexual arousal, gratification, or abuse, shall be punished by imprisonment in the state prison for three, four, or five years.

(b) As used in this section, "foreign object, substance, instrument, or device" shall not include any part of the body.
(Added by Stats.1978, c. 1313, p. ——, § 1.)

§ 290. Registration of sex offenders

Duty to register; time

Any person who, since the first day of July, 1944, has been or is hereafter convicted in the State of California of the offense of assault with intent to commit rape, the infamous crime against nature, or sodomy under Section 220, or of any offense defined in Section 266, 267, 268, 285, 286, 288, 288a, subdivision 1 of Section 647a, subdivision 2 or 3 of Section 261, subdivision (a) or (d) of Section 647, or subdivision 1 or 2 of Section 314, or of any offense involving lewd and lascivious conduct under Section 272; or any person who since such date has been or is hereafter convicted of the attempt to commit any of the above-mentioned offenses; or any person who since such date or at any time hereafter is discharged or paroled from a penal institution where he was confined because of the commission or attempt to commit one of the above-mentioned offenses; or any person who since such date or at any time hereafter is determined to be a mentally disordered sex offender under the provisions of Article 1 (commencing with Section 6300) of Chapter 2 of Part 2 of Division 6 of the Welfare and Institutions Code; or any person who has been since such date or is hereafter convicted in any other state of any offense which, if committed or attempted in this state, would have been punishable as one or more of the above-mentioned offenses shall within 30 days after the effective date of this section or within 30 days of his coming into any county or city, or city and county in which he resides or is temporarily domiciled for such length of time register with the chief of police of the city in which he resides or the sheriff of the county if he resides in an unincorporated area.

Notice of duty to register; prisoner or inmate

Any person who, after the first day of August, 1950, is discharged or paroled from a jail, prison, school, road camp, or other institution where he was confined because of the commission or attempt to commit one of the above-mentioned offenses or is released from a state hospital to which he was committed as a mentally disordered sex offender under the provisions of Article 1 (commencing with Section 6300) of Chapter 2 of Part 2 of Division 6 of the Welfare and Institutions Code shall, prior to such discharge, parole, or release, be informed of his duty to register under this section by the official in charge of the place of confinement or hospital and the official shall require the person to read and sign such form as may be required by the Department of Justice, stating that the duty of the person to register under this section has been explained to him. The official in charge of the place of confinement or hospital shall obtain the address where the person expects to reside upon his discharge, parole, or release and shall report such address to the Department of Justice. The official in charge of the place of confinement or hospital shall give one copy of the form to the person, and shall send two copies to the Department of Justice, which, in turn, shall forward one copy to the appropriate law enforcement agency having local jurisdiction where the person expects to reside upon his discharge, parole, or release.

Notice of duty to register; probationer or one paying fine

Any person who after the first day of August, 1950, is convicted in the State of California of the commission or attempt to commit any of the above-mentioned offenses and who is released on probation or discharged upon payment of a fine shall, prior to such release or discharge, be informed of his duty to register under this section by the court in which he has been convicted and the court shall require the person to read and sign such form as may be required by the Department of Justice, stating that the duty of the person to register under this section has been explained to him. The court shall obtain the address where the person expects to reside upon his release or discharge and shall report within three days such address to the Department of Justice. The court shall give one copy of the form to the person, and shall send two copies to the Department of Justice, which, in turn, shall forward one copy to the appropriate law enforcement agency having local jurisdiction where the person expects to reside upon his discharge, parole, or release.

Contents of registration

Such registration shall consist of (a) a statement in writing signed by such person, giving such information as may be required by the Department of Justice, and (b) the fingerprints and photograph of such person. Within three days thereafter the registering law enforcement agency shall forward such statement, fingerprints and photograph to the Department of Justice.

Change of address

If any person required to register hereunder changes his residence address he shall inform, in writing within 10 days, the law enforcement agency with whom he last registered of his new address. The law enforcement agency shall, within three days after receipt of such information, forward it to the Department of Justice. The Department of Justice shall forward appropriate registration data to the law enforcement agency having local jurisdiction of the new place of residence.

Violation; offense

Any person required to register under the provisions of this section who shall violate any of the provisions thereof is guilty of a misdemeanor.

Confidential records

The statements, photographs and fingerprints herein required shall not be open to inspection by the public or by any person other than a regularly employed peace or other law enforcement officer.

Mentally disordered sex offender defined

As used in this section "mentally disordered sex offender" includes any person who has been determined to be a sexual psychopath or a mentally disordered sex offender under any provision which upon the effective date of the amendment of this section enacted at the 1975–76 Regular Session of the Legislature is, or which prior to such date has been, contained in Division 6 (commencing with Section 6000) of the Welfare and Institutions Code.
(Amended by Stats.1975, c. 71, p. 134, § 12.)

§ 291. School employees; arrest for sex offense; notice to school authorities

Every sheriff or chief of police, upon the arrest for any of the offenses enumerated in Section 290 or in subdivision 1 of Section 261 of any school employee, shall do either of the following:

(1) If such school employee is a teacher in any of the public schools of this state, he shall immediately notify by telephone the superintendent of schools of the school district employing such teacher and shall immediately give written notice of the arrest to the

§ 291

Commission for Teacher Preparation and Licensing and to the superintendent of schools in the county wherein such person is employed. Upon receipt of such notice, the county superintendent of schools shall immediately notify the governing board of the school district employing such person.

(2) If such school employee is a nonteacher in any of the public schools of this state, he shall immediately notify by telephone the superintendent of schools of the school district employing such nonteacher and shall immediately give written notice of the arrest to the governing board of the school district employing such person.
(Amended by Stats.1976, c. 198, p. 516, § 17; Stats.1973, c. 489, p. 962, § 7.)

CRIMES AGAINST RELIGION AND MORALS

§ 303. Intoxicating liquors; employing person to encourage purchases; sale on commission

It shall be unlawful for any person engaged in the sale of alcoholic beverages, other than in the original package, to employ upon the premises where the alcoholic beverages are sold any person for the purpose of procuring or encouraging the purchase or sale of such beverages, or to pay any person a percentage or commission on the sale of such beverages for procuring or encouraging such purchase or sale. Violation of this section shall be a misdemeanor.
(Added by Stats.1935, c. 504, p. 1576, § 1.)

§ 303a. Begging or soliciting purchase of alcoholic beverages

It shall be unlawful, in any place of business where alcoholic beverages are sold to be consumed upon the premises, for any person to loiter in or about said premises for the purpose of begging or soliciting any patron or customer of, or visitor in, such premises to purchase any alcoholic beverage for the one begging or soliciting. Violation of this section shall be a misdemeanor.
(Added by Stats.1953, c. 1591, p. 3272, § 2.)

§ 308. Tobacco; selling or furnishing to minor under 18; punishment; posting copy of act by dealers

Every person, firm or corporation which sells or gives or in any way furnishes to another person who is in fact under the age of 18 years any tobacco, cigarette or cigarette papers or any other preparation of tobacco is guilty of a misdemeanor, and upon conviction thereof shall be punished for the first offense by a fine of not less than twenty-five dollars ($25) nor more than one hundred dollars ($100), or by imprisonment for not more than 60 days; and for the second offense by a fine of not less than fifty dollars ($50) nor more than two hundred dollars ($200), or by imprisonment for not more than 90 days; and for each subsequent offense by a fine of not less than one hundred dollars ($100) and not more than three hundred dollars ($300), or by imprisonment for not less than 90 days nor more than six months, or by both such fine and imprisonment.

Every person, firm or corporation which sells, or deals in tobacco or any preparation thereof, shall post conspicuously and keep so posted in his or their place of business a copy of this act, and any such person failing to do so shall upon conviction be punished by a fine of five dollars ($5) for the first offense and twenty-five dollars ($25) for each succeeding violation of this provision, or by imprisonment for not more than 30 days.

The Secretary of State is hereby authorized to have printed sufficient copies of this act to enable him to furnish dealers in tobacco with copies thereof upon their request for the same.
(Amended by Stats.1972, c. 618, p. 1138, § 115.)

§ 309. Admitting or keeping minors in house of prostitution

Any proprietor, keeper, manager, conductor, or person having the control of any house of prostitution, or any house or room resorted to for the purpose of prostitution, who shall admit or keep any minor of either sex therein; or any parent or guardian of any such minor, who shall admit or keep such minor, or sanction, or connive at the admission or keeping thereof, into, or in any such house, or room, shall be guilty of a misdemeanor.
(Added by Code Am.1880, c. 58, p. 35, § 1.)

§ 311. Definitions

As used in this chapter:

(a) "Obscene matter" means matter, taken as a whole, the predominant appeal of which to the average person, applying contemporary standards, is to prurient interest, i. e., a shameful or morbid interest in nudity, sex, or excretion; and is matter which taken as a whole goes substantially beyond customary limits of candor in description or representation of such matters; and is matter which taken as a whole is utterly without redeeming social importance.

(1) The predominant appeal to prurient interest of the matter is judged with reference to average adults unless it appears from the nature of the matter or the circumstances of its dissemination, distribution or exhibition, that it is designed for clearly defined deviant sexual groups, in which case the predominant appeal of the matter shall be judged with reference to its intended recipient group.

(2) In prosecutions under this chapter, where circumstances of production, presentation, sale, dissemination, distribution, or publicity indicate that matter is being commercially exploited by the defendant for the sake of its prurient appeal, such evidence is probative with respect to the nature of the matter and can justify the conclusion that the matter is utterly without redeeming social importance.

(3) In determining whether the matter taken as a whole goes substantially beyond customary limits of candor in description or representation of such matters the fact that the defendant knew that the matter depicts persons under the age of 16 years engaged in sexual conduct, as defined in subdivision (c) of Section 311.4, is a factor which can be considered in making such a determination.

(b) "Matter" means any book, magazine, newspaper or other printed or written material or any picture, drawing, photograph, motion picture, or other pictorial representation or any statute or other figure, or any recording, transcription or mechanical, chemical or electrical reproduction or any other articles, equipment, machines or materials.

(c) "Person" means any individual, partnership, firm, association, corporation or other legal entity.

(d) "Distribute" means to transfer possession of, whether with or without consideration.

(e) "Knowingly" means being aware of the character of the matter or live conduct.

(f) "Exhibit" means to show.

(g) "Obscene live conduct" means any physical human body activity, whether performed or engaged in alone or with other persons, including but not limited to singing, speaking, dancing, acting, simulating, or pantomiming, where, taken as a whole, the predominant appeal of such conduct to the average person, applying contemporary standards is to prurient interest, i. e., a shameful or morbid interest in nudity, sex, or excretion; and is conduct which taken as a whole goes substantially beyond customary limits of candor in description or representation of such matters; and is conduct which taken as a whole is utterly without redeeming social importance.

(1) The predominant appeal to prurient interest of the conduct is judged with reference to average adults unless it appears from the nature of the conduct or the circumstances of its production, presentation or exhibition, that it is designed for clearly defined deviant sexual groups, in which case the predominant appeal of the conduct shall be judged with reference to its intended recipient group.

(2) In prosecutions under this chapter; where circumstances of production, presentation advertising, or exhibition indicate that live conduct is being commercially exploited by the defendant for the sake of its prurient appeal, such evidence is probative with respect to the nature of the conduct and can justify the conclusion that the conduct is utterly without redeeming social importance.

(3) In determining whether the live conduct taken as a whole goes substantially beyond customary limits of candor in description or representation of such matters the fact that the defendant knew that the live conduct depicts persons under the age of 16 years engaged in sexual conduct, as defined in subdivision (c) of Section 311.4 is a factor which can be considered in making such a determination. (Amended by Stats.1978, c. 715, p. ——, § 1.)

Editors' Note

California's obscenity statute maintains the *Memoirs* definition which is the matter taken as a whole, to the average person applying contemporary standards, appeals to ones prurient interest, and which taken as a whole is utterly without redeeming social importance. The majority of other states follow the more relaxed definition as set forth in Miller v. Cal., 413 U.S. 15 (1973). This definition requires that the material when taken as a whole, to the average person, applying contemporary community standards, appeals to ones prurient interest, and is matter which taken as a whole depicts in a patently offensive way conduct which lacks serious literary, artistic, political, or scientific value. The essential difference between these standards is that pursuant to *Memoirs* it must be shown the matter is *utterly without* socially redeeming value. While *Miller*, provides that the material must lack serious literary, artistic, political, or scientific value.

Notes of Decisions

This section providing that, in obscenity prosecutions, evidence that matter in question was commercially exploited for sake of its prurient appeal could justify conclusion that matter was utterly without redeeming social importance was not unconstitutionally vague. People v. Kuhns (App.1976) 132 Cal.Rptr. 725.

Fact that obscene or other indecent exhibitions take place behind closed doors and are viewed only by those who choose to view them does not defeat the community's interest in regulating such exhibitions. People ex rel. Busch v. Projection Room Theater (1976) 130 Cal.Rptr. 328, 550 P.2d 600, 17 C.3d 42.

§ 311.2. Sending or bringing into state for sale or distribution, printing, exhibiting, distributing or possessing within state; exemptions

(a) Every person who knowingly sends or causes to be sent, or brings or causes to be brought, into this state for sale or distribution, or in this state possesses, prepares, publishes, or prints, with intent to distribute or to exhibit to others, or who offers to distribute, distributes, or exhibits to others, any obscene matter is guilty of a misdemeanor.

(b) Every person who knowingly sends or causes to be sent, or brings or causes to be brought, into this state for sale or distribution, or in this state possesses, prepares, publishes, or prints, with intent to distribute or to exhibit to others for commercial consideration, or who offers to distribute, distributes, or exhibits to others for commercial consideration, any obscene matter, knowing that such matter depicts a person under the age of 18 years personally engaging in or personally simulating sexual intercourse, masturbation, sodomy, bestiality, or oral copulation is guilty of a felony and shall be punished by imprisonment in state prison for two, three, or four years, or by a fine not exceeding fifty thousand dollars ($50,000), in the absence of a finding that the defendant would be incapable of paying such a fine, or by both such fine and imprisonment.

(c) The provisions of this section with respect to the exhibition of, or the possession with intent to exhibit, any obscene matter shall not apply to a motion picture operator or projectionist who is employed by a person licensed by any city or county and who is acting within the scope of his employment, provided that such operator or projectionist has no financial interest in the place wherein he is so employed.

(d) Except as otherwise provided in subdivision (c), the provisions of subdivision (a) or (b) with respect to the exhibition of, or the possession with intent to exhibit, any obscene matter shall not apply to any person who is employed by a person licensed by any city or county and who is acting within the scope of his employment, provided that such employed person has no financial interest in the place wherein he is so employed and has no control, directly or indirectly, over the exhibition of the obscene matter.
(Amended by Stats.1977, c. 1061, p. —, § 1.)

Editors' Note

This section makes it a felony to process, prepare, publish or print with the intent to distribute or exhibit to others, or offer to distribute or exhibit to others, obscene material depicting children under the age of 18 engaging or simulating to be engaging in sexual conduct.

Sexual conduct for purposes of this section is defined in subsection (b).

Notes of Decisions

This section making it a misdemeanor to possess with intent to distribute or to exhibit any obscene matter does not violate equal protection by exempting motion picture operators or projectionist but not exempting others such as a bookstore clerk, and usher, and ticket taker. People v. Haskin (1976) 127 Cal.Rptr. 426, 55 C.A.3d 231.

This section making it a misdemeanor to possess with intent to distribute or to exhibit any obscene matter is not unconstitutional on theory it does not comply with obscenity standards set forth in United States Supreme Court decision. [Miller v. California (1973) 413 U.S. 15, 93 S.Ct. 2607, 37 L.Ed.2d 419] Id.

§ 311.4. Employment of minor to perform prohibited acts

(a) Every person who, with knowledge that a person is a minor, or who, while in possession of such facts that he should reasonably know that such person is a minor, hires, employs, or uses such minor to do or assist in doing any of the acts described in Section 311.2, is guilty of a misdemeanor.

(b) Every person who, with knowledge that a person is a minor under the age of 16 years, or who, while in possession of such facts that he should reasonably know that such person is a minor under the age of 16 years, knowingly promotes, employs, uses, persuades, induces, or coerces a minor under the age of 16 years, or any parent or guardian of a minor under the age of 16 years under his or her control who knowingly permits such minor, to engage in or assist others to engage in either posing or modeling alone or with others for purposes of preparing a film, photograph, negative, slide, or live performance involving sexual conduct by a minor under the age of 16 years alone or with other persons or animals, for commercial purposes, is guilty of a felony and shall be punished by imprisonment in the state prison for three, four, or five years.

(c) As used in subdivision (b), "sexual conduct" means any of the following, whether actual or simulated: sexual intercourse, oral copulation, anal

intercourse, anal oral copulation, masturbation, bestiality, sexual sadism, sexual masochism, any lewd or lascivious sexual activity, or excretory functions performed in a lewd or lascivious manner, whether or not any of the above conduct is performed alone or between members of the same or opposite sex or between humans and animals. An act is simulated when it gives the appearance of being sexual conduct.
(Amended by Stats.1977, c. 1148, p. —, § 3.)

Editors' Note

This section makes it a felony to employ a child under the age of 16 or to promote, use, persuade, induce, or coerce a child under the age of 16 to pose or model alone, or with others, in the making of sexually explicit material.

Sexually explicit material is defined in subsection (c) of this section. It is important to note that Labor Code Sections 1309.5 and 1309.6 require that those who sell or distribute sexually explicit material depicting those under 16 years of age engaged in sexual conduct, keep a record of the names and addresses of those from whom they have acquired this material. Failure to keep these records is a misdemeanor. It is imperative that you recognize the disclosure of these records "by law enforcement officers, except in the performance of their duties, is a misdemeanor." Thus, beware that an inappropriate disclosure of the record keeping function of those who distribute sexually explicit material involving children may subject you to prosecution for a misdemeanor.

See below for the complete text of Labor Code Sections 1309.5 and 1309.6.

1309.5. (a) Every person who, with knowledge that a person is a minor under 16 years of age, or who, while in possession of such facts that he should reasonably know that such person is a minor under 16 years of age, knowingly sells or distributes for resale films, photographs, slides, or magazines which depict a minor under 16 years of age engaged in sexual conduct as defined in Section 311.4 of the Penal Code, shall determine the names and addresses of persons from whom such material is obtained, and shall keep a record of such names and addresses. Such records shall be kept for a period of three years after such material is obtained, and shall be kept confidential except that those records shall be available to law enforcement officers as described in Section 830.1 of the Penal Code upon request.

(b) Every retailer who knows or reasonably should know that such films, photographs, slides, or magazines depict a minor under the age of 16 years engaged in sexual conduct as defined in Section 311.4 of the Penal Code, shall keep a record of the names and addresses of persons from whom such material is acquired. Such records shall be kept for a period of three years after such material is acquired, and shall be kept confidential except that they shall be available to law enforcement officers as described in Section 830.1 of the Penal Code upon request.

(c) The failure to keep and maintain the records described in subdivisions (a) and (b) for a period three years after the obtaining or acquisition of such material is a misdemeanor. Disclosure of such records by law enforcement officers, except in the performance of their duties, is a misdemeanor.

1309.6. (a) Any person who violates any provision of Section 1309.5 shall be liable for a civil penalty not to exceed five thousand dollars ($5,000) for each violation, which shall be assessed and recovered in a civil action brought in the name of the people of the State of California by the Attorney General or by any district attorney, county counsel, or city attorney in any court of competent jurisdiction.

(b) If the action is brought by the Attorney General, one-half of the penalty collected shall be paid to the treasurer of the county in which the judgment was entered, and one-half to the State Treasurer. If brought by a district attorney or county counsel, the entire amount of penalty collected shall be paid to the treasurer of the county in which the judgment was entered. If brought by a city attorney or city prosecutor, one-half of the penalty shall be paid to the treasurer of the county and one-half to the city.

---

§ 311.5. Advertising or promoting sale or distribution; solicitation

Every person who writes, creates, or solicits the publication or distribution of advertising or other promotional material, or who in any manner promotes, the sale, distribution, or exhibition of matter represented or held out by him to be obscene, is guilty of a misdemeanor.
(Amended by Stats.1969, c. 249, p. 599, § 4.)

§ 311.6. Participation in, or production or presentation of, obscene live conduct in public place

Every person who knowingly engages or participates in, manages, produces, sponsors, presents or exhibits obscene live conduct to or before an assembly or audience consisting of at least one person or spectator in any public place or in any place exposed to public view, or in any place open to the public or to a segment thereof, whether or not an admission fee is charged, or whether or not attendance is conditioned upon the presentation of a membership card or other token, is guilty of a misdemeanor.
(Amended by Stats.1970, c. 1072, p. 1909, § 2.)

§ 311.7. Requiring receipt of obscene matter as condition to sale or delivery of papers, magazines, books, etc.; denying or threatening to deny franchise

Every person who, knowingly, as a condition to a sale, allocation, consignment, or delivery for resale of any paper, magazine, book, periodical, publication or other merchandise, requires that the purchaser or consignee receive any obscene matter or who denies or threatens to deny a franchise, revokes or threatens to revoke, or imposes any penalty, financial or otherwise, by reason of the failure of any person to accept obscene matter, or by reason of the return of such obscene matter, is guilty of a misdemeanor.
(Added by Stats.1961, c. 2147, p. 4428, § 5.)

§ 311.8. Defense

It shall be a defense in any prosecution for a violation of this chapter that the act charged was committed in aid of legitimate scientific or educational purposes.

(Added by Stats.1961, c. 2147, p. 4428, § 5.)

§ 311.9. Punishment

(a) Every person who violates Section 311.2 or 311.5, except subdivision (b) of Section 311.2, is punishable by fine of not more than one thousand dollars ($1,000) plus five dollars ($5) for each additional unit of material coming within the provisions of this chapter, which is involved in the offense, not to exceed ten thousand dollars ($10,000), or by imprisonment in the county jail for not more than six months plus one day for each additional unit of material coming within the provisions of this chapter, and which is involved in the offense, such basic maximum and additional days not to exceed 360 days in the county jail, or by both such fine and imprisonment. If such person has previously been convicted of any offense in this chapter, or of a violation of Section 313.1, a violation of Section 311.2 or 311.5, except subdivision (b) of Section 311.2, is punishable as a felony.

(b) Every person who violates Section 311.4 is punishable by fine of not more than two thousand dollars ($2,000) or by imprisonment in the county jail for not more than one year, or by both such fine and such imprisonment. If such person has been previously convicted of a violation of former Section 311.3 or Section 311.4, he is punishable by imprisonment in the state prison.

(c) Every person who violates Section 311.7 is punishable by fine of not more than one thousand dollars ($1,000) or by imprisonment in the county jail for not more than six months, or by both such fine and imprisonment. For a second and subsequent offense he shall be punished by a fine of not more than two thousand dollars ($2,000), or by imprisonment in the county jail for not more than one year, or by both such fine and imprisonment. If such person has been twice convicted of a violation of this chapter, a violation of Section 311.7 is punishable as a felony.

(Amended by Stats.1977, c. 1061, p. —, § 2.)

§ 312. Destruction of obscene material upon conviction

Upon the conviction of the accused, the court may, when the conviction becomes final, order any matter or advertisement, in respect whereof the accused stands convicted, and which remains in the possession or under the control of the district attorney or any law enforcement agency, to be destroyed, and the court may cause to be destroyed any such material in its possession or under its control.

(Added by Stats.1961, c. 2147, p. 4429, § 5.)

§ 313. Definitions

As used in this chapter:

(a) "Harmful matter" means matter, taken as a whole, the predominant appeal of which to the average person, applying contemporary standards, is to prurient interest, i. e., a shameful or morbid interest in nudity, sex, or excretion; and is matter which taken as a whole goes substantially beyond customary limits of candor in description or representation of such matters; and is matter which taken as a whole is utterly without redeeming social importance for minors.

(1) When it appears from the nature of the matter or the circumstances of its dissemination, distribution or exhibition that it is designed for clearly defined deviant sexual groups, the predominant appeal of the matter shall be judged with reference to its intended recipient group.

(Added by Stats.1969, c. 248, p. 596, § 1.)

§ 313.1. Distribution or exhibition to, or admittance of, a minor; sale or offer to sell from vending machine near school

(a) Every person who, with knowledge that a person is a minor, or who fails to exercise reasonable care in ascertaining the true age of a minor, knowingly distributes, sends, causes to be sent, exhibits, or offers to distribute or exhibit any harmful matter to the minor is guilty of a misdemeanor.

(b) Every person who misrepresents himself to be the parent or guardian of a minor and thereby causes the minor to be admitted to an exhibition of any harmful matter is guilty of a misdemeanor.

(c) Any person who, within 500 meters of any elementary school, junior high school, high school, or public playground, or any part thereof, knowingly sells or offers to sell, in any coin- or slug-operated vending machine or mechanically or electronically controlled vending machine which is located on a

public sidewalk, any harmful matter displaying to the public view photographs or pictorial representations of the commission of the following acts, is guilty of a misdemeanor: sodomy, oral copulation, sexual intercourse, masturbation, bestiality, or a photograph of an exposed penis in an erect and turgid state.
(Amended by Stats.1976, c. 1121, p. —, § 1.)

§ 313.4. Punishment

Every person who violates Section 313.1 is punishable by fine of not more than two thousand dollars ($2,000) or by imprisonment in the county jail for not more than one year, or by both such fine and imprisonment. If such person has been previously convicted of a violation of Section 313.1 or any section of Chapter 7.5 (commencing with Section 311) of Title 9 of Part 1 of this code, he is punishable by imprisonment in the state prison.
(Amended by Stats.1976, c. 1139, p. —, § 181, operative July 1, 1977.)

§ 314. Lewd or obscene conduct; indecent exposure; obscene exhibitions; punishment

Every person who willfully and lewdly, either:

1. Exposes his person, or the private parts thereof, in any public place, or in any place where there are present other persons to be offended or annoyed thereby; or,

2. Procures, counsels, or assists any person so to expose himself or take part in any model artist exhibition, or to make any other exhibition of himself to public view, or the view of any number of persons, such as is offensive to decency, or is adapted to excite to vicious or lewd thoughts or acts, is guilty of a misdemeanor.

Upon the second and each subsequent conviction under subdivision 1 of this section, or upon a first conviction under subdivision 1 of this section after a previous conviction under Section 288 of this code, every person so convicted is guilty of a felony, and is punishable by imprisonment in state prison.
(Amended by Stats.1976, c. 1139, p. —, § 182, operative July 1, 1977.)

Notes of Decisions

Nudity

Nudity in and of itself is not within proscription of this section relating to exposure of person or the private parts thereof. Eckl v. Davis (1975) 124 Cal.Rptr. 685, 51 C.A.3d 831.

Construction and application

To violate this section by willfully residing in a house of ill fame, one must do so voluntarily and with knowledge of the nature of the establishment; moreover, the evident purpose of this section in deterring the evil of prostitution requires that the prohibition against willful residence be limited to those who by their residence knowingly encourage or support the maintenance of that evil on the premises. Cartwright v. Board of Chiropractic Examiners (1976) 129 Cal.Rptr. 462, 548 P.2d 1134.

The legislature has expressly evidenced, by § 318.6 and this section relating to public exposure by employees or entertainers in food or beverage establishment, and to public exposure by participants in live acts, demonstrations or exhibitions, its intent to permit local regulation of the conduct therein described insofar as any such regulation might have otherwise invaded a field previously held to have been preempted by the state. Crownover v. Musick (1973) 107 Cal.Rptr. 681, 509 P.2d 497, 9 C.3d 405, certiorari denied 94 S.Ct. 1443, 415 U.S. 931, 39 L.Ed.2d 489.

Conviction of indecent exposure requires proof beyond a reasonable doubt that actor not only meant to expose himself, but intended by his conduct to direct public attention to his genitals for purpose of sexual arousal, gratification, or affront. In re Smith (1972) 102 Cal.Rptr. 335, 497 P.2d 807, 7 C.3d 362.

§ 315. Keeping or residing in house of ill-fame; common repute as evidence

Every person who keeps a house of ill-fame in this state, resorted to for the purposes of prostitution or lewdness, or who willfully resides in such house, is guilty of a misdemeanor; and in all prosecutions for keeping or resorting to such a house common repute may be received as competent evidence of the character of the house, the purpose for which it is kept or used, and the character of the women inhabiting or resorting to it.
(Amended by Stats.1905, c. 507, p. 668, § 1.)

§ 316. Keeping disorderly houses, etc., which disturb immediate neighborhood; innkeepers; landlords

Every person who keeps any disorderly house, or any house for the purpose of assignation or prostitution, or any house of public resort, by which the peace, comfort, or decency of the immediate neighborhood is habitually disturbed, or who keeps any inn in a disorderly manner; and every person who lets any apartment or tenement, knowing that it is to be used for the purpose of assignation or prostitution, is guilty of a misdemeanor.
(Amended by Code Am.1873–74, c. 614, p. 430, § 26.)

§ 318.5. Public exposure by employees or entertainers in food or beverage establishment; local regulations; exemptions

Nothing in this code shall invalidate an ordinance of, or be construed to prohibit the adoption of an ordinance by, a county or city, if such ordinance directly regulates the exposure of the genitals or buttocks of or the breasts of any person who acts as a waiter, waitress, or entertainer, whether or not the owner of the establishment in which the activity is performed employs or pays any compensation to such person to perform such activity, in an establishment which serves food, beverages, or food and beverages, including, but not limited to, alcoholic beverages, for consumption on the premises of such establishment.

The provisions of this section shall not apply to a theater, concert hall, or similar establishment which is primarily devoted to theatrical performances.

This section shall be known and may be cited as the "Quimby-Walsh Act."
(Added by Stats.1969, c. 1534, p. 3128, § 1.)

§ 318.6. Public exposure by participants in live acts, demonstrations or exhibitions; local regulations; exemptions

Nothing in this code shall invalidate an ordinance of, or be construed to prohibit the adoption of an ordinance by, a city or county, if such ordinance relates to any live acts, demonstrations, or exhibitions which occur in public places, places open to the public, or places open to public view and involve the exposure of the private parts or buttocks of any participant or the breasts of any female participant, and if such ordinance prohibits an act or acts which are not expressly authorized or prohibited by this code.

The provisions of this section shall not apply to a theater, concert hall, or similar establishment which is primarily devoted to theatrical performances.
(Added by Stats.1969, c. 1535, p. 3129, § 1.)

§ 319. Definition

Lottery defined. A lottery is any scheme for the disposal or distribution of property by chance, among persons who have paid or promised to pay any valuable consideration for the chance of obtaining such property or a portion of it, or for any share or any interest in such property, upon any agreement, understanding, or expectation that it is to be distributed or disposed of by lot or chance, whether called a lottery, raffle, or gift enterprise, or by whatever name the same may be known.
(Enacted 1872.)

§ 326.5. Bingo games for charity

(a) Neither this chapter nor Chapter 10 (commencing with Section 330) applies to any bingo game which is conducted in a city, county, or city and county pursuant to an ordinance enacted under Section 19 of Article IV of the State Constitution, provided, that such ordinance allows games to be conducted only by organizations exempted from the payment of the bank and corporation tax by Sections 23701a, 23701b, 23701d, 23701e, 23701f, 23701g, and 23701*l*, of the Revenue and Taxation Code and by mobilehome park associations and senior citizens organizations; and provided that the proceeds of such games are used only for charitable purposes.

(b) It is a misdemeanor for any person to receive or pay a profit, wage, or salary from any bingo game authorized by Section 19 of Article IV of the State Constitution.

(c) A violation of subdivision (b) of this section shall be punishable by a fine not to exceed ten thousand dollars ($10,000), which fine shall be deposited in the general fund of the city, county, or city and county which enacted the ordinance authorizing the bingo game. A violation of any provision of this section, other than subdivision (b), is a misdemeanor.

(d) The city, county, or city and county which enacted the ordinance authorizing the bingo game may bring an action to enjoin a violation of this section.

(e) No minors shall be allowed to participate in any bingo game.

(f) An organization authorized to conduct bingo games pursuant to subdivision (a) shall conduct a bingo game only on property owned or leased by it, and which property is used by such organization for an office of for performance of the purposes for which the organization is organized. Nothing in this subdivision shall be construed to require that the property owned or leased by the organization be used or leased exclusively by such organization.

(g) All bingo games shall be open to the public, not just to the members of the authorized organization.

(h) A bingo game shall be operated and staffed only by members of the authorized organization which organized it. Such members shall not receive a profit, wage, or salary from any bingo game. Only the organization authorized to conduct a bingo game shall operate such game, or participate in the promotion, supervision, or any other phase of such game.

(i) No individual corporation, partnership, or other legal entity except the organization authorized to conduct a bingo game shall hold a financial interest in the conduct of such bingo game.

(j) With respect to organizations exempt from payment of the bank and corporation tax by Section 23701d of the Revenue and Taxation Code, all profits derived from a bingo game shall be kept in a special fund or account and shall not be commingled with any other fund or account. Such profits shall be used only for charitable purposes. With respect to other organizations authorized to conduct bingo games pursuant to this section, all proceeds derived from a bingo game shall be kept in a special fund or account and shall not be commingled with any other fund or account. Such proceeds shall be used only for charitable purposes, except as follows:

(1) Such proceeds may be used for prizes.

(2) A portion of such proceeds, not to exceed 10 percent of the proceeds after the deduction for prizes, or five hundred dollars ($500) per month, whichever is less, may be used for rental of property, overhead, and administrative expenses.

(k) A city, county, or city and county may impose a license fee, on each organization which it authorizes to conduct bingo games. The fee, whether for the initial license or renewal, shall not exceed fifty dollars ($50). If an application for a license is denied, one-half of any license fee paid shall be refunded to the organization.

(*l*) No person shall be allowed to participate in a bingo game, unless the person is physically present at the time and place in which the bingo game is being conducted.

(m) The total value of prizes awarded during the conduct of any bingo games shall not exceed two hundred fifty dollars ($250) in cash or kind, or both, for each separate game which is held.

(n) As used in this section "bingo" means a game of chance in which prizes are awarded on the basis of designated numbers or symbols on a card which conform to numbers or symbols selected at random. It is the intention of the Legislature that bingo as defined in this subdivision applies exclusively to this section and shall not be applied in the construction or enforcement of any other provision of law.
(Amended by Stats.1977, c. 271, p. —, § 1.)

§ 337a. Bookmaking or pool-selling; keeping or occupying place with paraphernalia for recording wagers, etc.; stake holding; recording wagers; permitting unlawful use of room or enclosure; making or accepting wagers; punishment; application of section

Every person,

1. Who engages in pool selling or bookmaking, with or without writing, at anytime or place; or

2. Who, whether for gain, hire, reward, or gratuitously, or otherwise, keeps or occupies, for any period of time whatsoever, any room, shed, tenement, tent, booth, building, float, vessel, place, stand or enclosure, of any kind, or any part thereof, with a book or books, paper or papers, apparatus, device or paraphernalia, for the purpose of recording or registering any bet or bets, or any purported bet or bets, or wager or wagers, or any purported wager or wagers, or of selling pools, or purported pools, upon the result, or purported result, of any trial, or purported trial, or contest, or purported contest, of skill, speed or power of endurance of man or beast, or between men, beasts, or mechanical apparatus, or upon the result, or purported result, of any lot, chance, casualty, unknown or contingent event whatsoever; or

3. Who, whether for gain, hire, reward, or gratuitously, or otherwise, receives, holds, or forwards, or purports or pretends to receive, hold, or forward, in any manner whatsoever, any money, thing or consideration of value, or the equivalent or memorandum thereof, staked, pledged, bet or wagered, or to be staked, pledged, bet or wagered, or offered for the purpose of being staked, pledged, bet or wagered, upon the result, or purported result, of any trial, or purported trial, or contest, or purported contest, of skill, speed or power of endurance of man or beast, or between men, beasts, or mechanical apparatus, or upon the result, or purported result, of any lot, chance, casualty, unknown or contingent event whatsoever; or

4. Who, whether for gain, hire, reward, or gratuitously, or otherwise, at any time or place, records, or registers any bet or bets, wager or wagers, upon the result, or purported result, of any trial, or purported trial, or contest, or purported contest, of skill, speed or power of endurance of man or beast, or between men, beasts, or mechanical apparatus, or upon the result, or purported result, of any lot, chance, casualty, unknown or contingent event whatsoever; or

5. Who, being the owner, lessee or occupant of any room, shed, tenement, tent, booth, building, float, vessel, place, stand, enclosure or grounds, or any part thereof, whether for gain, hire, reward, or gratuitously, or otherwise, permits the same to be used or occupied for any purpose, or in any manner prohibited by subdivisions 1, 2, 3 or 4 of this section; or

§ 337a

6. Who lays, makes, offers or accepts any bet or bets, or wager or wagers, upon the result, or purported result, of any trial, or purported trial, or contest, or purported contest, of skill, speed or power of endurance of man or beast, or between men, beasts, or mechanical apparatus,

is punishable by imprisonment in the county jail for a period of not more than one year or in the state prison.

(a) In any accusatory pleading charging a violation of this section, if the defendant has been once previously convicted of a violation of any subdivision of this section, the previous conviction shall be charged in the accusatory pleading, and, if the previous conviction is found to be true by the jury, upon a jury trial, or by the court, upon a court trial, or is admitted by the defendant, the defendant shall, if he is not imprisoned in the state prison, be imprisoned in the county jail for a period of not more than one year or pay a fine of not less than five hundred dollars ($500) nor more than five thousand dollars ($5,000), or be punished by both such fine and imprisonment. Nothing in this paragraph shall prohibit a court from placing such a person on probation, provided, however, that such person shall be required to pay a fine of not less than five hundred dollars ($500) nor more than five thousand dollars ($5,000) or to be imprisoned in the county jail for a period of not more than one year as a condition thereof. In no event does the court have the power to absolve a person convicted hereunder from either being imprisoned or from paying a fine of not less than five hundred dollars ($500).

(b) In any accusatory pleading charging a violation of this section, if the defendant has been previously convicted two or more times of a violation of any subdivision of this section, each such previous conviction shall be charged in the accusatory pleadings; and if two or more of such previous convictions are found to be true by the jury, upon a jury trial, or by the court, upon a court trial, or are admitted by the defendant, the defendant shall, if he is not imprisoned in the state prison, be imprisoned in the county jail for a period of not more than one year or pay a fine of not less than one thousand dollars ($1,000) nor more than five thousand dollars ($5,000), or be punished by both such fine and imprisonment. Nothing in this paragraph shall prohibit a court from placing such a person on probation, provided however, that such person shall be required to pay a fine of not less than one thousand dollars ($1,000) nor more than five thousand dollars ($5,000) or to be imprisoned in the county jail for a period of not more than one year as a condition thereof. In no event does the court have the power to absolve a person convicted hereunder from either being imprisoned or from paying a fine of not less than one thousand dollars ($1,000).

Except where the existence of a previous conviction of any subdivision of this section was not admitted or not found to be true pursuant to this section, or the court finds that a prior conviction was invalid, the court shall not strike or dismiss any prior convictions alleged in the information or indictment.

This section shall apply not only to persons who may commit any of the acts designated in subdivisions 1 to 6 inclusive of this section, as a business or occupation, but shall also apply to every person or persons who may do in a single instance any one of the acts specified in said subdivisions 1 to 6 inclusive. (Amended by Stats.1978, c. 1164, p. —, § 1.)

Notes of Decisions

A "front office" is, for bookmaking purposes, a place staffed by a clerk who takes bets phoned in by bettors and who temporarily records them on objects which are quickly destructible. People v. Canard (1967) 65 Cal.Rptr. 15, 257 C.A.2d 444, certiorari denied 89 S.Ct. 231, 393 U.S. 912, 21 L.Ed.2d 198.

"Bookmaking" is the making of betting book and includes taking of bets. People v. Thompson (1962) 24 Cal.Rptr. 101, 206 C.A.2d 734; People v. Owens (1962) 23 Cal.Rptr. 449, 205 C.A.2d 775.

It is essential for conviction of violation of provision of this section proscribing the keeping or occupancy of any room containing paraphernalia for purpose of recording or registering any bets that person charged keep or occupy the room, that room contain specified paraphernalia, and that the occupancy and paraphernalia are for purpose of recording or registering bets. People v. Cuda (1960) 3 Cal.Rptr. 86, 178 C.A.2d 397.

§ 337b. Sporting events; offering or attempting to bribe player; punishment

Any person who gives, or offers or promises to give, or attempts to give or offer, any money, bribe, or thing of value, to any participant or player, or to any prospective participant or player, in any sporting event, contest, or exhibition of any kind whatsoever, except a wrestling exhibition as defined in Section 18607 of the Business and Professions Code, and specifically including, but without being limited to, such sporting events, contests, and exhibitions as baseball, football, basketball, boxing, horseracing, and wrestling matches, with the intention or understanding or agreement that such participant or player or such prospective participant or player shall not use his best efforts to win such sporting event, contest, or exhibition, or shall so conduct himself in such sporting event, contest, or exhibition that any other player, participant or team of players or participants shall thereby be assisted or enabled to win such sporting event, contest, or exhibition, or shall so conduct himself in such sporting event, contest, or exhibition as to limit his or his team's margin of victory in such sporting event, contest, or exhibition, is guilty of a felony, and shall be punished by imprisonment in the state prison, or by a fine not exceeding five thousand dollars ($5,000), or by both such fine and imprisonment.

(Amended by Stats.1976, c. 1139, p. —, § 184, operative July 1, 1977.)

§ 337c. Sporting events; player accepting or attempting to accept bribe; punishment

Any person who accepts, or attempts to accept, or offers to accept, or agrees to accept, any money, bribe or thing of value, with the intention or understanding or agreement that he will not use his best efforts to win any sporting event, contest, or exhibition of any kind whatsoever, except a wrestling exhibition as defined in Section 18607 of the Business and Professions Code, and specifically including, but without being limited to, such sporting events, contests, or exhibitions as baseball, football, basketball, boxing, horseracing, and wrestling matches, in which he is playing or participating or is about to play or participate in, or will so conduct himself in such sporting event, contest, or exhibition that any other player or participant or team of players or participants shall thereby be assisted or enabled to win such sporting event, contest, or exhibition, or will so conduct himself in such sporting event, contest, or exhibition as to limit his or his team's margin of victory in such sporting event, contest, or exhibition, is guilty of a felony, and shall be punished by imprisonment in the state prison, or by a fine not exceeding five thousand dollars ($5,000), or by both such fine and imprisonment.

(Amended by Stats.1976, c. 1139, p. —, § 185, operative July 1, 1977.)

§ 337d. Sporting events; offer or attempt to bribe official; punishment

Any person who gives, or offers to give, or promises to give, or attempts to give, any money, bribe or thing of value to any person who is umpiring, managing, directing, refereeing, supervising, judging, presiding or officiating at, or who is about to umpire, manage, direct, referee, supervise, judge, preside or officiate at any sporting event, contest, or exhibition of any kind whatsoever, and specifically including, but without being limited to, such sporting events, contests, and exhibitions as baseball, football, boxing, horseracing, and wrestling matches, with the intention or agreement or understanding that such person shall corruptly or dishonestly umpire, manage, direct, referee, supervise, judge, preside, or officiate at, any such sporting event, contest, or exhibition, or the players or participants thereof, with the intention or purpose that the result of the sporting event, contest, or exhibition will be affected or influenced thereby, is guilty of a felony and shall be punished by imprisonment in the state prison, or by a fine not exceeding five thousand dollars ($5,000), or by both such fine and imprisonment.

(Amended by Stats.1976, c. 1139, p. —, § 186, operative July 1, 1977.)

§ 337e. Sporting events; official receiving or attempting to receive bribe; punishment

Any person who as umpire, manager, director, referee, supervisor, judge, presiding officer or official receives or agrees to receive, or attempts to receive any money, bribe or thing of value, with the understanding or agreement that such umpire, manager, director, referee, supervisor, judge, presiding officer, or official shall corruptly conduct himself or shall corruptly umpire, manage, direct, referee, supervise, judge, preside, or officiate at, any sporting event, contest, or exhibition of any kind whatsoever, and specifically including, but without being limited to, such sporting events, contests, and exhibitions as baseball, football, boxing, horseracing, and wrestling matches, or any player or participant thereof, with the intention or purpose that the result of the sporting event, contest, or exhibition will be affected or influenced thereby, is guilty of a felony and shall be punished by imprisonment in the state prison, or by a fine not exceeding five thousand dollars ($5,000), or by both such fine and imprisonment.

(Amended by Stats.1976, c. 1139, p. —, § 187, operative July 1, 1977.)

§ 337i. Transmittal of racing information to gamblers

Every person who knowingly transmits information as to the progress or results of a horserace, or information as to wagers, betting odds, changes in betting odds, post or off times, jockey or player changes in any contest or trial, or purported contest or trial, involving humans, beasts, or mechanical

§ 337i

apparatus by any means whatsoever including, but not limited to telephone, telegraph, radio, and semaphore when such information is transmitted to or by a person or persons engaged in illegal gambling operations, is punishable by imprisonment in the county jail for a period of not more than one year or in the state prison.

This section shall not be construed as prohibiting a newspaper from printing such results or information as news, or any television or radio station from telecasting or broadcasting such results or information as news. This section shall not be so construed as to place in jeopardy any common carrier or its agents performing operations within the scope of a public franchise, or any gambling operation authorized by law.
(Amended by Stats.1976, c. 1139, p. —, § 189, operative July 1, 1977.)

CRIMES AGAINST PUBLIC HEALTH AND SAFETY

§ 377. False representation as physician to obtain prescription drugs

Every person who, in order to obtain for himself or another any drug that can be lawfully dispensed by a pharmacist only on prescription, falsely represents himself to be a physician or other person who can lawfully prescribe such drug, or falsely represents that he is acting on behalf of a person who can lawfully prescribe such drug, in a telephone communication with a pharmacist, is guilty of a misdemeanor.
(Added by Stats.1963, c. 1262, p. 2798, § 1.)

§ 397. Intoxicating liquors; sale to habitual drunkard or incompetent

Every person who sells or furnishes, or causes to be sold or furnished, intoxicating liquors to any habitual or common drunkard, or to any person who has been adjudged legally incompetent or insane by any court of this State and has not been restored to legal capacity, knowing such person to have been so adjudged, is guilty of a misdemeanor.
(Amended by Stats.1953, c. 146, p. 918, § 1.)

§ 398. Alcoholic beverages; sale, etc., between 2 and 6 a. m.

Every person engaged in the business of the sale or disposition of alcoholic beverages, who sells, gives or delivers, to any person, any alcoholic beverage between the hours of two o'clock a. m. and six o'clock a. m. of the same day, is guilty of a misdemeanor.
(Added by Stats.1937, c. 58, p. 153, § 2.)

CRIMES AGAINST THE PUBLIC PEACE

§ 403. Disturbance of public assembly or meeting

Every person who, without authority of law, willfully disturbs or breaks up any assembly or meeting, not unlawful in its character, other than such as is mentioned in Section 302 of the Penal Code and Section 29440 of the Elections Code, is guilty of a misdemeanor.
(Amended by Stats.1976, c. 1192, p. —, § 22.5.)

§ 404. Riots; definition

(a) Any use of force or violence, disturbing the public peace, or any threat to use such force or violence, if accompanied by immediate power of execution, by two or more persons acting together, and without authority of law, is a riot.

(b) As used in this section, disturbing the public peace may occur in any place of confinement. Place of confinement means any state prison, county jail, industrial farm, or road camp, or any city jail, industrial farm, or road camp.
(Amended by Stats.1978, c. 1186, p. —, § 1.)

§ 407. Unlawful assembly; definition

Whenever two or more persons assemble together to do an unlawful act, or do a lawful act in a violent, boisterous, or tumultuous manner, such assembly is an unlawful assembly.
(Amended by Stats.1969, c. 365, p. 890, § 1.)

Notes of Decisions

Proscriptions of this section must be limited to assemblies which are violent or which pose clear and present danger of imminent violence. In re Bozorg (1973) 108 Cal.Rptr. 465, 510 P.2d 1017, 9 C.3d 612, certiorari denied 94 S.Ct. 1959, 416 U.S. 950, 40 L.Ed.2d 300.

Legislature in its definitions of riot, rout, unlawful assembly, refusal to disperse and disturbing the peace, with the penalties connected therewith, has generally provided the means for officers to control any wilful and malicious obstruction of the citizens' free use of a public way. Rees v. City of Palm Springs (1961) 10 Cal.Rptr. 386, 188 C.A.2d 339.

The illegal purpose of group assembling to view "hot-rod" race renders the action of the group knowingly participating therein an "unlawful assembly" within statute providing that whenever two or more persons assemble together to do an unlawful act and separate without doing or advancing toward it or do an unlawful act in a violent, boisterous, or tumultuous manner such assembly is "unlawful assembly". Coverstone v. Davies (1952) 239 P.2d 876, 38 C.2d 315, certiorari denied 73 S.Ct. 50, 344 U.S. 840, 97 L.Ed. 653.

§ 408. Rout and unlawful assembly; punishment

Punishment of rout and unlawful assembly. Every person who participates in any rout or unlawful assembly is guilty of a misdemeanor.
(Enacted 1872.)

§ 409. Riot, rout, or unlawful assembly; remaining present after warning to disperse

Remaining present at place of riot, etc., after warning to disperse. Every person remaining present at the place of any riot, rout, or unlawful assembly, after the same has been lawfully warned to disperse, except public officers and persons assisting them in attempting to disperse the same, is guilty of a misdemeanor.
(Enacted 1872.)

§ 410. Magistrate or officer neglecting or refusing to disperse unlawful or riotous assembly

Magistrates neglecting or refusing to disperse rioters. If a magistrate or officer, having notice of an unlawful or riotous assembly, mentioned in this Chapter, neglects to proceed to the place of assembly, or as near thereto as he can with safety, and to exercise the authority with which he is invested for suppressing the same and arresting the offenders, he is guilty of a misdemeanor.
(Enacted 1872.)

§ 415. Fighting; noise; offensive words

Any of the following persons shall be punished by imprisonment in the county jail for a period of not more than 90 days, a fine of not more than two hundred dollars ($200), or both such imprisonment and fine:

(1) Any person who unlawfully fights in a public place or challenges another person in a public place to fight.

(2) Any person who maliciously and willfully disturbs another person by loud and unreasonable noise.

(3) Any person who uses offensive words in a public place which are inherently likely to provoke an immediate violent reaction.
(Amended by Stats.1976, c. 298, p. —, § 1.)

Notes of Decisions

A charge of disturbing the peace, wherein maximum lawful punishment is a fine not exceeding two hundred dollars or imprisonment in county jail for not more than 90 days, or both, is merely a "petty offense" for purposes of federal constitutional law, and therefore is not one as to which there is a right to trial by jury under the federal constitution. In re Gannon (1972) 103 Cal.Rptr. 224, 26 C.A.3d 731.

Where defendant, who walked through courthouse corridor wearing jacket bearing the words "Fuck the Draft" in a place where women and children were present, was convicted of disturbing the peace under this section prohibiting disturbing the peace by offensive conduct, the only "conduct" which the state sought to punish was the fact of communication; thus conviction rested solely upon "speech", not upon any separately identifiable conduct which allegedly was intended by defendant to be perceived by others as expressive of particular views but which, on its face, did not necessarily convey any message and hence arguably could be regulated without effectively repressing defendant's ability to express himself. Cohen v. California (U.S.1971) 91 S.Ct. 1780, 403 U.S. 15, 29 L.Ed.2d 284, rehearing denied 92 S.Ct. 26, 404 U.S. 876, 30 L.Ed.2d 124.

Phrases "disturb the peace" and "breach of the peace" as used in misdemeanor statute are substantially synonymous and are taken to mean disruption of public order by acts which are themselves violent or which tend to incite others to violence. In re Bushman (1970) 83 Cal.Rptr. 375, 463 P.2d 727, 1 C.3d 767.

Term "offensive" in describing conduct in disturbing the peace is not unconstitutionally vague and overbroad but has a well established meaning when used in connection with words which can cause a breach of the peace, and means conduct which incites violence or has a tendency to incite others to violence or a breach of the peace. People v. Cohen (1969) 81 Cal.Rptr. 503, 1 C.A.3d 94.

"Breach of the peace" and "disturbing the peace" are synonymous terms. Id.

Public peace is disturbed when acts complained of disturb public peace or tranquility enjoyed by members of community where good order reigns, or where acts are likely to produce violence, or where acts cause consternation and alarm in community; and it is not necessary that any act have in itself any element of violence in order to constitute breach of peace. People v. Green (1965) 44 Cal.Rptr. 438, 234 C.A.2d Supp. 871, certiorari denied 86 S.Ct. 576, 382 U.S. 993, 15 L.Ed.2d 480.

§ 415.5. Disturbance of peace of state college or university; punishment

(a) Any person who (1) unlawfully fights within any building or upon the grounds of any community college, state college, or state university or challenges another person within any such building or upon such grounds to fight, or (2) maliciously and willfully disturbs another person within any such building or upon such grounds by loud and unreasonable noise, or (3) uses offensive words within any such building or upon such grounds which are inherently likely to provoke an immediate violent reaction is guilty of a misdemeanor and shall be punished as follows:

(i) Upon a first conviction by a fine not exceeding two hundred dollars ($200) or by imprisonment in the county jail for a period of not more than 90 days, or by both such fine and imprisonment.

(ii) If the defendant has been previously convicted once of a violation of this section or of any offense defined in Chapter 1 (commencing with Section 626)

§ 415.5

of Title 15 of Part 1, by imprisonment in the county jail for a period of not less than 10 days or more than six months, or by both such imprisonment and a fine of not exceeding five hundred dollars ($500), and he shall not be released on probation, parole, or any other basis until he has served not less than 10 days.

(iii) If the defendant has been previously convicted two or more times of a violation of this section or of any offense defined in Chapter 1 (commencing with Section 626) of Title 15 of Part 1, by imprisonment in the county jail for a period of not less than 90 days or more than six months, or by both such imprisonment and a fine of not exceeding five hundred dollars ($500), and he shall not be released on probation, parole, or any other basis until he has served not less than 90 days.

(b) For the purpose of determining the penalty to be imposed pursuant to this section, the court may consider a written report from the Department of Justice containing information from its records showing prior convictions; and the communication is prima facie evidence of such convictions, if the defendant admits them, regardless of whether or not the complaint commencing the proceedings has alleged prior convictions.

(c) As used in this section "state university," "state college," and "community college" have the same meaning as these terms are given in Section 626.
(Amended by Stats.1976, c. 298, p. —, § 2.)

§ 416. Assembly for purpose of disturbing peace or committing unlawful act; refusal to disperse

Refusing to disperse upon lawful command. If two or more persons assemble for the purpose of disturbing the public peace, or committing any unlawful act, and do not disperse on being desired or commanded so to do by a public officer, the persons so offending are severally guilty of a misdemeanor.
(Enacted 1872.)

§ 417. Drawing, exhibiting, or using firearm or deadly weapon; self defense; peace officers

(a) Every person who, except in self-defense, in the presence of any other person, draws or exhibits any firearm, whether loaded or unloaded, or any other deadly weapon whatsoever, in a rude, angry or threatening manner, or who in any manner, unlawfully uses the same in any fight or quarrel is guilty of a misdemeanor.

(b) Every person who, in the immediate presence of a peace officer, draws or exhibits any firearm, whether loaded or unloaded, in a rude, angry or threatening manner, and who knows or reasonably should know that such victim is a peace officer engaged in the performance of his duties, and such peace officer is engaged in the performance of his duties is guilty of a felony punishable by imprisonment in the county jail not to exceed one year, or in the state prison.

As used in this section, "peace officers" refers to any person designated as a peace officer by Section 830.1, subdivisions (a) to (e), inclusive, of Section 830.2, and Section 830.5.
(Amended by Stats.1977, c. 667, p. —, § 1.)

TERRORISTS THREATS

§ 422. Felony; elements of crime; punishment

Any person who willfully threatens to commit a crime which will result in death or great bodily injury to another person, with intent to terrorize another or with reckless disregard of the risk of terrorizing another, and who thereby either:

(a) Causes another person reasonably to be in sustained fear for his or hers or their immediate family's safety;

(b) Causes the evacuation of a building, place of assembly, or facility used in public transportation;

(c) Interferes with essential public services; or

(d) Otherwise causes serious disruption of public activities, is guilty of a felony and shall be punished by imprisonment in the state prison.
(Added by Stats.1977, c. 1146, p. —, § 1.)

§ 422.5. Terrorize

As used in this title, "terrorize" means to create a climate of fear and intimidation by means of threats or violent action causing sustained fear for personal safety in order to achieve social or political goals.
(Added by Stats.1977, c. 1146, p. —, § 1.)

§ 424. Embezzlement and falsification of accounts by public officers; misappropriation; unauthorized loan, use or private profit; failure to pay over or transfer public moneys; punishment

Each officer of this state, or of any county, city, town, or district of this state, and every other person charged with the receipt, safekeeping, transfer, or disbursement of public moneys, who either:

1. Without authority of law, appropriates the same, or any portion thereof, to his own use, or to the use of another; or

2. Loans the same or any portion thereof; makes any profit out of, or uses the same for any purpose not authorized by law; or,

3. Knowingly keeps any false account, or makes any false entry or erasure in any account of or relating to the same; or,

4. Fraudulently alters, falsifies, conceals, destroys, or obliterates any such account; or,

5. Willfully refuses or omits to pay over, on demand, any public moneys in his hands, upon the presentation of a draft, order, or warrant drawn upon such moneys by competent authority; or,

6. Willfully omits to transfer the same, when such transfer is required by law; or,

7. Willfully omits or refuses to pay over to any officer or person authorized by law to receive the same, any money received by him under any duty imposed by law so to pay over the same;—

Is punishable by imprisonment in the state prison for two, three or four years, and is disqualified from holding any office in this state.

As used in this section, "public moneys" includes the proceeds derived from the sale of bonds or other evidence of indebtedness authorized by the legislative body of any city, county, district, or public agency. (Amended by Stats.1976, c. 1139, p. —, § 197, operative July 1, 1977.)

CRIMES AGAINST PROPERTY

§ 447a. Trailer coach; dwelling and appurtenances; punishment

Any person who willfully and maliciously sets fire to or burns or caused to be burned or who aids, counsels or procures the burning of any trailer coach, as defined in Section 635 of the Vehicle Code, or any inhabited house car, as defined in Section 362 of the Vehicle Code, or inhabited camper, as defined in Section 243 of the Vehicle Code, or any dwelling house, or any kitchen, shop, barn, stable or other outhouse that is parcel thereof, or belonging to or adjoining thereto, whether the property of himself or of another, shall be guilty of arson, and upon conviction thereof, be sentenced to the state prison for two, four, or six years. As used in this section, "inhabited" means currently being used for dwelling purposes, whether occupied or not.
(Amended by Stats.1978, c. 579, p. —. § 19.)

Notes of Decisions

Word "malice" in this section defining arson means deliberate and intentional firing of building, or other defined structure, as contrasted with an accidental or unintentional ignition thereof. People v. Andrews (1965) 44 Cal.Rptr. 94, 234 C.A.2d 69.

At common law, "arson" was the willful and malicious burning of the dwelling house of another, but "arson" has been extended by statute to include many acts of burning not involving special danger to the person. Ex parte Bramble (1948) 187 P.2d 411, 31 C.2d 43, certiorari denied 69 S.Ct. 1522, 337 U.S. 960, 93 L.Ed. 1759.

§ 448a. Private buildings other than dwelling; public buildings; punishment

Any person who willfully and maliciously sets fire to or burns or causes to be burned or who aids, counsels or procures the burning of any barn, stable, garage or other building, whether the property of himself or of another, not a parcel of a dwelling house; or any shop, storehouse, warehouse, factory, mill or other building, whether the property of himself or of another; or any church, meetinghouse, courthouse, workhouse, school, jail or other public building or any public bridge; shall, upon conviction thereof, be sentenced to the state prison for two, four, or six years.
(Amended by Stats.1978, c. 579, p. —, § 20.)

Editors' Note

Read People v. Beagle in table of cases included in this text.

§ 449a. Personal property; punishment

Any person who willfully and maliciously sets fire to or burns or causes to be burned or who aids, counsels or procures the burning of any barrack, cock, crib, rick or stack of hay, corn, wheat, oats, barley or other grain or vegetable product of any kind; or any field of standing hay or grain of any kind; or any pile of coal, wood or other fuel; or any pile of planks, boards, posts, rails or other lumber; or any streetcar, railway car, ship, boat or other watercraft, automobile or other motor vehicle; or any other personal property not herein specifically named except a trailer coach, as defined in Section 635 of the Vehicle Code; (such property being of the value of twenty-five dollars ($25) and the property of another person) shall upon conviction thereof, be sentenced to the state prison.
(Amended by Stats.1976, c. 1139, p. —, § 200, operative July 1, 1977.)

§ 449b. Malicious burning of bridge or of thing not subject to arson; punishment

Every person who willfully and maliciously burns any bridge exceeding in value fifty dollars ($50), or any structure, snowshed, vessel, or boat, not the subject of arson, or any tent, or any stack of hay or grain or straw of any kind, or any pile or baled hay or straw, or any pile of potatoes, or beans, or vegetables, or produce, or fruit of any kind, whether sacked, boxed, crated, or not, or any fence, or any railroad car, lumber, cordwood, railroad ties, telegraph or telephone poles, or shakes, or any tuleland or peat-ground of the value of twenty-five dollars ($25) or over, not the property of such person is punishable by imprisonment in the state prison.
(Amended by Stats.1976, c. 1139, p. —, § 201, operative July 1, 1977.)

§ 449c. Malicious burning of crops, grass, timber, brush, etc., punishment

Every person who willfully and maliciously burns any growing or standing grain, grass or tree, or any grass, forest, woods, timber, brush-covered land, or slashing, cutover land, not the property of such person is punishable by imprisonment in the state prison.
(Amended by Stats.1976, c. 1139, p. —, § 203, operative July 1, 1977.)

§ 450a. Personal property with intent to defraud insurers; punishment

Any person who willfully and with intent to injure or defraud the insurer sets fire to or burns or causes to be burned or who aids, counsels or procures the burning of any goods, wares, merchandise or other chattels or personal property of any kind, whether the property of himself or of another, which shall at the time be insured by any person or corporation against loss or damage by fire; shall upon conviction thereof, be sentenced to the state prison.
(Amended by Stats.1976, c. 1139, p. —, § 204, operative July 1, 1977.)

§ 451b. Local detention facility by prisoner in custody; maliciously starting unauthorized fire

(a) Any prisoner who is in custody in any local detention facility as defined in Section 6031.4 who maliciously starts an unauthorized fire is guilty of a misdemeanor.

(b) As used in this section, an "unauthorized fire" is one willfully set without the express or implied permission of the penal institution. It shall include, but not by way of limitation, fires started in mattresses, papers, rags, blankets, and paper cups without regard to the potential physical damage or harm that may naturally be expected to result therefrom.
(Added by Stats.1972, c. 916, p. 1636, § 1.)

§ 452. Possession of flammable, explosive or combustible material or substance, or device; intent; possession, manufacture or disposal of fire bomb

(a) Every person who possesses any flammable, explosive or combustible material or substance, or any device in an arrangement or preparation, with intent to willfully and maliciously use such material, substance or device to set fire to or burn any buildings or property mentioned in this chapter, is punishable by imprisonment in the state prison, or in the county jail, not exceeding one year.

(b) Every person who possesses, manufactures or disposes of a firebomb is guilty of a felony.

For the purposes of this subdivision, "disposes of" means to give, give away, loan, offer, offer for sale, sell, or transfer.

For the purposes of this subdivision, a "firebomb" is a breakable container containing a flammable liquid with a flashpoint of 150 degrees Fahrenheit or less, having a wick or similar device capable of being ignited, but no device commercially manufactured primarily for the purpose of illumination shall be deemed to be a firebomb for the purposes of this subdivision.

(c) Subdivisions (a) and (b) of this section shall not prohibit the authorized use or possession of any material, substance or device described therein by a member of the armed forces of the United States or by firemen, police officers, peace officers, or law enforcement officers authorized by the properly constituted authorities; nor shall those subdivisions prohibit the use or possession of any material, substance or device described therein when used solely for scientific research or educational purposes, or for disposal of brush under permit as provided for in Section 4494 of the Public Resources Code, or for any other lawful burning. Subdivision (b) of this section shall not prohibit the manufacture or disposal of a firebomb for the parties or purposes described in this subdivision.
(Amended by Stats.1976, c. 1139, p. —, § 205, operative July 1, 1977.)

§ 454. Violation of arson statutes during and within area of state of insurrection, state of disaster or extreme emergency; punishment

Every person who violates the provisions of Section 447a, 448a, 449a, 449b, 449c or 450a during and within the area of a state of insurrection or a state of emergency as proclaimed by the Governor pursuant to Section 143 of the Military and Veterans Code or pursuant to Section 8625 of the Government Code, provided that such state of emergency is proclaimed because of riot, is punishable by imprisonment in the state prison for three, five, or seven years. (Amended by Stats.1978, c. 579, p. —, § 21.)

§ 459. Definition

Every person who enters any house, room, apartment, tenement, shop, warehouse, store, mill, barn, stable, outhouse or other building, tent, vessel, railroad car, trailer coach, as defined in Section 635 of the Vehicle Code, any house car, as defined in Section 362 of the Vehicle Code, inhabited camper, as defined in Section 243 of the Vehicle Code, vehicle as defined by the Vehicle Code when the doors of such vehicle are locked, aircraft as defined by the Harbors and Navigation Code, mine or any underground portion thereof, with intent to commit grand or petit larceny or any felony is guilty of burglary. As used in this chapter, "inhabited" means currently being used for dwelling purposes, whether occupied or not. (Amended by Stats.1978, c. 579, p. —, § 22.)

Editors' Note

This section as amended in 1977 expands the definition of burglary to include house cars and campers when they are being used for dwelling purposes. This is the case whether or not someone is physically present in the vehicle at the time of the burglary.

Notes of Decisions

In general

Burglary is committed when person enters any house with intent to commit any felony. People v. Sears (1965) 44 Cal.Rptr. 330, 401 P.2d 938, 62 C.2d 737; People v. Bard (1968) 73 Cal.Rptr. 547, 447 P.2d 939, 70 C.2d 3.

Burglary is entering into a building with intent to commit theft or any felony. Reed v. Superior Court of Los Angeles County (1965) 47 Cal.Rptr. 815, 238 C.A.2d 321.

One who enters room or building with intent to commit a felony is guilty of burglary even though permission to enter has been extended to him personally or as a member of public, and entry need not constitute a trespass. People v. Sears (1965) 44 Cal.Rptr. 330, 401 P.2d 938, 62 C.2d 737.

Intruder's intent to commit theft was amply shown by his secret, noiseless entry in an unusual manner at an odd hour of night into homes where he was not an invited guest, the thefts of property, and his sudden flight on being discovered. People v. Corral (1964) 36 Cal.Rptr. 591, 224 C.A.2d 300.

Under this section, no breaking or use of force is required, and entry need not constitute a trespass; one who enters a room or building with intent to commit a felony is guilty of burglary even though permission to enter has been extended to him personally or as a member of the public. People v. Talbot (1966) 51 Cal.Rptr. 417, 414 P.2d 633, 64 C.2d 691, certiorari denied 87 S.Ct. 729, 385 U.S. 1015, 17 L.Ed.2d 551.

This section does not require breaking into any structure; burglary is committed if person enters store with intent to commit theft, although entry was made through public entrance during business hours. People v. Garcia (1963) 29 Cal.Rptr. 609, 214 C.A.2d 681.

A "breaking" is not one of the essential ingredients of crime of burglary. People v. Hickok (1962) 17 Cal.Rptr. 875, 198 C.A.2d 442.

Entry, in general

One may be guilty of violating section 484d et seq. without necessarily making any entry into store whatsoever since use or attempted use of credit card for purpose of obtaining goods, property, services, or anything of value need not be preceded by entry forbidden by this section. People v. Churchill (1967) 63 Cal.Rptr. 312, 255 C.A.2d 448.

The crime of burglary is complete when one enters the house of another with intent to commit a felony. People v. Morlock (1956) 292 P.2d 897, 46 C.2d 141.

Lateness of hour, numerous burglaries in area, and movement of defendant's vehicle behind apartment building constituted sufficient cause for police officer to stop defendant for routine interrogation, and when investigation thereafter established reasonable cause to believe defendant had committed felony, his subsequent arrest and incidental search of his person and vehicle were permissible. People v. Singletary (1968) 73 Cal.Rptr. 855, 268 C.A.2d 41.

Where, despite fact that driver of automobile used in robbery getaway could have been ticketed for speeding, vehicle was not stopped to make an arrest for moving violation but to conduct an investigation, and, if warranted, make an arrest for the robbery, incidental search of entire car for fruits of such robbery was justifiable. People v. Joines (1970) 89 Cal.Rptr. 661, 11 C.A.3d 259.

A person is guilty of burglary if he enters a room with intent to commit a theft, and such is so even though permission to enter has been extended to him personally or as a member of the public. People v. Edwards (1971) 99 Cal.Rptr. 516, 22 C.A.3d 598.

Inference of entry

Prosecution need only advance evidence from which a jury may reasonably infer entry with intent to steal to withstand reversal of conviction of burglary for failure of proof. People v. Earl (1973) 105 Cal.Rptr. 831, 29 C.A.3d 894.

Building or structure

Telephone booth with three walls, a door, roof and floor was a "building" within meaning of Penal Code section providing that "Every person who enters any building with intent to commit grand or petit larceny or any felony is guilty of burglary. People v. Nunez (1970) 86 Cal.Rptr. 707, 7 C.A.3d 655.

§ 460. Degrees; construction of section

1. Every burglary of an inhabited dwelling house or trailer coach as defined by the Vehicle Code, or the inhabited portion of any other building committed in the nighttime, is burglary of the first degree.

§ 460

2. All other kinds of burglary are of the second degree.

3. This section shall not be construed to supersede or affect Section 464 of the Penal Code.
(Amended by Stats.1978, c. 579, p. —, § 23.)

Notes of Decisions

A residence was an "inhabited dwelling house" for purposes of this section though resident was temporarily absent from premises. People v. Gilbert (1961) 10 Cal.Rptr. 799, 188 C.A.2d 723; People v. Tittle (1968) 65 Cal.Rptr. 576, 258 C.A.2d 518; People v. Valdez (1962) 21 Cal.Rptr. 764, 203 C.A.2d 559; People v. Hann (1930) 285 P. 1070, 104 C.A. 492; People v. Loggins (1955) 282 P.2d 961, 132 C.A.2d 736.

Word "inhabited", as used in this section, does not modify only "dwelling house"; the word also modifies the word "building". People v. Lewis (1969) 79 Cal.Rptr. 650.

To constitute burglary it is not necessary that theft or felony be actually committed, forcible entry with felonious intent to commit theft being sufficient even though burglar voluntarily abandons his unlawful purpose; and therefore, where defendant entered inhabited dwelling house with burglarious intent and in nighttime, it would be immaterial whether larcenous taking occurred during day or night. People v. Stewart (1952) 248 P.2d 768, 113 C.A.2d 687.

Where there are four different factual bases which make up offense of first-degree burglary, criminal process should disclose, either in pleadings or in verdict, and preferably in both, the exact crime for which defendant stands charged and convicted. People v. Taylor (1966) 55 Cal.Rptr. 521, 247 C.A.2d 11.

To constitute first degree burglary, theft must have been committed between sunset and sunrise. People v. Hanz (1961) 12 Cal.Rptr. 282, 190 C.A.2d 793, certiorari denied 82 S.Ct. 444, 368 U.S. 969, 7 L.Ed.2d 398.

§ 461. Punishment

Burglary is punishable as follows:

1. Burglary in the first degree: by imprisonment in the state prison for two, four, or six years.

2. Burglary in the second degree: by imprisonment in the county jail not exceeding one year or in the state prison.
(Amended by Stats.1978, c. 579, p. —, § 24.)

§ 463. Night-time defined

"Night-time" defined. The phrase "night-time," as used in this Chapter, means the period between sunset and sunrise.
(Enacted 1872.)

§ 464. Burglary with acetylene torch, etc., or explosives; punishment

Any person who, with intent to commit crime, enters, either by day or by night, any building, whether inhabited or not, and opens or attempts to open any vault, safe, or other secure place by use of acetylene torch or electric arc, burning bar, thermal lance, oxygen lance, or any other similar device capable of burning through steel, concrete, or any other solid substance, or by use of nitroglycerine, dynamite, gunpowder, or any other explosive, is guilty of a felony and, upon conviction, shall be punished by imprisonment in the state prison for a term of three, five, or seven years.
(Amended by Stats.1978, c. 579, p. —, § 25.)

§ 466. Burglars' tools; possession; intent; making or altering key; making, altering, or repairing thing for use in committing offense; building defined

Every person having upon him or in his possession a picklock, crow, keybit, or other instrument or tool with intent feloniously to break or enter into any building, railroad car, aircraft, or vessel, trailer coach, or vehicle as defined in the Vehicle Code, or who shall knowingly make or alter, or shall attempt to make or alter, any key or other instrument above named so that the same will fit or open the lock of a building, railroad car, aircraft, or vessel, trailer coach, or vehicle as defined in the Vehicle Code, without being requested so to do by some person having the right to open the same, or who shall make, alter, or repair any instrument or thing, knowing or having reason to believe that it is intended to be used in committing a misdemeanor or felony, is guilty of misdemeanor. Any of the structures mentioned in Section 459 shall be deemed to be a building within the meaning of this section.
(Amended by Stats.1977, c. 725, p. —, § 1; Stats.1977, c. 1147, p. —, § 2.)

§ 466.3. Possession of tool, device, etc. designed to open, break into, tamper with or damage coin-operated machine with intent to commit theft; punishment

(a) Whoever possesses a key, tool, instrument, explosive, or device, or a drawing, print, or mold of a key, tool, instrument, explosive, or device, designed to open, break into, tamper with, or damage a coin-operated machine as defined in subdivision (b), with intent to commit a theft from such machine, is punishable by imprisonment in the county jail for not more than one year, or by fine of not more than one thousand dollars ($1,000), or by both.

(b) As used in this section, the term "coin-operated machine" shall include any automatic vending machine or any part thereof, parking meter, coin telephone, coin laundry machine, coin dry cleaning ma-

chine, amusement machine, music machine, vending machine dispensing goods or services, or moneychanger.
(Added by Stats.1972, c. 1088, p. 2028, § 1.)

§ 466.5. Motor vehicle master key; motor vehicle wheel lock master key; unlawful possession; manufacture; sale

(a) Every person who, with the intent to use it in the commission of an unlawful act, possesses a motor vehicle master key or a motor vehicle wheel lock master key is guilty of a misdemeanor.

(b) Every person who, with the intent to use it in the commission of an unlawful act, uses a motor vehicle master key to open a lock or operate the ignition switch of any motor vehicle or uses a motor vehicle wheel lock master key to open a wheel lock on any motor vehicle is guilty of a misdemeanor.

(c) Every person who knowingly manufactures for sale, advertises for sale, offers for sale, or sells a motor vehicle master key or a motor vehicle wheel lock master key, except to persons who use such keys in their lawful occupations or businesses, is guilty of a misdemeanor.

(d) As used in this section:

(1) "Motor vehicle master key" means a key which will operate all the locks or ignition switches, or both the locks and ignition switches, in a given group of motor vehicle locks or motor vehicle ignition switches, or both motor vehicle locks and motor vehicle ignition switches, each of which can be operated by a key which will not operate one or more of the other locks or ignition switches in such group.

(2) "Motor vehicle wheel lock" means a device attached to a motor vehicle wheel for theft protection purposes which can be removed only by a key unit unique to the wheel lock attached to a particular motor vehicle.

(3) "Motor vehicle wheel lock master key" means a key unit which will operate all the wheel locks in a given group of motor vehicle wheel locks, each of which can be operated by a key unit which will not operate any of the other wheel locks in the group.
(Amended by Stats.1976, c. 138, p. —, § 1, urgency, eff. May 5, 1976.)

§ 466.6. Motor vehicle keys; making other than by duplication of existing key; information required for work orders; retention and inspection; misdemeanor

(a) Any person who makes a key capable of operating the ignition of a motor vehicle for another by any method other than by the duplication of an existing key, whether or not for compensation, shall obtain the name, address, telephone number, if any, date of birth, and driver's license number or identification number of the person requesting or purchasing the key; and the registration or identification number, license number, year, make, model, color, and vehicle identification number of the vehicle for which the key is to be made. Such information, together with the date the key was made and the signature of the person for whom the key was made, shall be set forth on a work order. A copy of each such work order shall be retained for one year and shall be open to inspection by any peace officer during business hours.

Any person who violates any provision of this subdivision is guilty of a misdemeanor.

(b) The provisions of this section shall include, but are not limited to, the making of a key from key codes or impressions.

(c) Nothing contained in this section shall be construed to prohibit the duplication of any key for a motor vehicle from another such key.
(Amended by Stats.1978, c. 119, p. —, § 1.)

§ 466.7. Motor vehicle keys; possession; knowledge of making without consent; misdemeanor

Every person who, with the intent to use it in the commission of an unlawful act, possesses a motor vehicle key with knowledge that such key was made without the consent of either the registered or legal owner of the motor vehicle or of a person who is in lawful possession of the motor vehicle, is guilty of a misdemeanor.
(Added by Stats.1977, c. 1147, p. —, § 4.)

§ 467. Deadly weapons; possession with intent to assault

Having possession of deadly weapons with intent to commit an assault. Every person having upon him any deadly weapon with intent to assault another, is guilty of a misdemeanor.
(Enacted 1872.)

§ 468. Sniperscopes; unlawful possession, etc.; authorized use

Any person who knowingly buys, sells, receives, disposes of, conceals, or has in his possession a sniperscope shall be guilty of a misdemeanor, punishable by a fine not to exceed one thousand dollars

§ 468

($1,000) or by imprisonment in the county jail for not more than one year, or by both such fine and imprisonment.

As used in this section, sniperscope means any attachment, device or similar contrivance designed for or adaptable to use on a firearm which, through the use of a projected infrared light source and electronic telescope, enables the operator thereof to visually determine and locate the presence of objects during the nighttime.

This section shall not prohibit the authorized use or possession of such sniperscope by a member of the armed forces of the United States or by police officers, peace officers, or law enforcement officers authorized by the properly constituted authorities for the enforcement of law or ordinances; nor shall this section prohibit the use or possession of such sniperscope when used solely for scientific research or educational purposes.
(Added by Stats.1958, 1st Ex.Sess., c. 76, p. 308, § 1.)

§ 469. Unauthorized making, duplicating or possession of key to public building

Any person who knowingly makes, duplicates, causes to be duplicated, or uses, or attempts to make, duplicate, cause to be duplicated, or use, or has in his possession any key to a building or other area owned, operated, or controlled by the State of California, any state agency, board, or commission, a county, city, or other public school or community college district without authorization from the person in charge of such building or area or his designated representative and with knowledge of the lack of such authorization is guilty of a misdemeanor.
(Added by Stats.1970, c. 1090, p. 1934, § 1, eff. Sept. 14, 1970.)

§ 470. Forgery, intent; documents of value; counterfeiting seal; uttering; falsification of records

Every person who, with intent to defraud, signs the name of another person, or of a fictitious person, knowing that he has no authority so to do, to, or falsely makes, alters, forges, or counterfeits, any charter, letters patent, deed, lease, indenture, writing obligatory, will, testament, codicil, bond, covenant, bank bill or note, post note, check, draft, bill of exchange, contract, promissory note, due bill for the payment of money or property, receipt for money or property, passage ticket, trading stamp, power of attorney, or any certificate of any share, right or interest in the stock of any corporation or association, or any controller's warrant for the payment of money at the treasury, county order or warrant, or request for the payment of money, or the delivery of goods or chattels of any kind, or for the delivery of any instrument of writing, or acquittance, release, or receipt for money or goods, or any acquittance, release, or discharge of any debt, account, suit, action, demand, or other thing, real or personal, or any transfer or assurance of money, certificate of shares of stock, goods, chattels, or other property whatever, or any letter of attorney, or other power to receive money, or to receive or transfer certificates of shares of stock or annuities, or to let, lease, dispose of, alien, or convey any goods, chattels, lands, or tenements, or other estate, real or personal, or any acceptance or indorsement of any bill of exchange, promissory note, draft, order, or any assignment of any bond, writing obligatory, promissory note, or other contract for money or other property; or counterfeits or forges the seal or handwriting of another; or utters, publishes, passes, or attempts to pass, as true and genuine, any of the above-named false, altered, forged, or counterfeited matters, as above specified and described, knowing the same to be false, altered, forged, or counterfeited, with intent to prejudice, damage, or defraud any person; or who, with intent to defraud, alters, corrupts or falsifies any record of any will, codicil, conveyance, or other instrument, the record of which is by law evidence, or any record of any judgment of a court or the return of any officer to any process of any court, is guilty of forgery.
(Amended by Stats.1968, c. 713, p. 1414, § 1.)

Notes of Decisions

Party who, without permission, used another's credit card to obtain airline tickets and signed invoice therefor could be convicted of forgery notwithstanding codification of credit card offenses. People v. Liberto (1969) 79 Cal.Rptr. 306, 274 A.C.A. 501.

Enumeration of specific kinds of instruments in this section creating felony of forgery is not exclusive in view of "catch-all" clause referring to forgery or counterfeiting of "the seal or handwriting of another." People v. Burkett (1969) 74 Cal.Rptr. 692, 271 A.C.A. 160.

This section was correctly applied against defendant charged with inducing homeowners to sign blank trust deed represented as being job completion form. People v. Carson (1966) 49 Cal.Rptr. 653, 240 C.A.2d 477.

Defendant was guilty of forgery where victims were induced by trick or device to sign trust deeds to their property without knowing they were signing such a document. People v. Bresin (1966) 53 Cal.Rptr. 687, 245 C.A.2d 232.

Mere presence of person at scene of crime is insufficient in itself to show that such person is aider or abettor, but presence of person at commission of felony by another is evidence to be considered in determining whether or not he was guilty of aiding and abetting. People v. Flores (1969) 75 Cal.Rptr. 231, 269 C.A.2d 666.

§ 470a. Forgery or counterfeiting of driver's license or identification card; intent; punishment

Every person who alters, falsifies, forges, duplicates or in any manner reproduces or counterfeits any driver's license or identification card issued by a governmental agency with the intent that such driver's license or identification card be used to facilitate the commission of any forgery, is punishable by imprisonment in the state prison, or by imprisonment in the county jail for not more than one year.
(Amended by Stats.1976, c. 1139, p. ——, § 209, operative July 1, 1977.)

§ 470b. Display or possession of forged driver's license or identification card; intent; punishment

Every person who displays or causes or permits to be displayed or has in his possession any driver's license or identification card of the type enumerated in Section 470a with the intent that such driver's license or identification card be used to facilitate the commission of any forgery, is punishable by imprisonment in the state prison, or by imprisonment in the county jail for not more than one year.
(Amended by Stats.1976, c. 1139, p. ——, § 210, operative July 1, 1977.)

§ 471. Forgery; false entries in records or returns

Making false entries in records or returns. Every person who, with intent to defraud another, makes, forges, or alters any entry in any book of records, or any instrument purporting to be any record or return specified in the preceding section, is guilty of forgery.
(Enacted 1872.)

§ 471.5. Alteration or modification of medical record with fraudulent intent; punishment

Any person who alters or modifies the medical record of any person, with fraudulent intent, is guilty of a misdemeanor.
(Added by Stats.1974, c. 888, p. 1889, § 10.)

§ 473. Forgery; punishment

Forgery is punishable by imprisonment in the state prison, or by imprisonment in the county jail for not more than one year.
(Amended by Stats.1976, c. 1139, p. ——, § 211, operative July 1, 1977.)

§ 474. Forgery; telegraph or telephone messages; intent; punishment

Every person who knowingly and willfully sends by telegraph or telephone to any person a false or forged message, purporting to be from a telegraph or telephone office, or from any other person, or who willfully delivers or causes to be delivered to any person any such message falsely purporting to have been received by telegraph or telephone, or who furnishes, or conspires to furnish, or causes to be furnished to any agent, operator, or employee, to be sent by telegraph or telephone, or to be delivered, any such message, knowing the same to be false or forged, with the intent to deceive, injure, or defraud another, is punishable by imprisonment in the state prison, or in the county jail not exceeding one year, or by fine not exceeding five thousand dollars ($5,000), or by both such fine and imprisonment.
(Amended by Stats.1976, c. 1139, p. ——, § 212, operative July 1, 1977.)

§ 475. Possession or receipt of forged bills and notes; intent; possession of blank bills and notes; intent; punishment

Every person who has in his possession, or receives from another person, any forged promissory note or bank bill, or bills, or any counterfeited trading stamp, or stamps, for the payment of money or property, with the intention to pass the same, or to permit, cause, or procure the same to be uttered or passed, with the intention to defraud any person, knowing the same to be forged or counterfeited, or has or keeps in his possession any blank or unfinished note or bank bill made in the form or similitude of any promissory note or bill for payment of money or property, made to be issued by any incorporated bank or banking company, or any blank or unfinished check, money order, or traveler's check, made in the form or similitude of any check, money order, or traveler's check, whether the parties thereto are real or fictitious, with intention to fill up and complete such blank and unfinished note or bill, check, money order, or traveler's check, or to permit, or cause, or procure the same to be filled up and completed in order to utter or pass the same, or to permit, or cause, or procure the same to be uttered or passed, to defraud any person, is punishable by imprisonment in the state prison, or by imprisonment in the county jail for not more than one year.
(Amended by Stats.1976, c. 1139, p. ——, § 213, operative July 1, 1977.)

§ 475a. Possession of completed check, money order, traveler's check, controller's warrant or county warrant with intent to defraud

Every person who has in his possession a completed check, money order, traveler's check, controller's warrant for the payment of money at the treasury, or county order or warrant, whether the parties thereto are real or fictitious, with intention to utter or pass the same, or to permit, cause, or procure the same to be uttered or passed, to defraud any person, is punishable by imprisonment in the state prison, or by imprisonment in the county jail for not more than one year.
(Amended by Stats.1976, c. 1139, p. —, § 214, operative July 1, 1977.)

§ 476. Making, possessing, uttering, etc., fictitious instruments; intent; punishment

Every person who makes, passes, utters, or publishes, with intention to defraud any other person, or who, with the like intention, attempts to pass, utter, or publish, or who has in his possession, with like intent to utter, pass, or publish, any fictitious bill, note, or check, purporting to be the bill, note, or check, or other instrument in writing for the payment of money or property of some bank, corporation, copartnership, or individual, when, in fact, there is no such bank, corporation, copartnership, or individual in existence, knowing the bill, note, check, or instrument in writing to be fictitious, is punishable by imprisonment in the county jail for not more than one year, or in the state prison.
(Amended by Stats.1976, c. 1139, p. —, § 215, operative July 1, 1977.)

§ 476a. Checks, drafts, or orders on banks; insufficient funds; intent to defraud; punishment; presumption from protest; credit defined; partial validity

(a) Any person who for himself or as the agent or representative of another or as an officer of a corporation, willfully, with intent to defraud, makes or draws or utters or delivers any check, or draft or order upon any bank or depositary, or person, or firm, or corporation, for the payment of money, knowing at the time of such making, drawing, uttering or delivering that the maker or drawer or the corporation has not sufficient funds in, or credit with said bank or depositary, or person, or firm, or corporation, for the payment of such check, draft or order and all other checks, drafts or orders upon such funds then outstanding, in full upon its presentation, although no express representation is made with reference thereto, is punishable by imprisonment in the county jail for not more than one year, or in the state prison.

(b) However, if the total amount of all such checks, drafts, or orders that the defendant is charged with and convicted of making, drawing, or uttering does not exceed one hundred dollars ($100), the offense is punishable only by imprisonment in the county jail for not more than one year, except that this subdivision shall not be applicable if the defendant has previously been convicted of a violation of Section 470, 475, or 476 of this code, or of this section of this code, or of the crime of petty theft in a case in which defendant's offense was a violation also of Section 470, 475, or 476 of this code or of this section or if the defendant has previously been convicted of any offense under the laws of any other state or of the United States which, if committed in this state, would have been punishable as a violation of Section 470, 475, or 476 of this code or of this section of this code or if he has been so convicted of the crime of petty theft in a case in which, if defendant's offense had been committed in this state, it would have been a violation also of Section 470, 475, or 476 of this code, or of this section.

(c) Where such check, draft, or order is protested, on the ground of insufficiency of funds or credit, the notice of protest thereof shall be admissible as proof of presentation, nonpayment and protest and shall be presumptive evidence of knowledge of insufficiency of funds or credit with such bank or depositary, or person, or firm, or corporation.

(d) The word "credit" as used herein shall be construed to mean an arrangement or understanding with the bank or depositary or person or firm or corporation for the payment of such check, draft or order.

(e) If any of the preceding paragraphs, or parts thereof, shall be found unconstitutional or invalid, the remainder of this section shall not thereby be invalidated, but shall remain in full force and effect.
(Amended by Stats.1976, c. 1139, p. —, § 216, operative July 1, 1977.)

Editors' Note

Read People v. Beagle in table of cases included in this text.

Notes of Decisions

Where defendant charged with writing checks without sufficient funds admitted that he knew he did not have sufficient funds, presentment to drawee bank was not necessary element of offense but sole issue was whether he intended to defraud bank which cashed checks. People v. Rubin (1963) 36 Cal.Rptr. 167, 223 C.A.2d 825, 9 A.L.R.3d 707.

Specific intent to defraud which is requisite in prosecution for issuing checks without sufficient funds may be inferred from all surrounding circumstances. People v. Costello (1963) 36 Cal.Rptr. 155, 223 C.A.2d 748.

Crime of forgery does not require proof of who actually created forged instrument since it also involves making or alteration of document without authority or the uttering of such document with intent to defraud. People v. Martin (1962) 25 Cal.Rptr. 610, 208 C.A.2d 867.

Make, draw, utter, or deliver

This section provides for separate offenses of drawing, uttering, or delivering a check upon a bank where drawer has insufficient funds, and the word "utter" meaning to put in circulation as money or currency, to cause to pass in trade, and "utterance" meaning, as putting in circulation, as false coin or forged notes. People v. Descant (1942) 124 P.2d 864, 51 C.A.2d 343.

Check, draft, or order

Counter checks, which were clearly orders on named bank for payment of money, were not "promissory notes" but where "checks" within this section prohibiting issuing check without sufficient funds, notwithstanding provision to effect that signer represented that amount drawn was on deposit to signer's credit in bank, free of any claims, and was assigned to payee and that signer guaranteed payment with exchange and costs in collecting. People v. Eisenberg (1963) 28 Cal.Rptr. 583, 213 C.A.2d 121.

One may be convicted of theft based upon representation that fraudulent check was good. People v. Mason (1973) 109 Cal.Rptr. 867, 34 C.A.3d 281.

§ 484. Theft defined

(a) Every person who shall feloniously steal, take, carry, lead, or drive away the personal property of another, or who shall fraudulently appropriate property which has been entrusted to him, or who shall knowingly and designedly, by any false or fraudulent representation or pretense, defraud any other person of money, labor or real or personal property, or who causes or procures others to report falsely of his wealth or mercantile character and by thus imposing upon any person, obtains credit and thereby fraudulently gets or obtains possession of money, or property or obtains the labor or service of another, is guilty of theft. In determining the value of the property obtained, for the purposes of this section, the reasonable and fair market value shall be the test, and in determining the value of services received the contract price shall be the test. If there be no contract price, the reasonable and going wage for the service rendered shall govern. For the purposes of this section, any false or fraudulent representation or pretense made shall be treated as continuing, so as to cover any money, property or service received as a result thereof, and the complaint, information or indictment may charge that the crime was committed on any date during the particular period in question. The hiring of any additional employee or employees without advising each of them of every labor claim due and unpaid and every judgment that the employer has been unable to meet shall be prima facie evidence of intent to defraud.

(b) Except as provided in Section 10855 of the Vehicle Code, intent to commit theft by fraud is presumed if one who has leased or rented the personal property of another pursuant to a written contract fails to return the personal property to its owner within 20 days after the owner has made written demand by certified or registered mail following the expiration of the lease or rental agreement for return of the property so leased or rented, or if one presents to the owner identification which bears a false or fictitious name or address for the purpose of obtaining the lease or rental agreement.

(c) The presumptions created by subdivision (b) are presumptions affecting the burden of producing evidence.

(d) Within 30 days after the lease or rental agreement has expired, the owner shall make written demand for return of the property so leased or rented. Notice addressed and mailed to the lessee or renter at the address given at the time of the making of the lease or rental agreement and to any other known address shall constitute proper demand. Where the owner fails to make such written demand the presumption created by subdivision (b) shall not apply.

(Amended by Stats.1967, c. 1335, p. 3167, § 1.)

Notes of Decisions

Larceny, embezzlement, and false pretenses were merged under single crime of theft in this section. People v. Leaverton (1930) 289 P. 890, 107 C.A. 51; People v. Stevenson (1930) 284 P. 487, 103 C.A. 82.

Theft includes embezzlement, theft by trick and device, and theft by false pretenses. People v. Riley (1963) 31 Cal.Rptr. 404, 217 C.A.2d 11.

Purpose behind consolidation of larcenous crimes into single crime of theft is to remove the technicalities previously existing in pleading and proof of these crimes, and indictments and informations charging crime of theft can now simply allege an unlawful taking. People v. Antoine (1960) 4 Cal.Rptr. 589, 180 C.A.2d 786.

§ 484

Elements of theft in general

Theft includes embezzlement, theft by trick and device, and theft by false pretenses. People v. Eitzen (1974) 117 Cal.Rptr. 772, 43 C.A.3d 253.

Amount of money received by defendant, and not ultimate loss to victim, was determinative of degree of theft charged against automobile dealer who allegedly sold vehicles on which mileage shown by odometers had been reduced. People v. Ross (1972) 100 Cal.Rptr. 703, 25 C.A.3d 190.

Taking of property with bona fide intent to recover liquidated claim may not be theft, but mere self help in recompense of unliquidated damages is "theft". People v. Holmes (1970) 84 Cal.Rptr. 889, 5 C.A.3d 21.

In prosecution for petty theft, prosecution must prove an unlawful taking and asportation of property of some intrinsic value with intent to deprive the owner thereof. People v. James (1957) 318 P.2d 175, 155 C.A.2d 604; People v. Dunn (1958) 330 P.2d 481, 164 C.A.2d 335.

Essential elements of grand theft are; taking of thing which is subject matter of crime from owner into possession of defendant without consent of owner or claim of right, asportation of subject matter, and taking and carrying away with intent to deprive owner of his property wholly and permanently. People v. Torres (1962) 20 Cal.Rptr. 315, 201 C.A.2d 290, certiorari denied 83 S.Ct. 89, 371 U.S. 850, 9 L.Ed.2d 86.

Obtaining money from others by false pretense, trick or artifice, or by appropriating it after it has been entrusted to defendant, is "theft." People v. Sears (1954) 269 P.2d 683, 124 C.A.2d 839.

Grand theft is committed when a person with a preconceived design to appropriate another's property to his own use obtains possession of it by fraud or trickery and such property need not be used by the thief. People v. Gatlin (1946) 170 P.2d 1013, 75 C.A.2d 288.

Lack of authority to sign his name may be established by testimony of credit card owner. People v. Liberto (1969) 79 Cal.Rptr. 306, 274 A.C.A. 501.

The elements of the offense proscribed by § 459 and that proscribed by § 484d et seq. dealing with credit card offenses are not identical even though coincidentally a particular defendant's acts may constitute a violation of both statutes. People v. Churchill (1967) 63 Cal.Rptr. 312, 255 C.A.2d 448.

Defendant who made clothing purchases of less than $50 each at two shops with stolen credit card was not subject to felony prosecution under § 459 in view of fact that the acts constituted offenses specifically prohibited as misdemeanors under the credit card statute (§ 484d et seq.) People v. Scott (1968) 66 Cal.Rptr. 432, 259 C.A.2d 589.

The taking of a pocketbook by means of force and fear and the threat of a deadly weapon was "robbery" and not "theft." People v. Melendrez (1938) 77 P.2d 870, 25 C.A.2d 490.

Intent, theft—In general

Intent to defraud is question of fact to be determined from all facts and circumstances of the case and may be inferred circumstantially. People v. Hedrick (1968) 71 Cal.Rptr. 352, 265 C.A.2d 392.

Taking of property is not theft in absence of an intent to steal. People v. Butler (1967) 55 Cal.Rptr. 511, 421 P.2d 703, 65 C.2d 569.

Felonious intent requisite to robbery is same intent common to offenses constituting theft. Id.

Time of formation of intent, theft

There is no larceny unless the taking is with specific intent, existing at the time of the taking, to appropriate property of another and permanently deprive him of its possession. People v. Turner (1968) 73 Cal.Rptr. 263, 267 C.A.2d 440.

Possession of stolen property

A defendant who is in possession of stolen property has a duty to explain his possession in order to remove effect of possession as a circumstance, taken with other suspicious facts, of guilt. People v. Wells (1961) 9 Cal.Rptr. 384, 187 C.A.2d 324.

§ 484b. Diversion of funds received to obtain or pay for services, labor, materials or equipment

Any person who receives money for the purpose of obtaining or paying for services, labor, materials or equipment and willfully fails to apply such money for such purpose by either willfully failing to complete the improvements for which funds were provided or willfully failing to pay for services, labor, materials or equipment provided incident to such construction, and wrongfully diverts the funds to a use other than that for which the funds were received, shall be guilty of a public offense and shall be punishable by a fine not exceeding five thousand dollars ($5,000), or by imprisonment in the state prison, or in the county jail not exceeding one year, or by both such fine and such imprisonment if the amount diverted is in excess of one thousand dollars ($1,000). If the amount diverted is less than one thousand dollars ($1,000), the person shall be guilty of a misdemeanor.
(Amended by Stats.1976, c. 1139, p. —, § 219, operative July 1, 1977.)

§ 484c. Submission of false voucher to obtain construction loan funds

Any person who submits a false voucher to obtain construction loan funds and does not use the funds for the purpose for which the claim was submitted is guilty of embezzlement.
(Added by Stats.1965, c. 1145, p. 2890, § 2.)

§ 484d. Definitions

As used in this section and Sections 484e to 484j, inclusive:

(1) "Cardholder" means any person to whom a credit card is issued or any person who has agreed with the card issuer to pay obligations arising from the issuance of a credit card to another person.

(2) "Credit card" means any card, plate, coupon book, or other credit device existing for the purpose of being used from time to time upon presentation to obtain money, property, labor, or services on credit.

(3) "Expired credit card" means a credit card which shows on its face it has elapsed.

(4) "Card issuer" means any person who issues a credit card or the agent of such person with respect to such card.

(5) "Retailer" means every person who is authorized by an issuer to furnish money, goods, services or anything else of value upon presentation of a credit card by a cardholder.

(6) A credit card is "incomplete" if part of the matter other than the signature of the cardholder which an issuer requires to appear on the credit card before it can be used by a cardholder has not been stamped, embossed, imprinted, or written on it.

(7) "Revoked credit card" means a credit card which is no longer authorized for use by the issuer, such authorization having been suspended or terminated and written notice thereof having been given to the cardholder.
(Amended by Stats.1971, c. 1019, p. 1963, § 5.)

§ 484e. Theft of credit card

(1) Every person who acquires a credit card from another without the cardholder's or issuer's consent or who, with knowledge that it has been so acquired, acquires the credit card, with intent to use it or to sell or transfer it to a person other than the issuer or the cardholder is guilty of petty theft.

(2) Every person who acquires a credit card that he knows to have been lost, mislaid, or delivered under a mistake as to the identity or address of the cardholder, and who retains possession with intent to use it or to sell it to transfer it to a person other than the issuer or the cardholder is guilty of petty theft.

(3) Every person who sells, transfers, conveys, or receives a credit card with the intent to defraud is guilty of petty theft.

(4) Every person other than the issuer, who within any consecutive 12-month period, acquires credit cards issued in the names of four or more persons which he has reason to know were taken or retained under circumstances which constitute a violation of subdivisions (1), (2), or (3) of this section is guilty of grand theft.
(Added by Stats.1967, c. 1395, p. 3259, § 3.)

§ 484f. Forgery of credit card

(1) Every person who, with intent to defraud, makes, alters, or embosses a card purporting to be a credit card or utters such a card is guilty of forgery.

(2) A person other than the cardholder or a person authorized by him who, with intent to defraud, signs the name of another or of a fictitious person to a credit card, sales slip, sales draft, or instrument for the payment of money which evidences a credit card transaction, is guilty of forgery.
(Added by Stats.1967, c. 1395, p. 3259, § 4.)

§ 484g. Theft by use of credit card obtained or retained in violation of section 484e

Every person, who with intent to defraud, (a) uses for the purpose of obtaining money, goods, services or anything else of value a credit card obtained or retained in violation of Section 484e or a credit card which he knows is forged, expired or revoked, or (b) obtains money, goods, services or anything else of value by representing without the consent of the cardholder that he is the holder of a credit card or by representing that he is the holder of a credit card and such card has not in fact been issued, is guilty of theft. If the value of all money, goods, services and other things of value obtained in violation of this section exceeds two hundred dollars ($200) in any consecutive six-month period, then the same shall constitute grand theft.
(Added by Stats.1967, c. 1395, p. 3259, § 5.)

§ 484h. Unlawfully furnishing money, goods or services by merchant on presentation of credit card obtained or retained in violation of section 484e

Every retailer who, with intent to defraud:

(a) Furnishes money, goods, services or anything else of value upon presentation of a credit card obtained or retained in violation of Section 484e hereof or a credit card which he knows is forged, expired or revoked, and who receives any payment therefor, is guilty of theft. If the payment received by the retailer for all money, goods, services and other things of value furnished in violation of this section exceeds two hundred dollars ($200) in any consecutive six-month period, then the same shall constitute grand theft.

(b) Fails to furnish money, goods, services or anything else of value which he represents in writing to the issuer that he has furnished, and who receives any payment therefor, is guilty of theft. If the difference between the value of all money, goods, services and anything else of value actually furnished and the payment or payments received by the retailer therefor upon such representation exceeds two hundred dollars ($200) in any consecutive six-month period, then the same shall constitute grand theft.
(Amended by Stats.1971, c. 1019, p. 1963, § 5.5.)

§ 484i. Unlawful possession of incomplete credit card

(a) Every person who possesses an incomplete credit card, with intent to complete it without the consent of the issuer is guilty of a misdemeanor.

(b) Every person who with intent to defraud possesses, with knowledge of its character, machinery, plates or any other contrivance designed for, and made use of in, the reproduction of instruments purporting to be the credit cards of an issuer who has not consented to the preparation of such credit cards, is punishable by imprisonment in the state prison, or by imprisonment in the county jail for not more than one year.

(Amended by Stats.1976, c. 1139, p. —, § 220, operative July 1, 1977.)

§ 484j. Publication of credit card number or code with intent it be used to avoid payment of lawful charge

Any person who publishes the number or code of an existing, canceled, revoked, expired or nonexistent credit card, or the numbering or coding which is employed in the issuance of credit cards, with the intent that it be used or with knowledge or reason to believe that it will be used to avoid the payment of any lawful charge, is guilty of a misdemeanor. As used in this section, "publishes" means the communication of information to any one or more persons, either orally, in person or by telephone, radio or television, or in a writing of any kind, including without limitation a letter or memorandum, circular or handbill, newspaper or magazine article, or book.

(Added by Stats.1971, c. 1019, p. 1964, § 6.)

§ 485. Theft; appropriation of lost property with knowledge or means of inquiry as to true owner

One who finds lost property under circumstances which give him knowledge of or means of inquiry as to the true owner, and who appropriates such property to his own use, or to the use of another person not entitled thereto, without first making reasonable and just efforts to find the owner and to restore the property to him, is guilty of theft.

(Amended by Stats.1927, c. 619, p. 1046, § 2.)

§ 486. Theft; degrees

Theft is divided into two degrees, the first of which is termed grand theft; the second, petty theft.

(Amended by Stats.1927, c. 619, p. 1047, § 3.)

§ 487. Grand theft defined

Grand theft is theft committed in any of the following cases:

1. When the money, labor or real or personal property taken is of a value exceeding two hundred dollars ($200); provided, that when domestic fowls, avocados, olives, citrus or deciduous fruits, nuts and artichokes are taken of a value exceeding fifty dollars ($50); provided, further, that where the money, labor, real or personal property is taken by a servant, agent or employee from his principal or employer and aggregates two hundred dollars ($200) or more in any 12 consecutive month period, then the same shall constitute grand theft.

2. When the property is taken from the person of another.

3. When the property taken is an automobile, firearm, horse, mare, gelding, any bovine animal, any caprine animal, mule, jack, jenny, sheep, lamb, hog, sow, boar, gilt, barrow or pig.

(Amended by Stats.1965, c. 161, p. 1125, § 1.)

Notes of Decisions

Defendant who misrepresented alleged termite damage to home and urgent need for extensive repairs and who thus obtained owner's signature to writing in which she agreed to pay corporation for designated work but which also provided that the contract should not be binding on corporation until accepted at home office and which never actually was accepted by corporation had attempted to commit the offense of taking property by false pretense, not grand theft. People v. Layman (1968) 66 Cal.Rptr. 267, 259 C.A.2d 404.

Elements necessary to prove grand theft are the taking of personal property valued in excess of $200 into possession of the criminal without consent of owner or under claim of right, asportation of the subject matter, and specific intent to deprive owner of his property wholly and permanently. People v. Walther (1968) 69 Cal.Rptr. 434, 263 C.A.2d 310.

Larceny by trick

A loan of money induced by a fraudulent representation that it will be used for a specific purpose accompanied by an intent to steal amounts to "larceny by trick and device." People v. Dedrick (1967) 57 Cal.Rptr. 740, 249 C.A.2d 750; People v. Lafka (1959) 344 P.2d 619, 174 C.A.2d 312.

Crime of "grand theft by trick and device" usually results when victim of a fraud intends not to pass complete title of his property, but that it shall be applied to a special purpose, while recipient of property intends to appropriate it to his own use. People v. Chamberlain (1950) 214 P.2d 600, 96 C.A.2d 178; People v. McCabe (1943) 141 P.2d 54, 60 C.A.2d 492; People v. Brown (1952) 249 P.2d 595, 114 C.A.2d 52; People v. Felsman (1967) 64 Cal.Rptr. 870, 257 C.A.2d 437.

Value

Written contractual obligation to pay in excess of $200 is property of value in excess of $200 as contemplated by definition of grand theft. People v. Parker (1967) 63 Cal.Rptr. 413, 255 C.A.2d 664; Buck v. Superior Court (1965) 42 Cal.Rptr. 527, 232 C.A.2d 153, 11

A.L.R.3d 1064, certiorari denied 86 S.Ct. 77, 382 U.S. 834, 15 L.Ed.2d 77.

The value of stolen articles for purpose of establishing a felony charge is fair market value and not value to any particular individual. People v. Latham (1941) 110 P.2d 101, 43 C.A.2d 35; People v. Lizarraga (1954) 264 P.2d 953, 122 C.A.2d 436.

Evidence of value of stolen property is element of grand theft that should warrant closest scrutiny by defense counsel when items stolen may have value dependent in large part on such factors as mark-up and type of store victimized, and it is open to defense counsel to show that list price in vicinity was lower than alleged price of stolen property. People v. Cook (1965) 43 Cal.Rptr. 646, 233 C.A.2d 435.

Market value of property stolen, is not dependent alone on wholesale or cost price. People v. Williams (1959) 337 P.2d 134, 169 C.A.2d 400.

§ 487a. Grand theft; stealing, transporting, appropriating, etc., carcass of animal

(a) Every person who shall feloniously steal, take, transport or carry the carcass of any bovine, caprine, equine, ovine, or suine animal or of any mule, jack, or jenny, which is the personal property of another, or who shall fraudulently appropriate such property which has been entrusted to him, is guilty of grand theft.

(b) Every person who shall feloniously steal, take, transport, or carry any portion of the carcass of any bovine, caprine, equine, ovine, or suine animal or of any mule, jack, or jenny, which has been killed without the consent of the owner thereof, is guilty of grand theft.
(Amended by Stats.1953, c. 1547, p. 3215, § 1.)

§ 487b. Grand theft; conversion of real property to personal property by severance

Every person who converts real estate of the value of fifty dollars ($50) or more into personal property by severance from the realty of another, and with felonious intent to do so, steals, takes, and carries away such property is guilty of grand theft and is punishable by imprisonment in the state prison.
(Amended by Stats.1976, c. 1139, p. —, § 221, operative July 1, 1977.)

§ 487c. Petty theft; conversion of real property to personal property by severance

Every person who converts real estate of the value of less than fifty dollars ($50) into personal property by severance from the realty of another, and with felonious intent to do so steals, takes, and carries away such property is guilty of petit theft and is punishable by imprisonment in the county jail for not more than one year, or by a fine not exceeding one thousand dollars ($1,000), or by both such fine and imprisonment.
(Added by Stats.1953, c. 32, p. 636, § 8.)

§ 487e. Grand theft; dog exceeding value of two hundred dollars

Every person who feloniously steals, takes, or carries away a dog of another which is of a value exceeding two hundred dollars ($200) is guilty of grand theft.
(Added by Stats.1967, c. 1218, p. 2980, § 1.)

§ 487f. Petty theft; dog not exceeding value of two hundred dollars

Every person who feloniously steals, takes, or carries away a dog of another which is of a value not exceeding two hundred dollars ($200) is guilty of petty theft.
(Added by Stats.1967, c. 1218, p. 2980, § 2.)

§ 487g. Grand theft; stealing dog for purposes of sale, medical research, or other commercial uses

Every person who feloniously steals, takes, or carries away a dog of another for purposes of sale, medical research, or other commercial uses, is guilty of grand theft.
(Added by Stats.1967, c. 1218, p. 2980, § 3.)

§ 488. Petty theft defined

Theft in other cases is petty theft.
(Amended by Stats.1927, c. 619, p. 1047, § 5.)

§ 489. Grand theft; punishment

Grand theft is punishable by imprisonment in the county jail for not more than one year or in the state prison.
(Amended by Stats.1976, c. 1139, p. —, § 223, operative July 1, 1977.)

§ 490. Petty theft; punishment

Petty theft is punishable by fine not exceeding one thousand dollars ($1,000), or by imprisonment in the county jail not exceeding six months, or both.
(Amended by Stats.1976, c. 1125, p. —, § 19.)

§ 490.5. Petty theft of retail merchandise; punishment

(a) Upon a first conviction for petty theft involving merchandise taken from a merchant's premises or a book or other library materials taken from a library facility, a person shall be punished by a mandatory

§ 490.5

fine of not less than fifty dollars ($50) and not more than one thousand dollars ($1,000) for each such violation; and may also be punished by imprisonment in the county jail, not exceeding six months, or both such fine and imprisonment.

(b) When an unemancipated minor's willful conduct would constitute petty theft involving merchandise taken from a merchant's premises or a book or other library materials taken from a library facility, any merchant or library facility who has been injured by such conduct may bring a civil action against the parent or legal guardian having control and custody of the minor. For the purposes of such actions the misconduct of the unemancipated minor shall be imputed to the parent or legal guardian having control and custody of the minor. The parent or legal guardian having control or custody of an unemancipated minor whose conduct violates this subdivision shall be jointly and severally liable with the minor to a merchant for the retail value of his merchandise, if not recovered in merchantable condition or to a library facility for the fair market value of its book or other library materials, plus damages of not less than fifty dollars ($50) nor more than five hundred dollars ($500) plus costs. Recovery of such damages may be had in addition to, and is not limited by, any other provision of law which limits the liability of a parent or legal guardian for the tortious conduct of a minor. An action for recovery of damages, pursuant to this subdivision, may be brought in small claims court if the total damages do not exceed the jurisdictional limit of such court, or in any other appropriate court; however, total damages, including the value of the merchandise or book or other library materials, shall not exceed five hundred dollars ($500) for each action brought under this section.

The provisions of this subdivision are in addition to other civil remedies and do not limit merchants or other persons to elect to pursue other civil remedies, except that the provisions of Section 1714.1 of the Civil Code shall not apply herein.

(c) In lieu of the fines prescribed by subdivision (a), any person may be required to perform public services designated by the court, provided that in no event shall any such person be required to perform less than the number of hours of such public service necessary to satisfy the fine assessed by the court as provided by subdivision (a) at the minimum wage prevailing in the state at the time of sentencing.

(d) All fines collected under this section shall be collected and distributed in accordance with Sections 1463 and 1463.1 of the Penal Code; provided, however, that a county may, by a majority vote of the members of its board of supervisors, allocate any amount up to, but not exceeding 50 percent of such fines to the county superintendent of schools for allocation to local school districts. The fines allocated shall be administered by the county superintendent of schools to finance public school programs, which provide counseling or other educational services designed to discourage shoplifting, theft, and burglary. Subject to rules and regulations as may be adopted by the Superintendent of Public Instruction, each county superintendent of schools shall allocate such funds to school districts within the county which submit project applications designed to further the educational purposes of this section. The costs of administration of this section by each county superintendent of schools shall be paid from the funds allocated to the county superintendent of schools.

(e)(1) A merchant may detain a person for a reasonable time for the purpose of conducting an investigation in a reasonable manner whenever the merchant has probable cause to believe the person to be detained is attempting to unlawfully take or has unlawfully taken merchandise from the merchant's premises.

A person employed by a library facility may detain a person for a reasonable time for the purpose of conducting an investigation in a reasonable manner whenever the person employed by a library facility has probable cause to believe the person to be detained is attempting to unlawfully remove or has unlawfully removed books or library materials from the premises of the library facility.

(2) In making the detention a merchant or a person employed by a library facility may use a reasonable amount of nondeadly force necessary to protect himself and to prevent escape of the person detained or the loss of property.

(3) During the period of detention any items which a merchant or any items which a person employed by a library facility has reasonable cause to believe are unlawfully taken from the premises of the merchant or library facility and which are in plain view may be examined by the merchant or person employed by a library facility for the purposes of ascertaining the ownership thereof.

(4) In any action for false arrest, false imprisonment, slander or unlawful detention brought by any

person detained by a merchant, it shall be a defense to such action that the merchant detaining such person had probable cause to believe that the person had stolen or attempted to steal merchandise and that the merchant acted reasonably under all the circumstances.

In any action for false arrest, false imprisonment, slander or unlawful detention brought by any person detained by a person employed by a library facility, it shall be a defense to such action that the person employed by a library facility detaining such person had probable cause to believe that the person had stolen or attempted to steal books or library materials and that the person employed by a library facility acted reasonably under all the circumstances.

(f) As used in this section:

(1) "Merchandise" means any personal property, capable of manual delivery, displayed, held or offered for retail sale by a merchant.

(2) "Merchant" means an owner or operator, and the agent, consignee, employee, lessee, or officer of an owner or operator, of any premises used for the retail purchase or sale of any personal property capable of manual delivery.

(3) The terms "book or other library materials" include any book, plate, picture, photograph, engraving, painting, drawing, map, newspaper, magazine, pamphlet, broadside, manuscript, document, letter, public record, microform, sound recording, audiovisual material in any format, magnetic or other tape, electronic data processing record, artifact, or other documentary, written or printed material regardless of physical form or characteristics, or any part thereof, belonging to, on loan to, or otherwise in the custody of a library facility.

(4) The term "library facility" includes any public library; any library of an educational, historical or eleemosynary institution, organization or society; any museum; any repository of public records.

(g) Any library facility shall post at its entrance and exit a conspicuous sign to read as follows:

In order to prevent the theft of books and library materials, state law authorizes the detention for a reasonable period of any person using these facilities suspected of committing "library theft" (Penal Code section 490.5).

(Amended by Stats.1978, c. 593, p. —, § 2.)

§ 490a. "Theft" substituted for larceny, embezzlement or stealing

Wherever any law or statute of this state refers to or mentions larceny, embezzlement, or stealing, said law or statute shall hereafter be read and interpreted as if the word "theft" were substituted therefor. (Added by Stats.1927, c. 619, p. 1047, § 7.)

§ 496. Receiving stolen property

1. Receiving; knowledge; concealment; punishment

1. Every person who buys or receives any property which has been stolen or which has been obtained in any manner constituting theft or extortion, knowing the property to be so stolen or obtained, or who conceals, sells, withholds or aids in concealing, selling, or withholding any such property from the owner, knowing the property to be so stolen or obtained, is punishable by imprisonment in a state prison, or in a county jail for not more than one year; provided, that where the district attorney or the grand jury determines that such action would be in the interests of justice, the district attorney or the grand jury, as the case may be, may, if the value of the property does not exceed two hundred dollars ($200), specify in the accusatory pleading that the offense shall be a misdemeanor, punishable only by imprisonment in the county jail not exceeding one year.

2. Secondhand dealers; inquiry; presumption

2. Every person whose principal business is dealing in or collecting used or secondhand merchandise or personal property, and every agent, employee or representative of such person, who buys or receives any property which has been stolen or obtained in any manner constituting theft or extortion, under such circumstances as should cause such person, agent, employee or representative to make reasonable inquiry to ascertain that the person from whom such property was bought or received had the legal right to sell or deliver it, without making such reasonable inquiry, shall be presumed to have bought or received such property knowing it to have been so stolen or obtained. This presumption may, however, be rebutted by proof.

3. Secondhand dealers; inquiry; burden of proof

3. When in a prosecution under this section it shall appear from the evidence that the defendant's principal business was as set forth in the preceding paragraph, that the defendant bought, received, or

§ 496

otherwise obtained, or concealed, withheld or aided in concealing or withholding from the owner, any property which had been stolen or obtained in any manner constituting theft or extortion, and that the defendant bought, received, obtained, concealed or withheld such property under such circumstances as should have caused him to make reasonable inquiry to ascertain that the person from whom he bought, received, or obtained such property had the legal right to sell or deliver it to him, then the burden shall be upon the defendant to show that before so buying, receiving, or otherwise obtaining such property, he made such reasonable inquiry to ascertain that the person so selling or delivering the same to him had the legal right to so sell or deliver it.

4. Damages and costs

4. Any person who has been injured by a violation of paragraph 1 of this section may bring an action for three times the amount of actual damages, if any, sustained by the plaintiff, costs of suit and reasonable attorney's fees.
(Amended by Stats.1976, c. 1139, p. —, § 224, operative July 1, 1977.)

Notes of Decisions

In general

Gist of offense of "receiving stolen property" is that purchase or receipt be with knowledge that property was stolen. People v. Salazar (1962) 26 Cal.Rptr. 456, 210 C.A.2d 89; People v. Smith (1945) 161 P.2d 941, 26 C.2d 854.

Where it is affirmatively established that defendant is the thief, he may not be prosecuted under this section proscribing receipt of stolen property if concealment and withholding of stolen goods have been part of activities connected with theft. People v. Marquez (1965) 47 Cal.Rptr. 166, 237 C.A.2d 627.

The crime of "receiving stolen property" congeals upon taking possession of stolen property with guilty knowledge, and the aiding and abetting of that crime would call for the performance of the criminal act with guilty knowledge of the wrongful purpose of the perpetrator. People v. Feldman (1959) 339 P.2d 888, 171 C.A.2d 15.

Purpose

This section, making it an offense to buy, receive, withhold or conceal stolen property, is directed at the traditional "fence" and those who lurk in background of criminal ways in order to provide thieves with market or depository for loot. People v. Tatum (1962) 25 Cal.Rptr. 832, 209 C.A.2d 179.

Elements of offense—In general

If, in convicting an accused of a violation of Veh.C. § 10851 proscribing the unlawful driving or taking of a vehicle, a jury finds that the accused intended only to temporarily deprive the owner of possession for the purpose of driving a vehicle, then the accused may also be guilty of a violation of this section if there is other evidence which establishes the elements of this crime, including evidence of the independent theft of the vehicle and the accused's knowledge thereof. People v. Jaramillo (1976) 129 Cal.Rptr. 306, 548 P.2d 706, 16 C.3d 752.

Elements of the crime of receiving stolen property are: that the particular property was stolen, that the accused received, concealed or withheld it from the owner thereof, and that the accused knew the property was stolen. People v. Katz (1975) 120 Cal.Rptr. 603, 47 C.A.3d 294.

To establish guilt of offense of receiving stolen property, it must be proved that property was stolen, that accused received it into his possession, and that he knew it was stolen. People v. Martin (1973) 108 Cal.Rptr. 809, 511 P.2d 1161, 9 C.3d 687, certiorari denied 94 S.Ct. 844, 414 U.S. 1113, 38 L.Ed.2d 740.

Conviction for receiving stolen property cannot withstand appellate scrutiny unless substantial evidence was presented to the trier of fact that (1) the property was received, concealed or withheld by the accused, (2) such property was obtained by theft or extortion, and (3) the accused knew that the property had been so obtained. People v. Kunkin (1973) 107 Cal.Rptr. 184, 507 P.2d 1392, 9 C.3d 245, 57 A.L.R.3d 1199.

Essential elements of receiving stolen property are: property must be stolen property; defendant must receive, conceal, or withhold it or aid in receiving, concealing or withholding it from its owner; and defendant must have knowledge that property is stolen property. People v. Schroeder (1968) 70 Cal.Rptr. 491, 264 C.A.2d 217; People v. Stuart (1969) 77 Cal.Rptr. 531, 272 A.C.A. 742; People v. Williams (1967) 61 Cal.Rptr. 238, 253 C.A.2d 952; People v. Siegfried (1967) 57 Cal.Rptr. 423, 249 C.A.2d 489; People v. Azevedo (1963) 32 Cal.Rptr. 748, 218 C.A.2d 483; People v. Bartfeld (1962) 22 Cal.Rptr. 618, 204 C.A.2d 701; People v. Candiotto (1960) 6 Cal.Rptr. 876, 183 C.A.2d 348; People v. Scaggs (1957) 314 P.2d 793, 153 C.A.2d 339; People v. Bateman (1931) 295 P. 530, 111 C.A. 109.

Value of property received is not a necessary element of proof in prosecution for receiving stolen property. People v. Superior Court for Los Angeles County (1969) 76 Cal.Rptr. 518, 271 A.C.A. 597; People v. Fitzpatrick (1889) 22 P. 215, 80 C. 538.

§ 496a. Junk and secondhand dealers; purchasing metals used in transportation or public utility service; determination of seller's right; punishment; record of transaction

(a) Every person who, being a dealer in or collector of junk, metals or secondhand materials, or the agent, employee, or representative of such dealer or collector, buys or receives any wire, cable, copper, lead, solder, mercury, iron or brass which he knows or reasonably should know is ordinarily used by or ordinarily belongs to a railroad or other transportation, telephone, telegraph, gas, water or electric light company or county, city, city and county or other political subdivision of this state engaged in furnishing public utility service without using due diligence to ascertain that the person selling or delivering the same has a legal right to do so, is guilty of criminally receiving such property, and is punishable, by imprisonment in a state prison, or in a county jail for not more than one year, or by a fine of not more than two hundred fifty dollars ($250), or by both such fine and imprisonment.

(b) Any person buying or receiving material pursuant to subdivision (a) shall obtain evidence of his identity from the seller including, but not limited to, such person's full name, signature, address, driver's license number, vehicle license number, and the license number of the vehicle delivering the material.

The record of the transaction shall include an appropriate description of the material purchased and such record shall be maintained pursuant to Section 21607 of the Business and Professions Code.
(Amended by Stats.1976, c. 1125, p. —, § 20; Stats.1976, c. 1139, p. —, § 225, operative July 1, 1977.)

§ 497. Bringing into state property stolen or received in another state

Every person who, in another state or country steals or embezzles the property of another, or receives such property knowing it to have been stolen or embezzled, and brings the same into this state, may be convicted and punished in the same manner as if such larceny, or embezzlement, or receiving, had been committed in this state.
(Amended by Stats.1905, c. 554, p. 718, § 1.)

§ 498. Theft of gas; evasion of payment; injury to or alteration of meter

Every person who shall willfully, with intent to injure or defraud, make or cause to be made, or uses or causes to be used, any pipe, tube, or other instrument or conduit in connection with any main, service pipe or other pipe or conduit owned or controlled by any other person for conducting or supplying illuminating or fuel gas, in such manner as to supply such or any illuminating or fuel gas to any burner, or outlet by or at which illuminating or fuel gas is consumed or otherwise used or wasted without passing through any meter provided for the measuring and registering the quantity of gas passing through such pipes, tubes or other conduits, or willfully acts in any other manner so as to evade, or cause the evasion of payment therefor, and every person who, with like intent, injures or alters any gas meter or register, or obstructs its action, is guilty of a misdemeanor.
(Amended by Stats.1909, c. 214, p. 329, § 1.)

§ 499. Theft of water

Every person who, with intent to injure or defraud, connects or causes to be connected, any pipe, tube, or other instrument, with any main, service-pipe, or other pipe, or conduit or flume for conducting water, for the purpose of taking water from such main, service-pipe, conduit or flume, without the knowledge of the owner thereof, and with intent to evade payment therefor, and every person who, with intent to injure or defraud, injures or alters any watermeter, watermeter seal, service valve, or other service connection, is guilty of a misdemeanor.
(Amended by Stats.1965, c. 103, p. 1045, § 1.)

§ 499b. Vehicle; taking for temporary use; punishment

Any person who shall, without the permission of the owner thereof, take any automobile, bicycle, motorcycle, or other vehicle or motorboat or vessel, for the purpose of temporarily using or operating the same, shall be deemed guilty of a misdemeanor, and upon conviction thereof, shall be punished by a fine not exceeding two hundred dollars ($200), or by imprisonment not exceeding three months, or by both such fine and imprisonment.
(Amended by Stats.1965, c. 1354, p. 3249, § 1.)

§ 499b.1. Vehicle; prior confinement for theft, unlawful driving or taking; subsequent conviction; punishment

(a) Any person who, having been convicted of a previous violation of Section 10851 of the Vehicle Code, or of subdivision (3) of Section 487, involving a vehicle or vessel, and having served a term therefor in any penal institution or having been imprisoned therein as a condition of probation for such offense, is subsequently convicted of a violation of Section 499b, involving a vehicle or vessel, is punishable for such subsequent offense by imprisonment in the county jail not exceeding one year or the state prison for 16 months, two, or three years.

(b) Any person convicted of a violation of Section 499b, who has been previously convicted under charges separately brought and tried two or more times of a violation of Section 499b, all such violations involving a vehicle or vessel, and who has been imprisoned therefore as a condition of probation or otherwise at least once, is punishable by imprisonment in the county jail for not more than one year or in the state prison for 16 months, two, or three years.
(Added by Stats.1978, c. 485, p. —, § 1.)

§ 503. Definition

"Embezzlement" defined. Embezzlement is the fraudulent appropriation of property by a person to whom it has been intrusted.
(Enacted 1872.)

§ 503

Notes of Decisions

Gist of "embezzlement" is appropriation to one's own use of property delivered for devotion to a particular purpose other than one's own enjoyment of it. People v. Kagan (1968) 70 Cal.Rptr. 732, 264 A.C.A. 781; People v. Parker (1965) 44 Cal.Rptr. 909, 235 C.A.2d 100; People v. Rath (1961) 16 Cal.Rptr. 641, 196 C.A.2d 638; People v. Miller (1961) 10 Cal.Rptr. 326, 188 C.A.2d 156; People v. Woolson (1960) 5 Cal.Rptr. 766, 181 C.A.2d 657; People v. Hodges (1957) 315 P.2d 38, 153 C.A.2d 788.

Essential elements of "embezzlement" are fiduciary relationship arising where one intrusts property to another, and fraudulent appropriation of that property by the latter. People v. Darling (1964) 41 Cal.Rptr. 219, 230 C.A.2d 615; Ex parte Holder (1920) 192 P. 90, 48 C.A. 468.

Property subject to embezzlement

Used money orders, which named defendant as sender and which were introduced, corroborated accomplice's testimony that money orders were employed by defendant, who was agent for sale of money orders and accomplice, charged with conspiracy and embezzling property of principal, to stock their superette and pay expenses in connection with operation thereof. People v. Harris (1969) 77 Cal.Rptr. 406, 272 A.C.A. 593.

§ 508. Clerk; agent; servant

When clerk, agent, or servant guilty of embezzlement. Every clerk, agent, or servant of any person who fraudulently appropriates to his own use, or secretes with a fraudulent intent to appropriate to his own use, any property of another which has come into his control or care by virtue of his employment as such clerk, agent, or servant, is guilty of embezzlement.

(Enacted 1872.)

§ 509. Distinct act of taking not necessary

Distinct act of taking. A distinct act of taking is not necessary to constitute embezzlement.

(Enacted 1872.)

§ 511. Defenses; claim of title; unlawful retention of property to offset or pay demands not excused

Claim of title a ground of defense. Upon any indictment for embezzlement, it is a sufficient defense that the property was appropriated openly and avowedly, and under a claim of title preferred in good faith, even though such claim is untenable. But this provision does not excuse the unlawful retention of the property of another to offset or pay demands held against him.

(Enacted 1872.)

§ 512. Defenses; mitigation of punishment; intent to restore property; time

The fact that the accused intended to restore the property embezzled, is no ground of defense or mitigation of punishment, if it has not been restored before an information has been laid before a magistrate, or an indictment found by a grand jury, charging the commission of the offense.

(Amended by Stats.1905, c. 520, p. 682, § 1.)

§ 513. Defenses; mitigation of punishment; restoration of property or tender before indictment or information

Whenever, prior to an information laid before a magistrate, or an indictment found by a grand jury, charging the commission of embezzlement, the person accused voluntarily and actually restores or tenders restoration of the property alleged to have been embezzled, or any part thereof, such fact is not a ground of defense, but it authorizes the court to mitigate punishment, in its discretion.

(Amended by Stats.1905, c. 520, p. 682, § 2.)

§ 514. Punishment; determination of value; defalcation of public funds; disfranchisement

Every person guilty of embezzlement is punishable in the manner prescribed for theft of property of the value or kind embezzled; and where the property embezzled is an evidence of debt or right of action, the sum due upon it or secured to be paid by it must be taken as its value; if the embezzlement or defalcation is of the public funds of the United States, or of this state, or of any county or municipality within this state, the offense is a felony, and is punishable by imprisonment in the state prison; and the person so convicted is ineligible thereafter to any office of honor, trust, or profit in this state.

(Amended by Stats.1976, c. 1139, p. ——, § 230, operative July 1, 1977.)

§ 518. Definition

Extortion is the obtaining of property from another, with his consent, or the obtaining of an official act of a public officer, induced by a wrongful use of force or fear, or under color of official right.

(Amended by Stats.1939, c. 601, p. 2017, § 1.)

Notes of Decisions

The crime of extortion involves "moral turpitude." Librarian v. State Bar (1952) 239 P.2d 865, 38 C.2d 328.

Where attorney made threats of action injurious to client and his wife to force payment of attorney's bill after client had filed bankruptcy petition, and attorney with a punitive motive wrote to immigration authorities to incite an investigation of client's wife as a supposed alien, attorney committed an action involving "moral turpitude" warranting suspension from the practice of law for six months, notwithstanding money may have been justly due the attorney. Lindenbaum v. State Bar (1945) 160 P.2d 9, 26 C.2d 565.

"Extortion" is obtaining of anything by illegal compulsion, and implies unwilling payment. Daniels v. U. S. (C.C.A.1927) 17 F.2d 339, certiorari denied 47 S.Ct. 591, 274 U.S. 744, 71 L.Ed. 1325.

"Extortion" is the obtaining of property from another, with his consent, induced by a wrongful use of force or fear, or under a color of official right, and "fear" such as will constitute extortion may be induced by threat to do an unlawful injury to person threatened, to accuse him of any crime, or to expose or to impute to him any disgrace or crime. People v. Goodman (1958) 323 P.2d 536, 159 C.A.2d 54.

§ 519. Fear used to extort; threats inducing

Fear, such as will constitute extortion, may be induced by a threat, either:

1. To do an unlawful injury to the person or property of the individual threatened or of a third person; or,

2. To accuse the individual threatened, or any relative of his, or member of his family, of any crime; or,

3. To expose, or to impute to him or them any deformity, disgrace or crime; or,

4. To expose any secret affecting him or them.
(Amended by Stats.1939, c. 601, p. 2017, § 2.)

Notes of Decisions

No precise or particular form of words is necessary in order to constitute a "threat" within § 518 et seq., rather threats can be made by innuendo and the circumstances under which the threat is uttered and relations between parties may be taken into consideration in making a determination of question involved. People v. Massengale (1968) 68 Cal.Rptr. 415, 261 C.A.2d 758.

Evidence was sufficient to support implied finding that defendant attempted to place owner of bar in fear of unlawful injury to his business or person if money was not paid to defendant and to sustain conviction of attempted extortion. People v. Camodeca (1959) 338 P.2d 903, 52 C.2d 142.

"Extortion" is the obtaining of property from another, with his consent, induced by a wrongful use of force or fear, or under a color of official right, and "fear" such as will constitute extortion may be induced by threat to do an unlawful injury to person threatened, to accuse him of any crime, or to expose or to impute to him any disgrace or crime. People v. Goodman (1958) 323 P.2d 536, 159 C.A.2d 54.

Threats to do only what party making them has legal right to do are not unlawful. McKay v. Retail Automobile Salesmen's Local Union No. 1067 (1940) 106 P.2d 373, 16 C.2d 311, certiorari denied 61 S.Ct. 939, 313 U.S. 566, 85 L.Ed. 1525.

§ 520. Punishment

Every person who extorts any money or other property from another, under circumstances not amounting to robbery, by means of force, or any threat, such as is mentioned in the preceding section, is punishable by imprisonment in the state prison for two, three or four years.
(Amended by Stats.1976, c. 1139, p. —, § 231, operative July 1, 1977.)

§ 521. Punishment; commission under color of official right

Punishment of extortion committed under color of official right. Every person who commits any extortion under color of official right, in cases for which a different punishment is not prescribed in this Code, is guilty of a misdemeanor.
(Enacted 1872.)

§ 522. Signature; obtaining by means of threats; punishment

Obtaining signature by means of threats. Every person who, by any extortionate means, obtains from another his signature to any paper or instrument, whereby, if such signature were freely given, any property would be transferred, or any debt, demand, charge, or right of action created, is punishable in the same manner as if the actual delivery of such debt, demand, charge, or right of action were obtained.
(Enacted 1872.)

Notes of Decisions

In general

No precise or particular form of words is necessary in order to constitute a "threat" within § 518 et seq., rather threats can be made by innuendo and the circumstances under which the threat is uttered and relations between parties may be taken into consideration in making a determination of question involved. People v. Massengale (1968) 68 Cal.Rptr. 415, 261 C.A.2d 758.

§ 523. Threatening letters; intent; punishment

Sending threatening letters with intent to extort money, etc. Every person who, with intent to extort any money or other property from another, sends or delivers to any person any letter or other writing, whether subscribed or not, expressing or implying, or adapted to imply, any threat such as is specified in Section 519, is punishable in the same manner as if such money or property were actually obtained by means of such threat.
(Enacted 1872.)

§ 524. Attempts; punishment

Every person who attempts, by means of any threat, such as is specified in Section 519 of this code, to extort money or other property from another is

§ 524

punishable by imprisonment in the county jail not longer than one year or in the state prison or by fine not exceeding five thousand dollars ($5,000), or by both such fine and imprisonment.
(Amended by Stats.1976, c. 1139, p. ——, § 232, operative July 1, 1977.)

Notes of Decisions

Essential elements of attempted extortion are the intent to commit the crime and a direct ineffectual act done toward its commission. People v. Asta (1967) 59 Cal.Rptr. 206, 251 C.A.2d 64.

Threat of disclosure of partially nude photographs of complainant, in connection with count charging defendant with attempted extortion in February, 1964, was reasonably inferable, as accompanying defendant's demand for money, from circumstances of prior incident involving actual payment to defendant in November 1963. People v. Peniston (1966) 51 Cal.Rptr. 744, 242 C.A.2d 719.

§ 537. Defrauding innkeepers, etc.

Any person who obtains any food or accommodations at an hotel, inn, restaurant, boardinghouse, lodginghouse, apartment house, bungalow court, motel, auto camp, or public or private campground, without paying therefor, with intent to defraud the proprietor or manager thereof, or who obtains credit at an hotel, inn, restaurant, boardinghouse, lodginghouse, apartment house, bungalow court, motel, auto camp, or public or private campground, by the use of any false pretense, or who, after obtaining credit, food, or accommodations, at an hotel, inn, restaurant, boardinghouse, lodginghouse, apartment house, bungalow court, motel, auto camp, or public or private campground, absconds, or surreptitiously, or by force, menace, or threats, removes any part of his baggage therefrom without paying for his food or accommodations is guilty of a misdemeanor.

Evidence that such person left the premises of such an hotel, inn, restaurant, boardinghouse, lodginghouse, apartment house, bungalow court, motel, auto camp, or public or private campground, without paying or offering to pay for such food or accommodation shall be prima facie evidence that such person obtained such food or accommodations with intent to defraud the proprietor or manager.
(Amended by Stats.1971, c. 198, p. 264, § 1.)

§ 537e. Articles from which serial number or identification mark has been removed; purchase, sale, possession; disposition by peace officers; exceptions

(a) Any person who knowingly buys, sells, receives, disposes of, conceals, or has in his possession a radio, piano, photograph, sewing machine, washing machine, typewriter, adding machine, comptometer, bicycle, a safe or vacuum cleaner, dictaphone, watch, watch movement, watch case, or any mechanical or electrical device, appliance, contrivance, material, piece of apparatus or equipment, from which the manufacturer's name plate, serial number or any other distinguishing number or identification mark has been removed, defaced, covered, altered or destroyed, is guilty of a misdemeanor.

(b) When property described in subdivision (a) comes into the custody of a peace officer it shall become subject to the provision of Chapter 12 (commencing with Section 1407), Title 10 of Part 2, relating to the disposal of stolen or embezzled property. Property subject to this section shall be considered stolen or embezzled property for the purposes of that chapter, and prior to being disposed of, shall have an identification mark, imbedded or engraved in, or permanently affixed to it.

(c) This section does not apply to those cases or instances where any of the changes or alterations enumerated in subdivision (a) have been customarily made or done as an established practice in the ordinary and regular conduct of business, by the original manufacturer, or by his duly appointed direct representative, or under specific authorization from the original manufacturer.
(Amended by Stats.1974, c. 269, p. 495, § 1.)

§ 538d. Impersonating an officer; wearing badge, etc.; intent

Any person other than one who by law is given the authority of a peace officer, who wilfully wears, exhibits, or uses the authorized badge, insigne, emblem, device, label, certificate, card, or writing, of a peace officer, with the intent of fraudulently personating a peace officer, or of fraudulently inducing the belief that he is a peace officer, is guilty of a misdemeanor.

Any person who wilfully wears, exhibits, or uses, or who wilfully makes, sells, loans, gives, or transfers to another, any badge, insigne, emblem, device, or any label, certificate, card, or writing, which falsely purports to be authorized for the use of one who by law is given the authority of a peace officer, or which so resembles the authorized badge, insigne, emblem, device, label, certificate, card, or writing of a peace officer as would deceive an ordinary reasonable person into believing that it is authorized for the use of one who by law is given the authority of a peace officer, is guilty of a misdemeanor.
(Added by Stats.1945, c. 1274, p. 2398, § 1.)

§ 548. Defrauding or prejudicing insurer; punishment

Every person who willfully burns or in any other manner injures, destroys, secretes, abandons, or disposes of any property which at the time is insured against loss or damage by fire, or theft, or embezzlement, or any casualty with intent to defraud or prejudice the insurer, whether the same be the property or in the possession of such person or any other person, is punishable by imprisonment in the state prison for two, three or four years.
(Amended by Stats.1976, c. 1139, p. —, § 240, operative July 1, 1977.)

§ 588a. Highways; throwing substances likely to injure persons, animals, or vehicles

Any person who throws or deposits any oil, glass bottle, glass nails, tacks, hoops, wire, cans, or any other substance likely to injure any person, animal or vehicle upon any public highway in the State of California shall be guilty of a misdemeanor; provided, however, that any person who willfully deposits any such substance upon any public highway in the State of California with the intent to cause great bodily injury to other persons using the highway shall be guilty of a felony.
(Amended by Stats.1963, c. 250, p. 1008, § 1.)

MALICIOUS MISCHIEF

§ 594. Vandalism; penalty

(a) Every person who maliciously injures or destroys any real or personal property not his own, in cases otherwise than those specified in this code, is guilty of vandalism.

(b) If the amount of injury or destruction is one thousand dollars ($1,000) or more, vandalism is punishable by (1) imprisonment for six months in the county jail, a fine of five hundred dollars ($500), or both or (2) imprisonment in the state prison not to exceed one year and one day, a fine of one thousand dollars ($1,000), or both such fine and imprisonment.

(c) If the amount of injury or destruction is less than one thousand dollars ($1,000), vandalism is punishable by imprisonment in the county jail for not more than six months, or by a fine of not more than five hundred dollars ($500), or by both such fine and imprisonment.
(Amended by Stats.1977, c. 165, p. —, § 8, urgency, eff. June 29, 1977, operative July 1, 1977.)

§ 594.5. Defacing property; punishment; repair or restitution as condition of probation; ordinance regulating aerosol containers

(a) Any person who, without the consent of the owner, willfully defaces, by paint or any other liquid, the property of another is guilty of a misdemeanor punishable by a fine of not more than five hundred dollars ($500), or not more than 30 days in the county jail, or both.

(b) A court may require as a condition of probation for any person guilty of violating this section, that he wash, paint, or repair the defaced property, or otherwise make restitution to the property owner. Nothing in this section shall be construed to limit the authority of a court to grant probation or provide conditions of probation.

(c) Nothing in this code shall invalidate an ordinance of, nor be construed to prohibit the adoption of an ordinance by, a city, city and county, or county, if such ordinance regulates the sale of aerosol containers of paint or other liquid substances capable of defacing property.
(Added by Stats.1974, c. 340, p. 671, § 2.)

§ 597. Cruelty to animals

(a) Every person who maliciously maims, wounds, tortures, or mutilates a living animal which is the property of another, or maliciously kills an animal which is the property of another, is guilty of an offense punishable by imprisonment in the state prison, or in a county jail for not more than one year.

(b) Except as otherwise provided in subdivision (a), every person who overdrives, overloads, drives when overloaded, overworks, tortures, torments, deprives of necessary sustenance, drink or shelter, cruelly beats, mutilates, or cruelly kills any animal, or causes or procures any animal to be so overdriven, overloaded, driven when overloaded, overworked, tortured, tormented, deprived of necessary sustenance, drink or shelter, or to be cruelly beaten, mutilated, or cruelly killed; and whoever, having the charge or custody of any animal, either as owned or otherwise, subjects any animal to needless suffering, or inflicts unnecessary cruelty upon the same, or in any manner abuses any animal, or fails to provide the same with proper food, drink, shelter or protection from the weather, or who drives, rides or otherwise uses the same when unfit for labor, is for every such offense, guilty of a misdemeanor.
(Amended by Stats.1976, c. 1139, p. —, § 250, operative July 1, 1977.)

§ 597.5. Fighting dogs; crime; misdemeanor; punishment

(a) Any person who does any of the following is guilty of a crime and is punishable by imprisonment in a state prison not to exceed one year and one day, or by imprisonment in a county jail not to exceed one year, or by a fine not to exceed fifty thousand dollars ($50,000), or by both such fine and imprisonment:

(1) Owns, possesses, keeps, or trains any dog, with the intent that such dog shall be engaged in an exhibition of fighting with another dog.

(2) For amusement or gain, causes any dog to fight with another dog, or causes any dogs to injure each other.

(3) Permits any act in violation of paragraph (1) or (2) to be done on any premises under his charge or control, or aids or abets any such act.

(b) Any person who is knowingly present, as a spectator, at any place, building, or tenement where preparations are being made for an exhibition of the fighting of dogs, with the intent to be present at such preparations, or is knowingly present at such exhibition or at any other fighting or injuring as described in paragraph (2) of subdivision (a), with the intent to be present at such exhibition, fighting, or injuring, is guilty of a misdemeanor.

(c) Nothing in this section shall prohibit any of the following:

(1) The use of dogs in the management of livestock, as defined by Section 14205 of the Food and Agricultural Code, by the owner of such livestock or his employees or agents or other persons in lawful custody thereof.

(2) The use of dogs in hunting as permitted by the Fish and Game Code including, but not limited to, Sections 3286, 3509, 3510, 4002, and 4756, and by the rules and regulations of the Fish and Game Commission.

(3) The training of dogs or the use of equipment in the training of dogs for any purpose not prohibited by law.

(Amended by Stats.1977, c. 165, p. —, § 9, urgency, eff. June 29, 1977, operative July 1, 1977.)

§ 597j. Cock; owning, possessing or keeping with intent to use for fighting; misdemeanor

Any person who owns, possesses or keeps any cock with the intent that such cock shall be used or engaged by himself or by his vendee or by any other person in any exhibition of fighting is guilty of a misdemeanor.

(Amended by Stats.1977, c. 307, p. —, § 1.)

§ 599aa. Seizure of fighting animals and birds, paraphernalia, etc.; affidavit of officer; custody of seized property; forfeiture and destruction or redelivery

Any authorized officer making an arrest under Section 597.5 shall, and any authorized officer making an arrest under Section 597b or 599a may, lawfully take possession of all birds or animals and all paraphernalia, implements or other property or things used or employed, or about to be employed, in the violation of any of the provisions of this code relating to the fighting of birds or animals. He shall state to the person in charge thereof at the time of such taking his name and residence. Such officer, after taking possession of such birds, animals, paraphernalia, implements or other property or things, shall file with the magistrate before whom the complaint is made against any person so arrested an affidavit stating therein the name of the person charged in such complaint, a description of the property so taken and the time and place of the taking thereof together with the name of the person for whom the same was taken and the name of the person who claims to own such property, if known, and that the affiant has reason to believe and does believe, stating the ground of such belief, that the property so taken was used or employed, or was about to be used or employed, in such violation of such provisions of this code. He shall thereupon deliver the property so taken to such magistrate, who shall, by order in writing, place the same in the custody of an officer or other proper person named and designated in such order, to be kept by him until the conviction or final discharge of such person complained against, and shall send a copy of such order without delay to the district attorney of the county. The officer or person so named and designated in such order shall immediately thereupon assume the custody of such property and shall retain the same, subject to the order of the court before which such person so complained against may be required to appear for trial. Upon the conviction of the person so charged, all property so seized shall be adjudged by the court to be forfeited and shall thereupon be destroyed or otherwise disposed of as the court may order. In the event of the acquittal or final discharge without conviction of the person so charged such court shall, on demand, direct the delivery of such property so held in custody to the owner thereof.

(Amended by Stats.1975, c. 1075, p. 2635, § 4.)

§ 599e. Killing unfit animals after notice by officer; offense of refusal to kill; killing by officer; exception

Every animal which is unfit, by reason of its physical condition, for the purpose for which such animals are usually employed, and when there is no reasonable probability of such animal ever becoming fit for the purpose for which it is usually employed, shall be by the owner or lawful possessor of the same, deprived of life within 12 hours after being notified by any peace officer, officer of said society, or employee of a pound or animal regulation department of a public agency who is a veterinarian, to kill the same, and such owner, possessor, or person omitting or refusing to comply with the provisions of this section shall, upon conviction, be deemed guilty of a misdemeanor, and after such conviction the court or magistrate having jurisdiction of such offense shall order any peace officer, officer of said society, or officer of a pound or animal regulation department of a public agency, to immediately kill such animal; provided, that this shall not apply to such owner keeping any old or diseased animal belonging to him on his own premises with proper care.
(Amended by Stats.1963, c. 1583, p. 3163, § 2.)

§ 602. Trespasses constituting misdemeanors; enumeration

Every person who willfully commits a trespass by any of the following acts is guilty of a misdemeanor:

(a) **Standing timber**

(a) Cutting down, destroying, or injuring any kind of wood or timber standing or growing upon the lands of another.

(b) **Carrying away timber**

(b) Carrying away any kind of wood or timber lying on such lands.

(c) **Injury to or severance from freehold**

(c) Maliciously injuring or severing from the freehold of another anything attached thereto, or the produce thereof.

(d) **Soil removal**

(d) Digging, taking, or carrying away from any lot situated within the limits of any incorporated city, without the license of the owner or legal occupant thereof, any earth, soil, or stone.

(e) **Soil removal from public property**

(e) Digging, taking, or carrying away from land in any city or town laid down on the map or plan of such city, or otherwise recognized or established as a street, alley, avenue, or park, without the license of the proper authorities, any earth, soil or stone.

(f) **Highway signs, etc.**

(f) Maliciously tearing down, damaging, mutilating, or destroying any sign, signboard or notice placed upon, or affixed to, any property belonging to the state, or to any city, county, city and county, town or village, or upon any property of any person, by the state or by an automobile association, which sign, signboard or notice is intended to indicate or designate a road or roads, or a highway or highways, or is intended to direct travelers from one point to another, or relates to fires, fire control, or any other matter involving the protection of the property, or putting up, affixing, fastening, printing, or painting upon any property belonging to the state, or to any city, county, town, or village, or dedicated to the public, or upon any property of any person, without license from the owner, any notice, advertisement, or designation of, or any name for any commodity, whether for sale or otherwise, or any picture, sign, or device intended to call attention thereto.

(g) **Oyster lands**

(g) Entering upon any lands owned by any other person whereon oysters or other shellfish are planted or growing; or injuring, gathering, or carrying away any oysters or other shellfish planted, growing, or being on any such lands, whether covered by water or not, without the license of the owner or legal occupant thereof; or destroying or removing, or causing to be removed or destroyed, any stakes, marks, fences, or signs intended to designate the boundaries and limits of any such lands.

(h) **Fences, gates and signs**

(h) Willfully opening, tearing down, or otherwise, destroying any fence on the enclosed land of another, or opening any gate, bar, or fence of another and willfully leaving it open without the written permission of the owner, or maliciously tearing down, mutilating, or destroying any sign, signboard, or other notice forbidding shooting on private property.

(i) **Fires**

(i) Building fires upon any lands owned by another where signs forbidding trespass are displayed at intervals not greater than one mile along the exterior boundaries and at all roads and trails entering such lands, without first having obtained written permission from the owner of such lands or his agent, or the person in lawful possession thereof.

(j) **Purpose to injure**

(j) Entering any lands, whether unenclosed or enclosed by fence, for the purpose of injuring any property or property rights or with the intention of interfering with, obstructing, or injuring any lawful business or occupation carried on by the owner of such land, his agent or by the person in lawful possession.

(k) **Posted lands**

(k) Entering any lands under cultivation or enclosed by fence, belonging to, or occupied by, another or entering upon uncultivated or unenclosed lands where signs forbidding trespass are displayed at intervals not less than three to the mile along all exterior boundaries and at all roads and trails entering such lands without the written permission of the owner of such land, his agent or of the person in lawful possession, and

(1) Refusing or failing to leave such lands immediately upon being requested by the owner of such land, his agent or by the person in lawful possession to leave such lands, or

(2) Tearing down, mutilating, or destroying any sign, signboard, or notice forbidding trespass or hunting on such lands, or

(3) Removing, injuring, unlocking, or tampering with any lock on any gate on or leading into such lands, or

(4) Discharging any firearm.

(*l*) **Occupation**

(*l*) Entering and occupying real property or structures of any kind without the consent of the owner, his agent, or the person in lawful possession thereof.

(m) **Driving on private land**

(m) Driving any vehicle, as defined in Section 670 of the Vehicle Code, upon real property belonging to or lawfully occupied by another and known not to be open to the general public, without the consent of the owner, his agent, or the person in lawful possession thereof.

(n) **Refusal to leave private property**

(n) Refusing or failing to leave land, real property, or structures belonging to or lawfully occupied by another and not open to the general public, upon being requested to leave by (1) a peace officer and the owner, his agent, or the person in lawful possession thereof, or (2) the owner, his agent, or the person in lawful possession thereof; provided, however, that clause (2) of this subdivision shall not be applicable to persons engaged in lawful labor union activities which are permitted to be carried out on the property by the California Agricultural Labor Relations Act, Part 3.5 (commencing with Section 1140) of Division 2 of the Labor Code, or by the National Labor Relations Act.

(*o*) **Closed lands**

(*o*) Entering upon any lands declared closed to entry as provided in Section 4256 of the Public Resources Code; provided, such closed areas shall have been posted with notices declaring such closure, at intervals not greater than one mile along the exterior boundaries or along roads and trails passing through such lands.

(p) **Refusal to leave public building**

(p) Refusing or failing to leave a public building of a public agency during those hours of the day or night when the building is regularly closed to the public upon being requested to do so by a regularly employed guard, watchman, or custodian of the public agency owning or maintaining the building or property, if the surrounding circumstances are such as to indicate to a reasonable man that such person has no apparent lawful business to pursue.

(q) **Skiing in closed area**

(q) Knowingly skiing in an area or on a ski trail which is closed to the public and which has signs posted indicating such closure.
(Amended by Stats.1978, c. 1392, p. —, § 1.)

§ 602.5. Unauthorized entry of property

Every person other than a public officer or employee acting within the course and scope of his employment in performance of a duty imposed by law, who enters or remains in any noncommercial dwelling house, apartment, or other such place without consent of the owner, his agent, or the person in lawful possession thereof, is guilty of a misdemeanor.
(Added by Stats.1961, c. 1186, p. 2920, § 1.)

§ 602.10. Obstruction of college or university teachers or students; punishment; physical force defined

Every person who, by physical force and with the intent to prevent attendance or instruction, willfully obstructs or attempts to obstruct any student or teacher seeking to attend or instruct classes at any of the campuses or facilities owned, controlled, or administered by the Regents of the University of California, the Trustees of the California State University and Colleges, or the governing board of a community college district or school district maintaining a community college shall be punished by a fine not exceeding five hundred dollars ($500), by imprisonment in a county jail for a period of not exceeding one year, or by both such fine and imprisonment.

As used in this section, "physical force" includes, but is not limited to, use of one's person, individually or in concert with others, to impede access to or movement within or otherwise to obstruct the students and teachers of the classes to which the premises are devoted.

(Amended by Stats.1972, c. 431, p. 795, § 50.)

§ 603. Forcibly entry; vandalism

Every person other than a peace officer engaged in the performance of his duties as such who forcibly and without the consent of the owner, representative of the owner, lessee or representative of the lessee thereof, enters a dwelling house, cabin, or other building occupied or constructed for occupation by humans, and who damages, injures or destroys any property of value in, around or appertaining to such dwelling house, cabin or other building, is guilty of a misdemeanor.

(Added by Stats.1941, c. 635, p. 2094, § 1.)

§ 606. Places of confinement; punishment

Every person who willfully and intentionally breaks down, pulls down, or otherwise destroys or injures any place of confinement, is punishable by fine not exceeding ten thousand dollars ($10,000), and by imprisonment in the state prison, except that where the damages or injury to any city, city and county or county place of confinement is determined to be two hundred dollars ($200) or less, he is guilty of a misdemeanor.

(Amended by Stats.1976, c. 1139, p. —, § 251, operative July 1, 1977.)

MISCELLANEOUS CRIMES

§ 626. Definitions

(a) As used in this chapter:

(1) "State university" means the University of California, and includes any affiliated institution thereof and any campus or facility owned, operated, or controlled by the Regents of the University of California.

(2) "State college" means any California state university or college, and includes any campus or facility owned, operated, or controlled by the Trustees of the California State University and Colleges.

(3) "Community college" means any school established pursuant to Chapter 3 (commencing with Section 25500) of Division 18.5 of the Education Code.

(4) "School" means any elementary school, junior high school, four-year high school, senior high school, adult school or any branch thereof, opportunity school, continuation high school, regional occupational center, evening high school, or technical school.

(5) "Chief administrative officer" means:

(i) The president of a state university or college, Chancellor of the California State University and Colleges, or the officer designated by the Regents of the University of California or pursuant to authority granted by the Regents of the University of California to administer and be the officer in charge of a campus or other facility owned, operated, or controlled by the Regents of the University of California, or the superintendent of a community college district or a school district maintaining a community college.

(ii) For a school: the principal of the school; or a person who possesses a standard supervision credential or a standard administrative credential and who is designated by the principal; or a person who carries out the same functions as a person who possesses such a credential and who is designated by the principal.

(b) For the purpose of determining the penalty to be imposed pursuant to this chapter, the court may consider a written report from the Department of Justice containing information from its records showing prior convictions; and the communication is prima facie evidence of such convictions, if the defendant admits them, regardless of whether or not the complaint commencing the proceedings has alleged prior convictions.

(Amended by Stats.1975, c. 678, p. 1490, § 55.)

§ 626.2. Entry upon campus or facility of state college or university after written notice of suspension or dismissal without permission; punishment

Every student or employee who, after a hearing, has been suspended or dismissed from a community college, state college, state university, or school for disrupting the orderly operation of the campus or facility of such institution, and as a condition of such suspension or dismissal has been denied access to the campus or facility, or both, of the institution for the period of the suspension or in the case of dismissal for a period not to exceed one year; who has been served by registered or certified mail, at the last address given by such person, with a written notice of such suspension or dismissal and condition; and who willfully and knowingly enters upon the campus or facility of the institution to which he has been denied access, without the express written permission of the chief administrative officer of the campus or facility, is guilty of a misdemeanor and shall be punished as follows:

(1) Upon a first conviction, by a fine of not exceeding five hundred dollars ($500), by imprisonment in the county jail for a period of not more than six months, or by both such fine and imprisonment.

(2) If the defendant has been previously convicted once of a violation of any offense defined in this chapter or Section 415.5, by imprisonment in the county jail for a period of not less than 10 days or more than six months, or by both such imprisonment and a fine of not exceeding five hundred dollars ($500), and he shall not be released on probation, parole, or any other basis until he has served not less than 10 days.

(3) If the defendant has been previously convicted two or more times of a violation of any offense defined in this chapter or Section 415.5, by imprisonment in the county jail for a period of not less than 90 days or more than six months, or by both such imprisonment and a fine of not exceeding five hundred dollars ($500), and he shall not be released on probation, parole, or any other basis until he has served not less than 90 days.

Knowledge shall be presumed if notice has been given as prescribed in this section. The presumption established by this section is a presumption affecting the burden of proof.

(Amended by Stats.1974, c. 988, p. 2070, § 2; Stats.1974, c. 1183, p. 2531, § 2.)

§ 626.4. Notice of withdrawal of consent; report; action on report; reinstatement of consent; hearing; unlawful entry upon campus or facility; punishment

(a) The chief administrative officer of a campus or other facility of a community college, state college, state university, or school, or an officer or employee designated by him to maintain order on such campus or facility, may notify a person that consent to remain on the campus or other facility under the control of the chief administrative officer has been withdrawn whenever there is reasonable cause to believe that such person has willfully disrupted the orderly operation of such campus or facility.

(b) Whenever consent is withdrawn by any authorized officer or employee other than the chief administrative officer, such officer or employee shall as soon as is reasonably possible submit a written report to the chief administrative officer. Such report shall contain all of the following:

(1) The description of the person from whom consent was withdrawn, including, if available, the person's name, address, and phone number.

(2) A statement of the facts giving rise to the withdrawal of consent.

If the chief administrative officer or, in his absence, a person designated by him for this purpose, upon reviewing the report, finds that there was reasonable cause to believe that such person has willfully disrupted the orderly operation of the campus or facility, he may enter written confirmation upon the report of the action taken by the officer or employee. If the chief administrative officer or, in his absence, the person designated by him, does not confirm the action of the officer or employee within 24 hours after the time that consent was withdrawn, the action of the officer or employee shall be deemed void and of no force or effect, except that any arrest made during such period shall not for this reason be deemed not to have been made for probable cause.

(c) Consent shall be reinstated by the chief administrative officer whenever he has reason to believe that the presence of the person from whom consent was withdrawn will not constitute a substantial and material threat to the orderly operation of the campus or facility. In no case shall consent be withdrawn for longer than 14 days from the date upon which consent was initially withdrawn. The person from whom consent has been withdrawn may submit a written request for a hearing on the withdrawal within the two-week period. Such written request shall state the address to which notice of hearing is to be sent. The chief administrative officer shall grant such a hearing not later than seven days from the date of receipt of such request and shall immediately mail a written notice of the time, place, and date of such hearing to such person.

(d) Any person who has been notified by the chief administrative officer of a campus or other facility of a community college, state college, state university, or school, or by an officer or employee designated by the chief administrative officer to maintain order on such campus or facility, that consent to remain on the campus or facility has been withdrawn pursuant to subdivision (a); who has not had such consent reinstated; and who willfully and knowingly enters or remains upon such campus or facility during the period for which consent has been withdrawn is guilty of a misdemeanor. This subdivision does not apply to any person who enters or remains on such campus or facility for the sole purpose of applying to the chief administrative officer for the reinstatement of consent or for the sole purpose of attending a hearing on the withdrawal.

(e) This section shall not affect the power of the duly constituted authorities of a community college, state college, state university, or school, to suspend, dismiss, or expel any student or employee at such university, college, or school.

(f) Any person convicted under this section shall be punished as follows:

(1) Upon a first conviction, by a fine of not exceeding five hundred dollars ($500), by imprisonment in the county jail for a period of not more than six months, or by both such fine and imprisonment.

(2) If the defendant has been previously convicted once of a violation of any offense defined in this chapter or Section 415.5, by imprisonment in the county jail for a period of not less than 10 days or more than six months, or by both such imprisonment and a fine of not exceeding five hundred dollars ($500), and he shall not be released on probation, parole, or any other basis until he has served not less than 10 days.

(3) If the defendant has been previously convicted two or more times of a violation of any offense defined in this chapter or Section 415.5, by imprisonment in the county jail for a period of not less than 90 days or more than six months, or by both such imprisonment and a fine of not exceeding five hundred dollars ($500), and he shall not be released on probation, parole, or any other basis until he has served not less than 90 days.

(g) This section shall not affect the rights of representatives of employee organizations to enter, or remain upon, school grounds while actually engaged in activities related to representation, as provided for in Article 5 (commencing with Section 13080) of Chapter 1, Division 10, Part 2, of the Education Code.

(Amended by Stats.1974, c. 988, p. 2071, § 3; Stats.1974, c. 1183, p. 2531, § 3.)

§ **626.6. Committing act, or entry upon campus or facility to commit act, likely to interfere with peaceful activities; direction to leave; refusal to leave or reentry; punishment**

In any case in which a person who is not a student or officer or employee of a community college, state college, state university, or school, and who is not required by his employment to be on the campus or any other facility owned, operated or controlled by the governing board of any such community college, state college, state university, or school, enters such campus or facility, and it reasonably appears to the chief administrative officer of such campus or facility or to an officer or employee designated by him to maintain order on such campus or facility that such person is committing any act likely to interfere with the peaceful conduct of the activities of such campus or facility or has entered such campus or facility for the purpose of committing any such act, the chief administrative officer or officer or employee designated by him to maintain order on such campus or facility may direct such person to leave such campus or facility, and if such person fails to do so or if such person willfully and knowingly reenters upon such campus or facility within 72 hours after being directed to leave, he is guilty of a misdemeanor and shall be punished as follows:

(1) Upon a first conviction by a fine of not exceeding five hundred dollars ($500), by imprisonment in the county jail for a period of not more than six months, or by both such fine and imprisonment.

(2) If the defendant has been previously convicted once of a violation of any offense defined in this chapter or Section 415.5, by imprisonment in the county jail for a period of not less than 10 days or more than six months, or by both such imprisonment and a fine of not exceeding five hundred dollars ($500), and shall not be released on probation, parole,

or any other basis until he has served not less than 10 days.

(3) If the defendant has been previously convicted two or more times of a violation of any offense defined in this chapter or Section 415.5, by imprisonment in the county jail for a period of not less than 90 days or more than six months, or by both such imprisonment and a fine of not exceeding five hundred dollars ($500), and he shall not be released on probation, parole, or any other basis until he has served not less than 90 days.

For purposes of this section, a representative of a school employee organization engaged in activities related to representation, as provided for in Article 5 (commencing with Section 13080) of Chapter 1, Division 10, Part 2, of the Education Code, shall be deemed a person required by his employment to be in a school building or on the grounds of a school.
(Amended by Stats.1974, c. 988, p. 2072, § 4; Stats.1974, c. 1183, p. 2533, § 4.)

§ 626.8. Disruptive presence at schools

(a) Any person who comes into any school building or upon any school ground, or street, sidewalk, or public way adjacent thereto, without lawful business thereon, and whose presence or acts interfere with the peaceful conduct of the activities of such school or disrupt the school or its pupils or school activities, and who remains there, or who reenters or comes upon such place within 72 hours, after being asked to leave by the chief administrative official of that school or, in the absence of the chief administrative official, the person acting as the chief administrative official, or by a member of the security patrol of the school district who has been given authorization, in writing, by the chief administrative official of that school to act as his agent in performing this duty, is guilty of a misdemeanor and shall be punished as follows:

(1) Upon a first conviction by a fine of not exceeding five hundred dollars ($500), by imprisonment in the county jail for a period of not more than six months, or by both such fine and imprisonment.

(2) If the defendant has been previously convicted once of a violation of any offense defined in this chapter or Section 415.5, by imprisonment in the county jail for a period of not less than 10 days or more than six months, or by both such imprisonment, and a fine of not exceeding five hundred dollars ($500), and he shall not be released on probation, parole, or any other basis until he has served not less than 10 days.

(3) If the defendant has been previously convicted two or more times of a violation of any offense defined in this chapter or Section 415.5, by imprisonment in the county jail for a period of not less than 90 days or more than six months, or by both such imprisonment and a fine of not exceeding five hundred dollars ($500), and he shall not be released on probation, parole, or any other basis until he has served not less than 90 days.

(b) As used in this section, "lawful business" means a reason for being present upon school property which is not otherwise prohibited by statute, by ordinance, or by any regulation adopted pursuant to statute or ordinance.
(Amended by Stats.1974, c. 988, p. 2073, § 5; Stats.1974, c. 1183, p. 2534, § 5.)

§ 626.9. Firearms; bringing into or possession of, upon or within public schools and grounds; exceptions

Any person, except a duly appointed peace officer as defined in Chapter 4.5 (commencing with Section 830) of Title 3 of Part 2, a full-time paid peace officer of another state or the federal government who is carrying out official duties while in California, any person summoned by any such officer to assist in making arrests or preserving the peace while he is actually engaged in assisting such officer, a member of the military forces of this state or the United States who is engaged in the performance of his duties, or a person holding a valid license to carry the firearm pursuant to Article 3 (commencing with Section 12050) of Chapter 1 of Title 2 of Part 4, who brings or possesses a firearm upon the grounds of any public school, including the University of California and the state university and colleges or within any public school, including the University of California and the state colleges, unless it is with the permission of the school authorities, shall be punished by imprisonment in the county jail for a period of not more than one year, a fine of not more than one thousand dollars ($1,000), or both such imprisonment and fine, or by imprisonment in the state prison.
(Amended by Stats.1976, c. 1139, p. ——, § 256, operative July 1, 1977.)

§ 626.10. Dirks, daggers, knives or razors; bringing into or possession of, upon or within public schools and grounds; exceptions

(a) Any person, except a duly appointed peace officer as defined in Chapter 4.5 (commencing with

Section 830) of Title 3 of Part 2, a full-time paid peace officer of another state or the federal government who is carrying out official duties while in this state, any person summoned by any such officer to assist in making arrests or preserving the peace while he is actually engaged in assisting any such officer, or a member of the military forces of this state or the United States who is engaged in the performance of his duties, who brings or possesses any dirk, dagger, knife having a blade longer than 3½ inches, folding knife with a blade that locks into place, or razor with an unguarded blade upon the grounds of, or within, any public school providing instruction in kindergarten or any of grades 1 through 12, inclusive, is guilty of a misdemeanor.

(b) Subdivision (a) shall not apply to any person who brings or possesses a knife having a blade longer than 3½ inches or razor with an unguarded blade under the grounds of, or within, a public school providing instruction in kindergarten or any of grades 1 through 12, inclusive, at the direction of a certificated or classified employee of the school for use in a school-sponsored activity or class.

(c) Subdivision (a) shall not apply to any person who brings or possesses a knife having a blade longer than 3½ inches or razor with an unguarded blade upon the grounds of, or within, a public school providing instruction in kindergarten or any of grades 1 through 12, inclusive, for a lawful purpose within the scope of his employment.

(d) Any certificated or classified employee of a public school providing instruction in kindergarten or any of grades 1 through 12, inclusive, may seize any of the weapons described in subdivision (a) from the possession of any person upon the grounds of, or within, the school if he knows or has reasonable cause to know the person is prohibited from bringing or possessing the weapon upon the grounds of, or within, the school.
(Added by Stats.1974, c. 103, p. 218, § 1.)

§ 626.11. Searches; evidence seized by teacher, official, employee or governing board member of state university, college or community college; admissibility in administrative disciplinary proceedings; nonvalidity of waiver of constitutional rights in dormitory rental

(a) Any evidence seized by a teacher, official, employee, or governing board member of any state university, state college, or community college, or by any person acting under his direction or with his consent in violation of standards relating to rights under the Fourth Amendment to the United States Constitution or under Section 13 of Article 1 of the State Constitution to be free from unreasonable searches and seizures, or in violation of state or federal constitutional rights to privacy, or any of them, are inadmissible in administrative disciplinary proceedings.

(b) Any provision in an agreement between a student and an educational institution specified in subdivision (a) relating to the leasing, renting, or use of a room of any student dormitory owned or operated by the institution by which the student waives a constitutional right under the Fourth Amendment to the United States Constitution or under Section 13 of Article 1 of the State Constitution, or under state or federal constitutional provision guaranteeing a right to privacy, or any of them, is contrary to public policy and void.

(c) Any evidence seized by a person specified in subdivision (a) after a nonconsensual entry not in violation of subdivision (a) into a dormitory room which evidence is not directly related to the purpose for which such entry was initially made is not admissible in administrative disciplinary proceedings.
(Added by Stats.1975, c. 867, p. 1939, § 1.)

§ 631. Wiretapping

(a) Prohibited acts; punishment; recidivists

(a) Any person who, by means of any machine, instrument, or contrivance, or in any other manner, intentionally taps, or makes any unauthorized connection, whether physically, electrically, acoustically, inductively, or otherwise, with any telegraph or telephone wire, line, cable, or instrument, including the wire, line, cable, or instrument of any internal telephonic communication system, or who willfully and without the consent of all parties to the communication, or in any unauthorized manner, reads, or attempts to read, or to learn the contents or meaning of any message, report, or communication while the same is in transit or passing over any such wire, line, or cable, or is being sent from, or received at any place within this state; or who uses, or attempts to use, in any manner, or for any purpose, or to communicate in any way, any information so obtained, or who aids, agrees with, employs, or conspires with any person or persons to unlawfully do, or permit, or cause to be done any of the acts or things mentioned above in this section, is punishable by a fine not exceeding two thousand five hundred dollars

§ 631

($2,500), or by imprisonment in the county jail not exceeding one year, or by imprisonment in the state prison, or by both such fine and imprisonment in the county jail or in the state prison. If such person has previously been convicted of a violation of this section or Section 632 or 636, he is punishable by fine not exceeding ten thousand dollars ($10,000), or by imprisonment in the county jail not exceeding one year, or by imprisonment in the state prison, or by both such fine and imprisonment in the county jail or in the state prison.

(b) **Exceptions**

(b) This section shall not apply (1) to any public utility engaged in the business of providing communications services and facilities, or to the officers, employees or agents thereof, where the acts otherwise prohibited herein are for the purpose of construction, maintenance, conduct or operation of the services and facilities of such public utility, or (2) to the use of any instrument, equipment, facility, or service furnished and used pursuant to the tariffs of such a public utility, or (3) to any telephonic communication system used for communication exclusively within a state, county, city and county, or city correctional facility.

(c) **Evidence**

(c) Except as proof in an action or prosecution for violation of this section, no evidence obtained in violation of this section shall be admissible in any judicial, administrative, legislative or other proceeding.
(Amended by Stats.1976, c. 1139, p. ——, § 257, operative July 1, 1977.)

§ 632. Eavesdropping on or recording confidential communications

(a) **Prohibited acts; punishment; recidivists**

(a) Every person who, intentionally and without the consent of all parties to a confidential communication, by means of any electronic amplifying or recording device, eavesdrops upon or records such confidential communication, whether such communication is carried on among such parties in the presence of one another or by means of a telegraph, telephone or other device, except a radio, shall be punishable by fine not exceeding two thousand five hundred dollars ($2,500), or by imprisonment in the county jail not exceeding one year, or by imprisonment in the state prison, or by both such fine and imprisonment in the county jail or in the state prison. If such person has previously been convicted of a violation of this section or Section 631 or 636, he is punishable by fine not exceeding ten thousand dollars ($10,000), or by imprisonment in the county jail not exceeding one year, or by imprisonment in the state prison, or by both such fine and imprisonment in the county jail or in the state prison.

(b) **Person**

(b) The term "person" includes an individual, business, association, partnership, corporation, or other legal entity, and an individual acting or purporting to act for or on behalf of any government or subdivision thereof, whether federal, state, or local, but excludes an individual known by all parties to a confidential communication to be overhearing or recording such communication.

(c) **Confidential communication**

(c) The term "confidential communication" includes any communication carried on in such circumstances as may reasonably indicate that any party to such communication desires it to be confined to such parties, but excludes a communication made in a public gathering or in any legislative, judicial, executive or administrative proceeding open to the public, or in any other circumstance in which the parties to the communication may reasonably except that the communication may be overheard or recorded.

(d) **Evidence**

(d) Except as proof in an action or prosecution for violation of this section, no evidence obtained as a result of eavesdropping upon or recording a confidential communication in violation of this section shall be admissible in any judicial, administrative, legislative or other proceeding.

(e) **Exceptions**

(e) This section shall not apply (1) to any public utility engaged in the business of providing communications services and facilities, or to the officers, employees or agents thereof, where the acts otherwise prohibited herein are for the purpose of construction, maintenance, conduct or operation of the services and facilities of such public utility, or (2) to the use of any instrument, equipment, facility, or service furnished and used pursuant to the tariffs of such a public utility, or (3) to any telephonic communication system used for communication exclusively within a state, county, city and county, or city correctional facility.

(f) Hearing aids

(f) This section does not apply to the use of hearing aids and similar devices, by persons afflicted with impaired hearing, for the purpose of overcoming the impairment to permit the hearing of sounds ordinarily audible to the human ear.
(Amended by Stats.1976, c. 1139, p. —, § 258, operative July 1, 1977.)

Notes of Decisions

Use of transmitting device, hidden on person of confederate of defendant charged with conspiracy to commit forgery, and of tape recorder in police officer's office to record conversation between the defendant and confederate, did not violate former § 653h, prohibiting unauthorized installation of dictographs. People v. Wootan (1961) 15 Cal.Rptr. 833, 195 C.A.2d 481.

§ 633. Law enforcement officers; authorized use of electronic, etc., equipment

Nothing in Section 631 or 632 shall be construed as prohibiting the Attorney General, any district attorney, or any assistant, deputy, or investigator of the Attorney General or any district attorney, or any officer of the California Highway Patrol, or any chief of police, assistant chief of police, or policeman of a city or city and county, or any sheriff, under sheriff, or deputy sheriff regularly employed and paid as such of a county, or any person acting pursuant to the direction of one of the above-named law enforcement officers acting within the scope of his authority, from overhearing or recording any communication which they could lawfully overhear or record prior to the effective date of this chapter.

Nothing in Section 631 or 632 shall be construed as rendering inadmissible any evidence obtained by the above-named persons by means of overhearing or recording any communication which they could lawfully overhear or record prior to the effective date of this chapter.
(Added by Stats.1967, c. 1509, p. 3586, § 1.)

§ 633.5. Recording communications relating to commission of extortion, kidnapping, bribery, felony involving violence against the person, or violation of § 653m

Nothing in Section 631 or 632 shall be construed as prohibiting one party to a confidential communication from recording such communication for the purpose of obtaining evidence reasonably believed to relate to the commission by another party to such communication of the crime of extortion, kidnapping, bribery, any felony involving violence against the person or a violation of Section 653m, and nothing in Section 631 or 632 shall be construed as rendering inadmissible in a prosecution for extortion, kidnapping, bribery, any felony involving violence against the person, or a violation of Section 653m, or any crime in connection therewith, any evidence so obtained.
(Added by Stats.1967, c. 1509, p. 3586, § 1.)

§ 634. Trespass for purpose of committing prohibited acts; punishment

Any person who trespasses on property for the purpose of committing any act, or attempting to commit any act, in violation of Section 631, 632 or 636 shall be punishable by fine not exceeding two thousand five hundred dollars ($2,500), or by imprisonment in the county jail not exceeding one year, or by imprisonment in the state prison, or by both such fine and imprisonment in the county jail or in the state prison. If such person has previously been convicted of a violation of this section or Section 631, 632 or 636, he is punishable by fine not exceeding ten thousand dollars ($10,000), or by imprisonment in the county jail not exceeding one year, or by imprisonment in the state prison, or by both such fine and imprisonment in the county jail or in the state prison.
(Amended by Stats.1976, c. 1139, p. —, § 259, operative July 1, 1977.)

§ 635. Manufacture, sale and possession of eavesdropping devices; punishment; recidivists; exceptions

(a) Every person who manufactures, assembles, sells, offers for sale, advertises for sale, possesses, transports, imports, or furnishes to another any device which is primarily or exclusively designed or intended for eavesdropping upon the communication of another is punishable by fine not exceeding two thousand five hundred dollars ($2,500), or by imprisonment in the county jail not exceeding one year, or by imprisonment in the state prison, or by both such fine and imprisonment in the county jail or in the state prison. If such person has previously been convicted of a violation of this section, he is punishable by a fine not exceeding ten thousand dollars ($10,000), or by imprisonment in the county jail not exceeding one year, or by imprisonment in the state prison, or by both such fine and imprisonment in the county jail or in the state prison.

(b) This section shall not apply to

(1) An act otherwise prohibited herein when performed by (i) a communication utility or an officer,

§ 635

employee or agent thereof for the purpose of construction, maintenance, conduct or operation of, or otherwise incident to the use of, the services or facilities of the utility, or (ii) a state, county or municipal law enforcement agency or an agency of the federal government, or (iii) a person engaged in selling such devices for use by, or resale to, agencies of a foreign government under terms approved by the federal government, communication utilities, state, county or municipal law enforcement agencies, or agencies of the federal government, or

(2) Possession by a subscriber to communication utilities service of such a device furnished by such utility pursuant to its tariffs.
(Amended by Stats.1976, c. 1139, p. —, § 260, operative July 1, 1977.)

§ 636.5. Police radio interception and divulgence prohibited; penalty

Any person not authorized by the sender, who intercepts any police radio service communication, and who divulges to any person he knows to be a suspect in the commission of any criminal offense, the existence, contents, substance, purport, effect or meaning of such communication concerning such offense with the intent that such suspect may avoid or escape from arrest, trial, conviction, or punishment is guilty of a misdemeanor.

Nothing in this section shall preclude prosecution of any person under Section 31 or 32.

As used in this section "police radio service communication" means a communication authorized by the Federal Communications Commission to be transmitted by a station in the police radio service.
(Added by Stats.1976, c. 1129, p. —, § 1.)

§ 637. Disclosure of telegraphic or telephonic message; punishment; exception

Every person not a party to a telegraphic or telephonic communication who willfully discloses the contents of a telegraphic or telephonic message, or any part thereof, addressed to another person, without the permission of such person, unless directed so to do by the lawful order of a court, is punishable by imprisonment in the state prison, or in the county jail not exceeding one year, or by fine not exceeding five thousand dollars ($5,000), or by both fine and imprisonment.
(Amended by Stats.1976, c. 1139, p. —, § 261, operative July 1, 1977.)

§ 637.3. Voice prints or other voice stress patterns; use of systems to record or examine without consent; damages

(a) No person or entity in this state shall use any system which examines or records in any manner voiceprints or other voice stress patterns of another person to determine the truth or falsity of statements made by such other person without his or her express written consent given in advance of the examination or recordation.

(b) This section shall not apply to any peace officer, as defined in Section 830, while he is carrying out his official duties.

(c) Any person who has been injured by a violator of this section may bring an action against the violator for his actual damages or one thousand dollars ($1,000), whichever is greater.
(Added by Stats.1978, c. 1251, p. —, § 1.)

§ 640a. Coin operated vending machines, etc.; use of slugs, counterfeited or foreign coins, etc.; manufacture or distribution of slugs

1. Any person who shall knowingly and wilfully operate, or cause to be operated, or who shall attempt to operate, or attempt to cause to be operated, any automatic vending machine, slot machine or other receptacle designed to receive lawful coin of the United States of America in connection with the sale, use or enjoyment of property or service, by means of a slug or any false, counterfeited, mutilated, sweated or foreign coin, or by any means, method, trick or device whatsoever not lawfully authorized by the owner, lessee or licensee of such machine or receptacle, or who shall take, obtain or receive from or in connection with any automatic vending machine, slot machine or other receptacle designed to receive lawful coin of the United States of America in connection with the sale, use or enjoyment of property or service, any goods, wares, merchandise, gas, electric current, article of value, or the use or enjoyment of any musical instrument, phonograph or other property, without depositing in and surrendering to such machine or receptacle lawful coin of the United States of America to the amount required therefor by the owner, lessee or licensee of such machine or receptacle shall be guilty of a misdemeanor.

2. Any person who, with intent to cheat or defraud the owner, lessee, licensee or other person entitled to the contents of any automatic vending machine, slot machine or other receptacle, depository

or contrivance designed to receive lawful coin of the United States of America in connection with the sale, use or enjoyment of property or service, or who, knowing or having cause to believe that the same is intended for unlawful use, shall manufacture for sale, or sell or give away any slug, device or substance whatsoever intended or calculated to be placed or deposited in any such automatic vending machine, slot machine or other such receptacle, depository or contrivance, shall be guilty of a misdemeanor.
(Amended by Stats.1957, c. 2096, p. 3720, § 1.)

§ 640b. Coin-box telephones; use of slugs, counterfeited or foreign coins, etc.; manufacture or distribution of slugs

1. Any person who knowingly, wilfully and with intent to defraud the owner, lessee or licensee of any coin-box telephone, shall operate or cause to be operated, attempt to operate, or attempt to cause to be operated, any coin-box telephone by means of any slug or any false, counterfeited, mutilated, sweated or foreign coin, or by any means, method, trick or device whatsoever not lawfully authorized by such owner, lessee or licensee, or any person who, knowingly, wilfully and with intent to defraud the owner, lessee or licensee of any coin-box telephone, shall take, obtain or receive from or in connection with any such coin-box telephone, the use or enjoyment of any telephone or telegraph facilities or service, without depositing in or surrendering to such coin-box telephone lawful coin of the United States of America to the amount required therefor by such owner, lessee or licensee, shall be guilty of a misdemeanor.

2. Any person who, with the intent to cheat or defraud the owner, lessee or licensee or other person entitled to the contents of any coin-box telephone, or who, knowing or having cause to believe that the same is intended for unlawful use, shall manufacture for sale, or sell or give away any slug, device or substance whatsoever intended or calculated to be placed or deposited in any such coin-box telephone, shall be guilty of a misdemeanor.
(Added by Stats.1957, c. 2096, p. 3720, § 2.)

§ 647. Disorderly conduct

Every person who commits any of the following acts is guilty of disorderly conduct, a misdemeanor:

(a) Who solicits any one to engage in or who engages in lewd or dissolute conduct in any public place or in any place open to the public or exposed to public view.

(b) Who solicits or who engages in any act of prostitution. As used in this subdivision, "prostitution" includes any lewd act between persons for money or other consideration.

(c) Who accosts other persons in any public place or in any place open to the public for the purpose of begging or soliciting alms.

(d) Who loiters in or about any toilet open to the public for the purpose of engaging in or soliciting any lewd or lascivious or any unlawful act.

(e) Who loiters or wanders upon the streets or from place to place without apparent reason or business and who refuses to identify himself and to account for his presence when requested by any peace officer so to do, if the surrounding circumstances are such as to indicate to a reasonable person that the public safety demands such identification.

(f) Who is found in any public place under the influence of intoxicating liquor, any drug, toluene, any substance defined as a poison in Schedule D of Section 4160 of the Business and Professions Code, or any combination of any intoxicating liquor, drug, toluene, or any such poison, in such a condition that he is unable to exercise care for his own safety or the safety of others, or by reason of his being under the influence of intoxicating liquor, any drug, toluene, any substance defined as a poison in Schedule D of Section 4160 of the Business and Professions Code, or any combination of any intoxicating liquor, drug, toluene, or any such poison, interferes with or obstructs or prevents the free use of any street, sidewalk, or other public way.

(ff) When a person has violated subdivision (f) of this section, a peace officer, if he is reasonably able to do so, shall place the person, or cause him to be placed, in civil protective custody. Such person shall be taken to a facility, designated pursuant to Section 5170 of the Welfare and Institutions Code, for the 72-hour treatment and evaluation of inebriates. A peace officer may place a person in civil protective custody with that kind and degree of force which would be lawful were he effecting an arrest for a misdemeanor without a warrant. No person who has been placed in civil protective custody shall thereafter be subject to any criminal prosecution or juvenile court proceeding based on the facts giving rise to such placement. This subdivision shall not apply to the following persons:

(1) Any person who is under the influence of any drug, or under the combined influence of intoxicating liquor and any drug.

§ 647

(2) Any person who a peace officer has probable cause to believe has committed any felony, or who has committed any misdemeanor in addition to subdivision (f) of this section.

(3) Any person who a peace officer in good faith believes will attempt escape or will be unreasonably difficult for medical personnel to control.

(g) Who loiters, prowls, or wanders upon the private property of another, in the nighttime, without visible or lawful business with the owner or occupant thereof.

(h) Who, while loitering, prowling, or wandering upon the private property of another, in the nighttime, peeks in the door or window of any inhabited building or structure located thereon, without visible or lawful business with the owner or occupant thereof.

(i) Who lodges in any building, structure, vehicle, or place, whether public or private, without the permission of the owner or person entitled to the possession or in control thereof.

In any accusatory pleading charging a violation of subdivision (b) of this section, if the defendant has been once previously convicted of a violation of that subdivision, the previous conviction shall be charged in the accusatory pleading; and, if the previous conviction is found to be true by the jury, upon a jury trial, or by the court, upon a court trial, or is admitted by the defendant, the defendant shall be imprisoned in the county jail for a period of not less than 45 days and shall not be eligible for release upon completion of sentence, on parole, or on any other basis until he has served a period of not less than 45 days in the county jail. In no such case shall the trial court grant probation or suspend the execution of sentence imposed upon the defendant.

In any accusatory pleading charging a violation of subdivision (b) of this section, if the defendant has been previously convicted two or more times of a violation of that subdivision, each such previous conviction shall be charged in the accusatory pleading; and, if two or more of such previous convictions are found to be true by the jury, upon a jury trial, or by the court, upon a court trial, or are admitted by the defendant, the defendant shall be imprisoned in the county jail for a period of not less than 90 days and shall not be eligible for release upon completion of sentence, on parole, or on any other basis until he has served a period of not less than 90 days in the county jail. In no such case shall the trial court grant probation or suspend the execution of sentence imposed upon the defendant.
(Amended by Stats.1977, c. 426, p. —, § 1.)

Notes of Decisions

Public place

Automobile parked on public street was "public place" within this section proscribing being found in public place under influence of intoxicating liquor. People v. Kelley (1969) 83 Cal.Rptr. 287, 3 C.A.3d 146.

A massage parlor which is open to common or general use is a "public place" at least with respect to portions used in common by its patrons and such premises are open to public within meaning of this section. Steinke v. Municipal Court for San Jose-Milpitas-Alviso Judicial Dist. (1969) 82 Cal.Rptr. 789, 2 C.A.3d 569.

A dance performed before an audience for entertainment cannot be held to violate statutory prohibitions of indecent exposure and lewd or dissolute conduct in absence of proof that the dance, tested in context of contemporary community standards, appealed to prurient interest of audience and affronted standards of decency generally accepted in the community. In re Giannini (1968) 72 Cal.Rptr. 655, 446 P.2d 535, 69 C.2d 563, certiorari denied 89 S.Ct. 1743, 395 U.S. 910, 23 L.Ed.2d 223.

Where, after midnight, police officers saw two known prostitutes with two men enter into apartment house known to be used for purposes of prostitution they had reasonable cause to believe that one or more public offenses were being committed in their presence and had right to arrest offenders. People v. Seals (1968) 69 Cal.Rptr. 861, 263 C.A.2d 575.

Identification, loitering

Words "loiter" and "wander" as used in this section to describe person who may be asked by police officer to identify himself and to account for his presence in prescribed circumstances are not so vague that men of common intelligence must necessarily guess at their meaning and differ as to their application. People v. Weger (1967) 59 Cal.Rptr. 661, 251 C.A.2d 584, certiorari denied 88 S.Ct. 774, 389 U.S. 1047, 19 L.Ed.2d 840.

Under this section, mere roaming from place to place by persons without visible means of support is no longer forbidden and to be guilty of offense one must also refuse to identify himself and to account for his presence when requested by police officer to do so if surrounding circumstances are such as to indicate to reasonable man that public safety demands such identification. People v. Weger (1967) 59 Cal.Rptr. 661, 251 C.A.2d 584, certiorari denied 88 S.Ct. 774, 389 U.S. 1047, 19 L.Ed.2d 840.

§ 647a. Vagrancy; annoying or molesting child under 18; punishment

Every person who annoys or molests any child under the age of 18 is a vagrant and is punishable upon first conviction by a fine not exceeding five hundred dollars ($500) or by imprisonment in the county jail for not exceeding six months or by both such fine and imprisonment and is punishable upon the second and each subsequent conviction or upon the first conviction after a previous conviction under Section 288 of this code by imprisonment in the state prison.
(Amended by Stats.1976, c. 1139, p. —, § 262, operative July 1, 1977.)

§ 647b. Loitering about adult schools; molesting of pupils

Every person who loiters about any school in which adults are in attendance at courses established pursuant to Chapter 5.5 (commencing with Section 5701) of Division 6 of the Education Code, and who annoys or molests any person in attendance therein shall be punished by a fine of not exceeding five hundred dollars ($500) or by imprisonment in the county jail for not exceeding six months, or by both such fine and imprisonment.

(Added by Stats.1965, c. 1706, p. 3840, § 2.)

§ 647c. Obstruction of street, sidewalk or other place open to public

Every person who willfully and maliciously obstructs the free movement of any person on any street, sidewalk, or other public place or on or in any place open to the public is guilty of a misdemeanor.

Nothing in this section affects the power of a county or a city to regulate conduct upon a street, sidewalk, or other public place or on or in a place open to the public.

(Amended by Stats.1968, c. 122, p. 335, § 3.)

§ 653f. Soliciting commission of certain offenses; punishment; degree of proof

(a) Every person who solicits another to offer or accept or join in the offer or acceptance of a bribe, or to commit or join in the commission of robbery, burglary, grand theft, receiving stolen property, extortion, rape by force and violence, perjury, subornation of perjury, forgery, kidnapping, arson or assault with a deadly weapon or instrument or by means of force likely to produce great bodily injury, is punishable by imprisonment in the county jail not more than one year or in the state prison, or by fine of not more than five thousand dollars ($5,000), or the amount which could have been assessed for commission of the offense itself, whichever is greater, or by both such fine and imprisonment.

(b) Every person who solicits another to commit or join in the commission of murder is punishable by imprisonment in the state prison for two, four, or six years.

(c) An offense charged in violation of subdivision (a) or (b) must be proven by the testimony of two witnesses, or of one witness and corroborating circumstances.

(Amended by Stats.1978, c. 579, p. —, § 26.)

§ 653m. Telephone calls with intent to annoy

(a) Every person who with intent to annoy telephones another and addresses to or about such other person any obscene language or addresses to such other person any threat to inflict injury to the person or property of the person addressed or any member of his family, is guilty of a misdemeanor.

(b) Every person who makes a telephone call with intent to annoy another and without disclosing his true identity to the person answering the telephone is, whether or not conversation ensues from making the telephone call, guilty of a misdemeanor.

(c) Any offense committed by use of a telephone as herein set out may be deemed to have been committed at either the place at which the telephone call or calls were made or at the place where the telephone call or calls were received.

(d) Subdivision (a) or (b) is violated when the person acting with intent to annoy makes a telephone call requesting a return call and performs the acts prohibited under such subdivision upon receiving the return call.

(Amended by Stats.1978, c. 1022, p. —, § 1.)

GENERAL PROVISIONS

§ 654. Offenses punishable in different ways by different provisions; double jeopardy

An act or omission which is made punishable in different ways by different provisions of this code may be punished under either of such provisions, but in no case can it be punished under more than one; an acquittal or conviction and sentence under either one bars a prosecution for the same act or omission under any other.

(Amended by Stats.1977, c. 165, p. —, § 11, urgency, eff. June 29, 1977, operative July 1, 1977.)

§ 663. Attempts; conviction though offense perpetrated; discretion of court

Attempts to commit crimes, when punishable. Any person may be convicted of an attempt to commit a crime, although it appears on the trial that the crime intended or attempted was perpetrated by such person in pursuance of such attempt, unless the Court, in its discretion, discharges the jury and directs such person to be tried for such crime.

(Enacted 1872.)

§ 663

Notes of Decisions

In order to justify conviction for attempt to commit crime, it is not necessary that overt act proved should be ultimate step towards commission of crime, and it is sufficient if it was first or some subsequent step in direct movement toward such consummation. People v. Seach (1963) 30 Cal.Rptr. 499, 215 C.A.2d 779.

Mere intention to commit a crime does not of itself amount to an "attempt", and some act done toward accomplishment of the intended crime is necessary, but if a person formulates the intent and then does something more which is the usual course of natural events would result in the commission of a crime, the attempt is complete, even though the intended crime could not have been completed, due to some extrinsic fact unknown to person who intended it. People v. Siu (1954) 271 P.2d 575, 126 C.A.2d 41.

Where defendant had no visible or lawful business in apartment house, manager observed him looking through window of apartment, defendant attempted to flee when manager approached him, he wore gloves and attempted to flee when told that police would be called, public offense of burglary was attempted in presence of manager who had authority to make citizen's arrest. People v. Garcia (1969) 78 Cal.Rptr. 775, 274 A.C.A. 116.

§ 664. Attempts; punishment

Every person who attempts to commit any crime, but fails, or is prevented or intercepted in the perpetration thereof, is punishable, where no provision is made by law for the punishment of such attempts, as follows:

1. If the offense so attempted is punishable by imprisonment in the state prison, the person guilty of such attempt is punishable by imprisonment in the state prison for one-half the term of imprisonment prescribed upon a conviction of the offense so attempted; provided, however, that if the crime attempted is one in which the maximum sentence is life imprisonment or death the person guilty of such attempt shall be punishable by imprisonment in the state prison for a term of five, seven, or nine years.

2. If the offense so attempted is punishable by imprisonment in a county jail, the person guilty of such attempt is punishable by imprisonment in a county jail for a term not exceeding one-half the term of imprisonment prescribed upon a conviction of the offense so attempted.

3. If the offense so attempted is punishable by a fine, the offender convicted of such attempt is punishable by a fine not exceeding one-half the largest fine which may be imposed upon a conviction of the offense so attempted.

4. If a crime is divided into degrees, an attempt to commit the crime may be of any such degree, and the punishment for such an attempt shall be determined as provided by this section.
(Amended by Stats.1978, c. 579, p. —, § 27; Stats.1978, c. 1166, p. —, §§ 1, 2.)

Notes of Decisions

"Attempt" defined

A specific intent and an ineffectual overt act directed at its consummation are the only two elements essential to an attempted crime. People v. Gibson (1949) 210 P.2d 747, 94 C.A.2d 468; People v. Petros (1914) 143 P. 246, 25 C.A. 236; People v. O'Bryan (1933) 23 P.2d 94, 132 C.A. 496; People v. Miller (1935) 42 P.2d 308, 2 C.2d 527, 98 A.L.R. 913; People v. Hickman (1939) 87 P.2d 80, 31 C.A.2d 4; People v. Benenato (1947) 175 P.2d 296, 77 C.A.2d 350; People v. Wallace (1947) 178 P.2d 771, 78 C.A.2d 726; People v. Neal (1950) 218 P.2d 556, 97 C.A.2d 668; People v. Buffum (1953) 256 P.2d 317, 40 C.2d 709; People v. Gallardo (1953) 257 P.2d 29, 41 C.2d 57.

Receiving stolen property

Defendant, who offered to and did purchase confidential telephone company lists which defendant erroneously believed had been stolen, could be convicted of an attempt to receive stolen property. People v. Meyers (1963) 28 Cal.Rptr. 753, 213 C.A.2d 518.

Armed robbery

Evidence sustained conviction for attempted robbery while armed with a deadly weapon. People v. Carter (1968) 65 Cal.Rptr. 845, 258 C.A.2d 628.

Theft

Police officer who for 45 minutes observed defendant place his hand on or unclasp purses of women had legal cause to arrest defendant charged with attempted grand theft from the person. People v. Euell (1968) 67 Cal.Rptr. 148, 260 C.A.2d 441.

§ 666. Petit theft; prior conviction of petit theft, grand theft, burglary or robbery; punishment

Every person who, having been convicted of petit theft, grand theft, burglary, or robbery and having served a term therefor in any penal institution or having been imprisoned therein as a condition of probation for such offense, is subsequently convicted of petit theft, then the person convicted of such subsequent offense is punishable by imprisonment in the county jail not exceeding one year, or in the state prison.
(Amended by Stats.1977, c. 296, p. —, § 1, urgency, eff. July 8, 1977, operative July 1, 1977.)

§ 667.5. Prior prison terms; enhancement of prison terms for new offenses

Enhancement of prison terms for new offenses because of prior prison terms shall be imposed as follows:

(a) Where one of the new offenses is one of the violent felonies specified in subdivision (c), in addition and consecutive to any other prison terms therefor, the court shall impose a three-year term for each prior separate prison term served by the defendant where the prior was one of the violent felonies specified in subdivision (c); provided that no additional term shall be imposed under this subdivision for any prison term served prior to a period of 10 years in which defendant remained free of both prison custody and the commission of an offense which results in a felony conviction.

(b) Except where subdivision (a) applies, where the new offense is any felony for which a prison sentence is imposed, in addition and consecutive to any other prison terms therefor, the court shall impose a one-year term for each prior separate prison term served for any felony; provided that no additional term shall be imposed under this subdivision for any prison term served prior to a period of five years in which defendant remained free of both prison custody and the commission of an offense which results in a felony conviction.

(c) For the purpose of this section, "violent felony" shall mean any of the following:

(1) Murder or voluntary manslaughter.

(2) Mayhem.

(3) Rape as defined in subdivisions (2) and (3) of Section 261.

(4) Sodomy by force, violence, duress, menace, or threat of great bodily harm.

(5) Oral copulation by force, violence, duress, menace, or threat of great bodily harm.

(6) Lewd acts on a child under 14 as defined in Section 288.

(7) Any felony punishable by death or imprisonment in the state prison for life.

(8) Any other felony in which the defendant inflicts great bodily injury on any person other than an accomplice which has been charged and proved as provided for in Section 12022.7 on or after July 1, 1977, or as specified prior to July 1, 1977, in Sections 213, 264, and 461, or any felony in which the defendant uses a firearm which use has been charged and proved as provided in Section 12022.5.

The Legislature finds and declares that these specified crimes merit special consideration when imposing a sentence to display society's condemnation for such extraordinary crimes of violence against the person.

(d) For the purposes of this section the defendant shall be deemed to remain in prison custody for an offense until the official discharge from such custody or until release on parole whichever first occurs including any time during which the defendant remains subject to reimprisonment for escape from such custody or is reimprisoned on revocation of parole. The additional penalties provided for prior prison terms shall not be imposed unless they are charged and admitted or found true in the action for the new offense.

(e) The additional penalties provided for prior prison terms shall not be imposed for any felony for which the defendant did not serve a prior separate term in state prison.

(f) A prior conviction of a felony shall include a conviction in another jurisdiction for an offense which if committed in California is punishable by imprisonment in state prison provided the defendant served one year or more in prison for such offense in the other jurisdiction. A prior conviction of a particular felony shall include a conviction in another jurisdiction for an offense which includes all of the elements of the particular felony as defined under California law provided the defendant served one year or more in prison for such offense in the other jurisdiction.

(g) A prior separate prison term for the purposes of this section shall mean a continuous completed period of prison incarceration imposed for the particular offense alone or in combination with concurrent or consecutive sentences for other crimes, including any reimprisonment on revocation of parole which is not accompanied by a new commitment to prison, and including any reimprisonment after escape from such incarceration.

(h) Serving a prison term includes any confinement time in any state prison or federal penal institution as punishment for commission of an offense, including confinement in a hospital or other institution or facility credited as service of prison time in the jurisdiction of such confinement.

(i) For the purposes of this section, a commitment to the State Department of Health as a mentally disordered sex offender following a conviction of a felony, which commitment exceeds one year in duration, shall be deemed a prior prison term.
(Amended by Stats.1977, c. 2, p. —, § 1, urgency, eff. Dec. 16, 1976, operative July 1, 1977; Stats.1977, c. 165, p. —, § 13, urgency eff. June 29, 1977, operative July 1, 1977.)

§ 668. Prior foreign conviction; punishment for subsequent offense

Every person who has been convicted in any other state, government, country, or jurisdiction of an offense for which, if committed within this state,

§ 668

such person could have been punished under the laws of this state by imprisonment in a state prison, is punishable for any subsequent crime committed within this state in the manner prescribed by law and to the same extent as if such prior conviction had taken place in a court of this state.
(Amended by Stats.1976, c. 1139, p. —, § 269, operative July 1, 1977.)

§ 669. Conviction of multiple offenses; direction for concurrent or consecutive terms; life term; proceeding on discovery of prior conviction after sentence for subsequent offense; duty of prison directors

When any person is convicted of two or more crimes, whether in the same proceeding or court or in different proceedings or courts, and whether by judgment rendered by the same judge or by different judges, the second or other subsequent judgment upon which sentence is ordered to be executed shall direct whether the terms of imprisonment or any of them to which he is sentenced shall run concurrently or consecutively; life sentences, whether with or without the possibility of parole, may be imposed to run consecutively with one another or with any other term of imprisonment for a felony conviction. Whenever a person is committed to prison on a life sentence which is ordered to run consecutive to any determinate term of imprisonment imposed pursuant to Sections 667.5, 1170, 1170.1, 12022, 12022.5, 12022.6, and 12022.7, the determinate term of imprisonment shall be served first and no part thereof shall be credited toward the person's eligibility for parole as calculated pursuant to Section 3046.

In the event that the court at the time of pronouncing the second or other judgment upon such person had no knowledge of a prior existing judgment or judgments, or having knowledge, fails to determine how the terms of imprisonment shall run in relation to each other, then, upon such failure so to determine, or upon such prior judgment or judgments being brought to the attention of the court at any time prior to the expiration of 60 days from and after the actual commencement of imprisonment upon the second or other subsequent judgments, the court shall, in the absence of the defendant and within 60 days of such notice, determine how the term of imprisonment upon said second or other subsequent judgment shall run with reference to the prior incompleted term or terms of imprisonment. Upon the failure of the court so to determine how the terms of imprisonment on the second or subsequent judgment shall run, the term of imprisonment on the second or subsequent judgment shall run concurrently.

The Department of Corrections shall advise the court pronouncing the second or other subsequent judgment of the existence of all prior judgments against the defendant, the terms of imprisonment upon which have not been completely served.
(Amended by Stats.1978, c. 579, p. —, § 28.)

§ 672. Offenses for which no fine prescribed; fine authorized in addition to imprisonment

Upon a conviction for any crime punishable by imprisonment in any jail or prison, in relation to which no fine is herein prescribed, the court may impose a fine on the offender not exceeding five hundred dollars ($500) in cases of misdemeanors or five thousand dollars ($5,000) in cases of felonies, in addition to the imprisonment prescribed.
(Amended by Stats.1949, c. 670, p. 1169, § 1.)

§ 673. Cruel, corporal or unusual punishments; treatment impairing health

It shall be unlawful to use in the reformatories, institutions, jails, state hospitals or any other state, county, or city institution any cruel, corporal or unusual punishment or to inflict any treatment or allow any lack of care whatever which would injure or impair the health of the prisoner, inmate, or person confined; and punishment by the use of the strait jacket, gag, thumbscrew, shower bath or the tricing up of a prisoner, inmate or person confined is hereby prohibited. Any person who violates the provisions of this section or who aids, abets, or attempts in any way to contribute to the violation of this section shall be guilty of a misdemeanor.
(Amended by Stats.1953, c. 615, p. 1861, § 1.)

Part 2
OF CRIMINAL PROCEDURE

§ 682. Prosecution by indictment or information; exceptions

Every public offense must be prosecuted by indictment or information, except:

1. Where proceedings are had for the removal of civil officers of the State;

2. Offenses arising in the militia when in actual service, and in the land and naval forces in the time

of war, or which the State may keep, with the consent of Congress, in time of peace;

3. Offenses tried in municipal and justice courts;

4. All misdemeanors of which jurisdiction has been conferred upon superior courts sitting as juvenile courts;

5. A felony to which the defendant has pleaded guilty to the complaint before a magistrate, where permitted by law.
(Amended by Stats.1951, c. 1608, p. 3613, § 9.)

§ 686.5. Release or acquittal of person arrested; return to place of arrest

In any case in which a person is arrested and released without trial or in which a person is arrested, tried, and acquitted, if such person is indigent and is released or acquitted at a place to which he has been transported by the arresting agency and which is more than 25 airline miles from the place of his arrest, the arresting agency shall, at his request, return or provide for return of such person to the place of his arrest.
(Added by Stats.1967, c. 1096, p. 2736, § 1.)

§ 688. Unnecessary restraint

No person charged with a public offense may be subjected, before conviction, to any more restraint than is necessary for his detention to answer the charge.
(Amended by Stats.1965, c. 299, p. 1368, § 140, operative Jan. 1, 1967.)

§ 689. Conviction only by verdict

No person can be convicted of a public offense unless by verdict of a jury, accepted and recorded by the court, by a finding of the court in a case where a jury has been waived, or by a plea of guilty.
(Amended by Stats.1951, c. 1674, p. 3830, § 2.)

§ 691. Words and phrases

The following words have in Part 2 of this code the signification attached to them in this section, unless it is otherwise apparent from the context:

1. The words "inferior court" or "inferior courts" include municipal courts and justices' courts.

2. The words "competent court" when used with reference to the jurisdiction over any public offense, mean any court the subject matter jurisdiction of which includes the offense so mentioned.

3. The words "jurisdictional territory" when used with reference to a court, mean the city and county, county, city, township or other limited territory over which the criminal jurisdiction of such court extends, as provided by law, and in case of a superior court mean the county in which such court sits.

4. The words "accusatory pleading" include an indictment, an information, an accusation, a complaint filed with a magistrate charging a public offense of which the superior court has original trial jurisdiction, and a complaint filed with an inferior court charging a public offense of which such inferior court has original trial jurisdiction.

5. The words "prosecuting attorney" include any attorney, whether designated as district attorney, city attorney, city prosecutor, prosecuting attorney, or by any other title, having by law the right or duty to prosecute, in behalf of the people, any charge of a public offense.

6. The word "county" includes county, city and county, and city.
(Amended by Stats.1965, c. 156, p. 1111, § 1.)

PREVENTION OF PUBLIC OFFENSES

§ 692. Parties authorized

Lawful resistance, by whom made. Lawful resistance to the commission of a public offense may be made:

1. By the party about to be injured;

2. By other parties.
(Enacted 1872.)

Notes of Decisions

One who as reasonable man is justified in believing that assailant intends to commit felony on him has right in defense of his person to use all force necessary to repel assault even to taking life of assailant, and is not bound to retreat. People v. Collins (1961) 11 Cal.Rptr. 504, 189 C.A.2d 575.

Person who uses reasonable force to protect himself or others against use of excessive force in making arrest is not guilty of any crime. People v. Soto (1969) 80 Cal.Rptr. 627, 276 C.A.2d 81.

Sections 243 and 834a outlawing resistance to unlawful arrests does not outlaw right to resist arrest by excessive force. People v. Curtis (1969) 74 Cal.Rptr. 713, 450 P.2d 33, 70 C.2d 347.

§ 693. Party about to be injured; circumstances in which authorized

By the party, in what cases and to what extent. Resistance sufficient to prevent the offense may be made by the party about to be injured:

1. To prevent an offense against his person, or his family, or some member thereof.

2. To prevent an illegal attempt by force to take or injure property in his lawful possession.
(Enacted 1872.)

Notes of Decisions

Evidence as to whether defendant was aggressor in altercation sustained conviction for voluntary manslaughter, over claim of self-defense. People v. Domingo (1962) 26 Cal.Rptr. 315, 210 C.A.2d 120.

The justification of self-defense requires that defendant was actually in fear of his life or serious bodily injury and that conduct of other party was such as to produce that state of mind in a reasonable person. People v. Sonier (1952) 248 P.2d 155, 113 C.A.2d 277.

A defendant's conduct must be judged, not on basis of what circumstances appeared to be to him, but on how a reasonable person would have acted under same circumstances, in determining whether defendant acted in self-defense. People v. Syed Shah (1949) 205 P.2d 1077, 91 C.A.2d 722; People v. Moody (1944) 143 P.2d 978, 62 C.A.2d 18.

§ 694. Other parties; circumstances in which authorized

By other parties, in what cases. Any other person, in aid or defense of the person about to be injured, may make resistance sufficient to prevent the offense.
(Enacted 1872.)

§ 697. Methods

Intervention of officers, in what cases. Public offenses may be prevented by the intervention of the officers of justice:

1. By requiring security to keep the peace;

2. By forming a police in cities and towns, and by requiring their attendance in exposed places;

3. By suppressing riots.
(Enacted 1872.)

§ 698. Justification of persons aiding officers

Persons acting in their aid justified. When the officers of justice are authorized to act in the prevention of public offenses, other persons, who, by their command, act in their aid, are justified in so doing.
(Enacted 1872.)

§ 723. Resistance to process; power of sheriff or other officer to overcome resistance

When a sheriff or other public officer authorized to execute process finds, or has reason to apprehend that resistance will be made to the execution of the process, the officer may command as many able-bodied inhabitants of the officer's county as he or she may think proper to assist in overcoming the resistance, and, if necessary, in seizing, arresting, and confining the persons resisting, their aiders and abettors.
(Amended by Stats.1976, c. 1171, p. ——, § 24.)

§ 724. Resistance to process; certification to court of resisters, aiders and abettors; contempt

The officer to certify to Court the name of the resisters, etc. The officer must certify to the Court from which the process issued the names of the persons resisting, and their aiders and abettors, to the end that they may be proceeded against for their contempt of Court.
(Enacted 1872.)

§ 726. Unlawful or riotous assemblies; command to disperse

Where any number of persons, whether armed or not, are unlawfully or riotously assembled, the sheriff of the county and his deputies, the officials governing the town or city, or the judges of the justice courts and constables thereof, or any of them, must go among the persons assembled, or as near to them as possible, and command them, in the name of the people of the State, immediately to disperse.
(Amended by Stats.1951, c. 1608, p. 3613, § 10.)

§ 727. Unlawful or riotous assemblies; arrest for failure to disperse; commanding aid

To arrest rioters if they do not disperse. If the persons assembled do not immediately disperse, such magistrates and officers must arrest them, and to that end may command the aid of all persons present or within the county.
(Enacted 1872.)

MODE OF PROSECUTION

§ 737. Offenses triable in superior court; prosecution by indictment or information; exceptions

All public offenses triable in the superior court must be prosecuted therein by indictment or information, except as provided in the Government Code, the Juvenile Court Law and Section 859a of this code.
(Added by Stats.1951, c. 1674, p. 3831, § 6.)

§ 738. Offenses triable in superior court; preliminary examination; order holding to answer; commencement by complaint

Before an information is filed there must be a preliminary examination of the case against the defendant and an order holding him to answer made under Section 872. The proceeding for a preliminary examination must be commenced by written complaint, as provided elsewhere in this code.
(Added by Stats.1951, c. 1674, p. 3831, § 6.)

§ 739. Offenses triable in superior court; information; filing; permissible charges; form

When a defendant has been examined and committed, as provided in Section 872, it shall be the duty of the district attorney of the county in which the offense is triable to file in the superior court of that county within 15 days after the commitment, an information against the defendant which may charge the defendant with either the offense or offenses named in the order of commitment or any offense or offenses shown by the evidence taken before the magistrate to have been committed. The information shall be in the name of the people of the State of California and subscribed by the district attorney.
(Added by Stats.1951, c. 1674, p. 3831, § 6.)

Notes of Decisions

Where the prosecution is supported only by testimony which the magistrate finds unworthy of belief, there is no sufficient cause to hold the accused for trial; but when the magistrate is confronted with a case where the credible evidence would support a finding of guilty, then, although the magistrate's personal opinion leads him to draw a different inference, there is nevertheless probable cause. Dudley v. Superior Court for Los Angeles County (1974) 111 Cal.Rptr. 797, 36 C.A.3d 977.

The district attorney is not bound by view of committing magistrate; he is free to file information charging highest offense which any reasonable construction of evidence adduced at preliminary hearing admits. People v. McKee (1968) 73 Cal.Rptr. 112, 267 C.A.2d 509.

§ 740. Offenses triable in inferior courts; prosecution by written complaint; oath; subscription; verification on information and belief

Except as otherwise provided by law, all public offenses triable in the inferior courts must be prosecuted by written complaint under oath subscribed by the complainant. Such complaint may be verified on information and belief.
(Added by Stats.1951, c. 1674, p. 3831, § 6.)

§ 777. General liability to punishment; offenses within state; federal offenses

Every person is liable to punishment by the laws of this State, for a public offense committed by him therein, except where it is by law cognizable exclusively in the courts of the United States; and except as otherwise provided by law the jurisdiction of every public offense is in any competent court within the jurisdictional territory of which it is committed.
(Amended by Stats.1951, c. 1674, p. 3831, § 8.)

§ 778. Offenses commenced without but consummated within state

When the commission of a public offense, commences without the State, is consummated within its boundaries by a defendant, himself outside the State, through the intervention of an innocent or guilty agent or any other means proceeding directly from said defendant, he is liable to punishment therefor in this State in any competent court within the jurisdictional territory of which the offense is consummated.
(Amended by Stats.1951, c. 1674, p. 3831, § 10.)

§ 778a. Offenses commenced within but consummated without state

Whenever a person, with intent to commit a crime, does any act within this state in execution or part execution of such intent, which culminates in the commission of a crime, either within or without this state, such person is punishable for such crime in this state in the same manner as if the same had been committed entirely within this state.
(Added by Stats.1905, c. 529, p. 692, § 2.)

§ 778b. Offense within state; principal or aider and abettor without state subsequently found in state

Every person who, being out of this state, causes, aids, advises, or encourages any person to commit a crime within this state, and is afterwards found within this state, is punishable in the same manner as if he had been within this state when he caused, aided, advised, or encouraged the commission of such crime.
(Added by Stats.1905, c. 529, p. 692, § 3.)

§ 781. Offenses in multiple jurisdictional territories

When a public offense is committed in part in one jurisdictional territory and in part in another, or the acts or effects thereof constituting or requisite to the

consummation of the offense occur in two or more jurisdictional territories, the jurisdiction of such offense is in any competent court within either jurisdictional territory.
(Amended by Stats.1951, c. 1674, p. 3832, § 11.)

§ 783. Offenses within state on vessel, train, motor vehicle, carrier, or aircraft

When a public offense is committed in this State, on board a vessel navigating a river, bay, slough, lake, or canal, or lying therein, in the prosecution of its voyage, or on a railroad train or car, motor vehicle, common carrier transporting passengers or on an aircraft prosecuting its trip, the jurisdiction is in any competent court, through, on, or over the jurisdictional territory of which the vessel, train, car, motor vehicle, common carrier or aircraft passes in the course of its voyage or trip, or in the jurisdictional territory of which the voyage or trip terminates.
(Amended by Stats.1951, c. 1674, p. 3832, § 13.)

§ 784. Kidnapping; false imprisonment; seizure for slavery; child stealing; abduction

The jurisdiction of a criminal action:

1. For forcibly and without lawful authority seizing and confining another, or inveigling or kidnapping another, with intent, against his or her will, to cause him or her to be secretly confined or imprisoned in this state, or to be sent out of the state, or from one county to another, or to be sold as a slave, or in any way held to service;

2. For decoying, taking, or enticing away any minor child, with intent to detain and conceal it from its parent, guardian, or other person having the lawful charge of the child;

3. For inveigling, enticing, or taking away any person for the purpose of concubinage or prostitution, as defined in subdivision (b) of Section 647;

Is in any competent court within the jurisdictional territory in which the offense was committed, or in the jurisdictional territory out of which the person upon whom the offense was committed was taken or within the jurisdictional territory in which an act was done by the defendant in instigating, procuring, promoting, or aiding in the commission of the offense, or in abetting the parties concerned therein.
(Amended by Stats.1975, c. 996, p. 2341, § 6.)

§ 786. Burglary, robbery, theft; property taken transported between jurisdictional territories

When property taken in one jurisdictional territory by burglary, robbery, theft, or embezzlement has been brought into another, the jurisdiction of the offense is in any competent court within either jurisdictional territory.
(Amended by Stats.1951, c. 1674, p. 3833, § 17.)

§ 789. Theft or receipt of stolen goods; offense committed out of state and property brought into state

The jurisdiction of a criminal action for stealing or embezzling, in any other state, the property of another, or receiving it knowing it to have been stolen or embezzled, and bringing the same into this State, is in any competent court into or through the jurisdictional territory of which such stolen or embezzled property has been brought.
(Amended by Stats.1951, c. 1674, p. 3833, § 18.)

§ 791. Accessory

In the case of an accessory, as defined in Section 32, in the commission of a public offense, the jurisdiction is in any competent court within the jurisdictional territory of which the offense of the accessory was committed, notwithstanding the principal offense was committed in another jurisdictional territory.
(Amended by Stats.1951, c. 1674, p. 3833, § 19.)

§ 792. Principal not present at commission of offense

The jurisdiction of a criminal action against a principal in the commission of a public offense, when such principal is not present at the commission of the offense is in the same court it would be under this code if he were so present and aiding and abetting therein.
(Amended by Stats.1951, c. 1674, p. 3833, § 20.)

§ 793. Jeopardy in another state or country

Conviction or acquittal in another State a bar, where the jurisdiction is concurrent. When an act charged as a public offense is within the jurisdiction of another State or country, as well as of this State, a conviction or acquittal thereof in the former is a bar to the prosecution or indictment therefor in this State.
(Enacted 1872.)

§ 794. Jeopardy in another court having jurisdiction

Where an offense is within the jurisdiction of two or more courts, a conviction or acquittal thereof in one court is a bar to a prosecution therefor in another.
(Amended by Stats.1951, c. 1674, p. 3833, § 21.)

§ 799. Murder, embezzlement of public moneys, kidnapping for ransom, etc., and falsification of public records; no limitation; time for commencement of prosecution

There is no limitation of time within which a prosecution for murder, the embezzlement of public moneys, a violation of Section 209, or the falsification of public records must be commenced. Prosecution for murder may be commenced at any time after the death of the person killed. Prosecution for the embezzlement of public money, a violation of Section 209, or the falsification of public records may be commenced at any time after the discovery of the crime.
(Amended by Stats.1970, c. 704, p. 1333, § 1.)

§ 800. Felonies in general, three year limit; acceptance of bribe by public official or employee, six year limit; grand theft, forgery, manslaughter, false claims, perjury, false documentary evidence or conflicts of interest, three year limit after discovery

An indictment for any felony, except murder, voluntary manslaughter, involuntary manslaughter, the embezzlement of public money, the acceptance of a bribe by a public official of a public employee, grand theft, forgery, the falsification of public records, a violation of Section 72, 118, 118a, 132, 134, or 209 of the Penal Code, Section 25540 or 25541 of the Corporations Code, or Section 1090 or 27443 of the Government Code, shall be found, an information filed, or case certified to superior court within three years after its commission. An indictment for the acceptance of a bribe by a public official or a public employee, a felony, shall be found, an information filed, or case certified to the superior court within six years after its commission. An indictment for grand theft, forgery, voluntary manslaughter, or involuntary manslaughter, a violation of Section 72, 118, 118a, 132 or 134, of the Penal Code, Section 25540 or 25541 of the Corporations Code, or Section 1090 or 27443 of the Government Code, shall be found, an information filed, or case certified to the superior court within three years after its discovery.
(Amended by Stats.1978, c. 663, p. —, § 8.)

Notes of Decisions

Where it was alleged that each theft with which defendant was charged was committed between November 11, 1966 and November 23, 1969, and where, under three-year statute of limitations, offenses could still have been prosecuted on November 10, 1969, amendment, on November 10, 1969, of statute of limitations was effective to extend the period within which the defendant could be charged. People v. Eitzen (1974) 117 Cal.Rptr. 772, 43 C.A.3d 253.

When an information shows on its face that prosecution of offense is barred by statute of limitations, defense may be raised at any time before or after judgment. People v. Witt (1975) 125 Cal.Rptr. 653, 53 C.A.3d 154, certiorari denied 96 S.Ct. 1518.

Within this section providing that three-year period of limitation on prosecution for grand theft and various other offenses shall be three years from the "discovery" of the offense, "discovery" imports a state of awareness and discovery of a loss, without discovery of a criminal agency is not enough. People v. Swinney (1975) 120 Cal.Rptr. 148, 46 C.A.3d 332.

§ 801. Misdemeanors; 1 year limit

An indictment for any misdemeanor must be found or an information or complaint filed within one year after its commission.
(Amended by Stats.1933, c. 648, p. 1678, § 1.)

§ 802. Computation of time; exclusion of period of defendant's absence from state

If, when or after the offense is committed, the defendant is out of the State, an indictment may be found, a complaint or an information filed or a case certified to the superior court, in any case originally triable in the superior court, or a complaint may be filed, in any case originally triable in any other court, within the term limited by law; and no time during which the defendant is not within this State, is a part of any limitation of the time for commencing a criminal action.
(Amended by Stats.1951, c. 1674, p. 3834, § 23.)

§ 803. Indictment "found" when presented and filed

Indictment found, when presented and filed. An indictment is found, within the meaning of this Chapter, when it is presented by the Grand Jury in open Court, and there received and filed.
(Enacted 1872.)

§ 806. Proceeding for examination before magistrate; complaint; formalities; contents; construction and effect

A proceeding for the examination before a magistrate of a person on a charge of an offense originally

§ 806

triable in a superior court must be commenced by written complaint under oath subscribed by the complainant and filed with the magistrate. Such complaint may be verified on information and belief. When the complaint is used as a pleading to which the defendant pleads guilty under Section 859a of this code, the complaint shall contain the same allegations, including the charge of prior conviction or convictions of crime, as are required for indictments and informations and, wherever applicable, shall be construed and shall have substantially the same effect as provided in this code for indictments and informations.
(Amended by Stats.1977, c. 1257, p. ——, § 119, urgency, eff. Jan. 3, 1977.)

§ 807. Magistrate defined

Magistrate defined. A magistrate is an officer having power to issue a warrant for the arrest of a person charged with a public offense.
(Enacted 1872.)

§ 808. Persons designated as magistrates

The following persons are magistrates:
1. The judges of the Supreme Court.
2. The judges of the courts of appeal.
3. The judges of the superior courts.
4. The judges of the municipal courts.
5. The judges of the justice courts.

(Amended by Stats.1967, c. 17, p. 848, § 107.)

§ 810. Availability of magistrate when court not in session; assistance of custodial officer; telephone call

(a) The presiding judge of the superior court, the presiding judge of each municipal court in a county, and the judge of each justice court in a county, shall, as often as is necessary, meet and designate on a schedule not less than one judge of the superior court, municipal court or justice court to be reasonably available on call as a magistrate for the setting of orders for discharge from actual custody upon bail, the issuance of search warrants, and for such other matters as may by the magistrate be deemed appropriate, at all times when a court is not in session in the county.

(b) The officer in charge of a jail, or a person he designates, in which an arrested person is held in custody shall assist the arrested person or his attorney in contacting the magistrate on call as soon as possible for the purpose of obtaining release on bail.

(c) Any telephone call made pursuant to this section by an arrested person while in custody or by such person's attorney shall not count or be considered as a telephone call for purposes of Section 851.5 of the Penal Code.
(Added by Stats.1973, c. 956, p. 1802, § 1.)

ARREST AND PEACE OFFICER STATUS

§ 813. Warrant; issuance

When a complaint is filed with a magistrate charging a public offense originally triable in the superior court of the county in which he sits, if such magistrate is satisfied from the complaint that the offense complained of has been committed and that there is reasonable ground to believe that the defendant has committed it, he must issue a warrant for the arrest of the defendant; provided, that a judge of the justice court who is not a member of the State Bar may issue such a warrant only upon the concurrence of the district attorney of the county in which he sits or the Attorney General.
(Amended by Stats.1978, c. 300, p. ——, § 1.)

Editors' Note

Read People v. Ramey, 16 Cal.3d 263, 127 Cal.Rptr. 629 (1976); People v. Amos, 70 Cal.App.3d 562, 139 Cal.Rptr. 30 (1977); People v. Superior Court (Simon) 7 Cal.3d 186, 101 Cal.Rptr. 837 (1972); and People v. Knutson, 60 Cal.App.3d 856, 131 Cal.Rptr. 846 (1976); included in Table of Cases included in this text regarding probable cause to arrest.

Notes of Decisions

In order for arrest warrant properly to issue, information in complaint or affidavit in support thereof must either state facts within personal knowledge of affiant or complainant directly supportive of allegations in complaint that defendant committed offense or, when such stated facts are not within personal knowledge of affiant or complainant, further state facts relating to identity and credibility of source of directly incriminating information. In re Walters (1975) 126 Cal.Rptr. 239, 543 P.2d 607, 15 C.3d 738.

In order for magistrate properly to issue arrest warrant, affidavit supporting warrant, or complaint itself, must recite competent facts that would lead man of ordinary caution and prudence conscientiously to entertain strong suspicion of guilt of accused. In re Walters (1975) 126 Cal.Rptr. 239, 543 P.2d 607, 15 C.3d 738.

If arrest warrant is based solely upon complaint or affidavit framed in terms of "information and belief" rather than upon affiant's personal knowledge, or solely upon complaint that is phrased in statutory language, warrant may be constitutionally inadequate if sufficient allegations of probable cause are not otherwise present. In re Walters (1975) 126 Cal.Rptr. 239, 543 P.2d 607, 15 C.3d 738.

A "warrant" is a process issued in the name of the state directed to any sheriff, constable, marshal or policeman commanding him to arrest and take into custody the named defendant. Pankewicz v. Jess (1915) 149 P. 997, 27 C.A. 340.

§ 814. Warrant; form

A warrant of arrest issued under Section 813 may be in substantially the following form:

County of _____

The people of the State of California to any peace officer of said State:

Complaint on oath having this day been laid before me that the crime of _____ (designating it generally) has been committed and accusing _____ (naming defendant) thereof, you are therefore commanded forthwith to arrest the above named defendant and bring him before me at _____ (naming the place), or in case of my absence or inability to act, before the nearest or most accessible magistrate in this county.

Dated at _____ (place) this _____ day of _____, 19___.

_____

(Signature and full official title of magistrate.)
(Amended by Stats.1951, c. 1674, p. 3834, § 28.)

§ 815. Warrant; contents

A warrant of arrest shall specify the name of the defendant or, if it is unknown to the magistrate, judge, justice, or other issuing authority, the defendant may be designated therein by any name. It shall also state the time of issuing it, and the city or county where it is issued, and shall be signed by the magistrate, judge, justice, or other issuing authority issuing it with the title of his office and the name of the court or other issuing agency.
(Amended by Stats.1970, c. 1490, p. 2969, § 1, eff. Sept. 19, 1970.)

Notes of Decisions

To meet constitutional requirements, "John Doe" warrant must describe person to be seized with reasonable particularity. People v. Montoya (1967) 63 Cal.Rptr. 73, 255 C.A.2d 137, certiorari denied 88 S.Ct. 1255, 390 U.S. 1007, 20 L.Ed.2d 109.

A warrant issued against defendant under an alias was not void on theory warrant was issued in a fictitious name, where alias was a name used by defendant, and therefore, following defendant's arrest under warrant, officers had a right to search defendant's apartment, and seizure of marijuana as a result of such search was legal. People v. McLean (1961) 16 Cal.Rptr. 347, 365 P.2d 403, 56 C.2d 660, certiorari denied 82 S.Ct. 1613, 370 U.S. 958, 8 L.Ed.2d 824.

§ 815a. Warrant; endorsement of amount of bail

At the time of issuing a warrant of arrest, the magistrate shall fix the amount of bail which in his judgment in accordance with the provisions of section 1275 will be reasonable and sufficient for the appearance of the defendant following his arrest, if the offense is bailable, and said magistrate shall endorse upon said warrant a statement signed by him, with the name of his office, dated at the county, city or town where it is made to the following effect "The defendant is to be admitted to bail in the sum of _____ dollars" (stating the amount).
(Added by Stats.1933, c. 242, p. 749, § 1.)

§ 816. Warrant; direction; execution

A warrant of arrest shall be directed generally to any peace officer, or to any public officer or employee authorized to serve process where the warrant is for a violation of a statute or ordinance which such person has the duty to enforce, in the state, and may be executed by any of those officers to whom it may be delivered.

When a warrant of arrest has been delivered to a peace officer and the person named in the warrant is otherwise lawfully in the custody of the peace officer, the warrant may be executed by the peace officer or by any clerk of a city or county jail authorized to act and acting under the peace officer's direction.
(Amended by Stats.1969, c. 1205, p. 2345, § 2.)

§ 818. Certain arrests for misdemeanors under Vehicle Code or local traffic ordinances; release on promise to appear

In any case in which, between sunset and sunrise, a peace officer serves upon a person, at his home, apartment, hotel room, or other place of permanent or temporary abode, a warrant of arrest for a misdemeanor offense under the Vehicle Code or under any local ordinance relating to stopping, standing, parking, or operation of a motor vehicle and where no written promise to appear has been filed and the warrant states on its face that a citation may be used in lieu of physical arrest, the peace officer may, instead of taking the person before a magistrate, prepare a notice to appear and release the person on his promise to appear, as prescribed by Sections 853.6 through 853.8 of the Penal Code. Issuance of a notice to appear and securing of a promise to appear shall be deemed a compliance with the directions of the warrant, and the peace officer issuing such notice to appear and obtaining such

§ 818

promise to appear shall endorse on the warrant "section 818, Penal Code, complied with" and return the warrant to the magistrate who issued it.
(Added by Stats.1963, c. 1529, p. 3115, § 1.)

§ 821. Arrest for felony; officer to take defendant before magistrate; arrest in another county; procedure

If the offense charged is a felony, and the arrest occurs in the county in which the warrant was issued, the officer making the arrest must take the defendant before the magistrate who issued the warrant or some other magistrate of the same county.

If the defendant is arrested in another county, the officer must, without unnecessary delay, inform the defendant in writing of his right to be taken before a magistrate in that county, note on the warrant that he has so informed defendant, and, upon being required by defendant, take him before a magistrate in that county, who must admit him to bail in the amount specified in the endorsement referred to in Section 815a, and direct the defendant to appear before the court or magistrate by whom the warrant was issued on or before a day certain which shall in no case be more than 10 days after such admittance to bail. If bail be forthwith given, the magistrate shall take the same and endorse thereon a memorandum of the aforesaid order for the appearance of the defendant, or, if the defendant so requires, he may be released on bail set on the warrant by the issuing court, as provided in Section 1269b of this code, without an appearance before a magistrate.

If the warrant on which the defendant is arrested in another county does not have bail set thereon, or if the defendant arrested in another county does not require the arresting officer to take him before a magistrate in that county for the purpose of being admitted to bail, or if such defendant, after being admitted to bail, does not forthwith give bail, the arresting officer shall immediately notify the law enforcement agency requesting the arrest in the county in which the warrant was issued that such defendant is in custody, and thereafter such law enforcement agency shall take custody of such defendant within five days in the county in which he was arrested and shall take such defendant before the magistrate who issued the warrant, or before some other magistrate of the same county.
(Amended by Stats.1965, c. 645, p. 1996, § 1.)

§ 822. Arrest for misdemeanor; officer to take defendant before magistrate; bail; direction to appear

If the offense charged is a misdemeanor, and the defendant is arrested in another county, the officer must, without unnecessary delay, inform the defendant in writing of his right to be taken before a magistrate in that county, note on the warrant that he has so informed defendant, and, upon being required by defendant, take him before a magistrate in that county, who must admit him to bail in the amount specified in the indorsement referred to in Section 815a, or if no bail is specified, the magistrate may set bail; if the defendant is admitted to bail the magistrate shall direct the defendant to appear before the court or magistrate by whom the warrant was issued on or before a day certain which shall in no case be more than 10 days after such admittance to bail. If bail be forthwith given, the magistrate shall take the same and indorse thereon a memorandum of the aforesaid order for the appearance of the defendant.

If the defendant arrested in another county on a misdemeanor charge does not require the arresting officer to take him before a magistrate in that county for the purpose of being admitted to bail, or if such defendant, after being admitted to bail, does not forthwith give bail, the arresting officer shall immediately notify the law enforcement agency requesting the arrest in the county in which the warrant was issued that such defendant is in custody, and thereafter such law enforcement agency shall take custody of such defendant within five days in the county in which he was arrested and shall take such defendant before the magistrate who issued the warrant, or before some other magistrate of the same county.

If a defendant is arrested in another county on a warrant charging the commission of a misdemeanor, upon which warrant the amount of bail is indorsed as provided in Section 815a, and defendant is held in jail in the county of arrest pending appearance before a magistrate, the officer in charge of the jail shall, to the same extent as provided by Section 1269b, have authority to approve and accept bail from defendant in the amount indorsed on the warrant, to issue and sign an order for the release of the defendant, and, on posting of such bail, shall discharge defendant from custody.
(Amended by Stats.1973, c. 620, p. 1143, § 1.)

§ 823. Proceedings on taking bail; certification; receipt for undertaking; discharge; delivery of warrant; disposition of undertaking

On taking the bail, the magistrate must certify that fact on the warrant, and deliver the warrant to the officer having charge of the defendant. The magistrate shall issue to defendant a receipt for the undertaking of bail. The officer must then discharge the defendant from arrest, and must, without delay, deliver the warrant to the clerk of the court at which the defendant is required to appear. If the undertaking of bail is in the form of a bond, the magistrate shall forward the bond to the court at which defendant is required to appear. If the undertaking is in the form of cash, the magistrate shall deposit the cash in the county treasury, notifying the county auditor thereof, and the county auditor shall, by warrant, transmit the amount of the undertaking to the court at which the defendant is required to appear. If authorized by the county auditor, the magistrate may deposit the money in a bank account pursuant to Section 68084 of the Government Code, and by check drawn on such bank account transmit the amount of the undertaking to the court at which the defendant is required to appear.
(Amended by Stats.1959, c. 133, p. 2023, § 1.)

§ 825. Appearance before magistrate; unnecessary delay; maximum time; right of attorney to visit prisoner; officer refusing to permit visit, offense, forfeiture

The defendant must in all cases be taken before the magistrate without unnecessary delay, and, in any event, within two days after his arrest, excluding Sundays and holidays; provided, however, that when the two days prescribed herein expire at a time when the court in which the magistrate is sitting is not in session, such time shall be extended to include the duration of the next regular court session on the judicial day immediately following.

After such arrest, any attorney at law entitled to practice in the courts of record of California, may, at the request of the prisoner or any relative of such prisoner, visit the person so arrested. Any officer having charge of the prisoner so arrested who willfully refuses or neglects to allow such attorney to visit a prisoner is guilty of a misdemeanor. Any officer having a prisoner in charge, who refuses to allow any attorney to visit the prisoner when proper application is made therefor, shall forfeit and pay to the party aggrieved the sum of five hundred dollars ($500), to be recovered by action in any court of competent jurisdiction.
(Amended by Stats.1961, c. 2209, p. 4554, § 1.)

Notes of Decisions

In general

Arraignment of defendant, who was arrested at 5:15 A.M. on Friday, November 21, 1975 and told that he was being arrested for possession of heroin and booked on that charge, on November 25, 1975, at 11:15 A.M. on complaint which charged him with being under influence of opiate and which was filed on November 24, 1975, was within time requirement of this section. People v. Johnson (Super.1976) 133 Cal.Rptr. 123.

Various statutes (Pen.C. §§ 686, 739, 825, 1381–1387) having specific limitation periods were enacted to protect fundamental right to a speedy trial, and such limitations should be closely followed unless demands of justice require otherwise. People v. Ortega Rodriguez (1971) 93 Cal.Rptr. 182, 15 C.A.3d 481.

Where defendant was arrested Saturday and Saturday and Sunday were judicial holidays, two-day period for arraignment did not commence until Monday and did not expire until midnight Tuesday and, since court was not then in session, defendant's arraignment Wednesday morning was proper. People v. Santos (1972) 102 Cal.Rptr. 678, 26 C.A.3d 397.

Searches and seizures

Defendant arrested on a warrant for a traffic offense may not be booked or searched until he has been given an opportunity to post bail, but when he has been given an opportunity and it appears that he cannot post bail, he may then be booked and searched since, in the absence of bail, he must be placed in jail pursuant to the warrant. People v. Collin (1973) 110 Cal.Rptr. 869, 35 C.A.3d 416.

§ 825.5. Right of physician or surgeon to visit prisoner

Any physician and surgeon, including a psychiatrist, licensed to practice in this state, who is employed by the prisoner or his attorney to assist in the preparation of the defense, shall be permitted to visit the prisoner while he is in custody.
(Added by Stats.1972, c. 1077, p. 2011, § 1.)

§ 827. Complaint of offense triable in another county; requirements of warrant; complaint to accompany warrant

When a complaint is filed with a magistrate of the commission of a public offense originally triable in the superior court of another county of the State than that in which he sits, but showing that the defendant is in the county where the complaint is filed, the same proceedings must be had as prescribed in this chapter, except that the warrant must require the defendant to be taken before the nearest or most accessible magistrate of the county in which the offense is triable, and the complaint must be delivered by the magistrate to the officer to whom the warrant is delivered.
(Amended by Stats.1951, c. 1674, p. 3835, § 33.)

§ 828. Offense triable in another county; magistrate before whom defendant taken; delivery of complaint and warrant; proceedings by magistrate

The officer who executes the warrant must take the defendant before the nearest or most accessible magistrate of the county in which the offense is triable, and must deliver to him the complaint and the warrant, with his return endorsed thereon, and the magistrate must then proceed in the same manner as upon a warrant issued by himself.
(Amended by Stats.1951, c. 1674, p. 3835, § 34.)

§ 829. Offense triable in inferior court of another county; admission to bail; transmittal of warrant, complaint, and undertaking

When a complaint is filed with a magistrate of the commission of a public offense triable in an inferior court of another county of the State than that in which he sits, but showing that the defendant is in the county where the complaint is filed, the officer must, upon being required by the defendant, take him before a magistrate of the county in which the warrant was issued, who must admit the defendant to bail in the amount specified in the endorsement referred to in Section 815a, and immediately transmit the warrant, complaint, and undertaking, to the clerk of the court in which the defendant is required to appear.
(Amended by Stats.1951, c. 1674, p. 3835, § 35.)

§ 830. Peace officers; persons included and excluded

Any person who comes within the provisions of this chapter and who otherwise meets all standards imposed by law on a peace officer is a peace officer, and notwithstanding any other provision of law, no person other than those designated in this chapter is a peace officer. The restriction of peace officer functions of any public officer or employee shall not affect his status for purposes of retirement.
(Added by Stats.1968, c. 1222, p. 2303, § 1.)

§ 830.1. Sheriffs, police, marshals, constables, inspectors and investigators of district attorneys

Any sheriff, undersheriff, or deputy sheriff, regularly employed and paid as such, of a county, any policeman of a city, any policeman of a district authorized by statute to maintain a police department, any marshal or deputy marshal of a municipal court, any constable or deputy constable, regularly employed and paid as such, of a judicial district, or any inspector or investigator regularly employed and paid as such in the office of a district attorney, is a peace officer. The authority of any such peace officer extends to any place in the state:

(a) As to any public offense committed or which there is probable cause to believe has been committed within the political subdivision which employs him; or

(b) Where he has the prior consent of the chief of police, or person authorized by him to give such consent, if the place is within a city or of the sheriff, or person authorized by him to give such consent, if the place is within a county; or

(c) As to any public offense committed or which there is probable cause to believe has been committed in his presence, and with respect to which there is immediate danger to person or property, or of the escape of the perpetrator of such offense.
(Amended by Stats.1977, c. 220, p. ——, § 1.)

§ 830.2. Highway patrol members; state police division members; national guard members; University of California police department members; state college police department members; B.A.R.T. police department members

(a) Any member of the California Highway Patrol is a peace officer whose authority extends to any place in the state; provided, that the primary duty of any such peace officer shall be the enforcement of the provisions of the Vehicle Code or of any other law relating to the use or operation of vehicles upon the highways, as that duty is set forth in the Vehicle Code. Provided further, that he shall not act as a peace officer in enforcing any other law except (i) when in pursuit of any offender or suspected offender or (ii) to make arrests for crimes committed in his presence or upon any highway or (iii) as provided in Sections 8597, 8598, and 8617 of the Government Code.

(b) Any member of the California State Police Division is a peace officer; provided, that the primary duty of any such peace officer shall be the protection of state properties and occupants thereof, and he shall not act as a peace officer in enforcing any law except (1) when in pursuit of any offender or suspected offender, (2) to make arrests for crimes committed in his presence or upon state properties, or (3) as provided in Sections 8597, 8598 and 8617 of the Government Code.

(c) Members of the California National Guard have the powers of peace officers when they are (1) called or ordered into active state service by the Governor pursuant to the provisions of Section 143 or 146 of the Military and Veterans Code, (2) serving within the area wherein military assistance is required, and (3) directly assisting civil authorities in any of the situations specified in Section 143 or 146. The authority of any such peace officer extends to the area wherein military assistance is required as to a public offense committed or which there is reasonable cause to believe has been committed within that area. The requirements of Section 1031 of the Government Code are not applicable under such circumstances.

(d) A member of the University of California Police Department appointed pursuant to Section 23501 of the Education Code is a peace officer whose authority extends to any place in the state; provided that the primary duty of any such peace officer shall be the enforcement of the law within the area specified in Section 23501 of the Education Code. Provided, further, that he shall not otherwise act as a peace officer in enforcing the law except (1) when in pursuit of any offender or suspected offender; (2) to make arrests otherwise lawful for crimes committed, or which there is probable cause to believe have been committed, in his presence or within the area specified in Section 23501 of the Education Code; or (3) when, while in uniform such officer, as a peace officer, is requested by a peace officer or other person to render such assistance as is appropriate under such circumstances to the officer or other person making such request, or to act upon his complaint.

Notwithstanding any other provisions of this code, including but not limited to Section 830.3, the provisions of this subdivision shall govern the authority and jurisdiction of a member of the University of California Police Department as a peace officer.

(e) A member of a state college police department appointed pursuant to Section 24651 of the Education Code is a peace officer whose authority extends to any place in the state; provided that the primary duty of any such peace officer shall be the enforcement of the law within the area specified in Section 24651 of the Education Code. Provided, further, that he shall not otherwise act as a peace officer in enforcing the law except (1) when in pursuit of any offender or suspected offender; (2) to make arrests otherwise lawful for crimes committed, or which there is probable cause to believe have been committed, in his presence or within the area specified in Section 24651 of the Education Code; or (3) when, while in uniform such officer, as a peace officer, is requested by a peace officer or other person to render such assistance as is appropriate under such circumstances to the officer or other person making such request, or to act upon his complaint.

Notwithstanding any other provisions of this code, including but not limited to Section 830.3, the provisions of this subdivision shall govern the authority and jurisdiction of a member of a state college police department as a peace officer.

(f) A member of the San Francisco Bay Area Rapid Transit District Police Department appointed pursuant to Section 28767.5 of the Public Utilities Code is a peace officer whose authority extends to any place in the state; provided, that the primary duty of any such peace officer shall be the enforcement of the law in or about properties owned, operated or administered by the district when performing necessary duties with respect to patrons, employees and properties of the district. Provided, further, that he shall not otherwise act as a peace officer in enforcing the law except (1) when in pursuit of any offender or suspected offender from within or about properties owned, operated or administered by the district when performing necessary duties with respect to patrons, employees and properties of the district; (2) to make arrests otherwise lawful for crimes committed, or which there is probable cause to believe have been committed, in his presence or within or about properties owned, operated or administered by the district; or (3) when, while in uniform such officer, as a peace officer, is requested by a peace officer or other person to render such assistance as is appropriate under such circumstances to the officer or other person making such request, or to act upon his complaint.

(Amended by Stats.1976, c. 1079, p. —, § 52; Stats.1976, c. 420, p. —, § 4.)

§ 830.3. Particular officers

(a) Officers of department of justice

(a) The Deputy Director, Assistant Directors, chiefs, assistant chiefs, special agents, and narcotics agents of the Department of Justice, and such investigators who are so designated by the Attorney General, are peace officers.

The authority of any such peace officer extends to any place in the state as to a public offense committed or which there is probable cause to believe has been committed within the state.

§ 830.3

(b) **District attorney's investigators**

(b) Any inspector or investigator regularly employed and paid as such in the office of a district attorney is a peace officer.

The authority of any such peace officer extends to any place in the state:

(1) As to any public offense committed, or which there is probable cause to believe has been committed, within the county which employs him; or

(2) Where he has the prior consent of the chief of police, or person authorized by him to give such consent, if the place is within a city or of the sheriff, or person authorized by him to give such consent, if the place is within a county; or

(3) As to any public offense committed or which there is probable cause to believe has been committed in his presence, and with respect to which there is immediate danger to person or property, or of the escape of the perpetrator of such offense.

(c) **Alcoholic beverage control officers**

(c) The Director of the Department of Alcoholic Beverage Control and persons employed by such department for the enforcement of the provisions of Division 9 (commencing with Section 23000) of the Business and Professions Code are peace officers; provided, that the primary duty of any such peace officer shall be the enforcement of the laws relating to alcoholic beverages, as that duty is set forth in Section 25755 of the Business and Professions Code. Any such peace officer is further authorized to enforce any penal provision of law while, in the course of his employment, he is in, on, or about any premises licensed pursuant to the Alcoholic Beverage Control Act.

(d) **Investigators for department of consumer affairs**

(d) The Chief and investigators of the Division of Investigation of the Department of Consumer Affairs, and investigators of the Board of Medical Quality Assurance, are peace officers; provided, that the primary duty of any such peace officer shall be the enforcement of the law as that duty is set forth in Section 160 of the Business and Professions Code.

(e) **Fish and game enforcement officers**

(e)(1) Members of the Wildlife Protection Branch of the Department of Fish and Game deputized pursuant to Section 856 of the Fish and Game Code are peace officers. The authority of any such peace officers extends to any place in the state as to a public offense committed or which there is probable cause to believe has been committed within the state.

(2) Other deputies of the Department of Fish and Game deputized pursuant to Section 851 of the Fish and Game Code, and county fish and game wardens deputized pursuant to Section 875 of such code, are peace officers, provided that the exclusive duty of such deputies or county fish and game wardens shall be the enforcement of the provisions of the Fish and Game Code and the regulations made pursuant thereto.

(f) **Forester and fire wardens**

(f) The State Forester and such employees or classes of employees of the Division of Forestry of the Department of Conservation and voluntary fire wardens as are designated by him pursuant to Section 4156 of the Public Resources Code are peace officers; provided, that the primary duty of any such peace officer shall be the enforcement of the law as that duty is set forth in Section 4156 of such code.

(g) **Department of motor vehicles; enforcement officers**

(g) Officers and employees of the Department of Motor Vehicles designated in Section 1655 of the Vehicle Code are peace officers; provided, that the primary duty of any such peace officer shall be the enforcement of the law as that duty is set forth in Section 1655 of such code.

(h) **California horse racing board; designated officers**

(h) The secretary, chief investigator, and racetrack investigators of the California Horse Racing Board are peace officers; provided, that the primary duty of any such peace officer shall be the enforcement of the provisions of Chapter 4 (commencing with Section 19400) of Division 8 of the Business and Professions Code and Chapter 10 (commencing with Section 330) of Title 9 of Part 1 of the Penal Code. Any such peace officer is further authorized to enforce any penal provision of law while, in the course of his employment, he is in, on, or about any horseracing enclosure licensed pursuant to the Horse Racing Law.

(i) **Regional park district police**

(i) Police officers of a regional park district, appointed or employed pursuant to Section 5561 of the Public Resources Code, and officers and employees of the Department of Parks and Recreation designated by the director pursuant to Section 5008 of such code are peace officers; provided, that the primary duty of any such peace officer shall be the enforcement of the law as such duties are set forth in Sections 5561 and 5008, respectively, of such code.

(j) **State fire marshals**

(j) The State Fire Marshal and assistant or deputy state fire marshals appointed pursuant to Section 13103 of the Health and Safety Code are peace officers; provided that the primary duty of any such peace officer shall be the enforcement of the law as that duty is set forth in Section 13104 of such code.

(k) **Arson investigators of fire protection agency; members of local agency fire department**

(k) Members of an arson-investigating unit, regularly employed and paid as such, of a fire protection agency of the state, of a county, city, or district, and members of a fire department or fire protection agency of the state, or a county, city, or district regularly paid and employed as such, are peace officers; provided, that the primary duty of arson investigators shall be the detection and apprehension of persons who have violated or who are suspected of having violated any fire law, and the primary duty, except as provided in Section 8597 of the Government Code, of fire department or fire protection agency members other than arson investigators when acting as peace officers shall be the enforcement of laws relating to fire prevention and fire suppression. Notwithstanding the provisions of Section 171c, 171d, 12027, or 12031, members of fire departments other than arson investigators are not peace officers for purposes of such sections except when designated as peace officers for such purposes by local ordinance or, if the local agency is not authorized to act by ordinance, by resolution.

(*l*) **Food and drug investigators**

(*l*) The Chief and such inspectors of the Bureau of Food and Drug as are designated by him pursuant to subdivision (a) of Section 216 of the Health and Safety Code are such peace officers; provided, that the exclusive duty of any such peace officer shall be the enforcement of the law as that duty is set forth in Section 216 of such code.

(m) **Park rangers of local agency**

(m) Persons designated by a local agency as park rangers, and regularly employed and paid as such, are peace officers; provided, that the primary duty of any such peace officer shall be the protection of park property and preservation of the peace therein.

Notwithstanding the provisions of Section 171c, 171d, 12027, or 12031, such park rangers are not peace officers for purposes of such sections except when designated as peace officers for such purposes by local ordinance or, if the local agency is not authorized to act by ordinance, by resolution.

(n) **Community college police**

(n) Members of a community college police department appointed pursuant to Section 25429 of the Education Code are peace officers; provided that the primary duty of any such peace officer shall be the enforcement of the law as prescribed in Section 25429 of the Education Code.

(o) **Investigators of labor law enforcement division**

(o) All investigators of the State Department of Health Services, Social Services, Mental Health, Developmental Services, and Alcohol and Drug Abuse and the Office of Statewide Health Planning and Development, are peace officers; provided that the primary duty of any such peace officer shall be the enforcement of the law relating to the duties of his department or office. Notwithstanding the provisions of Section 171c, 171d, 12027, or 12031, the investigators shall not carry firearms.

(p) **State department of health investigators**

(p) Persons designated as security officers by a municipal utility district pursuant to Section 12820 of the Public Utilities Code are peace officers while engaged in the performance of their duties as security officers.

(q) **Statewide authority; limitations on powers**

(q) The authority of any peace officer listed in subdivisions (c) through (p), inclusive, extends to any place in the state; provided, that except as otherwise provided in this section, Section 830.6 of this code, or Section 8597 of the Government Code, any such peace officer shall be deemed a peace officer only for purposes of his primary duty, and shall not act as a peace officer in enforcing any other law except:

(1) When in pursuit of any offender or suspected offender; or

(2) To make arrests for crimes committed, or which there is probable cause to believe have been committed, in his presence while he is in the course of his employment; or

(3) When, while in uniform, such officer is requested, as a peace officer, to render such assistance as is

§ 830.3

appropriate under the circumstances to the person making such request, or to act upon his complaint, in the event that no peace officer otherwise authorized to act in such circumstances is apparently and immediately available and capable of rendering such assistance or taking such action.
(Amended by Stats.1978, c. 429, p. ——, § 157.5; Stats.1978, c. 1138, p. ——, § 1.)

§ 830.5. Correctional, parole and probation officers

(a) Any parole officer of the State Department of Corrections, placement or parole officer of the Youth Authority, probation officer, or deputy probation officer is a peace officer. Except as otherwise provided in this subdivision, the authority of any such peace officer shall extend only (1) to conditions of parole or of probation by any person in this state on parole or probation; (2) to the escape of any inmate or ward from a state institution; (3) to the transportation of such persons; and (4) as provided in Section 8597 or 8598 of the Government Code, or when acting pursuant to Section 8617 of the Government Code. The authority of any parole officer of the State Department of Corrections shall further extend to violations of any penal provisions of law which are discovered in the course of and arise in connection with his employment.

(b) Any warden, superintendent, supervisor, or guard employed by the Department of Corrections, the Director of Corrections, any deputy director of the Department of Corrections, any superintendent, assistant superintendent, supervisor, or employee having custody of wards, of each institution of the Department of the Youth Authority, and any transportation officer of the Department of the Youth Authority, is a peace officer. The authority of any such peace officer shall extend only (1) as is necessary for the purpose of carrying out the duties of his employment, and (2) as provided in Section 8597 or 8598 of the Government Code, or when acting pursuant to Section 8617 of the Government Code. When he is carrying out his duties, any such supervisor, guard, officer, or employee who is engaged in transportation of prisoners or apprehension of prisoners or wards who have escaped is a peace officer whether acting within or without this state.

(c) When, pursuant to Nevada law, an officer or employee of the Nevada State Prison has in his custody in California a prisoner of the State of Nevada whom he is transporting from the Nevada State Prison or any honor or forest camp in Nevada to another point in Nevada for the purposes of firefighting or conservation work, such officer or employee of the Nevada State Prison shall have the power to maintain custody of the prisoner in California and to retake the prisoner if he should escape in California to the same extent as if such officer or employee were a peace officer appointed with California law and the prisoner had been committed to his custody in proceedings under California law.

(d) Any peace officer under this section shall have the same status of a peace officer provided for in subdivision (a) or (b) of Section 830.2 for the purpose of obtaining any group insurance benefits available to such peace officers.

(e) Any peace officer under this section shall have the full powers and duties of a peace officer as provided by Section 830.1 when acting pursuant to Section 8617 of the Government Code.
(Amended by Stats.1978, c. 642, p. ——, § 1.)

§ 830.5a. Department of Corrections; law enforcement liaison unit; authority

(a) Any agent of the law enforcement liaison unit of the Department of Corrections is a peace officer. The authority of any such peace officer shall extend only (1) to the investigation and apprehension of parole violators; (2) to the investigation and apprehension of any inmate or ward who has escaped from a state institution; (3) to any violation of a penal provision which arises and is discovered in the course of his performance of his employment duties; (4) to the transportation of such persons; (5) to the coordination of such activities with other criminal justice agencies; and (6) as provided in Section 8597 or 8598 of the Government Code, or when acting pursuant to Section 8617 of the Government Code.

(b) Any peace officer under this section shall have the same status of a peace officer provided for in subdivision (a) or (b) of Section 830.2 for the purpose of obtaining any group insurance benefits available to such peace officers.

(c) Any peace officer under this section shall have the full powers and duties of a peace officer as provided by Section 830.1 when acting pursuant to Section 8617 of the Government Code.
(Added by Stats.1974, c. 420, p. 1017.)

§ 830.10. Coroner and deputy coroners

(a) The coroner and deputy coroners, regularly employed and paid as such, of a county are peace officers. The primary duties of such peace officers are those set forth by Sections 27469 and 27491 through 27491.4, inclusive, of the Government Code. However, such coroner and deputy coroners shall not be authorized to carry concealable weapons capable of being concealed upon the person, unless they are authorized to do so by an ordinance or resolution of the county board of supervisors.

(b) The authority of any such peace officer extends to any place in the state; provided, that except as otherwise provided in Section 830.3 or Section 830.6 of this code, or Section 8597 of the Government Code, any such peace officer shall be deemed a peace officer only for purposes of his primary duty, and shall not act as a peace officer in enforcing any other law except:

(1) When in pursuit of any offender or suspected offender; or

(2) To make arrests for crimes committed, or which there is probable cause to believe have been committed, in his presence while he is in the course of his employment; or

(3) When, while in uniform, such officer is requested, as a peace officer, to render such assistance as is appropriate under the circumstances to the person making such request, or to act upon his complaint, in the event that no peace officer otherwise authorized to act in such circumstances is apparently and immediately available and capable of rendering such assistance or taking such action.

(Amended by Stats.1972, c. 618, p. 1139, § 116.)

§ 831. Custodial officers

(a) A custodial officer is a public officer, not a peace officer, employed by a law enforcement agency of a city having a population of over 2,000,000 who has the authority and responsibility for maintaining custody of prisoners and performs tasks related to the operation of a local detention facility used for the detention of persons usually pending arraignment or upon court order either for their own safekeeping or for the specific purpose of serving a sentence therein.

(b) A custodial officer shall have no right to carry or possess firearms in the performance of his prescribed duties.

(c) Every person, prior to actual assignment as a custodial officer, shall have satisfactorily completed the Commission on Peace Officer Standards and Training courses specified in Section 832 of the Penal Code and the Commission on Peace Officer Standards and Training course on jail operations.

(d) At any time 20 or more custodial officers are on duty, there shall be at least one peace officer, as described in Section 830.1 of the Penal Code, on duty at the same time to supervise the performance of the custodial officers.

(e) This section shall not be construed to confer any authority upon any custodial officer except while on duty.

(f) A custodial officer may use reasonable force in establishing and maintaining custody of persons delivered to him by a law enforcement officer; to make arrests for misdemeanors and felonies within the local detention facility pursuant to a duly issued warrant; to release without further criminal process persons arrested for intoxication; and to release misdemeanants on citation to appear in lieu of or after booking.

(Added by Stats.1974, c. 887, p. 1885, § 1.)

§ 832. Course of training in exercise of powers to arrest and in carrying and use of firearms

(a) Every person described in this chapter as a peace officer, shall receive a course of training in the exercise of his powers to arrest and a course of training in the carrying and use of firearms. The course of training in the carrying and use of firearms shall not be required of any peace officer whose employing agency prohibits the use of firearms. Such courses shall meet the minimum standards prescribed by the Commission on Peace Officer Standards and Training.

(b)(1) Every such peace officer described in this chapter, within 90 days following the date that he was first employed by any employing agency, shall, prior to the exercise of the powers of a peace officer, have satisfactorily completed the course of training as described in subdivision (a).

(2) Every peace officer described in Section 832.3 shall satisfactorily complete the training required by this section as part of the training and under the limitations set forth in Section 832.3.

(c) Persons described in this chapter as peace officers who have not so satisfactorily completed the courses described in subdivision (a) as specified in subdivision (b), shall not have the powers of a peace officer until they satisfactorily complete such courses.

(d) Any peace officer who on the effective date of this section possesses or is qualified to possess the

§ 832

basic certificate as awarded by the Commission on Peace Officer Standards and Training shall be exempted from the provisions of this section.
(Amended by Stats.1978, c. 1194, p. —, § 1.)

§ 832.1. Airport security personnel; training course

Any airport security officer, airport policeman, or airport special officer, regularly employed and paid by a city, county, city and county, or district who is a peace officer shall have completed a course of training relative to airport security approved by the Commission on Peace Officers Standards and Training. Any such airport officer so employed on the effective date of this section shall have completed the course of instruction required by this section by September 1, 1973. Any airport officer so employed after such effective date shall have completed the course of instruction within 90 days after such employment.

Any officer who has not satisfactorily completed such course within such prescribed time shall not continue to have the powers of a peace officer until they have satisfactorily completed such course.
(Amended by Stats.1975, c. 168, p. —, § 1.)

§ 832.3. Sheriffs, undersheriffs, deputy sheriffs, city and district policemen; employment after Jan. 1, 1975; completion of training course

(a) Except as provided in subdivision (b), any sheriff, undersheriff, or deputy sheriff of a county, any policeman of a city, and any policeman of a district authorized by statute to maintain a police department, who is first employed after January 1, 1975, for the purposes of the prevention and detection of crime and the general enforcement of the criminal laws of this state, shall successfully complete a course of training approved by the Commission on Peace Officer Standards and Training before exercising the powers of a peace officer, except while participating as a trainee in a supervised field training program approved by the Commission on Peace Officer Standards and Training.

(b) For the purpose of standardizing the training required in subdivision (a), the commission shall develop a training proficiency testing program, including a standardized examination which enables (1) comparisons between presenters of such training and (2) development of data base for subsequent training programs. Presenters approved by the commission to provide the training required in subdivision (a) shall administer the standardized examination to all graduates. Nothing in this subdivision shall make the completion of such examination a condition of successful completion of the training required in subdivision (a).

(c) Notwithstanding subdivision (c) of Section 84500 of the Education Code and any regulations adopted pursuant thereto, community colleges may give preference in enrollment to employed law enforcement trainees who shall complete training as prescribed by this section. At least 15 percent of each presentation shall consist of nonlaw enforcement trainees if they are available. Preference should only be given when the trainee could not complete the course within the time required by statute, and only when no other training program is reasonably available. Average daily attendance for such courses shall be reported for state aid.
(Amended by Stats.1978, c. 1193, p. —, §§ 1, 2; Stats.1978, c. 1260, p. —, §§ 1, 2.)

§ 832.4. Undersheriffs, deputy sheriffs, city and district policemen; employment after Jan. 1, 1974; basic certificate within 18 months

(a) Any undersheriff or deputy sheriff of a county, any policeman of a city, and any policeman of a district authorized by statute to maintain a police department, who is first employed after January 1, 1974, and is responsible for the prevention and detection of crime and the general enforcement of the criminal laws of this state, shall obtain the basic certificate issued by the Commission on Peace Officer Standards and Training within 18 months of his employment in order to continue to exercise the powers of a peace officer after the expiration of such 18-month period.

(b) Housing authority patrol officers of the City of Los Angeles shall be and shall remain a part of the Los Angeles City Housing Authority Retirement System and shall not become a part of any other peace officer retirement system or plan.
(Amended by Stats.1974, c. 1006, p. 2166, § 3.)

§ 832.5. Citizens' complaints against personnel; investigation; description of procedure; retention of records

(a) Each department or agency in this state which employs peace officers shall establish a procedure to investigate citizens' complaints against the personnel of such departments or agencies, and shall make a written description of the procedure available to the public.

(b) Complaints and any reports or findings relating thereto shall be retained for a period of at least five years.
(Amended by Stats.1978, c. 630, p. —, § 4.)

§ 832.7. Personnel records; confidentiality; discovery

Peace officer personnel records and records maintained pursuant to Section 832.5, or information obtained from such records, are confidential and shall not be disclosed in any criminal or civil proceeding except by discovery pursuant to Section 1043 of the Evidence Code. This section shall not apply to investigations or proceedings concerning the conduct of police officers or a police agency conducted by a grand jury or a district attorney's office.
(Added by Stats.1978, c. 630, p. —, § 5.)

§ 832.8. Personnel records

As used in Section 832.7, "personnel records" means any file maintained under that individual's name by his or her employing agency and containing records relating to:

(a) Personal data, including marital status, family members, educational and employment history, or similar information;

(b) Medical history;

(c) Election of employee benefits;

(d) Employee advancement, appraisal, or discipline;

(e) Complaints, or investigations of complaints, concerning an event or transaction in which he participated, or which he perceived, and pertaining to the manner in which he performed his duties; or

(f) Any other information the disclosure of which would constitute an unwarranted invasion of personal privacy.
(Added by Stats.1978, c. 630, p. —, § 6.)

§ 833. Possession of dangerous weapons; search; seizure; arrest

A peace officer may search for dangerous weapons any person whom he has legal cause to arrest, whenever he has reasonable cause to believe that the person possesses a dangerous weapon. If the officer finds a dangerous weapon, he may take and keep it until the completion of the questioning, when he shall either return it or arrest the person. The arrest may be for the illegal possession of the weapon.
(Added by Stats.1957, c. 2147, p. 3807, § 9.)

Editors' Note

Recent court decisions have broadened the ability to search for weapons even when the suspect has not been arrested, provided that the search is cursory and of the pat-down type.

The basis for any frisk is to prevent danger to the officer from an unanticipated assault. However, there must be some evidence that the officer reasonably believed he was confronting a person who had an instrumentality on his person capable of inflicting injury. Thus, the courts have held that the officer must be able to point to *particular facts* from which he reasonably believed in light of his experience that the individual he was dealing with was *armed and dangerous*.

It should be stressed that the officer need not be absolutely certain that the individual is armed. If an officer errs in this respect, it should be on the side of caution. Nonetheless, he may not indiscriminately frisk every individual he stops, and should be able to point to particular facts which gave rise to concern that the individual is armed and dangerous.

The following factors are among those which should be taken into consideration:

(1) The nature of the suspected crime and whether it involved a weapon.
(2) Whether it is day or night. The courts allow more latitude at night.
(3) Knowledge of the record or reputation of the person stopped.
(4) The number of officers making the stop.
(5) The number of suspects stopped.
(6) The demeanor of the suspects.
(7) Whether the suspect's clothes bulge in such a manner as to suggest the presence of weapons.
(8) Whether a suspect's companion is found to be armed.
(9) Whether the individual is stopped in a high crime area.
(10) Whether the suspect makes a furtive movement as if he were reaching for a weapon.

Not all of the above factors will, in themselves, justify a frisk. Merely because the officers have made a stop in the nighttime, or in a high crime area, for example, will not justify a frisk. If, on the other hand, the individual has been stopped pursuant to a report of an armed robbery, for example, a frisk will almost always be justified.

The courts have stressed that in determining whether the officer acted reasonably under the circumstances, weight will be given not to his suspicion or "hunch," but "to the specific reasonable inferences which he is entitled to draw from the facts in light of his experience." It should be again stressed that the officer's report should reflect the specific facts and inferences which justified the frisk.

The Scope of the Frisk

The purpose of the frisk is to discover guns, knives, clubs, or other hidden instruments that might be used to assault the officer. The scope of the search for weapons should be the minimum necessary to discovery the weapons and should be initially confined to a superficial pat-down for weapons. The officer should not ask the suspect to empty his pockets or pull up his sweater, for example, as the pat-down would suffice.

The officer may conduct a cursory search, not only of the individual's outer clothing, but of any area from which the individual might easily procure weapons, glove compartments, etc., *if* the officer reasonably suspects that a weapon is located there.

§ 833

Although the officer may have the right to pat down the suspect's outer clothing, he may not reach inside the clothing of the suspect or search further *unless he has reason to believe that the pat-down has disclosed the presence of a weapon.* The officer must feel some object which a prudent man could believe was an object usable as an instrument of assault. Absent this, the officer may not remove any object from the inside of the suspect's clothing, require the suspect to take the object out of his pocket, or demand that the suspect empty his pockets.

Thus, if the officer feels a hard object resembling a knife or a gun, he may remove the object from the suspect's pocket. If, on the other hand, the officer feels a soft bulge in the suspect's pocket, he may not take further action unless he reasonably believes, and is able to explain the reason for his belief, that the object is an actual, atypical weapon.

Read People v. Mosher, 1 Cal.3d 379, 82 Cal.Rptr. 379 (1969), in Table of Cases included in this text regarding stop and frisk.

Notes of Decisions

Officers could not arrest defendant for Vehicle Code infractions relating to driving without a driver's license, speeding, faulty brake lights, having a license plate on the vehicle that belonged to another vehicle, and for driving a vehicle that had no front license plate, which are all minor traffic violations. People v. Farley (1971) 98 Cal.Rptr. 89, 20 C.A.3d 1032.

An officer is not limited in a frisk or pat down search to locating "hard" weapons, but under certain circumstances can ascertain whether suspect possesses any other instrumentality which might be used to assault an officer or to effect an escape. People v. Armenta (1968) 73 Cal.Rptr. 819, 268 C.A.2d 248.

§ 834. Arrest defined; persons authorized to arrest

Arrest defined. By whom defined. An arrest is taking a person into custody, in a case and in the manner authorized by law. An arrest may be made by a peace officer or by a private person.
(Enacted 1872.)

Notes of Decisions

Essential elements of an "arrest" are: (1) taking a person into custody and (2) actual restraint of the person or his submission to custody. People v. Hatcher (1969) 82 Cal.Rptr. 323, 2 C.A.3d 71.

An arrest is more than a transient momentary incident; it continues through a transfer of custody of accused from a citizen to a peace officer; "arrest" is defined as the apprehending or detaining of person in order to be forthcoming to answer an alleged or suspected crime. People v. Harris (1967) 63 Cal.Rptr. 849, 256 C.A.2d 455.

Defendant who had been physically restrained with handcuffs, interrogated for a substantial period of time, and transported from scene of detention to site where crime was committed at time of interrogation in question was under "arrest". People v. Terry (1966) 50 Cal.Rptr. 120, 240 C.A.2d 681.

Stopping of person for interrogation does not necessarily constitute arrest. People v. Gibson (1963) 33 Cal.Rptr. 775, 220 C.A.2d 15.

Police officers stopping and interrogating a person outdoors at night does not constitute "arrest", though person interrogated may be momentarily detained. People v. Ellsworth (1961) 12 Cal.Rptr. 433, 190 C.A.2d 844.

When officer determines that there is probable cause to believe that a traffic offense has been committed and begins the process of citing the violator to appear in court, an "arrest" takes place, at least in the technical sense; while motorist who is actually taken into police custody for transportation before a magistrate is "under arrest" in the traditional sense of the term. People v. Superior Court of Los Angeles County (1972) 101 Cal.Rptr. 837, 496 P.2d 1205, 7 C.3d 186.

§ 834a. Resistance to arrest

If a person has knowledge, or by the exercise of reasonable care, should have knowledge, that he is being arrested by a peace officer, it is the duty of such person to refrain from using force or any weapon to resist such arrest.
(Added by Stats.1957, c. 2147, p. 3807, § 10.)

Notes of Decisions

Resistance to an unlawful arrest constitutes the misdemeanor offense of a battery, since the victim officer is not engaged in the performance of his duties; however, if the officer is making a lawful arrest, resistance becomes a felony; however, one may properly resist the use of excessive force regardless of whether the arrest is technically lawful or unlawful. People v. Henderson (1976) 129 Cal.Rptr. 844, 58 C.A.3d 349.

Arrestee does not have privilege to commit batteries on peace officers who make illegal arrest. People v. Muniz (1970) 84 Cal.Rptr. 501, 4 C.A.3d 562.

Illegality of arrest would not justify resistance on part of defendant accused of assault and battery on two peace officers. People v. Rhone (1968) 73 Cal.Rptr. 463, 267 C.A.2d 562.

This section was enacted to eliminate right of person improperly arrested to use force at time of arrest and to require him to seek his redress by resort to courts rather than by resort to violence. In re Bacon (1966) 49 Cal.Rptr. 322, 240 C.A.2d 34.

§ 835. Method of making arrest; amount of restraint

An arrest is made by an actual restraint of the person, or by submission to the custody of an officer. The person arrested may be subjected to such restraint as is reasonable for his arrest and detention.
(Amended by Stats.1957, c. 2147, p. 3805, § 1.)

Notes of Decisions

Custody or restraint authorized by law in an arrest may be effected by actual or constructive seizure or detention of person to be arrested, and person arrested may only be subjected to such restraint as is reasonable for his arrest and detention. People v. Superior Court In and For San Mateo County (1973) 110 Cal.Rptr. 504, 35 C.A.3d 1.

Essential elements of an "arrest" are: (1) taking a person into custody and (2) actual restraint of the person or his submission to custody. People v. Hatcher (1969) 82 Cal.Rptr. 323, 2 C.A.3d 71.

Defendant who had been physically restrained with handcuffs, interrogated for a substantial period of time, and transported from scene of detention to site where crime was committed at time of interrogation in question was under "arrest". People v. Terry (1966) 50 Cal.Rptr. 120, 240 C.A.2d 681.

Actual restraint and submission to custody sufficient to constitute an "arrest" existed where detectives accosted defendant at night on downtown street, told defendant to come with them, searched defendant's automobile, and took defendant to police station, even though defendant was not handcuffed. People v. Freeland (1963) 32 Cal.Rptr. 132, 218 C.A.2d 199.

§ 835a. Use of force to effect arrest, prevent escape, or overcome resistance

Any peace officer who has reasonable cause to believe that the person to be arrested has committed a public offense may use reasonable force to effect the arrest, to prevent escape or to overcome resistance.

A peace officer who makes or attempts to make an arrest need not retreat or desist from his efforts by reason of the resistance or threatened resistance of the person being arrested; nor shall such officer be deemed an aggressor or lose his right to self-defense by the use of reasonable force to effect the arrest or to prevent escape or to overcome resistance.
(Added by Stats.1957, c. 2147, p. 3807, § 11.)

§ 836. Peace officers; arrest under warrant; grounds for arrest without warrant

A peace officer may make an arrest in obedience to a warrant, or may, pursuant to the authority granted him by the provisions of Chapter 4.5 (commencing with Section 830) of Title 3 of Part 2, without a warrant, arrest a person:

1. Whenever he has reasonable cause to believe that the person to be arrested has committed a public offense in his presence.

2. When a person arrested has committed a felony, although not in his presence.

3. Whenever he has reasonable cause to believe that the person to be arrested has committed a felony, whether or not a felony has in fact been committed.
(Amended by Stats.1968, c. 1222, p. 2322, § 59.)

Editors' Note

An exception to subsection (1) is found in Section 40300.5 of the Vehicle Code which authorizes a peace officer to arrest without a warrant, a person involved in a traffic accident when the officer has reasonable cause to believe that such person has been operating a motor vehicle while intoxicated.

The courts have held the following factors to be significant in determining whether the officers properly arrested an individual. It should not be assumed that any of these factors, standing alone, necessarily justifies arresting the individual. For example, an individual may not be arrested merely because he is present in a high crime area. That fact, though, *taken with other facts*, may justify the arrest.

(1) Report of recent crime in the area. The kind of crime reported, as well as how recently it was reported, will be relevant.
(2) It is nighttime. Generally speaking, the courts allow more latitude in detention at night than in the day.
(3) The place is known as an area of frequent and current crimes, such as sales of narcotics.
(4) There is information that criminal activity was scheduled to take place of the type consistent with what the suspects are seen doing.
(5) There is knowledge that the suspect was previously convicted of the suspected crime.
(6) The suspect was driving a car in an erratic or suspicious fashion.
(7) The suspects were sitting in a parked car at an unusual time and place.
(8) The suspects gave cause to believe that they were violating motor vehicle laws.
(9) The suspects acted in an unusual manner at the approach of the officers.

Detentions

There are many occasions in which a peace officer does not have probable cause to make an arrest, however, he harbors a rational suspicion that the suspect may be involved in criminal activity. In these circumstances, the peace officer may detain the suspect for a short time to investigate further. If during this brief stop and questioning the officer becomes aware of other information relating to criminal activity, he might consider arresting the suspect, on the other hand the suspicious activity might prove to be perfectly harmless and the suspect would then be released.

Note: Read People v. Knutson, 60 Cal.App.3d 856, 131 Cal.Rptr. 846 (1976); People v. Moreno, 67 Cal.App.3d 962, 134 Cal.Rptr. 322 (1977); in Table of Cases included in this text regarding probable cause to detain.

Arrests

An arrest must be based on reasonable (or probable) cause to believe and conscientiously entertain an honest and strong suspicion that the accused has committed or attempted the commission of a crime.

Note: Read People v. Superior Court (Kiefer), 3 Cal.3d 807, 91 Cal.Rptr. 729 (1970); Kaplan v. Superior Court, 6 Cal.3d 150, 98 Cal.Rptr. 649 (1971); in Table of Cases included in this text regarding furtive gestures and probable cause to arrest and search.

Notes of Decisions

In general

Arrest cannot be made merely for investigation of crime and to be lawful arrest by peace officer can only be made pursuant to arrest warrant setting forth commission of specific crime, or without warrant if officer has reasonable cause to believe that person to be arrested has committed public offense in his presence, if person arrested has committed felony, though not in his presence, or if officer has reasonable cause to believe that person to be arrested has committed felony, whether or not felony has in fact been committed. People v. Superior Court for Los Angeles County (1971) 92 Cal.Rptr. 916, 15 C.A.3d 146.

§ 836   PENAL CODE

A police officer may lawfully arrest a person without a warrant if the person has committed a public offense in presence of arresting officer, or if arresting officer has reasonable cause to believe that person arrested has committed a felony. People v. Prather (1969) 74 Cal.Rptr. 82, 268 C.A.2d 748.

Arrest with warrant

Where police inspector's information that all-points bulletin and parole violator warrant had been issued for defendant was received from official sources, he was entitled to make arrest upon basis of that information. People v. Dubose (1971) 94 Cal.Rptr. 376, 17 C.A.3d 43.

Arrest without warrant in general

The two rationales which justify warrantless searches incident to arrest relate to the security of the arresting officers and the preservation of evidence, but such dual rationales for searches incident to arrest must be oriented solely to the threat posed by the arrestee, and the search for either weapons or evidence must be limited to arrestee's person and the area within his immediate control. Guidi v. Superior Court of Los Angeles County (1973) 109 Cal.Rptr. 684, 513 P.2d 908, 10 C.3d 1.

An arrest without warrant may be made if person arrested has committed a public offense in presence of arresting officer or if arresting officer has reasonable cause to believe that person arrested had committed a felony. People v. Tenney (1972) 101 Cal.Rptr. 419, 25 C.A.3d 16.

If police do not know whether crime has been committed and do not have probable cause to arrest suspect on specific charge, police do not possess valid authority to take suspect into custody. People v. Superior Court for Los Angeles County (1971) 92 Cal.Rptr. 916, 15 C.A.3d 146.

More evidence is required in support of probable cause to make lawful arrest without warrant than is required to justify issuance of search warrant. People v. Johnson (1970) 92 Cal.Rptr. 105, 13 C.A.3d 742.

Circumstances justifying arrest without warrant

A peace officer may make an arrest without a warrant whenever he has reasonable cause to believe that the person to be arrested has committed a public offense in his presence. People v. Garcia (1972) 105 Cal.Rptr. 584, 30 C.A.3d 266.

Though lack of registration card does not alone furnish probable cause for arrest of motorist for theft, it gives officer reasonable grounds to inquire further, and if motorist gives answers which are inconsistent, conflicting, or palpably false, such answers constitute further suspicious circumstance sufficient to support belief that the vehicle is stolen and to justify warrantless arrest. People v. Superior Court of Los Angeles County (1972) 101 Cal.Rptr. 837, 496 P.2d 1205, 7 C.3d 186.

Where informant was arrested as actual participant in crime involving same contraband with which defendant was implicated, and arresting officer observed marijuana being loaded into informer's vehicle after being told that informer had twice spoken to defendant as to its delivery, subsequently observed informant proceed by prearrangement to defendant's residence and leave shortly thereafter, and then received information from officer in touch with informant that delivery had been made, information furnished by such informant was sufficiently corroborated to raise reasonably honest and strong suspicion of defendant's guilt, and thus warrantless arrest, and subsequent search of defendant was proper. People v. Werber (1971) 97 Cal.Rptr. 150, 19 C.A.3d 598.

Informers, arrest without warrant

Though police officer went to defendant's apartment after receiving tip from an anonymous informant, where officer saw an automobile parked adjacent thereto which matched description given by witnesses to crime and upon further investigation, went to apartment and observed that defendant matched physical description of suspect, officer had reasonable cause to make a warrantless arrest of defendant. People v. Brooks (1975) 124 Cal.Rptr. 492, 51 C.A.3d 602, certiorari denied 96 S.Ct. 1469.

Fact that anonymous informer who caused police surveillance leading to defendant's arrest was "citizen informer" did not give information furnished by such informer any more probative force than information coming from a so-called reliable or tested informer. People v. Gonzales (1971) 95 Cal.Rptr. 291, 17 C.A.3d 848.

Information given by an untested informant may be sufficient to justify a warrantless arrest if corroborated in essential respects by other facts, sources or circumstances. People v. Fein (1971) 94 Cal.Rptr. 607, 484 P.2d 583, 4 C.3d 747.

Arrest and search may be made solely on basis of information received from single reliable informer. Pierson v. Superior Court (1970) 87 Cal.Rptr. 433, 8 C.A.3d 510.

Surveillance and investigation by officers, arrest without warrant

Officer's awareness that area in which defendants were apprehended was one where there had been high incidence of crime including several recent armed robberies, was factor, to be weighed with others, in determining whether precautionary frisk was reasonable. People v. Hill (1974) 117 Cal.Rptr. 393, 528 P.2d 1, 12 C.3d 731.

Reasonable or probable cause for arrest, in general

Where totality of ambient circumstances added up to reasonable and probable cause on narcotic agent's part to believe that hashish was being carried in one defendant's briefcase and in bag which other defendant carried off plane and handed to person waiting at airport in foreign vehicle without license plates, probable cause existed for warrantless arrest and for search of the briefcase and also for search of the bag made after the briefcase search had resulted in discovery of what appeared to be cakes of hashish. People v. Ramsey (1972) 105 Cal.Rptr. 445, 30 C.A.3d 364.

No exact formula exists for determining reasonable cause to make a warrantless arrest, and each case must be decided on facts and circumstances presented to officers at time they were required to act. People v. Fein (1971) 94 Cal.Rptr. 607, 484 P.2d 583, 4 C.3d 747.

Question of reasonable cause to make arrest and search without warrant must be tested by facts known to officers at time of search and if officers point to specific articulable facts and circumstances which would lead man of ordinary care and prudence to believe, or entertain strong suspicion, person arrested is guilty of felony, incidental search is reasonable although officer may be mistaken as to exact crime shown by facts. People v. Superior Court for Los Angeles County (1971) 92 Cal.Rptr. 916, 15 C.A.3d 146.

Accused's furtive actions during his attempt to escape when he was approached by officer, added to all other knowledge and information which previously had been imparted to officer, including that supplied by informer with respect to narcotics transactions, provided more than sufficient grounds for accused's arrest. People v. Cruz (1970) 85 Cal.Rptr. 918, 6 C.A.3d 384, certiorari denied 91 S.Ct. 377, 400 U.S. 966, 27 L.Ed.2d 386.

Totality of information, coming from a number of independent sources, may be sufficient to constitute reasonable or probable cause for an arrest without a warrant, even though no single item meets the test. People v. Superior Court for Los Angeles County (1969) 78 Cal.Rptr. 757, 274 C.A.2d 7.

Reasonable or probable cause for arrest is not determined by any exact formula and each case must be decided on its own facts and circumstances on total atmosphere of case. People v. Clark (1967) 63 Cal.Rptr. 622, 256 C.A.2d 6.

"Probable or reasonable cause" for an arrest for a felony under this section is such knowledge by arresting officer at the time of arrest of facts which would lead an ordinarily reasonable and prudent man then to conscientiously entertain an honest and strong suspicion that the person he was arresting had committed a felony. People v. Fritz (1967) 61 Cal.Rptr. 247, 253 C.A.2d 7, certiorari denied 88 S.Ct. 2066, 392 U.S. 910, 20 L.Ed.2d 1367.

Commission of felony, in general, reasonable cause

Felony arrest is lawful so long as arresting officer has reasonable cause to believe that the person arrested has committed a felony regardless of whether felony has in fact been committed. People v. Bianco (1975) 127 Cal.Rptr. 92, 55 C.A.3d Supp. 8.

Police officer may lawfully arrest person without warrant if arresting officer has reasonable cause to believe that person arrested has committed a felony. People v. Moore (1975) 124 Cal.Rptr. 290, 51 C.A.3d 610, certiorari denied 96 S.Ct. 2179.

Where officer who had been advised by informer that defendants were selling heroin from certain described premises where officer would find described vehicle and numerous people coming and going from house and officer after ascertaining that defendants resided on premises and familiarizing himself with defendant's picture kept house under surveillance and saw numerous people going in and out of the premises and at least on two occasions an exchange taking place and officer arrested one person who had just been in house for being under influence of heroin, officers had reasonable cause to believe that female defendant who was on premises had committed felony and search of premises was valid as incident to her lawful arrest. People v. Sotelo (1971) 95 Cal.Rptr. 486, 18 C.A.3d 9.

Probable cause for arrest may be defined as having more evidence for than against or supported by evidence which inclines mind to believe, but leaves some room for doubt; it is not limited to evidence that would be admissible at trial on issue of guilt. People v. Moore (1975) 124 Cal.Rptr. 290, 51 C.A.3d 610, certiorari denied 96 S.Ct. 2179.

While there is always a possibility that some additional person may be found in a house outside of which an arrest took place, mere possibility of additional persons in house, without more, is not enough to provide probable cause to search entire premises for additional suspects once suspect whom officers are seeking is arrested. Dillion v. Superior Court of Santa Barbara County (1972) 102 Cal.Rptr. 161, 497 P.2d 505, 7 C.3d 305.

Probable cause, in context of a warrantless arrest, has no other purpose than to impose legal limits upon types of suspicions upon which the law will allow a valid arrest to be predicated. Agar v. Superior Court for Los Angeles County (1971) 98 Cal.Rptr. 148, 21 C.A.3d 24.

"Probable cause" for arrest consists of having more evidence for than against supported by evidence which inclines mind to believe but leaves some room for doubt; it is not limited to evidence admissible at trial on issue of guilt; and test is not whether evidence upon which officer acts in making arrest is sufficient to convict, but only whether person should stand trial. Curry v. Superior Court of San Diego County (1970) 86 Cal.Rptr. 844, 7 C.A.3d 836.

Where one accused's statements implicating second accused were corroborated by blood on first accused's shoes and witnesses' description of first accused and were also corroborated by statements made by another informer, officers had probable cause to arrest second accused and arrest did not taint evidence subsequently seized. Clifton v. Superior Court In and For Humboldt County (1970) 86 Cal.Rptr. 612, 7 C.A.3d 245.

Burglary, commission of felony, probable cause

Evidence supported trial court's finding that probable cause existed for warrantless arrest of burglary suspect in his home. People v. Massey (1976) 130 Cal.Rptr. 581, 59 C.A.3d 777.

Where officers had rational suspicion that defendant might have been involved in burglary and, having stopped defendant, officers observed possible fruits of burglary as well as instrumentalities of burglary, officers had probable cause to arrest the defendant for burglary. People v. Taylor (App.1975) 120 Cal.Rptr. 762, 46 C.A.3d 513.

Officer who had been informed of theft of television set involving two men in stake bed truck and who observed such truck under circumstances warranting detention and observed square object on truck bed covered by blanket had reasonable cause to believe that truck had been used in burglary and that truck bed contained fruits of crime and was justified in patting square object through blanket to determine its nature and when he felt knob and reached opinion that object was in fact a television set and that tires on truck bed were stolen, there was probable cause to arrest occupants. People v. Amick (1973) 111 Cal.Rptr. 280, 36 C.A.3d 140.

Surveillance and investigation by officers, probable cause

Where officers knew that on day of murder the victim had telephoned woman and had arranged to meet her husband at certain residence to purchase some marijuana, that such woman had been at such residence at time of murder and had admitted murder victim and his companion into house and that woman accompanied body in trip to hospital but departed from automobile just before reaching hospital, such facts with others gave probable cause to arrest woman as participant in conspiracy or as aider and abettor. People v. Hill (1974) 117 Cal.Rptr. 393, 528 P.2d 1, 12 C.3d 731.

Probable cause to detain for investigation exists where (1) there is a rational suspicion by peace officer that some activity out of the ordinary is or has taken place, (2) some indication to connect the person under suspicion with the unusual activity, and (3) some suggestion that the activity is related to crime. People v. Juarez (1973) 110 Cal.Rptr. 865, 35 C.A.3d 631.

Police officer, who heard broadcast of a robbery which had just been committed, who knew from recent arrest report that one of the accused matched the general description of robber and who went to accused's home at which accused and another arrived in automobile, was justified in detaining accused and companion for purpose of interviewing them in parked automobile and information discovered during the detention, including the viewing of guns and ammunition in plain sight, provided probable cause to arrest accused and his companion and to conduct incidental search of automobile. People v. Sutton (1973) 110 Cal.Rptr. 635, 35 C.A.3d 264.

Temporary detention

Where defendant was first observed by two plainclothes officers to be driving erratically, and then, after defendant's vehicle had stopped and one officer approached and exhibited his badge, defendant pulled his vehicle into a driveway and backed out, forcing the officer to jump out of the way, and then started forward heading toward the officer, officers had probable cause to detain defendant. People v. Lozano (1976) 127 Cal.Rptr. 204, 57 C.A.3d 490.

Police officer had rational grounds for believing that juvenile was one of the four girls involved in robbery, and his temporary detention of her was thus lawful, where four girls at the scene of robbery had run away together, where, shortly after the robbery, they were seen together in its immediate vicinity, where three of the girls fit the description of three of the girls at the scene of the robbery, and where the juvenile, who was the fourth girl, though identified only by her race, sex and age, could quite reasonably be detained in order to discover whether she was one of the original group or a late joiner. Lynette G. v. Cabell (1976) 126 Cal.Rptr. 898, 54 C.A.3d 1087.

Where two police officers who were on patrol in a high-crime area noticed the two occupants of car which was parked at curb duck down out of sight as the police car's headlights flashed across the parked car, circumstances apparent to the officers were sufficient to cause a good-faith suspicion of criminal activity, and it was proper for police to detain occupants of the car for questioning. People v. Rios (1975) 124 Cal.Rptr. 737, 51 C.A.3d 1008.

Temporary detention of burglary suspect for questioning was not unduly prolonged while policeman checked by radio to determine whether warrants were outstanding against suspect, in view of seriousness of suspected crime of burglary. People v. Herrera (1975) 124 Cal.Rptr. 725, 52 C.A.3d 177.

Police officers' observation of marijuana plants growing in rear of residence justified further investigation with incident temporary detention of probable suspects. People v. Freund, 119 Cal.Rptr. 762.

Where defendant was in a residential area at 11:30 p. m. looking over fences into yard areas, probable cause existed for police officer to detain him for questioning. People v. Ketchum (1975) 119 Cal.Rptr. 368, 45 C.A.3d 328.

Where officer who, after observing defendant and another person stagger and enter vehicle, concluded that defendant and such other person were intoxicated stopped automobile being driven by such other person, and officer had observed defendant and driver bending down appearing to place something under seat, officer was justified in requesting occupants of automobile to alight. People v. Beal (1975) 118 Cal.Rptr. 272, 44 C.A.3d 216.

Where police officer observed, in high crime area, parked automobile in alley with trunk open, defendant emerging from between two residences carrying box obviously containing a large commercial type typewriter, the placing of box in trunk, and the driving of automobile to residence 150 to 200 feet away, adequate suspicious circumstances existed to justify temporary detention for purpose of inquiry, despite defendant's contention that observations of officer were consistent with innocent activity. People v. Wheeler (1974) 118 Cal.Rptr. 205, 43 C.A.3d 898.

Circumstances short of probable cause to make arrest may justify officer's investigatory detention of motorist and, if circumstances warrant, officer may conduct precautionary pat-down search for weapons. People v. Hill (1974) 117 Cal.Rptr. 393, 528 P.2d 1, 12 C.3d 731.

Initial frisk of passenger of pursued automobile was properly limited to patting of outer clothing, but where large roll of money was thereby visible inside open jacket pocket, discovery of the money was not product of an impermissibly excessive intrusion, nor was removal of three-inch by three-inch matchbox felt by officer in continuation of limited search, nor was examination of contents of the matchbox unjustified. Id.

Where police officer first saw defendant, in area in which groups of juveniles usually did not congregate, walking out of liquor store carrying paper bag toward officer and group of juveniles, and defendant, apparently upon noticing officer, made abrupt change of direction and deposited paper bag over retaining wall and started to walk toward group once again, defendant's conduct reasonably suggested possibility that he had possessed something which was in violation of law and officer was justified in detaining and questioning the other juveniles and defendant. People v. Superior Court In and For Monterey County (1973) 106 Cal.Rptr. 211, 30 C.A.3d 257.

A police officer may in appropriate circumstances and in an appropriate manner approach a person for purposes of investigating possibly criminal behavior even though there is no probable cause to make an arrest. People v. Orr (1972) 103 Cal.Rptr. 266, 26 C.A.3d 849.

Private university security officer who, while on patrol in midafternoon in neighborhood that had been scene of burglaries and indecent exposures, observed oddly dressed pedestrian turn his head as if to avoid confrontation acted in proper discharge of his duty in detaining person for further investigation. People v. Courtney (1970) 90 Cal.Rptr. 370, 11 C.A.3d 1185.

Stopping a person for questioning does not constitute an arrest but rather a temporary detention for purposes of investigation. People v. Anthony (1970) 86 Cal.Rptr. 767, 7 C.A.3d 751.

Where experienced narcotics officer was told by a deputy that he had reliable information that a certain person living at a specific address was involved with sale of heroin and that many persons who went there either made a purchase or used narcotics, and officer conducted a surveillance of premises and observed a male enter and exit the house, stopped and interviewed him and found he had evidence of narcotic usage, and subsequently in a similar surveillance officer observed accused enter premises and leave 15 minutes later, accused's detention and interrogation were not in violation of his rights under State and Federal Constitutions. People v. Garcia (1970) 86 Cal.Rptr. 628, 7 C.A.3d 314, certiorari denied 91 S.Ct. 888, 401 U.S. 914, 27 L.Ed.2d 814.

Pat-down search, detention

Pat-down search is intrusion which is constitutionally permissible only when investigating officer reasonably believes it is necessary for his own protection or safety of others. People v. Hill (1974) 117 Cal.Rptr. 393, 528 P.2d 1, 12 C.3d 731.

As far as reasonableness of pat down is concerned, there is no basis for differentiating between car passenger and driver, and it is reasonable for investigating officer to take precautionary measures with respect to all occupants of fleeing automobile. Id.

Where bartender notified police of defendant's presence at the bar with a gun, and, upon officer's arrival on the scene within two minutes, pointed to the defendant and informed the officer that defendant was the man with the gun, police officer properly acted on the information in performing pat down search. People v. Duren (1973) 107 Cal.Rptr. 157, 507 P.2d 1365, 9 C.3d 218.

In typical pedestrian traffic violation case, circumstances justifying a detention do not furnish probable cause to pat down pedestrian or his personal effects for weapons and those violations do not normally involve use of weapons. People v. Lawler (1973) 107 Cal.Rptr. 13, 507 P.2d 621, 9 C.3d 156.

Mere fact that defendant was observed apparently under the influence of something while lawfully crossing a street at an early hour in morning did not give police reasonable grounds to believe that he was armed and dangerous so that they could stop and pat him down for weapons. People v. Taylor (1972) 104 Cal.Rptr. 350, 501 P.2d 918, 8 C.A.3d 174.

Where male wearing black sweater had been seen walking away from automobile involved in hit-and-run accident, police officer on his way to scene of the accident saw defendant wearing a black sweater four blocks from the scene and asked him if he knew of a recent accident, and defendant replied he had been there but knew nothing about it, and where officer then required defendant to go with him to the scene for more investigation, patted defendant down before he was placed in police car, found switchblade knife and arrested him, such patdown was sensible precaution, and the arrest was lawful, and thus narcotics evidence subsequently found was admissible. People v. Ramos (1972) 102 Cal.Rptr. 502, 26 C.A.3d 108.

Victim as informer, reasonable cause

Citizen who purports to be victim or of to have witnessed crime is a reliable informant for purpose of establishing probable cause for arrest without a warrant even though his reliability has not been proven or tested. People v. Garber (1969) 80 Cal.Rptr. 214, 275 C.A.2d 119.

Although information provided by untested informer or by anonymous informer is not, without some showing justifying reliance, sufficient to justify an arrest, information from citizen who purports to be victim of robbery or assault may be sufficient even though his reliability has not been previously tested. People v. Hogan (1969) 80 Cal.Rptr. 28, 457 P.2d 868, 71 C.2d 888.

Corroboration of information from informer, reasonable cause

In view of nonreliable informer's accuracy with respect to subsidiary factors, he was sufficiently corroborated to furnish probable cause for arrest, by the matching of detailed descriptions of defendant given by informant and by victim respectively, and equivalence of date, time and location of the robbery and character of establishment robbed as given by informant and as disclosed on police report. People v. West (1969) 83 Cal.Rptr. 223, 3 C.A.3d 253.

Officer, who went to defendant's address in course of routine narcotic investigation three days after receiving information concerning presence of narcotics at defendant's address, and who upon entering defendant's apartment, detected odor of burnt marijuana and was given defendant's permission to search premises, had sufficient information in his possession to justify defendant's arrest, even if confidential communication by informant were entirely discounted, and defendant was not entitled to disclose of identity of informant on issue of probable cause. People v. Martin (1969) 82 Cal.Rptr. 414, 2 C.A.3d 121.

Information provided by a known informant of unproved reliability or by an anonymous informer is sufficient to warrant arrest without warrant if corroborated in essential respects by such other facts, sources or circumstances as would justify conclusion that reliance on the information is reasonable. People v. Davis (1969) 82 Cal.Rptr. 561, 2 C.A.3d 230.

Premises under defendant's control, search incident to arrest

People v. Hill (1968) 72 Cal.Rptr. 641, 446 P.2d 521, 69 C.2d 550 [main volume] affirmed 91 S.Ct. 1106, 401 U.S. 797, 28 L.Ed.2d 484.

Discovery and seizure of drugs in one of two adjacent houses which officers lawfully entered justified, under circumstances, arrest of all four occupants of the two houses on charges of possessing drugs and the limited search of both houses for other suspects. Bowyer v. Superior Court of Santa Cruz County (1974) 111 Cal.Rptr. 628, 37 C.A.3d 151, rehearing denied 112 Cal.Rptr. 266, 37 C.A.3d 151.

Movement of officer in apartment to point which enabled him to glance into kitchen area, where hashish was allegedly discovered, was justified as a cursory search for additional suspects necessary under the circumstances to allay a reasonable fear for his and his fellow officers' personal safety, where officer knew, inter alia, that traffickers included at least two other persons than those arrested in the apartment, when arrestees were in possession of ten pounds of hashish which had a street value in excess of $40,000, where informer had not looked into any room other than living room and bathroom, and where counter between kitchen and living room was high enough and long enough to shelter a lurking accomplice. Guidi v. Superior Court of Los Angeles County (1973) 109 Cal.Rptr. 684, 513 P.2d 908, 10 C.3d 1.

Vehicles, search incident to arrest

Since trunk of automobile was not an area into which occupants of the vehicle could reach in order to grab weapons or evidence, search of trunk of the automobile could not be justified as incident to the occupant's arrest for possession of marijuana which was found in the front seat of the automobile. Wimberly v. Superior Court of San Bernardino County (1976) 128 Cal.Rptr. 641, 547 P.2d 417, 16 C.3d 557.

Where police knew of defendant's parole violator status and were acting pursuant to a specific request from parole agents to apprehend defendant, the stopping of defendant's vehicle and warrantless arrest and search were not unlawful on theory that reliance on parole hold was a mere sham to support what was, in reality, only a police investigation. People v. Jochen (1975) 119 Cal.Rptr. 914, 46 C.A.3d 243.

Where police officer had probable cause to arrest defendant for receiving stolen merchandise at the time he opened defendant's automobile trunk, the opening of the trunk, even without consent, was a lawful search incident to an arrest, notwithstanding fact that arrest did not actually occur until immediately after recovery of the stolen merchandise. People v. Wheeler (1974) 118 Cal.Rptr. 205, 43 C.A.3d 898.

Search of defendants' automobile at police storage garage on morning following evening arrest was too remote in time and place to be justified as search incidental to arrest. People v. Hill (1974) 117 Cal.Rptr. 393, 528 P.2d 1, 12 C.3d 731.

Where officer's reasonable fear for his safety justified pat-down search of automobile occupants, who had stepped out of automobile, limited precautionary investigation of automobile to assure that there were no potential assailants hiding within was permissible. Id.

Where 18-year-old driver, whose vehicle was stopped for suspected violation of curfew ordinance, validly consented to search of vehicle after police officer advised him that his two juvenile passengers had record of prior arrests for burglary, evidence seized on search of vehicle was properly admitted in delinquency proceeding brought against one passenger, the probable cause requirement having been waived. In re Francis W. (App.1974) 117 Cal.Rptr. 277.

Search of defendant's automobile was not search incident to his arrest where automobile was not within his immediate control in sense that he could have obtained weapon or destructible evidence from it. People v. Dumas (1973) 109 Cal.Rptr. 304, 9 C.3d 788.

Where police officer detained defendant in parking lot at night near to recently burglarized business establishments, defendant gave elaborate explanation for his presence, and dust disturbances were noticed on door and window of unlocked vehicle which had personal property visible on front and rear seats, police officer's entry into the automobile was lawful, and contraband discovered in justifiable subsequent search was admissible. People v. Gale (1973) 108 Cal.Rptr. 852, 511 P.2d 1204, 9 C.3d 871.

§ 836.3. Arrest of escapees

A peace officer may make an arrest in obedience to a warrant delivered to him, or may, without a warrant, arrest a person who, while charged with or convicted of a misdemeanor, has escaped from any county or city jail, prison, industrial farm or industrial road camp or from the custody of the officer or person in charge of him while engaged on any county road or other county work or going to or returning

§ 836.3

from such county road or other county work or from the custody of any officer or person in whose lawful custody he is when such escape is not by force or violence.
(Added by Stats.1955, c. 609, p. 1101, § 1.)

§ 836.5. **Public officers and employees; arrest without warrant; grounds; civil liability; notice to appear; officers and employees of local agencies**

(a) A public officer or employee, when authorized by ordinance, may arrest a person without a warrant whenever he has reasonable cause to believe that the person to be arrested has committed a misdemeanor in his presence which is a violation of a statute or ordinance which such officer or employee has the duty to enforce.

(b) There shall be no civil liability on the part of, and no cause of action shall arise against, any public officer or employee acting pursuant to subdivision (a) and within the scope of his authority for false arrest or false imprisonment arising out of any arrest which is lawful or which the public officer or employee, at the time of the arrest, had reasonable cause to believe was lawful. No such officer or employee shall be deemed an aggressor or lose his right to self-defense by the use of reasonable force to effect the arrest, prevent escape, or overcome resistance.

(c) In any case in which a person is arrested pursuant to subdivision (a) and the person arrested does not demand to be taken before a magistrate, the public officer or employee making the arrest shall prepare a written notice to appear and release the person on his promise to appear, as prescribed by Chapter 5C (commencing with Section 853.6) of this title. The provisions of such chapter shall thereafter apply with reference to any proceeding based upon the issuance of a written notice to appear pursuant to this authority.

(d) The governing body of a local agency, by ordinance, may authorize those of its officers and employees who have the duty to enforce a statute or ordinance to arrest persons for violations of such statute or ordinance as provided in subdivision (a).

(e) For the purpose of this section, "ordinance" includes an order, rule, or regulation of any air pollution control district.
(Amended by Stats.1970, c. 114, p. 343, § 1.)

§ 837. **Private persons; authority to arrest**

Arrests by private persons. A private person may arrest another:

1. For a public offense committed or attempted in his presence.

2. When the person arrested has committed a felony, although not in his presence.

3. When a felony has been in fact committed, and he has reasonable cause for believing the person arrested to have committed it.
(Enacted 1872.)

Notes of Decisions

Construction and application

"Public offense," within meaning of this section includes misdemeanors. People v. Wilkins (1972) 104 Cal.Rptr. 89, 27 C.A.3d 763.

Corpus delicti

For there to be a valid arrest by private citizen under this section requirement that there in fact be a felony committed can only be met if there is evidence of the corpus delicti and it is an offense known by the arresting party to have been committed. People v. Aldapa (1971) 94 Cal.Rptr. 579, 17 C.A.3d 184.

Persons authorized to make arrest—In general

Even though evidence did evince commission of a burglary by victim so as to have given defendant cause as a private citizen to make an arrest of victim, use of deadly force to effect that arrest was not warranted, and victim's death during course of arrest could not be classified as justifiable, where crime committed by victim was not of the type which normally threatened death or great bodily harm in that it was committed during the daylight hours and in a business establishment which was open to the public and no confrontation aided by force was involved. People v. Piorkowski (1974) 115 Cal.Rptr. 830, 41 C.A.3d 324.

Fourth Amendment (U.S.C.A.Const. Amend. 4) prohibition against unreasonable searches and seizures did not apply to bondsman, who, in acting to protect his own private financial interest, arrested absconding defendant and reported finding amphetamine and hypodermic needle, which he took into his custody, to police. People v. Houle (1970) 91 Cal.Rptr. 874, 13 C.A.3d 892.

Arrest was not illegal because defendant was arrested in Orange County by police officers employed by the city of Long Beach, since, apart from authority vested in officers by § 817 (repealed. See, now, § 830 et seq.), an officer's power of arrest, when acting beyond limits of geographical unit by which he is appointed, becomes that which is conferred upon a private citizen in the same circumstances, and under this section a private person may arrest another when person arrested has committed a felony, although not in his presence. People v. Califano (App.1970) 85 Cal.Rptr. 292.

Officers outside jurisdiction

Arrest of defendant was not illegal by reason of fact that it was made by Los Angeles police in city of Burbank, where record indicated that a felony had been committed and that reasonable cause existed for believing that defendant had committed it, and power of officers to arrest under such circumstances was same as that of a private citizen. People v. Monson (1972) 105 Cal.Rptr. 92, 28 C.A.3d 935.

Police officer, who observed defendant asleep on cot in apartment, and who was informed by manager of apartment that the two female lessees would not spend the night there because a strange man was in the apartment, would have been authorized, as private citizen, to arrest defendant for taking up lodging in residence without owner's permission even though the officer was not within his jurisdiction. People v. Lyons (1971) 96 Cal.Rptr. 76, 18 C.A.3d 760.

Reasonable cause for arrest

A private person may arrest another for a public offense committed or attempted in his presence, when person arrested has committed a felony, although not in his presence, and when felony has been in fact committed and he has reasonable cause for believing that person arrested committed it. People v. Piorkowski (1974) 115 Cal.Rptr. 830, 41 C.A.3d 324.

Proof of commission of felony by person arrested by private citizen was not necessary under statute providing that a private person may arrest another when a felony has in fact been committed and he has reasonable cause for believing that person arrested has committed it. People v. Wilkins (1972) 104 Cal.Rptr. 89, 27 C.A.3d 763.

§ 838. Magistrate; oral order to officer or private person to arrest

Magistrates may order arrest. A magistrate may orally order a peace officer or private person to arrest any one committing or attempting to commit a public offense in the presence of such magistrate.
(Enacted 1872.)

§ 839. Authority to summon aid to make arrest

Persons making arrest may summon assistance. Any person making an arrest may orally summon as many persons as he deems necessary to aid him therein.
(Enacted 1872.)

Notes of Decisions

In general

School security officer who allegedly observed defendant assaulting elderly individual had right to delegate physical act of taking defendant into custody to police officer whom he had summoned and another school security guard. People v. Campbell (1972) 104 Cal.Rptr. 118, 27 C.A.3d 849.

§ 840. Time of arrest; felony; misdemeanor

An arrest for the commission of a felony may be made on any day and at any time of the day or night. An arrest for the commission of a misdemeanor or an infraction cannot be made between the hours of 10 o'clock p. m. of any day and 6 o'clock a. m. of the succeeding day, unless:

(1) The arrest is made without a warrant pursuant to Section 836 or 837.

(2) The arrest is made in a public place.

(3) The arrest is made when the person is in custody pursuant to another lawful arrest.

(4) The arrest is made pursuant to a warrant which, for good cause shown, directs that it may be served at any time of the day or night.
(Amended by Stats.1976, c. 436, p. —, § 1.)

§ 841. Formalities in making arrest; exceptions

The person making the arrest must inform the person to be arrested of the intention to arrest him, of the cause of the arrest, and the authority to make it, except when the person making the arrest has reasonable cause to believe that the person to be arrested is actually engaged in the commission of or an attempt to commit an offense, or the person to be arrested is pursued immediately after its commission, or after an escape.

The person making the arrest must, on request of the person he is arresting, inform the latter of the offense for which he is being arrested.
(Amended by Stats.1961, c. 1863, p. 3963, § 1.)

Notes of Decisions

In general

Where officer on probable cause has informed person of intention to arrest him, of cause of arrest and authority to make it, at scene of accident, officer is not bound to closely attend such person to exclusion of duty to obtain aid for accident victims and to prevent further traffic pileups and injuries, and if officer attends such necessary and humanitarian duties his failure to maintain close custody of suspect does not retroactively affect validity of arrest or provide immunity from operation of Veh.C. § 13353 providing for blood test. People v. Superior Court In and For San Mateo County (1973) 110 Cal.Rptr. 504, 35 C.A.3d 1.

Arresting officers' failure to comply with § 844 and this section requiring that officer announce his intention and demand admittance and explain purpose before making forcible entry was excused where officers reasonably believed that defendants had shot victim and were still armed and dangerous. People v. Braun (1973) 106 Cal.Rptr. 56, 29 C.A.3d 949.

Where defendant fled after school security officer had pulled him from elderly individual whom defendant allegedly was assaulting and police officer summoned by the school security officer pursued defendant security officer was not required to tell defendant that he was under arrest. People v. Campbell (1972) 104 Cal.Rptr. 118, 27 C.A.3d 849.

Engaged in commission of offense

Officers who did not have probable cause to make an arrest when they knocked acquired probable cause to arrest premises' occupants for being in place where marijuana was being smoked as soon as door was opened in response to their knocks and odor of marijuana emanated. People v. Peterson (1970) 88 Cal.Rptr. 597, 9 C.A.3d 627.

Defendant may not be heard to complain that he was not informed of cause of arrest when police officers had reasonable cause to believe that he was actually engaged in commission of an offense. People v. Bevins (1970) 85 Cal.Rptr. 876, 6 C.A.3d 421.

Compliance with requirements

Strict compliance with provision relating to prearrest procedures (§ 844 and this section) is not required and failure to comply therewith is excused if officer acts in good faith belief that compliance would increase his peril. People v. Braun (1973) 106 Cal.Rptr. 56, 29 C.A.3d 949.

§ 841

Demand and explanation, in general

Minimal compliance with this section requires an effort by officers prior to entry to communicate to persons inside that they seek to be admitted in order to discharge their duties as law enforcement officers. Young v. Superior Court of Tulare County (App.1976) 129 Cal.Rptr. 422.

Where original approach of police officers to premises occupied by defendant and companion was accompanied by announcement of identity of officers and announcement of officers' purpose to ascertain ownership of suspicious automobile parked outside premises, and where officers had already observed behavior of defendant's companion which provided probable cause to arrest companion for forging and counterfeiting driver's license, entry of officers did not violate any of defendant's or companion's rights under this section providing conditions of entry by officers into residences to make arrest. People v. Superior Court of Santa Clara County (1975) 125 Cal.Rptr. 504, 53 C.A.3d 40.

Knock and notice requirements apply, as a matter of policy, when entry of building is sought merely to investigate possible criminal activity. People v. Bruce (1975) 122 Cal.Rptr. 648, 49 C.A.3d 580.

Compliance with this section and § 1531 relating to police officer's right of entry into house of person to be arrested requires, at the very least, that police officers identify themselves prior to entry. People v. Keogh (1975) 120 Cal.Rptr. 817, 46 C.A.3d 919.

Evidence in prosecution for possession of heroin established that officers who conducted parole search of accused's apartment had informed accused's girl friend, who lived with accused, as to reason for officers' presence after she responded to officer's knock. People v. Thomas (1975) 119 Cal.Rptr. 739, 45 C.A.3d 749.

Under this section providing conditions of entry into residence by officers to make arrest, requirements that officer identity himself and that he demand entry were satisfied when officer loudly identified himself as police officer and pounded on door. People v. Hill (1974) 117 Cal.Rptr. 393, 528 P.2d 1, 12 C.3d 731.

Good cause

Mere fact that most people would be at home before 7:00 a. m. does not, in itself, constitute good cause for service of misdemeanor arrest warrant between the hours of 10:00 p. m. and 7:00 a. m. People v. Dinneen (1974) 119 Cal.Rptr. 186, 45 C.A.3d Supp. 5.

Fact that municipal court judges had been informed by marshals that, in many cases, misdemeanor warrants were not serviceable after 7:00 p. m. did not constitute good cause for service between the hours of 10:00 p. m. and 7:00 a. m. of warrants serviceable after 7:00 a. m. as well as warrants not so serviceable. Id.

§ 842. Exhibition of warrant on request

An arrest by a peace officer acting under a warrant is lawful even though the officer does not have the warrant in his possession at the time of the arrest, but if the person arrested so requests it, the warrant shall be shown to him as soon as practicable.
(Amended by Stats.1957, c. 2147, p. 3806, § 4.)

§ 843. Arrest under warrant; force permissible

What force may be used. When the arrest is being made by an officer under the authority of a warrant, after information of the intention to make the arrest, if the person to be arrested either flees or forcibly resists, the officer may use all necessary means to effect the arrest.
(Enacted 1872.)

Notes of Decisions

Officers can use force necessary to accomplish arrest and defend themselves. People v. Almarez (1961) 12 Cal.Rptr. 111, 190 C.A.2d 380.

An officer is not required to use force in entering a place to make an arrest, either with or without a warrant. People v. Rixner (1958) 321 P.2d 91, 157 C.A.2d 387.

Reasonable and necessary force used in effecting arrest did not render inadmissible, in abortion prosecution, evidence that defendant had stated, in response to question by arresting officers as to whether he had used certain implements, "Well, you see them there, don't you?" People v. Fowler (1953) 260 P.2d 89, 119 C.A.2d 657.

§ 844. Breaking open door or window to effect arrest; demand for admittance; explanation of purpose

To make an arrest, a private person, if the offense be a felony, and in all cases a peace officer, may break open the door or window of the house in which the person to be arrested is, or in which they have reasonable grounds for believing him to be, after having demanded admittance and explained the purpose for which admittance is desired.
(Amended by Code Am.1873–74, c. 614, p. 435, § 40.)

Notes of Decisions

Excuse from demand and explanation

Where defendant had on at least two prior occasions eluded arrest and defendant had demonstrated background of violence and an affinity for firearms, police officer with warrant for defendant's arrest was excused from complying with "knock and notice" rule. People v. Cox (App.1976) 130 Cal.Rptr. 440.

Noncompliance with this section governing forced entry into a home to effect an arrest may be excused when specific facts known to the officer before his entry are sufficient to support his good-faith belief that compliance would increase his peril, frustrate the arrest, or permit the destruction of evidence. People v. Bigham (1975) 122 Cal.Rptr. 252, 49 C.A.3d 73.

Exigent circumstances which may justify noncompliance with this section and § 1531 relating to police officer's right of entry into house of person to be arrested include peril to arresting officers, possibilities of escape or destruction of evidence. People v. Keogh (1975) 120 Cal.Rptr. 817, 46 C.A.3d 919.

Under this section, officers are justified in entering closed residence in order to make arrest if they have reasonable grounds for believing person to be arrested is inside and if they have demanded admittance and explained purpose for which admittance is sought. People v. Hill (1974) 117 Cal.Rptr. 393, 528 P.2d 1, 12 C.3d 731.

Where officers knowing only that shooting had very recently occurred found fresh bloodstains on fence and porch of dwelling and on automobile parked outside and observed through porch window what appeared to be bloodstains on floor inside, and officers received no response when knocking and announcing themselves, so that entering premises was only practical means of determining whether anyone inside needed assistance, warrantless entry was justified. Id.

If specific facts known to officer before he enters to search are sufficient to support his good-faith belief that compliance with knock-notice requirements will increase his peril or permit destruction of evidence, compliance therewith is excused. People v. Constancio (1974) 116 Cal.Rptr. 910, 42 C.A.3d 533.

Where undercover police officer's entry into defendant's room was not for the purpose of arresting anyone within the dwelling but was to observe and report on criminal behavior and assist in the accomplishing of the arrest of defendant by fellow officers, it was not necessary that the undercover officer divulge his true identity and the presence of the officer and the informer were not illegal because the undercover officer's presence in the room had been effectuated by trickery or ruse. People v. McCoy (1974) 115 Cal.Rptr. 559, 40 C.A.3d 854.

Noncompliance with announcement requirements of this section providing that a police officer may break open a door or window of dwelling house to make an arrest if person to be arrested is within dwelling or officer has reasonable grounds for believing him to be after officer demands admittance and explains purpose for which admittance is desired is excusable where there are reasonable grounds to believe that compliance would endanger arresting officer. People v. Bennetto (1974) 111 Cal.Rptr. 699, 517 P.2d 1163, 10 C.3d 695.

Evidence seized pursuant to unannounced entries is generally inadmissible; but failure to comply with § 1531 and this section requiring notice of authority and purpose does not compel application of exclusionary rule if specific facts known to the officer before his entry were sufficient to support his good-faith belief that compliance would increase his peril, frustrate arrest, or permit the destruction of evidence. Parsley v. Superior Court of Riverside County (1973) 109 Cal.Rptr. 563, 513 P.2d 611, 9 C.3d 934.

Where officers knocked and announced that they were from county sheriff's office and they were immediately fired upon through the door of the house, it was not necessary for the officers to announce the purpose for which they desired admittance. People v. Sommerhalder (1973) 107 Cal.Rptr. 289, 508 P.2d 289, 9 C.3d 290.

Arresting officers' failure to comply with § 841 and this section requiring that officer announce his intention and demand admittance and explain purpose before making forcible entry was excused where officers reasonably believed that defendants had shot victim and were still armed and dangerous. People v. Braun (1973) 106 Cal.Rptr. 56, 29 C.A.3d 949.

Where arresting officers were aware that defendant had shot two people minutes before they arrived to arrest him and had every reason to believe he was armed, strict compliance with this section was excused. People v. Goldbach (1972) 103 Cal.Rptr. 800, 27 C.A.3d 563.

Police who went to door of defendant's apartment in pursuit of defendant did not need search warrant, and since police were reasonable in believing that defendant was armed and dangerous, no demand and explanation for admittance before breaking in was necessary, and taking of notebook which officers felt might lead to defendant was not an unlawful search and seizure. People v. Carter (1972) 103 Cal.Rptr. 327, 26 C.A.3d 862.

Where officer had observed informant come out of open doorway of apartment, which was occupied by defendant, with contraband in his pocket, officer, who announced "police officers" several times before entering apartment, was excused from complying with requirement of this section that he explain before entering, purpose for which he desires admittance, in view of fact that surrounding circumstances made officer's purpose clear to occupants. People v. Lawrence (1972) 101 Cal.Rptr. 671, 25 C.A.3d 213.

Where police officer repeatedly identified himself and demanded admittance to defendant's residence, requirements of this section had been fulfilled and officer was not required to explain his purpose before entering and conducting search. People v. Turner (1976) 126 Cal.Rptr. 652, 54 C.A.3d 500.

Officers who knocked on door and demanded entrance as police officers with arrest warrant, and opened or forced doors when there was no response, complied with statutory announcement provision. Bowyer v. Superior Court of Santa Cruz County (1974) 111 Cal.Rptr. 628, 37 C.A.3d 151, rehearing denied 112 Cal.Rptr. 266, 37 C.A.3d 151.

Compliance with this section requiring that officer, before entering to make an arrest, first make demand for admittance and give explanation of purpose for which admittance is desired is achieved only when surrounding circumstances clearly indicate that elements of this section have been complied with. People v. Buckner (1973) 111 Cal.Rptr. 32, 35 C.A.3d 307.

Section 1531 and this section requiring notice of officer's authority and purpose prior to breaking door or window for purpose of executing search warrant or making an arrest serve purposes and policies of protecting privacy, protecting innocent persons on the premises, preventing violent confrontations, and protecting the police, and when police procedures fail to conform to the precise demands of the statute but nevertheless serve its policies, there is substantial compliance and insignificant defaults may be ignored. People v. Peterson (1973) 108 Cal.Rptr. 835, 511 P.2d 1187, 9 C.3d 717.

Where officers complied fully with stringent principles applicable to searches in relation to their initial entry into premises where they saw marijuana in plain sight, under which principles a search is not unreasonable if made with the consent of the cooccupant of the premises who officers reasonably and in good faith believe had authority to consent to their entry, activity of officers did not violate this section. People v. Superior Court of Los Angeles County (1973) 107 Cal.Rptr. 756, 31 C.A.3d 788.

Where police officers gave notice of demand for entrance by knocking three times, identified themselves, told defendant they wanted to talk to him, knew defendant possessed loaded revolver, heard sound of metal clicking, similar to closing of cylinder of revolver, coming from inside room, and where defendant did not open door until after third knock and attempted to slam it shut, police officers' entry by pushing door open was lawful and seizure of gun in plain view on table in room was lawful. People v. Garcia (1972) 105 Cal.Rptr. 584, 30 C.A.3d 266.

Forcible entry

Where police officers are in fresh pursuit of a suspect whom they have just arrested and who knows their identity, he is under arrest and they are pursuing him to take him into custody, the officers' forced entry to his home into which he has fled and inside of which he was attempting to bar entry, is effectuated in a manner which substantially complies with requirements of this section governing a forced entry to effectuate an arrest, even though the officers do not recite the statutory formalities. People v. Bigham (1975) 122 Cal.Rptr. 252, 49 C.A.3d 73.

A police officer may forcibly enter the door of a house to effect an arrest after (1) identifying himself as an officer, (2) explaining the purpose for which he desires to enter and (3) demanding entry. People v. Glasspoole (1975) 121 Cal.Rptr. 736, 48 C.A.3d 668.

Identification, compliance, with requirements, etc.

Identification alone can constitute substantial compliance with this section governing forced entry into a home to effect an arrest if prior to entry the surrounding circumstances make the officer's purpose clear to the occupants or show that demand for admittance would be futile. People v. Bigham (1975) 122 Cal.Rptr. 252, 49 C.A.3d 73.

§ 844

Failure to comply with requirements, breaking and entering

The attempted escape by defendant's cohort through side door of garage after officer opened main garage door did not justify noncompliance with knock and notice requirements inasmuch as the only avenues of escape were well covered and the escape attempt apparently occurred when officer opened the garage door, not beforehand. People v. Bruce (1975) 122 Cal.Rptr. 648, 49 C.A.3d 580.

Though slow burning of marijuana involved in its use probably would have resulted in its destruction during period normally required to obtain a warrant, such use did not make destruction imminent, during time required for compliance with this section governing breaking of a door or window to make an arrest; hence, possible destruction of marijuana through its use, which was essential to probable cause to arrest, did not justify officer's failure to satisfy statutory requisites before entering bedroom, door to which was closed. People v. Glasspoole (1975) 121 Cal.Rptr. 736, 48 C.A.3d 668.

Securing of house and detention of petitioner for three hours pending preparation and execution of search warrant did not remove taint of officers' initial illegal entry of house without complying with "knock-and-notice" provisions of this section where police entered the house for sole purpose of securing premises until a warrant could be obtained, and at that time efforts to obtain the warrant already had begun. Machado v. Superior Court, Stanislaus County (1975) 119 Cal.Rptr. 344, 45 C.A.3d 316.

Where entry into dwelling was effected nearly two hours after murder was committed and police officers were not in actual pursuit of any suspect, had no idea who or where the murderers were and no particular reason to believe that murderers were inside the house, the warrantless entry could not be justified as "hot pursuit." People v. Hill (1974) 117 Cal.Rptr. 393, 528 P.2d 1, 12 C.3d 731.

Entry governed by this section and § 1531 dealing with knock-notice requirement which does not comply therewith renders any search and seizure dependent thereon "unreasonable" within meaning of Fourth Amendment (U.S.C.A.Const. Amend. 4) and, as consequence, any evidence seized pursuant thereto inadmissible. People v. Constancio (1974) 116 Cal.Rptr. 910, 42 C.A.3d 533.

Inner door, breaking etc.

Requirements of this section apply to the inner doors of a house as well as to the outer doors. Blake v. Wernette (1976) 129 Cal.Rptr. 426, 57 C.A.3d 656.

Application of this section authorizing a peace officer to break open a door in order to effect an arrest is not limited to outer doors; notice requirement can apply equally to inner doors where the circumstances of the entry to the outer door do not give any notice to the occupants of closed inner room. People v. Glasspoole (1975) 121 Cal.Rptr. 736, 48 C.A.3d 668.

Belief of arresting officers

Where officer entertains reasonable and good-faith belief that compliance with "knock and notice" rule would increase his peril, frustrate arrest, or permit destruction of evidence, he may properly omit compliance. People v. Cox (App.1976) 130 Cal.Rptr. 440.

Even if police officers believed that criminal activity was in progress behind defendant's door, they were still required to identify themselves prior to entry. People v. Keogh (1975) 120 Cal.Rptr. 817, 46 C.A.3d 919.

This section providing that a police officer may break and enter a dwelling in order to effect an arrest if person to be arrested is within dwelling or there are reasonable grounds for believing him to be requires more than reasonable belief that person to be arrested owns or leases dwelling which is entered; there must be a reasonable belief that person is inside at time of entry. People v. Bennetto (1974) 111 Cal.Rptr. 699, 517 P.2d 1163, 10 C.3d 695.

Strict compliance with provision relating to prearrest procedures (§ 841 and this section) is not required and failure to comply therewith is excused if officer acts in good faith belief that compliance would increase his peril. People v. Braun (1973) 106 Cal.Rptr. 56, 29 C.A.3d 949.

Conduct of a marshal in taking position, ostensibly so as to cut off any possible escape, which enabled him not only to see bathroom occupant but also observe hashish pipe lying on chest directly below bathroom window ledge was such an unreasonable invasion of privacy in violation of Fourth Amendment rights that it could not be relied upon to establish reasonable grounds to believe subject of arrest warrants was in house, and order suppressing "fruits" of search conducted following marshals' entry into house on basis of one marshal's observations was justified. People v. Cagle (1971) 98 Cal.Rptr. 348, 21 C.A.3d 57.

Substantial compliance

Under doctrine of "substantial compliance," requirements of statute providing conditions of entry by officer into residence to make arrest will be deemed satisfied where police officers identify themselves, demand entry, and, although they fail to explain why they seek admittance, it is reasonably apparent to occupants why police wish to enter. People v. Superior Court of Santa Clara County (1975) 125 Cal.Rptr. 504, 53 C.A.3d 40.

Where, if woman sought by police had been inside residence, it would have been apparent to her that officers demanding admittance wished to seek her in connection with fatal shooting which had occurred in her presence only three days before, there was substantial compliance with requirement of this section that police officer entering residence to make arrest announce his purpose. People v. Hill (1974) 117 Cal.Rptr. 393, 528 P.2d 1, 12 C.3d 731.

Where landlady told officer that woman believed to be implicated in murder was inside residence, and officer had observed automobile believed to belong to woman and noted that porch light was on, he had reasonable cause to believe she was inside, within this section providing conditions of entry by officers to make arrest, though house lights were off and no one responded to officer's knocking, since officer could reasonably believe that woman was attempting to avoid apprehension by turning off lights and remaining silent. Id.

Where an inner door is voluntarily opened by an occupant, a forced entry by an arresting officer is permissible where a crime is being committed in his immediate presence; in such cases there is not the potential for violence inherent in unannounced entry through a previously closed door. People v. Glasspoole (1975) 121 Cal.Rptr. 736, 48 C.A.3d 668.

§ 845. Breaking open door or window to leave house entered for purpose of making arrest

Doors and windows may be broken, when. Any person who has lawfully entered a house for the purpose of making an arrest, may break open the door or window thereof if detained therein, when necessary for the purpose of liberating himself, and an officer may do the same, when necessary for the purpose of liberating a person who, acting in his aid, lawfully entered for the purpose of making an arrest, and is detained therein.

(Enacted 1872.)

§ 846. Disarming prisoner; delivery of weapons to magistrate

Weapons may be taken from persons arrested. Any person making an arrest may take from the person arrested all offensive weapons which he may have about his person, and must deliver them to the magistrate before whom he is taken.
(Enacted 1872.)

§ 847. Arrest by private person; duty to take prisoner before magistrate or deliver him to peace officer; liability for false arrest

A private person who has arrested another for the commission of a public offense must, without unnecessary delay, take the person arrested before a magistrate, or deliver him to a peace officer. There shall be no civil liability on the part of and no cause of action shall arise against any peace officer, acting within the scope of his authority, for false arrest or false imprisonment arising out of any arrest when:

(a) Such arrest was lawful or when such peace officer, at the time of such arrest had reasonable cause to believe such arrest was lawful; or

(b) When such arrest was made pursuant to a charge made, upon reasonable cause, of the commission of a felony by the person to be arrested; or

(c) When such arrest was made pursuant to the requirements of Penal Code Sections 142, 838 or 839.
(Amended by Stats.1957, c. 2147, p. 3806, § 5.)

§ 847.5. Fugitive admitted to bail in another state; affidavit; hearing; warrant for arrest; order for return

If a person has been admitted to bail in another state, escapes bail, and is present in this State, the bail bondsman or other person who is bail for such fugitive, may file with a magistrate in the county where the fugitive is present an affidavit stating the name and whereabouts of the fugitive, the offense with which the alleged fugitive was charged or of which he was convicted, the time and place of same, and the particulars in which the fugitive has violated the terms of his bail, and may request the issuance of a warrant for arrest of the fugitive, and the issuance, after hearing, of an order authorizing the affiant to return the fugitive to the jurisdiction from which he escaped bail. The magistrate may require such additional evidence under oath as he deems necessary to decide the issue. If he concludes that there is probable cause for believing that the person alleged to be a fugitive is such, he may issue a warrant for his arrest. The magistrate shall notify the district attorney of such action and shall direct him to investigate the case and determine the facts of the matter. When the fugitive is brought before him pursuant to the warrant, the magistrate shall set a time and place for hearing, and shall advise the fugitive of his right to counsel and to produce evidence at the hearing. He may admit the fugitive to bail pending the hearing. The district attorney shall appear at the hearing. If, after hearing, the magistrate is satisfied from the evidence that the person is a fugitive he may issue an order authorizing affiant to return the fugitive to the jurisdiction from which he escaped bail.

A bondsman or other person who is bail for a fugitive admitted to bail in another state who takes the fugitive into custody, except pursuant to an order issued under this section, is guilty of a misdemeanor.
(Added by Stats.1961, c. 2185, p. 4526, § 1.)

§ 848. Arrest by officer; compliance with warrant

Duty of officer arresting with warrant. An officer making an arrest, in obedience to a warrant, must proceed with the person arrested as commanded by the warrant, or as provided by law.
(Enacted 1872.)

§ 849. Arrest without warrant; duty to take prisoner before magistrate and file complaint; release from custody

(a) When an arrest is made without a warrant by a peace officer or private person, the person arrested, if not otherwise released, shall, without unnecessary delay, be taken before the nearest or most accessible magistrate in the county in which the offense is triable, and a complaint stating the charge against the arrested person shall be laid before such magistrate.

(b) Any peace officer may release from custody, instead of taking such person before a magistrate, any person arrested without a warrant whenever:

(1) He is satisfied that there are insufficient grounds for making a criminal complaint against the person arrested.

(2) The person arrested was arrested for intoxication only, and no further proceedings are desirable.

(3) The person was arrested only for being under the influence of a narcotic, drug, or restricted dangerous drug and such person is delivered to a facility or hospital for treatment and no further proceedings are desirable.

§ 849

(c) Any record of arrest of a person released pursuant to paragraphs (1) and (3) of subdivision (b) shall include a record of release. Thereafter, such arrest shall not be deemed an arrest, but a detention only.
(Amended by Stats.1971, c. 438, p. 898, § 154.)

§ 849.5. Arrest without filing of accusatory pleading; record; arrest deemed detention

In any case in which a person is arrested and released and no accusatory pleading is filed charging him with an offense, any record of arrest of the person shall include a record of release. Thereafter, the arrest shall not be deemed an arrest, but a detention only.
(Added by Stats.1975, c. 1117, p. 2709, § 1.)

Notes of Decisions

In general

Risk of improper uses of an arrest record have been greatly diminished by significant legislative and executive action; for example, the legislature has provided in effect that a substantial proportion of arrests not resulting in conviction shall not be recorded as arrests but simply as "detentions," and the legislature has taken a number of steps to insure that a record of arrest or detention be complete, i. e., that it also show the final disposition of the charge. Loder v. Municipal Court for San Diego Judicial Dist. of San Diego County (1976) 132 Cal.Rptr. 464, 553 P.2d 624.

§ 850. Telegraphic warrant; authorization; effect; proceedings under warrant

(a) A telegraphic copy of a warrant or an abstract of a warrant may be sent by telegraph, teletype, or any other electronic devices, to one or more peace officers, and such copy or abstract is as effectual in the hands of any officer, and he shall proceed in the same manner under it, as though he held the original warrant issued by a magistrate or the issuing authority or agency.

(b) An abstract of the warrant as herein referred to shall contain the following information: the warrant number, the charge, the court or agency of issuance, the subject's name, address and description, the bail, the name of the issuing magistrate or authority, and if the offense charged is a misdemeanor, whether the warrant has been certified for night service.
(Amended by Stats.1971, c. 194, p. 261, § 1.)

Notes of Decisions

In general

Statutory provisions that where no criminal complaint is filed any arrest shall be deemed a detention only (§ 849) and that releasing officer shall issue certificate describing action as a detention (§ 851.6) were not the equivalent of giving minors who were released without being formally charged with offense for which they were arrested the relief of having records sealed and being able to claim that they were never taken into custody, and failure to provide such relief constituted denial of equal protection. McMahon v. Municipal Court of Burbank Judicial Dist., Los Angeles County, 85 Cal.Rptr. 782, 6 C.A.3d 194.

An arrested person has the right to complete a telephone call to an attorney who may visit prisoner at either the prisoner's request or at the request of a relative or friend. People v. Downer (1962) 22 Cal.Rptr. 347, 372 P.2d 107, 57 C.2d 800.

Showing that accused, who was arrested for drunken driving, was afforded his statutory right at booking to make one telephone call did not show that he was given opportunity to procure physician to test his blood for alcoholic content. McCormick v. Municipal Court, Los Angeles Judicial Dist. (1961) 16 Cal.Rptr. 211, 195 C.A.2d 819.

Under this section, the right arises immediately after booking and lasts for indefinite time, until accused has no more need thereof. Ex parte Newbern (1961) 11 Cal.Rptr. 547, 360 P.2d 43, 55 C.2d 500.

Enumeration of attorney, employer, or a relative, as a person who may be called by a person arrested immediately after he is booked is permissive rather than exclusive, and local authorities may not deny an accused right to telephone anyone other than persons enumerated, and such right extends to a bail bondsman. Id.

§ 851. Telegraphic warrant; filing certified copy in telegraph office; return of original

Every officer causing telegraphic copies or abstracts of warrants to be sent, must certify as correct, and file in the telegraphic office from which such copies are sent, a copy of the warrant, and must return the original with a statement of his action thereunder.
(Amended by Stats.1965, c. 1990, p. 4518, § 1.)

§ 851.5. Right of arrested person to make telephone call; posting sign

(a) Immediately upon being booked, and, except where physically impossible, no later than three hours after arrest, an arrested person has the right to make at least two completed telephone calls, as described in subdivision (b).

The arrested person shall be entitled to make at least two such calls at no expense if the calls are completed to telephone numbers within the local calling area.

(b) At any police facility or place where an arrestee is detained, a sign containing the following information in bold block type shall be posted in a conspicuous place:

That the arrestee has the right to free telephone calls within the local dialing area, or at his own expense if outside the local area, to two of the following:

(1) An attorney of his choice or, if he has no funds, the public defender or other attorney assigned by the court to assist indigents, whose telephone number shall be posted. This phone call shall not be monitored, eavesdropped upon, or recorded.

(2) A bail bondsman.

(3) A relative or other person.

(c) These telephone calls shall be given immediately upon request, or as soon as practicable.

(d) This provision shall not abrogate a law enforcement officer's duty to advise a suspect of his right to counsel or of any other right.

(e) Any public officer or employee who willfully deprives an arrested person of any right granted by this section is guilty of a misdemeanor.
(Added by Stats.1975, c. 1200, p. 2966, § 2.)
Former section 851.5 was repealed by Stats.1975, c. 1200, p. 2966, § 1.

§ 851.6. Release of person arrested without warrant or filing of accusatory pleading; issuance of detention certificate; form; deletion from arrest records

(a) In any case in which a person is arrested and released pursuant to paragraph (1) or (3) of subdivision (b) of Section 849, the person shall be issued a certificate, signed by the releasing officer or his superior officer, describing the action as a detention.

(b) In any case in which a person is arrested and released and no accusatory pleading is filed charging him with an offense, the person shall be issued a certificate by the law enforcement agency which arrested him describing the action as a detention.

(c) The Attorney General shall prescribe the form and content of such certificate.

(d) Any reference to the action as an arrest shall be deleted from the arrest records of the arresting agency and of the Bureau of Criminal Identification and Investigation of the Department of Justice. Thereafter, any such record of the action shall refer to it as a detention.
(Amended by Stats.1975, c. 1117, p. 2709, § 1.5.)

§ 851.7. Petition to seal court records by person arrested for misdemeanor while a minor; grounds; exceptions

(a) Any person who has been arrested for a misdemeanor, with or without a warrant, while a minor, may, during or after minority, petition the court in which the proceedings occurred, or, if there were no court proceedings, the court in whose jurisdiction the arrest occurred, for an order sealing the records in the case, including any records of arrest and detention, if any of the following occurred:

(1) He was released pursuant to paragraph (1) of subdivision (b) of Section 849.

(2) Proceedings against him were dismissed, or he was discharged, without a conviction.

(3) He was acquitted.

(b) If the court finds that the petitioner is eligible for relief under subdivision (a), it shall issue its order granting the relief prayed for. Thereafter, the arrest, detention, and any further proceedings in the case shall be deemed not to have occurred, and the petitioner may answer accordingly any question relating to their occurrence.

(c) This section applies to arrests and any further proceedings that occurred before, as well as those that occur after, the effective date of this section.

(d) This section does not apply to any person taken into custody pursuant to Section 625 of the Welfare and Institutions Code, or to any case within the scope of Section 781 of the Welfare and Institutions Code, unless, after a finding of unfitness for the juvenile court or otherwise, there were criminal proceedings in the case, not culminating in conviction. If there were criminal proceedings not culminating in conviction, this section shall be applicable to such criminal proceedings if such proceedings are otherwise within the scope of this section.

(e) This section does not apply to arrests for, and any further proceedings relating to, any of the following:

(1) Offenses for which registration is required under Section 290.

(2) Offenses under Division 10 (commencing with Section 11000) of the Health and Safety Code.

(3) Offenses under the Vehicle Code or any local ordinance relating to the operation, stopping, standing, or parking of a vehicle.

(f) In any action or proceeding based upon defamation, a court, upon a showing of good cause, may order any records sealed under this section to be opened and admitted in evidence. The records shall be confidential and shall be available for inspection only by the court, jury, parties, counsel for the parties, and any other person who is authorized by the court to inspect them. Upon the judgment in the action or proceeding becoming final, the court shall order the records sealed.

§ 851.7

(g) This section shall apply in any case in which a person was under the age of 21 at the time of the commission of an offense as to which this section is made applicable if such offense was committed prior to March 7, 1973.
(Amended by Stats.1974, c. 401, p. 986, § 1.)

Notes of Decisions

Validity

This section permitting a minor who has been arrested for a misdemeanor to petition for an order sealing records in event proceedings against him are dismissed, or he is discharged, without a conviction is unconstitutional as amounting to a denial of equal protection insofar as it prohibits sealing of arrest records of narcotics offenses charged as misdemeanors. People v. Pruett (1975) 124 Cal.Rptr. 273, 51 C.A.3d 329.

In general

Application of this section providing that any minor who has been arrested for a misdemeanor, treated as an adult, but not convicted of offense, may at any time petition court to order the record in the case be sealed, and of Welf. & Inst.C. § 781 providing that a juvenile court record may be sealed when juvenile reaches his majority or upon expiration of five years from date on which jurisdiction of juvenile court terminates does not devolve upon any invidious discrimination between youths of different ages. T. N. G. v. Superior Court of City and County of San Francisco (1971) 94 Cal.Rptr. 813, 484 P.2d 981, 4 C.3d 767.

§ 851.8. Motion to seal records on acquittal if person appears to judge to be factually innocent; rights of defendant under order

Whenever a person is acquitted of a charge and it appears to the judge presiding at the trial wherein such acquittal occurred that the defendant was factually innocent of the charge, the judge may order that the records in the case be sealed, including any record of arrest or detention, upon the written or oral motion of any party in the case or the court, and with notice to all parties to the case. If such an order is made, the court shall give to the defendant a copy of such order and inform the defendant that he may thereafter state that he was not arrested for such charge and that he was found innocent of such charge by the court.
(Added by Stats.1975, c. 904, p. 2002, § 1.)

Notes of Decisions

In general

Arrest records and all other documents in the case may be sealed upon request whenever a person charged with any offense has been acquitted and it appears to the judge that he was "factually innocent"; and in that event, the court must inform the defendant that he may thereafter state that he was not arrested for such charge and that he was found innocent of such charge by the court. Loder v. Municipal Court for San Diego Judicial Dist. of San Diego County (1976) 132 Cal.Rptr. 464, 553 P.2d 624.

§ 852. Short title

This chapter may be cited as the Uniform Act on Fresh Pursuit.
(Added by Stats.1937, c. 301, p. 661, § 1.)

§ 852.1. Words and phrases

As used in this chapter:

(a) "State" means any State of the United States and the District of Columbia.

(b) "Peace officer" means any peace officer or member of any duly organized State, county, or municipal peace unit or police force of another State.

(c) "Fresh Pursuit" includes close pursuit and hot pursuit.
(Added by Stats.1937, c. 301, p. 661, § 1.)

§ 852.2. Foreign peace officer in fresh pursuit; authority to arrest and hold fugitive

Any peace officer of another State, who enters this State in fresh pursuit, and continues within this State in fresh pursuit, of a person in order to arrest him on the ground that he has committed a felony in the other State, has the same authority to arrest and hold the person in custody, as peace officers of this State have to arrest and hold a person in custody on the ground that he has committed a felony in this State.
(Added by Stats.1937, c. 301, p. 662, § 1.)

§ 853.5. Infractions; release procedures

Except as otherwise provided by law, in any case in which a person is arrested for an offense declared to be an infraction, the person may be released according to the procedures set forth by this chapter for the release of persons arrested for an offense declared to be a misdemeanor.
(Added by Stats.1971, c. 1379, p. 2729, § 3.)

§ 853.6. Notice to appear; contents; bail; warrant

(a) In any case in which a person is arrested for an offense declared to be a misdemeanor and does not demand to be taken before a magistrate, such person may, instead of being taken before a magistrate, be released according to the procedures set forth by this chapter. If the arresting officer or his superior determines that the person should be released, such officer or superior shall prepare in duplicate a written notice to appear in court, containing the name and address of such person, the offense charged, and the time and place where and when such person shall appear in court. If the person is not released prior to being booked and the officer in charge of the booking or his superior determines that the person should be released, such officer or superior shall prepare such written notice to appear in court.

(b) Unless waived by the person, the time specified in the notice to appear must be at least five (5) days after arrest.

(c) The place specified in the notice shall be the court of the magistrate before whom the person would be taken if the requirement of taking an arrested person before a magistrate were complied with, or shall be an officer authorized by such court to receive a deposit of bail.

(d) The officer shall deliver one copy of the notice to appear to the arrested person, and the arrested person, in order to secure release, must give his written promise so to appear in court by signing the duplicate notice which shall be retained by the officer. Thereupon the arresting officer shall forthwith release the person arrested from custody.

(e) The officer shall, as soon as practicable, file the duplicate notice with the magistrate specified therein. Thereupon the magistrate may fix the amount of bail which in his judgment, in accordance with the provisions of Section 1275 of the Penal Code, will be reasonable and sufficient for the appearance of the defendant and shall indorse upon the notice a statement signed by him in the form set forth in Section 815a of this code. The defendant may, prior to the date upon which he promised to appear in court, deposit with the magistrate the amount of bail thus set. Thereafter, at the time when the case is called for arraignment before the magistrate, if the defendant shall not appear, either in person or by counsel, the magistrate may declare the bail forfeited, and may in his discretion order that no further proceedings shall be had in such case, unless the defendant has been charged with violation of Section 374b or 374e of this code or of Section 11357, 11360, or 13002 of the Health and Safety Code, or a violation punishable under Section 5008.7 of the Public Resources Code, and he has previously been convicted of a violation of such section or punishable under such section, except in cases where the magistrate finds that undue hardship will be imposed upon the defendant by requiring him to appear, the magistrate may declare the bail forfeited and order that no further proceedings shall be had in such case.

Upon the making of such order that no further proceedings be had, all sums deposited as bail shall forthwith be paid into the county treasury for distribution pursuant to Section 1463 of this code.

(f) No warrant shall issue on such charge for the arrest of a person who has given such written promise to appear in court, unless and until he has violated such promise or has failed to deposit bail, to appear for arraignment, trial or judgment, or to comply with the terms and provisions of the judgment, as required by law.

(g) The officer shall indicate on the notice to appear whether he desires the arrested person to be booked as defined in subdivision 21 of Section 7 of this code. In such event, the magistrate shall, before the proceedings are finally concluded, order the defendant to be booked by the arresting agency.

(h) A peace officer may use the written notice to appear procedure set forth in this section for any misdemeanor offense in which the officer has arrested a person pursuant to Section 836 or in which he has taken custody of a person pursuant to Section 847.

(i) If the arrested person is not released pursuant to the provisions of this chapter prior to being booked by the arresting agency, then at the time of booking the arresting officer, the officer in charge of such booking or his superior officer, or any other person designated by a city or county for this purpose shall make an immediate investigation into the background of the person to determine whether he should be released pursuant to the provisions of this chapter. Such investigation shall include, but need not be limited to, the person's name, address, length of residence at that address, length of residence within this state, marital and family status, employment, length of that employment, prior arrest record, and such other facts relating to the person's arrest which would bear on the question of his release pursuant to the provisions of this chapter.

(j) Whenever any person is arrested by a peace officer for a misdemeanor, other than an offense described in subdivision (b) of Section 11357 or subdivision (c) of Section 11360 of the Health and Safety Code, and is not released with a written notice to appear in court pursuant to this chapter, the arresting officer shall indicate, on a form to be established by his employing law enforcement agency, which of the following was a reason for such nonrelease:

(1) The person arrested was so intoxicated that he could have been a danger to himself or to others.

(2) The person arrested required medical examination or medical care or was otherwise unable to care for his own safety.

(3) The person was arrested for one or more of the offenses listed in Section 40302 of the Vehicle Code.

(4) There were one or more outstanding arrest warrants for the person.

(5) The person could not provide satisfactory evidence of personal identification.

(6) The prosecution of the offense or offenses for which the person was arrested or the prosecution of any other offense or offenses would be jeopardized by immediate release of the person arrested.

(7) There was a reasonable likelihood that the offense or offenses would continue or resume, or that the safety of persons or property would be imminently endangered by release of the person arrested.

(8) The person arrested demanded to be taken before a magistrate or refused to sign the notice to appear.

(9) Any other reason, which shall be specifically stated on the form by the arresting officer.

Such form shall be filed with the arresting agency as soon as practicable and shall be made available to any party having custody of the arrested person, subsequent to the arresting officer, and to any person authorized by law to release him from custody before trial.

(Amended by Stats.1976, c. 270, p. ——, § 1.)

OF CRIMINAL PROCEDURE § 853.6

Official Forms

[Form for Uniform Misdemeanor and Traffic Citation]
REVERSE SIDE OF COURT COPY

BAIL:
The defendant is to be admitted to bail in the sum of _____ dollars.

_____
Judge

BOOKING: (To be ordered only on request of arresting officer)
The defendant is ordered to report to the [Name of the arresting agency] at [Address] and to be booked as provided by P.C. 853.6(g).

_____
Judge

(THIS SPACE FOR REMITTANCE CONTROL MACHINE ENTRIES)

[B2815]

§ 853.7

PENAL CODE

§ 853.7. Violation of promise to appear as misdemeanor

Official Forms

[Form for Uniform Traffic Citation]

REVERSE SIDE OF CITED PERSON'S COPY

IMPORTANT—READ CAREFULLY

WARNING:

Willful failure to appear as promised is a separate violation for which you may be arrested and punished by 6 MONTHS IN JAIL AND/OR $500.00 FINE, regardless of the disposition of the original charge (V.C. 40508). In addition, the Department of Motor Vehicles is REQUIRED TO WITHHOLD the issuance or renewal of your driver's license, and may revoke or suspend your driving privilege, if you violate your written promise to appear.

INFRACTIONS:

If the infraction box on the reverse side is checked, you may request a hearing by mailing a check or money order for the proper amount of deposit (see bail information below) by registered or certified mail at least 5 days before the required appearance date, indicating whether you wish the officer to be present. The court will notify you of your hearing date and time. Use of this procedure waives statutory limits on time for trial and failure to appear at trial is a misdemeanor.

BAIL INFORMATION:

The clerk of the court in which you have promised to appear is authorized to accept a deposit of bail to guarantee your appearance. For some offenses the court may accept this deposit by mail, and permit it to be forfeited, thereby relieving you of your duty to appear. (Under Veh. Code § 13103 a bail forfeiture is a conviction of the charged offense.)

A courtesy notice will be mailed to the address shown on your citation indicating whether an appearance is mandatory or indicating the required deposit which may be forfeited. If you do not receive such notice, you must contact the court, giving your citation date and number, or appear on or before the indicated appearance date. Make checks or money orders payable to the Clerk of the Court.

OFFICE OF THE CLERK:
 Hours:
 Address:
 Telephone:

JUVENILES:
You must appear with license at the date and time indicated, accompanied by parent or guardian.

DRIVERS LICENSE AND VEHICLE REGISTRATION VIOLATIONS:
You must bring a valid license or registration certificate at the time of your appearance if you have one or can lawfully obtain one, or have the correction certified below.

MECHANICAL DEFECTS:
If you are cited for a mechanical defect, you are directed to make the proper corrections and have that correction certified below or obtain other satisfactory evidence of correction. You may be required to explain to the judge any failure to make necessary corrections.

CERTIFICATE OF CORRECTION				
Section Violated	Signature of person certifying correction	Badge No.	Agency	Date

(THIS SPACE FOR REMITTANCE CONTROL MACHINE ENTRIES)

[B7161]

OF CRIMINAL PROCEDURE

§ 853.7

[Form for Uniform Misdemeanor and Traffic Citation]

REVERSE SIDE OF CITED PERSON'S COPY

IMPORTANT—READ CAREFULLY

WARNING:

Willful failure to appear as promised is a separate violation for which you may be arrested and punished by 6 MONTHS IN JAIL AND/OR $500.00 FINE, regardless of the disposition of the original charge (V.C. 40508, P.C. 853.7). In addition, the Department of Motor Vehicles is REQUIRED TO WITHHOLD the issuance or renewal of your driver's license, and may revoke or suspend your driving privilege, if you violate your written promise to appear when a traffic offense has been charged.

INFRACTIONS:

If the infraction box on the reverse side is checked, you may request a hearing by mailing a check or money order for the proper amount of deposit (see bail information below) by registered or certified mail at least 5 days before the required appearance date, indicating whether you wish the officer to be present. The court will notify you of your hearing date and time. Use of this procedure waives statutory limits on time for trial and failure to appear at trial is a misdemeanor.

BAIL INFORMATION:

The clerk of the court in which you have promised to appear is authorized to accept a deposit of bail to guarantee your appearance. For some offenses the court may accept this deposit by mail, and permit it to be forfeited, thereby relieving you of your duty to appear. (Under Veh. Code § 13103 a bail forfeiture is a conviction of the charged offense.)

A courtesy notice will be mailed to the address shown on your citation indicating whether an appearance is mandatory or indicating the required deposit which may be forfeited. If you do not receive such notice, you must contact the court, giving your citation date and number, or appear on or before the indicated appearance date. Make checks or money orders payable to the Clerk of the Court.

OFFICE OF THE CLERK:

  Hours:
  Address:
  Telephone:

JUVENILES:

You must appear with license at the date and time indicated, accompanied by parent or guardian.

DRIVERS LICENSE AND VEHICLE REGISTRATION VIOLATIONS:

You must bring a valid license or registration certificate at the time of your appearance if you have one or can lawfully obtain one, or have the correction certified below.

MECHANICAL DEFECTS:

If you are cited for a mechanical defect, you are directed to make the proper corrections and have that correction certified below or obtain other satisfactory evidence of correction. You may be required to explain to the judge any failure to make necessary corrections.

CERTIFICATE OF CORRECTION				
Section Violated	Signature of person certifying correction	Badge No.	Agency	Date

(THIS SPACE FOR REMITTANCE CONTROL MACHINE ENTRIES)

[B2811]

§ 853.9. Copy of written notice to appear as complaint; procedure

(a) Whenever written notice to appear has been prepared, delivered, and filed with the court pursuant to the provisions of Section 853.6 of this code, an exact and legible duplicate copy of the notice when filed with the magistrate, in lieu of a verified complaint, shall constitute a complaint to which the defendant may plead "guilty" or "nolo contendere."

If, however, the defendant violates his promise to appear in court, or does not deposit lawful bail, or pleads other than "guilty" or "nolo contendere" to the offense charged, a complaint shall be filed which shall conform to the provisions of this code and which shall be deemed to be an original complaint; and thereafter proceedings shall be had as provided by law, except that a defendant may, by an agreement in writing, subscribed by him and filed with the court, waive the filing of a verified complaint and elect that the prosecution may proceed upon a written notice to appear.

(b) Notwithstanding the provisions of subdivision (a) of this section, whenever the written notice to appear has been prepared on a form approved by the Judicial Council, an exact and legible duplicate copy of the notice when filed with the magistrate shall constitute a complaint to which the defendant may enter a plea and, if the notice to appear is verified, upon which a warrant may be issued. If the notice to appear is not verified, the defendant may, at the time of arraignment, request that a verified complaint be filed.

(Amended by Stats.1969, c. 43, p. 152, § 2.)

OF CRIMINAL PROCEDURE
Official Forms

§ 853.9

[Form for Uniform Traffic Citation]

FACE SIDE OF THE FORM

CITY OF

NOTICE TO APPEAR

NO. 0001

| DATE 19 | TIME M | DAY OF WEEK |

NAME (FIRST, MIDDLE, LAST)

RESIDENCE ADDRESS — CITY

BUSINESS ADDRESS — CITY

DRIVERS LICENSE NO. — STATE — CLASS — BIRTHDATE

SEX M F | HAIR | EYES | HEIGHT | WEIGHT | OTHER DES.

VEHICLE LICENSE NO. — STATE — PASSENGERS M F

YEAR OF VEH. | MAKE | MODEL | BODY STYLE | COLOR

REGISTERED OWNER OR LESSEE

ADDRESS OF OWNER OR LESSEE

VIOLATION(S) — CODE — SECTION — DESCRIPTION — ☐ INFRACTION

APPROX. SPEED | PF/MAX SPD. | VEH SPD LMT | SAFE SPD | CITY OF OCCUR

LOCATION OF VIOLATION(S)
ON

COMMENTS: (WEATHER, ROAD & TRAFFIC CONDITIONS)

I CERTIFY UNDER PENALTY OF PERJURY THAT THE FOREGOING IS TRUE AND CORRECT. EXECUTED AT THE PLACE AND ON THE DATE SHOWN ABOVE.
OFFICER   SERIAL NO.

N W E S

DIVISION OR AREA | DETAIL OR BEAT | COUNTY CODE | VACATION DATES TO

WITHOUT ADMITTING GUILT, I PROMISE TO APPEAR AT THE TIME AND PLACE CHECKED BELOW.

X SIGNATURE

BEFORE A JUDGE OR A CLERK OF THE MUNICIPAL OR JUSTICE COURT
TELEPHONE: ADDRESS
☐ JUVENILE COURT, TRAFFIC DIVISION
☐ DATE 19   TIME M   ☐ WITHIN 15 DAYS
☐ OR YOU MAY APPEAR ON THE NIGHT(S) OF   AT   P.M.

FORM APPROVED BY THE JUDICIAL COUNCIL OF CALIFORNIA.
REV. 1-1-76 V.C. 40500(B) 40513(B)   SEE REVERSE SIDE

▨ Grey areas indicate spaces subject to local or agency requirements.

[B7159]

§ 853.9

PENAL CODE

[Form for Uniform Misdemeanor Citation]

FACE SIDE OF THE FORM

CITY OF _____

NOTICE TO APPEAR

NO. 0001

| DATE 19 | TIME M | DAY OF WEEK |

NAME (FIRST, MIDDLE, LAST)

RESIDENCE ADDRESS _____ CITY _____

BUSINESS ADDRESS _____ CITY _____

DRIVERS LICENSE NO. _____ STATE _____ CLASS _____ BIRTHDATE _____

| SEX M F | HAIR | EYES | HEIGHT | WEIGHT | OTHER DES |

EMPLOYED BY _____ OCCUPATION _____

BIRTHPLACE _____ SOCIAL SECURITY NO. _____

VEHICLE LICENSE NO. _____ STATE _____

| YEAR OF VEH. | MAKE | MODEL | BODY STYLE | COLOR |

OFFENSE(S) | CODE | SECTION | DESCRIPTION

_____
_____
_____
_____
_____
_____

EVIDENCE SEIZED _____ BOOKING REQUIRED ☐

LOCATION OFFENSE(S) COMMITTED

☐ OFFENSE(S) NOT COMMITTED IN MY PRESENCE, CERTIFIED ON INFORMATION AND BELIEF. I CERTIFY UNDER PENALTY OF PERJURY THAT THE FOREGOING IS TRUE AND CORRECT. EXECUTED ON THE DATE SHOWN ABOVE AT

ISSUING OFFICER _____ CALIF. | SERIAL NO.
                              (PLACE)

NAME OF ARRESTING OFFICER - IF DIFFERENT FROM ABOVE | SERIAL NO. | VACATION DATES TO

WITHOUT ADMITTING GUILT, I PROMISE TO APPEAR AT THE TIME AND PLACE CHECKED BELOW.

X SIGNATURE _____

BEFORE A JUDGE OR A CLERK OF THE MUNICIPAL OR JUSTICE COURT
(ADDRESS)

| DATE 19 | TIME M | WITHIN 5 DAYS |

FORM APPROVED BY THE JUDICIAL COUNCIL OF CALIFORNIA. REV. 11-10-69 P.C. 853.9   SEE REVERSE SIDE

Grey areas indicate spaces subject to local or agency requirements.   [B2772]

OF CRIMINAL PROCEDURE § 853.9

[Form for Uniform Misdemeanor and Traffic Citation]
FACE SIDE OF THE FORM

CITY OF

NOTICE TO APPEAR

NO. 0001

| DATE 19 | TIME M | DAY OF WEEK |

NAME (FIRST, MIDDLE, LAST)

RESIDENCE ADDRESS — CITY

BUSINESS ADDRESS — CITY

DRIVERS LICENSE NO. — STATE — CLASS — BIRTHDATE

SEX M F | HAIR | EYES | HEIGHT | WEIGHT | OTHER DES.

VEHICLE LICENSE NO. — STATE — PASSENGERS M F

YEAR OF VEH. | MAKE | MODEL | BODY STYLE | COLOR

REGISTERED OWNER OR LESSEE

ADDRESS OF OWNER OR LESSEE

VIOLATION(S)   CODE   SECTION   DESCRIPTION   ☐ INFRACTION
                                              ☐ BOOKING REQUIRED

APPROX. SPEED | PF/MAX SPD. | VEH SPD LMT | SAFE SPD | CITY OF OCCUR

LOCATION OF VIOLATION(S)
ON

COMMENTS: (WEATHER, ROAD & TRAFFIC CONDITIONS)

☐ OFFENSE(S) NOT COMMITTED IN MY PRESENCE. CERTIFIED ON INFORMATION AND BELIEF.
I CERTIFY UNDER PENALTY OF PERJURY THAT THE FOREGOING IS TRUE AND CORRECT.
EXECUTED ON THE DATE SHOWN ABOVE AT

ISSUING OFFICER _____ CALIF.   SERIAL NO.
                      (PLACE)

NAME OF ARRESTING OFFICER, IF DIFFERENT FROM ABOVE | SERIAL NO. | VACATION DATES TO

WITHOUT ADMITTING GUILT, I PROMISE TO APPEAR AT THE TIME AND PLACE CHECKED BELOW.

X _____ SIGNATURE

BEFORE A JUDGE OR A CLERK OF THE MUNICIPAL OR JUSTICE COURT
TELEPHONE: ADDRESS
☐ JUVENILE COURT, TRAFFIC DIVISION
☐ DATE 19   TIME   M   ☐ WITHIN 15 DAYS
☐ OR YOU MAY APPEAR
   ON THE NIGHT(S) OF   AT   P.M.

FORM APPROVED BY THE JUDICIAL COUNCIL OF CALIFORNIA.
REV. 1-1-76 V.C. 40500(B) 40513(B) P.C. 853.9   SEE REVERSE SIDE

▒▒ **Grey areas indicate spaces subject to local or agency requirements.**   [B2812]

137

§ 853.9   PENAL CODE

[Form for Uniform Misdemeanor Citation]
FACE SIDE OF THE FORM

[Form image: Notice to Appear, No. 0001, with fields for City, Date, Time, Day of Week, Name, Residence Address, Business Address, Driver's License No., State, Class, Birthdate, Sex, Hair, Eyes, Height, Weight, Other Description, Employed By, Occupation, Birthplace, Social Security No., Vehicle License No., State, Year of Vehicle, Make, Model, Body Style, Color, Offense(s), Code, Section, Description, Evidence Seized, Booking Required, Location Offense(s) Committed, Issuing Officer, Place, Serial No., Name of Arresting Officer, Vacation Dates, Signature, Before a Judge or Clerk of the Municipal or Justice Court, Address, Date, Time, Within 5 Days. Form approved by the Judicial Council of California, Rev. 11-10-69 P.C. 853.9. See Reverse Side.]

Grey areas indicate spaces subject to local or agency requirements.
[A1090]

OF CRIMINAL PROCEDURE § 853.9

[Form for Uniform Misdemeanor and Traffic Citation]
FACE SIDE OF THE FORM

```
CITY OF _____

NOTICE TO APPEAR
                                            NO. 0001
DATE          TIME              DAY OF WEEK
        19              M
NAME (FIRST, MIDDLE, LAST)
RESIDENCE ADDRESS               CITY
BUSINESS ADDRESS                CITY
DRIVERS LICENSE NO.   STATE     CLASS  BIRTHDATE
SEX   HAIR    EYES    HEIGHT    WEIGHT  OTHER DES.
M F
VEHICLE LICENSE NO.   STATE     PASSENGERS
                                    M  F
YEAR OF VEH.  MAKE    MODEL   BODY STYLE  COLOR
REGISTERED OWNER OR LESSEE
ADDRESS OF OWNER OR LESSEE
VIOLATION(S)  CODE  SECTION  DESCRIPTION  ☐ INFRACTION
                                          ☐ BOOKING
                                            REQUIRED

APPROX. SPEED | PF/MAX SPD. | VEH SPD LMT | SAFE SPD | CITY OF OCCUR
LOCATION OF VIOLATION(S)
ON
COMMENTS: (WEATHER, ROAD & TRAFFIC CONDITIONS)

☐ OFFENSE(S) NOT COMMITTED IN MY PRESENCE. CERTIFIED ON INFORMATION AND BELIEF.
I CERTIFY UNDER PENALTY OF PERJURY THAT THE FOREGOING IS TRUE AND CORRECT.
EXECUTED ON THE DATE SHOWN ABOVE AT
ISSUING OFFICER                            SERIAL NO.
_____ CALIF.
            (PLACE)
NAME OF ARRESTING OFFICER, IF DIFFERENT FROM ABOVE | SERIAL NO. | VACATION DATES
                                                                      TO
WITHOUT ADMITTING GUILT, I PROMISE TO APPEAR AT THE TIME AND PLACE
CHECKED BELOW.

X SIGNATURE
BEFORE A JUDGE OR A CLERK OF THE MUNICIPAL OR JUSTICE COURT
    TELEPHONE:              ADDRESS
☐ JUVENILE COURT, TRAFFIC DIVISION
☐ DATE           TIME                      ☐ WITHIN
        19              M                    15 DAYS
☐ OR YOU MAY APPEAR
  ON THE NIGHT(S) OF            AT              P.M.
FORM APPROVED BY THE JUDICIAL COUNCIL OF CALIFORNIA.
REV. 1-1-76 V.C. 40500(B) 40513(B) P.C. 853.9   SEE REVERSE SIDE
```

▒▒▒ Grey areas indicate spaces subject to local or agency requirements.

139   [B7163]

§ 854. Authority to pursue and retake prisoner at any time or place

May be at any time or in any place in the State. If a person arrested escaped or is rescued, the person from whose custody he escaped or was rescued, may immediately pursue and retake him at any time and in any place within the State.
(Enacted 1872.)

§ 855. Authority to break doors or windows to retake prisoner if admittance refused

May break open door or window if admittance refused. To retake the person escaping or rescued, the person pursuing may break open an outer or inner door or window of a dwelling house, if, after notice of his intention, he is refused admittance.
(Enacted 1872.)

§ 868. Exclusion of public at defendant's request; prosecuting witness entitled to attendance of person of own choosing

The magistrate must also, upon the request of the defendant, exclude from the examination every person except his clerk, court reporter and bailiff, the prosecutor and his counsel, the Attorney General, the district attorney of the county, the investigating officer, the officer having custody of a prisoner witness while the prisoner is testifying, the defendant and his counsel, and the officer having the defendant in custody; provided, however, that a prosecuting witness may, in the discretion of the court, be entitled for moral support to the attendance of one person of his or her own choosing otherwise not a witness. The person so chosen shall not discuss prior to or during the preliminary hearing the testimony of the prosecuting witness with any person, other than the prosecuting witness, who is a witness in the examination. Nothing in this section shall affect the right to exclude witnesses as provided in Section 867 of the Penal Code.
(Amended by Stats.1976, c. 1178, p. —, § 2.)

GRAND JURY

§ 868.5. Rape, sodomy or oral copulation charges; attendance of person of prosecuting witness's own choosing during testimony; disclosure of testimony; exclusion of person chosen

Notwithstanding any other provision of law, a prosecuting witness in a case involving a violation of Section 261, 286, or 288a shall be entitled for support to the attendance of one person of his or her own choosing, at the preliminary hearing and at the trial, during the testimony of the prosecuting witness otherwise not a witness, and otherwise not a person described in Section 1070 of the Evidence Code unless such person who is described in Section 1070 of the Evidence Code is related to the prosecuting witness as a parent, child, or sibling and does not make notes during the hearing. At the request of the defendant or defendant's counsel, the court shall order the person so chosen not to communicate any or all of the testimony of the prosecuting witness to any person during or after the preliminary hearing and up to the conclusion of the trial. If the person so chosen attempts to influence or affect or influences or affects in any manner the testimony of the prosecuting witness during the giving of such testimony, the court shall exclude such person and allow the prosecuting witness to choose another person pursuant to this section. The defendant may move to exclude the person chosen for good cause, and the court shall hear the motion out of the presence of the jury, if any. If the court grants the motion the prosecuting witness may choose another person pursuant to this section. Nothing in this section shall affect the right to exclude witnesses as provided in Section 867.
(Added by Stats.1978, c. 1310, p. —, § 1.)

§ 888. Grand jury defined

A grand jury is a body of the required number of persons returned from the citizens of the county before a court of competent jurisdiction, and sworn to inquire of public offenses committed or triable within the county.
(Amended by Stats.1963, c. 259, p. 1018, § 1.)

§ 888.2. Required number defined

As used in this title as applied to a grand jury, "required number" means 23 in a county having a population exceeding four million and 19 in other counties.
(Added by Stats.1963, c. 259, p. 1018, § 2.)

§ 889. Indictment defined

An indictment is an accusation in writing, presented by the grand jury to a competent court, charging a person with a public offense.
(Added by Stats.1959, c. 501, p. 2443, § 2.)

§ 891. Recording, listening to or observing grand jury proceedings; misdemeanor

Every person who, by any means whatsoever, willfully and knowingly, and without knowledge and consent of the grand jury, records, or attempts to record, all or part of the proceedings of any grand jury while it is deliberating or voting, or listens to or observes, or attempts to listen to or observe, the proceedings of any grand jury of which he is not a member while such jury is deliberating or voting is guilty of a misdemeanor.

This section is not intended to prohibit the taking of notes by a grand jury in connection with and solely for the purpose of assisting him in the performance of his duties as such juror.

(Added by Stats.1959, c. 501, p. 2443, § 2.)

§ 895. Estimate of number of jurors needed; order

During the month preceding the beginning of the fiscal year of the county, the superior court of each county shall make an order designating the estimated number of grand jurors that will, in the opinion of the court, be required for the transaction of the business of the court during the ensuing fiscal year as provided in Section 905.5.

(Amended by Stats.1974, c. 393, p. 976, § 1.)

§ 896. Selection and listing by court; investigation; jurors

(a) Immediately after such order is made, the court shall select the grand jurors required by personal interview for the purpose of ascertaining whether they possess the qualifications prescribed by subdivision (a) of Section 893. If a person so interviewed, in the opinion of the court, possesses such qualifications, in order for his name to be listed he shall sign a statement declaring that he will be available for jury service for the number of hours usually required of a member of the grand jury in that county.

(b) The selections shall be made of men and women who are not exempt from serving and who are suitable and competent to serve as grand jurors pursuant to Sections 893, 898, and 899. The court shall list the persons so selected and required by the order to serve as grand jurors during the ensuing fiscal year of the county, or until a new list of grand jurors is provided, and shall at once place this list in the possession of the county clerk.

(Amended by Stats.1974, c. 393, p. 976, § 2.)

§ 899. Proportionate selection of names; separate list

The names for the grand jury list shall be selected from the different wards, judicial districts, or supervisorial districts of the respective counties in proportion to the number of inhabitants therein, as nearly as the same can be estimated by the persons making the list. The grand jury list shall be kept separate and distinct from the trial jury list. In a county of the first class, the names for such list may be selected from the county at large.

(Amended by Stats.1969, c. 64, p. 186, § 1.)

§ 907. Failure to obey summons; attachment and fine

Any grand juror summoned, who willfully and without reasonable excuse fails to attend, may be attached and compelled to attend and the court may also impose a fine not exceeding fifty dollars ($50), upon which execution may issue. If the grand jury was not personally served, the fine shall not be imposed until upon an order to show cause an opportunity has been offered the grand juror to be heard.

(Added by Stats.1959, c. 501, p. 2446, § 2.)

§ 915. Privacy; inquiry into offenses; discharge

When the grand jury has been impaneled, sworn, and charged, it shall retire to a private room, and inquire into the offenses cognizable by it. On the completion of the business before the grand jury, the court shall discharge it.

(Added by Stats.1959, c. 501, p. 2448, § 2.)

§ 917. Inquiry into public offenses; presentment by indictment

The grand jury may inquire into all public offenses committed or triable within the county and present them to the court by indictment.

(Added by Stats.1959, c. 501, p. 2448, § 2.)

§ 918. Individual jurors; declaration of knowledge of offenses; investigation

If a member of a grand jury knows, or has reason to believe, that a public offense, triable within the county, has been committed, he may declare it to his fellow jurors, who may thereupon investigate it.

(Amended by Stats.1976, c. 895, p. ——, § 1.)

§ 919. Authorization to inquire about prisoners not indicted and duty to inquire as to county prisons, and corrupt misconduct in public office

(a) The grand jury may inquire into the case of every person imprisoned in the jail of the county of a criminal charge and not indicted.

(b) The grand jury shall inquire into the condition and management of the public prisons within the county.

(c) The grand jury shall inquire into the willful or corrupt misconduct in office of public officers of every description within the county.
(Amended by Stats.1976, c. 895, p. ——, § 2.)

§ 921. Access to public prisons and public records

The grand jury is entitled to free access, at all reasonable times, to the public prisons, and to the examination, without charge, of all public records within the county.
(Added by Stats.1959, c. 501, p. 2449, § 2.)

§ 922. Proceedings for removal of district, county or city officers

The powers and duties of the grand jury in connection with proceedings for the removal of district, county, or city officers are prescribed in Article 3 (commencing with Section 3060), Chapter 7, Division 4, Title 1, of the Government Code.
(Added by Stats.1959, c. 501, p. 2449, § 2.)

§ 923. Investigation of matters of criminal nature; presentation by attorney general

Whenever the Attorney General considers the public interest requires, he may, with or without the concurrence of the district attorney, direct the grand jury to convene for the investigation and consideration of such matters of a criminal nature as he desires to submit to it. He may take full charge of the presentation of such matters to the grand jury, issue subpoenas, prepare indictments, and do all other things incident thereto to the same extent as the district attorney may do.
(Added by Stats.1959, c. 501, p. 2449, § 2.)

§ 924. Wilful disclosure of making of information or indictment; misdemeanor

Every grand juror who willfully discloses the fact of an information or indictment having been made for a felony, until the defendant has been arrested, is guilty of a misdemeanor.
(Added by Stats.1959, c. 501, p. 2449, § 2.)

§ 924.1. Wilful disclosure of evidence, statement of juror or vote; misdemeanor

Every grand juror who, except when required by a court, willfully discloses any evidence adduced before the grand jury, or anything which he himself or any other member of the grand jury has said, or in what manner he or any other grand juror has voted on a matter before them, is guilty of a misdemeanor.
(Added by Stats.1959, c. 501, p. 2449, § 2.)

§ 924.2. Secrecy of deliberations and voting; court order for disclosure of testimony

Each grand juror shall keep secret whatever he himself or any other grand juror has said, or in what manner he or any other grand juror has voted on a matter before them. Any court may require a grand juror to disclose the testimony of a witness examined before the grand jury, for the purpose of ascertaining whether it is consistent with that given by the witness before the court, or to disclose the testimony given before the grand jury by any person, upon a charge against such person for perjury in giving his testimony or upon trial therefor.
(Added by Stats.1959, c. 501, p. 2449, § 2.)

§ 924.3. Privilege of juror as to statements and vote; exception in case of perjury

A grand juror cannot be questioned for anything he may say or any vote he may give in the grand jury relative to a matter legally pending before the jury, except for a perjury of which he may have been guilty in making an accusation or giving testimony to his fellow jurors.
(Added by Stats.1959, c. 501, p. 2449, § 2.)

§ 934. Advice from judge, district attorney or county counsel

The grand jury, may, at all times, ask the advice of the court, or the judge thereof, or of the district attorney, or of the county counsel. Unless such advice is asked, the judge of the court, or county counsel as to civil matters, shall not be present during the sessions of the grand jury.
(Amended by Stats.1961, c. 1940, p. 4092, § 1.)

§ 935. Appearance of district attorney

The district attorney of the county may at all times appear before the grand jury for the purpose of giving information or advice relative to any matter cognizable by the grand jury, and may interrogate

witnesses before the grand jury whenever he thinks it necessary. When a charge against or involving the district attorney, or assistant district attorney, or deputy district attorney, or anyone employed by or connected with the office of the district attorney is being investigated by the grand jury, such district attorney, or assistant district attorney, or deputy district attorney, or all or anyone or more of them, shall not be allowed to be present before such grand jury when such charge is being investigated, in an official capacity but only as a witness, and he shall only be present while a witness and after his appearance as such witness shall leave the place where the grand jury is holding its session.
(Added by Stats.1959, c. 501, p. 2451, § 2.)

§ 936. Special counsel and investigators

When requested so to do by the grand jury of any county, the Attorney General may employ special counsel and special investigators, whose duty it shall be to investigate and present the evidence in such investigation to such grand jury.

The services of such special counsel and special investigators shall be a county charge of such county.
(Added by Stats.1959, c. 501, p. 2451, § 2.)

§ 939.2. Subpoena of witnesses; issuance

A subpoena requiring the attendance of a witness before the grand jury may be signed and issued by the district attorney, his investigator or, upon request of the grand jury, by any judge of the superior court, for witnesses in the state, in support of the prosecution, for those witnesses whose testimony, in his opinion is material in an investigation before the grand jury, and for such other witnesses as the grand jury, upon an investigation pending before them, may direct.
(Amended by Stats.1971, c. 1196, p. 2292, § 1.)

§ 939.3. Self-incrimination; procedure

In any investigation or proceeding before a grand jury for any felony offense when a person refuses to answer a question or produce evidence of any other kind on the ground that he may be incriminated thereby, proceedings may be had under Section 1324.
(Added by Stats.1959, c. 501, p. 2453, § 2.)

§ 939.7. Evidence for defendant, authority to exclude; weighing evidence; order for production of explanatory evidence

The grand jury is not required to hear evidence for the defendant, but it shall weigh all the evidence submitted to it, and when it has reason to believe that other evidence within its reach will explain away the charge, it shall order the evidence to be produced, and for that purpose may require the district attorney to issue process for the witnesses.
(Added by Stats.1959, c. 501, p. 2454, § 2.)

§ 939.8. Sufficiency of evidence to warrant indictment

The grand jury shall find an indictment when all the evidence before it, taken together, if unexplained or uncontradicted, would, in its judgment, warrant a conviction by a trial jury.
(Added by Stats.1959, c. 501, p. 2454, § 2.)

§ 939.91. Reports or declarations that on evidence jury could not find indictment or that witness called for purpose not involving charge against witness

(a) A grand jury which investigates a charge against a person, and as a result thereof cannot find an indictment against such person, shall, at the request of such person and upon the approval of the court which impaneled the grand jury, report or declare that a charge against such person was investigated and that the grand jury could not as a result of the evidence presented find an indictment. The report or declaration shall be issued upon completion of the investigation of the suspected criminal conduct, or series of related suspected criminal conduct, and in no event beyond the end of the grand jury's term.

(b) A grand jury shall, at the request of the person called and upon the approval of the court which impaneled the grand jury, report or declare that any person called before the grand jury for a purpose, other than to investigate a charge against such person, was called only as a witness to an investigation which did not involve a charge against such person. The report or declaration shall be issued upon completion of the investigation of the suspected criminal conduct, or series of related suspected criminal conduct, and in no event beyond the end of the grand jury's term.
(Added by Stats.1975, c. 467, p. 970, § 1.)

§ 940. Concurrence of jurors; number; endorsement

An indictment cannot be found without concurrence of at least 14 grand jurors in a county in which the required number of members of the grand jury prescribed by Section 888.2 is 23, and at least 12 grand jurors in other counties. When so found it must be endorsed, "A true bill," and the endorsement must be signed by the foreman of the grand jury.
(Amended by Stats.1963, c. 1520, p. 3100, § 1.)

§ 943. Names of witnesses; insertion or indorsement

Names of witnesses inserted at foot of indictment. When an indictment is found, the names of the witnesses examined before the Grand Jury, or whose depositions may have been read before them, must be inserted at the foot of the indictment, or indorsed thereon, before it is presented to the Court.
(Enacted 1872.)

§ 945. Defendant not in custody; procedure upon finding

Proceedings when defendant is not in custody. When an indictment is found against a defendant not in custody, the same proceedings must be had as are prescribed in Sections 979 to 984, inclusive, against a defendant who fails to appear for arraignment.
(Enacted 1872.)

PLEADINGS

§ 950. Accusatory pleading; title of action; statement of offense

The accusatory pleading must contain:

1. The title of the action, specifying the name of the court to which the same is presented, and the names of the parties;

2. A statement of the public offense or offenses charged therein.
(Amended by Stats.1951, c. 1674, p. 3836, § 43.)

§ 951. Indictment or information; form

An indictment or information may be in substantially the following form: The people of the State of California against A. B. In the superior court of the State of California, in and for the county of _____. The grand jury (or the district attorney) of the county of _____ hereby accuses A. B. of a felony (or misdemeanor), to wit: (giving the name of the crime, as murder, burglary, etc.), in that on or about the _____ day of _____, 19___, in the county of _____, State of California, he (here insert statement of act or omission, as for example, "murdered C. D.").
(Amended by Stats.1927, c. 613, p. 1043, § 1.)

§ 952. Statement of offense

In charging an offense, each count shall contain, and shall be sufficient if it contains in substance, a statement that the accused has committed some public offense therein specified. Such statement may be made in ordinary and concise language without any technical averments or any allegations of matter not essential to be proved. It may be in the words of the enactment describing the offense or declaring the matter to be a public offense, or in any words sufficient to give the accused notice of the offense of which he is accused. In charging theft it shall be sufficient to allege that the defendant unlawfully took the labor or property of another.
(Amended by Stats.1929, c. 159, p. 303, § 1.)

§ 953. Defendant charged by fictitious or erroneous name; insertion of true name

When a defendant is charged by a fictitious or erroneous name, and in any stage of the proceedings his true name is discovered, it must be inserted in the subsequent proceedings, referring to the fact of his being charged by the name mentioned in the accusatory pleading.
(Amended by Stats.1951, c. 1674, p. 3836, § 44.)

§ 954. Charge of multiple offenses or different statements of same offense; consolidation of accusatory pleadings; election not required; conviction on multiple charges; statement in verdict or finding; separate trials; acquittal on some counts

An accusatory pleading may charge two or more different offenses connected together in their commission, or different statements of the same offense or two or more different offenses of the same class of crimes or offenses, under separate counts, and if two or more accusatory pleadings are filed in such cases in the same court, the court may order them to be consolidated. The prosecution is not required to elect between the different offenses or counts set forth in the accusatory pleading, but the defendant may be convicted of any number of the offenses charged, and each offense of which the defendant is convicted must be stated in the verdict or the finding of the

court; provided, that the court in which a case is triable, in the interests of justice and for good cause shown, may in its discretion order that the different offenses or counts set forth in the accusatory pleading be tried separately or divided into two or more groups and each of said groups tried separately. An acquittal of one or more counts shall not be deemed an acquittal of any other count.
(Amended by Stats.1951, c. 1674, p. 3836, § 45.)

§ 955. Pleading time of offense

The precise time at which the offense was committed need not be stated in the accusatory pleading, but it may be alleged to have been committed at any time before the finding or filing thereof, except where the time is a material ingredient in the offense.
(Amended by Stats.1951, c. 1674, p. 3837, § 46.)

§ 959. Sufficiency of accusatory pleading

The accusatory pleading is sufficient if it can be understood therefrom:

1. That it is filed in a court having authority to receive it, though the name of the court be not stated.

2. If an indictment, that it was found by a grand jury of the county in which the court was held, or if an information, that it was subscribed and presented to the court by the district attorney of the county in which the court was held.

3. If a complaint, that it is made and subscribed by some natural person and sworn to before some officer entitled to administer oaths.

4. That the defendant is named, or if his name is unknown, that he is described by a fictitious name, with a statement that his true name is to the grand jury, district attorney, or complainant, as the case may be, unknown.

5. That the offense charged therein is triable in the court in which it is filed, except in case of a complaint filed with a magistrate for the purposes of a preliminary examination.

6. That the offense was committed at some time prior to the filing of the accusatory pleading.
(Amended by Stats.1951, c. 1674, p. 3837, § 49.)

§ 961. Pleading presumptions or matters judicially noticed unnecessary

Neither presumptions of law, nor matters of which judicial notice is authorized or required to be taken, need be stated in an accusatory pleading.
(Amended by Stats.1965, c. 299, p. 1368, § 142.)

§ 965. Forgery; misdescription of instrument; instrument destroyed or withheld by defendant

When an instrument which is the subject of an indictment or information for forgery has been destroyed or withheld by the act or the procurement of the defendant, and the fact of such destruction or withholding is alleged in the indictment, or information, and established on the trial, the misdescription of the instrument is immaterial.
(Amended by Code Am.1880, c. 47, p. 14, § 26.)

§ 969c. Defendant using weapon or armed with a firearm; allegation in each count; allegation of nature of weapon or firearm; multiple weapons or firearms; trial of issue

Whenever a defendant uses a weapon or was armed with a firearm under such circumstances as to bring such defendant within the operation of Section 12022 the fact that the defendant so used a weapon or was armed with a firearm may be charged in the accusatory pleading. This charge, if made, shall be added to and be a part of the count or each of the counts of the accusatory pleading which charge the offense at the time of the commission of which the defendant used a weapon or was armed with a firearm. That portion of any count which charges that the defendant used a weapon or was armed with a firearm shall be sufficient if it can be understood therefrom that at the time of his commission of the offense set forth in the count, the defendant used a weapon or was armed with a firearm. The nature of the weapon or firearm must be set forth. One such charge may name more than one weapon or firearm. If the defendant pleads not guilty of the offense charged in any count which alleges that the defendant used a weapon or was armed with a firearm, the question whether or not he used a weapon or was armed with a firearm as alleged must be tried by the court or jury which tries the issue upon the plea of not guilty. If the defendant pleads guilty of the offense charged the question whether or not he used a weapon or was armed with a firearm as alleged must be determined by the court before pronouncing judgment.
(Amended by Stats.1977, c. 165, p. —, § 13.3.)

§ 969d. Defendant using firearm; allegation in each count; nature of firearm; multiple firearms; trial of issue

Whenever a defendant used a firearm as recited in Section 12022.5, the fact that the defendant used a

§ 969d

firearm may be charged in the accusatory pleading. This charge, if made, shall be added to and be a part of the count or each of the counts of the accusatory pleading which charged the offense. That portion of any count which charges that the defendant used a firearm shall be sufficient if it can be understood therefrom that at the time of his commission of the offense set forth in the count the defendant used a firearm. The nature of the firearm must be set forth. One such charge may name more than one firearm. If the defendant pleads not guilty to the offense charged in any count which alleges that the defendant used a firearm, the question whether or not he used a firearm as alleged must be tried by the court or jury which tries the issue upon the plea of not guilty. If the defendant pleads guilty of the offense charged the question whether or not he used a firearm as alleged must be determined by the court before pronouncing judgment.
(Amended by Stats.1977, c. 165, p. —, § 13.5.)

§ 970. Several defendants; conviction or acquittal of one or more

When several defendants are named in one accusatory pleading, any one or more may be convicted or acquitted.
(Amended by Stats.1951, c. 1674, p. 3839, § 59.)

§ 971. Abrogation of distinction between accessories and principals, and between principals in first and second degree; effect upon pleadings

The distinction between an accessory before the fact and a principal, and between principals in the first and second degree is abrogated; and all persons concerned in the commission of a crime, who by the operation of other provisions of this code are principals therein, shall hereafter be prosecuted, tried and punished as principals and no other facts need be alleged in any accusatory pleading against any such person than are required in an accusatory pleading against a principal.
(Amended by Stats.1951, c. 1674, p. 3839, § 60.)

§ 972. Accessory; prosecution without regard to prosecution of principal

An accessory to the commission of a felony may be prosecuted, tried, and punished, though the principal may be neither prosecuted nor tried, and though the principal may have been acquitted.
(Amended by Code Am.1880, c. 47, p. 15, § 33.)

§ 976. Necessity; court; transfer; telephone calls

(a) When the accusatory pleading is filed, the defendant must be arraigned thereon before the court in which it is filed, unless the action is transferred to some other court for trial.

(b) In any county of the first or third class, if the defendant is to be arraigned in municipal court and is in custody, upon the approval of both the presiding judge of the municipal court in which the accusatory pleading is filed and the presiding judge of the municipal court within the county nearest to the place in which he is held in custody, he may also be arraigned before the municipal court within the county nearest to the place in which he is held in custody. Prior to being taken from the place where he is in custody to the place where he is to be arraigned, such defendant shall be allowed to make three completed telephone calls, at no expense to such defendant, in addition to any other telephone calls which such defendant is entitled to make pursuant to law.
(Amended by Stats.1975, c. 669, p. 1461, § 1.)

§ 977. Presence of defendant; exception

(a) In all cases in which the accused is charged with a misdemeanor only, he may appear by counsel only.

(b) In all cases in which a felony is charged, the accused must be present at the arraignment, at the time of plea, during the preliminary hearing, during those portions of the trial when evidence is taken before the trier of fact, and at the time of the imposition of sentence. The accused shall be personally present at all other proceedings unless he shall, with leave of court, execute in open court, a written waiver of his right to be personally present, approved by his counsel, which waiver must then be filed with the court; provided, however, that the court may specifically direct that defendant be personally present at any particular proceeding or portion thereof. The waiver shall be substantially in the following form:

"WAIVER OF DEFENDANT'S PERSONAL PRESENCE

"The undersigned defendant, having been advised of his right to be present at all stages of the proceedings, including but not limited to presentation of and arguments on questions of law, and to be confronted by and cross-examine all witnesses, hereby waives the right to be present at the hearing of any motion or other proceeding in this cause, including when the case is set for trial, when a continuance is ordered, when a motion to set aside the indictment or information pursuant to the provisions of the Penal Code, Section 995 and following is heard, when a motion for reduction of bail or for a personal recognizance release is heard, when a motion to reduce sentence is heard, and when questions of law are presented to or considered by the court. The undersigned defendant hereby requests the court to proceed during every absence of his which the court may permit pursuant to this waiver, and hereby agrees that his interest will be deemed represented at all times by the presence of his attorney the same as if the defendant himself were personally present in court, and further agrees that notice to his attorney that his presence in court on a particular day at a particular time is required will be deemed notice to him of the requirement of his appearance at said time and place.

"Dated: _____

_____
Defendant

_____
Address

"Approved:
"Dated _____
"_____
"Attorney for Defendant."

(Amended by Stats.1968, c. 1064, p. 2064, § 1.)

§ 979. Defendant discharged on bail or deposit; nonappearance; forfeiture; bench warrant

If the defendant has been discharged on bail or has deposited money or other property instead thereof, and does not appear to be arraigned when his personal presence is necessary, the court, in addition to the forfeiture of the undertaking of bail or of the money or other property deposited, may order the issuance of a bench warrant for his arrest.
(Amended by Stats.1951, c. 1674, p. 3840, § 65.)

§ 980. Bench warrant; issuance

At any time after the order for a bench warrant is made, whether the court is sitting or not, the clerk, or if there is no clerk, the judge or justice of the court, may, on application of the prosecuting attorney, issue a bench warrant to one or more counties.
(Amended by Stats.1951, c. 1674, p. 3840, § 66.)

§ 981. Bench warrant; form; felony case

The bench warrant upon the indictment or information must, if the offense is a felony, be substantially in the following form: County of _____. The People of the State of California to any Sheriff, Constable, Marshal, or Policeman in this State: An indictment having been found (or information filed) on the _____ day of _____, A.D. eighteen _____, in the Superior Court of the County of _____, charging C.D. with the crime of _____ (designating it generally); you are, therefore, commanded forthwith to arrest the above named C.D., and bring him before that Court (or if the indictment and information has been sent to another Court, then before that Court, naming it), to answer said indictment (or information), or if the Court be not in session, that you deliver him into the custody of the Sheriff of the County of _____.

Given under my hand, with the seal of said Court affixed, this _____ day of _____, A.D. ____.

By order of said Court.

[SEAL.]   E. F., Clerk.
(Amended by Code Am.1880, c. 47, p. 16, § 36.)

§ 982. Nonbailable offense; custody of defendant; bail upon habeas corpus; bailable offense; direction on bench warrant as to bail

The defendant, when arrested under a warrant for an offense not bailable, must be held in custody by the Sheriff of the county in which the indictment is found or information filed, unless admitted to bail after an examination upon a writ of habeas corpus; but if the offense is bailable, there must be added to the body of the bench warrant a direction to the following effect: "Or, if he requires it, that you take him before any magistrate in that county, or in the county in which you arrest him, that he may give bail to answer to the indictment (or information);" and the Court, upon directing it to issue, must fix the amount of bail, and an indorsement must be made thereon and signed by the Clerk, to the following

effect: "The defendant is to be admitted to bail in the sum of _____ dollars."
(Amended by Code Am.1880, c. 47, p. 16, § 37.)

§ 983. Bench warrant; service

The bench warrant may be served in any county in the same manner as a warrant of arrest.
(Amended by Stats.1951, c. 1674, p. 3840, § 67.)

§ 985. Increased bail on felony charge; custody until increased bail given

When the information or indictment is for a felony, and the defendant, before the filing thereof, has given bail for his appearance to answer the charge, the Court to which the indictment or information is presented, or in which it is pending, may order the defendant to be committed to actual custody, unless he gives bail in an increased amount, to be specified in the order.
(Amended by Code Am.1880, c. 47, p. 16, § 38.)

§ 986. Increased bail on felony charge; commitment of defendant or issuance of bench warrant

Defendant if present when order made, to be committed; if not, bench warrant to issue. If the defendant is present when the order is made, he must be forthwith committed. If he is not present, a bench warrant must be issued and proceeded upon in the manner provided in this Chapter.
(Enacted 1872.)

§ 995. Cases in which indictment or information must be set aside

The indictment or information must be set aside by the court in which the defendant is arraigned, upon his motion, in either of the following cases:

If it be an indictment:

1. Where it is not found, endorsed, and presented as prescribed in this code.

2. That the defendant has been indicted without reasonable or probable cause.

If it be an information:

1. That before the filing thereof the defendant had not been legally committed by a magistrate.

2. That the defendant had been committed without reasonable or probable cause.
(Amended by Stats.1949, c. 1311, p. 2298, § 1.)

Editors' Note

Read People v. Scoma in table of cases included in this text.

Notes of Decisions

There is sufficient evidence to require superior court to deny defendant's motion to dismiss information if evidence raises clear and distinct inference of existence of essential elements of crime charged. People v. McKee (1968) 73 Cal.Rptr. 112, 267 C.A.2d 509.

Information jointly charging two defendants with grand theft was not required to be set aside on statutory ground of lack of probable cause in view of competent evidence establishing that crime had been committed and connecting defendants to such crime. People v. Hardy (1969) 79 Cal.Rptr. 801, 275 C.A.2d 469.

An element of "reasonable or probable cause" within meaning of this section providing that information must be set aside where defendant has been committed without reasonable or probable cause is existence of competent substantial evidence to show commission of crime which it charged. People v. Firestine (1968) 74 Cal.Rptr. 168, 268 C.A.2d 533.

Seizure of forged checks at time of arrest of defendant as parole violator was valid, and evidence seized was sufficient probable cause for indictment for possession of forged checks, where there was no evidence that prior to entry and arrest defendant was being sought as either user or possessor of narcotics. People v. Beamon (1968) 73 Cal.Rptr. 604, 268 C.A.2d 61.

§ 996. Objections waived by failure to move to set aside indictment or information

If the motion to set aside the indictment or information is not made, the defendant is precluded from afterwards taking the objections mentioned in Section 995.
(Amended by Stats.1967, c. 138, p. 1193, § 5.)

§ 997. Motion to set aside; hearing; answer on denial of motion; exceptions; preliminary examination after resubmission

The motion must be heard at the time it is made, unless for cause the court postpones the hearing to another time. The court may entertain such motion prior to trial whether or not a plea has been entered and such plea need not be set aside in order to consider the motion. If the motion is denied, and the accused has not previously answered the indictment or information, either by demurring or pleading thereto, he shall immediately do so. If the motion is granted, the court must order that the defendant, if in custody, be discharged therefrom; or, if admitted to bail, that his bail be exonerated; or, if he has deposited money, or if money has been deposited by another or others instead of bail for his appearance, that the same be refunded to him or to the person or persons found by the court to have deposited said money on behalf of said defendant, unless it directs that the case be resubmitted to the same or another

grand jury, or that an information be filed by the district attorney; provided, that after such order of resubmission the defendant may be examined before a magistrate, and discharged or committed by him, as in other cases, if before indictment or information filed he has not been examined and committed by a magistrate.
(Amended by Stats.1968, c. 1064, p. 2065, § 2.)

§ 998. Resubmission of case; custody or bail; failure to find new indictment or file new information

If the Court directs the case to be resubmitted, or an information to be filed, the defendant, if already in custody, must so remain, unless he is admitted to bail; or, if already admitted to bail, or money has been deposited instead thereof, the bail or money is answerable for the appearance of the defendant to answer a new indictment or information; and, unless a new indictment is found or information filed before the next grand jury of the county is discharged, the Court must, on the discharge of such grand jury, make the order prescribed by the preceding section.
(Amended by Code Am.1880, c. 47, p. 17, § 44.)

§ 999. Order setting aside indictment or information not bar to subsequent prosecution

An order to set aside an indictment or information, as provided in this chapter, is no bar to a future prosecution for the same offense.
(Amended by Code Am.1880, c. 47, p. 18, § 45.)

§ 999b. Legislative findings and intent

The Legislature hereby finds a substantial and disproportionate amount of serious crime is committed against the people of California by a relatively small number of multiple and repeat felony offenders, commonly known as career criminals. In enacting this chapter, the Legislature intends to support increased efforts by district attorneys' offices to prosecute career criminals through organizational and operational techniques that have been proven effective in selected counties in this and other states.
(Added by Stats.1977, c. 1151, § 1.)

§ 999c. Career criminal prosecution program; allocation and award of funds; program, administrative guidelines and procedures; annual report

(a) There is hereby established in the Office of Criminal Justice Planning a program of financial and technical assistance for district attorneys' offices, designated the California Career Criminal Prosecution Program. All funds appropriated to the Office of Criminal Justice Planning for the purposes of this chapter shall be administered and disbursed by the executive director of such office in consultation with the California Council on Criminal Justice, and shall to the greatest extent feasible be coordinated or consolidated with federal funds that may be made available for these purposes.

(b) The executive director is authorized to allocate and award funds to counties in which career criminal prosecution units are established in substantial compliance with the policies and criteria set forth below in Sections 999d, 999e, 999f, and 999g.

(c) Such allocation and award of funds shall be made upon application executed by the county's district attorney and approved by its board of supervisors. Funds disbursed under this chapter shall not supplant local funds that would, in the absence of the California Career Criminal Prosecution Program, be made available to support the prosecution of felony cases.

(d) On or before April 1, 1978, and in consultation with the Attorney General, the executive director shall prepare and issue written program and administrative guidelines and procedures for the California Career Criminal Prosecution Program, consistent with this chapter. In addition to all other formal requirements that may apply to the enactment of such guidelines and procedures, a complete and final draft of them shall be submitted on or before March 1, 1978, to the chairpersons of the Criminal Justice Committee of the Assembly and the Judiciary Committee of the Senate of the California Legislature.

(e) Annually, commencing October 1, 1978, the executive director shall prepare a report to the Legislature describing in detail the operation of the statewide program and the results obtained of career criminal prosecution units of district attorneys' offices receiving funds under this chapter and under comparable federally-financed awards.
(Added by Stats.1977, c. 1151, p. —, § 1.)

§ 999d. Enhanced prosecution efforts and resources

Career criminal prosecution units receiving funds under this chapter shall concentrate enhanced prosecution efforts and resources upon individuals identified under selection criteria set forth in Section 999e. Enhanced prosecution efforts and resources shall include, but not be limited to:

(a) "Vertical" prosecutorial representation, whereby the prosecutor who makes the initial filing or appearance in a career criminal case will perform all subsequent court appearances on that particular case through its conclusion, including the sentencing phase;

(b) Assignment of highly qualified investigators and prosecutors to career criminal cases; and

(c) Significant reduction of caseloads for investigators and prosecutors assigned to career criminal cases.

(Added by Stats.1977, c. 1151, p. —, § 1.)

§ 999e. Persons subject to career criminal prosecution efforts; selection criteria

(a) An individual shall be the subject of career criminal prosecution efforts who is under arrest for the commission or attempted commission of one or more of the following felonies: robbery, burglary, arson, any unlawful act relating to controlled substances in violation of Section 11351 or 11352 of the Health and Safety Code, receiving stolen property, grand theft and grand theft auto; and who is either being prosecuted for three or more separate offenses not arising out of the same transaction involving one or more of such felonies, or has suffered at least one conviction during the preceding 10 years for any felony listed in paragraph (1) of this subdivision, or at least two convictions during the preceding 10 years for any felony listed in paragraph (2) of this subdivision:

(1) Robbery by a person armed with a deadly or dangerous weapon, burglary of the first degree, arson as defined in Section 447a or 448a, forcible rape, sodomy or oral copulation committed with force, lewd or lascivious conduct committed upon a child, kidnapping as defined in Section 209, or murder.

(2) Grand theft, grant theft auto, receiving stolen property, robbery other than that described in paragraph (1) above, burglary of the second degree, kidnapping as defined in Section 207, assault with a deadly weapon, or any unlawful act relating to controlled substances in violation of Section 11351 or 11352 of the Health and Safety Code.

For purposes of this chapter, the 10-year periods specified in this section shall be exclusive of any time which the arrested person has served in state prison.

(b) In applying the career criminal selection criteria set forth above, a district attorney may elect to limit career criminal prosecution efforts to persons arrested for any one or more of the felonies listed in subdivision (a) of this section if crime statistics demonstrate that the incidence of such one or more felonies presents a particularly serious problem in the county.

(c) In exercising the prosecutorial discretion granted by Section 999g, the district attorney shall consider the following: (1) the character, background, and prior criminal background of the defendant; and (2) the number and the seriousness of the offenses currently charged against the defendant.

(Added by Stats.1977, c. 1151, p. —, § 1.)

§ 999f. Policies; career criminal cases

Subject to reasonable prosecutorial discretion, each district attorney's office establishing a career criminal prosecution unit and receiving state support under this chapter shall adopt and pursue the following policies for career criminal cases:

(a) A plea of guilty or a trial conviction will be sought on the most serious offense charged in the accusatory pleading against an individual meeting career criminal selection criteria.

(b) All reasonable prosecutorial efforts will be made to resist the pretrial release of a charged defendant meeting career criminal selection criteria.

(c) All reasonable prosecutorial efforts will be made to persuade the court to impose the most severe authorized sentence upon a person convicted after prosecution as a career criminal.

(d) All reasonable prosecutorial efforts will be made to reduce the time between arrest and disposition of charge against an individual meeting career criminal selection criteria.

(e) The prosecution shall not negotiate an agreement with a career criminal:

(1) That permits the defendant to plead guilty or nolo contendere to an offense lesser in degree or in kind than the most serious offense charged in the information or indictment;

(2) That the prosecution shall not oppose the defendant's request for a particular sentence if below the maximum; or

(3) That a specific sentence is the appropriate disposition of the case if below the maximum.

(Added by Stats.1977, c. 1151, p. —, § 1.)

§ 999g. Exceptions to selection criteria and policies; specified circumstances; prosecutorial discretion

The selection criteria set forth in Section 999e and the policies of Section 999f shall be adhered to for each career criminal case unless, in the reasonable exercise of prosecutor's discretion, one or more of the following circumstances are found to apply to a particular case:

(a) The facts or available evidence do not warrant prosecution on the most serious offense charged.

(b) Prosecution of the most serious offense charged, if successful, would not add to the severity of the maximum sentence otherwise applicable to the case.

(c) Departure from such policies with respect to a particular career criminal defendant would substantially improve the likelihood of successful prosecution of one or more other felony cases.

(d) Extraordinary circumstances require the departure from such policies in order to promote the general purposes and intent of this chapter.
(Added by Stats.1977, c. 1151, p. —, § 1.)

§ 999h. Trier of fact; characterization of defendant as career criminal

The characterization of a defendant as a "career criminal" as defined by this chapter may not be communicated to the trier of fact.
(Added by Stats.1977, c. 1151, p. —, § 1.)

Editors' Note

This law appropriates state money to local career criminal prosecution units to concentrate prosecution efforts, and the most qualified deputies on recidivist offenders who have been arrested for the commission or attempted commission of robbery, burglary, arson, any unlawful act relating to controlled substances in violation of Section 11351 or 11352 of the Health and Safety Code, receiving stolen property, grand theft or grand theft auto. An offender will be the subject of career criminal prosecution efforts if he has one prior "violent" felony conviction or two prior "non-violent" felony convictions or has no priors but is being prosecuted for three or more separate offenses not arising out of the same transaction.

The additional funding will permit a career criminal deputy to have a caseload that is only half that of other deputies and this will enable the career criminal prosecutor to stay with career criminal cases from inception through conclusion. Thus, a career criminal prosecutor will become thoroughly familiar with each case and permit him or her to obtain a conviction on the most serious offense charged. Additionally, this law provides that a career criminal may not plea bargain his way out of the most serious offense charged. Moreover, the new legislation encourages District Attorneys to strongly resist pretrial release of a career criminal. This "no-bail" policy reflects the most recent indepth study on bail which indicates that a defendant's prior criminal record is the most significant factor in predicting whether a defendant will appear at trial.

§ 1000. Application of chapter to certain violations

(a) This chapter shall apply whenever a case is before any court upon an accusatory pleading for violation of Section 11350, 11357, 11364, 11365, 11377, or 11550 of the Health and Safety Code, or Section 11358 of the Health and Safety Code if the marijuana planted, cultivated, harvested, dried, or processed is for personal use, or Section 381 or subdivision (f) of Section 647 of the Penal Code, if for being under the influence of a controlled substance, or Section 4230 of the Business and Professions Code, and it appears to the district attorney that, except as provided in subdivision (b) of Section 11357 of the Health and Safety Code, all of the following apply to the defendant:

(1) The defendant has no conviction for any offense involving controlled substances prior to the alleged commission of the charged divertible offense.

(2) The offense charged did not involve a crime of violence or threatened violence.

(3) There is no evidence of a violation relating to narcotics or restricted dangerous drugs other than a violation of the sections listed in this subdivision.

(4) The defendant's record does not indicate that probation or parole has ever been revoked without thereafter being completed.

(5) The defendant's record does not indicate that he has been diverted pursuant to this chapter within five years prior to the alleged commission of the charged divertible offense.

(6) The defendant has no prior felony conviction within five years prior to the alleged commission of the charged divertible offense.

(b) The district attorney shall review his file to determine whether or not paragraphs (1) to (6), inclusive, of subdivision (a) are applicable to the defendant. If the defendant is found ineligible, the district attorney shall file with the court a declaration in writing or state for the record the grounds upon which the determination is based, and shall make this information available to the defendant and his attorney.
(Amended by Stats.1975, c. 1267, p. 3328, § 1.)

§ 1000.1. Determination of application to defendant; notification; investigation by probation department; admissibility of evidence

(a) If the district attorney determines that this chapter may be applicable to the defendant, he shall advise the defendant and his attorney in writing of such determination. This notification shall include:

(1) A full description of the procedures of diversionary investigation.

(2) A general explanation of the roles and authorities of the probation department, the district attorney, the community program, and the court in the diversion process.

(3) A clear statement that the court may decide in a hearing not to divert the defendant and that he may have to stand trial for the alleged offense.

(4) A clear statement that should the defendant fail in meeting the terms of his diversion, or should he be convicted of a misdemeanor which reflects the divertee's propensity for violence, or should the divertee be convicted of any felony, he may be required, after a court hearing, to stand trial for the original alleged offense.

(5) An explanation of criminal record retention and disposition resulting from participation in the diversion and the divertee's rights relative to answering questions about his arrest and diversion following successful completion of the diversion program.

(b) If the defendant consents and waives his right to a speedy trial the district attorney shall refer the case to the probation department. The probation department shall make an investigation and take into consideration the defendant's age, employment and service records, educational background, community and family ties, prior controlled substance use, treatment history, if any, demonstrable motivation and other mitigating factors in determining whether the defendant is a person who would be benefited by education, treatment, or rehabilitation. The probation department shall also determine which community programs the defendant would benefit from and which of those programs would accept the defendant. The probation department shall report its findings and recommendation to the court.

(c) No statement, or any information procured therefrom, made by the defendant to any probation officer or drug treatment worker, which is made during the course of any investigation conducted by the probation department or drug treatment program pursuant to subdivision (b), and prior to the reporting of the probation department's findings and recommendations to the court, shall be admissible in any action or proceeding brought subsequent to the investigation.

No statement, or any information procured therefrom, with respect to the specific offense with which the defendant is charged, which is made to any probation officer or drug program worker subsequent to the granting of diversion, shall be admissible in any action or proceeding.

In the event that diversion is either denied, or is subsequently revoked once it has been granted, neither the probation investigation nor statements or information divulged during that investigation shall be used in any sentencing procedures.
(Amended by Stats.1975, c. 1267, p. 3328, § 2.)

§ 1000.2. Hearing by court; diversion; exoneration of bail; progress reports

The court shall hold a hearing and, after consideration of the probation department's report and any other information considered by the court to be relevant to its decision, shall determine if the defendant consents to further proceedings under this chapter and waives his right to a speedy trial and if the defendant should be diverted and referred for education, treatment, or rehabilitation. If the court does not deem the defendant a person who would be benefited by diversion, or if the defendant does not consent to participate, the proceedings shall continue as in any other case.

At such time that a defendant's case is diverted, any bail bond or undertaking, or deposit in lieu thereof, on file by or on behalf of the defendant shall be exonerated, and the court shall enter an order so directing.

The period during which the further criminal proceedings against the defendant may be diverted shall be for no less than six months nor longer than two years. Progress reports shall be filed by the probation department with the court not less than every six months.
(Amended by Stats.1975, c. 357, p. 801, § 1; Stats.1975, c. 1267, p. 3330, § 3.)

Editors' Note

Labor Code Section 432.7 makes it a misdemeanor for any peace officer to disclose arrest, or pre-trial information, relating to a defendant who was diverted, when the disclosure is made with the intent of affecting a person's employment. Section 432.7 is also applicable to those diverted pursuant to Penal Code Section 1001.

§ 1000.3. Unsatisfactory performance in program by divertee; resumption of criminal proceedings; dismissal

If it appears to the probation department that the divertee is performing unsatisfactorily in the assigned program, or that the divertee is not benefiting from education, treatment, or rehabilitation, or that the divertee is convicted of a misdemeanor which reflects the divertee's propensity for violence, or if the divertee is convicted of a felony, after notice to the divertee, the court shall hold a hearing to determine whether the criminal proceedings should be reinstituted. If the court finds that the divertee is not performing satisfactorily in the assigned program, or that the divertee is not benefiting from diversion, or the court finds that the divertee has been convicted of a crime as indicated above, the criminal case shall be referred back to the court for resumption of the criminal proceedings. If the divertee has performed satisfactorily during the period of diversion, at the end of the period of diversion, the criminal charges shall be dismissed.
(Added by Stats.1975, c. 1267, p. 3330, § 5.)

§ 1000.5. Disposition of diverted cases, successful completion of program; record

Any record filed with the Department of Justice shall indicate the disposition in those cases diverted pursuant to this chapter. Upon successful completion of a diversion program the arrest upon which the diversion was based shall be deemed to have never occurred. The divertee may indicate in response to any question concerning his prior criminal record that he was not arrested or diverted for such offense. A record pertaining to an arrest resulting in successful completion of a diversion program shall not, without the divertee's consent, be used in any way which could result in the denial of any employment, benefit, license, or certificate.
(Added by Stats.1975, c. 1267, p. 3330, § 7.)

§ 1001. Legislative intent

It is the intent of the Legislature, that neither this chapter, Chapter 2.5 (commencing with Section 1000) of this title, nor any other provision of law be construed to preempt other current or future pretrial or precomplaint diversion programs. It is also the intent of the Legislature that current or future posttrial diversion programs not be preempted, except as provided in Section 13201, 13201.5, or 13352.5 of the Vehicle Code. Sections 1001.2 to 1001.11, inclusive, of this chapter shall apply only to pretrial diversion programs as defined in Section 1001.1 herein.
(Added by Stats.1977, c. 574, p. —, § 2, urgency, eff. Sept. 3, 1977.)

§ 1001.1. Pretrial diversion

As used in Sections 1001.2 to 1001.11, inclusive, of this chapter, pretrial diversion refers to the procedure of postponing prosecution either temporarily or permanently at any point in the judicial process from the point at which the accused is charged until adjudication.
(Added by Stats.1977, c. 574, p. —, § 2, urgency, eff. Sept. 3, 1977.)

§ 1001.2. Application of chapter

This chapter shall not apply to any pretrial diversion or posttrial programs for the treatment of problem drinking or alcoholism utilized for persons convicted of one or more offenses under Section 23102 of the Vehicle Code or to pretrial diversion programs established pursuant to Chapter 2.5 (commencing with Section 1000) of this title.
(Added by Stats.1977, c. 574, p. —, § 2, urgency, eff. Sept. 3, 1977.)

§ 1001.3. Admission of guilt; prohibition against requirement for placement in program

At no time shall a defendant be required to make an admission of guilt as a prerequisite for placement in a pretrial diversion program.
(Added by Stats.1977, c. 574, p. —, § 2, urgency, eff. Sept. 3, 1977.)

§ 1001.4. Hearing prior to termination

A divertee is entitled to a hearing, as set forth by law, before his or her pretrial diversion can be terminated for cause.
(Added by Stats.1977, c. 574, p. —, § 2, urgency, eff. Sept. 3, 1977.)

§ 1001.5. Statement by defendant or information procured therefrom; admissibility

No statement, or information procured therefrom, made by the defendant in connection with the determination of his or her eligibility for diversion, and no statement, or information procured therefrom, made by the defendant subsequent to the granting of diversion or while participating in such program, and no information contained in any report made with respect thereto, and no statement or other informa-

§ 1001.5

tion concerning the defendant's participation in such program shall be admissible in any action or proceeding. However, if a divertee is recommended for termination for cause, information regarding his or her participation in such program may be used for purposes of the termination proceedings.
(Added by Stats.1977, c. 574, p. —, § 2, urgency, eff. Sept. 3, 1977.)

§ 1001.6. Bail, undertaking or deposit; exoneration; order

At such time that a defendant's case is diverted, any bail bond or undertaking, or deposit in lieu thereof, on file by or on behalf of the defendant shall be exonerated, and the court shall enter an order so directing.
(Added by Stats.1977, c. 574, p. —, § 2, urgency, eff. Sept. 3, 1977.)

§ 1001.7. Dismissal of charges at end of diversion

If the divertee has performed satisfactorily during the period of diversion, the criminal charges shall be dismissed at the end of the period of diversion.
(Added by Stats.1977, c. 574, p. —, § 2, urgency, eff. Sept. 3, 1977.)

§ 1001.8. Record

Any record filed with the Department of Justice shall indicate the disposition of those cases diverted pursuant to this chapter.
(Added by Stats.1977, c. 574, p. —, § 2, urgency, eff. Sept. 3, 1977.)

§ 1001.9. Arrest; effect upon completion of program

Upon successful completion of a diversion program, the arrest upon which the diversion was based shall be deemed to have never occurred. The divertee may indicate in response to any question concerning his or her prior criminal record that he or she was not arrested or diverted for such offense. A record pertaining to an arrest resulting in successful completion of a diversion program shall not, without the divertee's consent, be used in any way which could result in the denial of any employment, benefit, license, or certificate.
(Added by Stats.1977, c. 574, p. —, § 2, urgency, eff. Sept. 3, 1977.)

§ 1001.10. Report to legislature; contents

A county or city which operates a diversion program, pursuant to this chapter, shall report to the Legislature annually regarding the implementation, administration and operation of such program. Such report shall include but not be limited to the following: the date the program commenced; the program's general eligibility criteria for divertees; the name of the county or other agency or agencies which establishes such eligibility criteria; other criteria or standards established for the program; the offense charged against the divertee; the number of individuals referred to the program; the number of individuals accepted by the program; the reasons for not accepting individuals referred to the program; the specific program completed by each successful divertee; the number of successful and unsuccessful terminations; the reason for unsuccessful termination; and the funding sources for the diversion organization. At no time shall the names, addresses, or other identifying information of the referred or participating divertees be used in these reports.
(Added by Stats.1977, c. 574, p. —, § 2, urgency, eff. Sept. 30, 1977.)

§ 1001.11. Duration of chapter

This chapter shall remain in effect until January 1, 1980, and on such date is repealed. However, if at the time this chapter is repealed a defendant has already been referred to and accepted by a diversion program or if a defendant is then participating in such a program, that defendant shall be allowed to continue in and complete such program.
(Added by Stats.1977, c. 574, p. —, § 2, urgency, eff. Sept. 3, 1977.)

§ 1016. Kinds of pleas; entry of multiple plea; presumption of sanity; change of plea; admission by plea of not guilty by reason of insanity without pleading not guilty

There are six kinds of pleas to an indictment or an information, or to a complaint charging an offense triable in any inferior court:

1. Guilty.

2. Not guilty.

3. Nolo contendere, subject to the approval of the court. The court shall ascertain whether the defendant completely understands that a plea of nolo contendere shall be considered the same as a plea of guilty and that, upon a plea of nolo contendere, the court shall find the defendant guilty. The legal effect of such a plea shall be the same as that of a plea of guilty, but the plea and any admissions required by the court during any inquiry it makes as to the voluntariness of and factual basis for the plea

may not be used against the defendant as an admission in any civil suit based upon or growing out of the act upon which the criminal prosecution is based.

4. A former judgment of conviction or acquittal of the offense charged.

5. Once in jeopardy.

6. Not guilty by reason of insanity.

A defendant who does not plead guilty may enter one or more of the other pleas. A defendant who does not plead not guilty by reason of insanity shall be conclusively presumed to have been sane at the time of the commission of the offense charged; provided, that the court may for good cause shown allow a change of plea at any time before the commencement of the trial. A defendant who pleads not guilty by reason of insanity, without also pleading not guilty, thereby admits the commission of the offense charged.

(Amended by Stats.1976, c. 1088, p. —, § 1.)

§ 1017. Place, form, and entry of plea

Every plea must be made in open court and may be oral or in writing, and must be entered upon the minutes of the court and must be taken down in shorthand by the official reporter if there is one present. The plea, whether oral or in writing, must be in substantially the following form:

1. If the defendant plead guilty: "The defendant pleads that he is guilty of the offense charged."

2. If he plead not guilty: "The defendant pleads that he is not guilty of the offense charged."

3. If he plead a former conviction or acquittal: "The defendant pleads that he has already been convicted (or acquitted) of the offense charged, by the judgment of the court of ———— (naming it), rendered at ———— (naming the place), on the ———— day of ————."

4. If he plead once in jeopardy: "The defendant pleads that he has been once in jeopardy for the offense charged (specifying the time, place, and court)."

5. If he plead not guilty by reason of insanity: "The defendant pleads that he is not guilty of the offense charged because he was insane at the time that he is alleged to have committed the unlawful act."

(Amended by Stats.1951, c. 1674, p. 3843, § 82.)

§ 1019. Plea of not guilty; issues

The plea of not guilty puts in issue every material allegation of the accusatory pleading, except those allegations regarding previous convictions of the defendant to which an answer is required by Section 1025.

(Amended by Stats.1951, c. 1674, p. 3844, § 83.)

§ 1023. Conviction, acquittal, or jeopardy; bar to subsequent prosecution

When the defendant is convicted or acquitted or has been once placed in jeopardy upon an accusatory pleading, the conviction, acquittal, or jeopardy is a bar to another prosecution for the offense charged in such accusatory pleading, or for an attempt to commit the same, or for an offense necessarily included therein, of which he might have been convicted under that accusatory pleading.

(Amended by Stats.1951, c. 1674, p. 3844, § 86.)

§ 1026. Pleas of insanity; separate trials; presumption of sanity; trial of sanity issue; verdict; sentence; confinement in state hospital or mental facility; outpatient status; restoration to sanity; transfers between facilities

When a defendant pleads not guilty by reason of insanity, and also joins with it another plea or pleas, he shall first be tried as if he had entered such other plea or pleas only, and in such trial he shall be conclusively presumed to have been sane at the time the offense is alleged to have been committed. If the jury shall find the defendant guilty, or if the defendant pleads only not guilty by reason of insanity, then the question whether the defendant was sane or insane at the time the offense was committed shall be promptly tried, either before the same jury or before a new jury in the discretion of the court. In such trial the jury shall return a verdict either that the defendant was sane at the time the offense was committed or that he was insane at the time the offense was committed. If the verdict or finding be that the defendant was sane at the time the offense was committed, the court shall sentence the defendant as provided by law. If the verdict or finding be that the defendant was insane at the time the offense was committed, the court unless it shall appear to the court that the defendant has fully recovered his sanity shall direct that the defendant be confined in a state hospital for the care and treatment of the mentally disordered or any other appropriate public or private mental health facility approved by the county mental health director, or the court may order the defendant to undergo outpatient treatment as specified in Section 1026.1 of the Penal Code. The court shall transmit a copy of its order to the county mental health director or his designee. If the defendant has been found guilty of murder, mayhem, a violation of Section 207 or 209 of the Penal Code in which the victim suffers intentionally inflicted great bodily injury, robbery in the first degree or in which the victim suffers great bodily injury, a violation of Section 447a of the Penal Code involving a trailer coach, as defined in Section 635 of the Vehicle Code, or any dwelling house, a violation of subdivision 2 or 3 of Section 261 of the Penal Code, a violation of Section 459 of the Penal Code in the first degree, assault with intent to commit murder, a violation of Section 220 of the Penal Code in which the victim suffers great bodily injury, a violation of Section 12303.1, 12303.2, 12303.3, 12308, 12309, or 12310 of the Penal Code, or if the defendant has been found guilty of a felony involving death, great bodily injury, or an act which poses a serious threat of bodily harm to another person, the court shall direct that the defendant be confined in a state hospital or other public or private mental health facility approved by the county mental health director for a minimum of 90 days before such defendant may be released on outpatient treatment pursuant to subdivision (f) of Section 7375 of the Welfare and Institutions Code. Prior to making such order directing that the defendant be confined in a state hospital or other facility or ordered to undergo outpatient treatment, the court shall order the county mental health director or his designee to evaluate the defendant and to submit to the court within 15 judicial days of such order his written recommendation as to whether the defendant should be required to undergo outpatient treatment or committed to a state hospital or another mental health facility. No person shall be admitted to a state hospital or other facility or accepted for outpatient treatment under this section without having been evaluated by the county mental health director or his or her designee. If, however, it shall appear to the court that the defendant has fully recovered his sanity such defendant shall be remanded to the custody of the sheriff until his sanity shall have been finally determined in the manner prescribed by law. A defendant committed to a state hospital or other facility or ordered to undergo outpatient treatment shall not be released from confinement or the required outpatient treatment unless and until the court which committed him shall, after notice and hearing, find and determine that his sanity has been restored. Nothing in this section contained shall prevent the transfer of such person from one state hospital to any other state hospital by proper authority nor the transfer of such patient to a hospital in another state in the manner provided by law, upon order of the superior court in the county from which he was committed, or in which he is detained.

If the defendant is committed or transferred to a state hospital pursuant to this section, the court may, upon receiving the written recommendation of the superintendent of the state hospital and the county mental health director that the defendant be transferred to a public or private mental health facility approved by the county mental health director, order the defendant transferred to such facility. If the defendant is committed or transferred to a public or private mental health facility approved by the county mental health director, the court may, upon receiving the written recommendation of the county mental health director, transfer the defendant to a state hospital or to another public or private mental health facility approved by the county mental health director. The defendant or prosecuting attorney, if he chooses to contest either kind of order of transfer, may petition the court for a hearing which shall be held if the court determines that sufficient grounds exist. At such hearing the prosecuting attorney or the defendant may present evidence bearing on the order of transfer. The court shall use the same standards as used in conducting probation revocation hearings pursuant to Section 1203.2 of the Penal Code.

Prior to making an order for transfer under this section, the court shall notify the defendant, the attorney of record for the defendant, the prosecuting attorney, and the county mental health director or his designee.

If the defendant is committed to a state hospital or other facility, the medical director of the facility shall, at six-month intervals, submit a report in writing to the court, the prosecuting attorney, and the attorney of record for the defendant setting forth the status and progress of the defendant. A copy of this report shall be furnished to the mental health director of the county of commitment.
(Amended by Stats.1978, c. 1291, p. ——, § 1.)

§ 1042.5. Trial of infraction

Trial of an infraction shall be by the court, but when a defendant has been charged with an infraction and with a public offense for which there is a

right to jury trial and a jury trial is not waived, the court may order that the offenses be tried together by jury or that they be tried separately with the infraction being tried by the court either in the same proceeding or a separate proceeding as may be appropriate.
(Added by Stats.1968, c. 1192, p. 2255, § 5.)

§ 1043. Presence of defendant; felony cases; misdemeanor cases; procedure

(a) Except as otherwise provided in this section, the defendant in a felony case shall be personally present at the trial.

(b) The absence of the defendant in a felony case after the trial has commenced in his presence shall not prevent continuing the trial to, and including, the return of the verdict in any of the following cases:

(1) Any case in which the defendant, after he has been warned by the judge that he will be removed if he continues his disruptive behavior, nevertheless insists on conducting himself in a manner so disorderly, disruptive, and disrespectful of the court that the trial cannot be carried on with him in the courtroom.

(2) Any prosecution for an offense which is not punishable by death in which the defendant is voluntarily absent.

(c) Any defendant who is absent from a trial pursuant to paragraph (1) of subdivision (b) may reclaim his right to be present at the trial as soon as he is willing to conduct himself consistently with the decorum and respect inherent in the concept of courts and judicial proceedings.

(d) Subdivisions (a) and (b) shall not limit the right of a defendant to waive his right to be present in accordance with Section 977.

(e) If the defendant in a misdemeanor case fails to appear in person at the time set for trial or during the course of trial, the court shall proceed with the trial, unless good cause for a continuance exists, if the defendant has authorized his counsel to proceed in his absence pursuant to subdivision (a) of Section 977.

If there is no authorization pursuant to subdivision (a) of Section 977 and if the defendant fails to appear in person at the time set for trial or during the course of trial, the court, in its discretion, may do one or more of the following, as it deems appropriate:

(1) Continue the matter.

(2) Order bail forfeited or revoke release on the defendant's own recognizance.

(3) Issue a bench warrant.

(4) Proceed with the trial if the court finds the defendant has absented himself voluntarily with full knowledge that the trial is to be held or is being held.

Nothing herein shall limit the right of the court to order the defendant to be personally present at the trial for purposes of identification unless counsel stipulate to the issue of identity.
(Amended by Stats.1977, c. 759, p. —, § 1; Stats.1977, c. 1152, p. —, § 2.)

Notes of Decisions

In general

This section providing that defendant must be personally present at trial is meant to require defendant's presence only at such stages of trial as affect his substantial rights, so that his presence is not necessary at proceedings which are merely preliminary or formal wherein no matters affecting his guilt or innocence are presented. People v. Boehm (1969) 75 Cal.Rptr. 590, 270 C.A.2d 13.

Requirement of Const. art. 1, § 13, cl. 3 and this section that a defendant be present at trial is limited to situation in which defendant's presence bears a reasonably substantial relation to the fullness of his opportunity to defend against the charge. In re Lessard (1965) 42 Cal.Rptr. 583, 399 P.2d 39, 62 A.C. 516.

The fact that this section requiring defendant to be personally present at a felony trial is apparently mandatory will not prevent a waiver of the right in a proper case. People v. Rogers (1957) 309 P.2d 949, 150 C.A.2d 403.

§ 1044. Control of proceedings by judge; restriction of evidence and argument to relevant and material matters

It shall be the duty of the judge to control all proceedings during the trial, and to limit the introduction of evidence and the argument of counsel to relevant and material matters, with a view to the expeditious and effective ascertainment of the truth regarding the matters involved.
(Added by Stats.1927, c. 607, p. 1040, § 1.)

§ 1048. Calendar; priorities; minor as victim or detained as material witness; continuance

The issues on the calendar must be disposed of in the following order, unless for good cause the court shall direct an action to be tried out of its order:

1. Prosecutions for felony, when the defendant is in custody.

2. Prosecutions for misdemeanor, when the defendant is in custody.

3. Prosecutions for felony, when the defendant is on bail.

4. Prosecutions for misdemeanor, when the defendant is on bail.

§ 1048

However, all criminal actions wherein a minor is detained as a material witness, or wherein the minor is the victim of the alleged offense, shall be given precedence over all other criminal actions in the order of trial. In such actions continuations shall be granted by the court only after a hearing and determination of the necessity thereof, and in any event, the trial shall be commenced within thirty days after arraignment, unless for good cause the court shall direct the action to be continued, after a hearing and determination of the necessity of such continuance.
(Amended by Stats.1949, c. 917, p. 1682, § 1.)

§ 1093. Order of procedure; change of order; powers of judge to comment and to charge as to law

The jury having been impaneled and sworn, unless waived, the trial must proceed in the following order, unless otherwise directed by the court:

1. If the accusatory pleading be for a felony, the clerk must read it, and state the plea of the defendant to the jury, and in cases where it charges a previous conviction, and the defendant has confessed the same, the clerk in reading it shall omit therefrom all that relates to such previous conviction. In all other cases this formality may be dispensed with.

2. The district attorney, or other counsel for the people, may make an opening statement in support of the charge. Whether or not the district attorney, or other counsel for the people, makes an opening statement, the defendant or his counsel may then make an opening statement, or may reserve the making of an opening statement until after introduction of the evidence in support of the charge.

3. The district attorney, or other counsel for the people shall then offer the evidence in support of the charge. The defendant or his counsel may then offer his evidence in support of the defense.

4. The parties may then respectively offer rebutting testimony only, unless the court, for good reason, in furtherance of justice, permit them to offer evidence upon their original case.

5. When the evidence is concluded, unless the case is submitted on either side, or on both sides, without argument, the district attorney, or other counsel for the people, and counsel for the defendant, may argue the case to the court and jury; the district attorney, or other counsel for the people, opening the argument and having the right to close.

6. The judge may then charge the jury, and must do so on any points of law pertinent to the issue, if requested by either party; and he may state the testimony, and he may make such comment on the evidence and the testimony and credibility of any witness as in his opinion is necessary for the proper determination of the case and he may declare the law. At the beginning of the trial or from time to time during the trial, and without any request from either party, the trial judge may give the jury such instructions on the law applicable to the case as he may deem necessary for their guidance on hearing the case. The trial judge may cause copies of instructions so given to be delivered to the jurors at the time they are given.
(Amended by Stats.1976, c. 488, p. —, § 1.)

§ 1094. Order of procedure; change of order

When order of trial may be departed from. When the state of the pleadings requires it, or in any other case, for good reasons, and in the sound discretion of the Court, the order prescribed in the last section may be departed from.
(Enacted 1872.)

§ 1095. Argument; number of counsel

If the offense charged is punishable with death, two counsel on each side may argue the cause. In any other case the court may, in its discretion, restrict the argument to one counsel on each side.
(Amended by Stats.1951, c. 1674, p. 3846, § 95.)

§ 1096. Presumption of innocence; effect; reasonable doubt

A defendant in a criminal action is presumed to be innocent until the contrary is proved, and in case of a reasonable doubt whether his guilt is satisfactorily shown, he is entitled to an acquittal, but the effect of this presumption is only to place upon the state the burden of proving him guilty beyond a reasonable doubt. Reasonable doubt is defined as follows: "It is not a mere possible doubt; because everything relating to human affairs, and depending on moral evidence, is open to some possible or imaginary doubt. It is that state of the case, which, after the entire comparison and consideration of all the evidence, leaves the minds of jurors in that condition that they can not say they feel an abiding conviction, to a moral certainty, of the truth of the charge."
(Amended by Stats.1927, c. 604, p. 1039, § 1.)

§ 1096a. Presumption of innocence; reasonable doubt; instruction

In charging a jury, the court may read to the jury section 1096 of this code, and no further instruction on the subject of the presumption of innocence or defining reasonable doubt need be given.
(Added by Stats.1927, c. 604, p. 1039, § 2.)

§ 1097. Reasonable doubt as to degree; conviction of lowest

When it appears that the defendant has committed a public offense, or attempted to commit a public offense, and there is reasonable ground of doubt in which of two or more degrees of the crime or attempted crime he is guilty, he can be convicted of the lowest of such degrees only.
(Amended by Stats.1978, c. 1166, p. ——, § 2.)

§ 1098. Defendants jointly charged; joint or separate trials; discretion

When two or more defendants are jointly charged with any public offense, whether felony or misdemeanor, they must be tried jointly, unless the court order separate trials. In ordering separate trials, the court in its discretion may order a separate trial as to one or more defendants, and a joint trial as to the others, or may order any number of the defendants to be tried at one trial, and any number of the others at different trials, or may order a separate trial for each defendant; provided, that where two or more persons can be jointly tried, the fact that separate accusatory pleadings were filed shall not prevent their joint trial.
(Amended by Stats.1955, c. 103, p. 568, § 1.)

§ 1103a. Perjury; proof required

No person shall be convicted of perjury where proof of falsity rests solely upon contradiction by testimony of a single person other than the defendant. Proof of falsity may be established by direct or indirect evidence.
(Amended by Stats.1969, c. 831, p. 1663, § 1.)

§ 1104. Conspiracy; necessity of alleging and proving overt act; proof of other overt acts

Upon a trial for conspiracy, in a case where an overt act is necessary to constitute the offense, the defendant cannot be convicted unless one or more overt acts are expressly alleged in the indictment or information, nor unless one of the acts alleged is proved; but other overt acts not alleged may be given in evidence.
(Amended by Code Am.1880, c. 47, p. 22, § 70.)

§ 1105. Murder; burden of proving mitigating circumstances, justification or excuse; exception; application

(a) Upon a trial for murder, the commission of the homicide by the defendant being proved, the burden of proving circumstances of mitigation, or that justify or excuse it, devolves upon him, unless the proof on the part of the prosecution tends to show that the crime committed only amounts to manslaughter, or that the defendant was justifiable or excusable.

(b) Nothing in this section shall apply to or affect any proceeding under Section 190.3 or 190.4.
(Amended by Stats.1977, c. 316, p. ——, § 20, urgency, eff. Aug. 11, 1977.)

§ 1111. Conviction on testimony of accomplice; corroboration; accomplice defined

A conviction can not be had upon the testimony of an accomplice unless it be corroborated by such other evidence as shall tend to connect the defendant with the commission of the offense; and the corroboration is not sufficient if it merely shows the commission of the offense or the circumstances thereof.

An accomplice is hereby defined as one who is liable to prosecution for the identical offense charged against the defendant on trial in the cause in which the testimony of the accomplice is given.
(Amended by Stats.1915, c. 457, p. 760, § 1.)

Notes of Decisions

Accomplices defined

Definition of "accomplice" includes, without being limited to, anyone who aids or abets the commission of a crime. People v. Bohmer (1975) 120 Cal.Rptr. 136, 46 C.A.3d 185, certiorari denied 96 S.Ct. 402, 423 U.S. 990, 46 L.Ed.2d 308.

To be included within the statutory definition of an accomplice, witness must have guilty knowledge and intent with regard to commission of crime. People v. Gordon (1973) 110 Cal.Rptr. 906, 516 P.2d 298, 10 C.3d 460.

For purpose of this section relating to testimony of an accomplice, an "accomplice" includes all persons concerned in commission of offense whether they directly commit the act constituting the offense or aid and abet in its commission. Id.

One is an "accomplice" if he is liable for prosecution for the same offense for which defendant is on trial. People v. Kageler (1973) 108 Cal.Rptr. 235, 32 C.A.3d 738.

For purposes of this section providing that a conviction cannot be had upon testimony of accomplice unless it be corroborated by such other evidence as shall tend to connect the defendant with the commission of the offense, an "accomplice" includes all persons concerned in commission of offense, whether they directly commit act constituting offense or aid and abet in its commission. People v. Scofield (1971) 95 Cal.Rptr. 405, 17 C.A.3d 1018.

§ 1111

To comply with this section requiring corroboration of testimony of accomplice, prosecution must produce independent evidence which, without aid or assistance from testimony of accomplice, tends to connect defendant with the crime charged. People v. Randono (1973) 108 Cal.Rptr. 326, 32 C.A.3d 164.

In order to corroborate testimony of an accomplice, prosecution must produce independent evidence which, without aid or assistance from the testimony of accomplice, tends to connect the defendant with the crime charged. People v. Perry (1972) 103 Cal.Rptr. 161, 499 P.2d 129, 7 C.3d 756.

Where witness who was facing charge of receiving stolen property as result of his involvement in the transaction did not testify to formation of any agreement prior to the theft and it was reasonably inferable that no agreement as to time and place of delivery was reached until after the theft was accomplished and it was inferable from defendant's inquiry after the theft as to when witness could get a buyer that no firm arrangements preceded the theft, defendant charged with grand theft did not meet burden of proving that witness was an accomplice whose testimony had to be corroborated. People v. Smith (1972) 102 Cal.Rptr. 625, 26 C.A.3d 404.

§ 1117. Discharge of jury for want of facts constituting offense; discharge of defendant and exoneration of bail; resubmission for new indictment or information; examination before magistrate

If the jury is discharged because the facts as charged do not constitute an offense punishable by law, the court must order that the defendant, if in custody, be discharged; or if admitted to bail, that his bail be exonerated; or, if he has deposited money or if money has been deposited by another or others instead of bail for his appearance, that the money be refunded to him or to the person or persons found by the court to have deposited said money on behalf of said defendant, unless in its opinion a new indictment or information can be framed upon which the defendant can be legally convicted, in which case it may direct the district attorney to file a new information, or (if the defendant has not been committed by a magistrate) direct that the case be submitted to the same or another grand jury; and the same proceedings must be had thereon as are prescribed in section 998; provided, that after such order or submission the defendant may be examined before a magistrate, and discharged or committed by him as in other cases.
(Amended by Stats.1935, c. 657, p. 1814, § 4.)

§ 1118. Trial by court without jury; entry of judgment of acquittal upon not guilty finding

In a case tried by the court without a jury, a jury having been waived, the court on motion of the defendant or on its own motion shall order the entry of a judgment of acquittal of one or more of the offenses charged in the accusatory pleading after the evidence of the prosecution has been closed if the court, upon weighing the evidence then before it, finds the defendant not guilty of such offense or offenses. If such a motion for judgment of acquittal at the close of the evidence offered by the prosecution is not granted, the defendant may offer evidence without first having reserved that right.
(Added by Stats.1967, c. 256, p. 1406, § 2.)

§ 1118.1. Trial by jury; entry of judgment of acquittal for insufficient evidence

In a case tried before a jury, the court on motion of the defendant or on its own motion, at the close of the evidence on either side and before the case is submitted to the jury for decision, shall order the entry of a judgment of acquittal of one or more of the offenses charged in the accusatory pleading if the evidence then before the court is insufficient to sustain a conviction of such offense or offenses on appeal. If such a motion for judgment of acquittal at the close of the evidence offered by the prosecution is not granted, the defendant may offer evidence without first having reserved that right.
(Added by Stats.1967, c. 256, p. 1406, § 3.)

§ 1118.2. Appealability of judgment bar to other prosecution for same offense

A judgment of acquittal entered pursuant to the provisions of Section 1118 or 1118.1 shall not be appealable and is a bar to any other prosecution for the same offense.
(Added by Stats.1967, c. 256, p. 1407, § 4.)

§ 1127c. Instruction as to flight; form

In any criminal trial or proceeding where evidence of flight of a defendant is relied upon as tending to show guilt, the court shall instruct the jury substantially as follows:

The flight of a person immediately after the commission of a crime, or after he is accused of a crime that has been committed, is not sufficient in itself to establish his guilt, but is a fact which, if proved, the jury may consider in deciding his guilt or innocence. The weight to which such circumstance is entitled is a matter for the jury to determine.

No further instruction on the subject of flight need be given.
(Added by Stats.1929, c. 875, p. 1939, § 1.)

§ 1129. Commitment of defendant on bail

When defendant on bail appears for trial he may be committed. When a defendant who has given bail appears for trial, the Court may, in its discretion, at any time after his appearance for trial, order him to be committed to the custody of the proper officer of the county, to abide the judgment or further order of the Court, and he must be committed and held in custody accordingly.
(Enacted 1872.)

§ 1131. Theft of money, bank notes, or securities; sufficiency of evidence to sustain allegations of description; proof where part of property returned

Upon a trial for larceny or embezzlement of money, bank notes, certificates of stock, or valuable securities, the allegation of the indictment or information, so far as regards the description of the property, is sustained, if the offender be proved to have embezzled or stolen any money, bank notes, certificates of stock, or valuable security, although the particular species of coin or other money, or the number, denomination, or kind of bank notes, certificates of stock, or valuable security, be not proved; and upon a trial for embezzlement, if the offender be proved to have embezzled any piece of coin or other money, any bank note, certificate of stock, or valuable security, although such piece of coin or other money, or such bank note, certificate of stock, or valuable security, may have been delivered to him in order that some part of the value thereof should be returned to the party delivering the same, and such part shall have been returned accordingly.
(Amended by Code Am.1880, c. 47, p. 24, § 78.)

§ 1168. Sentence to imprisonment in state prison; trial court sentencing; fixing of term or duration

(a) Every person who commits a public offense, for which any specification of three time periods of imprisonment in any state prison is now prescribed by law shall, unless such convicted person be placed on probation, a new trial granted, or the imposing of sentence suspended, be sentenced pursuant to Chapter 4.5 (commencing with Section 1170) of Title 7 of Part 2.

(b) For any person not sentenced under such provision, but who is sentenced to be imprisoned in the state prison, including imprisonment not exceeding one year and one day, the court imposing the sentence shall not fix the term or duration of the period of imprisonment.
(Amended by Stats.1977, c. 165, p. —, § 14.)

§ 1170. Legislative findings; determinate sentences; imposition; resentence

(a)(1) The Legislature finds and declares that the purposes of imprisonment for crime is punishment. This purpose is best served by terms proportionate to the seriousness of the offense with provision for uniformity in the sentences of offenders committing the same offense under similar circumstances. The Legislature further finds and declares that the elimination of disparity and the provision of uniformity of sentences can best be achieved by determinate sentences fixed by statute in proportion to the seriousness of the offense as determined by the Legislature to be imposed by the court with specified discretion.

(2) In any case in which the punishment prescribed by statute for a person convicted of a public offense is a term of imprisonment in the state prison of 16 months, two or three years; two, three, or four years; two, three, or five years; three, four, or five years; two, four, or six years; three, four, or six years; three, five, or seven years; three, six, or eight years; five, seven, or nine years; five, seven, or 11 years, or any other specification of three time periods, the court shall sentence the defendant to one of the terms of imprisonment specified unless such convicted person is given any other disposition provided by law, including a fine, jail, probation, or the suspension of imposition or execution of sentence or is sentenced pursuant to subdivision (b) of Section 1168 because he had committed his crime prior to July 1, 1977. In sentencing the convicted person, the court shall apply the sentencing rules of the Judicial Council. The court, unless it determines that there are circumstances in mitigation of the punishment prescribed, shall also impose any other term which it is required by law to impose as an additional term. Nothing in this article shall affect any provision of law which imposes the death penalty, which authorizes or restricts the granting of probation or suspending the execution or imposition of sentence, or expressly provides for imprisonment in the state prison for life. In any case in which the amount of preimprisonment credit under Section 2900.5 or any other provision of law is equal to or exceeds any sentence imposed pursuant to this chapter, the entire sentence, including any period of parole under Section 3000, shall be deemed to have been served and the defendant shall not be actually delivered to the custody of the

§ 1170

Director of Corrections. However, any such sentence shall be deemed a separate prior prison term under Section 667.5, and a copy of the judgment and other necessary documentation shall be forwarded to the Director of Corrections.

(b) When a judgment of imprisonment is to be imposed and the statute specifies three possible terms, the court shall order imposition of the middle term, unless there are circumstances in aggravation or mitigation of the crime. At least four days prior to the time set for imposition of judgment either party may submit a statement in aggravation or mitigation to dispute facts in the record or the probation officer's report, or to present additional facts. In determining whether there are circumstances that justify imposition of the upper or lower term, the court may consider the record in the case, the probation officer's report, other reports including reports received pursuant to Section 1203.03 and statements in aggravation or mitigation submitted by the prosecution or the defendant, and any further evidence introduced at the sentencing hearing. The court shall set forth on the record the facts and reasons for imposing the upper or lower term. The court may not impose an upper term by using the fact of any enhancement upon which sentence is imposed under Section 667.5, 1170.1, 12022, 12022.5, 12022.6, or 12022.7. A term of imprisonment shall not be specified if imposition of sentence is suspended.

(c) The court shall state the reasons for its sentence choice on the record at the time of sentencing. The court shall also inform the defendant that as part of the sentence after expiration of the term he may be on parole for a period as provided in Section 3000.

(d) When a defendant subject to this section or subdivision (b) of Section 1168 has been sentenced to be imprisoned in the state prison and has been committed to the custody of the Director of Corrections, the court may, within 120 days of the date of commitment on its own motion, or at any time upon the recommendation of the Director of Corrections or the Community Release Board, recall the sentence and commitment previously ordered and resentence the defendant in the same manner as if he had not previously been sentenced, provided the new sentence, if any, is no greater than the initial sentence. The resentence under this subdivision shall apply the sentencing rules of the Judicial Council so as to eliminate disparity of sentences and to promote uniformity of sentencing. Credit shall be given for time served.

(e) Any sentence imposed under this article shall be subject to the provisions of Sections 3000 and 3057 and any other applicable provisions of law.

(f) In all cases the Community Release Board shall, not later than one year after the commencement of the term of imprisonment, review the sentence and shall by motion recommend that the court recall the sentence and commitment previously ordered and resentence the defendant in the same manner as if he had not been previously sentenced if the board determines the sentence is disparate. The review under this section shall concern the decision to deny probation and the sentencing decisions enumerated in subdivisions (b), (c), (d), and (e) of Section 1170.3 and apply the sentencing rules of the Judicial Council and the information regarding the sentences in this state of other persons convicted of similar crimes so as to eliminate disparity of sentences and to promote uniformity of sentencing.
(Amended by Stats.1978, c. 579, p. ——, § 29.)

SENTENCING

§ 1170.1. Second or subsequent conviction of felony; felony while confined in state prison; additional sentences; limitation on enhancement and term of imprisonment

(a) Except as provided in subdivision (b) and subject to Section 654, when any person is convicted of two or more felonies, whether in the same proceeding or court or in different proceedings or courts, and whether by judgment rendered by the same or by a different court, and a consecutive term of imprisonment is imposed under Sections 669 and 1170, the aggregate term of imprisonment for all such convictions shall be the sum of the principal term, the subordinate term and any additional term imposed pursuant to Section 667.5. The principal term shall consist of the greatest term of imprisonment imposed by the court for any of the crimes, including any enhancements imposed pursuant to Section 12022, 12022.5, 12022.6, or 12022.7. The subordinate term for each consecutive offense shall consist of one-third of the middle term of imprisonment prescribed for each other felony conviction for which a consecutive term of imprisonment is imposed, and shall exclude any enhancements when the consecutive offense is not listed in subdivision (c) of Section 667.5, but shall include one-third of any enhancement imposed pursuant to Section 12022, 12022.5 or 12022.7 when the consecutive offense is listed in subdivision (c) of

Section 667.5. In no case shall the total of subordinate terms for consecutive offenses not listed in subdivision (c) of Section 667.5 exceed five years.

(b) In the case of any person convicted of one or more felonies committed while such person is confined in a state prison, or is subject to reimprisonment for escape from such custody and the law either requires the terms to be served consecutively or the court imposes consecutive terms, the term of imprisonment for all such convictions which such person is required to serve consecutively shall commence from the time such person would otherwise have been released from prison. If the new offenses are consecutive with each other, the principal and subordinate terms shall be calculated as provided in subdivision (a), except that the total of subordinate terms may exceed five years. The provisions of this subdivision shall be applicable in cases of convictions of more than one offense in different proceedings, and convictions of more than one offense in the same or different proceedings.

(c) When the court imposes a prison sentence for a felony pursuant to Section 1170 the court shall also impose the additional terms provided in Sections 667.5, 12022, 12022.5, 12022.6, and 12022.7, unless the additional punishment therefore is stricken pursuant to subdivision (g). The court shall also impose any other additional term which the court determines in its discretion or as required by law shall run consecutive to the term imposed under Section 1170. In considering the imposition of such additional terms, the court shall apply the sentencing rules of the Judicial Council.

(d) When two or more enhancements under Sections 12022, 12022.5, and 12022.7 may be imposed for any single offense, only the greatest enhancement shall apply; however, in cases of robbery, rape or burglary, or attempted robbery, rape or burglary the court may impose both (1) one enhancement for weapons as provided in either Section 12022 or 12022.5 and (2) an enhancement for great bodily injury as provided in Section 12022.7.

(e) The enhancements provided in Sections 667.5, 12022, 12022.5, 12022.6, and 12022.7 shall be pleaded and proven as provided by law.

(f) The term of imprisonment shall not exceed twice the number of years imposed by the trial court as the base term pursuant to subdivision (b) of Section 1170 unless the defendant stands convicted of a felony described in subdivision (c) of Section 667.5, or a consecutive sentence is being imposed pursuant to subdivision (b) of this section, or an enhancement is imposed pursuant to Section 12022, 12022.5, 12022.6 or 12022.7.

(g) Notwithstanding any other provision of law, the court may strike the additional punishment for the enhancements provided in Sections 667.5, 12022, 12022.5, 12022.6, and 12022.7 if it determines that there are circumstances in mitigation of the additional punishment and states on the record its reasons for striking the additional punishment.
(Amended by Stats.1977, c. 165, p. ——, § 17.)

§ 1170.2. Sentences for felony to state prison prior to effective date of this section; parole; release

(a) In the case of any inmate who committed a felony prior to July 1, 1977, who would have been sentenced under Section 1170 if he had committed it after July 1, 1977, the Community Release Board shall determine what the length of time of imprisonment would have been under Section 1170 without consideration of good-time credit and utilizing the middle term of the offense bearing the longest term of imprisonment of which the prisoner was convicted increased by any enhancements justified by matters found to be true and which were imposed by the court at the time of sentencing for such felony. Such matters include: being armed with a deadly or dangerous weapon as specified in Section 211a, 460, 3024, or 12022 prior to July 1, 1977, which may result in a one-year enhancement pursuant to the provisions of Section 12022; using a firearm as specified in Section 12022.5 prior to July 1, 1977, which may result in a two-year enhancement pursuant to the provisions of Section 12022.5; infliction of great bodily injury as specified in Section 213, 264, or 461 prior to July 1, 1977, which may result in a three-year enhancement pursuant to the provisions of Section 12022.7; any prior felony conviction as specified in any statute prior to July 1, 1977, which prior felony conviction is the equivalent of a prior prison term as defined in Section 667.5, which may result in the appropriate enhancement pursuant to the provisions of Section 667.5; and any consecutive sentence.

(b) If the calculation required under subdivision (a) is less than the time to be served prior to a release date set prior to July 1, 1977, or if a release date had not been set, the Community Release Board shall establish the prisoner's parole date, subject to subdivision (d), on the date calculated under subdivision (a) unless at least two of the members of the Community

§ 1170.2

Release Board after reviewing the prisoner's file, determine that due to the number of crimes of which the prisoner was convicted, or due to the number of prior convictions suffered by the prisoner, or due to the fact that the prisoner was armed with a deadly weapon when the crime was committed, or used a deadly weapon during the commission of the crime, or inflicted or attempted to inflict great bodily injury on the victim of the crime, the prisoner should serve a term longer than that calculated in subdivision (a), in which event the prisoner shall be entitled to a hearing before a panel consisting of at least two members of the Community Release Board as provided for in Section 3041.5. The Community Release Board shall notify each prisoner who is scheduled for such a hearing within 90 days of July 1, 1977, or within 90 days of the date the prisoner is received by or returned to the custody of the Department of Corrections, whichever is later. The hearing shall be held before April 1, 1978, or within 120 days of receipt of the prisoner, whichever is later. The board may by resolution extend this period an additional 90 days. However, such resolution shall have no force or effect if vetoed by resolution of either house of the Legislature. It is the intent of the Legislature that the hearings provided for in this subdivision shall be accomplished in the most expeditious manner possible. At such hearing the prisoner shall be entitled to be represented by legal counsel, a release date shall be set, and the prisoner shall be informed in writing of the extraordinary factors specifically considered determinative and on what basis the release date has been calculated. In fixing a term under this section the board shall be guided by, but not limited to, the term which reasonably could be imposed on a person who committed a similar offense under similar circumstances on or after July 1, 1977, and further, the board shall be guided by the following finding and declaration hereby made by the Legislature: that the necessity to protect the public from repetition of extraordinary crimes of violence against the person is the paramount consideration.

(c) Nothing in this section shall be deemed to keep an inmate in the custody of the Department of Corrections for a period of time longer than he would have been kept in its custody under the provisions of law applicable to him prior to July 1, 1977. Nothing in this section shall be deemed to require the release of an inmate sentenced to consecutive sentences under the provisions of law applicable to him prior to July 1, 1977, earlier than if he had been sentenced to concurrent sentences.

(d) In the case of any prisoner who committed a felony prior to July 1, 1977, who would have been sentenced under Section 1170 if the felony was committed on or after July 1, 1977, the good behavior and participation provisions of Article 2.5 (commencing with Section 2930) of Chapter 7 of Title 1 of Part 3 shall apply from July 1, 1977, and thereafter.

(e) In the case of any inmate who committed a felony prior to July 1, 1977, who would have been sentenced under Section 1168 if the felony was committed on or after July 1, 1977, the Community Release Board shall provide for release from prison as provided for by this code.

(f) In the case of any inmate who committed a felony prior to July 1, 1977, the length, conditions, revocation, and other incidents of parole shall be the same as if the prisoner had been sentenced for an offense committed on or after July 1, 1977.

(g) Nothing in this chapter shall affect the eligibility for parole under Article 3 (commencing with Section 3040) of Chapter 8 of Title 1 of Part 3 of an inmate sentenced pursuant to Section 1168 as operative prior to July 1, 1977, for a period of parole as specified in subdivision (b) of Section 3000.

(h) In fixing a term under this section, the Community Release Board shall utilize the terms of imprisonment as provided in Chapter 1139 of the Statutes of 1976, and Chapter 165 of the Statutes of 1977.

(Amended by Stats.1978, c. 329, p. ——, § 2; Stats.1978, c. 579, p. ——, § 30.)

§ 1170.3. Rules; criteria for consideration in sentencing to promote uniformity

The Judicial Council shall seek to promote uniformity in sentencing under Section 1170, by the adoption of rules providing criteria for the consideration of the trial judge at the time of sentencing regarding the court's decision to:

(a) Grant or deny probation.

(b) Impose the lower or upper prison term.

(c) Impose concurrent or consecutive sentences.

(d) Consider an additional sentence for prior prison terms.

(e) Impose an additional sentence for being armed with a deadly weapon, using a firearm, an excessive taking or damage, or the infliction of great bodily injury.

(Added by Stats.1976, c. 1139, p. ——, § 273, operative July 1, 1977.)

§ 1170.4. Collection analysis and distribution of information on sentencing practices

The Judicial Council shall collect, analyze, and quarterly distribute and publish relevant information to trial judges and other interested persons relating to sentencing practices in this state and other jurisdictions. Such information shall be taken into consideration by the Judicial Council in the adoption of rules pursuant to Section 1170.3.
(Amended by Stats.1977, c. 165, p. ——, § 18.5.)

§ 1170.5. Annual sentencing institutes

The Judicial Council shall conduct annual sentencing institutes for trial court judges pursuant to Section 68551 of the Government Code, toward the end of assisting the judge in the imposition of appropriate sentences.
(Added by Stats.1976, c. 1139, p. ——, § 273, operative July 1, 1977.)

§ 1170.6. Review and analysis of statutory sentences and operation of existing criminal penalties; report

The Judicial Council shall continually study and review the statutory sentences and the operation of existing criminal penalties and shall report to the Governor and to the appropriate policy committees of the Legislature its analysis regarding this subject matter and as to all proposed legislation affecting felony sentences. Such review and analysis shall take into consideration:

(a) The nature of the offense with the degree of danger the offense presents to society.

(b) The penalty of the offense as compared to penalties for offenses that are in their nature more serious.

(c) The penalty of the offense as compared to penalties for the same offense in other jurisdictions.

(d) The penalty of the offense as compared to recommendations for sentencing suggested by national commissions and other learned bodies.
(Added by Stats.1976, c. 1139, p. ——, § 273, operative July 1, 1977.)

§ 1191. Appointment of time for pronouncing judgment; reference to probation officer or placement in diagnostic facility; extension of time

In the superior court, after a plea, finding or verdict of guilty, or after a finding or verdict against the defendant on a plea of a former conviction or acquittal, or once in jeopardy, the court must appoint a time for pronouncing judgment, which must be within 28 days after the verdict, finding or plea of guilty, during which time the court shall refer the case to the probation officer for a report if eligible for probation and pursuant to Section 1203; provided, however, that the court may extend the time not more than 10 days for the purpose of hearing or determining any motion for a new trial, or in arrest of judgment, and may further extend the time until the probation officer's report is received and until any proceedings for granting or denying probation have been disposed of. If in the opinion of the court there is a reasonable ground for believing a defendant insane, the court may extend the time for pronouncing sentence until the question of insanity has been heard and determined, as provided in this code. If the court orders defendant placed in a diagnostic facility pursuant to Section 1203.03, the time otherwise allowed by this section for pronouncing judgment is extended by a period equal to (1) the number of days which elapse between the date of such order and the date on which notice is received from the Director of Corrections advising whether or not the Department of Corrections will receive defendant in such facility, and (2) if the director notifies the court that it will receive the defendant, the time which elapses until his return to the court from the facility.
(Amended by Stats.1977, c. 165, p. ——, § 19.)

§ 1192. Degree of offense; determination by court before passing sentence; effect of failure to determine degree

Upon a plea of guilty, or upon conviction by the court without a jury, of a crime or attempted crime distinguished or divided into degrees, the court must, before passing sentence, determine the degree. Upon the failure of the court to so determine, the degree of the crime or attempted crime of which the defendant is guilty, shall be deemed to be of the lesser degree.
(Amended by Stats.1978, c. 1166, p. ——, § 4.)

§ 1192.1. Specification of degree in plea of guilty to information or indictment

Upon a plea of guilty to an information or indictment accusing the defendant of a crime or attempted crime divided into degrees when consented to by the prosecuting attorney in open court and approved by the court, such plea may specify the degree thereof

§ 1192.1

and in such event the defendant cannot be punished for a higher degree of the crime or attempted crime than the degree specified.
(Amended by Stats.1978, c. 1166, p. ——, § 5.)

§ 1192.2. Specification of degree in plea of guilty before committing magistrate

Upon a plea of guilty before a committing magistrate as provided in Section 859a, to a crime or attempted crime divided into degrees, when consented to by the prosecuting attorney in open court and approved by such magistrate, such plea may specify the degree thereof and in such event, the defendant cannot be punished for a higher degree of the crime or attempted crime than the degree specified.
(Amended by Stats.1978, c. 1166, p. ——, § 6.)

§ 1192.4. Unaccepted and unapproved plea deemed withdrawn; admissibility in evidence; entry of additional pleas

If the defendant's plea of guilty pursuant to Section 1192.1 or 1192.2 is not accepted by the prosecuting attorney and approved by the court, the plea shall be deemed withdrawn and the defendant may then enter such plea or pleas as would otherwise have been available. The plea so withdrawn may not be received in evidence in any criminal, civil, or special action or proceeding of any nature, including proceedings before agencies, commissions, boards, and tribunals.
(Amended by Stats.1970, c. 1123, p. 1992, § 2.)

§ 1192.5. Plea of guilty or nolo contendere; specification of punishment and exercise of powers; procedure on approval; withdrawal

Upon a plea of guilty or nolo contendere to an accusatory pleading charging a felony, the plea may specify the punishment to the same extent as it may be specified by the jury on a plea of not guilty or fixed by the court on a plea of guilty, nolo contendere, or not guilty, and may specify the exercise by the court thereafter of other powers legally available to it.

Where such plea is accepted by the prosecuting attorney in open court and is approved by the court, the defendant, except as otherwise provided in this section, cannot be sentenced on such plea to a punishment more severe than that specified in the plea and the court may not proceed as to such plea other than as specified in the plea.

If the court approves of the plea, it shall inform the defendant prior to the making of the plea that (1) its approval is not binding, (2) it may, at the time set for the hearing on the application for probation or pronouncement of judgment, withdraw its approval in the light of further consideration of the matter, and (3) in such case, the defendant shall be permitted to withdraw his plea if he desires to do so. The court shall also cause an inquiry to be made of the defendant to satisfy itself that the plea is freely and voluntarily made, and that there is a factual basis for such plea.

If such plea is not accepted by the prosecuting attorney and approved by the court, the plea shall be deemed withdrawn and the defendant may then enter such plea or pleas as would otherwise have been available.

If such plea is withdrawn or deemed withdrawn, it may not be received in evidence in any criminal, civil, or special action or proceeding of any nature, including proceedings before agencies, commissions, boards, and tribunals.
(Amended by Stats.1974, c. 72, p. 158, § 1.)

§ 1194. Defendant in custody; method of bringing before court for judgment

When defendant in custody, how brought before the Court for judgment. When the defendant is in custody, the Court may direct the officer in whose custody he is to bring him before it for judgment, and the officer must do so.
(Enacted 1872.)

§ 1195. Defendant on bail or deposit; effect of appearance or nonappearance

If the defendant has been released on bail, or has deposited money or property instead thereof, and does not appear for judgment when his personal appearance is necessary, the court, in addition to the forfeiture of the undertaking of bail, or of the money or property deposited, must, on application of the prosecuting attorney, direct the issuance of a bench warrant for the arrest of the defendant.

If the defendant, who is on bail, does appear for judgment and judgment is pronounced upon him or probation is granted to him, then the bail shall be exonerated or, if money or property has been deposited instead of bail, it must be returned to the defendant or to the person or persons found by the court to have deposited said money or property on behalf of said defendant.
(Amended by Stats.1959, c. 1187, p. 3272, § 1.)

§ 1196. Bench warrant; issuance

The clerk, or the judge or justice, if there is no clerk, on application of the prosecuting attorney, must at any time after the order issue a bench warrant into one or more counties.
(Amended by Stats.1951, c. 1674, p. 3853, § 124.)

§ 1197. Bench warrant; form

The bench warrant must be substantially in the following form:

County of _____

The people of the State of California to any peace officer in this State: _____ (name of defendant) having been on the _____ day of _____, 19____, duly convicted in the _____ court of _____ (naming the court) of the crime of _____ (designating it generally), you are therefore commanded forthwith to arrest the above named defendant and bring him before that court for judgment.

Given under my hand with the seal of said court affixed, this _____ day of _____, 19____

By order of said court.

_____
(SEAL)   Clerk (or Judge, or Justice)
(Amended by Stats.1951, c. 1674, p. 3853, § 125.)

§ 1198. Bench warrant; service

The bench warrant may be served in any county in the same manner as a warrant of arrest.
(Amended by Stats.1951, c. 1674, p. 3853, § 126.)

§ 1199. Bench warrant; arrest of defendant; delivery to court

Whether the bench warrant is served in the county in which it was issued or in another county, the officer must arrest the defendant and bring him before the court, or deliver him to any peace officer of the county from which the warrant issued, who must bring him before said court according to the command thereof.
(Amended by Stats.1951, c. 1674, p. 3853, § 127.)

§ 1200. Arraignment of defendant for judgment; inquiry as to cause why judgment should not be pronounced

When the defendant appears for judgment he must be informed by the Court, or by the Clerk, under its direction, of the nature of the charge against him and of his plea, and the verdict, if any thereon, and must be asked whether he has any legal cause to show why judgment should not be pronounced against him.
(Amended by Code Am.1880, c. 47, p. 26, § 90.)

§ 1201. Causes against pronouncement of judgment; insanity; trial; pronouncement of judgment or commitment to state hospital; judgment after recovery of sanity; cause in arrest of judgment or for new trial

He may show, for cause against the judgment:

1. That he is insane; and if, in the opinion of the court, there is reasonable ground for believing him insane, the question of insanity must be tried as provided in chapter six, title ten, part two of this code. If, upon the trial of that question, the jury finds that he is sane, judgment must be pronounced, but if they find him insane, he must be committed to the state hospital for the care and treatment of the insane, until he becomes sane; and when notice is given of that fact, as provided in section one thousand three hundred and seventy-two, he must be brought before the court for judgment;

2. That he has good cause to offer, either in arrest of judgment or for a new trial; in which case the court may, in its discretion, order the judgment to be deferred, and proceed to decide upon the motion in arrest of judgment or for a new trial.
(Amended by Stats.1905, c. 571, p. 763, § 2.)

§ 1202.5. Theft and unlawful driving or taking of automobile or other vehicle; probation or suspension of sentence; reimbursement of or restitution to owner

(a) Notwithstanding the provisions of Section 1203 and subject to subdivision (b) of this section, no person convicted of violating Section 499b of this code, Section 10851 of the Vehicle Code, or Section 487 of this code for theft of an automobile or other vehicle, shall be granted probation or have the execution or imposition of sentence suspended when any pecuniary loss was sustained by the owner of the automobile or vehicle or the owner's assignee unless reimbursement for such loss or restitution is ordered as a condition of probation. If restitution is ordered, the court shall fix the amount of such loss by receiving such evidence as necessary.

Notwithstanding Section 1203.1,

(1) If restitution is ordered as a condition of probation, the court shall establish a reimbursement schedule not to exceed 10 years. If at any time

§ 1202.5

during this period, full restitution is made, the court shall refix the probationary period pursuant to the provisions of Section 1203.1.

(2) Payments shall be made to the owner of the automobile or vehicle or the owner's assignee through the probation officer of the county in which the defendant was convicted.

(3) The court may, in addition, order the defendant's California driver's license suspended for a period not to exceed 120 days.

(b) The court shall order restitution as a condition of probation pursuant to this section. If the defendant fails to make the restitution so ordered, his probation shall be revoked by the court pursuant to Section 1203.2, unless the defendant can show, at the revocation hearing, that he does not have the ability to pay.

(Added by Stats.1978, c. 1189, p. ——, § 1.)

§ 1202a. Judgment for imprisonment; direction for delivery of defendant; designation of institution by director of corrections; death sentence; orders designating places for reception of prisoners

If the judgment is for imprisonment in the State prison the judgment shall direct that the defendant be delivered into the custody of the Director of Corrections at the State prison or institution designated by the Director of Corrections as the place for the reception of persons convicted of felonies, except where the judgment is for death in which case the defendant shall be taken to the warden of the California State Prison at San Quentin.

Unless a different place or places are so designated by the Director of Corrections, the judgment shall direct that the defendant be delivered into the custody of the Director of Corrections at the California State Prison at San Quentin. The Director of Corrections shall designate a place or places for the reception of persons convicted of felonies by order, which order or orders shall be served by registered mail, return receipt requested, upon each judge of each superior court in the State. The Director of Corrections may change the place or places of commitment by the issuance of a new order. Nothing contained in this section affects any provision of Section 3400 of this code.

(Amended by Stats.1945, c. 91, p. 402, § 1.)

§ 1203. Probation; pre-sentence investigation, report and recommendations; mitigating circumstances; hearing by court; power to grant probation; summary denial in misdemeanor cases; offenses for which probation may not be granted; investigation and report where defendant ineligible; procedure for release to another state

(a) In every case in which a person is convicted of a felony and is eligible for probation, before judgment is pronounced, the court shall immediately refer the matter to the probation officer to investigate and report to the court, at a specified time, upon the circumstances surrounding the crime and the prior history and record of the person, which may be considered either in aggravation or mitigation of the punishment. The probation officer shall immediately investigate and make a written report to the court of his findings and recommendations, including his recommendations as to the granting or denying of probation and the conditions of probation, if granted. The probation officer shall also include in his report his determination of whether the defendant is a person who is required to pay a fine pursuant to Section 13967 of the Government Code. The probation officer shall also include in his report for the court's consideration whether the court shall require, as a condition of probation, restitution to the victim or to the Indemnity Fund if assistance has been granted to the victim pursuant to Article 1 (commencing with Section 13959) of Chapter 5 of Part 4 of Division 3 of Title 2 of the Government Code, a recommendation thereof, and if so, the amount thereof, and the means and manner of payment. The report shall be made available to the court and the prosecuting and defense attorneys at least nine days prior to the time fixed by the court for the hearing and determination of the report, and shall be filed with the clerk of the court as a record in the case at the time of the hearing. The time within which the report shall be made available and filed may be waived by written stipulation of the prosecuting and defense attorney which is filed with the court or an oral stipulation in open court which is made and entered upon the minutes of the court. At a time fixed by the court, the court shall hear and determine the application, if one has been made, or, in any case, the suitability of probation in the particular case. At the hearing, the court shall consider any report of the probation officer and shall make a statement that it has considered such report which shall be filed with the clerk of the court as a record in the case. If the court determines that there are circumstances in mitigation of the punishment prescribed by law or that the ends of justice would be subserved by granting probation to the person, it may place him on probation. If probation is denied, the clerk of the court shall immediately send a copy of the report to the Department of Corrections at the prison or other institution to which the person is delivered.

(b) If a defendant is not represented by an attorney, the court shall order the probation officer who makes the probation report to discuss its contents with the defendant.

(c) In every case in which a person is convicted of a misdemeanor, the court may either refer the matter to the probation officer for an investigation and a report or summarily grant or deny probation. If such a case is not referred to the probation officer, in sentencing the person, the court may consider any information concerning him which could have been included in a probation report. The court shall inform the person of the information to be considered and permit him to answer or controvert it. For this purpose, upon the request of the person, the court shall grant a continuance before the judgment is pronounced.

(d) Except in unusual cases where the interests of justice would best be served if the person is granted probation, probation shall not be granted to any of the following persons:

(1) Unless he had a lawful right to carry a deadly weapon, other than a firearm, at the time of the perpetration of the crime or his arrest, any person who has been convicted of arson, robbery, burglary, burglary with explosives, rape with force or violence, murder, assault with intent to commit murder, attempt to commit murder, trainwrecking, kidnapping, escape from the state prison, or a conspiracy to commit one or more of such crimes and was armed with such weapon at either of such times.

(2) Any person who used or attempted to use a deadly weapon upon a human being in connection with the perpetration of the crime of which he has been convicted.

(3) Any person who willfully inflicted great bodily injury or torture in the perpetration of the crime of which he has been convicted.

(4) Any person who has been previously convicted twice in this state of a felony or in any other place of a public offense which, if committed in this state, would have been punishable as a felony.

(5) Unless he has never been previously convicted once in this state of a felony or in any other place of a public offense which, if committed in this state, would have been punishable as a felony, any person who has been convicted of burglary with explosives, rape with force or violence, murder, attempt to commit murder, assault with intent to commit murder, trainwrecking, extortion, kidnapping, escape from the state prison, a violation of Section 286, 288, or 288a, or a conspiracy to commit one or more of such crimes.

(6) Any person who has been previously convicted once in this state of a felony or in any other place of a public offense which, if committed in this state, would have been punishable as a felony, if he committed any of the following acts:

(i) Unless he had a lawful right to carry a deadly weapon at the time of the perpetration of such previous crime or his arrest for such previous crime, he was armed with such weapon at either of such times.

(ii) He used or attempted to use a deadly weapon upon a human being in connection with the perpetration of such previous crime.

(iii) He willfully inflicted great bodily injury or torture in the perpetration of such previous crime.

(7) Any public official or peace officer of this state or any city, county, or other political subdivision who, in the discharge of the duties of his public office or employment, accepted or gave or offered to accept or give any bribe, embezzled public money, or was guilty of extortion.

(e) When probation is granted in a case which comes within the provisions of subdivision (d), the court shall specify on the record and shall enter on the minutes the circumstances indicating that the interests of justice would best be served by such a disposition.

(f) If a person is not eligible for probation, the judge may, in his discretion, refer the matter to the probation officer for an investigation of the facts relevant to the sentencing of the person. Upon such referral, the probation officer shall immediately investigate the circumstances surrounding the crime and the prior record and history of the person and make a written report to the court of his findings.

(g) In any case in which a defendant is convicted of a felony and a probation report is prepared pursuant to subdivision (a) or (f), the probation officer shall

§ 1203

obtain and include in such report a statement of the comments of the victim concerning the offense. The court may direct the probation officer not to obtain such a statement in any case where the victim has in fact testified at any of the court proceedings concerning the offense.

(h) No probationer shall be released to enter another state unless his case has been referred to the Administrator, Interstate Probation and Parole Compacts, pursuant to the Uniform Act for Out-of-State Probationer or Parolee Supervision (Article 3 (commencing with Section 11175) of Chapter 2 of Title I of Part 4).
(Amended by Stats.1978, c. 581, p. —, § 1; Stats.1978, c. 1262, p. —, §§ 1, 2.)

§ 1203.01. Statement of views respecting person convicted or sentenced; filing; transcript of sentencing proceedings; mailing of copies

Immediately after judgment has been pronounced, the judge and the district attorney, respectively, may cause to be filed with the clerk of the court a brief statement of their views respecting the person convicted or sentenced and the crime committed, together with such reports as the probation officer may have filed relative to the prisoner. The judge and district attorney shall cause such statements to be filed if no probation officer's report has been filed. The attorney for the defendant and the law enforcement agency that investigated the case may likewise file with the clerk of the court statements of their views respecting the defendant and the crime of which he was convicted. Forthwith after the filing of such statements and reports, the clerk of the court shall mail a copy thereof, certified by such clerk, along with a copy of the transcript of the proceedings at the time of the sentencing, with postage thereon prepaid, addressed to the Department of Corrections at the prison or other institution to which the person convicted is delivered. The clerk shall also mail a copy of any statement submitted by the court, district attorney, or law enforcement agency, pursuant to this section, with postage thereon prepaid, addressed to the attorney for the defendant, if any, and to the defendant in care of the Department of Corrections, and a copy of any statement submitted by the attorney for the defendant, with postage thereon prepaid, shall be mailed to the district attorney.
(Amended by Stats.1976, c. 876, p. —, § 1.)

§ 1203.02. Probation; inquiry into intoxication or addiction to use of intoxicating liquors; abstinence as a condition

The court, or judge thereof, in granting probation to a defendant convicted of any of the offenses enumerated in Section 290 of this code shall inquire into the question whether the defendant at the time the offense was committed was intoxicated or addicted to the excessive use of alcoholic liquor or beverages at that time or immediately prior thereto, and if the court, or judge thereof, believes that the defendant was so intoxicated, or so addicted, such court, or judge thereof, shall require as a condition of such probation that the defendant totally abstain from the use of alcoholic liquor or beverages.
(Amended by Stats.1951, c. 1608, p. 3614, § 14.)

§ 1203.03. Order placing defendant in diagnostic facility; observation and treatment; report; place of treatment; execution of order; credit on terms; remedial treatment

(a) In any case in which a defendant is convicted of an offense punishable by imprisonment in the state prison, the court, if it concludes that a just disposition of the case requires such diagnosis and treatment services as can be provided at a diagnostic facility of the Department of Corrections, may order that defendant be placed temporarily in such facility for a period not to exceed 90 days, with the further provision in such order that the Director of the Department of Corrections report to the court his diagnosis and recommendations concerning the defendant within the 90-day period.

(b) The Director of the Department of Corrections shall, within the 90 days, cause defendant to be observed and examined and shall forward to the court his diagnosis and recommendation concerning the disposition of defendant's case. Such diagnosis and recommendation shall be embodied in a written report and copies of the report shall be served only upon the defendant or his counsel, the probation officer, and the prosecuting attorney by the court receiving such report. After delivery of the copies of the report, the information contained therein shall not be disclosed to anyone else without the consent of the defendant. After disposition of the case, all copies of the report, except the one delivered to the defendant or his counsel, shall be filed in a sealed file and shall be available thereafter only to the defendant or his counsel, the prosecuting attorney, the court, the probation officer, or the Department of Corrections.

(c) Notwithstanding subdivision (b), the probation officer may retain a copy of the report for the purpose of supervision of the defendant if the defendant is placed on probation by the court. The report and information contained therein shall be confidential and shall not be disclosed to anyone else without the written consent of the defendant. Upon the completion or termination of probation, the copy of the report shall be returned by the probation officer to the sealed file prescribed in subdivision (b).

(d) The Department of Corrections shall designate the place to which a person referred to it under the provisions of this section shall be transported. After the receipt of any such person, the department may return the person to the referring court if the director of the department, in his discretion, determines that the staff and facilities of the department are inadequate to provide such services.

(e) The sheriff of the county in which an order is made placing a defendant in a diagnostic facility pursuant to this section, or any other peace officer designated by the court, shall execute the order placing such defendant in the center or returning him therefrom to the court. The expense of such sheriff or other peace officer incurred in executing such order is a charge upon the county in which the court is situated.

(f) It is the intention of the Legislature that the diagnostic facilities made available to the counties by this section shall only be used for the purposes designated and not in lieu of sentences to local facilities.

(g) Time spent by a defendant in confinement in a diagnostic facility of the Department of Corrections pursuant to this section or as an inpatient of the California Rehabilitation Center shall be credited on the term of imprisonment in state prison, if any, to which defendant is sentenced in the case.

(h) In any case in which a defendant has been placed in a diagnostic facility pursuant to this section and, in the course of his confinement, he is determined to be suffering from a remediable condition relevant to his criminal conduct, the department may, with the permission of defendant, administer treatment for such condition. If such treatment will require a longer period of confinement than the period for which defendant was placed in the diagnostic facility, the Director of Corrections may file with the court which placed defendant in the facility a petition for extension of the period of confinement, to which shall be attached a writing signed by defendant giving his consent to the extension. If the court finds the petition and consent in order, it may order the extension, and transmit a copy of the order to the Director of Corrections.
(Amended by Stats.1977, c. 165, p. —, § 21.)

§ 1203.04. Probation order and subsequent changes in status; copy to police department or law enforcement agency

Whenever a person is granted probation and placed under the care and supervision of the probation officer, the clerk of the court shall immediately submit a copy of the probation order and any subsequent changes in probationary status to the police department or other law enforcement agency which arrested the person or investigated the matter for the violation which supports the probation order.

This section shall apply to all persons who are on probation on or after the effective date of the enactment of this section at the 1970 Regular Session of the Legislature.
(Amended by Stats.1971, c. 70, p. 96, § 1.)

§ 1203.05. Report of probation officer; inspection; copies; petition or motion of court; subsequent arrest and accusation

(a) Except as provided in subdivision (b) or (c), after 30 days from the date judgment is pronounced or probation is granted, any report of the probation officer filed with the court may be inspected by court personnel and shall be made available only to persons authorized or required by law to inspect or receive copies of the report and shall not be open to public inspection.

(b) Any other person may inspect or receive copies of the report at any time by order of the court upon filing a petition therefor. In addition, the court, on its own motion, may at any time make the report public or disclose its contents.

(c) Any person is entitled to inspect or receive copies of a probation report that is not otherwise open to inspection or copying under subdivision (a) if another accusatory pleading, arising out of a subsequent arrest, is filed with respect to the person who is the subject of the report. In such a case, the report shall be open to inspection or copying until such time as there is a final disposition of the case. Thereafter, the report shall be subject to the applicable provisions of subdivision (a) or (b).
(Added by Stats.1971, c. 869, p. 1710, § 1.)

§ 1203.06. **Probation or suspension of execution or imposition of sentence prohibited for certain crimes; allegations of ineligibility; adjournment of proceedings**

Notwithstanding the provisions of Section 1203:

(a) Probation shall not be granted to, nor shall the execution or imposition of sentence be suspended for, any of the following persons:

(1) Any person who personally used a firearm during the commission or attempted commission of any of the following crimes:

(i) Murder.

(ii) Assault with intent to commit murder, in violation of Section 217.

(iii) Robbery, in violation of Section 211.

(iv) Kidnapping, in violation of Section 207.

(v) Kidnapping for ransom, extortion, or robbery, in violation of Section 209.

(vi) Burglary of the first degree, as defined in Section 460.

(vii) Rape by force or violence, in violation of subdivision (2) of Section 261.

(viii) Rape by threat of great and immediate bodily harm, in violation of subdivision (3) of Section 261.

(ix) Assault with intent to commit rape, the infamous crime against nature, or robbery, in violation of Section 220.

(x) Escape, in violation of Section 4530 or 4532.

(2) Any person previously convicted of a felony specified in subparagraphs (i) through (x) of paragraph (1), who is convicted of a subsequent felony and who was personally armed with a firearm at any time during its commission or attempted commission or was unlawfully armed with a firearm at the time of his arrest for the subsequent felony.

(b)(1) The existence of any fact which would make a person ineligible for probation under subdivision (a) shall be alleged in the accusatory pleading, and either admitted by the defendant in open court, or found to be true by the jury trying the issue of guilt or by the court where guilt is established by plea of guilty or nolo contendere or by trial by the court sitting without a jury.

(2) This subdivision does not prohibit the adjournment of criminal proceedings pursuant to Division 3 (commencing with Section 3000) or Division 6 (commencing with Section 6000) of the Welfare and Institutions Code.

(3) As used in subdivision (a) "used a firearm" means to display a firearm in a menacing manner, to intentionally fire it, or to intentionally strike or hit a human being with it.

(4) As used in subdivision (a) "armed with a firearm" means to knowingly carry a firearm as a means of offense or defense.

(Amended by Stats.1977, c. 165, p. —, § 22.)

Editors' Note

1203.07, 1203.08, 1203.09

This section mandates state prison for those convicted under the circumstances as set forth. Thus, probation, and suspension of the sentence is not possible, and the defendant must be sentenced to state prison.

---

§ 1203.07. **Narcotics violations; prohibition of probation or suspension of sentence**

(a) Notwithstanding the provisions of Section 1203, probation shall not be granted to, nor shall the execution or imposition of sentence be suspended for, any of the following persons:

(1) Any person who is convicted of violating Section 11351 of the Health and Safety Code by possessing for sale one-half ounce or more of a substance containing heroin.

(2) Any person who is convicted of violating Section 11352 of the Health and Safety Code by selling or offering to sell one-half ounce or more of a substance containing heroin.

(3) Any person convicted of violating Section 11351 of the Health and Safety Code by possessing heroin for sale or convicted of violating Section 11352 of the Health and Safety Code by selling or offering to sell heroin, and who has one or more prior convictions for violating Section 11351 or Section 11352 of the Health and Safety Code.

(b) The existence of any fact which would make a person ineligible for probation under subdivision (a) shall be alleged in the information or indictment, and either admitted by the defendant in open court, or found to be true by the jury trying the issue of guilt or by the court where guilt is established by plea of guilty or nolo contendere or by trial by the court sitting without a jury.

(Added by Stats.1975, c. 1087, p. 2651, § 6.)

§ 1203.08. Violent felonies; commission while on state prison parole; prohibition of probation or suspension of sentence

(a) Any person convicted of an offense punishable by imprisonment in a state prison but without an alternate sentence to the county jail shall not, in any case, be granted probation or have the execution or imposition of sentence suspended, if such offense was committed while the person was on state prison parole, pursuant to Section 3000, following a term of imprisonment imposed for a crime listed in subdivision (c) of Section 667.5.

(b) Any person convicted of an offense listed in subdivision (c) of Section 667.5, shall not, in any case, be granted probation or have the execution or imposition of sentence suspended, if such offense was committed while the person was on state prison parole, pursuant to Section 3000.

(c) The existence of any fact which would make a person ineligible for probation under subdivision (a) or (b) shall be alleged in the information or indictment, and either admitted by the defendant in open court, or found to be true by the jury trying the issue of guilt or by the court where guilt is established by plea of guilty or nolo contendere or by trial by the court sitting without a jury.
(Added by Stats.1977, c. 1153, p. —, § 1.)

§ 1203.09. Crimes against persons 60 years of age or older, blind persons, paraplegics or quadriplegics; denial of probation and suspension of sentence

(a) Notwithstanding any other provision of law, probation shall not be granted to, nor shall the execution or imposition of sentence be suspended for, any person who commits or attempts to commit one or more of the crimes listed in subdivision (b) against a person who is 60 years of age or older; or against a person who is blind, a paraplegic, or a quadriplegic, and such disability is known or reasonably should be known to the person committing the crime; and who during the course of the offense inflicts great bodily injury upon such person.

(b) Subdivision (a) applies to the following crimes:

(i) Murder.

(ii) Assault with intent to commit murder, in violation of Section 217.

(iii) Robbery, in violation of Section 211.

(iv) Kidnapping, in violation of Section 207.

(v) Kidnapping for ransom, extortion, or robbery, in violation of Section 209.

(vi) Burglary of the first degree, as defined in Section 460.

(vii) Rape by force or violence, in violation of subdivision (2) of Section 261.

(viii) Rape by threat of great and immediate bodily harm, in violation of subdivision (3) of Section 261.

(ix) Assault with intent to commit rape, sodomy, or robbery, in violation of Section 220.

(c) The existence of any fact which would make a person ineligible for probation under subdivision (a) shall be alleged in the information or indictment, and either admitted by the defendant in open court, or found to be true by the jury trying the issue of guilt or by the court where guilt is established by plea of guilty or nolo contendere or by trial by the court sitting without a jury.

(d) As used in this section "great bodily injury" means "great bodily injury" as defined in Section 12022.7.

(e) This section shall apply in all cases, including those cases where the infliction of great bodily injury is an element of the offense.
(Added by Stats.1977, c. 1150, p. —, § 1.)

§ 1203.1. Probation; suspension of sentence; conditions which may be imposed; supervisors authorized to provide public work; work to support dependents or pay fine; service of sentence at intermittent periods; objectives; violations; authority of probation officer; termination of probation; fingerprints; disposition of fines

The court or judge thereof, in the order granting probation, may suspend the imposing, or the execution of the sentence and may direct that such suspension may continue for such period of time not exceeding the maximum possible term of such sentence, except as hereinafter set forth, and upon such terms and conditions as it shall determine. The court, or judge thereof, in the order granting probation and as a condition thereof may imprison the defendant in the county jail for a period not exceeding the maximum time fixed by law in the instant case; provided, however, that where the maximum possible term of such sentence is five years or less, then such period of suspension of imposition or execution of sentence may, in the discretion of the court, continue for not over five years; may fine the

§ 1203.1

defendant in such sum not to exceed the maximum fine provided by law in such case; or may in connection with granting probation, impose either imprisonment in county jail, or fine, or both, or neither; may provide for reparation in proper cases; and may require bonds for the faithful observance and performance of any or all of the conditions of probation.

The court shall consider whether the defendant as a condition of probation shall make restitution to the victim or the Indemnity Fund if assistance has been granted to the victim pursuant to Article 1 (commencing with Section 13959) of Chapter 5 of Part 4 of Division 3 of Title 2 of the Government Code. In counties or cities and counties where road camps, farms, or other public work is available the court may place the probationer in such camp, farms, or other public work instead of in jail, and Section 25359 of the Government Code shall apply to probation and the court shall have the same power to require adult probationers to work, as prisoners confined in the county jail are required to work, at public work as therein provided; and supervisors of the several counties are hereby authorized to provide public work and to fix the scale of compensation of such adult probationers in their respective counties. In all cases of probation the court is authorized to require as a condition of probation that the probationer go to work and earn money for the support of his dependents or to pay any fine imposed or reparation condition, to keep an account of his earnings, to report the same to the probation officer and apply such earnings as directed by the court.

In all such cases if as a condition of probation a judge of the superior court sitting by authority of law elsewhere than at the county seat requires a convicted person to serve sentence at intermittent periods such sentence may be served on the order of the judge at the city jail nearest to the place at which the court is sitting, and the cost of his maintenance shall be a county charge.

The court may impose and require any or all of the above-mentioned terms of imprisonment, fine and conditions and other reasonable conditions, as it may determine are fitting and proper to the end that justice may be done, that amends may be made to society for the breach of the law, for any injury done to any person resulting from such breach and generally and specifically for the reformation and rehabilitation of the probationer, that should the probationer violate any of the terms or conditions imposed by the court in the instant matter, it shall have authority to modify and change any and all such terms and conditions and to reimprison the probationer in the county jail within the limitations of the penalty of the public offense involved. Upon the defendant being released from the county jail under the terms of probation as originally granted or any modification subsequently made, and in all cases where confinement in a county jail has not been a condition of the grant of probation, the court shall place the defendant or probationer in and under the charge of the probation officer and the court, for the period or term fixed for probation; provided, however, that upon the payment of any fine imposed and the fulfillment of all conditions of probation, probation shall cease at the end of the term of probation, or sooner, in the event of modification. In counties and cities and counties in which there are facilities for taking fingerprints, such marks of identification of each probationer must be taken and a record thereof kept and preserved.

Any other provision of law to the contrary notwithstanding, all fines collected by a county probation officer in any of the courts of this state, as a condition of the granting of probation, or as a part of the terms of probation, shall be paid into the county treasury and placed in the general fund, for the use and benefit of the county.

(Amended by Stats.1977, c. 1122, p. ——, § 5; Stats.1977, c. 1123, p. ——, § 6.)

§ 1203.1a. Temporary removal or release from custody preparatory to return to community

The probation officer of the county may authorize the temporary removal under custody or temporary release without custody of any inmate of the county jail, honor farm, or other detention facility, who is confined or committed as a condition of probation, after suspension of imposition of sentence or suspension of execution of sentence, for purposes preparatory to his return to the community, within 30 days prior to his release date, if he concludes that such an inmate is a fit subject therefor. Any such temporary removal shall not be for a period of more than three days. When an inmate is released for purposes preparatory to his return to the community, the probation officer may require the inmate to reimburse the county, in whole or in part, for expenses incurred by the county in connection therewith.

(Added by Stats.1971, c. 1357, p. 2676, § 1.)

§ 1203.2. **Rearrest of probationer; revocation of probation; tolling of probationary period; judgment; notice; commitment to youth authority; revocation of suspended sentence; setting aside revocation of probation**

(a) At any time during the probationary period of a person released on probation under the care of a probation officer pursuant to this chapter, any probation or peace officer may, without warrant or other process and at any time until the final disposition of the case, rearrest the person and bring him before the court or the court may, in its discretion, issue a warrant for his rearrest. Upon such rearrest, or upon the issuance of a warrant for rearrest the court may revoke and terminate such probation if the interests of justice so require and the court, in its judgment, has reason to believe from the report of the probation officer or otherwise that the person has violated any of the conditions of his probation, has become abandoned to improper associates or a vicious life, or has subsequently committed other offenses, regardless whether he has been prosecuted for such offenses. Such revocation, summary or otherwise, shall serve to toll the running of the probationary period.

(b) Upon its own motion or upon the petition of the probationer or the district attorney of the county in which the probationer is supervised, the court may modify, revoke, or terminate the probation of the probationer pursuant to this subdivision. The court shall give notice of its motion, and the district attorney shall give notice of his petition to the probationer, his attorney of record, and the probation officer; the probationer shall give notice of his petition to the probation officer; and notice of any such motion or petition shall be given to the district attorney in all cases. The court shall refer its motion or the petition to the probation officer. After the receipt of a written report from the probation officer, the court shall read and consider the report and either its motion or the petition and may modify, revoke, or terminate the probation of the probationer upon the grounds set forth in subdivision (a) if the interests of justice so require.

The notice required by this subdivision may be given to the probationer upon his first court appearance in such proceeding. Upon the agreement by the probationer in writing to the specific terms of a modification or termination of a specific term of probation, any requirement that the probationer make a personal appearance in court for the purpose of such modification or termination shall be waived. Prior to such modification or termination and waiver of appearance, the probationer shall be informed of his right to consult with counsel, and if indigent the right to secure court appointed counsel. If the probationer waives his right to counsel a written waiver shall be required. If probationer consults with counsel and thereafter agrees to a modification or termination of the term of probation and waiver of personal appearance, such agreement shall be signed by counsel showing approval for such modification or termination and waiver.

(c) Upon any revocation and termination of probation the court may, if the sentence has been suspended, pronounce judgment for any time within the longest period for which the person might have been sentenced. However, if the judgment has been pronounced and the execution thereof has been suspended, the court may revoke such suspension and order that the judgment shall be in full force and effect. In either case, the person shall be delivered over to the proper officer to serve his sentence, less any credits herein provided for.

(d) In any case of revocation and termination of probation, including, but not limited to, cases in which the judgment has been pronounced and the execution thereof has been suspended, upon such revocation and termination, the court may, in lieu of any other sentence, commit the person to the Department of the Youth Authority if he is otherwise eligible for such commitment.

(e) If probation has been revoked before the judgment has been pronounced, the order revoking probation may be set aside for good cause upon motion made before pronouncement of judgment. If probation has been revoked after the judgment has been pronounced, the judgment and the order which revoked the probation may be set aside for good cause within 30 days after the court has notice that the execution of the sentence has commenced. If an order setting aside the judgment, the revocation of probation, or both is made after the expiration of the probationary period, the court may again place the person on probation for such period and with such terms and conditions as it could have done immediately following conviction.
(Amended by Stats.1977, c. 358, p. ——, § 1.)

§ 1203.2a. **Sentencing probationer committed for another offense; report of commitment; commitment or sentence; term; sequence of sentences; absence of defendant; loss of jurisdiction**

If any defendant who has been released on probation is committed to a prison in this state for another

§ 1203.2a

offense, the court which released him on probation shall have jurisdiction to impose sentence, if no sentence has previously been imposed for the offense for which he was granted probation, in the absence of the defendant, on the request of the defendant made through his counsel, or by himself in writing, if such writing is signed in the presence of the warden or superintendent of the prison in which he is confined or the duly authorized representative of the warden or superintendent, and such warden or superintendent or his representative attests both that the defendant has made and signed such request and that he states that he wishes the court to impose sentence in the case in which he was released on probation, in his absence and without his being represented by counsel.

The probation officer may, upon learning of such defendant's imprisonment, and must within 30 days after being notified in writing by the defendant or his counsel, or the warden or superintendent or duly authorized representative of the prison in which the defendant is confined, report such commitment to the court which released him on probation.

Upon being informed by the probation officer of the defendant's confinement, or upon receipt from the warden, superintendent or duly authorized representative of any prison in this state of a certificate showing that the defendant is confined in prison, the court shall issue its commitment if sentence has previously been imposed. If sentence has not been previously imposed and if the defendant has requested the court through counsel or in writing in the manner herein provided to impose sentence in the case in which he was released on probation in his absence and without the presence of counsel to represent him, the court shall impose sentence and issue its commitment, or shall make other final order terminating its jurisdiction over the defendant in the case in which the order of probation was made. If the case is one in which sentence has previously been imposed, the court shall be deprived of jurisdiction over defendant if it does not issue its commitment or make other final order terminating its jurisdiction over defendant in the case within 60 days after being notified of the confinement. If the case is one in which sentence has not previously been imposed, the court is deprived of jurisdiction over defendant if it does not impose sentence and issue its commitment or make other final order terminating its jurisdiction over defendant in the case within 30 days after defendant has, in the manner prescribed by this section, requested imposition of sentence.

PENAL CODE

Upon imposition of sentence hereunder the commitment shall be dated as of the date upon which probation was granted and if the defendant is then in a state prison for an offense committed subsequent to the one upon which he has been on probation, the term of imprisonment of such defendant under a commitment issued hereunder shall commence upon the date upon which defendant was delivered to prison under commitment for his subsequent offense, unless the court shall order that the sentence for the prior offense shall commence upon termination of the sentence for said subsequent offense. In the event the probation officer fails to report such commitment to the court or the court fails to impose sentence as herein provided, the court shall be deprived thereafter of all jurisdiction it may have retained in the granting of probation in said case.
(Amended by Stats.1976, c. 376, p. —, § 1.)

§ 1203.3. Probation; revocation, modification, or termination; change of order respecting sentence; discharge of probationer

The court shall have authority at any time during the term of probation to revoke, modify, or change its order of suspension of imposition or execution of sentence. It may at any time when the ends of justice will be subserved thereby, and when the good conduct and reform of the person so held on probation shall warrant it, terminate the period of probation and discharge the person so held, but no such order shall be made without written notice first given by the court or the clerk thereof to the proper probation officer of the intention to revoke, modify, or change its order, and in all cases, if the court has not seen fit to revoke the order of probation and impose sentence or pronounce judgment, the defendant shall at the end of the term of probation or any extension thereof, be by the court discharged subject to the provisions of these sections.
(Amended by Stats.1937, c. 511, p. 1501, § 2.)

§ 1203.4. Discharged probationer; change of plea or vacation of verdict; dismissal of charge; release from penalties and disabilities; certificate of rehabilitation and pardon; application; pleading prior conviction in prosecution for subsequent offenses

(a) In any case in which a defendant has fulfilled the conditions of probation for the entire period of probation, or has been discharged prior to the termination of the period of probation, or in any other case in which a court, in its discretion and the interests of justice, determines that a defendant should be granted the relief available under this section, the defendant shall, at any time after the termination of the period of probation, if he is not then serving a sentence for any offense, on probation for any offense, or charged with the commission of any offense, be permitted by the court to withdraw his plea of guilty or plea of nolo contendere and enter a plea of not guilty; or, if he has been convicted after a plea of not guilty, the court shall set aside the verdict of guilty; and, in either case, the court shall thereupon dismiss the accusations or information against the defendant and he shall thereafter be released from all penalties and disabilities resulting from the offense of which he has been convicted, except as provided in Section 13555 of the Vehicle Code. The probationer shall be informed, in his probation papers, of this right and privilege and his right, if any, to petition for a certificate of rehabilitation and pardon. The probationer may make such application and change of plea in person or by attorney, or by the probation officer authorized in writing; provided, that, in any subsequent prosecution of the defendant for any other offense, the prior conviction may be pleaded and proved and shall have the same effect as if probation had not been granted or the accusation or information dismissed.

Dismissal of an accusation or information pursuant to this section does not permit a person to own, possess, or have in his custody or control any firearm capable of being concealed upon the person or prevent his conviction under Section 12021.

This subdivision shall apply to all applications for relief under this section which are filed on or after November 23, 1970.

(b) Subdivision (a) of this section does not apply to any misdemeanor which is within the provisions of subdivision (b) of Section 42001 of the Vehicle Code, or to any infraction.
(Amended by Stats.1978, c. 911, p. —, § 1.)

§ 1203.45. Petition for order sealing records; exceptions

(a) In any case in which a person was under the age of 18 years at the time of commission of a misdemeanor and is eligible for, or has previously received, the relief provided by Section 1203.4 or 1203.4a, such person, in a proceeding under Section 1203.4 or 1203.4a, or a separate proceeding, may petition the court for an order sealing the record of conviction and other official records in the case, including records of arrests resulting in the criminal proceeding and records relating to other offenses charged in the accusatory pleading, whether defendant was acquitted or charges were dismissed. If the court finds that such person was under the age of 18 at the time of the commission of the misdemeanor, and is eligible for relief under Section 1203.4 or 1203.4a or has previously received such relief, it may issue its order granting the relief prayed for. Thereafter such conviction, arrest, or other proceeding shall be deemed not to have occurred, and the petitioner may answer accordingly any question relating to their occurrence.

(b) This section applies to convictions which occurred before, as well as those which occur after, the effective date of this section.

(c) This section shall not apply to offenses for which registration is required under Section 290, to violations of Division 10 (commencing with Section 11000) of the Health and Safety Code, or to misdemeanor violations of the Vehicle Code relating to operation of a vehicle or of any local ordinance relating to operation, standing, stopping, or parking of a motor vehicle.

(d) This section does not apply to a person convicted of more than one offense, whether the second or additional convictions occurred in the same action in which the conviction as to which relief is sought occurred or in another action, except in the following cases:

(1) One of the offenses includes the other or others.

(2) The other conviction or convictions were for the following:

(i) Misdemeanor violations of Chapters 1 (commencing with Section 21000) to 9 (commencing with Section 22500), inclusive, or Chapters 12 (commencing with Section 23100) to 14 (commencing with Section 23340), inclusive, of Division 11 of the Vehicle Code, other than Sections 23101 to 23108, inclusive, or Section 23121.

(ii) Violation of any local ordinance relating to the operation, stopping, standing, or parking of a motor vehicle.

(3) The other conviction or convictions consisted of any combination of paragraphs (1) and (2).

(e) This section shall apply in any case in which a person was under the age of 21 at the time of the commission of an offense as to which this section is made applicable if such offense was committed prior to March 7, 1973.

(f) In any action or proceeding based upon defamation, a court, upon a showing of good cause, may order any records sealed under this section to be opened and admitted into evidence. The records shall be confidential and shall be available for inspection only by the court, jury, parties, counsel for the parties, and any other person who is authorized by the court to inspect them. Upon the judgment in the action or proceeding becoming final, the court shall order the records sealed.
(Amended by Stats.1974, c. 401, p. 987, § 2.)

§ 1203.5. Probation officers; officers appointed under juvenile court law as ex officio adult probation officers; exception

The offices of adult probation officer, assistant adult probation officer, and deputy adult probation officer are hereby created. The probation officers, assistant probation officers and deputy probation officers appointed in accordance with Chapter 2 (commencing with Section 500) of Division 2 of Part 1 of the Welfare and Institutions Code shall be ex officio adult probation officers, assistant adult probation officers and deputy adult probation officers except in any county or city and county whose charter provides for the separate office of adult probation officer. When the separate office of adult probation officer has been established he shall perform all the duties of probation officers except for matters under the jurisdiction of the juvenile court. Any adult probation officer may accept appointment as member of the Board of Corrections and serve in that capacity in addition to his duties as adult probation officer and may receive the per diem allowance authorized in Section 6025.1.
(Amended by Stats.1965, c. 1624, p. 3714, § 1.)

§ 1203.6. Adult probation officer; appointment and removal; salary; assistants, deputies and employees

The adult probation officer shall be appointed and may be removed for good cause by the judge of the superior court or, in a county with two superior court judges, by the judge who is senior in point of service. In the case of a superior court of more than two judges, a majority of the judges shall make the appointment, and may effect removal.

The salary of the probation officer shall be established by the board of supervisors.

The adult probation officer shall appoint and may remove all assistants, deputies and other persons employed in his department, and their compensation shall be established, according to the merit system or civil service system provisions of the county. If no merit system or civil service system exists in the county, the board of supervisors shall provide for appointment, removal, and compensation of such personnel.

This section is applicable in a charter county whose charter establishes the office of adult probation officer and provides that such officer shall be appointed in accordance with general law subject to the merit system provisions of the charter.
(Added by Stats.1965, c. 1624, p. 3715, § 3.)

§ 1203.9. Probation; transfer of cases; jurisdiction

(a) Whenever any person is released upon probation, the case may be transferred to any court of the same rank in any other county in which the person resides or to which the person moves, provided that the court of the receiving county shall first be given an opportunity to investigate and determine whether the person does reside in or has moved to that county. If the court finds that the person does not reside in or has not moved to that county it may refuse to accept the transfer. The court of the receiving county shall give the matter of investigating such transfers precedence over all actions or proceedings therein, except actions or proceedings to which special precedence is given by law, to the end that all such transfer shall be quickly completed.

(b) The order of transfer shall contain an order committing the probationer to the care and custody of the probation officer of the receiving county. A copy of the order shall be transmitted to the probation officer of that county, and thereafter the receiving court shall have entire jurisdiction over the case, with like power to again request transfer of the case whenever it seems proper.
(Amended by Stats.1972, c. 604, p. 1068, § 1.)

§ 1203.12. Probation officers; furnishing probationer with statement of terms and conditions; report of violations

The probation officer shall furnish to each person who has been released on probation, and committed to his care, a written statement of the terms and conditions of his probation unless such a statement has been furnished by the court, and shall report to

the court, or judge, releasing such person on probation, any violation or breach of the terms and conditions imposed by such court on the person placed in his care.
(Amended by Stats.1968, c. 1222, p. 2322, § 60.)

§ 1203.13. Probation officers; establishment and cooperation with public crime prevention councils

The probation officer of any county may establish, or assist in the establishment of, any public council or committee having as its object the prevention of crime, and may cooperate with or participate in the work of any such councils or committees for the purpose of preventing or decreasing crime, including the improving of recreational, health, and other conditions in the community.
(Added by Stats.1947, c. 876, p. 2056, § 1.)

§ 1203a. Probation; misdemeanor cases; maximum term

In all counties and cities and counties the courts therein, having jurisdiction to impose punishment in misdemeanor cases, shall have the power to refer cases, demand reports and to do and require all things necessary to carry out the purposes of Section 1203 of this code insofar as they are in their nature applicable to misdemeanors. Any such court shall have power to suspend the imposing or the execution of the sentence, and to make and enforce the terms of probation for a period not to exceed three years; provided, that when the maximum sentence provided by law exceeds three years imprisonment, the period during which sentence may be suspended and terms of probation enforced may be for a longer period than three years, but in such instance, not to exceed the maximum time for which sentence of imprisonment might be pronounced.
(Amended by Stats.1949, c. 504, p. 863, § 2.)

§ 1203b. Summary probation in misdemeanor and infraction cases; reports by probationer to court, not probation officers

All courts shall have power to grant probation summarily in misdemeanor and infraction cases without referring such cases to the probation officer; provided, however, that unless otherwise ordered by the court persons granted probation summarily shall report only to the court and the probation officer shall not be responsible in any way for supervising or accounting for such persons.
(Amended by Stats.1972, c. 618, p. 1143, § 119.)

§ 1204. Circumstances in aggravation or mitigation of punishment; hearing

The circumstances shall be presented by the testimony of witnesses examined in open court, except that when a witness is so sick or infirm as to be unable to attend, his deposition may be taken by a magistrate of the county, out of court, upon such notice to the adverse party as the court may direct. No affidavit or testimony, or representation of any kind, verbal or written, can be offered to or received by the court, or a judge thereof, in aggravation or mitigation of the punishment, except as provided in this and the preceding section. This section shall not be construed to prohibit the filing of a written report by a defendant or defendant's counsel on behalf of a defendant if such a report presents a study of his background and personality and suggests a rehabilitation program. If such a report is submitted, the prosecution or probation officer shall be permitted to reply to or to evaluate the program.
(Amended by Stats.1971, c. 1080, p. 2052, § 1.)

§ 1204.5. Judges; restriction on reading arrest reports, etc.

In any criminal action, after the filing of any complaint or other accusatory pleading and before a plea, finding, or verdict of guilty, no judge of any court shall read or consider any written report of any law enforcement officer or witness to any offense, or any information reflecting the arrest or conviction record of a defendant, or any affidavit or representation of any kind, verbal or written, except as provided in the rules of evidence applicable at the trial, or with the consent of the accused given in open court, or affidavits in connection with the issuance of a warrant or the hearing of any law and motion matter, or any application for an order fixing or changing bail, or a petition for a writ.
(Added by Stats.1968, c. 1362, p. 2599, § 1.)

§ 1205. Fine imposed with or without other punishment; imprisonment pending payment; maximum term; credit for each day of imprisonment; misdemeanors; payments; defaults

A judgment that the defendant pay a fine, with or without other punishment, may also direct that he be imprisoned until the fine is satisfied and may further direct that such imprisonment begin at and continue after the expiration of any imprisonment imposed as a part of the punishment or of any other imprisonment to which he may theretofore have been sentenced. Every such judgment shall specify the extent of the imprisonment for nonpayment of the fine, which shall not be more than one day for each thirty dollars ($30) of the fine, nor exceed in any case the term for which the defendant might be sentenced or imprisonment for the offense of which he has been convicted. A defendant held in custody for nonpayment of a fine shall be entitled to credit on the fine for each day he is so held in custody, at the rate specified in the judgment. When the defendant has been convicted of a misdemeanor, a judgment that the defendant pay a fine may also direct that he pay the fine within a limited time or in installments on specified dates and that in default of payment as therein stipulated he be imprisoned in the discretion of the court either until the defaulted installment is satisfied or until the fine is satisfied in full; but unless such direction is given in the judgment, the fine shall be payable forthwith.

Except as otherwise provided in case of fines imposed as conditions of probation, the defendant must pay the fine to the clerk of the court, or to the judge thereof if there is no clerk, unless the defendant is taken into custody for nonpayment of the fine, in which event payments made while he is in custody shall be made to the officer who holds him in custody and all amounts so paid shall be forthwith paid over by such officer to the court which rendered the judgment. The clerk shall report to the court every default in payment of a fine or any part thereof, or if there is no clerk, the court shall take notice of such default. If time has been given for payment of a fine or it has been made payable in installments, the court shall, upon any default in payment immediately order the arrest of the defendant and order him to show cause why he should not be imprisoned until the fine or installment thereof, as the case may be, is satisfied in full. If the fine, or installment, is payable forthwith and it is not so paid, the court shall without further proceedings, immediately commit the defendant to the custody of the proper officer to be held in custody until the fine or installment thereof, as the case may be, is satisfied in full. The provisions of this section shall apply to any violation of any of the codes or statutes of the State of California punishable by a fine or by a fine and imprisonment.
(Amended by Stats.1976, c. 1045, p. —, § 1.)

§ 1208. County jail prisoners; performance of work outside jails

(a) **Findings of county board; ordinance; confinement facility; custodian; contracts**

(a) The provisions of this section, insofar as they relate to employment, shall be operative in any county in which the board of supervisors by ordinance finds, on the basis of employment conditions, the state of the county jail facilities, and other pertinent circumstances, that the operation of this section, insofar as it relates to employment, in that county is feasible. The provisions of this section, insofar as they relate to education, shall be operative in any county in which the board of supervisors by ordinance finds, on the basis of education conditions, the state of the county jail facilities, and other pertinent circumstances, that the operation of this section, insofar as it relates to education, in that county is feasible. In any such ordinance the board shall prescribe whether the sheriff, the probation officer, the director of the county department of corrections, or the superintendent of a county industrial farm or industrial road camp in the county shall perform the functions of the work furlough administrator. The board may, in such ordinance, provide for the performance of any or all functions of the work furlough administrator by any one or more of such persons, acting separately or jointly as to any of such functions; and may, by a subsequent ordinance, revise such provisions within the authorization of this section. The board of supervisors may also terminate the operativeness of this section, either with respect to employment or education in the county if it finds by ordinance that because of changed circumstances, the operation of this section, either with respect to employment or education in that county is no longer feasible.

Notwithstanding any other provision of law, the board of supervisors may by ordinance designate a facility for confinement of prisoners classified for the work furlough program and designate the work furlough administrator as the custodian of the facility. The work furlough administrator may, with the approval of the board of supervisors, enter into contracts with appropriate public or nonprofit private agencies to provide a facility and services for the housing, sustenance, counseling, supervision, and related services for such inmates as are eligible for work furlough. No agency entering into such a contract may itself employ any person who is in the work furlough program. The sheriff or director of the county department of corrections, as the case may be, is authorized to transfer custody of such prisoners to the work furlough administrator to be confined in such facility for the period during which they are in the work furlough program.

(b) Continuation of employment; securing employment

(b) When a person is convicted of a misdemeanor and sentenced to the county jail, or is imprisoned therein for nonpayment of a fine, for contempt, or as a condition of probation for any criminal offense, or committed under the terms of Section 6404 or 6406 of the Welfare and Institutions Code as a habit-forming drug addict, the work furlough administrator may, if he concludes that such person is a fit subject therefor, direct that such person be permitted to continue in his regular employment, if that is compatible with the requirements of subdivision (d), or may authorize the person to secure employment for himself, unless the court at the time of sentencing or committing has ordered that such person not be granted work furloughs. The work furlough administrator may, if he concludes that such person is a fit subject therefor, direct that such person be permitted to continue in his regular educational program, if that is compatible with the requirements of subdivision (d), or may authorize the person to secure education for himself, unless the court at the time of sentencing has ordered that such person not be granted work furloughs.

(c) Arrangements; suitability of work; wages; labor disputes

(c) If the work furlough administrator so directs that the prisoner be permitted to continue in his regular employment or educational program, the administrator shall arrange for a continuation of such employment or education, so far as possible without interruption. If the prisoner does not have regular employment or a regular educational program, and the administrator has authorized the prisoner to secure employment or education for himself, the prisoner may do so, and the administrator may assist him in doing so. Any employment or education so secured must be suitable for the prisoner. Such employment or educational program, if such educational program includes earnings by the prisoner, must be at a wage at least as high as the prevailing wage for similar work in the area where the work is performed and in accordance with the prevailing working conditions in such area. In no event may any such employment or educational program involving earnings by the prisoner be permitted where there is a labor dispute in the establishment in which the prisoner is, or is to be, employed or educated.

(d) Confinement; release for medical treatment

(d) Whenever the prisoner is not employed or being educated and between the hours or periods of employment or education, he shall be confined in the facility designated by the board of supervisors for work furlough confinement unless the work furlough administrator directs otherwise. If the prisoner is injured during a period of employment or education, the work furlough administrator shall have the authority to release him from the facility for continued medical treatment by private physicians or at medical facilities at the expense of the employer, worker's compensation insurer, or the prisoner. Such release shall not be construed as assumption of liability by the county or work furlough administrator for medical treatment obtained.

The work furlough administrator may release any prisoner classified for the work furlough program for a period not to exceed 72 hours for medical, dental, or psychiatric care, or for family emergencies or pressing business which would result in severe hardship if the release were not granted, or to attend such activities as the administrator deems may effectively promote the prisoner's successful return to the community, including, but not limited to, an attempt to secure housing, employment, entry into educational programs, or participation in community programs.

(e) Earnings

(e) The earnings of the prisoner may be collected by the work furlough administrator, and it shall be the duty of the prisoner's employer to transmit such wages to the administrator at the latter's request. Earnings levied upon pursuant to writ of execution or in other lawful manner shall not be transmitted to the administrator. If the administrator has requested transmittal of earnings prior to levy, such request shall have priority. In a case in which the functions of the administrator are performed by a sheriff, and such sheriff receives a writ of execution for the earnings of a prisoner subject to this section but has not yet requested transmittal of the prisoner's earnings pursuant to this section, he shall first levy on the earnings pursuant to the writ. When an employer or educator transmits such earnings to the administrator pursuant to this subdivision he shall have no liability to the prisoner for such earnings. From such earnings the administrator shall pay the prisoner's board and personal expenses, both inside and outside the jail, and shall deduct so much of the costs of administration of this section as is allocable to such prisoner, and, in an amount determined by the administrator, shall pay the support of the prisoner's dependents, if any. If sufficient funds are available after making the foregoing payments, the administrator may, with the consent of the prisoner, pay, in whole or in part, the preexisting debts of the prisoner. Any balance shall be retained until the prisoner's discharge and thereupon shall be paid to him.

(f) **Time credits**

(f) The prisoner shall be eligible for time credits pursuant to Sections 4018, 4019, and 4019.2.

(g) **Violations**

(g) In the event the prisoner violates the conditions laid down for his conduct, custody, education, or employment, the work furlough administrator may order the balance of the prisoner's sentence to be spent in actual confinement.

(h) **Failure to return to place of confinement**

(h) Willful failure of the prisoner to return to the place of confinement not later than the expiration of any period during which he is authorized to be away from the place of confinement pursuant to this section is punishable as provided in Section 4532.

(i) **"Education", "educator" and "employment" defined**

(i) As used in this section, "education" includes vocational and educational training and counseling; and psychological, drug abuse, alcoholic and other rehabilitative counseling; "educator" includes a person or institution providing such training or counseling; and "employment" includes care of children, including the daytime care of children of the prisoner.

(j) **Citation**

(j) This section shall be known and may be cited as the "Cobey Work Furlough Law."
(Amended by Stats.1977, c. 545, p. ——, § 1.)

§ 1208.5. Inter-county work furlough agreements

The boards of supervisors of two or more counties having work furlough programs may enter into agreements whereby a person sentenced to, or imprisoned in, the jail of one county, but regularly employed in another county, may be transferred by the sheriff of the county in which he is confined to the jail of the county in which he is employed, in order that he may be enabled to continue in his regular employment in such other county through such county's work furlough program. Such agreement may make provision for the support of transferred persons by the county from which they are transferred. The board of supervisors of any county may, by ordinance, delegate the authority to enter into such agreements to the work furlough administrator.
(Amended by Stats.1975, c. 68, p. 130, § 1.)

§ 1214. Judgment for fine; issuance of execution

If the judgment is for a fine with or without imprisonment, execution may be issued thereon as on a judgment in a civil action.
(Amended by Stats.1905, c. 537, p. 698, § 1.)

§ 1215. Judgment for imprisonment or fine and imprisonment until paid; commitment; detention until compliance; supervision of probation officer upon suspension of sentence or execution; commitment upon revocation of probation

If the judgment is for imprisonment, or a fine and imprisonment until it be paid, the defendant must forthwith be committed to the custody of the proper officer and by him detained until the judgment is complied with. Where, however, the court has suspended sentence, or where, after imposing sentence, the court has suspended the execution thereof and placed the defendant on probation, as provided in section twelve hundred and three of the Penal Code, the defendant, if over the age of sixteen years, must forthwith be placed under the care and supervision of the probation officer of the court committing him, until the expiration of the period of probation and the compliance with the terms and conditions of the sentence, or of the suspension thereof. Where, however, the probation has been terminated as provided in section twelve hundred and three of the Penal Code, and the suspension of the sentence, or of the execution revoked, and the judgment pronounced, the defendant must forthwith be committed to the custody of the proper officer and be detained until the judgment be complied with.
(Amended by Stats.1903, c. 34, p. 35, § 2.)

§ 1216. Judgment for imprisonment in state prison; sheriff to deliver prisoner and abstract to warden; receipt

If the judgment is for imprisonment in the state prison, the sheriff of the county must, upon receipt of a certified abstract thereof, take and deliver the defendant to the warden of the state prison. He must also deliver to the warden the certified abstract of the judgment, and take from the warden a receipt for the defendant.
(Amended by Stats.1951, c. 460, p. 1489, § 2.)

§ 1242. Appeal by people; judgment for defendant unaffected until reversed

Effect of an appeal by the people. An appeal taken by the people in no case stays or affects the operation of a judgment in favor of the defendant, until judgment is reversed.
(Enacted 1872.)

§ 1243. Appeal from conviction; stay of judgment of death; discretion to order stay of other judgments or order of probation; certificate

An appeal to the Supreme Court or to a court of appeal from a judgment of conviction stays the execution of the judgment in all cases where sentence of death has been imposed, but does not stay the execution of the judgment or order granting probation in any other case unless the trial or appellate court shall so order. The granting or refusal of such order shall rest in the discretion of the court. If such order is made, the clerk of the court shall issue a certificate stating that such order has been made.
(Amended by Stats.1967, c. 17, p. 849, § 109.)

§ 1244. Stay pending appeal; sheriff to retain custody

Effect of an appeal by the defendant. If the certificate provided for in the preceding section is filed, the Sheriff must, if the defendant be in his custody, upon being served with a copy thereof, keep the defendant in his custody without executing the judgment, and detain him to abide the judgment on appeal.
(Enacted 1872.)

§ 1245. Stay pending appeal; suspension of further execution; restoration to original custody

If before the granting of the certificate, the execution of the judgment has commenced, the further execution thereof is suspended, and upon service of a copy of such certificate the defendant must be restored by the officer in whose custody he is, to his original custody.
(Amended by Stats.1905, c. 538, p. 701, § 6.)

§ 1268. Admission to bail defined

Admission to bail defined. Admission to bail is the order of a competent Court or magistrate that the defendant be discharged from actual custody upon bail.
(Enacted 1872.)

§ 1269. Taking of bail defined; entries by the clerk; destruction of bond

The taking of bail consists in the acceptance, by a competent court or magistrate, of the undertaking of sufficient bail for the appearance of the defendant, according to the terms of the undertaking, or that the bail will pay to the people of this State a specified sum. Upon filing, the clerk shall enter in the register of actions the date and amounts of such bond and the name or names of the surety or sureties thereon. In the event of the loss or destruction of such bond, such entries so made shall be prima facie evidence of the due execution of such bond as required by law.

Whenever any bail bond has been deposited in any criminal action or proceeding in a justice, municipal, or superior court or in any proceeding in habeas corpus in a superior court, either before or after the effective date of this amendment to this section, and it is made to appear to the satisfaction of the court by affidavit or by testimony in open court that more than three years have elapsed since the exoneration or release of said bail, the court must direct that such bond be destroyed.
(Amended by Stats.1955, c. 1348, p. 2427, § 1, eff. June 27, 1955.)

§ 1269a. Order for discharge on bail; necessity; contents; approval of undertaking; formalities; unauthorized release as offense

Except as otherwise provided by law, no defendant charged in a warrant of arrest with any public offense shall be discharged from custody upon bail except upon a written order of a competent court or magistrate admitting the defendant to bail in the amount specified in the indorsement referred to in Section 815a, and where an undertaking is furnished, upon a written order of such court or magistrate approving the undertaking. All such orders must be signed by such court or magistrate and delivered to the officer having custody of the defendant before the defendant is released. Any officer releasing any defendant upon bail otherwise than as herein provided shall be guilty of a misdemeanor.
(Amended by Stats.1941, c. 366, p. 1652, § 1.)

§ 1269b. Acceptance of bail; notice of appearance of prisoner; schedule of bail; discharge of prisoner; disposition of bail; forfeiture

(a) The officer in charge of a jail where an arrested person is held in custody, an officer of a sheriff's department or police department of a city who is in charge of a jail or employed at a fixed police

§ 1269b PENAL CODE

or sheriff's facility and is acting under an agreement with the agency which keeps the jail wherein an arrested person is held in custody, an employee of a sheriff's department or police department of a city who is assigned by such department to collect bail, the clerk of the justice or municipal court of the judicial district in which the offense was alleged to have been committed, and the clerk of the superior court in which the case against the defendant is pending shall have authority to approve and accept bail in such amount as fixed by the warrant of arrest or schedule of bail or order admitting to bail in cash or surety bond executed by a certified, admitted surety insurer as provided in the Insurance Code, to issue and sign an order for the release of the arrested person, and to set a time and place for the appearance of the arrested person before the appropriate court and give notice thereof.

(b) If a defendant has appeared before a judge of the court on the charge contained in the complaint, indictment, or information the bail shall be in the amount fixed by such judge at the time of such appearance; if no such appearance has been made, the bail shall be in the amount fixed in the warrant of arrest or, if no warrant of arrest has been issued, the amount of bail shall be pursuant to the uniform county wide schedule of bail for the county in which the defendant must appear, previously fixed and approved as provided in subdivisions (c) and (d).

(c) It is the duty of the superior, municipal and justice court judges in each county to prepare, adopt, and from time to time revise, by a majority vote, at a meeting called by the presiding judge of the superior court of the county, a uniform countywide schedule of bail for all bailable felony offenses.

(d) It is the duty of the municipal and justice court judges in each county to prepare, adopt, and from time to time revise, by a majority vote, at a meeting called by the presiding judge of the municipal court or the senior judge of the justice court at each county seat, a uniform, countywide schedule of bail for all misdemeanor and infraction offenses.

(e) Each countywide bail schedule shall contain a list of such offenses and the amounts of bail applicable thereto as the judges determine to be appropriate. If the schedules do not list all offenses specifically, they shall contain a general clause for designated amounts of bail as the judges of the county determined to be appropriate for all such offenses not specifically listed in the schedules. A copy of the countywide bail schedule shall be sent to the officer in charge of the county jail, to the officer in charge of each city jail within the county, to each superior, municipal and justice court judge and commissioner in the county, and to the Judicial Council.

(f) Upon posting such bail the defendant or arrested person shall be discharged from custody as to the offense on which the bail is posted.

All money and surety bonds so deposited with an officer authorized to receive bail shall be transmitted immediately to the judge or clerk of the court by which the order was made or warrant issued or bail schedule fixed. If, in the case of felonies, an indictment is filed, such judge or clerk of the court shall transmit all such money and surety bonds to the county clerk.

(g) If a defendant or arrested person so released fails to appear at the time and in the court so ordered upon his release from custody, the provisions of Sections 1305 and 1306 shall apply.

(Amended by Stats.1977, c. 579, p. ——, § 150; Stats.1977, c. 1257, p. ——, § 121, urgency, eff. Oct. 3, 1977.)

§ 1269c. Increase or reduction of bail in schedule; declaration by peace officers; application by defendant; determination by magistrate

In any case in which a defendant is arrested without a warrant for a bailable felony offense and a peace officer has reasonable cause to believe that the amount of bail set forth in the schedule of bail for that offense is insufficient to assure defendant's appearance, the peace officer shall prepare a declaration under penalty of perjury setting forth the facts and circumstances in support of his belief and file it with a magistrate, as defined in Section 808, in the county in which the offense is alleged to have been committed or having jurisdiction of the person of defendant, or a commissioner of such magistrate, requesting an order setting a higher bail. The defendant, either personally or through his attorney, friend, or member of family, also may make application to such magistrate for release on bail lower than that provided in the schedule of bail or on his own recognizance. The magistrate or commissioner to whom such application is made is authorized to set bail in such amount as he deems sufficient to assure the defendant's appearance, and to set such bail on such terms and conditions as he, in his discretion, deems appropriate, or he may authorize the defendant's release on his own recognizance. If, after such an application is made, no order changing the amount of bail is issued within eight hours after booking, the

defendant shall be entitled to be released on posting the amount of bail set forth in the applicable bail schedule.
(Added by Stats.1973, c. 810, p. 1445, § 3.)

§ 1270. Capital offenses; nonbailable when proof of guilt evident or presumption great; effect of indictment

Offense not bailable. A defendant charged with an offense punishable with death cannot be admitted to bail, when the proof of his guilt is evident or the presumption thereof great. The finding of an indictment does not add to the strength of the proof or the presumptions to be drawn therefrom.
(Enacted 1872.)

§ 1271. Before conviction; bail as of right

In what cases defendant may be admitted to bail before conviction. If the charge is for any other offense, he may be admitted to bail before conviction, as a matter of right.
(Enacted 1872.)

§ 1272. After conviction and pending probation or appeal; bail as of right; bail discretionary

After conviction of an offense not punishable with death, a defendant who has made application for probation or who has appealed may be admitted to bail:

1. As a matter of right, before judgment is pronounced pending application for probation in cases of misdemeanors, or when the appeal is from a judgment imposing a fine only.

2. As a matter of right, before judgment is pronounced pending application for probation in cases of misdemeanors, or when the appeal is from a judgment imposing imprisonment in cases of misdemeanors.

3. As a matter of discretion in all other cases.
(Amended by Stats.1971, c. 1790, p. 3856, § 3.)

§ 1273. Nature and conditions of bail; before conviction; after conviction and upon appeal

If the offense is bailable, the defendant may be admitted to bail before conviction:

First—For his appearance before the magistrate, on the examination of the charge, before being held to answer.

Second—To appear at the Court to which the magistrate is required to return the depositions and statement, upon the defendant being held to answer after examination.

Third—After indictment, either before the bench warrant is issued for his arrest, or upon any order of the Court committing him, or enlarging the amount of bail, or upon his being surrendered by his bail to answer the indictment in the Court in which it is found, or to which it may be transferred for trial.

And after conviction, and upon an appeal:

First—If the appeal is from a judgment imposing a fine only, on the undertaking of bail that he will pay the same, or such part of it as the appellate Court may direct, if the judgment is affirmed or modified, or the appeal is dismissed.

Second—If judgment of imprisonment has been given, that he will surrender himself in execution of the judgment, upon its being affirmed or modified, or upon the appeal being dismissed, or that in case the judgment be reversed, and that the cause be remanded for a new trial, that he will appear in the Court to which said cause may be remanded, and submit himself to the orders and process thereof.
(Amended by Code Am.1875–76, c. 80, p. 116, § 1.)

§ 1274. Bail discretionary; notice of application to district attorney

When bail is matter of discretion, notice of application must be given to District Attorney. When the admission to bail is a matter of discretion, the Court or officer to whom the application is made must require reasonable notice thereof to be given to the District Attorney of the county.
(Enacted 1872.)

§ 1277. Authority to admit to bail; committing magistrates; magistrates having habeas corpus jurisdiction

What magistrates may admit to bail. When the defendant has been held to answer upon an examination for a public offense, the admission to bail may be by the magistrate by whom he is so held, or by any magistrate who has power to issue the writ of habeas corpus.
(Enacted 1872.)

§ 1279. Qualifications of bail

The qualifications of bail are as follows:

1. Each of them must be a resident, householder, or freeholder within the state; but the court or magistrate may refuse to accept any person as bail

§ 1279

who is not a resident of the county where bail is offered;

2. They must each be worth the amount specified in the undertaking, exclusive of property exempt from execution, except that if any of the sureties is not worth the amount specified in the undertaking, exclusive of property exempt from execution, but owns any equity in real property, a hearing must be held before the magistrate to determine the value of such equity. Witnesses may be called and examined at such hearing and if the magistrate is satisfied that the value of the equity is equal to twice the amount of the bond such surety is justified. In any case, the court or magistrate, on taking bail, may allow more than two sureties to justify severally in amounts less than that expressed in the undertaking, if the whole justification be equivalent to that of sufficient bail.
(Amended by Stats.1931, c. 1172, p. 2481, § 1.)

§ 1295. Authority to make deposit in lieu of bail; discharge from custody

The defendant, or any other person, at any time after an order admitting defendant to bail or after the arrest and booking of a defendant for having committed a misdemeanor, instead of giving bail may deposit with the clerk of the court in which the defendant is held to answer or notified to appear for arraignment, the sum mentioned in the order, or if no order, in the schedule of bail previously fixed by the judges of said court, and upon delivering to the officer in whose custody defendant is a certificate of the deposit, defendant must be discharged from custody.

Where more than one such deposit is made with respect to any charge in any accusatory pleading based upon the acts supporting the original charge as a result of which an earlier deposit was made, the defendant shall receive credit in the amount of any such earlier deposit.
(Amended by Stats.1969, c. 1259, p. 2462, § 5.)

§ 1298. Deposit of state or federal bonds or real estate equity in lieu of bail; determination of value of equity; allowance; sale of bonds or equity and application of proceeds; duties of county treasurer

In lieu of a deposit of money, the defendant or any other person may deposit bonds of the United States or of the State of California of the face value of the cash deposit required, and such bonds shall be treated in the same manner as a deposit of money or the defendant may give as security any equity in real property which he owns. A hearing, at which witnesses may be called or examined, must be held before the magistrate to determine the value of such equity and if the magistrate finds that the value of such equity is equal to twice the amount of the cash deposit required he shall allow such bail. The clerk shall, under order of the court, when occasion arises therefor, sell the said bonds or the equity and apply the proceeds of such sale in the manner that a deposit of cash may be required to be applied.

The county treasurer shall, upon request of the judge, keep such deposit and return it to the clerk on order of the judge.
(Amended by Stats.1951, c. 1608, p. 3616, § 18.)

§ 1300. Persons authorized to surrender defendant; exoneration of bail or deposit; method of surrender; penalty for surrender without good cause

(a) At any time before the forfeiture of their undertaking, or deposit by a third person, the bail or the depositor may surrender the defendant in their exoneration, or he may surrender himself, to the officer to whose custody he was committed at the time of giving bail, in the following manner:

(1) A certified copy of the undertaking of the bail, or a certified copy of the certificate of deposit where a deposit is made, must be delivered to the officer who must detain the defendant in his custody thereon as upon a commitment, and by a certificate in writing acknowledge the surrender.

(2) The bail or depositor, upon surrendering the defendant, shall make reasonable effort to give notice to the defendant's last attorney of record, if any, of such surrender.

(3) The officer to whom the defendant is surrendered shall, within 48 hours of the surrender, bring the defendant before the court in which the defendant is next to appear on the case for which he has been surrendered. The court shall advise the defendant of his right to move the court for an order permitting the withdrawal of any previous waiver of time and shall advise him of the authority of the court, as provided in subdivision (b), to order return of the premium paid by the defendant or other person, or any part of it.

(4) Upon the undertaking, or certificate of deposit, and the certificate of the officer, the court in which the action or appeal is pending may, upon notice of five days to the district attorney of the county, with a

copy of the undertaking, or certificate of deposit, and the certificate of the officer, order that the bail or deposit be exonerated. However, if the defendant is released on his own recognizance or on another bond before the issuance of such an order, the court shall order that the bail or deposit be exonerated without prejudice to the court's authority under subdivision (b). On filing the order and papers used on the application, they are exonerated accordingly.

(b) Notwithstanding subdivision (a), if the court determines that good cause does not exist for the surrender of a defendant who has not failed to appear or has not violated any order of the court, it may, in its discretion, order the bail or the depositor to return to the defendant or other person who has paid the premium or any part of it, all of the money so paid or any part of it.
(Amended by Stats.1972, c. 1090, p. 2038, § 1.)

§ 1301. Arrest by bail or depositor for purpose of surrender

For the purpose of surrendering the defendant, the bail or any person who has deposited money or bonds to secure the release of the defendant, at any time before such bail or other person is finally discharged, and at any place within the state, may himself arrest defendant, or by written authority indorsed on a certified copy of the undertaking or a certified copy of the certificate of deposit, may empower any person of suitable age to do so.

Any bail or other person who so arrests a defendant in this state shall, without unnecessary delay, and, in any event, within 48 hours of the arrest, deliver the defendant to the court or magistrate before whom the defendant is required to appear or to the custody of the sheriff or police for confinement in the appropriate jail in the county or city in which defendant is required to appear. Any bail or other person who arrests a defendant outside this state shall, without unnecessary delay after the time defendant is brought into this state, and, in any event, within 48 hours after defendant is brought into this state, deliver the defendant to the custody of the court or magistrate before whom the defendant is required to appear or to the custody of the sheriff or police for confinement in the appropriate jail in the county or city in which defendant is required to appear.

Any bail or other person who willfully fails to deliver a defendant to the court, magistrate, sheriff, or police as required by this section is guilty of a misdemeanor.

The provisions of this section relating to the time of delivery of a defendant are for his benefit and, with the consent of the bail, may be waived by him. To be valid, such waiver shall be in writing, signed by the defendant, and delivered to such bail or other person within 48 hours after the defendant's arrest or entry into this state, as the case may be. The defendant, at any time and in the same manner, may revoke said waiver. Whereupon, he shall be delivered as provided herein without unnecessary delay and, in any event within 48 hours from the time of such revocation.

If any 48-hour period specified in this section terminates on a Saturday, Sunday, or holiday, delivery of a defendant by a bail or other person to the court or magistrate or to the custody of the sheriff or police may, without violating this section, take place before noon on the next day following which is not a Saturday, Sunday, or holiday.
(Amended by Stats.1965, c. 1859, p. 4301, § 1.)

§ 1302. Return of deposit on surrender; certificate; notice to district attorney

If money has been deposited instead of bail, and the defendant, at any time before the forfeiture thereof, surrenders himself to the officer to whom the commitment was directed, in the manner provided in the last two sections, the court must order a return of the deposit to the defendant or to the person or persons found by the court to have deposited said money on behalf of said defendant, upon the production of the certificate of the officer showing the surrender, and upon a notice of five days to the district attorney, with a copy of the certificate.
(Amended by Stats.1935, c. 657, p. 1815, § 9.)

§ 1318. Release for good cause; agreement to surrender self to custody of court

Upon good cause being shown, any court or magistrate who could release a defendant from custody upon his giving bail including a defendant arrested upon an out-of-county warrant may release such defendant on his own recognizance if it appears to such court or magistrate that such defendant will surrender himself to custody as agreed, by following the provisions of this article.
(Amended by Stats.1973, c. 620, p. 1144, § 2.)

§ 1318.2. Discretionary and permissive powers of court or magistrate

The powers granted to a court or magistrate by this article are purely discretionary and permissive. This article does not give any defendant the right to be released on his own recognizance.
(Added by Stats.1959, c. 1340, p. 3612, § 1.)

§ 1318.4. Filing written agreement; contents

To be released on his own recognizance the defendant shall file with the clerk of the court in which the magistrate or judge is presiding an agreement in writing duly executed by him, in which he agrees that:

(a) He will appear at all times and places as ordered by the court or magistrate releasing him and as ordered by any court in which, or any magistrate before whom, the charge is subsequently pending.

(b) If he fails to so appear and is apprehended outside of the State of California, he waives extradition.

(c) Any court or magistrate of competent jurisdiction may revoke the order of release and either return him to custody or require that he give bail or other assurance of his appearance as elsewhere provided by this chapter, upon a finding made in open court that he has failed to appear or has violated any condition of the order releasing him on his own recognizance, or that there has been a change of circumstances which increases the risk of failure to appear, or that additional facts have been presented which were not shown at the time of the original order releasing him on his own recognizance.
(Amended by Stats.1974, c. 202, p. 395, § 1.)

§ 1318.6. Bail or other security after release; commitment to actual custody of court

After a defendant has been released pursuant to this article, the court in which the charge is pending may require that the defendant either give bail in an amount specified by it or other security as elsewhere provided in this chapter upon a finding, made in open court that the defendant has failed to appear or has violated any condition of the order releasing him on his own recognizance, or that there has been a change of circumstances which increases the risk of failure to appear, or that additional facts have been presented which were not shown at the time of the original order releasing the defendant on his own recognizance. The court may order that the defendant be committed to actual custody unless he gives such bail or gives such other security.
(Amended by Stats.1974, c. 202, p. 396, § 2.)

§ 1318.8. Arrest of defendant; grounds

The court to which the committing magistrate returns the depositions, or in which an indictment, information or appeal is pending, or to which a judgment on appeal is remitted to be carried into effect, may, by an order entered upon its minutes, direct the arrest of any defendant who has been released upon his own recognizance and his commitment to the officer to whose custody he was committed at the time of such release, and his detention until legally discharged, in the following cases:

(a) When he has failed to appear as he agreed.

(b) When he was required to give bail or other security as provided in Section 1318.6 and has failed to do so.

(c) Upon an indictment being found or information filed in the cases provided in Section 985.
(Added by Stats.1959, c. 1340, p. 3613, § 1.)

§ 1319.2. Persons authorized to release defendant

This article does not authorize any clerk or other officer except the judge of a court or a magistrate to release a defendant upon his own recognizance.
(Added by Stats.1959, c. 1340, p. 3613, § 1.)

§ 1319.4. Felony offense; failure to appear; punishment

Every person who is charged with the commission of a felony who is released on his own recognizance pursuant to this article who willfully fails to appear as he has agreed, is guilty of a felony, and upon conviction thereof shall be punished by a fine not exceeding five thousand dollars ($5,000) or by imprisonment in the state prison, or in the county jail for not more than one year, or by both such fine and imprisonment.
(Amended by Stats.1976, c. 1139, p. —, § 274.5, operative July 1, 1977.)

§ 1319.6. Misdemeanor offense; failure to appear

Every person who is charged with the commission of a misdemeanor who is released on his own recognizance pursuant to this article who willfully fails to appear as he has agreed, is guilty of a misdemeanor.
(Added by Stats.1959, c. 1340, p. 3613, § 1.)

§ 1321. Competency; applicability of civil rules; exceptions

Who are competent witnesses. The rules for determining the competency of witnesses in civil actions are applicable also to criminal actions and proceedings, except as otherwise provided in this Code. (Enacted 1872.)

§ 1324. Self-incrimination; order compelling testimony; exemption from prosecution; perjury, false swearing, contempt, etc.

In any felony proceeding or in any investigation or proceeding before a grand jury for any felony offense if a person refuses to answer a question or produce evidence of any other kind on the ground that he may be incriminated thereby, and if the district attorney of the county in writing requests the superior court in and for that county to order that person to answer the question or produce the evidence, a judge of the superior court shall set a time for hearing and order the person to appear before the court and show cause, if any, why the question should not be answered or the evidence produced, and the court shall order the question answered or the evidence produced unless it finds that to do so would be clearly contrary to the public interest, or could subject the witness to a criminal prosecution in another jurisdiction, and that person shall comply with the order. After complying, and if, but for this section, he would have been privileged to withhold the answer given or the evidence produced by him, that person shall not be prosecuted or subjected to penalty or forfeiture for or on account of any fact or act concerning which, in accordance with the order, he was required to answer or produce evidence. But he may nevertheless be prosecuted or subjected to penalty or forfeiture for any perjury, false swearing or contempt committed in answering, or failing to answer, or in producing, or failing to produce, evidence in accordance with the order.
(Amended by Stats.1957, c. 2395, p. 4138, § 1.)

COMPELLING ATTENDANCE OF WITNESSES

§ 1326. Subpoena defined; persons authorized to issue

The process by which the attendance of a witness before a court or magistrate is required is a subpoena. It may be signed and issued by any of the following:

(1) A magistrate before whom a complaint is laid or his clerk, the district attorney or his investigator, or the public defender or his investigator, for witnesses in the state.

(2) The district attorney, his investigator, or, upon request of the grand jury, any judge of the superior court, for witnesses in the state, in support of an indictment or information, to appear before the court in which it is to be tried.

(3) The district attorney or his investigator, the public defender or his investigator, the clerk of the court in which a criminal action is to be tried, or, if there is no clerk, the judge of the court. The clerk or judge shall, at any time, upon application of the defendant, and without charge, issue as many blank subpoenas, subscribed by him, for witnesses in the state, as the defendant may require.

(4) The attorney of record for the defendant.
(Amended by Stats.1972, c. 543, p. 933, § 1.)

§ 1327. Subpoena; form

A subpoena authorized by Section 1326 shall be substantially in the following form:

The people of the State of California to A. B.:

You are commanded to appear before C. D., a judge of the Justice Court of _____ Judicial District, in _____ County (or as the case may be), at (naming the place), on (stating the day and hour), as a witness in a criminal action prosecuted by the people of the State of California against E. F.

Given under my hand this _____ day of _____, A.D. 19____. G. H., Judge of the Justice Court (or "J. K., District Attorney," or "J. K., District Attorney Investigator," or "D. E., Public Defender," or "D. E., Public Defender Investigator," or "F. G., Defense Counsel," or "By order of the court, L. M., Clerk," or as the case may be). If books, papers, or documents are required, a direction to the following effect must be contained in the subpoena: "And you are required, also, to bring with you the following" (describing intelligibly the books, papers, or documents required).
(Amended by Stats.1972, c. 543, p. 933, § 2.)

§ 1328. Subpoena; service; persons authorized; returns; method

A subpoena may be served by any person, but a peace officer must serve in his county any subpoena delivered to him for service, either on the part of the people or of the defendant, and must, without delay,

§ 1328

make a written return of the service, subscribed by him, stating the time and place of service. The service is made by delivering a copy of the subpoena to the witness personally.

Whenever any peace officer designated in Section 830 is required as a witness before any court or magistrate in any action or proceeding in connection with a matter regarding an event or transaction which he has perceived or investigated in the course of his duties, a subpoena requiring his attendance may be served either by delivering a copy to such peace officer personally or by delivering two copies to his immediate superior or agent designated by his immediate superior to receive such service. If service is made upon the immediate superior or agent designated by the immediate superior, the immediate superior or such agent shall deliver a copy of the subpoena to the peace officer as soon as possible and in no event later than such time as will enable the peace officer to comply with the subpoena.

If the immediate superior or his designated agent upon whom service is attempted to be made knows he will be unable to deliver a copy of the subpoena to the peace officer within such time as will allow the peace officer to comply with the subpoena, such immediate superior or agent may refuse to accept service of process and is excused from any duty, liability, or penalty arising in connection with such service, upon notifying the server of such fact.

If an immediate superior or his agent is tendered service of a subpoena less than five working days prior to the date of hearing, and he is not reasonably certain he can complete the service, he may refuse acceptance.

If an immediate superior or agent upon whom service has been made, subsequently determines that he will be unable to deliver a copy of the subpoena to the peace officer within such time as will allow the peace officer to comply with the subpoena, the immediate superior or agent shall notify the server or his office or agent not less than 48 hours prior to the hearing date indicated on the subpoena, and is thereby excused from any duty, liability, or penalty arising because of his failure to deliver a copy of the subpoena to the peace officer. The server, so notified, is therewith responsible for preparing the written return of service and for notifying the originator of the subpoena if required.

(Amended by Stats.1969, c. 311, p. 678, § 2.)

§ 1328.5. Peace officers; statement of business address in lieu of place of residence

Whenever any peace officer is a witness before any court or magistrate in any criminal action or proceeding in connection with a matter regarding an event or transaction which he has perceived or investigated in the course of his duties, where his testimony would become a matter of public record, and where he is required to state the place of his residence, he need not state the place of his residence, but in lieu thereof, he may state his business address.

(Added by Stats.1971, c. 636, p. ——, § 4.)

§ 1328a. Subpoena; telegraphic copy; effect

A telegraphic copy of a subpoena for a witness in a criminal proceeding may be sent by telegraph or teletype to one or more peace officers, and such copy is as effectual in the hands of any officer, and he must proceed in the same manner under it, as though he held the original subpoena issued.

(Added by Stats.1963, c. 803, p. 1833, § 1.)

§ 1328b. Subpoena; telegraphic copy; sending officer's duties

Every officer causing telegraphic copies of subpoenas to be sent, must certify as correct, and file in the telegraph office from which such copies are sent, a copy of the subpoena, and must return the original with a statement of his action thereunder.

(Added by Stats.1963, c. 803, p. 1833, § 2.)

§ 1328c. Subpoena; telegraphic copy; service and return

A peace officer must serve in his county or city any subpoena delivered to him by telegraph or teletype for service and must without delay make a return of the service by telegraph or teletype. Any officer making a return of service of a subpoena by telegraph or teletype must certify as to his actions in making the service and file in the telegraph office from which the return is sent a written statement with his signature in the same form as the return on an original subpoena. The service of a teletype subpoena is made by showing the original teletype to the witness personally and informing him of its contents and delivering to him a copy of the teletype.

(Added by Stats.1963, c. 803, p. 1833, § 3.)

§ 1329. Witnesses; fees and expenses; procedure for payment; rate

(a) When a person attends before a magistrate, grand jury, or court, as a witness in a criminal case, whether upon a subpoena or in pursuance of an undertaking, or voluntarily, the court, at its discretion, if the attendance of the witness be upon a trial may by an order upon its minutes, or in any criminal proceeding, by a written order, direct the county auditor to draw his warrant upon the county treasurer in favor of such witness for witness' fees at the rate of twelve dollars ($12) for each day's actual attendance and for a reasonable sum to be specified in the order for the necessary expenses of such witness. The court, in its discretion, may make an allowance under this section, or under Chapter 1 (commencing with Section 68070), Title 8, of the Government Code, as it may deem appropriate. The allowances are county charges.

(b) The court, in its discretion, may authorize payment to such a witness, if he is employed and if his salary is not paid by his employer during the time he is absent from his employment because of being such a witness, of a sum equal to his gross salary for such time, but such sum shall not exceed eighteen dollars ($18) per day. The sum is a county charge.

A person compensated under the provisions of this subdivision may not receive the payment of witness' fees as provided for in subdivision (a).
(Amended by Stats.1973, c. 1083, p. 2199, § 1.)

§ 1330. Witness; attendance; distance; indorsement of order on subpoena; subpoena duces tecum

No person is obliged to attend as a witness before a court or magistrate out of the county where the witness resides, or is served with the subpoena, unless the distance be less than 150 miles from his place of residence to the place of trial, or unless the judge of the court in which the offense is triable, or a justice of the Supreme Court, or a judge of a superior court, or, in the case of a minor concerning whom a petition has been filed pursuant to Article 7 (commencing with Section 650) of Chapter 2 of Part 1 of Division 2 of the Welfare and Institutions Code, by the judge of the juvenile court hearing the petition, upon an affidavit of the district attorney or prosecutor, or of the defendant, or his counsel, or in the case involving a minor in whose behalf a petition has been filed in the juvenile court, of the probation officer approving the filing of such petition or of any party to such action, or his counsel, stating that he believes the evidence of the witness is material, and his attendance at the examination, trial, or hearing is material and necessary, shall endorse on the subpoena an order for the attendance of the witness.

When a subpoena duces tecum is duly issued according to any other provision of law and is served upon a custodian of records or other qualified witness as provided in Article 4 (commencing with Section 1560) of Chapter 2 of Division 11 of the Evidence Code, and his personal attendance is not required by the terms of the subpoena, the limitations of this section shall not apply.
(Amended by Stats.1972, c. 393, p. 716, § 1.)

§ 1331. Witnesses; disobedience to subpoena; refusal to be sworn or to testify; contempt; liability to defendant; statutory damages

Disobedience to subpoena, etc. Disobedience to a subpoena, or a refusal to be sworn or to testify as a witness, may be punished by the Court or magistrate as a contempt. A witness disobeying a subpoena issued on the part of the defendant, unless he show good cause for his nonattendance, is liable to the defendant in the sum of one hundred dollars, which may be recovered in a civil action.
(Enacted 1872.)

§ 1331.5. Subpoenaed witness; agreement to appear at other time; contempt

Any person who is subpoenaed to appear at a session of court, or at the trial of an issue therein, may, in lieu of appearance at the time specified in the subpoena, agree with the party at whose request the subpoena was issued, to appear at another time or upon such notice as may be agreed upon. Any failure to appear pursuant to such agreement may be punished as a contempt, and a subpoena shall so state. The facts establishing such agreement and the failure to appear may be shown by the affidavit of any person having personal knowledge of the facts and the court may grant such continuance as may be appropriate.
(Added by Stats.1972, c. 393, p. 716, § 2.)

CRIMINAL INSANITY

§ 1367. Mentally incompetent persons; trial or punishment prohibited; application of §§ 1370, 1370.1

A person cannot be tried or adjudged to punishment while he is mentally incompetent. A defendant is mentally incompetent for purposes of this chapter 191 if, as a result of mental disorder or developmental disability, he is unable to understand the nature of the proceedings taken against him and to assist counsel in the conduct of a defense in a rational manner.

Section 1370 shall apply to a person who is incompetent as a result of a mental disorder. Section 1370.1 shall apply to a person who is incompetent as a result of a developmental disability and shall apply to a person who is incompetent as a result of a mental disorder, but is also developmentally disabled.
(Amended by Stats.1977, c. 695, p. —, § 1.)

§ 1368. Doubt as to defendant's mental competence; hearing; stay of criminal proceedings; discharge or retention of jury

(a) If, during the pendency of an action and prior to judgment, a doubt arises in the mind of the judge as to the mental competence of the defendant, he shall state that doubt in the record and inquire of the attorney for the defendant whether, in the opinion of the attorney, the defendant is mentally competent. If the defendant is not represented by counsel, the court shall appoint counsel. At the request of the defendant or his counsel or upon its own motion, the court shall recess the proceedings for as long as may be reasonably necessary to permit counsel to confer with the defendant and to form an opinion as to the mental competence of the defendant at that point in time.

(b) If counsel informs the court that he believes the defendant is or may be mentally incompetent, the court shall order that the question of the defendant's mental competence is to be determined in a hearing which is held pursuant to Sections 1368.1 and 1369. If counsel informs the court that he believes the defendant is mentally competent, the court may nevertheless order a hearing. Any hearing shall be held in the superior court.

(c) Except as provided in Section 1368.1, when an order for a hearing into the present mental competence of the defendant has been issued, all proceedings in the criminal prosecution shall be suspended until the question of the present mental competence of the defendant has been determined.

If a jury has been impaneled and sworn to try the defendant, the jury shall be discharged only if it appears to the court that undue hardship to the jurors would result if the jury is retained on call.

If the defendant is declared mentally incompetent, the jury shall be discharged.
(Amended by Stats.1974, c. 1511, p. 3317, § 3.)

§ 1369. Trial of issue of mental competence; order of proceedings

A trial by court or jury of the question of mental competence shall proceed in the following order:

(a) The court shall appoint a psychiatrist or licensed psychologist, and any other expert the court may deem appropriate, to examine the defendant. In any case where the defendant or his counsel informs the court that the defendant is not seeking a finding of mental incompetence, the court shall appoint two psychiatrists, licensed psychologists, or a combination thereof. One of the psychiatrists or licensed psychologists may be named by the defense and one may be named by the prosecution. If it is suspected the defendant is developmentally disabled, the court shall appoint the director of the regional center for the developmentally disabled established under Division 25 (commencing with Section 38000) of the Health and Safety Code, or the designee of the director, to examine the defendant. The court may order the developmentally disabled defendant to be confined for examination in a state hospital or any other residential facility designated by the director of the regional center.

(b)(1) The counsel for the defendant shall offer evidence in support of the allegation of mental incompetence.

(2) If the defense declines to offer any evidence in support of the allegation of mental incompetence, the prosecution may do so.

(c) The prosecution shall present its case regarding the issue of defendant's present mental competence.

(d) Each party may offer rebutting testimony, unless the court, for good reason in furtherance of justice, also permits other evidence in support of the original contention.

(e) When the evidence is concluded, unless the case is submitted without final argument, the prosecution shall make its final argument and the defense shall conclude with its final argument to the court or jury.

(f) In a jury trial, the court shall charge the jury, instructing them on all matters of law necessary for the rendering of a verdict. It shall be presumed that the defendant is mentally competent unless it is proved by a preponderance of the evidence that he is mentally incompetent. The verdict of the jury shall be unanimous.
(Amended by Stats.1977, c. 695, p. —, § 2.)

§ 1370. Resolution of question of mental competence; procedure after commitment to hospital or other facility; dismissal; conservatorship

(a) If the defendant is found mentally competent, the criminal process shall resume, the trial on the offense charged shall proceed, and judgment may be pronounced. If the defendant is found mentally incompetent, the trial or judgment shall be suspended until he becomes mentally competent, and the court shall order that (1) in the meantime, the defendant be delivered by the sheriff to a state hospital for the care and treatment of the mentally disordered or to any other available public or private mental health treatment facility approved by the county mental health director as will promote the defendant's speedy restoration of mental competence, or be ordered to undergo outpatient treatment as specified in Section 1370.3 and (2) upon his becoming competent, he be redelivered to the sheriff to be returned to court where the criminal process shall resume. The court shall transmit a copy of its order to the county mental health director or his designee.

If the defendant has been charged with murder, mayhem, a violation of Section 207 or 209 in which the victim suffers intentionally inflicted great bodily injury, robbery in the first degree or in which the victim suffers great bodily injury, a violation of Section 447a involving a trailer coach, as defined in Section 635 of the Vehicle Code, or any dwelling house, a violation of subdivision (2) and (3) of Section 261, a violation of Section 459 in the first degree, assault with intent to commit murder, a violation of Section 220 in which the victim suffers great bodily injury, a violation of Section 12303.1, 12303.3, 12308, 12309, or 12310, or if the defendant has been charged with a felony involving death, great bodily injury, or an act which poses a serious threat of bodily harm to another person, the court shall direct that the defendant be confined in a state hospital or other public or private mental health facility approved by the county mental health director for a minimum of 90 days before such defendant may be released on outpatient treatment pursuant to Section 1374. Prior to release on outpatient treatment, such defendant shall be returned to court for a hearing to determine whether the defendant is entitled to be admitted to bail or released upon his own recognizance.

Prior to making such order, the court shall order the county mental health director or his designee to evaluate the defendant and to submit to the court within 15 judicial days of such order his written recommendation as to whether the defendant should be required to undergo outpatient treatment, or committed to a state hospital or to any other mental health facility. No person shall be admitted to a state hospital or other facility or accepted for outpatient treatment under this section without having been evaluated by the county mental health director or his or her designee.

If the defendant is committed or transferred to a state hospital pursuant to this section, the court may, upon receiving the written recommendation of the superintendent of the state hospital and the county mental health director that the defendant be transferred to a public or private mental health facility approved by the county mental health director, order the defendant transferred to such facility. If the defendant is committed or transferred to a public or private mental health facility approved by the county mental health director, the court may, upon receiving the written recommendation of the county mental health director, transfer the defendant to a state hospital or to another public or private mental health facility approved by the county mental health director. In the event of dismissal of the criminal charges before the defendant recovers competence, the person shall be subject to the applicable provisions of the Lanterman-Petris-Short Act (Part 1 (commencing with Section 5000) of Division 5 of the Welfare and Institutions Code). The defendant or prosecuting attorney, if he chooses to contest either kind of order of transfer, may petition the court for a hearing, which shall be held if the court determines that sufficient grounds exist. At such hearing the prosecuting attorney or the defendant may present evidence bearing on the order of transfer. The court shall use the same standards as used in conducting probation revocation hearings pursuant to Section 1203.2.

Prior to making an order for transfer under this section, the court shall notify the defendant, the attorney of record for the defendant, the prosecuting attorney, and the county mental health director or his designee.

(b)(1) Within 90 days of a commitment made pursuant to subdivision (a), the superintendent of the state hospital or other facility to which the defendant is committed or from which the defendant is placed on outpatient treatment shall make a written report to the court and the county mental health director or his designee concerning the defendant's progress toward recovery of his mental competence. If the

§ 1370

defendant has not recovered his mental competence, but the report discloses a substantial likelihood the defendant will regain his mental competence in the foreseeable future, he shall remain in the state hospital or other facility or on outpatient treatment. Thereafter, at six-month intervals or until the defendant becomes mentally competent, the superintendent of the hospital or person in charge of the facility shall report to the court and the county mental health director or his designee regarding the defendant's progress toward recovery of his mental competence. If the report indicates that there is no substantial likelihood that the defendant will regain his mental competence in the foreseeable future, the committing court shall order him to be returned to the court for proceedings pursuant to paragraph (2) of subdivision (c). The court shall transmit a copy of its order to the county mental health director or his designee.

(2) If, after the defendant has been committed or has undergone outpatient treatment for 18 months, he is still hospitalized or on outpatient treatment pursuant to this section, he shall be returned to the committing court where a hearing shall be held pursuant to the procedures set forth in Section 1369. The court shall transmit a copy of its order to the county mental health director or his designee.

(3) If it is determined by the court that no treatment for the defendant's mental impairment is being conducted, the defendant shall be returned to the committing court.

(4) The superintendent or person in charge of the facility shall deliver the reports made pursuant to paragraph (1) to the committing court and to the county mental health director or his designee, which shall provide a copy thereof to the defendant, his attorney of record, and any other interested person specified by the defendant.

(c)(1) If, at the end of three years from the date of commitment or a period of commitment equal to the maximum term of imprisonment provided by law for the most serious offense charged in the information, indictment, or misdemeanor complaint, whichever is shorter, the defendant has not recovered his mental competence, he shall be returned to the committing court. The court shall notify the county mental health director or his designee of such return and of any resulting court orders.

(2) Whenever any defendant is returned to the court pursuant to paragraph (2) of subdivision (b) or paragraph (1) of subdivision (c) and it appears to the court that the defendant is gravely disabled as defined in paragraph (2) of subdivision (h) of Section 5008 of the Welfare and Institutions Code, the court shall order the conservatorship investigator of the county of commitment of the defendant to initiate conservatorship proceedings for such defendant pursuant to Chapter 3 (commencing with Section 5350) of Part 1 of Division 5 of the Welfare and Institutions Code. Any hearings required in the conservatorship proceedings shall be held in the superior court in the county which ordered the commitment. The court shall transmit a copy of the order directing initiation of conservatorship proceedings to the county mental health director or his designee.

(d) The criminal action remains subject to dismissal pursuant to Section 1385.

(e) If the criminal charge against the defendant is dismissed, the defendant shall be released from any commitment ordered under this section, but without prejudice to the initiation of any proceedings under the Lanterman-Petris-Short Act, Part 1 (commencing with Section 5000) of Division 5 of the Welfare and Institutions Code, which may be appropriate.
(Amended by Stats.1977, c. 691, p. —, § 2; Stats.1977, c. 695, p. —, § 3; Stats.1977, c. 1237, p. —, § 1.)

§ 1370.1. Developmental disability of defendant; procedure

(a) **Suspension of trial or judgment; state hospital, residential facility or outpatient treatment; return to mental competence; confinement for evaluation and treatment; contest of institutional transfers**

(a) If the defendant is found mentally competent, the criminal process shall resume, the trial on the offense charged shall proceed, and judgment may be pronounced. If the defendant is found mentally incompetent and is developmentally disabled, the trial or judgment shall be suspended until he becomes mentally competent, and the court shall order that (1) in the meantime, the defendant be delivered by the sheriff or other person designated by the court to a state hospital for the care and treatment of the developmentally disabled or any other available residential facility approved by the director of a regional center for the developmentally disabled established under Division 4.5 (commencing with Section 4500) of the Welfare and Institutions Code as will promote the defendant's speedy restoration of mental competence, or be ordered to undergo outpatient treatment as specified in Section 1370.3 and (2) upon his becoming competent, he be redelivered to the sheriff or other person designated by the court to be returned to court where the criminal process shall resume. The court shall transmit a copy of its order to the regional center director or his designee.

As used in this section, "developmental disability" means a disability which continues, or can be expected to continue, indefinitely and constitutes a substantial handicap for such individual. As defined by the Director of Developmental Services, this term shall include mental retardation, cerebral palsy, epilepsy, and autism. This term shall also include handicapping conditions found to be closely related to mental retardation or to require treatment similar to that required for mentally retarded individuals, but shall not include other handicapping conditions that are solely physical in nature.

If the defendant has been charged with murder, mayhem, a violation of Section 207 or 209 in which the victim suffers intentionally inflicted great bodily injury, robbery perpetrated by torture or by a person armed with a dangerous or deadly weapon or in which the victim suffers great bodily injury, a violation of Section 211a, a violation of Section 447a involving a trailer coach, as defined in Section 635 of the Vehicle Code, or any dwelling house, a violation of subdivision (2) or (3) of Section 261, a violation of Section 459 in the first degree, assault with intent to commit murder, a violation of Section 220 in which the victim suffers great bodily injury, a violation of Section 12303.1, 12303.3, 12308, 12309, or 12310, or if the defendant has been charged with a felony involving death, great bodily injury, or an act which poses a serious threat of bodily harm to another person, the court shall direct that the defendant be confined for evaluation and treatment in a state hospital or other residential facility approved by the regional center director for a minimum of 90 days before such defendant may be released on outpatient treatment pursuant to Section 1374. Prior to release on outpatient treatment, such defendant shall be returned to court for a hearing to determine whether the defendant is entitled to be admitted to bail or released upon his own recognizance.

Prior to making such order, the court shall order the regional center director or his designee to evaluate the defendant and to submit to the court within 15 judicial days of such order his written recommendation as to whether the defendant should be required to undergo outpatient treatment, or committed to a state hospital or to any other available residential facility approved by the regional center director.

If the defendant is committed or transferred to a state hospital pursuant to this section, the court may, upon receiving the written recommendation of the superintendent of the state hospital and the regional center director that the defendant be transferred to a residential facility approved by the regional center director, order the defendant transferred to such facility. If the defendant is committed or transferred to a residential facility approved by the regional center director, the court may, upon receiving the written recommendation of the regional center director, transfer the defendant to a state hospital or to another residential facility approved by the regional center director.

In the event of dismissal of the criminal charges before the defendant recovers competence, the person shall be subject to the applicable provisions of the Lanterman-Petris-Short Act (Part 1 (commencing with Section 5000) of Division 5 of the Welfare and Institutions Code) or to commitment or detention pursuant to a petition filed pursuant to Section 6502 of the Welfare and Institutions Code.

The defendant or prosecuting attorney, if he chooses to contest either kind of order or transfer, may petition the court for a hearing, which shall be held if the court determines that sufficient grounds exist. At such hearing the prosecuting attorney or the defendant may present evidence bearing on the order of transfer. The court shall use the same standards as used in conducting probation revocation hearings pursuant to Section 1203.2.

Prior to making an order for transfer under this section, the court shall notify the defendant, the attorney of record for the defendant, the prosecuting attorney, and the regional center director or his designee.

(b) **Progress reports; recovery of mental competence; return to committing court**

(b)(1) Within 90 days of a commitment made pursuant to subdivision (a), the superintendent of the state hospital or other facility to which the defendant is committed or from which the defendant is placed on outpatient treatment shall make a written report to the regional center director or his designee concerning the defendant's progress toward recovery of his mental competence which the regional center director or his designee shall immediately transmit to the court as part of the defendant's progress report.

§ 1370.1

If the defendant has not recovered his mental competence, but the report discloses a substantial likelihood the defendant will regain his mental competence in the foreseeable future, he shall remain in the state hospital or other facility or on outpatient treatment. Thereafter, at six-month intervals or until the defendant become mentally competent, the superintendent of the hospital or person in charge of the facility shall report to the regional center director or his designee regarding the defendant's progress toward recovery of his mental competence which the regional center director or his designee shall immediately transmit to the court as part of the defendant's progress report. If the report indicates that there is no substantial likelihood that the defendant will regain his mental competence in the foreseeable future, the committing court shall order him to be returned to the court for proceedings pursuant to paragraph (2) of subdivision (c). The court shall transmit a copy of its order to the regional center director or his designee.

(2) If, after the defendant has been committed or has undergone outpatient treatment for 18 months, he is still hospitalized or on outpatient treatment pursuant to this section, he shall be returned to the committing court where a hearing shall be held pursuant to the procedures set forth in Section 1369. The court shall transmit a copy of its order to the regional center director or his designee.

(3) If it is determined by the court that no treatment for the defendant's mental impairment is being conducted, the defendant shall be returned to the committing court.

(4) The regional center director or his designee shall deliver the reports made pursuant to paragraph (1) to the committing court and shall provide a copy thereof to the defendant, his attorney of record, and any other interested person specified by the defendant.

(c) Maximum commitment; failure to recover mental competence; return to committing court; dismissal of criminal action

(c)(1) If, at the end of three years from the date of commitment or a period of commitment equal to the maximum term of imprisonment provided by law for the most serious offense charged in the information, indictment, or misdemeanor complaint, whichever is shorter, the defendant has not recovered his mental competence, he shall be returned to the committing court. The court shall notify the regional center director or his designee of such return and of any resulting court orders.

(2) If it is found that the person is not subject to commitment or detention pursuant to the applicable provision of the Lanterman-Petris-Short Act (Part 1 (commencing with Section 5000) of Division 5 of the Welfare and Institutions Code) or to commitment or detention pursuant to a petition filed pursuant to Section 6502 of the Welfare and Institutions Code, the individual shall not be subject to further confinement pursuant to this article and the criminal action remains subject to dismissal pursuant to Section 1385.

(d) Dismissal of criminal action

(d) Notwithstanding any other provision of this section, the criminal action remains subject to dismissal pursuant to Section 1385. If at any time prior to the maximum period of time allowed for proceedings under this article, the regional center director concludes that the behavior of the defendant related to the defendant's criminal offense has been eliminated during time spent in court-ordered programs, the court may, upon recommendation of the regional center director, dismiss the criminal charges.
(Amended by Stats.1978, c. 429, p. —, § 159.)

§ 1370.2. Dismissal of misdemeanor charges against one mentally incompetent

If a person is adjudged mentally incompetent pursuant to the provisions of this chapter, the superior court may dismiss any misdemeanor charge pending against the mentally incompetent person. Ten days notice shall be given to the district attorney of any motion to dismiss pursuant to this section.
(Added by Stats.1974, c. 1511, p. 3320, § 7.)

§ 1370.3. Outpatient treatment; intent; hearings; progress reports; inpatient status

(a) If, in the evaluation ordered by the court under Section 1370, the county mental health director, or his designee, is of the opinion that the defendant is not a danger to the health and safety of others while on outpatient treatment and will benefit from such treatment, and has obtained the agreement of the person in charge of a mental health facility and of the defendant that the defendant will receive and submit to outpatient treatment and that the person in charge of the facility will designate a person to be the outpatient supervisor of the defendant, the court may order the defendant to undergo outpatient treatment. The court shall inform the prosecuting attorney and the defendant's attorney of record of its intent to make such an order, and shall make the evaluation and recommendation of the county mental health director, or his designee, available to them at least 15 days in advance of its order. The court may hold a hearing prior to ordering outpatient treatment, and (1) approve or disapprove of the plan or (2) take no action, in which case the plan shall be deemed approved. The court shall transmit a copy of its order to the county mental health director or his designee. At the request of the prosecuting attorney a hearing shall be held. Prior to filing such announcement of intent the county mental health director, or his designee, shall obtain the agreement of the person in charge of a mental health facility and of the defendant that the defendant will receive and submit to outpatient treatment and that the person in charge of the facility will designate a person to be the outpatient supervisor of the defendant. At 90-day intervals following the beginning of outpatient treatment, the outpatient supervisor shall make a report in writing to the court, the prosecuting attorney, the attorney of record for the defendant, and the county mental health director or his designee setting forth the status and progress of the defendant. The maximum period of such treatment shall not exceed one year. The court may at the end of such maximum period renew its approval for additional outpatient treatment upon the request of the county mental health director or his designee.

(b) When the outpatient supervisor is of the opinion that the defendant has recovered competence the supervisor shall communicate such opinion to the person in charge of the facility. If the person in charge of the facility concurs, he shall certify the opinion to the county mental health director or his designee, committing court, prosecuting attorney, and attorney of record for the defendant. The court shall calendar the case for further proceedings pursuant to Section 1372.

(c) If at any time during an outpatient treatment period the outpatient supervisor is of the opinion that the defendant requires extended inpatient treatment or refuses to accept further outpatient treatment, he shall communicate such opinion or refusal to the person in charge of the facility. If the person in charge of the facility concurs, he shall notify the committing court, the prosecuting attorney, the attorney of record for the defendant, and the county mental health director or his designee of his recommendation that the defendant be committed to undergo inpatient treatment in a state hospital or any other public or private mental health facility approved by the county mental health director. Within 15 judicial days, the court shall hold a hearing and shall either disapprove the recommendation or direct that the defendant be confined in a state hospital or other public or private mental health facility approved by the county mental health director.

(d) If at any time during an outpatient treatment period the prosecuting attorney is of the opinion that the defendant is a danger to the health and safety of others, while on outpatient treatment, he may petition the court for a hearing to determine whether the defendant shall be continued on outpatient treatment. The court shall calendar the case for further proceedings and the clerk shall notify the defendant, outpatient supervisor, the attorney of record for the defendant, and the county mental health director or his designee of the calendared date. Upon failure of the defendant to appear as noticed, if a proper affidavit of service and advisement has been filed with the court, the court may issue a body attachment for the defendant. If, after a hearing in open court conducted with the same standards used in probation revocation hearings pursuant to Section 1203.2, the judge of the committing court determines that the defendant is a danger to the health and safety of others, he shall commit the defendant to a state hospital for the care and treatment of the mentally disordered or to any public or private mental health facility approved by the county mental health director. The court shall transmit a copy of its order to the county mental health director or his designee. Such order shall be reviewable by a writ of habeas corpus only.

(e) An outpatient who requires inpatient treatment pending judicial determination of his outpatient status pursuant to subdivisions (c) and (d) shall receive such treatment subject to the provisions of Sections 5150, 5200, 5250, and 5300 of the Welfare and Institutions Code.

The person in charge of the facility in which an outpatient receives inpatient treatment shall notify the county mental health director or his designee of inpatient treatment provided to an outpatient under this section.
(Amended by Stats.1978, c. 1291, p. —, § 3.)

§ 1372. Restoration of competency; return to court

(a) If the superintendent of the hospital or facility to which the defendant is committed determines that

§ 1372

the defendant has regained his mental competence, he shall immediately certify that fact to the court, sheriff, and district attorney of the county in which defendant's case is pending and to defendant's attorney of record.

(b) If the defendant becomes mentally competent after a conservatorship has been established pursuant to the applicable provisions of the Lanterman-Petris-Short Act, Part 1 (commencing with Section 5000) of Division 5 of the Welfare and Institutions Code, and Section 1370, the conservator shall certify that fact to the sheriff and district attorney of the county in which defendant's case is pending, defendant's attorney of record, and the committing court.

(c) In the case of a defendant who is subject either to subdivision (a) or (b), the court shall order the sheriff to immediately return the defendant to the court in which the criminal charge is pending. Within two judicial days of the defendant's return the court shall hold a hearing to determine whether the defendant is entitled to be admitted to bail or released upon his own recognizance pending conclusion of the proceedings.
(Amended by Stats.1974, c. 1511, p. 3320, § 8.)

§ 1373. Transportation of defendant to and from hospital; county charge; recovery from estate or relative

The expense of sending the defendant to the state hospital or other facility, and of bringing him back, are chargeable to the county in which the indictment was found or information filed; but the county may recover them from the estate of the defendant, if he has any, or from a relative, bound to provide for and maintain him.
(Amended by Stats.1974, c. 1511, p. 3320, § 9.)

§ 1374. Outpatient treatment; intent; hearings; progress reports; inpatient status

(a) If the superintendent of a state hospital or other facility to which the defendant is committed or transferred is of the opinion that the defendant is not a danger to the health and safety of others, he may allow the defendant to be treated as an outpatient.

An announcement of intent to place the defendant on outpatient status shall be provided to the committing court, prosecuting attorney, and attorney of record for the defendant at least 15 days in advance of the change in status. The court may hold a hearing and (1) approve or disapprove of the plan or (2) take no action, in which case the plan shall be deemed to have been approved.

(b) Prior to filing such announcement of intent the superintendent shall obtain the agreement of the county mental health director, the person in charge of a mental health facility and of the defendant, that the defendant will receive and submit to outpatient treatment and that the person in charge of the facility will designate a person to be the outpatient supervisor of the defendant. At 90-day intervals following the beginning of outpatient treatment, the outpatient supervisor shall make a report in writing to the court, the state hospital or other facility to which the defendant was committed or transferred, the county mental health director or his designee, and to the person in charge of the mental health facility setting forth the status and progress of the defendant. The maximum period of such treatment shall not exceed one year. The court may at the end of such maximum period renew its approval for additional outpatient treatment upon the request of the superintendent of the state hospital or other facility. If the court does not so renew its approval, and the person has not been discharged from commitment, he shall be returned to the state hospital or other facility.

(c) When the outpatient supervisor is of the opinion that the defendant has recovered competence the supervisor shall communicate such opinion to the person in charge of the facility. If the person in charge of the facility concurs, he shall certify the opinion to the committing court, prosecuting attorney, attorney of record for the defendant, the county mental health director or his designee, and the director of the state hospital or other facility. The court shall calendar the case for further proceedings pursuant to Section 1372.

(d) If at any time during an outpatient treatment period the outpatient supervisor is of the opinion that the defendant requires extended inpatient treatment or refuses to accept further outpatient treatment, he shall communicate such opinion or refusal to the person in charge of the facility. If the person in charge of the facility concurs, he shall notify the committing court, the prosecuting attorney, the attorney of record for the defendant, and the county mental health director or his designee of his recommendation that the defendant be committed to a state hospital or any other public or private mental health facility approved by the county mental health director. Within 15 judicial days, the court shall hold a hearing and shall either disapprove the recommendation or direct that the defendant be confined in a state hospital or other public or private mental health facility approved by the county mental health director.

(e) If at any time during an outpatient treatment period the prosecuting attorney is of the opinion that the defendant is a danger to the health and safety of others while on outpatient treatment, he may petition the court for a hearing to determine whether the defendant shall be continued on outpatient treatment. The court shall calendar the case for further proceedings and the clerk shall notify the defendant, outpatient supervisor, the attorney of record for the defendant, and the county mental health director or his designee of the calendared date. Upon failure of the defendant to appear as noticed, if a proper affidavit of service and advisement has been filed with the court, the court may issue a body attachment for the defendant. If, after a hearing in open court conducted with the same standards used in probation revocation hearings pursuant to Section 1203.2, the judge of the committing court determines that the defendant is a danger to the health and safety of others, he shall order the defendant returned to the state hospital or other facility to which he was committed or transferred pursuant to Section 1370.

The court shall transmit a copy of its order to the county mental health director or his designee. Such order shall be reviewable by a writ of habeas corpus only.

(f) An outpatient who requires inpatient treatment pending determination of his outpatient status pursuant to subdivisions (b), (c), and (d) shall receive such treatment subject to the provisions of Sections 5150, 5200, 5250, and 5300 of the Welfare and Institutions Code.

The person in charge of the facility in which an outpatient receives inpatient treatment shall notify the county mental health director or his designee of inpatient treatment provided to an outpatient under this section.
(Amended by Stats.1978, c. 1291, p. ——, § 4.)

§ 1375.5. Credit on sentence for time spent in hospital or other facility

Time spent by a defendant in a hospital or other facility as a result of a commitment therein as a mentally incompetent pursuant to this chapter shall be credited on the term of any imprisonment, if any, for which the defendant is sentenced in the criminal case which was suspended pursuant to Section 1370 or 1370.1.

As used in this section, "time spent in a hospital or other facility" includes days a defendant is treated as an outpatient pursuant to Section 1374.
(Amended by Stats.1977, c. 695, p. ——, § 6.)

MISCELLANEOUS CRIMINAL PROCEDURE

§ 1385. Dismissal on court's own motion or application of prosecuting attorney; statement of reasons; dismissal prohibited for cause which would be ground of demurrer

The court may, either of its own motion or upon the application of the prosecuting attorney, and in furtherance of justice, order an action to be dismissed. The reasons of the dismissal must be set forth in an order entered upon the minutes. No dismissal shall be made for any cause which would be ground of demurrer to the accusatory pleading.
(Amended by Stats.1951, c. 1674, p. 3857, § 141.)

§ 1387. Dismissal as bar if felony previously dismissed or if misdemeanor; exception in felony cases if new evidence discovered

An order for the dismissal of an action pursuant to this chapter is a bar to any other prosecution for the same offense if it is a felony and the action has been previously dismissed pursuant to this chapter, or if it is a misdemeanor; except in those felony cases where subsequent to the dismissal of the felony the court finds that substantial new evidence has been discovered by the prosecution which would not have been known through the exercise of due diligence at or prior to the time of dismissal.
(Amended by Stats.1975, c. 1069, p. 2615, § 1.)

§ 1392. Summons; service; time

The summons must be served at least five days before the day of appearance fixed therein, by delivering a copy thereof and showing the original to the president or other head of the corporation, or to the secretary, cashier, managing agent, or an agent of the corporation designated for service of civil process.
(Amended by Stats.1973, c. 248, p. 639, § 1.)

§ 1393. Proceeding with charge; time

At the appointed time in the summons, the magistrate shall proceed with the charge in the same manner as in other cases.
(Amended by Stats.1971, c. 1591, p. 3206, § 3.)

§ 1394

§§ 1394, 1395. Repealed by Stats.1971, c. 1591, p. 3207, §§ 4, 5

§ 1396. Appearance by counsel; answer to accusatory pleading; exception; entry of plea on nonappearance

If an accusatory pleading is filed, the corporation may appear by counsel to answer the same, except that in the case of misdemeanors arising from operation of motor vehicles, or of infractions arising from operation of motor vehicles, a corporation may appear by its president, vice president, secretary or managing agent for the purpose of entering a plea of guilty. If it does not thus appear, a plea of not guilty shall be entered, and the same proceedings had thereon as in other cases.
(Amended by Stats.1973, c. 718, p. 1296, § 2.)

§ 1397. Fine; collection

Fine on conviction, how collected. When a fine is imposed upon a corporation on conviction, it may be collected by virtue of the order imposing it, by the Sheriff of the county, out of its real and personal property, in the same manner as upon an execution in a civil action.
(Enacted 1872.)

§ 1407. Property in custody of peace officer; holding subject to provisions of chapter

When property, alleged to have been stolen or embezzled, comes into the custody of a peace officer, he shall hold it subject to the provisions of this chapter relating to the disposal thereof.
(Amended by Stats.1975, c. 774, p. 1794, § 1.)

§ 1408. Property in custody of peace officer; order for delivery to owner; payment of expenses

On the application of the owner and on satisfactory proof of his ownership of the property, after reasonable notice and opportunity to be heard has been given to the person from whom custody of the property was taken and any other person as required by the magistrate, the magistrate before whom the complaint is laid, or who examines the charge against the person accused of stealing or embezzling it, shall order it to be delivered, without prejudice to the state, to the owner, on his paying the necessary expenses incurred in its preservation, to be certified by the magistrate. The order entitles the owner to demand and receive the property.
(Amended by Stats.1971, c. 799, p. 1553, § 1.)

§ 1409. Property in custody of magistrate; delivery to owner; proof of title; payment of expenses

If property stolen or embezzled comes into the custody of the magistrate, it shall be delivered, without prejudice to the state, to the owner upon his application to the court and on satisfactory proof of his title, after reasonable notice and opportunity to be heard has been given to the person from whom custody of the property was taken and any other person as required by the magistrate, and on his paying the necessary expenses incurred in its preservation, to be certified by the magistrate.
(Amended by Stats.1971, c. 799, p. 1553, § 2.)

§ 1410. Property not delivered to owner; proof of title; order for restoration by trial court

If the property stolen or embezzled has not been delivered to the owner, the court before which a trial is had for stealing or embezzling it, upon the application of the owner to the court and on proof of his title, after reasonable notice and opportunity to be heard has been given to the person from whom custody of the property was taken and any other person as required by the court, may order it to be restored to the owner without prejudice to the state.
(Amended by Stats.1971, c. 799, p. 1553, § 3.)

§ 1411. Unclaimed property delivered to county officer; notice; sale

If the ownership of the property stolen or embezzled and the address of the owner, and the address of the owner of a security interest therein, can be reasonably ascertained, the peace officer who took custody of the property shall notify the owner, and a person having a security interest therein, by letter of the location of the property and the method by which the owner may obtain it. Such notice shall be given upon the conviction of a person for an offense involving the theft, embezzlement or possession of such property, or if a conviction was not obtained, upon the making of a decision by the district attorney not to file the case or upon the termination of the proceedings in the case. Except as provided in Section 516 of the Welfare and Institutions Code, if the property stolen or embezzled is not claimed by the owner before the expiration of three months after the giving of such notice, or, in any case in which no such notice was given, before the expiration of six months from the conviction of a person for an offense involving the theft, embezzlement or possession of

such property, or if a conviction was not obtained, then from the time the property came into the possession of the peace officer or the case involving the person from whom it was obtained is disposed of, whichever is later, the magistrate or other officer having it in custody may, on the payment of the necessary expenses incurred in its preservation, deliver it to the county treasurer or other proper county officer, by whom it must be sold and the proceeds paid into the county treasury. If such property is transferred to the county purchasing agent it may be sold in the manner provided by Article 7 (commencing with Section 25500) of Chapter 5 of Part 2 of Division 2 of Title 3 of the Government Code for the sale of surplus personal property. If the county officer determines that any such property transferred to him for sale is needed for a public use, such property may be retained by the county and need not be sold. The magistrate or other officer having the property in custody may, however, provide for the sale of such property in the manner provided for the sale of unclaimed property which has been held for at least three months pursuant to Section 2080.4 of the Civil Code.
(Amended by Stats.1978, c. 121, p. —, § 1.)

§ 1412. Money or property taken from defendant on arrest; duplicate receipts; filing or delivery of receipts

Receipt by officers for money, etc., taken from a person arrested for a public offense. When money or other property is taken from a defendant, arrested upon a charge of a public offense, the officer taking it must at the time give duplicate receipts therefor, specifying particularly the amount of money or the kind of property taken; one of which receipts he must deliver to the defendant and the other of which he must forthwith file with the Clerk of the Court to which the depositions and statement are to be sent. When such property is taken by a police officer of any incorporated city or town, he must deliver one of the receipts to the defendant, and one, with the property, at once to the Clerk or other person in charge of the police office in such city or town.
(Enacted 1872.)

§ 1413. Person in charge of property section; record of property allegedly stolen or embezzled; delivery to owner; review by magistrate; liability

(a) The clerk or person having charge of the property section for any police department in any incorporated city or town, or for any sheriff's department in any county, shall enter in a suitable book a description of every article of property alleged to be stolen or embezzled, and brought into the office or taken from the person of a prisoner, and shall attach a number to each article, and make a corresponding entry thereof. He may engrave or imbed an identification number in property described in Section 537e for the purposes thereof.

(b) The clerk or person in charge of the property section may, upon satisfactory proof of the ownership of property held pursuant to Section 1407, and upon presentation of proper personal identification, deliver it to the owner. Such delivery shall be without prejudice to the state or to the person from whom custody of the property was taken or to any other person who may have a claim against the property. Prior to such delivery such clerk or person in charge of the property section shall make and retain a complete photographic record of such property. The person to whom property is delivered shall sign, under penalty of perjury, a declaration of ownership, which shall be retained by the clerk or person in charge of the property section. This subdivision shall not apply to any property subject to forfeiture under any provision of law. This subdivision shall not apply unless the clerk or person in charge of the property section has served upon the person from whom custody of the property was taken a notice of a claim of ownership and a copy of the satisfactory proof of ownership tendered and has allowed such person reasonable opportunity to be heard as to why such property should not be delivered to the person claiming ownership.

(c) The magistrate before whom the complaint is laid, or who examines the charge against the person accused of stealing or embezzling the property, or the court before which a trial is had for stealing or embezzling it, shall upon application by the person from whom custody of the property was taken, review the determination of the clerk or person in charge of the property section, and may order the property taken into the custody of the court upon a finding that the person to whom the property was delivered is not entitled thereto. Such court shall make its determination in the same manner as a determination is made when the matter is before the court pursuant to Sections 1408 to 1410, inclusive.

(e) The clerk or person in charge of the property section shall not be liable in damages for any official action performed hereunder in good faith.
(Amended by Stats.1975, c. 774, p. 1794, § 2.)

§ 1417. Exhibits introduced in criminal actions

All exhibits which have been introduced or filed in any criminal action or proceeding may be disposed of as provided in this chapter.
(Amended by Stats.1959, c. 1849, p. 4397, § 1.)

§ 1418. Time and manner of disposal

If the ownership of such exhibits and the address of the owner can be reasonably ascertained, the court shall notify the owner of the location thereof and the method by which the owner may obtain such exhibits. Such notice shall be given at the time the conviction, or, if none, the judgment or other termination of the proceedings, becomes final. After the expiration of three months from the time such notice is given, the court may, on application of the party entitled thereto, or an agent designated in writing by the owner, order all such exhibits, other than documentary exhibits, as may be released from the custody of the court without prejudice to the state, delivered to such party; provided, however, where the action or proceeding has resulted in an order granting probation, such delivery may be made any time after the final determination of an appeal of such order, taken under the provisions of Section 1237, or after the time for such appeal has elapsed but in no case sooner than the expiration of three months. In all cases in which the death penalty has been imposed no such order shall be made until the sentence of death has been carried out. If the party entitled to such exhibits is unknown, or fails to apply for the return of such exhibits, the procedure for their disposition shall be as follows:

Order designating exhibits to be released

After the expiration of six months from the time the conviction becomes final, or if the action or proceeding has not resulted in a conviction, at any time after the judgment has become final, the court in which the case was tried shall make an order specifying what exhibits may be released from the custody of the court without prejudice to the state. Upon receipt of such an order, the clerk of the court shall transfer the property to the county purchasing and stores agency or other proper county agency for sale to the public.

Order for return to owner

At any time prior to the time fixed for the transfer, the owner or any person entitled to the possession of any of such exhibits may obtain from the court an order returning them to him.

Sale for cash; proceeds

Articles not returned to their owners or to persons entitled to their possession at or prior to the time set for the transfer shall be sold by the proper receiving agency for cash; said articles shall be sold singly or in combinations. The money received from such sales shall be placed in the general fund of the county.

Deposit of money

Where the exhibit consists of money or currency and is unclaimed at the time of the transfer, the clerk shall not transfer it but shall immediately deposit it in the general fund of the county.

Sale by county purchasing agent; retention for public use

If any property is transferred to the county purchasing agent pursuant to this section it may be sold in the manner provided by Article 7 (commencing with Section 25500) of Chapter 5 of Part 2 of Division 2 of Title 3 of the Government Code for the sale of surplus personal property. If the county purchasing and stores agency or other proper county agency determines that any such property transferred to it for sale is needed for a public use, such property may be retained by the agency and need not be sold.
(Amended by Stats.1976, c. 369, p. —, § 2.)

§ 1418.5. Documentary exhibits

Order for release; application

The court may, on application of the party entitled thereto, or an agent designated in writing by the owner, order such documentary exhibits as may be released from the custody of the court without prejudice to the state delivered to such party any time after the final determination of the action or proceeding; provided, however, where the action or proceeding has resulted in an order granting probation, such delivery may be made any time after the final determination of an appeal of such order, taken under the provisions of Section 1237, or after the time for such appeal has elapsed.

Failure to apply for return

If the party entitled to such documentary exhibits is unknown, or fails to apply for the return of said exhibits, the procedure for their disposition shall be as follows:

Order for destruction; exceptions

After the expiration of six months from the time the conviction becomes final, or if the action or proceeding has not resulted in a conviction, at any time after the judgment has become final, the court in which the case was tried shall make an order requiring such exhibits to be destroyed; provided, that no such order shall be made authorizing the destruction of any documentary exhibit if the destruction of such exhibits would prejudice the state.

Death penalty cases

In all cases in which the death penalty has been imposed no such order shall be made until the sentence of death has been carried out.

Notice of proposed destruction; consent

No exhibit shall be destroyed or otherwise disposed of until 60 days after the clerk of the court has posted a notice conspicuously in three public places in the county, referring to the order for the disposition, describing briefly the exhibit, and indicating the date after which the exhibit will be destroyed or otherwise disposed of.
(Amended by Stats.1975, c. 774, p. 1795, § 4.)

§ 1418.6. Release of exhibits prior to final determination of action or proceedings; conditions

Notwithstanding Sections 1418 and 1418.5, the court may, on application of the party entitled thereto, or an agent designated in writing by the owner, order all such exhibits delivered to such party at any time prior to the final determination of the action or proceedings, upon stipulation of the parties if the following requirements are met:

(a) No prejudice will be suffered by either party.

(b) A full and complete photographic record is made of the material so released.

This section shall not apply to any material, the release of which is prohibited by Section 1419.
(Added by Stats.1975, c. 156, p. 287, § 1.)

§ 1419. Weapons, drugs, explosives, etc.

The provisions of Section 1418 shall not apply to any dangerous or deadly weapons, narcotic or poison drugs, explosives, or any property of any kind or character whatsoever the possession of which is prohibited by law, used by a defendant in the commission of the crime of which he was convicted, or with which he was armed or which he had upon his person at the time of his arrest.

Any such property filed as an exhibit shall be, by order of the trial court, destroyed or sold or otherwise disposed of under the conditions provided in such order.
(Added by Stats.1953, c. 51, p. 696, § 1.)

§ 1420. Deposit with county treasurer; publication of notice

All money received by a district attorney in any criminal action or proceeding, the owner or owners of which are unknown, and which remains unclaimed in the possession of the district attorney after final judgment in said criminal action or proceeding, may be deposited with the county treasurer. Upon the expiration of two years after such deposit, the county treasurer may cause a notice to be published in the county once a week for two successive weeks in a newspaper of general circulation published in the county.
(Added by Stats.1959, c. 2016, p. 4656, § 1.)

§ 1421. Contents of notice

The notice shall state the amount of money, the criminal action or proceeding in which the money was received by the district attorney, the fund in which it is held and that it is proposed that the money will become the property of the county on a designated date not less than 45 days nor more than 60 days after the first publication of the notice.
(Added by Stats.1959, c. 2016, p. 4656, § 1.)

§ 1422. Necessity of filing verified complaint; service; date money becomes property of county; transfer to general fund

Unless some person files a verified complaint seeking to recover all, or a designated part, of the money in a court of competent jurisdiction within the county in which the notice is published, and serves a copy of the complaint and the summons issued thereon upon the county treasurer before the date designated in the notice, upon that date the money becomes the property of the county and shall be transferred by the treasurer to the general fund.
(Added by Stats.1959, c. 2016, p. 4656, § 1.)

§ 1425. Repealed by Stats.1976, c. 1288, p. —, § 20

§ 1426a. Limitation of actions; misdemeanor complaint

A complaint for any misdemeanor triable in a justice court must be filed within one year after its commission.
(Amended by Stats.1951, c. 1608, p. 3620, § 30.)

§ 1427. Warrant; issuance; form; summons on offense by corporation; service; appearance and answer by corporation; nonappearance

(a) When a complaint is presented to a judge of an inferior court of the commission of a public offense appearing to be triable in his court, he must, if satisfied therefrom that the offense complained of has been committed and that there is reasonable ground to believe that the defendant has committed it, issue a warrant, for the arrest of the defendant.

(b) Such warrant of arrest and proceedings upon it shall be in conformity to the provisions of this code regarding warrants of arrest, and it may be in the following form:

County of _____

The people of the State of California, to any peace officer in this state:

Complaint upon oath having been this day made before me that the offense of _____ (designating it generally) has been committed and accusing _____ (name of defendant) thereof you are therefore commanded forthwith to arrest the above-named defendant and bring him forthwith before the _____ court of _____ (stating full title of court) at _____ (naming place).

Witness my hand and the seal of said court this _____ day of _____, 19____.

(Signed). _____

Judge of said court

If it appears that the offense complained of has been committed by a corporation, no warrant of arrest shall issue, but the judge must issue a summons substantially in the form prescribed in Section 1391. Such summons must be served at the time and in the manner designated in Section 1392 except that if the offense complained of is a violation of the Vehicle Code or a local ordinance adopted pursuant to the Vehicle Code, such summons may be served by deposit by the clerk of the court in the United States mail of an envelope enclosing the summons, which envelope shall be addressed to a person authorized to accept service of legal process on behalf of the defendant, and which envelope shall be mailed by registered mail or certified mail with a return receipt requested. Promptly upon such mailing, the clerk of the court shall execute a certificate of such mailing and place it in the file of the court for that case. At the time stated in the summons the corporation may appear by counsel and answer the complaint, except that in the case of misdemeanors arising from operation of motor vehicles, or of infractions arising from operation of motor vehicles, a corporation may appear by its president, vice president, secretary or managing agent for the purpose of entering a plea of guilty. If it does not appear, a plea of not guilty shall be entered, and the same proceedings had therein as in other cases.

(Amended by Stats.1973, c. 718, p. 1296, § 3.)

§ 1430. Copies of police, arrest, and crime reports; privileged matter

Upon the first court appearance of counsel, or upon a determination by a magistrate that the defendant can represent himself, the prosecuting attorney shall within two calendar days in all criminal cases triable in the municipal and justice courts, deliver to, or make accessible for inspection and copying by, the defendant or his counsel copies of police, arrest, and crime reports. Portions of such reports containing privileged information need not be disclosed if the defendant or his counsel has been notified that privileged information has not been disclosed. If the charges against the defendant are dismissed prior to the time the above-mentioned documents are delivered or made accessible, the prosecuting attorney need not deliver or make accessible such documents unless otherwise so compelled by law.

(Added by Stats.1975, c. 799, p. —, § 2.)

§ 1462. Municipal and justice court jurisdiction; restrictions

Each municipal and justice court shall have jurisdiction in all criminal cases amounting to misdemeanor, where the offense charged was committed within the county in which such municipal or justice court is established except those of which the juvenile court is given jurisdiction and those of which other courts are given exclusive jurisdiction. Each municipal and justice court shall have exclusive jurisdiction in all cases involving the violation of ordinances of cities or towns situated within the district in which such court is established.

(Amended by Stats.1976, c. 1288, p. —, § 21.)

§ 1462.1. Concurrent jurisdiction of municipal and justice courts

Text of Section operative until January 1, 1983.

Except as provided in Article 9 (commencing with Section 73640) of Chapter 10 of Title 8 of the Government Code, the jurisdiction of the municipal and justice courts is the same and concurrent.

The amendments to this section made during the 1977 portion of the 1977–78 Regular Session of the Legislature shall have no force or effect on or after January 1, 1983, unless a later enacted statute, which is chaptered before January 1, 1983, deletes or extends such date.
(Amended by Stats.1977, c. 1051, p. —, § 15.)

For text effective until January 1, 1983, see § 1462.1, ante

§ 1462.2. Trial of misdemeanor cases, determination of proper court; transfer of case

Except as otherwise provided in the Vehicle Code, the proper court for the trial of criminal cases amounting to misdemeanor shall be determined as follows: If there is a municipal or justice court, having jurisdiction of the subject matter of the case, established in the district within which the offense charged was committed, such court is the proper court for the trial of the case; otherwise, the court, having jurisdiction of the subject matter, nearest to the place where the offense was committed is the proper court for the trial of the case.

If an action or proceeding is commenced in a court having jurisdiction of the subject matter thereof other than the court herein designated as the proper court for the trial, the action may, notwithstanding, be tried in the court where commenced, unless the defendant, at the time he pleads, requests an order transferring the action or proceeding to the proper court. If after such request it appears that the action or proceeding was not commenced in the proper court, the court shall order the action or proceeding transferred to the proper court. The judge must, at the time of arraignment, inform the defendant of his right to be tried in the district wherein the offense was committed.
(Amended by Stats.1957, c. 1192, p. 2483, § 1.)

§ 1473. Persons authorized to prosecute writ; false evidence

(a) Every person unlawfully imprisoned or restrained of his liberty, under any pretense whatever, may prosecute a writ of habeas corpus, to inquire into the cause of such imprisonment or restraint.

(b) A writ of habeas corpus may be prosecuted for, but not limited to, the following reasons:

(1) False evidence that is substantially material or probative on the issue of guilt or punishment was introduced against a person at any hearing or trial relating to his incarceration; or

(2) False physical evidence, believed by a person to be factual, probative, or material on the issue of guilt, which was known by the person at the time of entering a plea of guilty, which was a material factor directly related to the plea of guilty by the person.

(c) Any allegation that the prosecution knew or should have known of the false nature of the evidence referred to in subdivision (b) is immaterial to the prosecution of a writ of habeas corpus brought pursuant to subdivision (b).

(d) Nothing in this section shall be construed as limiting the grounds for which a writ of habeas corpus may be prosecuted or as precluding the use of any other remedies.
(Amended by Stats.1975, c. 1047, p. 2466, § 2.)

§ 1474. Application by petition; signature; contents; verification

Application for, how made. Application for the writ is made by petition, signed either by the party for whose relief it is intended, or by some person in his behalf, and must specify:

1. That the person in whose behalf the writ is applied for is imprisoned or restrained of his liberty, the officer or person by whom he is so confined or restrained, and the place where, naming all the parties, if they are known, or describing them, if they are not known;

2. If the imprisonment is alleged to be illegal, the petition must also state in what the alleged illegality consists;

3. The petition must be verified by the oath or affirmation of the party making the application.
(Enacted 1872.)

§ 1475. Method of granting; grounds for discharge after remand; courts which may issue writ on subsequent applications; return; verification and contents of application; service

The writ of habeas corpus may be granted in the manner provided by law. If the writ has been granted by any court or a judge thereof and after the hearing thereof the prisoner has been remanded, he shall not be discharged from custody by the same or any other court of like general jurisdiction, or by a judge of the same or any other court of like general jurisdiction, unless upon some ground not existing in fact at the issuing of the prior writ. Should the prisoner desire to urge some point of law not raised in the petition for or at the hearing upon the return of the prior writ, then, in case such prior writ had been returned or returnable before a superior court or a judge thereof, no writ can be issued upon a second or other application except by the appropriate court of appeal or some judge thereof, or by the Supreme Court or some judge thereof, and in such an event such writ must not be made returnable before any superior court or any judge thereof. In the event, however, that the prior writ was returned or made returnable before a court of appeal or any judge thereof, no writ can be issued upon a second or other application except by the Supreme Court or some judge thereof, and such writ must be made returnable before said Supreme Court or some judge thereof.

Every application for a writ of habeas corpus must be verified, and shall state whether any prior application or applications have been made for a writ in regard to the same detention or restraint complained of in the application, and if any such prior application or applications have been made the later application must contain a brief statement of all proceedings had therein, or in any of them, to and including the final order or orders made therein, or in any of them, on appeal or otherwise.

Whenever the person applying for a writ of habeas corpus is held in custody or restraint by any officer of any court of this state or any political subdivision thereof, or by any peace officer of this state, or any political subdivision thereof, a copy of the application for such writ must in all cases be served upon the district attorney of the county wherein such person is held in custody or restraint at least 24 hours before the time at which said writ is made returnable and no application for such writ can be heard without proof of such service in cases where such service is required.

If such person is in custody for violation of an ordinance of a city which has a city attorney, a copy of the application for the writ must also be served on the city attorney of the city whose ordinance is the basis for the charge at least 24 hours before the time at which the writ is made returnable, provided that failure to serve such city attorney shall not deprive the court of jurisdiction to hear the application.
(Amended by Stats.1967, c. 17, p. 850, § 112.)

§ 1476. Endorsements upon petition; grant of writ; admission to bail

Any court or judge authorized to grant the writ, to whom a petition therefor is presented, must endorse upon the petition the hour and date of its presentation and the hour and date of the granting or denial of the writ, and must, if it appear that the writ ought to issue, grant the same without delay; and if the person by or upon whose behalf the application for the writ is made be detained upon a criminal charge, may admit him to bail, if the offense is bailable, pending the determination of the proceeding.
(Amended by Stats.1949, c. 1021, p. 1883, § 1.)

§ 1477. Direction and contents of writ

Writ, what to contain. The writ must be directed to the person having custody of or restraining the person on whose behalf the application is made, and must command him to have the body of such person before the Court or Judge before whom the writ is returnable, at a time and place therein specified.
(Enacted 1872.)

§ 1478. Service

If the writ is directed to the sheriff or other ministerial officer of the court out of which it issues, it must be delivered by the clerk to such officer without delay, as other writs are delivered for service. If it is directed to any other person, it must be delivered to the sheriff or a marshal, and be by him served upon such person by delivering the copy to him without delay, and make his return on the original to the court of issuance. If the person to whom the writ is directed cannot be found, or refuses admittance to the officer or person serving or delivering such writ, it may be served or delivered by leaving it at the residence of the person to whom it is directed, or by affixing it to some conspicuous place on the outside either of his dwelling house or of the place where the party is confined or under restraint.
(Amended by Stats.1968, c. 479, p. 1118, § 1.)

§ 1479. Disobedience of writ; attachment of person to whom writ directed; arrest; commitment

Proceedings upon disobedience to the writ. If the person to whom the writ is directed refuses, after service, to obey the same, the Court or Judge, upon affidavit, must issue an attachment against such person, directed to the Sheriff or Coroner, commanding him forthwith to apprehend such person and bring him immediately before such Court or Judge; and upon being so brought, he must be committed to the jail of the county until he makes due return to such writ, or is otherwise legally discharged.
(Enacted 1872.)

§ 1480. Return; contents; signature; verification

Return, what to contain. The person upon whom the writ is served must state in his return, plainly and unequivocally:

1. Whether he has or has not the party in his custody, or under his power or restraint;

2. If he has the party in his custody or power, or under his restraint, he must state the authority and cause of such imprisonment or restraint;

3. If the party is detained by virtue of any writ, warrant, or other written authority, a copy thereof must be annexed to the return, and the original produced and exhibited to the Court or Judge on the hearing of such return;

4. If the person upon whom the writ is served had the party in his power or custody, or under his restraint, at any time prior or subsequent to the date of the writ of habeas corpus, but has transferred such custody or restraint to another, the return must state particularly to whom, at what time and place, for what cause, and by what authority such transfer took place;

5. The return must be signed by the person making the same, and, except when such person is a sworn public officer, and makes such return in his official capacity, it must be verified by his oath.
(Enacted 1872.)

§ 1481. Production of body; exceptions

Body must be produced, when. The person to whom the writ is directed, if it is served, must bring the body of the party in his custody or under his restraint, according to the command of the writ, except in the cases specified in the next section.
(Enacted 1872.)

§ 1482. Hearing without production of body; illness or infirmity of person in custody; adjournment

When hearing may proceed without production of the body. When, from sickness or infirmity of the person directed to be produced, he cannot, without danger, be brought before the Court or Judge, the person in whose custody or power he is may state that fact in his return to the writ, verifying the same by affidavit. If the Court or Judge is satisfied of the truth of such return, and the return to the writ is otherwise sufficient, the Court or Judge may proceed to decide on such return, and to dispose of the matter as if such party had been produced on the writ, or the hearing thereof may be adjourned until such party can be produced.
(Enacted 1872.)

§ 1485. Discharge of person in custody; grounds

When Court may discharge the party. If no legal cause is shown for such imprisonment or restraint, or for the continuation thereof, such Court or Judge must discharge such party from the custody or restraint under which he is held.
(Enacted 1872.)

§ 1486. Remand of person in custody; grounds

When to remand party. The Court or Judge, if the time during which such party may be legally detained in custody has not expired, must remand such party, if it appears that he is detained in custody:

1. By virtue of process issued by any Court or Judge of the United States, in a case where such Court or Judge has exclusive jurisdiction; or,

2. By virtue of the final judgment or decree of any competent Court of criminal jurisdiction, or for any process issued upon such judgment or decree.
(Enacted 1872.)

§ 1487. Discharge of person in custody by virtue of process; grounds

Grounds of discharge in certain cases. If it appears on the return of the writ that the prisoner is in custody by virtue of process from any Court of this State, or Judge or officer thereof, such prisoner may be discharged in any of the following cases, subject to the restrictions of the last section:

1. When the jurisdiction of such Court or officer has been exceeded;

2. When the imprisonment was at first lawful, yet by some act, omission, or event which has taken place afterwards, the party has become entitled to a discharge;

3. When the process is defective in some matter of substance required by law, rendering such process void;

4. When the process, though proper in form, has been issued in a case not allowed by law;

5. When the person having the custody of the prisoner is not the person allowed by law to detain him;

6. Where the process is not authorized by any order, judgment, or decree of any Court, nor by any provision of law;

§ 1487

7. Where a party has been committed on a criminal charge without reasonable or probable cause.
(Enacted 1872.)

§ 1488. Defect in form of warrant of commitment not ground for discharge

If any person is committed to prison, or is in custody of any officer on any criminal charge, by virtue of any warrant of commitment of a magistrate, such person must not be discharged on the ground of any mere defect of form in the warrant of commitment.
(Amended by Stats.1951, c. 1608, p. 3618, § 25.)

§ 1490. Writ for purpose of giving bail; averments

Writ for purpose of bail. When a person is imprisoned or detained in custody on any criminal charge, for want of bail, such person is entitled to a writ of habeas corpus for the purpose of giving bail, upon averring that fact in his petition, without alleging that he is illegally confined.
(Enacted 1872.)

§ 1491. Writ for purposes of giving bail; taking and filing undertaking; amount of bail to be set immediately

Any judge before whom a person who has been committed upon a criminal charge may be brought on a writ of habeas corpus, if the same is bailable, may take an undertaking of bail from such person as in other cases, and file the same in the proper court. Whenever a writ of habeas corpus is returned to a court for hearing and the petitioner is charged with an offense other than a crime of violence or committed with a deadly weapon or involving the forcible taking or destruction of the property of another, but the prisoner does not stand convicted of any offense, the amount of the bail must be set immediately if no bail has theretofore been fixed.
(Amended by Stats.1933, c. 595, p. 1526, § 1.)

§ 1492. Party in custody not entitled to discharge and not bailed; remand to custody

Judge, when to remand. If a party brought before the Court or Judge on the return of the writ is not entitled to his discharge, and is not bailed, where such bail is allowable, the Court or Judge must remand him to custody or place him under the restraint from which he was taken, if the person under whose custody or restraint he was is legally entitled thereto.
(Enacted 1872.)

§ 1493. Illegal restraint or custody; commitment to legal custody

Person in illegal, may be committed to legal, custody. In cases where any party is held under illegal restraint or custody, or any other person is entitled to the restraint or custody of such party, the Judge or Court may order such party to be committed to the restraint or custody of such person as is by law entitled thereto.
(Enacted 1872.)

§ 1494. Custody pending judgment on return

Disposition of party, pending proceedings on return. Until judgment is given on the return, the Court or Judge before whom any party may be brought on such writ may commit him to the custody of the Sheriff of the county, or place him in such care or under such custody as his age or circumstances may require.
(Enacted 1872.)

§ 1495. Defect in form of writ; sufficiency; disobedience

Defect of form in the writ immaterial, when. No writ of habeas corpus can be disobeyed for defect of form, if it sufficiently appear therefrom in whose custody or under whose restraint the party imprisoned or restrained is, the officer or person detaining him, and the Court or Judge before whom he is to be brought.
(Enacted 1872.)

§ 1496. Discharge as bar to subsequent restraint for same cause; exceptions

Imprisonment after discharge, in what cases permitted. No person who has been discharged by the order of the Court or Judge upon habeas corpus can be again imprisoned, restrained, or kept in custody for the same cause, except in the following cases:

1. If he has been discharged from custody on a criminal charge, and is afterwards committed for the same offense, by legal order or process;

2. If, after a discharge for defect of proof, or for any defect of the process, warrant, or commitment in a criminal case, the prisoner is again arrested on sufficient proof and committed by legal process for the same offense.
(Enacted 1872.)

§ 1497. Warrant in lieu of writ; issuance; grounds; contents

Warrant may issue instead of writ, in certain cases. When it appears to any Court, or Judge, authorized by law to issue the writ of habeas corpus, that any one is illegally held in custody, confinement, or restraint, and that there is reason to believe that such person will be carried out of the jurisdiction of the Court or Judge before whom the application is made, or will suffer some irreparable injury before compliance with the writ of habeas corpus can be enforced, such Court or Judge may cause a warrant to be issued, reciting the facts, and directed to the Sheriff, Coroner, or Constable of the county, commanding such officer to take such person thus held in custody, confinement, or restraint, and forthwith bring him before such Court or Judge, to be dealt with according to law.
(Enacted 1872.)

§ 1505. Damages; refusal of officer or respondent to obey writ; recovery

If the officer or person to whom a writ of habeas corpus is directed, refuses obedience to the command thereof, he shall forfeit and pay to the person aggrieved a sum not exceeding five thousand dollars ($5,000), to be recovered by action in any court of competent jurisdiction.
(Amended by Stats.1959, c. 559, p. 2521, § 1.)

Editors' Note
Grounds for Lawful Searches.
(1) Pursuant to a warrant, (Penal Code Section 1525).
(2) Consent freely given by one who has the capacity.
(3) Search incident to a lawful arrest (Chimel v. California, 395 U.S. 752 (1969) see table of cases, in this text).
(4) Plain Sight (contraband in plain view).
(5) Exigent Circumstances (an emergency entrance, which is necessary to preserve life or property).
(6) Administrative searches for health and safety.

§ 1523. Definition

Search warrant defined. A search warrant is an order in writing, in the name of the people, signed by a magistrate, directed to a peace officer, commanding him to search for personal property, and bring it before the magistrate.
(Enacted 1872.)

Editors' Note
Read Aguilar v. Texas, People v. Hamilton, People v. Scoma in table of cases included in this text.

§ 1524. Issuance; grounds

(a) A search warrant may be issued upon any of the following grounds:

(1) When the property was stolen or embezzled.

(2) When the property or things were used as the means of committing a felony.

(3) When the property or things are in the possession of any person with the intent to use it as a means of committing a public offense, or in the possession of another to whom he may have delivered it for the purpose of concealing it or preventing its being discovered.

(4) When the property or things to be seized consist of any item or constitutes any evidence which tends to show a felony has been committed, or tends to show that a particular person has committed a felony.

(b) The property or things described in subdivision (a) may be taken on the warrant from any place, or from any person in whose possession it may be.

(c) No warrant shall issue for any item or items described in Section 1070 of the Evidence Code.
(Amended by Stats.1978, c. 1054, p. —, § 1.)

Editors' Note
A search warrant must indicate on what authority the warrant is being issued. The authority as set forth in Penal Code Section 1524 is statutory and may not be modified by judicial consent.
Subsections 2 and 4 apply only to factual situations involving the commission of felonies while Subsections 1 and 3 apply to the commission of either felonies or misdemeanors.

Notes of Decisions
In general

It is immaterial that affiant does not have personal knowledge of data included in affidavit filed in connection with application for search warrant so long as affidavit discloses that officer's informant had personal knowledge of facts related by him to officer, and that officer's informant was a person on whose statement the magistrate was entitled to rely. People v. Wilson (1967) 64 Cal.Rptr. 172, 256 C.A.2d 411, certiorari denied 88 S.Ct. 1653, 391 U.S. 903, 20 L.Ed.2d 418.

Lawless search and seizure by a private person acting in private capacity is not violation by a state or federal agency of constitutional guarantees. People v. Turner (1967) 57 Cal.Rptr. 854, 249 C.A.2d 909, certiorari denied 88 S.Ct. 348, 389 U.S. 963, 19 L.Ed.2d 375.

§ 1525

SEARCH WARRANTS

§ 1525. Issuance; probable cause; supporting affidavits

It cannot be issued but upon probable cause, etc. A search warrant cannot be issued but upon probable cause, supported by affidavit, naming or describing the person, and particularly describing the property and the place to be searched.
(Enacted 1872.)

Editors' Notes

In order for a search warrant to be valid, the supporting affidavit must contain sufficient information for the magistrate to independently believe that the items sought will be found at the place described in the affidavit, and that the information contained therein is reliable. When the information in the affidavit is based solely on the observance of the affiant, reliability is not usually in question. However, the factual sufficiency must be satisfied. The defiant must demonstrate personal knowledge and provide detailed information.

When the information is provided by an informant, you must be very careful to make certain not only of the factual sufficiency, but you must also establish the reliability of the informant. The two prong test set forth in Aguilar v. Texas, 378 U.S. 108, 114 (1964) must be met.

The "two-prong" test was restated by the California Supreme Court in People v. Superior Court *(Johnson)* (1972) 6 Cal.3d 704, 711: In order for an affidavit based on an informant's hearsay statement to be legally sufficient to support the issuance of a search warrant, two requirements must be met: (1) The affidavit must allege the informant's statement in language which is factual rather than conclusionary and must establish that the informant spoke with personal knowledge of the matters contained in the statement; and (2) the affidavit must contain some underlying factual information from which the magistrate issuing the warrant can reasonably conclude that the informant was credible or his information reliable. Analysis of the two prongs shows that each "prong" actually has two parts. The first prong requires that the informant's statement be factual *and* based upon *personal knowledge.*

The second prong requires that the affidavit show:
1. The informant himself is credible, *or*
2. That his information is reliable.

Read Aguilar v. Texas, 378 U.S. 108, 84 Superior Court 1509 (1964); People v. Hamilton, 71 Cal.2d 176, 77 Cal.Rptr. 785 (1969); in table of cases included in this text regarding informants and their reliability. Read People v. Superior Court (Kiefer), 3 Cal.3d 807, 91 Cal.Rptr. 729 (1970); Kaplan v. Superior Court, 6 Cal.3d 150, 98 Cal.Rptr. 649, (1971); in Table of Cases included in this text regarding furtive gestures and probable cause to arrest and search.

Notes of Decisions

In general

Good faith is immaterial and cannot serve to rehabilitate an otherwise defective search warrant. Lockridge v. Superior Court for Los Angeles County (1969) 80 Cal.Rptr. 223, 275 C.A.2d 612.

Magistrate's function is to determine if supporting affidavit shows probable cause to issue a search warrant. Charney v. Superior Court, San Diego County (1972) 104 Cal.Rptr. 213, 27 C.A.3d 888.

Probable cause—In general

Only the probability, and not prima facie showing, of criminal activity is standard of probable cause for issuance of search and seizure warrant. Monica Theater v. Municipal Court for Beverly Hills Judicial Dist. of Los Angeles County (1970) 88 Cal.Rptr. 71, 9 C.A.3d 1.

Phone call from deputy sheriff's wife stating deputy had marijuana in the trunk of his automobile provided department with probable cause to obtain a search warrant to search trunk of deputy's personal automobile which he used in his work and for which he was reimbursed. Salyer v. County of Los Angeles (1974) 116 Cal.Rptr. 27, 42 C.A.3d 866.

The requirement of probable cause before search warrant should be issued interposes the magistrate between the police officer's zealous pursuit of suspects and evidence and citizen's pursuit of privacy and freedom from unreasonable interference and the magistrate's function is to render neutral and detached judgment, not to serve as perfunctory rubber stamp for the police. Alexander v. Superior Court of Los Angeles County (1973) 107 Cal.Rptr. 483, 508 P.2d 1131, 9 C.3d 387.

For purposes of determining probable cause for issuance of search warrant, fact that husband and wife, in turning over to police a package of marijuana which wife assertedly had taken from garage on premises where defendant was later arrested, were exposing themselves to possible arrest for possession of marijuana, malicious prosecution, trespass or burglary provided strong indication that their information was credible. People v. Cohn (1973) 106 Cal.Rptr. 579, 30 C.A.3d 738.

When magistrate has found probable cause, courts should not invalidate search warrant by interpreting affidavit in hypertechnical rather than common sense manner and resolution of doubtful or marginal cases should be largely determined by preference to be accorded warrants. People v. Superior Court for Los Angeles County (App.1972) 100 Cal.Rptr. 539.

Reviewing court will accept in support of magistrate's determination of probable cause for issuance of search warrant evidence of less judicially competent or persuasive character than in case of determination by police officer of probable cause to search without warrant. In re Golia (1971) 94 Cal.Rptr. 323, 16 C.A.3d 775.

United States supreme court "two-prong test" [Aguilar v. Texas (1964) 378 U.S. 108, 84 S.Ct. 1509] that affidavit for search warrant may be based on hearsay information and need not reflect direct personal observation of affiant but that magistrate must be informed of some underlying circumstances on which informant based his conclusions and some of underlying circumstances from which officer concluded that informant, whose identity need not be disclosed, was credible or that his information was reliable, if satisfied as to primary confidential informant, need not be projected to declarant whose statements are recounted by confidential informant if that declarant is a suspect and the focus of the investigation. In re M. (1971) 93 Cal.Rptr. 679, 16 C.A.3d 96.

Deputy sheriff's search affidavit, which stated, inter alia, that he had been informed by agent of bureau of narcotic enforcement that on certain dates phone calls were initiated to defendant and in each instance a conversation was held with defendant concerning sale and purchase of heroin, that on other certain dates phone sale negotiations were consummated by defendant delivering a quantity of heroin to an undercover operator acting in employ and under direction of agent, and that in each instance state funds were used to purchase the heroin with serial numbers of all currency having been previously recorded, was sufficient. People v. Cain (1971) 93 Cal.Rptr. 388, 15 C.A.3d 687.

Where police had valid reason to believe that parcel containing marijuana would be delivered to defendant's premises by post office employee between certain hours on given day warrant to search defendant's premises for marijuana was validly issued notwithstanding that affidavit in support of warrant did not contain statement that officer knew at time he sought warrant that delivery had actually been made, and therefore search conducted pursuant to warrant was reasonable and consistent with all safeguards envisioned by federal and state constitutions. Alvidres v. Superior Court of Ventura County (1970) 90 Cal.Rptr. 682, 12 C.A.3d 575.

A search warrant may be issued by a magistrate only upon probable cause. People v. Kesey (1967) 58 Cal.Rptr. 625, 250 C.A.2d 669.

"Reasonable cause" and "probable cause", as used as standard for issuance of search warrant, arrest without warrant, commitment, or indictment, are synonymous. People v. Pease (1966) 51 Cal.Rptr. 448, 242 C.A.2d 442.

Sufficiency of probable cause

Citizen informant, who had witnessed the offense and was known by the peace officer, was sufficiently reliable for purpose of establishing probable cause for issuance of search warrant. People v. Glass (1976), 128 Cal.Rptr. 413, 56 C.A.3d 368.

Search warrant affidavit which alleged that, inter alia, defendant returned informant's telephone call, set up sale of cocaine, and at time of sale stated that informant, whose reliability was not challenged, need not state on telephone how much narcotics he wanted but "just come over after the call and I'll have it for you," was sufficient to establish probable cause for search of apartment allegedly being used by defendant, even ignoring portion of affidavit that stated that police officer recognized defendant's voice while listening, pursuant to federally authorized wiretap, to previous conversations between defendant and informer. People v. Howard (1976) 127 Cal.Rptr. 557, 55 C.A.3d 373.

Fourteen-year-old girl who stated to police officer that she had seen marijuana in bedroom used by her stepfather, that she was familiar with marijuana, and who gave statements which indicated that she was a witness to a crime was a "citizen-informant" and thus presumptively reliable even though she did admit that she had smoked marijuana; information supplied by her was sufficient to establish probable cause for issuance of search warrant without indication of her past reliability or corroboration of the information which she gave. People v. Schulle (1975) 124 Cal.Rptr. 585, 51 C.A.3d 809.

In examining affidavit to ascertain presence or absence of probable cause, courts are to interpret the affidavit in nontechnical, common-sense manner. People v. Superior Court for Colusa County (1975) 122 Cal.Rptr. 459, 49 C.A.3d 160.

Affidavit stating that confidential informant, whose reliability was well established, had told affiant-officer that he had seen a "quantity of paper bindles" containing heroin at defendant's residence at least once in the previous six days established probable cause to believe that heroin was still on the premises and authorized issuance of search warrant; disapproving Stoehr v. Superior Court, 34 Cal.App.3d 197, 109 Cal.Rptr. 756. People v. Mesa (1975) 121 Cal.Rptr. 473, 535 P.2d 337, 14 C.3d 466.

Even though apartment was listed in defendant's name and not in the name of suspected heroin seller, where informant had purchased heroin from seller on numerous occasions by calling seller at telephone number listed for defendant's apartment and where police observed seller leave defendant's apartment and go to prearranged location for delivery of heroin to informant, probable cause existed that seller was storing heroin in defendant's apartment, authorizing issuance of search warrant for apartment. People v. Hernandez (1974) 118 Cal.Rptr. 53, 43 C.A.3d 581.

Where, from facts described in affidavit for search warrant, other buildings on premises, namely, a garage with a bedroom over it, a shed converted to a bedroom, and a hothouse were all, in a nontechnical sense, appurtenances of main building, consisting of a two-story single-family residence, or so a police officer could reasonably believe, officer had reasonable cause to infer a connection between marijuana which he knew was in hothouse and renter of premises who, he could infer, was occupying house rather than one of bedrooms in outbuildings, and probable cause existed for issuance of warrant to search hothouse and main house, each of which was separately described in warrant, and evidence produced pursuant to searches was not subject to suppression. Houser v. Geary (C.A.1972) 465 F.2d 193, certiorari denied 93 S.Ct. 927, 409 U.S. 1113, 34 L.Ed.2d 696.

In light of the factual assertions contained in police officer's supporting affidavit, including a graphic and detailed description of the films described by him as obscene and an allegation that the films were exhibited in theater bearing a marquee announcing "Adult Film Novelties," the assertion of neither expertise nor contemporary community standards was necessary to justify issuance of search warrant. People v. Sarnblad (1972) 103 Cal.Rptr. 211, 26 C.A.3d 801.

Recitals in affidavit for search warrant that 13-year-old girl related to affiant that she was present on premises when her sister asked defendant where the "grass" was, that defendant brought out plastic bag, that cigarettes were rolled from substance in bag and smoked, that girl described odor of substance being smoked and its general physical characteristics, that complaints that premises were being frequented by hippie-types had been received and that known narcotics users and/or dealers frequented premises, were supportive of reasonable belief that narcotics would probably be found on premises and established probable cause for issuance of warrant. People v. Young (1970) 90 Cal.Rptr. 924, 12 C.A.3d 878.

To support reasonable belief and strong, conscientious suspicion that marijuana or dangerous drugs would be found in cabin would require only facts from which it could be inferred that defendant probably possessed such contraband and that defendant's connection with cabin was such as to make it probable that contraband could be found there. Frazzini v. Superior Court In and For Inyo County (1970) 87 Cal.Rptr. 32, 7 C.A.3d 1005.

Descriptions of persons

Phrase "unidentified persons" as used in search warrant did not describe with reasonable particularity the persons to be searched and warrant was invalid on its face as allowing an unlimited search of persons. People v. Tenney (1972), 101 Cal.Rptr. 419, 25 C.A.3d 16.

Description of property

Validity of search warrant was not affected by fact that supporting affidavit stated that parcel containing marijuana would be placed in normal mail channels and delivery made between 4:00 p. m. and 6:00 p. m. on stated date, whereas the package in fact was not placed in "normal" mail channels but was instead delivered by a specially selected mail carrier who required a return receipt upon delivery. People v. Sloss (1973) 109 Cal.Rptr. 583, 34 C.A.3d 74.

Though search warrant need not state owner or correct license number of automobile to be searched, it must, to support search of motor vehicle, at very least include some explicit description of particular vehicle or of place where vehicle is later found. People v. Dumas (1973) 109 Cal.Rptr. 304, 512 P.2d 1208, 9 C.3d 871.

§ 1525

Even if directive in warrant to search for "other hashish, marihuana, narcotics or narcotic paraphernalia" was inadequate to justify further search either because of lack of probable cause in the affidavit for search warrant, or because of overbreadth, directive to search for correspondence relating to smuggling was sustained by probable cause, and was not overbroad if construed as relating to known package which contained marihuana and was delivered to premises searched. People v. Superior Court In and For Santa Clara County (1972) 103 Cal.Rptr. 874, 27 C.A.3d 404.

Affidavit and search warrant, insofar as they described property to be seized as "evidences of indebtedness," telephone bills showing calls between petitioner and other persons and any papers showing names and addresses of associates of petitioner, was so broad as to be violative of constitutional and statutory provisions prohibiting a general exploratory warrant. Griffin v. Superior Court for Stanislaus County (1972) 103 Cal.Rptr. 379, 26 C.A.3d 672.

Description of place

Affidavit in support of search warrant was not insufficient on ground that it failed to connect defendant with the described marijuana and the subject premises where defendant was described in the affidavit as an occupant of the house in question and identified as the person who had furnished marijuana to the informant; in any event, warrant did not authorize a search of defendant's person but only a search of the premises. People v. Glass (1976) 128 Cal.Rptr. 413, 56 C.A.3d 368.

Description in search warrant must be sufficiently definite that officer conducting search can with reasonable effort ascertain and identify place intended, and nothing should be left to discretion of the officer. People v. Dumas (1973) 109 Cal.Rptr. 304, 512 P.2d 1208, 9 C.3d 871.

Fact that it was only after agent obtained warrant to search premises, address of which was discovered on illegal search of hat worn by one defendant, that agent received information that officer had followed two other defendants to residence did not invalidate search, where warrant was fair on its face and disclosed no illegality; it was permissible for the prosecution to give evidence dehors the affidavit, of the inevitable discovery of such information. People v. Aylwin (1973) 107 Cal.Rptr. 824, 31 C.A.3d 826.

Ignorance should not be substitute for necessity of particularly describing place to be searched, and of showing probable cause to believe that there is contraband at that place. People v. Sheehan (1972) 103 Cal.Rptr. 201, 28 C.A.3d 21.

Search warrant limiting search to four specifically described residences and to certain items satisfied particularization requirement. People v. Superior Court for Los Angeles County (App.1972) 100 Cal.Rptr. 539.

Fact that address on search warrant was "1360 Laurel Avenue" whereas petitioner's apartment was located at 1860 Laurel Avenue did not make warrant illegal where there was only one Laurel Avenue in the city which was one block long and all addresses on the block were in the 1800's. Tidwell v. Superior Court In and For Humboldt County (1971) 95 Cal.Rptr. 213, 17 C.A.3d 780.

§ 1526. Issuance; examination of complainant and witnesses; taking and subscribing affidavits; transcribed statements in lieu of written affidavit

(a) The magistrate may, before issuing the warrant, examine on oath the person seeking the warrant and any witnesses he may produce, and must take his affidavit or their affidavits in writing, and cause same to be subscribed by the party or parties making same.

(b) In lieu of the written affidavit required in subdivision (a), the magistrate may take an oral statement under oath which shall be recorded and transcribed. The transcribed statement shall be deemed to be an affidavit for the purposes of this chapter. In such cases, the recording of the sworn oral statement and the transcribed statement shall be certified by the magistrate receiving it and shall be filed with the clerk of the court. In the alternative in such cases, the sworn oral statement shall be recorded by a certified court reporter and the transcript of the statement shall be certified by the reporter, after which the magistrate receiving it shall certify the transcript which shall be filed with the clerk of the court.

(Amended by Stats.1972, c. 662, p. 1223, § 1.)

Notes of Decisions

In general

Sworn testimony which had not been recorded and transcribed as required by this section and thus did not appear in the record could not be considered for probable cause for issuance of search warrant. People v. Hill (1974) 117 Cal.Rptr. 393, 528 P.2d 1, 12 C.3d 731.

This section relating to magistrate's taking of oral statement and transcribing it in connection with issuance of search warrant should be interpreted to promote general purposes and policies of law and to produce result that is reasonable. People v. Peck (1974) 113 Cal.Rptr. 806, 38 C.A.3d 993.

Officer's sworn telephonic declarations in conversation with magistrate constituted an "affidavit" sufficient to support issuance of search warrant despite magistrate's delay in certifying the transcript and although officer did not sign written "affidavit" until day after search. Bowyer v. Superior Court of Santa Cruz County (1974) 111 Cal.Rptr. 628, 37 C.A.3d 151, rehearing denied 112 Cal.Rptr. 266, 37 C.A.3d 151.

This section is sufficiently broad to allow a telephone statement, provided it is recorded, as basis for issuance of a search warrant, and administering oath following statement, together with judge's inquiry as to truth of the statement just made, is not prejudicial error. People v. Aguirre (1972) 103 Cal.Rptr. 153, 26 C.A.3d Supp. 7.

Even if deposition, a sworn statement and an affidavit are synonymous, deposition and statement still have to be subscribed by person making them before they comply with statutory prerequisite for issuance of search warrant. Powelson v. Superior Court of Yolo County (1970) 88 Cal.Rptr. 8, 9 C.A.3d 357.

§ 1527. Affidavits; contents

The affidavit or affidavits must set forth the facts tending to establish the grounds of the application, or probable cause for believing that they exist.
Amended by Stats.1957, c. 1883, p. 3288, § 1.)

Editors' Note

Read Aguilar v. Texas, People v. Hamilton, People v. Scoma in table of cases included in this text.

The affidavit must set forth:
1. Statutory grounds for issuance of the search warrant.
2. The name of the affiant.
3. A description with reasonable particularity of the persons or places to be searched.
4. A description with reasonable particularity of the property to be seized.
5. A statement of probable cause based upon the affiance personal knowledge.

Notes of Decisions

Sufficiency of affidavits

Affidavit, which was executed by experienced narcotics investigator, which recited that when citizen informant had gone to described premises for purpose of installing water meter informant observed defendant smoking marijuana and also observed marijuana growing in the backyard and which also recited that following day affiant supplied informant with prerecorded funds and observed him enter residence and return a short time later with a bag of marijuana and that informant told affiant he had purchased the marijuana from defendant and that defendant removed it from a round can in the kitchen, was sufficient to establish probable cause for issuance of warrant to search the premises. People v. Glass (1976) 128 Cal.Rptr. 413, 56 C.A.3d 368.

Recital in affidavit, filed in support of search warrant, that defendant had acknowledged that he was experienced in the use of explosives and that there might be some explosives in his car was properly included within the affidavit in judging its sufficiency, as there was substantial evidence that the challenged incriminating statement was voluntarily given, not a product of interrogation in violation of defendant's Miranda rights. People v. McDaniel (1976) 127 Cal.Rptr. 467, 545 P.2d 843.

To be sufficient to support issuance of search warrant, affidavit based on an informant's hearsay statement must allege informant's statement in language which is factual rather than conclusional, must establish that informant spoke with personal knowledge of matters contained in the statement and must contain some underlying factual information from which magistrate can reasonably conclude that informant was credible or his information reliable. People v. Mesa (1975) 121 Cal.Rptr. 473, 535 P.2d 337, 14 C.3d 466.

While an affidavit for search warrant may be based upon hearsay information which does not reflect observations of affiant, an informant's statement which consists of double hearsay must meet both prongs of Aguilar test in regard to both hearsay assertions, e. g., statements of both informant and declarant. People v. Mardian (1975) 121 Cal.Rptr. 269, 47 C.A.3d 16.

Affidavit for search warrant was sufficient to satisfy prongs of Aguilar test where underlying circumstances upon which informants concluded that contraband was present in particular home were clearly set forth and reliability of informants was established both from details of their statements and from circumstances under which they were made. Id.

Affidavit in support of search warrant to effect that affiant-informant observed marijuana bricks in certain house, obtained bricks weighing approximately five pounds from certain described person and was subsequently given three pills, one of which was asserted to be LSD, and that he was subsequently arrested while in possession of bricks and pills, had not been convicted of crime of turpitude and had smoked marijuana and officer's affidavit which essentially repeated statements of informant's affidavit were not insufficient on their face, particularly in view of magistrate's extensive examination of informant. Theodore v. Superior Court of Orange County (1972) 104 Cal.Rptr. 226, 501 P.2d 234, 8 C.3d 77.

Where document which magistrate wrote out by hand and labeled "addendum" to affidavit for search warrant was in legal effect a nullity, and where affidavit, which was only document the magistrate was entitled to consider, was in his opinion insufficient to furnish probable cause, no legal basis existed for issuing search warrant, and thus search was illegal and evidence found was inadmissible in a prosecution on charges of possessing marijuana, possessing marijuana paraphernalia and maintaining a place for sale of narcotics. Charney v. Superior Court, San Diego County (1972) 104 Cal.Rptr. 213, 27 C.A.3d 888.

Where affidavit in support of search warrant showed source of the information on which affiant officer relied but did not demonstrate how information was conveyed to him but clear import of affidavit was that affiant officer received his separate pieces of information either from an officer to whom it had been first related or from an officer who first discovered the information by his own investigative means, or from a police department which had received information of a robbery, affidavit was constitutionally sufficient to afford basis for issuance of search warrant and failure of defendant's trial counsel to challenge it before trial did not result in constitutionally inadequate representation. People v. McDowell (1972) 104 Cal.Rptr. 181, 27 C.A.3d 864.

Affidavit for search warrant was properly found to set forth probable cause to believe that one mail parcel addressed to person living at premises designated in warrant and containing approximately three pounds fourteen ounces of marihuana would be located at the premises. People v. Superior Court In and For Santa Clara County (1972) 103 Cal.Rptr. 874, 27 C.A.3d 404.

Affidavit to effect that participant unknowingly dealing with affiant-undercover agent in contraband transaction had stated that 35 kilos of marijuana were at certain premises, and that person introduced to affiant by participant was observed to enter such premises and that 15 minutes later two men emerged from premises and placed large and small package in automobile trunk adequately supported issuance of search warrant, even if matter pertaining to observation of premises indicated, contrary to fact that observation was done by affiant's fellow officers, that such observation was made by affiant. People v. Christian (1972) 103 Cal.Rptr. 740, 27 C.A.3d 554, certiorari denied 93 S.Ct. 1915, 411 U.S. 937, 36 L.Ed.2d 398.

For search warrant affidavit based on informant's hearsay statement to be legally sufficient, affidavit must allege informant's statement in factual rather than conclusionary language, must establish that informant spoke with personal knowledge of matters contained in statement and must contain some underlying factual information from which issuing magistrate can reasonably conclude that informant was credible or his information reliable. People v. Senkir (1972) 103 Cal.Rptr. 138, 26 C.A.3d 411.

Even if other telephone conversations were unlawfully overheard by manager of apartment complex in which defendant lived, observations of detective during his surveillances were not the tainted fruit thereof, and did not have to be disregarded in determining sufficiency of affidavit for search warrant made by detective, where detective would undoubtedly have conducted surveillances and observed the same things as a result of information from reliable confidential informant coupled with report by manager of telephone conversation inadvertently overheard by her. People v. Buchanan (1972) 103 Cal.Rptr. 66, 26 C.A.3d 274.

Testimony of police officer in support of search warrant was constitutionally inadequate since it failed to reflect underlying circumstances from which judge could conclude that informant had personal knowledge of the information he gave the police and that the informant was credible or his information reliable; the officer's testimony merely indicated that he had a tip that he would find described truck containing marijuana at particular location and that described person would take possession of it; further, informant's hearsay statements were not buttressed by police observations of defendant's conduct which suggested no criminal activity. Halpin v. Superior Court of San Bernardino County (1972) 101 Cal.Rptr. 375, 495 P.2d 1295, 6 C.3d 885, certiorari denied 93 S.Ct. 318, 409 U.S. 982, 34 L.Ed.2d 246.

Where affidavit of informant was factual in nature, disclosed personal knowledge of informant and included statements which would incriminate not only defendant but informant himself, magistrate examined informant, and magistrate had benefit of listening to tape-recorded conversation between informant and defendant which corroborated statements made and information given in affidavits, magistrate was justified in relying on information supplied in affidavits. People v. Sanchez (1972) 101 Cal.Rptr. 193, 24 C.A.3d 664.

§ 1528. Issuance; magistrate satisfied as to grounds; formalities; command; duplicate original warrant

(a) If the magistrate is thereupon satisfied of the existence of the grounds of the application, or that there is probable cause to believe their existence, he must issue a search warrant, signed by him with his name of office, to a peace officer in his county, commanding him forthwith to search the person or place named, for the property or things specified, and to retain such property or things in his custody subject to order of the court as provided by Section 1536.

(b) The magistrate may orally authorize a peace officer to sign the magistrate's name on a duplicate original warrant. A duplicate original warrant shall be deemed to be a search warrant for the purposes of this chapter, and it shall be returned to the magistrate as provided for in Section 1537. In such cases, the magistrate shall enter on the face of the original warrant the exact time of the issuance of the warrant and shall sign and file the original warrant and the duplicate original warrant with the clerk of the court as provided for in Section 1541.
(Amended by Stats.1970, c. 809, p. 1531, § 2.)

§ 1529. Form

The warrant shall be in substantially the following form:

County of _____

The people of the State of California to any sheriff, constable, marshal, or policeman in the County of _____:

Proof, by affidavit, having been this day made before me by (naming every person whose affidavit has been taken), that (stating the grounds of the application, according to Section 1524, or, if the affidavit be not positive, that there is probable cause for believing that _____ stating the ground of the application in the same manner), you are therefore commanded, in the daytime (or at any time of the day or night, as the case may be, according to Section 1533), to make search on the person of C.D. (or in the house situated _____, describing it or any other place to be searched, with reasonable particularity, as the case may be) for the following property: (describing it with reasonable particularity); and if you find the same or any part thereof, to bring it forthwith before me (or this court) at (stating the place).

Given under my hand, and dated this _____ day of _____, A.D. 19__.

E. F., Judge of the Justice Court (or as the case may be).
(Amended by Stats.1971, c. 697, p. 1354, § 1.)

§ 1530. Service by officers; persons aiding officer

By whom served. A search warrant may in all cases be served by any of the officers mentioned in its directions, but by no other person, except in aid of the officer on his requiring it, he being present and acting in its execution.
(Enacted 1872.)

§ 1531. Execution; authority to break in after admittance refused

Officer may break open door, etc., to execute warrant. The officer may break open any outer or inner door or window of a house, or any part of a house, or anything therein, to execute the warrant, if, after notice of his authority and purpose, he is refused admittance.
(Enacted 1872.)

Notes of Decisions

Purpose

Purpose of "knock and notice" procedure is not to facilitate escape of suspected felons, to permit opportunity to destroy evidence, or to permit violent criminals to "get the drop" on police officers who are trying to make arrest. People v. Cox (App.1976) 130 Cal.Rptr. 440.

Section 844 and this section requiring notice of authority and purpose prior to forcing entry to execute arrest or search warrant are aimed at the protection of the privacy of people who are searched or arrested and at the prevention of violence brought on by a sudden and forcible entry. People v. Kasinger (1976) 129 Cal.Rptr. 483, 57 C.A.3d 975.

Section 844 and this section relating to police officer's right of entry into house of person to be arrested has common purpose of minimizing possibility of violent confrontations between police officers and private citizens occasioned by sudden unannounced entries by police officers into private dwellings. People v. Keogh (1975) 120 Cal.Rptr. 817, 46 C.A.3d 919.

Purposes and policies underlying regarding knock and notice procedures by law enforcement officers are the protection of the privacy of the individual and his home, protection of innocent persons who may also be present on premises where arrest is made, prevention of situations which are conducive to violent confrontations between occupant and individuals who enter his home without proper notice and protection of police who might be injured by a startled and fearful householder. People v. Freund, 119 Cal.Rptr. 762.

The purpose of § 844 and this section pertaining to forced entry to effect an arrest or to execute a search warrant is to prevent the sudden invasion of a home without warning which carries with it danger that through misunderstanding and misinterpretation officer and citizen may be seriously injured or even killed. Brown v. Superior Court In and For Alameda County (1973) 110 Cal.Rptr. 107, 34 C.A.3d 539.

When officers returned with search warrant it was unnecessary for them to knock and give notice, because house had been secured and there was no danger of violent confrontation. Ferdin v. Superior Court In and For Alameda County (1974) 112 Cal.Rptr. 66, 36 C.A.3d 774.

This section authorizing officer to break open any outer or inner door if, after notice of his authority and purpose, he is refused admittance applies to inner doors. People v. Webb (1973) 111 Cal.Rptr. 524, 36 C.A.3d 460.

Where brown bag was in plain sight of the officers who were executing search warrant, there was no search of defendant's person and the bag was subject to examination and seizure pursuant to the search warrant. Brown v. Superior Court In and For Alameda County (1973) 110 Cal.Rptr. 107, 34 C.A.3d 539.

This section and § 844 which deals with entries for the purpose of effecting an arrest are subject to similar construction. Id.

Where § 1533 provided for advance authorization by magistrate of nighttime service of search warrant, failure of this section to authorize advance approval of unannounced entry implied, under doctrine of inclusio unius est exclusio alterius, that the legislature intended not to permit warrants to excuse unannounced entry. Parsley v. Superior Court of Riverside County (1973) 109 Cal.Rptr. 563, 513 P.2d 611, 9 C.3d 934.

Advance judicial approval may not excuse noncompliance with statutory announcement requirements to the effect that officer generally may break open door or window in the execution of a search warrant (§ 844) or to effect an arrest (§ 1531) only if he is refused admittance after notice of his authority and purpose. Id.

Failure to comply with section

Entry governed by § 844 and this section dealing with knock-notice requirement which does not comply therewith renders any search and seizure dependent thereon "unreasonable" within meaning of Fourth Amendment (U.S.C.A.Const. Amend. 4) and, as consequence, any evidence seized pursuant thereto inadmissible. People v. Constancio (1974) 116 Cal.Rptr. 910, 42 C.A.3d 533.

This section which authorized officer to break open any outer or inner door to execute warrant if, after notice of his authority and purpose, he is refused admittance was not complied with where officers gave notice of their authority and purpose at one bedroom door but kicked in second bedroom door after knocking and waiting but without announcing their identity and purpose. People v. Webb (1973) 111 Cal.Rptr. 524, 36 C.A.3d 460.

A forced entry within five seconds of the notice of "authority and purpose" was not substantial compliance with this section providing the police officer executing search warrant may break open any outer or inner door or window of a house to execute the warrant, if, after notice of his authority and purpose, he is refused admittance. Brown v. Superior Court In and For Alameda County (1973) 110 Cal.Rptr. 107, 34 C.A.3d 539.

Compliance with section

Where police officer initiating search pursuant to probation condition, upon defendant's opening of inside door, opened screen door, displayed identification, and stated his purpose, he had substantially complied with statutory knock-notice requirements, and thus search was not unlawful. People v. Constancio (1974) 116 Cal.Rptr. 910, 42 C.A.3d 533.

Police officers who, in executing warrant for narcotics, approached defendant standing on the front porch of his house, informed defendant that they were investigating narcotics and had a search warrant to search for heroin, told defendant to let them in, and gave the defendant a copy of the warrant, substantially complied with this section which requires police officers to identify themselves and announce their purpose before entry into premises. People v. Murphy (1974) 116 Cal.Rptr. 889, 42 C.A.3d 81.

This section does not require the officers to give notice to all persons on the premises to be searched. Id.

Where police approaching defendant's apartment with search warrant had reliable information that defendant not only possessed weapons but habitually answered door armed with firearm, and upon approaching became aware of no further circumstances which would defeat inference of substantial possibility that defendant might apply deadly force to prevent apprehension, officers' failure to comply with statutory demand and notice requirements of this section did not require exclusion of evidence. People v. Dumas (1973) 109 Cal.Rptr. 304, 512 P.2d 1208, 9 C.3d 871.

Excuse from compliance with section

Where defendant had on at least two prior occasions eluded arrest and defendant had demonstrated background of violence and an affinity for firearms, police officer with warrant for defendant's arrest was excused from complying with "knock and notice" rule. People v. Cox (App.1976) 130 Cal.Rptr. 440.

The Parsley case, which was decided in August of 1973, which involved validity of search warrant issued in March of 1972 and which held that a magistrate is without power to authorize a "no-knock" forced entry, applied to warrant issued in April of 1973; hence, failure of officers to comply with this section authorizing a forced entry following notice of authority and purpose could not be predicated on the "no-knock" authorization contained in the warrant. People v. Henderson (1976) 129 Cal.Rptr. 844, 58 C.A.3d 349.

Where officers executing search warrant knew of defendant's arrest record, which indicated assaultive behavior and use of weapon as well as attempted disposal of contraband at time of narcotics arrest, such knowledge was sufficient to justify officers' "no-knock" forced entry, notwithstanding that arrest records did not reveal disposition of each case or that one officer testified that he did not determine the dispositions; hence, denial of pretrial suppression of evidence motion was proper. Id.

Exigent circumstances which may justify noncompliance with § 844 and this section relating to police officer's right of entry into

§ 1531 PENAL CODE

house of person to be arrested include peril to arresting officers, possibilities of escape or destruction of evidence. People v. Keogh (1975) 120 Cal.Rptr. 817, 46 C.A.3d 919.

If specific facts known to officer before he enters to search are sufficient to support his good-faith belief that compliance with knock-notice requirements will increase his peril or permit destruction of evidence, compliance therewith is excused. People v. Constancio (1974) 116 Cal.Rptr. 910, 42 C.A.3d 533.

Parole agent who was searching parolee's apartment pursuant to parolee's waiver of his Fourth Amendment rights (U.S.C.A.Const. Amend. 4) and who was invited in by occupant of apartment, was not required to comply with notice provisions of § 844 and this section. People v. Byrd (1974) 113 Cal.Rptr. 777, 38 C.A.3d 941.

Compliance with statutory "knock and notice" requirements of § 844 and this section is excused when officers have a reasonable belief that such compliance will permit destruction of evidence inside house and thereby frustrate their purposes. People v. Vargas (1974) 111 Cal.Rptr. 745, 36 C.A.3d 499.

Two exceptions to knock and notice rule are: (1) where there has been substantial compliance, and (2) where there is excused noncompliance. People v. Webb (1973) 111 Cal.Rptr. 524, 36 C.A.3d 460.

Where officers had information that occupant of apartment customarily carried a gun on his person, several handguns and a blackjack were found in a previous search, the policemen had been observed as they entered the building's front yard and the announcement, three to five seconds before the entry, that police officers with the search warrant were at the door alleviated probability of misunderstanding that persons other than law enforcement officers were invading the premises, strict compliance with this section was excused. Brown v. Superior Court In and For Alameda County (1973) 110 Cal.Rptr. 107, 34 C.A.3d 539.

Evidence seized pursuant to unannounced entries is generally inadmissible; but failure to comply with § 844 and this section requiring notice of authority and purpose does not compel application of exclusionary rule if specific facts known to the officer before his entry were sufficient to support his good-faith belief that compliance would increase his peril, frustrate arrest, or permit the destruction of evidence. Parsley v. Superior Court of Riverside County (1973) 109 Cal.Rptr. 563, 513 P.2d 611, 9 C.3d 934.

Forcible entry

People v. Vasquez (1969) 82 Cal.Rptr. 131, 1 C.A.3d 769 [main volume] certiorari denied 90 S.Ct. 1840, 398 U.S. 938, 26 L.Ed.2d 270.

People v. Garber (1969) 80 Cal.Rptr. 214, 275 C.A.2d 119 [main volume] certiorari denied 91 S.Ct. 1643, 402 U.S. 981, 29 L.Ed.2d 146.

Officers, who identified themselves outside defendant's door, who clearly stated their purpose, who demanded entrance, and who were refused, had the right to force an entry into defendant's dwelling when they were attempting to serve an arrest and search warrant. People v. Langley (1974) 116 Cal.Rptr. 80, 41 C.A.3d 339.

Where officers executing search warrant knocked on door of residence, gave notice of authority and purpose, and demanded that door be opened, and agent observed person, who appeared to be sleeping, reclining on couch inside house, and there was no refusal of admittance or action or inaction which could be understood by officers to indicate a refusal, there were no exigent circumstances excusing compliance with this section relating to execution of search warrant and officers' entry was illegal and evidence obtained inside house was product of illegal search. People v. Abdon (1975) 106 Cal.Rptr. 879, 30 C.A.2d 972.

Forcible entry of police officers, who, with warrant in hand appeared at defendant's house, knocked loudly and long on front door, several times identified themselves orally as officers, explained their purpose in seeking entrance to serve search warrant and demanded that door be opened, was not invalidated by virtue of officers' outward appearance, including sport clothes and goatee-type beard. People v. Schad (1971) 98 Cal.Rptr. 439, 21 C.A.3d 201.

Breaking

Entry through window which had no glass or screen but over which a cloth had been tied down to exclude light and the elements constituted a "breaking" within this section providing that officer executing search warrant may break open door or window if he is refused entrance after notice of his authority and purpose. Parsley v. Superior Court of Riverside County (1973) 109 Cal.Rptr. 563, 513 P.2d 611, 9 C.3d 934.

Where officer received consent to enter house and told one occupant of house of search warrant, officer's subsequent nonviolent entry of occupied bedroom through open door was not a "breaking" within this section and officer was not required to give notice of his authority and purpose before entering the bedroom. People v. Livermore (1973) 106 Cal.Rptr. 822, 30 C.A.3d 1073.

In executing search warrant pursuant to this section permitting breaking open door or window of house to execute search warrant, as distinguished from making of an arrest pursuant to § 844 permitting such a breaking to effect arrest, compliance with statutory requirement of giving notice of authority and purpose was not necessary, where evidence supported conclusion that no one was present on premises to be searched. Hart v. Superior Court In and For San Mateo County (1971) 98 Cal.Rptr. 565, 21 C.A.3d 496.

Inner and outer doors

This section applies to entries of closed outer and inner doors and to open outer doors. People v. Castaneda (1976) 129 Cal.Rptr. 755, 58 C.A.3d 165.

Though special circumstances may require compliance with this section, notice requirement is directed to initial entry of structure to which warrant is directed and, usually, does not apply to entry of each room or area within the premises. People v. Livermore (1973) 106 Cal.Rptr. 822, 30 C.A.3d 1073.

Destruction of evidence

Officers, armed with search warrant, were excused from observing statutory "knock and notice" requirements where they could have justifiably harbored a belief that words voiced from inside house were for purpose of shouting a warning of their presence and imminent entry and that evidence was about to be destroyed, and to have waited at front door for an indeterminate length of time for someone to come and be informed of their identity, authority and purpose would have completely frustrated days of police investigation. People v. Vargas (1974) 111 Cal.Rptr. 745, 36 C.A.3d 499.

Evidence in prosecution for possession of marijuana, barbiturates, and methamphetamine supported finding that full compliance with this section providing that officer may break open door or window of house to execute search warrant if, after notice of his authority and purpose, he is refused admittance was excused due to officers' good-faith belief that defendant was in process of attempting to dispose of evidence. People v. Pacheco (1972) 103 Cal.Rptr. 583, 27 C.A.3d 70.

Effect of violation of section

Failure of officers to comply with this section does not compel application of the exclusionary rule if the specific facts known to the officer before his entry are sufficient to support his good-faith belief that compliance will increase his peril, frustrate the search, or permit the destruction of evidence. Brown v. Superior Court In and For Alameda County (1973) 110 Cal.Rptr. 107, 34 C.A.3d 539.

Where officers' entry through front door of residence was illegal, the finding and seizure of marijuana plants found growing outside back door was tainted by the illegal entry. People v. Abdon (1973) 106 Cal.Rptr. 879, 30 C.A.3d 972.

Entry of house, in violation of this section, renders any following search and seizure unreasonable within purview of Fourth Amendment (U.S.C.A.Const. Amend. 14). People v. Pacheco (1972) 103 Cal.Rptr. 583, 27 C.A.3d 70.

Emergency situations

Record including showing that prior to events immediately preceding arrest of defendant for narcotics violation police had only a sketchy insubstantial basis of suspicion that defendant maintained his inventory of heroin at a certain residence, it was only when he left that residence to engage in his trade of selling heroin that there was reasonable cause to believe that residence was his warehouse, and as soon as proposition was ascertained police commenced lengthy process of securing a search warrant from a magistrate and police knew that illegal transaction had been arranged in part by telephone call in which defendant's wife had participated, and that when police knocked on the door the wife's conduct indicated that she had begun destruction of evidence, established an emergency so that evidence of contraband seized pursuant to search at the residence would not be suppressed. People v. Freeny (1974) 112 Cal.Rptr. 33, 37 C.A.3d 20.

Failure of officers to have taken an agent with them to defendant's residence who spoke Spanish was not a basis for concluding that officers deliberately created an emergency situation which gave rise to justification for entering home without compliance with statutory "knock and notice" requirements, where facts giving rise to justification for entry arose from shouting and voiced exclamations in front of home, not absence of a Spanish interpreter. People v. Vargas (1974) 111 Cal.Rptr. 745, 36 C.A.3d 499.

Exceptions to this section requiring that officer announce his authority and purpose and be refused admittance prior to breaking open door or window in the execution of search warrant pertain only to emergency situations existing at the time of entry. Parsley v. Superior Court of Riverside County (1973) 109 Cal.Rptr. 563, 513 P.2d 611, 9 C.3d 934.

Belief of officers

Where officer entertains reasonable and good-faith belief that compliance with "knock and notice" rule would increase his peril, frustrate arrest, or permit destruction of evidence, he may properly omit compliance. People v. Cox (App.1976) 130 Cal.Rptr. 440.

Even if police officers believed that criminal activity was in progress behind defendant's door, they were still required to identify themselves prior to entry. People v. Keogh (1975) 120 Cal.Rptr. 817, 46 C.A.3d 919.

§ 1532. Authority to break door or window to liberate officer or person aiding him

May break open door, etc., to liberate person acting in his aid. He may break open any outer or inner door or window of a house, for the purpose of liberating a person who, having entered to aid him in the execution of the warrant, is detained therein, or when necessary for his own liberation.
(Enacted 1872.)

§ 1533. Direction as to time for search; grounds for search at night

Upon a showing of good cause, the magistrate may, in his discretion, insert a direction in a search warrant that it may be served at any time of the day or night. In the absence of such a direction, the warrant shall be served only between the hours of 7 o'clock a. m. and 10 o'clock p. m.
(Amended by Stats.1970, c. 47, p. 65, § 1.)

Notes of Decisions

This section allowing execution of a search warrant between sunset and 10:00 p. m. without a showing of good cause for nighttime search, does not violate the warrant requirements of the state and federal constitutions; requirement of "good cause" for nighttime service of a warrant is essentially statutory requirement and not a constitutional requirement; there was nothing unreasonable or unconstitutional in legislative determination that search warrant may be executed between hours of 7:00 a. m. and 10:00 p. m. without a showing of good cause. People v. Glass (1976) 128 Cal.Rptr. 413, 56 C.A.3d 368.

Provision of this section that, upon a showing of good cause, magistrate may, in his discretion, insert a direction in a search warrant that it may be served at any time of day or night does not require a separate statement as to good cause for serving warrant in nighttime; if affidavit, read in a common sense manner and as a whole, reasonably supports inference that interests of justice are best served by authorization of nighttime service, provision for such service in warrant is proper. People v. Mardian (1975) 121 Cal.Rptr. 269, 47 C.A.3d 16.

Where informant, known to be reliable, reported that sales of marijuana were going on and that he had observed substantial amount of marijuana at premises to be searched, authorization for nighttime service of warrant was proper, and execution of warrant at night even though premises, which were lighted, were unoccupied was proper. People v. Peck (1974) 113 Cal.Rptr. 806, 38 C.A.3d 993.

§ 1534. Time limit for execution and return

(a) A search warrant shall be executed and returned within 10 days after date of issuance. A warrant executed within the 10-day period shall be deemed to have been timely executed and no further showing of timeliness need be made. After the expiration of 10 days, the warrant, unless executed, is void. The documents and records of the court relating to the warrant need not be open to the public until the execution and return of the warrant or the expiration of the 10-day period after issuance. Thereafter, if the warrant has been executed, the documents and records shall be open to the public as a judicial record.

(b) If a duplicate original search warrant has been executed, the peace officer who executed the warrant shall enter the exact time of its execution on its face.

(c) A search warrant may be made returnable before the issuing magistrate or his court.
(Amended by Stats.1971, c. 697, p. 1355, § 2.)

§ 1535. Receipt for property taken

Officer to give receipt for property taken. When the officer takes property under the warrant, he must give a receipt for the property taken (specifying it in detail) to the person from whom it was taken by him, or in whose possession it was found; or, in the absence of any person, he must leave it in the place where he found the property.
(Enacted 1872.)

§ 1536. Disposition of property taken; retention subject to order of court in which offense triable

All property or things taken on a warrant must be retained by the officer in his custody, subject to the order of the court to which he is required to return the proceedings before him, or of any other court in which the offense in respect to which the property or things taken is triable.
(Amended by Stats.1957, c. 1885, p. 3289, § 2.)

Notes of Decisions

Court derived its power to entertain motion for return of items seized pursuant to search warrant, which items were not introduced into evidence in prosecution for conspiracy to prepare, publish, distribute and exhibit obscene matter, and for possession of obscene material, from statute relating to disposition of property taken, as well as from its inherent power to control and prevent the abuse of its process. People v. Superior Court, Orange County (1972) 104 Cal.Rptr. 876, 28 C.A.3d 600.

An officer seizing and holding property under a search warrant does so on behalf of the court; possession by the officer in such case is, in contemplation of the law, possession by the court, and court would not lack power to entertain a summary proceeding for return of seized materials because such materials were not in custodia legis since they were not introduced into evidence. Id.

Fact that trial of prosecutions for conspiracy to prepare, publish, distribute and exhibit obscene matter, and for possession of obscene material, had been completed, resulting in acquittal of defendants, did not deprive superior court of the power to entertain a motion for return of seized materials which were not introduced into evidence, either pursuant to statute relating to disposition of property taken, or in exercise of court's inherent power to prevent abuse of court processes. Id.

Lower court had jurisdiction to entertain a nonstatutory motion for return of property seized from defendants, who were acquitted in obscenity prosecution, which property was not used in evidence in the prosecution, and the order to return was valid. Id.

During pendency of a criminal action, this section may provide the jurisdictional basis for a nonstatutory motion for release of property seized under a search warrant. Id.

§ 1537. Return; delivery to magistrate of inventory of property taken; verification of inventory; form

Return of warrant and delivery of inventory of property taken. The officer must forthwith return the warrant to the magistrate, and deliver to him a written inventory of the property taken, made publicly or in the presence of the person from whose possession it was taken, and of the applicant for the warrant, if they are present, verified by the affidavit of the officer at the foot of the inventory, and taken before the magistrate at the time, to the following effect: "I, R. S., the officer by whom this warrant was executed, do swear that the above inventory contains a true and detailed account of all the property taken by me on the warrant."
(Enacted 1872.)

§ 1538. Inventory of property taken; delivery of copies

Copy of inventory, to whom delivered. The magistrate must thereupon, if required, deliver a copy of the inventory to the person from whose possession the property was taken, and to the applicant for the warrant.
(Enacted 1872.)

§ 1538.5. Motion to return property or suppress evidence

(a) Grounds

(a) A defendant may move for the return of property or to suppress as evidence any tangible or intangible thing obtained as a result of a search or seizure on either of the following grounds:

(1) The search or seizure without a warrant was unreasonable.

(2) The search or seizure with a warrant was unreasonable because (i) the warrant is insufficient on its face; (ii) the property or evidence obtained is not that described in the warrant; (iii) there was not probable cause for the issuance of the warrant; (iv) the method of execution of the warrant violated federal or state constitutional standards; (v) there was any other violation of federal or state constitutional standards.

(b) First hearing

(b) When consistent with the procedures set forth in this section and subject to the provisions of Section 170 through 170.6 of the Code of Civil Procedure, the motion should first be heard by the magistrate who issued the search warrant if there is a warrant.

(c) Evidence

(c) Whenever a search or seizure motion is made in the municipal, justice or superior court as provided in this section, the judge or magistrate shall receive evidence on any issue of fact necessary to determine the motion.

(d) Effect of granting motion

(d) If a search or seizure motion is granted pursuant to the proceedings authorized by this section, the property or evidence shall not be admissible against the movant at any trial or other hearing unless further proceedings authorized by this section or Section 1238 or Section 1466 are utilized by the people.

(e) Return of property

(e) If a search or seizure motion is granted at a trial, the property shall be returned upon order of the court unless it is otherwise subject to lawful detention. If the motion is granted at a special hearing, the property shall be returned upon order of the court only if, after the conclusion of any further proceedings authorized by this section or Section 1238 or Section 1466, the property is not subject to lawful detention or if the time for initiating such proceedings has expired, whichever occurs last. If the motion is granted at a preliminary hearing, the property shall be returned upon order of court after 10 days unless the property is otherwise subject to lawful detention or unless, within that time, further proceedings authorized by this section or Section 1238 are utilized; if they are utilized, the property shall be returned only if, after the conclusion of such proceedings, the property is no longer subject to lawful detention.

(f) Felony; motion at preliminary hearing

(f) If the property or evidence relates to a felony offense initiated by a complaint, the motion may be made in the municipal or justice court at the preliminary hearing.

(g) Misdemeanor; pre-trial motion at special hearing

(g) If the property or evidence relates to a misdemeanor complaint, the motion shall be made in the municipal or justice court before trial and heard prior to trial at a special hearing relating to the validity of the search or seizure. If the property or evidence relates to a misdemeanor filed together with a felony, the procedure provided for a felony in this section and Sections 1238 and 1539 shall be applicable.

(h) Motion at trial

(h) If, prior to the trial of a felony or misdemeanor, opportunity for this motion did not exist or the defendant was not aware of the grounds for the motion, the defendant shall have the right to make this motion during the course of trial in the municipal, justice or superior court.

(i) Felony; renewal of motion at special hearing; review

(i) If the property or evidence obtained relates to a felony offense initiated by complaint and the defendant was held to answer at the preliminary hearing, or if the property or evidence relates to a felony offense initiated by indictment, the defendant shall have the right to renew or make the motion in the superior court at a special hearing relating to the validity of the search or seizure which shall be heard prior to trial and at least 10 days after notice to the people unless the people are willing to waive a portion of this time. The defendant shall have the right to litigate the validity of a search or seizure de novo on the basis of the evidence presented at a special hearing. After the special hearing is held in the superior court, any review thereafter desired by the defendant prior to trial shall be by means of an extraordinary writ of mandate or prohibition filed within 30 days after the denial of his motion at the special hearing.

(j) Relitigation of question after grant of motion; new evidence, review

(j) If the property or evidence relates to a felony offense initiated by complaint and the defendant's motion for the return of the property or suppression of the evidence at the preliminary hearing is granted, and if the defendant is not held to answer at the preliminary hearing, the people may file a new complaint or seek an indictment after the preliminary hearing, and the ruling at the prior hearing shall not be binding in any subsequent proceeding. If the property or evidence relates to a felony offense initiated by complaint and the defendant's motion for the return or suppression of the property or evidence at the preliminary hearing is granted, and if the defendant is held to answer at the preliminary hearing, the ruling at the preliminary hearing shall be binding upon the people unless, upon notice to the defendant and the court in which the preliminary hearing was held and upon the filing of an information, the people within 15 days after the preliminary hearing request in the superior court a special hear-

§ 1538.5

ing, in which case the validity of the search or seizure shall be relitigated de novo on the basis of the evidence presented at the special hearing, and the defendant shall be entitled, as a matter of right, to a continuance of the special hearing for a period of time up to 30 days. If defendant's motion is granted at a special hearing in the superior court, the people, if they have additional evidence relating to the motion and not presented at the special hearing, shall have the right to show good cause at the trial why such evidence was not presented at the special hearing and why the prior ruling at the special hearing should not be binding, or the people may seek appellate review as provided in subdivision (*o*), unless the court prior to the time such review is sought has dismissed the case pursuant to Section 1385. If the property or evidence seized relates solely to a misdemeanor complaint, and the defendant made a motion for the return of property or the suppression of evidence in the municipal court or justice court prior to trial, both the people and defendant shall have the right to appeal any decision of that court relating to that motion to the superior court of the county in which such inferior court is located, in accordance with the California Rules of Court provisions governing appeals from municipal and justice courts in criminal cases. If the people prosecute review by appeal or writ to decision, or any review thereof, in a felony or misdemeanor case, it shall be binding upon them.

(k) **Release of defendant pending resumption of proceedings in trial court**

(k) If the defendant's motion to return property or suppress evidence is granted and the case is dismissed pursuant to Section 1385, or the people appeal in a misdemeanor case pursuant to subdivision (j), the defendant shall be released pursuant to Section 1318 if he is in custody and not returned to custody unless the proceedings are resumed in the trial court and he is lawfully ordered by the court to be returned to custody.

If the defendant's motion to return property or suppress evidence is granted and the people file a petition for writ of mandate or prohibition pursuant to subdivision (*o*) or a notice of intention to file such a petition, the defendant shall be released pursuant to Section 1318 unless (1) he is charged with a capital offense in a case where the proof is evident and the presumption great, or (2) he is charged with a noncapital offense defined in Chapter 1 (commencing with Section 187) of Title 8 of Part 1 and the court

PENAL CODE

orders that the defendant be discharged from actual custody upon bail.

(*l*) **Stay; time for trial; dismissal; continuance; bail or release**

(*l*) If the defendant's motion to return property or suppress evidence is granted, the trial of a criminal case shall be stayed to a specified date pending the termination in the appellate courts of this state of the proceedings provided for in this section, Section 1238, or Section 1466 and, except upon stipulation of the parties, pending the time for the initiation of such proceedings. Upon the termination of such proceedings, the defendant shall be brought to trial as provided by Section 1382, and subject to the provisions of Section 1382, whenever the people have sought and been denied appellate review pursuant to subdivision (*o*), the defendant shall be entitled to have the action dismissed if he is not brought to trial within 30 days of the date of the order which is the last denial of the petition. Nothing contained in this subdivision shall prohibit a court, at the same time as it rules upon the search and seizure motion, from dismissing a case pursuant to Section 1385 when such dismissal is upon the court's own motion and is based upon an order at the special hearing granting defendant's motion to return property or suppress evidence. In a misdemeanor case, the defendant shall be entitled to a continuance of up to 30 days if he intends to file a motion to return property or suppress evidence and needs this time to prepare for the special hearing on the motion. In case of an appeal by the defendant in a misdemeanor case from the denial of such motion, he shall be entitled to bail as a matter of right, and, in the discretion of the trial or appellate court may be released on his own recognizance pursuant to Section 1318.4.

(m) **Exclusive pre-trial remedy; review on appeal after conviction**

(m) The proceedings provided for in this section, Section 995, Section 1238, and Section 1466 shall constitute the sole and exclusive remedies prior to conviction to test the unreasonableness of a search or seizure where the person making the motion for the return of property or the suppression of evidence is a defendant in a criminal case and the property or thing has been offered or will be offered as evidence against him. A defendant may seek further review of the validity of a search or seizure on appeal from a conviction in a criminal case notwithstanding the fact that such judgment of conviction is predicated upon a plea of guilty. Such review on appeal may be obtained by the defendant providing that at some stage of the proceedings prior to conviction he has moved for the return of property or the suppression of the evidence.

(n) **Motions on other grounds; existing law and procedure**

(n) Nothing contained in this section shall prohibit a person from making a motion, otherwise permitted by law, to return property, brought on the ground that the property obtained is protected by the free speech and press provisions of the Federal and State Constitutions. Nothing in this section shall be construed as altering (i) the law of standing to raise the issue of an unreasonable search or seizure; (ii) the law relating to the status of the person conducting the search or seizure; (iii) the law relating to the burden of proof regarding the search or seizure; (iv) the law relating to the reasonableness of a search or seizure regardless of any warrant which may have been utilized; or (v) the procedure and law relating to a motion made pursuant to Section 995 or the procedures which may be initiated after the granting or denial of such a motion.

(o) **People's petition for mandate or prohibition; notice of intention**

(o) Within 30 days after a defendant's motion is granted at a special hearing in the superior court, the people may file a petition for writ of mandate or prohibition, seeking appellate review of the ruling regarding the search or seizure motion. If the trial of a criminal case is set for a date which is less than 30 days from the granting of a defendant's motion at a special hearing in the superior court, the people, if they have not filed such a petition and wish to preserve their right to file such a petition, shall file in the superior court on or before the trial date or within 10 days after the special hearing, whichever occurs last, a notice of intention to file such a petition and shall serve a copy of the notice upon the defendant.
(Amended by Stats.1977, c. 137, p. —, § 1.)

Editors' Note

Read People v. Hawkins and People v. Mozzetti in table of cases included in this text.

Notes of Decisions

A motion, under this section, to return property or suppress evidence is directed not to identity of culprit but to legality of specific items of evidence obtained by a search and seizure; it is, in a sense, in the nature of a proceeding in rem against the evidence itself, and only connection which need be shown between the evidence and the moving party is a sufficient interest to give the latter standing to make the motion. People v. Gale (1973) 108 Cal.Rptr. 852, 511 P.2d 1204, 9 C.3d 788.

This section providing for pretrial suppression hearing dealing with issue of search and seizure does not provide an omnibus procedure for pretrial determination of rulings on evidentiary questions. People v. Rawlings (1974) 117 Cal.Rptr. 651, 42 C.A.3d 952.

Full body searches are impermissible when arrest will be disposed of by mere citation or when arrestee is to be transported to station house in police vehicle and there given opportunity to post bond. People v. Longwill (1975) 123 Cal.Rptr. 297, 538 P.2d 753, 14 C.3d 943.

Even though showing to be made, at motion to suppress, to support issuance of arrest warrant for parolee may in some cases be identical to that made at prerevocation hearing, such showing must be made at motion to suppress in view of this section specifically providing for such challenge and fact that state must establish probable cause in order to establish requisite jurisdiction over parolee. People v. Anderson (1975) 123 Cal.Rptr. 209, 49 C.A.3d 869.

Warrantless search of automobile trunk was unlawful, even though officers, after finding jewelry in glove compartment, had, for first time, reasonable cause to search trunk for more proceeds of burglary, since that cause rested on unlawful search of glove compartment and was fruit of that illegality and same lack of urgency that invalidated search of glove compartment still existed at time of search of trunk. People v. Jochen (1975) 119 Cal.Rptr. 914, 46 C.A.3d 243.

Where house was not itself an instrumentality used to commit crime nor was it evidence of crime, it was not seizable as being in plain sight. People v. Hill (1974) 117 Cal.Rptr. 393, 528 P.2d 1, 12 C.3d 731.

Even if law of Indiana prohibited defendant's wife from giving her consent to entry made by police into defendant's Indiana apartment where oscilloscope stolen in California burglary was found, oscilloscope and testimony concerning its discovery were admissible in California prosecution for that burglary, inasmuch as California's interest was entitled to superior recognition and, under law of California, officer had right to conclude that wife, possessing a key to apartment, had sufficient control over premises to have authority to invite police to enter and to examine articles in question. People v. Orlosky (1974) 115 Cal.Rptr. 598, 40 C.A.3d 935.

Where policeman watched defendant exit his automobile, move his hands under his jacket so that it appeared he was placing something behind his back, knock on front door of liquor store several times, look in numerous directions, including direction of police officer, enter vehicle and drive away, but area was not remote, lights were on in store, automobile was easily identifiable, hour was not late and defendant was not suspected of criminal activity, officer's detention of defendant was unlawful and handgun observed under seat of vehicle was properly suppressed. People v. Lathan (1974) 113 Cal.Rptr. 648, 38 C.A.3d 911.

Searches and seizures of allegedly obscene material, pursuant to two search warrants, were valid insofar as they were directed to two named magazines, where incriminating magazines, mock-up and pictures, discovered on arrested burglar, were shown to magistrate, where there was no claim that his determination that they were obscene was in error, and where the affidavits supporting the search warrants were sufficient to meet the other tests for a valid warrant. Fixler v. Superior Court (App.1974) 113 Cal.Rptr. 285.

§ 1538.5 PENAL CODE

Exclusionary rule founded on Fourth Amendment (U.S.C.A.Const. Amend. 4) is designed to prevent governmental action and does not extend to cases where evidence has been seized or obtained by private citizen unless that citizen was then acting as agent for government. People v. Wachter (1976) 130 Cal.Rptr. 279, 58 C.A.3d 911.

Where deputy sheriff who accompanied friend to defendant's farm because friend wanted to check on some chickens he had given to occupants of property was acting in his capacity as private citizen rather than as law enforcement officer when he entered defendant's premises and discovered presence of marijuana plants growing on plot not viewable from highway and when, upon his discovery, he communicated information as private citizen to proper law enforcement officials who subsequently issued lawful search warrant, deputy's actions were not subject to the "exclusionary rule" founded on the Fourth Amendment (U.S.C.A.Const. Amend. 4). Id.

Where officer who conducted pat-down search of defendant knew that small, round bottle in defendant's pocket was not a weapon, seizure of bottle after defendant stated that it contained pills was not justified and arrest of defendant for possession of the pills was illegal, and defendant's invitation to police to enter his apartment so that defendant could produce prescription for the pills could not be interpreted as voluntary consent validating officers' entry, and officers' entry into defendant's apartment and discovery of contraband was a direct product of the illegal arrest and invalid. People v. Leib (1976) 129 Cal.Rptr. 433, 548 P.2d 1105, 16 C.3d 869.

Officer's information as to previous activity of defendant in receiving stolen property was not probable cause for arrest, but where officer recognized defendant as driver of station wagon containing number of business machines and saw switch of automobiles and transfer of one machine in basement garage of residential complex and officer's independent investigation of official police records disclosed that defendant had been active as receiver of stolen property, there was probable cause for arrest and seizure of machines. People v. Martin (1973) 108 Cal.Rptr. 809, 511 P.2d 1161, 9 C.3d 687, certiorari denied 94 S.Ct. 844, 414 U.S. 1113, 38 L.Ed.2d 740.

Where seizure of alleged pornographic films had been legal, defendant in prosecution for possession and distribution of obscene material was not entitled to have reels of film returned pending judicial determination of their obscenity. People v. Burnstad (1973) 108 Cal.Rptr. 247, 32 C.A.3d 560.

Where interrogation, patdown and search which revealed contraband drugs occurred while motorist was illegally detained, evidence obtained should have been suppressed. People v. Grace (1973) 108 Cal.Rptr. 66, 32 C.A.3d 447.

Where officer, after entering defendant's home pursuant to defendant's request for aid, discovered bleeding woman in chair, and defendant changed his story as to what had happened, it was proper for police evidence technician, who arrived prior to defendant's accompanying officer to station, to conduct warrantless search of premises. People v. Wallace (1973) 107 Cal.Rptr. 659, 31 C.A.3d 865.

Dismissal of counts of information relating to burglary, possession of firearm by a felon, telephone tampering, and possession of equipment with serial numbers destroyed, together with defendant's stipulation relinquishing any property interest in items seized, rendered moot magistrate's prior order with respect to propriety of seizure of such items. People v. Chochos (1973) 107 Cal.Rptr. 410, 31 C.A.3d 445.

Where San Diego police received telephone call that man dressed in green shirt and brown jacket was at a certain bar with gun, officer arrived at the bar within two minutes, the bartender pointed defendant out as the man with the gun and defendant was dressed in green shirt and brown jacket and was leaving front door of the bar, the gun found on defendant's person during pat down search was not the product of illegal search and seizure but was the product of pat down search properly conducted following justifiable detention. People v. Duren (1973) 107 Cal.Rptr. 157, 507 P.2d 1365, 9 C.3d 218.

§ 1540. Restoration of property; property not described in warrant; no probable cause

Property, when to be restored to person from whom it was taken. If it appears that the property taken is not the same as that described in the warrant, or that there is no probable cause for believing the existence of the grounds on which the warrant was issued, the magistrate must cause it to be restored to the person from whom it was taken. (Enacted 1872.)

§ 1541. Magistrate without jurisdiction of offense; filing of warrant, return, affidavits and inventory with clerk of court having jurisdiction

The magistrate must annex the affidavit, or affidavits, the search warrant and return, and the inventory, and if he has not power to inquire into the offense in respect to which the warrant was issued, he must at once file such warrant and return and such affidavit, or affidavits, and inventory with the clerk of the court having power to so inquire. (Amended by Stats.1957, c. 1881, p. 3288, § 1.)

§ 1542. Search of defendant in presence of magistrate; grounds; retention of articles found

When magistrate may direct defendant to be searched in his presence. When a person charged with a felony is supposed by the magistrate before whom he is brought to have on his person a dangerous weapon, or anything which may be used as evidence of the commission of the offense, the magistrate may direct him to be searched in his presence, and the weapon or other thing to be retained, subject to his order, or to the order of the Court in which the defendant may be tried.
(Enacted 1872.)

FUGITIVES FROM JUSTICE

§ 1547. Reward; offer by governor; amount; payment

(a) The Governor may offer a reward of not more than ten thousand dollars ($10,000), payable out of the General Fund, for information leading to the arrest and conviction of any of the following:

(1) Any convict who has escaped from a state prison, prison camp, prison farm, or the custody of any prison officer or employee or as provided in Section 3059, 4530, or 4531.

(2) Any person who has committed, or is charged with the commission of, an offense punishable with death.

(3) Any person engaged in the robbery or hijacking of, or any attempt to rob or hijack, any person upon or in charge of, in whole or in part, any public conveyance engaged at the time in carrying passengers within this state.

(4) Any person who kills, assaults with a deadly weapon, or inflicts serious bodily harm upon a police officer who is acting in the line of duty.

(5) Any person who has committed a crime involving the burning or bombing of public property.

(b) The reward shall be paid to the person giving the information, immediately upon the conviction of the person so arrested.

(c) As used in this section, "hijacking" means an unauthorized person causing, or attempting to cause, by violence or threat of violence, a public conveyance to go to an unauthorized destination.
(Amended by Stats.1971, c. 1390, p. 2744, § 1.)

§ 1548. Words and phrases

As used in this chapter:

(a) "Governor" means any person performing the functions of Governor by authority of the law of this State.

(b) "Executive authority" means the Governor or any person performing the functions of Governor in a State other than this State.

(c) "State," referring to a State other than the State of California, means any other State or Territory, organized or unorganized, of the United States of America.

(d) "Laws of the United States" means: (1) those laws of the United States passed by Congress pursuant to authority given to Congress by the Constitution of the United States where the laws of the United States are controlling, and (2) those laws of the United States not controlling the several States of the United States but which are not in conflict with the provisions of this chapter.
(Added by Stats.1937, c. 554, p. 1582, § 2.)

§ 1548.1. Governor; duty to cause arrest and delivery

Subject to the provisions of this chapter, the Constitution of the United States, and the laws of the United States, it is the duty of the Governor of this State to have arrested and delivered up to the executive authority of any other State any person charged in that State with treason, felony, or other crime, who has fled from justice and is found in this State.
(Added by Stats.1937, c. 554, p. 1582, § 3.)

§ 1548.2. Demand for extradition; form and contents; documents to accompany demand; charge of crime; authentication

No demand for the extradition of a person charged with crime in another State shall be recognized by the Governor unless it is in writing alleging that the accused was present in the demanding State at the time of the commission of the alleged crime, and that thereafter he fled from that State. Such demand shall be accompanied by a copy of an indictment found or by information or by a copy of an affidavit made before a magistrate in the demanding State together with a copy of any warrant which was issued thereon; or such demand shall be accompanied by a copy of a judgment of conviction or of a sentence imposed in execution thereof, together with a statement by the executive authority of the demanding State that the person claimed has escaped from confinement or has violated the terms of his bail, probation or parole. The indictment, information, or affidavit made before the magistrate must substantially charge the person demanded with having committed a crime under the law of that State; and the copy of indictment, information, affidavit, judgment of conviction or sentence must be certified as authentic by the executive authority making the demand.
(Added by Stats.1937, c. 554, p. 1582, § 4.)

§ 1548.3. Demand for extradition; investigation by attorney general or district attorney; report

When a demand is made upon the Governor of this State by the executive authority of another State for the surrender of a person so charged with crime, the Governor may call upon the Attorney General or any district attorney in this State to investigate or assist in investigating the demand, and to report to him the situation and circumstances of the person so demanded, and whether he ought to be surrendered according to the provision of this chapter.
(Added by Stats.1937, c. 554, p. 1583, § 5.)

§ 1549.1. Surrender of person not in demanding state when committing act resulting in crime in demanding state; flight from, or presence in demanding state need not be shown

The Governor of this State may also surrender, on demand of the executive authority of any other State, any person in this State charged in such other State in the manner provided in section 1548.2 of this code with committing an act in this State, or in a third State, intentionally resulting in a crime in the State whose executive authority is making the demand. The provisions of this chapter, not otherwise inconsistent, shall apply to such cases, even though the accused was not in the demanding State at the time of the commission of the crime, and has not fled therefrom. Neither the demand, the oath, nor any proceedings under this chapter pursuant to this section need state or show that the accused has fled from justice from, or at the time of the commission of the crime was in, the demanding or other State.
(Added by Stats.1937, c. 554, p. 1583, § 7.)

§ 1549.2. Governor's warrant; direction; recitals

If a demand conforms to the provisions of this chapter, the Governor or agent authorized in writing by the Governor whose authorization has been filed with the Secretary of State shall sign a warrant of arrest, which shall be sealed with the State Seal, and shall be directed to any peace officer or other person whom he may entrust with the execution thereof. The warrant must substantially recite the facts necessary to the validity of its issuance.
(Amended by Stats.1967, c. 950, p. 2446, § 1.)

§ 1549.3. Governor's warrant; authority conferred

Such warrant shall authorize the peace officer or other person to whom it is directed:

(a) To arrest the accused at any time and any place where he may be found within the State;

(b) To command the aid of all peace officers or other persons in the execution of the warrant; and

(c) To deliver the accused, subject to the provisions of this chapter, to the duly authorized agent of the demanding State.
(Added by Stats.1937, c. 554, p. 1584, § 9.)

§ 1550. Arresting officer; power to command assistance; refusal to assist

Every peace officer or other person empowered to make the arrest hereunder shall have the same authority, in arresting the accused, to command assistance therefor as the persons designated in section 150 of this code. Failure or refusal to render such assistance is a violation of section 150 of this code.
(Added by Stats.1937, c. 554, p. 1584, § 10.)

§ 1550.1. Prisoner to be taken before magistrate; information as to demand, charge, and right to counsel; habeas corpus, time service

No person arrested upon such warrant shall be delivered over to the agent of the executive authority demanding him unless he first is taken forthwith before a magistrate, who shall inform him of the demand made for his surrender and of the crime with which he is charged, and that he has the right to demand and procure legal counsel. If the accused or his counsel desires to test the legality of the arrest, the magistrate shall fix a reasonable time to be allowed him within which to apply for a writ of habeas corpus. If the writ is denied or the accused is remanded to custody, and probable cause appears for an application for a writ of habeas corpus to another court, or justice or judge thereof, the order denying the writ or remanding the accused shall fix a reasonable time within which the accused may again apply for a writ of habeas corpus. When an application is made for a writ of habeas corpus as contemplated by this section, a copy of the application shall be served as provided in Section 1475 upon the district attorney of the county in which the accused is in custody, and upon the agent of the demanding state.
(Amended by Stats.1959, c. 725, p. 2713, § 1.)

§ 1550.2. Delivery of prisoner to agent of demanding state without appearance before magistrate; offense; punishment

Any officer or other person entrusted with a Governor's warrant who delivers to the agent of the demanding State a person in his custody under such Governor's warrant, in wilful disobedience to the preceding section, is guilty of a misdemeanor and, on conviction thereof, shall be fined not more than $1,000 or be imprisoned not more than six months, or both.
(Added by Stats.1937, c. 554, p. 1584, § 12.)

§ 1550.3. Confinement of prisoner under governor's warrant or of prisoner being taken through state; expense; evidence of authority

The officer or persons executing the Governor's warrant of arrest, or the agent of the demanding

State to whom the prisoner has been delivered may confine the prisoner in the jail of any county or city through which he may pass. The keeper of such jail must receive and safely keep the prisoner until the officer or person having charge of him is ready to proceed on his route. Such officer or person shall be charged with the expense of keeping the prisoner.

The officer or agent of a demanding State to whom a prisoner has been delivered following extradition proceedings in another State, or to whom a prisoner has been delivered after waiving extradition in such other State, and who is passing through this State with such a prisoner for the purpose of immediately returning such prisoner to the demanding State may confine the prisoner in the jail of any county or city through which he may pass. The keeper of such jail must receive and safely keep the prisoner until the officer or agent having charge of him is ready to proceed on his route. Such officer or agent shall be charged with the expense of keeping the prisoner. Such officer or agent shall produce and show to the keeper of such jail satisfactory written evidence of the fact that he is actually transporting such prisoner to the demanding State after a requisition by the executive authority thereof. Such prisoner shall not be entitled to demand a new requisition while in this State.
(Added by Stats.1937, c. 554, p. 1584, § 13.)

§ 1551. Complaint against fugitive; magistrate's warrant; attaching certified copy of complaint and affidavit to warrant

(a) Whenever any person within this State is charged by a verified complaint before any magistrate of this State with the commission of any crime in any other State, or, with having been convicted of a crime in that State and having escaped from confinement, or having violated the terms of his bail, probation or parole; or (b) whenever complaint is made before any magistrate in this State setting forth on the affidavit of any credible person in another State that a crime has been committed in such other State and that the accused has been charged in such State with the commission of the crime, or that the accused has been convicted of a crime in that State and has escaped from bail, probation or parole and is believed to be in this State; then the magistrate shall issue a warrant directed to any peace officer commanding him to apprehend the person named therein, wherever he may be found in this State, and to bring him before the same or any other magistrate who is available in or convenient of access to the place where the arrest is made. A certified copy of the sworn charge or complaint and affidavit upon which the warrant is issued shall be attached to the warrant.
(Added by Stats.1937, c. 554, p. 1585, § 14.)

§ 1551.1. Arrest without warrant; grounds; taking prisoner before magistrate; complaint

The arrest of a person may also be lawfully made by any peace officer, without a warrant, upon reasonable information that the accused stands charged in the courts of any other State with a crime punishable by death or imprisonment for a term exceeding one year. When so arrested the accused must be taken before a magistrate with all practicable speed and complaint must be made against him under oath setting forth the ground for the arrest as in the preceding section.
(Added by Stats.1937, c. 554, p. 1585, § 15.)

§ 1551.2. Proceedings for commitment of person arrested on magistrate's warrant or without warrant; evidence

Proceedings for the commitment of a person charged under sections 1551 and 1551.1 of this code shall be similar to those provided in this code for the commitment of a person charged with a public offense in this State except that an exemplified copy of an indictment found, an information, a verified complaint, or other judicial proceedings against such person in the State in which he is charged or alleged to have committed the offense may be received as evidence before the magistrate.
(Added by Stats.1937, c. 554, p. 1586, § 16.)

§ 1551.3. Notice of arrest of alleged fugitive

Immediately upon the arrest of the person charged, the magistrate must give notice thereof to the district attorney. The district attorney must immediately thereafter give notice to the executive authority of the State, or to the prosecuting attorney or presiding judge of the court of the city or county within the State having jurisdiction of the offense, to the end that a demand may be made for the arrest and surrender of the person charged.
(Added by Stats.1937, c. 554, p. 1586, § 17.)

§ 1552. Person arrested on magistrate's warrant or without warrant; commitment pending governor's warrant; bail

If at the hearing before the magistrate, it appears that the accused is the person charged with having

§ 1552

committed the crime alleged, the magistrate must, by a warrant reciting the accusation, commit him to the county jail for such a time, not exceeding thirty days and specified in the warrant, as will enable the arrest of the accused to be made under a warrant of the Governor on a requisition of the executive authority of the State having jurisdiction of the offense, unless the accused give bail as provided in section 1552.1, or until he shall be legally discharged.
(Added by Stats.1937, c. 554, p. 1586, § 18.)

§ 1552.1. Person arrested on magistrate's warrant or without warrant; bail

Unless the offense with which the prisoner is charged is shown to be an offense punishable by death or life imprisonment under the laws of the State in which it was committed, the magistrate may admit the person arrested to bail by bond or undertaking, with sufficient sureties, and in such sum as he deems proper, conditioned upon the appearance of such person before him at a time specified in such bond or undertaking and for his surrender upon the warrant of the Governor of this State.
(Added by Stats.1937, c. 554, p. 1586, § 19.)

§ 1552.2. Person arrested on magistrate's warrant or without warrant; expiration of time; discharge or recommitment; new bail; time limit

If the accused is not arrested under warrant of the Governor by the expiration of the time specified in the warrant, bond, or undertaking, a magistrate may discharge him or may recommit him for a further period of 60 days. In the latter event a justice of the Supreme Court or court of appeal or a judge of the superior court may again take bail for his appearance and surrender, as provided in Section 1552.1 but within a period not to exceed 60 days after the date of such new bond or undertaking.
(Amended by Stats.1967, c. 17, p. 851, § 115.)

§ 1553. Person arrested on magistrate's warrant or without warrant; non-appearance; forfeiture of bond; order for immediate arrest; recovery on bond

If the prisoner is admitted to bail, and fails to appear and surrender himself according to the conditions of his bond, the magistrate, by proper order, shall declare the bond forfeited and order his immediate arrest without warrant if he be within this State. Recovery may be had on such bond in the name of the people of the State as in the case of other bonds or undertakings given by a defendant in criminal proceedings.
(Added by Stats.1937, c. 554, p. 1587, § 21.)

§ 1553.1. Pendency of domestic prosecution; discretion to surrender or hold fugitive

If a criminal prosecution has been instituted against such person under the laws of this State and is still pending, the Governor, with the consent of the Attorney General, may surrender him on demand of the executive authority of another State or hold him until he has been tried and discharged or convicted and served his sentence in this State.
(Added by Stats.1937, c. 554, p. 1587, § 22.)

§ 1553.2. Inquiry into guilt or innocence; identification

The guilt or innocence of the accused as to the crime with which he is charged may not be inquired into by the Governor or in any proceeding after the demand for extradition accompanied by a charge of crime in legal form as above provided has been presented to the Governor, except as such inquiry may be involved in identifying the person held as the person charged with the crime.
(Added by Stats.1937, c. 554, p. 1587, § 23.)

§ 1554. Governor's warrant; recall; reissue

The Governor may recall his warrant of arrest or may issue another warrant whenever he deems it proper.
(Added by Stats.1937, c. 554, p. 1587, § 24.)

§ 1554.1. Governor's warrant; issuance to agent to receive person demanded from foreign state

Whenever the Governor of this State shall demand the return of a person charged with crime in this State or with escaping from confinement or violating the terms of his bail, probation or parole in this State, from the executive authority of any other State or of any foreign government or the chief justice or an associate justice of the Supreme Court of the District of Columbia authorized to receive such demand, he shall issue a warrant under the seal of this State to an agent, commanding him to receive the person so demanded and to convey him to the proper officer in the county in this State in which the offense was committed.
(Added by Stats.1937, c. 554, p. 1587, § 25.)

§ 1554.2. Application for requisition from foreign state; contents; verification; accompanying documents; filing; forwarding copies with requisition

(a) When the return to this State of a person charged with crime in this State is required, the district attorney shall present to the Governor his written application for a requisition for the return of the person charged. In such application there shall be stated the name of the person so charged, the crime charged against him, the approximate time, place and circumstances of its commission, and the State in which he is believed to be, including the location of the accused therein at the time the application is made. Such application shall certify that, in the opinion of the district attorney, the ends of justice require the arrest and return of the accused to this State for trial and that the proceeding is not instituted to enforce a private claim.

(b) When the return to this State is required of a person who has been convicted of a crime in this State and who has escaped from confinement or has violated the terms of his bail, probation or parole the district attorney of the county in which the offense was committed, the Adult Authority, the Director of Corrections, the California Institution for Women, the Youth Authority, or the sheriff of the county from which escape from confinement was made, shall present to the Governor a written application for a requisition for the return of such person. In such application there shall be stated the name of the person, the crime of which he was convicted, the circumstances of his escape or of the violation of the terms of his bail, probation or parole, and the State in which he is believed to be, including the location of such person therein at the time application is made.

(c) The application shall be verified, shall be executed in duplicate, and shall be accompanied by two certified copies of the indictment, the information, or the verified complaint made to the magistrate stating the offense with which the accused is charged, or the judgment of conviction or the sentence. The officer or board requesting the requisition may also attach such affidavits and other documents in duplicate as are deemed proper to be submitted with such application. One copy of the application, with the action of the Governor indicated by endorsement thereon, and one of the certified copies of the indictment, verified complaint, information, or judgment of conviction or sentence shall be filed in the office of the Secretary of State. The other copies of all papers shall be forwarded with the Governor's requisition.
(Amended by Stats.1945, c. 152, p. 635, § 1.)

§ 1555. Exemption of person extradited from civil process in certain actions; time

A person brought into this State on, or after waiver of extradition based on a criminal charge shall not be subject to service of process in civil actions arising out of the same facts as the criminal proceedings for which he is returned, until he has been convicted in the criminal proceeding, or, if acquitted, until he has had reasonable opportunity to return to the State from which he was extradited.
(Added by Stats.1937, c. 554, p. 1588, § 27.)

§ 1555.1. Waiver of extradition; method; advice as to rights; filing of waiver; delivery to agent of demanding state; voluntary return

Any person arrested in this State charged with having committed any crime in another State or alleged to have escaped from confinement, or broken the terms of his bail, probation or parole may waive the issuance and service of the Governor's warrant provided for in this chapter and all other procedure incidental to extradition proceedings, by subscribing in the presence of a magistrate within this State a writing which states that he consents to return to the demanding State; provided, however, that before such waiver shall be subscribed by such person, the magistrate shall inform him of his rights to require the issuance and service of a warrant of extradition as provided in this chapter.

If such waiver is executed, it shall forthwith be forwarded to the office of the Governor of this State and filed therein. The magistrate shall direct the officer having such person in custody to deliver such person forthwith to the duly authorized agent of the demanding State, and shall deliver to such agent a copy of such waiver.

Nothing in this section shall be deemed to limit the rights of the accused person to return voluntarily and without formality to the demanding State, nor shall this procedure of waiver be deemed to be an exclusive procedure or to limit the powers, rights or duties of the officers of the demanding State or of this State.
(Added by Stats.1937, c. 554, p. 1589, § 28.)

§ 1555.2. Chapter provisions not a waiver of state's rights or jurisdiction as to demanded person

Nothing in this chapter shall be deemed to constitute a waiver by this State of its right, power or privilege to try any demanded person for crime committed within this State, or of its right, power or privilege to regain custody of such person by extradition proceedings or otherwise for the purpose of trial, sentence or punishment for any crime committed

§ 1555.2

within this State; nor shall any proceedings had under this chapter which result in, or fail to result in, extradition be deemed a waiver by this State of any of its rights, privileges or jurisdiction in any manner whatsoever.
(Added by Stats.1937, c. 554, p. 1589, § 28.)

§ 1556. Prosecution of extradited person for other offenses

After a person has been brought back to this State by extradition proceedings, he may be tried in this State for other crimes which he may be charged with having committed in this State as well as for the crime or crimes specified in the requisition for his extradition.
(Added by Stats.1937, c. 554, p. 1589, § 29.)

§ 1556.1. Construction to effect uniformity

The provisions of this chapter shall be so interpreted and construed as to effectuate its general purposes to make uniform the law of those states which enact legislation based upon the Uniform Criminal Extradition Act.
(Added by Stats.1937, c. 554, p. 1589, § 30.)

§ 1557. Expense of returning fugitives; audit and payment; advances for or reimbursements of expenses

(a) This section shall apply when this state, or a city, county, or city and county employs a person to travel to a foreign jurisdiction outside this state for the express purpose of returning a fugitive from justice to this state when the Governor of this state, in the exercise of the authority conferred by Section 2, Article IV, of the Constitution of the United States, or by the laws of this state, has demanded the surrender of such fugitive from the executive authority of any state of the United States, or of any foreign government.

(b) Upon the approval of the Governor, the State Controller shall audit and pay out of the State Treasury as provided in subdivision (c) or (d) the accounts of the person employed to bring back such fugitive, including any money paid by such person for all of the following:

(1) Money paid to the authorities of a sister state for statutory fees in connection with the detention and surrender of such fugitive.

(2) Money paid to the authorities of the sister state for the subsistence of the fugitive while detained by such sister state without payment of which, the authorities of such state refuse to surrender such fugitive.

(3) Where it is necessary to present witnesses or evidence in the sister state, without which the sister state would not surrender the fugitive, the cost of producing such witnesses or evidence in the sister state.

(4) Where the appearance of witnesses has been authorized in advance by the Governor, who may authorize such appearance in unusual cases where the interests of justice would be served, the cost of producing witnesses to appear in the sister state on behalf of the fugitive in opposition to his extradition.

(c) No amount shall be paid out of the State Treasury to a city, county, or city and county except as specified herein.

(1) When a warrant has been issued by any magistrate after the filing of a complaint or the finding of an indictment and its presentation to the court and filing by the clerk, and the person named therein as defendant is a fugitive from justice, who has been found and arrested in any state of the United States or in any foreign government, the county auditor shall draw his warrant and the county treasurer shall pay to the person designated to return the fugitive, the amount of expenses estimated by the district attorney to be incurred in the return of such fugitive.

(2) If the person designated to return the fugitive is a city officer, the city officer authorized to draw warrants on the city treasury shall draw his warrant and the city treasurer shall pay to such person the amount of expenses estimated by the district attorney to be incurred in the return of such fugitive.

(3) The person designated to return the fugitive shall make no disbursements from any such fund so advanced without a receipt being obtained therefor showing the amount, the purpose for which the sum is expended, place, date, and to whom paid.

(4) Such receipts must be filed by such person with the county auditor or appropriate city officer or State Controller, as the case may be, together with an affidavit by such person that the expenditures represented by the receipts were necessarily made in the performance of duty, and when such advance has been made by the county or city treasurer to the person designated to return the fugitive, and has thereafter been audited by the State Controller, the payment thereof shall be made by the State Treasurer to the county or city treasurer, which has advanced the funds.

(5) In every case where the expenses of such person so employed to bring back such fugitive as herein provided, are less than the amount advanced on the recommendation of the district attorney, such persons so employed to bring back such fugitive shall return to the county or city treasurer, as appropriate, the difference in amount between the aggregate amount of receipts so filed by him, as herein employed, and the amount advanced to such person upon the recommendation of the district attorney.

(6) When no advance has been made to the person designated to return the fugitive, the sums expended by him, when audited by the State Controller, shall be paid by the State Treasurer to the person so designated.

(7) Any payments made out of the State Treasury pursuant to the provisions of this section shall be made from appropriations for the fiscal year in which such payments are made.

(d) Payments to state agencies will be made in accord with the rules of the Board of Control.
(Added by Stats.1974, c. 998, p. 2144, § 2.)

Part 3
OF IMPRISONMENT AND THE DEATH PENALTY

PRISONERS—MAINTENANCE AND RIGHTS

§ 2600. Deprivation of rights relating to security of institution and protection of public

A person sentenced to imprisonment in a state prison may, during any such period of confinement, be deprived of such rights, and only such rights, as is necessary in order to provide for the reasonable security of the institution in which he is confined and for the reasonable protection of the public.
(Added by Stats.1975, c. 1175, p. 2897, § 3.)

§ 2601. Retention of rights

Notwithstanding any other provision of law, each such person shall have the following civil rights:

(a) To inherit, own, sell, or convey real or personal property, including all written and artistic material produced or created by such person during the period of imprisonment; provided that, to the extent authorized in Section 2600, the Department of Corrections may restrict or prohibit sales or conveyances that are made for business purposes.

(b) To correspond, confidentially, with any member of the State Bar or holder of public office, provided that the prison authorities may open and inspect incoming mail to search for contraband.

(c) To purchase, receive, read, and permit other inmates to read any and all legal materials, newspapers, periodicals, and books accepted for distribution by the United States Post Office, except those which describe the making of any weapon, explosive, poison or destructive device. Nothing in this section shall be construed as limiting the right of prison authorities (1) to open and inspect any and all packages received by an inmate and (2) to establish reasonable restrictions as to the number of newspapers, magazines, and books that the inmate may have in his cell or elsewhere in the prison at one time.

(d) To have personal visits; provided that the department may provide such restrictions as are necessary for the reasonable security of the institution.

(e) To initiate civil actions.

(f) To marry.

(g) To create a power of appointment.

(h) To make a will.

(i) To receive all benefits provided for in Sections 3370 and 3371 of the Labor Code and in Section 5069 of this code.
(Amended by Stats.1976, c. 1347, p. —, § 8.)

§ 2930. Informing prisoners of prison rules, regulations and programs; entry in prisoner's central file

(a) The Department of Corrections shall inform every prisoner sentenced under Section 1170, not later than 14 days after reception in prison, of all applicable prison rules and regulations including the possibility of receiving a one-third reduction of the sentence for good behavior and participation. Within 14 days of the prisoner's arrival at the institution to which the prisoner is ultimately assigned by the Department of Corrections, the prisoner shall be informed of the range of programs offered by that institution and their availability at that institution. The prisoner's central file shall reflect compliance with the provisions of this section not later than 90 days after reception in prison.

(b) The department shall, within 90 days after July 1, 1977, inform every prisoner who committed a

§ 2930

felony before July 1, 1977, and who would have been sentenced under Section 1170 if the felony had been committed after July 1, 1977, of all applicable prison rules and regulations, which have not previously been provided, of the range of programs offered and their availability, and the possibility of receiving a reduction for good behavior and participation of one-third of the prisoner's remaining sentence after July 1, 1977. The inmate's central file shall reflect compliance with the provisions of this section.
(Amended by Stats.1977, c. 2, p. —, § 3, urgency, eff. Dec. 16, 1976, operative July 1, 1977; Stats.1977, c. 165, p. —, § 37, urgency, eff. June 29, 1977, operative July 1, 1977.)

§ 2931. **Reduction of term for good behavior and participation; documents outlining conditions; modifications**

(a) In any case in which an inmate was sentenced to the state prison pursuant to Section 1170, or if he committed a felony before July 1, 1977, and he would have been sentenced under Section 1170 if the felony had been committed after July 1, 1977, the Department of Corrections shall have the authority to reduce the term prescribed under such section by one-third for good behavior and participation consistent with subdivision (d) of Section 1170.2. A document shall be signed by a prison official and given to the inmate, at the time of compliance with Section 2930, outlining the conditions which the inmate shall meet to receive the credit. The conditions specified in such document may be modified upon any of the following:

(1) Mutual consent of the prisoner and the Department of Corrections.

(2) The transfer of the inmate from one institution to another.

(3) The department's determination of the prisoner's lack of adaptability or success in a specific program or assignment. In such case the inmate shall be entitled to a hearing regarding the department's decision.

(4) A change in custodial status.

(b) Total possible good behavior and participation credit shall result in a four-month reduction for each eight months served in prison or in a reduction based on this ratio for any lesser period of time. Three months of this four-month reduction, or a reduction based on this ratio for any lesser period, shall be based upon forbearance from any or all of the following activities:

(1) Assault with a weapon; or escape.

(2) Physically assaultive behavior; possession of a weapon without permission; possession of controlled substances without prescription; attempt to escape; or urging others, with the intent to cause a riot, to commit acts of force or violence, at a time and place under circumstances which produce a clear and present and immediate danger of a riot which results in acts of force or violence.

(3) Intentional destruction of state property valued in excess of fifty dollars ($50); falsification of a significant record or document; possession of escape tools without permission; or manufacture, sale or unauthorized possession or use of alcoholic beverages or any substance defined as a poison in Schedule D of Section 4160 of the Business and Professions Code. Activities specified in paragraph (1) may result in a maximum denial of good behavior credit or 45 days for each such prohibited activity. Activities specified in paragraph (2) may result in a maximum denial of good behavior credit of 30 days for each such prohibited activity. Activities specified in paragraph (3) may result in a maximum denial of good behavior credit of 15 days for each such prohibited activity. Nothing in this section shall prevent the Department of Corrections from seeking criminal prosecution for violations of law.

(c) One of the four months reduction, or a formula based on this ratio for a lesser period, shall be based solely upon participation in work, educational, vocational, therapeutic or other prison activities. Failure to succeed after demonstrating a reasonable effort in the specified activity shall not result in loss of participation credit. Failure to participate in the specified activities can result in a maximum loss of credit of 30 days for each failure to participate. However, those confined either by choice or due to behavior problems shall be given specified activities commensurate with the custodial status.
(Amended by Stats.1978, c. 380, p. —, § 125; Stats.1978, c. 532, p. —, § 1.)

§ 2932. **Denial of credit; procedures; notice of good behavior credit, participation credit and anticipated release date; conduct constituting crime**

(a) Not more than 90 days of good behavior credit nor more than 30 days of participation credit may be denied or lost during any eight-month period during which the misbehavior or failure to participate took place. Good behavior and participation credit shall be deemed to be earned in cases where the department fails to adhere to the time limitations of this section except as specified in subdivision (c). Any procedure not provided for by this section, but necessary to carry out the purposes of this section, shall be those procedures provided for by the Department of Corrections for serious disciplinary infractions if those procedures are not in conflict with this section.

(1) The Department of Corrections shall, using reasonable diligence to investigate, provide written notice to the prisoner. The written notice shall be given within five days after the discovery of information leading to charges that may result in a possible denial of good behavior or participation credit, but not later than 30 days after the alleged misbehavior took place, unless the evidence was not reasonably discoverable. The written notice shall include the specific charge, the date, the time, the place that the alleged misbehavior took place, the evidence relied upon, a written explanation of the procedures that will be employed at the proceedings and the prisoner's rights at such hearing, and in the case where the prisoner has been notified more than 30 days after the alleged misbehavior why the evidence was not reasonably discoverable within the 30 days or any sooner than it was discovered. Such hearing shall be conducted by an individual who shall be independent of the case and shall take place within 10 days of such written notice; unless for good cause shown by the Department of Corrections that extraordinary circumstances prevented the hearing from being conducted within 10 days and the prisoner is not prejudiced by the delay the Department of Corrections shall notify the prisoner in writing specifying the extraordinary circumstances and shall conduct the hearing as soon as possible but in no case later than 30 days after the initial written notice of possible good behavior or participation denial.

(2) The prisoner has the right to elect to be assigned an investigative employee who will gather information, talk to witnesses, prepare a written report and be present at the hearing.

(3) The prisoner may request witnesses to attend the hearing and they shall be called unless the person conducting the hearing has specific reasons to deny this request. Such specific reasons shall be set forth in writing and a copy of such document shall be presented to the prisoner.

(4) The person who will conduct the hearing shall determine if the prisoner shall need assistance with presentation of a defense at the hearing and if so, at the prisoner's discretion, the prisoner has the right to be assigned an employee of the Department of Corrections to assist in presenting the prisoner's defense.

(5) The prisoner has the right, under the direction of the person conducting the hearing, to question all witnesses.

(6) At the conclusion of the hearing the charge shall be dismissed if the facts do not support the charge, or the inmate may be found guilty on the basis of a preponderance of the evidence.

(7) If found guilty the prisoner shall be advised within 10 days in writing of the guilty finding and the specific evidence relied upon to reach this conclusion and the amount of good-time loss. The prisoner may appeal such decision through the Department of Corrections review procedure, and may, upon final notification of appeal denial, within 10 days of such notification demand review of the department's denial of credit to the Community Release Board, and the board may affirm, reverse, or modify the department's decision or grant a hearing before the board at which hearing the inmate will have the rights specified in Section 3041.5.

(b) Within 30 days of reception in prison, each prisoner shall be notified of the total amount of good behavior and participation credit which may be credited to his term and his anticipated good-time release date and shall be notified of any change in the anticipated release date.

(c) If the conduct the prisoner is charged with also constitutes a crime, the Department of Corrections may refer the case to criminal authorities for possible prosecution and notify the prisoner as provided in subdivision (a), in which case the time limitations specified in subdivision (a) shall not apply. If the district attorney has not filed an accusatory pleading against the prisoner within 60 days of such referral, the prisoner may request that a hearing be held in which case the department must hold the hearing within 15 days of such request.

In the case where the prisoner is prosecuted by the district attorney, the Department of Corrections shall not deny good behavior credit where the prisoner is found not guilty and may deny good behavior credit pursuant to the schedule specified in Section 2931 if the prisoner is found guilty.

(d) If good behavior or participation credit denial proceedings, or criminal prosecution prohibit the release of a prisoner who would have otherwise been

§ 2932

released, and the prisoner is found not guilty of the alleged misconduct, the amount of time spent incarcerated, in excess of what the period of incarceration would have been absent the alleged misbehavior, shall be deducted from the prisoner's parole period. (Amended by Stats.1977, c. 165, p. —, § 39, urgency, eff. June 29, 1977, operative July 1, 1977.)

§ 3000. Parole; conditions; counseling; convictions of child abuse or neglect; psychological evaluations

The Legislature finds and declares that the period immediately following incarceration is critical to successful reintegration of the offender into society and to positive citizenship. It is in the interest of public safety for the state to provide for the supervision of and surveillance of parolees and to provide educational, vocational, family and personal counseling necessary to assist parolees in the transition between imprisonment and discharge. A sentence pursuant to Section 1168 or 1170 shall include a period of parole, unless waived, as provided in this section. Notwithstanding any provision to the contrary in Article 3 (commencing with Section 3040) of this chapter:

(a) At the expiration of a term of imprisonment of one year and one day, or a term of imprisonment imposed pursuant to Section 1170, or at the expiration of such term as reduced pursuant to Section 2931, if applicable, the inmate shall be released on parole for a period not exceeding three years, unless the board for good cause waives parole and discharges the inmate from custody of the department.

(b) In the case of any inmate sentenced under Section 1168, the period of parole shall not exceed five years in the case of an inmate imprisoned under a life sentence, and shall not exceed three years in the case of an inmate whose prison sentence does not consist of imprisonment under a life sentence, unless in either case the board for good cause waives parole and discharges the inmate from custody of the department. This subdivision shall be also applicable to inmates who committed crimes prior to July 1, 1977, to the extent specified in Section 1170.2.

(c) The board shall consider the request of any inmate regarding the length of his parole and the conditions thereof.

(d) Upon successful completion of parole, or at the end of the maximum statutory period of parole specified for the inmate under subdivision (a) or (b), as the case may be, whichever is earlier, the inmate shall be discharged from custody. The date of the maximum statutory period of parole under this subdivision and subdivisions (a) and (b) shall be computed from the date of initial parole, or July 1, 1977, whichever is later, and shall be a period chronologically determined. Time during which parole is suspended because the prisoner has absconded or has been returned to custody as a parole violator shall not be credited toward such period of parole unless the prisoner is found not guilty of the parole violation. However, in no case, except as provided in Section 3064, may a prisoner sentenced pursuant to Section 1170 be retained under parole supervision or in custody for a period longer than four years from the date of his initial parole, and, except as provided in Section 3064, in no case may a prisoner sentenced pursuant to subdivision (b) of Section 1168 be retained under parole supervision or in custody for a period longer than seven years from the date of his initial parole.

(e) It is not the intent of this section to diminish resources presently allocated to the Department of Corrections for parole functions.

(f) The Department of Corrections shall meet with each inmate at least 30 days prior to his good time release date, unless such release date is within 30 days of July 1, 1977, and shall provide, under guidelines specified by the Community Release Board, the conditions of parole and the length of parole up to the maximum period of time provided by law. The inmate has the right to reconsideration of the length of parole and conditions thereof by the Community Release Board.
(Amended by Stats.1978, c. 582, p. —, § 1.)

§ 3022. Repealed by Stats.1977, c. 165, p. —, § 43.

COUNTY JAILS

§ 4000. Sheriffs as keepers; purposes

The common jails in the several counties of this State are kept by the sheriffs of the counties in which they are respectively situated, and are used as follows:

1. For the detention of persons committed in order to secure their attendance as witnesses in criminal cases;

2. For the detention of persons charged with crime and committed for trial;

3. For the confinement of persons committed for contempt, or upon civil process, or by other authority of law;

4. For the confinement of persons sentenced to imprisonment therein upon a conviction for crime.
(Added by Stats.1941, c. 106, p. 1119, § 15.)

§ 4001. Separation of different classes of prisoners; rooms required

Each county jail must contain a sufficient number of rooms to allow all persons belonging to either one of the following classes to be confined separately and distinctly from persons belonging to either of the other classes:

1. Persons committed on criminal process and detained for trial;

2. Persons already convicted of crime and held under sentence;

3. Persons detained as witnesses or held under civil process, or under an order imposing punishment for a contempt.
(Amended by Stats.1975, c. 592, p. —, § 1.)

§ 4002. Classes of prisoners not to be kept in same room

Persons committed on criminal process and detained for trial, persons convicted and under sentence, and persons committed upon civil process, must not be kept or put in the same room, nor shall male and female prisoners (except husband and wife) sleep, dress or undress, bathe, or perform eliminatory functions in the same room. Nothing in the section shall be construed to impose any requirement upon a county to confine male and female prisoners in the same or an adjoining facility or impose any duty upon a county to establish or maintain programs which involve the joint participation of male and female prisoners.
(Amended by Stats.1975, c. 592, p. —, § 2.)

§ 4003. Receipt for property taken from prisoner

Whenever any weapon or other personal property is taken from an arrested person, it shall be the duty of the desk clerk or other proper officer of any city, county or city and county jail, to which such person is committed for detention, to give a receipt to such person without delay for the property taken.
(Added by Stats.1941, c. 106, p. 1119, § 15.)

§ 4004. Commitment for examination or upon conviction; actual confinement; escape; orders for removal

A prisoner committed to the county jail for examination, or upon conviction for a public offense, must be actually confined in the jail until he is legally discharged; and if he is permitted to go at large out of the jail, except by virtue of a legal order or process, it is an escape; provided, however, that during the pendency of a criminal proceeding, the superior court or an inferior court, as the case may be, before which said proceeding is pending may make a legal order, good cause appearing therefor, for the removal of the prisoner from the county jail in custody of the sheriff. In judicial districts where there is a marshal, the marshal shall maintain custody of such prisoner while he is in the municipal court facility pursuant to such court order. The superior court of the county may make a legal order, good cause appearing therefor, for the removal of prisoners confined in the county jail, after conviction, in the custody of the sheriff.
(Amended by Stats.1968, c. 152, p. 377, § 1.)

§ 4004.5. City facilities for prisoners held for examination or during trial

A city may furnish facilities to be used for holding prisoners held for examination or during trial, without cost to the county or upon such terms as may be agreed upon by the governing body of such city and the board of supervisors, and the marshal or constable may keep such prisoners in their custody in such city jail.
(Added by Stats.1953, c. 1762, p. 3520, § 1.)

§ 4005. Prisoners of United States

The sheriff must receive, and keep in the county jail, any prisoner committed thereto by process or order issued under the authority of the United States, until he is discharged according to law, as if he had been committed under process issued under the authority of this State; provision being made by the United States for the support of such prisoner.
(Added by Stats.1941, c. 106, p. 1120, § 15.)

§ 4006. Prisoners of United States; safekeeping

A sheriff, to whose custody a prisoner is committed as provided in the last section, is answerable for his safekeeping in the courts of the United States, according to the laws thereof.
(Added by Stats.1941, c. 106, p. 1120, § 15.)

§ 4007. Use of jail in contiguous county; grounds; transfer of prisoner to state prison; grounds; notification of attorney general

When there is no jail in the county, or when the jail becomes unfit or unsafe for the confinement of prisoners, the judge of the superior court may, by a written order filed with the county clerk, designate the jail of a contiguous county for the confinement of the prisoners of his county, or of any of them, and may at any time modify or vacate such order.

When there are any reasonable grounds to believe that a prisoner may be forcibly removed from a county jail the sheriff may remove such prisoner to any California state prison for safekeeping and it is hereby made the duty of the warden of such prison to accept and detain such prisoner in his custody until his removal is ordered by the superior court of the county from which he was delivered. Immediately upon receiving such prisoner the warden shall advise the Attorney General of that fact in writing.

When a county prisoner requires medical treatment necessitating hospitalization which cannot be provided at the county jail or county hospital because of lack of adequate detention facilities, or when, because of his past or present behavior, such prisoner presents a serious custodial problem, with the consent of the Director of Corrections, the judge of the superior court may, upon request of the county sheriff, by a written order filed with the county clerk, designate, for the confinement of such prisoner, the nearest prison or correctional facility of this state which would be able to provide the necessary medical treatment or secure confinement of such prisoner, and may at any time modify or vacate such order. The rate of compensation for such medical treatment or confinement within a California state prison or correctional facility shall be established by the Department of Corrections of this state and shall be a charge against the county making the request for such treatment and confinement.

When there are any reasonable grounds to believe that there are prisoners in a county jail who are acting in concert and are likely to be a threat to other persons in the facility, or are likely to cause substantial damage to the facility, with the consent of the Director of Corrections, the judge of the superior court may, upon request of the county sheriff, by a written order filed with the county clerk, designate for the confinement of such persons the nearest state prison or correctional facility of the state which would, subject to space available, be able to secure confinement of such prisoners. The court shall immediately calendar the matter for a hearing to determine if the order shall continue or be rescinded. Such hearing shall be held within 48 hours of the initial order or the next judicial day, whichever occurs later. At such hearing, the prisoner shall be entitled to be present and to be represented by counsel. The court may at any time modify or vacate such order. The rate of compensation for such confinement within a California state prison or correctional facility shall be established by the Department of Corrections and shall be a charge against the county making the request for such confinement.
(Amended by Stats.1978, c. 837, p. —, §§ 1, 2.)

§ 4008. Use of jail of contiguous county; receipt of prisoners; duties of sheriff

A copy of the appointment, certified by the county clerk, must be served on the sheriff or keeper of the jail designated, who must receive into his jail all prisoners authorized to be confined therein, pursuant to the last section, and who is responsible for the safekeeping of the persons so committed, in the same manner and to the same extent as if he were sheriff to the county for whose use his jail is designated, and with respect to the persons so committed he is deemed the sheriff of the county from which they were removed.
(Added by Stats.1941, c. 106, p. 1120, § 15.)

§ 4009. Use of jail in contiguous county; revocation of order

When a jail is erected in a county for the use of which the designation was made, or its jail is rendered fit and safe for the confinement of prisoners, the judge of the superior court of that county must, by a written revocation, filed with the county clerk thereof, declare that the necessity for the designation has ceased, and that it is revoked.
(Added by Stats.1941, c. 106, p. 1120, § 15.)

§ 4010. Use of jail in contiguous county; revocation of order; removal of prisoners to proper jail

The county clerk must immediately serve a copy of the revocation upon the sheriff of the county, who must thereupon remove the prisoners to the jail of the county from which the removal was had.
(Added by Stats.1941, c. 106, p. 1120, § 15.)

§ 4011. Removal of prisoners for hospitalization; guards; costs

(a) When it is made to appear to a judge of superior court by affidavit of the sheriff or district attorney and oral testimony that a prisoner confined in any city or county jail requires medical or surgical treatment necessitating hospitalization, which treatment cannot be furnished or supplied at such city or county jail, the court in its discretion may order the removal of such person or persons from such city or county jail to the county hospital in such county; provided, if there is no county hospital in such county, then to any hospital designated by such court; and it shall be the duty of the sheriff to maintain the necessary guards, who may be private security guards, for the safekeeping of such prisoner, the expense of which shall be a charge against the county.

(b) The cost of such medical services and such hospital care and treatment shall be charged against the county subject to subdivisions (c) and (d), in the case of a prisoner in or taken from the county jail, or against the city in the case of a prisoner in or taken from the city jail, and the city or county may recover the same by appropriate action from the person so served or cared for, or any person or agency responsible for his care and maintenance. If the prisoner is in the county jail under contract with a city or under some other arrangement with the city to keep the city prisoner in the county jail, then the city shall be charged, subject to subdivisions (c) and (d), for the prisoner's care and maintenance with the same right of recovery against any responsible person or any other agency.

(c) When such prisoner is poor and indigent the cost of such medical services and such hospital care and treatment shall, in the case of persons removed from the city jail be paid out of the general fund of such city, and in the case of persons removed from the county jail to a hospital other than a county hospital, such cost shall be paid out of the general fund of such county or city and county. In the case of city jail prisoners removed to the county hospital, the cost of such hospital care and treatment to be paid by the city to the county, shall be the rate per day fixed by the board of supervisors of such county. Such board of supervisors may, but need not, fix different rates for different classes of patients, or for different wards, and any and all such rates may be changed by such board of supervisors at any time, but shall at all times approximate as nearly as may be, the average actual cost to the county of such hospital care and treatment either in such wards or for such classes of patients or otherwise.

(d) In the event such prisoner is financially able to pay for his care, support and maintenance, the medical superintendent of such hospital other than a county hospital may, with the approval of such judge of the superior court, enter into a special agreement with such person, or with his relatives or friends, for his care, support, maintenance, and other hospital expenses.

Any prisoner may decline such care or treatment and provide other care and treatment for himself at his own expense.
(Amended by Stats.1974, c. 505, p. 1181, § 1.)

§ 4011.5. Removal of prisoners; hospitalization; emergencies

Whenever it appears to a sheriff or jailer that a prisoner in a county jail or a city jail under his charge is in need of immediate medical or hospital care, and that the health and welfare of the prisoner will be injuriously affected unless he is forthwith removed to a hospital, the sheriff or jailer may authorize the immediate removal of the prisoner under guard to a hospital, without first obtaining a court order as provided in Section 4011. In any such case, however, if the condition of the prisoner prevents his return to the jail within 48 hours from the time of his removal, the sheriff or jailer shall apply to a judge of the superior court for an order authorizing the continued absence of the prisoner from the jail in the manner provided in Section 4011. The provisions of Section 4011 governing the cost of medical and hospital care of prisoners and the liability therefor, shall apply to the cost of, and the liability for, medical or hospital care of prisoners removed from jail pursuant to this section.
(Added by Stats.1945, c. 489, p. 988, § 1.)

§ 4011.9. Hospitalized prisoner; felony arrest, charge or conviction; removal of guard

Notwithstanding the provisions of Sections 4011 and 4011.5, when it appears that the prisoner in need of medical or surgical treatment necessitating hospitalization or in need of medical or hospital care was arrested for, charged with, or convicted of an offense constituting a felony, the court in proceedings under Section 4011 or the sheriff or jailer in action taken under Section 4011.5 may direct that the guard be removed from the prisoner while he is in the hospital,

§ 4011.9

if it reasonably appears that the prisoner is physically unable to effectuate an escape or the prisoner does not constitute a danger to life or property.
(Added by Stats.1976, c. 80, p. —, § 1.)

§ 4016.5. Parolee detention; reimbursement of county

When an alleged parole violator is detained in a county jail pursuant to an order of the Adult Authority under the authority granted by Section 3060 of the Penal Code, or pursuant to an order of the Governor under the authority granted by Section 3062, or pursuant to a valid exercise of a state parole officer's peace officer powers as specified in Section 830.5 of the Penal Code when such detention relates to violation of the conditions of parole and not a new criminal charge, the county shall be reimbursed for the costs of such detention by the Department of Corrections. Such reimbursement shall be expended for maintenance, upkeep, and improvement of jail conditions, facilities, and services. Before the county is reimbursed by the department, the total amount of all charges against that county authorized by law for services rendered by the department shall be first deducted from the gross amount of reimbursement authorized by this section. Such net reimbursement shall be calculated and paid monthly by the department. The department shall withhold all or part of such net reimbursement to a county whose jail facility or facilities do not conform to minimum standards for local detention facilities as authorized by Section 6030 of the Penal Code.
(Formerly § 4016. Renumbered § 4016.5 and amended by Stats.1976, c. 1079, p. —, § 57.)

§ 4018.6. Temporary removal for family emergencies or for preparation for return to community; limitation; reimbursement of county expenses

The sheriff of the county may authorize the temporary removal under custody or temporary release without custody of any inmate of the county jail, honor farm, or other detention facility for family emergencies or for purposes preparatory to his return to the community, if the sheriff concludes that such inmate is a fit subject therefor. Any such temporary removal shall not be for a period of more than three days. When an inmate is released for purposes preparatory to his return to the community, the sheriff may require the inmate to reimburse the county, in whole or in part, for expenses incurred by the county in connection therewith.
(Added by Stats.1975, c. 695, p. 1654, § 1.)

§ 4019. Application of section to certain prisoners; work performance and good behavior time credit

(a) The provisions of this section shall apply in all of the following cases:

(1) When a prisoner is confined in or committed to a county jail, industrial farm, or road camp, or any city jail, industrial farm, or road camp, including all days of custody from the date of arrest to the date on which the serving of the sentence commences, under a judgment of imprisonment, or a fine and imprisonment until the fine is paid in a criminal action or proceeding.

(2) When a prisoner is confined in or committed to the county jail, industrial farm, or road camp or any city jail, industrial farm, or road camp as a condition of probation after suspension of imposition of a sentence or suspension of execution of sentence, in a criminal action or proceeding.

(3) When a prisoner is confined in or committed to the county jail, industrial farm, or road camp or any city jail, industrial farm, or road camp for a definite period of time for contempt pursuant to a proceeding, other than a criminal action or proceeding.

(b) Subject to the provisions of subdivision (d), for each six-day period in which a prisoner is committed to a facility as specified in this section, one day shall be deducted from his period of confinement unless it appears by the record that the prisoner has refused to satisfactorily perform labor as assigned by the sheriff, chief of police, or superintendent of an industrial farm or road camp.

(c) For each six-day period in which a prisoner is committed to a facility as specified in this section, one day shall be deducted from his period of confinement unless it appears by the record that the prisoner has not satisfactorily complied with the reasonable rules and regulations established by the sheriff, chief of police, or superintendent of an industrial farm or road camp.

(d) Nothing in this section shall be construed to require the sheriff, chief of police, or superintendent of an industrial farm or road camp to assign labor to a prisoner if it appears from the record that the prisoner has refused to satisfactorily perform labor as assigned or that the prisoner has not satisfactorily complied with the reasonable rules and regulations of the sheriff, chief of police, or superintendent of any industrial farm or road camp.

(e) No deduction may be made under this section unless the person is committed for a period of six days or longer.
(Amended by Stats.1978, c. 1218, p. —, § 1.)

§ 4019.3. Credit for work

The board of supervisors may provide that each prisoner confined in or committed to a county jail shall be credited with a sum not to exceed two dollars ($2) for each eight hours of work done by him in such county jail.
(Amended by Stats.1975, c. 350, p. 797, § 1.)

§ 4021. Counties without female deputy sheriff; appointment of woman custodian; searches of or entrance into room occupied by person of opposite sex.

Whenever any female prisoner or prisoners are confined in any county jail in the state, and no regular jail female deputy sheriff has been appointed, there shall be designated by the sheriff some suitable woman who shall have immediate care of such female prisoner or prisoners, and who shall be paid out of the general fund of the county upon claims to be presented and allowed by the board of supervisors as other claims against the county. It shall be unlawful for any officer or jailer to search the person of any prisoner of the opposite sex, or to enter into the room or cell occupied by any prisoner of the opposite sex, except in the company of a deputy sheriff of the same sex as the prisoner.
(Amended by Stats.1975, c. 592, p. 1309, § 3.)

§ 4023.5. Female prisoners; use of materials for personal hygiene and birth control measures; family planning services; furnishing

(a) Any female confined in any local detention facility shall upon her request be allowed to continue to use materials necessary for (1) personal hygiene with regard to her menstrual cycle and reproductive system and (2) birth control measures as prescribed by her physician.

(b) Each and every female confined in any local detention facility shall be furnished by the county with information and education regarding the availability of family planning services.

(c) Family planning services shall be offered to each and every woman inmate at least 60 days prior to a scheduled release date. Upon request any woman inmate shall be furnished by the county with the services of a licensed physician or she shall be furnished by the county or by any other agency which contracts with the county with services necessary to meet her family planning needs at the time of her release.

(d) For the purposes of this section, "local detention facility" means any city, county, or regional facility used for the confinement of any female prisoner for more than 24 hours.
(Amended by Stats.1975, c. 1146, p. 2831, § 2.)

§ 4131.5. Battery upon person not confined or sentenced to same facility; punishment

Every person confined in, sentenced to, or serving a sentence in, a city, or county jail, industrial farm, or industrial road camp in this state, who commits a battery upon the person of an individual who is not himself a person confined or sentenced therein, is guilty of a public offense and is punishable by imprisonment in a state prison for not more than three years or in a county jail for not more than one year.
(Added by Stats.1976, c. 1120, p. —, § 1.)

OFFENSES BY PRISONERS

§ 4500. Assault with means of force likely to produce great bodily injury

Every person undergoing a life sentence in a state prison of this state, who, with malice aforethought, commits an assault upon the person of another with a deadly weapon or instrument, or by any means of force likely to produce great bodily injury is punishable with death or life imprisonment without possibility of parole. The penalty shall be determined pursuant to the provisions of Sections 190.3 and 190.4; however, in cases in which the person subjected to such assault does not die within a year and a day after such assault as a proximate result thereof, the punishment shall be imprisonment in the state prison for life without the possibility of parole for nine years.

For the purpose of computing the days elapsed between the commission of the assault and the death of the person assaulted, the whole of the day on which the assault was committed shall be counted as the first day.

Nothing in this section shall be construed to prohibit the application of this section when the assault was committed outside the walls of any prison if the person committing the assault was undergoing a life sentence in a state prison at the time of the commission of the assault and was not on parole.
(Amended by Stats.1977, c. 316, p. —, § 21, urgency, eff. Aug. 11, 1977.)

§ 4501. Assault with deadly weapon, etc.; prisoner for less than life; punishment

Every person confined in a state prison of this state except one undergoing a life sentence who commits an assault upon the person of another with a deadly weapon or instrument, or by any means of force likely to produce great bodily injury, shall be guilty of a felony and shall be imprisoned in the state prison for two, four, or six years to be served consecutively.
(Amended by Stats.1978, c. 579, p. —, § 33.)

§ 4501.5. Battery; prisoner for less than life; punishment

Every person confined in a state prison of this state who commits a battery upon the person of any individual who is not himself a person confined therein shall be guilty of a felony and shall be imprisoned in the state prison for two, three, or four years, to be served consecutively.
(Amended by Stats.1978, c. 579, p. —, § 34.)

§ 4502. Possession of deadly weapon; punishment

Every person confined in a state prison or who, while being conveyed to or from any state prison or while at any prison road camp, prison forestry camp, or other prison camps or prison farms or while being conveyed to or from any such place or while under the custody of prison officials, officers or employees, possesses or carries upon his person or has under his custody or control any instrument or weapon of the kind commonly known as a blackjack, slungshot, billy, sandclub, sandbag, or metal knuckles or any explosive substance or any dirk or dagger or sharp instrument, or any pistol, revolver or other firearm, is guilty of a felony and shall be punishable by imprisonment in a state prison for two, three, or four years to be served consecutively.
(Amended by Stats.1978, c. 579, p. —, § 35.)

§ 4503. Holding of hostages; offense; punishment

Any person confined therein who holds as hostage any person within any prison or facility under the jurisdiction of the Director of Corrections, or who by force or threat of force holds any person or persons against their will in defiance of official orders within any such prison or facility, shall be guilty of a felony and shall be imprisoned in the state prison for three, five, or seven years to be served consecutively.
(Amended by Stats.1978, c. 579, p. —, § 36.)

§ 4533. Keeper or other officer permitting; punishment

Every keeper of a prison, sheriff, deputy sheriff, constable, or jailor, or person employed as a guard, who fraudulently contrives, procures, aids, connives at, or voluntarily permits the escape of any prisoner in custody, is punishable by imprisonment in the state prison, and fine not exceeding ten thousand dollars ($10,000).
(Amended by Stats.1976, c. 1139, p. —, § 290, operative July 1, 1977.)

§ 4535. Carrying or sending into prison or jail things useful to aid escape; punishment

Every person who carries or sends into a prison or jail anything useful to aid a prisoner or inmate in making his escape, with intent thereby to facilitate the escape of any prisoner or inmate confined therein, is guilty of a felony.
(Amended by Stats.1976, c. 1139, p. —, § 291, operative July 1, 1977.)

§ 4550. Punishment

Every person who rescues or attempts to rescue, or aids another person in rescuing or attempting to rescue any prisoner from any prison, or prison road camp or any jail or county road camp, or from any officer or person having him in lawful custody, is punishable as follows:

1. If such prisoner was in custody upon a conviction of a felony punishable with death: by imprisonment in the state prison for two, three or four years;

2. If such prisoner was in custody otherwise than as specified in subsection 1 hereof: by imprisonment in the state prison, or by imprisonment in the county jail not to exceed one year.
(Amended by Stats.1976, c. 1139, p. —, § 292, operative July 1, 1977.)

UNAUTHORIZED COMMUNICATIONS WITH PRISONERS

§ 4570. Communication with prisoner without permission of officer in charge; bringing in or taking out letters, writing, literature, etc.

Every person who, without the permission of the warden or other officer in charge of any State prison, or prison road camp, or prison forestry camp, or other prison camp or prison farm or any other place where prisoners of the State prison are located under the custody of prison officials, officers or employees, or

any jail, or any county road camp in this State, communicates with any prisoner or person detained therein, or brings therein or takes therefrom any letter, writing, literature, or reading matter to or from any prisoner or person confined therein, is guilty of a misdemeanor.
(Amended by Stats.1943, c. 108, p. 808, § 1.)

§ 4570.5. False identification to secure admission to prison, jail, etc.

Every person who falsely identifies himself either verbally or by presenting any fraudulent written instrument to prison officials, officers, or employees of any state prison, prison road camp, or prison forestry camp, or other prison camp or prison farm, or any jail, or any county industrial farm, or any county road camp, for the purpose of securing admission to the premises or grounds of any such prison, camp, farm, or jail, and such person would not otherwise qualify for admission, is guilty of a misdemeanor.
(Added by Stats.1969, c. 424, p. 955, § 1.)

§ 4571. Ex-convict coming upon prison or camp grounds or adjacent lands

Every person who, having been previously convicted of a felony and confined in any State prison in this State, without the consent of the warden or other officer in charge of any State prison or prison road camp, or prison forestry camp, or other prison camp or prison farm or any other place where prisoners of the State prison are located under the custody of prison officials, officers or employees, or any jail or any county road camp in this State, comes upon the grounds of any such institution, or lands belonging or adjacent thereto, is guilty of a felony.
(Amended by Stats.1943, c. 108, p. 808, § 2.)

§ 4572. Tramps, vagrants, and known associates of thieves coming upon prison or camp grounds or adjacent lands and communicating with inmates

Any tramp, vagrant, or person who is a known associate of thieves, who comes into any State prison or prison road camp, or prison forestry camp, or other prison camp or prison farm or any other place where prisoners of the State prison are located under the custody of prison officials, officers or employees, or any jail or any county road camp in this State, or upon the grounds belonging or adjacent thereto, and communicates with any of the inmates of such institution, or place, without the consent of the supervising officer or other person having charge thereof, is guilty of a misdemeanor.
(Amended by Stats.1943, c. 108, p. 808, § 3.)

§ 4573. Narcotics or alcoholic beverages; bringing into prison, camp, jail, etc.

Except when otherwise authorized by law, or when authorized by the person in charge of the prison or other institution referred to in this section or by an officer of the institution empowered by the person in charge of the institution to give such authorization, any person, who knowingly brings or sends into, or knowingly assists in bringing into, or sending into, any state prison, prison road camp, prison forestry camp, or other prison camp or prison farm or any other place where prisoners of the state are located under the custody of prison officials, officers or employees, or into any county, city and county, or city jail, road camp, farm or other place where prisoners or inmates are located under custody of any sheriff, chief of police, peace officer, probation officer or employees, or within the grounds belonging to any such institution, any narcotic, the possession of which is prohibited by Division 10 (commencing with Section 11000) of the Health and Safety Code, any device, contrivance, instrument, or paraphernalia intended to be used for unlawfully injecting or consuming a narcotic, or any alcoholic beverage, is guilty of a felony.
(Amended by Stats.1970, c. 848, p. 1580, § 1.)

§ 4573.5. Unauthorized drugs; bringing into prison, camp, jail, etc.

Any person who knowingly brings into any state prison or other institution under the jurisdiction of the Department of Corrections, or into any prison camp, prison farm, or any other place where prisoners or inmates of such institutions are located under the custody of prison or institution officials, officers, or employees, or into any county, city and county or city jail, road camp, farm or any other institution or place where prisoners or inmates are being held under the custody of any sheriff, chief of police, peace officer, probation officer, or employees, or within the grounds belonging to any such institution or place, any drugs, other than narcotics, in any manner, shape, form, dispenser, or container, or any device, contrivance, instrument, or paraphernalia intended to be used for unlawfully injecting or consuming any drug other than narcotics, without having authority so to do by the rules of the Department of Correc-

§ 4573.5

tions, the rules of the prison, institution, camp, farm, place, or jail, or by the specific authorization of the warden, superintendent, jailer, or other person in charge of the prison, jail, institution, camp, farm, or place, is guilty of a felony.
(Amended by Stats.1970, c. 848, p. 1581, § 2.)

§ 4574. Firearms, deadly weapons or explosives; bringing into prison, camp, jail, etc.; punishment

Except when otherwise authorized by law, or when authorized by the person in charge of the prison or other institution referred to in this section or by an officer of the institution empowered by the person in charge of the institution to give such authorization, any person, who knowingly brings or sends into, or knowingly assists in bringing into, or sending into, any state prison or prison road camp or prison forestry camp, or other prison camp or prison farm or any other place where prisoners of the state prison are located under the custody of prison officials, officers or employees, or any jail or any county road camp in this state, or within the grounds belonging or adjacent to any such institution, any firearms, deadly weapons or explosives, and any person who, while lawfully confined in a jail or county road camp possesses therein any firearm, deadly weapon, or explosive, is guilty of a felony and punishable by imprisonment in the state prison for two, three, or four years.
(Amended by Stats.1978, c. 579, p. —, § 39.)

§ 4600. Punishment

Every person who willfully and intentionally breaks down, pulls down, or otherwise destroys or injures any jail, prison, or any public property in any jail or prison, is punishable by fine not exceeding ten thousand dollars ($10,000), and by imprisonment in the state prison, except that where the damage or injury to any city, city and county or county jail property is determined to be two hundred dollars ($200) or less, he is guilty of a misdemeanor.
(Amended by Stats.1978, c. 1186, p. —, § 2.)

POWERS AND DUTIES OF GOVERNOR

§ 4800. Constitutional authority

The general authority to grant reprieves, pardons and commutations of sentence is conferred upon the Governor by Section 8 of Article V of the Constitution of the State of California.
(Amended by Stats.1969, c. 43, p. 155, § 3.)

§ 4801. Report of names of deserving prisoners

The Community Release Board may report to the Governor from time to time the names of any and all persons imprisoned in any state prison who, in its judgment, ought to have a commutation of sentence or be pardoned and set at liberty on account of good conduct, or unusual term of sentence, or any other cause which, in their opinion, should entitle the prisoner to a pardon or commutation of sentence.
(Amended by Stats.1977, c. 165, p. —, § 65, urgency, eff. June 29, 1977, operative July 1, 1977.)

§ 4802. Application of second offender; reference

In the case of a person twice convicted of felony, the application for pardon or commutation of sentence shall be made directly to the Governor, who shall transmit all papers and documents relied upon in support of and in opposition to the application to the Community Release Board.
(Amended by Stats.1977, c. 165, p. —, § 66, urgency, eff. June 29, 1977, operative July 1, 1977.)

§ 4803. Statement of facts; recommendation of trial judge or district attorney

When an application is made to the Governor for pardon or commutation of sentence, or when an application has been referred to the Community Release Board, he or it may require the judge of the court before which the conviction was had, or the district attorney by whom the action was prosecuted, to furnish him or it, without delay, with a summarized statement of the facts proved on the trial, and of any other facts having reference to the propriety of granting or refusing said application, together with his recommendation for or against the granting of the same and his reason for such recommendation.
(Amended by Stats.1977, c. 165, p. —, § 67, urgency, eff. June 29, 1977, operative July 1, 1977.)

§ 4804. Notice to district attorney of application; proof of service

At least 10 days before the Governor acts upon an application for a pardon, written notice of the intention to apply therefor, signed by the person applying, must be served upon the district attorney of the county where the conviction was had, and proof, by affidavit, of the service must be presented to the Governor.
(Added by Stats.1941, c. 106, p. 1127, § 15.)

§ 4806. Notice of application dispensed with; circumstances

The provisions of Section 4804 are not applicable:

1. When there is imminent danger of the death of the person convicted or imprisoned;

2. When the term of imprisonment of the applicant is within 10 days of its expiration.
(Amended by Stats.1969, c. 597, p. 1228, § 1.)

§ 4807. Report to legislature

The Governor must, at the beginning of every session, communicate to the Legislature in addition to each case of reprieve, or pardon, as provided in Article V, Section 8, of the Constitution of California, each commutation, stating the name of the person convicted, the crime of which he was convicted, the sentence and its date, the date of the commutation and the reason for granting the same.
(Amended by Stats.1969, c. 597, p. 1228, § 2.)

§ 4807.2. Application; statement of compensation paid for procuring or assisting in procuring pardon or commutation

Every application for pardon or commutation of sentence shall be accompanied by a full statement of any compensation being paid to any person for procuring or assisting in procuring the pardon or commutation or the pardon or commutation shall be denied.
(Added by Stats.1943, c. 943, p. 2815, § 2.)

§ 4807.3. Compensation or gift for procuring or assisting in procuring pardon or commutation; statement by recipient; time for filing; failure to file; offense

Every person who receives or agrees to receive any compensation or who receives any gift for procuring or assisting in procuring a pardon or commutation of sentence for any applicant must file with the Governor a full statement of the amount and character of such compensation or gift within 10 days of the receipt thereof. Any failure to file a full statement as required by this section is a misdemeanor.
(Added by Stats.1943, c. 943, p. 2815, § 3.)

§ 4812. Applications; investigation, report and recommendations; assistance; examination of witnesses; administration of oaths

Upon request of the Governor the Community Release Board shall investigate and report on all applications for reprieves, pardons and commutation of sentence and shall make such recommendations to the Governor with reference thereto as to it may seem advisable. To that end the board shall examine and consider all applications so referred and all transcripts of judicial proceedings and all affidavits or other documents submitted in connection therewith, and shall have power to employ assistants and take testimony and to examine witnesses under oath and to do any and all things necessary to make a full and complete investigation of and concerning all applications referred to it. Members of the board and its administrative officer are, and each of them is, hereby authorized to administer oaths.
(Amended by Stats.1977, c. 165, p. ——, § 69, urgency, eff. June 29, 1977, operative July 1, 1977.)

§ 4813. Applications of second offenders; recommendation; transmittal of papers

In the case of applications of persons twice convicted of felony, the Community Release Board, after investigation, shall transmit its written recommendation upon such application to the Governor, together with all papers filed in connection with the application.
(Amended by Stats.1977, c. 165, p. ——, § 70, urgency, eff. June 29, 1977, operative July 1, 1977.)

§ 4850. Referrals to supreme court

No application which has not received a recommendation from the Community Release Board favorable to the applicant shall be forwarded to the Clerk of the Supreme Court, unless the Governor, notwithstanding the fact that the board has failed to make a recommendation favorable to the applicant, especially refers an application to the justices for their recommendation.
(Amended by Stats.1977, c. 165, p. ——, § 72, urgency, eff. June 29, 1977, operative July 1, 1977.)

§ 4852.01. Petition for certificate of rehabilitation and pardon; application of chapter

(a) Any person convicted of a felony who has been released from a state prison or other state penal institution or agency in California, whether discharged on completion of the term for which he was sentenced or released on parole prior to May 13, 1943, who has not been incarcerated in a state prison or other state penal institution or agency since his release and who presents satisfactory evidence of a three-year residence in this state immediately prior to the filing of the petition for a certificate of rehabilitation and pardon provided for by this chap-

§ 4852.01

ter, may file such petition pursuant to the provisions of this chapter.

(b) Any person convicted of a felony who, on May 13, 1943, was confined in a state prison or other institution or agency to which he was committed and any person convicted of a felony after that date who is committed to a state prison or other institution or agency may file a petition for a certificate of rehabilitation and pardon pursuant to the provisions of this chapter.

(c) Any person convicted of a felony the accusatory pleading of which has been dismissed pursuant to Section 1203.4 may file a petition for certificate of rehabilitation and pardon pursuant to the provisions of this chapter; provided the petitioner has not been incarcerated in any prison, jail, detention facility or other penal institution or agency since the dismissal of the accusatory pleading and is not on probation for the commission of any other felony, and petitioner presents satisfactory evidence of three years residence in this state prior to the filing of the petition.

(d) This chapter shall not apply to persons convicted of misdemeanors; to persons serving a mandatory life parole; to persons committed under death sentences; or to persons in the military service.
(Amended by Stats.1976, c. 434, p. —, § 2.)

§ 4852.03. Period of rehabilitation; determination of period

The period of rehabilitation shall begin to run upon the discharge of the petitioner from custody due to his completion of the term to which he was sentenced or upon his release on parole or probation, whichever is sooner. For purposes of this chapter, the period of rehabilitation shall constitute three years' residence in this state, plus a period of time determined by the following rules:

(1) To the three years there shall be added 30 days for each year of the term prescribed by statute as the maximum penalty of imprisonment for the crime of which the petitioner was convicted. When the maximum term includes the fractional part of a year, the period of rehabilitation shall be extended by a proportional part of the 30-day period.

(2) For the purposes of this chapter, crimes with maximum penalties of life imprisonment shall be regarded as carrying a maximum penalty of imprisonment for 50 years.

(3) Where the petitioner is convicted of multiple crimes, the maximum penalty for the purpose of computing the period of rehabilitation shall be determined as follows: (a) if the sentences are made to run concurrently, the greatest maximum penalty prescribed by statute for any of such crimes shall constitute the maximum penalty; (b) if the sentences are made to run consecutively, the sum of the maximum penalties prescribed by statute for all such crimes shall constitute the maximum penalty, but in no case shall the maximum penalty exceed the period prescribed for life imprisonment under subparagraph (2) of this section. The trial court hearing the application for the certificate of rehabilitation may, if the defendant was ordered to serve consecutive sentences, order that his statutory period of rehabilitation be extended for an additional period of time which when combined with the time already served will not exceed the period prescribed by statute for the sum of the maximum penalties for all such crimes.

(4) Any person who was discharged after completion of his term or was released on parole before May 13, 1943, is not subject to the periods of rehabilitation set forth in these rules.

Unless and until the period of rehabilitation, as stipulated herein, has passed, the petitioner shall be ineligible to file his petition for a certificate of rehabilitation with the court. Any certificate of rehabilitation which is issued and under which the petitioner has not fulfilled the requirements of this chapter shall be void.

A change of residence within this state does not interrupt the period of rehabilitation prescribed by this section.
(Amended by Stats.1976, c. 434, p. —, § 3.)

§ 4852.05. Conduct during rehabilitation period

During the period of rehabilitation the person shall live an honest and upright life, shall conduct himself with sobriety and industry, shall exhibit a good moral character, and shall conform to and obey the laws of the land.
(Added by Stats.1943, c. 400, p. 1923, § 1.)

§ 4852.06. Petition for ascertainment and declaration of rehabilitation and for certificate; time for filing

Except as provided in subdivision (a) of Section 4852.01, after the expiration of the minimum period of rehabilitation applicable to him (and, in the case of persons released upon parole or probation, after the termination of parole or probation), each person who

has complied with the requirements of Section 4852.-05 may file in the superior court of the county in which he then resides a petition for ascertainment and declaration of the fact of his rehabilitation and of matters incident thereto, and for a certificate of rehabilitation under this chapter. No such petition shall be filed until and unless the petitioner has continuously resided in this state, after leaving prison, for a period of not less than three years immediately preceding the date of filing the petition.
(Amended by Stats.1976, c. 434, p. —, § 4.)

§ 4852.07. Petition; notice of filing; officials to whom given; notice of time of hearing; time for service

The petitioner shall give notice of the filing of the petition to the district attorney of the county in which the petition is filed, to the district attorney of each county in which the petitioner was convicted of a felony or of a crime the accusatory pleading of which was dismissed pursuant to Section 1203.4, and to the office of the Governor, together with notice of the time of the hearing of the petition, at least 30 days prior to the date set for such hearing.
(Amended by Stats.1976, c. 434, p. —, § 5.)

§ 4852.12. Investigation and report by district attorney

(a) In any proceeding for the ascertainment and declaration of the fact of rehabilitation under this chapter, the court, upon the filing of the application for petition of rehabilitation, may request from the district attorney an investigation of the residence of the petitioner, the criminal record of the petitioner as shown by the records of the Department of Justice, any representation made to the court by the applicant, the conduct of the petitioner during his period of rehabilitation, including all matters mentioned in Section 4852.11, and any other information the court may deem necessary in making its determination. If so requested, the district attorney shall provide the court with a full and complete report of such investigations.

(b) In any proceeding for the ascertainment and declaration of the fact of rehabilitation under this chapter of a person convicted of a crime the accusatory pleading of which has been dismissed pursuant to Section 1203.4, the district attorney, upon request of the court, shall deliver to the court the criminal record of petitioner as shown by the records of the Department of Justice. The district attorney may investigate any representation made to the court by petitioner and may file with the court a report of the investigation including all matters known to the district attorney relating to the conduct and place and duration of residence of the petitioner during the period of rehabilitation and all known violations of law committed by petitioner.
(Amended by Stats.1976, c. 434, p. —, § 7.)

§ 4852.17. Report of certificate of rehabilitation or pardon; rights restored by pardon; exceptions

Whenever a person is issued a certificate of rehabilitation or granted a pardon from the Governor under this chapter, the fact shall be immediately reported to the Department of Justice by the court, Governor, officer, or governmental agency by whose official action the certificate is issued or the pardon granted. The Department of Justice shall immediately record the facts so reported on the former criminal record of the person, and transmit such facts to the Federal Bureau of Investigation at Washington, D. C. When the criminal record is thereafter reported by said department, it shall also report the fact that the person has received a certification of rehabilitation, or pardon, or both.

Whenever a person is granted a full and unconditional pardon by the Governor, based upon a certificate of rehabilitation, the pardon shall entitle the person to exercise thereafter all civil and political rights of citizenship, including but not limited to: (1) the right to vote; (2) the right to own, possess, and keep any type of firearm that may lawfully be owned and possessed by other citizens; except that this right shall not be restored, and Sections 12001 and 12021 of the Penal Code shall apply, if the person was ever convicted of a felony involving the use of a dangerous weapon.
(Amended by Stats.1972, c. 1377, p. 2836, § 75.)

§ 4853. Restoration of rights, privileges and franchises; exceptions

In all cases in which a full pardon has been granted by the Governor of this State or will hereafter be granted by said Governor to a person convicted of an offense to which said pardon applies, it shall operate to restore to such convicted person, all the rights, privileges, and franchises of which he has been deprived in consequence of said conviction or by reason of any matter involved therein; provided, that nothing herein contained shall abridge or impair the power or authority conferred by law on any board or

§ 4853

tribunal to revoke or suspend any such right, privilege or franchise for any act or omission not involved in said conviction; provided further, that nothing in this article shall affect any of the provisions of the Medical Practice Act or the power or authority conferred by law on the Board of Medical Examiners therein, or the power or authority conferred by law upon any board that issues a certificate which permits any person or persons to apply his or their art or profession on the person of another.
(Added by Stats.1941, c. 106, p. 1129, § 15.)

§ 4854. Firearms; restoration of rights; exceptions

In the granting of a pardon to a person, the Governor may provide that such person is entitled to exercise the right to own, possess and keep any type of firearm that may lawfully be owned and possessed by other citizens; except that this right shall not be restored, and Sections 12001 and 12021 of the Penal Code shall apply, if the person was ever convicted of a felony involving the use of a dangerous weapon.
(Added by Stats.1968, c. 878, p. 1668, § 1.)

§ 4900. Claim against state; persons authorized to present; presentation

Any person who, having been convicted of any crime against the State of California amounting to a felony, and having been imprisoned therefor in a State prison of this State shall hereafter be granted a pardon by the Governor of this State for the reason that the crime with which he was charged was either not committed at all or, if committed, was not committed by him, or who, being innocent of the crime with which he was charged for either of the foregoing reasons, shall have served the term or any part thereof for which he was imprisoned, may, under the conditions hereinafter provided, present a claim against the State to the State Board of Control for the pecuniary injury sustained by him through such erroneous conviction and imprisonment.
(Added by Stats.1941, c. 106, p. 1130, § 15.)

§ 4901. Claim against state; formalities; time for presentation

Such claim, accompanied by a statement of the facts constituting the claim, verified in the manner provided for the verification of complaints in civil actions, must be presented by the claimant to the Board of Control within a period of six months after judgment of acquittal or discharge given, or after pardon granted, or after release from imprisonment, and at least four months prior to the next meeting of the Legislature of this State; and no claim not so presented shall be considered by the Board of Control.
(Added by Stats.1941, c. 106, p. 1130, § 15.)

§ 4903. Hearing on claim; proof

On such hearing the claimant shall introduce evidence in support of the claim, and the Attorney General may introduce evidence in opposition thereto. The claimant must prove the facts set forth in the statement constituting the claim, including the fact that the crime with which he was charged was either not committed at all, or, if committed, was not committed by him, the fact that he did not, by any act or omission on his part, either intentionally or negligently, contribute to the bringing about of his arrest or conviction for the crime with which he was charged, and the pecuniary injury sustained by him through his erroneous conviction and imprisonment.
(Added by Stats.1941, c. 106, p. 1130, § 15.)

§ 4904. Report of findings to legislature; recommendation; limitation on amount of recovery

If the evidence shows that the crime with which the claimant was charged was either not committed at all, or, if committed, was not committed by the claimant, and that the claimant did not, by any act or omission either intentionally or negligently, contribute to the bringing about of his arrest or conviction, and that the claimant has sustained pecuniary injury through his erroneous conviction and imprisonment, the Board of Control shall report the facts of the case and its conclusions to the next Legislature of this state, with a recommendation that an appropriation be made by the Legislature for the purpose of indemnifying the claimant for such pecuniary injury; but the amount of the appropriation so recommended shall not exceed in any case, the sum of ten thousand dollars ($10,000).
(Amended by Stats.1969, c. 704, p. 1370, § 1.)

§ 5075. Community release board; members; term; chairman; vacancies

The Community Release Board shall be composed of nine members, each of whom shall be appointed by the Governor, with the advice and consent of the Senate, for a term of four years and until the appointment and qualification of his successor. Members shall be eligible for reappointment. Two of the original appointees shall be persons who were members of the Adult Authority immediately prior to July 1, 1977, and two shall be persons who were members of the Women's Board of Terms and Parole immediately prior to July 1, 1977.

The chairman of the board shall be designated by the Governor from time to time. The chairman shall be the administrative head of the board and shall exercise all duties and functions necessary to insure that the responsibilities of the board are successfully discharged. He shall be the appointing authority for all civil service positions of employment in the board.

The terms of the members shall expire as follows: two on March 15, 1978, two on March 15, 1979, two on March 15, 1980, and three on March 15, 1981. Successor members shall hold office for terms of four years, each term to commence on the expiration date of the term of the predecessor. The Governor shall fill every vacancy for the balance of the unexpired term. The selection of persons and their appointment by the Governor and confirmation by the Senate shall reflect as nearly as possible a cross-section of the racial, sexual, economic, and geographic features of the population of the state.

It is the further intent of this section that the board shall adopt such policies and practices as will permit continuing operations and improvements without any further increase in the number of its members.
(Amended by Stats.1977, c. 2, p. —, § 8, urgency, eff. Dec. 16, 1976, operative July 1, 1977.)

§ 6025. Membership; chairman; term of office; vice chairman; quorum; charges against members; removal

(a) The Board of Corrections shall be composed of 11 members, one of whom shall be the Secretary of the Health and Welfare Agency who shall be designated as the chairman, one of whom shall be the Director of Corrections, one of whom shall be the Director of the Youth Authority, and eight of whom shall be appointed by the Governor after consultation with, and with the advice of, the Secretary of the Health and Welfare Agency, and with the advice and consent of the Senate. There shall be one representative from each of the following categories:

(1) A member of a statewide parole board of this state.

(2) A county sheriff.

(3) A county supervisor or county administrative officer.

(4) A chief probation officer.

(5) An employee of a state correctional facility who is involved in either custody or care and treatment.

(6) An administrator of a local community-based correctional program.

(7) Two public members.

(b) Of the members first appointed by the Governor, two shall be appointed for a term of two years, three for a term of three years, and three for a term of four years. The length of the original term to be served by each such member first appointed shall be determined by lot. Their successors shall serve for a term of three years and until appointment and qualification of their successors, each term to commence on the expiration date of the term of the predecessor. The terms of the two persons last appointed as qualified persons, by the Governor with the advice and consent of the Senate, under the provisions of this section as it read prior to January 1, 1977, shall expire on that date.

(c) The board shall select a vice chairman from among its members. Six members of the board shall constitute a quorum.

(d) When the Board of Corrections is hearing charges against any member, the individual concerned shall not sit as a member of the board for the period of hearing of charges and the determination of recommendations to the Governor.

(e) If any appointed member is not in attendance for three consecutive meetings the board shall recommend to the Governor that the member be removed and the Governor shall make a new appointment, with the advice and consent of the Senate, for the remainder of the term.
(Amended by Stats.1976, c. 1237, p. —, § 1.)

§ 6027. Studies in criminology and penology; reports; recommendations

It shall be the duty of the Board of Corrections to make a study of the entire subject of crime, with particular reference to conditions in the State of California, including causes of crime, possible methods of prevention of crime, methods of detection of crime and apprehension of criminals, methods of prosecution of persons accused of crime, and the entire subject of penology, including standards and training for correctional personnel, and to report its findings, its conclusions and recommendations to the Governor and the Legislature at such times as they may require.
(Amended by Stats.1976, c. 1237, p. —, § 3.)

§ 6030. Local detention facilities; establishment of standards

(a) The Board of Corrections shall establish minimum standards for local detention facilities by July 1, 1972. The Board of Corrections shall review such standards biennially and make any appropriate revisions.

(b) The standards shall include, but not be limited to, the following: health and sanitary conditions, fire and life safety, security, rehabilitation programs, recreation, treatment of persons confined in local detention facilities, and personnel training.

(c) Such standards shall require that at least one person on duty at the facility is knowledgeable in the area of fire and life safety procedures.

(d) In establishing minimum standards, the Board of Corrections shall seek the advice of the following:

(1) For health and sanitary conditions:

The State Department of Health Services, physicians, psychiatrists, local public health officials, and other interested persons.

(2) For fire and life safety:

The State Fire Marshal, local fire officials, and other interested persons.

(3) For security, rehabilitation programs, recreation, and treatment of persons confined in local detention facilities:

The Department of Corrections, the Department of the Youth Authority, local juvenile justice commissions, local correction officials, experts in criminology and penology, and other interested persons.

(4) For personnel training:

The Commission on Peace Officer Standards and Training, psychiatrists, experts in criminology and penology, the Department of Corrections, the Department of the Youth Authority, local correctional officials, and other interested persons.
(Amended by Stats.1978, c. 1018, p. —, § 2.)

§ 6031.1. Biennial inspections; scope

Inspections of local detention facilities shall be made biennially. Inspections shall include, but not be limited to, the following:

(a) Health and safety inspections conducted pursuant to Section 459 of the Health and Safety Code.

(b) Fire suppression preplanning inspections by the local fire department.

(c) Security, rehabilitation programs, recreation, treatment of persons confined in local detention facilities, and personnel training by the staff of the Board of Corrections.

Reports of each facility's biennial inspection shall be furnished to the official in charge of the local detention facility, the local governing body, the grand jury, and the presiding or sole judge of the superior court in the county where the detention facility is located. Such reports shall set forth the areas wherein the local detention facility has complied and has failed to comply with the minimum standards established pursuant to Section 6030.
(Amended by Stats.1978, c. 1018, p. —, § 3.)

§ 6031.2. Inspection reports

The Board of Corrections shall file with the Legislature by March 31, 1974, and on March 31, in each even-numbered year thereafter, reports of the inspection of those local detention facilities that have not complied with the minimum standards established pursuant to Section 6030. The reports shall specify those areas in which the facility has failed to comply and the estimated cost to the facility necessary to accomplish compliance with the minimum standards.

The reports shall also include an evaluation of standards required of and training provided for correctional personnel. The reports shall specify those areas in which standards and training are, in the board's estimation, inadequate.
(Amended by Stats.1976, c. 1237, p. —, § 4.)

Part 4

PREVENTION OF CRIMES AND APPREHENSION OF CRIMINALS

§ 11050. Assignment of investigators; request

In any crime of statewide importance, the Attorney General may, upon the request of any district attorney, sheriff or chief of police, assign to such officer so requesting, an investigator or investigators for the investigation or detection of crimes, and the apprehension or prosecution of criminals.
(Amended by Stats.1972, c. 1377, p. 2836, § 80.)

§ 11106. Records of fingerprints, weapons transactions, pawned property, etc.; copies of records

In order to assist in the investigation of crime, the arrest and prosecution of criminals and the recovery of lost, stolen, or found property, the Attorney General shall keep and properly file a complete record of all copies of fingerprints, duplicate carbon copies of applications for licenses to carry concealed weapons and dealers' records of sales of deadly weapons, and reports of stolen, lost, found, pledged, or pawned property in any city or county of this State and shall furnish copies of any of such records to the officers mentioned in Section 11105 upon proper application therefor.
(Added by Stats.1953, c. 1385, p. 2966, § 1.)

§ 11107. Reports of sex crimes and of all felonies

Each sheriff or police chief executive shall furnish to the Department of Justice on standard forms approved by the department daily reports of those misdemeanors and felonies required by the Attorney General including but not limited to, forgery, fraud-bunco, bombings, receiving or selling stolen property, safe and commercial burglary, grand theft, child abuse, homicide, threats, and offenses involving lost, stolen, found, pledged or pawned property. These reports shall describe the nature and character of each such crime and note all particular circumstances of each such crime and include all additional or supplemental data. The Attorney General may also require that the report indicate whether or not the submitting agency considers the information to be confidential because it was compiled for the purpose of a criminal investigation of suspected criminal activities. The term "criminal investigation" includes the gathering and maintenance of information pertaining to suspected criminal activity.
(Amended by Stats.1978, c. 1135, p. ——, § 4.)

§ 11108. Reports of lost, stolen, found, pledged or pawned property

Each sheriff or police chief executive shall submit descriptions of serialized property which has been reported stolen, lost, found, recovered or under observation, directly into the appropriate Department of Justice automated property system for firearms, stolen bicycles, stolen vehicles, or other property, as the case may be.

Reports of stolen nonserialized property which has unique characteristics or inscriptions permitting accurate identification shall be sent by each sheriff or police chief executive directly to the Special Services Section of the department by letter or teletype.
(Added by Stats.1978, c. 1135, p. ——, § 6.)

§ 11110. Record on reports of suspected infliction of physical injury upon minor and arrests for and convictions of violation of section 273a

The Department of Justice shall maintain records of all reports of suspected infliction of physical injury upon a minor by other than accidental means and reports of arrest for, and convictions of, violation of Section 273a. On receipt from a city police department, sheriff or district attorney of a copy of a report of suspected infliction of physical injury upon a minor by other than accidental means received from a physician and surgeon, dentist, resident, intern, chiropractor, religious practitioner, registered nurse employed by a public health agency, school, or school district, director of a county welfare department, or any superintendent of schools of any public or private school system or any principal of any public or private school, the department shall transmit to the city police department, sheriff or district attorney, information detailing all previous reports of suspected infliction of physical injury upon the same minor or another minor in the same family by other than accidental means and reports of arrests for, and convictions of violation of Section 273a, concerning the same minor or another minor in the same family.

The department may adopt rules governing record-keeping and reporting under Section 11161.5.
(Amended by Stats.1972, c. 1377, p. 2838, § 83.)

§ 11111. Bicycles; stolen and lost; records; accessibility to law enforcement agencies

The Department of Justice shall maintain records relative to stolen and lost bicycles in the Criminal Justice Information System. Such records shall be accessible to authorized law enforcement agencies through the California Law Enforcement Telecommunications System.
(Amended by Stats.1974, c. 971, p. 2018, § 1.)

§ 11120. Record defined

As used in this article, "record" with respect to any person means the state summary criminal history information as defined in subdivision (a) of Section 11105, maintained under such person's name by the Department of Justice.
(Amended by Stats.1975, c. 1222, p. ——, § 3.)

§ 11122. Submission of application; fee

Any person desiring to examine a record relating to himself shall obtain from the chief of police of the city of his residence, or, if not a resident of a city, from the sheriff of his county of residence, or from the office of the department, an application form furnished by the department which shall require his fingerprints in addition to such other information as the department shall specify. The city or county, as applicable, may fix a reasonable fee for affixing the applicant's fingerprints to the form, and shall retain such fee for deposit in its treasury.
(Amended by Stats.1972, c. 1377, p. 2842, § 86.2.)

§ 11123. Submission of application; fee

The applicant shall submit the completed application directly to the department. The application shall be accompanied by a fee of five dollars ($5) or such higher amount, not to exceed ten dollars ($10) that the department determines equals the costs of processing the application and making a record available for examination. All fees received by the department under this section are hereby appropriated without regard to fiscal years for the support of the Department of Justice in addition to such other funds as may be appropriated therefor by the Legislature.
(Amended by Stats.1972, c. 1377, p. 2842, § 86.3.)

§ 11124. Notice of existence of record; time and place of inspection; examination; authority to take notes

When an application is received by the department, the department shall determine whether a record pertaining to the applicant is maintained. If such record is maintained, the department shall inform the applicant by mail of the existence of the record and shall either specify a time when the record may be examined at a suitable facility of the department or, if the applicant is unable to review the record at the time and place set by the department, authorize the applicant to review the record at any police department or sheriff's office which agrees to make the record available to the applicant. Upon verification of his identity, the applicant shall be allowed to examine the record pertaining to him, or a true copy thereof, for a period not to exceed one hour. The applicant may not retain or reproduce the record, but may make a written summary or notes in his own handwriting.
(Amended by Stats.1975, c. 667, p. —, § 1.)

§ 11125. Application of prisoner; place of examination of record

If the applicant is imprisoned in the state prison or confined in the county jail, his application shall be through the office in charge of records of the prison or jail. Such offices shall follow the provisions of this article applicable to cities and counties with respect to applications and fees. When an application is transmitted to the department pursuant to this section, the department shall make arrangements for the applicant to examine the record at his place of confinement. In all other respects, the provisions of Section 11124 shall govern the examination of the record.
(Amended by Stats.1972, c. 1377, p. 2842, § 86.5.)

§ 11126. Correction of record; written request for clarification; notice to applicant of determination; administrative adjudication; judicial review

(a) If the applicant desires to question the accuracy or completeness of any matter contained in the record, he may submit a written request, to the department in a form established by it. The request shall include a statement of the alleged inaccuracy or incompleteness in the record, and specify any proof or corroboration available. Upon receipt of such request, the department shall forward it to the person or agency which furnished the questioned information. Such person or agency shall, within 30 days of receipt of such written request for clarification, review its information and forward to the department the results of such review.

(b) If such agency concurs in the allegations of inaccurateness or incompleteness in the record, it shall correct its record and shall so inform the department, which shall correct the record accordingly. The department shall inform the applicant of its correction of the record under this subdivision within 30 days.

(c) If such agency denies the allegations of inaccurateness or incompleteness in the record, the matter shall be referred for administrative adjudication in accordance with Chapter 5 (commencing with Section 11500) of Part 1, Division 3, Title 2 of the Government Code for a determination of whether inaccuracy or incompleteness exists in the record. The agency from which the questioned information originated shall be the respondent in the hearing. If an inaccuracy or incompleteness is found in any record, the agency in charge of that record shall be directed to

correct it accordingly. Judicial review of the decision shall be governed by Section 11523 of the Government Code. The applicant shall be informed of the decision within 30 days of its issuance in accordance with Section 11518 of the Government Code.
(Amended by Stats.1972, c. 1377, p. 2843, § 86.6.)

§ 11127. Regulations

The department shall adopt all regulations necessary to carry out the provisions of this article.
(Amended by Stats.1972, c. 1377, p. 2843, § 86.7.)

§ 11140. Definitions

As used in this article:

(a) "Record" means the state summary criminal history information as defined in subdivision (a) of Section 11105, or a copy thereof, maintained under a person's name by the Department of Justice.

(b) "A person authorized by law to receive a record" means any person or public agency authorized by a court, statute, or decisional law to receive a record.
(Amended by Stats.1975, c. 1222, p. ——, § 5.)

§ 11141. Employee of justice department furnishing record or information to unauthorized person; misdemeanor

Any employee of the Department of Justice who knowingly furnishes a record or information obtained from a record to a person who is not authorized by law to receive the record or information is guilty of a misdemeanor.
(Added by Stats.1974, c. 963, p. 2008, § 1.)

§ 11142. Authorized person furnishing record or information to unauthorized person; misdemeanor

Any person authorized by law to receive a record or information obtained from a record who knowingly furnishes the record or information to a person who is not authorized by law to receive the record or information is guilty of a misdemeanor.
(Added by Stats.1974, c. 963, p. 2008, § 1.)

§ 11143. Unauthorized person receiving record or information; misdemeanor

Any person, except those specifically referred to in Section 1070 of the Evidence Code, who, knowing he is not authorized by law to receive a record or information obtained from a record, knowingly buys, receives, or possesses the record or information is guilty of a misdemeanor.
(Added by Stats.1974, c. 963, p. 2009, § 1.)

§ 11144. Dissemination of statistical or research information from a record

(a) It is not a violation of this article to disseminate statistical or research information obtained from a record, provided that the identity of the subject of the record is not disclosed.

(b) It is not a violation of this article to disseminate information obtained from a record for the purpose of assisting in the apprehension of a person wanted in connection with the commission of a crime.

(c) It is not a violation of this article to include information obtained from a record in (1) a transcript or record of a judicial or administrative proceeding or (2) any other public record when the inclusion of the information in the public record is authorized by a court, statute, or decisional law.
(Added by Stats.1974, c. 963, p. 2009, § 1.)

§ 11161.5. Injuries by other than accidental means, sexual molestation or § 273a injuries to minor; report by physician, teacher, social worker, etc.

(a) In any case in which a minor is brought to a physician and surgeon, dentist, resident, intern, podiatrist, chiropractor, marriage, family or child counselor, psychologist, or religious practitioner for diagnosis, examination or treatment, or is under his charge or care, or in any case in which a minor is observed by any registered nurse when in the employ of a public health agency, school, or school district and when no physician and surgeon, resident, or intern is present, by any superintendent, any supervisor of child welfare and attendance, or any certificated pupil personnel employee of any public or private school system or any principal of any public or private school, by any teacher of any public or private school, by any licensed day care worker, by an administrator of a public or private summer day camp or child care center, or by any social worker, by any peace officer, or by any probation officer, and it appears to the physician and surgeon, dentist, resident, intern, podiatrist, chiropractor, marriage, family or child counselor, psychologist, religious practitioner, registered nurse, school superintendent, supervisor of child welfare and attendance, certificated pupil personnel employee, school principal, teacher, licensed day care worker, administrator of a public or private summer day camp or child care center, social worker, peace officer, or probation officer, from observation of the minor that the minor has physical injury or injuries which appear to have been inflicted upon him by other than accidental means by any person, that the minor has been sexually molested, or that any injury prohibited by the terms of Section 273a has been inflicted upon the minor, he shall report such fact by telephone and in writing, within 36 hours, to both the local police authority having jurisdiction and to the juvenile probation department; or, in the alternative, either to the county welfare department, or to the county health department. The report shall state, if known, the name of the minor, his whereabouts and the character and extent of the injuries or molestation.

Whenever it is brought to the attention of a director of a county welfare department or health department that a minor has physical injury or injuries which appear to have been inflicted upon him by other than accidental means by any person, that a minor has been sexually molested, or that any injury prohibited by the terms of Section 273a has been inflicted upon a minor, he shall file a report without delay with the local police authority having jurisdiction and with the juvenile probation department as provided in this section.

No person shall incur any civil or criminal liability as a result of making any report authorized by this section unless it can be proven that a false report was made and the person knew or should have known that the report was false.

No person required to make a report pursuant to this section, nor any person taking photographs at his or her direction, shall incur any civil or criminal liability for taking photographs of a suspected victim of child abuse, or causing photographs to be taken of a suspected victim of child abuse, without parental consent, or for disseminating such photographs with the reports required by this section. However, the provisions of this section shall not be construed to grant immunity from such liability with respect to any other use of such photographs.

Copies of all written reports received by the local police authority shall be forwarded to the Department of Justice. If the records of the Department of Justice maintained pursuant to Section 11110 reveal any reports of suspected infliction of physical injury upon, sexual molestation of, or infliction of any injury prohibited by the terms of Section 273a upon, the same minor or any other minor in the same family by other than accidental means, or if the records reveal any arrest or conviction in other localities for a violation of Section 273a inflicted upon the same minor or any other minor in the same family, or if the records reveal any other pertinent information with respect to the same minor or any other minor in the same family, the local reporting agency and the local juvenile probation department shall be immediately notified of the fact.

Reports and other pertinent information received from the department shall be made available to: any licensed physician and surgeon, dentist, resident, intern, podiatrist, chiropractor, marriage, family or child counselor, psychologist, or religious practitioner with regard to his patient or client; any director of a county welfare department, school superintendent, supervisor of child welfare and attendance, certificated pupil personnel employee, or school principal having a direct interest in the welfare of the minor; and any probation department, juvenile probation department, or agency offering child protective services.

(b) If the minor is a person specified in Section 600 of the Welfare and Institutions Code and the duty of the probation officer has been transferred to the county welfare department pursuant to Section 576.5 of the Welfare and Institutions Code and the report is made to the local police authority having jurisdiction, then the report required by subdivision (a) of this section shall be made to the county welfare department.

(Amended by Stats.1978, c. 136, p. —, § 1.)

§ 11161.6. Injuries by other than accidental means, sexual molestation or § 273a injuries to minor; report by probation officer or other person

In any case in which a minor is observed by a probation officer or any person other than a person described in Section 11161.5 and it appears to the probation officer or person from observation of the minor that the minor has a physical injury or injuries which appear to have been inflicted upon him by other than accidental means by any person, that the minor has been sexually molested, or that any injury prohibited by the terms of Section 273a has been inflicted upon the minor, he may report such injury to the agencies designated in Section 11161.5.

No probation officer or person shall incur any civil or criminal liability as a result of making any report authorized by this section unless it can be proven that a false report was made and the probation officer or

person knew or should have known that the report was false.
(Amended by Stats.1976, c. 242, p. —, § 2.)

§ 11161.7. Injuries inflicted upon minors by other than accidental means; form for report by professional medical personnel

(a) The Department of Justice, in cooperation with the State Office of Child Abuse Prevention, shall adopt and cause to be printed, for dissemination through the various county welfare departments, a form which shall be used by reporting professional medical personnel in making reports required to be made pursuant to Section 11161.5.

(b) Failure by professional medical personnel to use such form in reporting an incident of possible child abuse shall not constitute a violation of Section 11162.
(Amended by Stats.1977, c. 958, p. —, § 2.)

§ 11161.8. Injuries or condition resulting from neglect or abuse; reports

Every person, firm, or corporation conducting any hospital in the state, or the managing agent thereof, or the person managing or in charge of such hospital, or in charge of any ward or part of such hospital, who receives a patient from a health facility, as defined in Section 1250 of the Health and Safety Code, who exhibits a physical injury or condition which, in the opinion of the admitting physician, reasonably appears to be the result of neglect or abuse, shall report such fact by telephone and in writing, within 36 hours, to both the local police authority having jurisdiction and the county health department.

Every physician and surgeon who has under his charge or care any such patient who exhibits a physical injury or condition which reasonably appears to be the result of neglect or abuse shall make such report. The report shall state the character and extent of the physical injury or condition.

No person shall incur any civil or criminal liability as a result of making any report authorized by this section.
(Added by Stats.1975, c. 719, p. 1710, § 1.)

§ 11401. Offense; punishment

Any person who:

1. By spoken or written words or personal conduct advocates, teaches or aids and abets criminal syndicalism or the duty, necessity or propriety of committing crime, sabotage, violence or any unlawful method of terrorism as a means of accomplishing a change in industrial ownership or control, or effecting any political change; or

2. Willfully and deliberately by spoken or written words justifies or attempts to justify criminal syndicalism or the commission or attempt to commit crime, sabotage, violence or unlawful methods of terrorism with intent to approve, advocate or further the doctrine of criminal syndicalism; or

3. Prints, publishes, edits, issues or circulates or publicly displays any book, paper, pamphlet, document, poster or written or printed matter in any other form, containing or carrying written or printed advocacy, teaching, or aid and abetment of, or advising, criminal syndicalism; or

4. Organizes or assists in organizing, or is or knowingly becomes a member of, any organization, society, group or assemblage of persons organized or assembled to advocate, teach or aid and abet criminal syndicalism; or

5. Willfully by personal act or conduct, practices or commits any act advised, advocated, taught or aided and abetted by the doctrine or precept of criminal syndicalism, with intent to accomplish a change in industrial ownership or control, or effecting any political change;

Is guilty of a felony and punishable by imprisonment in the state prison.
(Amended by Stats.1976, c. 1139, p. —, § 301, operative July 1, 1977.)

§ 12001.5. Manufacture, sale or possession of sawed-off shotguns not authorized

Except as provided in Section 12020, nothing in this chapter shall be construed as authorizing the manufacture, importation into the state, keeping for sale, offering for sale, or giving, lending, or possession of any sawed-off shotgun, as defined in Section 12020.
(Amended by Stats.1973, c. 732, p. 1316, § 1.)

§ 12002. Exemptions

(a) Nothing in this chapter prohibits police officers, special police officers, peace officers, or law enforcement officers from carrying any wooden club, baton, or any equipment authorized for the enforcement of law or ordinance in any city or county.

(b) Nothing in this chapter prohibits a uniformed security guard, regularly employed and compensated as such by a person engaged in any lawful business, while actually employed and engaged in protecting

§ 12002

and preserving property or life within the scope of his employment, from carrying any wooden club or baton of a type and substance approved by both the executive director of the California Crime Technological Research Foundation and the Department of Justice, if the uniformed security guard has satisfactorily completed a course of training in the carrying and use of the club or baton which has been approved by the Commission on Peace Officer Standards and Training.

(Amended by Stats.1974, c. 1214, p. 2623, § 4.)

§ 12020. Blackjacks, etc.; manufacture, sale or possession, concealed explosive or dagger; offense; punishment; exemption

(a) Any person in this state who manufactures or causes to be manufactured, imports into the state, keeps for sale, or offers or exposes for sale, or who gives, lends, or possesses any cane gun or wallet gun, any firearm which is not immediately recognizable as a firearm, any ammunition which contains or consists of any flechette darts, any bullet containing or carrying an explosive agent, or any instrument or weapon of the kind commonly known as a blackjack, slungshot, billy, nunchaku, sandclub, sandbag, sawed-off shotgun, or metal knuckles, or who carries concealed upon his person any explosive substance, other than fixed ammunition or who carries concealed upon his person any dirk or dagger, is guilty of a felony, and upon conviction shall be punishable by imprisonment in the county jail not exceeding one year or in a state prison. A bullet containing or carrying an explosive agent is not a destructive device as that term is used in Section 12301.

(b) Subdivision (a) shall not apply to any of the following:

(1) The manufacture, possession, transportation or use, with blank cartridges, of sawed-off shotguns solely as props for motion picture film or television program production when such is authorized by the Department of Justice pursuant to Article 6 (commencing with Section 12095) of this chapter and is not in violation of federal law.

(2) The possession of a nunchaku on the premises of a school which holds a regulatory or business license and teaches the arts of self-defense.

(3) The manufacture of a nunchaku for sale to, or the sale of a nunchaku to, a school which holds a regulatory or business license and teaches the arts of self-defense.

(4) Any antique firearm. For purposes of this section, the term "antique firearm" means any firearm not designed or redesigned for using rim fire or conventional center fire ignition with fixed ammunition and manufactured in or before 1898 (including any matchlock, flintlock, percussion cap, or similar type of ignition system or replica thereof, whether actually manufactured before or after the year 1898) and also any firearm using fixed ammunition manufactured in or before 1898, for which ammunition is no longer manufactured in the United States and is not readily available in the ordinary channels of commercial trade.

(5) Tracer ammunition manufactured for use in shotguns.

(c) Any person in this state who manufactures or causes to be manufactured, imports into the state, keeps for sale or offers or exposes for sale, or who gives, lends, or possesses any instrument, without handles, consisting of a metal plate having three or more radiating points with one or more sharp edges and designed in the shape of a polygon, trefoil, cross, star, diamond, or other geometric shape for use as a weapon for throwing is guilty of a felony and upon conviction shall be punishable by imprisonment in the county jail not exceeding one year or in a state prison.

(d)(1) As used in this section a "sawed-off shotgun" means any firearm (including any revolver) manufactured, designed, or converted to fire shotgun ammunition having a barrel or barrels of less than 18 inches in length, or a rifle having a barrel or barrels of less than 16 inches in length, or any weapon made from a rifle or shotgun (whether by manufacture, alteration, modification, or otherwise) if such weapon as modified has an overall length of less than 26 inches.

(2) As used in this section, a "nunchaku" means an instrument consisting of two or more sticks, clubs, bars or rods to be used as handles, connected by a rope, cord, wire or chain, in the design of a weapon used in connection with the practice of a system of self-defense such as karate.

(3) As used in this section a "wallet gun" means any firearm mounted or enclosed in a case, resembling a wallet, designed to be or capable of being carried in a pocket or purse, if such firearm may be fired while mounted or enclosed in such case.

(4) As used in this section a "cane gun" means any firearm mounted or enclosed in a stick, staff, rod,

crutch or similar device, designed to be or capable of being used as an aid in walking, if such firearm may be fired while mounted or enclosed therein.

(5) As used in this section, a "flechette dart" means a dart, capable of being fired from a firearm, which measures approximately one inch in length, with tail fins which take up five-sixteenths inch of the body.
(Amended by Stats.1978, c. 70, p. —, § 1.)

§ 12020.5. Advertising unlawful weapons prohibited

It shall be unlawful for any person, firm, corporation, or association, in any newspaper, magazine, circular, form letter, or open publication, published, distributed, or circulated in this state, or on any billboard, card, label, or other advertising medium, or by means of any other advertising device, to advertise the sale of any weapon or device whose possession is prohibited by Section 12020.
(Added by Stats.1976, c. 1127, p. —, § 1.)

§ 12021. Concealable firearms; prohibited ownership or possession; offense; punishment; exceptions

(a) Any person who has been convicted of a felony under the laws of the United States, of the State of California, or any other state, government, or country, or who is addicted to the use of any narcotic drug, who owns or has in his possession or under his custody or control any pistol, revolver, or other firearm capable of being concealed upon the person is guilty of a public offense, and shall be punishable by imprisonment in the state prison, or in a county jail not exceeding one year or by a fine not exceeding five hundred dollars ($500), or by both.

(b) Subdivision (a) shall not apply to a person who has been convicted of a felony under the laws of the United States unless:

(1) Conviction of a like offense under California law can only result in imposition of felony punishment; or

(2) The defendant was sentenced to a federal correctional facility for more than 30 days, or received a fine of more than one thousand dollars ($1,000), or received both such punishments.
(Amended by Stats.1976, c. 1139, p. —, § 303, operative July 1, 1977.)

§ 12022. Felony; commission or attempt; armed with a firearm or use of deadly or dangerous weapon; additional punishment

(a) Any person who is armed with a firearm in the commission or attempted commission of a felony shall, upon conviction of such felony or attempted felony, in addition and consecutive to the punishment prescribed for the felony or attempted felony of which he has been convicted, be punished by an additional term of one year, unless such arming is an element of the offense of which he was convicted. This additional term shall apply to any person who is a principal in the commission or attempted commission of a felony if one or more of the principals is armed with a firearm, whether or not such person is personally armed with a firearm.

(b) Any person who personally uses a deadly or dangerous weapon in the commission or attempted commission of a felony shall, upon conviction of such felony or attempted felony, in addition and consecutive to the punishment prescribed for the felony or attempted felony of which he has been convicted, be punished by an additional term of one year, unless use of a deadly or dangerous weapon is an element of the offense of which he was convicted.
(Amended by Stats.1977, c. 165, p. —, § 91, urgency, eff. June 29, 1977, operative July 1, 1977.)

§ 12022.5. Use of firearm in commission of felony or attempt; additional punishment

Any person who personally uses a firearm in the commission or attempted commission of a felony shall, upon conviction of such felony or attempted felony, in addition and consecutive to the punishment prescribed for the felony or attempted felony of which he has been convicted, be punished by an additional term of two years, unless use of a firearm is an element of the offense of which he was convicted.

The additional term provided by this section may be imposed in cases of assault with a deadly weapon under Section 245.
(Amended by Stats.1977, c. 165, p. —, § 92, urgency, eff. June 29, 1977, operative July 1, 1977.)

§ 12025. Carrying weapon concealed within vehicle or on person; offense; arms in holster or sheath

(a) Except as otherwise provided in this chapter, any person who carries concealed within any vehicle which is under his control or direction any pistol, revolver, or other firearm capable of being concealed upon the person without having a license to carry such firearm as provided in this chapter is guilty of a misdemeanor, and if he has been convicted previously of any felony or of any crime made punishable by this chapter, is guilty of a felony.

(b) Any person who carries concealed upon his person any pistol, revolver, or other firearm capable of being concealed upon the person without having a license to carry such firearm as provided in this chapter is guilty of a misdemeanor, except any person, having been convicted of a crime against the person, property or a narcotics or dangerous drug violation, who carries concealed upon his person any pistol, revolver, or other firearm capable of being concealed upon the person without having a license to carry such firearm as provided in this chapter is guilty of a public offense and is punishable by imprisonment in a state prison, or by imprisonment in a county jail not to exceed six months, or by fine not to exceed five hundred dollars ($500), or by both such fine and imprisonment, and if he has been convicted previously of any felony or of any crime made punishable by this chapter, is guilty of a felony.

(c) Firearms carried openly in belt holsters are not concealed within the meaning of this section, nor are knives which are carried openly in sheaths suspended from the waist of the wearer.
(Amended by Stats.1976, c. 1139, p. ——, § 306.5, operative July 1, 1977.)

§ 12027. Persons exempt

Section 12025 does not apply to or affect any of the following:

(a) **Peace officers**

(a) Peace officers listed in Section 830.1, 830.2, or subdivision (a) of Section 830.3, whether active or honorably retired, other duly appointed peace officers, full-time paid peace officers of other states and the federal government who are carrying out official duties while in California, or any person summoned by any such officers to assist in making arrests or preserving the peace while he is actually engaged in assisting such officer.

The agency from which a peace officer is honorably retired may, upon initial retirement of the peace officer, or at anytime subsequent thereto, deny or revoke, for good cause, the retired officer's privilege to carry a weapon as provided in this subdivision. Any peace officer who has been honorably retired shall be issued an identification certificate containing an endorsement by the issuing agency indicating whether or not the retired peace officer has the privilege to carry a weapon pursuant to this subdivision.

(b) **Merchants**

(b) The possession or transportation by any merchant of unloaded firearms as merchandise.

(c) **Members of armed forces**

(c) Members of the Army, Navy, or Marine Corps of the United States, or the National Guard, when on duty, or organizations which are by law authorized to purchase or receive such weapons from the United States or this state.

(d) **Authorized military or civil organizations**

(d) Duly authorized military or civil organizations while parading, or the members thereof when going to and from the places of meeting of their respective organizations.

(e) **Guards or messengers**

(e) Guards or messengers of common carriers, banks, and other financial institutions while actually employed in and about the shipment, transportation, or delivery of any money, treasurer, bullion, bonds, or other thing of value within this state.

(f) **Members of shooting clubs**

(f) Members of any club or organization organized for the purpose of practicing shooting at targets upon established target ranges, whether public or private, while such members are using any of the firearms referred to in this chapter upon such target ranges, or while going to and from such ranges.

(g) **Licensed hunters or fishermen**

(g) Licensed hunters or fishermen while engaged in hunting or fishing, or while going to or returning from such hunting or fishing expedition.

(h) **Members of antique gun clubs**

(h) Members of any club or organization organized for the purpose of collecting and displaying antique or historical pistols, revolvers or other firearms, while such members are displaying such weapons at meetings of such clubs or organizations or while going to and from such meetings, or individuals who collect such firearms not designed to fire, or incapable of firing fixed cartridges or fixed shot shells, or other firearms of obsolete ignition type for which ammunition is not readily available and which are generally

recognized as collector's items, provided such firearm is kept in the trunk. If the vehicle is not equipped with a trunk, such firearm shall be kept in a locked container in an area of the vehicle other than the utility or glove compartment.
(Amended by Stats.1974, c. 1090, p. 2316, § 1.)

§ 12028. Daggers or firearms as nuisance; surrender and destruction; restoration of stolen weapons to owner

(a) The unlawful concealed carrying upon the person or within the vehicle of the carrier of any of the weapons mentioned in Section 653k, 12020, or 12025 is a nuisance.

(b) A firearm of any nature used in the commission of any misdemeanor as provided in this code or any felony, or an attempt to commit any misdemeanor as provided in this code or any felony, is, upon a conviction of the defendant, a nuisance.

(c) Any weapon described in subdivision (a), or, upon conviction of defendant, any weapon described in subdivision (b), shall be surrendered to the sheriff of a county or the chief of police or other head of a municipal police department of any city or city and county. The officers to whom the weapons are surrendered, except upon the certificate of a judge of a court of record, or of the district attorney of the county, that the retention thereof is necessary or proper to the ends of justice, may annually, between the 1st and 10th days of July, in each year, offer the weapons, which the officers in charge of them consider to have value with respect to sporting, recreational, or collection purposes, for sale at public auction to persons licensed under federal law to engage in businesses involving any weapon purchased. If any weapon has been stolen and is thereafter recovered from the thief or his transferee, or is used in such a manner as to constitute a nuisance pursuant to subdivision (a) or (b) without the prior knowledge of its lawful owner that it would be so used, it shall not be so offered for sale but shall be restored to the lawful owner, as soon as its use as evidence has been served, upon his identification of the weapon and proof of ownership.

(d) If, under this section, a weapon is not of the type that can be sold to the public, generally, or is not sold pursuant to subdivision (c) the weapon shall, between the 1st and 10th days of July, next succeeding, be destroyed so that it can no longer be used as such weapon.

(e) This section shall not apply to any firearm in the possession of the Department of Fish and Game or which was used in the violation of any provision of law, or regulation thereunder, in the Fish and Game Code.

(f) No stolen weapon shall be sold or destroyed pursuant to subdivisions (c) or (d) unless reasonable notice is given to its lawful owner, if his identity and address can be reasonably ascertained.
(Amended by Stats.1971, c. 1271, p. 2490, § 2.)

§ 12029. Blackjacks, etc., as nuisances; confiscation and destruction; preparation as evidence

Except as provided in Section 12020, blackjacks, slungshots, billies, nunchakus, sandclubs, sandbags, metal knuckles, any instrument described in subdivision (c) of Section 12020, and sawed-off shotguns as defined in Section 12020 are nuisances. Such weapons shall be subject to confiscation and summary destruction whenever found within the state. Such weapons shall be destroyed in the same manner as other weapons described in Section 12028, except that upon the certification of a judge or of the district attorney that the ends of justice will be subserved thereby, such weapon shall be preserved until the necessity for its use ceases.
(Amended by Stats.1974, c. 141, p. 284, § 2.)

§ 12030. Firearms; delivery to armed forces or law enforcement agency

The officer having custody of any firearms which may be useful to the State Guard, the Coast Guard Auxiliary or to any military or naval agency of the federal or state government may upon the authority of the legislative body of the city, city and county, or county by which he is employed and the approval of the Adjutant General of the state deliver such firearms to the commanding officer of a unit of the State Guard, the Coast Guard Auxiliary or any other military agency of the state or federal government in lieu of destruction as required by this chapter. The officer delivering the firearms shall take a receipt for them containing a complete description thereof and shall keep the receipt on file in his office as a public record.

Any law enforcement agency which has custody of any firearms or any parts of any firearms which are subject to destruction as required by this chapter may, in lieu of destroying such weapons, retain and use any of them as may be useful in carrying out the official duties of such agency, or may turn over to the

§ 12030

criminalistics laboratory of the Department of Justice or the criminalistics laboratory of a police department, sheriff's office or district attorney's office any such weapons as may be useful in carrying out the official duties of their respective agencies.

Any firearm or part of any firearm which, rather than being destroyed, is used for official purposes pursuant to this section shall be destroyed by the agency using such weapon when it is no longer needed by the agency for use in carrying out its official duties.

Any law enforcement agency that retains custody of any firearm pursuant to this section or that destroys a firearm pursuant to Section 12028 shall notify the Department of Justice of such retention or destruction. This notification shall consist of a complete description of each firearm, including the name of the manufacturer or brand name, model, caliber, and serial number.
(Amended by Stats.1972, c. 1377, p. 2845, § 90.)

§ 12031. Carrying of loaded firearms; misdemeanor; exceptions

(a) Except as provided in subdivision (b), (c), or (d), every person who carries a loaded firearm on his person or in a vehicle while in any public place or on any public street in an incorporated city or in any public place or on any public street in a prohibited area of unincorporated territory is guilty of a misdemeanor.

(b) Subdivision (a) shall not apply to any of the following:

(1) Peace officers listed in Section 830.1 or 830.2, or subdivision (a) of Section 830.3, whether active or honorably retired, other duly appointed peace officers, full-time paid peace officers of other states and the federal government who are carrying out official duties while in California, or any person summoned by any such officers to assist in making arrests or preserving the peace while he is actually engaged in assisting such officer.

The agency from which a peace officer is honorably retired may, upon initial retirement of the peace officer, or at any time subsequent thereto, deny or revoke, for good cause, the retired officer's privilege to carry a weapon as provided in this paragraph. Any peace officer who has been honorably retired shall be issued an identification certificate containing an endorsement by the issuing agency indicating whether or not the retired peace officer has the privilege to carry a weapon pursuant to this paragraph.

(2) Members of the military forces of this state or of the United States engaged in the performance of their duties.

(3) Persons who are using target ranges for the purpose of practice shooting with a firearm or who are members of shooting clubs while hunting on the premises of such clubs.

(4) The carrying of concealable weapons by persons who are authorized to carry such weapons pursuant to Article 3 (commencing with Section 12050) of Chapter 1 of Title 2 of Part 4 of the Penal Code.

(c) Subdivision (a) shall not apply to any of the following who have completed a regular course in firearms training approved by the Commission on Peace Officer Standards and Training:

(1) Patrol special police officers appointed by the police commission of any city, county, or city and county under the express terms of its charter who also under the express terms of the charter (i) are subject to suspension or dismissal after a hearing on charges duly filed with the commission after a fair and impartial trial, (ii) must be not less than 18 years of age nor more than 40 years of age, (iii) must possess physical qualifications prescribed by the commission, and (iv) are designated by the police commission as the owners of a certain beat or territory as may be fixed from time to time by the police commission.

(2) The carrying of weapons by animal control officers or zookeepers, regularly compensated as such by a governmental agency when acting in the course and scope of their employment and when designated by a local ordinance or, if the governmental agency is not authorized to act by ordinance, by a resolution, either individually or by class, to carry such weapons, or by persons who are authorized to carry such weapons pursuant to Section 607f of the Civil Code, while actually engaged in the performance of their duties pursuant to such section.

(3) Harbor policemen designated pursuant to Section 663.5 of the Harbors and Navigation Code.

(d) Subdivision (a) shall not apply to any of the following who have been issued a certificate pursuant to Section 12033. Such certificate shall not be required of any person who is a peace officer, who has completed all training required by law for the exercise of his power as a peace officer, and who is employed while not on duty as such peace officer.

(1) Guards or messengers of common carriers, banks, and other financial institutions while actually employed in and about the shipment, transportation, or delivery of any money, treasure, bullion, bonds, or other thing of value within this state.

(2) Guards of contract carriers operating armored vehicles pursuant to California Highway Patrol and Public Utilities Commission authority (i) if hired prior to January 1, 1977; or (ii) if hired on or after January 1, 1977, if they have completed a course in the carrying and use of firearms as prescribed by the Department of Consumer Affairs.

(3) Private investigators, private patrol operators, and alarm company operators who are licensed pursuant to Chapter 11 (commencing with Section 7500) of Division 3 of the Business and Professions Code, while acting within the course and scope of their employment.

(4) Uniformed security guards or night watchmen employed by any public agency, while acting within the scope and in the course of their employment.

(5) Uniformed security guards, regularly employed and compensated as such by persons engaged in any lawful business, while actually engaged in protecting and preserving the property of their employers and uniformed alarm agents employed by an alarm company operator while on duty. Nothing in this paragraph shall be construed to prohibit cities and counties from enacting ordinances requiring alarm agents to register their name.

(6) Uniformed employees of private patrol operators and uniformed employees of private investigators licensed pursuant to Chapter 11 (commencing with Section 7500) of Division 3 of the Business and Professions Code while acting within the course and scope of their employment as private patrolmen or private investigators.

(e) In order to determine whether or not a firearm is loaded for the purpose of enforcing this section, peace officers are authorized to examine any firearm carried by anyone on his person or in a vehicle while in any public place or on any public street in an unincorporated city or prohibited area of an unincorporated territory. Refusal to allow a peace officer to inspect a firearm pursuant to the provisions of this section constitutes probable cause for arrest for violation of this section.

(f) As used in this section "prohibited area" means any place where it is unlawful to discharge a weapon.

(g) A firearm shall be deemed to be loaded for the purposes of this section when there is an unexpended cartridge or shell, consisting of a case which holds a charge of powder and a bullet or shot, in, or attached in any manner to, the firearm, including, but not limited to, in the firing chamber, magazine, or clip thereof attached to the firearm; except that a muzzle-loader firearm shall be deemed to be loaded when it is capped or primed and has a powder charge and ball or shot in the barrel or cylinder.

(h) Nothing in this section shall prevent any person engaged in any lawful business, including a nonprofit organization, or any officer, employee, or agent authorized by such person for lawful purposes connected with such business, from having a loaded firearm within such person's place of business, or any person in lawful possession of private property from having a loaded firearm on such property.

(i) Nothing in this section shall prevent any person from carrying a loaded firearm in an area within an incorporated city while engaged in hunting, during such time and in such area as the hunting is not prohibited by the city council.

(j) Nothing in this section is intended to preclude the carrying of any loaded firearm, under circumstances where it would otherwise be lawful, by a person who reasonably believes that the person or property of himself or another is in immediate danger and that the carrying of such weapon is necessary for the preservation of such person or property.

(k) Nothing in this section is intended to preclude the carrying of a loaded firearm by any person while engaged in the act of making or attempting to make a lawful arrest.

(*l*) Nothing in this section shall prevent any person from having a loaded weapon, if it is otherwise lawful, at his place of residence, including any temporary residence or campsite.
(Amended by Stats.1978, c. 380, p. ——, § 127; Stats.1978, c. 1023, p. ——, § 4.)

§ 12033. Security guard; certificate; completion of courses in firearms and powers of arrest; fee

The Department of Consumer Affairs may issue a certificate to any person referred to in subdivision (d) of Section 12031, upon notification by the school where the course was completed that the person has successfully completed a course in the carrying and use of firearms and a course of training in the exercise of the powers of arrest which meet the

§ 12033

standards prescribed by the department pursuant to Section 7514.1 of the Business and Professions Code.
(Amended by Stats.1978, c. 1023, p. ——, § 6.)

§ 12052. Fingerprints; necessity of taking; report pertaining to applicant; exception

The fingerprints of each applicant shall be taken and two copies on forms prescribed by the Department of Justice shall be forwarded to the department. Upon receipt of the fingerprints and the fee as prescribed in Section 12054, the department shall promptly furnish the forwarding licensing authority a report of all data and information pertaining to any applicant of which there is a record in its office. No license shall be issued by any licensing authority until after receipt of such report from the department.

Provided, however, that if the license applicant has previously applied to the same licensing authority for a license to carry concealed firearms and the applicant's fingerprints and fee have been previously forwarded to the Department of Justice, as herein provided, the licensing authority shall note such previous identification numbers and other data which would provide positive identification in the files of the Department of Justice on the copy of any subsequent license submitted to the department in conformance with Section 12053 and no additional application form or fingerprints shall be required.
(Amended by Stats.1972, c. 1377, p. 2845, § 91.)

§ 12053. Record of issuance; filing of copies

When any such license is issued a record thereof shall be maintained in the office of the licensing authority. Copies of each license issued shall be filed immediately by the issuing officer or authority with the Department of Justice.
(Amended by Stats.1972, c. 1377, p. 2846, § 92.)

§ 12054. Application fee; disposition

Each applicant for a new license or for the renewal of a license shall pay at the time of filing his application a fee determined by the Department of Justice to be sufficient to reimburse the Department of Justice for the direct costs of furnishing the report required by Section 12052. The officer receiving the application and the fee shall transmit the fee, with the fingerprints if required, to the Department of Justice. The fee charged shall not exceed ten dollars ($10). The licensing authority of any city or county may charge an additional fee, not to exceed three dollars ($3), for processing any such application, and shall transmit such additional fee, if any, to the city or county treasury.
(Amended by Stats.1972, c. 1377, p. 2846, § 93.)

§ 12070. Unlicensed business; offense

No person shall engage in the business of selling, transferring, advertising, offering, or exposing for sale or transfer, any pistol, revolver or other firearm capable of being concealed upon the person unless he has been issued a license pursuant to Section 12071. Any person violating this section is guilty of a misdemeanor. As used in this article, engaging in the business of selling or transferring concealable firearms does not include the infrequent sale or transfer, offering, exposing for sale, or advertising for sale any handgun at a gun show, swap meet or similar event.

As used in this section, "infrequent" means occasional and without regularity.
(Amended by Stats.1978, c. 899, p. ——, § 1.)

§ 12071. Retail licenses; business regulations

The duly constituted licensing authorities of any city or county shall accept applications for, and may grant licenses permitting the licensee to sell at retail within the county, city and county, city, town or other municipality pistols, revolvers, and other firearms capable of being concealed upon the person. If a license is granted it shall be in the form prescribed by the Attorney General, effective for not more than one year from the date of issue, and be subject to the following conditions, for breach of any of which the license shall be subject to forfeiture.

1. The business shall be carried on only in the building designated in the license.

2. The license or a copy thereof, certified by the issuing authority, shall be displayed on the premises where it can easily be seen.

3. No pistol or revolver shall be delivered.

(a) Within 15 days of the application for the purchase, and when delivered shall be unloaded and securely wrapped; nor

(b) Unless the purchaser either is personally known to the seller or shall present clear evidence of his identity.

4. No pistol or revolver, or imitation thereof, or placard advertising the sale or other transfer thereof, shall be displayed in any part of the premises where it can readily be seen from the outside.

(Amended by Stats.1975, c. 997, p. 2342, § 1.)

§ 12072. Prohibited transfers; delivery of weapon; transfer to stranger; offense

No person, corporation or dealer shall sell, deliver, or otherwise transfer any pistol, revolver, or other firearm capable of being concealed upon the person to any person whom he has cause to believe to be within any of the classes prohibited by Section 12021 from owning or possessing such firearms, nor to any minor, under the age of 18 years. In no event shall any such firearm be delivered to the purchaser within 15 days of the application for the purchase thereof, and when delivered such firearm shall be securely wrapped and shall be unloaded. Where neither party to the transaction holds a dealer's license, no person shall sell or otherwise transfer any such firearm to any other person within this state who is not personally known to the vendor. Any violation of the provisions of this section is a misdemeanor.
(Amended by Stats.1975, c. 997, p. 2342, § 2.)

§ 12073. Register of sales; contents; exemptions

Every person in the business of selling, leasing or otherwise transferring a pistol, revolver or other firearm, of a size capable of being concealed upon the person, whether such seller, lessor or transferor is a retail dealer, pawnbroker, or otherwise, except as provided by this chapter, shall keep a register in which shall be entered the time of sale, the date of sale, the name of the salesman making the sale, the place where sold, the make, model, manufacturer's number, caliber, or other marks of identification on such pistol, revolver or other firearm.

This section shall not apply to wholesale dealers in their business intercourse with retail dealers, nor to wholesale or retail dealers in the regular or ordinary transport of unloaded firearms as merchandise to other wholesale or retail dealers by mail, express or other mode of shipment, to points outside of the city or county wherein they are situated.
(Amended by Stats.1972, c. 501, p. 874, § 3.)

§ 12075. Register of sales; notice of issuance; nontransferable

The State Printer upon issuing a register shall forward to the Department of Justice the name and business address of the dealer together with the series and sheet numbers of the register. The register shall not be transferable. If the dealer moves his business to a different location he shall notify the department of such fact in writing within 48 hours.
(Amended by Stats.1972, c. 1377, p. 2846, § 94.)

§ 12076. Register of sales; violations; mailing copies; possession by unauthorized persons

The purchaser of any firearm capable of being concealed upon the person shall sign, and the dealer shall require him to sign his legal name and affix his residence address and date of birth to the register in, quadruplicate and the salesman shall affix his signature in quadruplicate on each sheet as a witness to the signature of the purchaser. Any person furnishing a fictitious name or address or knowingly furnishing an incorrect birth date and any person violating any of the provisions of this section is guilty of a misdemeanor.

Two copies of the original sheet of the register shall, on the date of sale, be placed in the mail, postage prepaid, and properly addressed to the Department of Justice at Sacramento and the third copy of the original shall be mailed, postage prepaid, to the chief of police, or other head of the police department of the city or county wherein the sale is made. Where the sale is made in a district where there is no municipal police department the third copy of the original sheet shall be mailed to the sheriff of the county wherein the sale is made.

If, on receipt of its two copies of the original sheet, it appears to the department that the purchaser resides in a district other than that to which a copy of the original sheet is required to be mailed, the department shall transmit one of its copies to the head of the municipal police department, if any, in the district in which the purchaser resides, or, if none, to the sheriff of the county in which he resides.

If the department determines that the purchaser is a person described in Section 12021 of this code or Section 8100 or 8103 of the Welfare and Institutions Code, it shall immediately notify the dealer of such fact.
(Amended by Stats.1972, c. 1377, p. 2846, § 95.)

§ 12079. Mail orders; record of order; fee

Any person, other than a dealer licensed under the provisions of Section 12071, or a manufacturer or wholesaler of weapons, who orders by mail any pistol, revolver, or firearm capable of being concealed upon the person shall, at least five days before ordering such weapon, file with the chief of police, or other head of the police department of the city, county, or city and county wherein such person maintains his residence or principal place of business, a record in

§ 12079

duplicate of such order. When such person resides or has his principal place of business where there is no municipal police department, then such record, in duplicate, shall be filed with the sheriff of the county where such person resides or maintains his principal place of business. Such record shall be substantially in the following form:

RECORD OF ORDER OF CONCEALABLE FIREARM

Name _____ Date of Birth _____
Permanent address _____
Height _____ feet _____ inches. Occupation _____
Color _____, skin _____, eyes _____, hair _____
Description of arm _____
               (state whether revolver or pistol)
Maker _____, caliber _____
Name and address of seller _____
Signature _____

The city, county, or city and county may charge a fee not exceeding one dollar ($1) for filing such record and shall send the duplicate of such record to the Department of Justice at Sacramento.

Within 14 days after receipt of such ordered weapon, the person who ordered such weapon shall transmit to the Department of Justice at Sacramento the serial number and a description of such weapon.

Any violation of this section is a misdemeanor.
(Amended by Stats.1972, c. 1377, p. 2849, § 98.)

§ 12090. Unauthorized alteration; punishment

Any person who changes, alters, removes or obliterates the name of the maker, model, manufacturer's number, or other mark of identification, including any distinguishing number or mark assigned by the Department of Justice on any pistol, revolver, or any other firearm, without first having secured written permission from the department to make such change, alteration or removal shall be punished by imprisonment in the state prison.
(Amended by Stats.1976, c. 1139, p. —, § 307, operative July 1, 1977.)

§ 12092. Assignment of number or mark

The Department of Justice upon request may assign a distinguishing number or mark of identification to any pistol or revolver whenever it is without a manufacturer's number, or other mark of identification or whenever the manufacturer's number or other mark of identification or the distinguishing number or mark assigned by the department has been destroyed or obliterated.
(Amended by Stats.1972, c. 1377, p. 2850, § 100.)

§ 12093. Stamping number or identifying indicium on firearm

Any person may place or stamp on any pistol, revolver, or other firearm any number or identifying indicium, provided the number or identifying indicium does not change, alter, remove, or obliterate the manufacturer's name, number, model, or other mark of identification. This section does not prohibit restoration by the owner of the name of the maker, model, or of the original manufacturer's number or other mark of identification when such restoration is authorized by the department, nor prevent any manufacturer from placing in the ordinary course of business the name of the maker, model, manufacturer's number, or other mark of identification upon a new firearm.
(Amended by Stats.1977, c. 253, p. —, § 1.)

§ 12094. Unmarked firearms; purchase, sale or possession; offense

Any person with knowledge of any change, alteration, removal, or obliteration described herein, who buys, receives, disposes of, sells, offers for sale, or has in his possession any pistol, revolver, or other firearm, which has had the name of the maker, model, or the manufacturer's number or other mark of identification including any distinguishing number or mark assigned by the Department of Justice changed, altered, removed, or obliterated is guilty of a misdemeanor.
(Amended by Stats.1974, c. 269, p. 495, § 3.)

§ 12095. Sawed-off shotguns as props; manufacture, possession, transportation or use; issuance of permit; duration of permit

If it finds that it does not endanger the public safety, the Department of Justice may issue permits initially valid for a period of one year, and renewable annually thereafter, for the manufacture, possession, transportation or use, with blank cartridges, of sawed-off shotguns solely as props for motion picture film or television program production upon a showing that good cause exists for the issuance thereof to the applicant for such a permit. No permit shall be issued to a person who is under 18 years of age.
(Added by Stats.1973, c. 732, p. 1318, § 4.)

§ 12096. Applications; fees

Applications for permits shall be filed in writing, signed by the applicant if an individual, or by a member or officer qualified to sign if the applicant is a firm or corporation, and shall state the name, business in which engaged, business address and a full description of the use to which the sawed-off shotguns are to be put.

Applications and permits shall be uniform throughout the state on forms prescribed by the Department of Justice.

Each applicant for a permit shall pay at the time of filing his application a fee determined by the Department of Justice, not to exceed fifty dollars ($50) for an initial application and ten dollars ($10) for an application to renew an existing permit.
(Added by Stats.1973, c. 732, p. 1318, § 4.)

§ 12097. Display; inspection; identification number for each sawed-off shotgun

(a) Every person, firm or corporation to whom a permit is issued shall keep it on his person or at the place where the sawed-off shotguns are kept. The permit shall be open to inspection by any peace officer or any other person designated by the authority issuing the permit.

(b) Every sawed-off shotgun possessed pursuant to the provisions of this article shall bear a unique identifying number. If a weapon does not bear a unique identifying number, the Department of Justice shall assign such a number which shall be placed or stamped on that weapon.
(Added by Stats.1973, c. 732, p. 1318, § 4.)

§ 12098. Revocation

Permits issued in accordance with this article may be revoked by the issuing authority at any time when it appears that the need for the sawed-off shotguns has ceased or that the holder of the permit has used the sawed-off shotguns for purposes other than those allowed by the permit or that the holder of the permit has not exercised great care in retaining custody of any weapons possessed under the permit.
(Added by Stats.1973, c. 732, p. 1318, § 4.)

§ 12220. Unauthorized sale, possession or transportation; punishment

Any person, firm or corporation, who within this state sells, offers for sale, possesses or knowingly transports any firearms of the kind commonly known as a machine gun, except as provided by this chapter, is guilty of a public offense and upon conviction thereof shall be punished by imprisonment in the state prison, or by a fine not to exceed five thousand dollars ($5,000), or by both such fine and imprisonment.
(Amended by Stats.1976, c. 1139, p. —, § 308, operative July 1, 1977.)

§ 12230. Authority to issue; showing necessary

The Department of Justice may issue permits for the possession and transportation or possession or transportation of such machineguns, upon a satisfactory showing that good cause exists for the issuance thereof to the applicant for such permit but no permit shall be issued to a person who is under 18 years of age.
(Amended by Stats.1972, c. 1377, p. 2850, § 102.)

§ 12231. Applications; contents; uniformity

Applications for permits shall be filed in writing, signed by the applicant if an individual, or by a member or officer qualified to sign if the applicant is a firm or corporation, and shall state the name, business in which engaged, business address and a full description of the use to which the firearms are to be put.

Applications and permits shall be uniform throughout the state on forms prescribed by the Department of Justice.
(Amended by Stats.1972, c. 1377, p. 2850, § 103.)

§ 12250. Authority to grant license; revocation; business regulations

The Department of Justice may grant licenses in a form to be prescribed by it effective for not more than one year from the date of issuance, to permit the sale at the place specified in the license of machineguns subject to all of the following conditions, upon breach of any of which the license shall be revoked:

1. The business shall be carried on only in the place designated in the license.

2. The license or a certified copy thereof must be displayed on the premises in a place where it may easily be read.

3. No machinegun shall be delivered to any person not authorized to receive the same under the provisions of this chapter.

4. A complete record must be kept of sales made under the authority of the license, showing the name and address of the purchaser, the descriptions and serial numbers of the weapons purchased, the number and date of issue of the purchaser's permit, if any, and the signature of the purchaser or purchasing

§ 12250

agent. This record shall be open to the inspection of any peace officer or other person designated by the Attorney General.
(Amended by Stats.1972, c. 1377, p. 2850, § 104.)

§ 12251. Unlawful possession of machinegun; injunction; destruction

It shall be a public nuisance to possess any machinegun in violation of this chapter, and the Attorney General, any district attorney or any city attorney may bring an action before the superior court to enjoin the possession of any such machinegun.

Any such machinegun found to be in violation of this chapter shall be surrendered to the Department of Justice, and the department shall destroy such machinegun so as to render it unusable and unrepairable as a machinegun, except upon the filing of a certificate with the department by a judge or district attorney stating that the preservation of such machinegun is necessary to serve the ends of justice.
(Amended by Stats.1972, c. 1377, p. 2851, § 105.)

§ 12303. Possession; other than fixed ammunition; punishment

Any person, firm, or corporation who, within this state, possesses any destructive device, other than fixed ammunition of a caliber greater than .60 caliber, except as provided by this chapter, is guilty of a public offense and upon conviction thereof shall be punished by imprisonment in the county jail for a term not to exceed one year, or in state prison, or by a fine not to exceed five thousand dollars ($5,000) or by both such fine and imprisonment.
(Amended by Stats.1976, c. 1139, p. —, § 309, operative July 1, 1977.)

§ 12303.1. Carrying or placement of explosive or destructive device on passenger vessel, aircraft, car or other vehicle; penalty

Every person who willfully does any of the following is guilty of a felony and is punishable by imprisonment in the state prison for two, four, or six years:

(a) Carries any explosive or destructive device on any vessel, aircraft, car, or other vehicle that transports passengers for hire.

(b) Places or carries any explosive or destructive device, while on board any such vessel, aircraft, car or other vehicle, in any hand baggage, roll, or other container.

(c) Places any explosive or destructive device in any baggage which is later checked with any common carrier.
(Amended by Stats.1978, c. 579, p. —, § 41.)

§ 12303.2. Possession of destructive devices or explosives in or near certain places; felony; punishment

Every person who recklessly or maliciously has in his possession any destructive device or any explosive on a public street or highway, in or near any theater, hall, school, college, church, hotel, other public building, or private habitation, in, on, or near any aircraft, railway passenger train, car, cable road or cable car, vessel engaged in carrying passengers for hire, or other public place ordinarily passed by human beings is guilty of a felony, and shall be punishable by imprisonment in the state prison for a period of two, four, or six years.
(Amended by Stats.1978, c. 579, p. —, § 42.)

§ 12303.3. Wrongful possession, explosion, etc., of destructive device or explosive with intent to injure or intimidate person or to injure or destroy property; felony; punishment

Every person who possesses, explodes, ignites, or attempts to explode or ignite any destructive device or any explosive with intent to injure, intimidate, or terrify any person, or with intent to wrongfully injure or destroy any property, is guilty of a felony, and shall be punished by imprisonment in the state prison for a period of three, five, or seven years.
(Amended by Stats.1978, c. 579, p. —, § 43.)

§ 12303.6. Sale or transportation; other than fixed ammunition; punishment

Any person, firm, or corporation who, within this state, sells, offers for sale, or knowingly transports any destructive device, other than fixed ammunition of a caliber greater than .60 caliber, except as provided by this chapter, is guilty of a felony and is punishable by imprisonment in the state prison for two, three or four years.
(Amended by Stats.1976, c. 1139, p. —, § 313, operative July 1, 1977.)

§ 12304. Sale, possession or transportation of fixed ammunition; punishment; subsequent conviction

Any person, firm or corporation who, within this state, sells, offers for sale, possesses or knowingly transports any fixed ammunition of a caliber greater than .60 caliber, except as provided in this chapter, is guilty of a public offense and upon conviction thereof shall be punished by imprisonment in the county jail for a term not to exceed six months or by a fine not to exceed one thousand dollars ($1,000), or by both such fine and imprisonment.

A second or subsequent conviction shall be punished by imprisonment in the county jail for a term not to exceed one year, or by imprisonment in the state prison, or by a fine not to exceed three thousand dollars ($3,000), or by both such fine and imprisonment.
(Amended by Stats.1976, c. 1139, p. —, § 314, operative July 1, 1977.)

§ 12305. Permits to conduct business; fee

Every dealer, manufacturer, importer, and exporter of any destructive device, or any motion picture or television studio using destructive devices in the conduct of its business, shall obtain a permit for the conduct of such business from the Department of Justice. Such permit shall be issued upon a satisfactory showing to him that good cause exists for the issuance thereof and after the payment of a fee of fifty dollars ($50). Such permit shall be valid for a period of one year only.
(Amended by Stats.1972, c. 1377, p. 2851, § 106.)

§ 12306. Permits; non-business purposes; fee

Any person, firm or corporation, other than those included in Section 12305, shall obtain a permit from the Department of Justice before possessing or transporting any destructive device. The department may issue such a permit upon a satisfactory showing that good cause exists for the issuance thereof, and after the payment of a fee of ten dollars ($10). The department shall issue a permit without payment of a fee upon a satisfactory showing that the possessor of such destructive devices is a bona fide collector of destructive devices. Such permit shall be valid for a period of one year only.
(Amended by Stats.1972, c. 1377, p. 2851, § 107.)

§ 12307. Unlawful possession; injunction; destruction

The possession of any destructive device in violation of this chapter shall be deemed to be a public nuisance and the Attorney General or district attorney of any city, county, or city and county may bring an action before the superior court to enjoin the possession of any such destructive device.

Any such destructive device found to be in violation of this chapter shall be surrendered to the Department of Justice, and the department shall destroy such destructive device so as to render it unusable and unrepairable as a destructive device, except upon the filing of a certificate with the department by a judge or district attorney stating that the preservation of such destructive device is necessary to serve the ends of justice.
(Amended by Stats.1972, c. 1377, p. 2851, § 108.)

§ 12308. Explosion, attempt to explode or ignite destructive device or explosive with intent to murder; felony; punishment

Every person who explodes, ignites, or attempts to explode or ignite any destructive device or any explosive with intent to commit murder is guilty of a felony, and shall be punished by imprisonment in the state prison for a period of five, seven, or nine years.
(Amended by Stats.1978, c. 579, p. —, § 44.)

§ 12309. Unlawful explosion or ignition of destructive device or explosive causing bodily injury; felony; punishment

Every person who willfully and maliciously explodes or ignites any destructive device or any explosive which causes bodily injury to any person is guilty of a felony, and shall be punished by imprisonment in the state prison for a period of five, seven, or nine years.
(Amended by Stats.1978, c. 579, p. —, § 45.)

§ 12312. Possession of materials with intent to make explosive or destructive device

Every person who possesses any substance, material, or any combination of substances or materials, with the intent to make any destructive device or any explosive without first obtaining a valid permit to make such destructive device or explosive, is guilty of a felony, and is punishable by imprisonment in the state prison for two, three, or four years.
(Amended by Stats.1978, c. 579, p. —, § 46.)

§ 12403. Exemptions; peace officers

Nothing in this chapter shall prohibit any person who is a peace officer as defined in Chapter 4.5 (commencing with Section 830) of Title 3 of Part 2 from purchasing, possessing, or transporting any tear gas weapon for official use in the discharge of his duties, if such weapon has been certified as acceptable under Article 5 (commencing with Section 12450)

§ 12403

of this chapter and if such person has satisfactorily completed a course of instruction approved by the Commission on Peace Officers Standards and Training in the use of tear gas.
(Amended by Stats.1977, c. 687, p. —, § 2.)

§ 12403.1. Exemptions; military and naval forces and federal law enforcement officers

Nothing in this chapter shall prohibit any member of the military and naval forces of this state or of the United States or any federal law enforcement officer from purchasing, possessing, or transporting any tear gas or tear gas weapon for official use in the discharge of his duties.
(Amended by Stats.1976, c. 1118, p. —, § 1.)

§ 12403.2. Repealed by Stats.1974, c. 420, p. 1019, § 3, urgency, eff. July 10, 1974

§ 12403.6. Employee of departments of justice or health; inapplicability of chapter

Provisions within this chapter shall not be construed to prohibit any Department of Justice or Department of Health employee, while acting within the scope of his duties, from possessing any tear gas or tear gas weapon for the purposes of examination, testing, or court appearance or any other official activity undertaken pursuant to the provisions of this chapter.
(Added by Stats.1976, c. 1118, p. —, § 2.)

§ 12403.7. Exemptions; weapons approved for self-defense; regulations; training

(a) Notwithstanding any other provision of law, any person may purchase, possess or use tear gas and tear gas weapons for the projection or release of tear gas if such tear gas and tear gas weapons are approved by the Department of Justice and are used solely for self-defense purposes, subject to the following requirements:

(1) No person convicted of a felony under the laws of the United States of the State of California, or any other state, government, or country shall purchase, possess, or use tear gas or tear gas weapons.

(2) No person who is addicted to any narcotic drug shall purchase, possess, or use tear gas or tear gas weapons.

(3) No person shall sell or furnish any tear gas or tear gas weapon to a minor.

(4)(i) No person shall purchase, possess or use any tear gas weapon which expels a projectile, or which expels the tear gas by any method other than an aerosol spray, or which is of a type, or size of container, other than authorized by regulation of the Department of Justice.

(ii) The department, with the cooperation of the State Department of Health Services, shall develop standards and promulgate regulations regarding the type of tear gas and tear gas weapons which may lawfully be purchased, possessed, and used pursuant to this section.

(iii) The regulations of the department shall include a requirement that every mace container and tear gas weapon which may be lawfully purchased, possessed, and used pursuant to this section have a label which states: "WARNING: The use of this substance or device for any purpose other than self-defense is a felony under California law. The contents are dangerous—use with care."

(5)(i) No person shall purchase, possess, or use any tear gas or any tear gas weapon who has not completed a course certified by the Department of Justice in the use of tear gas and tear gas weapons pursuant to which a card is issued identifying the person who has completed such a course. Such a course shall be taken in any training institution approved by the Department of Justice to offer tear gas training. Such a training institution is authorized to charge a fee covering the actual cost of such training.

(ii) The Department of Justice, in cooperation with the Commission on Peace Officer Standards and Training, shall develop standards for a course in the use of tear gas and tear gas weapons.

(6) No person shall purchase, possess or use any tear gas or tear gas weapon if such person has not been issued a permit by the police chief or sheriff having jurisdiction over the person's place of legal residence. The police chief or sheriff shall issue a permit to any person who has completed the course of training specified in paragraph (5), and who meets the following criteria:

(i) Is not a minor.

(ii) Has not been convicted of a felony.

(iii) Is not addicted to any narcotic drug.

(iv) Has not been convicted of any crime involving assault.

(v) Has not been convicted of misuse of tear gas under paragraph (8).

(7) If an application for a permit is denied, the police chief or sheriff denying such permit shall inform the applicant in writing of the reason for such denial.

The police chief or sheriff may charge a fee covering the actual cost of processing the application which shall also include the fee charged by the Department of Justice for noncriminal fingerprint card processing. The valid permit shall be carried on the person when carrying tear gas or tear gas weapons and shall be presented for examination to the vendor from whom any tear gas or tear gas weapons are purchased. The sale of tear gas or tear gas weapons by a vendor to a person who fails to present an identifying permit is a violation of Section 12420.

(8) Any person who has a valid permit, who uses tear gas or tear gas weapons except in self-defense or as authorized for training purposes by the department is guilty of a public offense and is punishable by imprisonment in a state prison for 16 months, or two or three years or in a county jail not to exceed one year or by fine not to exceed one thousand dollars ($1,000) or by both such fine and imprisonment.

(9) No person shall purchase, possess, or use any tear gas or tear gas weapon pursuant to this section prior to July 1, 1977.

(b) Such permit shall be valid for a period of seven years unless revoked because the person no longer meets the criteria specified under paragraph (6), and shall be nontransferable.

Applications and permits shall be uniform throughout the state on forms prescribed by the Department of Justice.

The Department of Justice may adopt and promulgate such regulations concerning the purchase and disposal of self-defense tear gas weapons, the standards for tear gas training courses, and the approval of facilities at which such training shall occur as are necessary to insure the safe use and possession of such tear gas weapons by permit holders.

(c) Any person who successfully completes training under this section for which the course and training facility must be approved by the Department of Justice is entitled to receive a certificate of completion issued by the Department of Justice. A fee shall be charged by the Department of Justice for the certificate. The fee shall be no more than is necessary to reimburse the Department of Justice for the costs of approving the courses, the facilities, maintaining control of the quality of the courses, and issuing the certificate of completion. The Department of Justice may provide by regulations the manner in which the fee is collected and paid.
(Amended by Stats.1978, c. 730, p. —, § 1.)

§ 12420. Sale, possession or transportation; punishment

Any person, firm, or corporation who within this state knowingly sells or offers for sale, possesses, or transports any tear gas or tear gas weapon, except as permitted under the provisions of this chapter, is guilty of a public offense and upon conviction thereof shall be punished by imprisonment in the state prison not to exceed two years or by a fine not to exceed two thousand dollars ($2,000), or by both.
(Amended by Stats.1976, c. 1118, p. —, § 3.)

§ 12422. Alteration of manufacturer's name, serial number or mark

Any person who changes, alters, removes or obliterates the name of the manufacturer, the serial number or any other mark of identification on any tear gas weapon is guilty of a public offense and, upon conviction, shall be punished by imprisonment in the state prison or by a fine of not more than two thousand dollars ($2,000) or by both.

Possession of any such weapon upon which the same shall have been changed, altered, removed, or obliterated, shall be presumptive evidence that such possessor has changed, altered, removed, or obliterated the same.
(Amended by Stats.1976, c. 1139, p. —, § 319, operative July 1, 1977.)

§ 12520. Possession; offense; punishment

Any person, firm or corporation who within this state possesses any device of the kind commonly known as a silencer for firearms is guilty of a felony and upon conviction thereof shall be punished by imprisonment in the state prison or by a fine not to exceed five thousand dollars ($5,000) or by both.
(Amended by Stats.1976, c. 1139, p. —, § 320, operative July 1, 1977.)

§ 12551. Sale to minors; misdemeanor

Every person who sells to a minor any firearm, air gun, or gas-operated gun, designed to fire a bullet, pellet or metal projectile, is guilty of a misdemeanor.
(Amended by Stats.1972, c. 579, p. 1010, § 40.)

§ 12552. Furnishing firearms, air guns, etc., to minors without parental consent

Every person who furnishes any firearm, air gun, or gas-operated gun, designed to fire a bullet, pellet or metal projectile, to any minor, without the express or implied permission of the parent or legal guardian of the minor, is guilty of a misdemeanor.
(Amended by Stats.1972, c. 579, p. 1010, § 41.)

§ 12560. Violation; penalty

Every person who has been convicted of a felony under the laws of the United States, of the State of California, or of any other state, government, or country and who used a firearm in the commission of such felony, who owns or has in his possession or under his custody or control any firearm is punishable by imprisonment in the state prison or in a county jail not exceeding one year or by a fine not exceeding five hundred dollars ($500), or by both such term of imprisonment and such fine.
(Amended by Stats.1976, c. 1139, p. —, § 321, operative July 1, 1977.)

§ 12580. Blowgun defined

"Blowgun," as used in this article, means a hollow tube designed and intended to be used as a tube through which a dart is propelled by the force of the breath of the user.
(Added by Stats.1972, c. 945, p. 1702, § 1.)

§ 12581. Blowgun ammunition defined

"Blowgun ammunition," as used in this article, means a dart designed and intended for use in a blowgun.
(Added by Stats.1972, c. 945, p. 1702, § 1, urgency, eff. Aug. 16, 1972.)

§ 12582. Manufacture, sale, offer for sale, possession or use

Any person who knowingly manufactures, sells, offers for sale, possesses, or uses a blowgun or blowgun ammunition in this state is guilty of a misdemeanor.
(Added by Stats.1972, c. 945, p. 1702, § 1.)

§ 12590. Prohibited acts; violations; penalty

(a) Any person who does any of the following acts while engaged in picketing, or other informational activities in a public place relating to a concerted refusal to work, is guilty of a misdemeanor:

(1) Carries concealed upon his person or within any vehicle which is under his control or direction any pistol, revolver, or other firearm capable of being concealed upon the person.

(2) Carries a loaded firearm upon his person or within any vehicle which is under his control or direction.

(3) Carries a deadly weapon, as defined in subdivision (f) of Section 3024.

(4) Wears the uniform of a peace officer, whether or not the person is a peace officer.

(b) This section shall not be construed to authorize or ratify any picketing or other informational activities not otherwise authorized by law.

(c) Section 12027 shall not be construed to authorize any conduct described in paragraph (1) of subdivision (a) of this section, nor shall subdivision (b) of Section 12031 be construed to authorize any conduct described in paragraph (2) of subdivision (a) of this section.
(Added by Stats.1976, c. 1004, p. —, § 1.)

§ 13200. Right of authorized access to individual record information not affected

Nothing in this chapter shall be construed to affect the right of access of any person or public agency to individual criminal offender record information that is authorized by any other provision of law.
(Added by Stats.1973, c. 992, p. 1914, § 1, operative July 1, 1978.)

§ 13201. Access to individual record information only if authorized by law

Nothing in this chapter shall be construed to authorize access of any person or public agency to individual criminal offender record information unless such access is otherwise authorized by law.
(Added by Stats.1973, c. 992, p. 1914, § 1, operative July 1, 1978.)

§ 13202. Public agencies and research bodies; aggregated information; removal of individual identification; costs

Every public agency or research body immediately concerned with the prevention or control of crime, the quality of criminal justice, or the custody or correction of offenders shall be provided with such aggregated criminal offender record information as is required for the performance of its duties, or the execution of research projects relating to the activities of criminal justice agencies or changes in legisla-

tive or executive policies, insofar as the technical or financial resources of statistical agencies permit, provided that all material identifying individuals has been removed, and provided that such agency or body pays the cost of the processing of such data when necessary.
(Added by Stats.1973, c. 992, p. 1914, § 1, operative July 1, 1978.)

§ 13300. **Furnishing to authorized persons; fingerprints on file without criminal history; fees**

(a) As used in this section:

(1) "Local summary criminal history information" means the master record of information compiled by any local criminal justice agency pursuant to Chapter 2 (commencing with Section 13100) of Title 3 of Part 4 of the Penal Code pertaining to the identification and criminal history of any person, such as name, date of birth, physical description, dates of arrests, arresting agencies and booking numbers, charges, dispositions, and similar data about such person.

(2) "Local summary criminal history information" does not refer to records and data compiled by criminal justice agencies other than that local agency, nor does it refer to records of complaints to or investigations conducted by, or records of intelligence information or security procedures of, the local agency.

(3) "Local agency" means a local criminal justice agency.

(b) A local agency shall furnish local summary criminal history information to any of the following, when needed in the course of their duties, provided that when information is furnished to assist an agency, officer, or official of state or local government, a public utility, or any entity, in fulfilling employment, certification, or licensing duties, the provisions of Chapter 1321 of the Statutes of 1974 and of Section 432.7 of the Labor Code shall apply:

(1) The courts of the state.

(2) Peace officers of the state as defined in Section 830.1, subdivisions (a) and (b) of Section 830.2, subdivisions (a), (b), and (j) of Section 830.3, subdivisions (a), (b), and (c) of Section 830.5, and Section 830.5a.

(3) District attorneys of the state.

(4) Prosecuting city attorneys of any city within the state.

(5) Probation officers of the state.

(6) Parole officers of the state.

(7) A public defender or attorney of record when representing a person in proceedings upon a petition for a certificate of rehabilitation and pardon pursuant to Section 4852.08.

(8) A public defender or attorney of record when representing a person in a criminal case and when authorized access by statutory or decisional law.

(9) Any agency, officer, or official of the state when such criminal history information is required to implement a statute, a regulation, or an ordinance that expressly refers to specific criminal conduct applicable to the subject person of the local summary criminal history information, and contains requirements or exclusions, or both, expressly based upon such specified criminal conduct.

(10) Any city or county, or city and county, or district, or any officer, or official thereof when access is needed in order to assist such agency, officer, or official in fulfilling employment, certification, or licensing duties, and when such access is specifically authorized by the city council, board of supervisors or governing board of the city, county, or district when such criminal history information is required to implement a statute, a regulation, or an ordinance that expressly refers to specific criminal conduct applicable to the subject person of the local summary criminal history information, and contains requirements or exclusions, or both, expressly based upon such specified criminal conduct.

(11) The subject of the local summary criminal history information.

(12) Any person or entity when access is expressly authorized by statute when such criminal history information is required to implement a statute, a regulation, or an ordinance that expressly refers to specific criminal conduct applicable to the subject person of the local summary criminal history information, and contains requirements or exclusions, or both, expressly based upon such specified criminal conduct.

(13) Any managing or supervising correctional officer of a county jail or other county correctional facility.

(c) The local agency may furnish local summary criminal history information, upon a showing of a compelling need, to any of the following, provided that when information is furnished to assist an agency, officer, or official of state or local government, a public utility, or any entity, in fulfilling employment, certification, or licensing duties, the

§ 13300

provisions of Chapter 1321 of the Statutes of 1974 and of Section 432.7 of the Labor Code shall apply:

(1) Any public utility as defined in Section 216 of the Public Utilities Code which operates a nuclear energy facility when access is needed in order to assist in employing persons to work at such facility, provided that, if the local agency supplies such data, it shall furnish a copy of such data to the person to whom the data relates.

(2) To a peace officer of the state other than those included in subdivision (b).

(3) To a peace officer of another country.

(4) To public officers (other than peace officers) of the United States, other states, or possessions or territories of the United States, provided that access to records similar to local summary criminal history information is expressly authorized by a statute of the United States, other states, or possessions or territories of the United States when such information is needed for the performance of their official duties.

(5) To any person when disclosure is requested by a probation, parole, or peace officer with the consent of the subject of the local summary criminal history information and for purposes of furthering the rehabilitation of the subject.

(6) The courts of the United States, other states or territories or possessions of the United States.

(7) Peace officers of the United States, other states, or territories, or possessions of the United States.

(8) To any individual who is the subject of the record requested when needed in conjunction with an application to enter the United States or any foreign nation.

(d) Whenever an authorized request for local summary criminal history information pertains to a person whose fingerprints are on file with the local agency and the local agency has no criminal history of that person, and the information is to be used for employment, licensing, or certification purposes, the fingerprint card accompanying such request for information, if any, may be stamped "no criminal record" and returned to the person or entity making the request.

(e) Whenever local summary criminal history information furnished pursuant to this section is to be used for employment, licensing, or certification purposes, the local agency shall charge the person or entity making the request a fee which it determines to be sufficient to reimburse the local agency for the cost of furnishing such information, provided that no fee shall be charged to any public law enforcement agency for local summary criminal history information furnished to assist it in employing, licensing, or certifying a person who is applying for employment with the agency as a peace officer, or criminal investigator. Any state agency required to pay a fee to the local agency for information received under this section may charge the applicant a fee sufficient to reimburse the agency for such expense.

(f) Whenever there is a conflict, the processing of criminal fingerprints shall take priority over the processing of applicant fingerprints.

(g) It is not a violation of this article to disseminate statistical or research information obtained from a record, provided that the identity of the subject of the record is not disclosed.

(h) It is not a violation of this article to include information obtained from a record in (1) a transcript or record of a judicial or administrative proceeding or (2) any other public record when the inclusion of the information in the public record is authorized by a court, statute, or decisional law.
(Amended by Stats.1978, c. 475, p. —, § 2.)

§ 13301. "Record"; "a person authorized by law to receive a record" defined

As used in this article

(a) "Record" means the master local summary criminal history information as defined in subdivision (a) of Section 13300, or a copy thereof.

(b) "A person authorized by law to receive a record" means any person or public agency authorized by a court, statute, or decisional law to receive a record.
(Added by Stats.1975, c. 1222, p. 3090, § 6, operative July 1, 1978.)

§ 13302. Furnishing to unauthorized person by employee of local agency

Any employee of the local criminal justice agency who knowingly furnishes a record or information obtained from a record to a person who is not authorized by law to receive the record or information is guilty of a misdemeanor.
(Added by Stats.1975, c. 1222, p. 3090, § 6, operative July 1, 1978.)

§ 13303. Furnishing to unauthorized person by authorized person

Any person authorized by law to receive a record or information obtained from a record who knowingly furnishes the record or information to a person who is not authorized by law to receive the record or information is guilty of a misdemeanor.

(Added by Stats.1975, c. 1222, p. 3090, § 6, operative July 1, 1978.)

§ 13304. Receipt, purchase or possession by unauthorized person

Any person, except those specifically referred to in Section 1070 of the Evidence Code, who, knowing he is not authorized by law to receive a record or information obtained from a record, knowingly buys, receives, or possesses the record or information is guilty of a misdemeanor.

(Added by Stats.1975, c. 1222, p. 3090, § 6, operative July 1, 1978.)

§ 13305. Statistical data, data for apprehension of purported criminal, and data in public records; authorized use

(a) It is not a violation of this article to disseminate statistical or research information obtained from a record, provided that the identity of the subject of the record is not disclosed.

(b) It is not a violation of this article to disseminate information obtained from a record for the purpose of assisting in the apprehension of a person wanted in connection with the commission of a crime.

(c) It is not a violation of this article to include information obtained from a record in (1) a transcript or record of a judicial or administrative proceeding or (2) any other public record when the inclusion of the information in the public record is authorized by a court, statute, or decisional law.

(Added by Stats.1975, c. 1222, p. 3090, § 6, operative July 1, 1978.)

VEHICLE CODE

As its name implies, the Vehicle Code is concerned with those laws relating to the sale, registration, equiping and safe operation of motor vehicles within the State of California. The Vehicle Code is the authorizing document for the Department of Motor Vehicles and the California Highway Patrol. It establishes responsibilities for accident investigation and sets forth special provisions for dealing with the prosecution of vehicle offenses. There are three volumes of the Vehicle Code in the complete set of West's Annotated California Codes. The provisions of primary interest to administration of justice students and practitioners are those sections dealing with vehicle registration, driver licensing, accident reporting, rules of the road (including driving under the influence of alcohol), vehicle equipment and offense prosecution. The sections selected for inclusion in this volume are intended to reflect these primary interest areas.

Division	Section
GENERAL PROVISIONS	1
1. WORDS AND PHRASES DEFINED	100
2. ADMINISTRATION	1500
3. REGISTRATION OF VEHICLES AND CERTIFICATES OF TITLE	4000
3.5 REGISTRATION AND TRANSFER OF VESSELS	9840
3.6 VEHICLE SALES	9950
4. SPECIAL ANTITHEFT LAWS	10500
5. OCCUPATIONAL LICENSING AND BUSINESS REGULATIONS	11100
6. DRIVERS' LICENSES	12500
6.5 MOTOR VEHICLE TRANSACTIONS WITH MINORS	15500
7. FINANCIAL RESPONSIBILITY LAWS	16000
9. CIVIL LIABILITY	17000
10. ACCIDENTS AND ACCIDENT REPORTS	20000
11. RULES OF THE ROAD	21000
12. EQUIPMENT OF VEHICLES	24000
13. TOWING AND LOADING EQUIPMENT	29000
14. TRANSPORTATION OF EXPLOSIVES	31600
14.5 TRANSPORTATION OF RADIOACTIVE MATERIALS	33000
14.7 FLAMMABLE LIQUIDS	34001
14.8 SAFETY REGULATIONS	34500
14.9 MOTOR VEHICLE DAMAGE CONTROL	34700
15. SIZE, WEIGHT, AND LOAD	35000
16. IMPLEMENTS OF HUSBANDRY	36000
16.5 OFF-HIGHWAY VEHICLES	38000
16.7 REGISTRATION AND LICENSING OF BICYCLES	39000
17. OFFENSES AND PROSECUTION	40000
18. PENALTIES AND DISPOSITION OF FEES, FINES, AND FORFEITURES	42000

GENERAL PROVISIONS

§ 15. "Shall" and "may"

"Shall" is mandatory and "may" is permissive. (Stats.1959, c. 3, p. 1524, § 15.)

§ 21. Uniformity of code

Except as otherwise expressly provided, the provisions of this code are applicable and uniform throughout the State and in all counties and municipalities therein, and no local authority shall enact or enforce any ordinance on the matters covered by this code unless expressly authorized herein. (Amended by Stats.1961, c. 2017, p. 4231, § 1.)

§ 31. False information to peace officer

No person shall give, either orally or in writing, information to a peace officer while in the performance of his duties under the provisions of this code when such person knows that the information is false. (Added by Stats.1965, c. 1264, p. 3140, § 1.)

Division 1
WORDS AND PHRASES DEFINED

§ 165. Authorized emergency vehicle

An authorized emergency vehicle is:

(a) Any publicly owned ambulance, lifeguard or lifesaving equipment or any privately owned ambulance used to respond to emergency calls and operated under a license issued by the Commissioner of the California Highway Patrol.

(b) Any publicly owned vehicle operated by the following persons, agencies or organizations:

(1) Any forestry or fire department of any public agency or fire department organized as provided in the Health and Safety Code.

(2) Any police department, including those of the University of California and the California State University and Colleges, sheriff's department, the California Highway Patrol, or the California State Police Division.

(3) The district attorney of any county or any district attorney investigator.

(4) Any constable or deputy constable engaged in law enforcement work.

(5) Peace officer personnel of the Department of Justice.

(6) Peace officer personnel of the state park system appointed pursuant to Section 5008 of the Public Resources Code.

(7) Peace officer personnel employed and compensated as members of a security patrol of a school district while carrying out the duties of their employment.

(8) Peace officer personnel of the Department of Corrections designated in subdivision (b) of Section 830.5 of, and in Section 830.5a of, the Penal Code.

(9) Housing authority patrol officers designated in paragraph (17) of subdivision (a) of Section 830.4 of the Penal Code.

(c) Any vehicle owned by the state, or any bridge and highway district, and equipped and used either for fighting fires, or towing or servicing other vehicles, caring for injured persons, or repairing damaged lighting or electrical equipment.

(d) Any state-owned vehicle used in responding to emergency fire, rescue or communications calls and operated either by the Office of Emergency Services or by any public agency or industrial fire department to which the Office of Emergency Services has assigned such vehicle.

(e) Any state-owned vehicle operated by a fish and game warden.

(f) Any vehicle owned or operated by any department or agency of the United States government:

(1) When such department or agency is engaged primarily in law enforcement work and the vehicle is used in responding to emergency calls, or

(2) When such vehicle is used in responding to emergency fire, ambulance or lifesaving calls.

(g) Any vehicle for which an authorized emergency vehicle permit has been issued by the Commissioner of the California Highway Patrol.
(Amended by Stats.1977, c. 1017, p. ——, § 1, urgency, eff. Sept. 23, 1977.)

§ 235. Business district

A "business district" is that portion of a highway and the property contiguous thereto (a) upon one side of which highway, for a distance of 600 feet, 50 percent or more of the contiguous property fronting thereon is occupied by buildings in use for business, or (b) upon both sides of which highway, collectively, for a distance of 300 feet, 50 percent or more of the contiguous property fronting thereon is so occupied. A business district may be longer than the distances specified in this section if the above ratio of buildings in use for business to the length of the highway exists.
(Stats.1959, c. 3, p. 1529, § 235.)

§ 240. Business and residence districts: determination

In determining whether a highway is within a business or residence district, the following limitations shall apply and shall qualify the definitions in Sections 235 and 515:

(a) No building shall be regarded unless its entrance faces the highway and the front of the building is within 75 feet of the roadway.

(b) Where a highway is physically divided into two or more roadways only those buildings facing each roadway separately shall be regarded for the purpose of determining whether the roadway is within a district.

(c) All churches, apartments, hotels, multiple dwelling houses, clubs, and public buildings, other than schools, shall be deemed to be business structures.

§ 240

(d) A highway or portion of a highway shall not be deemed to be within a district regardless of the number of buildings upon the contiguous property if there is no right of access to the highway by vehicles from the contiguous property.
(Stats.1959, c. 3, p. 1529, § 240.)

§ 305. Driver

A "driver" is a person who drives or is in actual physical control of a vehicle. The term "driver" does not include the tillerman or other person who, in an auxiliary capacity, assists the driver in the steering or operation of any articulated firefighting apparatus.
(Amended by Stats.1971, c. 213, p. 279, § 1.)

§ 377. Limit line

A "limit line" is a solid white line not less than 12 nor more than 24 inches wide, extending across a roadway or any portion thereof to indicate the point at which traffic is required to stop in compliance with legal requirements.
(Stats.1959, c. 3, p. 1534, § 377.)

§ 440. Official traffic control device

An "official traffic control device" is any sign, signal, marking, or device not inconsistent with this code, placed or erected by authority of a public body or official having jurisdiction, for the purpose of regulating, warning, or guiding traffic.
(Stats.1959, c. 3, p. 1535, § 440.)

§ 445. Official traffic control signal

An "official traffic control signal" is any device, whether manually, electrically or mechanically operated, by which traffic is alternately directed to stop and proceed and which is erected by authority of a public body or official having jurisdiction.
(Stats.1959, c. 3, p. 1535, § 445.)

§ 460. Owner

An "owner" is a person having all the incidents of ownership, including the legal title of a vehicle whether or not such person lends, rents, or creates a security interest in the vehicle; the person entitled to the possession of a vehicle as the purchaser under a security agreement; or the State, or any county, city, district, or political subdivision of the State, or the United States, when entitled to the possession and use of a vehicle under a lease, lease-sale, or rental-purchase agreement for a period of 30 consecutive days or more.
(Amended by Stats.1963, c. 1867, p. 3852, § 2.)

§ 505. Registered owner

A "registered owner" is a person registered by the department as the owner of a vehicle.
(Stats.1959, c. 3, p. 1536, § 505.)

§ 525. Right-of-way

"Right-of-way" is the privilege of the immediate use of the highway.
(Stats.1959, c. 3, p. 1536, § 525.)

§ 530. Roadway

A "roadway" is that portion of a highway improved, designed, or ordinarily used for vehicular travel.
(Stats.1959, c. 3, p. 1537, § 530.)

§ 555. Sidewalk

"Sidewalk" is that portion of a highway, other than the roadway, set apart by curbs, barriers, markings or other delineation for pedestrian travel.
(Amended by Stats.1959, c. 979, p. 3007, § 1.)

§ 587. Stop or stopping

"Stop or stopping" when prohibited shall mean any cessation of movement of a vehicle, whether occupied or not, except when necessary to avoid conflict with other traffic or in compliance with the direction of a police officer or official traffic control device or signal.
(Added by Stats.1961, c. 1917, p. 4036, § 1.)

§ 590. Street

"Street" is a way or place of whatever nature, publicly maintained and open to the use of the public for purposes of vehicular travel. Street includes highway.
(Stats.1959, c. 3, p. 1538, § 590.)

§ 627. Engineering and traffic survey

Engineering and traffic survey, as used in this code, means a survey of highway and traffic conditions in accordance with methods determined by the Department of Transportation for use by state and local authorities.

An engineering and traffic survey shall include, among other requirements deemed necessary by the department, consideration of the following:

(a) Prevailing speeds as determined by traffic engineering measurements.

(b) Accident records.

(c) Highway, traffic and roadside conditions not readily apparent to the driver.
(Amended by Stats.1974, c. 545, p. 1310, § 154.)

§ 670. Vehicle

A "vehicle" is a device by which any person or property may be propelled, moved, or drawn upon a highway, excepting a device moved exclusively by human power or used exclusively upon stationary rails or tracks.
(Amended by Stats.1975, c. 987, p. 2327, § 3.)

Division 2
ADMINISTRATION

§ 1500. Department of motor vehicles

There is in the Business and Transportation Agency the Department of Motor Vehicles.
(Amended by Stats.1969, c. 138, p. 371, § 277.)

§ 1656. Vehicle Code and synopsis

(a) The department shall publish the complete text of the California Vehicle Code together with other laws relating to the use of highways or the operation of motor vehicles at least once every two years and may republish the code and laws and distribute the same as may be deemed advisable without charge upon written request of any state or local governmental officer or agency, or of any federal agency. Paperback copies of the Vehicle Code may be distributed without charge to any public secondary school in this state in quantities not to exceed one for each driver training and education instructor and one for each public secondary school library. The department shall sell and distribute the California Vehicle Code to all other persons at a charge sufficient to pay the entire actual cost of publishing and distributing the code, except the charge shall not exceed three dollars ($3). In determining the amount of the charge, a fraction of a dollar shall be disregarded, unless it exceeds fifty cents ($0.50), in which case it shall be treated as one full dollar ($1). The receipts from the sale of such publications shall be deposited in the Motor Vehicle Account.

(b) The department shall publish a synopsis or summary of the laws regulating the operation of vehicles and the use of the highways and may deliver a copy thereof without charge with each original vehicle registration and with each original driver's license. The department shall publish such number of copies of the synopsis or summary in the Spanish language as the director determines are needed to meet the demand for such copies. The department shall furnish both English and Spanish copies to its field offices and to law enforcement agencies for general distribution and, when it does so, shall furnish the copies without charge.
(Amended by Stats.1978, c. 380, p. ——, § 142; Stats.1978, c. 818, p. ——, § 2.)

§ 2100. Department of California Highway Patrol

There is in the Business and Transportation Agency the Department of the California Highway Patrol.
(Amended by Stats.1969, c. 138, p. 371, § 279.)

§ 2409. Peace officer authority

All members of the California Highway Patrol have the powers of a peace officer as provided in Section 830.2 of the Penal Code.
(Amended by Stats.1971, c. 938, p. 1841, § 1.)

§ 2410. Traffic direction

Members of the California Highway Patrol are authorized to direct traffic according to law, and, in the event of a fire or other emergency, or to expedite traffic or insure safety, may direct traffic as conditions may require notwithstanding the provisions of this code.
(Stats.1959, c. 3, p. 1550, § 2410.)

§ 2411. Service of warrants

Members of the California Highway Patrol are authorized to serve all warrants relating to the enforcement of this code.
(Stats.1959, c. 3, p. 1550, § 2411.)

§ 2412. Accident investigation

All members of the California Highway Patrol may investigate accidents resulting in personal injuries or death and gather evidence for the purpose of prosecuting the person or persons guilty of any violation of the law contributing to the happening of such accident.
(Stats.1959, c. 3, p. 1550, § 2412.)

§ 2800. Obedience to traffic officers

It is unlawful to wilfully fail or refuse to comply with any lawful order, signal, or direction of any traffic officer or to refuse to submit to any lawful inspection under this code.
(Stats.1959, c. 3, p. 1552, § 2800.)

§ 2800.1. Flight from certain peace officers

Every person who, while operating a motor vehicle, hears a siren and sees at least one lighted lamp

exhibiting a red light emanating from a vehicle painted a distinctive color, distinctively marked, and operated by a member of the California Highway Patrol or any peace officer of any sheriff's or city police department wearing a complete, distinctive peace officer's uniform and appropriate badge, and who, with the intent to evade the officer, willfully disregards such siren and flashing light, and who flees or otherwise attempts to elude a pursuing peace officer's motor vehicle, is guilty of a misdemeanor.
(Added by Stats.1977, c. 1104, p. —, § 1.)

§ 2805. Inspection of vehicles, title or registration

(a) For the purpose of locating stolen vehicles, a member of the California Highway Patrol may inspect any vehicle of a type required to be registered under this code on a highway or in any public garage, repair shop, parking lot, new or used car lot, automobile dismantler's lot, vehicle shredding facility, vehicle leasing or rental lot, vehicle equipment rental yard, vehicle salvage pool, or other similar establishment, and may inspect the title or registration of vehicles, in order to establish the rightful ownership or possession of the vehicle.

(b) A member of the California Highway Patrol may also inspect, for the purposes specified in subdivision (a), implements of husbandry, special construction equipment, and special mobile equipment in the places described in subdivision (a) or when such a vehicle is incidentally operated or transported upon a highway.

(c) Whenever possible, inspections conducted pursuant to subdivision (a) or (b) shall be conducted at a time and in a manner so as to minimize any interference with, or delay of, business operations.
(Amended by Stats.1977, c. 325, p. —, § 1.)

§ 2810. Inspection to prevent theft

(a) A member of the California Highway Patrol may stop any vehicle transporting any timber products, livestock, poultry, or farm produce and inspect the bills of lading, shipping, delivery papers, or other evidence to determine whether the driver is in legal possession of the load, and upon reasonable belief that the driver of such vehicle is not in legal possession, shall take custody of the vehicle and load and turn the same over into the custody of the sheriff of the county wherein the timber products, livestock, poultry, farm produce, or any part thereof is apprehended.

(b) The sheriff shall receive and provide for the care and safekeeping of such timber products, livestock, poultry, farm produce, or any part thereof, and immediately, in co-operation with the department, proceed with the investigation and legal disposition thereof.

(c) Any expense incurred by the sheriff in the performance of his duties under this section shall be a legal charge against the county.
(Stats.1959, c. 3, p. 1553, § 2810.)

§ 2814. Passenger vehicle inspection

Every driver of a passenger vehicle shall stop and submit the vehicle to an inspection of the mechanical condition and equipment of the vehicle at any location where members of the California Highway Patrol are conducting tests and inspections of passenger vehicles and when signs are displayed requiring such stop.

The Commissioner of the California Highway Patrol may make and enforce regulations with respect to the issuance of stickers or other devices to be displayed upon passenger vehicles as evidence that the vehicles have been inspected and have been found to be in safe mechanical condition and equipped as required by this code and equipped with certified motor vehicle pollution control devices as required by Part 5 (commencing with Section 43000) of Division 26 of the Health and Safety Code which are correctly installed and in operating condition. Any sticker so issued shall be placed on the windshield within a seven-inch square as provided in Section 26708.

If, upon such inspection of a passenger vehicle, it is found to be in unsafe mechanical condition or not equipped as required by this code and the provisions of Part 5 (commencing with Section 43000) of Division 26 of the Health and Safety Code, the provisions of Article 2 (commencing with Section 40150) of Chapter 1 of Division 17 of this code shall apply.

The provisions of this section relating to motor vehicle pollution control devices apply to vehicles of the United States or its agencies, to the extent authorized by federal law.
(Amended by Stats.1975, c. 957, p. 2230, § 20.)

Division 3
REGISTRATION OF VEHICLES AND CERTIFICATES OF TITLE

§ 4000. Registration required; compliance with vehicular air pollution control provisions

(a) No person shall drive, move, or leave standing upon a highway any motor vehicle, trailer, semitrailer, pole or pipe dolly, logging dolly, or auxiliary dolly unless it is registered and the appropriate fees have been paid under this code.

(b) No person shall drive, move, or leave standing upon a highway any motor vehicle, as defined in Chapter 2 (commencing with Section 39010), Part 1, Division 26 of the Health and Safety Code, which has been registered in violation of Part 5 (commencing with Section 43000) of that Division 26.

(c) The provisions of this section shall not apply, following payment of fees due for registration, during such time that registration and transfer is being withheld by the Department of Motor Vehicles pending the investigation of any use tax due under the provisions of the Revenue and Taxation Code.

(d) When a vehicle is towed by a tow car on order of a sheriff, marshal, or other official acting pursuant to a court order or on order of a peace officer acting pursuant to the provisions of Chapter 10 (commencing with Section 22650) of Division 11, the provisions of subdivision (a) of this section shall not apply.
(Amended by Stats.1976, c. 1206, p. ——, § 14.)

§ 4002. Vehicles exempt under permit

When moved or operated under a permit issued by the department, registration is not required of:

(a) A vehicle not previously registered while being moved or operated from a dealer's, distributor's, or manufacturer's place of business to a place where essential parts of the vehicle are to be altered or supplied.

(b) A vehicle while being moved from a place of storage to another place of storage.

(c) A vehicle while being moved to or from a garage or repair shop for the purpose of repairs or alteration.

(d) A vehicle while being moved or operated for the purpose of dismantling or wrecking the same and permanently removing it from the highways.

(e) A vehicle, while being moved from one place to another for the purpose of inspection by the department, assignment of a vehicle identification number, inspection of pollution control devices, or weighing the vehicle.

(f) A vehicle, the construction of which has not been completed, until such time as the construction thereof is completed and final weights and costs can be determined for registration purposes.
(Amended by Stats.1977, c. 326, p. ——, § 1.)

Editors' Note

In addition, other sections create special exemptions for foreign commercial vehicles, special construction equipment, wheelchairs, cemetery equipment, forklifts, dollies, golf carts, snowmobiles and motorized bicycles.

§ 4454. Registration card kept with vehicle

(a) Every owner upon receipt of a registration card shall maintain the same or a facsimile copy thereof with the vehicle for which issued.

(b) The provisions of this section do not apply when a registration card is necessarily removed from the vehicle for the purpose of application for renewal or transfer of registration.
(Amended by Stats.1967, c. 410, p. 1629, § 1.)

§ 4457. Stolen, lost, or damaged cards and plates

If any registration card or license plate is stolen, lost, mutilated, or illegible, the owner of the vehicle for which the same was issued, as shown by the records of the department, shall immediately make application for and may, upon the applicant furnishing information satisfactory to the department, obtain a duplicate or a substitute or a new registration under a new registration number, as determined to be most advisable by the department.
(Stats.1959, c. 3, p. 1562, § 4457.)

§ 4458. Both plates lost or stolen

If both license plates have been lost by or stolen from the registered owner, he shall immediately notify the police department or sheriff's office of the city or county in which he resides and he shall immediately apply to the department for new plates in lieu of the plates stolen or lost and the department shall in every proper case, except in the case of plates which are exempt from fees, issue a pair of license plates of a different number and assign the registration number to the vehicle for which the plates are issued.
(Stats.1959, c. 3, p. 1563, § 4458.)

§ 4459. Stolen, lost or damaged certificate

If any certificate of ownership is stolen, lost, mutilated or illegible, the legal owner or, if none, then the owner of the vehicle for which the same was issued as shown by the records of the department shall immediately make application for and may, upon the applicant furnishing information satisfactory to the department, obtain a duplicate.
(Stats.1959, c. 3, p. 1563, § 4459.)

§ 4460. Seizure of documents and plates

The Department of Motor Vehicles and the Department of the California Highway Patrol or any regularly employed and salaried police officer or deputy sheriff may take possession of any certificate, card, permit, license, or license plate issued under this code upon expiration, revocation, cancellation, or suspension thereof or which is fictitious or which has been unlawfully or erroneously issued. Any license plate which is not attached to the vehicle for which issued, when and in the manner required under this code may be seized, and attachment to the proper vehicle may be made or required.

Any such document or license plate seized shall be delivered to the Department of Motor Vehicles.
(Amended by Stats.1967, c. 1110, p. 2754, § 2.)

§ 4461. Improper use of evidences of registration

No person shall lend any certificate of ownership, registration card, license plate, special plate, or permit issued to him if the person desiring to borrow the same would not be entitled to the use thereof nor shall any person knowingly permit the use of any of the same by one not entitled thereto.
(Stats.1959, c. 3, p. 1563, § 4461.)

§ 4462. Presentation and examination of registration card

(a) The driver of a motor vehicle shall present the registration or identification card or other evidence of registration of any or all vehicles under his immediate control for examination upon demand of any peace officer.

(b) No person shall display upon a vehicle, nor present to any peace officer, any registration card, identification card, temporary receipt, license plate, or permit not issued for such vehicle or not otherwise lawfully used thereon under this code.
(Amended by Stats.1967, c. 410, p. 1629, § 2.)

§ 4463. False evidences of registration

Every person who, with intent to defraud, alters, forges, counterfeits, or falsifies any certificate of ownership, registration card, certificate, license or special plate or permit provided for by this code or any comparable certificate of ownership, registration card, certificate, license or special plate or permit relating to motor vehicles provided for by any foreign jurisdiction or who alters, forges, counterfeits, or falsifies any such document or plate with intent to represent the same as issued by the department or who alters, forges, counterfeits, or falsifies with fraudulent intent any endorsement of transfer on a certificate of ownership, or who with fraudulent intent displays or causes or permits to be displayed or have in his possession any blank, incomplete, canceled, suspended, revoked, altered, forged, counterfeit, or false certificate of ownership, registration card, certificate, license or special plate or permit or who utters, publishes, passes, or attempts to pass, as true and genuine, any of the above-named false, altered, forged, or counterfeited matters knowing the same to be false, altered, forged, or counterfeited with intent to prejudice, damage, or defraud any person is guilty of a felony and upon conviction thereof shall be punished by imprisonment in the state prison, or in the county jail for not more than one year.
(Amended by Stats.1976, c. 1139, p. ——, § 335.)

§ 4464. Altered license plates

No person shall display upon a vehicle a license plate altered from its original markings.
(Added by Stats.1959, c. 1478, p. 3772, § 2.)

§ 4760. Failure to deposit bail for parking offenses

The department shall refuse to renew the registration of any vehicle whose registered owner or lessee has been sent or given a notice of violation relating to standing or parking pursuant to paragraph (2) of Section 41103 and has not complied with the provisions of paragraph (2) of Section 41103, unless he pays to the department, at the time he applies for renewal, the full amount of bail for offenses relating to standing or parking which he has failed to deposit as required by law, as shown by records of the department.
(Amended by Stats.1977, c. 804, p. ——, § 1.)

§ 5001. Regular series plates for law enforcement vehicles

The department may issue license plates for vehicles exempt from registration fees in the same series as plates issued for nonexempt vehicles. The plates may be issued for a one-year period and only upon the certification of the Attorney General that the issuance of the plates has been requested by the head of a criminal justice or a law enforcement agency of a city, county, or state or federal department, that the vehicle is assigned to persons responsible for investigating actual or suspected violations of the law or the

supervision of persons liberated from a state prison or other institution under the jurisdiction of the Department of Corrections by parole or the supervision of persons liberated from an institution under the jurisdiction of the Department of the Youth Authority by parole, and is intended for use in the line of duty.
(Amended by Stats.1978, c. 617, p. —, § 2.)

Division 3.5
REGISTRATION AND TRANSFER OF VESSELS
Division 3.6
VEHICLE SALES
Division 4
SPECIAL ANTITHEFT LAWS

§ 10500. Police reports

Every peace officer upon receiving a report based on reliable information that any vehicle registered under this code has been stolen, or taken or driven in violation of Section 10851, or that license plates for any vehicle have been lost or stolen, shall, immediately after receiving such information, report such information to the Department of Justice. An officer upon receiving information of the recovery of any vehicle or plates, which have been previously reported as stolen, taken or driven in violation of Section 10851, or lost, shall immediately report the fact of the recovery to such department. At the same time the recovering officer shall advise the Department of Justice and the original reporting police agency of the location and condition of such vehicle.
(Amended by Stats.1972, c. 98, p. 133, § 1.)

§ 10501. False report of theft

It is unlawful for any person to make or file a false or fraudulent report of theft of a vehicle required to be registered under this code with any law enforcement agency with intent to deceive.
(Stats.1959, c. 3, p. 1594, § 10501.)

§ 10750. Altering or changing vehicle numbers

(a) No person shall intentionally deface, destroy, or alter the motor number, other distinguishing number, or identification mark of a vehicle required or employed for registration purposes without written authorization from the department, nor shall any person place or stamp any serial, motor, or other number or mark upon a vehicle, except one assigned thereto by the department.

(b) This section does not prohibit the restoration by an owner of the original vehicle identification number when the restoration is authorized by the department, nor prevent any manufacturer from placing in the ordinary course of business numbers or marks upon new motor vehicles or new parts thereof.
(Amended by Stats.1970, c. 824, p. 1559, § 6.)

§ 10751. Manufacturer's serial or identification numbers

(a) No person shall knowingly buy, sell, offer for sale, receive, or have in his possession, any vehicle or component part thereof from which the manufacturer's serial or identification number has been removed, defaced, altered or destroyed, unless such vehicle or component part has attached thereto an identification number assigned or approved by the department in lieu of the manufacturer's number.

(b) Whenever such vehicle or component part comes into the custody of a peace officer it shall be destroyed, sold, or otherwise disposed of under the conditions as provided in an order by the court having jurisdiction. Nothing in this section shall, however, preclude the return of such vehicle or parts to the lawful owner thereof following presentation of satisfactory evidence of ownership and assignment of an identification number by the department. This subdivision shall not apply with respect to such vehicle or component part used as evidence in any criminal action or proceeding.

(c) This section shall not apply to a scrap metal processor engaged primarily in the acquisition, processing and shipment of ferrous and nonferrous scrap, and who receives dismantled vehicles from licensed dismantlers, or licensed junk collectors, or licensed junk dealers as scrap metal for the purpose of recycling the dismantled vehicles for their metallic content, the end product of which is the production of material for recycling and remelting purposes for steel mills, foundries, smelters and refiners.
(Added by Stats.1974, c. 8, p. 14, § 2.)

§ 10851. Theft and unlawful driving or taking of a vehicle

Any person who drives or takes a vehicle not his own, without the consent of the owner thereof, and with intent either permanently or temporarily to

§ 10851

deprive the owner thereof of his title to or possession of the vehicle, whether with or without intent to steal the same, or any person who is a party or accessory to or an accomplice in the driving or unauthorized taking or stealing is guilty of a public offense, and upon conviction thereof shall be punished by imprisonment in the state prison, or in the county jail for not more than one year or by a fine of not more than five thousand dollars ($5,000) or by both such fine and imprisonment. The consent of the owner of a vehicle to its taking or driving shall not in any case be presumed or implied because of such owner's consent on a previous occasion to the taking or driving of the vehicle by the same or a different person.
(Amended by Stats.1976, c. 1139, p. —, § 336.)

Law Review Commentaries

Theft and unlawful driving or taking of a vehicle. (1948) 21 So.Cal.L.R. 176. This article reads in part as follows:

"Prior to the amendment to California Motor Vehicle Code Section 503 by the 1947 session of the California Legislature, that section provided, in substance, that any person who takes a vehicle not his own, without the consent of the owner and in the absence thereof, and with intent either temporarily or permanently to deprive the owner of title or possession, with or without intent to steal, was guilty of a felony. This was practically the same offense, but with a different penalty, that was and still is proscribed by California Penal Code Section 499b (The Joy-ride statute). The Penal Code section provides that any person who shall, without the permission of the owner, take any vehicle for the purpose of temporarily using it is guilty of a misdemeanor. It is apparent that the provisions of these two sections practically duplicate each other. Therefore, it had been suggested that the passage of California Motor Vehicle Code Section 503 had repealed California Penal Code Section 499b by implication, on the ground that a later statute prescribing a different punishment for a particular offense repeals by implication a statute covering the same offense. Where this question had arisen in regard to these two sections, it was held that California Penal Code Section 499b had not been entirely repealed by California Motor Vehicle Code Section 503, in that the sections differ in two material respects: (1) In that California Motor Vehicle Section 503 is limited to cases in which the taking is in the absence of the owner, whereas California Penal Code Section 499b is not so limited; and (2) In that the felony covered by California Motor Vehicle Code Section 503 is not committed unless there is a specific intent to deprive the owner of title or possession, whereas this specific intent is not a requisite under California Penal Code Section 499b. Therefore, in order to charge an offense under California Penal Code Section 499b, it is necessary for the pleader to negate expressly an offense under California Motor Vehicle Section 503 by alleging either that the taking was in the presence of the owner or that there was no specific intent to deprive the owner of title or possession of the automobile.

"The 1947 Amendment of California Motor Vehicle Code Section 503 has eliminated the requirement that the taking be in the absence of the owner, but has left the remainder of the Section unchanged. This has served to accentuate the duplication of the two sections. The result is that they now differ in only one material respect—that is, the requirement of specific intent in California Motor Vehicle Code Section 503. In actuality, a situation in which the California Penal Code Section 499b would be applicable and California Motor Vehicle Code Section 503 inapplicable—a taking without intent to deprive the owner of possession, at least, temporarily—would be very rare. The conclusion seems inescapable that, for all practical purposes, the two sections are identical, and thus result in needless duplication."

Whether Vehicle Code § 503 is included in Penal Code § 487. (1949) 23 So.Cal.L.R. 107.

§ 10852. Breaking or removing vehicle parts

No person shall either individually or in association with one or more other persons, wilfully injure or tamper with any vehicle or the contents thereof or break or remove any part of a vehicle without the consent of the owner.
(Stats.1959, c. 3, p. 1597, § 10852.)

§ 10853. Malicious mischief to vehicle

No person shall with intent to commit any malicious mischief, injury, or other crime, climb into or upon a vehicle whether it is in motion or at rest, nor shall any person attempt to manipulate any of the levers, starting mechanism, brakes, or other mechanism or device of a vehicle while the same is at rest and unattended, nor shall any person set in motion any vehicle while the same is at rest and unattended.
(Stats.1959, c. 3, p. 1597, § 10853.)

Division 5
OCCUPATIONAL LICENSING AND BUSINESS REGULATIONS

Division 6
DRIVERS' LICENSES

§ 12500. Unlawful to drive unless licensed

(a) No person shall drive a motor vehicle upon a highway unless he then holds a driver's license issued under this code, except such persons as are expressly exempted under this code.

(b) No such person shall drive a motor vehicle or combination of vehicles that is not of a type for which he is licensed.
(Amended by Stats.1963, c. 74, p. 700, § 2.)

§ 12501. Persons exempt

The following persons are not required to obtain a driver's license:

(a) An officer or employee of the United States, while operating a motor vehicle owned or controlled by the United States on the business of the United States.

(b) Any person while driving or operating implements of husbandry incidentally operated or moved over a highway, except as provided in Section 36300.

(c) Any person driving or operating an off-highway motor vehicle subject to identification, as defined in Section 38012, while driving or operating such motor vehicle as provided in Section 38025.
(Amended by Stats.1972, c. 973, p. 1758, § 16.)

§ 12502. Nonresident driver

A nonresident over the age of 18 years having in his immediate possession a valid driver's license issued to him by a foreign jurisdiction of which he is a resident may operate a motor vehicle in this state without obtaining a license under this code except as provided in Section 12505.
(Amended by Stats.1971, c. 1748, p. 3763, § 54.5.)

§ 12503. Unlicensed nonresident

A nonresident over the age of 18 years whose home state or country does not require the licensing of drivers may operate a foreign vehicle owned by him for not to exceed 30 days without obtaining a license under this code.
(Amended by Stats.1971, c. 1748, p. 3763, § 55.)

§ 12504. Nonresident minors

(a) The provisions of Sections 12502 and 12503 shall apply to any nonresident over the age of 16 years but under the age of 18 years, but the maximum period during which such nonresident may operate a motor vehicle in this state without obtaining a driver's license shall be limited to a period of 10 days immediately following the entry of the nonresident into this state except as provided in subdivision (b) of this section.

(b) Any nonresident over the age of 16 years but under the age of 18 years who is a resident of a foreign jurisdiction which requires the licensing of drivers may continue to operate a motor vehicle in this state after 10 days from his date of entry into this state provided:

(1) He has a valid driver's license issued by such foreign jurisdiction in his immediate possession, and

(2) He has been issued and has in his immediate possession a nonresident minor's certificate, which is a certificate issued by the department upon filing "proof of ability to respond in damages," as defined in Section 16430, to a nonresident minor who holds a valid driver's license issued to him by his home state or country.

(c) Whenever any of the conditions for the issuance of a nonresident minor's certificate cease to exist, the department shall cancel and require the surrender to it of the nonresident minor's certificate.
(Amended by Stats.1971, c. 1748, p. 3763, § 56.)

§ 12505. Residence

(a) Any person entitled to an exemption under Section 12502, 12503, or 12504 may operate a motor vehicle in this state for not to exceed 10 days from the date he establishes residence in this state, except that he shall obtain a license upon becoming a resident before he is employed for compensation by another for the purpose of driving a motor vehicle on the highways.

(b) Subject to the provisions of Section 12504, any person over the age of 16 years who is the resident of a foreign jurisdiction other than a state, territory or possession of the United States, the District of Columbia, or the Commonwealth of Puerto Rico, having a valid driver's license issued to him by a jurisdiction having licensing standards deemed by the Department of Motor Vehicles equivalent to those of this state, may operate a motor vehicle in this state without obtaining a license, except that he shall obtain a license before he is employed for compensation by another for the purpose of driving a motor vehicle on the highways.

(c) Nothing in this section shall authorize the employment of a person in violation of Section 12515.
(Amended by Stats.1963, c. 209, p. 949, § 5.)

§ 12506. Temporary licenses

The department may issue a temporary driver's license to any person applying for a driver's license, or to any licensee whose license is required to be changed, added to, or modified. A temporary license shall permit the operation of a motor vehicle upon the highways for a period of 60 days, when the licensee has the license in his immediate possession, and while the department is completing its investigation and determination of all facts relative to the applicant's right to receive a license. The temporary license is invalid when the applicant's license has been issued or refused.
(Amended by Stats.1973, c. 891, p. 1661, § 1.)

§ 12507. License for persons under 18

Any person 16 years of age but less than 18, may apply for, and the department may issue a driver's license to such person upon successful completion of an examination as required by the department and upon compliance with one of the following:

(a) Satisfactory completion of approved courses in automobile driver education and driver training maintained pursuant to provisions of the Education Code in any secondary school of California, or equivalent instruction in a secondary school of another state.

(b) Satisfactory completion of six hours or more of behind-the-wheel instruction by a driving school or an independent driving instructor licensed under the provisions of Chapter 1 (commencing with Section 11100) of Division 5 of this code and either an accredited course in automobile driver education in any secondary school of California pursuant to provisions of the Education Code or satisfactory completion of equivalent professional instruction acceptable to the department. To be acceptable to the department the professional instruction shall meet minimum standards to be prescribed by the department, which standards shall be at least equal to the requirements for driver education and training contained in the rules and regulations adopted by the State Board of Education pursuant to provisions of the Education Code.
(Amended by Stats.1971, c. 438, p. 906, § 187.)

§ 12508. Limited term license

When in the opinion of the department it would be in the interest of safety, the department may issue, in individual cases, to any applicant for a driver's license, a license limited in duration to less than the regular term. Upon the expiration of a limited term license the department may extend its duration for an additional period without fee but the duration of the license and extensions shall not exceed the term of a regular license.
(Stats.1959, c. 3, p. 1615, § 12508.)

§ 12509. Instruction permits

(a) Except as otherwise provided in subdivision (f) of Section 12514, the department, for good cause, may issue an instruction permit to any physically and mentally qualified person who meets one of the following requirements and who applies to the department for an instruction permit:

(1) Is age 15 years and 6 months or over and has successfully completed approved courses in automobile driver education and driver training as provided in Section 12507.

(2) Is age 15 years and 6 months or over and has successfully completed an approved course in automobile driver education and is taking driver training as provided in Section 12507.

(3) Is age 15 years or over and is enrolled in an approved driver education course and is at the same time or during the same semester enrolled in an approved driver training course.

(4) Is over the age of 17 years and 6 months.

(b) An instruction permit issued pursuant to subdivision (a) shall entitle the applicant to operate a vehicle, subject to the limitations imposed by this section and any other provisions of law, upon the highways for a period not exceeding 12 months.

(c) Any person, while having in his immediate possession a valid permit issued pursuant to subdivision (a), may operate a motor vehicle, other than a motorcycle or a motorized bicycle, when either taking the driver training instruction of a kind referred to in Section 12507, or when practicing such instruction, and when accompanied by, and under the immediate supervision of, a California licensed driver 18 years of age or over whose driving privilege is not on probation. Except as provided in subdivision (d), such an accompanying licensed driver at all times shall occupy a position within the driver's compartment that would enable such accompanying licensed driver to assist the driver in controlling the vehicle as may be necessary to avoid a collision and to provide immediate guidance in the safe operation of such vehicle.

(d) Any person while having in his immediate possession a valid permit issued pursuant to subdivision (a), who is age 15 years and 6 months or over and who has successfully completed approved courses in automobile education and driver training as provided in Section 12507, and any person while having in his immediate possession a valid permit issued pursuant to subdivision (a) who is age 17 years and 6 months or over, may, in addition to operating a motor vehicle pursuant to subdivision (c), also operate a motorcycle or a motorized bicycle, except that such person shall not operate a motorcycle or a motorized bicycle during hours of darkness, shall stay off any freeways which have full control of access and no crossings at grade and shall not carry any passenger except an instructor licensed under Chapter 1 (commencing with Section 11100) of Division 5 of this code or a qualified instructor as defined in Section 18252.2 of the Education Code.

(e) No student shall take driver training instruction unless he is at the same time taking driver education instruction or has successfully completed driver education.

(f) The department may also issue an instruction permit to a person who has been issued a valid driver's license to authorize the person to obtain driver training instruction and to practice such instruction in order to obtain another class of driver's license or an endorsement.

(g) The department may further restrict permits issued under subdivision (a) as it may determine to be appropriate to assure the safe operation of a motor vehicle by the permittee.
(Amended by Stats.1977, c. 579, p. —, § 183.)

§ 12511. Licensee entitled to one license

No person shall have in his possession or otherwise under his control more than one valid driver's license issued under this code.
(Amended by Stats.1961, c. 1615, p. 3453, § 11.)

§ 12512. Age limit for drivers license

On or after July 1, 1967, except as provided in Sections 12507, 12513, and 12514, no driver's license shall be issued to any person under the age of 18 years.
(Amended by Stats.1965, c. 1035, p. 2673, § 3.)

§ 12804. Driver's examination; classification; certificates in lieu of driving test

(a) The examination shall include a test of the applicant's knowledge and understanding of the provisions of this code governing the operation of vehicles upon the highways, the ability to read and understand simple English used in highway traffic and directional signs, and his understanding of traffic signs and signals, including the bikeway signs, markers, and traffic control devices established by the Department of Transportation. The applicant shall be required to give an actual demonstration of his ability to exercise ordinary and reasonable control in operating a motor vehicle by driving the same under the supervision of an examining officer and submit to an examination appropriate to the type of motor vehicle or combination of vehicles he desires a license to drive, except that the department may waive the driving test part of the examination of an applicant who holds a valid license issued by another state, territory or possession of the United States, the District of Columbia, or the Commonwealth of Puerto Rico. The examination shall also include a test of the hearing and eyesight of the applicant and such other matters as may be necessary to determine the applicant's mental and physical fitness to operate a motor vehicle upon the highways and whether any ground exists for refusal of a license under this code. The examination for a class 1 or class 2 license under subdivision (b) of this section shall also include a report of a medical examination of the applicant given not more than two years prior to the date of the application by a physician licensed to practice medicine. The report shall be on a form approved by the department or by the Federal Highway Administration or the Federal Aviation Administration of the United States Department of Transportation. In establishing the requirements consideration may be given to the standards presently required of motor carrier drivers by the Federal Highway Administration of the United States Department of Transportation. Any physical defect of the applicant which in the opinion of the department is compensated to insure safe driving ability shall not prevent the issuance of a license to the applicant.

(b) In accordance with the following classifications any applicant for a driver's license shall be required to submit to an examination appropriate to the type of motor vehicle or combination of vehicles he desires a license to drive:

(1) Class 1. Any combination of vehicles and includes the operation of all vehicles under class 2 and class 3.

(2) Class 2. Any bus, any single vehicle with three or more axles, any such vehicles towing another vehicle weighing less than 6,000 pounds gross, and all vehicles covered under class 3.

(3) Class 3. A three-axle housecar, any two-axle vehicle, any such housecar or vehicle towing another vehicle weighing less than 6,000 pounds gross, and any two-axle vehicle weighing 4,000 pounds or more unladen when towing a trailer coach not exceeding 9,000 pounds gross, except a bus, two-wheel motorcycle, two-wheel motor-driven cycle, or "farm labor vehicle."

(4) Class 4. Any two-wheel motorcycle, any two-wheel motor-driven cycle, or any motorized bicycle. Authority to operate vehicles included in a class 4 license may be granted by endorsement on a class 1, 2

§ 12804

or 3 license upon completion of appropriate examination.

(c) Class 1 and class 2 drivers' licenses shall be valid for operating class 1 or class 2 vehicles only when a medical certificate approved by the department or the Federal Highway Administration or the Federal Aviation Administration of the United States Department of Transportation is in the licensee's immediate possession which has been issued within two years of the date of the operation of such vehicle, otherwise the license shall be valid only for operating class 3 vehicles and class 4 vehicles if so endorsed. A person holding a valid class 1 or class 2 driver's license on May 3, 1972, may operate class 1 or class 2 vehicles without a medical certificate until such time as the license expires.

(d) A farm labor vehicle driver certificate shall not be valid unless the driver is in possession of a medical certificate issued within the past two years.

(e) The department may accept a certificate of driving experience in lieu of a driving test on class 1 or 2 applications when such certificate is issued by an employer of the applicant provided the applicant has first qualified for a class 3 license and also met the other examination requirements for the license for which he is applying. Such certificate may be submitted as evidence of the applicant's experience or training in the operation of the types of equipment covered by the license for which he is applying.

(f) The department may accept a certificate of competence in lieu of a driving test on class 4 applications when such certificate is issued by a law enforcement agency for its officers who operate class 4 vehicles in their duties provided the applicant has also met the other examination requirements for the license for which he is applying.

(g) Notwithstanding the provisions of subdivision (b), any person holding a valid California driver's license of any class may operate a motorized bicycle without taking any special examination for the operation of a motorized bicycle, and without having a class 4 endorsement on such license.
(Amended by Stats.1978, c. 488, p. —, § 4.)

§ 12815. Licenses lost, destroyed, or mutilated

In the event a driver's license issued under this code is lost, destroyed or mutilated, the person to whom it was issued shall obtain a duplicate upon furnishing to the department (a) satisfactory proof of such loss, destruction, or mutilation and (b) if the licensee is a minor, evidence of permission to obtain a duplicate secured from the parents, guardian or person having custody of such minor. Any person who loses a driver's license and who, after obtaining a duplicate, finds the original license shall immediately destroy the original license.
(Amended by Stats.1970, c. 166, p. 409, § 2.)

§ 12951. Possession of license

(a) The licensee shall have the license issued to him in his immediate possession at all times when driving a motor vehicle upon a highway.

Any charge under this subdivision shall be dismissed when the person charged produces in court a driver's license duly issued to such person and valid at the time of his arrest, except that upon a third or subsequent charge the court in its discretion may dismiss the charge. When a temporary, interim, or duplicate driver's license is produced in court, the charge shall not be dismissed unless the court has been furnished proof by the Department of Motor Vehicles that such temporary, interim, or duplicate license was issued prior to the arrest, that the driving privilege and license had not been suspended or revoked, and that the person was eligible for such temporary, interim, or duplicate license.

(b) The driver of a motor vehicle shall present his license for examination upon demand of a peace officer enforcing the provisions of this code.
(Amended by Stats.1968, c. 1192, p. 2257, § 6.)

§ 13000. Issuance; contents; senior citizen notation; application

(a) The department may issue an identification card to any person attesting to the true name, correct age, and other identifying data as certified by the applicant for such identification card.

(b) Any person 62 years of age or older may apply for, and the department upon receipt of a proper application therefore shall issue, an identification card bearing the notation "Senior Citizen".

(c) Every application for an identification card shall be signed and verified by the applicant before a person authorized to administer oaths and shall be supported by such bona fide documentary evidence of the age and identity of such person as the department may require.

(d) Any person 62 years of age or older, and any other qualified person, may apply for, or possess, an identification card under the provisions of either subdivision (a) or (b), but not under both such provisions.
(Amended by Stats.1975, c. 1198, p. 2964, § 1.)

§ 13004. Unlawful acts

It is unlawful for any person:

(a) To display or cause or permit to be displayed or have in his possession any canceled, fictitious, fraudulently altered, or fraudulently obtained identification card.

(b) To lend his identification card to any other person or knowingly permit the use thereof by another.

(c) To display or represent any identification card not issued to him as being his card.

(d) To permit any unlawful use of an identification card issued to him.

(e) To do any act forbidden or fail to perform any act required by this article.

(f) To photograph, photostat, duplicate, or in any way reproduce any identification card or facsimile thereof in such a manner that it could be mistaken for a valid identification card, or to display or have in his possession any such photograph, photostat, duplicate, reproduction, or facsimile unless authorized by the provisions of this code.

(g) To alter any identification card in any manner not authorized by this code.
(Amended by Stats.1971, c. 1174, p. 2239, § 3.)

§ 13100. Cancellation

When used in reference to a driver's license, "cancellation" means that a driver's license certificate is terminated without prejudice and must be surrendered. Any person whose license has been canceled may immediately apply for a license. Cancellation of license may be made only when specifically authorized in this code, when application is made for a license to operate vehicles of a higher class, or when a license has been issued through error or voluntarily surrendered to the department.
(Amended by Stats.1974, c. 428, p. 1040, § 3.)

§ 13101. Revocation

When used in reference to a driver's license, "revocation" means that the person's privilege to drive a motor vehicle is terminated and a new driver's license may be obtained after the period of revocation.
(Stats.1959, c. 3, p. 1623, § 13101.)

§ 13102. Suspension; examination

When used in reference to a driver's license, "suspension" means that the person's privilege to drive a motor vehicle upon a highway is temporarily withdrawn. The department may, before terminating any suspension based upon a physical or mental condition of the licensee, require such examination of the licensee as deemed appropriate in relation to evidence of any condition which may affect the ability of the licensee to safely operate a motor vehicle.
(Amended by Stats.1976, c. 498, p. —, § 1.)

§ 13103. Equivalents of conviction

For purposes of this division, a plea of nolo contendere or a plea of guilty or judgment of guilty, whether probation is granted or not, a forfeiture of bail, or a finding reported under Section 1816, constitutes a conviction of any offense prescribed by this code, other than offenses relating to the unlawful parking of vehicles.
(Amended by Stats.1972, c. 1207, p. 2333, § 3.)

Editors' Note

Conditions allowing or requiring suspension or revocation of a driver's license include: speeding offenses, reckless driving, driving under the influence of alcohol/narcotic/drug, hit and run, failure to stop at railroad crossings as required, certain narcotic offense convictions, vehicle manslaughter, certain other vehicle felonies and refusal to submit to a blood/breath/urine test.

---

§ 13353. Chemical blood, breath, or urine tests

(a) Any person who drives a motor vehicle upon a highway shall be deemed to have given his consent to a chemical test of his blood, breath or urine for the purpose of determining the alcoholic content of his blood if lawfully arrested for any offense allegedly committed while the person was driving a motor vehicle under the influence of intoxicating liquor. The test shall be incidental to a lawful arrest and administered at the direction of a peace officer having reasonable cause to believe such person was driving a motor vehicle upon a highway while under the influence of intoxicating liquor. Such person shall be told that his failure to submit to or complete such a chemical test will result in the suspension of his privilege to operate a motor vehicle for a period of six months.

The person arrested shall have the choice of whether the test shall be of his blood, breath or urine, and he shall be advised by the officer that he has such choice. If the person arrested either is incapable, or states that he is incapable, of completing any chosen

§ 13353

test, he shall then have the choice of submitting to and completing any of the remaining tests or test, and he shall be advised by the officer that he has such choice.

Such person shall also be advised by the officer that he does not have the right to have an attorney present before stating whether he will submit to a test, before deciding which test to take, or during administration of the test chosen.

Any person who is dead, unconscious, or otherwise in a condition rendering him incapable of refusal shall be deemed not to have withdrawn his consent and such tests may be administered whether or not such person is told that his failure to submit to or complete the test will result in the suspension of his privilege to operate a motor vehicle.

(b) If any such person refuses the officer's request to submit to, or fails to complete, a chemical test, the department, upon receipt of the officer's sworn statement that he had reasonable cause to believe such person had been driving a motor vehicle upon a highway while under the influence of intoxicating liquor and that the person had refused to submit to, or failed to complete, the test after being requested by the officer, shall suspend his privilege to operate a motor vehicle for a period of six months. The officer's sworn statement shall be submitted on a form furnished or approved by the department. No such suspension shall become effective until 10 days after the giving of written notice thereof, as provided for in subdivision (c).

(c) The department shall immediately notify such person in writing of the action taken and upon his request in writing and within 15 days from the date of receipt of such request shall afford him an opportunity for a hearing in the same manner and under the same conditions as provided in Article 3 (commencing with Section 14100) of Chapter 3 of this division. For the purposes of this section the scope of the hearing shall cover the issues of whether the peace officer had reasonable cause to believe the person had been driving a motor vehicle upon a highway while under the influence of intoxicating liquor, whether the person was placed under arrest, whether he refused to submit to, or failed to complete, the test after being requested by a peace officer, and whether, except for the persons described in paragraph (a) above who are incapable of refusing, he had been told that his driving privilege would be suspended if he refused to submit to, or failed to complete, the test.

An application for a hearing made by the affected person within 10 days of receiving notice of the department's action shall operate to stay the suspension by the department for a period of 15 days during which time the department must afford a hearing. If the department fails to afford a hearing within 15 days, the suspension shall not take place until such time as the person is granted a hearing and is notified of the department's action as hereinafter provided. However, if the affected person requests that the hearing be continued to a date beyond the 15-day period, the suspension shall become effective immediately upon receipt of the department's notice that said request for continuance has been granted.

If the department determines upon a hearing of the matter to suspend the affected person's privilege to operate a motor vehicle, the suspension herein provided shall not become effective until five days after receipt by said person of the department's notification of such suspension.

(d) Any person who is afflicted with hemophilia shall be exempt from the blood test required by this section.

(e) Any person who is afflicted with a heart condition and is using an anticoagulant under the direction of a physician and surgeon shall be exempt from the blood test required by this section.

(f) A person lawfully arrested for any offense allegedly committed while the person was driving a motor vehicle under the influence of intoxicating liquor may request the arresting officer to have a chemical test made of the arrested person's blood, breath or urine for the purpose of determining the alcoholic content of such person's blood, and, if so requested, the arresting officer shall have the test performed.
(Amended by Stats.1978, c. 911, p. —, § 4.)

Editors' Note

Read People v. Hawkins and People v. Kraft in table of cases included in this text.

Notes of Decisions

Validity

The requirement that a driver charged with driving while under influence of intoxicating liquor submit to a chemical test does not violate his constitutional privilege against self-incrimination. Walker v. Department of Motor Vehicles (1969) 79 Cal.Rptr. 433, 274 C.A.2d 793; Fankhauser v. Orr (1968) 74 Cal.Rptr. 61, 268 C.A.2d 418.

Chemical tests prescribed by implied consent law do not violate driver's right against self-incrimination, nor his right to be free from illegal searches and seizures, nor his right to counsel. Westmoreland v. Chapman (1969) 74 Cal.Rptr. 363, 268 C.A.2d 1; Bush v. Bright (1968) 71 Cal.Rptr. 123, 264 C.A.2d 788.

Driver who was required to take sobriety test in form of blood test by this section which was not violative of Fifth Amendment (U.S.C.A.Const. Amend. 5) privilege against self-incrimination had no right to be informed that she was not required to take test. Newhouse v. Misterly (C.A.1969) 415 F.2d 514, certiorari denied 90 S.Ct. 1001, 397 U.S. 966, 25 L.Ed.2d 258.

This section providing for summary suspension of driver's license on sworn statement of arresting officer in case involving driving while intoxicated was valid. Funke v. Department of Motor Vehicles (1969) 81 Cal.Rptr. 662, 1 C.A.3d 449.

Delegation of power to motor vehicle department to make findings of fact pertinent to issues under implied consent law, including whether arrest of motorist is reasonable, did not constitute unconstitutional delegation of judicial functions to administrative agency. Finley v. Orr (1968) 69 Cal.Rptr. 137, 262 C.A.2d 656.

In general

While driver lawfully arrested for driving while intoxicated may choose from among three designated types of chemical tests required by this section, his obligation does not end when he has expressed such a choice; rather, he must go further and submit to the test. Cahall v. Department of Motor Vehicles, Division of Drivers' Licenses (1971) 94 Cal.Rptr. 182, 16 C.A.3d 491.

Upon inability of driver arrested for driving under influence of intoxicating liquors to submit to type of chemical test chosen by him, he was obliged, upon request so to do, to select another test with which he could comply, under this section providing for six-month suspension of privilege to operate motor vehicle. Quesada v. Orr (1971) 92 Cal.Rptr. 640, 14 C.A.3d 866.

Police officers, who, before doctor obtained blood sample from "defensive" accused arrested for drunk driving, placed accused on floor face down, applied a scissor lock on accused's legs, and held his arm up, used excessive force and exceeded limits of permissible police activity. People v. Kraft (1970) 84 Cal.Rptr. 280, 3 C.A.3d 890.

Under this section providing that any person who drives motor vehicle on a highway shall be deemed to have given his consent to a chemical test of his blood, breath or urine for purpose of determining alcoholic content, fact that police officer has reasonable cause to believe that person was driving on highway is not sufficient to support penalties imposed for failure to submit to test if motorist was not driving on highway. Weber v. Orr (1969) 79 Cal.Rptr. 297, 274 C.A.2d 288.

It is not act of obtaining driver's license that brings this section into play but instead act of driving motor vehicle on highway, and application of act to drivers who were issued licenses prior to enactment does not abridge drivers' constitutional rights. Serenko v. Bright (1968) 70 Cal.Rptr. 1, 263 C.A.2d 682.

Lawful arrest

Implied consent law becomes effective only when driver of motor vehicle is lawfully arrested. Spurlock v. Department of Motor Vehicles (1969) 82 Cal.Rptr. 42, 1 C.A.3d 821.

Taking of a blood sample for a test to determine defendant's sobriety without his consent cannot be regarded as an unreasonable search and seizure where the extraction is made in a medically approved manner and is incidental to a lawful arrest of one who is reasonably believed to have violated the law against driving while under the influence of intoxicants. People v. Kraft (Super.1969) 77 Cal.Rptr. 205, reversed 84 Cal.Rptr. 280, 3 C.A.3d 890.

Implied consent law with regard to chemical blood, breath, or urine tests complements, rather than supersedes, law making driving under influence of liquor, which proximately causes bodily injury to another, a felony and implied consent law does not call for exclusion of blood alcohol tests taken over defendant's refusal to submit, when such taking was in no way brutal or shocking to conscience and was incidental to lawful arrest. People v. Fite (1968) 73 Cal.Rptr. 666, 267 C.A.2d 685.

Where officers noted odor of alcohol on injured defendant's breath when she was removed from her automobile at scene of accident and there was probable cause to believe that defendant had committed a felony, it was proper to take a blood sample from defendant at the hospital and to admit evidence developed by its analysis which supported conclusion that she was under the influence of intoxicating liquor at time of accident, even though defendant had not been arrested when blood sample was taken and a warrant authorizing taking of blood sample had not been issued. People v. Glass (1968) 71 Cal.Rptr. 858, 266 C.A.2d 222.

There is a lawful arrest for purposes of this section when a suspect has been arrested after an accident for both drunkenness in a public place under Pen.C. § 647 and misdemeanor drunk driving under § 23102 where the officer who made the arrest arrives at the scene sometime after the occurrence of the accident and the suspect was identified as the driver by witnesses at the scene. 52 Ops.Atty.Gen. 250, 12-9-69.

Where officer observed that motorist's driving was jerky and that he was going across center line, and officer could smell alcohol on motorist's breath and noted slurred speech and bloodshot eyes, these observations and motorist's responses to routine field tests justified officer's arrest of motorist and invocation of procedures of the implied consent law, leading to six-month suspension of driver's license if motorist refused to take chemical blood-alcohol test. McDonnell v. Department of Motor Vehicles (1975) 119 Cal.Rptr. 804, 45 C.A.3d 653.

Where officer on probable cause has informed person of intention to arrest him, of cause of arrest and authority to make it, at scene of accident, officer is not bound to closely attend such person to exclusion of duty to obtain aid for accident victims and to prevent further traffic pileups and injuries, and if officer attends such necessary and humanitarian duties his failure to maintain close custody of suspect does not retroactively affect validity of arrest or provide immunity from operation of this section. People v. Superior Court In and For San Mateo County (1973) 110 Cal.Rptr. 504, 35 C.A.3d 1.

Police officer who followed erratically driven automobile until it was driven into driveway in residential area and who saw defendant as the only person around likely to have been the driver of automobile had reasonable cause to arrest defendant for driving while intoxicated, notwithstanding claim of defendant that officer did not actually see who was the driver of the erratically driven automobile. Noia v. Director, Dept. of Motor Vehicles (1973) 110 Cal.Rptr. 231, 34 C.A.3d 691.

Where deputy sheriff "stopped" motorist for alleged offense of drunk driving and summoned assistance of highway patrol and officer arrived in about 15 or 20 minutes, determined that motorist was under influence of alcohol and arrested motorist and asked him to submit to chemical test, officer had reasonable cause to believe motorist had committed the alleged offense, and, deputy sheriff having seen act constituting the offense and having participated in the arrest, arrest for misdemeanor was lawful and suspension of motorist's driver's license upon motorist's refusal to submit to test was proper. Freeman v. Department of Motor Vehicles (1969) 74 Cal.Rptr. 259, 449 P.2d 195, 70 C.2d 235.

§ 13353   VEHICLE CODE

Duty of officer

Where a motorist who has been given Miranda warnings manifests confusion by asserting his alleged right to an attorney prior to taking blood-alcohol test or deciding whether to take such test, it is incumbent on officer to explain that right to attorney does not apply to such tests. McDonnell v. Department of Motor Vehicles (1975) 119 Cal.Rptr. 804, 45 C.A.3d 653.

Refusal to submit to test—In general

In civil proceeding for suspension of person's driving privilege under implied consent law, driver does not enjoy right to consult with counsel, or to have counsel present, before deciding to submit to chemical tests prescribed by statute. Westmoreland v. Chapman (1969) 74 Cal.Rptr. 363, 268 C.A.2d 1; Reirdon v. Director, Dept. of Motor Vehicles (1968) 72 Cal.Rptr. 614, 266 C.A.2d 808.

Where driver arrested for drunk driving, after having been warned of his right to counsel and to remain silent and having been requested to submit to alternate chemical test when he was unable to give second urine specimen, did not request attorney but answered the request with "I'm not even going to give you an answer," police officer was justified in inferring that such reply was refusal to take another test, and such refusal was not result of confusion so as to vitiate the refusal under this section providing penalty of suspension of driver's license for six months. Cahall v. Department of Motor Vehicles, Division of Drivers' Licenses (1971) 94 Cal.Rptr. 182, 16 C.A.3d 491.

Fact that police officer did not present driver arrested for drunk driving with equipment or facilities necessary to accomplish blood or breathalyzer test was not basis for claim that driver did not refuse the tests under this section, where officer offered to have blood or breath test administered but driver, who had consented to urinalysis test but had been unable to provide second urine specimen, stated "I'm not even going to give you an answer." Id.

Where driver was advised of his choice of blood, breath, or urine test and chose the urine test, and was directed to restroom where with his back to open door he endeavored to produce urine specimen, where the driver asked arresting officer and laboratory attendant who remained behind him about 5 or 6 feet, to leave and to close the door, and after the officer refused and after about 15 minutes, stated that he would not take the test because he was too modest, and where blood and breath tests were again offered but were refused, the attempted administration of urine test conformed to requirements of this section providing for administration of chemical test for purpose of determining alcoholic content of blood and his driver's license was properly suspended for 6 months. Quesada v. Orr (1971) 92 Cal.Rptr. 640, 14 C.A.3d 866.

Determining factor as to whether motorist has refused to submit to chemical test required by this section is not state of suspect driver's mind, but is the fair meaning to be given his response to demand that he submit to the test. Maxsted v. Department of Motor Vehicles (1971) 92 Cal.Rptr. 579, 14 C.A.3d 982.

Motorist arrested for driving while under influence of intoxicating liquor was entitled by this section to submit to blood, breath or urine test to determine alcoholic content of blood, but his insistence upon taking all three tests amounted to refusal to submit to test. Kesler v. Department of Motor Vehicles (1969) 81 Cal.Rptr. 348, 459 P.2d 900, 1 C.3d 74, certiorari denied 90 S.Ct. 1121, 397 U.S. 989, 25 L.Ed.2d 396.

Refusal of motorist arrested for driving while intoxicated to submit to one of three blood alcohol tests provided by this section, predicated on motorist's insistence on taking all three tests, was not excused by arresting officer's failure to advise motorist that he could obtain additional test at his own expense; nor did such failure deprive motorist of due process of law. Id.

Statement of drunk driving suspect that he must first consult with counsel before deciding whether to submit to intoxication test constitutes refusal to submit. Maitland v. Chapman (1969) 80 Cal.Rptr. 729, 276 C.A.2d 296.

Motorist arrested for drunken driving did not have constitutional right to refuse to take blood alcohol test required by this section. Pepin v. Department of Motor Vehicles (1969) 79 Cal.Rptr. 657, 275 C.A.2d 9.

Insistence by motorist arrested for drunken driving upon consulting his attorney before taking blood alcohol test prescribed by this section supported finding that he refused to take test. Id.

Although it may well be that if one or two of the three tests (blood, urine or breath) for determining alcoholic content of blood is objectionable to licensee because of a valid technical deficiency he need not submit to a test which is not his first choice, nevertheless it is required that the licensee upon whom demand is properly made must point out the deficiency which has caused him to refuse his preferred test with clearness sufficient to permit police officers to decide on the validity of his protest and, if reasonable to do so, to take steps to meet the objection. Wegner v. Department of Motor Vehicles (1969) 76 Cal.Rptr. 920, 271 C.A.2d 838.

Motorist who was arrested for driving while under influence of intoxicating liquor and who refused to submit to chemical test to determine alcoholic content of his blood at time of arrest but who stated 30 or 45 minutes later that he would submit to test, at which time arresting officer, tending to other police duties, refused to return and no test was administered, could not successfully content that had officer administered test it would have been possible, through mathematical calculation, to determine from delayed test result the blood alcohol level at time of arrest, as scientific validity of such procedure was not established nor did this section make provision for such an inquiry. Zidell v. Bright (1968) 71 Cal.Rptr. 111, 264 C.A.2d 867.

Proceedings leading up to suspension of driving privilege upon refusal to take chemical blood, breath, or urine tests on arrest for drunken driving are civil in nature, rather than criminal. Fallis v. Department of Motor Vehicles (1968) 70 Cal.Rptr. 595, 264 C.A.2d 373.

A person lawfully arrested but believing himself innocent of charges cannot refuse blood alcohol test with impunity on theory that evidence as to his being under the influence of alcohol has been suppressed. Martin v. Department of Motor Vehicles (1976) 126 Cal.Rptr. 924, 524 C.A.3d 903.

Insistence on taking all three blood alcohol tests or none is a "refusal" within the implied consent law, as is an unequivocal "no" based on the uncommunicated belief that an attorney is on the way. McDonnell v. Department of Motor Vehicles (1975) 119 Cal.Rptr. 804, 45 C.A.3d 653.

Where motorist arrested for driving while under influence of intoxicating liquor was advised that she had right to remain silent, had right to attorney, was requested to submit to chemical test, was given choice of chemical test, was advised that refusal to submit to test would result in loss of driving privilege, and was advised she had no right to have attorney present before stating whether she would submit to test, motorist's refusal to reply to request to submit to test constituted refusal to submit to test under this section, even though motorist contended that she was confused by officer's advice that she had right to remain silent. Lampman v. Department of Motor Vehicles (1972) 105 Cal.Rptr. 101, 28 C.A.3d 922.

Motorist's belief that criminal conviction was necessary to bring about license suspension, not induced by police statements, did not excuse her refusal of test under implied consent law. Nidever v. Department of Motor Vehicles (1971) 98 Cal.Rptr. 665, 21 C.A.3d 850.

When a juvenile fails to select and complete one of the chemical tests for sobriety, it constitutes a refusal which will result in the suspension of his driving privilege even though such failure was based on advice or instructions of a parent. 54 Ops.Atty.Gen. 248, 11–23–71.

Unless motorist's arrest for driving motor vehicle while under influence of intoxicating liquor is confused or misled as to his rights, a refusal to take chemical test because of absence of counsel, or a consent to the test qualified by the requirement of the presence of counsel, will be deemed an absolute refusal. Goodman v. Orr (1971) 97 Cal.Rptr. 226, 19 C.A.3d 845.

Qualified consent, refusal to submit to test

Motorist, who was lawfully required as a condition to holding his license against suspension to take one of the three tests (blood, urine or breath) prescribed by this section for determining alcoholic content of blood, did not comply with this section by a consent which was made conditional upon the withdrawing of his blood by physician of his choice. Wegner v. Department of Motor Vehicles (1969) 76 Cal.Rptr. 920, 271 C.A.2d 838.

Driver may not qualify consent to submit to chemical test prescribed by implied consent law by condition that test be administered by or in the presence of his own physician inasmuch as such qualified consent amounts to refusal to take the test. Westmoreland v. Chapman (1969) 74 Cal.Rptr. 363, 268 C.A.2d 1.

Suspected drunk driver has refused to take blood alcohol test when he conditions his consent on having counsel present; he is not entitled to advice of counsel in connection with test. Rust v. Department of Motor Vehicles, Division of Driver's Licenses (1968) 73 Cal.Rptr. 366, 267 C.A.2d 545.

Motorist's statement to arresting officer that motorist would take chemical test to determine his sobriety on the condition that his attorney be present at taking of test amounted to "refusal" for purpose of suspension of his driving privilege under this section. Reirdon v. Director, Dept. of Motor Vehicles (1968) 72 Cal.Rptr. 614, 266 C.A.2d 808.

By imposing condition that her attorney be present before she would consent to taking one of three tests prescribed by this section to determine alcoholic content of blood, motorist in legal effect refused to take any test within purview of that section providing that refusal will result in suspension of driving privilege for period of six months. Ent v. State, Dept. of Motor Vehicles (1968) 71 Cal.Rptr. 726, 265 C.A.2d 936.

Licensee may not qualify his consent to submit to chemical blood, breath, or urine test on arrest for drunken driving by condition that test be administered by or in presence of his own physician, as such qualified consent amounts to refusal to take test. Fallis v. Department of Motor Vehicles (1968) 70 Cal.Rptr. 595, 264 C.A.2d 373.

Delay as constituting refusal to submit to test

Driver who was told at scene of his arrest for driving under influence of alcohol that a refusal to submit to one of three sobriety tests would probably result in suspension of his driver's license and was taken to police station where he was requested to submit to test and was told after attempting to consult his attorney before consenting to test that any further delay would constitute refusal to submit to test and that his driver's license would be suspended was adequately warned of consequences of his failure to submit to test and suspension of his license on basis of such refusal was proper. Janusch v. Department of Motor Vehicles (1969) 80 Cal.Rptr. 726, 276 C.A.2d 193.

Motorist who refused original demand to take chemical test to determine alcoholic content of his blood but consented to test four hours later did not comply with this section. Skinner v. Sillas (1976) 130 Cal.Rptr. 91, 58 C.A.3d 591.

Right to counsel, refusal to submit to test

Person arrested for driving motor vehicle while under influence of intoxicating liquor has no constitutional right to consult attorney before deciding whether he will submit to chemical tests for intoxication. Smith v. Department of Motor Vehicles (1969) 81 Cal.Rptr. 800, 1 C.A.3d 499; Lacy v. Orr (1969) 81 Cal.Rptr. 276, 276 C.A.2d 198; Lagomarsino v. Director of Dept. of Motor Vehicles (1969) 81 Cal.Rptr. 193, 276 C.A.2d 517; Maitland v. Chapman (1969) 80 Cal.Rptr. 729, 276 C.A.2d 296; West v. Dept. of Motor Vehicles (1969) 80 Cal.Rptr. 385, 275 C.A.2d 908; Pepin v. Department of Motor Vehicles (1969) 79 Cal.Rptr. 657, 275 C.A.2d 9; Whalen v. Municipal Court of City of Alhambra (1969) 79 Cal.Rptr. 523, 274 C.A.2d 809.

Motorist arrested for driving while intoxicated has no right to presence of counsel before blood alcohol test is taken. Funke v. Department of Motor Vehicles (1969) 81 Cal.Rptr. 662, 1 C.A.3d 449; Plumb v. Department of Motor Vehicles (1969) 81 Cal.Rptr. 639, 1 C.A.3d 256.

Rule that refusal of driver arrested for driving while intoxicated to take chemical test should be vitiated where he was confused by warnings as to his right to counsel and to remain silent and by demand for chemical test under this section does not apply when arresting officer explicitly informs arrestee that the rights to counsel and remain silent do not apply to taking of chemical test pursuant to this section. Cahall v. Department of Motor Vehicles, Division of Drivers' Licenses (1971) 94 Cal.Rptr. 182, 16 C.A.3d 491.

Petitioner was not entitled to counsel when he was called upon while in custody of police to decide whether he would submit or refuse to submit to chemical test to determine alcoholic content of blood. Finley v. Orr (1968) 69 Cal.Rptr. 137, 262 C.A.2d 656.

Person accused of driving while drunk has no constitutional right to refuse test designed to produce physical evidence in form of breath sample or blood or urine whether or not counsel is present and is not entitled to consult counsel before submitting to one of the tests and his statement that he will consent only after such consultation is refusal under statute. Janusch v. Department of Motor Vehicles (1969) 80 Cal.Rptr. 726, 276 C.A.2d 193.

Warning in general, refusal to submit to test

Arresting officer's admonition to motorist that his driver's license "could be suspended" if he failed to take one of the three tests required by law for persons arrested for drunk driving was insufficient under this section requiring warning that license will be or would be suspended in event of refusal. Giomi v. Director, Dept. of Motor Vehicles (1971) 93 Cal.Rptr. 613, 15 C.A.3d 905.

Where motorist who was arrested for driving while under influence of intoxicating liquor, warned of his Miranda rights and requested to submit to chemical test did not request an attorney but answered request to submit to test with an unqualified "no," there was no duty upon officer giving Miranda warnings to explain that right to counsel did not apply to suspect's statutory obligation to submit to chemical test, failure to so explain did not render driver's refusal "not an intelligent refusal" and department of motor vehicles properly ordered suspension of the driver's license. Maxsted v. Department of Motor Vehicles (1971) 92 Cal.Rptr. 579, 14 C.A.3d 982.

Where arresting officer read requirements of statute to petitioner that he was to submit to chemical test to determine alcoholic content of blood and refusal would result in suspension of driving privilege for six months, officer's subsequent statement to petitioner that "chances are" that he would lose his license if he refused did not vitiate compliance with this section and warning was sufficient. Smith v. Department of Motor Vehicles (1969) 81 Cal.Rptr. 800, 1 C.A.3d 499.

It is a question of fact whether Miranda warning so confused and misled motorist who has been asked to take a chemical test for intoxication that his demand for counsel prior to taking the test should not be regarded as an unjustified refusal. Lagomarsino v. Director of Dept. of Motor Vehicles (1969) 81 Cal.Rptr. 193, 276 C.A.2d 517.

The suspension of motorist driver's license for refusal to submit to a chemical test of the alcoholic contents of his blood, breath or urine following his arrest for driving under influence of intoxicating liquor was not improper on ground that the Miranda warning which advised him of his right to counsel during police interrogation led him to believe that he was entitled to counsel before and during the test, and that belief cancelled effect of statutory admonition that refusal to submit to test would result in suspension of license, where record disclosed that motorist had not been confused and misled by the Miranda warning. Walker v. Department of Motor Vehicles (1969) 79 Cal.Rptr. 433, 274 C.A.2d 793.

Fact that motorist arrested for drunken driving was first given Miranda warnings and thereafter asked if he would submit to chemical, blood, breath, or urine test, and thereafter motorist stated that he would not take any test unless given by his own doctor in presence of his attorney, did not violate motorist's constitutional rights and his statement constituted a refusal to take the test. Fallis v. Department of Motor Vehicles (1968) 70 Cal.Rptr. 595, 264 C.A.2d 373.

Where motorist arrested for operating vehicle under influence of intoxicating liquor refused to reply to officer's request to submit to chemical test, officer was not required to warn motorist that right to remain silent for purposes of self-incrimination did not include right to remain silent for purposes of driver licensing when chemical test was sought. Lampman v. Department of Motor Vehicles (1972) 105 Cal.Rptr. 101, 28 C.A.3d 922.

Warning by arresting officer, advising motorist that he was required to take one of three chemical tests of his choice and that if he refused to take one of such tests his driving privileges "could" be suspended for a period of six months, did not substantially comply with requirements of this section providing for mandatory suspension of driving privileges upon refusal by person arrested for driving while under the influence of intoxicating liquor to agree to submit to one of three chemical tests. Decker v. Department of Motor Vehicles (1972) 101 Cal.Rptr. 387, 495 P.2d 1307, 6 C.3d 903.

Right to counsel, warning, refusal to submit to tests

If after a Miranda warning, particularly if it is overbroad and encompasses the right to counsel at more than interrogation, suspected drunken driver replies to demand for chemical test with a request for counsel, trial court may fairly interpret that request as something other than a refusal, unless officer then informs suspect that the Miranda warning is inapplicable to the test, for purposes of determining whether driver's license can be suspended for refusal to take the test. Maxsted v. Department of Motor Vehicles (1971) 92 Cal.Rptr. 579, 14 C.A.3d 982.

Where following arrest for driving while intoxicated motorist was informed that he was entitled to be represented by an attorney at that time or at any other proceeding but was not informed that right to attorney did not entitle him to consult an attorney before taking blood-alcohol chemical test and refusal to take test was product of confusion and mistaken belief that he could refuse to do so until he had consulted an attorney, refusal to take test was not that refusal contemplated by this section. Rees v. Department of Motor Vehicles (1970) 87 Cal.Rptr. 456, 8 C.A.3d 746.

Where person arrested for driving motor vehicle while under influence of intoxicating liquor is confused and his replies to requests concerning willingness to submit to test to determine alcoholic content of blood indicate he is asserting a right which he mistakenly believes was just communicated to him to have attorney present, it is incumbent on arresting officer to elaborate on warning and to explicitly inform arrested person that he has no right to consult attorney before making decision that he will or will not submit to test. Smith v. Department of Motor Vehicles (1969) 81 Cal.Rptr. 800, 1 C.A.3d 499.

When driver asks to talk to his attorney before deciding whether or not to submit to one of sobriety tests required by this section and request comes after he has been told by officer that he has right to consult attorney, he cannot be deemed actually to have refused to submit to test if he, as matter of fact, honestly misconstrued officer's statement as right to make such call before reaching decision. Plumb v. Department of Motor Vehicles (1969) 81 Cal.Rptr. 639, 1 C.A.3d 256.

Where it becomes apparent that person arrested for driving while intoxicated is confused concerning right to counsel, it is incumbent upon officer to explain to arrestee that constitutional right to counsel is not applicable to decision he must make as to whether to take chemical test for intoxication and that he has no right to consult attorney before deciding whether or not to submit to chemical test. West v. Dept. of Motor Vehicles (1969) 80 Cal.Rptr. 385, 275 C.A.2d 908.

Where motorist who was arrested on drunken driving charge and who refused to submit to chemical test to determine alcoholic content of his blood until he could call his attorney was advised of his constitutional rights, including right to counsel, motorist could not be required to take test in absence of further explanation that his constitutional rights did not apply to decision to, or not to, submit to sobriety test, and suspension of driving license for refusal to submit to test was unauthorized. Weber v. Orr (1969) 79 Cal.Rptr. 297, 297 C.A.2d 288.

Where it becomes apparent that person arrested for driving while intoxicated is confused concerning right to counsel, it is incumbent upon officer to explain to arrested person that constitutional rights to counsel and to remain silent are not applicable to decision he must make as to whether to take chemical test for intoxication and that he has no right to consult attorney before deciding whether or not to submit to chemical. Wethern v. Orr (1969) 76 Cal.Rptr. 807, 271 C.A.2d 813.

Failure to advise motorist that he did not have right to attorney before deciding whether or not to take intoxication test rendered explanation of constitutional rights erroneous and misleading so that motorist who stated he wanted attorney did not refuse to take test within contemplation of statute authorizing six months' suspension of license for a refusal. Id.

Police officer, who warned defendant, arrested for drunken driving, of his right to an attorney, should have qualified his advice, when it became evident that defendant thought he was entitled to attorney before having to submit to requested blood alcohol test, to make it clear that the right to an attorney was inapplicable to requested blood alcohol test, and defendant's refusal to take test until he called his attorney did not constitute rejection warranting suspension of his driver's license. Rust v. Department of Motor Vehicles, Division of Driver's Licenses (1963) 73 Cal.Rptr. 366, 267 C.A.2d 545.

Motorist's refusal to submit to chemical test to determine his sobriety unless his attorney was present at test was effective refusal for purpose of suspension of his driving privilege under implied consent law, and that he could not assert that refusal was ineffective because he was confused by arresting officers' Miranda advice that he had right to counsel in connection with criminal charge of drunken driving, where he was clearly and unequivocally told that he had no right to presence of counsel at time test was being administered. Reirdon v. Director, Dept. of Motor Vehicles (1968) 72 Cal.Rptr. 614, 266 C.A.2d 808.

Even though motorist arrested for driving while under influence of intoxicating liquor demanded that counsel be present at taking of chemical test to determine alcoholic content of her blood, police were under no duty to warn her that she had no right to counsel at time of taking of test. Ent v. State, Dept. of Motor Vehicles (1968) 71 Cal.Rptr. 726, 265 C.A.2d 936.

Where defendant motorist who had been given Miranda warnings and implied consent admonition was advised by arresting officers that right to consult attorney did not apply to chemical test request but defendant refused to take test before he had consulted attorney, motorist's lack of understanding, whether engendered by his partial intoxication or attributable to his normal state of intelligence, did not affect the finality and effectiveness of his refusal to submit to chemical test. Goodman v. Orr (1971) 97 Cal.Rptr. 226, 19 C.A.3d 845.

Right to physician, warning, refusal to submit to test

Motorist, who was requested to take one of the three chemical sobriety tests under this section was not entitled to refuse to take any of the tests because he was not advised that he could employ a physician of his own choosing at his own expense to administer an additional chemical test. Lacy v. Orr (1969) 81 Cal.Rptr. 276, 276 C.A.2d 198.

Petitioner's insistence, after arrest for driving while under influence of intoxicating liquor, that drawing of blood for test of alcoholic content be performed by his own physician constituted refusal to submit to blood test and warranted suspension of driving privilege even though officer did not explain that petitioner had no right to have his physician withdraw the blood where petitioner's misconception was in no way police-initiated but rather was product of petitioner's own thinking. Beales v. State, Dept. of Motor Vehicles (1969) 76 Cal.Rptr. 662, 271 C.A.2d 594.

Persons incapable of refusal to submit to test

Provision of this section relating to chemical blood, breath, or urine tests, stating that any person who is dead, unconscious, or otherwise in a condition rendering him incapable of refusal shall be deemed not to have withdrawn his consent, does not confer any rights upon an intoxicated driver, but simply allows chemical test of a person who is dead, unconscious or otherwise unable to refuse, making it clear that even in such cases the earlier provision that the person shall be deemed to have given his consent shall nevertheless apply. Bush v. Bright (1968) 71 Cal.Rptr. 123, 264 C.A.2d 788.

Being too drunk to understand proffered information or explanations with respect to the implied consent law does not excuse refusal to take blood alcohol test. McDonnell v. Department of Motor Vehicles (1975) 119 Cal.Rptr. 804, 45 C.A.3d 653.

Time of test

It is common knowledge that intoxicating effect of alcohol diminishes with passage of time and that hence probative value of blood test diminishes as well. Lacy v. Orr (1969) 81 Cal.Rptr. 276, 276 C.A.2d 198.

Language of this section stating that chemical test to determine alcoholic content of blood shall be incidental to lawful arrest and administered at direction of officer having reasonable cause to believe motorist was driving under influence of intoxicating liquor and language that motorist may request arresting officer to have chemical test made and if so requested arresting officer shall have test performed, implies that decision of arresting officer whether to request test, and suspect's response thereto, should not be delayed. Zidell v. Bright (1968) 71 Cal.Rptr. 111, 264 C.A.2d 867.

Under this section, chemical test to determine blood alcohol content in arrested motorist must be taken as soon as possible after arresting for driving under the influence since alcohol in blood system dissipates quickly. Skinner v. Sillas (1976) 130 Cal.Rptr. 91, 58 C.A.3d 591.

Choice of test

Motorist has no right to be told of all three possible chemical tests under this section, as long as he is told of one and thereafter takes test of which he has been informed. Skinner v. Sillas (1976) 130 Cal.Rptr. 91, 58 C.A.3d 591.

Violation of portion of implied consent statute providing that a person arrested for any offense allegedly committed while driving under the influence of intoxicating liquor should have choice of whether test shall be of his blood, breath or urine and shall be advised by officer that he has such choice does not involve a violation of any constitutionally protected interest; thus, failure to advise defendant who was charged with drunk driving of his right of choice among the three tests did not render results of breathalyzer test taken by defendant inadmissible in prosecution for misdemeanor drunk driving. People v. Brannon (1973) 108 Cal.Rptr. 620, 32 C.A.3d 971.

Completion of test

If motorist elects to take one of three chemical tests under this section he must complete test or he will be deemed to have refused and failed to take it and, once he refuses to take one of the tests, there is no requirement that officers thereafter give him a test when he decides he is ready. Skinner v. Sillas (1976) 130 Cal.Rptr. 91, 58 C.A.3d 591.

Implied in "Implied Consent" statute (§ 13354 and this section) is requirement that one of described tests for intoxication be submitted to and completed expeditiously, and failure to complete test selected requires submission to, and completion of, one of other tests. Smith v. Cozens (1972) 101 Cal.Rptr. 787, 25 C.A.3d 300.

Evidence

Where requirement that driver take sobriety test in form of blood test was not violative of privilege against self-incrimination, it was not improper to allow evidence of her refusal to take test or to allow prosecutorial comment on her refusal, or for court to instruct on her refusal. Newhouse v. Misterly (C.A.1969) 415 F.2d 514, certiorari denied 90 S.Ct. 1001, 397 U.S. 966, 25 L.Ed.2d 258.

Evidence supported finding that motorist, who sought writ of mandamus to compel department of motor vehicles to annul order revoking his driver's license, and who subsequent to arrest gave clear and positive answers to questions including question whether he would take any of the three tests for determining alcoholic content of his blood on penalty of suspension of his driving privileges if he refused, was not in a condition rendering him incapable of refusing to submit to a chemical test. Hulshizer v. Department of Motor Vehicles (1969) 82 Cal.Rptr. 330, 1 C.A.3d 807.

Adequate evidence existed to support finding that motorist refused to take chemical test for intoxication, as against contention that his request for counsel was not a refusal to take the test. Lagomarsino v. Director of Dept. of Motor Vehicles (1969) 81 Cal.Rptr. 193, 276 C.A.2d 517.

§ 13353

Evidence in mandamus proceeding to compel department of motor vehicles to set aside order revoking driving privileges supported conclusion that drunk driving suspect was not misled into believing that he had right to refuse to take intoxication test because of warning of his rights to counsel and to remain silent. Maitland v. Chapman (1969) 80 Cal.Rptr. 729, 276 C.A.2d 296.

Under this section providing that arrested person shall be told that his failure to submit to a test will result in suspension of his license, it is a question of fact whether driver was given statutory advice, and whether he refused the test, and if evidence shows that officer made ambiguous or conflicting statements, that evidence has a bearing on whether the advice conforms substantially to statutory requirement, and whether response of driver indicated his confusion rather than his refusal to perform a statutory duty. Walker v. Department of Motor Vehicles (1969) 79 Cal.Rptr. 433, 274 C.A.2d 793.

Where blood sample was taken from defendant without force or violence, though defendant allegedly objected, result of blood test was not inadmissible on theory that by objecting, defendant agreed to accept penalty of suspension of his driver's license and thus could not be subjected to blood test. People v. Wren (1969) 76 Cal.Rptr. 673, 271 C.A.2d 788.

Evidence that petitioner after being arrested on suspicion of driving under the influence of intoxicating liquor was advised that if he refused to take one of three chemical tests provided for by implied consent law his license would be suspended, that petitioner refused to permit blood test to be taken because technician was not an M.D. and that petitioner refused to consent to other tests supported finding that petitioner refused to take test. Westmoreland v. Chapman (1969) 74 Cal.Rptr. 363, 268 C.A.2d 1.

Evidence supported finding that motorist, who was arrested for driving while intoxicated, who did not choose between blood, breath and urine tests for intoxication, but who did not expressly refuse to take a test, did not refuse to take test to determine his intoxication so as to warrant suspension of his driver's license. James v. State ex rel. Dept. of Motor Vehicles (1968) 73 Cal.Rptr. 452, 267 C.A.2d 750.

Motor vehicle department's admissible evidence before hearing officer at informal hearing to determine whether motorist's driver's license should be suspended for refusal to take chemical blood, breath, or urine test on arrest for drunken driving, consisting only of statement in form of conclusion that arresting officer had reasonable cause to arrest motorist was insufficient to overcome motorist's evidence to the contrary. Fallis v. Department of Motor Vehicles (1968) 70 Cal.Rptr. 595, 264 C.A.2d 373.

Although arresting officer's sworn statement and two police arrest records were not official records and were therefore improperly admitted in hearing for purpose of determining whether petitioner's driver's license should be suspended for failure to submit to blood, breath or urine chemical test after arrest for drunken driving, their admission did not provide grounds for writ of mandate to department of motor vehicles to vacate order suspending petitioner's license, as petitioner's own testimony provided sufficient evidence to support suspension order. Goss v. Department of Motor Vehicles (1968) 70 Cal.Rptr. 447, 264 C.A.2d 268.

Evidence produced by department of motor vehicles, in proceeding relating to suspension of driver's license, if itself insufficient, may be supplemented by testimony of licensee on his own behalf. August v. Department of Motor Vehicles (1968) 70 Cal.Rptr. 172, 264 C.A.2d 52.

Reception of testimony at driver's license suspension hearing with respect to petitioner's refusal to submit to chemical test for purpose of determining alcoholic content of blood did not violate petitioner's privilege against self-incrimination. Finley v. Orr (1968) 69 Cal. Rptr. 137, 262 C.A.2d 656.

§ 13354. Administration of tests

(a) Only a physician, registered nurse, licensed vocational nurse, duly licensed clinical laboratory technologist or clinical laboratory bioanalyst, or certified paramedic acting at the request of a peace officer may withdraw blood for the purpose of determining the alcoholic content therein. This limitation shall not apply to the taking of breath specimens. An emergency call for paramedic services shall take precedence over a peace officer's request for a paramedic to withdraw blood for determining its alcoholic content. A certified paramedic shall not withdraw blood for such purpose unless authorized by his or her employer to do so.

(b) The person tested may, at his own expense, have a physician, registered nurse, licensed vocational nurse, duly licensed clinical laboratory technologist or clinical laboratory bioanalyst or any other person of his own choosing administer a test, in addition to any administered at the direction of a peace officer, for the purpose of determining the amount of alcohol in his blood at the time alleged as shown by chemical analysis of his blood, breath or urine. The failure or inability to obtain an additional test by a person shall not preclude the admissibility in evidence of the test taken at the direction of a peace officer.

(c) Upon the request of the person tested full information concerning the test taken at the direction of the peace officer shall be made available to him or his attorney.

(d) No physician, registered nurse, licensed vocational nurse, duly licensed clinical laboratory technologist or clinical laboratory bioanalyst, or certified paramedic, or hospital, laboratory or clinic employing or utilizing the services of such physician, registered nurse, licensed vocational nurse, duly licensed laboratory technologist or clinical laboratory bioanalyst, or certified paramedic, owning or leasing the premises on which such tests are performed, shall incur any civil or criminal liability as a result of the proper administering of a blood test when requested in writing by a peace officer to administer such a test.

(e) If the test given under Section 13353 is a chemical test of urine, the person tested shall be given such privacy in the taking of the urine specimen as will insure the accuracy of the specimen and, at the same time, maintain the dignity of the individual involved.

(f) The Department of the California Highway Patrol, in cooperation with the State Department of Health Services or any other appropriate agency, shall adopt uniform standards for the withdrawal, handling, and preservation of blood samples prior to analysis.

(g) As used in this section, "certified paramedic" does not include any employee of a fire department.
(Amended by Stats.1978, c. 554, p. —, § 1.)

§ 14601. Driving when privileges suspended or revoked for certain offenses

(a) No person shall drive a motor vehicle upon a highway at any time when his driving privilege is suspended or revoked for reckless driving, driving while under the influence of alcohol or any drug, or under the combined influence of alcohol and any drug, any reason listed in subdivisions (b) through (f) of Section 12805 requiring the department to refuse to issue a license, negligent or incompetent operation of a motor vehicle as prescribed in subdivision (e) of Section 12809, or negligent operation as prescribed in Section 12810, and the person so driving has knowledge of such suspension or revocation. Knowledge shall be presumed if notice has been given by the department to such person. The presumption established by this subdivision is a presumption affecting burden of proof.

(b) Any person convicted under this section shall be punished upon a first conviction by imprisonment in the county jail for not less than five days nor more than six months and by fine of not more than five hundred dollars ($500), and upon a second or any subsequent conviction, within seven years of a prior conviction, by imprisonment in the county jail for not less than 10 days nor more than one year and by fine of not more than one thousand dollars ($1,000).

(c) If any person is convicted of a second or subsequent offense under this section within seven years of a prior conviction and is granted probation, it shall be a condition of probation that such person be confined in jail for at least 10 days.
(Amended by Stats.1972, c. 618, p. 1148, § 140.)

§ 14601.1. Driving when privilege revoked or suspended for other reasons

(a) No person shall drive a motor vehicle on a highway when his driving privilege is suspended or revoked for any reason other than those listed in Section 14601 when the person so driving has knowledge of either such fact. Knowledge shall be presumed if notice has been given by the department to such person. The presumption established by this subdivision is a presumption affecting the burden of proof.

(b) Any person convicted under this section shall be punished upon a first conviction by imprisonment in the county jail for not more than six months or by fine of not more than five hundred dollars ($500) or by both such fine and imprisonment, and upon a second or any subsequent conviction under this section or Section 14601, within seven years of a prior conviction, by imprisonment in the county jail for not less than five days nor more than one year and by fine of not more than one thousand dollars ($1,000).
(Amended by Stats.1972, c. 618, p. 1149, § 142.)

§ 14603. Violation of license restrictions

No person shall operate a vehicle in violation of the provisions of a restricted license issued to him.
(Stats.1959, c. 3, p. 1634, § 14603.)

§ 14606. Employment of person to drive motor vehicle; license and medical certificate

(a) No person shall employ or hire any person to drive a motor vehicle nor shall he knowingly permit or authorize the driving of a motor vehicle, owned by him or under his control, upon the highways by any person unless the person is then licensed for the appropriate class of vehicle to be driven.

(b) Whenever any person employs or hires any person, including a subhauler, to drive a class 1 or class 2 vehicle, the employer shall ascertain that such person has in his possession a medical certificate as provided in subdivision (c) of Section 12804 which has been issued within two years prior to the date of such employment or hiring. Whenever such person fails to qualify for such a medical certificate on reexamination, the employer shall report such failure to the department.
(Amended by Stats.1971, c. 1279, p. 2509, § 3.)

§ 14607. Permitting unlicensed minor to drive

No person shall cause or knowingly permit his child, ward, or employee under the age of 18 years to drive a motor vehicle upon the highways unless such child, ward, or employee is then licensed under this code.
(Amended by Stats.1971, c. 1748, p. 3764, § 59.)

§ 14610. Unlawful use of license

It is unlawful for any person:

(a) To display or cause or permit to be displayed or have in his possession any canceled, revoked, suspended, fictitious, fraudulently altered, or fraudulently obtained driver's license.

(b) To lend his driver's license to any other person or knowingly permit the use thereof by another.

(c) To display or represent any driver's license not issued to him as being his license.

(d) To fail or refuse to surrender to the department upon its lawful demand any driver's license which has been suspended, revoked or canceled.

(e) To permit any unlawful use of a driver's license issued to him.

(f) To do any act forbidden or fail to perform any act required by this division.

(g) To photograph, photostat, duplicate, or in any way reproduce any driver's license or facsimile thereof in such a manner that it could be mistaken for a valid license, or to display or have in his possession any such photograph, photostat, duplicate, reproduction, or facsimile unless authorized by the provisions of this code.

(h) To alter any driver's license in any manner not authorized by this code.
(Amended by Stats.1971, c. 1174, p. 2240, § 4.)

Division 6.5
MOTOR VEHICLE TRANSACTIONS WITH MINORS

§ 15500. Acquisition of vehicle by minor; drivers' license required

It is unlawful for any minor who does not possess a valid driver's license issued under this code to order, purchase or lease, attempt to purchase or lease, contract to purchase or lease, accept, or otherwise obtain, any vehicle of a type subject to registration.
(Added by Stats.1968, c. 1020, p. 1972, § 1.)

§ 15501. Unlawful for minor to present false driver's license

It is unlawful for any minor to present or offer to any person offering for sale or lease or to give or otherwise furnish thereto any motor vehicle of a type subject to registration, a driver's license which is false, fraudulent, or not actually his own for the purpose of ordering, purchasing or leasing, attempting to purchase or lease, contracting to purchase or lease, accepting, or otherwise obtaining such a vehicle.
(Added by Stats.1968, c. 1020, p. 1972, § 1.)

Division 7
FINANCIAL RESPONSIBILITY LAWS

§ 16000. Report required

The driver of every motor vehicle which is in any manner involved in an accident originating from the operation of a motor vehicle on any street or highway which accident has resulted in damage to the property of any one person in excess of three hundred fifty dollars ($350) or in bodily injury or in the death of any person shall within 15 days after the accident, report the accident on a form approved by the department to the office of the department at Sacramento, subject to the provisions of this chapter. A report shall not be required in the event that the motor vehicle involved in the accident was owned or leased by or under the direction of the United States, this state, or any political subdivision of this state or municipality thereof.
(Amended by Stats.1978, c. 997, p. —, § 1.)

§ 16005. Use of reports

(a) All reports and supplemental reports required by this chapter including insurance information forms shall be without prejudice to the individual so reporting and shall be for the confidential use of the department and any other state department requiring such information, except that the department shall upon request disclose from the reports:

(1) The names and addresses of persons involved in the accident.

(2) The registration numbers and descriptions of vehicles involved in the accident.

(3) The date, time, and location of the accident.

(4) Any suspension action taken by the department.

(5) The names and addresses of insurers.

(b) The information specified in subdivision (a) may be given to any person having a proper interest therein, including:

(1) The driver or drivers involved, or the employer, parent, or legal guardian thereof.

(2) The authorized representative of any person involved in the accident.

(3) Any person injured in the accident.

(4) The owners of vehicles or property damaged in the accident.

(5) Any law enforcement agency.

(6) Any court of competent jurisdiction.
(Added by Stats.1974, c. 1409, p. 3096, § 8.)

Editors' Note

The remaining sections within this Division deal with the detailed requirements of the State's Financial Responsibility Law. This law is designed to give monetary protection to persons injured while lawfully using the highways. Drivers involved in accidents must post a bond or show proof of insurance.

Division 9
CIVIL LIABILITY

§ 17004. Authorized emergency vehicles

A public employee is not liable for civil damages on account of personal injury to or death of any person or damage to property resulting from the operation, in the line of duty, of an authorized emergency vehicle while responding to an emergency call or when in the immediate pursuit of an actual or suspected violator of the law, or when responding to but not upon returning from a fire alarm or other emergency call.
(Amended by Stats.1965, c. 1527, p. 3620, § 5.)

§ 17300. Willful or negligent damage

Any person who willfully or negligently damages any street, highway, or appurtenances, including, but not limited to, guard rails, signs, traffic signals, and similar facilities, is liable for the cost of the repair or replacement thereof.

The liability stated in this section applies to an owner of a vehicle operated with his permission, as provided in Article 2 (commencing with Section 17150) and shall include liability for the cost of necessary safety precautions, such as warning traffic, the removal of debris resulting from accidents, or providing detours.

The Department of Transportation and local authorities in respect to highways under their respective jurisdictions are authorized to present claims for liability under this section and to bring actions for recovery thereon, and to settle and compromise in their discretion claims arising under this section.
(Amended by Stats.1974, c. 545, p. 1313, § 165.)

§ 17301. Damage by illegal operation of vehicle

(a) Any person driving any vehicle, object, or contrivance over a highway or bridge is liable for all damages which the highway or bridge may sustain as a result of any illegal operation, driving or moving of the vehicle, object, or contrivance, or as a result of operating, driving, or moving any vehicle, object, or contrivance weighing in excess of the maximum weight specified in this code which is operated under a special permit issued by the Department of Transportation.

(b) Whenever the driver is not the owner of the vehicle, object, or contrivance but is operating, driving, or moving the same with the express or implied permission of the owner, the owner and driver are jointly and severally liable for the damage.
(Amended by Stats.1974, c. 545, p. 1313, § 166.)

Division 10
ACCIDENTS AND ACCIDENT REPORTS

§ 20001. Duty to stop at scene of accident

The driver of any vehicle involved in an accident resulting in injury to any person, other than himself, or death of any person shall immediately stop the vehicle at the scene of the accident and shall fulfill the requirements of Sections 20003 and 20004.

Any person failing to comply with all the requirements of this section under such circumstances is guilty of a public offense and upon conviction thereof shall be punished by imprisonment in the state prison, or in the county jail for not to exceed one year or by fine of not to exceed five thousand dollars ($5,000) or by both.
(Amended by Stats.1976, c. 1139, p. ——, § 337.)

Notes of Decisions

Nature and elements of offense—In general

Omission, by driver involved in accident resulting in personal injury, to stop and perform acts required by this section, and knowledge by driver of injury are essential elements of offense proscribed by this section. People v. Rocovich (1969) 74 Cal.Rptr. 755, 269 C.A.2d 489.

Omission, by driver involved in accident resulting in personal injury, to give his name to victim, or to render to victim reasonable assistance, or to perform any one of the other acts required by this section constitutes the offense. People v. Limon (1967) 60 Cal.Rptr. 448, 252 C.A.2d 575.

§ 20001 VEHICLE CODE

An essential element of violation of this section requiring driver of vehicle involved in accident resulting in injury or death to stop immediately is failure of driver to stop immediately and furnish assistance and information required by § 20003. People v. Steinbach (1959) 333 P.2d 147, 166 C.A.2d 307.

This section requiring driver "involved in an accident" to stop, render assistance and give information is in no way made dependent upon whether or not control of a vehicle is retained or lost, or upon who may ultimately be found to have been most at fault. People v. Sell (1950) 215 P.2d 771, 96 C.A.2d 521.

Requirements of provisions of this section and § 20003 setting forth duties of driver of motor vehicle involved in accident causing injury and death to another define separate offenses. People v. Odom (1937) 66 P.2d 206, 19 C.A.2d 641.

Failure to perform any of five acts required of automobile driver after accident is punishable as separate offense. People v. Steele (1929) 280 P. 999, 100 C.A. 639.

Driver of automobile killing pedestrian was not relieved from duty to stop. People v. McKee (1926) 251 P. 675, 80 C.A. 200.

Failure to comply with any of the requirements of former Motor Vehicle Act, § 21, constituted a complete offense. People v. Huber (1923) 221 P. 695, 64 C.A. 352.

Knowledge and intent

Constructive knowledge of personal injury may be imputed to driver of vehicle where fact of personal injury is visible and obvious or where seriousness of collision would lead reasonable person to assume that there must have been resulting injuries, for purposes of felony hit-and-run driving statute. People v. Carter (1966) 52 Cal.Rptr. 207, 243 C.A.2d 239.

In absence of showing of actual knowledge of personal injury on part of motorist who was involved in collision or constructive knowledge thereof, he could not be properly convicted of felony hit-and-run driving. Id.

Knowledge of injury is essential element of crime of failure of a driver of vehicle involved in accident resulting in injury to stop, render aid, and leave identification. People v. Holford (1965) 45 Cal.Rptr. 167, 403 P.2d 423, 63 C.2d 74.

No competent evidence offered at preliminary hearing of driver accused of failure to perform duties of driver of vehicle involved in accident injuring another person established essential element of knowledge on part of driver that accident had occurred, and prohibition would issue requiring dismissal of charge on ground that driver was held to answer without reasonable or probable cause. Garabedian v. Superior Court of City and County of San Francisco (1963) 28 Cal.Rptr. 318, 378 P.2d 590, 59 C.2d 124.

Defendant's knowledge that another automobile involved in accident was wrecked and some other party therein injured was essential ingredient of proof in hit-and-run driving prosecution. People v. Mayo (1961) 15 Cal.Rptr. 366, 194 C.A.2d 527.

In prosecution for failure to perform duties of driver of vehicle involved in traffic accident injuring another person, question of knowledge of infliction of injury on part of accused was factual question for trial court. People v. Kuhn (1956) 292 P.2d 964, 139 C.A.2d 109.

Knowledge on part of accused of an infliction of injury upon another person is essential element of offense of failure to perform duties of driver of vehicle involved in traffic accident injuring another person. Id.

A specific intent is not a necessary element of offense of failing to stop and render aid after an automobile accident. People v. Henry (1937) 72 P.2d 915, 23 C.A.2d 155.

A motorist's declaration that he has no recollection of anything that may have occurred for an interval during which circumstantial evidence overwhelmingly indicates that his automobile was involved in an accident whereby another person was injured or killed is not determinative of the matter. Id.

Automobile driver is not criminally guilty of failing to render aid to injured person when he does not know of injury. People v. Rallo (1931) 6 P.2d 516, 119 C.A. 393.

Law requiring automobilist to stop and render aid was applicable only where automobilist knew accident happened. People v. Leutholtz (1929) 283 P. 292, 102 C.A. 493.

One controlling truck driver and knowing collision occurred is criminally liable for failure to stop and render assistance. People v. Maggio (1928) 266 P. 813, 90 C.A. 683.

Provisions of Motor Vehicle Act, § 141, requiring driver of automobile striking person to stop, render assistance, etc., do not apply to one ignorant of fact that automobile had struck another person. People v. Graves (1925) 240 P. 1019, 74 C.A. 415.

Independently of, as well as in view of, Pen.C. § 20, knowledge by driver of auto that he has collided with a vehicle is necessary to the offense under Pen.C. former § 367c of failure to stop and assist occupants of vehicle. People v. Fodera (1917) 164 P. 22, 33 C.A. 8.

Admissibility of evidence

In prosecution for leaving the scene of an accident without complying with requirements of law, evidence of statements of accused made to officer at time accused filed accident report were admissible although report itself was not admissible. People v. Misner (1954) 285 P.2d 938, 134 C.A.2d 377.

In action for death of pedestrian run over by truck at night while he was attempting to cross highway at place other than crosswalk, wherein negligence of truck driver was alleged by complaint in general terms, plaintiffs were entitled to introduce evidence to show that truck driver was negligent as a matter of law because he failed to stop after accident. Brooks v. E. J. Willig Truck Transp. Co. (1953) 255 P.2d 802, 40 C.2d 669.

In prosecution for failure to stop automobile and give required information to one injured thereby, a photograph, which constable testified was true representation of conditions on highway at place and time of accident, except for girl in photograph, was properly admitted, as illustrative of witness' testimony, over objection that he was not qualified to, and did not properly, identify photograph, though girl's presence therein was not explained. People v. Frank (1943) 141 P.2d 780, 60 C.A.2d 802.

In prosecution for failure to stop automobile and give required information to person injured thereby, error, if any, in admitting in evidence one of a series of six photographs, the rest of which were admitted without complaint, to illustrate testimony of constable, was not prejudicial to defendant. Id.

In prosecution of motorist for failing to stop after an accident resulting in injury to a bicyclist, statements of accused denying and then admitting she was driving the automobile involved in the collision were admissible as tending to prove consciousness of guilt. People v. Roche (1942) 121 P.2d 865, 49 C.A.2d 459.

In prosecution for failure to stop and give information and render aid to a bicyclist struck by motorist, statements of accused that she had observed girl on bicycle while driving, had heard a slight noise and felt her automobile skid, and that she looked back and saw the girl standing in the road brushing her clothes were admissible under evidence showing automobile in passing bicycle in the daytime struck the rear end and passed to its left, that motorist drove off rapidly and that the noise of the collision was heard some 50 feet away, there being no showing that accused suffered from impairment of her faculties. Id.

In prosecution for negligent homicide and for failure to stop and render aid after automobile accident, reception of journal article and diagram on question of intoxication as shown by alcoholic content of blood did not require reversal of conviction for failure to stop and render aid, even if reception was erroneous as violative of hearsay rule, in view of other evidence authorizing conviction without that evidence. People v. Henry (1937) 72 P.2d 915, 23 C.A.2d 155.

Admitting radiator emblem found near place of accident fitting into defendant's radiator in prosecution for manslaughter, driving while intoxicated, and failing to stop, was not error. People v. Leutholtz (1929) 283 P. 292, 102 C.A. 493.

Corpus delicti having been established by competent evidence, exclusive of any confession or admission by defendant, that latter's automobile collided with another car and proceeded without occupant rendering necessary assistance, defendant's admission that he was driving it at time was admissible in trial for violating Stats.1923, p. 562, § 141. People v. Halbert (1926) 248 P. 969, 78 C.A. 598.

In trial for failure to stop, render assistance, etc., after striking person with automobile, bottle of wine, which witnesses testified was thrown from defendant's machine shortly after accident, was admissible to show condition of defendant and his companions at time, and corroborate other evidence that they had indulged freely in intoxicating liquors just before collision. People v. Graves (1925) 240 P. 1019, 74 C.A. 415.

Nature and elements of offense, weight and sufficiency of evidence

In prosecution for hit and run driving, evidence was sufficient to establish requisite knowledge on defendant's part that accident had occurred resulting in injury to another. People v. Roberts (1963) 31 Cal.Rptr. 689, 217 C.A.2d 592.

In prosecution for a hit and run violation, where there was circumstantial evidence from which jury could conclude that automobile of defendant's wife sustained damage as a result of collision with another's motorcycle, who identified the defendant as driver of the automobile, evidence justified conviction on the ground that the defendant knew that the motorcyclist had been injured after a rear-end collision with the automobile and that the failure of defendant to stop was a deliberate one. People v. Blankenship (1959) 340 P.2d 34, 171 C.A.2d 173.

In prosecution for failure to stop, give information and render aid to injured bicyclist, evidence that motorist in overtaking the bicycle struck rear end of the bicycle and passed to the left in the daytime, that the noise of the collision was audible 50 feet away and motorist left scene rapidly, constituted a substantial showing motorist had knowledge her automobile had been involved in an accident resulting in personal injury. People v. Roche (1942) 121 P.2d 865, 49 C.A.2d 459.

Evidence that defendant's truck "sideswiped" automobile, that defendant knew that accident had occurred, and that defendant failed to stop his truck and render assistance to any persons injured in accident, warranted conviction for hit and run driving. People v. Bowlin (1937) 65 P.2d 840, 19 C.A.2d 397.

Evidence on prosecution under Pen.C. former § 367c, of driver of auto for not stopping and assisting occupants of vehicle collided with, was sufficient, as against claim of want of knowledge of collision. People v. Fodera (1917) 164 P. 22, 33 C.A. 8.

§ 20002. Duty where property damaged

(a) The driver of any vehicle involved in an accident resulting in damage to any property including vehicles shall immediately stop the vehicle at the scene of the accident and shall then and there either:

(1) Locate and notify the owner or person in charge of such property of the name and address of the driver and owner of the vehicle involved, or;

(2) Leave in a conspicuous place on the vehicle or other property damaged a written notice giving the name and address of the driver and of the owner of the vehicle involved and a statement of the circumstances thereof and shall without unnecessary delay notify the police department of the city wherein the collision occurred or, if the collision occurred in unincorporated territory, the local headquarters of the Department of the California Highway Patrol.

Any person failing to comply with all the requirements of this section is guilty of a misdemeanor and upon conviction thereof shall be punished by imprisonment in the county jail for not to exceed six months or by a fine of not to exceed five hundred dollars ($500) or by both.

(b) Any person who parks a vehicle which, prior to the vehicle again being driven, becomes a runaway vehicle and is involved in an accident resulting in damage to any property, attended or unattended, shall comply with the requirements of this section, relating to notification and reporting and will upon conviction thereof, be liable to the penalties of this section for failure to comply with said requirements. (Amended by Stats.1967, c. 652, p. 2009, § 2.)

Notes of Decisions

Validity

Byers v. Justice Court of Ukiah Judicial Dist. of Mendocino County (1969) 80 Cal.Rptr. 553, 458 P.2d 465, 71 C.2d 1039 [main volume] vacated 91 S.Ct. 1538, 402 U.S. 424, 29 L.Ed.2d 9.

Constitutional privilege against compulsory self-incrimination was not infringed by provision of this section which required motorist involved in accident to stop and give his name and address. California v. Byers (1971) 91 S.Ct. 1535, 402 U.S. 424, 29 L.Ed.2d 9.

Even if this section requiring motorist involved in accident to stop and give his name involved self-incrimination, disclosure was not "testimonial" within scope of privilege. (Per Chief Justice Burger with three Justices concurring and one concurring in result.) Id.

§ 20003. Duty upon injury or death

The driver of any vehicle involved in an accident resulting in injury to or death of any person shall also give his name, address, the registration number of the vehicle he is driving, the name of the owner, and upon request and if available exhibit his driver's license to the person struck or the driver or occupants of any vehicle collided with or shall give such information and exhibit his license to any traffic or police officer at the scene of the accident and shall

§ 20003

render to any person injured in the accident reasonable assistance, including the carrying or the making arrangements for the carrying of such person to a physician, surgeon or hospital for medical or surgical treatment if it is apparent that treatment is necessary or if such carrying is requested by the injured person.
(Stats.1959, c. 3, p. 1661, § 20003.)

§ 20004. Duty upon death

In the event of death of any person resulting from an accident, the driver of any vehicle involved after fulfilling the requirements of this division, and if there be no traffic or police officer at the scene of the accident to whom to give the information required by Section 20003, shall, without delay, report the accident to the nearest office of the Department of the California Highway Patrol or office of a duly authorized police authority and submit with the report the information required by Section 20003.
(Stats.1959, c. 3, p. 1661, § 20004.)

§ 20006. Driver without license

If the driver does not have his driver's license in his possession, he shall exhibit other valid evidences of identification to the occupants of a vehicle with which he collided.
(Stats.1959, c. 3, p. 1662, § 20006.)

§ 20009. Supplemental reports

The Department of the California Highway Patrol may require any driver, or the owner of a common carrier vehicle, involved in any accident of which a report must be made as provided in Section 20008 to file supplemental reports and may require witnesses of accidents to render reports to it whenever the original report is insufficient in the opinion of such department.
(Stats.1959, c. 3, p. 1663, § 20009.)

§ 20010. Driver unable to report

Whenever the driver of a vehicle is physically incapable of making a required accident report, any occupant in the vehicle at the time of the accident shall make the report or cause it to be made.
(Stats.1959, c. 3, p. 1663, § 20010.)

§ 20012. Reports confidential

All required accident reports, and supplemental reports, shall be without prejudice to the individual so reporting and shall be for the confidential use of the Department of Motor Vehicles and the Department of the California Highway Patrol, except that the Department of the California Highway Patrol or the law enforcement agency to whom the accident was reported shall disclose the entire contents of the reports, including, but not limited to, the names and addresses of persons involved in, or witnesses to, an accident, the registration numbers and descriptions of vehicles involved, the date, time and location of an accident, all diagrams, statements of the drivers involved in the accident and the statements of all witnesses, to any person who may have a proper interest therein, including, but not limited to, the driver or drivers involved, or the legal guardian thereof, the parent of a minor driver, the authorized representative of a driver, or to any person injured therein, the owners of vehicles or property damaged thereby, persons who may incur civil liability, including liability based upon a breach of warranty arising out of the accident, and any attorney who declares under penalty of perjury that he represents any of the above persons.
(Amended by Stats.1969, c. 19, p. 80, § 1.)

§ 20013. Reports as evidence

No such accident report shall be used as evidence in any trial, civil or criminal, arising out of an accident, except that the department shall furnish upon demand of any person who has, or claims to have, made such a report or upon demand of any court, a certificate showing that a specified accident report has or has not been made to the department solely to prove a compliance or failure to comply with the requirement that such a report be made to the department.
(Amended by Stats.1959, c. 1996, p. 4629, § 22.)

Editors' Note

Since the primary intent of the law requiring accident reports is to insure that information is made available to those involved, the written report itself may not be used as evidence. Testimony of direct observation of the accident scene, physical evidence of the accident and verbal statements of parties involved in the accident may be used as evidence. Section 20013 protects merely the report itself.

Division 11
RULES OF THE ROAD

§ 21000. Department

Wherever in this division "department" occurs, it means the Department of the California Highway Patrol.
(Stats.1959, c. 3, p. 1664, § 21000.)

§ 21001. Scope of division

The provisions of this division refer exclusively to the operation of vehicles upon the highways, unless a different place is specifically referred to.
(Stats.1959, c. 3, p. 1664, § 21001.)

§ 21050. Animals

Every person riding or driving an animal upon a highway has all of the rights and is subject to all of the duties applicable to the driver of a vehicle by this division and Division 10 (commencing with Section 20000), except those provisions which by their very nature can have no application.
(Amended by Stats.1967, c. 586, p. 1931, § 2.)

§ 21055. Exemption of authorized emergency vehicles

The driver of an authorized emergency vehicle is exempt from Chapter 2 (commencing with Section 21350), Chapter 3 (commencing with Section 21650), Chapter 4 (commencing with Section 21800), Chapter 5 (commencing with Section 21950), Chapter 6 (commencing with Section 22100), Chapter 7 (commencing with Section 22348), Chapter 8 (commencing with Section 22450), Chapter 9 (commencing with Section 22500), and Chapter 10 (commencing with Section 22650) of this division, and Article 3 (commencing with Section 38305) and Article 4 (commencing with Section 38312) of Chapter 5 of Division 16.5, under all of the following conditions:

(a) If the vehicle is being driven in response to an emergency call or while engaged in rescue operations or is being used in the immediate pursuit of an actual or suspected violator of the law or is responding to, but not returning from, a fire alarm, except that fire department vehicles are exempt whether directly responding to an emergency call or operated from one place to another as rendered desirable or necessary by reason of an emergency call and operated to the scene of the emergency or operated from one fire station to another or to some other location by reason of the emergency call.

(b) If the driver of the vehicle sounds a siren as may be reasonably necessary and the vehicle displays a lighted red lamp visible from the front as a warning to other drivers and pedestrians.

A siren shall not be sounded by an authorized emergency vehicle except when required under this section.
(Amended by Stats.1977, c. 1017, p. ——, § 2, urgency, eff. Sept. 23, 1977.)

§ 21200. Bicycle defined; rights and duties of rider

Every person riding a bicycle upon a roadway or any paved shoulder has all the rights and is subject to all the duties applicable to the driver of a vehicle by this division and Division 10 (commencing with Section 20000), except those provisions which by their very nature can have no application.
(Amended by Stats.1978, c. 421, p. ——, § 2.)

Editors' Note

The specific bicycle provisions have not been included in this text.

§ 21451. Green or "go"

Green alone or "go" on an official traffic control signal means both of the following:

(a) Vehicular traffic facing the signal shall proceed straight through or may turn right or left. Vehicular traffic may make a semicircular or U-turn except where such turn is prohibited by signs erected at such location. The semicircular or U-turn shall be made from the far left-hand lane that is lawfully available to traffic moving in the direction of travel from which the turn is commenced. However, vehicular traffic, including vehicles turning right or left, shall yield the right-of-way to other vehicles and to pedestrians lawfully within the intersection or an adjacent crosswalk at the time such signal was first exhibited.

(b) Pedestrians facing the signal may proceed across the roadway within any marked or unmarked crosswalk, but shall yield the right-of-way to all vehicles which were lawfully within the intersection at the time such signal was first exhibited.
(Amended by Stats.1977, c. 1017, p. ——, § 3 urgency, eff. Sept. 23, 1977.)

§ 21452. Yellow or "caution"

Yellow or "caution" on an official traffic control signal when shown following the green or "go" signals means that:

(a) Vehicular traffic facing the signal is thereby warned that the red or stop signal will be exhibited immediately thereafter and vehicular traffic will be required to stop when the red or stop signal is exhibited.

(b) No pedestrian shall enter the roadway or cross any part of a roadway or proceed from or to a safety zone against a yellow or "caution" signal.
(Stats.1959, c. 3, p. 1675, § 21452.)

§ 21453. Red or "stop"

Red alone or "stop" on an official traffic control signal means:

§ 21453

(a) Vehicular traffic facing the signal shall stop at a limit line wherever located. If there is no limit line, vehicular traffic facing the signal shall stop before entering a crosswalk on the near side of the intersection or, if none, then before entering an intersection. Vehicular traffic shall remain standing until green or "go" is shown alone, except as provided in the next succeeding paragraphs.

(b) The driver of a vehicle which is stopped as close as practicable at the entrance to the crosswalk on the near side of the intersection or, if none, then at the entrance to the intersection in obedience to a red or "stop" signal, may make a right turn but shall yield the right-of-way to pedestrians and other traffic proceeding as directed by the signal at said intersection, except that local authorities may by ordinance prohibit any such right turn against a red or "stop" signal at any intersection, which ordinance shall be effective when a sign is erected at such intersection giving notice thereof.

(c) The driver of a vehicle on a one-way street which intersects another one-way street on which traffic moves to the left shall stop in obedience to a red or "stop" signal but may then make a left turn into said one-way street, but shall yield the right-of-way to pedestrians and other traffic proceeding as directed by the signal at said intersection, except that local authorities may by ordinance prohibit any such left turn as above described, which ordinance shall be effective when a sign is erected at such intersection giving notice thereof.

(d) No pedestrian shall enter the roadway or cross any part of the roadway or proceed from or to a safety zone against a red or "stop" signal.
(Amended by Stats.1969, c. 246, p. 595, § 1.)

§ 21454. Green arrow

(a) A green arrow on an official traffic control signal means both of the following:

(1) Vehicular traffic facing the signal may make the movement indicated by the green arrow but shall yield the right-of-way to other vehicles and to pedestrians lawfully within the intersection or an adjacent crosswalk at the time such green arrow is exhibited.

(2) Vehicular traffic may make a semicircular or U-turn except where such turn is prohibited by signs erected at such location. The semicircular or U-turn shall be made from the far left-hand lane that is lawfully available to traffic moving in the direction of travel from which the turn is commenced.

(b) A green arrow may be displayed alone or with red, yellow, or green.

(c) It is unlawful to operate a traffic signal which is equipped with a green light and a red arrow which are shown simultaneously. A green arrow shall not be displayed so as to direct vehicular traffic in a manner as to conflict with another flow of vehicular traffic directed at the same time in another direction.

(d) In the event a flashing red or yellow signal replaces the green arrow, vehicular traffic facing the signal may make the movement which would have been indicated by the green arrow, but shall proceed pursuant to subdivision (a) of Section 21457 if the signal is a flashing red signal or pursuant to subdivision (b) of that section if the signal is a flashing yellow signal.
(Amended by Stats.1977, c. 1017, p. ——, § 4, urgency, eff. Sept. 23, 1977.)

§ 21456. Walk, wait, or don't walk

Whenever an official traffic control signal exhibiting the words "walk" or "wait" or "don't walk" are in place, the signals shall indicate as follows:

(a) Walk. A pedestrian facing the signal may proceed across the roadway in the direction of the signal or in a diagonal direction across the roadway within the intersection if so instructed by signs or signals installed at or near the intersection.

(b) Wait or Don't Walk. No pedestrian shall start to cross the roadway in the direction of such signal, but any pedestrian who has partially completed his crossing on the "walk" signal shall proceed to a sidewalk, safety zone or island while the "wait" or "don't walk" signal is showing.
(Stats.1959, c. 3, p. 1676, § 21456.)

§ 21456.1. Pedestrian traffic control

Whenever an official traffic control signal exhibiting the words "walk" or "wait" or "don't walk" is shown concurrently with official traffic control signals exhibiting the words "go," "caution" or "stop," or exhibiting different colored lights successively, one at a time or with arrows, a pedestrian facing such traffic control signals shall obey the "walk," "wait" or "don't walk" control signal as provided in Section 21456.
(Added by Stats.1961, c. 810, p. 2089, § 1.)

§ 21457. Flashing signals

Whenever a flashing red or yellow signal is used in an official traffic control device, it shall require obedience by vehicular traffic as follows:

(a) When a red lens is illuminated by rapid intermittent flashes, drivers of vehicles shall stop before entering the nearest crosswalk at an intersection or at a limit line when marked, and if there is no limit line or crosswalk, the driver shall stop at the entrance to the intersecting roadway. The right to proceed shall be subject to the rules provided in Section 21802.

(b) When a yellow lens is illuminated with rapid intermittent flashes, drivers of vehicles may proceed through the intersection or past the signal only with caution.
(Amended by Stats.1972, c. 46, p. 64, § 1.)

§ 21458. Curb markings

Whenever local authorities enact local parking regulations and indicate them by the use of paint upon curbs, the following colors only shall be used, and the colors indicate as follows:

(a) Red indicates no stopping, standing, or parking, whether the vehicle is attended or unattended, except that a bus may stop in a red zone marked or sign-posted as a bus loading zone.

(b) Yellow indicates stopping only for the purpose of loading or unloading passengers or freight for such time as may be specified by local ordinance.

(c) White indicates stopping only for loading or unloading of passengers for such time as may be specified by local ordinance or for the purpose of depositing mail in an adjacent mailbox.

(d) Green indicates time limit parking specified by local ordinance.

(e) Blue indicates parking limited exclusively to the vehicles of physically handicapped persons.

Regulations indicated as above provided shall be effective upon such days and during such hours or times as may be prescribed by local ordinances.
(Amended by Stats.1975, c. 688, p. ——, § 1.)

§ 21459. Distinctive roadway markings

(a) The Department of Transportation in respect to state highways and a local authority with respect to highways under its jurisdiction, is authorized to place and maintain upon highways distinctive roadway markings as described and with the effect set forth in Section 21460.

(b) The distinctive roadway markings shall be employed to designate any portion of a highway where the volume of traffic or the vertical or other curvature of the roadway renders it hazardous to drive on the left side of the marking or to indicate no driving to the left as provided in Section 21460, and shall not be employed for any other purpose.

(c) Any pavement marking other than as described in this section placed by the Department of Transportation or any local authority shall not be effective to indicate no driving over or to the left of the marking.
(Amended by Stats.1974, c. 545, p. 1318, § 185.)

§ 21460. Double lines

(a) When double parallel solid lines are in place, no person driving a vehicle shall drive to the left thereof, except as permitted in this section.

(b) When the double parallel lines, one of which is broken, are in place, no person driving a vehicle shall drive to the left thereof, except:

(1) That the driver on that side of the roadway in which the broken line is in place may cross over the double line or drive to the left thereof when overtaking or passing other vehicles.

(2) As provided in Section 21460.5.

(c) Either of the markings as specified in subdivision (a) or (b) shall not prevent a driver from turning to the left across any such marking at any intersection or into or out of a driveway, or making a U-turn under the rules governing such movement, and either of the markings shall be disregarded when authorized signs have been erected designating offcenter traffic lanes as permitted under Section 21657.

(d) Raised pavement markers may be used to simulate painted lines described in this section when such markers are placed in accordance with standards established by the Department of Transportation.
(Amended by Stats.1976, c. 482, p. ——, § 1.)

§ 21460.5. Two-way left-turn lanes; duration of section

Text of section operative until January 1, 1980

(a) The Department of Transportation and local authorities in their respective jurisdictions may designate a two-way left-turn lane on a highway. A two-way left-turn lane is a lane near the center of the highway set aside for use by vehicles making left turns in both directions from or into the highway.

(b) Until January 1, 1980, two-way left-turn lanes shall be designated by distinctive roadway markings consisting of either parallel dashed double yellow lines on each side of the lane, or parallel double lines, interior line dashed and exterior line solid, on each

§ 21460.5

side of the lane. The Department of Transportation may determine and prescribe standards and specifications governing length, width, and positioning of the distinctive pavement markings. All pavement markings designating a two-way left-turn lane shall conform to such standards and specifications.

(c) A vehicle shall not be driven in a designated two-way left-turn lane except when preparing for or making a left turn from or into a highway or when preparing for or making a U-turn when otherwise permitted by law. A left turn shall not be made from any other lane where a two-way left-turn lane has been designated.

(d) This section shall not prohibit driving across a two-way left-turn lane.

(e) Raised pavement markers may be used to simulate painted lines described in this section when such markers are placed in accordance with standards established by the Department of Transportation.

This section shall remain in effect until January 1, 1980, and as of such date is repealed.
(Amended by Stats.1976, c. 482, p. —, § 2.)

§ 21461. Obedience by driver to official traffic control devices

It shall be unlawful for any driver of a vehicle to fail to obey any sign or signal erected or maintained to indicate and carry out the provisions of this code or any local traffic ordinance or resolution adopted pursuant to a local traffic ordinance, or to fail to obey any device erected or maintained pursuant to Section 21352.
(Amended by Stats.1970, c. 827, p. 1561, § 1.)

§ 21461.5. Obedience by pedestrian to official traffic control devices

It shall be unlawful for any pedestrian to fail to obey any sign or signal erected or maintained to indicate or carry out the provisions of this code or any local traffic ordinance or resolution adopted pursuant to a local traffic ordinance, or to fail to obey any device erected or maintained pursuant to Section 21352.
(Added by Stats.1970, c. 827, p. 1561, § 2.)

§ 21462. Obedience to traffic control signals

The driver of any vehicle, the person in charge of any animal, any pedestrian, and the motorman of any streetcar shall obey the instructions of any official traffic signal applicable to him and placed as provided by law, unless otherwise directed by a police or traffic officer or when it is necessary for the purpose of avoiding a collision or in case of other emergency, subject to the exemptions granted by Section 21055.
(Stats.1959, c. 3, p. 1677, § 21462.)

§ 21463. Illegal operation of signals

No person shall operate a manually or traffic actuated signal other than for the purpose of permitting a pedestrian or vehicle to cross a roadway.
(Stats.1959, c. 3, p. 1678, § 21463.)

§ 21464. Interference with traffic devices

(a) No person shall without lawful authority deface, injure, attach any material or substance to, knock down, or remove, nor shall any person shoot at, any official traffic control device, traffic guidepost, traffic signpost, or historical marker placed or erected as authorized or required by law, nor shall any person without such authority deface, injure, attach any material or substance to, or remove, nor shall any person shoot at, any inscription, shield, or insignia on any such device, guide, or marker.

(b) No person shall use, nor shall any vehicle, other than an authorized emergency vehicle, be equipped with, any device capable of sending a signal that interrupts or changes the sequence patterns of an official traffic control signal unless such device or use is authorized by the Department of Transportation pursuant to Section 21350 or by local authorities pursuant to Section 21351.

(c) Any willful violation of subdivision (a) or (b) which results in injury to, or death of, a person shall be punished by imprisonment in the state prison, or imprisonment in a county jail for a period of not more than six months.
(Amended by Stats.1977, c. 805, p. —, § 1.)

§ 21465. Unauthorized traffic devices

No person shall place, maintain, or display upon, or in view of, any highway any unofficial sign, signal, device, or marking, or any sign, signal, device, or marking which purports to be or is an imitation of, or resembles, an official traffic control device or which attempts to direct the movement of traffic or which hides from view any official traffic control device.
(Amended by Stats.1967, c. 486, p. 1693, § 1.)

§ 21466. Light preventing recognition of official traffic control device

No person shall place or maintain or display upon or in view of any highway any light in such position as to prevent the driver of a vehicle from readily recognizing any official traffic control device.
(Amended by Stats.1970, c. 968, p. 1736, § 2.)

§ 21466.5. Light impairing driver's vision

No person shall place or maintain or display, upon or in view of any highway, any light of any color of such brilliance as to impair the vision of drivers upon the highway. A light source shall be considered vision impairing when its brilliance exceeds the values listed below.

The brightness reading of an objectionable light source shall be measured with a 1½-degree photoelectric brightness meter placed at the driver's point of view. The maximum measured brightness of the light source within 10 degrees from the driver's normal line of sight shall not be more than 1,000 times the minimum measured brightness in the driver's field of view, except that when the minimum measured brightness in the field of view is 10 foot-lamberts or less, the measured brightness of the light source in foot-lambert shall not exceed 500 plus 100 times the angle, in degrees, between the driver's line of sight and the light source.

The provisions of this section shall not apply to railroads as defined in Section 229 of the Public Utilities Code.
(Added by Stats.1970, c. 968, p. 1736, § 3.)

§ 21467. Prohibited signs and devices

Every prohibited sign, signal, device, or light is a public nuisance, and the Department of Transportation, members of the California Highway Patrol, and local authorities are hereby authorized and empowered without notice to remove the same, or cause the same to be removed, or the Director of Transportation, the commissioner, or local authorities may bring an action as provided by law to abate such nuisance.
(Amended by Stats.1974, c. 545, p. 1319, § 188.)

§ 21650. Right side of roadway

Upon all highways a vehicle shall be driven upon the right half of the roadway, except as follows:

(a) When overtaking and passing another vehicle proceeding in the same direction under the rules governing such movement.

(b) When placing a vehicle in a lawful position for, and when the vehicle is lawfully making, a left turn.

(c) When the right half of a roadway is closed to traffic under construction or repair.

(d) Upon a roadway restricted to one-way traffic.

(e) When the roadway is not of sufficient width.

(f) When the vehicle is necessarily traveling so slowly as to impede the normal movement of traffic, that portion of the highway adjacent to the right edge of the roadway may be utilized temporarily when in a condition permitting safe operation.
(Amended by Stats.1969, c. 136, p. 288, § 2.)

§ 21651. Divided highways

It is unlawful to drive any vehicle upon any highway which has been divided into two or more roadways by means of intermittent barriers or by means of a dividing section of not less than two feet in width either unpaved or delineated by curbs, lines, or other markings on the roadway except to the right of the barrier or dividing section, or to drive any vehicle over, upon, or across the dividing section, or to make any left turn or semicircular or U-turn on any such divided highway, except through an opening in the barrier designated and intended by public authorities for the use of vehicles or through a plainly marked opening in the dividing section.
(Stats.1959, c. 3, p. 1679, § 21651.)

§ 21652. Entering or leaving public highway via service road

When any service road has been constructed on or along any public highway and the main thoroughfare of the highway has been separated from the service road, it is unlawful for any person to drive any vehicle into the main thoroughfare from the service road or from the main thoroughfare into the service road except through an opening in the dividing curb, section, separation, or line.
(Amended by Stats.1963, c. 335, p. 1124, § 1.)

§ 21654. Slow-moving vehicles

(a) Notwithstanding the prima facie speed limits, any vehicle proceeding upon a highway at a speed less than the normal speed of traffic moving in the same direction at such time shall be driven in the right-hand lane for traffic or as close as practicable to the right-hand edge or curb, except when overtaking and passing another vehicle proceeding in the same direction or when preparing for a left turn at an intersection or into a private road or driveway.

§ 21654

(b) If a vehicle is being driven at a speed less than the normal speed of traffic moving in the same direction at such time, and is not being driven in the right-hand lane for traffic or as close as practicable to the right-hand edge or curb, it shall constitute prima facie evidence that the driver is operating the vehicle in violation of subdivision (a) of this section.

(c) The Department of Transportation, with respect to state highways, and local authorities, with respect to highways under their jurisdiction, may place and maintain upon highways official signs directing slow-moving traffic to use the right-hand traffic lane except when overtaking and passing another vehicle or preparing for a left turn.
(Amended by Stats.1974, c. 545, p. 1319, § 189.)

§ 21655. Designated lanes for certain vehicles

(a) Whenever the Department of Transportation or local authorities with respect to highways under their respective jurisdictions determines upon the basis of an engineering and traffic investigation that the designation of a specific lane or lanes for the travel of vehicles required to travel at reduced speeds would facilitate the safe and orderly movement of traffic, the department or local authority may designate specific lane or lanes for the travel of vehicles which are subject to the provisions of Section 22406 and shall erect signs at reasonable intervals giving notice thereof.

(b) Any vehicle subject to the provisions of Section 22406 shall be driven in the lane or lanes designated pursuant to subdivision (a) whenever signs have been erected giving notice of such designation. Except as otherwise provided in this subdivision, when specific lane or lanes have not been so designated, any such vehicle shall be driven in the right-hand lane for traffic or as close as practicable to the right edge or curb. If, however, specific lane or lanes have not been designated on a divided highway having four or more clearly marked lanes for traffic in one direction, any such vehicle may also be driven in the lane to the immediate left of such right-hand lane, unless otherwise prohibited under the provisions of this code. When overtaking and passing another vehicle proceeding in the same direction, such drivers shall use either the designated lane, the lane to the immediate left of the right-hand lane, or the right-hand lane for traffic as permitted under the provisions of this code.

This subdivision shall not apply to a driver who is preparing for a left- or right-hand turn or who is in the process of entering into or exiting from a highway or to a driver who must necessarily drive in a lane other than the right-hand lane to continue on his intended route.
(Amended by Stats.1975, c. 542, p. 1109, § 1.)

§ 21656. Turning out of slow-moving vehicles

On a two-lane highway where passing is unsafe because of traffic in the opposite direction or other conditions, a slow-moving vehicle, including a passenger vehicle, behind which five or more vehicles are formed in line, shall turn off the roadway at the nearest place designated as a turnout by signs erected by the authority having jurisdiction over the highway, or wherever sufficient area for a safe turnout exists, in order to permit the vehicles following it to proceed. As used in this section a slow-moving vehicle is one which is proceeding at a rate of speed less than the normal flow of traffic at the particular time and place.
(Amended by Stats.1965, c. 448, p. 1759, § 2.)

§ 21657. Designated traffic direction

The authorities in charge of any highway may designate any highway, roadway, part of a roadway, or specific lanes upon which vehicular traffic shall proceed in one direction at all or such times as shall be indicated by official traffic control devices. When a roadway has been so designated, a vehicle shall be driven only in the direction designated at all or such times as shall be indicated by traffic control devices.
(Amended by Stats.1969, c. 136, p. 288, § 4.)

§ 21658. Laned roadways

Whenever any roadway has been divided into two or more clearly marked lanes for traffic in one direction, the following rules apply:

(a) A vehicle shall be driven as nearly as practical entirely within a single lane and shall not be moved from the lane until such movement can be made with reasonable safety.

(b) Official signs may be erected directing slow-moving traffic to use a designated lane or allocating specified lanes to traffic moving in the same direction, and drivers of vehicles shall obey the directions of the traffic device.
(Amended by Stats.1975, c. 450, p. 948, § 1.)

§ 21659. Three-laned highways

Upon a roadway which is divided into three lanes a vehicle shall not be driven in the extreme left lane at any time, nor in the center lane except when overtak-

ing and passing another vehicle where the roadway ahead is clearly visible and the center lane is clear of traffic within a safe distance, or in preparation for a left turn, or where the center lane is at the time allocated exclusively to traffic moving in the direction the vehicle is proceeding and is signposted to give notice of such allocation. This section does not apply upon a one-way roadway.
(Stats.1959, c. 3, p. 1680, § 21659.)

§ 21660. Approaching vehicles

Drivers of vehicles proceeding in opposite directions shall pass each other to the right, and, except when a roadway has been divided into traffic lanes, each driver shall give to the other at least one-half of the main traveled portion of the roadway whenever possible.
(Stats.1959, c. 3, p. 1680, § 21660.)

§ 21661. Narrow roadways

Whenever upon any grade the width of the roadway is insufficient to permit the passing of vehicles approaching from opposite directions at the point of meeting, the driver of the vehicle descending the grade shall yield the right-of-way to the vehicle ascending the grade and shall, if necessary, back his vehicle to a place in the highway where it is possible for the vehicles to pass.
(Stats.1959, c. 3, p. 1680, § 21661.)

§ 21662. Mountain driving

The driver of a motor vehicle traveling through defiles or canyons or upon mountain highways shall hold the motor vehicle under control and as near the right-hand edge of the roadway as is reasonably possible and, except when driving entirely to the right of the center of the roadway, shall give audible warning with the horn of the motor vehicle upon approaching any curve where the view is obstructed within a distance of 200 feet along the highway.
(Amended by Stats.1959, c. 973, p. 3004, § 1.)

§ 21663. Driving on sidewalk

No person shall operate or move a motor vehicle upon a sidewalk except as may be necessary to enter or leave adjacent property.
(Added by Stats.1965, c. 1343, p. 3230, § 1.)

§ 21664. On-ramp exit

It is unlawful for the driver of any vehicle to make an exit from or to leave any freeway which has full control of access and no crossings at grade upon any on-ramp providing entrance to such freeway.
(Added by Stats.1965, c. 1100, p. 2747, § 1.)

§ 21700. Obstruction to driving

No person shall drive a vehicle when it is so loaded, or when there are in the front seat such number of persons as to obstruct the view of the driver to the front or sides of the vehicle or as to interfere with the driver's control over the driving mechanism of the vehicle.
(Amended by Stats.1965, c. 1500, p. 3523, § 7.)

§ 21701. Interference with driver or mechanism

No person shall wilfully interfere with the driver of a vehicle or with the mechanism thereof in such manner as to affect the driver's control of the vehicle. The provisions of this section shall not apply to a drivers' license examiner or other employee of the Department of Motor Vehicles when conducting the road or driving test of an applicant for a driver's license nor to a person giving instruction as a part of a course in driver training conducted by a public school, educational institution or a driver training school licensed by the Department of Motor Vehicles.
(Stats.1959, c. 3, p. 1681, § 21701.)

§ 21702. Limitation on driving hours

(a) No person shall drive upon any highway any vehicle designed or used for transporting persons for compensation for more than 10 consecutive hours nor for more than 10 hours spread over a total of 15 consecutive hours. Thereafter, such person shall not drive any such vehicle until eight consecutive hours have elapsed.

Regardless of aggregate driving time, no driver shall drive for more than 10 hours in any 24-hour period unless eight consecutive hours off duty have elapsed.

(b) No person shall drive upon any highway any vehicle designed or used for transporting merchandise, freight, materials or other property for more than 12 consecutive hours nor for more than 12 hours spread over a total of 15 consecutive hours. Thereafter, such person shall not drive any such vehicle until eight consecutive hours have elapsed.

Regardless of aggregate driving time, no driver shall drive for more than 12 hours in any 24-hour period unless eight consecutive hours off duty have elapsed.

(c) This section does not apply in any case of casualty or unavoidable accident or an act of God.

§ 21702

(d) In computing the number of hours under this section, any time spent by a person in driving such a vehicle outside this state shall, upon the vehicle entering this state, be included.

(e) Any person who violates any provision of this section is guilty of a misdemeanor and is punishable by a fine of not less than one hundred dollars ($100) nor more than five hundred dollars ($500) for each offense.

(f) This section shall not apply to the driver of a vehicle which is subject to the provisions of Section 34500.
(Amended by Stats.1967, c. 564, p. 1911, § 1.)

§ 21703. Following too closely

The driver of a motor vehicle shall not follow another vehicle more closely than is reasonable and prudent, having due regard for the speed of such vehicle and the traffic upon, and the condition of, the roadway.
(Stats.1959, c. 3, p. 1682, § 21703.)

Editors' Note

This section calls for "reasonable and prudent" action. This issue will be a court discretionary judgement matter determined by an assessment of evidence (testimony) presented.

---

§ 21705. Caravans

Motor vehicles being driven outside of a business or residence district in a caravan or motorcade, whether or not towing other vehicles, shall be so operated as to allow sufficient space and in no event less than 100 feet between each vehicle or combination of vehicles so as to enable any other vehicle to overtake or pass.
(Stats.1959, c. 3, p. 1682, § 21705.)

§ 21706. Following emergency vehicle

No motor vehicle, except an authorized emergency vehicle, shall follow within 300 feet of any authorized emergency vehicle being operated under the provisions of Section 21055.

This section shall not apply to a police or traffic officer when serving as an escort within the purview of Section 21057.
(Amended by Stats.1972, c. 46, p. 64, § 2.)

§ 21708. Fire hoses

No person shall drive or propel any vehicle or conveyance upon, over, or across, or in any manner damage any fire hose or chemical hose used by or under the supervision and control of any organized fire department. However, any vehicle may cross a hose provided suitable jumpers or other appliances are installed to protect the hose.
(Stats.1959, c. 3, p. 1683, § 21708.)

§ 21709. Safety zones

No vehicle shall at any time be driven through or within a safety zone.
(Stats.1959, c. 3, p. 1683, § 21709.)

§ 21710. Coasting prohibited

The driver of a motor vehicle when traveling on down grade upon any highway shall not coast with the gears of such vehicle in neutral.
(Stats.1959, c. 3, p. 1683, § 21710.)

§ 21711. Towed vehicles swerving

No person shall operate a train of vehicles when any vehicle being towed whips or swerves from side to side or fails to follow substantially in the path of the towing vehicle.
(Stats.1959, c. 3, p. 1683, § 21711. Amended by Stats.1959, c. 44, p. 1902, § 3.)

§ 21712. Unlawful riding and towing

(a) No person driving a motor vehicle shall knowingly permit any person to ride on any vehicle or upon any portion thereof not designed or intended for the use of passengers.

(b) No person shall ride on any vehicle or upon any portion thereof not designed or intended for the use of passengers.

(c) Subdivisions (a) and (b) shall not apply to any employee engaged in the necessary discharge of his duty or in the case of persons riding completely within or upon vehicle bodies in space intended for any load on the vehicle.

(d) No person shall drive a motor vehicle which is towing a trailer coach or camp trailer containing any passenger.

(e) No person shall knowingly drive a motor vehicle which is towing any person riding upon any bicycle, coaster, roller skates, sled, skis, or toy vehicle.

(f) Subdivision (d) shall not apply to a trailer coach being towed with a fifth-wheel device if the trailer coach is equipped with safety glazing materials wherever glazing materials are used in windows or doors, with an audible or visual signaling device which a passenger inside the trailer coach can use to

gain the attention of the motor vehicle driver, and with at least one unobstructed exit capable of being opened from both the interior and exterior of the trailer coach.
(Amended by Stats.1974, c. 578, p. 1397, § 1.)

§ 21750. Overtake and pass to left

The driver of a vehicle overtaking another vehicle proceeding in the same direction shall pass to the left at a safe distance without interfering with the safe operation of the overtaken vehicle, subject to the limitations and exceptions hereinafter stated.
(Amended by Stats.1961, c. 577, p. 1718, § 1.)

§ 21751. Passing without sufficient clearance

On a two-lane highway, no vehicle shall be driven to the left side of the center of the roadway in overtaking and passing another vehicle proceeding in the same direction unless the left side is clearly visible and free of oncoming traffic for a sufficient distance ahead to permit such overtaking and passing to be completely made without interfering with the same operation of any vehicle approaching from the opposite direction.
(Amended by Stats.1973, c. 50, p. 83, § 1.)

§ 21752. When driving on left prohibited

No vehicle shall be driven to the left side of the roadway under the following conditions:

(a) When approaching or upon the crest of a grade or a curve in the highway where the driver's view is obstructed within such distance as to create a hazard in the event another vehicle might approach from the opposite direction.

(b) When the view is obstructed upon approaching within 100 feet of any bridge, viaduct, or tunnel.

(c) When approaching within 100 feet of or when traversing any intersection or railroad grade crossing.

This section shall not apply upon a one-way roadway.
(Amended by Stats.1969, c. 417, p. 948, § 1.)

§ 21753. Yielding for passing

Except when passing on the right is permitted, the driver of an overtaken vehicle shall give way to the right in favor of the overtaking vehicle on audible signal and shall not increase the speed of his vehicle until completely passed by the overtaking vehicle.
(Stats.1959, c. 3, p. 1684, § 21753.)

§ 21754. Passing on the right

The driver of a motor vehicle may overtake and pass to the right of another vehicle only under the following conditions:

(a) When the vehicle overtaken is making or about to make a left turn.

(b) Upon a highway within a business or residence district with unobstructed pavement of sufficient width for two or more lines of moving vehicles in the direction of travel.

(c) Upon any highway outside of a business or residence district with unobstructed pavement of sufficient width and clearly marked for two or more lines of moving traffic in the direction of travel.

(d) Upon a one-way street.

(e) Upon a highway divided into two roadways where traffic is restricted to one direction upon each of such roadways.

The provisions of this section shall not relieve the driver of a slow moving vehicle from the duty to drive as closely as practicable to the right hand edge of the roadway.
(Stats.1959, c. 3, p. 1684, § 21754.)

§ 21755. Pass on right safely

The driver of a motor vehicle may overtake and pass another vehicle upon the right only under conditions permitting such movement in safety. In no event shall such movement be made by driving off the paved or main-traveled portion of the roadway.
(Stats.1959, c. 3, p. 1684, § 21755.)

§ 21758. Passing on grades

In the event any vehicle is being operated on any grade outside of a business or residence district at a speed of less than 20 miles per hour, no person operating any other motor vehicle shall attempt to overtake and pass such slow moving vehicle unless the overtaking vehicle is operated at a speed of at least 10 miles per hour in excess of the speed of the overtaken vehicle, nor unless the passing movement is completed within a total distance not greater than one-quarter of a mile.
(Stats.1959, c. 3, p. 1685, § 21758.)

§ 21759. Caution in passing animals

The driver of any vehicle approaching any horse drawn vehicle, any ridden animal, or any livestock shall exercise proper control of his vehicle and shall

reduce speed or stop as may appear necessary or as may be signalled or otherwise requested by any person driving, riding or in charge of the animal or livestock in order to avoid frightening and to safeguard the animal or livestock and to insure the safety of any person driving or riding the animal or in charge of the livestock.
(Stats.1959, c. 3, p. 1685, § 21759.)

§ 21800. Uncontrolled intersection

(a) The driver of a vehicle approaching an intersection shall yield the right-of-way to a vehicle which has entered the intersection from a different highway.

(b) When two vehicles enter an intersection from different highways at the same time the driver of the vehicle on the left shall yield the right-of-way to the driver of the vehicle on his right.

(c) This section shall not apply at intersections controlled by an official traffic control signal, stop sign, or yield right-of-way sign, or to vehicles approaching each other from opposite directions when the driver of one of the vehicles is intending to or is making a left turn.
(Stats.1959, c. 3, p. 1685, § 21800.)

Editors' Note

Violation of right-of-way laws must frequently be determined on the principle of "last clear chance".

§ 21801. Left turn right of way

(a) The driver of a vehicle intending to turn to the left at an intersection or into public or private property, or an alley, shall yield the right-of-way to all vehicles which have approached or are approaching from the opposite direction and which are so close as to constitute a hazard at any time during the turning movement and shall continue to yield the right-of-way to such approaching vehicles until such time as the left turn can be made with reasonable safety.

(b) A driver having so yielded and having given a signal when and as required by this code may turn left and the drivers of all other vehicles approaching from the opposite direction shall yield the right-of-way.
(Amended by Stats.1969, c. 312, p. 679, § 1.)

§ 21802. Approaching intersection entrance

(a) The driver of any vehicle approaching a stop sign at the entrance to, or within, an intersection shall stop as required by Section 22450 and shall then yield the right-of-way to other vehicles which have approached or are approaching so closely from another roadway as to constitute an immediate hazard and shall continue to yield the right-of-way to such approaching vehicles until such time as he can proceed with reasonable safety.

(b) A driver having so yielded may proceed and the drivers of all other approaching vehicles shall yield the right-of-way to the vehicle entering or crossing the intersection.

(c) This section shall have no application where stop signs are erected upon all approaches to an intersection.
(Amended by Stats.1969, c. 1101, p. 2100, § 2.)

§ 21803. Yield right-of-way

(a) The driver of any vehicle upon approaching any yield right-of-way sign shall yield the right-of-way to other vehicles which have entered the intersection from an intersecting street or which are approaching so closely on the intersecting street as to constitute an immediate hazard and shall continue to yield the right-of-way to such approaching vehicles until such time as he can proceed with reasonable safety.

(b) A driver, having so yielded, may then proceed and the drivers of all other vehicles approaching the intersection on the intersecting roadway shall yield the right-of-way to him.
(Amended by Stats.1969, c. 834, p. 1668, § 2.)

§ 21804. Entry onto highway

The driver of a vehicle about to enter or cross a highway from any public or private property, or from an alley, shall yield the right-of-way to all traffic, as defined in Section 620, approaching on the highway.
(Amended by Stats.1978, c. 122, p. —, § 1.)

§ 21805. Equestrian crossings

(a) The Department of Transportation, and local authorities, with respect to highways under their jurisdiction may designate any intersection of a highway and a bridle path or equestrian crossing by erecting on the highway at or near the approach to the intersection appropriate signs of a type approved by the Department of Transportation indicating the crossing and the crossmarks, safety devices or signals as the authorities may deem necessary to safeguard both the vehicular traffic and any equestrian at the crossing.

(b) The driver of a vehicle shall yield the right-of-way to any horseback rider crossing a roadway at an equestrian crossing designated by signs giving notice thereof as provided in this section.

(c) The provisions of subdivision (b) shall not relieve any horseback rider from the duty of using due care for his safety. No horseback rider shall suddenly leave a curb or other place of safety and proceed into the path of a vehicle which is so close as to constitute an immediate hazard.
(Amended by Stats.1973, c. 495, p. 970, § 1.)

§ 21806. Authorized emergency vehicles

Upon the immediate approach of an authorized emergency vehicle sounding a siren and having at least one lighted lamp exhibiting red light visible under normal atmospheric conditions from a distance of 1,000 feet to the front of such vehicle, except as otherwise directed by a traffic officer:

(a) The driver of every other vehicle shall yield the right-of-way and shall immediately drive to a position parallel to, and as close as possible to, the right-hand edge or curb of the highway clear of any intersection and thereupon stop and remain in such position until the authorized emergency vehicle has passed.

(b) The motorman of every street car shall immediately stop such car clear of any intersection and keep it in such position until the authorized emergency vehicle has passed.

(c) All pedestrians upon the highway shall remain in a place of safety or proceed to the nearest curb or place of safety until the authorized emergency vehicle has passed.
(Amended by Stats.1978, c. 252, p. ——, § 2.)

§ 21807. Effect of exemption

The provisions of Section 21806 shall not operate to relieve the driver of an authorized emergency vehicle from the duty to drive with due regard for the safety of all persons and property.
(Added by Stats.1961, c. 653, p. 1861, § 28.)

§ 21950. Right-of-way at crosswalks

(a) The driver of a vehicle shall yield the right-of-way to a pedestrian crossing the roadway within any marked crosswalk or within any unmarked crosswalk at an intersection, except as otherwise provided in this chapter.

(b) The provisions of this section shall not relieve a pedestrian from the duty of using due care for his safety. No pedestrian shall suddenly leave a curb or other place of safety and walk or run into the path of a vehicle which is so close as to constitute an immediate hazard.

(c) The provisions of subdivision (b) shall not relieve a driver of a vehicle from the duty of exercising due care for the safety of any pedestrian within any marked crosswalk or within any unmarked crosswalk at an intersection.
(Amended by Stats.1970, c. 1001, p. 1799, § 1.)

§ 21951. Vehicles stopped for pedestrians

Whenever any vehicle has stopped at a marked crosswalk or at any unmarked crosswalk at an intersection to permit a pedestrian to cross the roadway the driver of any other vehicle approaching from the rear shall not overtake and pass the stopped vehicle.
(Stats.1959, c. 3, p. 1687, § 21951.)

§ 21952. Right-of-way on sidewalk

The driver of any motor vehicle, prior to driving over or upon any sidewalk, shall yield the right-of-way to any pedestrian approaching thereon.
(Stats.1959, c. 3, p. 1687, § 21952.)

§ 21953. Tunnel or overhead crossing

Whenever any pedestrian crosses a roadway other than by means of a pedestrian tunnel or overhead pedestrian crossing, if a pedestrian tunnel or overhead crossing serves the place where the pedestrian is crossing the roadway, such pedestrian shall yield the right-of-way to all vehicles on the highway so near as to constitute an immediate hazard.

This section shall not be construed to mean that a marked crosswalk, with or without a signal device, cannot be installed where a pedestrian tunnel or overhead crossing exists.
(Amended by Stats.1972, c. 680, p. 1264, § 1.)

§ 21954. Pedestrians outside crosswalks

(a) Every pedestrian upon a roadway at any point other than within a marked crosswalk or within an unmarked crosswalk at an intersection shall yield the right-of-way to all vehicles upon the roadway so near as to constitute an immediate hazard.

(b) The provisions of this section shall not relieve the driver of a vehicle from the duty to exercise due care for the safety of any pedestrian upon a roadway.
(Amended by Stats.1971, c. 1015, p. 1955, § 1.)

§ 21955. Crossing between controlled intersections

Between adjacent intersections controlled by traffic control signal devices or by police officers, pedestrians shall not cross the roadway at any place except in a crosswalk.
(Stats.1959, c. 3, p. 1688, § 21955.)

§ 21956. Pedestrian on roadway

No pedestrian shall walk upon any roadway outside of a business or residence district otherwise than close to his left-hand edge of the roadway.
(Stats.1959, c. 3, p. 1688, § 21956.)

§ 21957. Hitchhiking

No person shall stand in a roadway for the purpose of soliciting a ride from the driver of any vehicle.
(Stats.1959, c. 3, p. 1688, § 21957.)

§ 22100. Turning upon a highway

Except as provided in Section 22101, the driver of any vehicle intending to turn upon a highway shall do so as follows:

(a) Right Turns. Both the approach for a right-hand turn and a right-hand turn shall be made as close as practicable to the right-hand curb or edge of the roadway except:

(1) Upon a highway having three marked lanes for traffic moving in one direction which terminates at an intersecting highway accommodating traffic in both directions, the driver of a vehicle in the middle lane may turn right into any lane lawfully available to traffic moving in such direction upon the roadway being entered.

(2) When a right-hand turn is made from a one-way highway at an intersection, a driver shall approach the turn as provided in subdivision (a) and shall complete the turn in any lane lawfully available to traffic moving in such direction upon the roadway being entered.

(b) Left Turns. The approach for a left turn shall be made as close as practicable to the left-hand edge of the extreme left-hand lane or portion of the roadway lawfully available to traffic moving in the direction of travel of such vehicle and, when turning at an intersection, the left turn shall not be made before entering the intersection. After entering the intersection, the left turn shall be made so as to leave the intersection in a lane lawfully available to traffic moving in such direction upon the roadway being entered, except:

(1) Upon a highway having three marked lanes for traffic moving in one direction which terminates at an intersecting highway accommodating traffic in both directions, the driver of a vehicle in the middle lane may turn left into any lane lawfully available to traffic moving in such direction upon the roadway being entered.
(Amended by Stats.1972, c. 1060, p. 1970, § 1.)

§ 22101. Regulation of turns at intersection

(a) The Department of Transportation or local authorities in respect to highways under their respective jurisdictions, may cause official traffic control devices to be placed or erected within or adjacent to intersections to regulate or prohibit turning movements at such intersections.

(b) When turning movements are required at an intersection notice of such requirement shall be given by erection of a sign, unless an additional clearly marked traffic lane is provided for the approach to the turning movement, in which event notice as applicable to such additional traffic lane shall be given by any official traffic control device.

(c) When right- or left-hand turns are prohibited at an intersection notice of such prohibition shall be given by erection of a sign.

(d) When official traffic control devices are placed as required in subdivisions (b) or (c), it shall be unlawful for any driver of a vehicle to disobey the directions of such official traffic control devices.
(Amended by Stats.1974, c. 545, p. 1321, § 193.)

§ 22102. U-turn in business district

No person in a business district shall make a U-turn, except at an intersection, or on a divided highway where an opening has been provided in accordance with Section 21651.
(Amended by Stats.1970, c. 620, p. 1231, § 2.)

§ 22103. U-turn in residence district

No person in a residence district shall make a U-turn when any other vehicle is approaching from either direction within 200 feet, except at an intersection when the approaching vehicle is controlled by an official traffic control device.
(Amended by Stats.1970, c. 620, p. 1231, § 3.)

§ 22105. Unobstructed view necessary for U-turn

No person shall make a U-turn upon any highway where the driver of such vehicle does not have an

unobstructed view for 200 feet in both directions along the highway and of any traffic thereon.
(Amended by Stats.1972, c. 64, p. 84, § 1.)

§ 22106. Starting parked vehicles or backing

No person shall start a vehicle stopped, standing, or parked on a highway, nor shall any person back a vehicle on a highway until such movement can be made with reasonable safety.
(Stats.1959, c. 3, p. 1689, § 22106.)

§ 22107. Turning movements and required signals

No person shall turn a vehicle from a direct course or move right or left upon a roadway until such movement can be made with reasonable safety and then only after the giving of an appropriate signal in the manner provided in this chapter in the event any other vehicle may be affected by the movement.
(Amended by Stats.1959, c. 1996, p. 4630, § 27.)

§ 22108. Duration of signal

Any signal of intention to turn right or left shall be given continuously during the last 100 feet traveled by the vehicle before turning.
(Stats.1959, c. 3, p. 1689, § 22108.)

§ 22109. Signal when stopping

No person shall stop or suddenly decrease the speed of a vehicle on a highway without first giving an appropriate signal in the manner provided in this chapter to the driver of any vehicle immediately to the rear when there is opportunity to give the signal.
(Stats.1959, c. 3, p. 1689, § 22109.)

§ 22110. Method of signaling

The signals required by this chapter shall be given either by means of the hand and arm or by a signal lamp, but when the body or load on any vehicle or combination of vehicles projects 24 inches or more to the left of the center of the steering wheel so that a hand and arm signal would not be visible both to the front and rear of such vehicle or combination of vehicles, or under any condition when a hand and arm signal would not be visible both to the front and rear of the vehicle or vehicles, then the vehicle or vehicles shall be equipped with, and signals shall be given by, a signal lamp, except that implements of husbandry need not be equipped with signal lamps, but drivers of implements of husbandry shall give a hand and arm signal when required by this chapter.
(Amended by Stats.1967, c. 859, p. 2300, § 1.)

§ 22111. Hand signals

All required signals given by hand and arm shall be given from the left side of a vehicle in the following manner:

(a) Left turn—hand and arm extended horizontally beyond the side of the vehicle.

(b) Right turn—hand and arm extended upward beyond the side of the vehicle, except that a bicyclist may extend the right hand and arm horizontally to the right side of the bicycle.

(c) Stop or sudden decrease of speed signal—hand and arm extended downward beyond the side of the vehicle.
(Amended by Stats.1976, c. 751, p. ——, § 15.)

§ 22112. School bus signal

The driver of a schoolbus shall operate the flashing red signal lamps required on such bus at all times when children are unloading from the schoolbus to cross a highway or when the bus is stopped for the purpose of loading children who must cross a highway to board the bus, except that such signal shall not be operated at any place where traffic is controlled by a traffic officer or official traffic control signal. The schoolbus signal lamps shall not be operated at any other time.
(Amended by Stats.1977, c. 553, p. ——, § 1.)

§ 22348. Temporary maximum speed limit

(a) Notwithstanding Sections 22349, 22356, or any other provision of this chapter to the contrary, no person shall drive a vehicle upon a highway at a speed greater than 55 miles per hour.

(b) Any vehicle subject to the provisions of Section 22406 shall be driven in a lane designated pursuant to Section 21655, or if no such lane has been designated, in the right-hand lane for traffic or as close as practicable to the right-hand edge or curb. When overtaking and passing another vehicle proceeding in the same direction, such drivers shall use either the designated lane, the lane to the immediate left of the right-hand lane, or the right-hand lane for traffic as permitted under the provisions of this code. If, however, specific lane or lanes have not been designated on a divided highway having four or more clearly marked lanes for traffic in one direction, any such vehicle may also be driven in the lane to the immediate left of such right-hand lane, unless otherwise prohibited under the provisions of this code. This subdivision shall not apply to a driver who is

§ 22348

preparing for a left- or right-hand turn or who is in the process of entering into or exiting from a highway or to a driver who must necessarily drive in a lane other than the right-hand lane to continue on his intended route.

(c) This section shall remain in effect 120 days from the date that the 55-mile-per-hour national maximum speed limit, as specified in Section 154 of Title 23 of the United States Code, is repealed.
(Amended by Stats.1978, c. 217, p. —, § 1.)

§ 22349. Maximum speed limit

Except as provided in Section 22356, no person shall drive a vehicle upon a highway at a speed greater than 65 miles per hour.
(Amended by Stats.1963, c. 1735, p. 3453, § 1.)

§ 22350. Basic speed law

No person shall drive a vehicle upon a highway at a speed greater than is reasonable or prudent having due regard for weather, visibility, the traffic on, and the surface and width of, the highway, and in no event at a speed which endangers the safety of persons or property.
(Amended by Stats.1963, c. 252, p. 1014, § 1.)

Editors' Note

Read People v. Wimberly in table of cases included in this text.

---

§ 22351. Speed law violations

(a) The speed of any vehicle upon a highway not in excess of the limits specified in Section 22352 or established as authorized in this code is lawful unless clearly proved to be in violation of the basic speed law.

(b) The speed of any vehicle upon a highway in excess of the prima facie speed limits in Section 22352 or established as authorized in this code is prima facie unlawful unless the defendant establishes by competent evidence that the speed in excess of said limits did not constitute a violation of the basic speed law at the time, place and under the conditions then existing.
(Stats.1959, c. 3, p. 1690, § 22351.)

§ 22352. Prima facie speed limits

The prima facie limits are as follows and the same shall be applicable unless changed as authorized in this code and, if so changed, only when signs have been erected giving notice thereof:

(a) Fifteen miles per hour:

(1) When traversing a railway grade crossing, if during the last 100 feet of the approach to the crossing the driver does not have a clear and unobstructed view of the crossing and of any traffic on the railway for a distance of 400 feet in both directions along such railway. This subdivision does not apply in the case of any railway grade crossing where human flagman is on duty or a clearly visible electrical or mechanical railway crossing signal device is installed but does not then indicate the immediate approach of a railway train or car.

(2) When traversing any intersection of highways if during the last 100 feet of his approach to the intersection the driver does not have a clear and unobstructed view of the intersection and of any traffic upon all of the highways entering the intersection for a distance of 100 feet along all such highways, except at an intersection protected by stop signs or yield right-of-way signs or controlled by official traffic control signals.

(3) On any alley.

(b) Twenty-five miles per hour:

(1) On any highway other than a state highway, in any business or residence district unless a different speed is determined by local authority under procedures set forth in this code.

(2) When passing a school building or the grounds thereof, contiguous to a highway and posted with a standard "SCHOOL" warning sign, while children are going to or leaving such school during opening or closing hours or during the noon recess period. Such prima facie limit shall also apply when passing any school grounds which are not separated from the highway by a fence, gate or other physical barrier while the grounds are in use by children and the highway is posted with a standard "SCHOOL" warning sign.
(Amended by Stats.1963, c. 397, p. 1203, § 1; Stats.1963, c. 409, p. 1214, § 3.)

§ 22354. Decrease of state highway limits

Whenever the Department of Transportation determines upon the basis of an engineering and traffic survey that the limit of 65 miles per hour is more than reasonable or safe upon any portion of a state highway where the limit of 65 miles is applicable, the department may determine and declare a prima facie speed limit of 60, 55, 50, 45, 40, 35, 30 or 25 miles per

hour, whichever is found most appropriate to facilitate the orderly movement of traffic and is reasonable and safe, which declared prima facie speed limit shall be effective when appropriate signs giving notice thereof are erected upon the highway.
(Amended by Stats.1974, c. 545, p. 1322, § 194.)

§ 22355. Variable speed limits

Whenever the Department of Transportation determines upon the basis of an engineering and traffic survey that the safe and orderly movement of traffic upon any state highway which is a freeway will be facilitated by the establishment of variable speed limits, the department may erect, regulate, and control signs upon the state highway which is a freeway, or any portion thereof, which signs shall be so designed as to permit display of different speed limits at various times of the day or night. Such signs need not conform to the standards and specifications established by regulations of the Department of Transportation pursuant to Section 21400, but shall be of sufficient size and clarity to give adequate notice of the applicable speed limit. The speed limit upon the freeway at a particular time and place shall be that which is then and there displayed upon such sign.
(Amended by Stats.1973, c. 78, p. 137, § 17.)

§ 22356. Increase of freeway limit

Whenever the Department of Transportation, after consultation with the Department of the California Highway Patrol, determines upon the basis of an engineering and traffic survey on existing freeway segments, or upon the basis of appropriate design standards and projected traffic volumes in the case of newly constructed freeway segments, that a speed greater than 65 miles per hour would facilitate the orderly movement of vehicular traffic and would be reasonable and safe upon any state highway or portion thereof which is a freeway with full control of access and without crossings at grade otherwise subject to a maximum speed limit of 65 miles per hour, the Secretary of the Business and Transportation Agency may declare a higher maximum speed of 70 miles per hour, and shall cause appropriate signs to be erected giving notice thereof.

No person shall drive a vehicle upon such highway at a speed greater than 70 miles per hour.
(Amended by Stats.1974, c. 545, p. 1322, § 195.)

§ 22358.3. Decrease on narrow street

Whenever a local authority determines upon the basis of an engineering and traffic survey that the prima facie speed limit of 25 miles per hour in a business or residence district or in a public park on any street having a roadway not exceeding 25 feet in width, other than a state highway, is more than is reasonable or safe, the local authority may, by ordinance or resolution, determine and declare a prima facie speed limit of 20 or 15 miles per hour, whichever is found most appropriate and is reasonable and safe. The declared prima facie limit shall be effective when appropriate signs giving notice thereof are erected upon the street.
(Amended by Stats.1972, c. 1095, p. 2056, § 3.)

§ 22358.4. Decrease of local limits near schools

Whenever a local authority determines upon the basis of an engineering and traffic survey that the prima facie speed limit of 25 miles per hour established by paragraph (2) of subdivision (b) of Section 22352 is more than is reasonable or safe, the local authority may, by ordinance or resolution, determine and declare a prima facie speed limit of 20 or 15 miles per hour, whichever is justified as the appropriate speed limit by such survey. No such ordinance or resolution shall be effective until appropriate signs giving notice thereof are erected upon the highway nor, in the case of a state highway, until such ordinance is approved by the Department of Transportation and such signs are erected upon the highway.
(Added by Stats.1974, c. 102, p. 217, § 1.)

§ 22363. Restrictions because of snow or ice conditions

Notwithstanding any speed limit that may be in effect upon the highway, the Department of Transportation in respect to state highways, or a local authority with respect to highways under its jurisdiction, may determine and declare a prima facie speed limit of 40, 35, 30, or 25 miles per hour, whichever is found most appropriate and is reasonable and safe based on the prevailing snow or ice conditions upon such highway or any portion thereof. Signs may be placed and removed as snow or ice conditions vary.
(Amended by Stats.1974, c. 545, p. 1322, § 196.)

§ 22364. Lane speed limits

Whenever the Department of Transportation determines upon the basis of an engineering and traffic survey that the safe and orderly movement of traffic

upon any state highway will be facilitated by the establishment of different speed limits for the various lanes of traffic, the department may place signs upon the state highway, or any portion thereof, which signs shall designate the speed limits for each of the lanes of traffic.
(Amended by Stats.1974, c. 545, p. 1322, § 197.)

§ 22400. Minimum speed law

(a) No person shall drive upon a highway at such a slow speed as to impede or block the normal and reasonable movement of traffic, except when reduced speed is necessary for safe operation or because upon a grade or in compliance with law.

(b) Whenever the Department of Transportation determines on the basis of an engineering and traffic survey that slow speeds on any part of a state highway consistently impede the normal and reasonable movement of traffic, the department may determine and declare a minimum speed limit below which no person shall drive a vehicle, except when necessary for safe operation or in compliance with law, when appropriate signs giving notice thereof are erected along the part of the highway for which a minimum speed limit is established.

Subdivision (b) of this section shall apply only to vehicles subject to registration.
(Amended by Stats.1974, c. 545, p. 1322, § 198.)

§ 22401. Traffic signals

Local authorities in timing traffic signals may so regulate the timing thereof as to permit the movement of traffic in an orderly and safe manner at speeds slightly at variance from the speed otherwise applicable under this code.
(Stats.1959, c. 3, p. 1694, § 22401.)

§ 22402. Bridges and structures

The Department of Transportation may, in the manner provided in Section 22404 determine the maximum speed, not less than five miles per hour, which can be maintained with safety to any bridge, elevated structure, tube, or tunnel on a state highway. Said department may also make a determination with reference to any other highway upon receiving a request therefor from the board of supervisors or road commissioner of the county, the governing body of the local authority having jurisdiction over the bridge, elevated structure, tube, or tunnel.
(Amended by Stats.1974, c. 545, p. 1323, § 199.)

§ 22403. Local bridges and structures

Any local authority may, in the manner provided in Section 22404, determine the maximum speed, not less than five miles per hour, which can be maintained with safety to any bridge, elevated structure, tube, or tunnel under its jurisdiction, or may request the Department of Transportation to make such determination.
(Amended by Stats.1974, c. 545, p. 1323, § 200.)

§ 22404. Revision of speed limit on bridges and structures

The Department of Transportation or local authority making a determination of the maximum safe speed upon a bridge, elevated structure, tube, or tunnel shall first make an engineering investigation and shall hold a public hearing.

Notice of the time and place of the public hearing shall be posted upon the bridge, elevated structure, tube, or tunnel at least five days before the date fixed for the hearing. Upon the basis of the investigation and all evidence presented at the hearing, the department or local authority shall determine by order in writing the maximum speed which can be maintained with safety to the bridge, elevated structure, tube or tunnel. Thereupon, the authority having jurisdiction over the bridge, elevated structure, tube, or tunnel shall erect and maintain suitable signs specifying the maximum speed so determined at a distance of not more than 500 feet from each end of the bridge, elevated structure, tube, tunnel, or any approach thereto.
(Amended by Stats.1974, c. 545, p. 1323, § 201.)

§ 22405. Violations on bridges and structures

(a) No person shall drive a vehicle on any bridge, elevated structure, tube, or tunnel constituting a part of a highway, at a speed which is greater than the maximum speed which can be maintained with safety to such structure.

(b) Upon the trial of any person charged with a violation of this section with respect to a sign erected under Section 22404, proof of the determination of the maximum speed by the Department of Transportation or local authority and the erection and maintenance of the speed signs shall constitute prima facie evidence of the maximum speed which can be maintained with safety to the bridge, elevated structure, tube, or tunnel.
(Amended by Stats.1974, c. 545, p. 1323, § 202.)

§ 22407. Decreasing maximum speed law for certain vehicles

Whenever the Department of Transportation or local authority determines upon the basis of engineering studies and a traffic survey that the speed of 55 miles per hour is more than is reasonable or safe for vehicles mentioned in subdivision (a) of Section 22406, which have a manufacturer's gross vehicle weight rating of 10,000 pounds or more, in descending a grade upon any portion of a highway, the department or local authority, with respect to highways under their respective jurisdiction, may determine and declare a speed limit of 50, 45, 40, 35, 30, 25, or 20 miles per hour, whichever is found most appropriate to facilitate the orderly movement of traffic and is reasonable and safe, which declared speed limit shall be effective for such vehicles when appropriate signs giving notice thereof are erected upon the highway.
(Amended by Stats.1973, c. 82, p. 143, § 1.)

§ 22450. Stop requirements

The driver of any vehicle approaching a stop sign at the entrance to, or within, an intersection, or railroad grade crossing shall stop at a limit line, if marked, otherwise before entering the crosswalk on the near side of the intersection.

If there is no limit line or crosswalk, the driver shall stop at the entrance to the intersecting roadway or railroad grade crossing.
(Amended by Stats.1969, c. 364, p. 890, § 1.)

§ 22451. Train signals

(a) The driver of any vehicle approaching a railroad grade crossing shall stop not less than 15 feet from the nearest rail and shall not proceed until he can do so safely, whenever the following conditions exist:

(1) A clearly visible electric or mechanical signal device or a flagman gives warning of the approach or passage of a train or car.

(2) An approaching train or car is plainly visible or is emitting an audible signal and, by reason of its speed or nearness, is an immediate hazard.

(b) No driver shall proceed through, around or under any railroad crossing gate while such gate is closed.
(Amended by Stats.1970, c. 608, p. 1189, § 1.)

§ 22454. School bus

The driver of any vehicle upon meeting or overtaking from either direction any schoolbus equipped with signs as required in this code which has stopped for the purpose of receiving or discharging any schoolchildren and displays a flashing red light signal visible from front and rear shall bring such vehicle to a stop immediately before passing the schoolbus and shall not proceed past the schoolbus until the red flashing signal ceases operation.

The driver of a vehicle upon a highway with separate roadways need not stop upon meeting or passing a schoolbus which is upon the other roadway. The driver of a vehicle need not stop upon meeting or passing a schoolbus when the schoolbus is stopped at an intersection where traffic is controlled by a traffic officer or official traffic control signal, or when the schoolbus is stopped at a place where traffic is controlled by a traffic officer or official traffic control signal.
(Amended by Stats.1971, c. 877, p. 1722, § 2.)

§ 22500. Prohibited stopping, standing, or parking

No person shall stop, park, or leave standing any vehicle whether attended or unattended, except when necessary to avoid conflict with other traffic or in compliance with the directions of a peace officer or official traffic control device, in any of the following places:

(a) Within an intersection except adjacent to curbs as may be permitted by local ordinance.

(b) On a crosswalk, except that a bus engaged as a common carrier or a taxicab may stop in an unmarked crosswalk to load or unload passengers when authorized by the legislative body of any city pursuant to ordinance.

(c) Between a safety zone and the adjacent right-hand curb or within the area between the zone and the curb as may be indicated by a sign or red paint on the curb, which sign or paint was erected or placed by local authorities pursuant to ordinance.

(d) Within 15 feet of the driveway entrance to any fire station. This paragraph shall not apply to any vehicle owned or operated by a fire department and clearly marked as a fire department vehicle.

(e) In front of a public or private driveway, except that a bus engaged as a common carrier, schoolbus, or a taxicab may stop to load or unload passengers when authorized by local authorities pursuant to ordinance.

§ 22500

In unincorporated territory, where the entrance of a private road or driveway is not delineated by an opening in a curb or by other curb construction, so much of the surface of the ground as is paved, surfaced, or otherwise plainly marked by vehicle use as a private road or driveway entrance, shall constitute a driveway.

(f) On a sidewalk, except electric carts when authorized by local ordinance, as specified in Section 21114.5.

(g) Alongside or opposite any street or highway excavation or obstruction when such stopping, standing, or parking would obstruct traffic.

(h) On the roadway side of any vehicle stopped, parked, or standing at the curb or edge of a highway.

(i) Alongside curb space authorized for the loading and unloading of passengers of a bus engaged as a common carrier in local transportation when indicated by a sign or red paint on such curb erected or painted by local authorities pursuant to ordinance.

(j) In a tube or tunnel, except vehicles of the authorities in charge, being used in the repair, maintenance, or inspection of the facility.

(k) Upon a bridge, except vehicles of the authorities in charge, being used in the repair, maintenance, or inspection of the facility, and except that a bus engaged as a common carrier in local transportation may stop to load or unload passengers upon a bridge where sidewalks are provided, when authorized by local authorities pursuant to ordinance, and except that local authorities pursuant to ordinance or the Department of Transportation pursuant to order, within their respective jurisdictions, may permit parking on bridges having sidewalks, and shoulders of sufficient width to permit parking without interfering with the normal movement of traffic on the roadway. Local authorities may by ordinance or resolution permit parking on such bridges on state highways in their respective jurisdictions if the ordinance or resolution is first approved in writing by the Department of Transportation. Parking shall not be permitted unless there are signs in place as may be necessary to indicate the provisions of local ordinances or the order of the Department of Transportation.
(Amended by Stats.1974, c. 545, p. 1324, § 203.)

§ 22502. Curb parking; local ordinances; exception

(a) Except as otherwise provided in this chapter every vehicle stopped or parked upon a roadway where there are adjacent curbs shall be stopped or parked with the right-hand wheels of such vehicle parallel with and within 18 inches of the right-hand curb, except that motorcycles shall be parked with at least one wheel or fender touching the right-hand curb. Where no curbs or barriers bound any two-way roadway, right-hand parallel parking is required unless otherwise indicated.

(b) The provisions of subdivision (a) or (e) do not apply to a commercial vehicle if a variation from the requirements of subdivision (a) or (e) is reasonably necessary to accomplish the loading or unloading of merchandise or passengers on, or from, such vehicle and while anything connected with such loading, or unloading, is being executed.

This subdivision shall not be construed to permit any vehicle to stop or park upon a roadway in a direction opposite to that in which traffic normally moves upon that half of the roadway on which such vehicle is stopped or parked.

(c) Notwithstanding the provisions of subdivision (b), local authorities may, by ordinance, prohibit commercial vehicles from stopping, parking, or standing on one side of a roadway in a business district with the wheels of such vehicle more than 18 inches from the curb. The ordinance shall be effective only if signs are placed in the areas to which it is applicable clearly indicating the prohibition.

(d) This section does not apply to vehicles of a public utility when such vehicles are being used in connection with the operation, maintenance, or repair of facilities of the public utility or are being used in connection with providing public utility service.

(e) Upon a one-way roadway, vehicles may be stopped or parked as provided in subdivision (a) or with the left-hand wheels parallel to and within 18 inches of the left-hand curb, except that motorcycles, if parked on the left-hand side, shall have either one wheel or one fender touching such curb. Where no curb or barriers bound any such one-way roadway, parallel parking on either side is required unless otherwise indicated.

The provisions of this subdivision shall not apply upon the roadways of a divided highway.
(Amended by Stats.1971, c. 448, p. 933, § 1.)

§ 22503.5. Two or three-wheeled motor vehicle parking regulations

Notwithstanding any other provision of this code, any local authority may, by ordinance or resolution,

establish special parking regulations for two-wheeled or three-wheeled motor vehicles.
(Amended by Stats.1972, c. 1095, p. 2056, § 4.)

§ 22504. Unincorporated area parking; school bus stops

(a) Upon any highway in unincorporated areas no person shall stop, park, or leave standing any vehicle, whether attended or unattended, upon the roadway when it is practicable to stop, park, or leave the vehicle off such portion of the highway, but in every event an unobstructed width of the highway opposite a standing vehicle shall be left for the free passage of other vehicles and a clear view of the stopped vehicle shall be available from a distance of 200 feet in each direction upon the highway. This section shall not apply upon a highway where the roadway is bounded by adjacent curbs.

(b) This section shall not apply to the driver of any vehicle which is disabled in such a manner and to such extent that it is impossible to avoid stopping and temporarily leaving the disabled vehicle on the roadway.

(c) When, in the judgment of the governing board of a school district, it is necessary for the safety of pupils being transported to and from schools to authorize a schoolbus stop at a place where there is not a clear view of the stop from a distance of 200 feet in each direction along the highway, such stop may be authorized by and with the approval of the California Highway Patrol. The Department of Transportation, in respect to state highways, and local authorities, in respect to highways under their jurisdiction, shall place sufficient signs along the highway to give adequate notice to motorists that they are approaching such bus stops.
(Amended by Stats.1974, c. 545, p. 1325, § 206.)

§ 22507. Local regulation

Local authorities may by ordinance or resolution prohibit or restrict the parking or standing of vehicles on certain streets or highways, or portions thereof, during all or certain hours of the day. Such ordinance or resolution may include a designation of certain streets upon which preferential parking privileges shall be given to residents and merchants adjacent to such streets under which such residents and merchants may be issued a permit which exempts them from the prohibition or restriction of such ordinance or resolution. With the exception of alleys, no such ordinance or resolution shall apply until signs or markings giving adequate notice thereof have been placed.
(Amended by Stats.1976, c. 1102, p. ——, § 1.)

§ 22507.5. Local regulation; overnight parking; commercial vehicles

Notwithstanding the provisions of Section 22507, local authorities may, by ordinance or resolution, prohibit or restrict the parking or standing of vehicles on certain streets or highways, or portions thereof, between the hours of 2 a. m. and 6 a. m., and may, by ordinance or resolution, prohibit or restrict the parking or standing, on any street, or portion thereof, in a residential district, of commercial vehicles having a manufacturer's gross vehicle weight rating of 10,000 pounds or more. Such ordinance or resolution relating to parking between the hours of 2 a. m. and 6 a. m. may provide for a system of permits for the purpose of exempting from the prohibition or restriction of such ordinance or resolution handicapped persons and residents of high-density, multiple-family dwelling areas or similar areas lacking adequate offstreet parking facilities. No such ordinance or resolution relating to the parking or standing of commercial vehicles in a residential district shall, however, be effective with respect to any commercial vehicle making pickups or deliveries of goods, wares, and merchandise from or to any building or structure located on the restricted streets or highways or for the purpose of delivering materials to be used in the actual and bona fide repair, alteration, remodeling, or construction of any building or structure upon the restricted streets or highways for which a building permit has previously been obtained.
(Amended by Stats.1976, c. 37, p. ——, § 1.)

§ 22507.8. Parking in spaces designated for disabled persons prohibited

(a) It is unlawful for any person to park or leave standing any vehicle in a stall or space designated for physically handicapped persons, if, immediately adjacent to and visible from such stall or space, there is posted a sign consisting of a profile view of a wheelchair with occupant in white on a blue background, unless the vehicle displays either one of the distinguishing license plates or a placard issued pursuant to Section 22511.5 or to disabled veterans, as specified in Section 9105.

(b) The provisions of subdivision (a) shall apply to all offstreet parking facilities owned or operated by the state, and to all offstreet parking facilities owned

§ 22507.8

or operated by a local authority if so designated by the local authority by ordinance or resolution. The provisions of subdivision (a) shall also apply to any privately owned and maintained offstreet parking facility as provided in Section 21107.8.
(Added by Stats.1976, c. 1096, p. ——, § 2.)

§ 22508. Parking meter zones

Local authorities shall not establish parking meter zones or fix the rate of fees for such zones except by ordinance. An ordinance establishing a parking meter zone shall describe the area which would be included within the zone.

Local authorities may by ordinance cause streets and highways to be marked with white lines designating parking spaces and require vehicles to park within the parking spaces.

No ordinance adopted by any local authority pursuant to this section with respect to any state highway shall become effective until the proposed ordinance has been submitted to and approved in writing by the Department of Transportation. The proposed ordinance shall be submitted to the department only by action of the local legislative body and the proposed ordinance shall be submitted in complete draft form.

Any ordinance adopted pursuant to this section establishing a parking meter zone or fixing rates of fees for such a zone shall be subject to local referendum processes in the same manner as if such ordinance dealt with a matter of purely local concern.
(Amended by Stats.1974, c. 545, p. 1326, § 208.)

§ 22509. Parking on hills

Local authorities within the reasonable exercise of their police powers may adopt rules and regulations by ordinance or resolution providing that no person driving, or in control of, or in charge of, a motor vehicle shall permit it to stand on any highway unattended when upon any grade exceeding 3 percent within any business or residence district without blocking the wheels of the vehicle by turning them against the curb or by other means.
(Stats.1959, c. 3, p. 1700, § 22509.)

§ 22513. Tow cars

The owner or operator of a tow car who complies with the requirements of this code relating to tow cars may stop or park such tow car upon a highway for the purpose of rendering assistance to a disabled vehicle, except that such person may not stop or park upon a freeway which has full control of access and no crossing at grade unless the tow car has been summoned to render assistance to a disabled vehicle.
(Amended by Stats.1967, c. 441, p. 1654, § 1.)

§ 22514. Fire hydrants

No person shall stop, park, or leave standing any vehicle within 15 feet of a fire hydrant except when local authorities indicate a different distance by signs or markings, and except when such vehicle is attended by a licensed driver who is seated in the front seat and who can immediately move such vehicle in case of necessity. This section shall not apply in respect to any vehicle owned or operated by a fire department and clearly marked as a fire department vehicle.
(Amended by Stats.1961, c. 1615, p. 3458, § 35.)

§ 22515. Unattended vehicles

No person driving, or in control of, or in charge of, a motor vehicle shall permit it to stand on any highway unattended without first effectively setting the brakes thereon and stopping the motor thereof.
(Stats.1959, c. 3, p. 1701, § 22515.)

§ 22516. Locked vehicle

No person shall leave standing a locked vehicle in which there is any person who cannot readily escape therefrom.
(Stats.1959, c. 3, p. 1701, § 22516.)

§ 22517. Opening and closing doors

No person shall open the door of a vehicle on the side available to moving traffic unless it is reasonably safe to do so and can be done without interfering with the movement of such traffic, nor shall any person leave a door open on the side of a vehicle available to moving traffic for a period of time longer than necessary to load or unload passengers.
(Amended by Stats.1963, c. 162, p. 895, § 1.)

§ 22520. Stopping on freeway

No person shall stop, park, or leave standing any vehicle upon a freeway which has full control of access and no crossings at grade except:

(a) When necessary to avoid injury or damage to persons or property.

(b) When required by law or in obedience to a peace officer or official traffic control device.

(c) Any person actually engaged in maintenance or construction on freeway property or any employee of a public agency actually engaged in the performance of official duties.

(d) Any vehicle which is so disabled that it is impossible to avoid temporarily stopping and any vehicle which has been summoned to render assistance to a vehicle or person, including a vehicle owned by the donor of free emergency assistance, which has been summoned by display upon or within a disabled vehicle of a placard or sign given to the driver of the disabled vehicle by the donor for the specific purpose of summoning assistance, other than towing service, from the donor.

(e) In locations where stopping, standing or parking is specifically permitted; provided, however, that buses may not stop on freeways unless sidewalks are provided with shoulders of sufficient width to permit stopping without interfering with the normal movement of traffic and without the possibility of crossing over fast lanes to reach the bus stop.

(f) Any person reporting a traffic accident or other situation or incident to a peace officer or any person specified in subdivision (c), either directly or by means of an emergency telephone or similar device.

(g) The owner or operator of a tow car operating under an agreement with the Department of the California Highway Patrol for the purpose of rapid removal of impediments to traffic.
(Amended by Stats.1973, c. 461, p. 930, § 1.)

§ 22521. Parking upon or near railroad track

No person shall park a vehicle upon any railroad track or within 7½ feet of the nearest rail.
(Added by Stats.1968, c. 625, p. 1309, § 1.)

§ 22650. Prohibition of removal

It is unlawful for any peace officer or any unauthorized person to remove any unattended vehicle from a highway to a garage or to any other place, except as provided in this code.
(Stats.1959, c. 3, p. 1701, § 22650.)

§ 22651. Circumstances permitting removal

Any member of the California Highway Patrol; any regularly employed and salaried deputy of the sheriff's office of a county in which a vehicle is located; any regularly employed and salaried officer of a police department in a city in which a vehicle is located; any regularly employed and salaried officer of the University of California Police Department on or about a campus or in or about other grounds or properties owned, operated, controlled, or administered by the Regents of the University of California on or in which a vehicle is located; any regularly employed and salaried officer of a California state university and college police department on or about a campus or in or about other grounds or properties owned, operated, controlled, or administered by the Trustees of the California State University and Colleges on or in which a vehicle is located; any regularly employed and salaried employee, who is engaged in directing traffic or enforcing parking laws and regulations, of a city or a county in which a vehicle is located; or any police officer appointed or employed by the board of directors of a regional park district on or about lands, grounds, or properties owned, operated, or administered by the regional park district on or in which a vehicle is located; may remove a vehicle from a highway under any of the following circumstances:

(a) When any vehicle is left unattended upon any bridge, viaduct, or causeway or in any tube or tunnel where the vehicle constitutes an obstruction to traffic.

(b) When any vehicle is parked or left standing upon a highway in such a position as to obstruct the normal movement of traffic or in such a condition as to create a hazard to other traffic upon the highway.

(c) When any vehicle is found upon a highway and report has previously been made that the vehicle has been stolen or complaint has been filed and a warrant thereon issued charging that the vehicle has been embezzled.

(d) When any vehicle is illegally parked so as to block the entrance to a private driveway and it is impractical to move such vehicle from in front of the driveway to another point on the highway.

(e) When any vehicle is illegally parked so as to prevent access by firefighting equipment to a fire hydrant and it is impracticable to move such vehicle from in front of the fire hydrant to another point on the highway.

(f) When any vehicle, except any highway maintenance or construction equipment, is left unattended for more than four hours upon the right-of-way of any freeway which has full control of access and no crossings at grade.

(g) When the person or persons in charge of a vehicle upon a highway are by reason of physical injuries or illness incapacitated to such an extent as to be unable to provide for its custody or removal.

(h) When an officer arrests any person driving or in control of a vehicle for an alleged offense and the

§ 22651

officer is by this code or other law required or permitted to take, and does take, the person arrested before a magistrate without unnecessary delay.

(i) When any vehicle registered in a foreign jurisdiction is found upon a highway and it is known to have been issued five or more notices of parking violation over a period of five or more days, to which the owner or person in control of the vehicle has not responded, the vehicle may be impounded until such person furnishes to the impounding law enforcement agency evidence of his identity and an address within this state at which he can be located and satisfactory evidence that bail has been deposited for all notices of parking violation issued for the vehicle. A notice of parking violation issued to such a vehicle shall be accompanied by a warning that repeated violations may result in the impounding of the vehicle. In lieu of requiring satisfactory evidence that such bail has been deposited, the impounding law enforcement agency may, in its discretion, issue a notice to appear for the offenses charged, as provided in Article 2 (commencing with Section 40500) of Chapter 2 of Division 17. In lieu of either furnishing satisfactory evidence that such bail has been deposited or accepting the notice to appear, such person may demand to be taken without unnecessary delay before a magistrate within the county in which the offenses charged are alleged to have been committed and who has jurisdiction of the offenses and is nearest or most accessible with reference to the place where the vehicle is impounded.

(j) When any vehicle is found illegally parked and there are no license plates or other evidence of registration displayed, the vehicle may be impounded until the owner or person in control of the vehicle furnishes the impounding law enforcement agency evidence of his identity and an address within this state at which he can be located.

(k) When any vehicle is parked or left standing upon a highway for 72 or more consecutive hours in violation of a local ordinance authorizing removal.

(*l*) When any vehicle is illegally parked on a highway in violation of any local ordinance forbidding standing or parking and the use of a highway or a portion thereof is necessary for the cleaning, repair, or construction of the highway, or for the installation of underground utilities, and signs giving notice that such a vehicle may be removed are erected or placed at least 24 hours prior to the removal by local authorities pursuant to the ordinance.

(m) Wherever the use of the highway or any portion thereof is authorized by local authorities for a purpose other than the normal flow of traffic or for the movement of equipment, articles, or structures of unusual size, and the parking of any vehicle would prohibit or interfere with such use or movement, and signs giving notice that such a vehicle may be removed are erected or placed at least 24 hours prior to the removal by local authorities pursuant to the ordinance.

(n) Whenever any vehicle is parked or left standing where local authorities by resolution or ordinance have prohibited such parking and have authorized the removal of vehicles. No vehicle may be removed unless signs are posted giving notice of the removal. (Amended by Stats.1977, c. 73, p. ——, § 1; Stats.1977, c. 486, p. ——, § 2; Stats.1977, c. 1129, p. ——, § 2.)

Editors' Note

Read People v. Mozzetti in table of cases included in this text.

Notes of Decisions

Arrest of driver

Deputy sheriff who arrested driver and occupant of automobile for intoxication properly refused to release automobile and surrender its possession to one who was stranger to the officer and who had no identification in his possession where ownership of vehicle had not been determined because of absence of registration certificate. Martinez v. Superior Court for Los Angeles County (1970) 87 Cal.Rptr. 6, 7 C.A.3d 569.

Custodial possession of an automobile is not an inevitable concomitant of arrest of the driver. Virgil v. Superior Court, Placer County (1968) 73 Cal.Rptr. 793, 268 C.A.2d 127.

Where defendant was legally under arrest for commission of misdemeanor hit-run violation, box of recording tapes which had been stolen from another automobile was in plain sight of officer standing outside of hit-run automobile at time of alleged "search" defendant was a burglary suspect, and act of officer in allowing witness a closer inspection of property might well have immediately exculpated defendant from further suspicion of that offense, officer's picking up the box of stereo tapes for witness' closer inspection was reasonably incidental to defendant's earlier arrest. People v. Harris (1967) 63 Cal.Rptr. 849, 256 C.A.2d 455.

Police officer is authorized to remove vehicle from highway to nearest garage when he arrests any person driving or in control of vehicle for an alleged offense or where such officer is by the Vehicle Code or other law required to take person arrested immediately before a magistrate. People v. Simpson (1959) 339 P.2d 156, 170 C.A.2d 524.

An arresting officer has no authority to remove the vehicle of an arrested person from a highway except under the conditions and for the reasons set forth in this section. 28 Ops.Atty.Gen. 185.

Searches and seizures—In general

Where automobile had been reported stolen and defendant who had been driving it had confessed to bank robbery, search of automobile and seizure of stolen bank money and guns believed to have been used in robbery was proper and evidence seized was admissible. Schoepflin v. U. S. (C.A.1968) 391 F.2d 390, certiorari denied 89 S.Ct. 146, 393 U.S. 865, 21 L.Ed.2d 133.

Denial, in prosecution for possessing amphetamine, a restricted, dangerous drug, for sale, of motion to suppress brown paper bag found in defendant's trunk and containing amphetamine tablets was not error on theory that cataloging of contents of defendant's truck violated his constitutional rights, where arrest of defendant for drunk driving took place at night passenger had disappeared and there was no one to whom the truck could be entrusted. People v. Padilla (1971) 93 Cal.Rptr. 554, 15 C.A.3d 1010.

Officer who arrested defendant for drunken driving had reasonable cause to search defendant's vehicle as incident to lawful arrest. Martinez v. Superior Court of Los Angeles County (1970) 87 Cal.Rptr. 6, 7 C.A.3d 569.

Where police officers had received radio report of robbery, private citizen reported to officer that apparent robber had spoken to driver of automobile near scene of crime, officers had probable cause to make search of the vehicle. People v. Sesser (1969) 75 Cal.Rptr. 297, 269 C.A.2d 707.

Constitution does not permit an otherwise unreasonable search of an automobile simply because police have statutory authority to arrest and take an accused before a magistrate plus the right to cause automobile to be removed from the highway. Virgil v. Superior Court, Placer County (1968) 73 Cal.Rptr. 793, 268 C.A.2d 127.

Taking of defendant's automobile into custody and searching it was not necessary or legal and violated his Fourth and Fourteenth Amendment rights where defendant was arrested for speeding and given a ticket for reckless driving, search had no relation to the traffic violation, traffic violation did not involve any forfeiture of the automobile and there was nothing which would reasonably have justified search, which produced growing marijuana plants in a pan under front seat of automobile. Id.

Where search of defendant's automobile did not produce any evidence which was used to convict defendant of burglary nor lead to production of any such evidence, reversal of conviction would not be required even if search of defendant's automobile made after defendant's arrest was illegal. People v. Bright (1967) 59 Cal.Rptr. 372, 251 C.A.2d 395.

This section permitting officer to remove a vehicle from highway upon arrest of motorist and § 22850 permitting storage of such a vehicle in place designated or maintained by governmental agency did not authorize making of search of automobile in police impound lot without warrant. People v. Burke (1964) 39 Cal.Rptr. 531, 394 P.2d 67, 61 C.2d 575.

Liquor taken from automobile of defendant, who had been arrested by police officer pursuant to warrants for defendant's arrest for traffic offenses, and who was later charged with second degree burglary of market from which liquor was taken was product of legal search. People v. Garcia (1963) 29 Cal.Rptr. 609, 214 C.A.2d 681.

Since arrest of defendant motorist on outstanding traffic warrant was lawful, defendant properly was taken to police station for booking, and the booking search of his person, which yielded amphetamine tablets and seconal capsules, was reasonable and lawful; however, the drugs, bullets and firearms found in defendant's automobile were seized as the result of an unlawful search, since, under the circumstances, including the fact that the vehicle was not stolen or subject to forfeiture or illegally parked or unable to be locked, the deputies' custodial care of the automobile after defendant's arrest was neither necessary nor proper. People v. Landa (1973) 106 Cal.Rptr. 329, 30 C.A.3d 487.

Where defendant, properly arrested for running red light, was capable of moving his automobile and no reason appeared why he could not have taken charge of his own vehicle and driven under direction of officer to nearby place of safekeeping before he was taken before magistrate, police custodial care of defendant's vehicle, whose contents were inventoried and whose trunk was found to contain unlocked suitcase carrying plastic bag of marijuana, was neither necessary nor proper and evidence discovered in such illegal search was properly suppressed. People v. Nagel (1971) 95 Cal.Rptr. 129, 17 C.A.3d 492.

Warrantless search of unlocked suitcase observed on rear seat of automobile following removal of vehicle from roadway subsequent to automobile accident and seizure of quantity of marijuana from suitcase was not justified where search was not incident to lawful arrest, based on probable cause to believe that vehicle contained contraband or justified by peculiar nature of police custody involved, notwithstanding that search was part of routine police inventory of contents of vehicle preparatory to placing vehicle in storage. Mozzetti v. Superior Court of Sacramento County (1971) 94 Cal.Rptr. 412, 484 P.2d 84, 4 C.3d 699.

Inventory, searches and seizures

Where defendant and his passenger appeared to be intoxicated at time of arrest and defendant's ability to consent to release of his automobile was impaired, defendant was unable to produce registration or driver's license and police did not know true relationship of defendant with man who identified himself as a relative, deputy sheriff and city officer who was called to scene of arrest were entitled to remove the automobile from the alley which it blocked and to inventory the automobile and allegedly stolen items discovered during inventory were not product of unreasonable search and seizure. Martinez v. Superior Court for Los Angeles County (1970) 87 Cal.Rptr. 6, 7 C.A.3d 569.

With right of police to impound an automobile a concomitant right to inventory its contents arises, and inventory must be reasonably related to its purpose which is protection of automobile owner from loss, and police or other custodian from liability or unjust claim; and right to inventory extends to open areas of vehicle including such areas under seat and other places where property is ordinarily kept such as glove compartment and trunk, but not hidden places. People v. Andrews (1970) 85 Cal.Rptr. 908, 6 C.A.2d 428.

Where police officer made customary inventory of contents of automobile in good faith in connection with impounding the automobile, and was not looking for evidence to be used in criminal prosecution, and where officer opened trunk to look for spare tire pursuant to standard checklist, he properly opened duffel bag, which was found in trunk, to inventory the contents thereof, and drugs and other evidence found in the bag were lawfully obtained. People v. Marchese (1969) 80 Cal.Rptr. 525, 275 C.A.2d 1007.

Where two officers saw automobile being driven 15 miles per hour over speed limit and weaving back and forth, and officers formed opinion that driver and passenger were intoxicated, arrested driver, removed automobile and proceeded to inventory automobile as required by this section, marijuana discovered during inventory was properly seized by officers. People v. Superior Court of Sacramento County (1969) 80 Cal.Rptr. 209, 275 C.A.2d 631.

Inventory of vehicle is permissible when there is no reasonable alternative to towing and storage, and evidence which comes to light during course of such inventory is properly admitted into evidence. Id.

Evidence discovered by police while making inventory of contents of impounded vehicle was not product of improper search. People v. Sesser (1969) 75 Cal.Rptr. 297, 269 C.A.2d 707.

Police officer, who, on investigating accident, saw occupants of automobile removed by ambulance, who found contents of vehicle thrown about as result of upset, who had no reason to believe that contraband was in vehicle, who was not looking for narcotics, and who was not requested to make search was not required to obtain search warrant before making inventory of contents of automobile. People v. Roth (1968) 68 Cal.Rptr. 49, 261 C.A.2d 430.

Police had right to seize and hold hit-run automobile for purpose of retaining the necessary evidence, and since defendant was under arrest for hit-run violation it was duty of officers to take him before a magistrate without unnecessary delay, and for that reason officers were authorized to remove the automobile from street and to impound it, and having such custody, officers might properly make an inventory of its contents for protection of defendant, the garageman and the police. People v. Harris (1967) 63 Cal.Rptr. 849, 256 C.A.2d 455.

People v. Andrews (1970) 85 Cal.Rptr. 908, 6 C.A.3d 428 [main volume] certiorari denied 91 S.Ct. 152, 40 U.S. 908, 27 L.Ed.2d 147.

While police may take note of any personal property in plain sight within an automobile being taken into custody, only objects plainly visible without probing may be listed in the inventory or other police report, and a search into a closed suitcase or package or bag constitutes an unreasonable search. People v. Landa (1973) 106 Cal.Rptr. 329, 30 C.A.3d 487.

California Supreme Court decision (Mozzetti v. Superior Court, 94 Cal.Rptr. 412, 4 Cal.3d 699, 484 P.2d 84) that police procedure of inventorying vehicle to be impounded, involves a substantial invasion of privacy of vehicle owner and is a "search" governed by Fourth Amendment (U.S.C.A.Const. Amend. 4) requirements of reasonableness is to be given retrospective effect with respect to all cases not final on April 30, 1971, the date it was decided. People v. Heredia (1971) 97 Cal.Rptr. 488, 20 C.A.3d 194.

Impounded vehicle, searches and seizures

Burden was upon prosecution to justify search which produced growing marijuana plants in a pan under front seat of automobile of defendant arrested for speeding and given ticket for reckless driving, and it was therefore prosecution's burden to show that impounding of automobile was necessary. Virgil v. Superior Court, Placer County (1968) 73 Cal.Rptr. 793, 268 C.A.2d 127.

Officer was not entitled on basis of two traffic violations of having obscured front license plate and failing to have valid driver's license in his possession to place motorist under arrest and take him before magistrate; officer's only right was to give him notice to appear as prescribed in § 40500, and officer had no right to impound defendant's vehicle and search of vehicle was not justified as incidental to such process. People v. Van Sanden (1968) 73 Cal.Rptr. 359, 267 C.A.2d 662.

Search, without warrant, of defendant's vehicle, which had been left at scene of crime, was permissible on ground that vehicle had been impounded as vehicle abandoned on public street and police were therefore justified in itemizing its contents for protection of owner, garageman, and police. People v. Laursen (1968) 71 Cal.Rptr. 71, 264 C.A.2d 932.

Constitution does not permit otherwise unreasonable search of automobile simply because police have statutory authority to impound it. People v. Upton (1968) 65 Cal.Rptr. 103, 257 C.A.2d 677.

After arresting defendant for possession of prohibited instruments found in automobile, officers had right to impound automobile and had custody of automobile, articles found therein were properly in their possession, and no new seizure occurred when trunk of impounded automobile was pried open and money allegedly taken in burglary was found. People v. Odegard (1962) 21 Cal.Rptr. 515, 203 C.A.2d 427.

Search made of interior of defendant's automobile at time and place of arrest made because of unsatisfactory explanation of defendant's reasons for being about building in area where numerous burglaries had been perpetrated and because of suspicious circumstances was lawful as search incident to arrest, but search of trunk of automobile after defendant was taken to police station and automobile was towed to police impound lot was too remote in time and place to be lawful when conducted without warrant, and evidence obtained as result thereof was improperly admitted. People v. Burke (1964) 39 Cal.Rptr. 531, 394 P.2d 67, 61 C.2d 575.

Officer who was conducting inventory for valuables incident to impounding of defendant's car pursuant to this section, who was not given key to trunk but who opened it by pushing in lock and lifting lid with fingers conducted an unreasonable search of trunk and trial court erred prejudicially in denying motion to suppress amphetamine tablets found in trunk, requiring reversal of conviction based on guilty plea to charge of violation of Health & S.C. §§ 11530.5, 11911. People v. Heredia (1971) 97 Cal.Rptr. 488, 20 C.A.3d 194.

Burden of proof

Since officers who arrested defendant motorist had no search warrant, the people had the burden of demonstrating justification for the officers' taking custody of defendant's automobile after his arrest and taking an official inventory of its contents. People v. Landa (1973) 106 Cal.Rptr. 329, 30 C.A.3d 487.

§ 22653. Removal from private property

(a) Any peace officer, other than an employee directing traffic or enforcing parking laws and regulations, specified in Section 22651 may remove a vehicle from private property when the vehicle is found on private property and a report has previously been made that the vehicle has been stolen or a complaint has been filed and a warrant thereon issued charging that the vehicle has been embezzled.

(b) Any member of the California Highway Patrol; any regularly employed and salaried deputy of sheriff's office of a county; any regularly employed and salaried officer of a police department of a city; any regularly employed and salaried officer of the California State Police; any regularly employed and salaried officer of the University of California Police Department; or any regularly employed or salaried officer of a California state university and college police department, may, after a reasonable period of time, remove a vehicle from private property if the vehicle has been involved in, and left at the scene of, a traffic accident and no owner is available to grant permission to remove the vehicle. This subdivision does not authorize the removal of a vehicle where the owner has been contacted and has refused to grant permission to remove the vehicle.

(c) Nothing in this section is intended to expand the territorial jurisdiction of peace officers beyond the provisions of Sections 830.1 and 830.2 of the Penal Code.

(Amended by Stats.1978, c. 427, p. —, § 1.)

§ 22654. Authorization for moving a vehicle

(a) Whenever any peace officer or other employee directing traffic or enforcing parking laws and regulations, as specified in Section 22651, finds a vehicle standing upon a highway in violation of Sections 22500 and 22504, the officer or employee may move the vehicle or require the driver or other person in charge of the vehicle to move it to the nearest available position off the roadway or to the nearest parking location, or may remove and store the vehicle if moving it off the roadway to a parking location is impracticable.

(b) Whenever such an officer or employee finds a vehicle standing upon a street in violation of a traffic ordinance enacted by local authorities to prevent flooding of adjacent property, he or she may move the vehicle or require the driver or person in charge of the vehicle to move it to the nearest available location in the vicinity where parking is permitted.

(c) Any state, county, or city authority charged with the maintenance of any highway may move any vehicle which is disabled or abandoned or which constitutes an obstruction to traffic from the place where it is located on a highway as may be necessary to keep the highway open or safe for public travel. In addition, employees of the Department of Transportation may remove any disabled vehicle which constitutes an obstruction to traffic on a freeway from the place where it is located to the nearest available location where parking is permitted; and if the vehicle is unoccupied, the department shall comply with the notice requirements of subdivision (d) of this section.

(d) Any state, county, or city authority charged with the maintenance or operation of any highway, highway facility, or public works facility, in cases necessitating the prompt performance of any work on or service to such highway, highway facility, or public works facility, may move to the nearest available location where parking is permitted, any unattended vehicle which obstructs or interferes with the performance of such work or service or may remove and store such a vehicle if moving it off the roadway to a location where parking is permitted would be impracticable. If the vehicle is moved to another location where it is not readily visible from its former parked location or it is stored, the person causing such movement or storage of the vehicle shall immediately, by the most expeditious means, notify the owner of the vehicle of its location. If for any reason the vehicle owner cannot be so notified, the person causing the vehicle to be moved or stored shall immediately, by the most expeditious means, notify the police department of the city in which the vehicle was parked, or, if the vehicle had been parked in an unincorporated area of a county, notify the sheriff's department and nearest office of the California Highway Patrol in that county. No vehicle may be removed and stored pursuant to this subdivision unless signs indicating that no person shall stop, park, or leave standing any vehicle within the areas marked by the signs because such work or service would be done, were placed at least 24 hours prior to such movement or removal and storage.
(Amended by Stats.1977, c. 73, p. ——, § 4.)

§ 22655. Impounding vehicle for investigation

When any member of the California Highway Patrol, or any regularly employed and salaried officer of a police department in a city, or sheriff's department authorized to enforce the provisions of this code pursuant to Section 26613 of the Government Code, or any regularly employed and salaried officer of the California State Police on or about state grounds or properties, or any regularly employed and salaried officer of the University of California Police Department on or about a campus or in or about other grounds or properties owned, operated, controlled or administered by the Regents of the University of California, or any regularly employed and salaried officer of a California state university and college police department on or about a campus or in or about other grounds or properties owned, operated, controlled or administered by the Trustees of the California State University and Colleges, or any police officer appointed or employed by the board of directors of a regional park district on or about lands or properties owned, operated, or administered by the regional park district, has reasonable cause to believe that a motor vehicle on a highway has been involved in a hit-and-run accident, and the operator of the vehicle has failed to stop and comply with the provisions of Sections 20002, through 20006, inclusive, the officer may remove the vehicle from the highway for the purpose of inspection. Unless sooner released, the vehicle shall be released upon the expiration of 48 hours after such removal from the highway upon demand of the owner. When determining the 48-hour period, weekends and holidays shall not be included.
(Amended by Stats.1978, c. 505, p. ——, § 1.)

§ 22656. Removal from railroad right of way

Any member of the California Highway Patrol, or any regularly employed and salaried officer of a railroad, commissioned by the Governor pursuant to Section 8226 of the Public Utilities Code, or any regularly employed and salaried deputy of the sheriff's office of a county in which a vehicle is located, or any regularly employed and salaried officer of a police department in a city in which a vehicle is located, or any regularly employed and salaried officer of the California State Police on or about state grounds or properties on or in which a vehicle is located, or any regularly employed and salaried officer of the University of California Police Department on or about a campus or in or about other grounds or properties owned, operated, controlled or administered by the Regents of the University of California on or in which a vehicle is located, or any regularly employed and salaried officer of a California state university or college police department on or about a campus or in or about other grounds or properties owned, operated, controlled or administered by the Trustees of the California State University and Colleges on or in which a vehicle is located, or any regularly employed and salaried officer of a transit district security force on or about parking lots owned by the transit district or in or about other grounds or properties owned, operated, controlled or administered by the board of directors of the transit district on or in which a vehicle is located, or any police officer appointed or employed by the board of directors of a regional park district on or about lands or properties owned, operated, or administered by such regional park district on or in which a vehicle is located, may remove a vehicle from a railroad right-of-way if the vehicle is parked upon any railroad track or within 7½ feet of the nearest rail.
(Amended by Stats.1978, c. 182, p. ——, § 1.)

§ 22658. Removal from private property

(a) The owner or person in lawful possession of any private property may, subsequent to giving notice to the city police or county sheriff, whichever is appropriate, cause the removal of a vehicle parked on such property to the nearest public garage if there is displayed in plain view on the property a sign prohibiting public parking and containing the telephone number of the local traffic law enforcement agency. The person causing removal of such vehicle shall comply with the requirements of Sections 22852 and 22853 relating to notice in the same manner as applicable to an officer removing a vehicle from private property. The provisions of this section shall not limit or affect any right or remedy which the owner or person in lawful possession of private property may have by virtue of other provisions of law authorizing the removal of a vehicle parked upon such property.

(b) The owner of a vehicle removed from private property pursuant to subdivision (a) may recover for any damage to the vehicle resulting from any intentional or negligent act of any person causing the removal of, or removing, the vehicle.
(Amended by Stats.1971, c. 1698, p. 3639, § 1.)

§ 22659. Removal of vehicles by State Police

Any officer of the California State Police or any person duly authorized by the state agency in possession of property owned by the State, or rented or leased from others by the State and any officer of the California State Police providing policing services to property of a district agricultural association may, subsequent to giving notice to the city police or county sheriff, whichever is appropriate, cause the removal of a vehicle from such property to the nearest public garage, under any of the following circumstances:

(a) When the vehicle is illegally parked in locations where signs are posted giving notice of violation and removal.

(b) When an officer arrests any person driving or in control of a vehicle for an alleged offense and the officer is by this code or other law required to take the person arrested before a magistrate without unnecessary delay.

(c) When any vehicle is found upon such property and report has previously been made that the vehicle has been stolen or complaint has been filed and a warrant thereon issued charging that the vehicle has been embezzled.

(d) When the person or persons in charge of a vehicle upon such property are by reason of physical injuries or illness incapacitated to such an extent as to be unable to provide for its custody or removal.

The person causing removal of such vehicle shall comply with the requirements of Sections 22852 and 22853 relating to notice.
(Amended by Stats.1963, c. 518, p. 1396, § 1.)

§ 22660. Local ordinances

Notwithstanding any other provision of law, a city, county, or city and county may adopt an ordinance

establishing procedures for the abatement and removal, as public nuisances, of abandoned, wrecked, dismantled, of inoperative vehicles or parts thereof from private or public property, not including highways; and for the recovery, pursuant to Section 25845 or 38773.5 of the Government Code, or assumption by the local authority, of costs of administration and such removal.
(Amended by Stats.1976, c. 29, p. —, § 1.)

§ 22700. Abandonment prohibited

(a) No person shall abandon a vehicle upon any highway.

(b) No person shall abandon a vehicle upon public or private property without the express or implied consent of the owner or person in lawful possession or control of the property.
(Amended by Stats.1965, c. 1135, p. 2788, § 6.)

§ 22701. Presumption

The abandonment of any vehicle in a manner as provided in Section 22700 shall constitute a prima facie presumption that the last registered owner of record, not having complied with the provisions of Section 5900, is responsible for such abandonment and is thereby liable for the cost of removal and disposition of the vehicle.
(Added by Stats.1965, c. 1135, p. 2789, § 8.)

§ 22702. Removal of abandoned vehicles

(a) Any member of the California Highway Patrol or any regularly employed and salaried deputy sheriff or other employee of the county designated to perform this function by the board of supervisors in which a vehicle is located or any regularly employed and salaried police officer or other employee of the city designated to perform this function by the city council, in which a vehicle is located who has reasonable grounds to believe that the vehicle has been abandoned, may remove the vehicle from a highway or from public or private property.

(b) Any member of the California State Police who has reasonable grounds to believe that a vehicle has been abandoned upon property owned by the state, or rented or leased from others by the state, or property of a district agricultural association as to which the California State Police is providing policing services, may remove the vehicle from such property.

(c) Any regularly employed and salaried officer or other employee of the University of California Police Department who has reasonable grounds to believe that a vehicle has been abandoned on or about a campus or in or about other grounds or properties owned, operated, controlled or administered by the Regents of the University of California may remove the vehicle from such property.

(d) Any policeman appointed or employed by the board of directors of a regional park district who has reasonable grounds to believe that a vehicle has been abandoned upon property owned by the regional park district or rented or leased from others by the regional park district, may remove the vehicle from such property.

(e) Any regularly employed and salaried officer or other employee of a California state university or college police department who has reasonable grounds to believe that a vehicle has been abandoned on or about a campus or in or about other grounds or properties owned, operated, controlled or administered by the Trustees of the California State University and Colleges, may remove the vehicle from such property.

(f) Any person performing a franchise or contract awarded pursuant to subdivision (a) of Section 22710, may remove a vehicle from a highway or place to which it has been removed pursuant to subdivision (c) of Section 22654 or from public or private property, after a determination by a member of the California Highway Patrol or any regularly employed and salaried deputy or other employee of the sheriff's office of a county in which such vehicle is located or any regularly employed and salaried officer or other employee of a police department in a city in which such vehicle is located that such vehicle is abandoned.

(g) The public agency employing the officer shall make an appraisal of any such vehicle either prior to or within five days after removal.

(h) A county or city employee, other than an employee of a sheriff's department or a city police department, designated to remove vehicles pursuant to this section may do so only after he has mailed or personally delivered a written report identifying the vehicle and its location to the office of the Department of the California Highway Patrol located nearest to the vehicle.

(i) Any regularly employed and salaried officer of a transit district security force who has reasonable grounds to believe that a vehicle has been abandoned on property owned by the transit district or rented or leased from others by the transit district, may remove the vehicle from such property.
(Amended by Stats.1974, c. 797, p. 1746, § 3.)

§ 22850. Storage of vehicle; mileage

Whenever an officer or employee removes a vehicle from a highway, or from public or private property, unless otherwise provided, he shall take the vehicle to the nearest garage or other place of safety or to a garage designated or maintained by the governmental agency of which the officer or employee is a member, where the vehicle shall be placed in storage.

At the time of such removal, the officer or employee shall determine the amount of mileage on the vehicle.
(Amended by Stats.1975, c. 239, p. 629, § 1.)

Editors' Note

Read People v. Mozzetti in table of cases included in this text. The Vehicle Code also regulates private parking lots. These sections have not been included in this text.

---

§ 23101. Influence of alcohol and drugs causing death or injury

Text of section operative until July 1, 1980

(a) It is unlawful for any person, while under the influence of intoxicating liquor, or under the combined influence of intoxicating liquor and any drug, to drive a vehicle upon a highway and when so driving do any act forbidden by law or neglect any duty imposed by law in the driving of such vehicle, which act or neglect proximately causes death or bodily injury to any person other than himself.

(b) It is unlawful for any person, while under the influence of intoxicating liquor, or under the combined influence of intoxicating liquor and any drug, to drive a vehicle other than on a highway and when so driving do any act, or neglect any duty imposed by law, which act or neglect proximately causes death or bodily injury to any person other than himself.

(c) Any person convicted under this section shall be punished by imprisonment in the state prison, or in the county jail for not less than 90 days nor more than one year, and by fine of not less than two hundred seventy-five dollars ($275) nor more than five thousand dollars ($5,000).

(d) If any person is convicted of an offense under this section within five years of a prior conviction of a violation of Section 23102 or 23105 and is granted probation, it shall be a condition of probation that such person be confined in jail for at least 5 days but not more than one year and pay a fine of at least two hundred seventy-five dollars ($275) but not more than five thousand dollars ($5,000). If any person is convicted of an offense under this section within five years of a prior conviction of a violation of this section or Section 23106, and is granted probation, it shall be a condition of probation that such person be confined in jail for at least 90 days but not more than one year, and pay a fine of at least two hundred seventy-five dollars ($275) but not more than five thousand dollars ($5,000).

(e) In no event does the court have the power to absolve a person who is convicted of an offense under this section within five years of a prior conviction of a violation of this section or Section 23102, 23105, or 23106 from the obligation of spending the minimum time in confinement as provided in this section and of paying a fine of at least two hundred seventy-five dollars ($275), except as provided in subdivision (f).

(f) Except in unusual cases where the interests of justice demand an exception, the court shall not strike a prior conviction of an offense under this section or Section 23102, 23105, or 23106 for purposes of sentencing in order to avoid imposing as part of the sentence or term of probation the minimum time in confinement and the minimum fine, as provided in this section. When such a prior conviction is stricken by the court for purposes of sentencing, the court shall specify the reason or reasons for such striking order. On appeal by the people from such an order striking such a prior conviction, it shall be conclusively presumed that such order was made only for the reasons specified in such order, and such order shall be reversed if there is no substantial basis in the record for any of such reasons.

This section shall remain in effect only until July 1, 1980, and as of that date is repealed.
(Amended by Stats.1978, c. 790, p. ——, § 3.)

Editors' Note

Read People v. Hawkins in table of cases included in this text.

Notes of Decisions

In general

The mere act of driving a motor vehicle on a public highway while intoxicated is an unlawful act, but whether it is a felony or a misdemeanor depends on the facts and circumstances in the case. People v. Levens (1938) 82 P.2d 698, 28 C.A.2d 455; People v. Freeman (1936) 60 P.2d 333, 16 C.A.2d 101.

If minor driver's employer allegedly procured minor's drunkenness at a Christmas party and despite minor's drunkenness guided him to his automobile, placed him in automobile, and directed him to drive home, employer procured the improper illegal driving and would be responsible for injuries to third persons caused by minor's driving while intoxicated. Brockett v. Kitchen Boyd Motor Co. (1968) 70 Cal.Rptr. 136, 264 C.A.2d 69.

Intoxication, nature and elements of offense

In prosecution of defendant who, while allegedly under influence of intoxicating liquor, drove his vehicle across center line of highway and collided with another automobile resulting in injuries to occupant of other automobile, it was unnecessary for state to prove that defendant was drunk and it was only necessary to show that alcohol had appreciably impaired his ability to drive in a prudent manner. People v. Baxter (1959) 332 P.2d 334, 165 C.A.2d 648.

In prosecution for driving motor vehicle while under influence of intoxicating liquor resulting in bodily injury to another person, it is not necessary to prove any specific degree of intoxication. People v. Markham (1957) 314 P.2d 217, 153 C.A.2d 260.

To warrant conviction for driving automobile while "under influence of intoxicating liquor", a finding that intoxicating liquor had so far affected the nervous system, brain or muscles of accused as to impair to an appreciable degree the ability to operate vehicle in a manner like that of an ordinarily prudent and cautious person in full possession of his faculties using reasonable care and under like conditions, would be sufficient. People v. Haeussler (1953) 260 P.2d 8, 41 C.2d 252, certiorari denied 74 S.Ct. 533, 347 U.S. 931, 98 L.Ed. 1082.

Persons may be "under influence of intoxicating liquor", within meaning of this section, without having been affected to extent commonly associated with intoxication, or drunkenness. Id.

Motorist could not be held liable in automobile collision case merely because she drank intoxicating liquor before collision, if liquor did not affect her driving in any appreciable degree, and fact that she drank the liquor should not bias or prejudice jury. Christensen v. Harmonson (1952) 247 P.2d 956, 113 C.A.2d 175.

In prosecution for driving automobile while intoxicated, it is a matter of common knowledge that some persons react to influence of intoxicating liquors by becoming dull, rather than by becoming frenzied. People v. Mullins (1924) 226 P. 622, 66 C.A. 475.

Where intoxicating liquor has so far affected the nervous system, brain, or muscles of the driver of an automobile as to impair to an appreciable degree his ability to operate an automobile in a manner that an ordinarily prudent and cautious man in the full possession of his faculties using reasonable care would drive a similar vehicle under like conditions, the driver is "under the influence of intoxicating liquor," within Stats.1919, p. 214, § 17, denouncing the driving of an automobile while "under the influence of intoxicating liquor." People v. Dingle (1922) 205 P. 705, 56 C.A. 445.

Proximate cause

To establish offense of driving while under influence of intoxicant in unlawful manner, proximately causing injury to another, requires proof that defendant, while driving vehicle under influence of intoxicant, committed act forbidden by law or neglected duty imposed by law, and that such act or omission was proximate cause of injury to some person. People v. Schumacher (1961) 14 Cal.Rptr. 924, 194 C.A.2d 335.

Defendant, who while driving automobile, crossed center line of highway and collided with another automobile causing injury to occupant thereof violated law in driving of his vehicle and violation of law was proximate cause of bodily injury within contemplation of this section concerning driving while under influence of liquor. People v. Baxter (1959) 332 P.2d 334, 165 C.A.2d 648.

Bodily injury

"Bodily injury" as used in this section means harm or hurt to the body and requires more than shaking up, fright or minor headache, and is not so indefinite and uncertain a term as to fail to give a basis for criminal conviction. People v. Lares (1968) 68 Cal.Rptr. 144, 261 C.A.2d 657.

Arrest

Police officer who observed driver driving five miles per hour slower than posted speed limit, weaving from side to side of road, and swerving to avoid automobiles parked at curb had reasonable ground to believe that driver was intoxicated and was justified in stopping him for investigation. Cornforth v. Department of Motor Vehicles (1970) 83 Cal.Rptr. 762, 3 C.A.3d 550.

Officer who came upon automobile collision scene where he discovered defendant driver, who had crossed into wrong lane, unconscious, detected odor of alcohol on defendant's breath, and observed vodka bottles in defendant's vehicle, had probable cause to "mentally" place defendant under arrest for driving while under influence of intoxicating alcoholic beverages. People v. Lane (1966) 49 Cal.Rptr. 712, 240 C.A.2d 634.

Police officer who noted defendant had "strong alcohol" on his breath, that his speech was slurry, and that his eyes were watery, after officer arrived at scene of automobile collision, had probable cause to arrest defendant for drunk driving and was therefore justified in taking a urine sample to determine defendant's blood alcohol level. People v. Lachman (1972) 100 Cal.Rptr. 710, 23 C.A.3d 1094.

Tests, admissibility of evidence

Evidence of blood test wherein blood sample used was taken from unconscious defendant was admissible in prosecution for driving while intoxicated, where police officer had with probable cause "mentally" placed defendant under arrest, as product of search incident to lawful arrest. People v. Lane (1966) 49 Cal.Rptr. 712, 240 C.A.2d 634.

Upon observing partially filled bottle of beer on front floor of defendant's automobile, which had collided on wrong side of highway with another automobile, officers had reasonable ground to believe that defendant caused collision and was under influence of alcohol, obtaining of blood sample from defendant while he was unconscious was not unlawful search and sample and its analysis were admissible. People v. Pack (1962) 19 Cal.Rptr. 186, 199 C.A.2d 857.

In prosecution culminating in conviction for driving while under the influence of liquor, trial court erred in admitting result of blood test into evidence before permitting defendant to testify on voir dire as to issue of consent; but in view of admonition of court and other evidence, which was so strong that jury would have found defendant guilty even without evidence of results of blood tests, reversal was not required. People v. Cavallero (1960) 2 Cal.Rptr. 687, 178 C.A.2d 5.

In prosecution for driving motor vehicle while under influence of intoxicating liquor causing bodily injury to another, testimony concerning results of blood alcohol test given two hours after accident was admissible without necessity of other testimony as to sobriety of defendant. People v. Markham (1957) 314 P.2d 217, 153 C.A.2d 260.

In prosecution for driving automobile while under influence of intoxicating liquor causing bodily injury to another, any objections that defendant might have had to admissibility of blood alcohol test were waived when he made no objection to admissibility of results of such test. Id.

In prosecution for driving motor vehicle while under influence of liquor, resulting in bodily injury, and for manslaughter while driving

§ 23101

vehicle, admission in evidence of testimony relative to results of tests on sample of blood taken from defendant while he was unconscious did not violate any of defendant's constitutional rights. People v. Lewis (1957) 313 P.2d 972, 152 C.A.2d 824.

The taking of a blood sample for an alcoholic test without consent of the defendant could not be regarded as an unreasonable search and seizure where the extraction was made in a medically approved manner and was incident to the lawful arrest of the defendant who was reasonably believed to have violated this section, statute providing that one who drives an automobile while under the influence of intoxicating liquor and causes personal injury is guilty of a felony, and blood test was admissible in later prosecution. People v. Duroncelay (1957) 312 P.2d 690, 48 C.2d 766.

Even if violence was applied to defendant to induce his cooperation in taking intoximeter test, results of intoximeter test were lawful and admissible in prosecution of defendant for driving an automobile while under the influence of intoxicating liquor and in an unlawful manner proximately causing bodily injury to another. People v. Kiss (1954) 269 P.2d 924, 125 C.A.2d 138.

In prosecution for driving an automobile while under the influence of intoxicating liquor in an unlawful manner proximately causing bodily injury to another, admission of testimony of forensic chemist that the contents of a balloon used in making intoximeter test can determine whether another is under the influence of intoxicating liquors, and that intoximeter results showed defendant's blood alcohol concentrate to be sufficient to place a person under the influence of alcohol, was proper. Id.

Where sample of accused's blood was taken for analysis of alcoholic content, after automobile accident, and evidence thereby obtained was used in obtaining conviction for manslaughter and driving while intoxicated, stipulation at trial that blood sample was taken with defendant's consent, precluded defendant from objecting that admission of results of blood test forced him to give self-incriminating evidence, and deprived him of due process. People v. Quarles (1954) 266 P.2d 68, 123 C.A.2d 1.

In prosecution for driving motor vehicle while under influence of intoxicating liquor, any error in admitting evidence as to defendant's taking of intoximeter test and chemist's testimony respecting his findings in connection therewith and effect of such findings was not prejudicial to defendant, in view of other strong and convincing evidence of his intoxication at time of automobile collision resulting in prosecution. People v. Hernandez (1953) 262 P.2d 367, 121 C.A.2d 55.

§ 23102. Influence of alcohol or alcohol and drugs

Text of section operative until July 1, 1980

(a) It is unlawful for any person who is under the influence of intoxicating liquor, or under the combined influence of intoxicating liquor and any drug, to drive a vehicle upon any highway.

(b) It is unlawful for any person who is under the influence of intoxicating liquor, or under the combined influence of intoxicating liquor and any drug, to drive a vehicle upon other than a highway.

The department shall not be required to provide patrol or enforce the provisions of this subdivision.

(c) Any person convicted under this section shall be punished upon a first conviction by imprisonment in the county jail for not less than 48 hours nor more than six months or by fine of not less than two hundred seventy-five dollars ($275) nor more than five hundred dollars ($500) or by both such fine and imprisonment. If, however, any person so convicted consents to, and does participate in and successfully completes, a driver improvement program or treatment program for persons who are habitual users of alcohol, or both such programs, as designated by the court, the court shall punish such person by a fine of not less than one hundred seventy-five dollars ($175) nor more than five hundred dollars ($500) or by imprisonment in the county jail for not less than 48 hours nor more than six months or by both such fine and imprisonment.

(d) Any person convicted of an offense under this section within five years of a prior conviction of an offense under this section or Section 23105 shall be punished by imprisonment in the county jail for not less than 48 hours nor more than one year and by a fine of not less than two hundred seventy-five dollars ($275) nor more than one thousand dollars ($1,000). Any person convicted of an offense under this section within five years of a prior conviction of a violation of Section 23101 or 23106 shall be punished by imprisonment in the county jail for not less than five days nor more than one year and by a fine of not less than two hundred seventy-five dollars ($275) nor more than one thousand dollars ($1,000).

(e) If any person is convicted of an offense under this section within five years of a prior conviction under this section or under Section 23105 and is granted probation, it shall be a condition of probation that such person be confined in jail for at least 48 hours but not more than one year and pay a fine of at least two hundred seventy-five dollars ($275) but not more than one thousand dollars ($1,000). If any person is convicted of an offense under this section within five years of a prior conviction under Section 23101 or 23106 and is granted probation, it shall be a condition of probation that such person be confined in jail for not less than five days nor more than one year and by a fine of not less than two hundred seventy-five dollars ($275) nor more than one thousand dollars ($1,000).

(f) In no event does the court have the power to absolve a person who is convicted of an offense under this section within five years of a prior conviction under this section or Section 23101, 23105, or 23106 from the obligation of spending the minimum time in confinement in the county jail as provided in this section and of paying a fine of at least two hundred seventy-five dollars ($275), except as provided in subdivision (g).

(g) Except in unusual cases where the interests of justice demand an exception, the court shall not strike a prior conviction of an offense under this section for purposes of sentencing in order to avoid imposing as part of the sentence or term of probation the minimum time in confinement in the county jail and the minimum fine, as provided in this section.

When such a prior conviction is stricken by the court for purposes of sentencing, the court shall specify the reason or reasons for such striking order.

On appeal by the people from such an order striking such a prior conviction it shall be conclusively presumed that such order was made only for the reasons specified in such order and such order shall be reversed if there is no substantial basis in the record for any of such reasons.

(h) The court may order that any person convicted under this section, who is to be punished by imprisonment in jail, be imprisoned on days other than days of regular employment of the person, as determined by the court.

(i) If the person convicted under this section is under the age of 21 years and the vehicle used in any such violation is registered to such person, the vehicle may be impounded at the owner's expense for not less than one day nor more than 30 days.

This section shall remain in effect only until July 1, 1980, and as of such date is repealed.
(Amended by Stats.1978, c. 790, p. ——, § 4.)

Editors' Note
Read People v. Kraft and Schmerber v. California in table of cases included in this text.

Notes of Decisions
Constitutional rights

Provision of § 23126 establishing that blood alcohol level of .10% as determined in test given after defendant is arrested for driving under influence of intoxicating liquor establishes that defendant is presumptively under influence of alcohol was not unconstitutional on theory that it deprived defendant of presumption of innocence and of right to remain silent. People v. Schrieber (1975) 119 Cal.Rptr. 812, 45 C.A.3d 917.

Municipal court judge, who, when confronted with fact that accused was, without benefit of counsel, determined to plead guilty to driving under influence of intoxicating liquor, reiterated advice in respect to accused's right to counsel and some other rights, was not required to repeat advice as to each of accused's constitutional rights which had been covered when group was advised of such rights at mass arraignment. James v. Ventura County Municipal Court, Camarillo Dept. (1975) 119 Cal.Rptr. 606, 45 C.A.3d 557.

By entry of guilty plea, in prosecution for misdemeanor drunk driving, after collective advice regarding constitutional rights had been given to assembled defendants, defendant expressly waived such rights. Hartman v. Municipal Court for Northern Judicial Dist. of San Mateo County (1973) 111 Cal.Rptr. 126, 35 C.A.3d 891.

Conviction for misdemeanor drunk driving could not stand where the record was devoid of any evidence that plaintiff who pleaded guilty, intelligently waived his privilege against self-incrimination, his right to confront his accusers, and his right to a jury trial. Cooper v. Justice Court of El Centro Judicial Dist., Imperial County (1972) 104 Cal.Rptr. 543, 28 C.A.3d 286.

Elements

Evidence of breathalyzer or other chemical test is not necessary element of prosecution for drunk driving. People v. Hitch (1974) 117 Cal.Rptr. 9, 527 P.2d 361, 12 C.3d 641.

Drugs

Where defendant was charged with driving while under the influence of intoxicating liquor, penciled notation "w/drugs" which appeared in the clerk's minutes was irrelevant and neither added nor detracted from the fact that defendant was properly arraigned on the charge of driving under the influence of intoxicating liquor and pleaded guilty thereto, and in no way resulted in any denial of or any failure to explain any constitutional safeguards, despite contention that such notation created a stigma that defendant would not have accepted by guilty plea had he known it would attach to him. Smith v. Municipal Court of Los Angeles Judicial Dist., Los Angeles County Judicial Dist. (App.1976) 131 Cal.Rptr. 200.

In prosecution for driving while under the influence of intoxicating liquor, it is legally immaterial whether the violation was with or without drugs; the only purpose of defining the offense in terms of both circumstances is to eliminate as a possible defense the claim that a drug, medically prescribed or otherwise, rather than liquor, was the substance which influenced or affected driving. Id.

Tests—In General

Provision of § 23126 establishing that blood alcohol level of .10% as determined in test after defendant is arrested for driving while under influence of intoxicating liquor establishes that defendant is presumptively under influence of alcohol was not unconstitutional for failing to fix ultimate time as to period in which prescribed test must be taken, since the greater of the elapse of time, the greater the likelihood that alcohol in defendant's system would become dissipated by normal body processes. People v. Schrieber (1975) 119 Cal.Rptr. 812, 45 C.A.3d 917.

Where defendant motorist who had been given Miranda warnings and implied consent admonition was advised by arresting officers that right to consult attorney did not apply to chemical test request but defendant refused to take test before he had consulted attorney, motorist's lack of understanding, whether engendered by his partial intoxication or attributable to his normal state of intelligence, did not affect the finality and effectiveness of his refusal to submit to chemical test. Goodman v. Orr (1971) 97 Cal.Rptr. 226, 19 C.A.3d 845.

Blood tests

Physician's withdrawal, at direction of police officer, of blood sample from body of person accused of criminal offense of driving

§ 23102

automobile while under influence of intoxicating liquor and admission of blood analysis in evidence did not deny accused due process of law under Fourteenth Amendment (U.S.C.A.Const. Amend. 14). Schmerber v. State of California (1966) 86 S.Ct. 1826, 384 U.S. 757, 16 L.Ed.2d 908.

Police officers, who, before doctor obtained blood sample from "defensive" accused arrested for drunk driving, placed accused on floor face down, applied a scissor lock on accused's legs, and held his arm up, used excessive force and exceeded limits of permissible police activity. People v. Kraft (1970) 84 Cal.Rptr. 280, 3 C.A.3d 890.

Legislature did not intend, by enactment of implied consent law, to preclude the taking of blood samples as an incident to a lawful arrest of persons refusing. People v. Kraft (Super.1969) 77 Cal.Rptr. 205, reversed on other grounds 84 Cal.Rptr. 280, 3 C.A.3d 890.

Petitioner's insistence, after arrest for driving while under influence of intoxicating liquor, that drawing of blood for test of alcoholic content be performed by his own physician constituted refusal to submit to blood test and warranted suspension of driving privilege even though officer did not explain that petitioner had no right to have his physician withdraw the blood where petitioner's misconception was in no way police-initiated but rather was product of petitioner's own thinking. Beales v. State, Dept. of Motor Vehicles (1969) 76 Cal.Rptr. 662, 271 C.A.2d 594.

Where police officers found motorist unconscious behind steering wheel of automobile, and physical evidence indicated that motorist's automobile had struck parked vehicle, and officers detected strong smell of alcoholic beverage about person of motorist and her automobile and a police officer, who had no warrant, requested doctor at hospital to take blood sample from still unconscious motorist, and doctor did so, result of blood test could be used in prosecution of motorist for misdemeanor of driving while intoxicated. In re McDonald (1967) 58 Cal.Rptr. 29, 249 C.A.2d 960.

Motorist who was charged with drunk driving was not denied due process of law because she was refused opportunity to phone her doctor, who was almost two hours driving time away, to make a blood test when she was released from jail 20 minutes to a half an hour after being brought there and could have phoned her doctor then or could have had test made at local hospital. Application of Howard (1962) 25 Cal.Rptr. 590, 208 C.A.2d 709.

Law enforcement agencies have no duty or obligation to cause blood sample to be made to determine alcoholic content of blood of one accused of drunken driving. McCormick v. Municipal Court, Los Angeles Judicial Dist. (1961) 16 Cal.Rptr. 211, 195 C.A.2d 819.

The right of a defendant suspected of being under influence of intoxicating liquor to have reasonable opportunity to call a doctor of his own choice and at his own expense to give him a blood test does not prevent police from making their own test of defendant's blood even before arrival of his doctor. People v. Dawson (1960) 7 Cal.Rptr. 384, 184 C.A.2d Supp. 881.

The police may make test of blood of defendant suspected of being under influence of intoxicating liquor even without his consent and if defendant refuses to submit to such a police test the fact of his refusal may be proved at trial and jury may be instructed accordingly. Id.

Defendant had no right to unilaterally seek pretrial ruling on purely evidentiary question of admissibility of results of gas chromatograph test conducted by police officer who was not trained in accordance with regulation governing the administering of breath tests and had no right to move for dismissal of prosecution for driving under influence of intoxicating liquor based upon pretrial ruling suppressing results of gas chromatograph administered to determine amount of alcohol in defendant's system. People v. Rawlings (1974) 117 Cal.Rptr. 651, 42 C.A.3d 952.

Violation of portion of implied consent statute providing that a person arrested for any offense allegedly committed while driving under the influence of intoxicating liquor should have choice of whether test shall be of his blood, breath or urine and shall be advised by officer that he has such choice does not involve a violation of any constitutionally protected interest; thus, failure to advise defendant who was charged with drunk driving of his right of choice among the three tests did not render results of breathalyzer test taken by defendant inadmissible in prosecution for misdemeanor drunk driving. People v. Brannon (1973) 108 Cal.Rptr. 620, 32 C.A.3d 971.

Arrest

In view of fact that time had to be taken to bring accused to hospital from scene of accident where he had been arrested for driving automobile while under influence of intoxicating liquor and that percentage of alcohol in blood of accused would begin to diminish shortly after his drinking stopped, officer might reasonably have believed that he was confronted with emergency in which delay necessary to obtain search warrant threatened destruction of evidence and attempt, without warrant, to secure evidence of blood-alcohol content by officer's directing physician in hospital to take blood sample from accused was an appropriate incident to accused's arrest. Schmerber v. State of California (1966) 86 S.Ct. 1826, 384 U.S. 757, 16 L.Ed.2d 908.

Deputy sheriffs who had witnessed defendant's automobile weave from center lane to curb outside city and defendant's failure to make proper stop at intersection on city-county border and who had observed defendant with strong odor of alcohol on his breath stagger after being stopped inside city, had probable cause to believe that public offenses had been committed in their presence, both in county and city, that there was danger to both persons and property, and that perpetrator would escape unless stopped, and arrest of defendant was legally effected inside city under Pen.C. § 830.1 giving peace officer such authority under those circumstances. People v. Tennessee (1970) 84 Cal.Rptr. 697, 4 C.A.3d 788.

Police officer who observed driver driving five miles per hour slower than posted speed limit, weaving from side to side of road, and swerving to avoid automobiles parked at curb had reasonable ground to believe that driver was intoxicated and was justified in stopping him for investigation. Cornforth v. Department of Motor Vehicles (1970) 83 Cal.Rptr. 762, 3 C.A.3d 550.

Where officer had report that vehicle fitting description of vehicle he stopped had recently been involved in collision with light pole and officer detected odor of alcohol on driver's breath and found her unable to satisfactorily perform roadside sobriety test, officer had probable cause to arrest driver. Spurlock v. Department of Motor Vehicles (1969) 82 Cal.Rptr. 42, 1 C.A.3d 821.

In order for arrest for traffic violation to be proper, offense must have been committed in arresting officer's presence. Id.

Where officers arrived on scene of automobile accident in less than one minute after receiving radio alert, and they found motorist unconscious behind steering wheel of automobile which was stopped partly on lawn and sidewalk of private residence, and they detected a strong smell of alcoholic beverage about person of motorist and automobile, and physical evidence indicated that automobile had struck a legally parked, unoccupied vehicle, there was sufficient evidence for arrest without a warrant of motorist for misdemeanor driving of automobile while intoxicated. In re McDonald (1967) 58 Cal.Rptr. 29, 249 C.A.2d 960.

Arrests of driver and passenger were lawful where they were intoxicated. People v. Robinson (1965) 44 Cal.Rptr. 762, 402 P.2d 834, 62 C.A.2d 889.

RULES OF THE ROAD § 23102

Arrest of defendant for driving while under influence of intoxicating liquor and for driving without an operator's license in his possession was unlawful, where arresting officer did not see defendant driving automobile and arrived at scene of accident several minutes after it occurred and while defendant was standing in highway. People v. Walker (1962) 21 Cal.Rptr. 692, 203 C.A.2d 552.

There is a lawful arrest for purposes of § 13353 when a suspect has been arrested after an accident for both drunkenness in a public place under Pen.C. § 647 and misdemeanor drunk driving under this section where the officer who made the arrest arrives at the scene sometime after the occurrence of the accident and the suspect was identified as the driver by witnesses at the scene. 52 Ops.Atty.Gen. 250, 12-9-69.

Where highway patrol academy cadets stopped respondent's erratically driven car and recorded its make, description and license, where respondent, without permission, drove away and eluded cadets and officer radioed by them, where, after brief search and location of car, the officer and cadets approached home where it was found and inquired as to ownership, where respondent, after the cadets mistakenly identified another, volunteered that he was the driver, and where his physical appearance supplied evidence of intoxication, the officer had reasonable cause to believe that drunk driving had been committed, and the facts satisfied warrantless arrest requirement of the offense occurring in his presence. Packer v. Director, Dept. of Motor Vehicles (1976) 128 Cal.Rptr. 907, 57 C.A.3d 206.

Section 40300.5 permitting warrantless arrest of a person involved in a traffic accident when officer has reasonable cause to believe that such person has been driving while under influence of intoxicating liquor or under combined influence of intoxicating liquor and any drug was applicable to arrest for violation of Pen.C. § 367d making it a misdemeanor to drive under influence of intoxicating liquor or under combined influence of intoxicating liquor and any drug even though alleged offense occurred on a private access road rather than a public highway. People v. Ashley (1971) 95 Cal.Rptr. 509, 17 C.A.3d 1122.

Searches and seizures

When there is valid arrest of motorist for driving while under influence of intoxicating liquor, or, because driver or passenger of vehicle is found to be under influence of intoxicating liquor in any public place, officer, as incident to such arrest, may search the offender and the automobile in which he was observed for purpose of discovering evidence of the crime. People v. Superior Court for Marin County (1971) 92 Cal.Rptr. 545, 14 C.A.3d 935.

Police officer, who arrested driver of petitioner's automobile for custodial offense of driving while under influence of intoxicating liquor, acted properly in searching driver's person for purpose of discovering weapon or destructible evidence prior to placing him in police automobile. Pugh v. Superior Court, Riverside County (1970) 91 Cal.Rptr. 168, 12 C.A.3d 1184.

Where defendant and his passenger appeared to be intoxicated at time of arrest and defendant's ability to consent to release of his automobile was impaired, defendant was unable to produce registration or driver's license and police did not know true relationship of defendant with man who identified himself as a relative, deputy sheriff and city officer who was called to scene of arrest were entitled to remove the automobile from the alley which it blocked and to inventory the automobile and allegedly stolen items discovered during inventory were not product of unreasonable search and seizure. Martinez v. Superior Court for Los Angeles County (1970) 87 Cal.Rptr. 6, 7 C.A.3d 569.

Where defendant was intoxicated at time of his arrest and was unable to produce any indicia of ownership of automobile, deputy sheriff and city officer called to assist deputy were entitled to inventory contents of automobile defendant was driving in order to protect the officers, the true owner of the contents of the vehicle and any person who accepted responsibility of safeguarding vehicle and its contents. Id.

Once a motor vehicle has been properly stopped for routine check, officers are not required to bind themselves to what may be obvious, nor refrain from search if defendant voluntarily consents. People v. De La Torre (1967) 64 Cal.Rptr. 804, 257 C.A.2d 162.

Search of automobile made incident to lawful arrest of driver for operating vehicle while under influence of alcoholic beverage and pursuant to customary procedure of inventorying contents of automobile preliminary to its lawful impounding was properly occasioned, even though driver protested having his automobile stored and requested that it be left in parking lot where he was arrested so that a friend of his could pick it up. People v. Gil (1967) 56 Cal.Rptr. 88, 248 C.A.2d 189.

Any citizen, guilty or innocent, threatened with imminent impounding of his automobile might well violently protest in order to try to avoid expense involved and, therefore, driver's violent protest against storing his automobile after his arrest for drunk driving could not justify arresting officer's lifting of floor mat and discovery of marijuana. Id.

Search of automobile incident to arrest of driver for driving while under influence of alcoholic beverage could not be constitutionally justified by fact that search uncovered marijuana; but, on the other hand, search was not necessarily constitutionally vulnerable because it turned up evidence of crime different from one which occasioned search. Id.

Where officers observed defendant's vehicle make an unsafe lane change and swerve over double yellow line and detected strong smell of alcohol on defendant's breath, search of the vehicle for the possible presence of liquor containers was proper. People v. Fulk (1974) 114 Cal.Rptr. 567, 39 C.A.3d 851.

Although officer had not seen automobile accident in which defendant was involved, did not smell odor of alcohol, was unable to identify any one intoxicant to exclusion of others, and intended to book defendant on misdemeanor violation of this section, where officer had reasonable cause to believe defendant had been driving a motor vehicle while under influence of one or more of four kinds of intoxicants, including combined influence of liquor and any drug, search of defendant's person to find evidence of offense was a lawful incident of arrest. People v. Howell (1972) 105 Cal.Rptr. 748, 30 C.A.3d 228.

Where defendant was arrested for driving while under the influence of alcohol or some other drug, arresting officer was both entitled and duty bound to search defendant's person for evidence of the crime which might disclose the nature of the drug causing the intoxication. People v. Gomez (1972) 103 Cal.Rptr. 453, 26 C.A.3d 928.

Where it was necessary to take defendant to police station to take breathalyzer test after he had been arrested for drunk driving, warrantless search of his person at police station was permissible and, therefore, amphetamines found in such search were admissible. People v. Wilken (1971) 97 Cal.Rptr. 925, 20 C.A.3d 872.

Presumptions

Bad faith destruction of test ampoule and its contents and reference ampoule used in breathalyzer test raises inference that ampoules could demonstrate innocence, and in such an instance dismissal may well be proper sanction. People v. Hitch (1974) 117 Cal.Rptr. 9, 527 P.2d 361, 12 C.3d 641.

§ 23103. Reckless driving

Text of section operative until July 1, 1980

Any person who drives any vehicle upon a highway in willful or wanton disregard for the safety of persons or property is guilty of reckless driving and upon conviction thereof shall be punished by imprisonment in the county jail for not less than five days nor more than 90 days or by fine of not less than fifty dollars ($50) nor more than two hundred fifty dollars ($250) or by both such fine and imprisonment, except as provided in Section 23104.

This section shall remain in effect only until July 1, 1980, and as of that date is repealed.
(Amended by Stats.1978, c. 790, p. ——, § 5.)

§ 23104. Reckless driving: bodily injury

Text of section operative until July 1, 1980

Whenever reckless driving of a vehicle proximately causes bodily injury to any person, the person driving the vehicle shall upon conviction thereof be punished by imprisonment in the county jail for not less than 30 days nor more than six months or by fine of not less than one hundred twenty-five dollars ($125) nor more than five hundred dollars ($500) or by both.

This section shall remain in effect only until July 1, 1980, and as of that date is repealed.
(Amended by Stats.1978, c. 790, p. ——, § 6.)

§ 23105. Influence of drug or addiction

Text of section operative until July 1, 1980

(a) It is unlawful for any person who is under the influence of any drug to drive a vehicle upon any highway.

(b) It is unlawful for any person who is under the influence of any drug to drive a vehicle upon other than a highway.

The department shall not be required to provide patrol or enforce the provisions of this subdivision.

(c) It is unlawful for any person who is addicted to the use of any drug, except such a person who is participating in a methadone maintenance treatment program approved pursuant to Article 3 (commencing with Section 4350) of Chapter 1 of Part 1 of Division 4 of the Welfare and Institutions Code, to drive a vehicle upon any highway.

(d) Any person convicted under this section shall be punished upon a first conviction by imprisonment in the county jail for not less than 48 hours nor more than six months or by fine of not less than two hundred seventy-five dollars ($275) nor more than five hundred dollars ($500) or by both such fine and imprisonment. If, however, any person so convicted consents to participate, and does participate in and successfully completes, a driver improvement program or a treatment program for persons who are habitual users of drugs, or both such programs, as designated by the court, a court shall punish such person by fine of not less than one hundred seventy-five dollars ($175) nor more than five hundred dollars ($500) or by imprisonment in the county jail for not less than 48 hours nor more than six months or by both such fine and imprisonment.

(e) Any person convicted of an offense under this section within five years of a prior conviction of an offense under this section or Section 23102 shall be punished by imprisonment in the county jail for not less than 48 hours nor more than one year and by a fine of not less than two hundred seventy-five dollars ($275) nor more than one thousand dollars ($1,000). Any person convicted of an offense under this section within five years of a prior conviction of a violation of Section 23101 or 23106 shall be punished by imprisonment in the county jail for not less than five days nor more than one year and by a fine of not less than two hundred seventy-five dollars ($275) nor more than one thousand dollars ($1,000).

(f) If any person is convicted of an offense under this section within five years of a prior conviction under this section or under Section 23102 and is granted probation, it shall be a condition of probation that such person be confined in jail for at least 48 hours but not more than one year and pay a fine of at least two hundred seventy-five dollars ($275) but not more than one thousand dollars ($1,000). If any person is convicted of an offense under this section within five years of a prior conviction under Section 23101 or 23106 and is granted probation, it shall be a condition of probation that such person be confined in jail for not less than five days nor more than one year and by a fine of not less than two hundred seventy-five dollars ($275) nor more than one thousand dollars ($1,000).

(g) In no event does the court have the power to absolve a person who is convicted of an offense under this section within five years of a prior conviction under this section or Section 23101, 23102, or 23106 from the obligation of spending the minimum time in confinement in the county jail as provided in this section and of paying a fine of at least two hundred seventy-five dollars ($275), except as provided in subdivision (h).

(h) Except in unusual cases where the interests of justice demand an exception, the court shall not strike a prior conviction of an offense under this section for purposes of sentencing in order to avoid imposing as part of the sentence or term of probation the minimum time in confinement in the county jail and the minimum fine, as provided in this section.

When such a prior conviction is stricken by the court for purposes of sentencing, the court shall specify the reason or reasons for such striking order.

On appeal by the people from such an order striking such a prior conviction it shall be conclusively presumed that such order was made only for the reasons specified in such order and such order shall be reversed if there is no substantial basis in the record for any of such reasons.

(i) The court may order that any person convicted under this section, who is to be punished by imprisonment in jail, be imprisoned on days other than days of regular employment of the person, as determined by the court.

(j) If the person convicted under this section is under the age of 21 years and the vehicle used in any such violation is registered to such person, the vehicle may be impounded at the owner's expense for not less than one day nor more than 30 days.

This section shall remain in effect only until July 1, 1980, and as of that date is repealed.
(Amended by Stats.1978, c. 790, p. —, § 7.)

§ 23106. Influence of drugs causing death or injury

Text of section operative until July 1, 1980

(a) It is unlawful for any person, while under the influence of any drug, to drive a vehicle upon a highway and when so driving do any act forbidden by law or neglect any duty imposed by law in the driving of such vehicle, which act or neglect proximately causes death or bodily injury to any person other than himself.

(b) It is unlawful for any person, while under the influence of any drug, to drive a vehicle other than on a highway and when so driving do any act, neglect any duty imposed by law, which act or neglect proximately causes death or bodily injury to any person other than himself.

(c) Any person convicted under this section shall be punished by imprisonment in the state prison, or in the county jail for not less than 90 days nor more than one year, and by fine of not less than two hundred seventy-five dollars ($275) nor more than five thousand dollars ($5,000).

(d) If any person is convicted of an offense under this section within five years of a prior conviction under Section 23102 or 23105 and is granted probation, it shall be a condition of probation that such person be confined in jail for at least five days but not more than one year and pay a fine of at least two hundred seventy-five dollars ($275) but not more than five thousand dollars ($5,000). If any person is convicted of an offense under this section within five years of a prior conviction of a violation of this section or Section 23101 and is granted probation, it shall be a condition of probation that such person be confined in jail for at least 90 days but not more than one year and pay a fine of at least two hundred seventy-five dollars ($275) but not more than five thousand dollars ($5,000).

(e) In no event does the court have the power to absolve a person who is convicted of an offense under this section within five years of a prior conviction of a violation of this section or Section 23101, 23102, or 23105 from the obligation of spending the minimum time in confinement as provided in this section and of paying a fine of at least two hundred seventy-five dollars ($275), except as provided in subdivision (f).

(f) Except in unusual cases where the interests of justice demand an exception, the court shall not strike a prior conviction of an offense under this section or Section 23101, 23102, or 23105 for purposes of sentencing in order to avoid imposing as part of the sentence or term of probation the minimum time in confinement and the minimum fine, as provided in this section. When such a prior conviction is stricken by the court for purposes of sentencing, the court shall specify the reason or reasons for such striking order. On appeal by the people from such an order striking such a prior conviction, it shall be conclusively presumed that such order was made only for the reasons specified in such order, and such order shall be reversed if there is no substantial basis in the record for any of such reasons.

This section shall remain in effect only until July 1, 1980, and as of that date is repealed.
(Amended by Stats.1978, c. 790, p. —, § 8.)

§ 23107. Defense to drug violations

The fact that any person charged with a violation of Section 23105 or 23106 is or has been entitled to use such drug under the laws of this state shall not constitute a defense against any violation of the sections.
(Amended by Stats.1971, c. 1530, p. 3028, § 19.)

§ 23109. Speed contests and exhibitions of speed

(a) No person shall engage in any motor vehicle speed contest on a highway, and no person shall aid or abet in any motor vehicle speed contest on any highway.

(b) No person shall engage in any motor vehicle exhibition of speed on a highway, and no person shall aid or abet in any motor vehicle exhibition of speed on any highway.

(c) No person shall for the purpose of facilitating or aiding or as an incident to any motor vehicle speed contest or exhibition upon a highway in any manner obstruct or place any barricade or obstruction or assist or participate in placing any barricade or obstruction upon any highway.

(d) Any person who violates this section shall upon conviction thereof be punished by imprisonment in the county jail for not more than 90 days or by fine of not more than two hundred fifty dollars ($250) or by both such fine and imprisonment.
(Amended by Stats.1967, c. 607, p. 1956, § 1.)

Notes of Decisions
Construction and application

Officer's testimony, in prosecution for illegal possession of marijuana indicated probable cause for stopping defendant for speed in excess of the prima facie limits in a residential zone. People v. Anderson (1968) 71 Cal.Rptr. 827, 266 C.A.2d 125.

Excessive acceleration of automobile on highway in highly developed and populated area in such manner as to cause tires to scream loudly and to lose traction on highway constituted "exhibition of speed on highway" within proscription of this section. People v. Grier (1964) 38 Cal.Rptr. 11, 226 C.A.2d 360.

Even if observer is required before person can be found guilty of violating provision of this section proscribing exhibitions of speed on highway, such observer need not be known to exhibitor. Id.

Violation of this section prohibiting racing of motor vehicles, while establishing prima facie evidence of negligence as a matter of law, is subject to limitation that recovery may be had only if violation is proximate cause of injury. Agovino v. Kunze (1960) 5 Cal.Rptr. 534, 181 C.A.2d 591.

Acceleration so rapid as to break the traction between a vehicle's tires and the pavement may constitute an exhibition of speed within the meaning of this section, regardless of whether another vehicle is involved, or whether the posted speed limit is violated. 38 Ops.Atty. Gen. 102.

Section 590, defining street or highway as a way or place publicly maintained and open to use of public for purposes of vehicular travel, includes roadway within park, so that under this section, which makes it a misdemeanor for any person to engage in vehicle speed exhibitions on highway, all persons who engage in such contests on such roadway are subject to prosecution for misdemeanor. 23 Ops.Atty.Gen. 143.

In view of city charter provision giving recreation and park commission complete control of Golden Gate Park area, determination by commission to close park road to general vehicular traffic and to devote it temporarily to motor vehicle speed contest constituted a withdrawal of the avenues of the park from their status of highways and constituted them solely a part of the park so that the city in so using the roadway was not guilty of violation of this section, prohibiting motor vehicle speed contests on highways. Id.

Racing in general

Speed contests are forbidden by law. Callahan v. City and County of San Francisco (1967) 57 Cal.Rptr. 639, 249 C.A.2d 696.

In manslaughter prosecution, where defendant was guilty of reckless speeding, and was racing his automobile on a public street with automobile of a codefendant, mere fact that his vehicle did not strike another automobile, and death was caused by collision of codefendant's automobile with such other vehicle, did not mean that defendant was not criminally liable under Pen.Code, § 192, on any theory that his actions were not the proximate cause of the death, in view of showing that defendant and codefendant were jointly engaged in a series of acts which led directly to the fatal collision. People v. Kemp (1957) 310 P.2d 680, 150 C.A.2d 654.

Searches and seizures

In order to justify thorough search of one who has been arrested for a serious traffic offense such as engaging in a speed contest, it is not necessary to decide whether his violation of law was a "jailable offense," which would allow a jailhouse search and, therefore, by anticipation a search in the field, and as long as officer has taken alleged offender into custody and is about to transport him, whether to a magistrate only (if arrestee is able to make bail) or to some place of detention until he shall have made bail, he may search person of arrestee to protect against weapons and against disposing of contraband during transportation. Morel v. Superior Court of San Mateo County (1970) 89 Cal.Rptr. 297, 10 C.A.3d 913.

Evidence

In automobile passenger's action against defendant driver for injuries sustained in collision between passenger's automobile and one driven by a third party on theory that third party and defendant were racing their vehicles at time of collision and that defendant's negligence was the proximate cause of accident, there was substantial evidence to present a jury question as to whether defendant was negligent in racing vehicle with third party at time of accident and whether such negligence was a proximate cause of collision. Agovino v. Kunze (1960) 5 Cal.Rptr. 534, 181 C.A.2d 591.

Evidence sustained finding that minor had violated this section. In re Harvill (1959) 335 P.2d 1016, 168 C.A.2d 490.

§ 23110. Throwing substance at vehicles

(a) Any person who throws any substance at a vehicle or any occupant thereof on a highway is guilty of a misdemeanor.

(b) Any person who with intent to do great bodily injury maliciously and willfully throws or projects

any rock, brick, bottle, metal or other missile, or projects any other substance capable of doing serious bodily harm at such vehicle or occupant thereof is guilty of a felony and upon conviction shall be punished by imprisonment in the state prison.
(Amended by Stats.1976, c. 1119, p. ——, § 2.)

§ 23111. Throwing substances on highways or adjoining areas

No person in any vehicle and no pedestrian shall throw or discharge from or upon any road or highway or adjoining area, public or private, any lighted or nonlighted cigarette, cigar, match, or any flaming or glowing substance. This section shall be known as the Paul Buzzo Act.
(Amended by Stats.1970, c. 1548, p. 3151, § 8.)

§ 23112. Throwing, depositing, or dumping matter on highway

(a) No person shall throw or deposit, nor shall the registered owner or the driver, if such owner is not then present in the vehicle, aid or abet in the throwing or depositing upon any highway any bottle, can, garbage, glass, nail, offal, paper, wire, any substance likely to injure or damage traffic using the highway, or any noisome, nauseous, or offensive matter of any kind.

(b) No person shall place, deposit, or dump, or cause to be placed, deposited, or dumped, any rocks, refuse, garbage, or dirt in or upon any highway, including any portion of the right-of-way thereof, without the consent of the state or local agency having jurisdiction over the highway.

(c) Any person who violates this section shall upon conviction thereof be punished by a fine of not less than twenty-five dollars ($25). No part of such fine shall be suspended. The court may permit the fine required by this section to be paid in installments if the court determines that the defendant is unable to pay the fine in one lump sum.
(Amended by Stats.1976, c. 213, p. ——, § 2.)

§ 23114. Spilling loads on highways

No vehicle shall be driven or moved on any highway unless the vehicle is so constructed, covered, or loaded as to prevent any of its contents or load other than clear water or feathers from live birds from dropping, sifting, leaking, blowing, spilling, or otherwise escaping therefrom.
(Amended by Stats.1965, c. 455, p. 1765, § 1.)

§ 23115. Rubbish vehicles

No vehicle loaded with garbage, swill, cans, bottles, wastepapers, ashes, refuse, trash, or rubbish, or any other noisome, nauseous, or offensive matter, or anything being transported to a dump site for disposal shall be driven or moved upon any highway unless the load is totally covered in a manner which will prevent the load or any part of the load from spilling or falling from the vehicle. This section does not prohibit a rubbish vehicle from being without cover while in the process of acquiring its load in circumstances wherein no law, administrative regulation, or local ordinance requires such cover.

This section does not apply to any vehicle engaged in transporting wet waste fruit or vegetable matter, or waste products from a food processing establishment, nor to any highway maintenance vehicle operated by, or operated under contract with, any local authority or the state, and engaged in transporting snow, mud, earthen slide material, rock, portland cement, or asphaltic concrete paving and structural materials, to a dump site for disposal.
(Amended by Stats.1975, c. 1166, p. 2884, § 1.)

§ 23120. Temple width of glasses

No person shall operate a motor vehicle while wearing glasses having a temple width of one-half inch or more if any part of such temple extends below the horizontal center of the lens so as to interfere with lateral vision.
(Added by Stats.1959, c. 531, p. 2498, § 1.)

§ 23121. Drinking in motor vehicle

No person shall drink any alcoholic beverage in any motor vehicle when such vehicle is upon any highway. As used in this chapter, alcoholic beverage shall have the same meaning as in Section 23004 of the Business and Professions Code.
(Added by Stats.1961, c. 1903, p. 4010, § 1.)

§ 23122. Possession of opened container

No person shall have in his possession on his person, while in a motor vehicle upon a highway, any bottle, can, or other receptacle, containing any alcoholic beverage which has been opened, or a seal broken, or the contents of which have been partially removed.
(Amended by Stats.1968, c. 238, p. 549, § 1.)

§ 23123. Storage of opened container

It is unlawful for the registered owner of any motor vehicle, or the driver if the registered owner is

§ 23123

not then present in the vehicle, to keep in a motor vehicle, when such vehicle is upon any highway, any bottle, can, or other receptacle containing any alcoholic beverage which has been opened, or a seal broken, or the contents of which have been partially removed, unless such container is kept in the trunk of the vehicle, or kept in some other area of the vehicle not normally occupied by the driver or passengers, if the vehicle is not equipped with a trunk. A utility compartment or glove compartment shall be deemed to be within the area occupied by the driver and passengers.

This section shall not apply to the living quarters of a housecar or camper.
(Amended by Stats.1968, c. 238, p. 549, § 2.)

§ 23123.5. Possession of alcohol in vehicle; persons under 21

(a) No person under the age of 21 years shall knowingly drive any motor vehicle carrying any alcoholic beverage, unless such person is accompanied by a parent or legal guardian or is employed by a licensee under the Alcoholic Beverage Control Act (Division 9, commencing with Section 23000, of the Business and Professions Code), and is driving the motor vehicle during regular hours and in the course of his employment.

(b) No passenger in any motor vehicle who is under the age of 21 years shall knowingly possess or have under his control any alcoholic beverage, unless such passenger is accompanied by a parent or legal guardian or is employed by a licensee under the Alcoholic Beverage Control Act (Division 9, commencing with Section 23000, of the Business and Professions Code), and such possession or control is during regular hours and in the course of his employment.

(c) If the vehicle used in any violation of subdivision (a) or (b) is registered to such person under the age of 21 years, the vehicle may be impounded at the owner's expense for not less than one day nor more than 30 days for each violation.

(d) Any such person under 21 years of age found guilty under this section shall also have his driver's license suspended for not less than 15 days nor more than 30 days.
(Amended by Stats.1972, c. 881, p. 1559, § 2.)

§ 23125. Possession of alcoholic beverage; exceptions

(a) The provisions of Sections 23121 and 23122 shall not apply to passengers in any bus, taxicab or the living quarters of a housecar or camper nor shall Section 23123 apply to the driver or owner of a bus or taxicab.

(b) The provisions of Sections 23121, 23122, and 23123 shall not apply to any person who, upon the recommendation of a doctor, carries alcoholic beverages in his motor vehicle for medicinal purposes. Such sections shall also not apply to any clergyman who carries alcoholic beverages in his motor vehicle for religious purposes.
(Amended by Stats.1968, c. 238, p. 549, § 4.)

§ 23126. Driving while intoxicated; presumption

(a) Upon the trial of any criminal action, or preliminary proceeding in a criminal action, arising out of acts alleged to have been committed by any person while driving a vehicle while under the influence of intoxicating liquor, the amount of alcohol in the person's blood at the time of the test as shown by chemical analysis of his blood, breath, or urine shall give rise to the following presumptions affecting the burden of proof:

(1) If there was at that time less than 0.05 percent by weight of alcohol in the person's blood, it shall be presumed that the person was not under the influence of intoxicating liquor at the time of the alleged offense.

(2) If there was at that time 0.05 percent or more but less than 0.10 percent by weight of alcohol in the person's blood, such fact shall not give rise to any presumption that the person was or was not under the influence of intoxicating liquor, but such fact may be considered with other competent evidence in determining whether the person was under the influence of intoxicating liquor at the time of the alleged offense.

(3) If there was at that time 0.10 percent or more by weight of alcohol in the person's blood, it shall be presumed that the person was under the influence of intoxicating liquor at the time of the alleged offense.

(b) Percent by weight of alcohol in the blood shall be based upon grams of alcohol per 100 milliliters of blood.

(c) The foregoing provisions shall not be construed as limiting the introduction of any other competent evidence bearing upon the question whether the person was under the influence of intoxicating liquor at the time of the alleged offense.
(Added by Stats.1969, c. 231, p. 565, § 1.)

§ 23127. Trails and paths

No person shall operate an unauthorized motor vehicle on any state, county, city, private, or district hiking or horseback riding trail or bicycle path that is clearly marked by an authorized agent or owner with signs at all entrances and exits and at intervals of not more than one mile indicating no unauthorized motor vehicles are permitted on the hiking or horseback riding trail or bicycle path, except bicycle paths which are contiguous or adjacent to a roadway dedicated solely to motor vehicle use.

For the purpose of this section "unauthorized motor vehicle" means any motor vehicle that is driven upon a hiking or horseback riding trail or bicycle path without the written permission of an agent or the owner of the trail or path.

This section does not apply to the operation of an authorized emergency or maintenance vehicle on a hiking or horseback riding trail or bicycle path whenever necessary in furtherance of the purpose for which the vehicle has been classed as an authorized emergency vehicle. Any person who violates this section is guilty of a misdemeanor.
(Amended by Stats.1973, c. 951, p. 1790, § 1.)

§ 23128. Snowmobiles

It is unlawful for any person to operate a snowmobile in the following manner:

(a) On a highway except as provided in Section 38025.

(b) In a careless or negligent manner so as to endanger a person or property.

(c) For the purpose of pursuing deer or other game mammal with intent to harass such animals.

(d) For the purpose of violating Section 602 of the Penal Code.
(Formerly § 23337, added by Stats.1969, c. 1075, p. 2064, § 9. Renumbered § 23128 and amended by Stats.1972, c. 973, p. 1759, § 17, urgency, eff. Aug. 16, 1972.)

§ 23129. Camper mounted on motor vehicle; exit requirements

No person shall drive a motor vehicle upon which is mounted a camper containing any passengers unless there is at least one unobstructed exit capable of being opened from both the interior and exterior of such camper.
(Added by Stats.1972, c. 432, p. 797, § 1.)

§ 23130. Noise limits

(a) No person shall operate either a motor vehicle or combination of vehicles of a type subject to registration at any time or under any condition of grade, load, acceleration, or deceleration in such a manner as to exceed the following noise limit for the category of motor vehicle within the speed limits specified in this section:

	Speed limit of 35 mph or less	Speed limit of more than 35 mph
(1) Any motor vehicle with a manufacturer's gross vehicle weight rating of more than 10,000 pounds and any combination of vehicles towed by such motor vehicle	86 dbA	90 dbA
	Speed limit of 45 mph or less	Speed limit of more than 45 mph
(2) Any motorcycle other than a motor-driven cycle	82 dbA	86 dbA
(3) Any other motor vehicle and any combination of vehicles towed by such motor vehicle.	76 dbA	82 dbA

(b) The noise limits established by this section shall be based on a distance of 50 feet from the center of the lane of travel within the speed limit specified in this section. The Department of the California Highway Patrol may provide for measuring at distances other than 50 feet from the center of the lane of travel. In such a case, the measurement shall be corrected so as to provide for measurements equivalent to the noise limit established by this section measured at 50 feet.

(c) The department shall adopt regulations establishing the test procedures and instrumentation to be utilized. These procedures shall allow, to the extent feasible, noise measurement and enforcement action to be accomplished in reasonably confined areas such as residential areas of urban cities.

(d) This section applies to the total noise from a vehicle or combination of vehicles and shall not be construed as limiting or precluding the enforcement of any other provisions of this code relating to motor vehicle exhaust noise.

(e) For the purpose of this section, a motortruck, truck tractor, or bus that is not equipped with an identification plate or marking bearing the manufacturer's name and manufacturer's gross vehicle weight rating shall be considered as having a manu-

§ 23130

facturer's gross vehicle weight rating of more than 10,000 pounds if the unladen weight is more than 5,000 pounds.

(f) No person shall have a cause of action relating to the provisions of this section against a manufacturer of a vehicle or a component part thereof on a theory based upon breach of express or implied warranty unless it is alleged and proved that such manufacturer did not comply with noise limit standards of the Vehicle Code applicable to manufacturers and in effect at the time such vehicle or component part was first sold for purposes other than resale.
(Amended by Stats.1975, c. 993, p. 2337, § 1.)

§ 23130.5. Vehicular noise limits; 35 m. p. h. or less speed zone

(a) Notwithstanding the provisions of subdivision (a) of Section 23130, the noise limits, within a speed zone of 35 miles per hour or less on level streets, or streets with a grade not exceeding plus or minus 1 percent, for the following categories of motor vehicles, or combinations of vehicles, which are subject to registration, shall be:

(1) Any motor vehicle with a manufacturer's gross vehicle weight rating of 6,000 pounds or more and any combination of vehicles towed by such motor vehicle .... 82 dbA

(2) Any motorcycle other than a motor-driven cycle .... 77 dbA

(3) Any other motor vehicle and any combination of vehicles towed by such motor vehicle .... 74 dbA

No person shall operate such a motor vehicle or combination of vehicles in such a manner as to exceed the noise limits specified in this section.

The provisions of subdivisions (c), (d), (e), and (f) of Section 23130 shall apply to this section.

(b) Measurements shall not be made within 200 feet of any intersection controlled by an official traffic control device, or within 200 feet of the beginning or end of any grade in excess of plus or minus 1 percent. Measurements shall be made when it is reasonable to assume that the vehicle flow is at a constant rate of speed, and measurement shall not be made under congested traffic conditions which require noticeable acceleration or deceleration.

(c) Test procedures and instrumentation to be utilized shall be in accordance with regulations of the Department of the California Highway Patrol, except that measurement shall not be conducted within 200 feet of any intersection controlled by an official traffic control device, or within 200 feet of the beginning or end of a grade.

(d) The noise limits established by this section shall be based on a distance of 50 feet from the center of the lane of travel within the speed limit specified in this section. The Department of the California Highway Patrol may provide for measuring at distances closer than 50 feet from the center of the lane of travel. In such a case, the measuring devices shall be so calibrated as to provide for measurements equivalent to the noise limit established by this section measured at 50 feet.

Vehicles equipped with at least two snowtread tires are exempt from this section.
(Amended by Stats.1974, c. 359, p. 690, § 1.)

§ 23253. Obedience to officers

All persons in or upon any vehicular crossing must at all times comply with any lawful order, signal, or direction by voice or hand of any member of the California Highway Patrol or an employee of the Department of Transportation who is a peace officer.
(Amended by Stats.1974, c. 545, p. 1332, § 220.)

Division 12
EQUIPMENT OF VEHICLES

§ 24002. Vehicle not equipped or unsafe

It is unlawful to operate any vehicle or combination of vehicles which is in an unsafe condition, which is not equipped as required by this code, or which is not safely loaded.
(Stats.1959, c. 3, p. 1713, § 24002.)

§ 24003. Vehicle with unlawful lights

No vehicle shall be equipped with any lamp or illuminating device not required or permitted in this code, nor shall any lamp or illuminating device be mounted inside a vehicle unless specifically permitted by this code. This section does not apply to:

(a) Interior lamps such as door, brake and instrument lamps, and map, dash, and dome lamps designed and used for the purpose of illuminating the interior of the vehicle.

(b) Lamps needed in the operation or utilization of those vehicles mentioned in Section 25801, or vehicles used by public utilities in the repair or maintenance of their service, or used only for the illumination of cargo space of a vehicle while loading or unloading.

(c) Approved warning lamps mounted inside an authorized emergency vehicle.
(Amended by Stats.1963, c. 547, p. 1427, § 1.)

§ 24004. Unlawful operation after notice by officer

No person shall operate any vehicle or combination of vehicles after notice by a traffic officer that the vehicle is in an unsafe condition or is not equipped as required by this code, except as may be necessary to return the vehicle or combination of vehicles to the residence or place of business of the owner or driver or to a garage, until the vehicle and its equipment have been made to conform with the requirements of this code.

The provisions of this section shall not apply to an employee who does not know that such notice has been issued, and in such event the provisions of Section 40001 shall be applicable.
(Amended by Stats.1965, c. 306, p. 1403, § 1.)

§ 24005. Sale, transfer or installment of unlawful equipment

It is unlawful for any person to sell, offer for sale, lease, install, or replace, either for himself or as the agent or employee of another, or through such agent or employee, any glass, lighting equipment, signal devices, brakes, vacuum or pressure hose, muffler, exhaust, or any kind of equipment whatsoever for use, or with knowledge that any such equipment is intended for eventual use, in any vehicle, that is not in conformity with this code or regulations made thereunder.
(Amended by Stats.1971, c. 734, p. 1460, § 1.)

§ 24008. Modification of vehicles

It is unlawful to operate any passenger vehicle, or commercial vehicle under 4,000 pounds, which has been modified from the original design so that any portion of such vehicle other than the wheels has less clearance from the surface of a level roadway than the clearance between the roadway and the lowermost portion of any rim of any wheel in contact with such roadway.
(Amended by Stats.1961, c. 1562, p. 3383, § 1.)

§ 24008.5. Unsafe vehicle modification

An "unsafe condition" within the meaning of Section 24002 includes, but is not limited to, the raising of the center of gravity or other modification of a vehicle so as to unsafely affect its operation or stability.
(Added by Stats.1969, c. 300, p. 671, § 1.)

§ 24250. Lighting during darkness

During darkness, a vehicle shall be equipped with lighted lighting equipment as required for the vehicle by this chapter.
(Stats.1959, c. 3, p. 1714, § 24250.)

§ 24252. Lighting equipment requirements

(a) All lighting equipment of a required type installed on a vehicle shall at all times be maintained in good working order. Lamps shall be equipped with bulbs of the correct voltage rating corresponding to the nominal voltage at the lamp socket.

(b) The voltage at any tail, stop, license plate, side marker or clearance lamp socket on a vehicle shall not be less than 85 percent of the design voltage of the bulb. Voltage tests shall be conducted with the engine operating.

(c) Two or more lamp or reflector functions may be combined, provided each function required to be approved meets the specifications determined and published by the department.

(1) No turn signal lamp may be combined optically with a stoplamp unless the stoplamp is extinguished when the turn signal is flashing.

(2) No clearance lamp may be combined optically with any taillamp or identification lamp.
(Amended by Stats.1968, c. 980, p. 1866, § 2.)

§ 24253. Taillamps which remain lighted

(a) All motor vehicles manufactured and first registered after January 1, 1970, shall be equipped so all taillamps are capable of remaining lighted for a period of at least one-quarter hour with the engine inoperative. This requirement shall be complied with by an energy storing system which is recharged by energy produced by the vehicle.

(b) All motorcycles manufactured and first registered after January 1, 1971, shall be equipped so all taillamps, when turned on, will remain lighted automatically for a period of at least one-quarter hour if the engine stops.
(Amended by Stats.1970, c. 217, p. 470, § 1.)

§ 24400. Headlamps on motor vehicles

During darkness, every motor vehicle other than a motorcycle, shall be equipped with at least two lighted headlamps, with at least one on each side of the front of the vehicle, and, except as to vehicles registered prior to January 1, 1930, they shall be located directly above or in advance of the front axle of the vehicle. The headlamps and every light source in any headlamp unit shall be located at a height of not more than 54 inches nor less than 24 inches.
(Stats.1959, c. 3, p. 1715, § 24400.)

§ 24401. Dimmed lights on parked vehicles

Whenever any motor vehicle is parked or standing upon a highway any headlamp that is lighted shall be dimmed or on the lower beam.
(Stats.1959, c. 3, p. 1715, § 24401.)

§ 24404. Spotlamps

(a) A motor vehicle may be equipped with not to exceed two white spotlamps, which shall not be used in substitution of headlamps.

(b) No spotlamp shall be equipped with any lamp source exceeding 32 standard candlepower or 30 watts nor project any glaring light into the eyes of an approaching driver.

(c) Every spotlamp shall be so directed when in use: That no portion of the main substantially parallel beam of light will strike the roadway to the left of the prolongation of the left side line of the vehicle.

That the top of the beam will not strike the roadway at a distance in excess of 300 feet from the vehicle.

(d) This section does not apply to spotlamps on authorized emergency vehicles.

(e) No spotlamp when in use shall be directed so as to illuminate any other moving vehicle.
(Amended by Stats.1967, c. 544, p. 1893, § 2.)

§ 24408. Beam indicator

(a) Every new motor vehicle registered in this state after January 1, 1940, which has multiple-beam road lighting equipment shall be equipped with a beam indicator, which shall be lighted whenever the uppermost distribution of light from the headlamps is in use, and shall not otherwise be lighted.

(b) The indicator shall be so designed and located that when lighted it will be readily visible without glare to the driver of the vehicle so equipped. Any such lamp on the exterior of the vehicle shall have a light source not exceeding two candlepower, and the light shall not show to the front or sides of the vehicle.
(Amended by Stats.1970, c. 422, p. 834, § 1.)

§ 24409. Use of multiple beams

Whenever a motor vehicle is being operated during darkness, the driver shall use a distribution of light, or composite beam, directed high enough and of sufficient intensity to reveal persons and vehicles at a safe distance in advance of the vehicle, subject to the following requirements and limitations:

(a) Whenever the driver of a vehicle approaches an oncoming vehicle within 500 feet, he shall use a distribution of light or composite beam so aimed that the glaring rays are not projected into the eyes of the oncoming driver.

The lowermost distribution of light specified in this article shall be deemed to avoid glare at all times regardless of road contour.

(b) Whenever the driver of a vehicle follows another vehicle within 300 feet to the rear, he shall use the lowermost distribution of light specified in this article.
(Amended by Stats.1965, c. 37, p. 915, § 1.)

§ 24410. Single beams

Headlamps arranged to provide a single distribution of light not supplemented by auxiliary driving lamps are permitted on motor vehicles manufactured and sold prior to September 19, 1940, in lieu of multiple-beam road lighting equipment if the single distribution of light complies with the following requirements and limitations:

(a) The headlamps shall be so aimed that when the vehicle is not loaded none of the high-intensity portion of the light shall at a distance of 25 feet ahead project higher than a level of five inches below the level of the center of the lamp from which it comes, and in no case higher than 42 inches above the level on which the vehicle stands at a distance of 75 feet ahead.

(b) The intensity shall be sufficient to reveal persons and vehicles at a distance of at least 200 feet.
(Stats.1959, c. 3, p. 1716, § 24410.)

§ 24600. Taillamps generally

During darkness every motor vehicle which is not in combination with any other vehicle and every vehicle at the end of a combination of vehicles shall be equipped with lighted taillamps mounted on the rear as follows:

(a) Every such vehicle shall be equipped with one or more taillamps.

(b) Every such vehicle, other than a motorcycle, manufactured and first registered on or after January 1, 1958, shall be equipped with not less than two taillamps, except that trailers and semitrailers manufactured after July 23, 1973, which are less than 30 inches wide, may be equipped with one taillamp which shall be mounted at or near the vertical centerline of the vehicles. If such a vehicle is equipped with two taillamps, they shall be mounted as specified in subdivision (d).

(c) Every such vehicle or vehicle at the end of a combination of vehicles, subject to subdivision (a) of Section 22406 shall be equipped with not less than two taillamps.

(d) When two taillamps are required, at least one shall be mounted at the left and one at the right side respectively at the same level.

(e) Taillamps shall be red in color and shall be plainly visible from all distances within 500 feet to the rear except that taillamps on vehicles manufactured after January 1, 1969, shall be plainly visible from all distances within 1,000 feet to the rear.

(f) Taillamps on vehicles manufactured on or after January 1, 1969, shall be mounted not lower than 15 inches nor higher than 72 inches, except that a tow car, in addition to being equipped with the required taillamps, may also be equipped with two taillamps which may be mounted not lower than 15 inches nor higher than the maximum allowable vehicle height and as far forward as the rearmost portion of the driver's seat in the rearmost position. Such additional taillamps on a tow car shall be lighted whenever the headlamps are lighted.
(Amended by Stats.1976, c. 154, p. —, § 2.)

§ 24601. Lamp

Either the taillamp or a separate lamp shall be so constructed and placed as to illuminate with a white light the rear license plate during darkness and render it clearly legible from a distance of 50 feet to the rear. When the rear license plate is illuminated by a lamp other than a required taillamp, the two lamps shall be turned on or off only by the same control switch at all times.
(Amended by Stats.1965, c. 1313, p. 3200, § 4.)

§ 24603. Stoplamps

Every motor vehicle which is not in combination with any other vehicle and every vehicle at the end of a combination of vehicles shall at all times be equipped with stoplamps mounted on the rear as follows:

(a) Every such vehicle shall be equipped with one or more stoplamps.

(b) Every such vehicle, other than a motorcycle, manufactured and first registered on or after January 1, 1958, shall be equipped with two stoplamps, except that trailers and semitrailers manufactured after July 23, 1973, which are less than 30 inches wide, may be equipped with one stoplamp which shall be mounted at or near the vertical centerline of the trailer. If such vehicle is equipped with two stoplamps, they shall be mounted as specified in subdivision (d).

(c) Stoplamps on vehicles manufactured on or after January 1, 1969, shall be mounted not lower than 15 inches nor higher than 72 inches, except that a tow car, in addition to being equipped with the required stoplamps, may also be equipped with two stoplamps which may be mounted not lower than 15 inches nor higher than the maximum allowable vehicle height and as far forward as the rearmost portion of the driver's seat in the rearmost position.

(d) Where two stoplamps are required, at least one shall be mounted at the left and one at the right side, respectively, at the same level.

(e) Stoplamps on vehicles manufactured on or after January 1, 1979, shall emit a red light. Stoplamps on vehicles manufactured before January 1, 1979, shall emit a red or yellow light. All stoplamps shall be plainly visible and understandable from a distance of 300 feet to the rear both during normal sunlight and at nighttime, except that stoplamps on a vehicle of a size required to be equipped with clearance lamps shall be visible from a distance of 500 feet during such times.

(f) Stoplamps shall be actuated upon application of the service (foot) brake and the hand control head for air, vacuum, or electric brakes. In addition, all stoplamps may be activated by a mechanical device designed to function only upon sudden release of the accelerator while the vehicle is in motion. Such mechanical device shall be approved by, and comply with specifications and regulations established by, the department.

§ 24603

(g) Any vehicle may be equipped with supplemental stoplamps mounted to the rear of the rearmost portion of the driver's seat in its rearmost position in addition to the lamps required to be mounted on the rear of the vehicle. The supplemental stoplamp on that side of a vehicle toward which a turn will be made may flash as part of the supplemental turn signal lamp.
(Amended by Stats.1978, c. 252, p. —, § 3.)

§ 24604. Lamp or flag on projections

Whenever the load upon any vehicle extends, or whenever any integral part of any vehicle projects, to the rear four feet or more beyond the bed or body of the vehicle, there shall be displayed at the extreme end of the load or projecting part of the vehicle during darkness, in addition to the required taillamp, two red lights with a bulb rated not in excess of six candlepower plainly visible from a distance of at least 500 feet to the sides and rear. At any other time there shall be displayed at the extreme end of the load or projecting part of the vehicle a red flag or cloth not less than 16 inches square.
(Amended by Stats.1965, c. 1313, p. 3200, § 6.)

§ 24606. Backup lamps

(a) Every motor vehicle, other than a motorcycle, of a type subject to registration and manufactured on and after January 1, 1969, shall be equipped with one or more backup lamps either separately or in combination with another lamp. Any vehicle may be equipped with backup lamps.

(b) Backup lamps shall be so directed as to project a white light illuminating the highway to the rear of the vehicle for a distance not to exceed 75 feet. A backup lamp may project incidental red, amber, or white light through reflectors or lenses that are adjacent or close to, or a part of, the lamp assembly.

(c) Backup lamps shall not be lighted except when the vehicle is about to be or is backing or except in conjunction with a lighting system which activates the lights for a temporary period after the ignition system is turned off.
(Amended by Stats.1968, c. 980, p. 1869, § 8.)

§ 24607. Reflectors

Every vehicle subject to registration under this code shall at all times be equipped with red reflectors mounted on the rear as follows:

(a) Every vehicle shall be equipped with at least one reflector so maintained as to be plainly visible at night from all distances within 350 to 100 feet from the vehicle when directly in front of the lawful upper headlamp beams.

(b) Every vehicle, other than a motorcycle, manufactured and first registered on or after January 1, 1965, shall be equipped with at least two reflectors meeting the visibility requirements of subdivision (a), except that trailers and semitrailers manufactured after July 23, 1973, which are less than 30 inches wide, may be equipped with one reflector which shall be mounted at or near the verticle centerline of the trailer. If such vehicle is equipped with two reflectors, they shall be mounted as specified in subdivision (d).

(c) Every motortruck having an unladen weight of more than 5,000 pounds, every trailer coach, every camp trailer, every vehicle or vehicle at the end of a combination of vehicles subject to subdivision (a) of Section 22406, and every vehicle 80 or more inches in width manufactured on or after January 1, 1969, shall be equipped with at least two reflectors maintained so as to be plainly visible at night from all distances within 600 feet to 100 feet from the vehicle when directly in front of lawful upper headlamp beams.

(d) When more than one reflector is required, at least one shall be mounted at the left side and one at the right side, respectively, at the same level. Required reflectors shall be mounted not lower than 15 inches nor higher than 60 inches, except that a tow car, in addition to being equipped with the required reflectors, may also be equipped with two reflectors which may be mounted not lower than 15 inches nor higher than the maximum allowable vehicle height and as far forward as the rearmost portion of the driver's seat in the rearmost position. Additional reflectors of a type approved by the department may be mounted at any height.

(e) Reflectors on truck tractors may be mounted on the rear of the cab. Any reflector installed on a vehicle as part of its original equipment prior to January 1, 1941, need not be of an approved type provided it meets the visibility requirements of subdivision (a).
(Amended by Stats.1976, c. 154, p. —, § 4.)

§ 24608. Reflectors on front and sides

(a) Motortrucks, trailers, semitrailers, and buses 80 or more inches in width manufactured on or after January 1, 1968, shall be equipped with an amber reflector on each side at the front and a red reflector on each side at the rear. Any vehicle may be so equipped.

(b) Motortrucks, trailers, semitrailers, housecars, and buses 80 or more inches in width and 30 or more feet in length manufactured on or after January 1, 1968, shall be equipped with an amber reflector mounted on each side at the approximate midpoint of the vehicle. Any such vehicle manufactured prior to January 1, 1968, may be so equipped.

(c) Required reflectors on the sides of vehicles shall be mounted not lower than 15 inches nor higher than 60 inches. Additional reflectors of a type approved by the department may be mounted at any height.

(d) Reflectors required or permitted in subdivisions (a) and (b) shall be so maintained as to be plainly visible at night from all distances within 600 feet to 100 feet from the vehicle when directly in front of lawful upper headlamp beams.

(e) Area reflectorizing material may be used in lieu of the reflectors required or permitted in subdivisions (a) and (b), provided each installation is of sufficient size to meet the photometric requirement for such reflectors.
(Amended by Stats.1975, c. 854, p. 1919, § 2.)

§ 24609. Vehicle reflectors

Any vehicle may be equipped with white or amber reflectors upon the front of the vehicle, but they shall be mounted not lower than 15 inches nor higher than 60 inches.
(Added by Stats.1969, c. 341, p. 716, § 4.)

§ 24800. Lighted parking lamps

No vehicle shall be driven at any time with the parking lamps lighted except when the lamps are being used as turn signal lamps or when the headlamps are also lighted.
(Amended by Stats.1961, c. 58, p. 1011, § 45.)

§ 24801. Parking lamps

Parking lamps are those lamps permitted by Section 25106, or any lamps mounted on the front of a vehicle, designed to be displayed primarily when the vehicle is parked.
(Stats.1959, c. 3, p. 1719, § 24801.)

§ 24802. Lamps on parked vehicle

No lights need be displayed upon a vehicle which is:

(a) Parked off the roadway and not in a hazardous position on the highway; or

(b) Parked with a wheel within 18 inches of a curb; or

(c) Parked within a business or residence district with a wheel within 18 inches of a curb or edge of the roadway.
(Amended by Stats.1977, c. 620, p. ——, § 2.)

§ 24950. Turn signal system required

Whenever any motor vehicle is towing a trailer coach or a camp trailer the combination of vehicles shall be equipped with a lamp-type turn signal system.
(Amended by Stats.1971, c. 1536, p. 3044, § 5.)

§ 24951. Turn signal system

(a) Any vehicle may be equipped with a lamp-type turn signal system capable of clearly indicating any intention to turn either to the right or to the left.

(b) The following vehicles shall be equipped with a lamp-type turn signal system meeting the requirements of this chapter.

(1) Motortrucks, truck tractors, buses and passenger vehicles, other than motorcycles, manufactured and first registered on or after January 1, 1958.

(2) Trailers and semitrailers manufactured and first registered between December 31, 1957, and January 1, 1969, having a gross weight of 6,000 pounds or more.

(3) Trailers and semitrailers 80 or more inches in width manufactured on or after January 1, 1969.

(4) Motorcycles manufactured and first registered on or after January 1, 1973, except motor-driven cycles whose speed attainable in one mile is 30 miles per hour or less.

The requirements of this subdivision shall not apply to special mobile equipment, or auxiliary dollies.

(c) Turn signal lamps on vehicles manufactured on or after January 1, 1969, shall be mounted not lower than 15 inches.
(Amended by Stats.1975, c. 475, p. 984, § 1.)

§ 24952. Requirement of signals

A lamp-type turn signal shall be plainly visible and understandable in normal sunlight and at nighttime from a distance of at least 300 feet to the front and rear of the vehicle, except that turn signal lamps on vehicles of a size required to be equipped with

clearance lamps shall be visible from a distance of 500 feet during such times.
(Amended by Stats.1965, c. 1012, p. 2644, § 4.)

§ 24953. Lamps of turn signals

(a) Any turn signal system used to give a signal of intention to turn right or left shall project a flashing white or amber light visible to the front and a flashing red or amber light visible to the rear.

(b) Side-mounted turn signal lamps of an approved type projecting a flashing amber light to either side may be used to supplement the front and rear turn signals. Side-mounted turn signal lamps mounted to the rear of the center of the vehicle may project a flashing red light no part of which shall be visible from the front.

(c) In addition to any required turn signal lamps, any vehicle may be equipped with supplemental rear turn signal lamps mounted to the rear of the rearmost portion of the driver's seat in its rearmost position.
(Amended by Stats.1972, c. 203, p. 425, § 1.)

§ 25100. Clearance and side-marker lamps

(a) Except as provided in subdivisions (b) and (d), every vehicle 80 inches or more in overall width shall be equipped during darkness as follows:

(1) At least one amber clearance lamp at each side mounted on a forward-facing portion of the vehicle and visible from the front and at least one red clearance lamp at each side mounted on a rearward-facing portion of the vehicle and visible from the rear.

(2) At least one amber side-marker lamp on each side near the front and at least one red side-marker lamp on each side near the rear.

(3) At least one amber side-marker lamp on each side at or near the center on trailers and semitrailers 30 feet or more in length and which are manufactured and first registered after January 1, 1962. Any such vehicle manufactured and first registered prior to January 1, 1962, may be so equipped.

(4) At least one amber side-marker lamp mounted at approximate midpoint of housecars, motortrucks, and buses 30 or more feet in length and manufactured on or after January 1, 1969. Any such vehicle manufactured prior to January 1, 1969, may be so equipped.

(5) Combination clearance and side-marker lamps mounted as side-marker lamps and meeting the visibility requirements for both types of lamps may be used in lieu of required individual clearance or side-marker lamps.

(b) The following vehicles when 80 inches or more in overall width and not equipped as provided in subdivision (a) shall be equipped during darkness as follows:

(1) Truck tractors shall be equipped with at least one amber clearance lamp at each side on the front of the cab or sleeper and may be equipped with amber side-marker lamps on each side.

(2) Truck tractors manufactured on or after January 1, 1969, shall be equipped with one amber side-marker lamp on each side near the front.

(3) Pole or pipe dollies, or logging dollies shall be equipped with at least one combination clearance and side-marker lamp on each side showing red to the front, side, and rear.

(4) Vehicles, except truck tractors, which are 80 inches or more in width over a distance not exceeding three feet from front to rear shall be equipped with at least one amber combination clearance lamp and side-marker lamp on each side visible from the front, side, and rear if the projection is near the front of the vehicle and at least one such red lamp if the projection is near the rear of the vehicle.

(5) Towing motor vehicles engaged in driveaway-towaway operations shall be equipped with at least one amber clearance lamp at each side on the front and at least one amber side-marker lamp on each side near the front.

(6) Towed motor vehicles engaged in driveaway-towaway operations shall be equipped with at least one amber side-marker lamp on each side of intermediate vehicles, and the rearmost vehicle shall be equipped with at least one red side-marker lamp on each side and at least one red clearance lamp at each side on the rear.

(7) Trailers and semitrailers designed for transporting single boats in a cradle-type mounting and for launching the boat from the rear of the trailer need not be equipped with front and rear clearance lamps provided amber clearance lamps showing to the front and red clearance lamps showing to the rear are located on each side at or near the midpoint between the front and rear of the trailer to indicate the extreme width of the trailer.

(c) Loads extending beyond the side of a vehicle where the overall width of the vehicle and load is 80 inches or more shall be equipped with an amber combination clearance and side-marker lamp on the side at the front and a red combination clearance and side-marker lamp on the side at the rear. In lieu of the foregoing requirement, projecting loads not exceeding three feet from front to rear at the extreme width shall be equipped with at least one amber combination clearance and side-marker lamp on the side visible from the front, side, and rear if the projection is near the front of the vehicle and at least one such red lamp if the projection is near the rear of the vehicle.

(d) Clearance and side-marker lamps are not required on auxiliary dollies or on passenger vehicles other than a housecar.

(e) Clearance lamps shall be visible from all distances between 500 feet and 50 feet to the front or rear of the vehicle, and side-marker lamps shall be visible from all distances between 500 feet and 50 feet to the side of the vehicle.

(f) Clearance lamps shall, so far as is practicable, be mounted to indicate the extreme width of the vehicle. Side-marker lamps shall be mounted not lower than 15 inches on vehicles manufactured on and after January 1, 1968. Combination clearance and side-marker lamps required on loads shall be mounted so the lenses project to the outer extremity of the vehicle or load.
(Amended by Stats.1976, c. 900, p. —, § 1.)

§ 25101. Repealed by Stats.1974, c. 635, p. 1490, § 5

§ 25102. Lamps on sides of vehicles

In addition to the lamps otherwise permitted by this chapter, any motor vehicle may be equipped with lamps on the sides thereof, visible from the side of the vehicle but not from the front or rear thereof, which lamps, together with mountings or receptacles, shall be set into depressions or recesses in the body of the vehicle and shall not protrude beyond or outside the body of the vehicle. The light source in each of the lamps shall not exceed two candlepower and shall emit diffused light of any color, except that the color red is permitted only on authorized emergency vehicles.
(Stats.1959, c. 3, p. 1721, § 25102.)

§ 25103. Projecting load

Whenever the load upon any vehicle extends from the left side of the vehicle one foot or more to the left of the front hub cap on the left side there shall be displayed at the extreme left side of the load during darkness a lighted lantern or other light plainly visible from a distance of at least 300 feet to the left side and the front and rear of the vehicle.

The lamp shall not contain a bulb rated in excess of six candlepower
(Stats.1959, c. 3, p. 1721, § 25103.)

§ 25104. Wide vehicles

Any vehicle operating other than during darkness and wider than permitted under Sections 35100 to 35108, inclusive, shall display a red flag or cloth not less than 16 inches square at the extreme left front and left rear of the vehicle or equipment.
(Stats.1959, c. 3, p. 1721, § 25104.)

§ 25105. Courtesy lamps; door-mounter lamps/reflectors; exterior lamps

(a) Any motor vehicle may be equipped with running board or door-mounted courtesy lamps. The bulbs in the lamps shall not exceed six standard candlepower and shall emit either a green or white light without glare. The beams of the lamps shall not be visible to the front or rear of the vehicle.

(b) Any motor vehicle may be equipped with inside door-mounted red lamps or red reflectorizing devices or material visible to the rear of the vehicle when the doors are open. The bulbs in the lamps shall not exceed six standard candlepower.

(c) Any bus, housecar, or camper may be equipped with exterior lamps for the purpose of lighting the entrances and exits of such vehicles, which lamps may be lighted only when such vehicles are not in motion. The lamp source of such exterior lamps shall not exceed 32 standard candlepower, or 30 watts, nor project any glaring light into the eyes of an approaching driver.
(Amended by Stats.1977, c. 287, p. —, § 4.)

§ 25106. Cowl or fender lamps; side-marker or combination clearance and side-marker lamps

(a) Any motor vehicle may be equipped with lighted white or amber cowl or fender lamps on the front. Any vehicle may be equipped with not more than one amber side lamp on each side near the front, nor more than one red side lamp on each side near the rear. The light source of each such lamp shall not exceed four standard candlepower.

(b) Lamps approved as side-marker or combination clearance and side-marker lamps may be installed on the sides of vehicles at any location, but any lamp

installed within 24 inches of the rear of the vehicle shall be red, and any lamp installed at any other location shall be amber.
(Amended by Stats.1978, c. 252, p. —, § 4.)

§ 25107. Cornering lamps on fenders

Any motor vehicle may be equipped with not more than two cornering lamps designed and of sufficient intensity for the purpose of revealing objects only in the direction of turn while the vehicle is turning or while the turn signal lamps are operating to signal an intention to turn. The lamps shall be designed so that no glaring light is projected into the eyes of an approaching driver.
(Amended by Stats.1965, c. 1313, p. 3202, § 10.)

§ 25108. Pilot indicators

(a) Any motor vehicle may be equipped with not more than two amber turn signal pilot indicators mounted on the exterior. The light output from any such indicator shall not exceed 5 candlepower unless provision is made for operating the indicator at reduced intensity during darkness in which event the light output shall not exceed 5 candlepower during darkness or 15 candlepower at any other time. The center of the beam shall be projected toward the driver.

(b) Other exterior pilot indicators of any color may be used for monitoring exterior lighting devices, provided that the area of each indicator is less than 0.20 square inches, the intensity of each indicator does not exceed 0.10 candlepower and the color red is not visible to the front.
(Amended by Stats.1967, c. 440, p. 1653, § 2.)

§ 25109. Running lamps

Any motor vehicle may be equipped with two white or amber running lamps mounted on the front, one at each side, which shall not be lighted during darkness except while the motor vehicle is parked.

§ 25110. Utility flood and loading lamps

(a) The following vehicles may be equipped with utility flood or loading lamps mounted on the rear, and sides, which project a white light illuminating an area to the side or rear of the vehicle for a distance not to exceed 75 feet at the level of the roadway:

(1) Tow cars which are used to tow disabled vehicles may display such utility flood lights but only during the period of preparation for towing at the location from which a disabled vehicle is to be towed.

(2) Ambulances used to respond to emergency calls may display such utility flood and loading lights but only at the scene of an emergency or while loading or unloading patients.

(3) Firefighting equipment designed and operated exclusively as such may display such utility flood lamps only at the scene of an emergency.

(b) Lamps permitted under subdivision (a) shall not be lighted during darkness, except while the vehicle is parked, nor project any glaring light into the eyes of an approaching driver.
(Added by Stats.1975, c. 551, p. 1125, § 1.)

§ 25305. Use of fusees

(a) No person shall place, deposit, or display upon or adjacent to any highway any lighted fusee, except as a warning to approaching vehicular traffic or railroad trains, or both, of an existing hazard upon or adjacent to the highway or highway-railroad crossing.

(b) It is unlawful to use any fusee which produces other than a red light. The provisions of this subdivision shall not apply to any railroad, as defined in Section 229 of the Public Utilities Code.
(Added by Stats.1971, c. 84, p. 112, § 1.)

§ 25500. Use of reflectorizing material

(a) Area reflectorizing material may be displayed on any vehicle, provided: the color red is not displayed on the front; designs do not tend to distort the length or width of the vehicle; and designs do not resemble official traffic control devices, except that alternate striping resembling a barricade pattern may be used.

No vehicle shall be equipped with area reflectorizing material contrary to these provisions.

(b) The provisions of this section shall not apply to license plate stickers or tabs affixed to license plates as authorized by the Department of Motor Vehicles.
(Amended by Stats.1971, c. 1536, p. 3044, § 7.)

§ 25650. Headlights on motorcycles

Every motorcycle during darkness shall be equipped with at least one and not more than two lighted headlamps which shall conform to the requirements and limitations of this division.
(Stats.1959, c. 3, p. 1727, § 25650.)

§ 25650.5. Headlamps on motorcycles manufactured after 1974

Every motorcycle manufactured and first registered on and after January 1, 1978, shall be equipped with at least one and not more than two headlamps which automatically turn on when the engine of the motorcycle is started and which remain lighted as long as the engine is running.
(Amended by Stats.1978, c. 252, p. —, § 7.)

§ 25651. Headlamps on motor-driven cycles

The headlamp upon a motor-driven cycle may be of the single-beam or multiple-beam type, but in either event, when the vehicle is operated during darkness, the headlamp shall comply with the requirements and limitations as follows:

(a) The headlamp shall be of sufficient intensity to reveal a person or a vehicle at a distance of not less than 100 feet when the motor-driven cycle is operated at any speed less than 25 miles per hour and at a distance of not less than 200 feet when operated at a speed of 25 to not exceeding 35 miles per hour, and at a distance of 300 feet when operated at a speed greater than 35 miles per hour.

(b) In the event the motor-driven cycle is equipped with a multiple-beam headlamp, the upper beam shall meet the minimum requirements set forth above and the lowermost beam shall meet the requirements applicable to a lowermost distribution of light as set forth in subdivision (b) of Section 24407.

(c) In the event the motor-driven cycle is equipped with a single-beam lamp, it shall be so aimed that when the vehicle is loaded none of the high intensity portion of light, at a distance of 25 feet ahead, shall project higher than the level of the center of the lamp from which it comes.
(Amended by Stats.1959, c. 1996, p. 4635, § 35.)

§ 25950. Color of lamps and reflectors

Unless provided otherwise, the color of lamps and reflectors upon a vehicle shall be as follows:

(a) All lamps and reflectors visible from in front of a vehicle shall be white or yellow, except as follows:

(1) Rear side-marker lamps required by Section 25100 may show red to the front.

(2) The color of foglamps described in Section 24403 may be in the color spectrum from white to yellow.

(b) All lamps and reflectors visible from the rear of a vehicle shall be red, except that stoplamps on vehicles manufactured before January 1, 1979, and turn signal lamps and front side-marker lamps required by Section 25100, may show yellow to the rear.

This section applies to the color of a lamp whether lighted or unlighted, and to any reflector exhibiting or reflecting perceptible light of 0.05 candlepower or more per foot-candle of incident illumination, except that taillamps, stoplamps, and turn signal lamps that are visible to the rear may be white when unlighted on vehicles manufactured before January 1, 1974. Any taillamp, stoplamp, backup lamp, or turn signal lamp may have an unlighted lens color that is darker than the lighted color, and any such lamps that are in addition to the minimum required number may be white or yellow when unlighted.

§ 25951. Direction of beam

Any lighted lamp or device upon a motor vehicle other than headlamps, spotlamps, signal lamps, or auxiliary driving lamps, warning lamps which projects a beam of light of an intensity greater than 300 candlepower shall be so directed that no part of the beam will strike the level of the roadway at a distance of more than 75 feet from the vehicle.
(Amended by Stats.1965, c. 1313, p. 3203, § 12.)

§ 25952. Lamps and reflectors on loads

(a) Lamps, reflectors, and area reflectorizing material of a type required or permitted on a vehicle may be mounted on a load carried by the vehicle in lieu of, or in addition to, such equipment on the vehicle. Such equipment shall be mounted on the load in a manner that would comply with the requirements of this code and regulations adopted pursuant to this code if the load were an integral part of the vehicle.

(b) Lamps on vehicles carried as a load shall not be lighted unless such lamps are mounted in accordance with subdivision (a).
(Added by Stats.1969, c. 341, p. 716, § 6.)

§ 26450. Required brake system

Every motor vehicle shall be equipped with a service brake system and every motor vehicle, other than a motorcycle, shall be equipped with a parking brake system. Both the service brake and parking brake shall be separately applied.

If the two systems are connected in any way, they shall be so constructed that failure of any one part,

except failure in the drums, brakeshoes, or other mechanical parts of the wheel brake assemblies, shall not leave the motor vehicle without operative brakes.
(Amended by Stats.1967, c. 369, p. 1597, § 1.)

§ 26451. Parking brake system

The parking brake system of every motor vehicle shall comply with the following requirements:

(a) The parking brake shall be adequate to hold the vehicle or combination of vehicles stationary on any grade on which it is operated under all conditions of loading on a surface free from snow, ice or loose material. In any event the parking brake shall be capable of locking the braked wheels to the limit of traction.

(b) The parking brake shall be applied either by the driver's muscular efforts, by spring action, or by other energy which is isolated and used exclusively for the operation of the parking brake or the combination parking brake and emergency stopping system.

(c) The parking brake shall be held in the applied position by mechanical means, spring devices, or captive air pressure in self-contained cells, which self-contained cells do not lose more than five pounds of air pressure during a 30-day period from their standard operating pressure potential as established by the manufacturer. The force to hold the vehicle parked shall be applied through mechanical linkage to the braked wheels when a spring device or captive air pressure in self-contained cells is used.
(Amended by Stats.1967, c. 1427, p. 3355, § 1.)

§ 26452. Brakes after engine failure

All motor vehicles shall be so equipped as to permit application of the brakes at least once for the purpose of bringing the vehicle to a stop within the legal stopping distance after the engine has become inoperative.
(Stats.1959, c. 3, p. 1734, § 26452.)

§ 26454. Control and stopping requirements

(a) The service brakes of every motor vehicle or combination of vehicles shall be adequate to control the movement of and to stop and hold such vehicle or combination of vehicles under all conditions of loading on any grade on which it is operated.

(b) Every motor vehicle or combination of vehicles, at any time and under all conditions of loading, shall, upon application of the service brake, be capable of stopping from an initial speed of 20 miles per hour according to the following requirements:

	Maximum Stopping Distance (feet)
(1) Any passenger vehicle	25
(2) Any single motor vehicle with a manufacturer's gross vehicle weight rating of less than 10,000 lbs.	30
(3) Any combination of vehicles consisting of a passenger vehicle or any motor vehicle with a manufacturer's gross vehicle weight rating of less than 10,000 lbs. in combination with any trailer, semitrailer or trailer coach	40
(4) Any single motor vehicle with a manufacturer's gross vehicle weight rating of 10,000 lbs. or more or any bus	40
(5) All other combinations of vehicles	50

(Amended by Stats.1965, c. 443, p. 1751, § 4.)

§ 26456. Stopping tests

Stopping distance requirement tests shall be conducted on a substantially level, dry, smooth, hard-surface road that is free from loose material and where the grade does not exceed plus or minus 1 percent. Stopping distance shall be measured from the instant brake controls are moved and from an initial speed of approximately 20 miles per hour. No test of brake performance shall be made upon a highway at a speed in excess of 25 miles per hour.
(Stats.1959, c. 3, p. 1735, § 26456.)

§ 26700. Windshields

Every passenger vehicle, other than a motorcycle, and every bus, motortruck or truck tractor, and every firetruck, fire engine or other fire apparatus, whether publicly or privately owned, shall be equipped with an adequate windshield.
(Amended by Stats.1967, c. 379, p. 1604, § 1.)

§ 26707. Condition and use of windshield wipers

Windshield wipers required by this code shall be maintained in good operating condition and shall provide clear vision through the windshield for the driver. Wipers shall be operated under conditions of fog, snow, or rain and shall be capable of effectively clearing the windshield under all ordinary storm or load conditions while the vehicle is in operation.
(Stats.1959, c. 3, p. 1736, § 26707.)

§ 26708. Material obstructing or reducing driver's view

(a) No person shall drive any motor vehicle with any object or material placed, displayed, installed, affixed, or applied upon the windshield, or side or rear windows, or with any object or material so placed, displayed, installed, affixed, or applied in or upon the vehicle as to obstruct or reduce the driver's clear view through the windshield or side windows.

(b) This section shall not apply to:

(1) Rearview mirrors.

(2) Adjustable nontransparent sunvisors which are mounted forward of the side windows and are not attached to the glass.

(3) Signs, stickers, or other materials which are displayed in a seven-inch square in the lower corner of the windshield farthest removed from the driver or signs, stickers, or other materials which are displayed in a five-inch square in the lower corner of the windshield nearest the driver.

(4) Side windows which are to the rear of the driver.

(5) Direction, destination, or termini signs upon a passenger common carrier motor vehicle, providing such signs do not interfere with the driver's clear view of approaching traffic.

(6) Rear window wiper motor.

(7) Rear trunk lid handle or hinges.

(8) The rear window or windows, when the motor vehicle is equipped with outside mirrors on both the left- and right-hand sides of the vehicle that are so located as to reflect to the driver a view of the highway through each mirror for a distance of at least 200 feet to the rear of the vehicle.

(c) Notwithstanding subdivision (a), transparent material may be installed, affixed, or applied to the topmost portion of the windshield if:

(1) The bottom edge of the material is at least 29 inches above the undepressed driver's seat when measured from a point five inches in front of the bottom of the backrest with the driver's seat in its rearmost and lowermost position with the vehicle on a level surface.

(2) The material is not red or amber in color.

(3) There is no opaque lettering on the material and any other lettering does not affect primary colors or distort vision through the windshield.

(4) The material does not reflect sunlight or headlight glare into the eyes of occupants of oncoming or following vehicles to any greater extent than the windshield without the material.

(Amended by Stats.1978, c. 222, p. ——, § 1; Stats.1978, c. 222, p. ——, § 2; Stats.1978, c. 500, p. ——, § 1, Stats.1978, c. 500, p. ——, § 2.)

§ 26708.5. Transparent materials

It is unlawful for any person to place, install, affix, or apply any transparent material upon the windshield, or side or rear windows, of any motor vehicle if such material alters the color or reduces the light transmittance of such windshield or side or rear windows, except as provided in subdivision (b) of Section 26708.

This section shall not, however, apply to factory-installed tinted glass or the equivalent replacement thereof.

(Added by Stats.1972, c. 528, p. 912, § 2.)

§ 26709. Mirrors

(a) Every motor vehicle registered in a foreign jurisdiction and every motorcycle subject to registration in this state shall be equipped with a mirror so located as to reflect to the driver a view of the highway for a distance of at least 200 feet to the rear of such vehicle.

Every motor vehicle subject to registration in this state, except a motorcycle, shall be equipped with not less than two such mirrors, including one affixed to the left-hand side.

(b) The following described types of motor vehicles, of a type subject to registration, shall be equipped with mirrors on both the left- and right-hand sides of the vehicle so located as to reflect to the driver a view of the highway through each mirror for a distance of at least 200 feet to the rear of such vehicle:

(1) A motor vehicle so constructed or loaded as to obstruct the driver's view to the rear.

(2) A motor vehicle towing a vehicle and the towed vehicle or load thereon obstructs the driver's view to the rear.

(3) A bus or trolley coach.

(c) The provisions of subdivision (b) shall not apply to a passenger vehicle when the load obstructing the driver's view consists of passengers.

(Amended by Stats.1970, c. 74, p. 87, § 1.)

§ 26710. Defective windshields and rear windows

It is unlawful to operate any motor vehicle upon a highway when the windshield or rear window is in such a defective condition as to impair the driver's vision either to the front or rear.

In the event any windshield or rear window fails to comply with this code the officer making the inspection shall direct the driver to make the windshield and rear window conform to the requirements of this code within 48 hours. The officer may also arrest the driver and give him notice to appear and further require the driver or the owner of the vehicle to produce in court satisfactory evidence that the windshield or rear window has been made to conform to the requirements of this code.
(Stats.1959, c. 3, p. 1737, § 26710.)

§ 27000. Horns or warning devices

Every motor vehicle when operated upon a highway shall be equipped with a horn in good working order and capable of emitting sound audible under normal conditions from a distance of not less than 200 feet, but no horn shall emit an unreasonably loud or harsh sound. An authorized emergency vehicle used in responding to fire calls may be equipped with, and use in conjunction with the siren on such vehicle, an air horn which emits sounds that do not comply with the requirements of this section.
(Amended by Stats.1965, c. 1015, p. 2650, § 1.)

§ 27001. Use of horns; theft alarm system

(a) The driver of a motor vehicle when reasonably necessary to insure safe operation shall give audible warning with his horn.

(b) The horn shall not otherwise be used, except as a theft alarm system which operates as specified in Article 13 (commencing with Section 28085) of this chapter.
(Amended by Stats.1977, c. 993, p. —, § 2.)

§ 27002. Sirens

No vehicle shall be equipped with, nor shall any person use upon a vehicle any siren, except that an authorized emergency vehicle shall be equipped with a siren of a type approved by the department.
(Amended by Stats.1961, c. 653, p. 1863, § 50.)

§ 27150. Adequate muffler required

(a) Every motor vehicle subject to registration shall at all times be equipped with an adequate muffler in constant operation and properly maintained to prevent any excessive or unusual noise, and no muffler or exhaust system shall be equipped with a cutout, bypass, or similar device.

(b) Except as provided in Division 16.5 (commencing with Section 38000) with respect to off-highway motor vehicles subject to identification, every passenger vehicle operated off the highways shall at all times be equipped with an adequate muffler in constant operation and properly maintained so as to meet the requirements of Article 2.5 (commencing with Section 27200), and no muffler or exhaust system shall be equipped with a cutout, bypass, or similar device.

(c) The provisions of subdivision (b) shall not be applicable to passenger vehicles being operated off the highways in an organized racing or competitive event conducted under the auspices of a recognized sanctioning body or by permit issued by the local governmental authority having jurisdiction.
(Amended by Stats.1977, c. 579, p. —, § 188; Stats.1977, c. 558, § 1.)

§ 27150.1. Sale of exhaust systems; misdemeanor

On and after the effective date of regulations and standards adopted by the commissioner pursuant to Section 27150.2, no person engaged in a business which involves the selling of motor vehicle exhaust systems, or parts thereof, including, but not limited to, mufflers, shall offer for sale, sell, or install, a motor vehicle exhaust system, or part thereof, including, but not limited to, a muffler, unless it meets such regulations and standards.

A violation of this section shall constitute a misdemeanor.
(Amended by Stats.1973, c. 610, p. 1131, § 1.)

§ 27151. Modification of exhaust systems

No person shall modify the exhaust system of a motor vehicle in a manner which will amplify or increase the noise emitted by the motor of such vehicle, above that emitted by the muffler originally installed on the vehicle and the original muffler shall comply with all of the requirements of this chapter. No person shall operate a motor vehicle with an exhaust system so modified.
(Amended by Stats.1971, c. 503, p. 995, § 1, operative May 3, 1972.)

§ 27152. Exhaust pipes

The exhaust gases from a motor vehicle shall not be directed to the side of the vehicle between 2 feet and 11 feet above the ground.
(Stats.1959, c. 3, p. 1738, § 27152.)

§ 27153. Exhaust products

No motor vehicle shall be operated in a manner resulting in the escape of excessive smoke, flame, gas, oil, or fuel residue.

The provisions of this section apply to motor vehicles of the United States or its agencies, to the extent authorized by federal law.
(Amended by Stats.1971, c. 739, p. 1465, § 5, operative May 3, 1972.)

§ 27153.5. January 1, 1971, motor vehicle exhaust standards

(a) No motor vehicle first sold or registered as a new motor vehicle on or after January 1, 1971, shall discharge into the atmosphere at elevation of less than 4,000 feet any air contaminant for a period of more than 10 seconds which is:

(1) As dark or darker in shade as that designated as No. 1 on the Ringelmann Chart, as published by the United States Bureau of Mines, or

(2) Of such opacity as to obscure an observer's view to a degree equal to or greater than does smoke described in paragraph (1) of this subdivision.

(b) No motor vehicle first sold or registered prior to January 1, 1971, shall discharge into the atmosphere at elevation of less than 4,000 feet any air contaminant for a period of more than 10 seconds which is:

(1) As dark or darker in shade than that designated as No. 2 on the Ringelmann Chart, as published by the United States Bureau of Mines, or

(2) Of such opacity as to obscure an observer's view to a degree equal to or greater than does smoke described in paragraph (1) of this subdivision.

(c) The provisions of this section apply to motor vehicles of the United States or its agencies, to the extent authorized by federal law.
(Amended by Stats.1973, c. 216, p. 596, § 1.)

§ 27154. Gases and fumes

The cab of any motor vehicle shall be reasonably tight against the penetration of gases and fumes from the engine or exhaust system. The exhaust system, including the manifold, muffler, and exhaust pipes shall be so constructed as to be capable of being maintained and shall be maintained in a reasonably gastight condition.
(Stats.1959, c. 3, p. 1738, § 27154.)

§ 27156. Air pollution control devices

No person shall operate or leave standing upon any highway any motor vehicle which is required to be equipped with a motor vehicle pollution control device under Part 5 (commencing with Section 43000) of Division 26 of the Health and Safety Code or any other certified motor vehicle pollution control device required by any other state law or any rule or regulation adopted pursuant to such law, or required to be equipped with a motor vehicle pollution control device pursuant to the National Emission Standards Act (42 U.S.C., Secs. 1857f–1 to 1857f–7, inclusive) and the standards and regulations promulgated thereunder, unless the motor vehicle is equipped with the required motor vehicle pollution control device which is correctly installed and in operating condition. No person shall disconnect, modify, or alter any such required device.

No person shall install, sell, offer for sale, or advertise any device, apparatus, or mechanism intended for use with, or as a part of, any required motor vehicle pollution control device or system which alters or modifies the original design or performance of any such motor vehicle pollution control device or system.

When the court finds that a person has willfully violated this section, he shall be fined the maximum amount that may be imposed in the case, and no part of the fine may be suspended.

"Willfully," as used in this section, has the same meaning as the meaning of that word prescribed in Section 7 of the Penal Code.

No person shall operate a vehicle after notice by a traffic officer that such vehicle is not equipped with the required certified motor vehicle pollution control device correctly installed in operating condition, except as may be necessary to return the vehicle to the residence or place of business of the owner or driver or to a garage, until the vehicle has been properly equipped with such a device.

The notice to appear issued or complaint filed for a violation of this section shall require that the person to whom the notice to appear is issued or against whom the complaint is filed produce proof of correction pursuant to Section 40150 or proof of exemption pursuant to Section 4000.1 or 4000.2.

This section shall not apply to an alteration, modification, or modifying device, apparatus, or mechanism found by resolution of the State Air Resources Board either:

§ 27156

(1) To not reduce the effectiveness of any required motor vehicle pollution control device; or

(2) To result in emissions from any such modified or altered vehicle which are at levels which comply with existing state or federal standards for that model year of the vehicle being modified or converted.

The provisions of this section apply to motor vehicles of the United States or its agencies, to the extent authorized by federal law.
(Amended by Stats.1976, c. 231, p. —, § 7.)

§ 27304. Driver training vehicles

All vehicles owned and utilized in driver training by a driver training school licensed under the provisions of Chapter 1 (commencing with Section 11100) of Division 5 or in a course in automobile driver training in any secondary school maintained under the Education Code shall be equipped with a seatbelt for the driver and each passenger. Such seatbelt shall either comply with regulations adopted pursuant to Section 2402.5 or be of a type approved by the department.

It shall be unlawful for any driver or passenger to operate or ride in such a vehicle while it is being operated for the purposes of driver training, unless such person is utilizing an installed seatbelt in the proper manner.
(Amended by Stats.1972, c. 618, p. 1151, § 149.)

§ 27400. Wearing of headsets or earplugs

No person operating any motor vehicle shall wear any headset covering, or any earplugs in, both ears. The provisions of this section shall not apply to:

(a) Law enforcement personnel when on duty.

(b) Any person engaged in the operation of either special construction equipment or equipment for use in the maintenance of any highway.

(c) Any person engaged in the operation of refuse collection equipment who is wearing a safety headset or safety earplugs.
(Amended by Stats.1977, c. 348, p. —, § 1.)

§ 27450. Thickness of solid tire

When any vehicle is equipped with any solid tire, the solid tire shall have a minimum thickness of resilient rubber as follows:

(a) If the width of the tire is three inches but less than six inches, one inch thick.

(b) If the width of the tire is six inches but not more than nine inches, 1¼ inches thick.

(c) If the width of the tire is more than nine inches, 1½ inches thick.
(Stats.1959, c. 3, p. 1738, § 27450.)

§ 27451. Measurement of solid tire

The rubber of a solid tire shall be measured between the surface of the roadway and the nearest metal part of the base flange to which the tire is attached at the point where the concentrated weight of the vehicle bears upon the surface of the roadway.
(Stats.1959, c. 3, p. 1738, § 27451.)

§ 27452. Condition of solid tire

The required thickness of rubber shall extend evenly around the entire periphery of the tire. The entire solid tire shall be securely attached to the channel base and shall be without flat spots or bumpy rubber.
(Stats.1959, c. 3, p. 1739, § 27452.)

§ 27454. Protuberances on tires

No tire on any vehicle upon any state highway shall have on its periphery any block, stud, flange, cleat, ridge, bead, or any other protuberance of metal or wood which projects beyond the tread of the traction surface of the tire.

This section does not apply to the following:

(a) Tire chains of reasonable size used to prevent skidding when upon wet surfaces or when upon snow or ice.

(b) Pneumatic tires which have embedded therein wire not to exceed 0.075 of an inch in diameter and which are so constructed that under no conditions will the percentage of metal in contact with the roadway exceed 5 percent of the total tire area in contact with the roadway, except that during the first 1,000 miles of use or operation of any such tire, the metal in contact with the roadway may exceed 5 percent of the tire area in contact with the roadway, but shall in no event exceed 20 percent of such area.

(c) Vehicles operated upon unimproved roadways when necessary in the construction or repair of highways.

(d) Traction engines or tractors when operated under the conditions of a permit first obtained from the Department of Transportation.

(e) Pneumatic tires containing metal-type studs of tungsten carbide or other suitable material and which

are so inserted or constructed that under no conditions will the number of studs or the percentage of metal in contact with the roadway exceed 3 percent of the total tire area in contact with the roadway, between the first day of October and the first day of May. This subdivision shall remain in effect until May 1, 1981, and shall have no force or effect after that date.
(Amended by Stats.1978, c. 190, p. —, § 1.)

§ 27455. Inner tubes

(a) On and after January 1, 1975, no person shall sell or offer for sale an inner tube for use in a radial tire unless, at the time of manufacture, the tube valve stem is colored red or is distinctly marked in accordance with rules and regulations adopted by the department, taking into consideration the recommendations of manufacturers of inner tubes.

(b) No person shall install an inner tube in a radial tire unless the inner tube is designed for use in a radial tire.
(Added by Stats.1973, c. 741, p. 1338, § 1.)

§ 27459. Tire chains or snow-tread tires

No person shall operate any motor vehicle, trailer or semitrailer upon any portion of a highway without tire chains when such portion of the highway is signed for the requirement of such chains. In any case where a passenger vehicle or motortruck having an unladen weight of 6,000 pounds or less may be required by the Department of Transportation or local authorities to be equipped with tire chains such chains shall be placed on at least two drive wheels or, the department or local authorities may provide, in the alternative, that the vehicle may be equipped with snow-tread tires on at least two drive wheels when the weather and surface conditions at the time are such that the stopping, tractive, and cornering abilities of the tires are adequate. The snow-tread tires shall be of a type and design manufactured for use on ice and snow as a replacement for tire chains and shall be in good condition.
(Amended by Stats.1974, c. 591, p. 1411, § 1.)

§ 27459.5. Sale of tire chains

No person shall sell, offer for sale, lease, install, or replace on a vehicle for use on a highway, any tire chains which are not in compliance with regulations for tire chains adopted by the commissioner.
(Added by Stats.1974, c. 135, p. 272, § 2.)

§ 27460. Four-wheel drive vehicles

Any passenger vehicle or motortruck having an unladen weight of 6,500 pounds or less and operated and equipped with four-wheel drive and with snow-tread tires on all four drive wheels may be operated upon any portion of a highway without tire chains, notwithstanding the fact that such highway is signed for the requirement of chains and provided that tire chains for at least one set of drive wheels are carried in or upon such vehicle. The snow-tread tires shall meet the requirements specified in Section 27459 of this code, and such vehicle shall not, when so operated, tow another vehicle except as may be necessary to move a disabled vehicle from the roadway.

No person shall use such tires on four-wheel drive vehicles in place of tire chains whenever weather and roadway conditions at the time are such that the stopping, tractive and cornering abilities of the tires are not adequate or whenever the Department of Transportation or local authorities, in their respective jurisdictions, place signs prohibiting their operation unless equipped with tire chains.
(Amended by Stats.1974, c. 591, p. 1412, § 2.)

§ 27460.5. Sale of recut or regrooved tires

No person shall knowingly sell or offer or expose for sale any motor vehicle tire except a commercial vehicle tire, or any motor vehicle equipped with any tire except a commercial vehicle tire, which has been recut or regrooved. For purposes of this section a recut or regrooved tire is an unretreaded or unrecapped tire into which new grooves have been cut or burned.
(Added by Stats.1965, c. 1518, p. 3612, § 1.)

§ 27461. Use of recut or regrooved tires

No person shall cause or permit the operation of and no driver shall knowingly operate any motor vehicle except a commercial vehicle, on any street or highway, which is equipped with one or more recut or regrooved tires. For purposes of this section a recut or regrooved tire is an unretreaded or unrecapped tire into which new grooves have been cut or burned.
(Added by Stats.1965, c. 1518, p. 3612, § 2.)

§ 27465. Tread depth of pneumatic tires

(a) No dealer or person holding a retail seller's permit shall sell, offer for sale, expose for sale, or install on a vehicle axle for use on a highway, a pneumatic tire when the tire is so worn that less than one thirty-second ($\frac{1}{32}$) of an inch tread depth remains

§ 27465

in any two adjacent grooves at any location on the tire. This subdivision shall not apply to any person who installs on a vehicle, as part of an emergency service rendered to a disabled vehicle upon a highway, a spare tire with which such disabled vehicle was equipped.

(b) No person shall use on a highway a pneumatic tire on a vehicle axle when the tire is so worn that less than one thirty-second ($1/32$) of an inch tread depth remains in any two adjacent grooves at any location on the tire, except when temporarily installed on a disabled vehicle as specified in subdivision (a).

(c) The measurement of tread depth shall not be made where tie bars, humps, or fillets are located.

(d) The requirements of this section shall not apply to implements of husbandry.

(e) The department, if it determines that such action is appropriate and in keeping with reasonable safety requirements, may adopt regulations establishing more stringent tread depth requirements than those specified in this section for those vehicles defined in Sections 322, 323, and 545, and may adopt regulations establishing tread depth requirements different from those specified in this section for those vehicles listed in Section 34500.
(Amended by Stats.1977, c. 77, p. —, § 1, urgency, eff. May 26, 1977; Stats.1977, c. 733, p. —, § 1.)

§ 27500. Pneumatic tire standard regulations

(a) The department may adopt regulations relating to standards for pneumatic tires of a vehicle type as it determines necessary to provide for public safety.

(b) In adopting these regulations, the department shall consider as evidence of generally accepted standards, the rules and regulations which have been adopted by the Federal Highway Administration and Rubber Manufacturers Association.
(Amended by Stats.1970, c. 216, p. 469, § 3.)

§ 27501. Pneumatic tires which do not conform to regulations

(a) No dealer or person holding a retail seller's permit shall sell, offer for sale, expose for sale, or install on a vehicle for use on a highway, a pneumatic tire which is not in compliance with regulations adopted pursuant to Section 27500. This subdivision shall not apply to any person who installs on a vehicle, as part of an emergency service rendered to a vehicle upon a highway, a spare tire with which such disabled vehicle was equipped.

(b) No person shall use on a highway a pneumatic tire which is not in conformance with such regulations.
(Amended by Stats.1976, c. 70, p. —, § 3.)

§ 27600. Fenders and mudguards

No person shall operate any motor vehicle having three or more wheels, any trailer, or semitrailer unless equipped with fenders, covers, or devices, including flaps or splash aprons, or unless the body of the vehicle or attachments thereto afford adequate protection to effectively minimize the spray or splash of water or mud to the rear of the vehicle and all such equipment or such body or attachments thereto shall be at least as wide as the tire tread. This section does not apply to those vehicles exempt from registration, trailers and semitrailers having an unladen weight of under 1,500 pounds, or any vehicles manufactured and first registered prior to January 1, 1971, having an unladen weight of under 1,500 pounds.
(Amended by Stats.1970, c. 215, p. 468, § 1.)

§ 27601. Radiator ornaments

On and after January 1, 1939, no person shall sell any new motor vehicle, nor shall any person operate any motor vehicle sold as a new motor vehicle in this State after January 1, 1939, which is equipped with a radiator cap or radiator ornament upon the top thereof which extends or protrudes to the front of the face of the radiator grill of the motor vehicle.
(Stats.1959, c. 3, p. 1739, § 27601.)

§ 27602. Television

No person shall drive a motor vehicle which is equipped with a television receiver, screen, or other means of visually receiving a television broadcast which is located in the motor vehicle at any point forward of the back of the driver's seat, or which is visible to the driver while operating the motor vehicle.
(Stats.1959, c. 3, p. 1739, § 27602.)

§ 27700. Required equipment

Tow cars shall:

(a) Be equipped with one or more brooms, and the driver of the tow car engaged to remove a disabled vehicle from the scene of an accident shall remove all glass and debris deposited upon the roadway by the disabled vehicle which is to be towed.

(b) Be equipped with and carry a shovel, and whenever practical the tow car driver engaged to remove any disabled vehicle shall spread dirt upon that portion of the roadway where oil or grease has been deposited by such disabled vehicle.

(c) Be equipped with at least one fire extinguisher of the dry chemical or carbon dioxide type with an aggregate rating of at least 4–B, C units and bearing the approval of a laboratory nationally recognized as properly equipped to make such approval.
(Amended by Stats.1961, c. 529, p. 1632, § 1.)

§ 27800. **Passengers; equipment and usage**

It is unlawful for a driver of a motorcycle or a motorized bicycle to carry any other person thereon, except on a seat securely fastened to the machine at the rear of the driver and provided with footrests, or in a sidecar attached to a motorcycle and designed for the purpose of carrying a passenger. Every passenger on a motorcycle or a motorized bicycle shall keep his feet on the footrests while such vehicle is in motion.
(Amended by Stats.1978, c. 421, p. —, § 5.)

§ 27801. **Required position of equipment**

No person shall drive any two-wheel motorcycle:

(a) Equipped with a seat so positioned that the driver, when sitting astride the seat, cannot reach the ground with his feet.

(b) Equipped with handlebars so positioned that the hands of the driver, when upon the grips, are at or above his shoulder height when sitting astride the seat.
(Amended by Stats.1971, c. 207, p. 271, § 1.)

§ 27802. **Safety helmet regulations; motorcycles and motorized bicycles**

(a) The department shall adopt reasonable regulations establishing specifications and standards for safety helmets offered for sale, or sold, for use by drivers and passengers of motorcycles and motorized bicycles as it determines are necessary for the safety of such drivers and passengers. In developing the regulations, the department shall consider all standards which have been developed and adopted as a requirement by other states.

(b) No person shall sell, or offer for sale, for use by a driver or passenger of a motorcycle or motorized bicycle any safety helmet which is not of a type approved by the department.
(Amended by Stats.1977, c. 655, p. —, § 1.)

§ 28050. **True mileage driven**

It is unlawful for any person to advertise for sale, to sell, to use, or to install on any part of a motor vehicle or on an odometer in a motor vehicle any device which causes the odometer to register any mileage other than the true mileage driven. For the purposes of this section the true mileage driven is that mileage driven by the car as registered by the odometer within the manufacturer's designed tolerance.
(Added by Stats.1967, c. 1109, p. 2754, § 1.)

§ 28050.5. **Operation with nonfunctional odometer prohibited**

It is unlawful for any person with the intent to defraud to operate a motor vehicle on any street or highway knowing that the odometer of such vehicle is disconnected or nonfunctional.
(Added by Stats.1967, c. 1210, p. 2754, § 1.)

§ 28051. **Unlawful to alter indicated mileage**

It is unlawful for any person to disconnect, turn back, advance, or reset the odometer of any motor vehicle with the intent to alter the number of miles indicated on the odometer gauge.
(Amended by Stats.1973, c. 774, p. 1388, § 4.)

§ 28051.5. **Device to turn back or reset odometer**

It is unlawful for any person to advertise for sale, to sell, or to use, any device designed primarily for the purpose of turning back or resetting the odometer of any motor vehicle to reduce the number of miles indicated on the odometer gauge.
(Added by Stats.1970, c. 841, p. 1576, § 1.)

Division 13
TOWING AND LOADING EQUIPMENT

§ 28071. **Passenger vehicle bumper requirements**

Every passenger vehicle registered in this state shall be equipped with a front bumper and with a rear bumper. As used in this section, "bumper" means any device designed and intended by a manufacturer to prevent the front or rear of the body of the vehicle from coming into contact with any other motor vehicle. This section shall not apply to any passenger vehicle that is required to be equipped with an energy absorption system pursuant to either state or federal law, or to any passenger vehicle which was not equipped with a front or rear bumper, or both, at the time that it was first sold and registered under the laws of this or any other state or foreign jurisdiction.
(Amended by Stats.1973, c. 451, p. 917, § 1.)

§ 28080. **Camper passenger signaling device**

(a) Every motor vehicle upon which a camper is mounted shall be equipped with an audible or visual signaling device which can be activated from inside

§ 28080

the camper and which is constructed so as to allow any person inside the camper to gain the attention of the driver of the motor vehicle. In no event shall a horn, as required by Section 27000, be used to comply with this subdivision.

(b) No person shall drive a motor vehicle upon which is mounted a camper containing any passenger unless the motor vehicle is equipped as required by subdivision (a).
(Added by Stats.1973, c. 292, p. 700, § 1.)

§ 28081. When signaling device not required

The provisions of Section 28080 shall not apply to either of the following:

(a) Any motor vehicle upon which a camper is mounted if a person is able to move between the cab portion of the motor vehicle and the camper.

(b) Any motor vehicle upon which a camper is mounted, which motor vehicle is equipped with a sliding or removable rear window which can be opened or removed by a person inside such camper.
(Added by Stats.1973, c. 292, p. 700, § 1.)

§ 29003. Hitch, coupling device, or connection

(a) Every hitch or coupling device used as a means of attaching the towed and towing vehicles shall be properly and securely mounted and be structurally adequate for the weight drawn. The mounting of the hitch or coupling device on the towing and towed vehicle shall include sufficient reinforcement or bracing of the frame to provide sufficient strength and rigidity to prevent undue distortion of the frame.

(b) The drawbar, tongue, or other connection between the towing and towed vehicles shall be securely attached and structurally adequate for the weight drawn.
(Added by Stats.1969, c. 338, p. 712, § 5.)

§ 29004. Towed vehicle

(a) Every towed vehicle shall be coupled to the towing vehicle by means of a safety chain, cable, or equivalent device in addition to the regular drawbar, tongue or other connection.

(b) All safety connections and attachments shall be of sufficient strength to control the towed vehicle in event of failure of the regular hitch, coupling device, drawbar, tongue or other connection.

(c) No more slack shall be left in a safety chain, cable or equivalent device than is necessary to permit proper turning. When a drawbar, as defined in Section 300, is used as the towing connection, the safety chain, cable or equivalent device shall be connected to the towed and towing vehicle and to the drawbar so as to prevent the drawbar from dropping to the ground if the drawbar fails.

(d) The requirement of subdivision (a) does not apply to a semitrailer having a connecting device composed of a fifth wheel and kingpin assembly, nor to a towed motor vehicle when steered by a person who holds a license for the type of vehicle being towed.
(Added by Stats.1969, c. 338, p. 712, § 7.)

§ 29005. Drawbar length

When one vehicle is towing another, the drawbar or other connection shall not exceed 15 feet.
(Added by Stats.1961, c. 58, p. 1012, § 50.1.)

§ 29006. Coupling of towed vehicles

(a) No person shall operate a vehicle towing another motor vehicle upon a freeway unless the towing vehicle is coupled to the towed vehicle by a rigid structure attached securely to both vehicles by nonrigid means.

(b) The requirements of subdivision (a) are not applicable to a vehicle towing a motor vehicle which has been disabled and is being towed from the point of disablement to the nearest and most accessible exit from the freeway.
(Added by Stats.1970, c. 334, p. 731, § 1.)

Division 14
TRANSPORTATION OF EXPLOSIVES

Division 14.5
TRANSPORTATION OF RADIOACTIVE MATERIALS

Division 14.7
FLAMMABLE LIQUIDS

Division 14.8
SAFETY REGULATIONS

Division 14.9
MOTOR VEHICLE DAMAGE CONTROL

§ 34715. Energy-absorption system

No new passenger vehicle, except a passenger vehicle certified by its manufacturer as having been

manufactured prior to September 1, 1973, shall be sold or registered on and after September 1, 1973, unless it has a manufacturer's warranty that it is equipped with an appropriate energy-absorption system that meets the requirement for energy absorption systems set by the National Highway Traffic Safety Administration.
(Amended by Stats.1977, c. 880, p. —, § 2.)

Division 15

SIZE, WEIGHT, AND LOAD

§ 35100. Total outside width; exceptions

(a) The total outside width of any vehicle or the load thereon shall not exceed 96 inches, except as otherwise provided in this chapter.

(b) Notwithstanding the provisions of subdivision (a), the total outside width of any load on a vehicle may exceed a width of 96 inches but shall not exceed a width of 100 inches, except as otherwise provided in this chapter.

(c) The amendments to this section enacted at the 1973–74 Regular Session of the Legislature increasing the permissible width of loads from 96 to 100 inches shall have no application to highways which are a part of the national system of interstate and defense highways (as referred to in Section 108 of the Federal Aid Highway Act of 1956) when such application would prevent this state from receiving any federal funds for highway purposes, and in such event the provisions of law applicable to the maximum permissible width of any such load in effect on December 31, 1974, shall remain applicable to such load.
(Amended by Stats.1974, c. 972, p. 2022, § 1.)

§ 35250. Maximum height; exceptions

No vehicle shall exceed a height of 13 feet and 6 inches measured from the surface upon which the vehicle stands, except as follows:

(a) The boom or mast of a forklift truck may not exceed a height of 14 feet.

(b) A double-deck bus may not exceed a height of 14 feet, 3 inches. Any double-deck bus which exceeds a height of 13 feet, 6 inches shall only be operated on those highways where such operation is deemed to be safe by the entity operating the bus.
(Amended by Stats.1975, c. 240, p. 630, § 1.)

§ 35400. General limitations

Text of section operative until January 1, 1980

(a) No vehicle shall exceed a length of 40 feet.

(b) This section does not apply to:

(1) A vehicle used in a combination of vehicles when the excess length is caused by auxiliary parts, equipment, or machinery not used as space to carry any part of the load, except that the combination of vehicles shall not exceed the length provided for combination vehicles.

(2) A vehicle when the excess length is caused by any parts necessary to comply with the fender and mudguard regulations of this code.

(3) An articulated bus, except that such bus shall not exceed a length of 60 feet.

(4) An articulated trolley coach, except that such trolley coach shall not exceed a length of 50 feet.

(5) A semitrailer while being towed by a motortruck or truck tractor, if the distance from the kingpin to the rearmost axle of the semitrailer does not exceed 38 feet; provided, that the semitrailer does not, exclusive of attachments, extend forward of the rear of the cab of the motortruck or truck tractor.

(6) A bus when the excess length is caused by the projection of a front safety bumper or a rear safety bumper, or both. Such safety bumper shall not cause the length of the vehicle to exceed the maximum legal limit by more than one foot in the front and one foot in the rear. For the purposes of this chapter, "safety bumper" means any device which may be fitted on an existing bumper or which replaces the bumper and is so constructed, treated, or manufactured so that it absorbs energy upon impact.

(7) A bus when the excess length is caused by a device, located in front of the front axle, for lifting wheelchairs into the bus. Such a device shall not cause the length of the bus to be extended by more than 18 inches exclusive of any front safety bumper.

(8) A vehicle designed and used exclusively for drilling water wells, except that such vehicle shall not exceed a length of 48 feet. The provisions of this paragraph shall only apply to such vehicles when operated upon highways within counties wherein the governing board has declared that a drought condition exists and that a severe underground water shortage condition exists. The provisions of this paragraph shall apply only to those vehicles operating under permit on the date the amendment to this

section at the 1977–78 Regular Session of the Legislature became operative.

This section shall remain in effect only until January 1, 1980, and as of that date is repealed. (Amended by Stats.1978, c. 64, p. —, § 1.)

§ 35401. Combinations of vehicles

(a) Except as provided in subdivision (b), no combination of vehicles coupled together, including any attachments thereto, shall exceed a total length of 65 feet.

(b) The following combinations of vehicles coupled together, including any attachments thereto, shall not exceed a total length of 60 feet:

(1) A truck tractor and semitrailer.

(2) A truck tractor, auxiliary dolly and semitrailer.

(3) A motortruck and semitrailer, if the pivot point of the semitrailer connection is less than two feet to the rear of the center of the rearmost axle of the motortruck, or the distance from the pivot point to the center of the rearmost axle of the semitrailer exceeds 34 feet.

(c) Any city or county may, by ordinance, prohibit a combination of vehicles of a total length in excess of 60 feet upon highways under their respective jurisdiction. Such an ordinance shall not be effective until appropriate signs are erected indicating either the streets affected by the ordinance or the streets not affected, as the local authorities determine will best serve to give notice of the ordinance.

The Legislature in enacting this section does not intend to reduce, and this section shall not be construed to reduce, any maximum total length of any combination of vehicles permitted under the statutes as they existed on January 1, 1974. (Added by Stats.1974, c. 479, p. 1111, § 2.)

§ 35410. Projections to the rear

The load upon any motor vehicle alone or an independent load only upon a trailer or semitrailer shall not extend to the rear beyond the last point of support for a greater distance than that equal to two-thirds of the length of the wheelbase of the vehicle carrying such load, except that the wheelbase of a semitrailer shall be considered as the distance between the rearmost axle of the towing vehicle and the rearmost axle of the semitrailer. (Stats.1959, c. 3, p. 1761, § 35410.)

§ 35413. Tires on front of vehicles

No person shall drive a motor vehicle upon a highway with any tire fastened in front of the vehicle, unless such tire is securely mounted in a tire carrier firmly attached to the vehicle in a manner approved and specified by the California Highway Patrol. (Amended by Stats.1961, c. 155, p. 1161, § 1.)

Division 16
IMPLEMENTS OF HUSBANDRY
Division 16.5
OFF–HIGHWAY VEHICLES

Editors' Note

The Off-Highway Vehicle Division established laws regulating the use and operation of off-road vehicles including jeeps, motorcycles and dune buggies. Such vehicles must be issued an identification number. A separate set of "rules of the road" has been enacted. Off-road vehicle equipment standards have also been established. Only the major provisions of this Division have been included in this volume.

§ 38280. Federal, state, and local authority

Federal, state, or local authorities having jurisdiction over public lands may place or cause to be placed and maintained, such appropriate signs, signals and other traffic control devices as may be necessary to properly indicate and carry out any provision of law or any duly adopted regulation of such governmental authority or to warn or guide traffic. (Added by Stats.1976, c. 1093, p. —, § 26.)

§ 38300. Unlawful to disobey sign, signal, or traffic control device

It is unlawful for the driver of any vehicle to disobey any sign, signal, or traffic control device placed or maintained pursuant to Section 38280. (Added by Stats.1976, c. 1093, p. —, § 26.)

§ 38301. Unlawful to violate special regulations

It is unlawful to operate a vehicle in violation of special regulations which have been promulgated by the governmental agency having jurisdiction over public lands, including, but not limited to, regulations governing access, routes of travel, plants, wildlife, wildlife habitat, water resources, and historical sites. (Added by Stats.1976, c. 1093, p. —, § 26.)

§ 38302. Unlawful to place unauthorized signs

It is unlawful for any person to place or erect any sign, signal, or traffic control device for off-highway traffic upon public lands unless authorized by law.
(Added by Stats.1976, c. 1093, p. —, § 26.)

§ 38304. Ability to reach and operate controls

The operator of an off-highway motor vehicle shall be able to reach and operate all controls necessary to safely operate the vehicle.
(Added by Stats.1976, c. 1093, p. —, § 26.)

§ 38305. Basic speed law

No person shall drive an off-highway motor vehicle at a speed greater than is reasonable or prudent and in no event at a speed which endangers the safety of other persons or property.
(Added by Stats.1976, c. 1093, p. —, § 26.)

§ 38310. Prima facie speed limit

The prima facie speed limit within 50 feet of any campground, campsite, or concentration of people or animals shall be 15 miles per hour unless changed as authorized by this code and, if so changed, only when signs have been erected giving notice thereof.
(Added by Stats.1976, c. 1093, p. —, § 26.)

§ 38312. Starting parked vehicles

No person shall place in motion an off-highway motor vehicle that is stopped, standing, or parked until such movement can be made with reasonable safety.
(Added by Stats.1976, c. 1093, p. —, § 26.)

§ 38314. Turning movements

No person shall turn an off-highway motor vehicle from a direct course or move right or left until such movement can be made with reasonable safety.
(Added by Stats.1976, c. 1093, p. —, § 26.)

§ 38316. Reckless driving

(a) It is unlawful for any person to drive any off-highway motor vehicle with a willful and wanton disregard for the safety of other persons or property.

(b) Any person who violates this section shall, upon conviction thereof, be punished by imprisonment in the county jail for not less than five days nor more than 90 days or by fine of not less than twenty-five dollars ($25) nor more than two hundred fifty dollars ($250) or by both such fine and imprisonment, except as provided in Section 38317.
(Added by Stats.1976, c. 1093, p. —, § 26.)

§ 38317. Reckless driving causing bodily injury

Whenever reckless driving of an off-highway motor vehicle proximately causes bodily injury to any person, the person driving the vehicle shall, upon conviction thereof, be punished by imprisonment in the county jail for not less than 30 days nor more than six months or by fine of not less than one hundred dollars ($100) nor more than five hundred dollars ($500) or by both such fine and imprisonment.
(Added by Stats.1976, c. 1093, p. —, § 26.)

§ 38318. Throwing substances at off-highway motor vehicles

(a) Any person who throws any substance at an off-highway motor vehicle or occupant thereof is guilty of a misdemeanor.

(b) Any person who with intent to do great bodily injury maliciously and willfully throws or projects any rock, brick, bottle, metal, or other missile or projects any other substance capable of doing serious bodily harm or discharges a firearm at such vehicle or occupant thereof is guilty of a felony and upon conviction shall be punished by imprisonment for not less than one year nor more than five years in the state prison.
(Added by Stats.1976, c. 1093, p. —, § 26.)

§ 38318.5. Malicious placement of cable, chain, or rope

Any person who, with intent to do great bodily injury, erects or places any cable, chain, rope, fishing line or other similar material which is unmarked, or intentionally placed, or both, for malicious purpose is guilty of a felony and upon conviction thereof shall be punished by imprisonment for not less than one year nor more than five years in the state prison.
(Added by Stats.1976, c. 1093, p. —, § 26.)

§ 38319. Operation causing damage

No person shall operate, nor shall an owner permit the operation of, an off-highway motor vehicle in a manner likely to cause malicious or unnecessary damage to the land, wildlife, wildlife habitat or vegetative resources.
(Added by Stats.1976, c. 1093, p. —, § 26.)

§ 38320. Throwing, depositing, or dumping matter

(a) No person shall throw or deposit, nor shall the registered owner or the driver, if such owner is not

§ 38320

then present in the vehicle, aid or abet in the throwing or depositing, upon any area, public or private, any bottle, can, garbage, glass, nail, offal, paper, wire, any substance likely to injure or kill wild or domestic animal or plant life or damage traffic using such area, or any noisome, nauseous or offensive matter of any kind.

(b) No person shall place, deposit or dump, or cause to be placed, deposited or dumped, any rocks or dirt in or upon any area, public or private, without the consent of the property owner or public agency having jurisdiction over the area.

(c) Any person who violates this section shall, upon conviction thereof, be punished by a fine of not less than twenty-five dollars ($25). No part of such fine shall be suspended. The court may permit the fine required by this section to be paid in installments if the court determines that the defendant is unable to pay the fine in one lump sum.
(Added by Stats.1976, c. 1093, p. —, § 26.)

§ 38321. Removal of material

(a) Any person who drops, dumps, deposits, places, or throws, or causes or permits to be dropped, dumped, deposited, placed, or thrown, upon any area, any material described in Section 38320, shall immediately remove the material or cause it to be removed.

(b) If such person fails to comply with the provisions of this section, the governmental agency responsible for the maintenance of the area, or the property owner of the land on which the material has been deposited, may remove such material and collect, by civil action, if necessary, the actual cost of the removal operation in addition to any other damages authorized by law from the person who did not comply with the requirements of this section.
(Added by Stats.1976, c. 1093, p. —, § 26.)

Division 16.7

REGISTRATION AND LICENSING OF BICYCLES

Editors' Note

This Division provides authorization for local government to license and register bicycles and forms the basis for the development of record systems to assist in the recovery and return of stolen bicycles. Specific sections are not included in this volume.

Division 17

OFFENSES AND PROSECUTION

§ 40000.1. Infractions

Except as otherwise provided in this article, it is unlawful and constitutes an infraction for any person to violate, or fail to comply with any provision of this code, or any local ordinance adopted pursuant to this code.
(Added by Stats.1971, c. 1178, p. 2245, § 3.)

§ 40000.3. Felonies and offenses punishable either as felonies or misdemeanor violation of court order punishable as contempt

A violation expressly declared to be a felony, or a public offense which is punishable, in the discretion of the court, either as a felony or misdemeanor, or a willful violation of a court order which is punishable as contempt pursuant to subdivision (a) of Section 42003, is not an infraction.
(Amended by Stats.1973, c. 1162, p. 2419, § 1.5.)

§ 40000.5. Misdemeanors

A violation of any of the following provisions shall constitute a misdemeanor, and not an infraction:

Section 20, relating to false statements.

Section 27, relating to impersonating a member of the California Highway Patrol.

Section 31, relating to giving false information.

Paragraph (4) of subdivision (a), or subdivision (b), or both, of Section 221, relating to proper evidence of clearance for dismantling.
(Amended by Stats.1976, c. 937, p. —, § 3.)

§ 40000.7. Misdemeanors

A violation of any of the following provisions shall constitute a misdemeanor, and not an infraction:

Section 2416, relating to regulations for emergency vehicles.

Section 2800, relating to failure to obey an officer's lawful order or submit to a lawful inspection.

Section 2800.1, relating to fleeing from a peace officer.

Section 2801, relating to failure to obey a fireman's lawful order.

Section 2803, relating to unlawful vehicle or load.

Section 2815, relating to failure to obey a crossing guard's traffic signal or direction.

Section 5753, relating to delivery of certificates of ownership and registration when committed by a dealer or any person while a dealer within the preceding 12 months.

Section 5901, relating to dealers and lessor-retailers giving notice.

Section 5901.1, relating to lessors giving notice and failure to pay fee.

Section 8803, relating to return of canceled, suspended, or revoked documents and license plates of a dealer, manufacturer, transporter, dismantler or salesman.
(Amended by Stats.1978, c. 272, p. —, § 3.)

§ 40000.8. Misdemeanors

A violation of any of the following provisions shall constitute a misdemeanor, and not an infraction:

Chapter 2 (commencing with Section 9850), Division 3.5, relating to the registration of vessels.
(Added by Stats.1972, c. 618, p. 1151, § 152.)

§ 40000.9. Misdemeanors

A violation of any of the following provisions shall constitute a misdemeanor, and not an infraction:

Section 10501, relating to false report of vehicle theft.

Sections 10750 and 10751, relating to altered or defaced vehicle identifying numbers.

Section 10851.5, relating to theft of binder chains.

Sections 10852 and 10853, relating to injuring or tampering with a vehicle.

Section 10854, relating to unlawful use of stored vehicle.
(Added by Stats.1971, c. 1178, p. 2246, § 7.)

§ 40000.11. Misdemeanors

A violation of any of the following provisions shall constitute a misdemeanor, and not an infraction:

Division 5 (commencing with Section 11100), relating to occupational licensing and business regulations.

Section 12500, subdivision (a), relating to unlicensed drivers.

Section 12951, subdivision (b), relating to refusal to display license.

Section 13004, relating to unlawful use of identification card.

Section 14601, relating to driving when suspended.

Section 14601.1, relating to driving when suspended.

Section 14610, relating to unlawful use of driver's license.

Section 15501, relating to use of false or fraudulent license by minor.
(Added by Stats.1971, c. 1178, p. 2246, § 8.)

§ 40000.13. Misdemeanors

A violation of any of the following provisions shall constitute a misdemeanor, and not an infraction:

Section 16560, relating to interstate highway carriers.

Section 20002, relating to duties at accidents.
(Added by Stats.1971, c. 1178, p. 2246, § 9.)

§ 40000.15. Misdemeanors

A violation of any of the following provisions shall constitute a misdemeanor, and not an infraction:

Section 23102, relating to driving under the influence.

Sections 23103 and 23104, relating to reckless driving.

Section 23105, relating to driving under the influence.

Section 23109, relating to speed contests or exhibitions.

Section 23110, subdivision (a), relating to throwing at vehicles.

Section 23253, relating to officers on vehicular crossings.

Section 23332, relating to trespassing.

Section 27150.1, relating to sale of exhaust systems.
(Amended by Stats.1973, c. 1162, p. 2420, § 6.)

§ 40000.19. Misdemeanors

A violation of any of the following provisions shall constitute a misdemeanor, and not an infraction:

Division 14 (commencing with Section 31600), relating to transportation of explosives.

Division 14.5 (commencing with Section 33000), relating to transportation of radioactive materials.

Division 14.7 (commencing with Section 34001), relating to flammable liquids.
(Added by Stats.1971, c. 1178, p. 2247, § 11.)

§ 40000.21. Misdemeanors

A violation of any of the following provisions shall constitute a misdemeanor, and not an infraction:

(a) Section 34506, subdivision (a), relating to the hours of service of drivers.

(b) Section 34506, subdivision (b), relating to the transportation of hazardous materials.

(c) Section 34506, subdivision (c), relating to schoolbuses.

(Amended by Stats.1977, c. 406, p. ——, § 14, urgency, eff. Aug. 27, 1977.)

§ 40000.23. Misdemeanors

A violation of any of the following provisions shall constitute a misdemeanor, and not an infraction:

Chapter 5 (commencing with Section 35550), Division 15, relating to weight restrictions, except in cases of weight violations where the amount of excess weight is less than 4,501 pounds.
(Added by Stats.1971, c. 1178, p. 2247, § 13.)

§ 40000.24. Misdemeanors

A violation of any of the following provisions shall constitute a misdemeanor and not an infraction:

Section 38316, relating to reckless driving.

Section 38317, relating to reckless driving with injury.

Section 38319, relating to protection of the environment.

Section 38320, relating to the depositing of matter.
(Added by Stats.1976, c. 1093, p. ——, § 29.)

§ 40000.25. Misdemeanors

A violation of any of the following provisions shall constitute a misdemeanor, and not an infraction:

Section 40005, relating to owner's responsibility.

Section 40504, relating to false signatures.

Section 40508, relating to failure to appear or to pay fine.

Section 40519, relating to failure to appear.

Section 40614, relating to use of a fictitious name.

Section 40616, relating to a willful violation of a notice to correct.

Section 42005, relating to failure to attend traffic school.
(Amended by Stats.1978, c. 1350, p. ——, § 1.)

§ 40001. Owner's responsibility

(a) It is unlawful for the owner, or any other person, employing or otherwise directing the driver of any vehicle to cause the operation of the vehicle upon a highway in any manner contrary to law.

(b) It is unlawful for an owner to request, cause, or permit the operation of any vehicle:

(1) Which is not registered or for which any fee has not been paid under this code.

(2) Which is not equipped as required in this code.

(3) Which does not comply with the size, weight, or load provisions of this code.

(4) Which does not comply with the regulations promulgated pursuant to this code, or with applicable city or county ordinances adopted pursuant to this code.

(5) Which is not in compliance with the provisions of Chapter 4 (commencing with Section 39080) of Division 26 of the Health and Safety Code and the rules and regulations of the Motor Vehicle Pollution Control Board and the State Air Resources Board.

Whenever the owner or lessee is prosecuted for a violation pursuant to the provisions of this section the court may, on the request of the owner or lessee, take appropriate steps to make the driver of the vehicle, or any other person who directs the loading, maintenance or operation of the vehicle, a codefendant.

In the event such codefendant is held solely responsible and found guilty, the court may dismiss the charge against the owner or lessee.
(Amended by Stats.1968, c. 49, p. 197, § 15.)

§ 40002. Prosecution of persons owning or controlling vehicles

(a) Whenever a written notice to appear has been mailed to an owner of a vehicle or other person referred to in Section 40001, an exact and legible duplicate copy of the notice when filed with the magistrate, in lieu of a verified complaint, shall constitute a complaint to which the defendant may plead "guilty."

If, however, the defendant fails to appear in court or does not deposit lawful bail, or pleads other than "guilty" of the offense charged, a complaint shall be filed which shall conform to the provisions of Chapter 2 (commencing with Section 948) of Title 5, Part 2 of the Penal Code, and which shall be deemed to be an original complaint, and thereafter proceedings shall be had as provided by law, except that a defendant may, by an agreement in writing, subscribed by him and filed with the court, waive the filing of a verified complaint and elect that the prosecution may proceed upon a written notice to appear.

(b) A warrant of arrest shall not issue against an owner of a vehicle or other person referred to in Section 40001 following the filing of a complaint for an offense under that section if the owner or person was not driving the vehicle involved unless he is given notice of the offense against him and is informed that unless he appears in the court designated in the notice within 10 days after service of the notice and answers the charge, a warrant or citation to appear will be issued against him. The notice shall be given as prescribed by Section 22.
(Amended by Stats.1963, c. 1322, p. 2843, § 2.)

§ 40003. Prosecution of employees

Whenever an employee is prosecuted for a violation of any provision of this code, or regulations promulgated pursuant to this code, relating to the size, weight, registration, equipment, or loading of a vehicle while operating a vehicle he was employed to operate, and which is owned by his employer, the court shall on the request of the employee take appropriate proceedings to make the owner of the vehicle a codefendant. In the event it is found that the employee had reasonable grounds to believe that the vehicle operated by him as an employee did not violate such provisions, and in the event the owner is found guilty under the provisions of Section 40001, the court may dismiss the charges against the employee.

In those cases in which the charges against the employee are dismissed, the abstract of the record of the court required by Section 1803 shall clearly indicate that such charges were dismissed and that the owner of the vehicle was found guilty under Section 40001.
(Amended by Stats.1967, c. 819, p. 2245, § 1.)

§ 40004. Period for commencement of criminal actions

(a) The period for commencing criminal action against any person having filed or caused to be filed any false, fictitious, altered, forged or counterfeit document with the Department of Motor Vehicles or the Department of the California Highway Patrol shall, if the offense is a misdemeanor, expire one year from time of discovery of such act.

(b) The period for commencing criminal action against any person having filed or caused to be filed any false, fictitious, altered, forged or counterfeit document with the Department of Motor Vehicles or the Department of the California Highway Patrol shall, if the offense is a felony, expire three years from time of discovery of such act.

(c) The time allowed for commencing criminal proceedings as provided in subdivisions (a) and (b) of this section shall not extend beyond five years from the date of commission of the act.
(Added by Stats.1968, c. 1192, p. 2262, § 12.)

§ 40005. Employer's failure

Whenever a driver is cited for a violation of any provision of this code, or regulations promulgated pursuant to this code, relating to the size, weight, equipment, registration, fees, or loading of a vehicle, while operating a vehicle he was employed or otherwise directed to operate, and which is not owned by him, and the driver gives the citation to the owner or any other person referred to in Section 40001, if the owner or other person undertakes to answer the charge or otherwise to cause its disposition without any further action by the driver and then fails to act in accordance with the undertaking as a consequence of which a warrant is issued for the arrest of the driver, the owner or other person is guilty of a misdemeanor.
(Added by Stats.1965, c. 294, p. 1292, § 1.)

§ 40150. Proof of correction

Whenever any vehicle or combination of vehicles is found to be in an unsafe mechanical condition or is not equipped as required by this code, and a notice to appear is issued or a complaint filed for such violation, the notice to appear or the complaint may require that the person to whom the notice to appear is issued or against whom the complaint is filed shall produce in court satisfactory evidence that the vehicle or its equipment has been made to conform with the requirements of this code.
(Amended by Stats.1961, c. 1728, p. 3738, § 1.)

§ 40151. Lighting equipment

(a) Whenever any lighting equipment or device is not of a type approved by the Department of the California Highway Patrol, the officer making the inspection shall direct the driver to remove the lighting equipment or device within 24 hours.

§ 40151

(b) Whenever any lighting equipment or device is a type approved by the department but by reason of faulty adjustment or otherwise fails to comply with this code, the officer making the inspection shall direct the driver to make it comply with this code within 48 hours.
(Stats.1959, c. 3, p. 1774, § 40151.)

§ 40300. Application of chapter

The provisions of this chapter shall govern all peace officers in making arrests for violations of this code without a warrant for offenses committed in their presence, but the procedure prescribed herein shall not otherwise be exclusive of any other method prescribed by law for the arrest and prosecution of a person for an offense of like grade.
(Stats.1959, c. 3, p. 1774, § 40300.)

§ 40300.5. Arrest without warrant

Notwithstanding any other provision of law, a peace officer may, without a warrant, arrest a person involved in a traffic accident when the officer has reasonable cause to believe that such person had been driving while under the influence of intoxicating liquor or any drug, or under the combined influence of intoxicating liquor and any drug.
(Amended by Stats.1977, c. 16, p. —, § 1.)

§ 40301. Procedure

Except as provided in this chapter, whenever a person is arrested for any violation of this code declared to be a felony, he shall be dealt with in like manner as upon arrest for the commission of any other felony.
(Stats.1959, c. 3, p. 1774, § 40301.)

§ 40302. Mandatory appearance

Whenever any person is arrested for any violation of this code, not declared to be a felony, the arrested person shall be taken without unnecessary delay before a magistrate within the county in which the offense charged is alleged to have been committed and who has jurisdiction of the offense and is nearest or most accessible with reference to the place where the arrest is made in any of the following cases:

(a) When the person arrested fails to present his driver's license or other satisfactory evidence of his identity for examination.

(b) When the person arrested refuses to give his written promise to appear in court.

(c) When the person arrested demands an immediate appearance before a magistrate.

(d) When the person arrested is charged with violating Section 23102 or 23105.
(Amended by Stats.1971, c. 1530, p. 3028, § 21.)

Editors' Note

This section requires that the violator of specified conditions be taken before a magistrate. In addition, case law has limited searches to officer safety transportation pat downs under the conditions outlined in a, b and c of this section.

Notes of Decisions

Identity

Police officer was justified in stopping automobile at 10:30 p. m. because of missing front license plate and front headlight and asking driver to produce his license or other identification and vehicle registration; the driver was properly detained when he failed to present for examination his driver's license or other satisfactory evidence of his identity. People v. Peffer (App.1972), 103 Cal.Rptr. 16.

Social security card was not satisfactory evidence of identity of driver under this section where such card on its face bears a number, name and signature but no description of or information concerning the holder, and where it also contains on its face a statement that the card is for social security and tax purposes and is not for identification. People v. Farley (1971) 98 Cal.Rptr. 89, 20 C.A.3d 1032.

Arrest

Where person arrested for traffic violation not amounting to a felony is taken into custody for transportation before a magistrate, either under § 40303 giving officer option to follow such procedure or under this section making such procedure mandatory, arrestee must be transported directly to a magistrate or to one of the other officials listed in the § 40307 and must immediately be released on bail or written promise to appear, and cannot lawfully be subjected to the routine booking process used in the case of a nontraffic misdemeanant. People v. Superior Court of Los Angeles County (1972), 101 Cal.Rptr. 837, 496 P.2d 1205, 7 C.3d 186.

Although defendant arrested following vehicle inspection when it was determined that there were outstanding city warrants had right to post bail, search of defendant's purse during booking procedure was not illegal inasmuch as it appeared that defendant did not have enough money on her person to post bail and some detention would have been necessary before defendant could arrange bail. People v. Rhodes (1972) 100 Cal.Rptr. 487, 23 C.A.3d 257.

Where defendant, although originally stopped on traffic violation, was subsequently observed by officer, after her vehicle had been stopped, to do very poorly on several coordination and reaction tests although officer was unable to detect any odor of alcohol about defendant's person, officer had probable cause to arrest defendant for driving under influence of a narcotic and subsequent routine search of defendant's person at jail by matrons who discovered three plastic bags containing seconal and amphetamine pills was neither unreasonable nor unlawful. People v. Munsey (1971) 95 Cal.Rptr. 811, 18 C.A.3d 440.

Searches and seizures

Defendant arrested on a warrant for a traffic offense may not be booked or searched until he has been given an opportunity to post bail, but when he has been given an opportunity and it appears that he cannot post bail, he may then be booked and searched since, in the absence of bail, he must be placed in jail pursuant to the warrant. People v. Collin (1973) 110 Cal.Rptr. 869, 35 C.A.3d 416.

Where officer stopped vehicle for minor vehicle infraction, driver presented no identification and no evidence of registration and none was found in vehicle, officer suspected vehicle was stolen, passenger was uncooperative and gave evasive answer when officer asked him driver's name and encounter took place at 10:30 in the evening, officer, who harbored fearful anxiety for his own safety, was justified in asking passenger to alight from vehicle and in conducting pat down search; fact that officer had not ascertained whether vehicle was stolen was not significant as a search for weapons was properly made whether or not he had probable cause to arrest. People v. Peffer (App.1972), 103 Cal.Rptr. 16.

Where defendant, while operating an automobile, was stopped for equipment violation and officer took him into custody for transportation before a magistrate upon his failure to produce identification or registration for the car, search of defendant could not be justified as an incident to officer's decision to take defendant before a magistrate. People v. Superior Court of Los Angeles County (1972) 101 Cal.Rptr. 837, 496 P.2d 1205, 7 C.3d 186.

Where a person arrested for a traffic violation not amounting to a felony is taken into custody for purposes of transportation before a magistrate, he cannot be searched as an incident of that procedure, either in the field or at a police station; disapproving Morel v. Superior Court, 10 Cal.App.3d 913, 89 Cal.Rptr. 297, and its progeny. Id.

Warrantless search of automobile which defendant had been driving at time he was arrested for driving with no license in his possession, officer's opening of unlocked attache case found lying on rear seat of automobile and seizure of marijuana found within the case could not be justified either on theory that officers had authority to inventory contents of vehicle as part of impound procedure or on theory that there was reasonable cause to search automobile as incident to arrest of defendant. People v. Denman (1971) 97 Cal.Rptr. 23, 19 C.A.3d 632.

Where defendant, properly arrested for running red light, was capable of moving his automobile and no reason appeared why he could not have taken charge of his own vehicle and driven under direction of officer to nearby place of safekeeping before he was taken before magistrate, police custodial care of defendant's vehicle, whose contents were inventoried and whose trunk was found to contain unlocked suitcase carrying plastic bag of marijuana was neither necessary nor proper and evidence discovered in such illegal search was properly suppressed. People v. Nagel (1971) 95 Cal.Rptr. 129, 17 C.A.3d 492.

§ 40303. Optional appearance before a magistrate

Whenever any person is arrested for any of the following offenses and the arresting officer is not required to take the person without unnecessary delay before a magistrate, the arrested person shall, in the judgment of the arresting officer, either be given a 10 days' notice to appear as herein provided or be taken without unnecessary delay before a magistrate within the county in which the offense charged is alleged to have been committed and who has jurisdiction of the offense and is nearest or most accessible with reference to the place where the arrest is made.

(a) Section 10852 or 10853, relating to injuring or tampering with a vehicle.

(b) Section 23103 or 23104, relating to reckless driving.

(c) Section 2800, insofar as it relates to a failure or refusal of the driver of a vehicle to stop and submit to an inspection or test of the lights upon the vehicle under Section 2804 hereof, which is punishable as a misdemeanor.

(d) Section 2800, insofar as it relates to a failure or refusal of the driver of a vehicle to stop and submit to a brake test which is punishable as a misdemeanor.

(e) Section 2800, relating to the refusal to submit vehicle and load to an inspection, measurement, or weighing as prescribed in Section 2802 or a refusal to adjust the load or obtain a permit as prescribed in Section 2803.

(f) Section 20002, relating to failure to stop in the event of an accident involving damage to property.

(g) Section 23109, relating to participating in speed contests or exhibition of speed.

(h) Sections 14601 and 14601.1, relating to driving while license is suspended or revoked.

(i) When the person arrested has attempted to evade arrest.

(j) Section 23332, relating to persons upon vehicular crossings.

(k) Section 2813, relating to the refusal to stop and submit a vehicle to an inspection of its size, weight, and equipment.

(*l*) Section 2146.5, as it relates to a pedestrian who, after being cited for a violation of Section 21461.5, is within 24 hours, again found upon the freeway in violation of Section 21461.5 and thereafter refuses to leave the freeway after being lawfully ordered to do so, by a peace officer, and having been informed that his failure to leave could result in his arrest.

(m) Section 2800, as it relates to a pedestrian who, after having been cited for a violation of Section 2800 for failure to obey a lawful order of a peace officer issued pursuant to Section 21962, is within 24 hours again found upon the bridge or overpass and thereafter refuses to leave after being lawfully ordered to do so by a peace officer and after having been informed that his failure to leave could result in his arrest.

(Amended by Stats.1976, c. 1082, p. —, § 1.)

Editors' Note

This section allows only a pat down search for the officer's safety during transportation when the violator is taken into custody. A

§ 40303

booking search is not justified until the violator has had an opportunity to post bail.

Notes of Decisions

Arrest

When officer determines that there is probable cause to believe that a traffic offense has been committed and begins the process of citing the violator to appear in court, an "arrest" takes place, at least in the technical sense; while motorist who is actually taken into police custody for transportation before a magistrate is "under arrest" in the traditional sense of the term. People v. Superior Court of Los Angeles County (1972) 101 Cal.Rptr. 837, 496 P.2d 1205, 7 C.3d 186.

Where person arrested for traffic violation not amounting to a felony is taken into custody for transportation before a magistrate, either under this section giving officer option to follow such procedure or under § 40302 making such procedure mandatory, arrestee must be transported directly to a magistrate or to one of the other officials listed in § 40307 and must immediately be released on bail or written promise to appear, and cannot lawfully be subjected to the routine booking process used in the case of a nontraffic misdemeanant. Id.

Where petitioner was told he was being arrested for reckless driving, and there was no evidence to establish that police had in mind a baggie containing marijuana which was thrown out window of automobile being driven by petitioner, subsequent booking-search could not be justified on theory that petitioner was actually arrested and booked for possession of the baggie. Agar v. Superior Court for Los Angeles County (1971) 98 Cal.Rptr. 148, 21 C.A.3d 24.

Other offenses

Unless police officer believed that crime of possession of marijuana had been committed by petitioner who was told he was being arrested for reckless driving and was booked for reckless driving, issue of probable cause to support arrest for possession of a baggie containing marijuana did not arise. Agar v. Superior Court for Los Angeles County (1971) 98 Cal.Rptr. 148, 21 C.A.3d 24.

Searches and seizures

Where a person arrested for a traffic violation not amounting to a felony is taken into custody for purposes of transportation before a magistrate, he cannot be searched as an incident of that procedure, either in the field or at a police station; disapproving Morel v. Superior Court, 89 Cal.Rptr. 297, 10 C.A.3d 913, and its progeny. People v. Superior Court of Los Angeles County (1972) 101 Cal.Rptr. 837, 496 P.2d 1205, 7 C.3d 186.

Even though arrest for reckless driving was based upon probable cause, subsequent booking-search was illegal, in view of this section providing that when an officer makes a stop for reckless driving the officer is given option of either issuing offender a ten days' notice to appear or of taking offender without unnecessary delay before a magistrate, and where there was no evidence to suggest that defendant could not have made bail and would have had to have been jailed. Agar v. Superior Court for Los Angeles County (1971) 98 Cal.Rptr. 148, 21 C.A.3d 24.

§ 40304. Discretionary procedure

Whenever any person is arrested by any member of the California Highway Patrol for any violation of any state law regulating the operation of vehicles or the use of the highways declared to be a misdemeanor but which offense is not specified in this code, he shall, in the judgment of the arresting officer, either be given a 10-day notice to appear in the manner provided in this chapter or be taken without unnecessary delay before a magistrate within the county in which the offense charged is alleged to have been committed and who has jurisdiction of the offense and is nearest or most accessible with reference to the place where the arrest is made, or, upon demand of the person arrested, before a magistrate in the judicial district in which the offense is alleged to have been committed.

(Stats.1959, c. 3, p. 1775, § 40304.)

§ 40305. Offense by nonresident

Whenever a nonresident is arrested for violating any section of this code while driving a motor vehicle and does not furnish satisfactory evidence of identity and an address within this State at which he can be located, he may, in the discretion of the arresting officer, be taken immediately before a magistrate within the county where the offense charged is alleged to have been committed, and who has jurisdiction over the offense and is nearest or most accessible with reference to the place where the arrest is made. If the magistrate is not available at the time of the arrest and the arrested person is not taken before any other person authorized to receive a deposit of bail, and if the arresting officer does not have the authority or is not required to take the arrested person before a magistrate or other person authorized to receive a deposit of bail by some other provision of law, the nonresident shall be released from custody upon giving a written promise to appear as provided in Article 2 (commencing with Section 40500).

(Amended by Stats.1961, c. 314, p. 1357, § 1.)

§ 40306. Misdemeanor and infraction procedure before magistrate

(a) Whenever a person is arrested for a misdemeanor or an infraction and is taken before a magistrate, the arresting officer shall file with the magistrate a complaint stating the offense with which the person is charged.

(b) The person taken before a magistrate shall be entitled to at least five days continuance of his case in which to plead and prepare for trial and the person shall not be required to plead or be tried within the five days unless he waives such time in writing or in open court.

(c) The person taken before a magistrate shall thereupon be released from custody upon his own recognizance or upon such bail as the magistrate may fix.
(Amended by Stats.1968, c. 1192, p. 2262, § 13.)

§ 40307. Magistrate unavailable

When an arresting officer attempts to take a person arrested for a misdemeanor or infraction of this code before a magistrate and the magistrate or person authorized to act for him is not available, the arresting officer shall take the person arrested, without unnecessary delay, before:

(a) The clerk of the magistrate who shall admit him to bail in accordance with a schedule fixed as provided in Section 1269b of the Penal Code, or

(b) The officer in charge of the most accessible county or city jail or other place of detention within the county who shall admit him to bail in accordance with a schedule fixed as provided in Section 1269b of the Penal Code or may, in lieu of bail, release the person on his written promise to appear as provided in subdivisions (a) through (f) of Section 853.6 of the Penal Code.

Whenever a person is taken into custody pursuant to subdivision (a) of Section 40302 and is arrested for a misdemeanor or infraction of this code pertaining to the operation of a motor vehicle, the officer in charge of the most accessible county or city jail or other place of detention within the county may detain the person arrested for a reasonable period of time, not to exceed two hours, in order to verify his identity.
(Amended by Stats.1974, c. 593, p. 1419, § 1.)

§ 40309. Posting of bail by mail

Whenever a citation is issued for overtime parking in accordance with the provisions of Sections 41102 and 41103 of this code, the amount fixed as bail for the violation charged may be forwarded by United States mail to the person authorized to receive a deposit of bail. Bail forwarded by mail shall be effective only when actually received, and the presumption that a letter duly directed and mailed was received, shall not apply. The provisions of Section 40512 of this code are applicable to bail posted pursuant to this section.
(Added by Stats.1960, 1st Ex.Sess., c. 40, p. 384, § 1.)

§ 40309.5. Written notice of bail

Every written notice of a violation of an ordinance of a city or county relating to parking offenses shall be accompanied by a written notice of the bail due for that violation and the address of the person authorized to receive a deposit of bail, to whom payments thereof may be sent, and a statement in bold print that payments of the bail for such parking offenses may be sent through the mail.
(Amended by Stats.1970, c. 846, p. 1578, § 1.)

§ 40311. Arraignment for other violations

Whenever a person is arrested under authority of a warrant, the court to which such person is taken shall, with his consent, have jurisdiction to arraign him at that time for any other alleged violation of this code or an ordinance relating to traffic offenses for which he has been issued a written notice to appear in court, notwithstanding the fact that the time for appearance specified in such notice has not yet arrived.
(Added by Stats.1959, c. 977, p. 3006, § 1.)

§ 40500. Notice; form; construction

(a) Whenever a person is arrested for any violation of this code not declared to be a felony, or for a violation of an ordinance of a city or county relating to traffic offenses and he is not immediately taken before a magistrate, as provided in this chapter, the arresting officer shall prepare in triplicate a written notice to appear in court or before a person authorized to receive a deposit of bail, containing the name and address of the person, the license number of his vehicle, if any, the name and address, when available, of the registered owner or lessee of the vehicle, the offense charged and the time and place when and where he shall appear.

(b) The Judicial Council shall prescribe the form of the notice to appear.

(c) Nothing in this section shall be construed so as to require the law enforcement agency or the arresting officer issuing the notice to appear to inform any person arrested pursuant to this section of the amount of bail required to be deposited for the offense charged.
(Amended by Stats.1975, c. 1257, p. 3295, § 1.)

§ 40501. Time to appear

The time specified in the notice to appear must be at least 10 days after such arrest.
(Stats.1959, c. 3, p. 1777, § 40501.)

§ 40502. Place to appear

The place specified in the notice to appear shall be either:

(a) Before a magistrate within the county in which the offense charged is alleged to have been committed and who has jurisdiction of the offense and is nearest or most accessible with reference to the place where the arrest is made.

(b) Upon demand of the person arrested, before a municipal court judge or other magistrate having jurisdiction of the offense at the county seat of the county in which the offense is alleged to have been committed or before a magistrate in the judicial district in which the offense is alleged to have been committed.

(c) Before a person authorized to receive a deposit of bail.

The clerk and deputy clerks of the municipal and justice courts are persons authorized to receive bail in accordance with a schedule of bail approved by the judges of said courts.

(d) Before the juvenile court, a juvenile court referee, or a juvenile traffic hearing officer within the county in which the offense charged is alleged to have been committed, if the person arrested appears to be under the age of 18 years. The juvenile court shall by order designate the proper person before whom such appearance is to be made.

If the place specified in the notice to appear is within a district or city and county where a department of the municipal court is to hold a night session within a period of not more than 10 days after the arrest, the notice to appear shall contain, in addition to the above, a statement notifying the person arrested that he may appear before such a night session of the court.
(Amended by Stats.1965, c. 1705, p. 3838, § 2.)

§ 40503. Speed charge

Every notice to appear or notice of violation and every complaint or information charging a violation of any provision of this code regulating the speed of vehicles upon a highway shall specify the approximate speed at which the defendant is alleged to have driven and exactly the prima facie or maximum speed limit applicable to the highway at the time and place of the alleged offense and shall state any other speed limit alleged to have been exceeded if applicable to the particular type of vehicle or combination of vehicles operated by the defendant.
(Amended by Stats.1969, c. 1056, p. 2039, § 1.)

§ 40504. Delivery of notice

(a) The officer shall deliver one copy of the notice to appear to the arrested person and the arrested person in order to secure release must give his written promise to appear in court or before a person authorized to receive a deposit of bail by signing two copies of the notice which shall be retained by the officer. Thereupon the arresting officer shall forthwith release the person arrested from custody.

(b) Any person who signs a written promise to appear with a false or fictitious name is guilty of a misdemeanor regardless of the disposition of the charge upon which he was originally arrested.
(Amended by Stats.1963, c. 802, p. 1833, § 1.)

§ 40505. Copy of notice

Whenever any traffic or police officer delivers a notice to appear or notice of violation charging an offense under this code to any person, it shall include all information set forth upon the copy of the notice filed with a magistrate and no traffic or police officer shall set forth on any notice filed with a magistrate or attach thereto or accompany the notice with any written statement giving information or containing allegations which have not been delivered to the person receiving the notice to appear or notice of violation.
(Amended by Stats.1969, c. 1056, p. 2039, § 2.)

§ 40506. Filing copies

The officer shall, as soon as practicable, file a copy of the notice with the magistrate or before a person authorized by the magistrate or judge to receive a deposit of bail specified therein, and a copy with the commissioner, chief of police, sheriff or other superior officer of the arresting officer.
(Stats.1959, c. 3, p. 1778, § 40506.)

§ 40507. Appearance by counsel

A written promise to appear in court may be complied with by an appearance by counsel.
(Stats.1959, c. 3, p. 1778, § 40507.)

§ 40508. Violation of promise to appear

(a) Any person willfully violating his written promise to appear in court or before a person authorized to receive a deposit of bail is guilty of a misdemeanor regardless of the disposition of the charge upon which he was originally arrested.

(b) Any person willfully failing to pay a lawfully imposed fine for a violation of any provision of this code or a local ordinance adopted pursuant to this code within the time authorized by the court and without lawful excuse having been presented to the court on or before the date the fine is due is guilty of a misdemeanor regardless of the full payment of the fine after such time.

(c) If a person convicted of an infraction fails to pay a fine or any installment thereof within the time authorized by the court, the court may, except as otherwise provided in this paragraph, impound the person's driver's license and order him not to drive for a period not to exceed 30 days. Before returning the license to the person the court shall endorse on the reverse side of the license that the person was ordered not to drive, the period for which such order was made, and the name of the court making the order. If the defendant satisfies the court that impounding his driver's license and ordering him not to drive will affect his livelihood, the court shall order that the person limit his driving for a period not to exceed 30 days to such driving as is essential in the court's determination to the person's employment, including his driving to and from his place of employment if other means of transportation are not reasonably available. The court shall provide for the endorsement of such limitation on the person's license. The impounding of the license and ordering the person not to drive or the order limiting the person's driving does not constitute a suspension of the license, but a violation of the order constitutes contempt of court.
(Amended by Stats.1968, c. 1192, p. 2262, § 15.)

§ 40509. Deposit of bail; parking violations

(a) Whenever any person has for a period of 15 or more days violated his written promise to appear in court or before the person authorized to receive a deposit of bail or violated an order to appear in court or to pay a fine pursuant to subdivision (a) of Section 42003 the magistrate or clerk of the court may give notice of such fact to the department. Such notice shall be given not less than 30 days nor more than 60 days after issuance of a warrant. Whenever thereafter the case in which such promise was given is adjudicated or the person who has violated the court order appears in court or otherwise satisfies the order of the court, the magistrate or clerk of the court hearing the case shall sign and file with the department a certificate to that effect.

(b) Whenever any person has for a period of 15 or more days willfully failed to pay a lawfully imposed fine within the time authorized by the court, the magistrate or clerk of such court may give notice of such fact to the department for any violation which is required to be reported pursuant to Section 1803. Whenever thereafter the fine is fully paid, the magistrate or clerk of such court shall sign and file with the department a certificate showing that the fine has been paid.
(Amended by Stats.1971, c. 1532, p. 3037, § 3.)

§ 40510. Deposit of bail; payment by personal check

The defendant may, prior to the date upon which he promised to appear, deposit bail with the magistrate or the person authorized to receive a deposit of bail.

For any offense which is not declared to be a felony, such deposit of bail may be by the personal check of the person who has signed a written promise to appear, if he furnishes to the person authorized to receive a deposit of bail satisfactory evidence of residence in this state and if such personal check is drawn on a banking institution located in this state.
(Amended by Stats.1970, c. 299, p. 572, § 1.)

§ 40511. Fixing bail

If bail has not been previously fixed and approved by the judges of the court in accordance with a schedule of bail, the magistrate shall fix the amount of bail which in his judgment, in accordance with Section 1275 of the Penal Code, will be reasonable and sufficient for the appearance of the defendant and shall endorse upon the notice a statement signed by him in the form set forth in Section 815a of the Penal Code.
(Stats.1959, c. 3, p. 1778, § 40511.)

§ 40512. Forfeiture of bail

If at the time when the case is called for arraignment before the magistrate the defendant does not appear, either in person or by counsel, the magistrate may declare the bail forfeited and may in his discretion order that no further proceedings be had in the case, unless the defendant has been charged with violation of Section 23111 or 23112, or subdivision (a) of Section 23113, and he has been previously convicted of the same, except in cases where the magistrate finds that undue hardship will be imposed upon the defendant by requiring him to appear, the magistrate may declare the bail forfeited and order that no further proceedings shall be had in such case.

§ 40512

Upon the making of the order that no further proceedings be had, all sums deposited as bail shall forthwith be paid into the city or county treasury, as the case may be.
(Amended by Stats.1970, c. 1548, p. 3151, § 9.)

§ 40512.5. Optional bail forfeiture

If at the time when the case is called for trial the defendant does not appear either in person or by counsel and has not requested in writing that the trial proceed in his absence, the court may declare the bail forfeited and may in its discretion order that no further proceedings be had in the case, or the court may act pursuant to Section 1043 of the Penal Code. However, if the defendant has been charged with violation of Section 23111 or 23112, or subdivision (a) of Section 23113, and he has been previously convicted of a violation of the same section, the court may declare the bail forfeited, but shall issue a bench warrant for the arrest of the person charged, except in cases where the magistrate finds that undue hardship will be imposed upon the defendant by requiring him to appear, the magistrate may declare the bail forfeited and order that no further proceedings shall be had in such case.
(Amended by Stats.1970, c. 1548, p. 3151, § 10.)

§ 40513. Filing of complaint

(a) Whenever written notice to appear has been prepared, delivered, and filed with the court, or whenever notice has been given pursuant to the provisions of Section 41102, an exact and legible duplicate copy of the notice when filed with the magistrate, in lieu of a verified complaint, shall constitute a complaint to which the defendant may plead "guilty" or "nolo contendere."

If, however, the defendant violates his promise to appear in court or does not deposit lawful bail, or pleads other than "guilty" or "nolo contendere" to the offense charged, a complaint shall be filed which shall conform to the provisions of Chapter 2 (commencing with Section 948) of Title 5, Part 2 of the Penal Code, and which shall be deemed to be an original complaint, and thereafter proceedings shall be had as provided by law, except that a defendant may, by an agreement in writing, subscribed by him and filed with the court, waive the filing of a verified complaint and elect that the prosecution may proceed upon a written notice to appear.

(b) Notwithstanding the provisions of subdivision (a) of this section, whenever the written notice to appear has been prepared on a form approved by the Judicial Council, an exact and legible duplicate copy of the notice when filed with the magistrate shall constitute a complaint to which the defendant may enter a plea and, if the notice to appear is verified, upon which a warrant may be issued. If the notice to appear is not verified, the defendant may, at the time of arraignment, request that a verified complaint be filed.
(Amended by Stats.1968, c. 906, p. 1697, § 2.)

§ 40514. Issuance of warrant

No warrant shall issue on the charge for the arrest of a person who has given his written promise to appear in court or before a person authorized to receive a deposit of bail, unless he has violated the promise or has failed to deposit bail, to appear for arraignment, trial or judgment, or to comply with the terms and provisions of the judgment, as required by law.
(Stats.1959, c. 3, p. 1779, § 40514.)

§ 40515. Issuance of warrant for violation of promise to appear

(a) When a person signs a written promise to appear at the time and place specified in the written promise to appear and has not posted bail, the magistrate may issue and have delivered for execution a warrant for his arrest within 20 days after his failure to appear before the magistrate, or if the person promises to appear before an officer authorized to accept bail other than a magistrate and fails to do so on or before the date on which he promised to appear, then, within 20 days after the delivery of the written promise to appear by the officer to a magistrate having jurisdiction over the offense.

(b) When the person violates his promise to appear before an officer authorized to receive bail other than a magistrate, the officer shall immediately deliver to a magistrate having jurisdiction over the offense charged the written promise to appear and the complaint, if any, filed by the arresting officer.
(Amended by Stats.1971, c. 1042, p. 1998, § 1.)

§ 40516. Expense to departments

(a) The expenses incurred by the Department of the California Highway Patrol and the Department of Motor Vehicles in executing any warrant issued as a result of a notice to appear issued by a member of the California Highway Patrol shall be a legal charge against the city or county in which jurisdiction the warrant was issued except where the commissioner authorizes the acceptance of a warrant for execution within 30 days of the date of its issuance.

(b) The commissioner or director shall certify to the Controller the cost of executing warrants on behalf of each city or county under this section. The departments shall be reimbursed for costs as provided in Section 11004.5 of the Revenue and Taxation Code.

(c) The peace officer to whom a warrant has been delivered for execution, upon demand, shall transfer the warrant, if it has not been executed within 30 days of the date of its issuance, to any member of the California Highway Patrol or to the Department of Motor Vehicles for execution.
(Amended by Stats.1959, c. 1996, p. 4640, § 52.)

§ 40517. Change of venue

(a) Whenever any person has given his written promise to appear, or has received a written notice of violation, or has received written notice to appear, or against whom a complaint has been filed charging a violation of this code punishable as a misdemeanor requiring such person to appear before a justice court judge who is not at the county seat of the county wherein the offense is alleged to have been committed, he may demand a transfer of the case to a municipal court judge or other magistrate having jurisdiction of the offense at the county seat upon filing with such justice court judge an affidavit that he believes that a fair trial without excessive penalties cannot be had before such justice court judge. In the event that a trial date has been set before such justice court judge, such affidavit must be filed at least 10 days prior to the trial date.

(b) Thereupon the justice court judge with whom the affidavit is filed shall be without jurisdiction to proceed with the case and shall immediately transfer the case and all papers in connection therewith for further proceedings before a municipal court judge or other magistrate having jurisdiction of such offense at the county seat.

(c) The foregoing method of securing a change of venue is in addition to any other method provided by law for obtaining a change of venue.
(Amended by Stats.1969, c. 1056, p. 2040, § 3.)

§ 40519. Trial scheduling; written not guilty plea

(a) Any person who has received a written notice to appear for an infraction may, prior to the time at which he is required to appear, make a deposit and declare his intention to plead not guilty to the clerk of the court named in the notice to appear. The deposit shall be in the amount of bail established pursuant to the provisions of Section 1269b of the Penal Code, together with any assessment required by Section 42006 or 42050 of this code, for the offense charged, and shall be used for the purpose of guaranteeing the appearance of the defendant at the time and place scheduled by the clerk for arraignment and for trial, and to apply toward the payment of any fine or assessment prescribed by the court in the event of conviction. The case shall thereupon be set for arraignment and trial on the same date, unless the defendant requests separate arraignment.

(b) Any person who has received a written notice to appear for an infraction may, prior to the time at which he is required to appear, plead not guilty in writing in lieu of appearing in person. The written plea shall be directed to the court named in the notice to appear and, if mailed, shall be sent by certified or registered mail postmarked not later than five days prior to the day upon which appearance is required. Such written plea and request to the court shall be accompanied by a deposit consisting of the amount of bail established pursuant to the provisions of Section 1269b of the Penal Code, together with any assessment required by Section 42006 or 42050 of this code, for that offense, which amount shall be used for the purpose of guaranteeing the appearance of the defendant at the time and place set by the court for trial and to apply toward the payment of any fine or assessment prescribed by the court in the event of conviction. Thereafter, the case shall be conducted in the same manner as if the defendant had appeared in person, had made his plea in open court, and had deposited such sum as bail. The court or the clerk of the court shall notify the accused of the time and place of trial by first-class mail postmarked at least 10 days prior to the time set for the trial. Any person using this procedure shall be deemed to have waived his right to be tried within the statutory period.

(c) Any person using the procedure set forth in subdivision (a) or (b) shall be deemed to have given his written promise to appear at the time designated by the court for trial, and failure to appear at the trial shall constitute a misdemeanor.

(d) This section shall become operative on July 1, 1976.
(Added by Stats.1975, c. 1257, p. 3296, § 3.)

§ 40521. Forfeited bail and penalty assessment: deposit by mail

(a) Except when personal appearance is required by the bail schedule established under Section 1269b of the Penal Code, a person to whom a notice to appear has been issued under Section 40500 who intends to forfeit bail and to pay any penalty assessment may forward by United States mail the amount fixed as bail, together with the appropriate amount of any penalty assessment, to the person authorized to receive a deposit of bail. Notwithstanding the provisions of Section 40510, such amounts may be paid in the form of a personal check of the person who has signed a written promise to appear and drawn on a banking institution located in this state, a bank cashier's check, or a money order. Bail and any penalty assessment shall be paid not later than the day of appearance set forth in the notice to appear.

(b) Bail forwarded by mail shall be effective only when the funds are actually received.

(c) The provisions of Section 40512 are applicable to bail paid pursuant to this section. Upon the making of the order pursuant to Section 40512 that no further proceedings be had, the amount paid as bail shall be paid into the city or county treasury, as the case may be, and the penalty assessment shall be transmitted to the State Treasury in the manner provided in Section 42052.
(Added by Stats.1976, c. 127, p. —, § 1.)

§ 40600. Notice of violation; reasonable cause for issuance

(a) Notwithstanding any other provision of law, a peace officer who has successfully completed at least 40 hours of instruction in a course or courses of instruction, approved by the Commission on Peace Officer Standards and Training, in the investigation of traffic accidents may prepare in triplicate, on a form approved by the Judicial Council, a written notice of violation when the peace officer has reasonable cause to believe that any person involved in a traffic accident has violated a provision of this code not declared to be a felony or a violation of a local ordinance and the violation was a factor in the occurrence of the traffic accident.

(b) A notice of violation shall contain the name and address of the person, the license number of his vehicle, if any, the name and address, when available, of the registered owner or lessee of the vehicle, the offense charged, and the time and place when and where he may appear in court or before a person authorized to receive a deposit of bail. The time specified shall be at least 10 days after such notice of violation is delivered.

(c) The preparation and delivery of a notice of violation does not constitute an arrest.

(d) For the purposes of this article, a peace officer will be deemed to have reasonable cause to issue a written notice of violation if, as a result of his investigation, he has evidence, either testimonial or real, or a combination of testimonial and real, that would be sufficient to issue a written notice to appear if he had personally witnessed the events he investigated.

(e) As used in this section, "peace officer" means a member of the California Highway Patrol; a sheriff, undersheriff, or deputy sheriff of a county; a policeman of a city; or a policeman of a district authorized by statute to maintain a police department.

(f) The provisions of this article shall have no application to the procedures specified in Article 2 (commencing with Section 40500).

(g) This section shall apply to the procedures specified in Chapter 2.5 (commencing with Section 40650) of this division except that the notice of violation shall be as set forth and approved by the Traffic Adjudication Board.
(Amended by Stats.1978, c. 722, p. —, § 2.)

§ 40601. Place to appear

The place specified in the notice of violation shall be either:

(a) Before a magistrate within the county in which the offense charged is alleged to have been committed and who has jurisdiction of the offense and is nearest or most accessible with reference to the place where the offense charged is alleged to have been committed.

(b) Upon demand of the person receiving the notice of violation, before a municipal court judge or other magistrate having jurisdiction of the offense at the county seat of the county in which the offense is alleged to have been committed or before a magistrate in the judicial district in which the offense is alleged to have been committed.

(c) Before a person authorized to receive a deposit of bail.

The clerk and deputy clerks of the municipal and justice courts are persons authorized to receive bail in accordance with a schedule of bail approved by the judges of said courts.

(d) Before the juvenile court, a juvenile court referee, or a juvenile traffic hearing officer within the county in which the offense charged is alleged to have been committed, if the person receiving the notice of violation appears to be under the age of 18 years. The juvenile court shall by order designate the proper person before whom such appearance is to be made.

If the place specified in the notice of violation is within a district or city and county where a department of the municipal court is to hold a night session within a period of not more than 10 days after such notice of violation is delivered, the notice of violation shall contain, in addition to the above, a statement notifying the person receiving such notice that he may appear before such a night session of the court.
(Added by Stats.1969, c. 1056, p. 2040, § 4.)

§ 40602. Delivery of notice

The officer shall deliver one copy of the notice of violation to the person named therein.
(Added by Stats.1969, c. 1056, p. 2040, § 4.)

§ 40603. Filing of complaint

When a notice of violation has been prepared, delivered, and filed with the court, in lieu of a verified complaint, the notice of violation shall constitute a complaint to which the defendant may plead "guilty" or "nolo contendere." If, however, the defendant does not appear, or deposit lawful bail, or pleads other than "guilty" or "nolo contendere" to the offense charged, a verified complaint may be filed which shall conform to the provisions of Chapter 2 (commencing with Section 948) of Title 5, Part 2 of the Penal Code, and which shall be deemed to be an original complaint, and thereafter proceedings shall be had as provided by law, except that a defendant may, by an agreement in writing, subscribed by him and filed with the court, waive the filing of a verified complaint and elect that the prosecution may proceed upon the written notice of violation.
(Added by Stats.1969, c. 1056, p. 2040, § 4.)

§ 40604. Issuance of warrant

Before any warrant for arrest may issue following the filing of a complaint charging the offense for which the written notice of violation was issued pursuant to Section 40600, a notice of the filing of the complaint shall be issued and served upon the person charged with the offense by personal delivery or by certified mail, postage prepaid and return receipt requested, addressed to the person at the address shown in the accident report. The notice shall contain the name and address of the person, the license number of the vehicle involved, the name and address, when available, of the registered owner or lessee of the vehicle, the offense shown on the written notice of violation, and the approximate time of the commission of the offense. The notice shall inform the person that, unless he appears in the court designated in the notice within 10 days after the service of the notice and answers the charges against him, a warrant will issue for his arrest. Proof of service shall be made by the affidavit of any person over 18 years of age making the service showing the time, place, and manner of service and facts showing that the service was made in accordance with this section. If service is made by mail, no warrant for arrest may issue unless the proof of service includes evidence satisfactory to the court establishing actual delivery to the person by a signed return receipt or other evidence.
(Added by Stats.1974, c. 794, p. 1738, § 4.)

§ 40800. Vehicle and uniform used by officers

Every traffic officer on duty for the exclusive or main purpose of enforcing the provisions of Division 10 or 11 of this code shall wear a full distinctive uniform, and if the officer while so on duty uses a motor vehicle, it must be painted a distinctive color specified by the commissioner.

This section does not apply to an officer assigned exclusively to the duty of investigating and securing evidence in reference to any theft of a vehicle or failure of a person to stop in the event of an accident or violation of Section 23109 or in reference to any felony charge, or to any officer engaged in serving any warrant when the officer is not engaged in patrolling the highways for the purpose of enforcing the traffic laws.
(As amended by Stats.1961, c. 202, p. 1212, § 2.)

§ 40801. Speed trap prohibition

No peace officer or other person shall use a speed trap in arresting, or participating or assisting in the arrest of, any person for any alleged violation of this code nor shall any speed trap be used in securing evidence as to the speed of any vehicle for the purpose of an arrest or prosecution under this code.
(Stats.1959, c. 3, p. 1780, § 40801.)

§ 40802. Speed trap defined

Text of section operative until January 1, 1982

A "speed trap" is either of the following:

(a) A particular section of a highway measured as to distance and with boundaries marked, designated, or otherwise determined in order that the speed of a vehicle may be calculated by securing the time it takes the vehicle to travel the known distance.

(b) A particular section of a highway with a prima facie speed limit provided by this code or by local ordinance pursuant to paragraph (1) of subdivision (b) of Section 22352, or established pursuant to Section 22354, 22357, 22358, or 22358.3, which speed limit is not justified by an engineering and traffic survey conducted within five years prior to the date of the alleged violation, and where enforcement involves the use of radar or other electronic devices which measure the speed of moving objects. The provisions of this subdivision do not apply to local streets and roads.

For purposes of this section, local streets and roads shall be defined by the latest functional usage and federal-aid system maps as submitted to the Federal Highway Administration. When these maps have not been submitted, the following definition shall be used: A local street or road primarily provides access to abutting residential property and shall meet the following three conditions:

1. Roadway width of not more than 40 feet.

2. Not more than ½ mile of uninterrupted length. Interruptions shall include official traffic control devices as defined in Section 445.

3. Not more than one traffic lane in each direction.

This section shall remain in effect only until January 1, 1982, and as of that date is repealed.
(Amended by Stats.1978, c. 1210, p. —, § 1.)

§ 40803. Speed trap evidence

No evidence as to the speed of a vehicle upon a highway shall be admitted in any court upon the trial of any person for an alleged violation of this code when the evidence is based upon or obtained from or by the maintenance or use of a speed trap.
(Stats.1959, c. 3, p. 1781, § 40803.)

§ 40804. Testimony based on speed trap

(a) In any prosecution under this code upon a charge involving the speed of a vehicle, any officer or other person shall be incompetent as a witness if the testimony is based upon or obtained from or by the maintenance or use of a speed trap.

(b) Every officer arresting, or participating or assisting in the arrest of, a person so charged while on duty for the exclusive or main purpose of enforcing the provisions of Divisions 10 and 11 is incompetent as a witness if at the time of such arrest he was not wearing a distinctive uniform, or was using a motor vehicle not painted the distinctive color specified by the commissioner.

This section does not apply to an officer assigned exclusively to the duty of investigating and securing evidence in reference to any theft of a vehicle or failure of a person to stop in the event of an accident or violation of Section 23109 or in reference to any felony charge or to any officer engaged in serving any warrant when the officer is not engaged in patrolling the highways for the purpose of enforcing the traffic laws.
(Amended by Stats.1978, c. 84, p. —, § 1.)

§ 40805. Admission of speed trap evidence

Every court shall be without jurisdiction to render a judgment of conviction against any person for a violation of this code involving the speed of a vehicle if the court admits any evidence or testimony secured in violation of, or which is inadmissible under this article.
(Stats.1959, c. 3, p. 1781, § 40805.)

§ 40806. Police reports

In the event a defendant charged with an offense under this code pleads guilty, the trial court shall not at any time prior to pronouncing sentence receive or consider any report, verbal or written, of any police or traffic officer or witness of the offense without fully informing the defendant of all statements in the report or statement of witnesses, or without giving the defendant an opportunity to make answer thereto or to produce witnesses in rebuttal, and for such purpose the court shall grant a continuance before pronouncing sentence if requested by the defendant.
(Stats.1959, c. 3, p. 1781, § 40806.)

§ 40807. Use of evidence regarding departmental action

No record of any action taken by the department against a person's privilege to operate a motor vehicle, nor any testimony regarding the proceedings at, or concerning, or produced at, any hearing held in connection with such action, shall be admissible as evidence in any court in any criminal action.

No provision of this section shall in any way limit the admissibility of such records or testimony as is necessary to enforce the provisions of this code relating to operating a motor vehicle without a valid driver's license or when the driving privilege is suspended or revoked, the admissibility of such records or testimony in any prosecution for failure to disclose any matter at such a hearing when required by law to do so, or the admissibility of such records and testimony when introduced solely for the purpose of impeaching the credibility of a witness.
(Added by Stats.1977, c. 804, p. —, § 4.)

§ 41100. Speed restriction signs

In any action involving the question of unlawful speed of a vehicle upon a highway which has been signposted with speed restriction signs of a type complying with the requirements of this code, it shall be presumed that existing facts authorize the erection of the signs and that the prima facie speed limit on the highway is the limit stated on the signs. This presumption may be rebutted.
(Stats.1959, c. 3, p. 1782, § 41100.)

§ 41101. Official signs and traffic control devices

(a) Whenever a traffic sign or traffic control device is placed in a position approximately conforming to the requirements of this code, it shall be presumed to have been placed by the official act or direction of lawful authority, unless the contrary is established by competent evidence.

(b) Any sign or traffic control device placed pursuant to this code and purporting to conform to the lawful requirements pertaining to it shall be presumed to comply with the requirements of this code unless the contrary is established by competent evidence.
(Stats.1959, c. 3, p. 1782, § 41101.)

§ 41102. Unattended vehicle; prima facie evidence

(a) In any prosecution against the registered owner of a motor vehicle charging a violation of any regulation governing the standing or parking of a vehicle under this code or any ordinance enacted by local authorities, proof by the people of the State of California that the particular vehicle described in the complaint was parked in violation of any provision of this code or such ordinance, together with proof that the defendant named in the complaint was at the time of parking the registered owner of the vehicle, shall constitute prima facie evidence that the registered owner of the vehicle was the person who parked or placed the vehicle at the point where, and for the time during which, the violation occurred, but for the purposes of this subdivision proof that a person is the registered owner of a vehicle is not prima facie evidence that the registered owner has violated any other provision of law. Proof of a written lease of, or rental agreement for, a particular vehicle described in the complaint, on the date and time of such violation, which lease or rental agreement includes the name and address of the person to whom the vehicle is leased or rented, a copy of which was delivered to the court giving the notice required in paragraph 2 of Section 41103 within 30 days after date of giving of such notice, shall rebut the prima facie evidence that the registered owner was the person who parked or placed the vehicle at the time and place where the violation occurred. The above provisions shall apply only when the procedure required by Section 41103 is complied with.

(b) In any prosecution against the lessee or renter of a motor vehicle charging a violation of any regulation governing the standing or parking of a vehicle under this code or any ordinance enacted by local authorities, proof by the people of the State of California that the particular vehicle described in the complaint was parked in violation of any provision of this code or such ordinance, together with proof that the defendant named in the complaint was at the time of parking the lessee or renter of the vehicle, shall constitute prima facie evidence that the lessee or renter of the vehicle was the person who parked or placed the vehicle at the point where, and for the time during which, the violation occurred, but for the purposes of this subdivision, proof that a person is the lessee or renter of a vehicle is not prima facie evidence that the lessee or renter has violated any other provision of law.

(c) In any prosecution charging a violation of any provision of this code requiring the display of any evidence of registration, with respect to an unattended vehicle, proof by the people of the State of California that the particular vehicle described in the complaint failed to properly display such evidence of registration, together with proof that the defendant named in the complaint was at the time the registered owner of the vehicle, shall constitute prima facie evidence that the registered owner of the vehicle was responsible for the vehicle at the time the violation occurred. No other prima facie evidence shall be created by this subdivision. The above

§ 41102

provisions shall apply only when the procedure required by Section 41103 is complied with.

(d) Any charge under this section shall be dismissed when the person charged has made a bona fide sale or transfer of the vehicle and has delivered possession thereof to the purchaser and has complied with the requirements of subdivision (a) or (b) of Section 5602 prior to the date of the alleged violation and has advised the court of the name and address of the purchaser, and of the date of sale.
(Amended by Stats.1971, c. 237, p. 363, § 1.)

§ 41103. Parking violation; notice procedure

The method of giving notice for the purposes of the provisions of Section 41102 is as follows:

(1) During the time of the violation a notice thereof shall be securely attached to the vehicle setting forth the violation, including reference to the section of this code or of such ordinance so violated, the approximate time thereof, and the location where such violation occurred and fixing a time and place for appearance by the registered owner or the lessee or renter in answer to such notice.

Such notice shall be attached to such vehicle either on the steering post or front door handle thereof or in such other conspicuous place upon the vehicle as to be easily observed by the person in charge of such vehicle upon his return thereto.

(2) Before any notice of noncompliance may be forwarded to the department under Section 41103.5 or any warrant for the arrest of a resident of this state may be issued following the filing of a complaint charging such a violation, a notice of the violation shall be given to the person so charged. Such notice shall contain the information required in paragraph (1) and shall also inform such registered owner or the lessee or renter that unless he appears in the court designated in such notice within 10 days after service of such notice and answers such charge, or completes and files an affidavit of nonownership, the renewal of his registration is contingent upon his compliance with the notice of violation and that, failing such compliance, a warrant or citation to appear may be issued against him.

Such notice shall contain or be accompanied by an affidavit of nonownership. In addition to any other required information, such notice shall also provide information as to what constitutes nonownership, information as to the effect of executing such affidavit, and instructions for mailing or returning the affidavit to the court. Upon receipt of evidence satisfactory to the court that the person charged with violating Section 41102 has made a bona fide sale or transfer of the vehicle and has delivered possession thereof to the purchaser prior to the date of the alleged violation, the court shall obtain verification from the department that the person charged has complied with the requirements of subdivision (a) or (b) of Section 5602, and, if the person has complied with subdivision (a) or (b) of Section 5602, the charges against the person under Section 41102 shall be dismissed.

Such notice shall be given, either by personal delivery thereof to such owner, lessee or renter, or by deposit in the United States mail of an envelope with postage prepaid, which envelope shall contain such notice and shall be addressed to such owner, lessee or renter at his address as shown by the records of the department or the leasing or renting agency. The giving of notice by personal delivery is complete upon delivery of a copy of such notice to such person. The giving of notice by mail is complete upon the expiration of 10 days after the deposit of such notice.

Proof of giving such notice may be made by the certificate of any traffic or police officer or affidavit of any person over 18 years of age naming the person to whom such notice was given and specifying the time, place and manner of the giving thereof.

(3) Before any warrant for the arrest of a nonresident of this state may be issued following the filing of a complaint charging such a violation, a notice of the violation shall be given to the person so charged. Such notice shall contain the information required in paragraph (1) and shall also inform such registered owner or the lessee or renter that unless he appears in the court to be designated in such notice within 10 days after service of such notice and answers such charge, or completes and files an affidavit of nonownership, a warrant or citation to appear will be issued against him.
(Amended by Stats.1977, c. 804, p. —, § 5.)

§ 41400. Prior conviction or acquittal

Whenever any person is charged with a violation of this code, it is a sufficient defense to such charge if it appears that in a criminal prosecution in another state or by the Federal Government, founded upon the act or omission in respect to which he is on trial, he has been convicted or acquitted.
(Stats.1959, c. 3, p. 1783, § 41400.)

§ 41401. Federal law

No person shall be prosecuted for a violation of any provision of this code if the violation was required by a law of the federal government, by any rule, regulation, directive or order of any agency of the federal government, the violation of which is subject to penalty under an act of Congress, or by any valid order of military authority.
(Amended by Stats.1973, c. 78, p. 140, § 24.)

§ 41402. Emergency Services Act

No person shall be prosecuted for a violation of any provision of this code when violation of such provision is required in order to comply with any regulation, directive, or order of the Governor promulgated under the California Emergency Services Act.
(Amended by Stats.1971, c. 438, p. 909, § 196.)

§ 41500. Non-felony offenses of persons in custody

(a) No person shall be subject to prosecution for any nonfelony offense arising out of the operation of a motor vehicle or violation of this code as a pedestrian which is pending against him at the time of his commitment to the custody of the Director of Corrections or the Department of the Youth Authority.

(b) Notwithstanding any other provisions of law to the contrary, no driver's license shall be suspended or revoked, nor shall the issuance or renewal of such license be refused as a result of a pending nonfelony offense occurring prior to the time a person was committed to the custody of the Director of Corrections or the Department of the Youth Authority or as a result of a notice received by the department pursuant to subdivision (a) of Section 40509 when the offense which gave rise to the notice occurred prior to the time a person was committed to the custody of the Director of Corrections or the Department of Youth Authority.

(c) The department shall remove from its records any notice received by it pursuant to subdivision (a) of Section 40509 upon receipt of satisfactory evidence that a person was committed to the custody of the Director of Corrections or the Department of the Youth Authority after the offense which gave rise to the notice occurred.

(d) The provisions of this section shall not apply to any nonfelony offense wherein the department is required by this code to immediately revoke or suspend the privilege of any person to drive a motor vehicle upon receipt of a duly certified abstract of the record of any court showing that the person has been convicted of such nonfelony offense.

(e) The provisions of subdivisions (a), (b), and (c) shall not apply to any offense committed by a person while he is temporarily released from custody pursuant to law or while he is on parole.
(Amended by Stats.1975, c. 545, p. 1111, § 1.)

§ 41600. Arrest quota defined

For purposes of this chapter, "arrest quota" means any requirement regarding the number of arrests made, or the number of citations issued, by a peace officer, or the proportion of such arrests made and citations issued by a peace officer relative to the arrests made and citations issued by another peace officer or group of officers.
(Added by Stats.1976, c. 1111, p. ——, § 1.)

§ 41061. Citation defined

For purposes of this chapter, "citation" means a notice to appear, notice of violation, or notice of parking violation.
(Added by Stats.1976, c. 1111, p. ——, § 1.)

§ 41602. Arrest quota prohibited

No state or local agency employing peace officers engaged in the enforcement of this code or any local ordinance adopted pursuant to this code, may establish any policy requiring any peace officer to meet an arrest quota.
(Added by Stats.1976, c. 1111, p. ——, § 1.)

§ 41603. Evaluation of peace officer's performance

No state or local agency employing peace officers engaged in the enforcement of this code shall use the number of arrests or citations issued by a peace officer as the sole criteria for promotion, demotion, dismissal, or the earning of any benefit provided by the agency. Any such arrests or citations, and their ultimate dispositions, may only be considered in evaluating the overall performance of a peace officer. Such an evaluation may include, but shall not be limited to, criteria such as attendance, punctuality, work safety, complaints by citizens, commendations, demeanor, formal training, and professional judgment.
(Amended by Stats.1977, c. 579, p. ——, § 189.)

Division 18
PENALTIES AND DISPOSITION OF FEES, FINES, AND FORFEITURES

§ 42000. Felony

Unless a different penalty is expressly provided by this code, every person convicted of a felony for a violation of any provision of this code shall be punished by a fine of not less than one thousand dollars ($1,000) or more than five thousand dollars ($5,000) or by imprisonment in the state prison or by both such fine and imprisonment.
(Amended by Stats.1976, c. 1139, p. —, § 342.)

§ 42001. Infractions and special misdemeanors

(a) Except as provided in Section 42001.5, every person convicted of an infraction for a violation of this code or of any local ordinance adopted pursuant to this code shall be punished upon a first conviction by a fine not exceeding fifty dollars ($50) and for a second conviction within a period of one year by a fine of not exceeding one hundred dollars ($100) and for a third or any subsequent conviction within a period of one year by a fine of not exceeding two hundred fifty dollars ($250).

(b) Every person convicted of a misdemeanor violation of Sections 2800, 2801, and 2803 insofar as they affect failure to stop and submit to inspection of equipment or for an unsafe condition endangering any person, and Section 2800.1, shall be punished upon a first conviction by a fine not exceeding fifty dollars ($50) or by imprisonment in the county jail for not exceeding five days and for a second conviction within a period of one year by a fine of not exceeding one hundred dollars ($100) or by imprisonment in the county jail for not exceeding 10 days, or by both such fine and imprisonment and for a third or any subsequent conviction within a period of one year by a fine of not exceeding five hundred dollars ($500) or by imprisonment in the county jail for not exceeding six months or by both such fine and imprisonment.

(c) Notwithstanding the provisions of subdivision (a), every pedestrian convicted of an infraction for a violation of this code or of any local ordinance adopted pursuant to this code shall be punished by a fine not exceeding fifty dollars ($50).

(d) Subdivision (a) shall have no application to any violation punishable pursuant to Section 42001.7, any violation by a pedestrian, or Article 2 (commencing with Section 42030) of Chapter 1 of this division relating to weight violations.
(Amended by Stats.1978, c. 421, p. —, § 7; Stats.1978, c. 626, p. —, § 3.)

§ 42001.5. Abandoning vehicle; parking in disabled person's space

(a) Every person convicted of an infraction for a violation of Section 22700 shall be punished by a fine of not less than fifty dollars ($50).

(b) Every person convicted of an infraction for a violation of Section 22507.8 shall be punished upon a first conviction by a fine of not less than twenty-five dollars ($25).
(Amended by Stats.1977, c. 590, p. —, § 2.)

§ 42001.7. Littering

Every person convicted of a violation of Section 23111 or 23112, or subdivision (a) of Section 23113, shall be punished by a mandatory fine of not less than ten dollars ($10) nor more than five hundred dollars ($500) upon a first conviction, by a mandatory fine of not less than twenty-five dollars ($25) nor more than five hundred dollars ($500) upon a second conviction, and by a mandatory fine of not less than fifty dollars ($50) nor more than five hundred dollars ($500) upon a third or subsequent conviction.

The court may, in addition to the fine imposed upon a second or subsequent conviction, require as a condition of probation, in addition to any other condition of probation, that any person convicted of a violation of this section pick up litter at a time and place within the jurisdiction of the court for not less than four hours upon a second conviction and for not less than eight hours upon a third or subsequent conviction.
(Added by Stats.1970, c. 1548, p. 3152, § 11.)

§ 42002. General misdemeanors

Unless a different penalty is expressly provided by this code, every person convicted of a misdemeanor for a violation of any of the provisions of this code shall be punished by a fine of not exceeding five hundred dollars ($500) or by imprisonment in the county jail for not exceeding six months, or by both such fine and imprisonment.
(Stats.1959, c. 3, p. 1785, § 42002.)

§ 42050. Assessment for driver education and peace officers' training

To reimburse the General Fund for amounts appropriated therefrom for the laboratory phases of driver education pursuant to Section 17305 of the Education Code, and to augment the Peace Officers' Training Fund to the extent designated in Section 42052, there shall be levied a penalty assessment on all offenses involving a violation of a section of this code or any local ordinance adopted pursuant to this code, except offenses relating to parking or registration or offenses by pedestrians or bicyclists, or where an order is made to pay a sum to the general fund of a county pursuant to subdivision (3)(c) of Section 564 of the Welfare and Institutions Code, in the following amounts:

(a) Where a fine is
    imposed .....$5 for each $20 of fine, or fraction thereof.

(b) If sentence is
    suspended ...$5 if jail only, otherwise based on the amount of the fine levied, as in subdivision (a).

(c) If bail is forfeited ....$5 for each $20 of bail, or fraction thereof.

(d) Where multiple offenses are involved ......The penalty assessment shall be based on the total fine or bail for all offenses, or $5 for each jail sentence.

When a fine is suspended, in whole or in part, the penalty assessment shall be reduced in proportion to the suspension.
(Amended by Stats.1974, c. 1265, p. 2745, § 2.)

§ 42052. Disposition of assessment

After a determination by the court of the amount due under Section 42050, the clerk of the court shall collect the same and transmit it to the county treasury. It shall then be transmitted to the State Treasury in the same manner as fines collected for the state by a county. Upon order of the State Controller, the money shall be deposited in the State Treasury as follows:

(a) Seventy-five percent of each such penalty assessment shall be deposited in the Driver Training Penalty Assessment Fund, which fund is continued in existence, to be used exclusively to reimburse the General Fund as provided in Section 42050.

(b) Twenty-five percent of each such penalty assessment shall be deposited in the Peace Officers' Training Fund.
(Amended by Stats.1973, c. 1059, p. 2099, § 5.)

§ 42053. Waiver of assessment

In any case where a person convicted of any violation of this code punishable by fine and the levy of the driver training penalty assessment is imprisoned until the fine is satisfied, the judge may waive all or any part of the penalty assessment the payment of which would work a hardship on the person convicted or his immediate family.
(Stats.1959, c. 3, p. 1787, § 42053.)

HEALTH AND SAFETY CODE

The Health and Safety Code was formulated in 1939, when the legislature consolidated and revised laws relating to the preservation of the public health and safety. The Health and Safety Code also contains laws pertaining to the safety and protection of property and the handling of dead bodies.

The sections of this Code which will be of prime concern to peace officers will be found in Division Ten, commencing with Section 11000; it is these sections which are concerned with controlling narcotics and controlled substances. Division Ten in 1972, was amended substantially, and retitled "The Uniform Controlled Substances Act," which now closely parallels the federal scheduling of controlled substances.

The control of explosives is also included within this Code as Division 11, and presented here for your information.

Division	Section
GENERAL PROVISIONS	1
1. ADMINISTRATION OF PUBLIC HEALTH	100
2. LICENSING PROVISIONS	1200
3. PEST ABATEMENT	1700
4. COMMUNICABLE DISEASE PREVENTION AND CONTROL	3000
5. SANITATION	3700
6. SANITARY DISTRICTS	6400
7. DEAD BODIES	7000
8. CEMETERIES	8100
9. VITAL STATISTICS	10000
10. UNIFORM CONTROLLED SUBSTANCES ACT	11000
10.5 RESTRICTED DANGEROUS DRUGS	11901
10.6 COMMUNITY NARCOTICS AND DANGEROUS DRUG TREATMENT SERVICES [REPEALED]	11920
10.8 STATE OFFICE OF NARCOTICS AND DRUG ABUSE	11940
10.9 METHYLAMINE AND PHENYLACETONE	11991
11. EXPLOSIVES	12000
12. FIRES AND FIRE PROTECTION	13000
13. HOUSING	15000
14. POLICE PROTECTION	20000
15. POISONS [REPEALED]	
16. VENEREAL DISEASE [REPEALED]	
17-19. BLANK	
20. MISCELLANEOUS HEALTH AND SAFETY PROVISIONS	24000
21. SHERMAN FOOD, DRUG, AND COSMETIC LAW	26000
22. MISCELLANEOUS PROVISIONS RELATING TO FOODS, RESTAURANTS, AND HAZARDOUS SUBSTANCES	27000
23. HOSPITAL DISTRICTS	32000
23.5 ENDOWMENT HOSPITALS	32500
24. COMMUNITY DEVELOPMENT AND HOUSING	33000
25. SERVICES FOR THE MENTALLY RETARDED	38000
30. REPEALS	40000

Division 10

UNIFORM CONTROLLED SUBSTANCES ACT

§ 11000. Short title

This division shall be known as the "California Uniform Controlled Substances Act."
(Added by Stats.1972, c. 1407, p. 2987, § 3.)

§ 11001. Application of definitions

Unless the context otherwise requires, the definitions in this chapter govern the construction of this division.
(Added by Stats.1972, c. 1407, p. 2987, § 3.)

§ 11002. Administer

"Administer" means the direct application of a controlled substance, whether by injection, inhalation, ingestion, or any other means, to the body of a patient for his immediate needs or to the body of a research subject by any of the following:

(a) A practitioner or, in his presence, by his authorized agent.

(b) The patient or research subject at the direction and in the presence of the practitioner.
(Added by Stats.1972, c. 1407, p. 2987, § 3.)

§ 11003. Agent

"Agent" means an authorized person who acts on behalf of or at the direction of a manufacturer, distributor, or dispenser. It does not include a common or contract carrier, public warehouseman, or employee of the carrier or warehouseman.
(Added by Stats.1972, c. 1407, p. 2988, § 3.)

§ 11004. Attorney general

"Attorney General" means the Attorney General of the State of California.
(Added by Stats.1972, c. 1407, p. 2988, § 3.)

§ 11005. Board of pharmacy

"Board of Pharmacy" means the California State Board of Pharmacy.
(Added by Stats.1972, c. 1407, p. 2988, § 3.)

§ 11006.5. Concentrated cannabis

"Concentrated cannabis" means the separated resin, whether crude or purified, obtained from marijuana.
(Added by Stats.1975, c. 248, p. —, § 1.)

§ 11007. Controlled substance

(a) Except for the purposes of Chapter 4 (commencing with Section 11150) of this division, "controlled substance" means a drug, substance, or immediate precursor which are included in Schedules I through V, inclusive, pursuant to Chapter 2 (commencing with Section 11053).

(b) As used in Chapter 4 (commencing with Section 11150) of this division and any provisions of this division specifying penalties for offenses defined in Chapter 4 (commencing with Section 11150), except for those offenses which are punishable under Section 11371, "controlled substance" means any drug, substance, or immediate precursor which is included in one of the five schedules contained in the Federal Controlled Substances Act (Title II, P.L. 91–513), as such schedules may be revised from time to time to add, delete, or transfer substances from one schedule to another, whether by congressional enactment or by administrative rule of the United States Attorney General adopted pursuant to Section 201 of such act. Whenever reference is made in Chapter 4 (commencing with Section 11150) of this division to a controlled substance classified in a particular schedule, the reference shall be deemed to be to a federal controlled substance classified in the designated federal schedule, as such schedules may be so revised from time to time.
(Amended by Stats.1976, c. 1035, p. —, § 1.)

§ 11008. Customs broker

"Customs broker" means a person in this state who is authorized to act as a broker for any of the following:

(a) A person in this state who is licensed to sell, distribute, or otherwise possess any controlled substance.

(b) A person in any other state who ships any controlled substance into this state.

(c) A person in this state or any other state who ships or transfers any controlled substance through this state.
(Added by Stats.1972, c. 1407, p. 2988, § 3.)

§ 11009. Deliver or delivery

"Deliver" or "delivery" means the actual, constructive, or attempted transfer from one person to another of a controlled substance, whether or not there is an agency relationship.
(Added by Stats.1972, c. 1407, p. 2988, § 3.)

§ 11010. Dispense

"Dispense" means to deliver a controlled substance to an ultimate user or research subject by or pursuant to the lawful order of a practitioner, including the prescribing, furnishing, packaging, labeling, or compounding necessary to prepare the substance for that delivery.
(Added by Stats.1972, c. 1407, p. 2987, § 3.)

§ 11011. Dispenser

"Dispenser" means a practitioner who dispenses.
(Added by Stats.1972, c. 1407, p. 2988, § 3.)

§ 11012. Distribute

"Distribute" means to deliver other than by administering or dispensing a controlled substance.
(Added by Stats.1972, c. 1407, p. 2988, § 3.)

§ 11013. Distributor

"Distributor" means a person who distributes. The term distributor also includes warehousemen handling or storing controlled substances and customs brokers.
(Added by Stats.1972, c. 1407, p. 2988, § 3.)

§ 11014. Drug

"Drug" means (a) substances recognized as drugs in the official United States Pharmacopoeia, official Homeopathic Pharmacopoeia of the United States, or official National Formulary, or any supplement to any of them; (b) substances intended for use in the diagnosis, cure, mitigation, treatment, or prevention of disease in man or animals; (c) substances (other than food) intended to affect the structure or any function of the body of man or animals; and (d) substances intended for use as a component of any article specified in subdivision (a), (b), or (c) of this section. It does not include devices or their components, parts, or accessories.
(Added by Stats.1972, c. 1407, p. 2988, § 3.)

§ 11015. Federal bureau

"Federal bureau" means the Bureau of Narcotics and Dangerous Drugs of the United States Department of Justice, or its successor agency.
(Added by Stats.1972, c. 1407, p. 2988, § 3.)

§ 11016. Furnish

"Furnish" has the same meaning as provided in Section 4048.5 of the Business and Professions Code.
(Added by Stats.1972, c. 1407, p. 2989, § 3.)

§ 11017. Manufacturer

"Manufacturer" has the same meaning as provided in Section 4034 of the Business and Professions Code.
(Added by Stats.1972, c. 1407, p. 2987, § 3.)

§ 11018. Marijuana

"Marijuana" means all parts of the plant Cannabis sativa L., whether growing or not; the seeds thereof; the resin extracted from any part of the plant; and every compound, manufacture, salt, derivative, mixture, or preparation of the plant, its seeds or resin. It does not include the mature stalks of the plant, fiber produced from the stalks, oil or cake made from the seeds of the plant, any other compound, manufacture, salt, derivative, mixture, or preparation of the mature stalks (except the resin extracted therefrom), fiber, oil, or cake, or the sterilized seed of the plant which is incapable of germination.
(Added by Stats.1972, c. 1407, p. 2989, § 3.)

Notes of Decisions

Section 11360 and this section, which prohibit sale of "marijuana" and which define "marijuana" as "Cannabis sativa L." were sufficient to forewarn defendant convicted of selling marijuana of crimes for which he was charged even though he argued that the marijuana which he sold might not be "Cannabis sativa L." but might be another type of marijuana. People v. Van Alstyne (1975) 121 Cal.Rptr. 363, 46 C.A.3d 900, certiorari denied 96 S.Ct. 798, 423 U.S. 1060, 46 L.Ed.2d 652.

Possession of any part of marijuana plant whether it be of a male or female plant, which differ as to their resin content potential, may be prosecuted but if prosecution is based upon possession of parts of plant other than resin or seed such as leaves and stems, marijuana must be in quantity sufficient for use in smoking. People v. Pohle (1971) 97 Cal.Rptr. 364, 20 C.A.3d 78.

Possession of resin extracted from any part of marijuana plant may be prosecuted but if such prosecution is based upon possession of resin alone, there must be quantity sufficient for use to which such resin may be put. Id.

In a prosecution for possession of marijuana, prosecution is not required to establish that particular marijuana possessed by defendant has a potential to produce a narcotic effect on one using it; prosecution is required only to establish that substance possessed is marijuana and that it is of a quantity which can be potentiated by consumption in any of the manners customarily employed by users rather than useless traces or debris of narcotic. People v. Piper (1971) 96 Cal.Rptr. 643, 19 C.A.3d 248.

§ 11019. Narcotic drug

"Narcotic drug" means any of the following, whether produced directly or indirectly by extraction from substances of vegetable origin, or independently by means of chemical synthesis, or by a combination of extraction and chemical synthesis:

(a) Opium and opiate, and any salt, compound, derivative, or preparation of opium or opiate.

(b) Any salt, compound, isomer, derivative, or preparation thereof which is chemically equivalent or identical with any of the substances referred to in subdivision (a), but not including the isoquinoline alkaloids of opium.

(c) Opium poppy and poppy straw.

(d) Coca leaves and any salt, compound, derivative, or preparation of coca leaves, and any salt, compound, isomer, derivative, or preparation thereof which is chemically equivalent or identical with any of these substances, but not including decocainized coca leaves or extractions of coca leaves which do not contain cocaine or ecgonine.
(Added by Stats.1972, c. 1407, p. 2989, § 3.)

Notes of Decisions

Since 1972 amendment of § 11001 (repealed. Now, this section) under which marijuana was eliminated as a "narcotic" and was also not classified as a dangerous drug, was enacted prior to the time decision by board of medical examiners, which entered disciplinary order against petitioner physician who was convicted of the misdemeanor of possessing marijuana, became final petitioner was entitled to the benefit thereof and, accordingly, the board would be ordered to dismiss the proceeding and to vacate, annul and expunge its decision. Weissbuch v. Board of Medical Examiners (1974) 116 Cal.Rptr. 479, 41 C.A.3d 924.

§ 11020. Opiate

"Opiate" means any substance having an addiction-forming or addiction-sustaining liability similar to morphine or being capable of conversion into a drug having addiction-forming or addiction-sustaining liability. It does not include, unless specifically designated as controlled under Chapter 2 (commencing with Section 11053) of this division, the dextrorotatory isomer of 3-methoxy-n-methylmorphinan and its salts (dextromethorphan). It does include its racemic and levorotatory forms.
(Added by Stats.1972, c. 1407, p. 2989, § 3.)

§ 11021. Opium poppy

"Opium poppy" means the plant of the species Papaver somniferum L., except its seeds.
(Added by Stats.1972, c. 1407, p. 2989, § 3.)

§ 11022. Person

"Person" means individual, corporation, government or governmental subdivision or agency, business trust, estate, trust, partnership, or association, or any other legal entity.
(Added by Stats.1972, c. 1407, p. 2989, § 3.)

§ 11023. Pharmacy

"Pharmacy" has the same meaning as provided in Section 4035 of the Business and Professions Code.
(Added by Stats.1972, c. 1407, p. 2989, § 3.)

§ 11024. Physician, dentist, podiatrist, pharmacist, veterinarian

"Physician," "dentist," "podiatrist," "pharmacist," and "veterinarian" mean persons who are licensed to practice their respective professions in this state.
(Added by Stats.1972, c. 1407, p. 2989, § 3.)

§ 11025. Poppy straw

"Poppy straw" means all parts, except the seeds, of the opium poppy, after mowing.
(Added by Stats.1972, c. 1407, p. 2990, § 3.)

§ 11026. Practitioner

"Practitioner" means any of the following:

(a) A physician, dentist, veterinarian, podiatrist, or pharmacist acting within the scope of a project authorized under Article 18 (commencing with Section 429.70) of Chapter 2 of Part 1 of Division 1, or registered nurse acting within the scope of a project authorized under Article 18 (commencing with Section 429.70) of Chapter 2 of Part 1 of Division 1, or physician's assistant acting within the scope of a project authorized under Article 18 (commencing with Section 429.70) of Chapter 2 of Part 1 of Division 1, scientific investigator, or other person licensed, registered or otherwise permitted to distribute, dispense, conduct research with respect to or to administer a controlled substance in the course of professional practice or research in this state.

(b) A pharmacy, hospital, or other institution licensed, registered, or otherwise permitted to distribute, dispense, conduct research with respect to or to administer a controlled substance in the course of professional practice or research in this state.
(Amended by Stats.1977, c. 843, p. —, § 16.)

§ 11027. Prescription

"Prescription" means an oral order for a controlled substance given individually for the person for whom prescribed, directly from the prescriber to the furnisher or indirectly by means of a written order of the prescriber.
(Amended by Stats.1976, c. 896, p. —, § 2.)

§ 11029. Production

"Production" includes the manufacture, planting, cultivation, growing, or harvesting of a controlled substance.
(Added by Stats.1972, c. 1407, p. 2990, § 3.)

§ 11030. Ultimate user

"Ultimate user" means a person who lawfully possesses a controlled substance for his own use or for the use of a member of his household or for administering to an animal owned by him or by a member of his household.
(Added by Stats.1972, c. 1407, p. 2990, § 3.)

§ 11031. Wholesaler

"Wholesaler" has the same meaning as provided in Section 4038 of the Business and Professions Code.
(Added by Stats.1972, c. 1407, p. 2990, § 3.)

§ 11032. Narcotics, restricted dangerous drugs and marijuana; construction of terms used in other divisions

Whenever reference is made to the term "narcotics" in any provision of law outside of this division, unless otherwise expressly provided, it shall be construed to mean controlled substances classified in Schedules I and II, as defined in this division. Whenever reference is made to "restricted dangerous drugs" outside of this division, unless otherwise expressly provided, it shall be construed to mean controlled substances classified in Schedules III and IV. Whenever reference is made to the term "marijuana" in any provision of law outside of this division, unless otherwise expressly provided, it shall be construed to mean marijuana as defined in this division.
(Added by Stats.1972, c. 1407, p. 2990, § 3.)

§ 11053. Alternative names

The controlled substances listed or to be listed in the schedules in this chapter are included by whatever official, common, usual, chemical, or trade name designated.
(Added by Stats.1972, c. 1407, p. 2990, § 3.)

§ 11054. Schedule I, substances included

(a) Except for purposes of Chapter 4 (commencing with Section 11150) of this division, the controlled substances listed in this section are included in Schedule I.

(b) Any of the following opiates, including their isomers, esters, ethers, salts, and salts of isomers, esters, and ethers, unless specifically excepted, whenever the existence of these isomers, esters, ethers and salts is possible within the specific chemical designation:

(1) Acetylmethadol.
(2) Allylprodine.
(3) Alphacetylmethadol.
(4) Alphameprodine.
(5) Alphamethadol.
(6) Benzethidine.
(7) Betacetylmethadol.
(8) Betameprodine.
(9) Betamethadol.
(10) Betaprodine.
(11) Clonitazene.
(12) Dextromoramide.
(13) Dextrorphan.
(14) Diampromide.
(15) Diethylthiambutene.
(16) Dimenoxadol.
(17) Dimepheptanol.
(18) Dimethylthiambutene.
(19) Dioxaphetyl butyrate.
(20) Dipipanone.
(21) Ethylmethylthiambutene.
(22) Etonitazene.
(23) Etoxeridine.
(24) Furethidine.
(25) Hydroxypethidine.
(26) Ketobemidone.
(27) Levomoramide.
(28) Levophenacylmorphan.
(29) Morpheridine.
(30) Noracymethadol.
(31) Norlevorphanol.
(32) Normethadone.
(33) Norpipanone.
(34) Phenadoxone.
(35) Phenampromide.
(36) Phenomorphan.
(37) Phenoperidine.
(38) Piritramide.
(39) Proheptazine.
(40) Properidine.
(41) Propiran.
(42) Racemoramide.
(43) Trimeperidine.

(c) Any of the following opium derivatives, their salts, isomers and salts of isomers, unless specifically excepted, whenever the existence of these salts, isomers and salts of isomers is possible within the specific chemical designation:

(1) Acetorphine.
(2) Acetyldihydrocodeine.
(3) Benzylmorphine.
(4) Codeine methylbromide.
(5) Codeine-N-oxide.
(6) Cyprenorphine.
(7) Desomorphine.
(8) Dihydromorphine.
(9) Etorphine.
(10) Heroin.
(11) Hydromorphinol.
(12) Methyldesorphine.
(13) Methyldihydromorphine.

(14) Morphine methylbromide.
(15) Morphine methylsulfonate.
(16) Morphine-N-oxide.
(17) Myrophine.
(18) Nicocodeine.
(19) Nicomorphine.
(20) Normorphine.
(21) Phoclodine.
(22) Thebacon.

(d) Any material, compound, mixture, or preparation which contains any quantity of the following hallucinogenic substances, their salts, isomers and salts of isomers, unless specifically excepted, whenever the existence of these salts, isomers, and salts of isomers is possible within the specific chemical designation:

(1) 3, 4-methylenedioxy amphetamine.
(2) 5-methoxy-3, 4-methylenedioxy amphetamine.
(3) 3, 4, 5-trimethoxy amphetamine.
(4) Bufotenine.
(5) Diethyltryptamine.
(6) Dimethyltryptamine.
(7) 4-methyl-2, 5-dimethoxylamphetamine.
(8) Ibogaine.
(9) Lysergic acid diethylamide.
(10) Marijuana.
(11) Mescaline.
(12) Peyote.
(13) N-ethyl-3-piperidyl benzilate.
(14) N-methyl-3-piperidyl benzilate.
(15) Psilocybin.
(16) Psilocyn.
(17) Tetrahydrocannabinols.

(Amended by Stats.1976, c. 1035, p. —, § 2.)

§ 11055. Schedule II, substances included

(a) Except for purposes of Chapter 4 (commencing with Section 11150) of this division, the controlled substances listed in this section are included in Schedule II.

(b) Any of the following substances, except those narcotic drugs listed in other schedules, whether produced directly or indirectly by extraction from substances of vegetable origin, or independently by means of chemical synthesis, or by combination of extraction and chemical synthesis:

(1) Opium and opiate, and any salt, compound, derivative, or preparation of opium or opiate, with the exception of naloxone hydrochloride (N-allyl-14-hydroxy-nordihydromorphinone hydrochloride), but including the following:

(i) Raw opium.
(ii) Opium extracts.
(iii) Opium fluid extracts.
(iv) Powdered opium.
(v) Granulated opium.
(vi) Tincture of opium.
(vii) Apomorphine.
(viii) Codeine.
(ix) Ethylmorphine.
(x) Hydrocodone.
(xi) Hydromorphone.
(xii) Metopon.
(xiii) Morphine.
(xiv) Oxycodone.
(xv) Oxymorphone.
(xvi) Thebaine.

(2) Any salt, compound, isomer, derivative, or preparation thereof which is chemically equivalent or identical with any of the substances referred to in paragraph (1), but not including the isoquinoline alkaloids of opium.

(3) Opium poppy and poppy straw.

(4) Coca leaves and any salt, compound, derivative, or preparation of coca leaves, and any salt, compound, derivative, or preparation thereof which is chemically equivalent or identical with any of these substances, but not including decocainized coca leaves or extractions which do not contain cocaine or ecgonine.

(c) Any of the following opiates, including their isomers, esters, ethers, salts, and salts of isomers, whenever the existence of these isomers, esters, ethers and salts is possible within the specific chemical designation:

(1) Alphaprodine.
(2) Anileridine.
(3) Bezitramide.
(4) Dihydrocodeine.
(5) Diphenoxylate.
(6) Fentanyl.
(7) Isomethadone.
(8) Levomethorphon.
(9) Levorphanol.
(10) Metazocine.
(11) Methadone.
(12) Methadone—intermediate, 4-cyano-2-dimethylamino-4, 4-diphenyl butane.
(13) Moramide—intermediate, 2-methyl-3-morpholino-1, 1-diphenyl-propane-carboxylic acid.

(14) Pethidine.

(15) Pethidine—intermediate—A, 4-cyano-1-methyl-4-phenylpiperidine.

(16) Pethidine—intermediate—B, ethyl-4-phenylpiperidine-4-carboxylate.

(17) Pethidine—intermediate—C, 1-methyl-4-phenylpiperidine-4-carboxylic acid.

(18) Phenazocine.

(19) Piminodine.

(20) Racemethorphan.

(21) Racemorphan.

(d) Any material, compound, mixture, or preparation which contains any quantity of the following substances having a potential for abuse associated with a stimulant effect on the central nervous system:

(1) Amphetamine, its salts, optical isomers, and salts of its optical isomers.

(2) Phenmetrazine and its salts.

(3) Any substance which contains any quantity of methamphetamine, including its salts, isomers, and salts of isomers.

(4) Methylphenidate.

(e) Any material, compound, mixture, or preparation which contains any quantity of phencyclidine having a potential for abuse associated with a depressant effect on the central nervous system.
(Amended by Stats.1978, c. 699, p. —, § 1.)

§ 11056. Schedule III, substances included

(a) Except for purposes of Chapter 4 (commencing with Section 11150) of this division, the controlled substances listed in this section are included in Schedule III.

(b) Unless listed in another schedule, any material, compound, mixture, or preparation which contains any quantity of the following substances having a potential for abuse associated with a depressant effect on the central nervous system:

(1) Any substance which contains any quantity of a derivative of barbituric acid, or any salt of a derivative of barbituric acid, except those substances which are specifically listed in other schedules.

(2) Chlorhexadol.

(3) Glutethimide.

(4) Lysergic acid.

(5) Lysergic acid amide.

(6) Methaqualone and its salts.

(7) Methyprylon.

(8) Sulfondiethylmethane.

(9) Sulfonethylmethane.

(10) Sulfonmethane.

(c) Nalorphine.

(d) Any material, compound, mixture, or preparation containing limited quantities of any of the following narcotic drugs, or any salts thereof:

(1) Not more than 1.8 grams of codeine, or any of its salts, per 100 milliliters or not more than 90 milligrams per dosage unit, with an equal or greater quantity of an isoquinoline alkaloid of opium.

(2) Not more than 1.8 grams of codeine, or any of its salts, per 100 milliliters or not more than 90 milligrams per dosage unit, with one or more active, nonnarcotic ingredients in recognized therapeutic amounts.

(3) Not more than 300 milligrams of dihydrocodeinone, or any of its salts, per 100 milliliters or not more than 15 milligrams per dosage unit, with a fourfold or greater quantity of an isoquinoline alkaloid of opium.

(4) Not more than 300 milligrams of dihydrocodeinone, or any of its salts, per 100 milliliters or not more than 15 milligrams per dosage unit, with one or more active, nonnarcotic ingredients in recognized therapeutic amounts.

(5) Not more than 1.8 grams of dihydrocodeine, or any of its salts, per 100 milliliters or not more than 90 milligrams per dosage unit, with one or more active, nonnarcotic ingredients in recognized therapeutic amounts.

(6) Not more than 300 milligrams of ethylmorphine, or any of its salts, per 100 milliliters or not more than 15 milligrams per dosage unit, with one or more ingredients in recognized therapeutic amounts.

(7) Not more than 500 milligrams of opium per 100 milliliters or per 100 grams, or not more than 25 milligrams per dosage unit, with one or more active, nonnarcotic ingredients in recognized therapeutic amounts.

(8) Not more than 50 milligrams of morphine, or any of its salts, per 100 milliliters or per 100 grams with one or more active, nonnarcotic ingredients in recognized therapeutic amounts.
(Amended by Stats.1978, c. 699, p. —, § 2.)

§ 11057. Schedule IV, substances included

(a) Except for purposes of Chapter 4 (commencing with Section 11150) of this division, the controlled substances listed in this section are included in Schedule IV.

(b) Any material, compound, mixture, or preparation which contains any quantity of the following substances having a potential for abuse associated with a depressant effect on the central nervous system:

(1) Barbital.
(2) Chloral betaine.
(3) Chloral hydrate.
(4) Ethchlorvynol.
(5) Ethinamate.
(6) Methohexital.
(7) Meprobamate.
(8) Methylphenobarbital.
(9) Paraldehyde.
(10) Petrichloral.
(11) Phenobarbital.

(Amended by Stats.1976, c. 1035, p. ——, § 5.)

§ 11058. Schedule V, substances included

(a) Except for purposes of Chapter 4 (commencing with Section 11150) of this division, the controlled substances listed in this section are included in Schedule V.

(b) Any compound, mixture, or preparation containing limited quantities of any of the following narcotic drugs, which also contains one or more nonnarcotic active medicinal ingredients in sufficient proportion to confer upon the compound, mixture, or preparation, valuable medicinal qualities other than those possessed by the narcotic drug alone:

(1) Not more than 200 milligrams of codeine, or any of its salts, per 100 milliliters or per 100 grams.

(2) Not more than 100 milligrams of dihydrocodeine, or any of its salts, per 100 milliliters or per 100 grams.

(3) Not more than 100 milligrams of ethylmorphine, or any of its salts, per 100 milliliters or per 100 grams.

(4) Not more than 2.5 milligrams of diphenoxylate and not less than 25 micrograms of atrophine sulfate per dosage unit.

(5) Not more than 100 milligrams of opium per 100 milliliters or per 100 grams.

(Amended by Stats.1976, c. 1035, p. ——, § 6.)

§ 11100. Transferor's report; exceptions

(a) Any manufacturer, wholesaler, retailer, or other person who sells, transfers, or otherwise furnishes any of the following substances to any person in this state shall submit a report to the State Department of Justice of all such transactions:

(1) Phenyl-2-propanone
(2) Methylamine
(3) D-lysergic acid
(4) Ergotamine tartrate
(5) Diethyl malonate
(6) Malonic acid
(7) Ethyl malonate
(8) Barbituric acid
(9) Piperidine

(b) The Department of Justice may adopt rules and regulations in accordance with Chapter 4.5 (commencing with Section 11371) of Division 3 of Title 2 of the Government Code that add substances to subdivision (a) if the substance is a precursor to a controlled substance and delete substances from subdivision (a). However, no regulation adding or deleting a substance shall have any effect beyond March 1 of the year following the calendar year during which the regulation was adopted.

(c) This section shall not apply to any of the following:

(1) Any pharmacist or other authorized person who sells or furnishes such substance upon the prescription of a physician, dentist, podiatrist, or veterinarian.

(2) Any physician, dentist, podiatrist, or veterinarian who administers or furnishes such substance to his patients.

(3) Any manufacturer or wholesaler licensed by the Board of Pharmacy who sells, transfers, or otherwise furnishes such substance to a licensed pharmacy, physician, dentist, podiatrist, or veterinarian.

(d) Any manufacturer, wholesaler, retailer, or other persons who sells, transfers, or otherwise furnishes any substance listed in subdivision (a) to a person in this state shall, within 72 hours thereafter, submit a report of such transaction to the Department of Justice. However, the Department of Justice may authorize the submission of such reports on a monthly basis with respect to repeated, regular transactions between the furnisher and the recipient involving the

§ 11100

same substance if the Department of Justice determines that: (1) a pattern of regular supply of such substance exists as between the manufacturer, wholesaler, retailer, or other person who sells, transfers, or otherwise furnishes such substance and the recipient of the substance, and (2) the recipient has established a record of utilization of such substance for lawful purposes.
(Amended by Stats.1976, c. 1117, p. —, § 1.)

§ 11101. Transferor's reporting form

The State Department of Justice shall provide a common reporting form for the substances in Section 11100 which contains at least the following information:

(a) Name of the substance.

(b) Quantity of the substance sold, transferred, or furnished.

(c) The date the substance was sold, transferred, or furnished.

(d) The name and address of the person buying or receiving such substance.

(e) The name and address of the manufacturer, wholesaler, retailer, or other person selling, transferring, or furnishing such substance.
(Amended by Stats.1974, c. 1072, p. —, § 2.)

§ 11102. Regulations

The Department of Justice may adopt all regulations necessary to carry out the provisions of this part.
(Added by Stats.1974, c. 1072, p. —, § 3.)

§ 11103. Theft, loss and discrepancy reports

The theft or loss of any substance regulated pursuant to Section 11100 discovered by any licensee or any person regulated by the provisions of this chapter shall be reported to the Department of Justice within three days after such discovery.

Any difference between the quantity of any substance regulated pursuant to Section 11100 received and the quantity shipped shall be reported to the Department of Justice within three days of the receipt of actual knowledge of the discrepancy.

Any report made pursuant to this section shall also include the name of the common carrier or person who transports the substance and date of shipment of the substance.
(Amended by Stats.1974, c. 1072, p. —, § 6.)

§ 11104. Furnishing § 11100 (a) substance for manufacturing purposes; felony

Any manufacturer, wholesaler, retailer, or other person who sells, transfers, or otherwise furnishes any of the substances listed in subdivision (a) of Section 11100 with knowledge that the recipient will use the substance to unlawfully manufacture a controlled substance is guilty of a felony.
(Added by Stats.1978, c. 699, p. —, § 2.3.)

§ 11105. Reports or records to department of justice; certification of accuracy; perjury

Any person submitting a report or record to the Department of Justice pursuant to the requirements of this article shall certify the accuracy of information contained therein under penalty of perjury.
(Added by Stats.1978, c. 699, p. —, § 2.5.)

§ 11150. Persons authorized to write prescriptions

No person other than a physician, dentist, podiatrist, or veterinarian, or pharmacist acting within the scope of a project authorized under Article 18 (commencing with Section 429.70) of Chapter 2 of Part 1 of Division 1, or registered nurse acting within the scope of a project authorized under Article 18 (commencing with Section 429.70) of Chapter 2 of Part 1 of Division 1, or physician's assistant acting within the scope of a project authorized under Article 18 (commencing with Section 429.70) of Chapter 2 of Part 1 of Division 1 shall write a prescription.
(Amended by Stats.1977, c. 843, p. —, § 18.)

§ 11150.5. Schedule references deemed to be to federal schedule

The provisions of this chapter shall be applicable to controlled substances subject to the Federal Controlled Substances Act (Title II, P.L. 91–513), as provided in subdivision (b) of Section 11007. References in this chapter to controlled substances classified in a particular schedule shall be deemed to be a reference to the federal schedule of such number, rather than a reference to the schedules set forth in Chapter 2 (commencing with Section 11053) of this division.
(Added by Stats.1976, c. 1035, p. —, § 7.)

§ 11151. Prescriptions by unlicensed person authorized to practice

A prescription written by an unlicensed person lawfully practicing medicine pursuant to Section 2147.5 of the Business and Professions Code, shall be

filled only at a pharmacy maintained in the hospital which employs such unlicensed person.
(Added by Stats.1972, c. 1407, p. 3001, § 3.)

§ 11152. Nonconforming prescriptions

No person shall write, issue, fill, compound, or dispense a prescription that does not conform to this division.
(Added by Stats.1972, c. 1407, p. 3001, § 3.)

§ 11153. Responsibility of practitioner and pharmacist; order to provide an addict with controlled substance

The responsibility for the proper prescribing and dispensing of controlled substances is upon the practitioner, but a corresponding liability rests with the pharmacist who fills the prescription. An order purporting to be a prescription issued to an addict or habitual user of controlled substances, which is not in the course of professional treatment nor part of an authorized methadone maintenance program, for the purpose of providing the user with controlled substances, sufficient to keep him comfortable by maintaining his customary use, is not a prescription within the meaning and intent of this division; and the person filling such an order, as well as the person issuing it, may be charged with violation of the law.
(Added by Stats.1972, c. 1407, p. 3001, § 3.)

Notes of Decisions

Within section 11162.5 (repealed. Now, this section) prohibiting prescribing narcotics, not in course of professional treatment but sufficient to keep addict comfortable by maintaining his customary use, language, sufficient, etc., does not describe part of substantive offense but merely describes specific intent required and prosecution need not show that defendant prescribed precise amount needed to keep person comfortable according to particular size and duration of his habit. People v. Anderson (1972) 105 Cal.Rptr. 664, 29 C.A.3d 551.

§ 11154. Prescription, administration or furnishing controlled substances, restrictions

Except in the regular practice of his profession, no person shall prescribe, administer, dispense, or furnish, a controlled substance to or for any person who is not under his treatment for a pathology or condition other than addiction to a controlled substance, except as provided in this division.
(Added by Stats.1972, c. 1407, p. 3002, § 3.)

Notes of Decisions

Section 11163 (repealed. Now, this section) was constitutional. People v. Bowman (1958) 320 P.2d 70, 156 C.A.2d 784.

This section penalizing "except in the regular practice of his profession" the administering or furnishing of a narcotic to any person who is not under the treatment of a physician for a condition other than a narcotic addiction is not invalid because the quoted phrase is too uncertain to give notice of what constitutes the act sought to be prohibited. People v. Nunn (1956) 296 P.2d 813, 46 C.2d 460, certiorari denied and appeal dismissed 77 S.Ct. 126, 352 U.S. 883, 1 L.Ed.2d 82, rehearing denied 77 S.Ct. 260, 352 U.S. 945, 1 L.Ed.2d 240.

Section 11163 (repealed. Now, this section) forbidding certain narcotics prescriptions was not enacted to protect persons not under physician's treatment for pathology from faulty diagnosis or improvident administration of narcotics, but rather to prevent one having access to narcotics from making them available, other than for legitimate purpose, to one under treatment for a pathology. People v. Braddock (1954) 264 P.2d 521, 41 C.2d 794, certiorari denied 75 S.Ct. 27, 348 U.S. 837, 99 L.Ed. 660.

In prosecution charging licensed medical doctor with prescribing narcotics to persons not under his treatment for pathology, prosecution was required to prove that defendant was a licensed physician and was entitled to prove that he had knowledge of narcotic laws, and if proof of such facts implied other misconduct by physician no prejudicial error occurred, absent evidence of bad faith, and where the implication was dispelled by admonition to jury by court and by explanatory statements and questions of prosecutor. People v. Baker (1974) 113 Cal.Rptr. 248, 39 C.A.3d 550.

In prosecution for unlawfully prescribing narcotics, state need not, as part of its case in chief, prove that a defendant physician did not act in good faith. People v. Fong (1954) 277 P.2d 859, 129 C.A.2d 667.

§ 11155. Physician surrendering controlled substance privileges; prohibited acts

Any physician, who by court order or order of any state or governmental agency, or who voluntarily surrenders his controlled substance privileges, shall not possess, administer, dispense, or prescribe a controlled substance unless and until such privileges have been restored, and he has obtained current registration from the appropriate federal agency as provided by law.
(Added by Stats.1972, c. 1407, p. 3002, § 3.)

§ 11156. Addicts; restriction on prescription, administration or dispensation

No person shall prescribe for or administer, or dispense a controlled substance to an addict or habitual user, or to any person representing himself as such, except as permitted by this division.
(Added by Stats.1972, c. 1407, p. 3002, § 3.)

Notes of Decisions

Section 11164 (repealed, now this section) was constitutional. People v. Bowman (1958) 320 P.2d 70, 156 C.A.2d 784.

This section is not unconstitutional on the ground that the legislature cannot deprive a doctor of the right to prescribe for any patient including one who may be an addict and that the section leaves the subject of who constitutes an addict to speculation and conjecture. People v. Nunn (1956) 296 P.2d 813, 46 C.2d 460,

§ 11156

certiorari denied and appeal dismissed 77 S.Ct. 126, 352 U.S. 883, 1 L.Ed.2d 82, rehearing denied 77 S.Ct. 260, 352 U.S. 945, 1 L.Ed.2d 240.

Under this section, prohibiting the prescribing of narcotics to addict except "where the patient's addiction is complicated by the presence of incurable disease," burden of proving addict was suffering from incurable disease or condition shifted to defendant doctor in narcotics case after prosecution showed that defendant knowingly contributed to addiction of patient. People v. Lawrence (1962) 18 Cal.Rptr. 196, 198 C.A.2d 54.

In prosecution of a physician for a narcotics violation a narcotics inspector's act in giving a false name and address and in telling physician the inspector was using "H" when buying narcotics from the physician were not illegal in view that inspector was immune from prosecution and a conviction resulting from use of the evidence secured by such acts was not against public policy and a denial of due process of law. People v. Nunn (1956) 296 P.2d 813, 46 C.2d 460, certiorari denied and appeal dismissed 77 S.Ct. 126, 352 U.S. 883, 1 L.Ed.2d 82, rehearing denied 77 S.Ct. 260, 352 U.S. 945, 1 L.Ed.2d 240.

As used in this section inhibiting the dispensing of narcotics to person representing himself as an addict, word "dispense" does not refer only to filling of prescriptions, but was intended to prohibit the giving or distributing of narcotics. Davis v. Board of Medical Examiners (1952) 239 P.2d 78, 108 C.A.2d 346.

§ 11157. False or fictitious prescription

No person shall issue a prescription that is false or fictitious in any respect.
(Added by Stats.1972, c. 1407, p. 3002, § 3.)

Notes of Decisions

It does not follow from fact that offense is punishable under this section prohibiting fictitious prescriptions that such act may not also amount to a violation of § 11163 (repealed. See, now, § 11154), prohibiting prescription of narcotics for persons not under treatment. People v. Braddock (1954) 264 P.2d 521, 41 C.2d 794, certiorari denied 75 S.Ct. 27, 348 U.S. 837, 99 L.Ed. 660.

A "prescription" is a written instrument ordinarily used in ordering a drug or medical remedy. People v. Whitlow (1952) 249 P.2d 35, 113 C.A.2d 804.

§ 11158. Prescriptions for schedule II, III, IV and V substances; practitioners authorized to administer controlled substances

Except as provided in Section 11159, no controlled substance classified in Schedule II shall be dispensed without a prescription meeting the requirements of this chapter. Except as provided in Section 11159 or when dispensed directly to an ultimate user by a practitioner, other than a pharmacist or pharmacy, no controlled substance classified in Schedule III, IV, or V may be dispensed without a prescription meeting the requirements of this chapter.

Except as otherwise prohibited or limited by law, a practitioner specified in Section 11150, may administer controlled substances in the regular practice of his profession.
(Added by Stats.1976, c. 896, p. ——, § 6.)

§ 11159. Order for use by hospital patient; form and contents; record

An order for controlled substances for use by a patient in a county or licensed hospital shall be exempt from all requirements of this article, but shall be in writing on the patient's record, signed by the prescriber, dated, and shall state the name and quantity of the controlled substance ordered and the quantity actually administered. The record of such orders shall be maintained as a hospital record for a minimum of seven years.
(Added by Stats.1972, c. 1407, p. 3002, § 3.)

§ 11161. Official blanks; state issuance; unauthorized possession

Prescription blanks shall be issued by the Department of Justice in serially numbered groups of 100 forms each in triplicate, and shall be furnished free of cost to any person authorized to write a prescription, and such prescription blanks shall not be transferable. Any person possessing any such prescription blank otherwise than as herein provided is guilty of a misdemeanor.
(Amended by Stats.1975, c. 678, p. ——, § 41.)

§ 11162. Official blanks; form and contents

The prescription blanks shall be printed on distinctive paper, serial number of the group being shown on each form, and also each form being serially numbered.
(Added by Stats.1972, c. 1407, p. 2987, § 3.)

§ 11163. Official blanks; number issued at one time

Not more than one such prescription group shall in any case be issued or furnished by the Department of Justice to the same prescriber at one time.
(Amended by Stats.1975, c. 678, p. ——, § 42.)

§ 11164. Execution and contents of prescriptions for schedule II, III, IV and V controlled substances; oral prescriptions

Except as provided in Section 11167, no person shall prescribe a controlled substance, nor shall any person fill, compound, or dispense such a prescription unless it complies with the requirements of this section.

(a) Each prescription for a controlled substance classified in Schedule II which is a narcotic drug shall be wholly written in ink or indelible pencil in the handwriting of the prescriber upon the official prescription form issued by the Department of Justice. Such prescriptions shall be prepared in triplicate, signed and dated by the prescriber, and shall contain the name and address of the person for whom the controlled substance is prescribed, the name and quantity of the controlled substance prescribed, directions for use, and the address, category of professional licensure, and the federal controlled substance registration of the prescriber. The original and one copy of such a prescription shall be delivered to the pharmacist filling the prescription. The original shall be retained by the pharmacist and the copy, properly endorsed by him, shall be transmitted to the Department of Justice at the end of the month in which the prescription was filled.

(b) Each prescription for a controlled substance classified in Schedule II which is not a narcotic drug or for a controlled substance classified in Schedule III, IV, or V, except as authorized by subdivision (c), shall be subject to the following requirements:

(1) The prescription shall be signed and dated by the prescriber and shall contain the name of the person for whom the controlled substance is prescribed, the name and quantity of controlled substance prescribed, and directions for use. With respect to prescriptions for controlled substances classified in Schedule II which are not narcotic drugs, and any controlled substance classified in Schedule III, the signature, date, and information required by this paragraph shall be wholly written in ink or indelible pencil in the handwriting of the prescriber.

(2) In addition, the prescription shall contain the name, address, telephone number, category of professional licensure, and federal controlled substance registration number of the prescriber. The information required by this paragraph shall be either preprinted upon the prescription blank, typewritten, rubber stamped, or printed by hand. Notwithstanding any provision in this section, the prescriber's address, telephone number, category of professional licensure, or federal controlled substances registration number need not appear on the prescription if such information is readily retrievable in the pharmacy.

(3) The prescription shall also contain the address of the person for whom the controlled substance is prescribed. If the prescriber does not specify such address on the prescription, the pharmacist filling the prescription or an employee acting under his direction shall write or type the address on the prescription or maintain such information in a readily retrievable form in the pharmacy.

(c) Any controlled substance classified in Schedule III, IV, or V may be dispensed upon an oral prescription, which shall be reduced to writing by the pharmacist filling the prescription or by such other person as is expressly authorized by provisions of the Business and Professions Code. The date of issue of the prescription and all the information required for a written prescription by subdivision (b) shall be included in such written record of the prescription. The pharmacist need not reduce to writing the address, telephone number, license classification, or federal registry number of the prescriber or the address of the patient if such information is readily retrievable in the pharmacy. Pursuant to authorization of the prescriber, any employee of the prescriber on his behalf may orally transmit a prescription for a controlled substance classified in Schedule IV or V, if in such cases the written record of the prescription required by this subdivision specifies the name of the employee of the prescriber transmitting the prescription.

(Amended by Stats.1978, c. 1103, p. —, § 5.)

§ 11165. Separate prescription blanks; written prescriptions containing controlled substances

Each written prescription for a controlled substance or for any material, compound, mixture, or preparation containing one or more controlled substances shall be set forth on a separate prescription blank.

(Added by Stats.1976, c. 896, p. —, § 11.)

§ 11166. Time for tender and filling of prescriptions; Schedule II controlled substances; filling forged or altered prescriptions for controlled substances

No person shall fill a prescription for a controlled substance classified in Schedule II which is tendered to him after the seventh day following the date of issue. No person shall knowingly fill a forged or altered prescription for a controlled substance except for the addition of the address of the person for whom the controlled substance is prescribed as provided by paragraph (3) of subdivision (b) of Section 11164.

(Added by Stats.1976, c. 896, p. —, § 13.)

§ 11167. Epidemics, accidents or calamities; oral prescriptions for Schedule II controlled substances; use of other than official form for written prescriptions

In the event of an epidemic or accident or calamity, any controlled substance classified in Schedule II may be dispensed upon an oral prescription if failure to issue such a prescription might result in loss of life or intense suffering. Prior to filling such a prescription, the pharmacist shall reduce it to writing. The date of issue of the prescription and all the information required for a written prescription by Section 11164 shall be included in such written record of the prescription.

Additionally, in such an emergency a prescriber may issue a written prescription for a controlled substance classified in Schedule II which is a narcotic drug upon a form other than the official prescription form issued by the Department of Justice. However, such a prescription shall in all other respects comply with the requirements of subdivision (a) of Section 11164.

When an emergency oral or written prescription is issued pursuant to this section, the prescriber shall within 72 hours submit the prescription in the form required by Section 11164 to the pharmacy or pharmacist filling the prescription. If the prescriber does not provide such a prescription within 72 hours, the pharmacist filling the emergency prescription shall immediately so inform the Department of Justice.
(Added by Stats.1976, c. 896, p. ——, § 15.)

§ 11168. Prescription book; retention

The prescription book containing the prescriber's copies of prescriptions issued shall be retained by the prescriber which shall be preserved for three years. (Formerly § 11166, added by Stats.1972, c. 1407, p. 3003, § 3. Renumbered § 11168 and amended by Stats.1976, c. 896, p. ——, § 12.)

§ 11170. Controlled substances for self use

No person shall prescribe, administer, or furnish a controlled substance for himself.
(Added by Stats.1972, c. 1407, p. 3003, § 3.)

§ 11171. Prescription, administration or furnishing controlled substance

No person shall prescribe, administer, or furnish a controlled substance except under the conditions and in the manner provided by this division.
(Added by Stats.1972, c. 1407, p. 3003, § 3.)

§ 11172. Antedating or postdating prescription

No person shall antedate or postdate a prescription.
(Added by Stats.1972, c. 1407, p. 3003, § 3.)

§ 11173. Fraud, deceit, misrepresentations

(a) No person shall obtain or attempt to obtain controlled substances, or procure or attempt to procure the administration of or prescription for controlled substances, (1) by fraud, deceit, misrepresentation, or subterfuge; or (2) by the concealment of a material fact.

(b) No person shall make a false statement in any prescription, order, report, or record, required by this division.

(c) No person shall, for the purpose of obtaining controlled substances, falsely assume the title of, or represent himself to be, a manufacturer, wholesaler, pharmacist, physician, dentist, veterinarian, registered nurse, physician's assistant, or other authorized person.

(d) No person shall affix any false or forged label to a package or receptacle containing controlled substances.
(Amended by Stats.1977, c. 843, p. ——, § 19.)

§ 11174. False name or address

No person shall, in connection with the prescribing, furnishing, administering, or dispensing of a controlled substance, give a false name or false address.
(Added by Stats.1972, c. 1407, p. 3004, § 3.)

Notes of Decisions

Although owner of automobile unlawfully gave false name and address in purchasing a cough syrup which contained codeine but for which a prescription was not needed, automobile was not subject to forfeiture for allegedly being used to unlawfully transport a narcotic, since possession of cough syrup was not unlawful. People v. One 1962 Chevrolet Bel Air (1967) 56 Cal.Rptr. 878, 248 C.A.2d 725.

Neither an offense under § 11168 (repealed, now § 11171), requiring conformance with narcotic provisions in prescription, administration and furnishing of narcotics, nor offense under § 11225 (repealed. See, now § 11190), relating to facts required to be shown by narcotic records, was necessarily included offense within § 11170 (repealed. See, now, § 11173) or former § 11170.5 (now this section), proscribing use of false statements in prescriptions or false names or addresses in connection with prescribing or dispensing narcotic, under either language of indictment or facts and circumstances as shown by evidence and court properly declined to give lesser included offenses charge. People v. Meyer (1963) 31 Cal.Rptr. 285, 216 C.A.2d 618.

A defendant charged in language of provision of § 11170 (repealed. See, now, § 11173) proscribing false statements in prescriptions or provision of this section proscribing false names and addresses in connection with prescribing narcotics need not be shown to have violated § 11225 (repealed. See, now, § 11190) prescribing contents of records which must be kept to commit offense charged and, accordingly, misdemeanor of violating the latter provision is not necessarily included offense in felony charge under the former two provisions. Id.

§ 11175. Possession of noncomplying prescriptions; unlawfully obtained controlled substances

No person shall obtain or possess a prescription that does not comply with this division, nor shall any person obtain a controlled substance by means of a prescription which does not comply with this division or possess a controlled substance obtained by such a prescription.
(Amended by Stats.1976, c. 896, p. —, § 17.)

§ 11179. Filing and retention of prescriptions

A person who fills a prescription shall keep it on file for at least three years from the date of filling it.
(Amended by Stats.1976, c. 896, p. —, § 21.)

§ 11180. Possession of controlled substance obtained by nonconforming prescription

No person shall obtain or possess a controlled substance obtained by a prescription that does not comply with this division.
(Added by Stats.1972, c. 1407, p. 3004, § 3.)

§ 11190. Duty to keep record; contents

Every practitioner, other than a pharmacist, who issues a prescription, or dispenses or administers a controlled substance classified in Schedule II shall make a record that, as to the transaction, shows all of the following:

(a) The name and address of the patient.

(b) The date.

(c) The character and quantity of controlled substances involved.

The prescriber's record shall show the pathology and purpose for which the prescription is issued, or the controlled substance administered, prescribed, or dispensed.
(Amended by Stats.1976, c. 1015, p. —, § 1.)

§ 11191. Preservation of record; violations

The record shall be preserved for three years.

Every person who violates any provision of this section is guilty of a misdemeanor.
(Amended by Stats.1976, c. 896, p. —, § 23.)

§ 11192. Prima facie evidence of violation

In a prosecution for a violation of Section 11190, proof that a defendant received or has had in his possession at any time a greater amount of controlled substances than is accounted for by any record required by law or that the amount of controlled substances possessed by a defendant is a lesser amount than is accounted for by any record required by law is prima facie evidence of a violation of the section.
(Amended by Stats.1976, c. 637, p. —, § 1.)

§ 11195. Receipt for pharmacist's copy of prescription removed by officer

Whenever the pharmacist's copy of a controlled substance prescription is removed by a peace officer, agent of the Attorney General, or inspector of the Board of Pharmacy, or investigator of the Division of Investigation of the Department of Consumer Affairs for the purpose of investigation or as evidence, the officer or inspector or investigator shall give to the pharmacist a receipt in lieu thereof.
(Added by Stats.1972, c. 1407, p. 3005, § 3.)

§ 11200. Restrictions and prohibitions

No person shall refill a controlled substance prescription more than six months after the date thereof or cause such a prescription to be refilled more than five times, unless renewed by the prescriber. No prescription for a Schedule II substance may be refilled.
(Added by Stats.1972, c. 1407, p. 3005, § 3.)

§ 11205. Controlled substance prescription file

The owner of a pharmacy or any person who purchases a controlled substance upon federal order forms as required pursuant to the provisions of the Federal "Comprehensive Drug Abuse Prevention and Control Act of 1970," (P.L. 91–513, 84 Stat. 1236), relating to the importation, exportation, manufacture, production, compounding, distribution, dispensing, and control of controlled substances, and who sells controlled substances obtained upon such federal order forms in response to prescriptions shall maintain and file such prescriptions in a separate file apart from noncontrolled substances prescriptions. Such files shall be preserved for a period of three years.
(Amended by Stats.1976, c. 896, p. —, § 24.)

§ 11206. Contents of controlled substance prescription file

The prescription file shall constitute a record that as to the transactions shall show all of the following:

(a) The name and address of the patient.

(b) The date.

(c) The character, quantity, and directions for use of the controlled substance involved.

(d) The name, address, telephone number, category of professional licensure, and the federal controlled substance registration number of the prescriber. (Amended by Stats.1976, c. 896, p. ——, § 25.)

§ 11207. Compounding, preparation, filling or dispensing of controlled substance prescriptions; registered or intern pharmacists

No person other than a registered pharmacist under the laws of this state or an intern pharmacist, as defined in Section 4038.1 of the Business and Professions Code, who is under the personal supervision of a pharmacist, shall compound, prepare, fill or dispense a prescription for a controlled substance. (Amended by Stats.1976, c. 896, p. ——, § 26.)

§ 11208. Evidence

In a prosecution under this division, proof that a defendant received or has had in his possession at any time a greater amount of controlled substances than is accounted for by any record required by law or that the amount of controlled substances possessed by the defendant is a lesser amount than is accounted for by any record required by law is prima facie evidence of guilt.
(Added by Stats.1972, c. 1407, p. 3006, § 3.)

§ 11210. Conditions authorizing prescription; quantity; duration

A physician, surgeon, dentist, veterinarian, or podiatrist, or pharmacist acting within the scope of a project authorized under Article 18 (commencing with Section 429.70) of Chapter 2 of Part 1 of Division 1, or registered nurse acting within the scope of a project authorized under Article 18 (commencing with Section 429.70) of Chapter 2 of Part 1 of Division 1, or physician's assistant acting within the scope of a project authorized under Article 18 (commencing with Section 429.70) of Chapter 2 of Part 1 of Division 1 may prescribe for, furnish to, or administer controlled substances to his patient when the patient is suffering from a disease, ailment, injury, or infirmities attendant upon old age, other than addiction to a controlled substance.

The physician, surgeon, dentist, veterinarian, or podiatrist, or pharmacist acting within the scope of a project authorized under Article 18 (commencing with Section 429.70) of Chapter 2 of Part 1 of Division 1, or registered nurse acting within the scope of a project authorized under Article 18 (commencing with Section 429.70) of Chapter 2 of Part 1 of Division 1, or physician's assistant acting within the scope of a project authorized under Article 18 (commencing with Section 429.70) of Chapter 2 of Part 1 of Division 1 shall prescribe, furnish, or administer controlled substances only when in good faith he believes the disease, ailment, injury, or infirmity, requires such treatment.

The physician, surgeon, dentist, veterinarian or podiatrist, or pharmacist acting within the scope of a project authorized under Article 18 (commencing with Section 429.70) of Chapter 2 of Part 1 of Division 1, or registered nurse acting within the scope of a project authorized under Article 18 (commencing with Section 429.70) of Chapter 2 of Part 1 of Division 1, or physician's assistant acting within the scope of a project authorized under Article 18 (commencing with Section 429.70) of Chapter 2 of Part 1 of Division 1 shall prescribe, furnish, or administer controlled substances only in such quantity and for such length of time as are reasonably necessary. (Amended by Stats.1977, c. 843, p. ——, § 20.)

§ 11221. Physicians' reports of treatment

The physician prescribing, furnishing, or administering any narcotic controlled substance in the treatment of an addict for addiction shall within five days after the first treatment report by registered mail, over his signature, to the Attorney General stating the name and address of the patient, and the name and quantities of narcotic controlled substances prescribed.

The report shall state the progress of the patient under the treatment.

The physician shall in the same manner further report on the 15th day of the treatment and on the 30th day of the treatment, and thereafter shall make such further reports as are requested in writing by the Attorney General.
(Added by Stats.1972, c. 1407, p. 3009, § 3.)

§ 11222. Arrested persons; medical aid; methadone maintenance

In any case in which a person is taken into custody by arrest or other process of law and is lodged in a jail or other place of confinement, and there is reasonable cause to believe that such person is addicted to a controlled substance, it is the duty of the person in charge of the place of confinement to provide the person so confined with medical aid as necessary to ease any symptoms of withdrawal from the use of controlled substances.

In any case in which a person, who is participating in a methadone maintenance program, is incarcerated in a jail or other place of confinement, he shall, in the discretion of the director of such program, be entitled to continue in such program until conviction.
(Added by Stats.1972, c. 1407, p. 3010, § 3.)

§ 11240. Human beings

No veterinarian shall prescribe, administer, or furnish a controlled substance for himself or any other human being.
(Added by Stats.1972, c. 1407, p. 3010, § 3.)

§ 11250. Authorized retail sales by pharmacists; execution of orders required by federal law

No prescription is required in case of the sale of controlled substances at retail in pharmacies by pharmacists to any of the following:

(a) Physicians.

(b) Dentists.

(c) Podiatrists.

(d) Veterinarians.

(e) Pharmacists acting within the scope of a project authorized under Article 18 (commencing with Section 429.70) of Chapter 2 of Part 1 of Division 1, or registered nurses acting within the scope of a project authorized under Article 18 (commencing with Section 429.70) of Chapter 2 of Part 1 of Division 1, or physician's assistants acting within the scope of a project authorized under Article 18 (commencing with Section 429.70) of Chapter 2 of Part 1 of Division 1.

In any sale mentioned in this article, there shall be executed any written order that may otherwise be required by federal law relating to the production, importation, exportation, manufacture, compounding, distributing, dispensing, or control of controlled substances.
(Amended by Stats.1977, c. 843, p. ——, § 21.)

§ 11350. Possession of designated controlled substances; punishment

Except otherwise provided in this division, every person who possesses (1) any controlled substance specified in subdivision (b) or (c) of Section 11054, specified in paragraph (11), (12), or (17) of subdivision (d) of Section 11054, or specified in subdivision (b) or (c) of Section 11055, or (2) any controlled substance classified in Schedule III, IV, or V which is a narcotic drug, unless upon the written prescription of a physician, dentist, podiatrist, or veterinarian licensed to practice in this state, shall be punished by imprisonment in the state prison.
(Amended by Stats.1976, c. 1139, p. ——, § 65, operative July 1, 1977.)

Historical Note

1975 Amendment. Prohibited granting probation or suspending execution or imposition of sentence as specified at end of subds. (a), (b), and (c).

1976 Amendment. Deleted, following "state prison" the words "for a period of not less than two years or more than 10 years"; and deleted subds. (b) to (d).

Notes of Decisions

Exclusive possession or control is not necessary for a conviction of possessing narcotics. People v. Rice (1976) 131 Cal.Rptr. 330, 59 C.A.3d 998.

To prove unlawful possession of narcotics, it is not necessary to show exclusive possession of premises on which drug is found or to show physical possession of the drug. People v. Thomas (1975) 119 Cal.Rptr. 739, 45 C.A.3d 749.

Validity

Prohibition by this section against possession of heroin does not violate constitutional prohibition against cruel and unusual punishment. People v. Bowens (1964) 40 Cal.Rptr. 435, 229 C.A.2d 590.

Alleged deleterious effects upon Indian community from use of peyote in religious ceremony observed by Navajo Indians did not constitute compelling state interest such as would warrant abridgement of Indians' constitutional right to freedom of religion. People v. Woody (1964) 40 Cal.Rptr. 69, 394 P.2d 813, 61 C.A. 813.

Construction and application

Under "criminal acts" test, possession of heroin placed in bush for sale to co-defendant and separate and distinct possession of balloon of heroin found in defendant's pocket after his arrest were two separate acts and defendant was properly convicted of possession of heroin found in his pocket and possession of heroin in bush for sale, despite contention that defendant merely possessed single large quantity which was split up between bush and his pocket. People v. Martin (1971) 95 Cal.Rptr. 250, 17 C.A.3d 661.

Legislature, in segregating various offenses relating to prohibited narcotics and paraphernalia associated with their use, did not intend to promulgate rule that would preclude conviction upon charge of possession of persons discovered to be in possession of usable quantity of contraband if, as result of his own efforts, he was able to place all but small unusable quantity thereof beyond reach of police

§ 11350

before he could be effectively prevented from disposing of physical evidence. People v. Garcia (1967) 56 Cal.Rptr. 217, 248 C.A.2d 284.

Conviction of county jail inmate for possession of narcotics was proper under provision of former section 11500. People v. Clark (1966) 51 Cal.Rptr. 7, 241 C.A.2d 775.

California could not constitutionally apply this section proscribing use of peyote so as to prevent Indian tribe from using peyote as sacramental symbol similar to bread and wine used in Christian churches. People v. Woody (1964) 40 Cal.Rptr. 69, 394 P.2d 813, 61 C.2d 716.

Elements of possession generally

Unlawful possession of narcotics is established by proof that accused exercised dominion and control over contraband, that he had knowledge of his presence, and that accused had knowledge that the material was a narcotic. People v. Foster (1971) 97 Cal.Rptr. 94, 19 C.A.3d 649; People v. Schroeder (1968) 70 Cal.Rptr. 491, 264 C.A.2d 217; People v. Showers (1968) 68 Cal.Rptr. 459, 440 P.2d 939, 68 C.2d 639.

Unlawful possession of narcotics is established by proof (1) that the accused exercised dominion and control over the contraband, (2) that he had knowledge of its presence, and (3) that he had knowledge of its narcotic character; the three elements may be proved by circumstantial evidence and reasonable inferences drawn from such evidence. People v. Fitzwater (1968) 67 Cal.Rptr. 190, 260 C.A.2d 478, certiorari denied 89 S.Ct. 378, 393 U.S. 953, 21 L.Ed.2d 364; People v. Schumacher (1967) 64 Cal.Rptr. 494, 256 C.A.2d 858.

To justify conviction for possession of heroin, state must prove that accused exercised dominion and control over drug with knowledge of its presence and narcotic character. People v. Camerano (1968) 67 Cal.Rptr. 446, 260 C.A.2d 861; People v. Mora (1965) 42 Cal.Rptr. 725, 232 C.A.2d 400.

Neither exclusive possession of premises nor physical possession of drug is essence of offense of illegal possession of narcotics. People v. McCottry (1962) 23 Cal.Rptr. 309, 205 C.A.2d 698; People v. Williams (1961) 16 Cal.Rptr. 842, 196 C.A.2d 845.

Knowledge as element

Knowledge of narcotic character of substance is essential element of offense of possession of narcotic. People v. Juvera (1963) 29 Cal.Rptr. 653, 214 C.A.2d 569; People v. Jackson (1958) 331 P.2d 218, 164 C.A.2d 772; People v. Castellanos (1958) 320 P.2d 152, 157 C.A.2d 36; People v. Hancock (1958) 319 P.2d 731, 156 C.A.2d 305; People v. Candiotto (1954) 275 P.2d 500, 128 C.A.2d 347.

It is not scientific measurement and detection which is ultimate test of known possession of narcotic, but rather defendant's awareness of its presence. People v. White (1965) 41 Cal.Rptr. 604, 231 C.A.2d 82; People v. Sullivan (1965) 44 Cal.Rptr. 524, 234 C.A.2d 562; People v. Aguilar (1963) 35 Cal.Rptr. 516, 223 A.C.A. 120.

Defendant's knowledge of narcotic character of substance possessed can be inferred from evidence of other acts of similar nature committed by him. Hacker v. Superior Court of Tulare County (1968) 73 Cal.Rptr. 907, 268 C.A.2d 387.

In order to convict defendant of possession of narcotics, prosecution must prove that defendant had knowledge that whatever substance was possessed was narcotic. People v. Perez (1968) 72 Cal.Rptr. 746, 267 C.A.2d 275.

All surrounding facts and circumstances may be considered in determining knowing possession of narcotics, including defendant's conduct, admissions, contrary statements or explanations. People v. Schumacher (1967) 64 Cal.Rptr. 494, 256 C.A.2d 858.

Amount of substance

Conviction for possession of narcotics must be based on proof of possession of quantity sufficient for sale or consumption. People v. Morales (1968) 66 Cal.Rptr. 234, 259 C.A.2d 290, certiorari denied 89 S.Ct. 469, 393 U.S. 988, 21 L.Ed.2d 450.

Essential element of crime of possession of heroin was that the capsule handed to defendant contained heroin. People v. Ihm (1966) 55 Cal.Rptr. 599, 247 C.A.2d 388.

In penalizing a person who possesses narcotic, legislature proscribed possession of substance that has a narcotic potential and condemned commodity that can be used as such but did not refer to useless traces or residue of such substance. People v. Leal (1966) 50 Cal.Rptr. 777, 413 P.2d 665, 64 C.2d 504.

Element of possession of defendant, charged with possession of heroin, was established by proof of any recognizable quantity of the narcotic. People v. Dominguez (1965) 46 Cal.Rptr. 23, 236 C.A.2d 464.

Knowledge of presence, sufficiency of evidence

Evidence on issue of knowledge of presence of heroin in automobile occupied by defendant and of its narcotic character was sufficient to support conviction of possessing and transporting a narcotic. People v. Richardson (1970) 85 Cal.Rptr. 607, 6 C.A.3d 70.

Evidence that defendant while under influence of narcotic was passenger in automobile being driven by person who was also under influence of narcotic in which vehicle narcotics were found in glove compartment was insufficient to establish that defendant had knowledge of presence of narcotics or to sustain conviction for unlawful possession. People v. Boddie (1969) 80 Cal.Rptr. 83, 274 C.A.2d 408.

Evidence sustained finding in prosecution for possession of narcotics that defendant knew of presence of narcotics in motel room. People v. Amiotte (1963) 30 Cal.Rptr. 102, 215 C.A.2d 176, certiorari denied 84 S.Ct. 521, 375 U.S. 987, 11 L.Ed.2d 474.

Requisite knowledge of presence of narcotics in pocket of defendant charged with possession of heroin and of nature thereof as narcotics were matters which could properly and sufficiently be established by circumstantial evidence. People v. Lopez (1960) 8 Cal.Rptr. 184, 185 C.A.2d 301.

In a prosecution for unlawful possession of narcotics found in locked automobile owned by defendant, who was in possession of the only known keys to the automobile which was admittedly parked by the defendant a considerable distance from his home, evidence sustained implied finding that defendant intentionally had possession, with knowledge, of the narcotics found in his automobile. People v. Brajevich (1959) 344 P.2d 815, 174 C.A.2d 438.

Knowledge may be inferred from all surrounding facts and circumstances. People v. Flores (1958) 327 P.2d 932, 162 C.A.2d 222.

§ 11351. Possession for sale of designated controlled substances; punishment

Except as otherwise provided in this division, every person who possesses for sale (1) any controlled substance specified in subdivision (b) or (c) of Section 11054, specified in paragraph (11), (12), or (17) of subdivision (d) of Section 11054, or specified in subdivision (b) or (c) of Section 11055, or (2) any controlled substance classified in Schedule III, IV, or V which is a narcotic drug, shall be punished by imprisonment in the state prison for two, three or four years.

(Amended by Stats.1976, c. 1139, p. —, § 66, operative July 1, 1977.)

Editors' Note

Penal Code Section 1203.7 mandates that those convicted of violating Health and Safety Code Sections 11351 or 11352 by selling or possessing for sale a substance containing ½ ounce or more of heroin shall not receive probation, but instead be sentenced to state prison or committed to the California Rehabilitation Center.

Notes of Decisions

To support a conviction of possession of amphetamines for sale, it must be shown that accused exercised control or had right to exercise control over the controlled substance that he had knowledge of presence of such substance, that he had knowledge of its nature and that he had specific intent to sell the same; such elements may be established by circumstantial evidence and any reasonable inferences drawn therefrom. People v. Glass (1975) 118 Cal.Rptr. 797, 44 C.A.3d 772.

Elements of crime of possession of heroin for sale are actual or constructive possession of the narcotic for the purpose or intent of selling it, with knowledge of its presence and with knowledge that the material is heroin. Williams v. Superior Court For San Joaquin County (1974) 112 Cal.Rptr. 485, 38 C.A.3d 412.

Elements of crime of unlawfully possessing heroin for sale require that defendant exercise dominion and control over narcotic, have knowledge of narcotic's presence and knowledge that material was narcotic, but constructive possession is all that is necessary and that may be proved by circumstantial evidence. People v. Wilson (1967) 64 Cal.Rptr. 172, 256 A.C.A. 458, certiorari denied 88 S.Ct. 1653, 391 U.S. 903, 20 L.Ed.2d 418.

Possession, elements of crime

Possession of commercial quantity of heroin furnishes circumstantial evidence of specific intent to sell heroin. People v. Long (1974) 117 Cal.Rptr. 200, 42 C.A.3d 751.

Fact that quantity of heroin and type of packaging found alongside defendant's back yard fence indicated it was intended for sale supported conviction of unlawful possession of a controlled substance for sale since the heroin was in defendant's custody and control. People v. Langley (1974) 116 Cal.Rptr. 80, 41 C.A.3d 339.

Where defendant was arrested in an apartment in which a dish containing heroin and narcotic paraphernalia was found and where defendant had in his pants pocket three balloons of heroin, the mere possession of the narcotic constituted substantial evidence that defendant knew of its nature. People v. Acuna (1973) 111 Cal.Rptr. 878, 35 C.A.3d 987.

Probable cause, arrest

Under evidence that defendant had been contacted to deliver narcotics, had left his residence immediately after the contact, and had proceeded to place where narcotics were to be exchanged for cash, the totality of circumstances represented probable cause to believe defendant was in course of doing what he had said he was going to do, i. e., deliver heroin, so that police had probable cause to arrest defendant. People v. Freeny (1974) 112 Cal.Rptr. 33, 37 C.A.3d 20.

Officers, who had been advised that a person had entered house to buy narcotics, had reasonable cause to believe him in possession of drugs where officers had been reliably informed that house was scene of numerous sales and person appeared in company of known drug user and, when confronted with officers on leaving, he thrust his hand into his pocket, retreated from police, and shouted warning to person inside. Pierson v. Superior Court (1970) 87 Cal.Rptr. 433, 8 C.A.3d 510.

Where informant told officer that one of the defendants was selling both marijuana and heroin in certain block on certain street and was using certain described motor vehicles, and officer verified reliability of informant, and officer saw that defendant walk to rear of residence in that block and entered a shed, after which he drove away in one of described motor vehicles, and several hours later officer saw two of described motor vehicles back up to shed and saw persons carrying articles into shed, information possessed by officer constituted reasonable cause to believe that such defendant had committed a felony and authorized arrest of such defendant without a warrant. People v. Marquez (1968) 66 Cal.Rptr. 615, 259 C.A.2d 593, certiorari denied 89 S.Ct. 386, 393 U.S. 955, 21 L.Ed.2d 367.

Where defendant was observed to have had numerous puncture marks on right arm, severely pinpointed eyes and slurred speech, probable cause for his arrest on ground that he was under influence of narcotics was established and search of defendant's apartment was reasonable incident of arrest and thus justified. People v. Hirsch (1967) 60 Cal.Rptr. 451, 252 C.A.2d 420.

Probable cause, searches and seizures

Officers who were advised by reliable informant that specified male and another person, probably a girl, would be coming to informer's apartment for purpose of delivering heroin, with high probability that other person might be carrying it, and who after being given prearranged signal by informer, arrived at front door where they observed male and female had probable cause to search female. People v. Fourshey (1974) 113 Cal.Rptr. 275, 38 C.A.3d 426.

In light of fact that untested informant's information had been corroborated by correctness of his prediction that alien, who admitted to being a runner for petitioner, would receive heroin from petitioner on a certain evening, and by fact that package which was handed to him was placed by alien below or to side of right front seat of car, a place where it would not be readily seen, and then by fact that alien drove, after he had received the package, to a certain place where informant had said the heroin would be delivered to a named recipient, narcotics officers had probable cause to search alien's vehicle. Ferdin v. Superior Court In and For Alameda County (1974) 112 Cal.Rptr. 66, 36 C.A.3d 774.

Circumstances that co-defendant was in possession of marijuana after leaving apartment, that known narcotics violators were seen going to apartment and that landlady had smelled marijuana gave police officers reasonable cause, for purpose of search without warrant, to believe that proscribed narcotics were on premises. People v. Newell (1969) 77 Cal.Rptr. 771, 272 C.A.2d 638.

Probable cause for issuance of search warrant existed, where two reliable informants stated that defendant had been selling heroin at a market and affiant police officer had personally verified that defendant, or someone answering his description, drove an automobile to lot near market and, after parking, headed in direction of market. People v. Gallardo (1966) 52 Cal.Rptr. 777, 244 C.A.2d 105.

Actions of defendant, following officer's knock on door and demand for admittance, in throwing balloons out of apartment window gave reasonable cause for forcible entry by officer and search disclosing heroin, empty balloons, sundry articles of the kind usually employed in cutting and packaging heroin, and bindle containing marijuana. People v. Padilla (1966) 49 Cal.Rptr. 340, 240 C.A.2d 114.

§ 11352. Transportation, sale, giving away, etc. of designated controlled substances; punishment

Except as otherwise provided in this division, every person who transports, imports into this state, sells,

§ 11352

furnishes, administers, or gives away, or offers to transport, import into this state, sell, furnish, administer, or give away, or attempts to import into this state or transport (1) any controlled substance specified in subdivision (b) or (c) of Section 11054, specified in paragraph (11), (12), or (17) of subdivision (d) of Section 11054, or specified in subdivision (b) or (c) of Section 11055, or (2) any controlled substance classified in Schedule III, IV, or V which is a narcotic drug, unless upon the written prescription of a physician, dentist, podiatrist, or veterinarian licensed to practice in this state, shall be punished by imprisonment in the state prison for three, four, or five years.
(Amended by Stats.1976, c. 1139, p. —, § 67, operative July 1, 1977.)

Editors' Note

Penal Code Section 1203.07 mandates that those convicted of violating Health and Safety Code Sections 11351 or 11352 by selling or possessing for sale a substance containing ½ ounce or more of heroin shall not receive probation, but instead be sentenced to state prison or committed to the California Rehabilitation Center.

Notes of Decisions

Nature and elements of offense—In general

Precedents which established elements of crimes of possession for sale of narcotics and offering to sell narcotics are applicable to elements of crimes of possession for sale of dangerous drugs and offering to sell dangerous drugs, including benzedrine, where language defining crimes involving dangerous drugs is the same as the language used to define comparable offenses involving narcotics. People v. Allen (1967) 62 Cal.Rptr. 235, 254 C.A.2d 597.

It is not necessary that buyer have narcotic deal directly with seller and fact that parties deal with each other through third party is sufficient to sustain conviction for illegal sale of narcotics. People v. Rivera (1962) 21 Cal.Rptr. 182, 202 C.A.2d 839.

Activities of defendants in procuring narcotics in exchange for money involved making sale of narcotics and was violation of this section, making it unlawful to sell, furnish or give away narcotics, even if defendants furnished the narcotics in role of agents between purchaser and supplier or seller and buyer. People v. Richards (1962) 17 Cal.Rptr. 845, 198 C.A.2d 465.

Under this section the requirement of a direct, unequivocal act toward a sale necessary for an attempt to make a sale is not an implied element of an offer to sell. People v. Brown (1961) 9 Cal.Rptr. 816, 357 P.2d 1072, 55 C.2d 64, certiorari denied 81 S.Ct. 1932, 366 U.S. 970, 6 L.Ed.2d 1259.

Defendant cannot be punished for both transportation of heroin and sale of same narcotics where only transportations proved are necessarily incident to the sales. People v. Castiel (1957) 315 P.2d 79, 153 C.A.2d 653.

Intent, nature and elements of offense

Specific intent is a requirement for crime of offering to sell heroin. People v. Mora (App.1974) 117 Cal.Rptr. 262; People v. Longino (1963) 35 Cal.Rptr. 367, 222 C.A.2d 734; People v. Brown (1961) 9 Cal.Rptr. 816, 357 P.2d 1049, 55 C.2d 64, certiorari denied 81 S.Ct. 1932, 366 U.S. 970, 6 L.Ed.2d 1259.

If specific intent to sell narcotic is present, offense of offering to sell narcotic is complete at time of offer, and delivery is not essential element. People v. Medina (1972) 103 Cal.Rptr. 721, 27 C.A.3d 473.

Breach of this section pertaining to sale of narcotics occurs when there is offer to sell narcotic, accompanied by specific intent to sell and actual delivery is not required. People v. Monteverde (1965) 46 Cal.Rptr. 206, 236 C.A.2d 630.

A specific intent to sell a narcotic is an essential element of the crime of offering to make such a sale, and persons who offer to sell narcotics with no intention of performing are not engaged in narcotics traffic and are not guilty of violation of this section. People v. Camarillo (1964) 37 Cal.Rptr. 178, 225 C.A.2d 127.

§ 11352.5. Sale of heroin; fine in addition to imprisonment

The court shall impose a fine not exceeding fifty thousand dollars ($50,000), in the absence of a finding that the defendant would be incapable of paying such a fine, in addition to any term of imprisonment provided by law for any of the following persons:

(1) Any person who is convicted of violating Section 11351 of the Health and Safety Code by possessing for sale one-half ounce or more of a substance containing heroin.

(2) Any person who is convicted of violating Section 11352 of the Health and Safety Code by selling or offering to sell one-half ounce or more of a substance containing heroin.

(3) Any person convicted of violating Section 11351 of the Health and Safety Code by possessing heroin for sale or convicted of violating Section 11352 of the Health and Safety Code by selling or offering to sell heroin, and who has one or more prior convictions for violating Section 11351 or Section 11352 of the Health and Safety Code.
(Added by Stats.1976, c. 1132, p. —, § 1.)

§ 11353. Adult inducing minor to violate provisions; use or employment of minors; punishment

Every person 18 years of age or over who in any voluntary manner solicits, induces, encourages, or intimidates any minor with the intent that the minor shall knowingly violate any provision of this chapter or Section 11550 with respect to (1) a controlled substance which is specified in subdivision (b) or (c) of Section 11054, specified in paragraph (11), (12), or (17) of subdivision (d) of Section 11054, or specified in subdivision (b) or (c) of Section 11055 or, (2) any controlled substance classified in Schedule III, IV, or V which is a narcotic drug, who hires, employs, or uses a minor to knowingly and unlawfully transport, carry, sell, give away, prepare for sale, or peddle any such controlled substance, or who unlawfully sells, furnishes, administers, gives, or offers to sell, furnish, administer, or give, any such controlled substance to a minor shall be punished by imprisonment in the state prison for a period of three, four, or five years. (Amended by Stats.1976, c. 1139, p. ——, § 68, operative July 1, 1977.)

Notes of Decisions

Age of defendant

It will not be necessary for prosecution in every instance to prove actual age of defendant charged with furnishing narcotic to minor as there will be occasions when his physical appearance will be such that jury could not entertain a reasonable doubt that he was over the age of 21 years, but in any event the information or indictment must contain the necessary language as to age and in jury trials the jury must be properly instructed as to all elements of the offense. People v. Montalvo (1971) 93 Cal.Rptr. 581, 482 P.2d 205, 4 C.3d 328, 49 A.L.R.3d 518.

Minors

Person married at 18 and later divorced came within provision of Civil Code § 25 that all persons under 21 years of age are minors, and was "minor" within this section, proscribing furnishing of narcotics to minor, and such person did not come within exception specifying that persons attain majority status by being 18 and married. People v. Vassar (1962) 24 Cal.Rptr. 481, 207 C.A.2d 318.

Minor involved in offense of using minor for purpose of transporting narcotics was not an accomplice of person committing such offense, and instruction requested in prosecution for such offense, that testimony of accomplice was required to be corroborated was properly refused. People v. De Paula (1954) 276 P.2d 600, 43 C.2d 643.

Minor involved in offense of using minor for purpose of transporting narcotics is regarded as a victim, not as an accomplice whose testimony it is necessary to corroborate. Id.

Where facts testified to by minor, involved in offense of using minor for purpose of transporting heroin, where within knowledge and power of accused to dispute, jury could consider accused's failure to explain or deny such testimony as tending to indicate the truth thereof and as indicating that among inferences that could reasonably be drawn therefrom, those unfavorable to accused were the more probable. Id.

§ 11354. Minor inducing another minor to violate provisions; use or employment of minors; punishment; juvenile court

(a) Every person under the age of 18 years who in any voluntary manner solicits, induces, encourages, or intimidates any minor with the intent that the minor shall knowingly violate any provision of this chapter or Section 11550, who hires, employs, or uses a minor to knowingly and unlawfully transport, carry, sell, give away, prepare for sale, or peddle (1) any controlled substance specified in subdivision (b) or (c) of Section 11054, specified in paragraph (11), (12), or (17) of subdivision (d) of Section 11054, or specified in subdivision (b) or (c) of Section 11055 or (2) any controlled substance classified in Schedule III, IV, or V which is a narcotic drug, or who unlawfully sells, furnishes, administers, gives, or offers to sell, furnish, administer, or give, any such controlled substance to a minor shall be punished by imprisonment in the state prison.

(b) This section is not intended to affect the jurisdiction of the juvenile court.
(Amended by Stats.1976, c. 1139, p. ——, § 69, operative July 1, 1977.)

§ 11355. Sale or furnishing substance falsely represented to be a controlled substance; punishment

Every person who agrees, consents, or in any manner offers to unlawfully sell, furnish, transport, administer, or give (1) any controlled substance specified in subdivision (b) or (c) of Section 11054, specified in paragraph (10), (11), (12), or (17) of subdivision (d) of Section 11054, or specified in subdivision (b) or (c) of Section 11055 or, (2) any controlled substance classified in Schedule III, IV, or V which is a narcotic drug to any person, or offers, arranges, or negotiates to have any such controlled substance unlawfully sold, delivered, transported, furnished, administered, or given to any person and then sells, delivers, furnishes, transports, administers, or gives, or offers, arranges, or negotiates to have sold, delivered, transported, furnished, administered, or given to any person any other liquid, substance or material in lieu of any such controlled substance shall be punished by imprisonment in the county jail for not more than one year, or in the state prison. (Amended by Stats.1976, c. 1139, p. ——, § 70, operative July 1, 1977.)

Notes of Decisions

This section which makes it illegal to agree to sell a narcotic and then to deliver instead a nonnarcotic substance was designed to discourage anyone from engaging or appearing to engage in narcotics traffic rather than to define the contractual rights of the pusher and his victim. People v. Ernst (1975) 121 Cal.Rptr. 857, 48 C.A.3d 785.

Sale of substitute in lieu of restricted dangerous drug is a general intent crime and thus defendant's specific intent to sell substance other than a controlled substance did not have to be shown to establish her violation of this section; overruling People v. Contreras, 226 Cal.App.2d 700, 38 Cal.Rptr. 338, and People v. Sweet, 257 Cal.App.2d 167, 65 Cal.Rptr. 31. People v. Lechlinski (1976) 131 Cal.Rptr. 701, 60 C.A.3d 766.

Apparent tender of narcotics for which parties had negotiated and accepted invitation to sample an amount sufficient to satisfy the buyer constituted adequate delivery of the substance to require defendants to plead to information which charged them with agreeing to sell a narcotic and instead delivering a nonnarcotic substance. People v. Ernst (1975) 121 Cal.Rptr. 857, 48 C.A.3d 785.

§ 11357. Unauthorized possession; punishment; prior convictions

(a) Except as authorized by law, every person who possesses any concentrated cannabis shall be punished by imprisonment in the county jail for a period of not more than one year or by a fine of not more than five hundred dollars ($500), or by both such fine and imprisonment, or shall be punished by imprisonment in the state prison.

(b) Except as authorized by law, every person who possesses not more than one avoirdupois ounce of marijuana, other than concentrated cannabis, is guilty of a misdemeanor and shall be punished by a fine of not more than one hundred dollars ($100). Notwithstanding other provisions of law, if such person has been previously convicted three or more times of an offense described in this subdivision during the two-year period immediately preceding the date of commission of the violation to be charged, the previous convictions shall also be charged in the accusatory pleading and, if found to be true by the jury upon a jury trial or by the court upon a court trial or if admitted by the person, the provisions of Sections 1000.1 and 1000.2 of the Penal Code shall be applicable to him, and the court shall divert and refer him for education, treatment, or rehabilitation, without a court hearing or determination or the concurrence of the district attorney, to an appropriate community program which will accept him. If the person is so diverted and referred he shall not be subject to the fine specified in this subdivision. If no community program will accept him, the person shall be subject to the fine specified in this subdivision. In any case in which a person is arrested for a violation of this subdivision and does not demand to be taken before a magistrate, such person shall be released by the arresting officer upon presentation of satisfactory evidence of identity and giving his written promise to appear in court, as provided in Section 853.6 of the Penal Code, and shall not be subjected to booking.

(c) Except as authorized by law, every person who possesses more than one avoirdupois ounce of marijuana, other than concentrated cannabis, shall be punished by imprisonment in the county jail for a period of not more than six months or by a fine of not more than five hundred dollars ($500), or by both such fine and imprisonment.
(Amended by Stats.1976, c. 1139, p. ——, § 71, operative July 1, 1977.)

Editors' Note

This section which became effective on January 1, 1976, makes the possession of less than one ounce of marijuana punishable by a maximum fine of $100. Although this offense remains a misdemeanor, it does not subject the defendant to arrest. Simple possession is a citable misdemeanor unless there are other factors present which justify a physical arrest.

Possession in excess of one ounce may be prosecuted as an arrestable misdemeanor subject to imprisonment in the county jail for no more than six months or a $500 fine.

Health and Safety Code Section 11361.51 provides for the destruction, after two years, of all records which relate to the conviction for simple possession of marijuana.

§ 11358. Unauthorized cultivation, harvesting or processing; punishment

Every person who plants, cultivates, harvests, dries, or processes any marijuana or any part thereof, except as otherwise provided by law, shall be punished by imprisonment in the state prison.
(Amended by Stats.1976, c. 1139, p. ——, § 72, operative July 1, 1977.)

Notes of Decisions

Searches and seizures

In light of duty of law enforcement officer to promptly report felonious conduct that comes to his knowledge, affidavit in support of search warrant which revealed that deputy sheriff had observed marijuana plants growing on defendant's property and informed authorities of such on August 23, 1975, alleged facts from which it could be inferred that marijuana was observed by deputy at time closely proximate to his call to authorities and that marijuana was still present at time affidavit was made, and thus affidavit was not insufficient to support issuance of warrant as result of absence of specific date in affidavit. People v. Wachter (1976) 130 Cal.Rptr. 279, 58 C.A.3d 911.

Where deputy sheriff who accompanied friend to defendant's farm because friend wanted to check on some chickens he had given to occupants of property was acting in his capacity as private citizen rather than as law enforcement officer when he entered defendant's premises and discovered presence of marijuana plants growing on plot not viewable from highway and when, upon his discovery, he communicated information as private citizen to proper law enforcement officials who subsequently issued lawful search warrant, deputy's actions were not subject to the "exclusionary rule" founded on the Fourth Amendment (U.S.C.A.Const. Amend. 4). Id.

Officer who placed 25 power spotting telescope on tripod on county-owned property immediately to rear of defendant's residence and who observed four marijuana plants growing in planter located inside rear window of residence did not unreasonably invade defendant's privacy. Id.

Use of binoculars by officer to confirm what he believed from unaided observation and report of another police officer to be growing marijuana plants on sun deck of defendants' residence did not invade defendants' reasonable expectation of privacy so as to invalidate either warrant or search, where marijuana plants were seen in plain and unobstructed view from a neighbor's backyard. People v. Vermouth (1974) 116 Cal.Rptr. 675, 42 C.A.3d 353.

Officer's observation of marijuana plants growing in petitioner's backyard from second floor bedroom of house next door after receiving a complaint from next door neighbor was not a violation of petitioner's reasonable expectation of privacy, and officer's subsequent search of yard with consent of petitioner after informing her that he was there to investigate possible cultivation of marijuana was legal, rendering marijuana uncovered as a result thereof admissible in evidence, where yard was vulnerable to observation by any of petitioner's neighbors, and, in essence was open to public view, and marijuana plants were in plain view, both to neighbors and to police. Dillon v. Superior Court of Santa Barbara County (1972) 102 Cal.Rptr. 161, 497 P.2d 505, 7 C.3d 305.

§ 11359. Possession for sale; punishment

Every person who possesses for sale any marijuana, except as otherwise provided by law, shall be punished by imprisonment in the state prison.
(Amended by Stats.1976, c. 1139, p. ——, § 73, operative July 1, 1977.)

Notes of Decisions
Elements of offense

Police officers' observation of marijuana seeds on floor of vehicle next to smoking pipe and their detection of the odor of burnt marijuana was sufficient to raise reasonable belief that the occupants of the automobile had recently smoked marijuana and thus provided basis for officers to believe that the occupants of the vehicle were aware of the nature and existence of the contraband found in their vehicle and that there might be other marijuana in the vehicle. Wimberly v. Superior Court of San Bernardino County (1976) 128 Cal.Rptr. 641, 547 P.2d 417, 16 C.3d 557.

Arrest

Where deputy had received information from informant that earlier in the day informant had bought eight kilos of marijuana from defendant at his residence and that defendant had at least eight more kilos and had been informed by two other deputies that the latter had observed defendant in a "loaded" condition on several occasions, the deputy learned from police records that defendant resided at address given him by fellow deputy and from police photograph that defendant matched description supplied by informant and when deputy approached defendant's residence with intention of talking to him defendant ran toward the garage yelling "Jesus Christ, the cops," there was sufficient probable cause for arrest. People v. Bigham (1975) 122 Cal.Rptr. 252, 49 C.A.3d 73.

Motorists and motor vehicles, search

Police officer's observance of erratic driving of automobile, of marijuana seeds adjacent to smoking pipe on the floor of the automobile, of odor of burnt marijuana and burnt residue in the pipe, and small quantity of marijuana secreted in jacket indicated only that the occupants of the vehicle were casual users of marijuana and thus did not give probable cause for search of the trunk for additional contraband; disapproving, to extent that it is contrary, People v. Superior Court (Courie), 118 Cal.Rptr. 586, 44 Cal.App.3d 207. Wimberly v. Superior Court of San Bernardino County (1976) 128 Cal.Rptr. 641, 547 P.2d 417, 16 C.3d 557.

Police officer's detection of strong odor of unburned marijuana emanating from occupants and automobile stopped for speeding in early morning hours on remote section of interstate highway furnished probable cause to search interior of automobile in which a small quantity of marijuana was found and the trunk in which a large quantity of marijuana was found since odor of marijuana was detected prior to entry into the automobile thereby establishing probable cause without any question of previous infringement of defendant's rights. People v. Cook (1975) 119 Cal.Rptr. 500, 532 P.2d 148, 13 C.3d 663, certiorari denied 96 S.Ct. 135, 423 U.S. 870, 46 L.Ed.2d 100.

Police officer who arrested defendant for driving under the influence of marijuana and for illegally using marijuana and who subsequently discovered in the passenger portion of the automobile a burning marijuana cigarette with a moist end and over two ounces of marijuana hidden in the glove compartment, had probable cause to search the trunk of the automobile and three and one-half kilos discovered in the trunk were admissible. People v. Superior Court for Los Angeles County (1974) 118 Cal.Rptr. 586, 44 C.A.3d 207.

Search of trunk of defendant's automobile following defendant's arrest for driving under the influence of marijuana and for illegally using marijuana based on police officers' observations that defendant had been driving erratically, was beyond the permissible scope of a search incident to arrest. Id.

§ 11360. Transportation, sale, import, give away, etc.; punishment

(a) Except as otherwise provided by this section or as authorized by law, every person who transports, imports into this state, sells, furnishes, administers, or gives away, or offers to transport, import into this state, sell, furnish, administer, or give away, or attempts to import into this state or transport any marijuana shall be punished by imprisonment in the state prison for a period of two, three or four years.

(b) Except as authorized by law, every person who gives away, offers to give away, transports, offers to transport, or attempts to transport not more than one avoirdupois ounce of marijuana, other than concentrated cannabis, is guilty of a misdemeanor and shall be punished by a fine of not more than one hundred dollars ($100). In any case in which a person is arrested for a violation of this subdivision and does not demand to be taken before a magistrate, such person shall be released by the arresting officer upon presentation of satisfactory evidence of identity and giving his written promise to appear in court, as provided in Section 853.6 of the Penal Code, and shall not be subjected to booking.
(Amended by Stats.1976, c. 1139, p. ——, § 74, operative July 1, 1977.)

Notes of Decisions

Word "transport" within this section pertaining to offense of transportation of marijuana refers to transporting for personal use as well as to transporting for purpose of sale or distribution. People v. Rogers (1971) 95 Cal.Rptr. 601, 486 P.2d 129, 5 C.3d 129.

§ 11360

Arrest

Where police officer received telephone call from person identifying himself as police officer in another city informing him of specific details as to suitcase allegedly containing marijuana which was to arrive on given airline flight, and circumstances were such that officer could reasonably believe that informant was actually police officer, and information was later verified by officer's own investigations, officer had reasonable cause, without warrant, to arrest persons who claimed suitcase on its arrival. People v. Villalva (1973) 109 Cal.Rptr. 16, 33 C.A.3d 362.

Where officer was involved in narcotic buying program which required his identity to be secret while he continued his investigations and defendant did not show that delay was for any unlawful purpose or prejudiced him, delay of five months between time of alleged offense and time of arrest did not warrant dismissal of information. People v. Wright (1969) 82 Cal.Rptr. 859, 2 C.A.3d 732.

Arrest of student, purportedly an agent of defendant who was charged with possession and sale of marijuana, was lawful where arresting officers acted on information received from undercover officer who had prior dealings with student and who, on day of arrest, had arranged to make a marijuana purchase from student and information obtained from student could be used in making arrest of student's supplier. People v. Tovar (1966) 49 Cal.Rptr. 79, 239 C.A.2d 644.

§ 11361. Adults employing or selling to minors; punishment

Every person 18 years of age or over who hires, employs, or uses a minor in unlawfully transporting, carrying, selling, giving away, preparing for sale, or peddling any marijuana, who unlawfully sells, furnishes, administers, gives, or offers to sell, furnish, administer, or give any marijuana to a minor, or who induces a minor to use marijuana in violation of law shall be punished by imprisonment in the state prison for a period of three, four, or five years.
(Amended by Stats.1976, c. 1139, p. ——, § 75, operative July 1, 1977.)

§ 11361.5. Destruction of arrest and conviction records; applicable offenses; method; records not applicable; costs

(a) Records of any court of this state, any public or private agency that provides services upon referral under Section 1000.2 of the Penal Code, or of any state agency or local public agency pertaining to the arrest or conviction of any person for a violation of subdivision (b) or (c) of Section 11357 or subdivision (c) of Section 11360, shall not be kept beyond two years from the date of such a conviction, or from the date of the arrest if there was no conviction. It shall be the duty of each court and each such agency having custody of such records to provide for the timely destruction thereof in accordance with the provisions of subdivision (c). The requirements of this subdivision shall not apply to records of any conviction occurring prior to January 1, 1976, or records of any arrest not followed by a conviction occurring prior to such date.

(b) This subdivision shall be applicable only to records of convictions and arrests not followed by conviction occurring prior to January 1, 1976, for any of the following offenses:

(1) Any violation of Section 11357 or a statutory predecessor thereof.

(2) Unlawful possession of a device, contrivance, instrument or paraphernalia used for unlawfully smoking marijuana, in violation of Section 11364, as it existed prior to January 1, 1976, or a statutory predecessor thereof.

(3) Unlawful visitation or presence in a room or place in which marijuana is being unlawfully smoked or used, in violation of Section 11365, as it existed prior to January 1, 1976, or a statutory predecessor thereof.

(4) Unlawfully using or being under the influence of marijuana, in violation of Section 11550, as it existed prior to January 1, 1976, or a statutory predecessor thereof.

Any person subject to such an arrest or conviction may apply to the Department of Justice for destruction of records pertaining thereto if two years or more have elapsed since the date of the conviction, or since the date of the arrest if not followed by a conviction. The application shall be submitted upon a form supplied by the Department of Justice and shall be accompanied by a fee, which shall be established by the department in such amount as will defray the cost of administering this subdivision and costs incurred by the state under subdivision (e), but which shall not exceed thirty-seven dollars and fifty cents ($37.50). The application form shall be made available at every local police or sheriff's department and from the Department of Justice and may require such information as the department determines is necessary for purposes of identification.

The department may request, but not require, the applicant to include a self-administered fingerprint upon the application. If the department is unable to sufficiently identify the applicant for purposes of this subdivision without such fingerprint or without additional fingerprints, it shall so notify the applicant and shall request the applicant to submit such fingerprints as may be required to effect identification, including a complete set if necessary, or, alternatively, to abandon the application and request a refund of all or a portion of the fee submitted with the application, as provided in this section. If the applicant fails or refuses to submit fingerprints in accordance with the department's request within such reasonable time as shall be established by the department or if the applicant requests a refund of the fee, the department shall promptly mail a refund to the applicant at the address specified in the application or at such other address as may be specified by the applicant. However, if the department has notified the applicant that election to abandon the application will result in forfeiture of a specified amount which is a portion of the fee, the department may retain such portion of the fee as the department may determine will defray the actual costs of processing the application, provided, the amount of such portion retained shall not exceed ten dollars ($10).

Upon receipt of a sufficient application, the Department of Justice shall destroy records of the department, if any, pertaining to such arrest or conviction in the manner prescribed by subdivision (c) and shall notify the Federal Bureau of Investigation, the law enforcement agency which arrested the applicant, and, if the applicant was convicted, the probation department which investigated the applicant and the Department of Motor Vehicles, of the application. Each state or local agency receiving such a notice from the Department of Justice shall destroy records of such agency, if any, pertaining to the arrest or conviction specified in the notice, in the manner prescribed by subdivision (c). The application form and the notices from the department to the agencies specified in this subdivision shall be destroyed by the department or agency, as the case may be, at the time the other records of the arrest or conviction are destroyed.

(c) Destruction of records of arrest or conviction pursuant to subdivision (a) or (b) of this section shall be accomplished by permanent obliteration of all entries or notations upon such records pertaining to the arrest or conviction, and the record shall be prepared again so that it appears that the arrest or conviction never occurred. However, where (1) the only entries upon the record pertain to such arrest or conviction and (2) the record can be destroyed without necessarily effecting the destruction of other records, then the document constituting the record shall be physically destroyed.

(d) Notwithstanding subdivision (a) or (b), written transcriptions of oral testimony in court proceedings and published judicial appellate reports shall not be subject to the provisions of this section. Additionally, no records shall be destroyed pursuant to subdivision (a) if the defendant or a codefendant has filed a civil action against the peace officers or law enforcement jurisdiction which made the arrest or instituted the prosecution and if the agency which is the custodian of such records has received a certified copy of the complaint in such civil action, until the civil action has finally been resolved. Immediately following the final resolution of the civil action, records subject to subdivision (a) of this section shall be destroyed pursuant to subdivision (a) if more than two years has elapsed from the date of the conviction or arrest without conviction.

(e) Costs incurred by local agencies in complying with the provisions of subdivision (b) shall be reimbursed as provided in Section 2231 of the Revenue and Taxation Code.
(Amended by Stats.1976, c. 952, p. ——, § 1.)

§ 11361.7. Accuracy, relevancy, timeliness and completeness of record subject to destruction; alteration of records; questions on prior criminal record; application of section

(a) Any record subject to destruction or permanent obliteration pursuant to Section 11361.5, or more than two years of age, or a record of a conviction for an offense specified in subdivision (a) or (b) of Section 11361.5 which became final more than two years previously, shall not be considered to be accurate, relevant, timely, or complete for any purposes by any agency or person. The provisions of this subdivision shall be applicable for purposes of the Privacy Act of 1974 (5 U.S.C. Section 552a) to the fullest extent permissible by law, whenever any information or record subject to destruction or permanent obliteration under Section 11361.5 was obtained by any state agency, local public agency, or any public or private agency that provides services upon referral under Section 1000.2 of the Penal Code, and is thereafter shared with or disseminated to any agency of the federal government.

(b) No public agency shall alter, amend, assess, condition, deny, limit, postpone, qualify, revoke, surcharge, or suspend any certificate, franchise, incident, interest, license, opportunity, permit, privilege, right, or title of any person because of an arrest or conviction for an offense specified in subdivision (a) or (b) of Section 11361.5, or because of the facts or events leading to such an arrest or conviction, on or after the date the records of such arrest or conviction

§ 11361.7

are required to be destroyed by subdivision (a) of Section 11361.5, or two years from the date of such conviction or arrest without conviction with respect to arrests and convictions occurring prior to January 1, 1976. As used in this subdivision, "public agency" includes, but is not limited to, any state, county, city and county, city, public or constitutional corporation or entity, district, local or regional political subdivision, or any department, division, bureau, office, board, commission or other agency thereof.

(c) Any person arrested or convicted for an offense specified in subdivision (a) or (b) of Section 11361.5 may, two years from the date of such a conviction, or from the date of the arrest if there was no conviction, indicate in response to any question concerning his prior criminal record that he was not arrested or convicted for such offense.

(d) The provisions of this section shall be applicable without regard to whether destruction or obliteration of records has actually been implemented pursuant to Section 11361.5.
(Added by Stats.1976, c. 952, p. —, § 2.)

§ 11362. "Felony offense" and offense "punishable as a felony" defined

As used in this article "felony offense," and offense "punishable as a felony" refer to an offense for which the law prescribes imprisonment in the state prison as either an alternative or the sole penalty, regardless of the sentence the particular defendant received.
(Added by Stats.1972, c. 1407, p. 3018, § 3.)

§ 11363. Planting, cultivating and harvesting; punishment

Every person who plants, cultivates, harvests, dries, or processes any plant of the genus Lophophora, also known as peyote, or any part thereof shall be punished by imprisonment in the county jail for a period of not more than one year or the state prison.
(Amended by Stats.1976, c. 1139, p. —, § 76, operative July 1, 1977.)

Editors' Note

Subsection (d) will preclude the destruction of all records relating to convictions for simple possession of marijuana if the arrest is the subject of a civil suit against the peace officer, and he has filed a certified copy of the complaint with the holder of the records. Thus in order to prevent the destruction of all records relating to the arrest or conviction, which is the subject of a civil suit, *the peace officer must* file a copy of the complaint with the agency that is the custodian of the records.

Notes of Decisions

In general

Where defendant agreed to plead guilty to charge of possession of marijuana in return for probationary sentence of three years, he was estopped to assert right to destruction of records of such conviction pending satisfactory completion of probationary period, or completion of any sentence that might be imposed for violation of that probation. People v. Chapman (App.1976) 132 Cal.Rptr. 831.

Proper procedure for seeking destruction of records of conviction of possession of marijuana is to file petition with superior court in proceeding independent from criminal case involving conviction. Id.

This section authorizing destruction of records of conviction of possession of marijuana was unconstitutional insofar as it was interpreted to compel destruction of any record of court of record, or any copy thereof in official possession of any officer of executive department, pertaining to conviction, judgment or commitment in any proceeding in which there was unexpired sentence or grant of probation which had not yet been completed. Id.

Where prior convictions for possession of marijuana constitute part of the basis for a sentence presently being served under §§ 11350 et seq., 11360, 11363 or Pen.C. § 3024, records of such convictions cannot be destroyed under this section. 59 Ops.Atty.Gen. 30, 1–16–76.

Time for destruction

The legislature did not intend destruction under this section to occur before two years has elapsed from the date of conviction, or from the date of arrest, if there was no conviction. 59 Ops.Atty.Gen. 30, 1–16–76.

§ 11364. Opium pipes; instruments for injecting or smoking controlled substances

It is unlawful to possess an opium pipe or any device, contrivance, instrument or paraphernalia used for unlawfully injecting or smoking (1) a controlled substance specified in subdivision (b) or (c) of Section 11054, specified in paragraph (11), (12), or (17) of subdivision (d) of Section 11054, or specified in subdivision (b) or (c) of Section 11055 or (2) a controlled substance which is a narcotic drug classified in Schedule III, IV, or V.
(Amended by Stats.1975, c. 248, p. —, § 6.)

§ 11365. Presence in room or place where designated controlled substances smoked or used

It is unlawful to visit or to be in any room or place where any controlled substances which are specified in subdivision (b) or (c) of Section 11054, specified in paragraph (11), (12), or (17) of subdivision (d) of Section 11054, or specified in subdivision (b) or (c) of Section 11055, or which are narcotic drugs classified in Schedule III, IV, or V, are being unlawfully smoked or used with knowledge that such activity is occurring.
(Amended by Stats.1975, c. 248, p. —, § 7.)

§ 11366. Opening or maintenance of unlawful places; punishment

Every person who opens or maintains any place for the purpose of unlawfully selling, giving away, or using any controlled substance which is (1) specified in subdivision (b) or (c) of Section 11054, specified in paragraph (10), (11), (12), or (17) of subdivision (d) of Section 11054, or specified in subdivision (b) or (c) of Section 11055, or (2) which is a narcotic drug classified in Schedule III, IV, or V, shall be punished by imprisonment in the county jail for a period of not more than one year or the state prison.
(Amended by Stats.1976, c. 1139, p. —, § 77, operative July 1, 1977.)

§ 11367. Immunity from prosecution

All duly authorized peace officers, while investigating violations of this division in performance of their official duties, and any person working under their immediate direction, supervision or instruction, are immune from prosecution under this division.
(Added by Stats.1972, c. 3019, p. 2987, § 3.)

Notes of Decisions

In general

Where defendant did not show that he was acting under immediate direction of peace officer when engaged in transactions of allegedly furnishing marijuana and selling marijuana and did not show that he was ever requested to engage in narcotics transactions to gain information for peace officer, trial court did not err in failing to instruct, on its own motion, as to immunity from prosecution. People v. Lo Cicero (1969) 80 Cal.Rptr. 913, 459 P.2d 241, 71 C.2d 1186.

In prosecution of a physician for a narcotics violation, a narcotics inspector's act in giving a false name and address and in telling physician the inspector was using "H" when buying narcotics from the physician were not illegal in view that inspector was immune from prosecution and a conviction resulting from use of the evidence secured by such acts was not against public policy and a denial of due process of law. People v. Nunn (1956) 296 P.2d 813, 46 C.2d 460, certiorari denied and appeal dismissed 77 S.Ct. 126, 352 U.S. 883, 1 L.Ed.2d 82, rehearing denied 77 S.Ct. 260, 352 U.S. 945, 1 L.Ed.2d 240.

§ 11368. Forged or altered prescriptions; punishment

Every person who forges or alters a prescription or who issues or utters an altered prescription, or who issues or utters a prescription bearing a forged or fictitious signature for any narcotic drug, or who obtains any narcotic drug by any forged, fictitious, or altered prescription, or who has in possession any narcotic drug secured by such forged, fictitious, or altered prescription, shall for the first offense be punished by imprisonment in the county jail for not less than six months nor more than one year, or in the state prison.
(Amended by Stats.1976, c. 1139, p. —, § 78, operative July 1, 1977.)

§ 11369. Arrest of alien; notice to federal agency

When there is reason to believe that any person arrested for violation of Section 11350, 11352, 11353, 11355, 11357, 11360, 11361, 11363, 11366, 11368 or 11550, may not be a citizen of the United States, the arresting agency shall notify the appropriate agency of the United States having charge of deportation matters.
(Added by Stats.1972, c. 1407, p. 3019, § 3.)

§ 11370. Probation or suspension of sentence; prior convictions

(a) Any person convicted of violating Section 11350, 11353, 11355, 11357, 11359, 11360, 11361, 11363, 11366, or 11368, or of committing any offense referred to in those sections, shall not, in any case, be granted probation by the trial court or have the execution of the sentence imposed upon him suspended by the court, if he has been previously convicted of any offense described in subdivision (c).

(b) Any person who was 18 years of age or over at the time of the commission of the offense and is convicted for the first time of selling, furnishing, administering, or giving a controlled substance which is (1) specified in subdivision (b) or (c) of Section 11054, specified in paragraph (11), (12), or (17) of subdivision (d) of Section 11054, or specified in subdivision (b) or (c) of Section 11055, or, (2) which is a narcotic drug classified in Schedule III, IV, or V, to a minor or inducing a minor to use such a controlled substance in violation of law shall not, in any case, be granted probation by the trial court or have the execution of the sentence imposed upon him suspended by the court.

(c) Any previous conviction of any of the following offenses, or of an offense under the laws of another state or of the United States which, if committed in this state, would have been punishable as such an offense, shall render a person ineligible for probation or suspension of sentence pursuant to subdivision (a) of this section:

(1) Any felony offense described in this division involving a controlled substance specified in subdivision (b) or (c) of Section 11054, specified in paragraph (10), (11), (12), or (17) of subdivision (d) of Section 11054, or specified in subdivision (b) or (c) of Section 11055.

§ 11370

(2) Any felony offense described in this division involving a narcotic drug classified in Schedule III, IV, or V.
(Amended by Stats.1975, c. 1087, p. 2650, § 4.)

§ 11371. Prescription violations; inducing minor to violate provisions; punishment

Any person who shall violate any of the provisions of Section 11152, 11153, 11154, 11155, or 11156 with respect to (1) a controlled substance specified in subdivision (b) or (c) of Section 11054, specified in paragraph (10), (11), (12), or (17) of subdivision (d) of Section 11054, or specified in subdivision (b) or (c) of Section 11055, or (2) a controlled substance which is a narcotic drug classified in Schedule III, IV, or V, or who in any voluntary manner solicits, induces, encourages or intimidates any minor with the intent that such minor shall commit any such offense, shall be punished by imprisonment in the state prison or in a county jail not exceeding one year, or by a fine not exceeding twenty thousand dollars ($20,000), or by both such fine and imprisonment.
(Amended by Stats.1976, c. 1139, p. —, § 80.5, operative July 1, 1977.)

§ 11371.1. Fraud and false representation; inducing minor to violate provisions; punishment

Any person who shall violate any of the provisions of Section 11173 or 11174 with respect to (1) a controlled substance specified in subdivision (b) or (c) of Section 11054, specified in paragraph (10), (11), (12), or (17) of subdivision (d) of Section 11054, or specified in subdivision (b) or (c) of Section 11055, or (2) a controlled substance which is a narcotic drug classified in Schedule III, IV, or V, or who in any voluntary manner solicits, induces, encourages or intimidates any minor with the intent that such minor shall commit any such offense, shall be punished by imprisonment in the state prison, or in a county jail not exceeding one year.
(Added by Stats.1976, c. 1136, p. —, § 4.)

§ 11372. Fines

In addition to the term of imprisonment provided by law for persons convicted of violating Section 11350, 11351, 11352, 11353, 11355, 11359, 11360, or 11361 of this code, the trial court may impose a fine not exceeding twenty thousand dollars ($20,000) for each such offense. In no event shall such fine be levied in lieu of or in substitution for the term of imprisonment provided by law for any of such offenses.
(Added by Stats.1972, c. 3020, p. 2987, § 3.)

§ 11373. Education or treatment as a condition of probation

Whenever any person is granted probation by the trial court after conviction for possession of any controlled substance classified in Schedule I or II, such trial court shall, as a condition of probation, order such person to secure education or treatment from a local community agency designated by such court, if such service is available and the person is likely to benefit from the service.

If such defendant is a minor, the trial court shall also order his parents or guardian to participate in such education or treatment to the extent the court determines will aid the education or treatment of the minor.

If a minor is found by a juvenile court to have been in possession of any controlled substance classified in Schedule I or II, in addition to any other order it may make, such juvenile court shall order the minor to receive education or treatment from a local community agency designated by such court, if such service is available and the person is likely to benefit from the service, and it shall also order his parents or guardian to participate in such education or treatment to the extent the court determines will aid the education or treatment of the minor.
(Added by Stats.1972, c. 1407, p. 3020, § 3.)

§ 11374. Violation of or failure to comply with provisions; misdemeanor

Every person who violates or fails to comply with any provision of this division, except one for which a penalty is otherwise in this division specifically provided, is guilty of a misdemeanor punishable by a fine in a sum not less than thirty dollars ($30) nor more than five hundred dollars ($500), or by imprisonment for not less than 15 nor more than 180 days, or by both.
(Added by Stats.1972, c. 1407, p. 3021, § 3.)

§ 11376. Education or treatment as a condition of probation

Whenever any person is granted probation by the trial court after conviction for possession of any controlled substance which is (1) classified in Schedule III, IV, or V and which is not a narcotic drug or (2) which is specified in subdivision (d) of Section 11054, except paragraphs (10), (11), (12), and (17) of such subdivision, or specified in subdivision (d) of

Section 11055, such trial court shall, as a condition of probation, order such person to secure education or treatment from a local community agency designated by such court, if such service is available and the person is likely to benefit from the service.

If such defendant is a minor, the trial court shall also order his parents or guardian to participate in such education or treatment to the extent the court determines will aid the education or treatment of the minor.

If a minor is found by a juvenile court to have been in possession of any such controlled substance, in addition to any other order it may make, such juvenile court shall order the minor to receive education or treatment from the local community agency designated by such court, if such service is available and the person is likely to benefit from the service, and it shall also order his parents or guardian to participate in such education or treatment to the extent the court determines will aid the education or treatment of the minor.
(Amended by Stats.1973, c. 1078, p. 2183, § 21, eff. Oct. 1, 1973.)

§ 11377. Unauthorized possession; punishment

(a) Except as otherwise provided in Article 8 (commencing with Section 4211) of Chapter 9 of Division 2 of the Business and Professions Code, every person who possesses any controlled substance which is (1) classified in Schedule III, IV, or V, other than any substance specified in paragraph (6) of subdivision (b) of Section 11056, and which is not a narcotic drug or (2) which is specified in subdivision (d) of Section 11054, except paragraphs (10), (11), (12), and (17) of such subdivision, or specified in subdivision (d) or (e) of Section 11055, unless upon the prescription of a physician, dentist, podiatrist, or veterinarian, or pharmacist acting within the scope of a project authorized under Article 18 (commencing with Section 429.70) of Chapter 2 of Part 1 of Division 1, or registered nurse acting within the scope of a project authorized under Article 18 (commencing with Section 429.70) of Chapter 2 of Part 1 of Division 1, or physician's assistant acting within the scope of a project authorized under Article 18 (commencing with Section 429.70) of Chapter 2 of Part 1 of Division 1 licensed to practice in this state, shall be punished by imprisonment in the county jail for a period of not more than one year or the state prison.

(b) Except as otherwise provided in Article 8 (commencing with Section 4211) of Chapter 9 of Division 2 of the Business and Professions Code, every person who possesses any controlled substance specified in paragraph (6) of subdivision (b) of Section 11056, unless upon prescription of a physician, dentist, podiatrist, or veterinarian, or pharmacist acting within the scope of a project authorized under Article 18 (commencing with Section 429.70) of Chapter 2 of Part 1 of Division 1, or registered nurse acting within the scope of a project authorized under Article 18 (commencing with Section 429.70) of Chapter 2 of Part 1 of Division 1, or physician's assistant acting within the scope of a project authorized under Article 18 (commencing with Section 429.70) of Chapter 2 of Part 1 of Division 1, licensed to practice in this state, shall be punished by a fine of not exceeding five hundred dollars ($500), or by imprisonment in the county jail for not exceeding six months, or by both such fine and imprisonment.
(Amended by Stats.1978, c. 699, p. —, § 3.)

§ 11378. Possession for sale; punishment

Except as otherwise provided in Article 8 (commencing with Section 4211) of Chapter 9 of Division 2 of the Business and Professions Code, every person who possesses for sale any controlled substance which is (1) classified in Schedule III, IV, or V, and which is not a narcotic drug or (2) which is specified in subdivision (d) of Section 11054, except paragraphs (10), (11), (12), and (17) of such subdivision, or specified in subdivision (d) of Section 11055, shall be punished by imprisonment in the state prison.
(Amended by Stats.1976, c. 1139, p. —, § 82, operative July 1, 1977.)

§ 11378.5. Phencyclidine; possession for sale; punishment

Except as otherwise provided in Article 8 (commencing with Section 4211) of Chapter 9 of Division 2 of the Business and Professions Code, every person who possesses for sale any controlled substance which is specified in subdivision (e) of Section 11055, shall be punished by imprisonment in the state prison for a period of three, four, or five years.
(Added by Stats.1978, c. 699, p. —, § 4.)

§ 11379. Transportation, sale, manufacture, etc.; punishment

Except as otherwise provided in Article 8 (commencing with Section 4211) of Chapter 9 of Division 2 of the Business and Professions Code, every person who transports, imports into this state, sells, manufactures, compounds, furnishes, administers, or gives

away, or offers to transport, import into this state, sell, manufacture, compound, furnish, administer, or give away, or attempts to import into this state or transport any controlled substance which is (1) classified in Schedule III, IV, or V and which is not a narcotic drug or (2) which is specified in subdivision (d) of Section 11054 except paragraphs (10), (11), (12), and (17) of such subdivision, or specified in subdivision (d) of Section 11055, unless upon the prescription of a physician, dentist, podiatrist, or veterinarian, or pharmacist acting within the scope of a project authorized under Article 18 (commencing with Section 429.70) of Chapter 2 of Part 1 of Division 1, or registered nurse acting within the scope of a project authorized under Article 18 (commencing with Section 429.70) of Chapter 2 of Part 1 of Division 1, or physician's assistant acting within the scope of a project authorized under Article 18 (commencing with Section 429.70) of Chapter 2 of Part 1 of Division 1 licensed to practice in this state, shall be punished by imprisonment in the state prison for a period of two, three, or four years.
(Amended by Stats.1977, c. 843, p. —, § 24.)

§ 11379.5. Phencyclidine; transportation, sale, manufacture, etc.; punishment

Except as otherwise provided in Article 8 (commencing with Section 4211) of Chapter 9 of Division 2 of the Business and Professions Code, every person who transports, imports into this state, sells, manufactures, compounds, furnishes, administers, or gives away, or offers to transport, import into this state, sell, manufacture, compound, furnish, administer, or give away, or attempts to import into this state or transport any controlled substance which is specified in subdivision (e) of Section 11055, unless upon the prescription of a physician, dentist, podiatrist, or veterinarian licensed to practice in this state, shall be punished by imprisonment in the state prison for a period of three, four, or five years.
(Added by Stats.1978, c. 699, p. —, § 5.)

Notes of Decisions

If specific intent to sell narcotic is present, offense of offering to sell narcotic is complete at time of offer, and delivery is not essential element. People v. Medina (1972) 103 Cal.Rptr. 721, 27 C.A.3d 473.

The elements of the offense of selling or offering to sell a restricted dangerous drug are the same as those of the offense of selling or offering to sell narcotics. People v. Innes (1971) 93 Cal.Rptr. 829, 16 C.A.3d 175.

Possession of dangerous drugs for sale may be found to be joint in appropriate circumstances and, although fact of access by several persons is a matter to be considered, no sharp line can be drawn to distinguish congeries of facts which will or will not permit a finding of joint or constructive possession based on access. People v. Hunt (1971) 93 Cal.Rptr. 197, 481 P.2d 205, 4 C.3d 231.

Violation of this section making the offering to sell dangerous drugs a crime is complete when a person offers to sell the proscribed drugs, with specific intent to make a sale. People v. Allen (1967) 62 Cal.Rptr. 235, 254 C.A.2d 597.

Delivery is not an essential element of the offense of offering to sell dangerous drugs. Id.

§ 11380. Adult using minor as agent; inducing minor to violate provisions; furnishing to minor; punishment

(a) Every person 18 years of age or over who violates any provision of this chapter involving controlled substances which are (1) classified in Schedule III, IV, or V and which are not narcotic drugs or (2) which are specified in subdivision (d) of Section 11054, except paragraphs (10), (11), (12), and (17) of such subdivision, or specified in subdivision (d) of Section 11055, by the use of a minor as agent, who solicits, induces, encourages, or intimidates any minor with the intent that the minor shall violate any provision of this article involving such controlled substances or who unlawfully furnishes, offers to furnish, or attempts to furnish such controlled substances to a minor shall be punished by imprisonment in the state prison for a period of three, four or five years.

(b) Nothing contained in this section shall apply to a registered pharmacist furnishing controlled substances pursuant to a prescription.
(Amended by Stats.1976, c. 1139, p. —, § 84, operative July 1, 1977.)

§ 11380.5. Phencyclidine; adult using minor or agent; inducing minor to violate provisions; furnishing to minor; punishment

(a) Every person 18 years of age or over who violates any provision of this chapter involving controlled substances which are specified in subdivision (e) of Section 11055, by the use of a minor as agent, who solicits, induces, encourages, or intimidates any minor with the intent that the minor shall violate any provision of this article involving such controlled substances or who unlawfully furnishes, offers to furnish, or attempts to furnish such controlled substances to a minor shall be punished by imprisonment in the state prison for a period of three, four, or five years.

(b) Nothing contained in this section shall apply to a registered pharmacist furnishing controlled substances pursuant to a prescription.
(Added by Stats.1978, c. 699, p. —, § 6.)

§ 11381. "Felony offense" and offense "punishable as a felony" defined

As used in this article "felony offense" and offense "punishable as a felony" refer to an offense for which the law prescribes imprisonment in the state prison as either an alternative or the sole penalty, regardless of the sentence the particular defendant received.
(Added by Stats.1972, c. 1407, p. 3024, § 3.)

§ 11382. Sale or furnishing substance falsely represented to be a controlled substance; punishment

Every person who agrees, consents, or in any manner offers to unlawfully sell, furnish, transport, administer, or give any controlled substance which is (1) classified in Schedule III, IV, or V and which is not a narcotic drug, or (2) which is specified in subdivision (d) of Section 11054, except paragraphs (10), (11), (12), and (17) of such subdivision, or specified in subdivision (d) or (e) of Section 11055, to any person, or offers, arranges, or negotiates to have any such controlled substance unlawfully sold, delivered, transported, furnished, administered, or given to any person and then sells, delivers, furnishes, transports, administers, or gives, or offers, or arranges, or negotiates to have sold, delivered, transported, furnished, administered, or given to any person any other liquid, substance, or material in lieu of any such controlled substance shall be punished by imprisonment in the county jail for not more than one year, or in the state prison.
(Amended by Stats.1978, c. 699, p. —, § 7.)

§ 11382.5. Identification of manufacturer of controlled substances; exception; application to pharmacists

All controlled substances in Schedules I, II, III, IV, and V, in solid or capsule form, except for such controlled substances in the possession or inventory of a wholesaler, retailer, or pharmacist on January 1, 1975, shall not be sold, furnished, or distributed in this state unless they have on the controlled substance if in solid form, or on the capsule if in capsule form, an identifying device, insignia, or mark of the manufacturer of such controlled substance. However, the exception for such controlled substances in the possession or inventory of a wholesaler, retailer, or pharmacist shall not be available to any wholesaler, retailer, or pharmacist under the control or jurisdiction of a manufacturer of controlled substances.

This section shall not apply to a pharmacist who, in accordance with applicable state law, compounds such controlled substance in the course of his practice as a pharmacist for direct dispensing by him upon a prescription of any person licensed to prescribe such controlled substances.
(Added by Stats.1974, c. 926, p. —, § 1.)

§ 11383. Possession with intent to manufacture methamphetamine; offense; punishment; exception

(a) Any person who possesses both methylamine and phenyl–2–propanone (phenylacetone) at the same time with the intent to manufacture methamphetamine is guilty of a felony and shall be punished by imprisonment in the state prison.

(b) Any person who possesses both piperidine and cyclohexanone at the same time, or a combination product thereof, with intent to manufacture phencyclidine (PCP) is guilty of a felony and shall be punished by imprisonment in the state prison for three, four, or five years.

(c) For purposes of this section, possession of immediate precursors sufficient for the manufacture of methylamine, phenyl–2–propanone, piperidine, or cyclohexanone shall be deemed to be possession of such a derivative substance.

(d) The provisions of subdivision (a), (b), and (c) shall not apply to drug manufacturers licensed by this state or persons authorized by regulation of the Board of Pharmacy to possess such substances or combinations of substances.
(Amended by Stats.1978, c. 699, p. —, § 8.)

§ 11384. Regulations by board of pharmacy

The Board of Pharmacy shall, by regulation, authorize such persons to possess any combinations of substance specified in subdivision (a) or (b) of Section 11383 as it determines need and will use such substance for a lawful purpose.
(Amended by Stats.1976, c. 1116, p. —, § 3.)

§ 11450. Agents and employees of attorney general

The Attorney General may, in conformity with the State Civil Service Act, part 2 (commencing with Section 18500), Division 5, Title 2 of the Government Code, employ such agents, chemists, clerical, and other employees as are necessary for the conduct of the affairs of the Department of Justice in carrying out its responsibilities specified in this division.
(Amended by Stats.1974, c. 1403, p. —, § 5.)

§ 11470. Property subject to forfeiture

The following are subject to forfeiture:

(a) All controlled substances which have been manufactured, distributed, dispensed, or acquired in violation of this division.

(b) All raw materials, products and equipment of any kind which are used, or intended for use, in manufacturing, compounding, processing, delivering, importing, or exporting any controlled substance in violation of this division.

(c) All property which is used, or intended for use, as a container for property described in subdivision (a) or (b).

(d) All books, records, and research products and materials, including formulas, microfilm, tapes, and data which are used, or intended for use, in violation of this division.

(e) The interest of any registered owner of a boat, airplane, or any vehicle other than an implement of husbandry, as defined in Section 36000 of the Vehicle Code, or a vehicle which may be lawfully driven upon the highway with a class 3 or class 4 license, as prescribed in Section 12804 of the Vehicle Code, used, in direct relation to the particular offense for which the owner or defendant is arrested and convicted, to unlawfully transport for sale any controlled substance.
(Amended by Stats.1977, c. 771, p. —, § 1.)

§ 11471. Seizure of property subject to forfeiture

Property subject to forfeiture under this division may be seized by the Attorney General upon process issued by any court having jurisdiction over the property. Seizure without process may be made if any of the following situations exist:

(a) The seizure is incident to an arrest or a search under a search warrant.

(b) The property subject to seizure has been the subject of a prior judgment in favor of the state in a criminal injunction or forfeiture proceeding based upon this division.

(c) The Attorney General has probable cause to believe that the property is directly or indirectly dangerous to health or safety.

(d) The Attorney General has probable cause to believe that the property was used or is intended to be used in violation of this division.
(Added by Stats.1972, c. 1407, p. 3026, § 3.)

§ 11472. Institution of proceedings

In the event of seizure pursuant to Section 11471, proceedings under Section 11473 shall be instituted promptly.
(Added by Stats.1972, c. 1407, p. 2087, § 3.)

§ 11473. Seizure by peace officer; search warrant

Controlled substances and any device, contrivance, instrument, or paraphernalia used for unlawfully using or administering a controlled substance, which are possessed in violation of this division, may be seized by any peace officer and in the aid of such seizure a search warrant may be issued as prescribed by law.
(Added by Stats.1972, c. 1407, p. 3026, § 3.)

§ 11474. Order for destruction; delivery of seized property

All seizures under provisions of this chapter, except seizures of vehicles, boats, or airplanes, shall, upon conviction of the owner or defendant, be ordered destroyed by the judge of the court in which conviction was had and the judge shall turn all such evidence over to the Attorney General for destruction or disposition.
(Amended by Stats.1976, c. 1407, p. —, § 2.)

§ 11475. Schedule I substances as contraband; forfeiture

Controlled substances listed in Schedule I that are possessed, transferred, sold, or offered for sale in violation of this division are contraband and shall be seized and summarily forfeited to the state. Controlled substances listed in Schedule I, which are seized or come into the possession of the state, the owners of which are unknown, are contraband and shall be summarily forfeited to the state.
(Added by Stats.1972, c. 1407, p. 3026, § 3.)

§ 11476. Plants from which schedule I and II substances derived; seizure and forfeiture

Species of plants from which controlled substances in Schedules I and II may be derived which have been planted or cultivated in violation of this division, or of which the owners or cultivators are unknown, or which are wild growths, may be seized and summarily forfeited to the state.
(Added by Stats.1972, c. 1407, p. 3027, § 3.)

§ 11477. Plants; authority for seizure and forfeiture

The failure, upon demand by the Attorney General, or his authorized agent, of the person in occupancy or in control of land or premises upon which the species of plants are growing or being stored, to produce an appropriate registration, or proof that he is the holder thereof, constitutes authority for the seizure and forfeiture of the plants.
(Added by Stats.1972, c. 1407, p. 3027, § 3.)

§ 11487. Reports to attorney general of amounts, kind, and disposition of controlled substances; duration of section

Each city, county, or state agency coming into possession of a controlled substance pursuant to the provisions of this chapter shall report semiannually to the Attorney General the amounts, kind, and disposition of controlled substances so seized.

The reports provided for by this section shall be in a form and contain such information as determined necessary by the Attorney General.

The Attorney General shall issue an annual report to the Governor and Legislature correlating and summarizing the reports provided for by this section.

This section shall remain in effect only until January 1, 1980, and as of such date is repealed, unless a later enacted statute, which is chaptered before January 1, 1980, deletes or extends such date.
(Added by Stats.1976, c. 1134, p. —, § 1.)

§ 11490. Arrest or attempt to arrest; seizure of vehicle, boat or airplane used to unlawfully transport for sale; disposition

Any peace officer of this state, upon making or attempting to make an arrest for a violation of Section 11351, 11352, 11355, 11359, 11360, 11378, or 11379, insofar as the offense involves sale, transportation for sale, or possession for sale, may seize any vehicle, boat, or airplane used to unlawfully transport for sale any controlled substance. If he does not hold the vehicle, boat, or airplane for evidence, he shall immediately deliver such vehicle, boat, or airplane to the State Department of Justice to be held as evidence until a forfeiture has been declared or a release ordered; otherwise he shall return the vehicle, boat, or airplane to the registered owner.
(Added by Stats.1976, c. 1407, p. —, § 3.)

§ 11491. Determination of disposition; notice of seizure and intended forfeiture proceedings; rights of bona fide purchaser; acquisition of interest after notice

(a) Within 15 days after such seizure, if the Department of Justice determines that the factual circumstances do not warrant that the vehicle, boat, or airplane come within subdivision (e) of Section 11470, or if for any other reason it decides not to seek forfeiture, it shall return the vehicle, boat, or airplane to the arresting officer who shall return it to the registered owner. If the Department of Justice does not return the vehicle, boat, or airplane to the arresting officer, it shall cause an investigation to be made as to any claimant to the vehicle, boat, or airplane whose right, title, interest, or lien is of record in the Department of Motor Vehicles or appropriate federal agency. Except as provided in subdivision (b), if the department finds that any person, other than the registered owner, is the legal owner thereof, and such ownership interest did not arise subsequent to the date and time of arrest or seizure of the vehicle, boat, or airplane, it shall forthwith send a notice of the seizure to such legal owner at his address appearing on the records of the Department of Motor Vehicles or appropriate federal agency. Notice of seizure and intended forfeiture proceedings shall be filed with the county clerk and shall be served on all owners whose interest will be affected thereby.

(b) A bona fide purchaser without notice of the arrest or seizure whose interest was acquired subsequent to the arrest or seizure shall be entitled to participate in the forfeiture proceedings to establish his claim.

(c) An assignee, purchaser, or holder in due course who had notice of the arrest or seizure at the time he acquired his interest and who sells, assigns, or conveys such interest is guilty of a fraudulent conveyance as provided for in Section 531 of the Penal Code, and civilly liable under Section 3439.07 of the Civil Code.
(Added by Stats.1976, c. 1407, p. —, § 4.)

§ 11491.1. Notice to owners; contents

Actual notice shall be given to each owner whose right, title, or interest is of record in the Department of Motor Vehicles or appropriate federal agency, by mailing a copy of the notice by registered mail to the address as given upon the records of the Department of Motor Vehicles or appropriate federal agency; and

§ 11491.1

to each owner whose name and address is known, to the last known address of the owner.

All other owners, whose addresses are unknown, but who are believed to have an interest in the vehicle, boat, or airplane, by one publication in a newspaper of general circulation in the county where the seizure was made.

All notices shall set forth the time within which an answer is required to be filed pursuant to Section 11491.2.
(Added by Stats.1976, c. 1407, p. ——, § 5.)

§ 11491.2. Answer by owner or holder of security interest

Within 10 days after receipt of actual notice or within 30 days of the publication of the notice, any owner of any right, title, or interest in, or lien upon, a seized vehicle, boat, or airplane may file a verified answer to the fact of the use of the vehicle, boat, or airplane alleged in the notice of seizure and of the intended forfeiture proceeding; and any person holding a valid lien, mortgage, security interest, or interest under a conditional sales contract may file a verified answer to the facts set forth in the notice and setting forth, if such be the fact, that he acquired his interest prior to the date of seizure without actual knowledge that the vehicle, boat, or airplane was to be used in the manner set forth in subdivision (e) of Section 11470.
(Added by Stats.1976, c. 1407, p. ——, § 6.)

§ 11491.3. Answers; extension of time; prohibition

No extensions of time shall be granted for the purpose of filing the answer.
(Added by Stats.1976, c. 1407, p. ——, § 7.)

§ 11491.4. Answer not filed; declaration of forfeiture; right to convey clear title

If, at the end of the times set forth in Section 11491.2, there is no verified answer on file, the court, upon motion, shall declare the vehicle, boat, or airplane forfeited to the state upon conviction as provided in Section 11492. Notwithstanding any other provision of law, a certified copy of said declaration of forfeiture, duly filed with the Department of Motor Vehicles or appropriate federal agency, shall constitute authority for the state to convey clear title to the vehicle, boat, or airplane to any purchaser thereof in the manner provided in Sections 11493.1 and 11494.
(Added by Stats.1976, c. 1407, p. ——, § 8.)

§ 11491.5. Answer filed; hearing; date; priority

If a verified answer is filed, the forfeiture proceeding shall be set for hearing on a day not less than 30 days therefrom, and the proceeding shall have priority over other civil cases.
(Added by Stats.1976, c. 1407, p. ——, § 9.)

§ 11491.6. Notice of hearing

Notice of the hearing shall be given in the same manner as provided in Section 11491.1.
(Added by Stats.1976, c. 1407, p. ——, § 10.)

§ 11491.7. Burden of proof

At the hearing, the state shall have the burden of establishing beyond a reasonable doubt that the owner of the vehicle, boat, or airplane, or the owner of an interest in such vehicle, boat, or airplane, consented to the use of such vehicle, boat, or airplane with the knowledge that it would be used for a violation of this chapter.
(Amended by Stats.1977, c. 771, p. ——, § 2.)

§ 11492. Forfeiture decree; inapplicability to interested party without knowledge of use; necessity of conviction

No legal or registered title or interest in the vehicle, boat, or airplane shall be affected by the forfeiture decree under this article unless the state has proved that the owner of such interest consented to the use of such vehicle, boat, or airplane with knowledge that it was used for the purpose charged. No forfeiture shall be ordered unless and until a conviction is had for an offense set forth in Section 11490.
(Amended by Stats.1977, c. 771, p. ——, § 3.)

§ 11493. Forfeiture hearing; continuance; conduct; findings; determination of rights of owner or lienholder

The forfeiture hearing may be continued until after a verdict of guilt on the related charges has been decided. The forfeiture hearing shall be conducted in accordance with Sections 600 to 630, inclusive, of the Code of Civil Procedure if a trial by jury, and by Sections 631 to 636, inclusive, of the Code of Civil Procedure if by court. Unless the court or jury finds that the vehicle, boat, or airplane was used in violation of this chapter, the court shall order the vehicle, boat, or airplane released to the person entitled thereto.

If the court or jury finds that the vehicle, boat, or airplane was used in violation of this chapter, but does not find that a person holding a valid lien, mortgage, security interest, or interest under a conditional sales contract acquired his interest with actual knowledge that the vehicle, boat, or airplane was to be used for a purpose for which forfeiture is permitted and if the amount due him is equal to, or in excess of, the appraised value of the vehicle, boat, or airplane, the court shall order the vehicle, boat, or airplane released to him. If the amount due him is less than the appraised value of the vehicle, boat, or airplane, he may pay to the Department of General Services the amount of the registered owner's equity, which shall be deemed to be the difference between the appraised value and the amount of the lien, mortgage, security interest, or interest under a conditional sales contract. Upon such payment, the state shall relinquish all claims to the vehicle, boat, or airplane. If the holder of the interest elects not to make such payment to the Department of General Services, the vehicle, boat, or airplane shall be deemed forfeited to the Department of General Services and the ownership certificate shall be forwarded. Appraised value is to be determined as of the date judgment is entered on a wholesale basis either by agreement between the legal owner and the Department of General Services, or if such persons cannot agree, then by the inheritance tax appraiser for the county in which the action is brought.
(Amended by Stats.1977, c. 771, p. ——, § 4.)

§ 11493.1. Sale at public auction; failure of holder of security interest to make payment

If the amount due to a person holding a valid lien, mortgage, security interest, or interest under a conditional sales contract is less than the value of the vehicle, boat, or airplane, and the person elects not to make payment to the Department of General Services, the vehicle, boat, or airplane shall be sold at public auction by the Department of General Services.
(Added by Stats.1976, c. 1407, p. ——, § 14.)

§ 11494. Notice of sale; publication

The Department of General Services shall publish a notice of the sale by one publication in a newspaper published and circulated in the city, community, or locality where the sale is to take place.
(Added by Stats.1976, c. 1407, p. ——, § 15.)

§ 11495. Proceeds of sale; distribution

In all cases where a vehicle, boat, or airplane is seized pursuant to this chapter and is forfeited to the state and turned over to and sold by the Department of General Services, the proceeds of the sale shall be distributed as follows, in the order indicated:

(a) To the bona fide or innocent purchaser, conditional sales vendor, or mortgagee of the vehicle, boat, or airplane, if any, up the amount of his interest in the vehicle, boat, or airplane, when the court declaring the forfeiture orders a distribution to such person.

(b) The balance, if any, to accumulate, and from time to time, as the proceeds become sufficient, to be distributed:

1. To the Department of General Services for all expenditures made or incurred by it in connection with the sale, including expenditure for any necessary repairs, storage, or transportation, of any vehicle, boat, or airplane seized under this article.

2. To the Attorney General for all expenditures made or incurred by him in connection with the forfeiture proceedings of any vehicle, boat, or airplane seized under this article, including, but not limited to, expenditures for witness fees, reporters' fees, transcripts, printing, traveling, and investigation.

3. To the state for all expenditures for traveling, investigation, storage, and other expenses made or incurred by the Department of Justice after the seizure, and in connection with the forfeiture of any vehicle, boat, or airplane seized under this article.

4. The remainder, if any, from any vehicle, boat, or airplane seized by a state officer, to the State Treasury, for credit to the General Fund.

5. The remainder, if any, from any vehicle, boat, or airplane seized by an officer of a county or a city, to the State Controller, for transfer to the General Fund of the county or city for any expenditures for the investigation, storage, and other expenses made or incurred by the county or city in connection with such seizure.

6. The remainder, if any, to the State Treasury, for credit to the General Fund.
(Amended by Stats.1978, c. 78, p. ——, § 1.)

§ 11499. Decisional law relating to search and seizure; chapter not construed to extend or change

Nothing in this chapter shall be construed to extend or change decisional law as it relates to the topic of search and seizure.
(Added by Stats.1977, c. 771, p. —, § 5.)

§ 11550. Unlawful acts; exception; burden of defense; punishment; probation

No person shall use, or be under the influence of any controlled substance which is (1) specified in subdivision (b) or (c) of Section 11054, specified in paragraph (11), (12), or (17) of subdivision (d) of Section 11054, or specified in subdivision (b) or (c) of Section 11055, or (2) which is a narcotic drug classified in Schedule III, IV, or V, excepting when administered by or under the direction of a person licensed by the state to dispense, prescribe, or administer controlled substances. It shall be the burden of the defense to show that it comes within the exception. Any person convicted of violating any provision of this section is guilty of a misdemeanor and shall be sentenced to serve a term of not less than 90 days nor more than one year in the county jail. The court may place a person convicted hereunder on probation for a period not to exceed five years and shall in all cases in which probation is granted require as a condition thereof that such person be confined in the county jail for at least 90 days. In no event does the court have the power to absolve a person who violates this section from the obligation of spending at least 90 days in confinement in the county jail.
(Amended by Stats.1975, c. 248, p. —, § 8.)

Notes of Decisions

In general

In absence of any evidence that defendant knows he may be charged with being under the influence of controlled substance, conduct of police in telling him he is charged with possession of controlled substance on police theory that defendant is in "internal possession" of such a substance will support trial court's finding that defendant has been misled to his prejudice and thus deprived of due process or speedy trial rights; even if defendant does know that he is suspected of or may be charged with being under the influence of controlled substance, other circumstances may also support finding of prejudice. People v. Johnson, (Super.1976) 133 Cal.Rptr. 123.

Where defendant, who was arrested and charged with possession of heroin, was offered opportunity to promptly give urine specimen and have it analyzed and defendant refused such test, due process rights of defendant, who was subsequently charged with being under influence of opiate, were not violated by any refusal to give him a urine test. Id.

Under influence of narcotics, arrest

Although there was no evidence that booking procedure whereby defendant was charged with possession of heroin on police theory that he was in "internal possession" of heroin misled defendant, where trial court could have reasonably inferred that if defendant had not been told that charges against him were dismissed and defendant had been arraigned on charge of being under influence of opiate at earlier date, counsel would have instructed him to have medical examination at time when it might have produced useful results, dismissal of charge of being under the influence was justified. People v. Johnson (Super.1976) 133 Cal.Rptr. 123.

Current use

The "use" proscribed by this section pertaining to use of controlled substance is a current use, not a use in the past. People v. Velasquez (1976) 126 Cal.Rptr. 656, 54 C.A.3d 695.

In prosecution for using heroin, testimony which supported no usage closer than the five to seven-day period testified to by people's expert could not support finding of a current addiction and use. Id.

§ 11551. Tests to determine use of controlled substances as condition of probation or parole; cost of administration; regulations

(a) Whenever any court in this state grants probation to a person who the court has reason to believe is or has been a user of controlled substances, the court may require as a condition to probation that the probationer submit to periodic tests by a city or county health officer, or by a physician and surgeon appointed by the city or county health officer with the approval of the Attorney General, to determine, by whatever means is available, whether the probationer is addicted to a controlled substance.

In any case provided for in this subdivision, the city or county health officer, or the physician and surgeon appointed by the city or county health officer with the approval of the Attorney General shall report the results of the tests to the probation officer.

(b) In any case in which a person is granted parole by a county parole board and the person is or has been a user of controlled substances, a condition of the parole may be that the parolee undergo periodic tests as provided in subdivision (a) and that the county or city health officer, or the physician and surgeon appointed by the city or county health officer with the approval of the Attorney General, shall report the results to the board.

(c) In any case in which any state agency grants a parole to a person who is or has been a user of controlled substances, it may be a condition of the parole that the parolee undergo periodic tests as provided in subdivision (a) and that the county or city health officer, or the physician and surgeon appointed by the city or county health officer with the approval of the Attorney General, shall report the results of the tests to such state agency.

(d) The cost of administering tests pursuant to subdivisions (a) and (b) shall be a charge against the county. The cost of administering tests pursuant to subdivision (c) shall be paid by the state.

(e) The state department, in conjunction with the Attorney General, shall issue regulations governing the administering of the tests provided for in this section and providing the form of the report required by this section.
(Added by Stats.1972, c. 1407, p. 3031, § 3.)

§ 11552. Arrested persons; tests to determine use of controlled substances

In any case in which a person has been arrested for a criminal offense and is suspected of being addicted to a controlled substance, a law enforcement officer having custody of such person may, with the written consent of such person, request the city or county health officer, or physician appointed by such health officer pursuant to Section 11551, to administer to the arrested person a test to determine, by whatever means is available whether the arrested person is addicted to a controlled substance, and such health officer or physician may administer such test to such arrested person.
(Added by Stats.1972, c. 1407, p. 3032, § 3.)

§ 11570. Nuisance

Every building or place used for the purpose of unlawfully selling, serving, storing, keeping, or giving away controlled substances as defined in this division, and every building or place wherein or upon which such acts take place, is a nuisance which shall be enjoined, abated, and prevented, whether it is a public or private nuisance.
(Added by Stats.1972, c. 1407, p. 3034, § 3.)

§ 11571. Action to abate; injunction

Whenever there is reason to believe that such a nuisance is kept, maintained or exists in any county, the district attorney of the county, in the name of the people, shall, or any citizen of the state resident in the county, in his own name, may, maintain an action to abate and prevent the nuisance and perpetually to enjoin the person conducting or maintaining it, and the owner, lessee, or agent of the building or place, in or upon which the nuisance exists, from directly or indirectly maintaining or permitting the nuisance.
(Added by Stats.1972, c. 1407, p. 3034, § 3.)

§ 11580. Violation of injunction or abatement order; penalty

A violation or disobedience of the injunction or order for abatement is punishable as a contempt of court by a fine of not less than two hundred dollars ($200) nor more than one thousand dollars ($1,000), or by imprisonment in the county jail for not less than one nor more than six months, or by both.
(Added by Stats.1972, c. 1407, p. 3035, § 3.)

§ 11581. Removal and sale of property; closing of building or place; duration

If the existence of the nuisance is established in the action, an order of abatement shall be entered as a part of the judgment, which order shall direct the removal from the building or place of all fixtures, musical instruments, and other movable property used in conducting, maintaining, aiding, or abetting the nuisance and shall direct their sale in the manner provided for the sale of chattels under execution.

The order shall provide for the effectual closing of the building or place against its use for any purpose, and for keeping it closed for a period of one year, unless sooner released, as provided in this division.
(Added by Stats.1972, c. 1407, p. 3035, § 3.)

§ 11590. Persons required to register

(a) Any person who, on or after the effective date of this section, is convicted in the State of California of any offense defined in Section 11350, 11351, 11352, 11353, 11354, 11355, 11357, 11358, 11359, 11360, 11361, 11363, 11366, 11368, or 11550, or any person who is, on or after such date, discharged or paroled from a penal institution where he was confined because of the commission of any such offense, or any person who is, on or after such date, convicted in any other state of any offense which, if committed or attempted in this state, would have been punishable as one or more of the above-mentioned offenses, shall within 30 days after the effective date of this section or within 30 days of his coming into any county or city, or city and county in which he resides or is temporarily domiciled for such length of time, register with the chief of police of the city in which he resides or the sheriff of the county if he resides in an unincorporated area.

(b) Any person who, on or after the effective date of this section is convicted in any federal court of any offense which, if committed or attempted in this state would have been punishable as one or more of the offenses enumerated in subdivision (a) shall within 30 days after the effective date of this section

§ 11590

or within 30 days of his coming into any county or city, or city and county in which he resides or is temporarily domiciled for such length of time, register with the chief of police of the city in which he resides or the sheriff of the county if he resides in an unincorporated area.

(c) This section does not apply to a conviction of a misdemeanor under Section 11357 or 11360.
(Amended by Stats.1975, c. 248, p. —, § 9.)

§ 11591. School employee; arrest for controlled substance offense; notice to school authorities

Every sheriff or chief of police, upon the arrest for any of the controlled substance offenses enumerated in Section 11590, or Section 11364, insofar as that section relates to paragraph (9) of subdivision (d) of Section 11054, of any school employee, shall do either of the following:

(1) If such school employee is a teacher in any of the public schools of this state, he shall immediately notify by telephone the superintendent of schools of the school district employing such teacher and shall immediately give written notice of the arrest to the Commission for Teacher Preparation and Licensing and to the superintendent of schools in the county wherein such person is employed. Upon receipt of such notice, the county superintendent of schools shall immediately notify the governing board of the school district employing such person.

(2) If such school employee is a nonteacher in any of the public schools of this state, he shall immediately notify by telephone the superintendent of schools of the school district employing such nonteacher and shall immediately give written notice of the arrest to the governing board of the school district employing such person.

(3) If such school employee is a teacher in any private school of this state, he shall immediately notify by telephone the private school authority employing such teacher and shall immediately give written notice of the arrest to the private school authority employing such teacher.
(Amended by Stats.1973, c. 489, p. 962, § 6.)

§ 11594. Registration requirements; change of address; duration; violations; confidential information

The registration required by Section 11590 shall consist of (a) a statement in writing signed by such person, giving such information as may be required by the Department of Justice, and (b) the fingerprints and photograph of such person. Within three days thereafter the registering law enforcement agency shall forward such statement, fingerprints and photograph to the Department of Justice.

If any person required to register hereunder changes his residence address he shall inform, in writing within 10 days, the law enforcement agency with whom he last registered of his new address. The law enforcement agency shall, within three days after receipt of such information, forward it to the Department of Justice. The Department of Justice shall forward appropriate registration data to the law enforcement agency having local jurisdiction of the new place of residence.

All registration requirements set forth in this article shall terminate five years after the discharge from prison, release from jail or termination of probation or parole of the person convicted. Nothing in this section shall be construed to conflict with the provisions of Section 1203.4 of the Penal Code concerning termination of probation and release from penalties and disabilities of probation.

Any person required to register under the provisions of this section who shall knowingly violate any of the provisions thereof is guilty of a misdemeanor.

The statements, photographs and fingerprints herein required shall not be open to inspection by the public or by any person other than a regularly employed peace or other law enforcement officer.
(Amended by Stats.1974, c. 1403, p. —, § 11.)

Division 11
EXPLOSIVES

§ 12000. Explosives defined

For the purposes of this part, the term "explosives" shall mean any substance, or combination of substances, the primary or common purpose of which is detonation or rapid combustion and which is capable of a relatively instantaneous or rapid release of gas and heat, or any substance, the primary purpose of which, when combined with others, is to form a substance capable of a relatively instantaneous or rapid release of gas and heat. The term "explosives" shall include, but shall not necessarily be limited to, any of the following:

(a) Dynamite, nitroglycerine, picric acid, lead azide, fulminate of mercury, black powder, smokeless powder, propellant explosives, detonating primers, blasting caps, or commercial boosters.

(b) Substances determined to be class A and class B explosives as classified by the United States Department of Transportation.

(c) Nitro carbo nitrate substances (blasting agent) as classified by the United States Department of Transportation.

(d) Any material designated as an explosive by the State Fire Marshal. Such designation shall be made pursuant to the classification standards established by the United States Department of Transportation. The State Fire Marshal shall adopt regulations in accordance with the provisions of Chapter 4.5 (commencing with Section 11371), Part 1, Division 3, Title 2 of the Government Code to establish procedures for the classification and designation of explosive materials or explosive devices that are not under the jurisdiction of the United States Department of Transportation.

(e) Certain class C explosives as designated by the United States Department of Transportation when listed in regulations adopted by the State Fire Marshal.

For the purposes of this part, the term "explosives" shall not include any destructive device, as defined in Section 12301 of the Penal Code, nor shall it include ammunition or small arms primers manufactured for use in shotguns, rifles, and pistols.
(Amended by Stats.1970, c. 1421, p. 2699, § 1; Stats.1970, c. 1425, p. 2175, § 1.)

§ 12080. Sale, gift, or transportation of unclassified explosives prohibited; authorization for transportation

(a) No person shall sell, give away, or transport any explosive which has not been classified as provided in Section 12000.

(b) The State Fire Marshal, upon receiving an application from any interested party, with the concurrence of the chief in the area affected, and if he determines that such action may be taken without jeopardizing the public welfare and safety, may authorize the transportation of unclassified explosives provided all other provisions of this part are met.
(Added by Stats.1967, c. 1497, p. 3496, § 2.)

§ 12082. Sale, furnishing or giving away to minors; ineligibility for permit

No explosives shall be sold, furnished, or given away to any person under 21 years of age, whether such person is acting for himself or for another person, nor shall any such person be eligible to obtain any permit to receive explosives governed by the provisions of this part.

The reference to "under 21 years of age" in this section is unaffected by Section 1 of Chapter 1748 of the Statutes of 1971 or any other provision of that chapter.
(Amended by Stats.1972, c. 1011, p. 1874, § 2.)

§ 12083. Unauthorized entry of place containing explosives

With the exception of the chief, the owner, a person authorized to enter by the owner, or the owner's agent, no person shall enter any explosive manufacturing plant, magazine, or vehicle containing explosives.
(Added by Stats.1967, c. 1497, p. 3497, § 2.)

§ 12084. Discharge of firearms

No person shall willfully discharge any firearm within 500 feet of any magazine or any explosive manufacturing plant.
(Added by Stats.1967, c. 1497, p. 3497, § 2.)

§ 12086. Theft or loss of explosives; report

Any theft or loss of explosives, whether from a storage magazine, a vehicle in which they are being transported, or from a site on which they are being used, or from any other location, shall immediately be reported by the person having control of such explosives to the local police or county sheriff. The local police or county sheriff shall immediately transmit a report of such theft or loss of explosives to the State Bureau of Criminal Identification and Investigation at Sacramento.
(Amended by Stats.1970, c. 1425, p. 2717, § 6.)

§ 12120. Unlawful to sell, give, or deliver explosive to person not possessing valid permit

No person shall knowingly sell, give away, deliver, or otherwise dispose of any explosive to any person who does not possess a valid permit as required pursuant to Section 12101.

The provisions of this section and subdivisions (e) and (f) of Section 12122 do not apply to transactions by the Department of Defense or to the transactions

§ 12120

of an agency or organization acting pursuant to contract with the Department of Defense.
(Amended by Stats.1968, c. 662, p. 1342, § 8.)

§ 12303. Lawful possession of explosive defined

"Lawful possession of an explosive," as used in this chapter, means possessing explosives in accordance with the stated purpose and conditions of a valid permit obtained pursuant to the provisions of this part, unless such person is specifically excepted from the permit requirements by the provisions of this part.
(Amended by Stats.1970, c. 1421, p. 2707, § 23; Stats.1970, c. 1425, p. 2723, § 23.)

§ 12305. Unlawful possession; felony

Every person not in the lawful possession of an explosive who knowingly has any explosive in his possession is guilty of a felony.
(Added by Stats.1967, c. 1497, p. 3502, § 2.)

BUSINESS AND PROFESSIONS CODE

The Business and Professions Code is currently contained in eight volumes of West's Annotated California Codes. The Bus & Prof.C. is the basic authorizing document for the State Department of Consumer Affairs and a variety of California Boards and regulatory bodies charged with the responsibilities of maintaining professional conduct and licensing standards. In addition to setting professional standards, the Bus & Prof.C. sets out the causes and procedures for revocation of professional and business licensure.

A partial list of businesses and professions impacted by the Bus. & Prof.C. include: dentistry, nursing, pharmacy, accountants, attorneys, barbers, collection agencies, contractors, private detectives, funeral directors, social workers, tax preparers, real estate salespeople and real estate agents. The Bus. & Prof.C. also sets weight and measure standards and regulates the sale of alcoholic beverages.

Although each business or profession is treated separately in the code, a generalized list of unprofessional conduct or behavior can be given here to indicate the causes for license denial or revocation and the type of investigative activities which may be conducted by the licensing authority. Unprofessional conduct may include:

1. falsification of documents or records,
2. misrepresentation of identity,
3. prior conviction of certain crimes,
4. practice without a license,
5. unauthorized use of title,
6. abuse or alteration of license,
7. unlawful advertising,
8. abuse of drugs, narcotics and/or alcohol.

The following selected sections of the Bus & Prof.C. are of primary interest to administration of justice students.

Division	Section	Division	Section
GENERAL PROVISIONS	1	4. REAL ESTATE	10000
1. DEPARTMENT OF CONSUMER AFFAIRS	100	5. WEIGHTS AND MEASURES	12001
		6. BUSINESS RIGHTS	14000
1.5 DENIAL, SUSPENSION AND REVOCATION OF LICENSES	475	7. GENERAL BUSINESS REGULATIONS	16000
		8. SPECIAL BUSINESS REGULATIONS	18400
2. HEALING ARTS	500	9. ALCOHOLIC BEVERAGES	23000
3. PROFESSIONS AND VOCATIONS GENERALLY	5000	30. REPEALS	30000

Division 1
DEPARTMENT OF CONSUMERS AFFAIRS

§ 100. Existence of department

There is in the state government, in the Agriculture and Services Agency, a Department of Consumer Affairs.

(Amended by Stats.1971, c. 716, p. 1388, § 4.)

§ 101. Composition of department

The department is comprised of:

(a) The Board of Dental Examiners of California.
(b) The Board of Medical Quality Assurance of the State of California.
(c) The State Board of Optometry.
(d) The California State Board of Pharmacy.
(e) The Board of Examiners in Veterinary Medicine.
(f) The State Board of Accountancy.
(g) The California State Board of Architectural Examiners.
(h) The State Board of Barber Examiners.
(i) The State Board of Registration for Professional Engineers.
(j) The Contractors' State License Board.
(k) The State Board of Cosmetology.
(*l*) The State Board of Funeral Directors and Embalmers.
(m) The Structural Pest Control Board.
(n) The Bureau of Home Furnishings.
(*o*) The Board of Registered Nursing.
(p) The State Board of Fabric Care.
(q) The Board of Chiropractic Examiners.
(r) The Board of Behavioral Science Examiners.
(s) The State Athletic Commission.
(t) The Cemetery Board.
(u) The State Board of Guide Dogs for the Blind.
(v) The Bureau of Collection and Investigative Services.
(w) The Certified Shorthand Reporters Board.
(x) The Board of Vocational Nurse and Psychiatric Technician Examiners of the State of California.
(y) The California State Board of Landscape Architects.
(z) The Bureau of Repair Services.
(aa) The Bureau of Employment Agencies.
(ab) The Board of Osteopathic Examiners.
(ac) The Division of Investigation.
(ad) The Bureau of Automotive Repair.
(ae) The State Board of Registration for Geologists and Geophysicists.
(af) The State Board of Examiners of Nursing Home Administrators.
(ag) Any other boards, offices, or officers subject to its jurisdiction by law.

(Amended by Stats.1977, c. 141, p. —, § 1, urgency, eff. June 29, 1977.)

§ 108. Functions of boards

Each of the boards comprising the department exists as a separate unit, and has the functions of setting standards, holding meetings, and setting dates thereof, preparing and conducting examinations, passing upon applicants, conducting investigations of violations of laws under its jurisdiction, issuing citations and holding hearings for the revocation of licenses, and the imposing of penalties following such hearings, in so far as these powers are given by statute to each respective board.

(Stats.1937, c. 399, p. 1233, § 108.)

§ 119. License offenses

Any person who does any of the following is guilty of a misdemeanor:

(a) Displays or causes or permits to be displayed or has in his possession any canceled, revoked, suspended, fictitious, or fraudulently altered license, or any document simulating a license or purporting to be or to have been issued as a license.

(b) Lends his license to any other person or knowingly permits the use thereof by another.

(c) Displays or represents any license not issued to him as being his license.

(d) Fails or refuses to surrender to the issuing authority upon its lawful demand any license which has been suspended, revoked, or canceled.

(e) Permits any unlawful use of a license issued to him.

(f) Photographs, photostats, duplicates, or in any way reproduces any license or facsimile thereof in such a manner that it could be mistaken for a valid license, or displays or has in his possession any such photograph, photostat, duplicate, reproduction, or facsimile unless authorized by the provisions of this code.

As used in this section, "license" includes "certificate," "permit," "authority," and "registration" or any other indicia giving authorization to engage in a business or profession regulated by this code or referred to in Sections 1000 and 3600.

(Added by Stats.1965, c. 1083, p. 2730, § 1.)

§ 160. Chief and investigators; authority of peace officers

The Chief and all investigators of the Division of Investigation of the department and all investigators of the Board of Medical Quality Assurance have the authority of peace officers while engaged in exercising the powers granted or performing the duties imposed upon them or the division in investigating the laws administered by the various boards comprising the department or commencing directly or indirectly any criminal prosecution arising from any investigation conducted under these laws. All persons herein referred to shall be deemed to be acting within the scope of employment with respect to all acts and matters in this section set forth.
(Amended by Stats.1975, 2nd Ex.Sess., c. 2, p. —, § 1.)

Division 1.5
DENIAL, SUSPENSION AND REVOCATION OF LICENSES

§ 480. Acts disqualifying applicant

(a) A board may deny a license regulated by this code on the grounds that the applicant has one of the following:

(1) Been convicted of a crime; or

(2) Done any act involving dishonesty, fraud or deceit with the intent to substantially benefit himself or another, or substantially injure another; or

(3) Done any act which if done by a licentiate of the business or profession in question, would be grounds for suspension or revocation of license.

The board may deny a license pursuant to this subdivision only if the crime or act is substantially related to the qualifications, functions or duties of the business or profession for which application is made.

(b) Notwithstanding any other provision of this code, no person shall be denied a license solely on the basis that he has been convicted of a crime if he has obtained a certificate of rehabilitation under Section 4852.01 and following of the Penal Code, and if his probation has been terminated and the information or accusation has been dismissed pursuant to Section 1203.4 of the Penal Code.

(c) A board may deny a license regulated by this code on the ground that the applicant knowingly made a false statement of fact required to be revealed in the application for such license.
(Amended by Stats.1976, c. 947, p. —, § 1.)

§ 481. Criteria; crime or act substantially related to qualifications, etc.

Each board under the provisions of this code shall develop criteria to aid it, when considering the denial, suspension or revocation of a license, to determine whether a crime or act is substantially related to the qualifications, functions, or duties of the business or profession it regulates.
(Added by Stats.1974, c. 1321, p. 2875, § 6.)

Division 2
HEALING ARTS

§ 4143. Unlawful possession; exceptions; disposition of used needle or syringe

(a) It is unlawful for any person to have in his possession or under his control any hypodermic needle or hypodermic syringe.

(b) The provisions of this section do not apply to persons who have acquired possession and control of a hypodermic needle or hypodermic syringe in accordance with the provisions of this code authorizing and regulating the furnishing, possession and use of such needles and syringes.

Any used hypodermic needle or hypodermic syringe which is to be disposed of shall be destroyed in such a manner as to render such unit or units unfit for reuse in any manner. Such destruction may include, but is not limited to, grinding and disposal in sewerage systems where such disposal is authorized by the appropriate agency with jurisdiction over such sewerage system.
(Amended by Stats.1972, c. 883, p. 1561, § 1.)

§ 4211. Dangerous drug

"Dangerous drug" means any drug unsafe for self-medication, except preparations of drugs defined in subdivisions (e), (f), (h), and (i) hereof, designed for the purpose of feeding or treating animals (other than man) or poultry, and so labeled, and includes the following:

(a) Any hypnotic drug. "Hypnotic drug" includes acetylurea derivatives, barbituric acid derivatives, chloral, paraldehyde, sulfomethane derivatives, or any compounds or mixtures or preparations that may be used for producing hypnotic effects.

(b) Aminopyrine, or compounds or mixtures thereof.

(c) Amphetamine, desoxyephedrine, or compounds or mixtures thereof except preparations for use in the nose and unfit for internal use.

(d) Cinchophen, neocinchophen, or compounds or mixtures thereof.

(e) Diethyl-stilbestrol, or compounds or mixtures thereof.

(f) Ergot, cottonroot, or their contained or derived active compounds or mixtures thereof.

(g) Oils of croton, rue, savin or tansy or their contained or derived compounds or mixtures thereof.

(h) Sulfanilamide or substituted sulfanilamides, or compounds or mixtures thereof, except preparations for topical application only containing not more than five percent (5%) strength.

(i) Thyroid and its contained or derived active compounds or mixtures thereof.

(j) Phenylhydantoin derivatives.

(k) Any drug which bears the legend: "Caution: federal law prohibits dispensing without prescription;" or, any device which bears the statement: "Caution: federal law restricts this device to sale by or on the order of a _____," the blank to be filled in with the designation of the practitioner licensed to use or order use of the device. However, this section, nor any other provision of law, shall not prohibit the sale of such devices to skilled nursing facilities or intermediate care facilities licensed pursuant to Chapter 2 (commencing with Section 1250) of Division 2 of the Health and Safety Code.

(*l*) Hypnotic drugs when combined and compounded with non hypnotic drugs.

(m) Any narcotic antagonist drug which has been found by the federal government to have currently accepted medical use in treatment in the United States and to have no potential for abuse or abuse liability.
(Amended by Stats.1977, c. 479, p. ——, § 2.)

§ 4230. Possession of drug without prescription

No person shall have in possession any preparation included in subdivision (a) or (c) of Section 4211 except that furnished to such person upon the prescription of a physician, dentist, podiatrist, or veterinarian, or pharmacist acting within the scope of a project authorized under Article 18 (commencing with Section 429.70) of Chapter 2 of Part 1 of Division 1 of the Health and Safety Code, or registered nurse acting within the scope of a project authorized under Article 18 (commencing with Section 429.70) of Chapter 2 of Part 1 of Division 1 of the Health and Safety Code, or physician's assistant acting within the scope of a project authorized under Article 18 (commencing with Section 429.70) of Chapter 2 of Part 1 of Division 1 of the Health and Safety Code. The provisions of this section do not apply to the possession of any drug defined in subdivision (a) or (c) of Section 4211 by a manufacturer or wholesaler or a pharmacy or physician or podiatrist or dentist or veterinarian or laboratory or pharmacist acting within the scope of a project authorized under Article 18 (commencing with Section 429.70) of Chapter 2 of Part 1 of Division 1 of the Health and Safety Code, or registered nurse acting within the scope of a project authorized under Article 18 (commencing with Section 429.70) of Chapter 2 of Part 1 of Division 1 of the Health and Safety Code, or physician's assistant acting within the scope of a project authorized under Article 18 (commencing with Section 429.70) of Chapter 2 of Part 1 of Division 1 of the Health and Safety Code when in stock in containers correctly labeled with the name and address of the supplier or producer.
(Amended by Stats.1977, c. 843, p. ——, § 10.)

§ 4390. Forgery of prescription; offense; punishment

Every person who signs the name of another, or of a fictitious person, or falsely makes, alters, forges, utters, publishes, passes, or attempts to pass, as genuine, any prescription for any drugs is guilty of a forgery and upon conviction thereof shall be punished by imprisonment in the state prison, or by imprisonment in the county jail for not more than one year.

Every person who has in his possession any drugs secured by such forged prescription shall be punished by imprisonment in the state prison, or by imprisonment in the county jail for not more than one year.
(Amended by Stats.1976, c. 1139, p. ——, § 3.)

Division 3
PROFESSIONS AND VOCATIONS GENERALLY
Division 4
REAL ESTATE
Division 5
WEIGHTS AND MEASURES

§ 12024. Short quantity; offense

Every person, who by himself, or through or for another, sells any commodity in less quantity than he represents it to be is guilty of a misdemeanor.
(Added by Stats.1939, c. 43, p. 447, § 1.)

§ 12024.1. Misrepresentation of charge for service; offense

Every person, by himself, or through or for another, who willfully misrepresents a charge for service rendered on the basis of weight, time, measure, or count is guilty of a misdemeanor.

(Added by Stats.1969, c. 731, p. 1466, § 1.)

§ 12024.2. Computation of untrue value at time of sale; misdemeanor; infraction; punishment

(a) It shall be unlawful for any person to compute at the time of sale of a commodity a value which is not a true extension of a price per unit which at that time is advertised, posted or quoted.

A violation of this subdivision shall constitute a misdemeanor, punishable by a fine of not less than twenty-five dollars ($25) nor more than one thousand dollars ($1,000) or by imprisonment in the county jail for a period not exceeding one year or by both, if the violation is intentional or grossly negligent, or when the difference between the value actually computed and the total true value of the commodity offered for sale (pursuant to the advertised, posted or quoted price per unit) is more than one dollar ($1) greater than the total true value of the commodity offered for sale, or if the defendant has been convicted of two or more violations of this section within the 24-month period immediately preceding the third offense and such prior convictions are admitted by defendant or alleged in the accusatory pleading. For this purpose, a bail forfeiture shall be deemed to be a conviction of the offense charged.

(b) A violation of this section shall constitute an infraction when the difference between the value actually computed and the total true value of the commodity offered for sale (pursuant to the advertised, posted or quoted price per unit) is not more than one dollar ($1) greater than the total true value of the commodity offered for sale. Such violation shall be punishable by a fine of not more than fifty dollars ($50) for a first offense within the 24-month period immediately preceding the commission of the offense and a fine of not more than one hundred dollars ($100) for a second offense within the 24-month period immediately preceding the commission of the offense.

(Amended by Stats.1977, c. 778, p. —, § 1, urgency, eff. Sept. 13, 1977.)

§ 12024.6. False advertising

No person, firm, corporation, or association shall advertise, solicit, or represent by any means, a product for sale or purchase if it is intended to entice a consumer into a transaction different from that originally represented.

(Added by Stats.1975, c. 907, p. 2008, § 1.)

Editors' Note

These sections (12024–12024.6) represent increased legislative attention directed toward protecting the consumer in the marketplace.

Division 6
BUSINESS RIGHTS
Division 7
GENERAL BUSINESS REGULATIONS

§ 16000. Authority to license for regulation; powers

The legislative bodies of incorporated cities may, in the exercise of their police power, and for the purpose of regulation, as herein provided, and not otherwise, license any kind of business not prohibited by law transacted and carried on within the limits of their jurisdictions, including all shows, exhibitions and lawful games, and may fix the rates of such license fee and provide for its collection by suit or otherwise.

(Added by Stats.1941, c. 61, p. 718, § 1.)

Editors' Note

Section 16000 grants authority to cities to regulate local businesses. This section is the basis for local ordinances regulating the conduct and licensing of pool halls, theatres, pawn shops, dance halls, taxi cabs, restaurants, massage parlors, adult bookstores and other municipal businesses. Section 16100, which is not included in this text, provides similar authorization to local county governments.

Division 8
SPECIAL BUSINESS REGULATIONS
Division 9
ALCOHOLIC BEVERAGES

§ 25602. Sales to drunkard or intoxicated person

(a) Every person who sells, furnishes, gives, or causes to be sold, furnished, or given away, any alcoholic beverage to any habitual or common drunkard or to any obviously intoxicated person is guilty of a misdemeanor.

(b) No person who sells, furnishes, gives, or causes to be sold, furnished, or given away, any alcoholic beverage pursuant to subdivision (a) of this section shall be civilly liable to any injured person or the estate of such person for injuries inflicted on that person as a result of intoxication by the consumer of such alcoholic beverage.

(c) The Legislature hereby declares that this section shall be interpreted so that the holdings in cases such as Vesely v. Sager (5 Cal.3d 153), Bernhard v. Harrah's Club (16 Cal.3d 313) and Coulter v. Superior Court (—— Cal.3d ——) be abrogated in favor of prior judicial interpretation finding the consumption of alcoholic beverages rather than the serving of alcoholic beverages as the proximate cause of injuries inflicted upon another by an intoxicated person.
(Amended by Stats.1978, c. 929, p. ——, § 1.)

§ 25603. Bringing alcoholic beverage into prison, jail, or reformatory

Every person, not authorized by law, who brings into any state prison, city or county jail, city and county jail, or reformatory in this State, or within the grounds belonging to any such institution, any alcoholic beverage is guilty of a felony.
(Added by Stats.1953, c. 152, p. 1020, § 1.)

§ 25658. Minors; selling or furnishing to; purchases or consumption by; permitting consumption

(a) Every person who sells, furnishes, gives, or causes to be sold, furnished, or given away, any alcoholic beverage to any person under the age of 21 years is guilty of a misdemeanor.

(b) Any person under the age of 21 years who purchases any alcoholic beverage, or any person under the age of 21 years who consumes any alcoholic beverage in any on-sale premises, is guilty of a misdemeanor and shall be punished by a fine of not less than one hundred dollars ($100), no part of which shall be suspended.

(c) Any on-sale licensee who knowingly permits a person under the age of 21 years to consume any alcoholic beverage in the on-sale premises, whether or not the licensee has knowledge that the person is under the age of 21 years, is guilty of a misdemeanor.
(Amended by Stats.1959, c. 866, p. 2901, § 1.)

§ 25660.5. Minors; selling or furnishing false evidence of majority and identity to

Any person who sells, gives, or furnishes to any person under the age of 21 years any false or fraudulent written, printed, or photostatic evidence of the majority and identity of such person or who sells, gives or furnishes to any person under the age of 21 years evidence of majority and identification of any other person is guilty of a misdemeanor.
(Amended by Stats.1965, c. 1216, p. 3035, § 1.)

§ 25661. False evidence of age and identity; use; possession

Any person under the age of 21 years who presents or offers to any licensee, his agent or employee, any written, printed, or photostatic evidence of age and identity which is false, fraudulent or not actually his own for the purpose of ordering, purchasing, attempting to purchase or otherwise procuring or attempting to procure, the serving of any alcoholic beverage, or who has in his possession any false or fraudulent written, printed, or photostatic evidence of age and identity, is guilty of a misdemeanor and shall be punished by a fine of at least one hundred dollars ($100), no part of which shall be suspended.
(Amended by Stats.1959, c. 868, p. 2902, § 1.)

§ 25662. Possession of beverage by minor

Any person under the age of 21 years who has any alcoholic beverage in his possession on any street or highway or in any public place or in any place open to the public is guilty of a misdemeanor. This section does not apply to possession by a person under the age of 21 years making a delivery of an alcoholic beverage in pursuance of the order of his parent or in pursuance of his employment.
(Amended by Stats.1963, c. 396, p. ——, § 1.)

Notes of Decisions

In general

Where minor defendant's automobile was initially stopped because of defective license plate lamp and it was further observed that he was in possession of an alcoholic beverage, defendant was chargeable only with possession of alcoholic beverage in a vehicle and police did not have probable cause to arrest defendant for contributing to delinquency of his minor companion in the automobile or to incarcerate and make strip search which disclosed marijuana. People v. Superior Court for Marin County (1971) 92 Cal.Rptr. 545, 14 C.A.3d 935.

Defendant, a minor, who was found in possession of alcoholic beverages in his vehicle at the time he was stopped for a defective equipment violation was chargeable with violation of Veh.C. § 23123.5 prohibiting the possession by a minor of alcoholic beverage in a motor vehicle under his control and defendant could not be arrested nor prosecuted under this section prohibiting a minor from having any alcoholic beverage in his possession on any street or highway or in any public place. Id.

Arrest

Where police officer first noticed defendant walking out of liquor store with paper bag in hand toward officer and group of juveniles and where defendant, apparently upon noticing officer, made abrupt change of direction and deposited paper bag over retaining wall and started to walk toward group once again, officer was justified in investigating the contents of the paper bag and in arresting defendant, rather than issuing citation, when examination of the contents of bag disclosed violation of this section proscribing possession of alcoholic beverages by a minor in a public place. People v. Superior Court In and For Monterey County (1973) 106 Cal.Rptr. 211, 30 C.A.3d 257.

§ 25665. Minors entering and remaining on premises

Any licensee under an on-sale license issued for public premises, as defined in Section 23039, who permits a person under the age of 21 years to enter and remain in the licensed premises without lawful business therein is guilty of a misdemeanor. Any person under the age of 21 years who enters and remains in the licensed public premises without lawful business therein is guilty of a misdemeanor and shall be punished by a fine of not less than one hundred dollars ($100), no part of which shall be suspended.

(Amended by Stats.1959, c. 867, p. 2901, § 1.)

Division 30

REPEALS

WELFARE AND INSTITUTIONS CODE

The Welfare and Institutions Code contains the law relating to and providing for protection, care, and assistance to children, aged persons and others. The Code has been extensively revised, particularly in the fields of juvenile court law, narcotics addiction, mental health, and public social services.

Division	Section
GENERAL PROVISIONS	1
1. ADMINISTRATION OF WELFARE AND INSTITUTIONS	100
2. CHILDREN	200
2.5 YOUTHS	1700
3. NARCOTIC ADDICTS	3000
4. STATE DEPARTMENT OF HEALTH	4000
5. COMMUNITY MENTAL HEALTH SERVICES	5000
6. ADMISSIONS AND JUDICIAL COMMITMENTS	6000
6.5 CO-ORDINATION OF PROGRAMS FOR THE HANDICAPPED CHILDREN [REPEALED].	
7. MENTAL INSTITUTIONS	7000
8. MISCELLANEOUS	8000
8.5 AGING	9000
9. PUBLIC SOCIAL SERVICES	10000
10. STATE DEPARTMENT OF REHABILITATION	19000
11. OFFICE OF ALCOHOLISM	19900
20. REPEALS	20000

GENERAL PROVISIONS

§ 1. Title of code

This act shall be known as the Welfare and Institutions Code.
(Stats.1937, c. 369, p. 1005, § 1.)

§ 19. Purpose of code

It is the purpose of this code, in establishing programs and services which are designed to provide protection, support or care of children, to provide protective services to the fullest extent deemed necessary by the juvenile court, probation department or other public agencies designated by the board of supervisors to perform the duties prescribed by this code to insure that the rights or physical, mental or moral welfare of children are not violated or threatened by their present circumstances or environment. Such essential services may be provided irrespective of whether the child or the family of the child is otherwise known to the responsible local agency.
(Amended by Stats.1967, c. 90, p. 1003, § 2.)

Division 1

ADMINISTRATION OF WELFARE AND INSTITUTIONS

Division 2

CHILDREN

Editors' Note

Division 2 carries the major laws related to dependent children and wards of the court. The major chapter incorporates the juvenile court law which was the subject of major revision in 1976. The sections included in this volume give full attention to the juvenile justice procedural process extending from the peace officer powers to take a child into custody to the responsibilities of probation and judicial authorities.

§ 201. Construction

The provisions of this chapter, insofar as they are substantially the same as existing statutory provisions relating to the same subject matter, shall be construed as restatements and continuations thereof, and not as new enactments.
(Added by Stats.1976, c. 1068, p. —, § 1.5.)

§ 202. Purpose; liberal construction

(a) The purpose of this chapter is to secure for each minor under the jurisdiction of the juvenile court such care and guidance, preferably in his own home, as will serve the spiritual, emotional, mental, and physical welfare of the minor and the best interests of the state; to protect the public from criminal conduct by minors; to impose on the minor a sense of responsibility for his own acts; to preserve and strengthen the minor's family ties whenever possible, removing him from the custody of his parents only when necessary for his welfare or for the safety and protection of the public; and, when the minor is removed from his own family, to secure for him custody, care, and discipline as nearly as possible equivalent to that which should have been given by his parents. This chapter shall be liberally construed to carry out these purposes.

(b) The purpose of this chapter also includes the protection of the public from the consequences of criminal activity, and to such purpose probation officers, peace officers, and juvenile courts shall take into account such protection of the public in their determinations under this chapter.
(Amended by Stats.1977, c. 910, p. —, § 1.)

§ 203. Order adjudging minor ward of juvenile court; effect; proceedings

An order adjudging a minor to be a ward of the juvenile court shall not be deemed a conviction of a crime for any purpose, nor shall a proceeding in the juvenile court be deemed a criminal proceeding.
(Added by Stats.1976, c. 1068, p. —, § 1.5.)

§ 206. Contact or association with habitual delinquents or truants; separate segregated facilities; record of arrest

No person taken into custody solely upon the ground that he is a person described in Section 300 or adjudged to be such and made a dependent child of the juvenile court pursuant to this chapter solely upon that ground shall, in any detention under this chapter, be brought into direct contact or personal association with any person taken into custody on the ground that he is a person described by Section 601 or 602, or who has been made a ward of the juvenile court on either such ground.

Separate, segregated facilities for such persons alleged to be within the description of Section 300, or persons adjudged to be such and made dependent children of the court pursuant to this chapter solely upon that ground shall be provided by the board of supervisors. Such separate, segregated facilities may be provided in the juvenile hall or elsewhere.

The facilities required by such section shall, with regard to minors alleged or adjudged to come within subdivision (a), (b), or (d) of Section 300 be nonsecure.

The facilities provided to minors alleged or adjudged to come within subdivision (c) of Section 300 shall be secure.

No record of the detention of such a person shall be made or kept by any law enforcement agency or the Bureau of Criminal Identification and Investigation as a record of arrest.
(Amended by Stats.1978, c. 1168, p. —, § 1.)

§ 207. Place of detention

(a) No court, judge, referee, or peace officer shall knowingly detain in any jail or lockup any person under the age of 18 years, unless a judge of the juvenile court shall determine that there are no other proper and adequate facilities for the care and detention of such person, or unless such person has been transferred by the juvenile court to another court for proceedings not under the Juvenile Court Law and has been charged with or convicted of a felony. If any person under the age of 18 years is transferred by the juvenile court to another court and is charged with or convicted of a felony as herein provided and is not released pending hearing, such person may be committed to the care and custody of a sheriff, constable, or other peace officer who shall keep such person in the juvenile hall or in such other suitable place as such latter court may direct, provided that no such person shall be detained in or committed to any hospital except for medical or other remedial care and treatment or observation.

(b) Notwithstanding the provisions of subdivision (a), no minor shall be detained in any jail, lockup, juvenile hall, or other secure facility who is taken into custody solely upon the ground that he is a person described by Section 601 or adjudged to be such or made a ward of the juvenile court solely upon that ground, except as provided in subdivision (c). If any such minor, other than a minor described in subdivision (c), is detained, he shall be detained in a sheltered-care facility or crisis resolution home as provided for in Section 654, or in a nonsecure facility provided for in subdivision (a), (b), (c), or (d) of Section 727.

(c) A minor taken into custody upon the ground that he is a person described in Section 601, or adjudged to be a ward of the juvenile court solely upon that ground, may be held in a secure facility, other than a facility in which adults are held in secure custody, in any of the following circumstances:

(1) For up to 12 hours after having been taken into custody for the purpose of determining if there are

any outstanding wants, warrants, or holds against the minor in cases where the arresting officer or probation officer has cause to believe that such wants, warrants, or holds exists.

(2) For up to 24 hours after having been taken into custody, in order to locate the minor's parent or guardian as soon as possible and to arrange the return of the minor to his parent or guardian.

(3) For up to 24 hours after having been taken into custody, in order to locate the minor's parent or guardian as soon as possible and to arrange the return of the minor to his parent or guardian, whose parent or guardian is a resident outside of the state wherein the minor was taken into custody, except that such period may be extended to no more than 72 hours when the return of the minor cannot reasonably be accomplished within 24 hours due to the distance of the parents or guardian from the county of custody, difficulty in locating the parents or guardian, or difficulty in locating resources necessary to provide for the return of the minor.

(d) Any minor detained in juvenile hall pursuant to subdivision (c) may not be permitted to come or remain in contact with any person detained on the basis that he has been taken into custody upon the ground that he is a person described in Section 602 or adjudged to be such or made a ward of the juvenile court upon that ground.

(e)[1] Every county shall keep a record of each minor detained under subdivision in the same facility provided they are not permitted to come or remain in contact within that facility.

(e) Every county shall keep a record of each minor detained under subdivision (c), the place and length of time of such detention, and the reasons why such detention was necessary. Every county shall report, on a monthly basis, this information to the Department of the Youth Authority, on forms to be provided by that agency.

The Youth Authority shall not disclose the name of the detainee, or any personally identifying information contained in reports sent to the Youth Authority under this subdivision.
(Amended by Stats.1978, c. 1061, p. ——, § 1.)

§ 208. Detention or sentence to adult institutions; contact with adults; adults committed for sex offenses

(a) When any person under 18 years of age is detained in or sentenced to any institution in which adults are confined, it shall be unlawful to permit such person to come or remain in contact with such adults.

(b) No person who is a ward or dependent child of the juvenile court who is detained in or committed to any state hospital or other state facility shall be permitted to come or remain in contact with any adult person who has been committed to any state hospital or other state facility as a mentally disordered sex offender under the provisions of Article 1 (commencing with Section 6300) of Chapter 2 of Part 2 of Division 6, or with any adult person who has been charged in an accusatory pleading with the commission of any sex offense for which registration of the convicted offender is required under Section 290 of the Penal Code and who has been committed to any state hospital or other state facility pursuant to Section 1026 or 1370 of the Penal Code.

(c) As used in this section, "contact" does not include participation in supervised group therapy or other supervised treatment activities, participation in work furlough programs, or participation in hospital recreational activities which are directly supervised by employees of the hospital, so long as living arrangements are strictly segregated and all precautions are taken to prevent unauthorized associations.
(Amended by Stats.1977, c. 806, p. ——, § 1.)

§ 214. Written promise to appear; failure to perform; misdemeanor

In each instance in which a provision of this chapter authorizes the execution by any person of a written promise to appear or to have any other person appear before the probation officer or before the juvenile court, any willful failure of such promissor to perform as promised constitutes a misdemeanor and is punishable as such if at the time of the execution of such written promise the promissor is given a copy of such written promise upon which it is clearly written that failure to appear or to have any other person appear as promised is punishable as a misdemeanor.
(Added by Stats.1976, c. 1068, p. ——, § 1.5.)

§ 215. Probation officer and department of probation defined

As used in this chapter, unless otherwise specifically provided, the term "probation officer" shall mean the juvenile probation officer or the person who is both the juvenile probation officer and the adult

---

1. So in printer's copy.

probation officer, and shall include any social worker in a county welfare department when supervising dependent children of the juvenile court pursuant to Section 272 by order of the court under Section 300, and the term "department of probation" shall mean the department of juvenile probation or the department wherein the services of juvenile and adult probation are both performed.
(Added by Stats.1976, c. 1068, p. ——, § 1.5.)

§ 245. Jurisdiction; name

Each superior court shall exercise the jurisdiction conferred by this chapter, and while sitting in the exercise of such jurisdiction, shall be known and referred to as the juvenile court.
(Added by Stats.1976, c. 1068, p. ——, § 4.)

§ 280. Duties of officers in court; social study of minor; contents

Except where waived by the probation officer, judge or referee and the minor, the probation officer shall be present in court to represent the interests of each person who is the subject of a petition to declare such person to be a ward or dependent child upon all hearings or rehearings of his case, and shall furnish to the court such information and assistance as the court may require. If so ordered, he shall take charge of such person before and after any hearing or rehearing.

It shall be the duty of the probation officer to prepare for every hearing on the disposition of a case as provided by Section 356 or 702 a social study of the minor, containing such matters as may be relevant to a proper disposition of the case. Such social study shall include a recommendation for the disposition of the case.
(Added by Stats.1976, c. 1068, p. ——, § 5.)

§ 281. Investigation; reports

The probation officer shall upon order of any court in any matter involving the custody, status, or welfare of a minor or minors, make an investigation of appropriate facts and circumstances and prepare and file with the court written reports and written recommendations in reference to such matters. The court is authorized to receive and consider the reports and recommendations of the probation officer in determining any such matter.
(Added by Stats.1976, c. 1068, p. ——, § 5.)

§ 281.5. Removal of minor from custody of parent or guardian; placement with relative of minor; recommendation

If a probation officer determines to recommend to the court that a minor alleged to come within Section 300, 601, or 602, or adjudged to come within Section 300, 601, or 602 should be removed from the physical custody of his parent or guardian, the probation officer shall give primary consideration to recommending to the court that the minor be placed with a relative of the minor, if such placement is in the best interests of the minor and will be conducive to reunification of the family.
(Added by Stats.1977, c. 236, p. ——, § 1.)

§ 283. Powers of peace officer

Every probation officer, assistant probation officer, and deputy probation officer shall have the powers and authority conferred by law upon peace officers listed in Section 830.5 of the Penal Code.
(Added by Stats.1976, c. 1068, p. ——, § 5.)

§ 284. Reports to youth authority

All probation officers shall make such special and periodic reports to the Youth Authority as the authority may require and upon forms furnished by the authority.
(Added by Stats.1976, c. 1068, p. ——, § 5.)

§ 285. Reports to bureau of criminal statistics

All probation officers shall make such periodic reports to the Bureau of Criminal Statistics as the bureau may require and upon forms furnished by the bureau, provided that no personally identifying information shall be transmitted regarding any proceeding under Section 300.
(Amended by Stats.1977, c. 884, p. ——, § 1.)

§ 300. Persons subject to jurisdiction

Any person under the age of 18 years who comes within any of the following descriptions is within the jurisdiction of the juvenile court which may adjudge such person to be a dependent child of the court:

(a) Who is in need of proper and effective parental care or control and has no parent or guardian, or has no parent or guardian willing to exercise or capable of exercising such care or control, or has no parent or guardian actually exercising such care or control. No parent shall be found to be incapable of exercising proper and effective parental care or control solely because of a physical disability, including, but not limited to, a defect in the visual or auditory functions of his or her body, unless the court finds that the disability prevents the parent from exercising such care or control.

(b) Who is destitute, or who is not provided with the necessities of life, or who is not provided with a home or suitable place of abode.

(c) Who is physically dangerous to the public because of a mental or physical deficiency, disorder or abnormality.

(d) Whose home is an unfit place for him by reason of neglect, cruelty, depravity, or physical abuse of either of his parents, or of his guardian or other person in whose custody or care he is.
(Amended by Stats.1978, c. 539, p. —, § 1.)

§ 301. Retention of jurisdiction

The court may retain jurisdiction over any person who is found to be a dependent child of the juvenile court until such ward or dependent child attains the age of 21 years.
(Added by Stats.1976, c. 1068, p. —, § 6.)

§ 305. Temporary custody; peace officer; warrant

A peace officer may, without a warrant, take into temporary custody a minor:

(a) Who is under the age of 18 years when such officer has reasonable cause for believing that such minor is a person described in Section 300.

(b) Who is a dependent child of the juvenile court or concerning whom an order has been made under Section 320 or 356 when such officer has reasonable cause for believing that person has violated an order of the juvenile court or has escaped from any commitment ordered by the juvenile court, or

(c) Who is under the age of 18 years and who is found in any street or public place suffering from any sickness or injury which requires care, medical treatment, hospitalization, or other remedial care.
(Added by Stats.1976, c. 1068, p. —, § 7.)

§ 307. Alternative proceedings; release; notice to appear; taking minor before probation officer

An officer who takes a minor into temporary custody under the provisions of Section 305 shall thereafter proceed as follows:

(a) He may release such minor; or

(b) He may prepare in duplicate a written notice to appear before the probation officer of the county in which such minor was taken into custody at a time and place specified in the notice. The notice shall also contain a concise statement of the reasons such minor was taken into custody. He shall deliver one copy of the notice to such minor or to a parent, guardian, or responsible relative of such minor and may require such minor or his parent, guardian, or relative, or both, to sign a written promise that either or both will appear at the time and place designated in the notice. Upon the execution of the promise to appear, he shall immediately release such minor. He shall, as soon as practicable, file one copy of the notice with the probation officer; or

(c) He may take such minor without unnecessary delay before the probation officer of the county in which such person was taken into custody, or in which such person resides, or in which the acts take place or the circumstances exist which are alleged to bring the minor within the provisions of Section 300, and deliver the custody of such minor to the probation officer.

In determining which disposition of the minor he will make, the officer shall prefer the alternative which least restricts the minor's freedom of movement, provided such alternative is compatible with the best interests of the minor and the community.
(Added by Stats.1976, c. 1068, p. —, § 7.)

§ 308. Notice to parent or guardian; right to make telephone calls

(a) When an officer takes a minor before a probation officer pursuant to this article, he shall take immediate steps to notify the minor's parent, guardian, or a responsible relative that such minor is in custody and the place where he is being held.

(b) Immediately after being taken to a probation officer pursuant to this article and, except where physically impossible, no later than three hours after he has been taken into custody, the minor has the right to make at least two telephone calls from the place where he is being held, one call completed to his parent or guardian, a responsible relative, or his employer, and another call completed to an attorney. The calls shall be at his own expense and in the presence of a public officer or employee. Any public officer or employee who willfully deprives a minor taken into custody of his right to make such telephone calls is guilty of a misdemeanor.
(Amended by Stats.1978, c. 1168, p. —, § 2.)

§ 309. Investigation; release of minor

(a) Upon delivery to the probation officer of a minor who has been taken into temporary custody under the provisions of this article, the probation officer shall immediately investigate the circumstances of the minor and the facts surrounding his being taken into custody and shall immediately release such minor to the custody of his parent, guardian, or responsible relative unless one or more of the following conditions exist:

(1) The minor is in need of proper and effective parental care or control and has no parent, guardian, or responsible relative; or has no parent, guardian, or responsible relative willing to exercise or capable of exercising such care or control; or has no parent, guardian, or responsible relative actually exercising such care or control.

(2) The minor is destitute or is not provided with the necessities of life or is not provided with a home or suitable place of abode.

(3) The minor is provided with a home which is an unfit place for him by reason of neglect, cruelty, depravity or physical abuse of either of his parents, or of his guardian or other person in whose custody or care he is.

(4) Continued detention of the minor is a matter of immediate and urgent necessity for the protection of the minor or the person or property of another.

(5) The minor is likely to flee the jurisdiction of the court.

(6) The minor has violated an order of the juvenile court.

(7) The minor is physically dangerous to the public because of a mental or physical deficiency, disorder or abnormality.

(b) In any case in which there is reasonable cause for believing that a minor who is under the care of a physician or surgeon or a hospital, clinic, or other medical facility and cannot be immediately moved is a person described in subdivision (d) of Section 300, the minor shall be deemed to have been taken into temporary custody and delivered to the probation officer for the purposes of this chapter while he is at the office of the physician or surgeon or such medical facility.
(Added by Stats.1976, c. 1068, p. ——, § 7.)

§ 310. Written promise to appear

As a condition for the release of such minor, the probation officer may require such minor or his parent, guardian, or relative, or both, to sign a written promise that either or both of them will appear before the probation officer at a suitable place designated by the probation officer at a specified time.
(Amended by Stats.1978, c. 1168, p. ——, § 3.)

§ 311. Filing petition; notice of hearing; privileges and rights of minors

(a) If the probation officer determines that the minor shall be retained in custody, he shall immediately file a petition pursuant to Section 332 with the clerk of the juvenile court who shall set the matter for hearing on the detention hearing calendar. The probation officer shall thereupon notify each parent or each guardian of the minor of the time and place of such hearing if the whereabouts of each parent or guardian can be ascertained by due diligence, and the probation officer shall serve those persons entitled to notice of the hearing under the provisions of Section 335 with a copy of the petition and notify such persons of the time and place of the detention hearing. Such notice may be given orally.

(b) In such hearing the minor has a privilege against self-incrimination and has a right to confrontation by, and cross-examination of, any person examined by the court as provided in Section 319.
(Added by Stats.1976, c. 1068, p. ——, § 7.)

§ 312. Notice of hearings

Upon reasonable notification by counsel representing the minor, his parents or guardian, the clerk of the court shall notify such counsel of the hearings in the manner provided for notice to the parent or guardian of the minor under this chapter.
(Added by Stats.1976, c. 1068, p. ——, § 7.)

§ 313. Release within 48 hours; exceptions; written explanation for custody over 6 hours

(a) Whenever a minor is taken into custody by a peace officer or probation officer, except when such minor willfully misrepresents himself as 18 or more years of age, such minor shall be released within 48 hours after having been taken into custody, excluding nonjudicial days, unless within said period of time a petition to declare him a dependent child has been filed pursuant to the provisions of this chapter.

(b) Whenever a minor who has been held in custody for more than six hours by the probation officer is subsequently released and no petition is filed, the

probation officer shall prepare a written explanation of why the minor was held in custody for more than six hours. The written explanation shall be prepared within 72 hours after the minor is released from custody and filed in the record of the case. A copy of the written explanation shall be sent to the parents, guardian, or other person having care or custody of the minor.
(Added by Stats.1976, c. 1068, p. —, § 7.)

§ 314. Misrepresentation of age

When a minor willfully misrepresents himself to be 18 or more years of age when taken into custody by a peace officer or probation officer, and this misrepresentation effects a material delay in investigation which prevents the filing of a petition pursuant to the provisions of this chapter, such petition or complaint shall be filed within 48 hours from the time his true age is determined, excluding nonjudicial days. If, in such cases, the petition is not filed within the time prescribed by this section, the minor shall be immediately released from custody.
(Added by Stats.1976, c. 1068, p. —, § 7.)

§ 315. Detention hearing; release

Unless sooner released, a minor taken into custody under the provisions of this article shall be brought before a judge or referee of the juvenile court for a hearing (which shall be referred to as a "detention hearing") to determine whether the minor shall be further detained, as soon as possible but in any event before the expiration of the next judicial day after a petition to declare such minor a ward or dependent child has been filed. If the minor is not brought before a judge or referee of the juvenile court within the period prescribed by this section, he shall be released from custody.
(Added by Stats.1976, c. 1068, p. —, § 7.)

§ 316. Informing minor as to reasons for custody; nature of proceedings; right to counsel

Upon his appearance before the court at the detention hearing, such minor and his parent or guardian, if present, shall first be informed of the reasons why the minor was taken into custody, the nature of the juvenile court proceedings, and the right of such minor and his parent or guardian to be represented at every stage of the proceedings by counsel.
(Added by Stats.1976, c. 1068, p. —, § 7.)

§ 317. Appointment of counsel

When it appears to the court that the minor or his parent or guardian desires counsel but is unable to afford and cannot for that reason employ counsel, the court may appoint counsel. In any case in which it appears to the court that there is such a conflict of interest between a parent or guardian and child that one attorney could not properly represent both, the court shall appoint counsel, in addition to counsel already employed by a parent or guardian or appointed by the court to represent the minor or parent or guardian. In a county where there is no public defender the court may fix the compensation to be paid by the county for service of such appointed counsel.
(Added by Stats.1976, c. 1068, p. —, § 7.)

§ 318. Appointment of counsel; continuation of representation

(a) Notwithstanding the provisions of Section 317, when a minor who is alleged to be a person described in subdivision (d) of Section 300 appears before the juvenile court at a detention hearing, the court shall appoint counsel. The court may appoint the district attorney to represent the minor pursuant to Section 351.

(b) The counsel appointed by the court shall represent the minor at the detention hearing and at all subsequent proceedings before the juvenile court.

(c) Any counsel upon entering an appearance on behalf of a minor shall continue to represent that minor unless relieved by the court upon the substitution of other counsel or for cause.
(Added by Stats.1976, c. 1068, p. —, § 7.)

§ 319. Examination of minor; order releasing minor from custody

The court will examine such minor, his parent, guardian, or other person having relevant knowledge, hear such relevant evidence as the minor, his parent or guardian or their counsel desires to present, and, unless it appears that such minor has violated an order of the juvenile court or has escaped from the commitment of the juvenile court or that it is a matter of immediate and urgent necessity for the protection of such minor or the person or property of another that he be detained or that such minor is likely to flee the jurisdiction of the court, the court shall make its order releasing such minor from custody.
(Added by Stats.1976, c. 1068, p. —, § 7.)

§ 320. Order detaining minor in juvenile hall; period of detention

If it appears upon the hearing that such minor has violated an order of the juvenile court or has escaped from a commitment of the juvenile court or that it is a matter of immediate and urgent necessity for the protection of such minor or the person or property of another that he be detained, or that such minor is likely to flee the jurisdiction of the court, the court may make its order that such minor be detained in a suitable place designated by the juvenile court for a period not to exceed 15 judicial days and shall enter said order together with its findings of fact in support thereof in the records of the court.
(Amended by Stats.1978, c. 1168, p. —, § 4.)

§ 323. Order requiring reappearance of minor, parent or guardian

Upon any hearing or rehearing under the provisions of this article, the court may order such minor or any parent or guardian of such minor who is present in court to again appear before the court or the probation officer at a time and place specified in said order.
(Added by Stats.1976, c. 1068, p. —, § 7.)

§ 325. Filing of petition

A proceeding in the juvenile court to declare a minor a dependent child of the court is commenced by the filing with the court, by the probation officer, of a petition, in conformity with the requirements of this article.
(Added by Stats.1976, c. 1068, p. —, § 8.)

§ 327. Venue

Either the juvenile court in the county in which a minor resides or in the county where the minor is found or in the county in which the acts take place or the circumstances exist which are alleged to bring such minor within the provisions of Section 300, is the proper court to commence proceedings under this chapter.
(Added by Stats.1976, c. 1068, p. —, § 8.)

§ 328. Reasonable cause; investigation

Whenever the probation officer has cause to believe that there was or is within the county, or residing therein, a person within the provisions of Section 300, the probation officer shall immediately make such investigation as he deems necessary to determine whether proceedings in the juvenile court should be commenced.
(Added by Stats.1976, c. 1068, p. —, § 8.)

§ 329. Application to commence proceedings; affidavit; allegations; indorsement by probation officer

Whenever any person applies to the probation officer to commence proceedings in the juvenile court, such application shall be in the form of an affidavit alleging that there was or is within the county, or residing therein, a minor within the provisions of Section 300, and setting forth facts in support thereof. The probation officer shall immediately make such investigation as he deems necessary to determine whether proceedings in the juvenile court should be commenced. If the probation officer does not take action under Section 330 and does not file a petition in the juvenile court within three weeks after such application, he shall endorse upon the affidavit of applicant his decision not to proceed further and his reasons therefor and shall immediately notify the applicant of the action taken or the decision rendered by him under this section. The probation officer shall retain the affidavit and his endorsement thereon for a period of 30 days after such notice to applicant.
(Added by Stats.1976, c. 1068, p. —, § 8.)

§ 330. Program of supervision

In any case in which a probation officer, after investigation of an application for petition or other investigation he is authorized to make, concludes that a minor is within the jurisdiction of the juvenile court or will probably soon be within such jurisdiction, he may, in lieu of filing a petition or subsequent to dismissal of a petition already filed, and with consent of the minor's parent or guardian, undertake a program of supervision of the minor, for not to exceed six months, and attempt thereby to adjust the situation which brings the minor within the jurisdiction of the court or creates the probability that he will soon be within such jurisdiction. Nothing in this section shall be construed to prevent the probation officer from filing a petition at any time within said six-month period.

The program of supervision of the minor undertaken pursuant to this section may call for the minor to obtain care and treatment for the misuse of restricted dangerous drugs or addiction to narcotics from a county mental health service or other appropriate community agency.
(Added by Stats.1976, c. 1068, p. —, § 8.)

§ 331. Failure of probation officer to file petition and take action; review

When any person has applied to the probation officer, pursuant to Section 329, to commence juvenile court proceedings and the probation officer fails to file a petition within three weeks after such application, such person may, within one month after making such application, apply to the juvenile court to review the decision of the probation officer, and the court may either affirm the decision of the probation officer or order him to commence juvenile court proceedings.

(Added by Stats.1976, c. 1068, p. ——, § 8.)

§ 334. Time for hearing

Upon the filing of the petition, the clerk of the juvenile court shall set the same for hearing within 30 days, except that in the case of a minor detained in custody at the time of the filing of the petition, the petition must be set for hearing within 15 judicial days from the date of the order of the court directing such detention.

(Added by Stats.1976, c. 1068, p. ——, § 8.)

§ 335. Notice of hearing

Upon the filing of the petition, the clerk of the juvenile court shall issue a notice, to which shall be attached a copy of the petition, and he shall cause the same to be served upon the minor, if the minor is 14 or more years of age, and upon each of the persons described in subdivision (e) of Section 332 whose residence addresses are set forth in said petition and thereafter before the hearing upon all such persons whose residence addresses become known to the clerk. The clerk shall issue a copy of the petition to the attorney for the minor's parent or guardian and to the district attorney, if the district attorney has notified the clerk of the court that he wishes to receive such petition, containing the time, date, and place of the hearing.

(Added by Stats.1976, c. 1068, p. ——, § 8.)

§ 336. Contents of notice

The notice shall contain:

(a) The name and address of the person to whom the notice is directed.

(b) The date, time, and place of the hearing on the petition.

(c) The name of the minor upon whose behalf the petition has been brought.

(d) Each section and subdivision under which the proceeding has been instituted.

(e) A statement that the minor and his parent or guardian or adult relative, as the case may be, to whom notice is required to be given, are entitled to have an attorney present at the hearing on the petition, and that, if the parent or guardian or such adult relative is indigent and cannot afford an attorney, and the minor or his parent or guardian or such adult relative desires to be represented by an attorney, such parent or guardian or adult relative shall promptly notify the clerk of the juvenile court.

(Added by Stats.1976, c. 1068, p. ——, § 8.)

§ 337. Personal service; service by mail

(a) If the minor is detained the clerk of the juvenile court shall cause the notice and copy of the petition to be served on all persons required to receive such notice and copy of the petition, either personally or by certified mail with request for return receipt, as soon as possible after filing of the petition and at least five days prior to the time set for hearing, unless such hearing is set less than five days from the filing of the petition, in which case, such notice and copy of the petition must be served at least 24 hours prior to the time set for hearing.

(b) If the minor is not detained the clerk of the juvenile court shall cause the notice and copy of the petition to be served on all persons required to receive such notice and copy of the petition, either personally, by certified mail with request for return receipt, or by first-class mail, at least 10 days prior to the time set for hearing. If such a person is known to reside outside of the county, the clerk of the juvenile court shall mail the notice and copy of the petition, by certified mail with request for return receipt or by first-class mail, to such person, as soon as possible after filing of the petition and at least 10 days before the time set for hearing. Failure to respond to the notice by certified mail with request for return receipt or by first-class mail shall in no way result in arrest or detention. In the instance of failure to appear after notice by certified or first-class mail, the court shall direct that the notice and copy of the petition is to be personally served on all persons required to receive such notice and copy of the petition. Personal service of the notice and copy of the petition outside of the county at least 10 days before the time set for hearing is equivalent to such service by certified or first-class mail. Service may be waived by any person by a voluntary appearance

entered in the minutes of the court or by a written waiver of service filed with the clerk of the court at or prior to the hearing.
(Added by Stats.1976, c. 1068, p. —, § 8.)

§ 338. Notice; citation; issuance and service

In addition to the notice provided in Sections 335 and 336 the juvenile court may issue its citation directing any parent or guardian of the person concerning whom a petition has been filed to appear at the time and place set for any hearing under the provisions of this chapter, including a hearing under the provisions of Section 257, and directing any person having custody or control of the minor concerning whom the petition has been filed to bring such minor with him. The notice shall in addition state that a parent or guardian may be required to participate in a counseling program with the minor concerning whom the petition has been filed. Personal service of such citation shall be made at least 24 hours before the time stated therein for such appearance.
(Added by Stats.1976, c. 1068, p. —, § 8.)

§ 339. Warrant of arrest against parent or guardian

In case such citation cannot be served, or the person served fails to obey it, or in any case in which it appears to the court that the citation will probably be ineffective, a warrant of arrest may issue on the order of the court either against the parent, or guardian, or the person having the custody of the minor, or with whom the minor is living.
(Added by Stats.1976, c. 1068, p. —, § 8.)

§ 340. Warrant of arrest against minor

Whenever a petition has been filed in the juvenile court alleging that a minor comes within the provisions of Section 300 and praying for a hearing thereon, or whenever any subsequent petition has been filed praying for a hearing in the matter of said minor and it appears to the court that the conduct and behavior of the said minor may endanger the health, person, welfare, or property of himself or others, or that the circumstances of his home environment may endanger the health, person, welfare or property of said minor, a warrant of arrest may be issued immediately for the minor.
(Added by Stats.1976, c. 1068, p. —, § 8.)

§ 341. Subpoenas

Upon request of the probation officer, district attorney, the minor or the minor's parent, guardian, or custodian, the court or the clerk of the court shall issue, and, on the court's own motion, it may issue subpoenas requiring attendance and testimony of witnesses and production of papers at any hearing under the provisions of this chapter. When a person attends a juvenile court hearing as a witness upon a subpoena at its discretion, the court may by an order on its minutes, direct the county auditor to draw his warrant upon the county treasurer in favor of such witness for witness fees in the amount and manner prescribed by Section 68093 of the Government Code. The fees are county charges.
(Added by Stats.1976, c. 1068, p. —, § 8.)

§ 345. Special or separate session; presence of persons on trial or awaiting trial

All cases under the provisions of this chapter shall be heard at a special or separate session of the court, and no other matter shall be heard at such session. No person on trial, awaiting trial, or under accusation of crime, other than a parent, guardian, or relative of the minor, shall be permitted to be present at any such session, except as a witness.

Cases in which the minor is detained and the sole allegation is that the minor is a person described in Section 300 shall be granted precedence on the calendar of the court for the day on which the case is set for hearing.
(Added by Stats.1976, c. 1068, p. —, § 9.)

§ 346. Admission of public and persons having interest in case

Unless requested by the minor concerning whom the petition has been filed and any parent or guardian present, the public shall not be admitted to a juvenile court hearing. The judge or referee may nevertheless admit such persons as he deems to have a direct and legitimate interest in the particular case or the work of the court.
(Added by Stats.1976, c. 1068, p. —, § 9.)

§ 349. Presence of minor and person entitled to notice; right to counsel

A minor who is the subject of a juvenile court hearing and any person entitled to notice of the hearing under the provisions of Section 335, is entitled to be present at such hearing. Any such minor and any such person has the right to be represented at such hearing by counsel of his own choice.
(Added by Stats.1976, c. 1068, p. —, § 9.)

§ 350. Control and conduct of proceedings

The judge of the juvenile court shall control all proceedings during the hearings with a view to the expeditious and effective ascertainment of the jurisdictional facts and the ascertainment of all information relative to the present condition and future welfare of the person upon whose behalf the petition is brought. Except where there is a contested issue of fact or law, the proceedings shall be conducted in an informal nonadversary atmosphere with a view to obtaining the maximum cooperation of the minor upon whose behalf the petition is brought and all persons interested in his welfare with such provisions as the court may make for the disposition and care of such minor.
(Added by Stats.1976, c. 1068, p. ——, § 9.)

§ 351. Appearance by district attorney; consent of court

In a juvenile court hearing, where the minor who is the subject of the hearing is represented by counsel, the district attorney shall, with the consent or at the request of the juvenile court judge, appear and participate in the hearing to assist in the ascertaining and presenting of the evidence. Where the petition in a juvenile court proceeding alleges that a minor is a person described in subdivision (a), (b), or (d) of Section 300, and either of the parents, or the guardian, or other person having care or custody of the minor, or who resides in the home of the minor, is charged in a pending criminal prosecution based upon unlawful acts committed against the minor, the district attorney shall, with the consent or at the request of the juvenile court judge, represent the minor in the interest of the state at the juvenile court proceeding. The terms and conditions of such representation shall be with the consent or approval of the judge of the juvenile court.
(Added by Stats.1976, c. 1068, p. ——, § 9.)

§ 352. Continuance of hearing under this chapter

(a) Upon request of counsel for the minor, the court may continue any hearing under this chapter beyond the time limit within which the hearing is otherwise required to be held.

(b) In any case in which the minor is represented by counsel and no objection is made to an order continuing any such hearing beyond the time limit within which the hearing is otherwise required to be held, the absence of such an objection shall be deemed a consent to the continuance.
(Added by Stats.1976, c. 1068, p. ——, § 9.)

§ 353. Reading petition; advising minor of right to counsel; appointment of counsel; continuance

At the beginning of the hearing on a petition filed pursuant to Article 8 (commencing with Section 325) of this chapter, the judge or clerk shall first read the petition to those present and upon request of the minor upon whose behalf the petition has been brought or upon the request of any parent, relative or guardian, the judge shall explain any term of allegation contained therein and the nature of the hearing, its procedures, and possible consequences. The judge shall ascertain whether the minor and his parent or guardian or adult relative, as the case may be, has been informed of the right of the minor to be represented by counsel, and if not, the judge shall advise the minor and such person, if present, of the right to have counsel present and where applicable, of the right to appointed counsel. If such person is unable to afford counsel and desires to have the minor represented by counsel, the court may in a case in which the minor is alleged to be within the provisions of Section 300, appoint counsel to represent the minor. The court shall continue the hearing for not to exceed seven days, as necessary to make an appointment of counsel, or to enable counsel to acquaint himself with the case, or to determine whether the parent or guardian or adult relative is unable to afford counsel at his own expense, and shall continue the hearing as necessary to provide reasonable opportunity for the minor and the parent or guardian or adult relative to prepare for the hearing.
(Added by Stats.1976, c. 1068, p. ——, § 9.)

§ 354. Continuance of hearing on petition filed pursuant to article 8 of this chapter

Except where a minor is in custody, any hearing on a petition filed pursuant to Article 8 (commencing with Section 325) of this chapter may be continued by the court for not more than 10 days in addition to any other continuance authorized in this chapter whenever the court is satisfied that an unavailable and necessary witness will be available within such time.
(Added by Stats.1976, c. 1068, p. ——, § 9.)

§ 355. Description of minor; reception of evidence; extrajudicial admissions or confessions; objections to evidence

At the hearing, the court shall first consider only the question whether the minor is a person described

by Section 300, and for this purpose, any matter or information relevant and material to the circumstances or acts which are alleged to bring him within the jurisdiction of the juvenile court is admissible and may be received in evidence; however, proof by a preponderance of evidence, legally admissible in the trial of civil cases must be adduced to support a finding that the minor is a person described by Section 300. If the minor is not represented by counsel at the hearing, it shall be deemed that objections that could have been made to the evidence were made.
(Added by Stats.1976, c. 1068, p. —, § 9.)

§ 356. Finding and order; dismissal; discharge; continuance to receive social study or other evidence; detention order

After hearing such evidence, the court shall make a finding, noted in the minutes of the court, whether or not the minor is a person described by Section 300. If it finds that the minor is not such a person, it shall order that the petition be dismissed and the minor be discharged from any detention or restriction theretofore ordered. If the court finds that the minor is such a person, it shall make and enter its findings and order accordingly and shall then proceed to hear evidence on the question of the proper disposition to be made of the minor. Prior to doing so, it may continue the hearing, if necessary, to receive the social study of the probation officer or to receive other evidence on its own motion or the motion of a parent or guardian for not to exceed 10 judicial days if the minor is detained during such continuance, and if the minor is not detained, it may continue the hearing to a date not later than 30 days after the date of filing of the petition. The court may, for good cause shown continue the hearing for an additional 15 days, if the minor is not detained. The court may make such order for detention of the minor or his release from detention, during the period of the continuance, as is appropriate.
(Added by Stats.1976, c. 1068, p. —, § 9.)

§ 358. Evidence as to proper disposition of minor; reception of social study in evidence

After finding that a minor is a person described in Section 300, the court shall hear evidence on the question of the proper disposition to be made of the minor. The court shall receive in evidence the social study of the minor made by the probation officer and such other relevant and material evidence as may be offered, and in any judgment and order of disposition, shall state the social study made by the probation officer has been read and considered by the court.
(Added by Stats.1976, c. 1068, p. —, § 9.)

§ 359. Minor using narcotics or restricted dangerous drug; continuance of hearing; 72 hour treatment and evaluation; report; disposition; reimbursement of expenditure

Whenever a minor who appears to be a danger to himself or others as a result of the use of narcotics (as defined in Section 11001 of the Health and Safety Code), or a restricted dangerous drug (as defined in Section 11901 of the Health and Safety Code), is brought before any judge of the juvenile court, the judge may continue the hearing and proceed pursuant to this section. The court may order the minor taken to a facility designated by the county and approved by the State Department of Mental Health as a facility for 72-hour treatment and evaluation. Thereupon the provisions of Section 11922 of the Health and Safety Code shall apply, except that the professional person in charge of the facility shall make a written report to the court concerning the results of the evaluation of the minor.

If the professional person in charge of the facility for 72-hour evaluation and treatment reports to the juvenile court that the minor is not a danger to himself or others as a result of the use of narcotics or restricted dangerous drugs or that the minor does not require 14-day intensive treatment, or if the minor has been certified for not more than 14 days of intensive treatment and the certification is terminated, the minor shall be released if the juvenile court proceedings have been dismissed; referred for further care and treatment on a voluntary basis, subject to the disposition of the juvenile court proceedings; or returned to the juvenile court, in which event the court shall proceed with the case pursuant to this chapter.

Any expenditure for the evaluation or intensive treatment of a minor under this section shall be considered an expenditure made under Part 2 (commencing with Section 5600) of Division 5, and shall be reimbursed by the state as are other local expenditures pursuant to that part.
(Amended by Stats.1978, c. 380, p. —, § 151.)

§ 360. Order adjudging minor a dependent child of the court

After receiving and considering the evidence on the proper disposition of the case, the court, if the court

has found that the minor is a person described by Section 300, may order and adjudge the minor to be a dependent child of the court.
(Added by Stats.1976, c. 1068, p. —, § 10.)

§ 361. Parental control; removal from custody

In all cases wherein a minor is adjudged a dependent child of the court, the court may limit the control to be exercised over such dependent child by any parent or guardian and shall by its order clearly and specifically set forth all such limitations, but no dependent child shall be taken from the physical custody of a parent or guardian unless upon the hearing the court finds one of the following facts:

(a) That the parent or guardian is incapable of providing or has failed or neglected to provide proper maintenance, training, and education for the minor.

(b) That the welfare of the minor requires that his custody be taken from his parent or guardian.
(Added by Stats.1976, c. 1068, p. —, § 10.)

§ 362. Order for care, supervision, custody, maintenance and support of dependent child; counseling

(1) When a minor is adjudged a dependent child of the court on the ground that he is a person described by Section 300, the court may make any and all reasonable orders for the care, supervision, custody, conduct, maintenance, and support of such minor, including medical treatment, subject to further order of the court.

The court may order the care, custody, control and conduct of such minor to be under the supervision of the probation officer or may commit such minor to the care, custody and control of:

(a) Some reputable person of good moral character who consents to such commitment.

(b) Some association, society, or corporation embracing within its objects the purpose of caring for such minors, with the consent of such association, society, or corporation.

(c) The probation officer, to be boarded out or placed in some suitable family home or suitable private institution, subject to the requirements of Chapter 2 (commencing with Section 1250) or Chapter 3 (commencing with Section 1500) of Division 2 of the Health and Safety Code; provided, however, that pending action by the State Department of Health Services or State Department of Social Services, the placement of a minor in a home certified as meeting minimum standards for boarding homes by the probation officer shall be legal for all purposes.

(d) Any other public agency organized to provide care for needy or neglected children.

When a minor is adjudged a dependent child of the court, on the ground that he is a person described by Section 300 and the court orders that a parent or guardian shall retain custody of such minor subject to the supervision of the probation officer, the parent or guardian may be required, and may be ordered, to participate in a counseling program to be provided by an appropriate agency designated by the court. When a minor is adjudged a dependent child of the court on the ground that he is a person described by subdivision (d) of Section 300 and the court orders that a parent or guardian shall retain custody of such minor subject to the supervision of the probation officer, the parent or guardian shall be required to participate in a counseling program to be provided by an appropriate agency, designated by the court.

(2) The juvenile court may direct any and all reasonable orders to the parents and guardians of the minor who is the subject of any proceedings under this chapter as the court deems necessary and proper to carry out the provisions of subdivision (1).
(Amended by Stats.1978, c. 380, p. —, § 152.)

§ 363. Reduction of assistance of person legally responsible for care of minor removed from unfit home

If the parent or person legally responsible for the care of any minor who is found to be a person described in subdivision (d) of Section 300 receives public assistance or care, any portion of which is attributable to the minor, a copy of the order of the court providing for the removal of the minor from his home shall be furnished to the appropriate social services official, who shall reduce the public assistance and care furnished the parent or other person by the amount attributable to the minor.
(Added by Stats.1976, c. 1068, p. —, § 10.)

§ 364. Retention by parent or guardian of minor allegedly living in unfit home; subsequent proceedings

In any case in which the court has ordered that a parent or guardian shall retain physical custody of a minor who is found to be a person described in subdivision (d) of Section 300, subject to supervision of the probation officer, whenever the probation officer subsequently receives a report of acts or

circumstances which indicate that there is reasonable cause to believe that the minor is a person described in subdivision (d) of Section 300, he shall commence proceedings under this chapter. If, as a result of the proceedings required, the court finds that the minor is a person described in subdivision (d) of Section 300, the court shall remove such minor from the care, custody, and control of his parent or guardian and shall commit such minor to the care, custody, and control of those persons or organizations enumerated in Section 362.
(Added by Stats.1976, c. 1068, p. —, § 10.)

§ 366. Continuation of hearing; duties of probation officer; notice

Every hearing in which an order is made adjudging a minor a dependent child of the juvenile court pursuant to Section 300 and every subsequent hearing in which such an order is made, except a hearing at which the court orders the termination of its jurisdiction over such minor, shall be continued to a specific future date not more than one year after the date of such order. The continued hearing shall be placed on the appearance calendar and the probation officer shall make an investigation, file a supplemental report and make his recommendation for disposition. The court shall advise all persons present of the date of the future hearing and of their right to be present, to be represented by counsel and to show cause, if they have cause, why the jurisdiction of the court over the minor should be terminated. Notice of hearing shall be mailed by the probation officer to the same persons as in an original proceeding and to counsel of record by certified mail addressed to the last known address of the person to be notified, or shall be personally served on such persons, not earlier than 30 days preceding the date to which the hearing was continued.
(Added by Stats.1976, c. 1068, p. —, § 10.)

§ 367. Detention until execution of commitment order; review of detention of minor

(a) Whenever a person has been adjudged a dependent child of the juvenile court and has been committed or otherwise disposed of as provided in this chapter for the care of dependent children of the juvenile court, the court may order that said dependent child be detained in a suitable place designated as the court seems fit until the execution of the order of commitment or of other disposition.

(b) In any case in which a minor is detained for more than 15 days pending the execution of the order of commitment or of any other disposition, the court shall periodically review the case to determine whether the delay is reasonable. Such periodic reviews shall be held at least every 15 days, commencing from the time the minor was initially detained pending the execution of the order of commitment or of any other disposition, and during the course of each review the court shall inquire regarding the action taken by the probation department to carry out its order, the reasons for the delay, and the effect of the delay upon the minor.
(Amended by Stats.1978, c. 1168, p. —, § 5.)

§ 385. Changing, modifying or setting aside orders; procedural requirements

Any order made by the court in the case of any person subject to its jurisdiction may at any time be changed, modified, or set aside, as the judge deems meet and proper, subject to such procedural requirements as are imposed by this article.
(Added by Stats.1976, c. 1068, p. —, § 12.)

§ 386. Notice of application

No order changing, modifying, or setting aside a previous order of the juvenile court shall be made either in chambers, or otherwise, unless prior notice of the application therefor has been given by the judge or the clerk of the court to the probation officer and to the minor's counsel of record, or, if there is no counsel of record, to the minor and his parent or guardian.
(Added by Stats.1976, c. 1068, p. —, § 12.)

§ 387. Removing dependent child from parent's custody; placement or commitment

Hearing.

An order changing or modifying a previous order by removing a minor from the physical custody of a parent, guardian, relative or friend and directing placement in a foster home, or commitment to a private institution or commitment to a county institution, shall be made only after noticed hearing upon a supplemental petition.

(a) **Supplemental petition; contents.**

(a) The supplemental petition shall be filed by the probation officer in the original matter and shall contain a concise statement of facts sufficient to support the conclusion that the previous disposition has not been effective in the rehabilitation of the minor.

(b) Filing; notice; hearing.

(b) Upon the filing of such supplemental petition, the clerk of the juvenile court shall immediately set the same for hearing within 30 days, and the probation officer shall cause notice thereof to be served upon the persons and in the manner prescribed by Sections 335 and 337.

(c) Detention pending adjudication.

(c) An order for the detention of the minor pending adjudication of the petition may be made only after a hearing is conducted pursuant to Article 7 (commencing with Section 305) of this chapter.
(Added by Stats.1976, c. 1068, p. ——, § 12.)

§ 388. Petition to change, modify or set aside order or terminate jurisdiction of court; grounds; verification; contents; hearing

Any parent or other person having an interest in a child who is a dependent child of the juvenile court or the child himself through a properly appointed guardian may, upon grounds of change of circumstance or new evidence, petition the court in the same action in which the child was found to be a dependent child of the juvenile court for a hearing to change, modify, or set aside any order of court previously made or to terminate the jurisdiction of the court. The petition shall be verified and, if made by a person other than the child, shall state the petitioner's relationship to or interest in the child and shall set forth in concise language any change of circumstance or new evidence which are alleged to require such change of order or termination of jurisdiction.

If it appears that the best interests of the child may be promoted by the proposed change of order or termination of jurisdiction, the court shall order that a hearing be held and shall give prior notice, or cause prior notice to be given, to such persons and by such means as prescribed by Section 386, and, in such instances as the means of giving notice is not prescribed by such sections, then by such means as the court prescribes.
(Added by Stats.1976, c. 1068, p. ——, § 12.)

§ 389. Petition for sealing records; notice; hearing; grounds for and effect of order; inspection of records

(a) In any case in which a petition has been filed with a juvenile court to commence proceedings to adjudge a person a dependent child of the court, in any case in which a person is cited to appear before a probation officer or is taken before a probation officer pursuant to Section 307, or in any case in which a minor is taken before any officer of a law enforcement agency, the person or the county probation officer may, five years or more after the jurisdiction of the juvenile court has terminated as to the person, or, in a case in which no petition is filed, five years or more after the person was cited to appear before a probation officer or was taken before a probation officer pursuant to Section 307 or was taken before any officer of a law enforcement agency, or, in any case, at any time after the person has reached the age of 18 years, petition the court for sealing of the records, including records of arrest, relating to the person's case, in the custody of the juvenile court and probation officer and any other agencies, including law enforcement agencies, and public officials as petitioner alleges, in his petition, to have custody of such records. The court shall notify the district attorney of the county and the county probation officer, if he is not the petitioner of the petition, and such district attorney or probation officer or any of their deputies or any other person having relevant evidence may testify at the hearing on the petition. If, after hearing, the court finds that since such termination of jurisdiction or action pursuant to Section 307, as the case may be, he has not been convicted of a felony or of any misdemeanor involving moral turpitude and that rehabilitation has been attained to the satisfaction of the court, it shall order sealed all records, papers, and exhibits in the person's case in the custody of the juvenile court, including the juvenile court record, minute book entries, and entries on dockets, and other records relating to the case in the custody of such other agencies and officials as are named in the order. Thereafter, the proceedings in such case shall be deemed never to have occurred, and the person may properly reply according to any inquiry about the events, records of which are ordered sealed. The court shall send a copy of the order to each agency and official named therein, and each such agency and official shall seal records in its custody as directed by the order, shall advise the court of its compliance, and thereupon shall seal the copy of the court's order for sealing of records that it or he received. The person who is the subject of the records sealed pursuant to this section may petition the superior court to permit inspection of the records by persons named in the petition, and the superior court may so order. Otherwise, except as provided in subdivision (b), such records shall not be open to inspection.

(b) In any action or proceeding based upon defamation, a court, upon a showing of good cause, may order any records sealed under this section to be opened and admitted into evidence. The records shall be confidential and shall be available for inspection only by the court, jury, parties, counsel for the parties, and any other person who is authorized by the court to inspect them. Upon the judgment in the action or proceeding becoming final, the court shall order the records sealed.
(Added by Stats.1976, c. 1068, p. —, § 12.)

§ 390. Dismissal of petition; grounds

A judge of the juvenile court in which a petition was filed, at any time before the minor reaches the age of 21 years, may dismiss the petition or may set aside the findings and dismiss the petition if the court finds that the interests of justice and the welfare of the minor require such dismissal, or if it finds that the minor is not in need of treatment or rehabilitation. The court shall have jurisdiction to order such dismissal or setting aside of the findings and dismissal regardless of whether the minor is, at the time of such order, a dependent child of the court.
(Added by Stats.1976, c. 1068, p. —, § 12.)

§ 395. Appealable orders, judgments or decrees; stay; precedence

A judgment or decree of a juvenile court or final order of a referee which becomes effective without approval of a judge of the juvenile court assuming jurisdiction and declaring any person to be a person described in Section 300, or on denying a motion made pursuant to Section 262, may be appealed from in the same manner as any final judgment, and any subsequent order may be appealed from as from an order after judgment; but no such order or judgment shall be stayed by such appeal, unless suitable provision is made for the maintenance, care, and custody of such person pending the appeal, and unless such provision is approved by an order of the juvenile court. Such appeal shall have precedence over all other cases in the court to which the appeal is taken.

An appellant unable to afford counsel shall be provided a free copy of the transcript.
(Added by Stats.1976, c. 1068, p. —, § 13.)

§ 601. Minors habitually disobedient or truant

(a) Any person under the age of 18 years who persistently or habitually refuses to obey the reasonable and proper orders or directions of his parents, guardian, or custodian, or who is beyond the control of such person, or who is under the age of 18 years when he violated any ordinance of any city or county of this state establishing a curfew based solely on age is within the jurisdiction of the juvenile court which may adjudge such person to be a ward of the court.

(b) If a school attendance review board determines that the available public and private services are insufficient or inappropriate to correct the habitual truancy of the minor, or to correct the minor's persistent or habitual refusal to obey the reasonable and proper orders or directions of school authorities, or if the minor fails to respond to directives of a school attendance review board or to services provided, the minor is then within the jurisdiction of the juvenile court which may adjudge such person to be a ward of the court; provided, that it is the intent of the Legislature that no minor who is adjudged a ward of the court pursuant solely to this subdivision shall be removed from the custody of the parent or guardian except during school hours.
(Amended by Stats.1976, c. 1071, p. —, § 11.)

§ 601.1. Referral of habitually disobedient or truant minors to school attendance review board

Any person under the age of 18 years who persistently or habitually refuses to obey the reasonable and proper orders or directions of school authorities, and is thus beyond the control of such authorities, or who is a habitual truant from school within the meaning of any law of this state, shall, prior to any referral to the juvenile court of the county, be referred to a school attendance review board pursuant to Section 48263 of the Education Code.
(Amended by Stats.1978, c. 380, p. —, § 153.)

§ 601.2. Failure of parent, guardian, or person in charge of minor to respond to directives of school attendance review board; disposition of minor

In the event that a parent or guardian or person in charge of a minor described in Section 601.1 fails to respond to directives of the school attendance review board or to services offered on behalf of the minor, the school attendance review board shall direct that the minor be referred to the probation department or to the county welfare department under Section 300, and the school attendance review board may require the school district to file a complaint against the parent, guardian, or other person in charge of such minor as provided in Section 48291 or Section 48454 of the Education Code.
(Amended by Stats.1978, c. 380, p. —, § 154.)

§ 602. Minors violating laws defining crime; minors failing to obey court order

Any person who is under the age of 18 years when he violates any law of this state or of the United States or any ordinance of any city or county of this state defining crime other than an ordinance establishing a curfew based solely on age, is within the jurisdiction of the juvenile court, which may adjudge such person to be a ward of the court.
(Amended by Stats.1976, c. 1071, p. —, § 12.)

§ 603. Preliminary examination; trying case upon accusatory pleading

No court shall have jurisdiction to conduct a preliminary examination or to try the case of any person upon an accusatory pleading charging such person with the commission of a public offense or crime when such person was under the age of 18 years at the time of the alleged commission thereof unless the matter has first been submitted to the juvenile court by petition as provided in Article 7 (commencing with Section 650), and said juvenile court has made an order directing that such person be prosecuted under the general law.
(Added by Stats.1961, c. 1616, p. 3472, § 2.)

§ 604. Suspension of proceedings; certification to juvenile court; finding; transmittal of pleadings

(a) Whenever a case is before any court upon an accusatory pleading and it is suggested or appears to the judge before whom such person is brought that the person charged was, at the date the offense is alleged to have been committed, under the age of 18 years, such judge shall immediately suspend all proceedings against such person on such charge; he shall examine into the age of such person, and if, from such examination, it appears to his satisfaction that such person was at the date the offense is alleged to have been committed under the age of 18 years, he shall forthwith certify to the juvenile court of his county:

(1) That such person (naming him) is charged with such crime (briefly stating its nature);

(2) That such person appears to have been under the age of 18 years at the date the offense is alleged to have been committed, giving date of birth when known;

(3) That proceedings have been suspended against such person on such charge by reason of his age, with the date of such suspension.

To such certification, the judge shall attach, a copy of the accusatory pleading.

(b) When a court certifies a case to the juvenile court pursuant to subdivision (a), it shall be deemed that jeopardy has not attached by reason of the proceedings prior to certification, but the court may not resume proceedings in the case, nor may a new proceeding under the general law be commenced in any court with respect to the same matter unless the juvenile court has found that the minor is not a fit subject for consideration under the Juvenile Court Law and has ordered that proceedings under the general law resume or be commenced.

(c) The certification and accusatory pleading shall be promptly transmitted to the clerk of the juvenile court. Upon receipt thereof, the clerk of the juvenile court shall immediately notify the probation officer who shall immediately proceed in accordance with Article 16 (commencing with Section 650) to cause the filing of a petition pursuant to Section 656, except that such petition need not be verified.
(Amended by Stats.1977, c. 1241, p. —, § 1.7.)

§ 605. Statute of limitations; suspension

Whenever a petition is filed in a juvenile court alleging that a minor is a person within the description of Section 602, and while the case is before the juvenile court, the statute of limitations applicable under the general law to the offense alleged to bring the minor within such description is suspended.
(Added by Stats.1961, c. 1616, p. 3473, § 2.)

§ 606. Subjecting minor to criminal prosecution

When a petition has been filed in a juvenile court, the minor who is the subject of the petition shall not thereafter be subject to criminal prosecution based on the facts giving rise to the petition unless the juvenile court finds that the minor is not a fit and proper subject to be dealt with under this chapter and orders that criminal proceedings be resumed or instituted against him.
(Added by Stats.1961, c. 1616, p. 3473, § 2.)

§ 607. Retention of jurisdiction

(a) The court may retain jurisdiction over any person who is found to be a ward or dependent child of the juvenile court until such ward or dependent child attains the age of 21 years, except as provided in subdivision (b).

(b) The court may retain jurisdiction over any person who is found to be a person described in Section 602 of this code by reason of the violation, when he was 16 years of age or older, of any of the offenses listed in subdivision (b) of Section 707 until such person attains the age of 23 years if the person was committed to the Youth Authority.
(Amended by Stats.1976, c. 1071, p. —, § 13.)

§ 625. Temporary custody; peace officer; warrant

A peace officer may, without a warrant, take into temporary custody a minor:

(a) Who is under the age of 18 years when such officer has reasonable cause for believing that such minor is a person described in Section 601 or 602, or

(b) Who is a ward of the juvenile court or concerning whom an order has been made under Section 636 or 702, when such officer has reasonable cause for believing that person has violated an order of the juvenile court or has escaped from any commitment ordered by the juvenile court, or

(c) Who is under the age of 18 years and who is found in any street or public place suffering from any sickness or injury which requires care, medical treatment, hospitalization, or other remedial care.

In any case where a minor is taken into temporary custody on the ground that there is reasonable cause for believing that such minor is a person described in Section 601 or 602, or that he has violated an order of the juvenile court or escaped from any commitment ordered by the juvenile court, the officer shall advise such minor that anything he says can be used against him and shall advise him of his constitutional rights, including his right to remain silent, his right to have counsel present during any interrogation, and his right to have counsel appointed if he is unable to afford counsel.
(Amended by Stats.1976, c. 1068, p. —, § 24.)

§ 626. Alternative proceedings; release; notice to appear; taking minor before probation officer

An officer who takes a minor into temporary custody under the provisions of Section 625 shall thereafter proceed as follows:

(a) He may release such minor; or

(b) He may prepare in duplicate a written notice to appear before the probation officer of the county in which such minor was taken into custody at a time and place specified in the notice. The notice shall also contain a concise statement of the reasons such minor was taken into custody. He shall deliver one copy of the notice to such minor or to a parent, guardian, or responsible relative of such minor and may require such minor or his parent, guardian, or relative, or both, to sign a written promise that either or both will appear at the time and place designated in the notice. Upon the execution of the promise to appear, he shall immediately release such minor. He shall, as soon as practicable, file one copy of the notice with the probation officer; or

(c) He may take such minor without unnecessary delay before the probation officer of the county in which such person was taken into custody, or in which such person resides, or in which the acts take place or the circumstances exist which are alleged to bring the minor within the provisions of Section 601 or 602, and deliver the custody of such minor to the probation officer. In no case shall he delay the delivery of the minor to the probation officer for more than 24 hours if such minor has been taken into custody without a warrant on the belief that he has committed a misdemeanor.

In determining which disposition of the minor he will make, the officer shall prefer the alternative which least restricts the minor's freedom of movement, provided such alternative is compatible with the best interests of the minor and the community.
(Amended by Stats.1978, c. 1372, p. —, § 2.)

§ 627. Notice to parent or guardian; right to make telephone calls

(a) When an officer takes a minor before a probation officer at a juvenile hall or to any other place of confinement pursuant to this article, he shall take immediate steps to notify the minor's parent, guardian, or a responsible relative that such minor is in custody and the place where he is being held.

(b) Immediately after being taken to a place of confinement pursuant to this article and, except where physically impossible, no later than three hours after he has been taken into custody, the minor has the right to make at least two telephone calls from the place where he is being held, one call completed to his parent or guardian, a responsible relative, or his employer, and another call completed to an attorney. The calls shall be at his own expense and in the presence of a public officer or employee. Any public officer or employee who willfully deprives a minor taken into custody of his right to make such telephone calls is guilty of a misdemeanor.
(Amended by Stats.1971, c. 1030, p. —, § 1.)

§ 627.5. Advice as to constitutional rights

In any case where a minor is taken before a probation officer pursuant to the provisions of Section 626 and it is alleged that such minor is a person described in Section 601 or 602, the probation officer shall immediately advise the minor and his parent or guardian that anything the minor says can be used against him and shall advise them of the minor's constitutional rights, including his right to remain silent, his right to have counsel present during any interrogation, and his right to have counsel appointed if he is unable to afford counsel. If the minor or his parent or guardian requests counsel, the probation officer shall notify the judge of the juvenile court of such request and counsel for the minor shall be appointed pursuant to Section 634.
(Added by Stats.1967, c. 1355, p. 3193, § 2.)

§ 628. Investigation; release of minor

(a) Upon delivery to the probation officer of a minor who has been taken into temporary custody under the provisions of this article, the probation officer shall immediately investigate the circumstances of the minor and the facts surrounding his being taken into custody and shall immediately release such minor to the custody of his parent, guardian, or responsible relative unless one or more of the following conditions exist:

(1) The minor is in need of proper and effective parental care or control and has no parent, guardian, or responsible relative; or has no parent, guardian, or responsible relative willing to exercise or capable of exercising such care or control; or has no parent, guardian, or responsible relative actually exercising such care or control.

(2) The minor is destitute or is not provided with the necessities of life or is not provided with a home or suitable place of abode.

(3) The minor is provided with a home which is an unfit place for him by reason of neglect, cruelty, depravity or physical abuse of either of his parents, or of his guardian or other person in whose custody or care he is.

(4) Continued detention of the minor is a matter of immediate and urgent necessity for the protection of the minor or reasonable necessity for the protection of the person or property of another.

(5) The minor is likely to flee the jurisdiction of the court.

(6) The minor has violated an order of the juvenile court.

(7) The minor is physically dangerous to the public because of a mental or physical deficiency, disorder or abnormality.

(b) In any case in which there is reasonable cause for believing that a minor who is under the care of a physician or surgeon or a hospital, clinic, or other medical facility and cannot be immediately moved is a person described in subdivision (d) of Section 300, the minor shall be deemed to have been taken into temporary custody and delivered to the probation officer for the purposes of this chapter while he is at the office of the physician or surgeon or such medical facility.
(Amended by Stats.1977, c. 579, p. ——, § 195.)

§ 628.1. Release of minor to home supervision

If the minor meets one or more of the criteria for detention under Section 628, but the probation officer believes that 24-hour secure detention is not necessary in order to protect the minor or the person or property of another, or to ensure that the minor does not flee the jurisdiction of the court, the probation officer shall proceed according to this section.

Unless one of the conditions described in paragraph (1), (2), or (3) of subdivision (a) of Section 628 exists, the probation officer shall release such minor to his parent, guardian, or responsible relative on home supervision. As a condition for such release, the probation officer shall require the minor to sign a written promise that he understands and will observe the specific conditions of home supervision release. Such conditions may include curfew and school attendance requirements related to the protection of the minor or the person or property of another, or to the minor's appearances at court hearings. A minor who violates a specific condition of home supervision release which he has promised in writing to obey may be taken into custody and placed in secure detention, subject to court review at a detention hearing.

A minor on home supervision shall be entitled to the same legal protections as a minor in secure detention, including a detention hearing.
(Added by Stats.1976, c. 1071, p. ——, § 16.)

§ 629. Written promise to appear

As a condition for the release of such minor, the probation officer may require such minor or his parent, guardian, or relative, or both, to sign a written promise that either or both of them will

appear before the probation officer at the juvenile hall or other suitable place designated by the probation officer at a specified time.
(Added by Stats.1961, c. 1616, p. 3474, § 2.)

§ 630. Filing petition; notice of hearing; privileges and rights of minor

(a) If the probation officer determines that the minor shall be retained in custody, he shall immediately proceed in accordance with Article 16 (commencing with Section 650), to cause the filing of a petition pursuant to Section 656 with the clerk of the juvenile court who shall immediately set the matter for hearing on the detention calendar. Immediately upon filing the petition with the clerk of the juvenile court, if the minor is alleged to be a person described in Section 601 or 602, the probation officer or the prosecuting attorney, as the case may be, shall serve such minor with a copy of the petition and notify him of the time and place of the detention hearing. The probation officer, or the prosecuting attorney, as the case may be, shall thereupon notify each parent or each guardian of the minor of the time and place of such hearing if the whereabouts of each parent or guardian can be ascertained by due diligence. Such notice may be given orally.

(b) In such hearing, the minor has a privilege against self-incrimination and has a right to confrontation by, and cross-examination of, any person examined by the court as provided in Section 635.
(Amended by Stats.1977, c. 1241, p. ——, § 2.)

§ 630.1. Notice of hearings

Upon reasonable notification by counsel representing the minor, his parents or guardian, the clerk of the court shall notify such counsel of the hearings in the manner provided for notice to the parent or guardian of the minor under this chapter.
(Added by Stats.1967, c. 507, p. 1852, § 1.)

§ 631. Release within 48 hours; exceptions; written explanation for custody over 6 hours

(a) Except as provided in subdivision (b), whenever a minor is taken into custody by a peace officer or probation officer, except when such minor willfully misrepresents himself as 18 or more years of age, such minor shall be released within 48 hours after having been taken into custody, excluding nonjudicial days, unless within said period of time a petition to declare him a ward had been filed pursuant to the provisions of this chapter or a criminal complaint against him has been filed in a court of competent jurisdiction.

(b) Whenever a minor is taken into custody by a peace officer or probation officer without a warrant on the belief that the minor has committed a misdemeanor, except when such minor misrepresents himself as 18 or more years of age, such minor shall be released within 48 hours after having been taken into custody or on the next judicial day, whichever is later, unless a petition has been filed to declare the minor to be a ward and the minor has been ordered detained by a judge or referee of the juvenile court pursuant to Section 635.

(c) Whenever a minor who has been held in custody for more than six hours by the probation officer is subsequently released and no petition is filed, the probation officer shall prepare a written explanation of why the minor was held in custody for more than six hours. The written explanation shall be prepared within 72 hours after the minor is released from custody and filed in the record of the case. A copy of the written explanation shall be sent to the parents, guardian, or other person having care or custody of the minor.
(Amended by Stats.1978, c. 1372, p. ——, § 3.)

§ 631.1. Misrepresentation of age

When a minor willfully misrepresents himself to be 18 or more years of age when taken into custody by a peace officer or probation officer, and this misrepresentation effects a material delay in investigation which prevents the filing of a petition pursuant to the provisions of this chapter or the filing of a criminal complaint against him in a court of competent jurisdiction within 48 hours, such petition or complaint shall be filed within 48 hours from the time his true age is determined, excluding nonjudicial days. If, in such cases, the petition or complaint is not filed within the time prescribed by this section, the minor shall be immediately released from custody.
(Amended by Stats.1972, c. 579, p. 1018, § 54.)

§ 632. Detention hearing; release

Unless sooner released, a minor taken into custody under the provisions of this article shall be brought before a judge or referee of the juvenile court for a hearing (which shall be referred to as a "detention hearing") to determine whether the minor shall be further detained, as soon as possible but in any event before the expiration of the next judicial day after a

petition to declare such minor a ward or dependent child has been filed. A minor taken into custody without a warrant on the belief that he has committed a misdemeanor shall be brought before a judge or referee of the juvenile court for a hearing to determine whether the minor shall be further detained as soon as possible but in no event beyond 48 hours or before the expiration of the next judicial day after having been taken into custody, whichever is later, after a petition to declare such minor a ward has been filed. If the minor is not brought before a judge or referee of the juvenile court within the period prescribed by this section, he shall be released from custody.
(Amended by Stats.1978, c. 1372, p. —, § 4.)

§ 633. Informing minor as to reasons for custody; nature of proceedings; right to counsel

Upon his appearance before the court at the detention hearing, such minor and his parent or guardian, if present, shall first be informed of the reasons why the minor was taken into custody, the nature of the juvenile court proceedings, and the right of such minor and his parent or guardian to be represented at every stage of the proceedings by counsel.
(Added by Stats.1961, c. 1616, p. 3475, § 2.)

§ 634. Appointment of counsel

When it appears to the court that the minor or his parent or guardian desires counsel but is unable to afford and cannot for that reason employ counsel, the court may appoint counsel. In a case in which the minor is alleged to be a person described in Section 601 or 602, the court shall appoint counsel for the minor if he appears at the hearing without counsel, whether he is unable to afford counsel or not, unless there is an intelligent waiver of the right of counsel by the minor; and, in the absence of such waiver, if the parent or guardian does not furnish counsel and the court determines that the parent or guardian has the ability to pay for counsel, the court shall appoint counsel at the expense of the parent or guardian. In any case in which it appears to the court that there is such a conflict of interest between a parent or guardian and child that one attorney could not properly represent both, the court shall appoint counsel, in addition to counsel already employed by a parent or guardian or appointed by the court to represent the minor or parent or guardian. In a county where there is no public defender the court may fix the compensation to be paid by the county for service of such appointed counsel.
(Amended by Stats.1971, c. 667, p. —, § 2.)

§ 635. Examination of minor; order releasing minor from custody; factors in determination

The court will examine such minor, his parent, guardian, or other person having relevant knowledge, hear such relevant evidence as the minor, his parent or guardian or their counsel desires to present, and, unless it appears that such minor has violated an order of the juvenile court or has escaped from the commitment of the juvenile court or that it is a matter of immediate and urgent necessity for the protection of such minor or reasonably necessary for the protection of the person or property of another that he be detained or that such minor is likely to flee to avoid the jurisdiction of the court, the court shall make its order releasing such minor from custody.

The circumstances and gravity of the alleged offense may be considered, in conjunction with other factors, to determine whether it is a matter of immediate and urgent necessity for the protection of the minor or reasonably necessary for the protection of the person or property of another that the minor be detained.
(Amended by Stats.1977, c. 1241, p. —, § 3.)

§ 636. Order detaining minor in juvenile hall or on home supervision; criteria

If it appears upon the hearing that such minor has violated an order of the juvenile court or has escaped from a commitment of the juvenile court or that it is a matter of immediate and urgent necessity for the protection of such minor or reasonably necessary for the protection of the person or property of another that he be detained or that such minor is likely to flee to avoid the jurisdiction of the court, the court may make its order that such minor be detained in the juvenile hall or other suitable place designated by the juvenile court for a period not to exceed 15 judicial days and shall enter said order together with its findings of fact in support thereof in the records of the court. The circumstances and gravity of the alleged offense may be considered, in conjunction with other factors, to determine whether it is a matter of immediate and urgent necessity for the protection of the minor or the person or property of another that the minor be detained.

If the court finds that the criteria of Section 628.1 are applicable, the court may, and after the operative date of that section the court shall, place the minor on

home supervision for a period not to exceed 15 judicial days, and shall enter such order together with its findings of fact in support thereof in the records of the court. If the court releases the minor on home supervision, the court may continue, modify, or augment any conditions of release previously imposed by the probation officer, or may impose new conditions on a minor released for the first time. If there are new or modified conditions, the minor shall be required to sign a written promise to obey such conditions pursuant to Section 628.1.
(Amended by Stats.1976, c. 1070, p. —, § 2; Stats.1976, c. 1071, p. —, § 37.)

§ 636.2. Nonsecure detention facilities; operation; criteria for detention therein

The probation officer may operate and maintain nonsecure detention facilities, or may contract with public or private agencies offering such services, for those minors who are not considered escape risks and are not considered a danger to themselves or to the person or property of another. Criteria to be considered for detention in such facilities shall include, but not be limited to: (a) the nature of the offense, (b) the minor's previous record including escapes from secure detention facilities, (c) lack of criminal sophistication, and (d) the age of the minor. A minor detained in such facilities who leaves the same without permission may be housed in a secure facility following his apprehension, pending a detention hearing pursuant to Section 632.
(Amended by Stats.1977, c. 1241, p. —, § 3.5.)

§ 637. Rehearing; continuance

When a hearing is held under the provisions of this article and no parent or guardian of such minor is present and no parent or guardian has had actual notice of the hearing, a parent or guardian of such minor may file his affidavit setting forth such facts with the clerk of the juvenile court and the clerk shall immediately set the matter for rehearing at a time within 24 hours, excluding Sundays and nonjudicial days from the filing of the affidavit. Upon the rehearing, the court shall proceed in the same manner as upon the original hearing.

If the minor or, if the minor is represented by an attorney, the minor's attorney, requests evidence of the prima facie case, a rehearing shall be held within three judicial days to consider evidence of the prima facie case. If the prima facie case is not established, the minor shall be released from detention.

When the court ascertains that the rehearing cannot be held within three judicial days because of the unavailability of a witness, a reasonable continuance may be granted for a period not to exceed five judicial days.
(Amended by Stats.1975, c. 1266, p. 3324, § 1.)

§ 638. Continuance; motion

Upon motion of the minor or a parent or guardian of such minor, the court shall continue any hearing or rehearing held under the provisions of this article for one day, excluding Sundays and nonjudicial days.
(Added by Stats.1961, c. 1616, p. 3476, § 2.)

§ 639. Order requiring reappearance of minor, parent or guardian

Upon any hearing or rehearing under the provisions of this article, the court may order such minor or any parent or guardian of such minor who is present in court to again appear before the court or the probation officer at a time and place specified in said order.
(Added by Stats.1961, c. 1616, p. 3476, § 2.)

§ 650. Filing of petition

(a) A proceeding in the juvenile court to declare a minor a dependent child of the court or a ward of the court under Section 601 is commenced by the filing with the court, by the probation officer, of a petition, in conformity with the requirements of this article.

(b) A proceeding in the juvenile court to declare a minor a ward under Section 602 of the court is commenced by the filing with the court, by the prosecuting attorney as petitioner, of a petition, in conformity with the requirements of this article.
(Amended by Stats.1976, c. 1068, p. —, § 32; Stats.1976, c. 1071, p. —, § 20.)

§ 651. Venue

Either the juvenile court in the county in which a minor resides or in the county where the minor is found or in the county in which the acts take place or the circumstances exist which are alleged to bring such minor within the provisions of Section 601 or 602, is the proper court to commence proceedings under this chapter.
(Amended by Stats.1976, c. 1068, p. —, § 34.)

§ 652. Reasonable cause; investigation

Whenever the probation officer has cause to believe that there was or is within the county, or residing therein, a person within the provisions of

Section 601 or 602, the probation officer shall immediately make such investigation as he deems necessary to determine whether proceedings in the juvenile court should be commenced.
(Amended by Stats.1976, c. 1068, p. ——, § 35.)

§ 653. Application to commence proceedings; affidavit; allegations; indorsement by probation officer

Whenever any person applies to the probation officer to commence proceedings in the juvenile court, such application shall be in the form of an affidavit alleging that there was or is within the county, or residing therein, a minor within the provisions of Section 300, 601, or 602, or that a minor committed an offense described in Section 602 within the county, and setting forth facts in support thereof. The probation officer shall immediately make such investigation as he deems necessary to determine whether proceedings in the juvenile court should be commenced. If the probation officer determines that proceedings pursuant to Section 650 should be commenced to declare a person described in Section 602 to be a ward of the juvenile court, the probation officer shall cause the affidavit to be taken to the prosecuting attorney. The prosecuting attorney shall within his discretionary power institute proceedings in accordance with his role as public prosecutor pursuant to subdivision (b) of Section 650 of this code and Section 26500 of the Government Code.

If the probation officer does not take action under Section 654 and does not file a petition in juvenile court within 21 court days after such application, or in the case of an affidavit alleging that a minor committed an offense described in Section 602 or alleging that a minor is within Section 602, does not cause the affidavit to be taken to the prosecuting attorney with 21 court days after such application, he shall endorse upon the affidavit of applicant his decision not to proceed further and his reasons therefor and shall immediately notify the applicant of the action taken or the decision rendered by him under this section. The probation officer shall retain the affidavit and his indorsement thereon for a period of 30 days after such notice to applicant.
(Amended by Stats.1978, c. 380, p. ——, § 155.)

§ 654. Program of supervision

In any case in which a probation officer, after investigation of an application for petition or other investigation he is authorized to make concludes that a minor is within the jurisdiction of the juvenile court or will probably soon be within such jurisdiction, he may, in lieu of filing a petition to declare a minor a dependent child of the court or a minor or a ward of the court under Section 601 or requesting that a petition be filed by the prosecuting attorney to declare a minor a ward of the court under Section 602 or subsequent to dismissal of a petition already filed, and with consent of the minor and the minor's parent or guardian, delineate specific programs of supervision for the minor, for not to exceed six months, and attempt thereby to adjust the situation which brings the minor within the jurisdiction of the court or creates the probability that he will soon be within such jurisdiction. Nothing in this section shall be construed to prevent the probation officer from filing a petition or requesting the prosecuting attorney to file a petition at any time within said six-month period. If the probation officer determines that the minor has not involved himself in the specific programs within 60 days, the probation officer shall immediately file a petition or request that a petition be filed by the prosecuting attorney. However, when in the judgment of the probation officer the interest of the minor and the community can be protected, the probation officer shall make a diligent effort to proceed under this section.

The program of supervision of the minor undertaken pursuant to this section may call for the minor to obtain care and treatment for the misuse of restricted dangerous drugs or addiction to narcotics from a county mental health service or other appropriate community agency.

Further, this section shall authorize the probation officer with consent of the minor and the minor's parent or guardian to provide the following services in lieu of filing a petition:

(a) Maintain and operate sheltered-care facilities, or contract with private or public agencies to provide such services. Such placement shall be limited to a maximum of 90 days. Counseling services shall be extended to the sheltered minor and his family during this period of diversion services. The minor and his parents may be required to make full or partial reimbursement for the services rendered the minor and his family during the diversion process. Referrals for sheltered-care diversion may be made by the minor, his family, schools, law enforcement or any other private or public social service agency.

(b) Maintain and operate crisis resolution homes, or contract with private or public agencies offering such services. Residence at such facilities shall be limited to 20 days during which period individual and family counseling shall be extended the minor and his family. Failure to resolve the crisis within the 20-day period may result in the minor's referral to a sheltered-care facility for a period not to exceed 90 days. Referrals shall be accepted from the minor, his family, schools, law enforcement or any other private or public social service agency. The minor, his parents, or both, may be required to reimburse the county for the cost of services rendered at a rate to be determined by the county board of supervisors.

(c) Maintain and operate counseling and educational centers, or contract with private and public agencies, societies or corporations whose purpose is to provide vocational training or skills. Such centers may be operated separately or in conjunction with crisis resolution homes to be operated by the probation officer. The probation officer shall be authorized to make referrals to the appropriate existing private or public agencies offering similar services when available.

At the conclusion of the program of supervision undertaken pursuant to this section, the probation officer shall prepare and maintain a followup report of the actual program measures taken.
(Amended by Stats.1978, c. 380, p. —, § 156.)

§ 655. Failure of probation officer to commence proceedings; review

(a) When any person has applied to the probation officer, pursuant to Section 653, to request commencement of juvenile court proceedings to declare a minor a ward of the court under Section 602 and the probation officer does not cause the affidavit to be taken to the prosecuting attorney pursuant to Section 653 within 21 court days after such application, such person may, within 30 court days after making such application, apply to the prosecuting attorney to review the decision of the probation officer, and the prosecuting attorney may either affirm the decision of the probation officer or commence juvenile court proceedings.

(b) When any person has applied to the probation officer, pursuant to Section 653, to commence juvenile court proceedings to declare a minor a dependent child of the court or a ward of the court under Section 601 and the probation officer fails to file a petition within 21 court days after such application, such person may within 30 court days after making such application, apply to the juvenile court to review the decision of the probation officer, and the court may either affirm the decision of the probation officer or order him to commence juvenile court proceedings.
(Amended by Stats.1977, c. 1241, p. —, § 7.)

§ 656. Petition; verification; contents

A petition to commence proceedings in the juvenile court to declare a minor a ward of the court shall be verified and must contain:

(a) The name of the court to which the same is addressed.

(b) The title of the proceeding.

(c) The code section or sections and subdivision or subdivisions under which the proceedings are instituted.

(d) The name, age, and address, if any, of the minor upon whose behalf the petition is brought.

(e) The name or names and residence address, if known to petitioner, of all parents and guardians of such minor. If there is no parent or guardian residing within the state, or if his place of residence is not known to petitioner, the petition must also contain the name and residence address, if known, of any adult relative residing within the county, or, if there be none, the adult relative residing nearest to the location of the court.

(f) A concise statement of facts, separately stated, to support the conclusion that the minor upon whose behalf the petition is being brought is a person within the definition of each of the sections and subdivisions under which the proceedings are being instituted.

(g) The fact that the minor upon whose behalf the petition is brought is detained in custody or is not detained in custody, and if he is detained in custody, the date and the precise time the minor was taken into custody.
(Amended by Stats.1976, c. 1068, p. —, § 37.)

§ 656.1. Specification of crime in petition

Any petition alleging that the minor is a person described by Section 602 shall specify as to each count whether the crime charged is a felony or a misdemeanor.
(Added by Stats.1976, c. 1071, p. —, § 24.5.)

§ 656.5. Unverified petition; dismissal without prejudice

Any petition filed in juvenile court to commence proceedings pursuant to this chapter that is not verified may be dismissed without prejudice by such court.
(Added by Stats.1972, c. 897, p. 1594, § 1.)

§ 657. Time for hearing; waiver of jurisdictional hearing

Upon the filing of the petition, the clerk of the juvenile court shall set the same for hearing within 30 days, except that in the case of a minor detained in custody at the time of the filing of the petition, the petition must be set for hearing within 15 judicial days from the date of the order of the court directing such detention.

At the detention hearing, or any time thereafter, a minor who is alleged to come within the provisions of Section 601 or 602, may, with the consent of counsel, admit in court the allegations of the petition and waive the jurisdictional hearing.
(Amended by Stats.1971, c. 1389, p. —, § 4.)

§ 658. Notice of hearing

Upon the filing of the petition, the clerk of the juvenile court shall issue a notice, to which shall be attached a copy of the petition, and he shall cause the same to be served upon the minor, if the minor is eight or more years of age, and upon each of the persons described in subdivision (e) of Section 656 whose residence addresses are set forth in said petition and thereafter before the hearing upon all such persons whose residence addresses become known to the clerk. The clerk shall issue a copy of the petition, to the minor's attorney and to the district attorney, if the district attorney has notified the clerk of the court that he wishes to receive such petition, containing the time, date, and place of the hearing.
(Amended by Stats.1976, c. 1068, p. —, § 38.)

§ 659. Contents of notice

The notice must contain:

(a) The name and address of the person to whom the notice is directed.

(b) The date, time, and place of the hearing on the petition.

(c) The name of the minor upon whose behalf the petition has been brought.

(d) Each section and subdivision under which the proceeding has been instituted.

(e) A statement that the minor and his parent or guardian or adult relative, as the case may be, to whom notice is required to be given, are entitled to have an attorney present at the hearing on the petition, and that, if the parent or guardian or such adult relative is indigent and cannot afford an attorney, and the minor or his parent or guardian or such adult relative desires to be represented by an attorney, such parent or guardian or adult relatives shall promptly notify the clerk of the juvenile court.
(Amended by Stats.1963, c. 917, p. 2167, § 8.)

§ 660. Personal service; service by mail

(a) If the minor is detained the clerk of the juvenile court shall cause the notice and copy of the petition to be served on all persons required to receive such notice and copy of the petition, either personally or by certified mail with request for return receipt, as soon as possible after filing of the petition and at least five days prior to the time set for hearing, unless such hearing is set less than five days from the filing of the petition, in which case, such notice and copy of the petition must be served at least 24 hours prior to the time set for hearing.

(b) If the minor is not detained the clerk of the juvenile court shall cause the notice and copy of the petition to be served on all persons required to receive such notice and copy of the petition, either personally, by certified mail with request for return receipt, or by first-class mail, at least 10 days prior to the time set for hearing. If such person is known to reside outside of the county, the clerk of the juvenile court shall mail the notice and copy of the petition, by certified mail with request for return receipt or by first-class mail, to such person, as soon as possible after filing of the petition and at least 10 days before the time set for hearing. Failure to respond to the notice by certified mail with request for return receipt or by first-class mail shall in no way result in arrest or detention. In the instance of failure to appear after notice by certified or first-class mail, the court shall direct that the notice and copy of the petition is to be personally served on all persons required to receive such notice and copy of the petition. Personal service of the notice and copy of the petition outside of the county at least 10 days before the time set for hearing is equivalent to such service by certified or first-class mail. Service may be waived by any person by a voluntary appearance entered in the minutes of the court or by a written waiver of service filed with the clerk of the court at or prior to the hearing.

(c) For purposes of this section, service on the minor's attorney shall constitute service on the minor's parent or guardian.
(Amended by Stats.1976, c. 1068, p. —, § 39.)

§ 661. Notice; citation; issuance and service

In addition to the notice provided in Sections 658 and 659, the juvenile court may issue its citation directing any parent or guardian of the person concerning whom a petition has been filed to appear at the time and place set for any hearing under the provisions of this chapter, including a hearing under the provisions of Section 257, and directing any person having custody or control of the minor concerning whom the petition has been filed to bring such minor with him. The notice shall in addition state that a parent or guardian may be required to participate in a counseling program with the minor concerning whom the petition has been filed. Personal service of such citation shall be made at least 24 hours before the time stated therein for such appearance.
(Amended by Stats.1976, c. 1068, p. —, § 40.)

§ 662. Warrant of arrest against parent or guardian

In case such citation cannot be served, or the person served fails to obey it, or in any case in which it appears to the court that the citation will probably be ineffective, a warrant of arrest may issue on the order of the court either against the parent, or guardian, or the person having the custody of the minor, or with whom the minor is.
(Added by Stats.1961, c. 1616, p. 3480, § 2.)

§ 663. Warrant of arrest against minor

Whenever a petition has been filed in the juvenile court alleging that a minor comes within the provisions of Section 601 or 602 of this code and praying for a hearing thereon, or whenever any subsequent petition has been filed praying for a hearing in the matter of said minor and it appears to the court that the conduct and behavior of the said minor may endanger the health, person, welfare, or property of himself or others, or that the circumstances of his home environment may endanger the health, person, welfare or property of said minor, a warrant of arrest may be issued immediately for the minor.
(Amended by Stats.1976, c. 1068, p. —, § 41.)

§ 664. Subpoenas

Upon request of the probation officer, district attorney, the minor or the minor's parent, guardian, or custodian, the court or the clerk of the court shall issue, and, on the court's own motion, it may issue subpoenas requiring attendance and testimony of witnesses and production of papers at any hearing under the provisions of this chapter. When a person attends a juvenile court hearing as a witness upon a subpoena at its discretion, the court may by an order on its minutes, direct the county auditor to draw his warrant upon the county treasurer in favor of such witness for witness fees in the amount and manner prescribed by Section 68093 of the Government Code. The fees are county charges.
(Amended by Stats.1967, c. 507, p. 1852, § 2.)

§ 675. Special or separate session; presence of persons on trial or awaiting trial

All cases under the provisions of this chapter shall be heard at a special or separate session of the court, and no other matter shall be heard at such session. No person on trial, awaiting trial, or under accusation of crime, other than a parent, guardian, or relative of the minor, shall be permitted to be present at any such session, except as a witness.
(Amended by Stats.1976, c. 1068, p. —, § 43.)

§ 676. Admission of public and persons having interest in case

Unless requested by the minor concerning whom the petition has been filed and any parent or guardian present, the public shall not be admitted to a juvenile court hearing. The judge or referee may nevertheless admit such persons as he deems to have a direct and legitimate interest in the particular case or the work of the court.
(Added by Stats.1961, c. 1616, p. 3480, § 2.)

§ 679. Presence of minor and person entitled to notice; right to counsel

A minor who is the subject of a juvenile court hearing and any person entitled to notice of the hearing under the provisions of Section 658, is entitled to be present at such hearing. Any such minor and any such person has the right to be represented at such hearing by counsel of his own choice or, if unable to afford counsel, has the right to be represented by counsel appointed by the court.
(Amended by Stats.1976, c. 1068, p. —, § 44.)

§ 680. Control and conduct of proceedings

The judge of the juvenile court shall control all proceedings during the hearings with a view to the expeditious and effective ascertainment of the jurisdictional facts and the ascertainment of all information relative to the present condition and future welfare of the person upon whose behalf the petition

is brought. Except where there is a contested issue of fact or law, the proceedings shall be conducted in an informal nonadversary atmosphere with a view to obtaining the maximum cooperation of the minor upon whose behalf the petition is brought and all persons interested in his welfare with such provisions as the court may make for the disposition and care of such minor.
(Added by Stats.1961, c. 1616, p. 3481, § 2.)

§ 681. Appearance by district attorney; consent of court

(a) In a juvenile court hearing which is based upon a petition that alleges that the minor upon whose behalf the petition is being brought is a person within the description of Section 602, the prosecuting attorney shall appear on behalf of the people of the State of California.

(b) In a juvenile court hearing which is based upon a petition that alleges that the minor upon whose behalf the petition is being brought is a person within the description of Section 601 and the minor who is the subject of the hearing is represented by counsel, the prosecuting attorney may, with the consent or at the request of the juvenile court judge, or at the request of the probation officer with the consent of the juvenile court judge, appear and participate in the hearing to assist in the ascertaining and presenting of the evidence. Where the petition in a juvenile court proceeding alleges that a minor is a person described in subdivision (a), (b), or (d) of Section 300, and either of the parents, or the guardian, or other person having care or custody of the minor, or who resides in the home of the minor, is charged in a pending criminal prosecution based upon unlawful acts committed against the minor, the prosecuting attorney shall, with the consent or at the request of the juvenile court judge, represent the minor in the interest of the state at the juvenile court proceeding. The terms and conditions of such representation shall be with the consent or approval of the judge of the juvenile court.
(Amended by Stats.1978, c. 380, p. ——, § 157.)

§ 682. Continuance of hearing under this chapter

(a) Upon request of counsel for the minor, the court may continue any hearing under this chapter beyond the time limit within which the hearing is otherwise required to be held.

(b) In any case in which the minor is represented by counsel and no objection is made to an order continuing any such hearing beyond the time limit within which the hearing is otherwise required to be held, the absence of such an objection shall be deemed a consent to the continuance.
(Added by Stats.1971, c. 698, p. ——, § 3.)

§ 702. Finding and order; dismissal; discharge; continuance to receive social study or other evidence; detention order

After hearing such evidence, the court shall make a finding, noted in the minutes of the court, whether or not the minor is a person described by Section 300, 601, or 602. If it finds that the minor is not such a person, it shall order that the petition be dismissed and the minor be discharged from any detention or restriction theretofore ordered. If the court finds that the minor is such a person, it shall make and enter its findings and order accordingly, and shall then proceed to hear evidence on the question of the proper disposition to be made of the minor. Prior to doing so, it may continue the hearing, if necessary, to receive the social study of the probation officer or to receive other evidence on its own motion or the motion of a parent or guardian for not to exceed 10 judicial days if the minor is detained during such continuance, and if the minor is not detained, it may continue the hearing to a date not later than 30 days after the date of filing of the petition. The court may, for good cause shown continue the hearing for an additional 15 days, if the minor is not detained. The court may make such order for detention of the minor or his release from detention, during the period of the continuance, as is appropriate.

If the minor is found to have committed an offense which would in the case of an adult be punishable alternatively as a felony or a misdemeanor, the court shall declare the offense to be a misdemeanor or felony.
(Amended by Stats.1977, c. 579, p. ——, § 203.)

§ 702.5. Privilege against self incrimination; confrontation by and cross-examination of witnesses

In any hearing conducted pursuant to Section 701 or 702 to determine whether a minor is a person described in Section 601 or 602, the minor has a privilege against self-incrimination and has a right to confrontation by, and cross-examination of, witnesses.
(Added by Stats.1967, c. 1355, p. 3196, § 11.)

§ 706. Evidence as to proper disposition of minor; reception of social study in evidence

After finding that a minor is a person described in Section 601 or 602, the court shall hear evidence on the question of the proper disposition to be made of the minor. The court shall receive in evidence the social study of the minor made by the probation officer and such other relevant and material evidence as may be offered, and in any judgment and order of disposition, shall state the social study made by the probation officer has been read and considered by the court.

(Amended by Stats.1976, c. 1068, p. —, § 50.)

§ 707. Fitness hearing

(a) In any case in which a minor is alleged to be a person described in Section 602 by reason of the violation, when he was 16 years of age or older, of any criminal statute or ordinance except those listed in subdivision (b), upon motion of the petitioner made prior to the attachment of jeopardy the court shall cause the probation officer to investigate and submit a report on the behavioral patterns and social history of the minor being considered for unfitness. Following submission and consideration of the report, and of any other relevant evidence which the petitioner or the minor may wish to submit the juvenile court may find that the minor is not a fit and proper subject to be dealt with under the juvenile court law if it concludes that the minor would not be amenable to the care, treatment and training program available through the facilities of the juvenile court, based upon an evaluation of the following criteria:

(1) The degree of criminal sophistication exhibited by the minor.

(2) Whether the minor can be rehabilitated prior to the expiration of the juvenile court's jurisdiction.

(3) The minor's previous delinquent history.

(4) Success of previous attempts by the juvenile court to rehabilitate the minor.

(5) The circumstances and gravity of the offense alleged to have been committed by the minor.

A determination that the minor is not a fit and proper subject to be dealt with under the juvenile court law may be based on any one or a combination of the factors set forth above, which shall be recited in the order of unfitness. In any case in which a hearing has been noticed pursuant to this section, the court shall postpone the taking of a plea to the petition until the conclusion of the fitness hearing, and no plea which may already have been entered shall constitute evidence at such hearing.

(b) In any case in which a minor is alleged to be a person described in Section 602 by reason of the violation, when he was 16 years of age or older, of one of the following offenses:

(1) Murder;

(2) Arson of an inhabited building;

(3) Robbery while armed with a dangerous or deadly weapon;

(4) Rape with force or violence or threat of great bodily harm;

(5) Kidnapping for ransom;

(6) Kidnapping for purpose of robbery;

(7) Kidnapping with bodily harm;

(8) Assault with intent to murder or attempted murder;

(9) Assault with a firearm or destructive device;

(10) Assault by any means of force likely to produce great bodily injury;

(11) Discharge of a firearm into an inhabited or occupied building.

(12) Any offense described in Section 1203.09 of the Penal Code, upon motion of the petitioner made prior to the attachment of jeopardy the court shall cause the probation officer to investigate and submit a report on the behavioral patterns and social history of the minor being considered for unfitness. Following submission and consideration of the report, and of any other relevant evidence which the petitioner or the minor may wish to submit the juvenile court shall find that the minor is not a fit and proper subject to be dealt with under the juvenile court law unless it concludes that the minor would be amenable to the care, treatment and training program available through the facilities of the juvenile court based upon an evaluation of the following criteria:

(i) The degree of criminal sophistication exhibited by the minor, and

(ii) Whether the minor can be rehabilitated prior to the expiration of the juvenile court's jurisdiction, and

(iii) The minor's previous delinquent history, and

(iv) Success of previous attempts by the juvenile court to rehabilitate the minor, and

(v) The circumstances and gravity of the offenses alleged to have been committed by the minor.

A determination that the minor is a fit and proper subject to be dealt with under the juvenile court law shall be based on a finding of amenability after consideration of the criteria set forth above, and reasons therefor shall be recited in the order. In any case in which a hearing has been noticed pursuant to this section, the court shall postpone the taking of a plea to the petition until the conclusion of the fitness hearing and no plea which may already have been entered shall constitute evidence at such hearing. (Amended by Stats.1977, c. 1150, p. —, § 2.)

§ 707.1. Minors declared not fit and proper subject under juvenile court law; criminal prosecution

If the minor is declared not a fit and proper subject to be dealt with under the juvenile court law, the district attorney or other appropriate prosecuting officer shall acquire the authority to file an accusatory pleading against the minor in a court of criminal jurisdiction. The case shall proceed from that point according to the laws applicable to a criminal case, provided, that unless the juvenile court specifically orders the individual minor delivered to the custody of the sheriff upon a finding that the safety of the public or of the inmates of the juvenile hall cannot be otherwise protected, the minor, if detained, shall remain in the juvenile hall pending final disposition by the criminal court. If a prosecution has been commenced in another court but has been suspended while juvenile court proceedings are being held, it shall be ordered that the proceedings upon such prosecution resume.

(Added by Stats.1975, c. 1266, p. 3325, § 5.)

§ 707.2. Remand of minors to Youth Authority for evaluation and report prior to sentence

Prior to sentence, the court of criminal jurisdiction may remand the minor to the custody of the California Youth Authority for not to exceed 90 days for the purpose of evaluation and report concerning his amenability to training and treatment offered by the Youth Authority. No minor who was under the age of 18 years when he committed any criminal offense and who has been found not a fit and proper subject to be dealt with under the juvenile court law shall be sentenced to the state prison unless he has first been remanded to the custody of the California Youth Authority for evaluation and report pursuant to this section and the court finds after having read and considered the report submitted by the Youth Authority that the minor is not a suitable subject for commitment to the Youth Authority.

(Amended by Stats.1976, c. 1069, p. —, § 1.)

§ 725. Judgment; placing minor on probation; adjudging minor ward of court or dependent child of court

After receiving and considering the evidence on the proper disposition of the case, the court may enter judgment as follows:

(a) If the court has found that the minor is a person described by Section 601 or 602, it may, without adjudging such minor a ward of the court, place the minor on probation, under the supervision of the probation officer, for a period not to exceed six months.

(b) If the court has found that the minor is a person described by Section 601 or 602 it may order and adjudge the minor to be a ward of the court.

(Amended by Stats.1976, c. 1068, p. —, § 52.)

§ 726. Parental or guardian control; limitations; removal from physical custody; findings and order; maximum period of physical confinement; jurisdiction

In all cases wherein a minor is adjudged a ward or dependent child of the court, the court may limit the control to be exercised over such ward or dependent child by any parent or guardian and shall by its order clearly and specifically set forth all such limitations, but no ward or dependent child shall be taken from the physical custody of a parent or guardian unless upon the hearing the court finds one of the following facts:

(a) That the parent or guardian is incapable of providing or has failed or neglected to provide proper maintenance, training, and education for the minor.

(b) That the minor has been tried on probation in such custody and has failed to reform.

(c) That the welfare of the minor requires that his custody be taken from his parent or guardian.

In any case in which the minor is removed from the physical custody of his parent or guardian as the result of an order of wardship made pursuant to Section 602, the order shall specify that the minor may not be held in physical confinement for a period in excess of the maximum term of imprisonment which could be imposed upon an adult convicted of the offense or offenses which brought or continued the minor under the jurisdiction of the juvenile court.

As used in this section and in Section 731, "maximum term of imprisonment" means the longest of the three time periods set forth in paragraph (2) of subdivision (a) of Section 1170 of the Penal Code, but without the need to follow the provisions of subdivision (b) of Section 1170 of the Penal Code or to consider time for good behavior or participation pursuant to Sections 2930, 2931, and 2932 of the Penal Code, plus enhancements which must be proven if pled.

If the court elects to aggregate the period of physical confinement on multiple counts, or multiple petitions, including previously sustained petitions adjudging the minor a ward within Section 602, the "maximum term of imprisonment" shall be specified in accordance with subdivision (a) of Section 1170.1 of the Penal Code.

If the charged offense is a misdemeanor or a felony not included within the scope of Section 1170 of the Penal Code, the "maximum term of imprisonment" is the longest term of imprisonment prescribed by law.

"Physical confinement" means placement in a juvenile hall, ranch, camp, forestry camp or secure juvenile home pursuant to Section 730, or in any institution operated by the Youth Authority.

Nothing in this section shall be construed to limit the power of the court to retain jurisdiction over a minor and to make appropriate orders pursuant to Section 727 for the period permitted by Section 607.
(Amended by Stats.1977, c. 1238, p. ——, § 1, urgency, eff. Oct. 1, 1977.)

§ 730. Minor violating criminal law; ward of court; commitment to juvenile home; requiring ward to work

When a minor is adjudged a ward of the court on the ground that he is a person described by Section 602, the court may order any of the types of treatment referred to in Section 727, and as an additional alternative, may commit the minor to a juvenile home, ranch, camp or forestry camp. If there is no county juvenile home, ranch, camp or forestry camp within the county, the court may commit the minor to the county juvenile hall.

When such ward is placed under the supervision of the probation officer or committed to his care, custody and control, the court may make any and all reasonable orders for the conduct of such ward including the requirement that he go to work and earn money for the support of his dependents or to effect reparation and in either case that he keep an account of his earnings and report the same to the probation officer and apply such earnings as directed by the court. The court may impose and require any and all reasonable conditions that it may determine fitting and proper to the end that justice may be done and the reformation and rehabilitation of the ward enhanced.
(Amended by Stats.1976, c. 1071, p. ——, § 29.5.)

§ 731. Person violating laws; ward of court; commitment to youth authority

When a minor is adjudged a ward of the court on the ground that he is a person described by Section 602, the court may order any of the types of treatment referred to in Sections 727 and 730, and, in addition may order the ward to make restitution or to participate in uncompensated work programs or may commit the ward to a sheltered-care facility or may order that the ward and his family or guardian participate in a program of professional counseling as arranged and directed by the probation officer as a condition of continued custody of such minor or may commit the minor to the Youth Authority.

A minor committed to the Youth Authority may not be held in physical confinement for a period of time in excess of the maximum period of imprisonment which could be imposed upon an adult convicted of the offense or offenses which brought or continued the minor under the jurisdiction of the juvenile court. Nothing in this section limits the power of the Youth Authority to retain the minor on parole status for the period permitted by Section 1769.
(Amended by Stats.1978, c. 380, p. ——, § 165.)

§ 731.5. Minor violating Section 490.5 of Penal Code; public services

In addition to the provisions of Section 731, if a minor's conduct constitutes a violation of Section 490.5 of the Penal Code, the court may require the minor to perform public services designated by the court.
(Added by Stats.1976, c. 1131, p. ——, § 2.)

Editors' Note

Petty theft of retail merchandise, see Penal Code § 490.5.

---

§ 734. Conditions of commitment to Youth Authority

No ward of the juvenile court shall be committed to the Youth Authority unless the judge of the court is

fully satisfied that the mental and physical condition and qualifications of the ward are such as to render it probable that he will be benefited by the reformatory educational discipline or other treatment provided by the Youth Authority.
(Added by Stats.1961, p. 1616, p. 3487, § 2.)

§ 735. Summary of facts accompanying commitment papers

Accompanying the commitment papers, the court shall send to the Director of the Youth Authority a summary of all the facts in the possession of the court, covering the history of the ward committed and a statement of the mental and physical condition of the ward.
(Added by Stats.1961, c. 1616, p. 3488, § 2.)

§ 737. Detention until execution of commitment order; review of detention of minor

(a) Whenever a person has been adjudged a ward of the juvenile court, and has been committed or otherwise disposed of as provided in this chapter for the care of wards of the juvenile court, the court may order that said ward be detained in the detention home, or in the case of a ward of the age of 18 years or more, in the county jail or otherwise as to the court seems fit until the execution of the order of commitment or of other disposition.

(b) In any case in which a minor is detained for more than 15 days pending the execution of the order of commitment or of any other disposition, the court shall periodically review the case to determine whether the delay is reasonable. Such periodic reviews shall be held at least every 15 days, commencing from the time the minor was initially detained pending the execution of the order of commitment or of any other disposition, and during the course of each review the court shall inquire regarding the action taken by the probation department to carry out its order, the reasons for the delay, and the effect of the delay upon the minor.
(Amended by Stats.1976, c. 1068, p. ——, § 61.)

§ 742. Informing alleged victim of crime of final disposition upon request

Upon the request of an alleged victim of a crime, the probation officer shall, within 60 days of the final disposition of a case within which a petition has been filed pursuant to Section 602, inform such person by letter of the final disposition of the case. "Final disposition" means dismissal, acquittal, or findings made pursuant to Section 731.
(Added by Stats.1976, c. 1070, p. ——, § 4.)

§ 775. Changing, modifying or setting aside orders; procedural requirements

Any order made by the court in the case of any person subject to its jurisdiction may at any time be changed, modified, or set aside, as the judge deems meet and proper, subject to such procedural requirements as are imposed by this article.
(Added by Stats.1961, c. 1616, p. 3491, § 2.)

§ 776. Notice of application

No order changing, modifying, or setting aside a previous order of the juvenile court shall be made either in chambers, or otherwise, unless prior notice of the application therefor has been given by the judge or the clerk of the court to the probation officer and prosecuting attorney and to the minor's counsel of record, or, if there is no counsel of record, to the minor and his parent or guardian.
(Amended by Stats.1977, c. 1241, p. ——, § 8.)

§ 777. Removal of minor from physical custody; placement or commitment; noticed hearing upon supplemental petition

An order changing or modifying a previous order by removing a minor from the physical custody of a parent, guardian, relative or friend and directing placement in a foster home, or commitment to a private institution or commitment to a county institution, or an order changing or modifying a previous order by directing commitment to the Youth Authority shall be made only after noticed hearing upon a supplemental petition.

(a) The supplemental petition shall be filed by the probation officer, where a minor has been declared a ward of the court under Section 601, and by the prosecuting attorney at the request of the probation officer where a minor has been declared a ward under Section 602, in the original matter and shall contain a concise statement of facts sufficient to support the conclusion that the previous disposition has not been effective in the rehabilitation or protection of the minor.

(b) Upon the filing of such supplemental petition, the clerk of the juvenile court shall immediately set the same for hearing within 30 days, and the probation officer shall cause notice thereof to be served upon the persons and in the manner prescribed by Sections 658 and 660.

(c) An order for the detention of the minor pending adjudication of the petition may be made only after a hearing is conducted pursuant to Article 15 (commencing with Section 625) of this chapter.
(Amended by Stats.1977, c. 1241, p. —, § 9, urgency, eff. Oct. 1, 1977.)

§ 778. Petition to change, modify or set aside order or terminate jurisdiction of court; grounds; verification; content; hearing

Any parent or other person having an interest in a child who is a ward of the juvenile court or the child himself through a properly appointed guardian may, upon grounds of change of circumstance or new evidence, petition the court in the same action in which the child was found to be a ward of the juvenile court for a hearing to change, modify, or set aside any order of court previously made or to terminate the jurisdiction of the court. The petition shall be verified and, if made by a person other than the child, shall state the petitioner's relationship to or interest in the child and shall set forth in concise language any change of circumstance or new evidence which are alleged to require such change of order or termination of jurisdiction.

If it appears that the best interests of the child may be promoted by the proposed change of order or termination of jurisdiction, the court shall order that a hearing be held and shall give prior notice, or cause prior notice to be given, to such persons and by such means as prescribed by Sections 776 and 779, and, in such instances as the means of giving notice is not prescribed by such sections, then by such means as the court prescribes.
(Amended by Stats.1976, c. 1068, p. —, § 69.)

§ 779. Changing, modifying or setting aside order of commitment to youth authority; notice

The court committing a ward to the Youth Authority may thereafter change, modify, or set aside the order of commitment. Ten days' notice of the hearing of the application therefor shall be served by United States mail upon the Director of the Youth Authority. In changing, modifying, or setting aside such order of commitment, the court shall give due consideration to the effect thereof upon the discipline and parole system of the Youth Authority or of the correctional school in which the ward may have been placed by the Youth Authority. Except as in this section provided, nothing in this chapter shall be deemed to interfere with the system of parole and discharge now or hereafter established by law, or by rule of the Youth Authority, for the parole and discharge of wards of the juvenile court committed to the Youth Authority, or with the management of any school, institution, or facility under the jurisdiction of the Youth Authority. Except as in this section provided, nothing in this chapter shall be deemed to interfere with the system of transfer between institutions and facilities under the jurisdiction of the Youth Authority.

However, before any inmate of a correctional school may be transferred to a state hospital, he shall first be returned to a court of competent jurisdiction and, after hearing, may be committed to a state hospital for the insane in accordance with law.
(Added by Stats.1961, c. 1616, p. 3492, § 2.)

§ 781. Petition for sealing records; notice; hearing; grounds for and effect of order; inspection of records

(a) In any case in which a petition has been filed with a juvenile court to commence proceedings to adjudge a person a ward of the court, in any case in which a person is cited to appear before a probation officer or is taken before a probation officer pursuant to Section 626, or in any case in which a minor is taken before any officer of a law enforcement agency, the person or the county probation officer may, five years or more after the jurisdiction of the juvenile court has terminated as to the person, or, in a case in which no petition is filed, five years or more after the person was cited to appear before a probation officer or was taken before a probation officer pursuant to Section 626 or was taken before any officer of a law enforcement agency, or, in any case, at any time after the person has reached the age of 18 years, petition the court for sealing of the records, including records of arrest, relating to the person's case, in the custody of the juvenile court and probation officer and any other agencies, including law enforcement agencies, and public officials as petitioner alleges, in his petition, to have custody of such records. The court shall notify the district attorney of the county and the county probation officer, if he is not the petitioner of the petition, and such district attorney or probation officer or any of their deputies or any other person having relevant evidence may testify at the hearing on the petition. If, after hearing, the court finds that since such termination of jurisdiction or action pursuant to Section 626, as the case may be, he has not been convicted of a felony or of any misdemeanor involving moral turpitude and that rehabilitation has been attained to the satisfaction of the court, it shall order sealed all records, papers, and exhibits in the person's case in the custody of the juvenile court, including the juvenile court record, minute book entries, and entries on dockets, and other records relating to the case in the custody of such other agencies and officials as are named in the order. Thereafter, the proceedings in such case shall be deemed never to have occurred, and the person may properly reply accordingly to any inquiry about the events, records of which are ordered sealed. The court shall send a copy of the order to each agency and official named therein, and each such agency and official shall seal records in its custody as directed by the order, shall advise the court of its compliance, and thereupon shall seal the copy of the court's order for sealing of records that it or he received. The person who is the subject of records sealed pursuant to this section may petition the superior court to permit inspection of the records by persons named in the petition, and the superior court may so order. Otherwise, except as provided in subdivision (b), such records shall not be open to inspection.

(b) In any action or proceeding based upon defamation, a court, upon a showing of good cause, may order any records sealed under this section to be opened and admitted into evidence. The records shall be confidential and shall be available for inspection only by the court, jury, parties, counsel for the parties, and any other person who is authorized by the court to inspect them. Upon the judgment in the action or proceeding becoming final, the court shall order the records sealed.

(Amended by Stats.1976, c. 1068, p. —, § 70.)

§ 782. Dismissal of petition; grounds

A judge of the juvenile court in which a petition was filed, at any time before the minor reaches the age of 21 years, may dismiss the petition or may set aside the findings and dismiss the petition if the court finds that the interests of justice and the welfare of the minor require such dismissal, or if it finds that the minor is not in need of treatment or rehabilitation. The court shall have jurisdiction to order such dismissal or setting aside of the findings and dismissal regardless of whether the minor is, at the time of such order, a ward or dependent child of the court.

(Added by Stats.1971, c. 607, p. —, § 1.)

§ 800. Appealable orders, judgments or decrees; stay; precedence

A judgment or decree of a juvenile court or final order of a referee which becomes effective without approval of a judge of the juvenile court assuming jurisdiction and declaring any person to be a person described in Section 601 or 602, or on denying a motion made pursuant to Section 567, may be appealed from in the same manner as any final judgment, and any subsequent order may be appealed from as from an order after judgment; but no such order or judgment shall be stayed by such appeal, unless suitable provision is made for the maintenance, care, and custody of such person pending the appeal, and unless such provision is approved by an order of the juvenile court. Such appeal shall have precedence over all other cases in the court to which the appeal is taken.

An appellant unable to afford counsel shall be provided a free copy of the transcript.

All appeals shall be initiated by the filing of a notice of appeal in conformity with the requirements of Section 1240.1 of the Penal Code.

(Amended by Stats.1978, c. 1385, p. —, § 3.)

§ 825. Juvenile court record

The order and findings of the superior court in each case under the provisions of this chapter shall be entered in a suitable book or other form of written record which shall be kept for that purpose and known as the "juvenile court record."

(Added by Stats.1961, c. 1616, p. 3494, § 2.)

§ 826. Destruction of records, papers and exhibits; destroy defined

After five years from the date on which the jurisdiction of the juvenile court over a minor is terminated, the judge or clerk of the juvenile court, or the probation officer, may destroy all records and papers in the proceedings concerning the minor. Exhibits shall be destroyed as provided under Sections 1418, 1418.5, and 1419 of the Penal Code. For the purpose of this section, "destroy" means destroy or dispose of for the purpose of destruction.

The juvenile court record, any minute book entries, dockets, and judgment dockets shall be microfilmed or photocopied prior to destruction. Every such reproduction shall be deemed and considered an original. A transcript, exemplification, or certified copy of any reproduction shall be deemed and considered a transcript, exemplification, or certified copy, as the case may be, of the original.

(Amended by Stats.1977, c. 239, p. —, § 1.)

§ 826.5. Destruction of records, papers and exhibits; microfilm or photocopies; reproductions as originals

(a) Notwithstanding the provisions of Section 826, at any time within a period of five years after the jurisdiction of the juvenile court over a minor is terminated, the judge or clerk of the juvenile court or the probation officer may destroy all records and papers, the juvenile court record, any minute book entries, dockets, and judgment dockets in the proceedings concerning the minor if the records and papers, juvenile court record, any minute book entries, dockets, and judgment dockets are microfilmed or photocopied prior to destruction. Exhibits shall be destroyed as provided under Sections 1418, 1418.5, and 1419 of the Penal Code. For the purposes of this section, "destroy" means destroy or dispose of for the purpose of destruction.

(b) Every reproduction shall be deemed and considered an original. A transcript, exemplification, or certified copy of any reproduction shall be deemed and considered a transcript, exemplification, or certified copy, as the case may be, of the original.
(Amended by Stats.1977, c. 239, p. —, § 2.)

§ 827. Inspection of petition and reports of probation officer

Except as provided in Section 828, a petition filed in any juvenile court proceeding, reports of the probation officer, and all other documents filed in any such case or made available to the probation officer in making his report, or to the judge, referee or other hearing officer, and thereafter retained by the probation officer, judge, referee, or other hearing officer, may be inspected only by court personnel, the minor who is the subject of the proceeding, his parents or guardian, the attorneys for such parties, and such other persons as may be designated by court order of the judge of the juvenile court upon filing a petition therefor.
(Amended by Stats.1972, c. 1139, p. 2206, § 1.)

§ 828. Disclosure of information gathered by law enforcement agency

Except as provided in Sections 389 and 781 of this code or 1203.45 of the Penal Code, any information gathered by a law enforcement agency relating to the taking of a minor into custody may be disclosed to another law enforcement agency, or to any person or agency which has a legitimate need for the information for purposes of official disposition of a case. When the disposition of a taking into custody is available, it must be included with any information disclosed.
(Amended by Stats.1976, c. 1068, p. —, § 73.)

§ 840. Establishment of program in each county; home supervision defined

There shall be in each county probation department a program of home supervision to which minors described by Section 628.1 shall be referred. Home supervision is a program in which persons who would otherwise be detained in the juvenile hall are permitted to remain in their homes pending court disposition of their cases, under the supervision of a deputy probation officer, probation aide, or probation volunteer.
(Amended by Stats.1977, c. 1241, p. —, § 9.5.)

§ 841. Probation officer or aide; assignment and duties

The duties of a deputy probation officer, or a probation aide or volunteer under the supervision of a deputy probation officer, assigned to home supervision are to assure the minor's appearance at probation officer interviews and court hearings and to assure that the minor obeys the conditions of his release and commits no public offenses pending final disposition of his case. A deputy probation officer assigned to home supervision shall have a caseload of no more than 10 minors. Whenever possible, a minor shall be assigned to a deputy probation officer, probation aide, or volunteer who resides in the same community as the minor.
(Amended by Stats.1978, c. 1157, p. —, § 2.)

§ 850. Establishment; maintenance; designation

The board of supervisors in every county shall provide and maintain, at the expense of the county, in a location approved by the judge of the juvenile court or in counties having more than one judge of the juvenile court, by the presiding judge of the juvenile court, a suitable house or place for the detention of wards and dependent children of the juvenile court and of persons alleged to come within the jurisdiction of the juvenile court. Such house or place shall be known as the "juvenile hall" of the county. Wherever, in any provision of law, reference is made to detention homes for juveniles, such reference shall be deemed and construed to refer to the juvenile halls provided for in this article.
(Added by Stats.1961, c. 1616, p. 3494, § 2.)

§ 851. Nature; conduct

The juvenile hall shall not be in, or connected with, any jail or prison, and shall not be deemed to be nor be treated as a penal institution. It shall be conducted in all respects as nearly like a home as possible.
(Added by Stats.1961, c. 1616, p. 3494, § 2.)

§ 856. Establishment of schools; school facilities

The board of supervisors may provide for the establishment of a public elementary school and of a public secondary school in connection with any juvenile hall, juvenile house, day center, juvenile ranch, or juvenile camp, for the education of the children in such facilities.
(Amended by Stats.1977, c. 430, p. —, § 2.)

§ 871. Minor under custody or commitment; escape; misdemeanor

Any person under the custody of a probation officer in a county juvenile hall, or committed to a county juvenile home, ranch, camp, or forestry camp, who escapes or attempts to escape from such county juvenile hall, home, ranch, camp, or forestry camp, is guilty of a misdemeanor.
(Added by Stats.1968, c. 536, p. 1188, § 3.)

§ 881. Establishment; commitment; operation and administration

The board of supervisors of any county may, by ordinance, establish juvenile homes, ranches, camps, or forestry camps, within or without the county, to which persons made wards of the court on the ground of fitting the description in Section 602 may be committed. As far as possible, the provisions of this chapter relating to commitments to the probation officer shall apply to commitments to such juvenile homes, except that where any ward proves to be unfit to remain in any such home, in the opinion of the superintendent or director thereof, said superintendent or director shall make recommendation to the probation department for consideration for other commitment. Complete operation and authority for the administration shall be vested in the county.
(Amended by Stats.1976, c. 1071, p. —, § 32.5.)

§ 886. Maximum number of children

No juvenile home or camp established pursuant to the provisions of this article shall receive or contain more than 100 children at any one time.
(Added by Stats.1961, c. 1616, p. 3497, § 2.)

Division 2.5
YOUTHS

§ 1700. Purpose of chapter; liberal interpretation

The purpose of this chapter is to protect society more effectively by substituting for retributive punishment methods of training and treatment directed toward the correction and rehabilitation of young persons found guilty of public offenses. To this end it is the intent of the Legislature that the chapter be liberally interpreted in conformity with its declared purpose.
(Added by Stats.1941, c. 937, p. 2522, § 1.)

§ 1710. Department

There is in the Human Relations Agency the Department of the Youth Authority.
(Amended by Stats.1969, c. 138, p. 374, § 294.)

§ 1711. Members

The authority shall consist of eight members who shall devote their entire time to its work. The appointing authority shall ensure that there is a representation of persons of both sexes on the authority.
(Amended by Stats.1975, c. 1129, p. 2775, § 6.)

§ 1711.3. Powers and duties of board and director; delegation of powers

The Youth Authority Board shall meet with the Director of the Department of Youth Authority not less than four times a year for the purpose of discussing policy and offering advice on policy pertaining to care and treatment of wards. The director may advise the Youth Authority Board in the establishment of general policies relating to the functions and duties of the Youth Authority Board.

The following powers and duties shall be exercised and performed by the Youth Authority Board as such, or may be delegated to a panel, member, or case hearing representative as provided in Section 1711.5 of this code: return of persons to the court of commitment for redisposition by the court, discharge of commitment, orders to parole and condition thereof, revocation or suspension of parole, recommendation for treatment program, determination of the date of next appearance, return of nonresident persons to the jurisdiction of the state of legal residence.

The case of each ward shall be heard immediately after the case study of the ward has been completed and at such other times as is necessary to exercise the powers and duties listed above.

All other powers, duties, and functions pertaining to the care and treatment of wards provided by any provision of law shall be exercised and performed by the director. The director may make and enforce all rules appropriate to the proper accomplishment of his functions.

The director may delegate the powers and duties vested in him by this section, in accordance with Section 7 of this code.
(Amended by Stats.1963, c. 1352, p. 2880, § 4.)

§ 1711.5. Performance of functions by full board, panels or referees; delegation of authority; appeals

The Youth Authority Board shall formulate general policies governing the performance of its functions by the full board, or, pursuant to delegation, by panels, or referees. Where the board performs its functions meeting en banc in either public or executive sessions to decide matters of general policy, at least five members shall be present and no such action shall be valid unless it is concurred in by a majority vote of those present.

Case hearing representatives may be employed to participate with the board in the hearing of cases and to whom authority may be delegated as provided below in this section.

The board may delegate its authority to hear, consider, and act upon cases to members or case hearing representatives, sitting either on a panel or as a referee. A panel may consist of two or more members, or a member and a case hearing representative, or two case hearing representatives. Two members of a panel shall constitute a quorum, and no action of the panel shall be valid unless concurred in by a majority vote of those present.

When delegating its authority, the board may, in its discretion, condition finality of the decision of the panel or referee to whom authority is delegated on concurrence of a member or members of the board. In determining whether, in any case, it shall delegate its authority and the extent of delegation, the board shall take into account the degree of complexity of the issues presented by the case.

The board shall adopt rules under which a person under the jurisdiction of the Youth Authority or other persons, as specified in the rules, may appeal any decision of a case hearing representative. The board shall consider and act upon the appeal in accordance with such rules.
(Amended by Stats.1972, c. 532, p. 923, § 3.)

§ 1731. Determination of age

When in any criminal proceeding in a court of this State a person has been convicted of a public offense for which the court has power under this chapter to commit to the Authority, the court shall determine whether the person was less than 21 years of age at the time of the apprehension from which the criminal proceeding resulted. Proceedings in a juvenile court in respect to a juvenile are not criminal proceedings as that phrase is used in this chapter.
(Amended by Stats.1944, 3d Ex.Sess., c. 2, p. 22, § 3.)

§ 1731.5. Reference of persons to authority; description; certification; commitment

After certification to the Governor as provided in this article a court may commit to the authority any person convicted of a public offense who comes within subdivisions (a), (b), and (c), or subdivisions (a), (b), and (d), below:

(a) Is found to be less than 21 years of age at the time of apprehension.

(b) Is not sentenced to death, imprisonment for life, imprisonment for 90 days or less, or the payment of a fine, or after having been directed to pay a fine, defaults in the payment thereof, and is subject to imprisonment for more than 90 days under the judgment.

(c) Is not granted probation.

(d) Was granted probation and probation is revoked and terminated.

The Youth Authority shall accept a person committed to it pursuant to this article if it believes that the person can be materially benefited by its reformatory and educational discipline, and if it has adequate facilities to provide such care.
(Amended by Stats.1969, c. 785, p. 1602, § 2.)

§ 1737. Recall of commitment and resentencing; credit for time served

When a person has been committed to the custody of the authority, if it is deemed warranted by a diagnostic study and recommendation approved by the director, the judge who ordered the commitment or, if the judge is not available, the presiding or sole judge of the court, within 120 days of the date of commitment on his own motion, or the court, at any

§ 1737

time thereafter upon recommendation of the director, may recall the commitment previously ordered and resentence the person as if he had not previously been sentenced. The time served while in custody of the authority shall be credited toward the term of any person resentenced pursuant to this section.
(Amended by Stats.1975, c. 1103, p. 2676, § 1.)

§ 1737.1. Return of person to committing court

Whenever any person who has been charged with or convicted of a public offense in adult court and committed to the authority appears to the authority, either at the time of his presentation or after having become an inmate of any institution or facility subject to the jurisdiction of the authority, to be an improper person to be retained in any such institution or facility, or to be so incorrigible or so incapable of reformation under the discipline of the authority as to render his detention detrimental to the interests of the authority and the other persons committed thereto, the authority may return him to the committing court. In the case of a person convicted of a public offense, said court may then commit him to a state prison or sentence him to a county jail as provided by law for punishment of the offense of which he was convicted. The maximum term of imprisonment for a person committed to a state prison under this section shall be a period equal to the maximum term prescribed by law for the offense of which he was convicted less the period during which he was under the control of the Youth Authority. The Adult Authority may, after seeking the advice of the Youth Authority, allow any such person time credit reductions from his term of confinement according to the table set forth in Section 2920 of the Penal Code for the time during which such person was under the control of the Youth Authority. This section shall not apply to commitments from juvenile court.
(Amended by Stats.1976, c. 1071, p. —, § 33.)

§ 1766.5. Grievances; system for resolution; requirements

The director shall establish and maintain a fair, simple and expeditious system for resolution of grievances of all persons committed to the Youth Authority regarding the substance or application of any written or unwritten policy, rule or regulation of the department or of an agent or contractor of the department or any decision, behavior or action by an employee, agent or contractor or by other person committed to the Youth Authority. The system shall:

(a) Provide for the participation of employees of the department and of persons committed to the Youth Authority on as equal a basis and at the most decentralized level reasonably possible and feasible in the design, implementation and operation of the system;

(b) Provide, to the extent reasonably possible, for the selection by their peers of persons committed to the Youth Authority as participants in the design, implementation and operation of the system;

(c) Provide, within specific time limits, for written responses with written reasons in support thereof to all grievances at all decision levels within the system;

(d) Provide for priority processing of grievances which are of an emergency nature, including, but not limited to, matters which would, by passage of time required for normal processing, be made moot and matters in which delay would subject the grievant to substantial risk of personal injury or other damage;

(e) Provide for the right of grievants to be represented by another person committed to the Youth Authority, by an employee, or by any other person, including a volunteer who is a regular participant in departmental operations;

(f) Provide for safeguards against reprisals against any grievant or participant in the resolution of a grievance;

(g) Provide, at one or more decision levels of the process, for a full hearing of the grievance at which all parties to the controversy and their representatives shall have the opportunity to be present and to present evidence and contentions regarding the grievance;

(h) Provide a method of appeal of grievance decisions available to all parties to the grievance, including, but not limited to, final right of appeal to advisory arbitration of the grievance by a neutral person not employed by the department, the decision of such arbitrator to be adopted by the department unless such decision is in violation of law, would result in physical danger to any persons, would require expenditure of funds not reasonably available for such purpose to the department, or, in the personal judgment of the director, would be detrimental to the public or to the proper and effective accomplishment of the duties of the department;

(i) Provide for the monitoring of the system by the department with an annual report regarding the operation of the system to be filed with the Legisla-

ture, with the Attorney General and with the State Public Defender, and further provide, pursuant to contract or other appropriate means, for an annual evaluation of the system by a public or private agency independent of the department to the extent necessary to ascertain whether the requirements of this section are being met. The results of which evaluation shall be filed with the department, the Legislature, the Attorney General, and the State Public Defender.
(Added by Stats.1976, c. 710, p. —, § 1.)

§ 1769. Discharge of persons committed by juvenile court

(a) Every person committed to the authority by a juvenile court shall, except as provided in subdivision (b), be discharged upon the expiration of a two-year period of control or when the person reaches his 21st birthday, whichever occurs later, unless an order for further detention has been made by the committing court pursuant to Article 6 (commencing with Section 1800).

(b) Every person committed to the authority by a juvenile court who has been found to be a person described in Section 602 by reason of the violation, when such person was 16 years of age or older, of any of the offenses listed in subdivision (b) of Section 707, shall be discharged upon the expiration of a two-year period of control or when the person reaches his or her 23rd birthday, whichever occurs later, unless an order for further detention has been made by the committing court pursuant to Article 6 (commencing with Section 1800).
(Amended by Stats.1976, c. 1071, p. —, § 34.)

Division 3
NARCOTIC ADDICTS

§ 3000. Legislative intent

It is the intent of the Legislature that persons addicted to narcotics, or who by reason of repeated use of narcotics are in imminent danger of becoming addicted, shall be treated for such condition and its underlying causes, and that such treatment shall be carried out for nonpunitive purposes not only for the protection of the addict, or person in imminent danger of addiction, against himself, but also for the prevention of contamination of others and the protection of the public. Persons committed to the program provided for in this chapter who are uncooperative with efforts to treat them or are otherwise unresponsive to treatment nevertheless should be kept in the program for purposes of control. It is the further intent of the Legislature that persons committed to this program who show signs of progress after an initial or subsequent periods of treatment and observation be given reasonable opportunities to demonstrate ability to abstain from the use of narcotics under close supervision in outpatient status outside of the rehabilitation center provided for in Chapter 2 (commencing with Section 3300) of this division. Determinations of progress of persons committed to the program should be based upon criteria to be established by the Director of Corrections with the advice of clinically trained and experienced personnel.

The enactment of the preceding provisions of this section shall not be construed to be evidence that the intent of the Legislature was otherwise before such enactment.
(Added by Stats.1965, c. 1226, p. 3062, § 2.)

§ 3001. Detention, treatment and rehabilitation facility within department of corrections; purpose

The narcotic detention, treatment and rehabilitation facility referred to herein shall be one within the Department of Corrections whose principal purpose shall be the receiving, control, confinement, employment, education, treatment and rehabilitation of persons under the custody of the Department of Corrections or any agency thereof who are or have been addicted to narcotics or who by reason of repeated use of narcotics are in imminent danger of becoming addicted.
(Added by Stats.1965, c. 1226, p. 3063, § 2.)

§ 3002. Escape or attempted escape; punishment; exception

Every person committed pursuant to this chapter or former Chapter 11 (commencing with Section 6399) of Title 7 of the Penal Code who escapes or attempts to escape from lawful custody is guilty of a crime punishable by imprisonment in the state prison. This section does not apply to unauthorized absence from a halfway house.
(Amended by Stats.1976, c. 1139, p. —, § 344.5 operative July 1, 1977.)

§ 3009. Narcotic addict

A "narcotic addict," as used in this division refers to any person, adult or minor, who is addicted to the unlawful use of any narcotic as defined in Division 10 of the Health and Safety Code, except marijuana.
(Added by Stats.1965, c. 1227, p. 3075, § 13.)

Division 4
STATE DEPARTMENT OF HEALTH

Division 5
COMMUNITY MENTAL HEALTH SERVICES

Editors' Note

Division 5 contains the laws related to community mental health services, including procedures authorizing peace officers to detain mentally disordered persons and inebriates.

§ 5001. Legislative intent

The provisions of this part shall be construed to promote the legislative intent as follows:

(a) To end the inappropriate, indefinite, and involuntary commitment of mentally disordered persons, developmentally disabled persons, and persons impaired by chronic alcoholism, and to eliminate legal disabilities;

(b) To provide prompt evaluation and treatment of persons with serious mental disorders or impaired by chronic alcoholism;

(c) To guarantee and protect public safety;

(d) To safeguard individual rights through judicial review;

(e) To provide individualized treatment, supervision, and placement services by a conservatorship program for gravely disabled persons;

(f) To encourage the full use of all existing agencies, professional personnel and public funds to accomplish these objectives and to prevent duplication of services and unnecessary expenditures;

(g) To protect mentally disordered persons and developmentally disabled persons from criminal acts.
(Amended by Stats.1977, c. 1167, p. ——, § 1.)

§ 5004. Protection from criminal acts

Mentally disordered persons and developmentally disabled persons shall receive protection from criminal acts equal to that provided any other resident in this state.
(Added by Stats.1977, c. 1167, p. ——, § 2.)

§ 5150. Dangerous or gravely disabled person; taking into custody; application; basis of probable cause; liability

When any person, as a result of mental disorder, is a danger to others, or to himself, or gravely disabled, a peace officer, member of the attending staff, as defined by regulation, of an evaluation facility designated by the county, or other professional person designated by the county may, upon probable cause, take, or cause to be taken, the person into custody and place him in a facility designated by the county and approved by the State Department of Mental Health as a facility for 72-hour treatment and evaluation.

Such facility shall require an application in writing stating the circumstances under which the person's condition was called to the attention of the officer, member of the attending staff, or professional person, and stating that the officer, member of the attending staff, or professional person has probable cause to believe that the person is, as a result of mental disorder, a danger to others, or to himself, or gravely disabled. If the probable cause is based on the statement of a person other than the officer, member of the attending staff, or professional person, such person shall be liable in a civil action for intentionally giving a statement which he knows to be false.
(Amended by Stats.1977, c. 1252, p. ——, § 554, operative July 1, 1978.)

§ 5151. Detention for evaluation; services provided

If the facility for 72-hour treatment and evaluation admits the person, it may detain him or her for evaluation and treatment for a period not to exceed 72 hours. Saturdays, Sundays, and holidays may be excluded from the 72-hour period if the Department of Mental Health certifies for each facility that evaluation and treatment services cannot reasonably be made available on those days. The certification by the department is subject to renewal every two years. The department shall adopt regulations defining criteria for determining whether a facility can reasonably be expected to make evaluation and treatment services available on Saturdays, Sundays, and holidays.

If in the judgment of the professional person in charge of the facility providing evaluation and treatment, or his designee, the person can be properly served without being detained, he shall be provided evaluation, crisis intervention, or other inpatient or outpatient services on a voluntary basis.
(Amended by Stats.1978, c. 1294, p. —, § 2.)

§ 5152. Evaluation; treatment and care; release or other disposition

Each person admitted to a facility for 72-hour treatment and evaluation under the provisions of this article shall receive an evaluation as soon after he is admitted as possible and shall receive such treatment and care as his condition requires for the full period that he is held. Such person shall be released before 72 hours have elapsed if, in the opinion of the professional person in charge of the facility, or his designee, the person no longer requires evaluation or treatment.

Persons who have been detained for evaluation and treatment shall be released, referred for further care and treatment on a voluntary basis, certified for intensive treatment, or a conservator or temporary conservator shall be appointed pursuant to this part as required.
(Amended by Stats.1970, c. 1627, p. 3441, § 9.)

§ 5152.1. Notification to county mental health director and peace officer; conditions

The professional person in charge of the facility providing 72-hour evaluation and treatment, or his designee, shall notify the county mental health director or his designee and the peace officer who makes the written application pursuant to Section 5150 if both of the following conditions apply:

(a) The peace officer requests such notification at the time he makes the application and he certifies in writing that the person has been referred to the facility under circumstances in which a criminal charge might be filed.

(b) The person admitted pursuant to such application is not detained by the facility or is detained for a period less than the full period of allowable detention in the 72-hour facility.
(Added by Stats.1975, c. 960, p. 2643, § 3.)

§ 5152.2. Methods for prompt notification to peace officers

Each law enforcement agency within a county shall arrange with the county mental health director a method for giving prompt notification to peace officers pursuant to Section 5152.1.
(Added by Stats.1975, c. 960, p. 2643, § 4.)

§ 5153. Plain clothes officers; vehicles

Whenever possible, officers charged with apprehension of persons pursuant to this article shall dress in plain clothes and travel in unmarked vehicles.
(Amended by Stats.1969, c. 722, p. 1422, § 6.)

§ 5154. Exemption from liability

The professional person in charge of the facility providing 72-hour treatment and evaluation, his designee, and the peace officer responsible for the detainment of the person shall not be held civilly or criminally liable for any action by a person released at or before the end of 72 hours pursuant to this article.
(Amended by Stats.1968, c. 1374, p. 2644, § 19.)

§ 5157. Information to be given person taken into custody; contents; record of advisement

(a) Each person, at the time he or she is first taken into custody under provisions of Section 5150, shall be provided, by the person who takes such other person into custody, the following information orally. The information shall be in substantially the following form:

My name is _____.
I am a _____.
    (peace officer, mental health professional)
with _____.
         (name of agency)
You are not under criminal arrest, but I am taking you for examination by mental health professionals at _____.
         (name of facility)

You will be told your rights by the mental health staff.

If taken into custody at his or her residence, the person shall also be told the following information in substantially the following form:

You may bring a few personal items with you which I will have to approve. You can make a phone call and/or leave a note to tell your friends and/or family where you have been taken.

§ 5157

(b) The designated facility shall keep, for each patient evaluated, a record of the advisement given pursuant to subdivision (a) which shall include:

(1) Name of person detained for evaluation.

(2) Name and position of peace officer or mental health professional taking person into custody.

(3) Date.

(4) Whether advisement was completed.

(5) If not given or completed, the mental health professional at the facility shall either provide the information specified in subdivision (a), or include a statement of good cause, as defined by regulations of the State Department of Health, which shall be kept with the patient's medical record.

(c) Each person admitted to a designated facility for 72-hour evaluation and treatment shall be given the following information by admission staff at the evaluation unit. The information shall be given orally and in writing and in a language or modality accessible to the person. The written information shall be available in the person's native language or the language which is the person's principal means of communication. The information shall be in substantially the following form:

My name is _____.
My position here is _____.

You are being placed into the psychiatric unit because it is our professional opinion that as a result of mental disorder, you are likely to:

(check applicable)
    harm yourself _____
    harm someone else _____
    be unable to take care of your own
        food, clothing, and housing needs _____

We feel this is true because

_____

(herewith a listing of the facts upon which the allegation of dangerous or gravely disabled due to mental disorder is based, including pertinent facts arising from the admission interview.)

You will be held on the ward for a period up to 72 hours.

This does not include weekends or holidays.

Your 72-hour period will begin _____
                          (day and time.)

During these 72 hours you will be evaluated by the hospital staff, and you may be given treatment, including medications. It is possible for you to be released before the end of the 72 hours. But if the staff decides that you need continued treatment you can be held for a longer period of time. If you are held longer than 72 hours you have the right to a lawyer and a qualified interpreter and a hearing before a judge. If you are unable to pay for the lawyer, then one will be provided free.

(d) For each patient admitted for 72-hour evaluation and treatment, the facility shall keep with the patient's medical record a record of the advisement given pursuant to subdivision (c) which shall include:

(1) Name of person performing advisement.

(2) Date.

(3) Whether advisement was completed.

(4) If not completed, a statement of good cause.

If the advisement was not completed at admission, the advisement process shall be continued on the ward until completed. A record of the matters prescribed by subdivisions (a), (b), and (c) shall be kept with the patient's medical record.
(Added by Stats.1977, c. 1021, p. —, § 1.)

§ 5170. Dangerous or gravely disabled person; taking into civil protective custody

When any person is a danger to others, or to himself, or gravely disabled as a result of inebriation, a peace officer, member of the attending staff, as defined by regulation, of an evaluation facility designated by the county, or other person designated by the county may, upon reasonable cause, take, or cause to be taken, the person into civil protective custody and place him in a facility designated by the county and approved by the State Department of Alcohol and Drug Abuse as a facility for 72-hour treatment and evaluation of inebriates.
(Amended by Stats.1978, c. 429, p. —, § 204.)

§ 5170.5. Right to make telephone calls

Any person placed in an evaluation facility has, immediately after he is taken to an evaluation facility and except where physically impossible, no later than three hours after he is placed in such facility or taken to such unit, the right to make, at his own expense, at least two completed telephone calls. If the person placed in the evaluation facility does not have money upon him with which to make such calls, he shall be allowed free at least two completed local toll free or collect telephone calls.
(Amended by Stats.1974, c. 1024, p. 2223, § 2.)

§ 5171. Detention for evaluation; services provided

If the facility for 72-hour treatment and evaluation of inebriates admits the person, it may detain him for evaluation and detoxification treatment, and such other treatment as may be indicated, for a period not to exceed 72 hours. Saturdays, Sundays and holidays shall be included for the purpose of calculating the 72-hour period. However, a person may voluntarily remain in such facility for more than 72 hours if the professional person in charge of the facility determines the person is in need of and may benefit from further treatment and care, provided any person who is taken or caused to be taken to the facility shall have priority for available treatment and care over a person who has voluntarily remained in a facility for more than 72 hours.

If in the judgment of the professional person in charge of the facility providing evaluation and treatment, the person can be properly served without being detained, he shall be provided evaluation, detoxification treatment or other treatment, crisis intervention, or other inpatient or outpatient services on a voluntary basis.
(Amended by Stats.1971, c. 1581, p. —, § 6.)

§ 5172. Evaluation; treatment and care; release or other disposition

Each person admitted to a facility for 72-hour treatment and evaluation under the provisions of this article shall receive an evaluation as soon after he is admitted as possible and shall receive such treatment and care as his condition requires for the full period that he is held. Such person shall be released before 72 hours have elapsed if, in the opinion of the professional person in charge of the facility, the person no longer requires evaluation or treatment.

Persons who have been detained for evaluation and treatment shall be released, referred for further care and treatment on a voluntary basis, or, if the person, as a result of impairment by chronic alcoholism, is a danger to others or to himself, or gravely disabled, he may be certified for intensive treatment, or a conservator or temporary conservator shall be appointed for him pursuant to this part as required.
(Amended by Stats.1971, c. 1443, p. —, § 1.)

§ 5172.1. Voluntary application by inebriate for admission

Any person who is a danger to others, or to himself, or gravely disabled as a result of inebriation, may voluntarily apply for admission to a 72-hour evaluation and detoxification treatment facility for inebriates.
(Added by Stats.1971, c. 1581, p. —, § 7.)

§ 5173. Exemption from liability

The professional person in charge of the facility providing 72-hour treatment and evaluation, and the peace officer responsible for the detainment of the person shall not be held civilly or criminally liable for any action by a person released at or before the end of 72 hours pursuant to this article.
(Added by Stats.1969, c. 1472, p. 3016, § 2.)

§ 5176. Counties to which article applicable; designation of facilities and capacities

This article shall apply only to those counties wherein the board of supervisors has adopted a resolution stating that suitable facilities exist within the county for the care and treatment of inebriates and persons impaired by chronic alcoholism, designating the facilities to be used as facilities for 72-hour treatment and evaluation of inebriates and for the extensive treatment of persons impaired by chronic alcoholism, and otherwise adopting the provisions of this article.

Each county Short-Doyle plan for a county to which this article is made applicable shall designate the specific facility or facilities for 72-hour evaluation and detoxification treatment of inebriates and for intensive treatment of persons impaired by chronic alcoholism and for the treatment of such persons on a voluntary basis under this article, and shall specify the maximum number of patients that can be served at any one time by each such facility.
(Amended by Stats.1974, c. 1024, p. 2223, § 4.)

Division 6
ADMISSIONS AND JUDICIAL COMMITMENTS

§ 6300. Definitions

As used in this article, "mentally disordered sex offender" means any person who by reason of mental defect, disease, or disorder, is predisposed to the commission of sexual offenses to such a degree that he is dangerous to the health and safety of others. Wherever the term "sexual psychopath" is used in any code, such term shall be construed to refer to and mean a "mentally disordered sex offender."
(Added by Stats.1967, c. 1667, p. 4107, § 37.)

§ 6302. Certification for hearing and examination after conviction

(a) General provisions; failure to register under Penal Code § 290

(a) When a person is convicted of any sex offense, the trial judge, on his own motion, or on motion of the prosecuting attorney, or on application by affidavit by or on behalf of the defendant, if it appears to the satisfaction of the court that there is probable cause for believing such a person is a mentally disordered sex offender within the meaning of this chapter, may adjourn the proceeding or suspend the sentence, as the case may be, and may certify the person for hearing and examination by the superior court of the county to determine whether the person is a mentally disordered sex offender within the meaning of this article.

As used in this section the term "sex offense" means any offense for which registration is required by Section 290 of the Penal Code; or any felony or misdemeanor which is shown by clear proof or the stipulation of the defendant to have been committed primarily for purposes of sexual arousal or gratification.

When an affidavit is filed under (a) it shall be substantially in the form specified for the affidavit in Section 6251 of this code. The title and body of the affidavit shall refer to such person as "an alleged mentally disordered sex offender" and shall state fully the facts upon which the allegation that the person is a mentally disordered sex offender is based. If the person is then before the court or is in custody, the court may order that the person be detained in a place of safety until the issue and service of an order for examination and detention as provided by this article.

(b) Child under 14; misdemeanor

(b) When a person is convicted of a sex offense involving a child under 14 years of age and it is a misdemeanor, and the person has been previously convicted of a sex offense in this or any other state, the court shall adjourn the proceeding or suspend the sentence, as the case may be, and shall certify the person for hearing and examination by the superior court of the county to determine whether the person is a mentally disordered sex offender within the meaning of this article.

(c) Child under 14; felony

(c) When a person is convicted of a sex offense involving a child under 14 years of age and it is a felony, the court shall adjourn the proceeding or suspend the sentence, as the case may be, and shall certify the person for hearing and examination by the superior court of the county to determine whether the person is a mentally disordered sex offender within the meaning of this article.

(d) Certification; statement

(d) When the court certifies the person for hearing and examination by the superior court of the county to determine whether the person is a mentally disordered sex offender, the court shall transmit to the superior court its certification to that effect, accompanied by a statement of the court's reasons for finding that there is probable cause for believing such person is a mentally disordered sex offender within the meaning of this article in cases certified under (a), or a statement of the facts making such certification mandatory under (b) or (c).

The judge or justice presiding in such court, whenever it is deemed necessary or advisable, may issue and deliver to some peace officer for service, an order directing that the person be apprehended and taken before a judge of the superior court for a hearing and examination to determine whether the person is a mentally disordered sex offender. The officer shall thereupon apprehend and detain the person until a hearing and examination can be had. At the time of the apprehension a copy of the affidavit if one was filed, the certification, accompanied by the court's statement, and the warrant shall be personally delivered to the person and copies thereof shall also be delivered to the superior court to which the person was certified and to the district attorney of the county.

The order for examination and detention shall be substantially in the form provided by Section 6252 of this code.

(Amended by Stats.1976, c. 1101, p. —, § 2.)

§ 6800. Poor and indigent committed persons; care of patients; effect of delivery to hospital

All peace officers and other persons having similar duties relating to judicially committed poor persons shall see that all poor and indigent committed persons within their respective municipalities are speedily granted the relief conferred by this part. When so ordered by a superior court judge, they shall see that such committed persons are, without unnecessary delay, transferred to the proper state hospitals provided for their care and treatment. Before sending a

person to any such hospital, they shall see that he is in a state of bodily cleanliness and comfortably clothed with clean clothes. The department may by order direct that any person whom it deems unsuitable therefor shall not be employed as an attendant for any committed person. After the patient has been delivered to the proper officers of the hospital, the care and custody of the county or municipality from which he is sent ceases.
(Amended by Stats.1968, c. 1374, p. 2686, § 111.)

Division 7
MENTAL INSTITUTIONS

§ 7325. Arrest; peace officer; notification

When any patient committed by a court to a state hospital or other institution on or before June 30, 1969, or when any patient who is judicially committed on or after July 1, 1969, or when any patient who is involuntarily detained pursuant to Part 1 (commencing with Section 5000) of Division 5 escapes from any state hospital, any hospital or facility operated by or under the Veterans' Administration of the United States government, or any facility designated by a county pursuant to such Part 1, or any facility into which the patient has been placed by his conservator appointed pursuant to Chapter 3 (commencing with Section 5350), Part 1, Division 5, of this code, or when a judicially committed patient's return from leave of absence has been authorized or ordered by the State Department of Mental Health or the facility of the Veterans' Administration, any peace officer, upon written request of the state hospital, veterans' facility, or the facility designated by a county, or the patient's conservator appointed pursuant to Chapter 3 (commencing with Section 5350), Part 1, Division 5, of this code, shall without the necessity of a warrant or court order, or any officer or employee of the State Department of Mental Health designated to perform such duties may, apprehend, take into custody and deliver him to the state hospital or to a facility of the Veterans' Administration, or the facility designated by a county, or to any person or place authorized by the State Department of Mental Health, or by the Veterans' Administration, or the local director of the county mental health program of the county in which is located the facility designated by the county, or the patient's conservator appointed pursuant to Chapter 3 (commencing with Section 5350), Part 1, Division 5, of this code, as the case may be, to receive him.

Every officer or employee of the State Department of Mental Health designated to apprehend or return such patients shall have the powers and privileges of peace officers so far as necessary to enforce the provisions of this section.

As used in this section "any peace officer" means the persons specified in Section 830.1 of the Penal Code.

The written notification of the escape required by this section shall include the name and physical description of the patient, his home address, the degree of dangerousness of the patient and any additional information which is necessary to apprehend and return the patient. Any officer or employee of a state hospital, hospital or facility operated by or under the Veterans' Administration, or any facility designated by a county pursuant to Part 1 (commencing with Section 5000) of Division 5 shall provide any peace officer with any information concerning any patient who escapes from such hospital or facility in order to assist in the apprehension and return of the patient.

The person in charge of such hospital or facility, or his designee, may provide telephonic notification of the escape to the law enforcement agency of the county or city in which the hospital or facility is located. If such notification is given, the time and date of notification, the person notified, and the person making the notification shall be noted in the written notification required by this section.
(Amended by Stats.1977, c. 1252, p. —, § 680, operative July 1, 1978.)

§ 7326. Assisting escape; offense

Any person who willfully assists any judicially committed or remanded patient of a state hospital to escape, to attempt to escape therefrom, or to resist being returned from a leave of absence shall be punished by imprisonment in the state prison, a fine of not more than five thousand dollars ($5,000) or both such imprisonment and fine; or by imprisonment in a county jail for a period of not more than one year, a fine of not more than one thousand dollars ($1,000) or both such imprisonment and fine.
(Amended by Stats.1976, c. 1139, p. —, § 346.)

Division 8
MISCELLANEOUS

§ 8101. Sale or gift to mental patient; punishment

Any person who shall knowingly supply, sell, give, or allow possession or control of any deadly weapon

as defined in Section 12022 of the Penal Code to any person who is a mental patient in any public or private hospital or institution or on leave of absence from any such hospital or institution shall be punishable by imprisonment in a state prison, or in a county jail for a period of not exceeding one year, by a fine of not exceeding five hundred dollars ($500), or by both such fine and imprisonment.
(Amended by Stats.1976, c. 1139, p. —, § 348.)

§ 8102. Confiscation and custody of firearms

Whenever a person who has been detained or apprehended for examination of his mental condition, or who is a mental patient in any hospital or institution or who is on leave of absence from such hospital or institution, is found to own, have in his possession or under his control, any firearm whatsoever, said firearm shall be confiscated by any law enforcement agency or peace officer, who shall retain custody of said firearm until the release without commitment of the person or the restoration to capacity of the person, or until the appointment of a guardian for the person, or shall make such other disposition of the firearm as ordered by the court.
(Added by Stats.1967, c. 1667, p. 4183, § 42.)

§ 8103. Certificate for possession of firearms; examination; review of denial; violations

No person who has been adjudicated by a court to be a danger to others as a result of a mental disorder or mental illness, after October 1, 1955, shall have in his possession or under his custody or control any firearm unless there has been issued to such person a certificate as hereafter described in this section and such person has not, subsequent to the issuance of such certificate, again been adjudicated by a court to be a danger to others as a result of a mental disorder or mental illness.

A certificate meeting the requirements of this section must be a written statement that is either part of a broader certificate of competency or a separate document and that is issued, on application of the person who was so adjudicated, either at the time of release from treatment under such adjudication or at a later date, by the medical director of any California state hospital, stating that in the opinion of the person issuing the certificate based either on his own knowledge or on the opinions of members of his staff or on records of the institution, the applicant is a person who may possess a firearm without endangering others. If a person applies to a medical director of a California state hospital for such a certificate and the applicant has not been treated in that hospital, or if the medical director believes that a current mental examination is necessary to enable him to determine whether or not such a certificate shall be issued, the medical director shall cause such person to be examined by a member of the staff of the hospital and may otherwise investigate the case. The medical director may charge a reasonable fee for such examination and investigation.

Refusal of a medical director to issue a certificate of competency or separate document as described in the preceding provisions of this section is reviewable by mandamus in the superior court of the county of which the applicant is a resident or the county in which the hospital of which the medical director is head. Upon a showing to the satisfaction of the court of abuse of discretion by the medical director the court shall issue its writ directing the medical director to issue its certificate or document.

No person who has been found, pursuant to Section 1026 of the Penal Code, not guilty by reason of insanity of murder, mayhem, a violation of Section 207 or 209 of the Penal Code in which the victim suffers intentionally inflicted great bodily injury, robbery in which the victim suffers great bodily injury, a violation of Section 447a of the Penal Code involving a trailer coach, as defined in Section 635 of the Vehicle Code, or any dwelling house, a violation of subdivision 2 or 3 of Section 261 of the Penal Code, a violation of Section 459 of the Penal Code in the first degree, assault with intent to commit murder, a violation of Section 220 of the Penal Code in which the victim suffers great bodily injury, a violation of Section 12303.1, 12303.2, 12303.3, 12308, 12309, or 12310 of the Penal Code, or of a felony involving death, great bodily injury, or an act which poses a serious threat of bodily harm to another person, shall have in his possession or under his custody or control any firearm.

Every person who possesses or has under his custody or control any firearm in violation of this section is guilty of a misdemeanor.
(Amended by Stats.1978, c. 187, p. —, § 1.)

§ 8104. Maintenance of records; availability to department of justice

The State Department of Mental Health shall keep and maintain records necessary to identify any person who comes within any of the provisions of this chapter. Such records shall be made available to the

Department of Justice upon request. The Department of Justice shall make such requests only with respect to its duties with regard to applications for permits for explosives as defined in Section 12000 of the Health and Safety Code, concealable weapons as defined in Section 12001 of the Penal Code, machineguns as defined in Section 12200 of the Penal Code and destructive devices as defined in Section 12301 of the Penal Code. Such records shall not be furnished or made available to any person unless the department determines that disclosure of any information in such records is necessary to carry out its duties with respect to applications for permits for explosives, destructive devices, concealable weapons, and machineguns.
(Amended by Stats.1977, c. 1252, p. —, § 707, operative July 1, 1978.)

Division 8.5
AGING
Division 9
PUBLIC SOCIAL SERVICES

§ 11476. Absent or unmarried parents; reference to and duties of district attorney; effect of court order on agreements; reciprocal agreements; collection through federal courts or agencies

It shall be the duty of the county department to refer all cases where a parent is absent from the home, or where the parents are unmarried and parentage has not been determined by a court of competent jurisdiction, to the district attorney immediately at the time the application for assistance, or certificate of eligibility, is signed by the applicant or recipient. If an applicant is found to be ineligible, such applicant shall be notified in writing that the referral of case to the district attorney may be terminated at such applicant's request. The county department shall cooperate with the district attorney and shall make available to him all pertinent information as provided in Section 11478.

Upon referral from the county department, the district attorney shall investigate the question of nonsupport or paternity and shall take all steps necessary to obtain support for the needy child and determine paternity in the case of a child born out of wedlock. Upon the advice of the county department that a child is being considered for adoption, the district attorney shall delay the investigation and other actions with respect to the case until advised that the adoption is no longer under consideration. The granting of aid to an applicant shall not be delayed or contingent upon investigation by the district attorney.

Where a court order has been obtained, any contractual agreement for support between the district attorney or the county department and the noncustodial parent shall be deemed null and void to the extent that it is not consistent with the court order.

Whenever a family which has been receiving aid to families with dependent children ceases to receive assistance, the district attorney shall:

(1) Continue to enforce support payments from the noncustodial parent for a period not to exceed three months from the month following the month in which such family ceased to receive assistance and pay all amounts so collected to the family; and

(2) At the end of such three-month period, if after written notice to the individual, the district attorney is requested to do so by the individual on whose behalf the enforcement efforts will be made, continue to enforce such support payments from the noncustodial parent.

The district attorney shall, where appropriate, utilize reciprocal arrangements adopted with other states in securing support from an absent parent for any child. In individual cases where utilization of reciprocal arrangements has proven ineffective, the district attorney may forward to the Attorney General a request to utilize federal courts in order to obtain or enforce orders for child support. If reasonable efforts to collect amounts assigned pursuant to Welfare and Institutions Code Section 11477 have failed, the district attorney may forward a certified copy of such court order to the Attorney General with a request that the case be forwarded to the Treasury Department for collection. The Attorney General, where appropriate shall forward such requests to the Secretary of Health, Education, and Welfare, or his designated representative.
(Amended by Stats.1976, c. 1034, p. —, § 2.)

§ 11480. Receipt or use of aid for purpose other than support

Any person other than a needy child, who willfully and knowingly receives or uses any part of an aid grant paid pursuant to this chapter for a purpose other than support of the needy children and the caretaker involved, is guilty of a misdemeanor.
(Added by Stats.1965, c. 1784, p. 4018, § 5.)

§ 11482. False representation to obtain aid; unlawfully receiving or attempting to receive aid

Any person other than a needy child, who willfully and knowingly, with the intent to deceive, makes a false statement or representation or knowingly fails to disclose a material fact to obtain aid, or who, knowing he is not entitled thereto, attempts to obtain aid or to continue to receive aid to which he is not entitled, or a larger amount than that to which he is legally entitled, is guilty of a misdemeanor.
(Added by Stats.1965, c. 1784, p. 4018, § 5.)

§ 12850. Repealed by Stats.1974, c. 75, p. 170, § 12

§ 14026. Furnishing, giving or lending Medi-Cal card or labels to unauthorized person; misrepresentation as Medi-Cal beneficiary; penalty

It is a misdemeanor for a Medi-Cal beneficiary to furnish, give or lend his Medi-Cal card or labels to any person other than a provider of service as required under Medi-Cal regulations.

It is a misdemeanor for any person who knows he is not eligible for Medi-Cal benefits to represent himself to any health care provider as a Medi-Cal beneficiary.
(Added by Stats.1972, c. 1043, p. 1921, § 1.)

§ 18910. Violations

Whoever knowingly uses, transfers, acquires, or possesses food stamps or authorizations to purchase food stamps in any manner not authorized by this chapter or by the Food Stamp Act of 1964 (Public Law 88–525 and all amendments made thereto) is guilty of a misdemeanor if the face value of the food stamps or the authorizations to purchase food stamps is two hundred dollars ($200) or less; or exceeds his cost, if any, to purchase them by two hundred dollars ($200) or less; or is guilty of a felony if the face value of the food stamps or the authorizations to purchase food stamps exceeds by more than two hundred dollars ($200) his cost, if any, to purchase them.

Whoever knowingly uses, transfers, acquires, or possesses blank authorizations to purchase food stamps in any manner not authorized by this chapter with the intent to defraud is guilty of a felony.

Whoever counterfeits or alters or knowingly uses, transfers, acquires, or possesses counterfeited or altered authorizations to purchase food stamps or food stamps in any manner not authorized by the Food Stamp Act of 1964 (Public Law 88–525 and all amendments made thereto) or the federal regulations pursuant to the act is guilty of forgery.

Whoever fraudulently appropriates food stamps or authorizations to purchase food stamps with which he has been entrusted pursuant to his duties as a public employee is guilty of embezzlement of public funds.

In no event shall separate offenses, which by themselves would be punishable as misdemeanors, be accumulated for prosecution as a felony.
(Amended by Stats.1974, c. 75, p. 171, § 15.)

Division 10
STATE DEPARTMENT OF REHABILITATION

Division 11
OFFICE OF ALCOHOLISM

Division 20
REPEALS

EVIDENCE CODE

The Evidence Code is a combination dictionary and rule book containing definitions of special words and rules controlling the admissibility of evidence. In few, if any, areas of the law is there as great a need for immediate and accurate information as there is in the law of evidence. Questions involving the admissibility of evidence are important and are frequently related to behavior of police officers at the scene of a criminal incident. Knowledge of the rules of evidence becomes a vital link in moving a criminal investigation from a general inquiry of an unsolved crime, to the fixing of criminal responsibility beyond a reasonable doubt. Characteristic of any attempt to develop a set of rules covering all circumstances, the Evidence Code not only sets general rules, but then follows those rules with qualified exceptions. You will find the phrase, "except as otherwise provided by law" used in several sections of the Evidence Code. As a criminal justice agent you should be concerned with developing knowledge of both the general rule and the exceptions. California's Evidence Code was enacted in 1965. The current code was developed by the California Law Revision Commission after extensive review of the common law, statute law in other codes, court decisions, the Uniform Rules of Evidence and past practices.

§ 105 EVIDENCE CODE

Division	Section
1. PRELIMINARY PROVISIONS AND CONSTRUCTION	1
2. WORDS AND PHRASES DEFINED	100
3. GENERAL PROVISIONS	300
4. JUDICIAL NOTICE	450
5. BURDEN OF PROOF; BURDEN OF PRODUCING EVIDENCE; PRESUMPTIONS AND INFERENCES	500
6. WITNESSES	700
7. OPINION TESTIMONY AND SCIENTIFIC EVIDENCE	800
8. PRIVILEGES	900
9. EVIDENCE AFFECTED OR EXCLUDED BY EXTRINSIC POLICIES	1100
10. HEARSAY EVIDENCE	1200
11. WRITINGS	1400

Division 1
PRELIMINARY PROVISIONS AND CONSTRUCTION

Division 2
WORDS AND PHRASES DEFINED

Editors' Note

The words and phrases defined in this Division are very important to an understanding of other portions of the Evidence Code.

§ 105. "Action"

"Action" includes a civil action and a criminal action.
(Stats.1965, c. 299, § 105.)

§ 110. "Burden of producing evidence"

"Burden of producing evidence" means the obligation of a party to introduce evidence sufficient to avoid a ruling against him on the issue.
(Stats.1965, c. 299, § 110.)

§ 115. "Burden of proof"

"Burden of proof" means the obligation of a party to establish by evidence a requisite degree of belief concerning a fact in the mind of the trier of fact or the court. The burden of proof may require a party to raise a reasonable doubt concerning the existence or nonexistence of a fact or that he establish the existence or nonexistence of a fact by a preponderance of the evidence, by clear and convincing proof, or by proof beyond a reasonable doubt.

Except as otherwise provided by law, the burden of proof requires proof by a preponderance of the evidence.
(Stats.1965, c. 299, § 115.)

§ 130. "Criminal action"

"Criminal action" includes criminal proceedings.
(Stats.1965, c. 299, § 130.)

§ 135. "Declarant"

"Declarant" is a person who makes a statement.
(Stats.1965, c. 299, § 135.)

§ 140. "Evidence"

"Evidence" means testimony, writings, material objects, or other things presented to the senses that are offered to prove the existence or nonexistence of a fact.
(Stats.1965, c. 299, § 140.)

§ 145. "The hearing"

"The hearing" means the hearing at which a question under this code arises, and not some earlier or later hearing.
(Stats.1965, c. 299, § 145.)

§ 150. "Hearsay evidence"

"Hearsay evidence" is defined in Section 1200.
(Stats.1965, c. 299, § 150.)

§ 160. "Law"

"Law" includes constitutional, statutory, and decisional law.
(Stats.1965, c. 299, § 160.)

§ 165. "Oath"

"Oath" includes affirmation or declaration under penalty of perjury.
(Stats.1965, c. 299, § 165.)

§ 170. "Perceive"

"Perceive" means to acquire knowledge through one's senses.
(Stats.1965, c. 299, § 170.)

§ 175. "Person"

"Person" includes a natural person, firm, association, organization, partnership, business trust, corporation, or public entity.
(Stats.1965, c. 299, § 175.)

§ 180. "Personal property"

"Personal property" includes money, goods, chattels, things in action, and evidences of debt.
(Stats.1965, c. 299, § 180.)

§ 185. "Property"

"Property" includes both real and personal property.
(Stats.1965, c. 299, § 185.)

§ 190. "Proof"

"Proof" is the establishment by evidence of a requisite degree of belief concerning a fact in the mind of the trier of fact or the court.
(Stats.1965, c. 299, § 190.)

§ 195. "Public employee"

"Public employee" means an officer, agent, or employee of a public entity.
(Stats.1965, c. 299, § 195.)

§ 200. "Public entity"

"Public entity" includes a nation, state, county, city and county, city, district, public authority, public agency, or any other political subdivision or public corporation, whether foreign or domestic.
(Stats.1965, c. 299, § 200.)

§ 205. "Real property"

"Real property" includes lands, tenements, and hereditaments.
(Stats.1965, c. 299, § 205.)

§ 210. "Relevant evidence"

"Relevant evidence" means evidence, including evidence relevant to the credibility of a witness or hearsay declarant, having any tendency in reason to prove or disprove any disputed fact that is of consequence to the determination of the action.
(Stats.1965, c. 299, § 210.)

§ 220. "State"

"State" means the State of California, unless applied to the different parts of the United States. In the latter case, it includes any state, district, commonwealth, territory, or insular possession of the United States.
(Stats.1965, c. 299, § 220.)

§ 225. "Statement"

"Statement" means (a) oral or written verbal expression or (b) nonverbal conduct of a person intended by him as a substitute for oral or written verbal expression.
(Stats.1965, c. 299, § 225.)

§ 230. "Statute"

"Statute" includes a treaty and a constitutional provision.
(Stats.1965, c. 299, § 230.)

§ 235. "Trier of fact"

"Trier of fact" includes (a) the jury and (b) the court when the court is trying an issue of fact other than one relating to the admissibility of evidence.
(Stats.1965, c. 299, § 235.)

§ 240. "Unavailable as a witness"

(a) Except as otherwise provided in subdivision (b), "unavailable as a witness" means that the declarant is:

(1) Exempted or precluded on the ground of privilege from testifying concerning the matter to which his statement is relevant;

(2) Disqualified from testifying to the matter;

(3) Dead or unable to attend or to testify at the hearing because of then existing physical or mental illness or infirmity;

(4) Absent from the hearing and the court is unable to compel his attendance by its process; or

(5) Absent from the hearing and the proponent of his statement has exercised reasonable diligence but has been unable to procure his attendance by the court's process.

(b) A declarant is not unavailable as a witness if the exemption, preclusion, disqualification, death, inability, or absence of the declarant was brought about by the procurement or wrongdoing of the proponent of his statement for the purpose of preventing the declarant from attending or testifying.
(Stats.1965, c. 299, § 240.)

§ 250. "Writing"

"Writing" means handwriting, typewriting, printing, photostating, photographing, and every other

§ 250

means of recording upon any tangible thing any form of communication or representation, including letters, words, pictures, sounds, or symbols, or combinations thereof.

(Stats.1965, c. 299, § 250.)

Division 3

GENERAL PROVISIONS

§ 300. Applicability of code

Except as otherwise provided by statute, this code applies in every action before the Supreme Court or a court of appeal, superior court, municipal court, or justice court, including proceedings in such actions conducted by a referee, court commissioner, or similar officer, but does not apply in grand jury proceedings.

(As amended Stats.1967, c. 17, p. 836, § 35.)

§ 310. Questions of law for court

(a) All questions of law (including but not limited to questions concerning the construction of statutes and other writings, the admissibility of evidence, and other rules of evidence) are to be decided by the court. Determination of issues of fact preliminary to the admission of evidence are to be decided by the court as provided in Article 2 (commencing with Section 400) of Chapter 4.

(b) Determination of the law of an organization of nations or of the law of a foreign nation or a public entity in a foreign nation is a question of law to be determined in the manner provided in Division 4 (commencing with Section 450).

(Stats.1965, c. 299, § 310.)

Editors' Note

Trial courts (judges) have considerable discretion in matters of evidence. Examples of this discretion include:
1. Determination of the competency of witnesses to testify
2. Qualifying expert witnesses
3. Ruling upon the use of hypothetical questions
4. Interpreting "reasonableness"
5. Determining relevance of evidence
6. Determining voluntariness of confessions
7. Ruling on the admission or exclusion of evidence
8. Determining the order of proof.

§ 311. Procedure when foreign or sister-state law cannot be determined

If the law of an organization of nations, a foreign nation or a state other than this state, or a public entity in a foreign nation or a state other than this state, is applicable and such law cannot be determined, the court may, as the ends of justice require, either:

(a) Apply the law of this state if the court can do so consistently with the Constitution of the United States and the Constitution of this state; or

(b) Dismiss the action without prejudice or, in the case of a reviewing court, remand the case to the trial court with directions to dismiss the action without prejudice.

(Stats.1965, c. 299, § 311.)

§ 312. Jury as trier of fact

Except as otherwise provided by law, where the trial is by jury:

(a) All questions of fact are to be decided by the jury.

(b) Subject to the control of the court, the jury is to determine the effect and value of the evidence addressed to it, including the credibility of witnesses and hearsay declarants.

(Stats.1965, c. 299, § 312.)

Editors' Note

This section places the fact finding responsibility in a jury trial upon the jury. Case law has consistently held that it is the jury's task to resolve the facts of a case even in the face of substantial conflicts in evidence presented by each party in the action.

§ 320. Power of court to regulate order of proof

Except as otherwise provided by law, the court in its discretion shall regulate the order of proof.

(Stats.1965, c. 299, § 320.)

§ 350. Only relevant evidence admissible

No evidence is admissible except relevant evidence.

(Stats.1965, c. 299, § 350.)

Notes of Decisions

In general

General rule in criminal cases is that evidence tending logically, naturally and by reasonable inference to establish any fact material for prosecution or to overcome any material matter sought to be proved by defense is admissible on behalf of prosecution, and that weight of such evidence is for jury no matter how weak it may be, if it tends to prove issue before the jury. People v. Slocum (1975) 125 Cal.Rptr. 442, 52 C.A.3d 867, certiorari denied 96 S.Ct. 2635.

§ 351. Admissibility of relevant evidence

Except as otherwise provided by statute, all relevant evidence is admissible.
(Stats.1965, c. 299, § 351.)

Editors' Note

Case law has developed in a variety of areas testing the relevancy of certain types of evidence. Cases have supported the use of clothing, blood stains, weapons, shells and bullets, diagrams, maps, charts, experiments, fingerprints, footprints, human organ specimens, chemical tests and analysis results, stolen property, masks, instruments of crime, models, photographs, sound and visual recordings and writings, as relevant evidence in appropriate cases.

The "except as otherwise provided by statute" provision of this section allows for exclusion of some evidence which may be relevant yet is still inadmissible as a result of some other statutory law. Hearsay evidence (see Evidence Code § 1200) and certain privileged communications (see Evidence Code § 900) are examples of statutes causing the exclusion of evidence. Evidence obtained by police search and seizure may be excluded according to the provisions of Penal Code § 1538.5.

Other causes for statutory exclusion are covered in Evidence Code § 352.

In addition to statutory exclusions, California case law has created an "exclusionary rule" to prevent admissibility of evidence obtained in violation of the State Constitution (See People v. Cahan, 44 C.2d 434). Several other cases have denied admissibility to (1) lie detector tests (2) truth serum tests.

Notes of Decisions

Lie detector tests have no place in California law. Gideon v. Gideon (1957) 314 P.2d 1011, 153 C.A.2d 541.

Results of lie detector tests are not admissible in evidence in a criminal prosecution. People v. Porter (1955) 288 P.2d 561, 136 C.A.2d 461.

The results of a test made under truth serum is not admissible in a criminal case. People v. Jones (1959) 343 P.2d 577, 52 C.2d 636, certiorari denied 80 S.Ct. 364, 361 U.S. 926, 4 L.Ed.2d 350.

§ 352. Discretion of court to exclude evidence

The court in its discretion may exclude evidence if its probative value is substantially outweighed by the probability that its admission will (a) necessitate undue consumption of time or (b) create substantial danger of undue prejudice, of confusing the issues, or of misleading the jury.
(Stats.1965, c. 299, § 352.)

Editors' Note

Read People v. Beagle in table of cases included in this text. In addition to statutory and case limitations on the admissibility of evidence, this section grants judicial discretion to exclude some evidence.

Notes of Decisions
In general

In prosecution of alleged leader of communal "family" and three of his alleged followers for conspiracy and murder, testimony that there was "X" on asserted leader's forehead and, on following day, "X's" were observed on foreheads of other three defendants was admissible to show affinity between defendants as well as asserted leadership. People v. Manson (1976) 132 Cal.Rptr. 265, 61 C.A.3d 102.

It is exclusive province of trial court in criminal cases to determine whether probative value of proffered evidence outweighs its possible prejudicial effect. People v. Demond (1976) 130 Cal.Rptr. 590, 59 C.A.3d 574.

Editors' Note

Evidence consuming undue amounts of time would include cumulative evidence.

Notes of Decisions
Cumulative evidence

In prosecution for conspiracy and murder, trial court's refusal to authorize jury view of scene of crimes was not error, in view of presence of diagrams and photographic evidence adequately depicting the scenes. People v. Manson (1976) 132 Cal.Rptr. 265, 61 C.A.3d 102.

Trial court has discretion to refuse to admit cumulative evidence. Horn v. General Motors Corp. (1976) 131 Cal.Rptr. 78.

Editors' Note

The issue of undue prejudice is frequently raised in criminal cases in relation to the admissibility of gruesome photographs.

Notes of Decisions
Photographs

Repugnant photographs of scene of crime may not be introduced in evidence where their sole purpose is to inflame jury against accused, but such pictures are admissible if they have some evidentiary value; the matter being one for sound discretion of trial court. People v. Schiers (1958) 324 P.2d 981, 160 C.A.2d 364, hearing denied 329 P.2d 1, 160 C.A.2d 364.

It is error to receive in evidence photographs of a homicide victim designed primarily to arouse the passions of jury, but such photographs are admissible when relevant to issues before court and their probative value is not outweighed by danger of prejudice to defendant. People v. Cheary (1957) 309 P.2d 431, 48 C.2d 301.

Photographs should not be offered or admitted in evidence in the criminal trial for any purpose other than that of helping the jury. People v. Logan (1953) 260 P.2d 20, 41 C.2d 279.

Admission of photographs of homicide victim is within sound discretion of trial court. People v. Burns (1952) 241 P.2d 308, 109 C.A.2d 524, hearing denied 242 P.2d 9, 109 C.A.2d 524.

In homicide prosecution, trial judge abused his discretion in admitting in evidence photographs of victim, taken after autopsy, where it was obvious that only purpose of exhibiting such photographs was to inflame jury's emotions against defendant. Id.

In prosecution for murder, admission of two photographs to which objection was made was abuse of discretion where, in light of many other photographs of deceased victim, probative value of such photographs, which were gruesome, revolting and shocking to ordinary sensibilities, was substantially outweighed by danger of undue prejudice to defendant. People v. Gibson (1976) 128 Cal.Rptr. 302, 56 C.A.3d 119.

Where photographs and motion picture of grave sites and exhumation of bodies were in part gory but were not cumulative as evidence and permitting prosecution to show that bodies sustained no damage in recovery process, such evidence was admissible in murder prosecution. People v. Moran (1974) 114 Cal.Rptr. 413, 39 C.A.3d 398.

Admission of photographs which depicted portions of body of deceased, which were relevant on issue of manner in which decedent met her death and which were utilized by medical expert in explaining his findings to the jury was not an abuse of discretion. People v. Parks (1973) 108 Cal.Rptr. 34, 32 C.A.3d 143.

Admitting into evidence, in murder prosecution, three color photographs of decedent was not improper, where the photographs aided the jury in reconstructing the physical surroundings of the crime as well as the manner in which the victim's wounds were inflicted, and where defendant made no specific showing that the photographs were so duplicative or inflammatory that their admission into evidence constituted an abuse of court's discretion. People v. Hathcock (1973) 105 Cal.Rptr. 540, 504 P.2d 476, 8 C.3d 599.

Admission of photographs of victim lies solely within discretion of trial judge and his ruling will not be reversed unless their probative value is clearly outweighed by their prejudicial effect. People v. Murphy (1972) 105 Cal.Rptr. 138, 503 P.2d 594, 8 C.3d 349, certiorari denied 94 S.Ct. 173, 414 U.S. 833, 38 L.Ed.2d 68.

§ 353. Effect of erroneous admission of evidence

A verdict or finding shall not be set aside, nor shall the judgment or decision based thereon be reversed, by reason of the erroneous admission of evidence unless:

(a) There appears of record an objection to or a motion to exclude or to strike the evidence that was timely made and so stated as to make clear the specific ground of the objection or motion; and

(b) The court which passes upon the effect of the error or errors is of the opinion that the admitted evidence should have been excluded on the ground stated and that the error or errors complained of resulted in a miscarriage of justice.
(Stats.1965, c. 299, § 353.)

§ 354. Effect of erroneous exclusion of evidence

A verdict or finding shall not be set aside, nor shall the judgment or decision based thereon be reversed, by reason of the erroneous exclusion of evidence unless the court which passes upon the effect of the error or errors is of the opinion that the error or errors complained of resulted in a miscarriage of justice and it appears of record that:

(a) The substance, purpose, and relevance of the excluded evidence was made known to the court by the questions asked, an offer of proof, or by any other means;

(b) The rulings of the court made compliance with subdivision (a) futile; or

(c) The evidence was sought by questions asked during cross-examination or recross-examination.
(Stats.1965, c. 299, § 354.)

§ 355. Limited admissibility

When evidence is admissible as to one party or for one purpose and is inadmissible as to another party or for another purpose, the court upon request shall restrict the evidence to its proper scope and instruct the jury accordingly.
(Stats.1965, c. 299, § 355.)

§ 356. Entire act, declaration, conversation, or writing may be brought out to elucidate part offered

Where part of an act, declaration, conversation, or writing is given in evidence by one party, the whole on the same subject may be inquired into by an adverse party; when a letter is read, the answer may be given; and when a detached act, declaration, conversation, or writing is given in evidence, any other act, declaration, conversation, or writing which is necessary to make it understood may also be given in evidence.
(Stats.1965, c. 299, § 356.)

§ 400. "Preliminary fact"

As used in this article, "preliminary fact" means a fact upon the existence or nonexistence of which depends the admissibility or inadmissibility of evidence. The phrase "the admissibility or inadmissibility of evidence" includes the qualification or disqualification of a person to be a witness and the existence or nonexistence of a privilege.
(Stats.1965, c. 299, § 400.)

§ 401. "Proffered evidence"

As used in this article, "proffered evidence" means evidence, the admissibility or inadmissibility of which is dependent upon the existence or nonexistence of a preliminary fact.
(Stats.1965, c. 299, § 401.)

§ 402. Procedure for determining foundational and other preliminary facts

(a) When the existence of a preliminary fact is disputed, its existence or nonexistence shall be determined as provided in this article.

(b) The court may hear and determine the question of the admissibility of evidence out of the presence or hearing of the jury; but in a criminal action, the court shall hear and determine the question of the admissibility of a confession or admission of the defendant out of the presence and hearing of the jury if any party so requests.

(c) A ruling on the admissibility of evidence implies whatever finding of fact is prerequisite thereto; a separate or formal finding is unnecessary unless required by statute.
(Stats.1965, c. 299, § 402.)

§ 403. Determination of foundational and other preliminary facts where relevancy, personal knowledge, or authenticity is disputed

(a) The proponent of the proffered evidence has the burden of producing evidence as to the existence of the preliminary fact, and the proffered evidence is inadmissible unless the court finds that there is evidence sufficient to sustain a finding of the existence of the preliminary fact, when:

(1) The relevance of the proffered evidence depends on the existence of the preliminary fact;

(2) The preliminary fact is the personal knowledge of a witness concerning the subject matter of his testimony;

(3) The preliminary fact is the authenticity of a writing; or

(4) The proffered evidence is of a statement or other conduct of a particular person and the preliminary fact is whether that person made the statement or so conducted himself.

(b) Subject to Section 702, the court may admit conditionally the proffered evidence under this section, subject to evidence of the preliminary fact being supplied later in the course of the trial.

(c) If the court admits the proffered evidence under this section, the court:

(1) May, and on request shall, instruct the jury to determine whether the preliminary fact exists and to disregard the proffered evidence unless the jury finds that the preliminary fact does exist.

(2) Shall instruct the jury to disregard the proffered evidence if the court subsequently determines that a jury could not reasonably find that the preliminary fact exists.
(Stats.1965, c. 299, § 403.)

§ 404. Determination of whether proffered evidence is incriminatory

Whenever the proffered evidence is claimed to be privileged under Section 940, the person claiming the privilege has the burden of showing that the proffered evidence might tend to incriminate him; and the proffered evidence is inadmissible unless it clearly appears to the court that the proffered evidence cannot possibly have a tendency to incriminate the person claiming the privilege.
(Stats.1965, c. 299, § 404.)

§ 406. Evidence affecting weight or credibility

This article does not limit the right of a party to introduce before the trier of fact evidence relevant to weight or credibility.
(Stats.1965, c. 299, § 406.)

§ 410. "Direct evidence"

As used in this chapter, "direct evidence" means evidence that directly proves a fact, without an inference or presumption, and which in itself, if true, conclusively establishes that fact.
(Stats.1965, c. 299, § 410.)

§ 411. Direct evidence of one witness sufficient

Except where additional evidence is required by statute, the direct evidence of one witness who is entitled to full credit is sufficient for proof of any fact.
(Stats.1965, c. 299, § 411.)

§ 412. Party having power to produce better evidence

If weaker and less satisfactory evidence is offered when it was within the power of the party to produce stronger and more satisfactory evidence, the evidence offered should be viewed with distrust.
(Stats.1965, c. 299, § 412.)

§ 413. Party's failure to explain or deny evidence

In determining what inferences to draw from the evidence or facts in the case against a party, the trier of fact may consider, among other things, the party's failure to explain or to deny by his testimony such evidence or facts in the case against him, or his willful suppression of evidence relating thereto, if such be the case.
(Stats.1965, c. 299, § 413.)

Division 4
JUDICIAL NOTICE

§ 450. Judicial notice may be taken only as authorized by law

Judicial notice may not be taken of any matter unless authorized or required by law.
(Stats.1965, c. 299, § 450.)

Notes of Decisions

Effect of judicial notice

Judicial notice is a kind of evidence and may be relied upon to contradict other evidence and to support findings of fact and a judgment based thereon. Mack v. State Bd. of Ed. (1964) 36 Cal.Rptr. 677, 224 C.A.2d 370; Del Bosque v. Kakoo Singh (1937) 65 P.2d 951, 19 C.A.2d 487.

The doctrine of "judicial notice" was adopted as a judicial shortcut to avoid necessity for the formal introduction of evidence in certain cases where there is no real need for such evidence. Communist Party of U. S. of America v. Peek (1942) 127 P.2d 889, 20 C.2d 536; Varcoe v. Lee (1919) 181 P. 223, 180 C. 338.

§ 451. Matters which must be judicially noticed

Judicial notice shall be taken of:

(a) The decisional, constitutional, and public statutory law of this state and of the United States and the provisions of any charter described in Section 3, 4, or 5 of Article XI of the California Constitution.

(b) Any matter made a subject of judicial notice by Section 11383, 11384, or 18576 of the Government Code or by Section 1507 of Title 44 of the United States Code.

(c) Rules of professional conduct for members of the bar adopted pursuant to Section 6076 of the Business and Professions Code and rules of practice and procedure for the courts of this state adopted by the Judicial Council.

(d) Rules of pleading, practice, and procedure prescribed by the United States Supreme Court, such as the Rules of the United States Supreme Court, the Federal Rules of Civil Procedure, the Federal Rules of Criminal Procedure, the Admiralty Rules, the Rules of the Court of Claims, the Rules of the Customs Court, and the General Orders and Forms in Bankruptcy.

(e) The true signification of all English words and phrases and of all legal expressions.

(f) Facts and propositions of generalized knowledge that are so universally known that they cannot reasonably be the subject of dispute.
(Amended by Stats.1972, c. 764, p. 1373, § 1.)

Comment—Assembly Committee on Judiciary

Judicial notice of the matters specified in Section 451 is *mandatory*, whether or not the court is requested to notice them. Although the court errs if it fails to take judicial notice of the matters specified in this section, such error is not necessarily reversible error. Depending upon the circumstances, the appellate court may hold that the error was "invited" (and, hence, is not reversible error) or that points not urged in the trial court may not be advanced on appeal. These and similar principles of appellate practice are not abrogated by this section.

Section 451 includes matters both of law and of fact. The matters specified in subdivisions (a), (b), (c), and (d) are all matters that, broadly speaking, can be considered as a part of the "law" applicable to the particular case. The court can reasonably be expected to discover and apply this law even if the parties fail to provide the court with references to the pertinent cases, statutes, regulations and rules. Other matters that also might properly be considered as a part of the law applicable to the case (such as the law of foreign nations and certain regulations and ordinances) are included under Section 452, rather than under Section 451, primarily because of the difficulty of ascertaining such matters. Subdivision (e) of Section 451 requires the court to judicially notice "the true signification of all English words and phrases and of all legal expressions." These are facts that must be judicially noticed in order to conduct meaningful proceedings. Similarly, subdivision (f) of Section 451 covers "universally known" facts.

Listed below are the matters that must be judicially noticed under Section 451.

California and federal law. The decisional, constitutional, and public statutory law of California and of the United States must be judicially noticed under subdivision (a). This requirement states existing law as found in subdivision 3 of Code of Civil Procedure Section 1875 (superseded by the Evidence Code).

Charter provisions of California cities and counties. Judicial notice must be taken under subdivision (a) of the provisions of charters adopted pursuant to Section 7½ or 8 of Article XI of the California Constitution. Notice of these provisions is mandatory under the State Constitution. Cal.Const., Art. XI, § 7½ (county charter), § 8 (charter of city or city and county).

Regulations of California and federal agencies. Judicial notice must be taken under subdivision (b) of the rules, regulations, orders, and standards of general application adopted by California state agencies and filed with the Secretary of State or printed in the California Administrative Code or the California Administrative Register. This is existing law as found in Government Code Sections 11383 and 11384. Under subdivision (b), judicial notice must also be taken of the rules of the State Personnel Board. This, too, is existing law under Government Code Section 18576.

Subdivision (b) also requires California courts to judicially notice documents published in the Federal Register (such as (1) presidential proclamations and executive orders having general applicability and legal effect and (2) orders, regulations, rules, certificates, codes of fair competition, licenses, notices, and similar instruments, having general applicability and legal effect, that are issued, prescribed, or promulgated by federal agencies). There is no clear holding that this is existing California law. Although Section 307 of Title 44 of the United States Code provides that the "contents of the Federal Register shall be judicially noticed," it is not clear that this *requires* notice by state courts. See Broadway Fed. etc. Loan Ass'n v. Howard, 133 Cal.App.2d 382, 386 note 4, 285 P.2d 61, 64 note 4 (1955) (referring to 44 U.S.C.A. §§ 301–314). *Compare* Note, 59 Harv.L. Rev. 1137, 1141 (1946) (doubt expressed that notice is required), *with*

Knowlton, *Judicial Notice*, 10 Rutgers L.Rev. 501, 504 (1956) ("it would seem that this provision is binding upon the state courts"). Livermore v. Beal, 18 Cal.App.2d 535, 542–543, 64 P.2d 987, 992 (1937), suggests that California courts are required to judicially notice pertinent federal official action, and California courts have judicially noticed the contents of various proclamations, orders, and regulations of federal agencies. *E. g.,* Pacific Solvents Co. v. Superior Court, 88 Cal.App.2d 953, 955, 199 P.2d 740, 741 (1948) (orders and regulations); People v. Mason, 72 Cal.App.2d 699, 706–707, 165 P.2d 481, 485 (1946) (presidential and executive proclamations) (disapproved on other grounds in People v. Friend, 50 Cal.2d 570, 578, 327 P.2d 97, 102 (1958)); Downer v. Grizzly Livestock & Land Co., 6 Cal.App.2d 39, 42, 43 P.2d 843, 845 (1935) (rules and regulations). Section 451 makes the California law clear.

Rules of court. Judicial notice of the California Rules of Court is required under subdivision (c). These rules, adopted by the Judicial Council, are as binding on the parties as procedural statutes. Cantillon v. Superior Court, 150 Cal.App.2d 184, 309 P.2d 890 (1957). See Albermont Petroleum, Ltd. v. Cunningham, 186 Cal.App.2d 84, 9 Cal.Rptr. 405 (1960). Likewise, the rules of pleading, practice, and procedure promulgated by the United States Supreme Court are required to be judicially noticed under subdivision (d).

The rules of the California and federal courts which are required to be judicially noticed under subdivisions (c) and (d) are, or should be, familiar to the court or easily discoverable from materials readily available to the court. However, this may not be true of the court rules of sister states or other jurisdictions nor, for example, of the rules of the various United States Courts of Appeals or local rules of a particular superior court. See Albermont Petroleum, Ltd. v. Cunningham, 186 Cal.App.2d 84, 9 Cal.Rptr. 405 (1960). Judicial notice of these rules is permitted under subdivision (e) of Section 452 but is not required unless there is compliance with the provisions of Section 453.

State Bar Rules of Professional Conduct. The Rules of Professional Conduct of the State Bar of California are, in effect, rules of the Supreme Court, for they must be approved by that court. Barton v. State Bar, 209 Cal. 677, 289 P. 818 (1930). Subdivision (e), therefore, requires the court to take judicial notice of these rules to the same extent that it takes notice of other rules of court.

Words, phrases, and legal expressions. Subdivision (e) requires the court to take judicial notice of "the true signification of all English words and phrases and of all legal expressions." This restates the same matter covered in subdivision 1 of Code of Civil Procedure Section 1875. Under existing law, however, it is not clear that judicial notice of these matters is mandatory.

"Universally known" facts. Subdivision (f) requires the court to take judicial notice of indisputable facts and propositions universally known. "Universally known" does not mean that every man on the street has knowledge of such facts. A fact known among persons of reasonable and average intelligence and knowledge will satisfy the "universally known" requirement. *Cf.* People v. Tossetti, 107 Cal.App. 7, 12, 289 P. 881, 883 (1930).

Subdivision (f) should be contrasted with subdivisions (g) and (h) of Section 452, which provide for judicial notice of indisputable facts and propositions that are matters of common knowledge or are capable of immediate and accurate determination by resort to sources of reasonably indisputable accuracy. Subdivisions (g) and (h) permit notice of facts and propositions that are indisputable but are not "universally" known.

Judicial notice does not apply to facts merely because they are known to the judge to be indisputable. The facts must fulfill the requirements of subdivision (f) of Section 451 or subdivision (g) or (h) of Section 452. If a judge happens to know a fact that is not widely enough known to be subject to judicial notice under this division, he may not "notice" it.

It is clear under existing law that the court may judicially notice the matters specified in subdivision (f); it is doubtful, however, that the court *must* notice them. See Varcoe v. Lee, 180 Cal. 338, 347, 181 P. 223, 227 (1919) (dictum). Since subdivision (f) covers universally known facts, the parties ordinarily will expect the court to take judicial notice of them; the court should not be permitted to ignore such facts merely because the parties fail to make a formal request for judicial notice.

§ 452. Matters which may be judicially noticed

Judicial notice may be taken of the following matters to the extent that they are not embraced within Section 451:

(a) The decisional, constitutional, and statutory law of any state of the United States and the resolutions and private acts of the Congress of the United States and of the Legislature of this state.

(b) Regulations and legislative enactments issued by or under the authority of the United States or any public entity in the United States.

(c) Official acts of the legislative, executive, and judicial departments of the United States and of any state of the United States.

(d) Records of (1) any court of this state or (2) any court of record of the United States or of any state of the United States.

(e) Rules of court of (1) any court of this state or (2) any court of record of the United States or of any state of the United States.

(f) The law of an organization of nations and of foreign nations and public entities in foreign nations.

(g) Facts and propositions that are of such common knowledge within the territorial jurisdiction of the court that they cannot reasonably be the subject of dispute.

(h) Facts and propositions that are not reasonably subject to dispute and are capable of immediate and accurate determination by resort to sources of reasonably indisputable accuracy.
(Stats.1965, c. 299, § 452.)

Comment—Assembly Committee on Judiciary

Section 452 includes matters both of law and of fact. The court *may* take judicial notice of these matters, even when not requested to do so; it is *required* to notice them if a party requests it and satisfies the requirements of Section 453.

The matters of law included under Section 452 may be neither known to the court nor easily discoverable by it because the sources of information are not readily available. However, if a party requests it and furnishes the court with "sufficient information" for it to take judicial notice, the court must do so if proper notice has been given to each adverse party. See Evidence Code § 453. Thus, judicial notice of these matters of law is mandatory only if counsel adequately discharges his responsibility for informing the court as to the law applicable to the case. The simplified process of judicial notice can then be applied to all of the law applicable to the case, including such law as ordinances and the law of foreign nations.

Although Section 452 extends the process of judicial notice to some matters of law which the courts do not judicially notice under existing law, the wider scope of such notice is balanced by the assurance that the matter need not be judicially noticed unless adequate information to support its truth is furnished to the court. Under Section 453, this burden falls upon the party requesting that judicial notice be taken. In addition, the parties are entitled under Section 455 to a reasonable opportunity to present information to the court as to the propriety of taking judicial notice and as to the tenor of the matter to be noticed.

Listed below are the matters that may be judicially noticed under Section 452 (and must be noticed if the conditions specified in Section 453 are met).

Law of sister states. Subdivision (a) provides for judicial notice of the decisional, constitutional, and statutory law in force in sister states. California courts now take judicial notice of the law of sister states under subdivision 3 of Section 1875 of the Code of Civil Procedure. However, Section 1875 seems to preclude notice of sister-state law as interpreted by the intermediate-appellate courts of sister states, whereas Section 452 permits notice of relevant decisions of *all* sister-state courts. If this be an extension of existing law, it is a desirable one, for the courts of sister states generally can be considered as responsive to the need for properly determining the law as are equivalent courts in California. The existing law also is not clear as to whether a request for judicial notice of sister-state law is required and whether judicial notice is mandatory. On the necessity for a request for judicial notice, see Comment, 24 Cal.L. Rev. 311, 316 (1936). On whether judicial notice is mandatory, see In re Bartges, 44 Cal.2d 241, 282 P.2d 47 (1955), and the opinion of the Supreme Court in denying a hearing in Estate of Moore, 7 Cal. App.2d 722, 726, 48 P.2d 28, 29 (1935).

Law of territories and possessions of the United States. Subdivision (a) also provides for judicial notice of the decisional, constitutional, and statutory law in force in the territories and possessions of the United States. See the broad definition of "state" in Evidence Code § 220. It is not clear under existing California law whether this law is treated as sister-state law or foreign law. See Witkin, California Evidence § 45 (1958).

Resolutions and private acts. Subdivision (a) provides for judicial notice of resolutions and private acts of the Congress of the United States and of the legislature of any state, territory, or possession of the United States. See the broad definition of "state" in Evidence Code § 220.

The California law on this matter is not clear. Our courts are authorized by subdivision 3 of Code of Civil Procedure Section 1875 to take judicial notice of private statutes of this State and the United States, and they probably would take judicial notice of resolutions of this State and the United States under the same subdivision. It is not clear whether such notice is compulsory. It may be that judicial notice of a private act pleaded in a criminal action pursuant to Penal Code Section 963 is mandatory, whereas judicial notice of the same private act may be discretionary when pleaded in a civil action pursuant to Section 459 of the Code of Civil Procedure.

Although no case in point has been found, California courts probably would not take judicial notice of a resolution or private act of a sister state or territory or possession of the United States. Although Section 1875 is not the exclusive list of the matters that will be judicially noticed, the courts did not take judicial notice of a private statute prior to the enactment of Section 1875. Ellis v. Eastman, 32 Cal. 447 (1867).

Regulations, ordinances, and similar legislative enactments. Subdivision (b) provides for judicial notice of regulations and legislative enactments, adopted by or under the authority of the United States or of any state, territory, or possession of the United States, including public entities therein. See the broad definition of "public entity" in Evidence Code § 200. The words "regulations and legislative enactments" include such matters as "ordinances" and other similar legislative enactments. Not all public entities legislate by ordinance.

This subdivision changes existing law. Under existing law, municipal courts take judicial notice of ordinances in force within their jurisdiction. People v. Cowles, 142 Cal.App.2d Supp. 865, 867, 298 P.2d 732, 733–734 (1956); People v. Crittenden, 93 Cal.App.2d Supp. 871, 877, 209 P.2d 161, 165 (1949). In addition, an ordinance pleaded in a criminal action pursuant to Penal Code Section 963 must be judicially noticed. On the other hand, neither the superior court nor a district court of appeal will take judicial notice in a civil action of municipal or county ordinances. Thompson v. Guyer-Hays, 207 Cal.App.2d 366, 24 Cal.Rptr. 461 (1962); County of Los Angeles v. Bartlett, 203 Cal.App.2d 523, 21 Cal.Rptr. 776 (1962); Becerra v. Hochberg, 193 Cal.App.2d 431, 14 Cal.Rptr. 101 (1961). It seems safe to assume that ordinances of sister states and of territories and possessions of the United States would not be judicially noticed under existing law.

Judicial notice of certain regulations of California and federal agencies is mandatory under subdivision (b) of Section 451. Subdivision (b) of Section 452 provides for judicial notice of California and federal regulations that are not included under subdivision (b) of Section 451 and, also, for judicial notice of regulations of other states and territories and possessions of the United States.

Both California and federal regulations have been judicially noticed under subdivision 3 of Code of Civil Procedure Section 1875. 18 Cal.Jur.2d Evidence § 24. Although no case in point has been found, it is unlikely that regulations of other states or of territories or possessions of the United States would be judicially noticed under existing law.

Official acts of the legislative, executive, and judicial departments. Subdivision (c) provides for judicial notice of the official acts of the legislative, executive, and judicial departments of the United States and any state, territory, or possession of the United States. See the broad definition of "state" in Evidence Code § 220. Subdivision (c) states existing law as found in subdivision 3 of Code of Civil Procedure Section 1875. Under this provision, the California courts have taken judicial notice of a wide variety of administrative and executive acts, such as proceedings and reports of the House Committee on Un-American Activities, records of the State Board of Education, and records of a county planning commission. See Witkin, California Evidence § 49 (1958), and 1963 Supplement thereto.

Court records and rules of court. Subdivisions (d) and (e) provide for judicial notice of the court records and rules of court of (1) any court of this State or (2) any court of record of the United States or of any state, territory, or possession of the United States. See the broad definition of "state" in Evidence Code § 220. So far as court records are concerned, subdivision (d) states existing law. Flores v. Arroyo, 56 Cal.2d 492, 15 Cal.Rptr. 87, 364 P.2d 263 (1961). While the provisions of subdivision (c) of Section 452 are broad enough to include court records, specific mention of these records in subdivision (d) is desirable in order to eliminate any uncertainty in the law on this point. See the Flores case, *supra.*

Subdivision (e) may change existing law so far as judicial notice of rules of court is concerned, but the provision is consistent with the modern philosophy of judicial notice as indicated by the holding in Flores v. Arroyo, *supra*. To the extent that subdivision (e) overlaps with subdivisions (c) and (d) of Section 451, notice is, of course, mandatory under Section 451.

Foreign law. Subdivision (f) provides for judicial notice of the law of organizations of nations, foreign nations, and public entities in foreign nations. See the broad definition of "public entity" in Evidence Code § 200. Subdivision (f) should be read in connection with Sections 310, 311, 453, and 454. These provisions retain the substance of the existing law which was enacted in 1957 upon recommendation of the California Law Revision Commission. Code Civ.Proc. § 1875. See 1 Cal.Law Revision Comm'n. Rep., Rec. & Studies, Recommendation and Study Relating to Judicial Notice of the Law of Foreign Countries at I–1 (1957).

Subdivision (f) refers to "the law" of organizations of nations, foreign nations, and public entities in foreign nations. This makes all law, in whatever form, subject to judicial notice.

Matters of "common knowledge" and verifiable facts. Subdivision (g) provides for judicial notice of matters of common knowledge within the court's territorial jurisdiction that are not subject to dispute. "Territorial jurisdiction," in this context, refers to the county in which a superior court is located or the judicial district in which a municipal or justice court is located. The fact of which notice is taken need not be something physically located within the court's territorial jurisdiction, but common knowledge of the fact must exist within the court's territorial jurisdiction. Subdivision (g) reflects existing case law. Varcoe v. Lee, 180 Cal. 338, 181 Pac. 223 (1919); 18 Cal.Jur.2d Evidence § 19 at 439–440. The California courts have taken judicial notice of a wide variety of matters of common knowledge. Witkin, California Evidence §§ 50–52 (1958).

Subdivision (h) provides for judicial notice of indisputable facts immediately ascertainable by reference to sources of reasonably indisputable accuracy. In other words, the facts need not be actually known if they are readily ascertainable and indisputable. Sources of "reasonably indisputable accuracy" include not only treatises, encyclopedias, almanacs, and the like, but also persons learned in the subject matter. This would not mean that reference works would be received in evidence or sent to the jury room. Their use would be limited to consultation by the judge and the parties for the purposes of determining whether or not to take judicial notice and determining the tenor of the matter to be noticed.

Subdivisions (g) and (h) include, for example, facts which are accepted as established by experts and specialists in the natural, physical, and social sciences, if those facts are of such wide acceptance that to submit them to the jury would be to risk irrational findings. These subdivisions include such matters listed in Code of Civil Procedure Section 1875 as the "geographical divisions and political history of the world." To the extent that subdivisions (g) and (h) overlap subdivision (f) of Section 451, notice is, of course, mandatory under Section 451.

The matters covered by subdivisions (g) and (h) are included in Section 452, rather than Section 451, because it seems reasonable to put the burden on the parties to bring adequate information before the court if judicial notice of these matters is to be mandatory. See Evidence Code § 453 and the Comment thereto.

Under existing law, courts take judicial notice of the matters that are included under subdivisions (g) and (h), either pursuant to Section 1875 of the Code of Civil Procedure or because such matters are matters of common knowledge which are certain and indisputable. Witkin, California Evidence §§ 50–52 (1958). Notice of these matters probably is not compulsory under existing law.

§ 453. Compulsory judicial notice upon request

The trial court shall take judicial notice of any matter specified in Section 452 if a party requests it and:

(a) Gives each adverse party sufficient notice of the request, through the pleadings or otherwise, to enable such adverse party to prepare to meet the request; and

(b) Furnishes the court with sufficient information to enable it to take judicial notice of the matter. (Stats.1965, c. 299, § 453.)

Comment—Law Revision Commission

Section 453 provides that the court must take judicial notice of any matter specified in Section 452 if a party requests that such notice be taken, furnishes the court with sufficient information to enable it to take judicial notice of the matter, and gives each adverse party sufficient notice of the request to prepare to meet it.

Section 453 is intended as a safeguard and not as a rigid limitation on the court's power to take judicial notice. The section does not affect the discretionary power of the court to take judicial notice under Section 452 where the party requesting that judicial notice be taken fails to give the requisite notice to each adverse party or fails to furnish sufficient information as to the propriety of taking judicial notice or as to the tenor of the matter to be noticed. Hence, when he considers it appropriate, the judge may take judicial notice under Section 452 and may consult and use any source of pertinent information, whether or not furnished by the parties. However, where the matter noticed under Section 452 is one that is of substantial consequence to the action—even though the court may take judicial notice under Section 452 when the requirements of Section 453 have not been satisfied—the party adversely affected must be given a reasonable opportunity to present information as to the propriety of taking judicial notice and as to the tenor of the matter to be noticed. See Evidence Code § 455 and the Comment thereto.

The "notice" requirement. The party requesting the court to judicially notice a matter under Section 453 must give each adverse party sufficient notice, through the pleadings or otherwise, to enable him to prepare to meet the request. In cases where the notice given does not satisfy this requirement, the court may decline to take judicial notice. A somewhat similar notice to the adverse parties is required under subdivision 4 of Section 1875 of the Code of Civil Procedure when a request for judicial notice of the law of a foreign country is made. Section 453 broadens this existing requirement to cover all matters specified in Section 452.

The notice requirement is an important one since judicial notice is binding on the jury under Section 457. Accordingly, the adverse parties should be given ample notice so that they will have an opportunity to prepare to oppose the taking of judicial notice and to obtain information relevant to the tenor of the matter to be noticed.

Since Section 452 relates to a wide variety of facts and law, the notice requirement should be administered with flexibility in order to insure that the policy behind the judicial notice rules is properly implemented. In many cases, it will be reasonable to expect the notice to be given at or before the time of the pretrial conference. In other cases, matters of fact or law of which the court should take judicial notice may come up at the trial. Section 453 merely requires reasonable notice, and the reasonableness of the notice given will depend upon the circumstances of the particular case.

The "sufficient information" requirement. Under Section 453, the court is not required to resort to any sources of information not provided by the parties. If the party requesting that judicial notice be taken under Section 453 fails to provide the court with "sufficient information," the judge may decline to take judicial notice. For example, if the party requests the court to take judicial notice of the specific gravity of gold, the party requesting that notice be taken must furnish the judge with definitive information as to the specific gravity of gold. The judge is not required to undertake the necessary research to determine the fact, though, of course, he is not precluded from doing such research if he so desires.

Section 453 does not define "sufficient information"; this will necessarily vary from case to case. While the parties will understandably use the best evidence they can produce under the circumstances, mechanical requirements that are ill-suited to the individual case should be avoided. The court justifiably might require that the party requesting that judicial notice be taken provide expert testimony to clarify especially difficult problems.

Burden on party requesting that judicial notice be taken. Where a request is made to take judicial notice under Section 453, the court may decline to take judicial notice unless the party requesting that notice be taken persuades the judge that the matter is one that properly may be noticed under Section 452 and also persuades the judge as to the tenor of the matter to be noticed. The degree of the judge's persuasion regarding a particular matter is determined by the subdivision of Section 452 which authorizes judicial notice of the matter. For example, if the matter is claimed to be a fact of common knowledge under paragraph (g) of Section 452, the party must persuade the judge that the fact is of such common knowledge within the territorial jurisdiction of the court that it cannot reasonably be subject to dispute, *i. e.,* that no reasonable person having the same information as is available to the judge could rationally disbelieve the fact. On the other hand, if the matter to be noticed is a city ordinance under paragraph (b) of Section 452, the party must persuade the judge that a valid ordinance exists and also as to its tenor; but the judge need not believe that no reasonable person could conclude otherwise.

Without regard to the evidence supplied by the party requesting that judicial notice be taken, the judge's determination to take judicial notice of a matter specified in Section 452 will be upheld on appeal if the matter was properly noticed. The reviewing court may resort to any information, whether or not available at the trial, in order to sustain the proper taking of judicial notice. See Evidence Code § 459. On the other hand, even though a party requested that judicial notice be taken under Section 453 and gave notice to each adverse party in compliance with subdivision (a) of Section 453, the decision of the judge not to take judicial notice will be upheld on appeal unless the reviewing court determines that the party furnished information to the judge that was so persuasive that no reasonable judge would have refused to take judicial notice of the matter.

§ 454. Information that may be used in taking judicial notice

(a) In determining the propriety of taking judicial notice of a matter, or the tenor thereof:

(1) Any source of pertinent information, including the advice of persons learned in the subject matter, may be consulted or used, whether or not furnished by a party.

(2) Exclusionary rules of evidence do not apply except for Section 352 and the rules of privilege.

(b) Where the subject of judicial notice is the law of an organization of nations, a foreign nation, or a public entity in a foreign nation and the court resorts to the advice of persons learned in the subject matter, such advice, if not received in open court, shall be in writing.

(Stats.1965, c. 299, § 454.)

§ 455. Opportunity to present information to court

With respect to any matter specified in Section 452 or in subdivision (f) of Section 451 that is of substantial consequence to the determination of the action:

(a) If the trial court has been requested to take or has taken or proposes to take judicial notice of such matter, the court shall afford each party reasonable opportunity, before the jury is instructed or before the cause is submitted for decision by the court, to present to the court information relevant to (1) the propriety of taking judicial notice of the matter and (2) the tenor of the matter to be noticed.

(b) If the trial court resorts to any source of information not received in open court, including the advice of persons learned in the subject matter, such information and its source shall be made a part of the record in the action and the court shall afford each party reasonable opportunity to meet such information before judicial notice of the matter may be taken.

(Stats.1965, c. 299, § 455.)

§ 456. Noting for record denial of request to take judicial notice

If the trial court denies a request to take judicial notice of any matter, the court shall at the earliest practicable time so advise the parties and indicate for the record that it has denied the request.

(Stats.1965, c. 299, § 456.)

§ 457. Instructing jury on matter judicially noticed

If a matter judicially noticed is a matter which would otherwise have been for determination by the jury, the trial court may, and upon request shall, instruct the jury to accept as a fact the matter so noticed.

(Stats.1965, c. 299, § 457.)

§ 458. Judicial notice by trial court in subsequent proceedings

The failure or refusal of the trial court to take judicial notice of a matter, or to instruct the jury with respect to the matter, does not preclude the trial court in subsequent proceedings in the action from taking judicial notice of the matter in accordance with the procedure specified in this division. (Stats.1965, c. 299, § 458.)

§ 459. Judicial notice by reviewing court

(a) The reviewing court shall take judicial notice of (1) each matter properly noticed by the trial court and (2) each matter that the trial court was required to notice under Section 451 or 453. The reviewing court may take judicial notice of any matter specified in Section 452. The reviewing court may take judicial notice of a matter in a tenor different from that noticed by the trial court.

(b) In determining the propriety of taking judicial notice of a matter, or the tenor thereof, the reviewing court has the same power as the trial court under Section 454.

(c) When taking judicial notice under this section of a matter specified in Section 452 or in subdivision (f) of Section 451 that is of substantial consequence to the determination of the action, the reviewing court shall comply with the provisions of subdivision (a) of Section 455 if the matter was not theretofore judicially noticed in the action.

(d) In determining the propriety of taking judicial notice of a matter specified in Section 452 or in subdivision (f) of Section 451 that is of substantial consequence to the determination of the action, or the tenor thereof, if the reviewing court resorts to any source of information not received in open court or not included in the record of the action, including the advice of persons learned in the subject matter, the reviewing court shall afford each party reasonable opportunity to meet such information before judicial notice of the matter may be taken. (Stats.1965, c. 299, § 459.)

§ 460. Appointment of expert by court.

Where the advice of persons learned in the subject matter is required in order to enable the court to take judicial notice of a matter, the court on its own motion or on motion of any party may appoint one or more such persons to provide such advice. If the court determines to appoint such a person, he shall be appointed and compensated in the manner provided in Article 2 (commencing with Section 730) of Chapter 3 of Division 6. (Stats.1965, c. 299, § 460.)

Division 5
BURDEN OF PROOF; BURDEN OF PRODUCING EVIDENCE; PRESUMPTIONS AND INFERENCES

§ 500. Party who has the burden of proof

Except as otherwise provided by law, a party has the burden of proof as to each fact the existence or nonexistence of which is essential to the claim for relief or defense that he is asserting. (Stats.1965, c. 299, § 500.)

Comment—Law Revision Commission

As used in Section 500, the burden of proof means the obligation of a party to produce a particular state of conviction in the mind of the trier of fact as to the existence or nonexistence of a fact. See Evidence Code §§ 115, 190. If this requisite degree of conviction is not achieved as to the existence of a particular fact, the trier of fact must assume that the fact does not exist. Morgan, Basic Problems of Evidence 19 (1957); 9 Wigmore, Evidence § 2485 (3d ed. 1940). Usually, the burden of proof requires a party to convince the trier of fact that the existence of a particular fact is more probable than its nonexistence—a degree of proof usually described as proof by a preponderance of the evidence. Evidence Code § 115; Witkin, California Evidence § 59 (1958). However, in some instances, the burden of proof requires a party to produce a substantially greater degree of belief in the mind of the trier of fact concerning the existence of the fact—a burden usually described by stating that the party must introduce clear and convincing proof (Witkin, California Evidence § 60 (1958)) or, with respect to the prosecution in a criminal case, proof beyond a reasonable doubt (Penal Code § 1096).

The defendant in a criminal case sometimes has the burden of proof in regard to a fact essential to negate his guilt. However, in such cases, he usually is not required to persuade the trier of fact as to the existence of such fact; he is merely required to raise a reasonable doubt in the mind of the trier of fact as to his guilt. Evidence Code § 501; People v. Bushton, 80 Cal. 160, 22 Pac. 127 (1889). If the defendant produces no evidence concerning the fact, there is no issue on the matter to be decided by the jury; hence, the jury may be instructed that the nonexistence of the fact must be assumed. See, e. g., People v. Harmon, 89 Cal.App.2d 55, 58, 200 P.2d 32, 34 (1948) (prosecution for narcotics possession; jury instructed "that the burden of proof is upon the defendant that he possessed a written prescription and that in the absence of such evidence it must be assumed that he had no such prescription"). See also People v. Boo Doo Hong, 122 Cal. 606, 607, 55 Pac. 402, 403 (1898).

Section 1981 of the Code of Civil Procedure (superseded by Evidence Code Section 500) provides that the party holding the affirmative of the issue must produce the evidence to prove it and that the burden of proof lies on the party who would be defeated if no evidence were given on either side. This section has been criticized as establishing a meaningless standard:

§ 500

The "affirmative of the issue" lacks any substantial objective meaning, and the allocation of the burden actually requires the application of several rules of practice and policy, not entirely consistent and not wholly reliable. [Witkin, California Evidence § 56 at 72–73 (1958).]

That the burden is on the party having the affirmative [or] that a party is not required to prove a negative . . . is no more than a play on words, since practically any proposition may be stated in either affirmative or negative form. Thus a plaintiff's exercise of ordinary care equals absence of contributory negligence, in the minority of jurisdictions which place this element in plaintiff's case. In any event, the proposition seems simply not to be so. [Cleary, Presuming and Pleading: An Essay on Juristic Immaturity, 12 Stan.L.Rev. 5, 11 (1959).]

"The basic rule, which covers most situations, is that whatever facts a party must affirmatively plead he also has the burden of proving." Witkin, California Evidence § 56 at 73 (1958). Section 500 follows this basic rule. However, Section 500 is broader, applying to issues not necessarily raised in the pleadings.

Under Section 500, the burden of proof as to a particular fact is normally on the party to whose case the fact is essential. "[W]hen a party seeks relief the burden is upon him to prove his case, and he cannot depend wholly upon the failure of the defendant to prove his defenses." Cal. Employment Comm'n v. Malm, 59 Cal.App.2d 322, 323, 138 P.2d 744, 745 (1943). And, "as a general rule, the burden is on the defendant to prove new matter alleged as a defense . . , even though it requires the proof of a negative." Wilson v. California Cent. R.R., 94 Cal. 166, 172, 29 Pac. 861, 864 (1892).

Section 500 does not attempt to indicate what facts may be essential to a particular party's claim for relief or defense. The facts that must be shown to establish a cause of action or a defense are determined by the substantive law, not the law of evidence.

The general rule allocating the burden of proof applies "except as otherwise provided by law." The exception is included in recognition of the fact that the burden of proof is sometimes allocated in a manner that is at variance with the general rule. In determining whether the normal allocation of the burden of proof should be altered, the courts consider a number of factors: the knowledge of the parties concerning the particular fact, the availability of the evidence to the parties, the most desirable result in terms of public policy in the absence of proof of the particular fact, and the probability of the existence or nonexistence of the fact. In determining the incidence of the burden of proof, "the truth is that there is not and cannot be any one general solvent for all cases. It is merely a question of policy and fairness based on experience in the different situations." 9 Wigmore, Evidence § 2486 at 275 (3d ed. 1940).

Under existing California law, certain matters have been called "presumptions" even though they do not fall within the definition contained in Code of Civil Procedure Section 1959 (superseded by Evidence Code Section 600). Both Section 1959 and Evidence Code Section 600 define a presumption to be an assumption or conclusion of fact that the law requires to be drawn from the proof or establishment of some other fact. Despite the statutory definition, subdivisions 1 and 4 of the Code of Civil Procedure Section 1963 (superseded by Sections 520 and 521 of the Evidence Code) provide presumptions that a person is innocent of crime or wrong and that a person exercises ordinary care for his own concerns. Similarly, some cases refer to a presumption of sanity. It is apparent that these so-called presumptions do not arise from the establishment or proof of a fact in the action. In fact, they are not presumptions at all but are preliminary allocations of the burden of proof in regard to the particular issue. This preliminary allocation of the burden of proof may be satisfied in particular cases by proof of a fact giving rise to a presumption that does affect the burden of proof. For example, the initial burden of proving negligence may be satisfied in a particular case by proof that undamaged goods were delivered to a bailee and that such goods were lost or damaged while in the bailee's possession. Upon such proof, the bailee would have the burden of proof as to his lack of negligence. George v. Bekins Van & Storage Co., 33 Cal.2d 834, 205 P.2d 1037 (1949). *Cf.* Com. Code § 7403.

Because the assumptions referred to above do not meet the definition of a presumption contained in Section 600, they are not continued in this code as presumptions. Instead, they appear in the next article in several sections allocating the burden of proof on specific issues. See Article 2 (Sections 520–522).

§ 501. Burden of proof in criminal action generally

Insofar as any statute, except Section 522, assigns the burden of proof in a criminal action, such statute is subject to Penal Code Section 1096. (Stats.1965, c. 299, § 501.)

Comment—Law Revision Commission

A statute assigning the burden of proof may require the party to whom the burden is assigned to raise a reasonable doubt in the mind of the trier of fact or to persuade the trier of fact by a preponderance of evidence, by clear and convincing proof, or by proof beyond a reasonable doubt. See Evidence Code § 115.

Sections 520–522 (which assign the burden of proof on specific issues) may, at times, assign the burden of proof to the defendant in a criminal action. Elsewhere in the codes are other sections that either specifically allocate the burden of proof to the defendant in a criminal action or have been construed to allocate the burden of proof to the defense. For example, Health and Safety Code Section 11721 provides specifically that, in a prosecution for the use of narcotics, it is the burden of the defense to show that the narcotics were administered by or under the direction of a person licensed to prescribe and administer narcotics. Health and Safety Code Section 11500, on the other hand, prohibits the possession of narcotics but provides an exception for narcotics possessed pursuant to a prescription. The courts have construed this section to place the burden of proof on the defense to show that the exception applies and that the narcotics were possessed pursuant to a prescription. People v. Marschalk, 206 Cal.App.2d 346, 23 Cal.Rptr. 743 (1962); People v. Bill, 140 Cal.App. 389, 392–394, 35 P.2d 645, 647–648 (1934).

Section 501 is intended to make it clear that the statutory allocations of the burden of proof appearing in this chapter and elsewhere in the codes are subject to Penal Code Section 1096, which requires that a criminal defendant be proved guilty beyond a reasonable doubt, *i. e.*, that the statutory allocations do not (except on the issue of insanity) require the defendant to persuade the trier of fact of his innocence. Under Evidence Code Section 522, as under existing law, the defendant must prove his insanity by a preponderance of the evidence. People v. Daugherty, 40 Cal.2d 876, 256 P.2d 911 (1953). However, where a statute allocates the burden of proof to the defendant on any other issue relating to the defendant's guilt, the defendant's burden, as under existing law, is merely to raise a reasonable doubt as to his guilt. People v. Bushton, 80 Cal. 160, 22 Pac. 127 (1889). Section 501 also makes it clear that, when a statute assigns the burden of proof to the prosecution in a criminal action, the prosecution must discharge that burden by proof beyond a reasonable doubt.

PROOF; PRESUMPTIONS AND INFERENCES § 600

Notes of Decisions

Reasonable doubt

In criminal action, burden is placed on people to establish beyond a reasonable doubt guilt only of defendant therein, leaving issues which do not particularly relate to his guilt to be made according to preponderance of evidence. People v. McGill (1935) 51 P.2d 433, 10 C.A.2d 155.

Generally, doctrine of reasonable doubt extends to evidence by which every material issue of corpus delicti is sought to be proved. Id.

A "reasonable doubt" is not a mere possible doubt, but is the absence of an abiding conviction to a moral certainty of the truth of the charge. People v. Miller (1916) 154 P. 468, 171 C. 649.

§ 502. Instructions on burden of proof

The court on all proper occasions shall instruct the jury as to which party bears the burden of proof on each issue and as to whether that burden requires that a party raise a reasonable doubt concerning the existence or nonexistence of a fact or that he establish the existence or nonexistence of a fact by a preponderance of the evidence, by clear and convincing proof, or by proof beyond a reasonable doubt. (Stats.1965, c. 299, § 502.)

§ 520. Claim that person guilty of crime or wrongdoing

The party claiming that a person is guilty of crime or wrongdoing has the burden of proof on that issue. (Stats.1965, c. 299, § 520.)

§ 521. Claim that person did not exercise care

The party claiming that a person did not exercise a requisite degree of care has the burden of proof on that issue. (Stats.1965, c. 299, § 521.)

§ 522. Claim that person is or was insane

The party claiming that any person, including himself, is or was insane has the burden of proof on that issue. (Stats.1965, c. 299, § 522.)

§ 550. Party who has the burden of producing evidence

(a) The burden of producing evidence as to a particular fact is on the party against whom a finding on that fact would be required in the absence of further evidence.

(b) The burden of producing evidence as to a particular fact is initially on the party with the burden of proof as to that fact. (Stats.1965, c. 299, § 550.)

Comment—Law Revision Commission

Section 550 deals with the allocation of the burden of producing evidence. At the outset of the case, this burden will coincide with the burden of proof. 9 Wigmore, Evidence § 2487 at 279 (3d ed. 1940). However, during the course of the trial, the burden may shift from one party to another, irrespective of the incidence of the burden of proof. For example, if the party with the initial burden of producing evidence establishes a fact giving rise to a presumption, the burden of producing evidence will shift to the other party, whether or not the presumption is one that affects the burden of proof. In addition, a party may introduce evidence of such overwhelming probative force that no person could reasonably disbelieve it in the absence of countervailing evidence, in which case the burden of producing evidence would shift to the opposing party to produce some evidence. These principles are in accord with well-settled California law. See Discussion in Witkin, California Evidence §§ 53–56 (1958). See also 9 Wigmore, Evidence § 2487 (3d ed. 1940).

§ 600. Presumption and inference defined

(a) A presumption is an assumption of fact that the law requires to be made from another fact or group of facts found or otherwise established in the action. A presumption is not evidence.

(b) An inference is a deduction of fact that may logically and reasonably be drawn from another fact or group of facts found or otherwise established in the action.
(Stats.1965, c. 299, § 600.)

Comment—Assembly Committee on Judiciary

The definition of a presumption in Section 600 is substantially the same as that contained in Code of Civil Procedure Section 1959: "A presumption is a deduction which the law expressly directs to be made from particular facts." Section 600 was derived from Rule 13 of the Uniform Rules of Evidence and supersedes Code of Civil Procedure Section 1959.

The second sentence of subdivision (a) may be unnecessary in light of the definition of "evidence" in Section 140—"testimony, writings, material objects, or other things presented to the senses that are offered to prove the existence or nonexistence of a fact." Presumptions, then, are not "evidence" but are conclusions that the law requires to be drawn (in the absence of a sufficient contrary showing) when some other fact is proved or otherwise established in the action.

Nonetheless, the second sentence has been added here to repudiate specifically the rule of Smellie v. Southern Pac. Co., 212 Cal. 540, 299 Pac. 529 (1931). That case held that a presumption is evidence that must be weighed against conflicting evidence; and in Scott v. Burke, 39 Cal.2d 388, 247 P.2d 313 (1952), the Supreme Court held that conflicting presumptions must be weighed against each other. These decisions require the jury to perform an intellectually impossible task. The jury is required to weigh the testimony of witnesses and other evidence as to the circumstances of a particular event against the fact that the law requires an opposing conclusion in the absence of contrary evidence and to determine which "evidence" is of greater probative force. Or else, the jury is required to accept the fact that the law requires two opposing conclusions and to determine which required conclusion is of greater probative force.

Moreover, the doctrine that a presumption is evidence imposes upon the party with the burden of proof a much higher burden of proof than is warranted. For example, if a party with the burden of proof has a presumption invoked against him and if the presumption remains in the case as evidence even though the jury believes that he has produced a preponderance of the evidence, the effect is that he must produce some additional but unascertainable quantum of proof in order to dispel the effect of the presumption. See Scott v. Burke, 39 Cal.2d 388, 405–406, 247 P.2d 313, 323–324 (1952) (dissenting opinion). The doctrine that a presumption is evidence gives no guidance to the jury or to the parties as to the amount of this additional proof. The most that should be expected of a party in a civil case is that he prove his case by a preponderance of the evidence (unless some specific presumption or rule of law requires proof of a particular issue by clear and convincing evidence). The most that should be expected of the prosecution in a criminal case is that it establish the defendant's guilt beyond a reasonable doubt. To require some additional quantum of proof, unspecified and uncertain in amount, to dispel a presumption which persists as evidence in the case unfairly weights the scales of justice against the party with the burden of proof.

To avoid the confusion engendered by the doctrine that a presumption is evidence, this code describes "evidence" as the matters presented in judicial proceedings and uses presumptions solely as devices to aid in determining the facts from the evidence presented.

The definition of "inference" in subdivision (b) restates in substance the definition contained in Code of Civil Procedure Sections 1958 and 1960. Under the Evidence Code, an inference is not itself evidence; it is the result of reasoning from evidence.

In the sections that follow, the Evidence Code classifies presumptions and lists a number of specific presumptions. Some presumptions that have been listed in the Code of Civil Procedure have not been listed as presumptions in the Evidence Code. But the fact that a statutory presumption has been repealed will not preclude the drawing of any appropriate inferences from the facts that would have given rise to the presumption. And, in appropriate cases, the court may instruct the jury on the propriety of drawing particular inferences.

Editors' Note

A review of Penal Code § 496 and § 12091 may be helpful as examples of laws creating presumptions or allowing inferences.

---

§ 601. Classification of presumptions

A presumption is either conclusive or rebuttable. Every rebuttable presumption is either (a) a presumption affecting the burden of producing evidence or (b) a presumption affecting the burden of proof. (Stats.1965, c. 299, § 601.)

Comment—Law Revision Commission

Under existing law, some presumptions are conclusive. The court or jury is required to find the existence of the presumed fact regardless of the strength of the opposing evidence. The conclusive presumptions are specified in Section 1962 of the Code of Civil Procedure (superseded by Article 2 (Sections 620–624) of this chapter).

Under existing law, too, all presumptions that are not conclusive are rebuttable presumptions. Code Civ.Proc. § 1961 (superseded by Evidence Code § 601). However, the existing statutes make no attempt to classify the rebuttable presumptions.

For several decades, courts and legal scholars have wrangled over the purpose and function of presumptions. The view espoused by Professors Thayer (Thayer, Preliminary Treatise on Evidence 313–352 (1898)) and Wigmore (9 Wigmore, Evidence §§ 2485–2491 (3d ed. 1940)), accepted by most courts (see Morgan, Presumptions, 10 Rutgers L.Rev. 512, 516 (1956)), and adopted by the American Law Institute's Model Code of Evidence, is that a presumption is a preliminary assumption of fact that disappears from the case upon the introduction of evidence sufficient to sustain a finding of the nonexistence of the presumed fact. In Professor Thayer's view, a presumption merely reflects the judicial determination that the same conclusionary fact exists so frequently when the preliminary fact exists that, once the preliminary fact is established, proof of the conclusionary fact may be dispensed with unless there is actually some contrary evidence:

> Many facts and groups of facts often recur, and when a body of men with a continuous tradition has carried on for some length of time this process of reasoning upon facts that often repeat themselves, they cut short the process and lay down a rule. To such facts they affix, by a general declaration, the character and operation which common experience has assigned to them. [Thayer, Preliminary Treatise on Evidence 326 (1898).]

Professors Morgan and McCormick argue that a presumption should shift the burden of proof to the adverse party. Morgan, Some Problems of Proof 81 (1956); McCormick, Evidence § 317 at 671–672 (1954). They believe that presumptions are created for reasons of policy and argue that, if the policy underlying a presumption is of sufficient weight to require a finding of the presumed fact when there is no contrary evidence, it should be of sufficient weight to require a finding when the mind of the trier of fact is in equilibrium, and, *a fortiori*, it should be of sufficient weight to require a finding if the trier of fact does not believe the contrary evidence.

The classification of presumptions in the Evidence Code is based on a third view suggested by Professor Bohlen in 1920. Bohlen, The Effect of Rebuttable Presumptions of Law Upon the Burden of Proof, 68 U.Pa.L.Rev. 307 (1920). Underlying the presumptions provisions of the Evidence Code is the conclusion that the Thayer view is correct as to some presumptions, but that the Morgan view is right as to others. The fact is that presumptions are created for a variety of reasons, and no single theory or rationale of presumptions can deal adequately with all of them. Hence, the Evidence Code classifies all rebuttable presumptions as either (1) presumptions affecting the burden of producing evidence (essentially Thayer presumptions), or (2) presumptions affecting the burden of proof (essentially Morgan presumptions).

Sections 603 and 605 set forth the criteria by which the two classes of rebuttable presumptions may be distinguished, and Sections 604, 606, and 607 prescribe their effect. Articles 3 and 4 (Sections 630–668) classify many presumptions found in California law; but many other presumptions, both statutory and common law, must await classification by the courts in accordance with the criteria contained in Sections 603 and 605.

The classification scheme contained in the Evidence Code follows a distinction that appears in the California cases. Thus, for example, the courts have at times held that presumptions do not affect the burden of proof. Estate of Eakle, 33 Cal.App.2d 379, 91 P.2d 954 (1939) (presumption of undue influence); Valentine v. Provident Mut. Life Ins. Co., 12 Cal.App.2d 616, 55 P.2d 1243 (1936) (presumption of death from seven years' absence). And at other times the courts have held that certain presumptions do affect the burden of proof. Estate of Nickson, 187 Cal. 603, 203 Pac. 106 (1921) ("clear and convincing proof" required to overcome presumption of community property); Estate of Walker, 180 Cal. 478, 181 Pac. 792 (1919) ("clear and satisfactory proof" required to overcome presumption of legitimacy). The cases have not, however, explicitly recognized the distinction, nor have they applied it consistently. Compare Estate of Eakle, *supra* (presumption of undue influence does not affect burden of proof), *with* Estate of Witt, 198 Cal. 407, 245 Pac. 197 (1926) (presumption of undue influence must be overcome with "the clearest and most satisfactory evidence"). The Evidence Code clarifies the law relating to presumptions by identifying the distinguishing factors, and it provides a measure of certainty by classifying a number of specific presumptions.

Editors' Note

Presumptions exist in many of the Codes other than the Evidence Code. Some examples include:
1. Penal Code § 1016—presumption of sanity
2. Penal Code § 1096—presumption of innocence
3. Vehicle Code § 23126—presumption of influence of alcohol from chemical test results

§ 602. Statute making one fact prima facie evidence of another fact

A statute providing that a fact or group of facts is prima facie evidence of another fact establishes a rebuttable presumption.

(Stats.1965, c. 299, § 602.)

Comment—Law Revision Commission

Section 602 indicates the construction to be given to the large number of statutes scattered through the codes that state that one fact or group of facts is prima facie evidence of another fact. See, e. g., Agric.Code § 18, Com.Code § 1202, Rev. & Tax.Code § 6714. In some instances, these statutes have been enacted for reasons of public policy that require them to be treated as presumptions affecting the burden of proof. See People v. Schwartz, 31 Cal.2d 59, 63, 187 P.2d 12, 14 (1947); People v. Mahoney, 13 Cal.2d 729, 732–733, 91 P.2d 1029, 1030–1031 (1939). It seems likely, however, that in many instances such statutes are not intended to affect the burden of proof but only the burden of producing evidence. Section 602 provides that these statutes are to be regarded as rebuttable presumptions. Hence, unless some specific language applicable to the particular statute in question indicates whether it affects the burden of proof or only the burden of producing evidence, the courts will be required to classify these statutes as presumptions affecting the burden of proof or the burden of producing evidence in accordance with the criteria set forth in Sections 603 and 605.

§ 603. Presumption affecting the burden of producing evidence defined

A presumption affecting the burden of producing evidence is a presumption established to implement no public policy other than to facilitate the determination of the particular action in which the presumption is applied.

(Stats.1965, c. 299, § 603.)

§ 604. Effect of presumption affecting burden of producing evidence

The effect of a presumption affecting the burden of producing evidence is to require the trier of fact to assume the existence of the presumed fact unless and until evidence is introduced which would support a finding of its nonexistence, in which case the trier of fact shall determine the existence or nonexistence of the presumed fact from the evidence and without regard to the presumption. Nothing in this section shall be construed to prevent the drawing of any inference that may be appropriate.

(Stats.1965, c. 299, § 604.)

§ 605. Presumption affecting the burden of proof defined

A presumption affecting the burden of proof is a presumption established to implement some public policy other than to facilitate the determination of the particular action in which the presumption is applied, such as the policy in favor of establishment of a parent and child relationship, the validity of marriage, the stability of titles to property, or the security of those who entrust themselves or their property to the administration of others.

(Amended by Stats.1975, c. 1244, p. 3201, § 12.)

§ 606. Effect of presumption affecting burden of proof

The effect of a presumption affecting the burden of proof is to impose upon the party against whom it operates the burden of proof as to the nonexistence of the presumed fact.

(Stats.1965, c. 299, § 606.)

§ 607. Effect of certain presumptions in a criminal action

When a presumption affecting the burden of proof operates in a criminal action to establish presumptively any fact that is essential to the defendant's guilt, the presumption operates only if the facts that give rise to the presumption have been found or otherwise established beyond a reasonable doubt and, in such case, the defendant need only raise a reasonable doubt as to the existence of the presumed fact.

(Stats.1965, c. 299, § 607.)

§ 620. Conclusive presumptions

The presumptions established by this article, and all other presumptions declared by law to be conclusive, are conclusive presumptions.
(Stats.1965, c. 299, § 620.)

Editors' Note

The conclusive presumptions which follow § 620 deal with issues of legitimacy, facts recited in written instruments and estoppel. These presumptions rarely impact criminal cases and have not been included in this text.

---

§ 630. Presumptions affecting the burden of producing evidence

The presumptions established by this article, and all other rebuttable presumptions established by law that fall within the criteria of Section 603, are presumptions affecting the burden of producing evidence.
(Stats.1965, c. 299, § 630.)

§ 631. Money delivered by one to another

Money delivered by one to another is presumed to have been due to the latter.
(Stats.1965, c. 299, § 631.)

§ 637. Ownership of things possessed

The things which a person possesses are presumed to be owned by him.
(Stats.1965, c. 299, § 637.)

§ 640. Writing truly dated

A writing is presumed to have been truly dated.
(Stats.1965, c. 299, § 640.)

§ 641. Letter received in ordinary course of mail

A letter correctly addressed and properly mailed is presumed to have been received in the ordinary course of mail.
(Stats.1965, c. 299, § 641.)

§ 660. Presumptions affecting the burden of proof

The presumptions established by this article, and all other rebuttable presumptions established by law that fall within the criteria of Section 605, are presumptions affecting the burden of proof.
(Stats.1965, c. 299, § 660.)

§ 664. Official duty regularly performed

It is presumed that official duty has been regularly performed. This presumption does not apply on an issue as to the lawfulness of an arrest if it is found or otherwise established that the arrest was made without a warrant.
(Stats.1965, c. 299, § 664.)

§ 665. Ordinary consequences of voluntary act

A person is presumed to intend the ordinary consequences of his voluntary act. This presumption is inapplicable in a criminal action to establish the specific intent of the defendant where specific intent is an element of the crime charged.
(Stats.1965, c. 299, § 665.)

§ 666. Judicial action lawful exercise of jurisdiction

Any court of this state or the United States, or any court of general jurisdiction in any other state or nation, or any judge of such a court, acting as such, is presumed to have acted in the lawful exercise of its jurisdiction. This presumption applies only when the act of the court or judge is under collateral attack.
(Stats.1965, c. 299, § 666.)

§ 667. Death of person not heard from in seven years

A person not heard from in seven years is presumed to be dead.
(Stats.1965, c. 299, § 667.)

§ 668. Unlawful intent

An unlawful intent is presumed from the doing of an unlawful act. This presumption is inapplicable in a criminal action to establish the specific intent of the defendant where specific intent is an element of the crime charged.
(Stats.1965, c. 299, § 668.)

Notes of Decisions

Criminal intent in general

To render person guilty of public offense in which specific intent is not ingredient, it is sufficient that he intentionally committed forbidden act, and it is not essential to prove that person charged entertained any intent to violate law and it is presumed that unlawful act was done with unlawful intent. Dunn v. Municipal Court, Eureka Judicial Dist. (1963) 34 Cal.Rptr. 251, 220 C.A.2d 858.

Before a person may be found guilty of a crime it is not essential that the proof should show that such person entertained any intent to violate the law since it is sufficient that he intentionally committed forbidden act. People v. Bateman (1959) 345 P.2d 334, 175 C.A.2d 69.

When the intent is not made an affirmative element of the crime, the law imputes that the act knowingly was done with criminal intent, though the offender was honestly mistaken as to the meaning of the law violated. People v. McCalla (1923) 220 P. 436, 63 C.A. 783, error dismissed 45 S.Ct. 461, 267 U.S. 585, 69 L.Ed. 799.

When the intent is not made an affirmative element of a crime, the law imputes that the act knowingly done was with criminal intent, and it need not be alleged nor proven. People v. Wolfrom (1911) 115 P. 1088, 15 C.A. 732.

The intent essential under Pen.C., § 20, to constitute a crime, is evidenced by the acts of accused, and the presumptions arising therefrom, which presumption attaches successively to each act as done, regardless of the original intent. People v. White (1907) 90 P. 471, 5 C.A. 329.

A charge relating to presumptions, as follows: "That an unlawful act was done with unlawful intent, and that a person intends the ordinary consequences of his voluntary act. The effect of these rules is that when the doing of an act is proven which, if there be guilty intent, would be a violation of law, the burden of proving the act to have been without such intent is in most cases upon the accused,"—was erroneous. People v. Ribolsi (1891) 26 P. 1082, 89 C. 492.

Specific intent

Where a specific intent is made an element of the crime charged, the specific intent cannot be presumed from the doing of the unlawful act, but must be proved as a fact. People v. Neal (1940) 104 P.2d 555, 40 C.A.2d 115.

Person is presumed to intend to do things which he does, and especially so when they are done in commission of a crime, excepting where intent must be proved as necessary element. People v. Head (1935) 50 P.2d 832, 9 C.A.2d 647.

Where specific intent is an essential ingredient of an offense, the intent must be proved like any other fact in the case, and no presumption of law arises as to the existence of such intent. People v. Maciel (1925) 234 P. 877, 71 C.A. 213.

§ 669. Failure to exercise due care

(a) The failure of a person to exercise due care is presumed if:

(1) He violated a statute, ordinance, or regulation of a public entity;

(2) The violation proximately caused death or injury to person or property;

(3) The death or injury resulted from an occurrence of the nature which the statute, ordinance, or regulation was designed to prevent; and

(4) The person suffering the death or the injury to his person or property was one of the class of persons for whose protection the statute, ordinance, or regulation was adopted.

(b) This presumption may be rebutted by proof that:

(1) The person violating the statute, ordinance, or regulation did what might reasonably be expected of a person of ordinary prudence, acting under similar circumstances, who desired to comply with the law; or

(2) The person violating the statute, ordinance, or regulation was a child and exercised the degree of care ordinarily exercised by persons of his maturity, intelligence, and capacity under similar circumstances, but the presumption may not be rebutted by such proof if the violation occurred in the course of an activity normally engaged in only by adults and requiring adult qualifications.

(Added by Stats.1967, c. 650, p. 2004, § 1.)

Division 6

WITNESSES

§ 700. General rule as to competency

Except as otherwise provided by statute, every person is qualified to be a witness and no person is disqualified to testify to any matter.

(Stats.1965, c. 299, § 700.)

Comment—Law Revision Commission

Section 700 makes it clear that all grounds for disqualification of witnesses must be based on statute. There can be no nonstatutory grounds for disqualification. The section is similar to and supersedes Section 1879 of the Code of Civil Procedure, which provides that "all persons . . . who, having organs of sense, can perceive, and perceiving, can make known their perceptions to others, may be witnesses."

Just as Code of Civil Procedure Section 1879 is limited by various statutory restrictions on the competency of witnesses, the broad rule stated in Section 700 is also substantially qualified by statutory restrictions appearing in the Evidence Code and in other California codes. See, e. g., Evidence Code § 701 (mental or physical capacity to be a witness), § 702 (requirement of personal knowledge), § 703 (judge as a witness), § 704 (juror as a witness), §§ 900–1070 (privileges), § 1150 (continuing existing law limiting use of juror's evidence concerning jury misconduct); Vehicle Code § 40804 (speed trap evidence).

§ 701. Disqualification of witness

A person is disqualified to be a witness if he is:

(a) Incapable of expressing himself concerning the matter so as to be understood, either directly or through interpretation by one who can understand him; or

(b) Incapable of understanding the duty of a witness to tell the truth.

(Stats.1965, c. 299, § 701.)

§ 702. Personal knowledge of witness

(a) Subject to Section 801, the testimony of a witness concerning a particular matter is inadmissible unless he has personal knowledge of the matter.

§ 702

Against the objection of a party, such personal knowledge must be shown before the witness may testify concerning the matter.

(b) A witness' personal knowledge of a matter may be shown by any otherwise admissible evidence, including his own testimony.
(Stats.1965, c. 299, § 702.)

§ 703. Judge as witness

(a) Before the judge presiding at the trial of an action may be called to testify in that trial as a witness, he shall, in proceedings held out of the presence and hearing of the jury, inform the parties of the information he has concerning any fact or matter about which he will be called to testify.

(b) Against the objection of a party, the judge presiding at the trial of an action may not testify in that trial as a witness. Upon such objection, the judge shall declare a mistrial and order the action assigned for trial before another judge.

(c) The calling of the judge presiding at a trial to testify in that trial as a witness shall be deemed a consent to the granting of a motion for mistrial, and an objection to such calling of a judge shall be deemed a motion for mistrial.

(d) In the absence of objection by a party, the judge presiding at the trial of an action may testify in that trial as a witness.
(Stats.1965, c. 299, § 703.)

§ 704. Juror as witness

(a) Before a juror sworn and impaneled in the trial of an action may be called to testify before the jury in that trial as a witness, he shall, in proceedings conducted by the court out of the presence and hearing of the remaining jurors, inform the parties of the information he has concerning any fact or matter about which he will be called to testify.

(b) Against the objection of a party, a juror sworn and impaneled in the trial of an action may not testify before the jury in that trial as a witness. Upon such objection, the court shall declare a mistrial and order the action assigned for trial before another jury.

(c) The calling of a juror to testify before the jury as a witness shall be deemed a consent to the granting of a motion for mistrial, and an objection to such calling of a juror shall be deemed a motion for mistrial.

(d) In the absence of objection by a party, a juror sworn and impaneled in the trial of an action may be compelled to testify in that trial as a witness.
(Stats.1965, c. 299, § 704.)

§ 710. Oath required

Every witness before testifying shall take an oath or make an affirmation or declaration in the form provided by law.
(Stats.1965, c. 299, § 710.)

§ 711. Confrontation

At the trial of an action, a witness can be heard only in the presence and subject to the examination of all the parties to the action, if they choose to attend and examine.
(Stats.1965, c. 299, § 711.)

§ 720. Qualification as an expert witness

(a) A person is qualified to testify as an expert if he has special knowledge, skill, experience, training, or education sufficient to qualify him as an expert on the subject to which his testimony relates. Against the objection of a party, such special knowledge, skill, experience, training, or education must be shown before the witness may testify as an expert.

(b) A witness' special knowledge, skill, experience, training, or education may be shown by any otherwise admissible evidence, including his own testimony.
(Stats.1965, c. 299, § 720.)

Editors' Note

The qualification of an expert witness is a matter within the discretion of the court. Particular subjects have not been granted acceptance as matters subject to expert testimony.

Notes of Decisions

Lie detectors

Courts have not found established scientific certainty in lie detector tests sufficient to justify submission of their results to jury. People v. King (1968) 72 Cal.Rptr. 478, 266 A.C.A. 466.

Voice print analysis

Testimony by head of voice identification unit of a state police force, who was the only witness to testify on issue of general acceptance in the scientific community of voice print analysis and who was one of the leading proponents of the analysis, to the effect that he had prepared or reviewed 180,000 voice spectrograms during the course of a university study in a controlled experimental situation and that the scientific community involved in voice print analysis generally accepted the technique as extremely reliable was insufficient to demonstrate scientific acceptance of the technique as generally reliable and thus to permit admission of voice print analysis in defendant's trial. People v. Kelly (1976) 130 Cal.Rptr. 144, 549 P.2d 1240.

§ 721. Cross-examination of expert witness

(a) Subject to subdivision (b), a witness testifying as an expert may be cross-examined to the same extent as any other witness and, in addition, may be fully cross-examined as to (1) his qualifications, (2) the subject to which his expert testimony relates, and (3) the matter upon which his opinion is based and the reasons for his opinion.

(b) If a witness testifying as an expert testifies in the form of an opinion, he may not be cross-examined in regard to the content or tenor of any scientific, technical, or professional text, treatise, journal, or similar publication unless:

(1) The witness referred to, considered, or relied upon such publication in arriving at or forming his opinion; or

(2) Such publication has been admitted in evidence.
(Stats.1965, c. 299, § 721.)

§ 722. Credibility of expert witness

(a) The fact of the appointment of an expert witness by the court may be revealed to the trier of fact.

(b) The compensation and expenses paid or to be paid to an expert witness by the party calling him is a proper subject of inquiry by any adverse party as relevant to the credibility of the witness and the weight of his testimony.
(Stats.1965, c. 299, § 722.)

§ 723. Limit on number of expert witnesses

The court may, at any time before or during the trial of an action, limit the number of expert witnesses to be called by any party.
(Stats.1965, c. 299, § 723.)

§ 730. Appointment of expert by court

When it appears to the court, at any time before or during the trial of an action, that expert evidence is or may be required by the court or by any party to the action, the court on its own motion or on motion of any party may appoint one or more experts to investigate, to render a report as may be ordered by the court, and to testify as an expert at the trial of the action relative to the fact or matter as to which such expert evidence is or may be required. The court may fix the compensation for such services, if any, rendered by any person appointed under this section, in addition to any service as a witness, at such amount as seems reasonable to the court.
(Stats.1965, c. 299, § 730.)

§ 760. "Direct examination"

"Direct examination" is the first examination of a witness upon a matter that is not within the scope of a previous examination of the witness.
(Stats.1965, c. 299, § 760.)

§ 761. "Cross-examination"

"Cross-examination" is the examination of a witness by a party other than the direct examiner upon a matter that is within the scope of the direct examination of the witness.
(Stats.1965, c. 299, § 761.)

§ 762. "Redirect examination"

"Redirect examination" is an examination of a witness by the direct examiner subsequent to the cross-examination of the witness.
(Stats.1965, c. 299, § 762.)

§ 763. "Recross-examination"

"Recross-examination" is an examination of a witness by a cross-examiner subsequent to a redirect examination of the witness.
(Stats.1965, c. 299, § 763.)

§ 764. "Leading question"

A "leading question" is a question that suggests to the witness the answer that the examining party desires.
(Stats.1965, c. 299, § 764.)

§ 765. Court to control mode of interrogation

The court shall exercise reasonable control over the mode of interrogation of a witness so as (a) to make such interrogation as rapid, as distinct, and as effective for the ascertainment of the truth, as may be, and (b) to protect the witness from undue harassment or embarrassment.
(Stats.1965, c. 299, § 765.)

§ 766. Responsive answers

A witness must give responsive answers to questions, and answers that are not responsive shall be stricken on motion of any party.
(Stats.1965, c. 299, § 766.)

§ 767. Leading questions

Except under special circumstances where the interests of justice otherwise require:

(a) A leading question may not be asked of a witness on direct or redirect examination.

(b) A leading question may be asked of a witness on cross-examination or recross-examination.
(Stats.1965, c. 299, § 767.)

§ 768. Writings

(a) In examining a witness concerning a writing, it is not necessary to show, read, or disclose to him any part of the writing.

(b) If a writing is shown to a witness, all parties to the action must be given an opportunity to inspect it before any question concerning it may be asked of the witness.
(Stats.1965, c. 299, § 768.)

§ 769. Inconsistent statement or conduct

In examining a witness concerning a statement or other conduct by him that is inconsistent with any part of his testimony at the hearing, it is not necessary to disclose to him any information concerning the statement or other conduct.
(Stats.1965, c. 299, § 769.)

§ 770. Evidence of inconsistent statement of witness

Unless the interests of justice otherwise require, extrinsic evidence of a statement made by a witness that is inconsistent with any part of his testimony at the hearing shall be excluded unless:

(a) The witness was so examined while testifying as to give him an opportunity to explain or to deny the statement; or

(b) The witness has not been excused from giving further testimony in the action.
(Stats.1965, c. 299, § 770.)

§ 771. Production of writing used to refresh memory

(a) Subject to subdivision (c), if a witness, either while testifying or prior thereto, uses a writing to refresh his memory with respect to any matter about which he testifies, such writing must be produced at the hearing at the request of an adverse party and, unless the writing is so produced, the testimony of the witness concerning such matter shall be stricken.

(b) If the writing is produced at the hearing, the adverse party may, if he chooses, inspect the writing, cross-examine the witness concerning it, and introduce in evidence such portion of it as may be pertinent to the testimony of the witness.

(c) Production of the writing is excused, and the testimony of the witness shall not be stricken, if the writing:

(1) Is not in the possession or control of the witness or the party who produced his testimony concerning the matter; and

(2) Was not reasonably procurable by such party through the use of the court's process or other available means.
(Stats.1965, c. 299, § 771.)

Comment—Assembly Committee on Judiciary

Section 771 grants to an adverse party the right to inspect any writing used to refresh a witness' recollection, whether the writing is used by the witness while testifying or prior thereto. . . . In a criminal case, the defendant can compel the prosecution to produce any written statement of a prosecution witness relating to matters covered in the witness' testimony. People v. Estrada, 54 Cal.2d 713, 7 Cal.Rptr. 897, 355 P.2d 641 (1960). . . .

§ 772. Order of examination

(a) The examination of a witness shall proceed in the following phases: direct examination, cross-examination, redirect examination, recross-examination, and continuing thereafter by redirect and recross-examination.

(b) Unless for good cause the court otherwise directs, each phase of the examination of a witness must be concluded before the succeeding phase begins.

(c) Subject to subdivision (d), a party may, in the discretion of the court, interrupt his cross-examination, redirect examination, or recross-examination of a witness, in order to examine the witness upon a matter not within the scope of a previous examination of the witness.

(d) If the witness is the defendant in a criminal action, the witness may not, without his consent, be examined under direct examination by another party.
(Stats.1965, c. 299, § 772.)

§ 773. Cross-examination

(a) A witness examined by one party may be cross-examined upon any matter within the scope of the direct examination by each other party to the action in such order as the court directs.

(b) The cross-examination of a witness by any party whose interest is not adverse to the party calling him is subject to the same rules that are applicable to the direct examination.
(Stats.1965, c. 299, § 773.)

§ 774. Re-examination

A witness once examined cannot be reexamined as to the same matter without leave of the court, but he may be reexamined as to any new matter upon which he has been examined by another party to the action. Leave may be granted or withheld in the court's discretion.
(Stats.1965, c. 299, § 774.)

§ 775. Court may call witnesses

The court, on its own motion or on the motion of any party, may call witnesses and interrogate them the same as if they had been produced by a party to the action, and the parties may object to the questions asked and the evidence adduced the same as if such witnesses were called and examined by an adverse party. Such witnesses may be cross-examined by all parties to the action in such order as the court directs.
(Stats.1965, c. 299, § 775.)

§ 777. Exclusion of witness

(a) Subject to subdivisions (b) and (c), the court may exclude from the courtroom any witness not at the time under examination so that such witness cannot hear the testimony of other witnesses.

(b) A party to the action cannot be excluded under this section.

(c) If a person other than a natural person is a party to the action, an officer or employee designated by its attorney is entitled to be present.
(Stats.1965, c. 299, § 777.)

§ 778. Recall of witness

After a witness has been excused from giving further testimony in the action, he cannot be recalled without leave of the court. Leave may be granted or withheld in the court's discretion.
(Stats.1965, c. 299, § 778.)

§ 780. General rule as to credibility

Except as otherwise provided by statute, the court or jury may consider in determining the credibility of a witness any matter that has any tendency in reason to prove or disprove the truthfulness of his testimony at the hearing, including but not limited to any of the following:

(a) His demeanor while testifying and the manner in which he testifies.

(b) The character of his testimony.

(c) The extent of his capacity to perceive, to recollect, or to communicate any matter about which he testifies.

(d) The extent of his opportunity to perceive any matter about which he testifies.

(e) His character for honesty or veracity or their opposites.

(f) The existence or nonexistence of a bias, interest, or other motive.

(g) A statement previously made by him that is consistent with his testimony at the hearing.

(h) A statement made by him that is inconsistent with any part of his testimony at the hearing.

(i) The existence or nonexistence of any fact testified to by him.

(j) His attitude toward the action in which he testifies or toward the giving of testimony.

(k) His admission of untruthfulness.
(Stats.1965, c. 299, § 780.)

Notes of Decisions
Impeaching credibility in general
Extrajudicial statements made during interrogation by defendant regarding his striking of victim with brick and his killing of victim, although received in violation of Miranda decision regarding the advising of an accused of his constitutional rights, were admissible to impeach credibility of defendant whose testimony was inconsistent with statements. People v. Castaneda (1975) 125 Cal.Rptr. 9, 52 C.A.3d 334.

§ 782. Rape; evidence of sexual conduct of complaining witness; procedure for admissibility

(a) In any prosecution under Section 261, or 264.1 of the Penal Code, or for assault with intent to commit, attempt to commit, or conspiracy to commit any crime defined in any such section, if evidence of sexual conduct of the complaining witness is offered to attack the credibility of the complaining witness under Section 780, the following procedure shall be followed:

(1) A written motion shall be made by the defendant to the court and prosecutor stating that the defense has an offer of proof of the relevancy of evidence of the sexual conduct of the complaining witness proposed to be presented and its relevancy in attacking the credibility of the complaining witness.

§ 782

(2) The written motion shall be accompanied by an affidavit in which the offer of proof shall be stated.

(3) If the court finds that the offer of proof is sufficient, the court shall order a hearing out of the presence of the jury, if any, and at such hearing allow the questioning of the complaining witness regarding the offer of proof made by the defendant.

(4) At the conclusion of the hearing, if the court finds that evidence proposed to be offered by the defendant regarding the sexual conduct of the complaining witness is relevant pursuant to Section 780, and is not inadmissible pursuant to Section 352 of this code, the court may make an order stating what evidence may be introduced by the defendant, and the nature of the questions to be permitted. The defendant may then offer evidence pursuant to the order of the court.

(b) As used in this section, "complaining witness" means the alleged victim of the crime charged, the prosecution of which is subject to this section.
(Added by Stats.1974, c. 569, p. 1388, § 1.)

Notes of Decisions

Validity

Provision of this section imposing a procedural limitation on the admissibility of evidence of sexual conduct of the alleged victim of a rape or a related offense offered to attack her credibility is not unconstitutionally vague, nor could the provision, as applied by the trial judge in the instant case, have conceivably tended to incriminate defendant, despite his claim of a violation of his privilege against self-incrimination. People v. Blackburn (1976) 128 Cal.Rptr. 864, 56 C.A.3d 685.

Offer of proof

Rape defendant's offer of proof, as a predicate for the admissibility of evidence of sexual conduct by the alleged victim in order to attack her credibility, was insufficient, since the barred impeachment evidence concerned only the collateral matter of the accuracy of the victim's testimony at the preliminary hearing in an area of improper cross-examination. People v. Blackburn (1976) 128 Cal. Rptr. 864, 56 C.A.3d 685.

§ 785. Parties may attack or support credibility

The credibility of a witness may be attacked or supported by any party, including the party calling him.
(Stats.1965, c. 299, § 785.)

§ 786. Character evidence generally

Evidence of traits of his character other than honesty or veracity, or their opposites, is inadmissible to attack or support the credibility of a witness.
(Stats.1965, c. 299, § 786.)

§ 787. Specific instances of conduct

Subject to Section 788, evidence of specific instances of his conduct relevant only as tending to prove a trait of his character is inadmissible to attack or support the credibility of a witness.
(Stats.1965, c. 299, § 787.)

Editors' Note

Read People v. Beagle in table of cases included in this text.

§ 788. Prior felony conviction

For the purpose of attacking the credibility of a witness, it may be shown by the examination of the witness or by the record of the judgment that he has been convicted of a felony unless:

(a) A pardon based on his innocence has been granted to the witness by the jurisdiction in which he was convicted.

(b) A certificate of rehabilitation and pardon has been granted to the witness under the provisions of Chapter 3.5 (commencing with Section 4852.01) of Title 6 of Part 3 of the Penal Code.

(c) The accusatory pleading against the witness has been dismissed under the provisions of Penal Code Section 1203.4, but this exception does not apply to any criminal trial where the witness is being prosecuted for a subsequent offense.

(d) The conviction was under the laws of another jurisdiction and the witness has been relieved of the penalties and disabilities arising from the conviction pursuant to a procedure substantially equivalent to that referred to in subdivision (b) or (c).
(Stats.1965, c. 299, § 788.)

Editors' Note

Read People v. Beagle in table of cases included in this text.

§ 789. Religious belief

Evidence of his religious belief or lack thereof is inadmissible to attack or support the credibility of a witness.
(Stats.1965, c. 299, § 789.)

§ 790. Good character of witness

Evidence of the good character of a witness is inadmissible to support his credibility unless evidence of his bad character has been admitted for the purpose of attacking his credibility.
(Stats.1965, c. 299, § 790.)

§ 791. Prior consistent statement of witness

Evidence of a statement previously made by a witness that is consistent with his testimony at the hearing is inadmissible to support his credibility unless it is offered after:

(a) Evidence of a statement made by him that is inconsistent with any part of his testimony at the hearing has been admitted for the purpose of attacking his credibility, and the statement was made before the alleged inconsistent statement; or

(b) An express or implied charge has been made that his testimony at the hearing is recently fabricated or is influenced by bias or other improper motive, and the statement was made before the bias, motive for fabrication, or other improper motive is alleged to have arisen.

(Stats.1965, c. 299, § 791.)

Division 7
OPINION TESTIMONY AND SCIENTIFIC EVIDENCE

§ 800. Opinion testimony by lay witness

If a witness is not testifying as an expert, his testimony in the form of an opinion is limited to such an opinion as is permitted by law, including but not limited to an opinion that is:

(a) Rationally based on the perception of the witness; and

(b) Helpful to a clear understanding of his testimony.

(Stats.1965, c. 299, § 800.)

§ 801. Opinion testimony by expert witness

If a witness is testifying as an expert, his testimony in the form of an opinion is limited to such an opinion as is:

(a) Related to a subject that is sufficiently beyond common experience that the opinion of an expert would assist the trier of fact; and

(b) Based on matter (including his special knowledge, skill, experience, training, and education) perceived by or personally known to the witness or made known to him at or before the hearing, whether or not admissible, that is of a type that reasonably may be relied upon by an expert in forming an opinion upon the subject to which his testimony relates, unless an expert is precluded by law from using such matter as a basis for his opinion.

(Stats.1965, c. 299, § 801.)

§ 802. Statement of basis of opinion

A witness testifying in the form of an opinion may state on direct examination the reasons for his opinion and the matter (including, in the case of an expert, his special knowledge, skill, experience, training, and education) upon which it is based, unless he is precluded by law from using such reasons or matter as a basis for his opinion. The court in its discretion may require that a witness before testifying in the form of an opinion be first examined concerning the matter upon which his opinion is based.

(Stats.1965, c. 299, § 802.)

§ 803. Opinion based on improper matter

The court may, and upon objection shall, exclude testimony in the form of an opinion that is based in whole or in significant part on matter that is not a proper basis for such an opinion. In such case, the witness may, if there remains a proper basis for his opinion, then state his opinion after excluding from consideration the matter determined to be improper.

(Stats.1965, c. 299, § 803.)

§ 805. Opinion on ultimate issue

Testimony in the form of an opinion that is otherwise admissible is not objectionable because it embraces the ultimate issue to be decided by the trier of fact.

(Stats.1965, c. 299, § 805.)

§ 870. Opinion as to sanity

A witness may state his opinion as to the sanity of a person when:

(a) The witness is an intimate acquaintance of the person whose sanity is in question;

(b) The witness was a subscribing witness to a writing, the validity of which is in dispute, signed by the person whose sanity is in question and the opinion relates to the sanity of such person at the time the writing was signed; or

(c) The witness is qualified under Section 800 or 801 to testify in the form of an opinion.

(Stats.1965, c. 299, § 870.)

Comment—Law Revision Commission

* * * Section 870 does not disturb the present rule that permits a witness to testify to a person's rational or irrational appearance or

conduct, even though the witness is not qualified under Section 870 to express an opinion on the person's sanity. See Pfingst v. Goetting, 96 Cal.App.2d 293, 215 P.2d 93 (1950).

Division 8
PRIVILEGES

§ 911. General rule as to privileges

Except as otherwise provided by statute:

(a) No person has a privilege to refuse to be a witness.

(b) No person has a privilege to refuse to disclose any matter or to refuse to produce any writing, object, or other thing.

(c) No person has a privilege that another shall not be a witness or shall not disclose any matter or shall not produce any writing, object, or other thing. (Stats.1965, c. 299, § 911.)

§ 912. Waiver of privilege

(a) Except as otherwise provided in this section, the right of any person to claim a privilege provided by Section 954 (lawyer-client privilege), 980 (privilege for confidential marital communications), 994 (physician-patient privilege), 1014 (psychotherapist-patient privilege), 1033 (privilege of penitent), or 1034 (privilege of clergyman) is waived with respect to a communication protected by such privilege if any holder of the privilege, without coercion, has disclosed a significant part of the communication or has consented to such disclosure made by anyone. Consent to disclosure is manifested by any statement or other conduct of the holder of the privilege indicating his consent to the disclosure, including his failure to claim the privilege in any proceeding in which he has the legal standing and opportunity to claim the privilege.

(b) Where two or more persons are joint holders of a privilege provided by Section 954 (lawyer-client privilege), 994 (physician-patient privilege), or 1014 (psychotherapist-patient privilege), a waiver of the right of a particular joint holder of the privilege to claim the privilege does not affect the right of another joint holder to claim the privilege. In the case of the privilege provided by Section 980 (privilege for confidential marital communications), a waiver of the right of one spouse to claim the privilege does not affect the right of the other spouse to claim the privilege.

(c) A disclosure that is itself privileged is not a waiver of any privilege.

(d) A disclosure in confidence of a communication that is protected by a privilege provided by Section 954 (lawyer-client privilege), 994 (physician-patient privilege), or 1014 (psychotherapist-patient privilege), when such disclosure is reasonably necessary for the accomplishment of the purpose for which the lawyer, physician, or psychotherapist was consulted, is not a waiver of the privilege.
(Stats.1965, c. 299, § 912.)

Comment—Senate Committee on Judiciary

This section covers in some detail the matter of waiver of those privileges that protect confidential communications.

Subdivision (a). Subdivision (a) states the general rule with respect to the manner in which a privilege is waived. Failure to claim the privilege where the holder of the privilege has the legal standing and the opportunity to claim the privilege constitutes a waiver. This seems to be the existing law. See City & County of San Francisco v. Superior Court, 37 Cal.2d 227, 233, 231 P.2d 26, 29 (1951); Lissak v. Crocker Estate Co., 119 Cal. 442, 51 P. 688 (1897). There is, however, at least one case that is out of harmony with this rule. People v. Kor, 129 Cal.App.2d 436, 277 P.2d 94 (1954) (defendant's failure to claim privilege to prevent a witness from testifying to a communication between the defendant and his attorney held not to waive the privilege to prevent the attorney from similarly testifying).

Subdivision (b). A waiver of the privilege by a joint holder of the privilege does not operate to waive the privilege for any of the other joint holders of the privilege. This codifies existing law. See People v. Kor, 129 Cal.App.2d 436, 277 P.2d 94 (1954); People v. Abair, 102 Cal.App.2d 765, 228 P.2d 336 (1951).

Subdivision (c). A privilege is not waived when a revelation of the privileged matter takes place in another privileged communication. Thus, for example, a person does not waive his lawyer-client privilege by telling his wife in confidence what it was that he told his attorney. Nor does a person waive the marital communication privilege by telling his attorney in confidence in the course of the attorney-client relationship what is was that he told his wife. And a person does not waive the lawyer-client privilege as to a communication by relating it to another attorney in the course of a separate relationship. A privileged communication should not cease to be privileged merely because it has been related in the course of another privileged communication. The theory underlying the concept of waiver is that the holder of the privilege has abandoned the secrecy to which he is entitled under the privilege. Where the revelation of the privileged matter takes place in another privileged communication, there has not been such an abandonment. Of course, this rule does not apply unless the revelation was within the scope of the relationship in which it was made; a client consulting his lawyer on a contract matter who blurts out that he told his doctor that he had a venereal disease has waived the privilege, even though he intended the revelation to be confidential, because the revelation was not necessary to the contract business at hand.

Subdivision (d). Subdivision (d) is designed to maintain the confidentiality of communications in certain situations where the communications are disclosed to others in the course of accomplishing the purpose for which the lawyer, physician, or psychotherapist was consulted. For example, where a confidential communication from a client is related by his attorney to a physician, appraiser, or other expert in order to obtain that person's assistance so that the attorney will better be able to advise his client, the disclosure is not a waiver of the privilege, even though the disclosure is made with the client's knowledge and consent. Nor would a physician's or psychotherapist's keeping of confidential records necessary to diagnose or treat a patient, such as confidential hospital records, be a waiver of the privilege, even though other authorized persons have access to the records. Similarly, the patient's presentation of a physician's prescription to a registered pharmacist would not constitute a waiver of the physician-patient privilege because such disclosure is reasonably necessary for the accomplishment of the purpose for which the physician is consulted. See also Evidence Code § 992. Communications such as these, when made in confidence, should not operate to destroy the privilege even when they are made with the consent of the client or patient. Here, again, the privilege holder has not evidenced any abandonment of secrecy. Hence, he should be entitled to maintain the confidential nature of his communications to his attorney or physician despite the necessary further disclosure.

Subdivision (d) may change California law. Green v. Superior Court, 220 Cal.App.2d 121, 33 Cal.Rptr. 604 (1963) (hearing denied), held that the physician-patient privilege did not provide protection against disclosure by a pharmacist of information concerning the nature of drugs dispensed upon prescription. See also Himmelfarb v. United States, 175 F.2d 924 (9th Cir. 1949) (applying the California law of privileges and holding that a lawyer's revelation to an accountant of a client's communication to the lawyer waived the client's privilege if such revelation was authorized by the client).

§ 913. Comment on, and inferences from, exercise of privilege

(a) If in the instant proceeding or on a prior occasion a privilege is or was exercised not to testify with respect to any matter, or to refuse to disclose or to prevent another from disclosing any matter, neither the presiding officer nor counsel may comment thereon, no presumption shall arise because of the exercise of the privilege, and the trier of fact may not draw any inference therefrom as to the credibility of the witness or as to any matter at issue in the proceeding.

(b) The court, at the request of a party who may be adversely affected because an unfavorable inference may be drawn by the jury because a privilege has been exercised, shall instruct the jury that no presumption arises because of the exercise of the privilege and that the jury may not draw any inference therefrom as to the credibility of the witness or as to any matter at issue in the proceeding.
(Stats.1965, c. 299, § 913.)

§ 914. Determination of claim of privilege; limitation on punishment for contempt

(a) The presiding officer shall determine a claim of privilege in any proceeding in the same manner as a court determines such a claim under Article 2 (commencing with Section 400) of Chapter 4 of Division 3.

(b) No person may be held in contempt for failure to disclose information claimed to be privileged unless he has failed to comply with an order of a court that he disclose such information. This subdivision does not apply to any governmental agency that has constitutional contempt power, nor does it apply to hearings and investigations of the Industrial Accident Commission, nor does it impliedly repeal Chapter 4 (commencing with Section 9400) of Part 1 of Division 2 of Title 2 of the Government Code. If no other statutory procedure is applicable, the procedure prescribed by Section 1991 of the Code of Civil Procedure shall be followed in seeking an order of a court that the person disclose the information claimed to be privileged.
(Stats.1965, c. 299, § 914.)

Comment—Assembly Committee on Judiciary

Subdivision (a) makes the general provisions concerning preliminary determinations on admissibility of evidence (Sections 400–406) applicable when a presiding officer who is not a judge is called upon to determine whether or not a privilege exists. Subdivision (a) is necessary because Sections 400–406, by their terms, apply only to determinations by a court.

Subdivision (b) is needed to protect persons claiming privileges in nonjudicial proceedings. Because such proceedings are often conducted by persons untrained in law, it is desirable to have a judicial determination of whether a person is required to disclose information claimed to be privileged before he can be held in contempt for failing to disclose such information. What is contemplated is that, if a claim of privilege is made in a nonjudicial proceeding and is overruled, application must be made to a court for an order compelling the witness to answer. Only if such order is made and is disobeyed may a witness be held in contempt. That the determination of privilege in a judicial proceeding is a question for the judge is well-established California law. See, e. g., Holm v. Superior Court, 42 Cal.2d 500, 507, 267 P.2d 1025, 1029 (1954).

Subdivision (b), of course, does not apply to any body—such as the Public Utilities Commission—that has constitutional power to impose punishment for contempt. See, e. g., Cal.Const., Art. XII, § 22. Nor does this subdivision apply to witnesses before the State Legislature or its committees. See Govt.Code §§ 9400–9414. Likewise, subdivision (b) does not apply to hearings and investigations of the State Industrial Accident Commission.

§ 915. Disclosure of privileged information in ruling on claim of privilege

(a) Subject to subdivision (b), the presiding officer may not require disclosure of information claimed to be privileged under this division in order to rule on the claim of privilege.

(b) When a court is ruling on a claim of privilege under Article 9 (commencing with Section 1040) of Chapter 4 (official information and identity of informer) or under Section 1060 (trade secret) and is unable to do so without requiring disclosure of the

§ 915

information claimed to be privileged, the court may require the person from whom disclosure is sought or the person authorized to claim the privilege, or both, to disclose the information in chambers out of the presence and hearing of all persons except the person authorized to claim the privilege and such other persons as the person authorized to claim the privilege is willing to have present. If the judge determines that the information is privileged, neither he nor any other person may ever disclose, without the consent of a person authorized to permit disclosure, what was disclosed in the course of the proceedings in chambers.
(Stats.1965, c. 299, § 915.)

Comment—Law Revision Commission

Subdivision (a) states the general rule that revelation of the information asserted to be privileged may not be compelled in order to determine whether or not it is privileged. This codifies existing law. See Collette v. Sarrasin, 184 Cal. 283, 288–289, 193 Pac. 571, 573 (1920); People v. Glen Arms Estate, Inc., 230 Cal.App.2d 841, 846 note 1, 41 Cal.Rptr. 303, 305 note 1 (1964).

Subdivision (b) provides an exception to this general rule for information claimed to be privileged under Section 1040 (official information), Section 1041 (identity of an informer), or Section 1060 (trade secret). These privileges exist only if the interest in maintaining the secrecy of the information outweighs the interest in seeing that justice is done in the particular case. In at least some cases, it will be necessary for the judge to examine the information claimed to be privileged in order to balance these competing considerations intelligently. See People v. Glen Arms Estate, Inc., 230 Cal.App.2d 841, 846 note 1, 41 Cal.Rptr. 303, 305 note 1 (1964), and the cases cited in 8 Wigmore, Evidence § 2379 at 812 note 6 (McNaughton rev. 1961). And see United States v. Reynolds, 345 U.S. 1, 7–11 (1953), and pertinent discussion thereof in 8 Wigmore, Evidence § 2379 (McNaughton rev. 1961). Even in these cases, Section 915 undertakes to give adequate protection to the person claiming the privilege by providing that the information be disclosed in confidence to the judge and requiring that it be kept in confidence if it is found to be privileged.

The exception in subdivision (b) applies only when a court is ruling on the claim of privilege. Thus, in view of subdivision (a), disclosure of the information cannot be required, for example, in an administrative proceeding.

§ 916. Exclusion of privileged information where persons authorized to claim privilege are not present

(a) The presiding officer, on his own motion or on the motion of any party, shall exclude information that is subject to a claim of privilege under this division if:

(1) The person from whom the information is sought is not a person authorized to claim the privilege; and

(2) There is no party to the proceeding who is a person authorized to claim the privilege.

(b) The presiding officer may not exclude information under this section if:

(1) He is otherwise instructed by a person authorized to permit disclosure; or

(2) The proponent of the evidence establishes that there is no person authorized to claim the privilege in existence.
(Stats.1965, c. 299, § 916.)

Comment—Assembly Committee on Judiciary

Section 916 is needed to protect the holder of a privilege when he is not available to protect his own interest. For example, a third party—perhaps the lawyer's secretary—may have been present when a confidential communication to a lawyer was made. In the absence of both the holder himself and the lawyer, the secretary could be compelled to testify concerning the communication if there were no provision such as Section 916 which requires the presiding officer to recognize the privilege.

Section 916 is designed to protect only privileged information that the holder of the privilege could protect by claiming the privilege at the hearing. It is not designed to protect unprivileged information. For example, if the statement offered in evidence is a declaration against the penal interest of the declarant, Section 916 does not authorize the presiding officer to exclude the evidence on the ground of the declarant's privilege against self-incrimination. If the declarant were present, his self-incrimination privilege would merely preclude his giving self-incriminating testimony at the hearing; it could not be asserted to prevent the disclosure of previously made self-incriminating statements.

The erroneous exclusion of information pursuant to Section 916 on the ground that it is privileged might amount to prejudicial error. On the other hand, the erroneous failure to exclude information pursuant to Section 916 could *not* amount to prejudicial error. See Evidence Code § 918.

Section 916 may be declarative of the existing law. No case in point has been found, but see the language in People v. Atkinson, 40 Cal. 284, 285 (1870) (attorney-client privilege).

§ 917. Presumption that certain communications are confidential

Whenever a privilege is claimed on the ground that the matter sought to be disclosed is a communication made in confidence in the course of the lawyer-client, physician-patient, psychotherapist-patient, clergyman-penitent, or husband-wife relationship, the communication is presumed to have been made in confidence and the opponent of the claim of privilege has the burden of proof to establish that the communication was not confidential.
(Stats.1965, c. 299, § 917.)

Comment—Assembly Committee on Judiciary

A number of sections provide privileges for communications made "in confidence" in the course of certain relationships. Although there appear to have been no cases involving the question in California, the general rule elsewhere is that a communication made in the course of such a relationship is presumed to be confidential and the party objecting to the claim of privilege has the burden of showing that it was not. See generally, with respect to the marital communication privilege, 8 Wigmore, Evidence § 2336 (McNaughton rev. 1961). See also Blau v. United States, 340 U.S. 332, 333–335 (1951) (holding that marital communications are presumed to be confidential). In adopting by statute a revised version of the privileges article of the Uniform Rules of Evidence, New Jersey included such a provision in its statement of the lawyer-client privilege. N.J.Rev.Stat. § 2A:84A–20(3), added by N.J.Laws 1960, Ch. 52, p. 452.

If the privilege claimant were required to show that the communication was made in confidence, he would be compelled, in many cases, to reveal the subject matter of the communication in order to establish his right to the privilege. Hence, Section 917 is included to establish a presumption of confidentiality, if this is not already the existing law in California. See Sharon v. Sharon, 79 Cal. 633, 678, 22 Pac. 26, 40 (1889) (attorney-client privilege); Hager v. Shindler, 29 Cal. 47, 63 (1865) ("*Prima facie*, all communications made by a client to his attorney or counsel [in the course of that relationship] must be regarded as confidential.").

To overcome the presumption, the proponent of the evidence must persuade the presiding officer that the communication was not made in confidence. Of course, if the facts show that the communication was not intended to be kept in confidence, the communication is not privileged. See Solon v. Lichtenstein, 39 Cal.2d 75, 244 P.2d 907 (1952). And the fact that the communication was made under circumstances where others could easily overhear is a strong indication that the communication was not intended to be confidential and is, therefore, unprivileged. See Sharon v. Sharon, 79 Cal. 633, 677, 22 Pac. 26, 39 (1889); People v. Castiel, 153 Cal.App.2d 653, 315 P.2d 79 (1957).

§ 918. Effect of error in overruling claim of privilege

A party may predicate error on a ruling disallowing a claim of privilege only if he is the holder of the privilege, except that a party may predicate error on a ruling disallowing a claim of privilege by his spouse under Section 970 or 971.
(Stats.1965, c. 299, § 918.)

§ 919. Admissibility where disclosure erroneously compelled; claim of privilege; coercion

(a) Evidence of a statement or other disclosure of privileged information is inadmissible against a holder of the privilege if:

(1) A person authorized to claim the privilege claimed it but nevertheless disclosure erroneously was required to be made; or

(2) The presiding officer did not exclude the privileged information as required by Section 916.

(b) If a person authorized to claim the privilege claimed it, whether in the same or a prior proceeding, but nevertheless disclosure erroneously was required by the presiding officer to be made, neither the failure to refuse to disclose nor the failure to seek review of the order of the presiding officer requiring disclosure indicates consent to the disclosure or constitutes a waiver and, under these circumstances, the disclosure is one made under coercion.
(Amended by Stats.1974, c. 227, p. 426, § 1.)

Law Revision Commission Comment 1974 Amendment

Subdivision (b) has been added to Section 919 to make clear that, after disclosure of privileged information has been erroneously required to be made by order of a trial court or other presiding officer, neither the failure to refuse to disclose nor the failure to challenge the order (by, for example, a petition for a writ of habeas corpus or other special writ or by an appeal from a contempt order) amounts to a waiver and the disclosure is one made under coercion for the purposes of Sections 912(a) and 919(a)(1). See Section 905 (defining "presiding officer"). The addition of subdivision (b) will preclude any possibility of a contrary interpretation of Sections 912 and 919 based on the language found in Markwell v. Sykes, 173 Cal.App.2d 642, 649–650, 343 P.2d 769, 773–774 (1959). See Recommendation Relating to Erroneously Ordered Disclosure of Privileged Information, 11 Cal.L.Revision Comm'n Reports 1163 (1973).

The phrase "whether in the same or a prior proceeding" has been included in subdivision (b) to avoid any implication that might be drawn from the original Law Revision Commission Comment to Section 919 that subdivision (a)(1) applies only where the privilege was claimed in a prior proceeding. The protection afforded by Section 919, of course, also applies where a claim of privilege is made at an earlier stage in the same proceeding and the presiding officer erroneously overruled the claim and ordered disclosure of the privileged information to be made.

§ 930. Privilege not to be called as a witness and not to testify

To the extent that such privilege exists under the Constitution of the United States or the State of California, a defendant in a criminal case has a privilege not to be called as a witness and not to testify.
(Stats.1965, c. 299, § 930.)

Editors' Note

Read Miranda v. Arizona in table of cases included in this text.

Comment—Law Revision Commission

Section 930 recognizes that the defendant in a criminal case has a constitutional privilege not to be called as a witness and not to testify. Cal.Const., Art. I, § 13. See Killpatrick v. Superior Court, 153 Cal.App.2d 146, 314 P.2d 164 (1957); People v. Talle, 111 Cal.App.2d 650, 245 P.2d 633 (1952). Section 930 also recognizes that the defendant may have a similar privilege under the United States Constitution. See Malloy v. Hogan, 378 U.S. 1 (1964).

§ 940. Privilege against self-incrimination

To the extent that such privilege exists under the Constitution of the United States or the State of

§ 940

California, a person has a privilege to refuse to disclose any matter that may tend to incriminate him.
(Stats.1965, c. 299, § 940.)

Editors' Note

Read Miranda v. Arizona in table of cases included in this text.

§ 950. "Lawyer"

As used in this article, "lawyer" means a person authorized, or reasonably believed by the client to be authorized, to practice law in any state or nation.
(Stats.1965, c. 299, § 950.)

§ 951. "Client"

As used in this article, "client" means a person who, directly or through an authorized representative, consults a lawyer for the purpose of retaining the lawyer or securing legal service or advice from him in his professional capacity, and includes an incompetent (a) who himself so consults the lawyer or (b) whose guardian or conservator so consults the lawyer in behalf of the incompetent.
(Stats.1965, c. 299, § 951.)

§ 952. "Confidential communication between client and lawyer"

As used in this article, "confidential communication between client and lawyer" means information transmitted between a client and his lawyer in the course of that relationship and in confidence by a means which, so far as the client is aware, discloses the information to no third persons other than those who are present to further the interest of the client in the consultation or those to whom disclosure is reasonably necessary for the transmission of the information or the accomplishment of the purpose for which the lawyer is consulted, and includes a legal opinion formed and the advice given by the lawyer in the course of that relationship.
(As amended by Stats.1967, c. 650, p. 2006, § 3.)

§ 953. "Holder of the privilege"

As used in this article, "holder of the privilege" means:

(a) The client when he has no guardian or conservator.

(b) A guardian or conservator of the client when the client has a guardian or conservator.

(c) The personal representative of the client if the client is dead.

(d) A successor, assign, trustee in dissolution, or any similar representative of a firm, association, organization, partnership, business trust, corporation, or public entity that is no longer in existence.
(Stats.1965, c. 299, § 953.)

§ 954. Lawyer-client privilege

Subject to Section 912 and except as otherwise provided in this article, the client, whether or not a party, has a privilege to refuse to disclose, and to prevent another from disclosing, a confidential communication between client and lawyer if the privilege is claimed by:

(a) The holder of the privilege;

(b) A person who is authorized to claim the privilege by the holder of the privilege; or

(c) The person who was the lawyer at the time of the confidential communication, but such person may not claim the privilege if there is no holder of the privilege in existence or if he is otherwise instructed by a person authorized to permit disclosure.

The relationship of attorney and client shall exist between a law corporation as defined in Article 10 (commencing with Section 6160) of Chapter 4 of Division 3 of the Business and Professions Code and the persons to whom it renders professional services, as well as between such persons and members of the State Bar employed by such corporation to render services to such persons. The word "persons" as used in this subdivision includes partnerships, corporations, associations and other groups and entities.
(Amended by Stats.1968, c. 1375, p. 2695, § 2.)

§ 955. When lawyer required to claim privilege

The lawyer who received or made a communication subject to the privilege under this article shall claim the privilege whenever he is present when the communication is sought to be disclosed and is authorized to claim the privilege under subdivision (c) of Section 954.
(Stats.1965, c. 299, § 955.)

§ 956. Exception: Crime or fraud

There is no privilege under this article if the services of the lawyer were sought or obtained to enable or aid anyone to commit or plan to commit a crime or a fraud.
(Stats.1965, c. 299, § 956.)

§ 970. Privilege not to testify against spouse

Except as otherwise provided by statute, a married person has a privilege not to testify against his spouse in any proceeding.
(Stats.1965, c. 299, § 970.)

§ 971. Privilege not to be called as a witness against spouse

Except as otherwise provided by statute, a married person whose spouse is a party to a proceeding has a privilege not to be called as a witness by an adverse party to that proceeding without the prior express consent of the spouse having the privilege under this section unless the party calling the spouse does so in good faith without knowledge of the marital relationship.
(Stats.1965, c. 299, § 971.)

§ 972. When privilege not applicable

A married person does not have a privilege under this article in:

(a) A proceeding brought by or on behalf of one spouse against the other spouse.

(b) A proceeding to commit or otherwise place his spouse or his spouse's property, or both, under the control of another because of the spouse's alleged mental or physical condition.

(c) A proceeding brought by or on behalf of a spouse to establish his competence.

(d) A proceeding under the Juvenile Court Law, Chapter 2 (commencing with Section 500) of Part 1 of Division 2 of the Welfare and Institutions Code.

(e) A criminal proceeding in which one spouse is charged with:

(1) A crime against the person or property of the other spouse or of a child of either, whether committed before or during marriage.

(2) A crime against the person or property of a third person committed in the course of committing a crime against the person or property of the other spouse, whether committed before or during marriage.

(3) Bigamy.

(4) A crime defined by Section 270 or 270a of the Penal Code.
(Amended by Stats.1975, c. 71, p. 132, § 2.)

§ 973. Waiver of privilege.

(a) Unless erroneously compelled to do so, a married person who testifies in a proceeding to which his spouse is a party, or who testifies against his spouse in any proceeding, does not have a privilege under this article in the proceeding in which such testimony is given.

(b) There is no privilege under this article in a civil proceeding brought or defended by a married person for the immediate benefit of his spouse or of himself and his spouse.
(Stats.1965, c. 299, § 973.)

§ 980. Privilege for confidential marital communications

Subject to Section 912 and except as otherwise provided in this article, a spouse (or his guardian or conservator when he has a guardian or conservator), whether or not a party, has a privilege during the marital relationship and afterwards to refuse to disclose, and to prevent another from disclosing, a communication if he claims the privilege and the communication was made in confidence between him and the other spouse while they were husband and wife.
(Stats.1965, c. 299, § 980.)

§ 981. Exception: Crime or fraud

There is no privilege under this article if the communication was made, in whole or in part, to enable or aid anyone to commit or plan to commit a crime or a fraud.
(Stats.1965, c. 299, § 981.)

§ 982. Exception: Commitment or similar proceeding

There is no privilege under this article in a proceeding to commit either spouse or otherwise place him or his property, or both, under the control of another because of his alleged mental or physical condition.
(Stats.1965, c. 299, § 982.)

§ 985. Exception: Certain criminal proceedings

There is no privilege under this article in a criminal proceeding in which one spouse is charged with:

(a) A crime committed at any time against the person or property of the other spouse or of a child of either.

(b) A crime committed at any time against the person or property of a third person committed in the course of committing a crime against the person or property of the other spouse.

(c) Bigamy.

(d) A crime defined by Section 270 or 270a of the Penal Code.

(Amended by Stats.1975, c. 71, p. 133, § 3.)

§ 987. Exception: Communication offered by spouse who is criminal defendant

There is no privilege under this article in a criminal proceeding in which the communication is offered in evidence by a defendant who is one of the spouses between whom the communication was made.

(Stats.1965, c. 299, § 987.)

§ 992. "Confidential communication between patient and physician"

As used in this article, "confidential communication between patient and physician" means information, including information obtained by an examination of the patient, transmitted between a patient and his physician in the course of that relationship and in confidence by a means which, so far as the patient is aware, discloses the information to no third persons other than those who are present to further the interest of the patient in the consultation or those to whom disclosure is reasonably necessary for the transmission of the information or the accomplishment of the purpose for which the physician is consulted, and includes a diagnosis made and the advice given by the physician in the course of that relationship.

(As amended by Stats.1967, c. 650, p. 2006, § 4.)

§ 998. Exception: Criminal proceeding

There is no privilege under this article in a criminal proceeding.

(Stats.1965, c. 299, § 998.)

§ 1010. "Psychotherapist"

As used in this article, "psychotherapist" means:

(a) A person authorized, or reasonably believed by the patient to be authorized, to practice medicine in any state or nation who devotes, or is reasonably believed by the patient to devote, a substantial portion of his time to the practice of psychiatry;

(b) A person licensed as a psychologist under Chapter 6.6 (commencing with Section 2900) of Division 2 of the Business and Professions Code;

(c) A person licensed as a clinical social worker under Article 4 (commencing with Section 9040) of Chapter 17 of Division 3 of the Business and Professions Code, when he is engaged in applied psychotherapy of a nonmedical nature.

(d) A person who is serving as a school psychologist and holds a credential authorizing such service issued by the state.

(e) A person licensed as a marriage, family and child counselor under Chapter 4 (commencing with Section 17800) of Part 3, Division 5 of the Business and Professions Code.

(Amended by Stats.1974, c. 546, p. 1359, § 16.)

§ 1011. "Patient"

As used in this article, "patient" means a person who consults a psychotherapist or submits to an examination by a psychotherapist for the purpose of securing a diagnosis or preventive, palliative, or curative treatment of his mental or emotional condition or who submits to an examination of his mental or emotional condition for the purpose of scientific research on mental or emotional problems.

(Stats.1965, c. 299, § 1011.)

§ 1012. "Confidential communication between patient and psychotherapist"

As used in this article, "confidential communication between patient and psychotherapist" means information, including information obtained by an examination of the patient, transmitted between a patient and his psychotherapist in the course of that relationship and in confidence by a means which, so far as the patient is aware, discloses the information to no third persons other than those who are present to further the interest of the patient in the consultation, or those to whom disclosure is reasonably necessary for the transmission of the information or the accomplishment of the purpose for which the psychotherapist is consulted, and includes a diagnosis made and the advice given by the psychotherapist in the course of that relationship.

(Amended by Stats.1970, c. 1397, p. 2627, § 2.)

§ 1013. "Holder of the privilege"

As used in this article, "holder of the privilege" means:

(a) The patient when he has no guardian or conservator.

(b) A guardian or conservator of the patient when the patient has a guardian or conservator.

(c) The personal representative of the patient if the patient is dead.

(Stats.1965, c. 299, § 1013.)

§ 1014. Psychotherapist-patient privilege; application to individuals and entities

Subject to Section 912 and except as otherwise provided in this article, the patient, whether or not a party, has a privilege to refuse to disclose, and to prevent another from disclosing, a confidential communication between patient and psychotherapist if the privilege is claimed by:

(a) The holder of the privilege;

(b) A person who is authorized to claim the privilege by the holder of the privilege; or

(c) The person who was the psychotherapist at the time of the confidential communication, but such person may not claim the privilege if there is no holder of the privilege in existence or if he is otherwise instructed by a person authorized to permit disclosure.

The relationship of a psychotherapist and patient shall exist between a psychological corporation as defined in Article 9 (commencing with Section 2995) of Chapter 6.6 of Division 2 of the Business and Professions Code or a licensed clinical social workers corporation as defined in Article 5 (commencing with Section 9070) of Chapter 17 of Division 3 of the Business and Professions Code, and the patient to whom it renders professional services, as well as between such patients and psychotherapists employed by such corporations to render services to such patients. The word "persons" as used in this subdivision includes partnerships, corporations, associations and other groups and entities.
(Amended by Stats.1972, c. 1286, p. 2569, § 6.)

§ 1015. When psychotherapist required to claim privilege

The psychotherapist who received or made a communication subject to the privilege under this article shall claim the privilege whenever he is present when the communication is sought to be disclosed and is authorized to claim the privilege under subdivision (c) of Section 1014.
(Stats.1965, c. 299, § 1015.)

§ 1016. Exception: Patient-litigant exception

There is no privilege under this article as to a communication relevant to an issue concerning the mental or emotional condition of the patient if such issue has been tendered by:

(a) The patient;

(b) Any party claiming through or under the patient;

(c) Any party claiming as a beneficiary of the patient through a contract to which the patient is or was a party; or

(d) The plaintiff in an action brought under Section 376 or 377 of the Code of Civil Procedure for damages for the injury or death of the patient.
(Stats.1965, c. 299, § 1016.)

§ 1017. Exception: Court-appointed psychotherapist

There is no privilege under this article if the psychotherapist is appointed by order of a court to examine the patient, but this exception does not apply where the psychotherapist is appointed by order of the court upon the request of the lawyer for the defendant in a criminal proceeding in order to provide the lawyer with information needed so that he may advise the defendant whether to enter or withdraw a plea based on insanity or to present a defense based on his mental or emotional condition.
(As amended by Stats.1967, c. 650, p. 2007, § 6.)

§ 1018. Exception: Crime or tort

There is no privilege under this article if the services of the psychotherapist were sought or obtained to enable or aid anyone to commit or plan to commit a crime or a tort or to escape detection or apprehension after the commission of a crime or a tort.
(Stats.1965, c. 299, § 1018.)

§ 1024. Exception: Patient dangerous to himself or others

There is no privilege under this article if the psychotherapist has reasonable cause to believe that the patient is in such mental or emotional condition as to be dangerous to himself or to the person or property of another and that disclosure of the communication is necessary to prevent the threatened danger.
(Stats.1965, c. 299, § 1024.)

§ 1025. Exception: Proceeding to establish competence

There is no privilege under this article in a proceeding brought by or on behalf of the patient to establish his competence.
(Stats.1965, c. 299, § 1025.)

§ 1026. Exception: Required report

There is no privilege under this article as to information that the psychotherapist or the patient is required to report to a public employee or as to information required to be recorded in a public office, if such report or record is open to public inspection.
(Stats.1965, c. 299, § 1026.)

§ 1027. Privilege nonexistent; patient child under 16 or victim of crime

There is no privilege under this article if all of the following circumstances exist:

(a) The patient is a child under the age of 16.

(b) The psychotherapist has reasonable cause to believe that the patient has been the victim of a crime and that disclosure of the communication is in the best interest of the child.
(Added by Stats.1970, c. 1397, p. 2627, § 3.)

§ 1030. "Clergyman"

As used in this article, "clergyman" means a priest, minister, religious practitioner, or similar functionary of a church or of a religious denomination or religious organization.
(Stats.1965, c. 299, § 1030.)

§ 1031. "Penitent"

As used in this article, "penitent" means a person who has made a penitential communication to a clergyman.
(Stats.1965, c. 299, § 1031.)

§ 1032. "Penitential communication"

As used in this article, "penitential communication" means a communication made in confidence, in the presence of no third person so far as the penitent is aware, to a clergyman who, in the course of the discipline or practice of his church, denomination, or organization, is authorized or accustomed to hear such communications and, under the discipline or tenets of his church, denomination, or organization, has a duty to keep such communications secret.
(Stats.1965, c. 299, § 1032.)

§ 1033. Privilege of penitent

Subject to Section 912, a penitent, whether or not a party, has a privilege to refuse to disclose, and to prevent another from disclosing, a penitential communication if he claims the privilege.
(Stats.1965, c. 299, § 1033.)

§ 1034. Privilege of clergyman

Subject to Section 912, a clergyman, whether or not a party, has a privilege to refuse to disclose a penitential communication if he claims the privilege.
(Stats.1965, c. 299, § 1034.)

§ 1040. Privilege for official information

(a) As used in this section, "official information" means information acquired in confidence by a public employee in the course of his duty and not open, or officially disclosed, to the public prior to the time the claim of privilege is made.

(b) A public entity has a privilege to refuse to disclose official information, and to prevent another from disclosing such information, if the privilege is claimed by a person authorized by the public entity to do so and:

(1) Disclosure is forbidden by an act of the Congress of the United States or a statute of this state; or

(2) Disclosure of the information is against the public interest because there is a necessity for preserving the confidentiality of the information that outweighs the necessity for disclosure in the interest of justice; but no privilege may be claimed under this paragraph if any person authorized to do so has consented that the information be disclosed in the proceeding. In determining whether disclosure of the information is against the public interest, the interest of the public entity as a party in the outcome of the proceeding may not be considered.
(Stats.1965, c. 299, § 1040.)

Comment—Assembly Committee on Judiciary

* * * The official information privilege provided in Section 1040 does not extend to the identity of an informer. Section 1041 provides special rules for determining when the government has a privilege to keep secret the identity of an informer.

§ 1041. Privilege for identity of informer

(a) Except as provided in this section, a public entity has a privilege to refuse to disclose the identity of a person who has furnished information as provided in subdivision (b) purporting to disclose a violation of a law of the United States or of this state or a public entity in this state, and to prevent another from disclosing such identity, if the privilege is claimed by a person authorized by the public entity to do so and:

(1) Disclosure is forbidden by an act of the Congress of the United States or a statute of this state; or

(2) Disclosure of the identity of the informer is against the public interest because there is a necessity for preserving the confidentiality of his identity that outweighs the necessity for disclosure in the interest of justice; but no privilege may be claimed under this paragraph if any person authorized to do so has consented that the identity of the informer be disclosed in the proceeding. In determining whether disclosure of the identity of the informer is against the public interest, the interest of the public entity as a party in the outcome of the proceeding may not be considered.

(b) This section applies only if the information is furnished in confidence by the informer to:

(1) A law enforcement officer;

(2) A representative of an administrative agency charged with the administration or enforcement of the law alleged to be violated; or

(3) Any person for the purpose of transmittal to a person listed in paragraph (1) or (2).

(c) There is no privilege under this section to prevent the informer from disclosing his identity. (Stats.1965, c. 299, § 1041.)

Notes of Decisions

In general

Whether nondisclosure to defendant of confidential informant's identity is erroneous depends on particular circumstances of each case, taking into consideration crime charged, possible defenses, possible significance of informant's testimony and other relevant factors. People v. O'Brien (App.1976) 132 Cal.Rptr. 616.

Defendant was not entitled to disclosure of informant's identity on issue of guilt or innocence where defendant did not show even a "reasonable probability" that the informant could provide testimony material to some theory of defense; assertion that since informant stated that two individuals were selling drugs and witness had never been to their residence the informant might testify that any contact he had made was through only one such individual did not warrant disclosure since defendant was charged with possession for sale based on personal possession of heroin when arrested and neither informant nor the contact could have furnished relevant information. People v. Rodgers (1976) 126 Cal.Rptr. 719, 54 C.A.3d 508.

In prosecution for possession of narcotics for sale, trial court's finding that defendants were entitled to disclosure of identity of informer was sustained by evidence which, inter alia, presented possibility that undisclosed informer might have given testimony in favor of either defendant which would have thrown onus of control or right to control narcotics found in the premises on the other defendant or on some third person present in residence when informer was there. People v. Tolliver (1975) 125 Cal.Rptr. 905, 53 C.A.3d 1036.

Person who merely identified a voice on a tape recording and who did not approach the authorities and inform them of criminal conduct but was approached by the authorities was nonetheless an "informant" whose identity the people had a right to refuse to disclose under this section granting privilege with respect to identity of informers. People v. Kelly (1975) 122 Cal.Rptr. 393, 49 C.A.3d 214.

Within this section granting public entities privilege to refuse to disclose identity of person who has furnished information purporting to disclose a violation of law, the covered disclosure includes the identity of the perpetrator. Id.

Under this section, it is not necessary to invocation of privilege by the people that contact between the informer and the officials was initiated by the informer rather than by the police. Id.

Defendant, convicted of violating Pen.C. § 12220 forbidding possession of machine gun and Pen.C. § 12021 forbidding ex-felons from possessing concealable firearms, failed to demonstrate any reasonable possibility that informant, whose personal observations were basis of affidavit for warrant for search of defendant's house for narcotics and dangerous drugs, might have aided in exonerating defendant who only made the bare suggestion, in attempting to compel disclosure of informant, that informant might establish that someone other than defendant possessed weapons found as a result of search pursuant to warrant. People v. Kilpatrick (1973) 107 Cal.Rptr. 367, 31 C.A.3d 431.

When a person who actively cooperates with the police becomes an eyewitness to a narcotics violation the police and prosecution must undertake reasonable efforts in good faith to locate the informer so that either party or the court itself could, if it so desired, subpoena him as a witness. People v. Goliday (1973) 106 Cal.Rptr. 113, 505 P.2d 537, 8 C.3d 771.

Where in camera hearing indicated that knowledge which informant had could not benefit defendant, who was charged with possession of marijuana, barbiturates and methamphetamine, and informant had given information leading to arrest of at least 50 persons and asserted that he had been harassed by suspects informed on and that he was afraid for himself and family if his identity and address became public, defendant was not entitled to disclosure of identity of informant. People v. Pacheco (1972) 103 Cal.Rptr. 583, 27 C.A.3d 70.

Where in camera hearing was held after defendant duly moved for disclosure of identity of informant whose "tip" had resulted in defendant's arrest and prosecution had claimed privilege, proceedings were reported, and reporter's transcript was sealed and transmitted to court of appeal as required by § 1042, defendant, under entire record, was not improperly denied disclosure of name of informant. People v. Doran (App.1972) 100 Cal.Rptr. 886.

Absent showing of theory of defense or other pertinent material, court cannot determine existence of a reasonable possibility that evidence to be obtained from anonymous informer may be helpful to defendant. People v. Sewell (1970) 83 Cal.Rptr. 895, 3 C.A.3d 1035.

Fact that police were without motive to harm defendant when they made no effort to learn residence of an informer to establish a way by which to locate him and did so merely to foster security of informer was not sufficient on which to justify prosecution's failure to disclose information concerning "identity" of informer. Eleazer v. Superior Court of Los Angeles County (1970) 83 Cal.Rptr. 586, 464 P.2d 42, 1 C.3d 847.

All defendants are required to do to show right to pretrial discovery of identity of informant is to demonstrate reasonable possibility that informant could give evidence on issue of guilt which might result in exoneration and defendants need not state facts showing materiality of testimony. Honore v. Superior Court of Alameda County (1969) 74 Cal.Rptr. 233, 449 P.2d 169, 70 C.2d 162.

Where no information contained in officer's affidavit on which search warrant was issued was relied on by prosecutor on issue of guilt and informers were neither participants nor eyewitnesses to crime of which defendants were convicted and defendants did not

§ 1041   EVIDENCE CODE

demonstrate how informers were material witnesses on issue of guilt, denying defendants' motion to strike officer's testimony on ground that officer refused to identify informants was not error. People v. De Leon (1968) 67 Cal.Rptr. 45, 260 C.A.2d 143, certiorari denied 89 S.Ct. 407, 393 U.S. 969, 21 L.Ed.2d 380.

Where disclosure of identity of informer was relevant and helpful to defense or essential to fair determination of cause inasmuch as informer was participant in sale of heroin to officer and witness to transactions, privilege against nondisclosure of identity of informer could not be invoked, but even so, prosecution was under no obligation to produce informant as witness when prosecution fully complied with request for disclosure by giving all information it had relative to identity and whereabouts of informer. People v. Lara (1967) 61 Cal.Rptr. 303, 253 C.A.2d 600.

Burden of proof

Where defendant demonstrates reasonable possibility that anonymous informant whose identity he seeks could give evidence on issue of his guilt which might result in defendant's exoneration, defendant has discharged burden of proving that informant would be "material witness," and is entitled to disclosure. People v. O'Brien (App.1976) 132 Cal.Rptr. 616.

To obtain disclosure of an informant's identity, defendant is not required to show that the informer was either a participant in crime charged or an eyewitness thereto; nor is it required that defendant establish that the informer would give favorable testimony. People v. Tolliver (1975) 125 Cal.Rptr. 905, 53 C.A.3d 1036.

Although defendant seeking to discover identity of informant bears burden of demonstrating that informant would be material witness on issue of guilt and nondisclosure of his identity would deprive defendant of fair trial, burden is discharged when defendant demonstrates reasonable possibility that anonymous informant whose identity is sought could give evidence on issue of guilt which might result in defendant's exoneration. People v. Borunda (1974) 113 Cal.Rptr. 825, 522 P.2d 5, 11 C.3d 523.

Defendant seeking to discover identity of informant has burden of showing that in view of evidence in particular case informant would be a material witness on issue of guilt and that nondisclosure would deprive him of a fair trial; burden is discharged by demonstrating a reasonable possibility that informant might be able to exonerate defendant. People v. Kilpatrick (1973) 107 Cal.Rptr. 367, 31 C.A.3d 431.

Defendant seeking to discover identity of informant bears burden of demonstrating that, in view of evidence, informer would be material witness on issue of guilt and nondisclosure of his identity would deprive defendant of fair trial. Theodor v. Superior Court of Orange County (1972) 104 Cal.Rptr. 226, 501 P.2d 234, 8 C.3d 77.

Discretion of court

In determining whether to require disclosure of identity of an informer, public interest in protecting flow of information and individual's right to prepare his defense must be balanced, and whether proper balance renders nondisclosure erroneous must depend on particular circumstances of each case, taking into consideration crime charged, possible defenses, possible significance of informer's testimony and other relevant factors. People v. Pacheco (1972) 103 Cal.Rptr. 583, 27 C.A.3d 70.

Rule regarding privileged communications makes informer testimony admissible to establish reasonable cause for arrest or search although judge exercises his discretion to forbid nondisclosure of informer's identity, if informer is shown to be reliable, and such rule is constitutional. People v. Hirsch (1967) 60 Cal.Rptr. 451, 252 C.A.2d 420.

Evidence produced by search of defendants who were arrested pursuant to information received by sheriff's office from treasury department official who, in turn, received such information from reliable informer was not rendered inadmissible by prosecution's failure to disclose name of informer since, in light of circumstances testified to by treasury department official who testified to informer's reliability and who was subjected to cross-examination, it was within sound discretion of trial judge to permit evidence to be so introduced. People v. Sanders (1967) 58 Cal.Rptr. 259, 250 C.A.2d 123.

Official confidence

Where there was nothing to indicate that informer himself had either been in defendant's apartment or in some other way had been personally involved in heroin being placed or kept in hiding there, although inference to such effect could be drawn from detailed nature of information which informer furnished, trial court in prosecution for possession of heroin correctly sustained officer's claim of privilege as to name of informer. People v. Johnson (1970) 92 Cal.Rptr. 105, 13 C.A.3d 742.

Testimony of police officer, who arrested one of the defendants for possession of marijuana and heroin for purpose of sale, on cross-examination that he would not reveal name of his informant because to do so would destroy usefulness of informant and imperil his life supported trial court's finding that refusal to name informant was justified under this section. People v. Marquez (1968) 66 Cal.Rptr. 615, 259 C.A.2d 593, certiorari denied 89 S.Ct. 386, 393 U.S. 955, 21 L.Ed.2d 367.

Materiality of identity

Under evidence that abandoned truck discovered by police had been used to transport stolen safe, that truck was taken into custody, that truck was stolen from storage yard, that confidential informant told police that truck was located in private garage, that lessee of garage had received telephone call from defendant asking lessee to paint truck, and that truck was discovered at lessee's shop shortly thereafter, informant could not have been "material witness" to burglary with which defendant was charged, and thus defendant was not entitled to disclosure of informant's identity. People v. O'Brien (App.1976) 132 Cal.Rptr. 616.

Within rule that privilege for nondisclosure of an informant's identity does not apply if the informer is a material witness for a defendant, "material witness" means an informant with respect to whom there is a reasonable possibility that he could give evidence bearing on the defendant's guilt that might exonerate defendant of the criminal charge. People v. Tolliver (1975) 125 Cal.Rptr. 905, 53 C.A.3d 1036.

Remedy of defendant who desired disclosure of identity of confidential informant was by motion in the trial court where evidence would have been taken on the question of the materiality of the informant's testimony on the issue of guilt. People v. Flemmings (1973) 109 Cal.Rptr. 661, 34 C.A.3d 63.

Since two witness informers, who allegedly were neither paid nor regular police agents, might have supported defendant's plea of innocence to charge of unlawful sale of secobarbital and amphetamine tablets by testifying that defendant declined to sell restricted drugs to police officer, the prosecution, therefore, owed a duty to disclose the "identity" of the two informers at the preliminary hearing as well as at the trial. People v. Goliday (1973) 106 Cal.Rptr. 113, 505 P.2d 537, 8 C.3d 771.

If defendant makes adequate showing that informer may be material witness on issue of guilt or innocence, disclosure of identity of informer should be compelled or case dismissed. Theodor v. Superior Court of Orange County (1972) 104 Cal.Rptr. 226, 501 P.2d 234, 8 C.3d 77.

Demonstration of reasonable possibility that anonymous informer who had supplied information constituting probable cause which is basis of search warrant can give evidence on issue of guilt which might result in defendant's exoneration so as to compel disclosure of informer's identity requires articulation of theory of defense based upon defense or prosecution evidence presented at trial or upon declarations filed in support of motion to disclose and not mere speculation on part of defendant. People v. Sewell (1970) 83 Cal.Rptr. 895, 3 C.A.3d 1035.

"Identity" of informer, which prosecution is required to reveal when informer is a material witness to crime, includes his name as well as all pertinent information which might assist defense in locating him. Eleazer v. Superior Court of Los Angeles County (1970) 83 Cal.Rptr. 586, 464 P.2d 42, 1 C.3d 847.

Where informant had visited defendant's apartment sometime between 3 and 8 p.m. of day preceding search of apartment and reported to officer that four persons were seen in apartment and it was possible that marijuana found in search was brought into apartment by those four persons rather than by defendants, testimony of informer as to identity and activities of those four persons "might" result in defendants' exoneration, and in order to secure defendants a fair trial disclosure of informer's identity would be compelled. Honore v. Superior Court of Alameda County (1969) 74 Cal.Rptr. 233, 449 P.2d 169, 70 C.2d 162.

Defendant who claimed entrapment was not entitled to disclosure of names of informers whose information was used by officer to obtain search warrant, where no evidence of entrapment was produced, issue was not raised at trial and defendant rested on defense that contraband belonged to another. People v. De Leon (1968) 67 Cal.Rptr. 45, 260 C.A.2d 143, certiorari denied 89 S.Ct. 407, 393 U.S. 969, 21 L.Ed.2d 380.

When it appears from evidence that informer is a material witness on issue of guilt, and accused seeks disclosure on cross-examination, the people must either disclose his identity or incur a dismissal. People v. Garcia (1967) 64 Cal.Rptr. 110, 434 P.2d 366, 67 C.2d 830.

Disclosure in interest of justice

Where defendant makes adequate showing that confidential informer may be material witness on issue of his guilt or innocence, disclosure of informer's identity should be compelled or case dismissed. People v. O'Brien (App.1976) 132 Cal.Rptr. 616.

The right to the disclosure of identity of material witness arises in trial court when the defendant demonstrates the reasonable possibility that the testimony of the anonymous informant, whose identity is sought, might result in defendant's exoneration. People v. Flemmings (1973) 109 Cal.Rptr. 661, 34 C.A.3d 63.

Necessary showing to compel disclosure of identity of informant that there was a reasonable possibility that informant might be able to exonerate defendant must go beyond mere fact that informant obviously possessed knowledge of defendant's criminal activities. People v. Kilpatrick (1973) 107 Cal.Rptr. 367, 31 C.A.3d 431.

The official identity of informant privilege must yield when it is shown that the informant whose identity is sought is a material witness for the defense and nondisclosure would deprive defendant of a fair trial; in such cases, it is clear that the balance is struck in favor of defendant, and disclosure must be ordered on pain of dismissal; only after it is first determined that the informant is not a material witness to guilt or innocence and disclosure be denied. People v. Goliday (1973) 106 Cal.Rptr. 113, 505 P.2d 537, 8 C.3d 771.

Where there was discrepancy in physical description supplied by informant's affidavit in support of search warrant and defendant's appearance, unusual credit arrangement and accessibility of others to house which was subject of search warrant bore on whether defendant was in possession of drugs and informant, who was material witness on such issues, may have been both participant and eyewitness to charged offenses of possession of marijuana and restricted dangerous drugs and of possession of marijuana and restricted dangerous drugs for purpose of sale, disclosure of identity of informant was required. Theodor v. Superior Court of Orange County (1972) 104 Cal.Rptr. 226, 501 P.2d 234, 8 C.3d 77.

Right of public entity to refuse disclosure of an informant's identity may not be exercised where defendant demonstrates reasonable possibility that anonymous informant could give evidence on issue of guilt which might exonerate him. People v. Singletary (1969) 81 Cal.Rptr. 79, 276 C.A.2d 601.

When it appears from evidence that informer is a material witness on issue of guilt, and accused seeks disclosure on cross-examination, people must either disclose his identity or incur a dismissal. Honore v. Superior Court of Alameda County (1969) 74 Cal.Rptr. 233, 449 P.2d 169, 70 C.2d 162.

Refusal to require disclosure of identity of informants in prosecution for possession of heroin for sale and for possession of marijuana deprived defendant of a fair trial and required reversal where informants were neither participants in the alleged crime nor were eyewitnesses thereto, and warrant and affidavit in support thereof related to persons other than defendant, who alleged that he was in apartment where narcotics were found merely as a visitor attempting to get a "fix" and who denied that he was a resident of the apartment. People v. Garcia (1967) 64 Cal.Rptr. 110, 434 P.2d 366, 67 C.2d 830.

Refusal to disclose

People were privileged to refuse to disclose identity of informant. People v. Rodgers (1976) 126 Cal.Rptr. 719, 54 C.A.3d 508.

Criminal participation by informer

Person who was both an eyewitness to, and participant in, alleged sale of seconal made by defendant was a "material witness" on issue of guilt, so that prosecution was required to disclose witness' "identity," which included his name as well as all pertinent information which might have assisted defense to locate him. Eleazer v. Superior Court of Los Angeles County (1970) 83 Cal.Rptr. 586, 464 P.2d 42, 1 C.3d 847.

When an informant participates in the criminal act he is no longer simply an informer; rather, he then becomes a material witness to the criminal act and, in fact, he is similar to a feigned accomplice. People v. Garcia (1967) 64 Cal.Rptr. 110, 434 P.2d 366, 67 C.2d 830.

Preliminary hearing

Stipulation that the entire preliminary transcript and exhibits were admissible subject to whatever objections either side might make clearly indicated that objections to evidence made at preliminary examination were waived unless restated at trial so that failure to order disclosure of identity of informants was not error where defendant did not make such a request in trial court. People v. Campuzano (1967) 61 Cal.Rptr. 695, 254 C.A.2d 52.

Waiver

Mere inadvertent mention of informant's name by police officer during preliminary examination was not in itself sufficient to cause waiver of privilege against nondisclosure of agent's identity. People v. Borunda (1974) 113 Cal.Rptr. 825, 522 P.2d 5, 11 C.3d 523.

§ 1042. Adverse order or finding in certain cases

(a) Except where disclosure is forbidden by an act of the Congress of the United States, if a claim of

§ 1042

privilege under this article by the state or a public entity in this state is sustained in a criminal proceeding, the presiding officer shall make such order or finding of fact adverse to the public entity bringing the proceeding as is required by law upon any issue in the proceeding to which the privileged information is material.

(b) Notwithstanding subdivision (a), where a search is made pursuant to a warrant valid on its face, the public entity bringing a criminal proceeding is not required to reveal to the defendant official information or the identity of an informer in order to establish the legality of the search or the admissibility of any evidence obtained as a result of it.

(c) Notwithstanding subdivision (a), in any preliminary hearing, criminal trial, or other criminal proceeding, any otherwise admissible evidence of information communicated to a peace officer by a confidential informant, who is not a material witness to the guilt or innocence of the accused of the offense charged, is admissible on the issue of reasonable cause to make an arrest or search without requiring that the name or identity of the informant be disclosed if the judge or magistrate is satisfied, based upon evidence produced in open court, out of the presence of the jury, that such information was received from a reliable informant and in his discretion does not require such disclosure.

(d) When, in any such criminal proceeding, a party demands disclosure of the identity of the informant on the ground the informant is a material witness on the issue of guilt, the court shall conduct a hearing at which all parties may present evidence on the issue of disclosure. Such hearing shall be conducted outside the presence of the jury, if any. During the hearing, if the privilege provided for in Section 1041 is claimed by a person authorized to do so or if a person who is authorized to claim such privilege refuses to answer any question on the ground that the answer would tend to disclose the identity of the informant, the prosecuting attorney may request that the court hold an in camera hearing. If such a request is made, the court shall hold such a hearing outside the presence of the defendant and his counsel. At the in camera hearing, the prosecution may offer evidence which would tend to disclose or which discloses the identity of the informant to aid the court in its determination whether there is a reasonable possibility that nondisclosure might deprive the defendant of a fair trial. A reporter shall be present at the in camera hearing. Any transcription of the proceedings at the in camera hearing, as well as any physical evidence presented at the hearing, shall be ordered sealed by the court, and only a court may have access to its contents. The court shall not order disclosure, nor strike the testimony of the witness who invokes the privilege, nor dismiss the criminal proceeding, if the party offering the witness refuses to disclose the identity of the informant, unless, based upon the evidence presented at the hearing held in the presence of the defendant and his counsel and the evidence presented at the in camera hearing, the court concludes that there is a reasonable possibility that nondisclosure might deprive the defendant of a fair trial.
(Amended by Stats.1969, c. 1412, p. 2891, § 1.)

Notes of Decisions

In general

In prosecution for possession of narcotics for sale, trial court's finding that defendants were entitled to disclosure of identity of informer was sustained by evidence which, inter alia, presented possibility that undisclosed informer might have given testimony in favor of either defendant which would have thrown onus of control or right to control narcotics found in the premises on the other defendant or on some third person present in residence when informer was there. People v. Tolliver (1975) 125 Cal.Rptr. 905, 53 C.A.3d 1036.

At in camera hearing held to examine official personnel file of policeman who allegedly precipitated violence which resulted in defendant being charged with assault on a police officer, it was not necessary that defense or prosecution be represented as to do so would destroy the privilege of confidentiality of such records which the in camera hearing was designed to protect. People v. Woolman (1974) 115 Cal.Rptr. 324, 40 C.A.3d 652.

The people's right to request an in camera hearing does not arise only after trial court has first found that a prima facie case for disclosure of identity of informer has been made by a defendant, since this section expressly provides that the very purpose of the in camera hearing is "to aid the court in its determination whether there is reasonable possibility that nondisclosure might deprive the defendant of a fair trial." Williams v. Superior Court for San Joaquin County (1974) 112 Cal.Rptr. 485, 38 C.A.3d 412.

Full cross-examination of prosecution witnesses concerning informant reliability is not only necessary for a proper exercise of the court's discretion in refusing to compel disclosure of the informant's identity but appears to be a constitutional prerequisite to invoking the informant privilege. Parsley v. Superior Court of Riverside County (1973) 109 Cal.Rptr. 563, 513 P.2d 611, 9 C.3d 934.

Where in camera hearing was held after defendant duly moved for disclosure of identity of informant whose "tip" had resulted in defendant's arrest and prosecution had claimed privilege, proceedings were reported, and reporter's transcript was sealed and transmitted to court of appeal as required by this section, defendant, under entire record, was not improperly denied disclosure of name of informant. People v. Doran (App.1972) 100 Cal.Rptr. 886.

Where defendant accused of selling methedrine secured a subpoena duces tecum calling for production of records of the state bureau of narcotics enforcement of cases in which defendant supplied information to bureau agents, and the bureau invoked privilege against harmful disclosure of official information and the prosecution moved to quash the subpoena, a ruling should have been withheld pending inquiry into a possible middle ground, and the court should have ruled after and not before state's counteroffer. People v. Superior Court for Sacramento County (1971) 97 Cal.Rptr. 118, 19 C.A.3d 522.

Person who was both an eyewitness to, and participant in, alleged sale of seconal made by defendant was a "material witness" on issue of guilt, so that prosecution was required to disclose witness' "identity," which included his name as well as all pertinent information which might have assisted defense to locate him. Eleazer v. Superior Court of Los Angeles County (1970) 83 Cal.Rptr. 586, 464 P.2d 42, 1 C.3d 847.

The defendant need not prove that the informer would give testimony favorable to the defense in order to compel disclosure of his identity, nor need he prove that the informer was a participant in or even an eyewitness to the crime; the defendant's burden extends only to a showing that in view of the evidence, the informer would be a material witness on issue of guilt and nondisclosure of his identity would deprive the defendant of a fair trial. Price v. Superior Court of San Diego County (1970) 83 Cal.Rptr. 369, 463 P.2d 721, 1 C.3d 836.

To compel disclosure of identity of informer, accused has burden of showing a reasonable possibility that the anonymous informant whose identity is sought could give evidence on issue of guilt that might result in defendant's exoneration and that showing must encompass more than speculation. People v. Martin (1969) 82 Cal.Rptr. 414, 2 C.A.3d 121.

Where only evidence offered by prosecution in 1963 trial as to reliability of informer or credibility of his information was the officer's opinion that informer was reliable, without any showing of the underlying circumstances or any factual proof as to reliability and credibility, information obtained from informant could not be used to establish probable cause for arrest and search. People v. Johnson (1968) 68 Cal.Rptr. 441, 440 P.2d 921, 68 C.2d 629.

Search warrant, based on information supplied to affiant by informer who on two previous occasions had allegedly given affiant information leading to arrest of individuals whose cases were still pending, was valid on its face, and precluded defendant from discovering through cross-examination of affiant, title of pending cases in which informant proved reliable. People v. Cain (1968) 67 Cal.Rptr. 922, 261 C.A.2d 383.

Testimony of police officer, who arrested one of the defendants for possession of marijuana and heroin for purpose of sale, on cross-examination that he would not reveal name of his informant because to do so would destroy usefulness of informant and imperil his life supported trial court's finding that refusal to name informant was justified under this section. People v. Marquez (1968) 66 Cal.Rptr. 615, 259 C.A.2d 593, certiorari denied 89 S.Ct. 386, 393 U.S. 955, 21 L.Ed.2d 367.

Refusal to require disclosure of identity of informants in prosecution for possession of heroin for sale and for possession of marijuana deprived defendant of a fair trial and required reversal where informants were neither participants in the alleged crime nor were eyewitnesses thereto, and warrant and affidavit in support thereof related to persons other than defendant, who alleged that he was in apartment where narcotics were found merely as a visitor attempting to get a "fix" and who denied that he was a resident of the apartment. People v. Garcia (1967) 64 Cal.Rptr. 110, 434 P.2d 366, 67 C.2d 830.

When it appears from evidence that informer is a material witness on issue of guilt, and accused seeks disclosure on cross-examination, the people must either disclose his identity or incur a dismissal. Id.

Where disclosure of identity of informer was relevant and helpful to defense or essential to fair determination of cause inasmuch as informer was participant in sale of heroin to officer and witness to transactions, privilege against nondisclosure of identity of informer could not be invoked, but even so, prosecution was under no obligation to produce informant as witness when prosecution fully complied with request for disclosure by giving all information it had relative to identity and whereabouts of informer. People v. Lara (1967) 61 Cal.Rptr. 303, 253 C.A.2d 600.

On question of constitutionality of former C.C.P. § 1881.1 (Repealed) which provided that evidence of information communicated to peace officer by a confidential informant, who is not material witness to guilt or innocence of accused, shall be admissible on issue of reasonable cause to make an arrest or search without requiring name or identity of informant to be disclosed if judge is satisfied that such information was received from reliable informer and does not require such disclosure, no distinction need be made between a proceeding to suppress evidence, a preliminary hearing, and the criminal trial. People v. Sanders (1967) 58 Cal.Rptr. 259, 250 C.A.2d 123.

Election between disclosure and adverse order or finding

Where defendant shows good cause in support of discovery motion, upon assertion of people's conditional privilege of confidentiality of records, trial court must then weigh whether necessity for preserving confidentiality of information sought by defendant outweighs necessity for disclosure in interest of justice. In re Valerie E. (1975) 123 Cal.Rptr. 242, 50 C.A.3d 213.

Where defendant accused of selling methedrine secured a subpoena duces tecum calling for production of certain records of state bureau of narcotics enforcement of cases in which defendant had supplied information to bureau agents, and prosecution made a counteroffer which defense counsel refused to accept, trial court should have ascertained whether the offer reasonably fulfilled defendant's needs and, if it did, should have forced the defense to accept the offer on pain of an adverse ruling, and failure to do so was error. People v. Superior Court for Sacramento County (1971) 97 Cal.Rptr. 118, 19 C.A.3d 522.

Material witness

Within rule that privilege for nondisclosure of an informant's identity does not apply if the informer is a material witness for a defendant, "material witness" means an informant with respect to whom there is a reasonable possibility that he could give evidence bearing on the defendant's guilt that might exonerate defendant of the criminal charge. People v. Tolliver (1975) 125 Cal.Rptr. 905, 53 C.A.3d 1036.

Reasonable cause

In case in which minor was charged with committing battery against two police officers, request by minor for all information regarding citizen complaints for excessive force against two police officers involved was sufficiently specific to justify discovery. In re Valerie E. (1975) 123 Cal.Rptr. 242, 50 C.A.3d 213.

Information received from informant that certain person was selling heroin in his hotel room did not furnish officers with probable cause for arrest or search of alleged seller in hall of hotel, and alleged seller's consent to entry of his hotel room by officers was invalid and heroin found in seller's hotel room in possession of defendant was product of officers' unlawful conduct and was inadmissible. People v. Johnson (1968) 68 Cal.Rptr. 441, 440 P.2d 921, 68 C.2d 629.

Evidence produced by search of defendants who were arrested pursuant to information received by sheriff's office from treasury department official who, in turn, received such information from reliable informer was not rendered inadmissible by prosecution's failure to disclose name of informer since, in light of circumstances testified to by treasury department official who testified to informer's reliability and who was subjected to cross-examination, it was within sound discretion of trial judge to permit evidence to be so introduced. People v. Sanders (1967) 58 Cal.Rptr. 259, 250 C.A.2d 123.

Peace officer

Proper application of former C.C.P. § 1881.1 (Repealed) which provided that evidence of information communicated to peace officer by confidential informant, who is not a material witness to guilt or innocence of accused, shall be admissible on issue of reasonable cause to make arrest or search without disclosure of name or identity of informant if judge is satisfied that information was received from a reliable informant and does not require such disclosure does not exclude from definition of "peace officer" an officer of Customs Bureau and as to information received by him in his official capacity and bearing upon his official duties he may be accorded the testimonial privilege permitted by former C.C.P. § 1881.1 (Repealed). People v. Sanders (1967) 58 Cal.Rptr. 259, 250 C.A.2d 123.

Informer

Informer was not a "material witness" whose identity the people were constitutionally obliged to disclose where he merely identified voice on a tape recording of an extortionate telephone conversation. People v. Kelly (1975) 122 Cal.Rptr. 393, 49 C.A.3d 214.

Informer was not shown to be a material witness whose name should be disclosed on theory that he might have been biased, that he might have possessed an interest or stake in the criminal activity, or that he might be impeachable, where defendant set out no support for such assertion and provided no reason to believe that informer was involved with the criminal activity. Id.

Disclosure of informant can only be ordered upon a showing that informant would be material witness on issue of guilt. People v. Castro (1974) 117 Cal.Rptr. 295, 42 C.A.3d 960.

Refusal of police to identify informant did not, by itself, or with added fact that police had promised informant they would not disclose his identity, lead to conclusion that police could not have sought to prosecute defendant for sale or possession of heroin so as to have precluded an arrest for sale or possession of heroin inasmuch as officers' knowledge of sale, and necessary possession as part of offense, was not erased. People v. McClure (1974) 113 Cal.Rptr. 815, 39 C.A.3d 64.

Evidence suggesting that officers possessed knowledge from a confidential informant that person in house to be entered was known to answer the door while armed with a firearm was incompetent and thus inadmissible at preliminary hearing to justify entry without announcement of authority and purpose, where court neither compelled disclosure of informant's identity nor exercised discretion based on evidence produced in open court that informant was reliable, and, on the contrary, restricted cross-examination of testifying police officers concerning informant's reliability. Parsley v. Superior Court of Riverside County (1973) 109 Cal.Rptr. 563, 513 P.2d 611, 9 C.3d 934.

Defendant was not denied due process in hearing on his application for probation by police officer's testimony as to sale of commercial quantity of heroin by defendant to a confidential informant and reports that defendant was a "big dealer" in heroin, nor by denial of his motion for disclosure of identity of confidential informant, where defendant identified the individual who he claimed was the informant and attempted to impeach him, and where the purchase by the informant was observed by police officers and, in addition, statement that defendant was a "big dealer" was supported by other independent evidence of defendant's commercial activity. People v. Peterson (1973) 108 Cal.Rptr. 835, 511 P.2d 1187, 9 C.3d 717.

Where prior to trial defendant moved to discover name of informant court followed proper procedure when after an in-camera session with officer who prepared affidavit for search warrant court determined that the identity of informant was not material to the defense and then had officer take stand at trial and claim privilege following which officer was extensively cross-examined by counsel for all defendants. People v. Kilpatrick (1973) 107 Cal.Rptr. 367, 31 C.A.3d 431.

If police inspired illegal eavesdropping on telephone call from defendant to another or unauthorized entry into the other's room, they should not be permitted to use information so obtained and where informant was a percipient witness on issue of manner in which information was obtained and there was no contention that informant was a proved and reliable informant, it was an abuse of discretion to fail to order disclosure of identity of informant. People v. Shipstead (App.1971) 96 Cal.Rptr. 513, 19 C.A.3d 58.

This section providing for evidentiary hearing does not require that defendant present evidence thereat in support of his request for disclosure of informer's identity. People v. Johnson (1970) 92 Cal.Rptr. 105, 13 C.A.3d 742.

Prosecution was not required to disclose identity of informer who had supplied information constituting probable cause which was basis for warrant authorizing search of defendant's apartment in order to allow defendant to cross-examine informer for purpose of attacking such probable cause where warrant was valid on its face. People v. Sewell (1970) 83 Cal.Rptr. 895, 3 C.A.3d 1035.

Where affidavit in support of petition for warrant authorizing search of defendant's apartment stated that reliable informer had observed marijuana in defendant's apartment but did not state that informer was percipient witness to particular possession of contraband disclosed by search, defendant who presented no evidence or declaration in support of his motion to disclose identity of informer failed to demonstrate reasonable possibility that informer could have given evidence which might have resulted in defendant's exoneration and prosecution was not required to disclose identity of informer. Id.

Fact that police were without motive to harm defendant when they made no effort to learn residence of an informer to establish a way by which to locate him and did so merely to foster security of informer was not sufficient on which to justify prosecution's failure to disclose information concerning "identity" of informer. Eleazer v. Superior Court of Los Angeles County (1970) 83 Cal.Rptr. 586, 464 P.2d 42, 1 C.3d 847.

Where role of informer was simply that of pointing finger of suspicion at defendant, thereby putting wheels of investigation in motion, and he in no way participated in criminal acts for which defendant three days later was arrested, there was no basis to compel disclosure of identity of informer on the issue of guilt. People v. Martin (1969) 82 Cal.Rptr. 414, 2 C.A.3d 121.

Refusing to require disclosure of informant was not an abuse of discretion in prosecution for narcotics violations where the informant was neither a participant nor a witness to the crime, and no showing was made that informant would be a material witness on issue of defendant's guilt or innocence or that informer's testimony could in any manner benefit the cause of defendant. People v. Castillo (1969) 80 Cal.Rptr. 211, 274 C.A.2d 508, certiorari denied 91 S.Ct. 1670, 402 U.S. 984, 29 L.Ed.2d 149.

Hearing, disclosure of informer

Defendants were not denied constitutional rights of confrontation, cross-examination, compulsory process or effective use of counsel by fact that trial court, prior to denying defendants' request for disclosure of identity of informant, held in camera hearing to determine whether informant was material witness, especially where record of such hearing was maintained so that defendants could obtain appellate review. People v. O'Brien (App.1976) 132 Cal.Rptr. 616.

When at pretrial hearing in prosecution for possession for sale of heroin, defendant moved to compel disclosure of identity of confidential informant, trial court erred in refusing to hold, at People's request, an in camera hearing at which People would produce informant for questioning. People v. Aguilera (App.1976) 131 Cal.Rptr. 603.

Defendant was not entitled to disclosure of informant's identity on issue of guilt or innocence where defendant did not show even a "reasonable probability" that the informant could provide testimony material to some theory of defense; assertion that since informant stated that two individuals were selling drugs and witness had never been to their residence the informant might testify that any contact he had made was through only one such individual did not warrant disclosure since defendant was charged with possession for sale based on personal possession of heroin when arrested and neither informant nor the contact could have furnished relevant information. People v. Rodgers (App.1976) 126 Cal.Rptr. 719.

At hearing in support of motion for disclosure of informant's identity, hearsay exclusionary rule is not a complete barrier; thus, affidavit to support search warrant which recited informant's communication to police officer was admissible evidence. People v. Tolliver (1975) 125 Cal.Rptr. 905, 53 C.A.3d 1036.

In holding statutory hearing in camera, outside hearing of defendant and counsel, with respect to whether informer was a material witness whose identity should be disclosed, there was no reversible error in holding hearing without requiring informant's presence. People v. Kelly (1975) 122 Cal.Rptr. 393, 49 C.A.3d 214.

Right to disclosure of informer

Under evidence that abandoned truck discovered by police had been used to transport stolen safe, that truck was taken into custody, that truck was stolen from storage yard, that confidential informant told police that truck was located in private garage, that lessee of garage had received telephone call from defendant asking lessee to paint truck, and that truck was discovered at lessee's shop shortly thereafter, informant could not have been "material witness" to burglary with which defendant was charged, and thus defendant was not entitled to disclosure of informant's identity. People v. O'Brien (App.1976) 132 Cal.Rptr. 616.

Where there is reasonable possibility that informant could give evidence on issue of guilt which might result in defendant's exoneration of crime charged, defendant's interest outweighs the public interest in nondisclosure and court must order disclosure or make other appropriate orders if People exercise nondisclosure privilege. People v. Aguilera (App.1976) 131 Cal.Rptr. 603.

Prosecution cannot successfully invoke privilege for nondisclosure of an informant's identity if the defendant demonstrates a reasonable possibility that the informer could give evidence on the issue of guilt that might result in defendant's exoneration. People v. Tolliver (1975) 125 Cal.Rptr. 905, 53 C.A.3d 1036.

Confrontation guaranteed by the Sixth Amendment applies only to trial, and did not apply to hearing with respect to whether informant was a material witness whose identity had to be disclosed. People v. Kelly (1975) 122 Cal.Rptr. 393, 49 C.A.3d 214.

Defendant has the constitutional right of knowing informer's identity when he shows a reasonable possibility that the informer will be a material witness on the issue of guilt. Id.

Standards, disclosure of informer

Where defendant makes adequate showing that confidential informer may be material witness on issue of his guilt or innocence, disclosure of informer's identity should be compelled or case dismissed. People v. O'Brien (App.1976) 132 Cal.Rptr. 616.

Whether nondisclosure to defendant of confidential informant's identity is erroneous depends on particular circumstances of each case, taking into consideration crime charged, possible defenses, possible significance of informant's testimony and other relevant factors. Id.

In cases involving question of whether informant should be disclosed, court must resolve conflict between public interest in maintaining confidentiality of police informants and defendant's interest in access to information which might tend to exonerate him. People v. Aguilera (App.1976) 131 Cal.Rptr. 603.

Where defendant had consented to submit to warrantless searches as condition of probation, he was not entitled to question reliability of informant who supplied information which led police to make such warrantless search. People v. Turner (1976) 126 Cal.Rptr. 652, 54 C.A.3d 500.

To obtain disclosure of an informant's identity, defendant is not required to show that the informer was either a participant in crime charged or an eyewitness thereto; nor is it required that defendant establish that the informer would give favorable testimony. People v. Tolliver (1975) 125 Cal.Rptr. 905, 53 C.A.3d 1036.

Errors of trial court in stating too stringent a standard in determining whether informer is a material witness whose identity must be disclosed by the government were not prejudicial where informer was not shown to possess evidence bearing on guilt and was not a material witness under appropriate, less stringent standard. People v. Kelly (1975) 122 Cal.Rptr. 393, 49 C.A.3d 214.

In determining whether informant is a material witness whose identity must be disclosed, there is no requirement that the government in opposing disclosure show that informant was reliable. Id.

Speculation may be part of the standard "a reasonable probability," for showing that informer is a material witness whose identity must be disclosed. Id.

§ 1050. Privilege to protect secrecy of vote

If he claims the privilege, a person has a privilege to refuse to disclose the tenor of his vote at a public election where the voting is by secret ballot unless he voted illegally or he previously made an unprivileged disclosure of the tenor of his vote.
(Stats.1965, c. 299, § 1050.)

§ 1060. Privilege to protect trade secret

If he or his agent or employee claims the privilege, the owner of a trade secret has a privilege to refuse to disclose the secret, and to prevent another from disclosing it, if the allowance of the privilege will not tend to conceal fraud or otherwise work injustice.
(Stats.1965, c. 299, § 1060.)

§ 1070. Newsmen's refusal to disclose news source

(a) A publisher, editor, reporter, or other person connected with or employed upon a newspaper, magazine, or other periodical publication, or by a press association or wire service, or any person who has been so connected or employed, cannot be adjudged in contempt by a judicial, legislative, administrative body, or any other body having the power to issue subpoenas, for refusing to disclose, in any proceeding as defined in Section 901, the source of any information procured while so connected or employed for publication in a newspaper, magazine or other periodical publication, or for refusing to disclose any unpublished information obtained or prepared in gathering, receiving or processing of information for communication to the public.

(b) Nor can a radio or television news reporter or other person connected with or employed by a radio or television station, or any person who has been so connected or employed, be so adjudged in contempt for refusing to disclose the source of any information procured while so connected or employed for news or news commentary purposes on radio or television, or for refusing to disclose any unpublished information obtained or prepared in gathering, receiving or processing of information for communication to the public.

(c) As used in this section, "unpublished information" includes information not disseminated to the public by the person from whom disclosure is sought, whether or not related information has been disseminated and includes, but is not limited to, all notes, outtakes, photographs, tapes or other data of whatever sort not itself disseminated to the public through a medium of communication, whether or not published information based upon or related to such material has been disseminated.
(Amended by Stats.1974, c. 1456, p. 3184, § 2.)

Notes of Decisions

In general

Question of propriety of denial of habeas corpus relief to petitioner, a reporter who was committed to prison for civil contempt after refusing to disclose names of persons from whom he had received information during criminal trial, in violation of court's order concerning publicity, was a substantial one and, in interest of justice, petitioner would be released on personal recognizance pending decision of his case by the court of appeals. Farr v. Pitchess (1973) 93 S.Ct. 593, 409 U.S. 1243, 34 L.Ed.2d 655.

California "Shield Law" for the news media was inapplicable to civil contempt proceeding brought against radio station newsman who, after a grant of immunity, refused to comply with federal grand jury subpoena duces tecum which directed him to appear before the grand jury and bring the original copy of the communique he had received from the New World Liberation Front pertaining to certain bombings and threats of bombings. In re Lewis (D.C.1974) 384 F.Supp. 133.

In determining the applicability of the newsperson's privilege, court must, as it does with the privilege against self-incrimination, consider not only the offered evidence, but also the matters disclosed and argued, the implications of the question, the setting in which it is asked, and all other relevant factors. Rosato v. Superior Court of Fresno County (1975) 124 Cal.Rptr. 427, 51 C.A.3d 190, certiorari denied 96 S.Ct. 3200.

If copy of transcript of grand jury testimony, which had been ordered sealed by court, and which had come into the hands of newsman, contained telltale markings or variations which would tend to reveal that the transcript had been obtained from a protected source, i. e., from a person not specifically subject to order prohibiting specific court officers from releasing the transcript for public dissemination, newsman's refusal to produce the copy of the transcript which had been given him or to answer questions concerning telltale variations or markings on the transcript would have been properly sustained in view of "shield law." Id.

Inherent power of the judiciary, as a separate and coequal branch of the tripartite governmental structure, to control its own proceedings and officers places limitations on the newsman's privilege. Id.

Where newspaper reporter who had been held in contempt for failure to disclose the source of his story about a trial was afforded an opportunity to comply with the order after court of appeal decision holding reporters' statutory exemption from contempt to be unconstitutional, reporter was not denied due process by virtue of an unexpected interpretation rejecting the ground which he believed exempted him from the court order. In re Farr (1974) 111 Cal.Rptr. 649, 36 C.A.3d 577.

This section could not be applied to shield petitioner from contempt for failure to reveal names of attorneys of record in criminal trial and another person who furnished him with copies of statement disclosing that the defendants planned other murders; such application of this section would result in an unconstitutional interference by the legislative branch with power of court to control its own proceedings and officers. Farr v. Superior Court of Los Angeles County (1971) 99 Cal.Rptr. 342, 22 C.A.3d 60, certiorari denied 93 S.Ct. 430, 409 U.S. 1011, 34 L.Ed.2d 305.

Legislative intent

Legislature, in enacting newsman's "shield law," recognized the importance of maintaining a free flow of information and intended that the statute be given a broad, rather than a narrow, construction. Rosato v. Superior Court of Fresno County (1975) 124 Cal.Rptr. 427, 51 C.A.3d 190, certiorari denied 96 S.Ct. 3200.

Privilege

Absent any constitutional or other limitation on the exercise of a newsman's "shield" privilege, it extends not only to the identity of a source but to the disclosure of any information, in whatever form, which might tend to reveal the source of the information. Rosato v. Superior Court of Fresno County (1975) 124 Cal.Rptr. 427, 51 C.A.3d 190, certiorari denied 96 S.Ct. 3200.

Newsman's "shield law" does not shield newsmen from testifying about criminal activity in which they have participated or which they have observed. Id.

Radio station manager

Propriety vel non of questions propounded to newsmen, who refused to answer them, concerning who, if anyone, had violated trial court's protective and seal orders concerning grand jury testimony discussed and decided in light of California "shield law." Rosato v. Superior Court of Fresno County (1975) 124 Cal.Rptr. 427, 51 C.A.3d 190, certiorari denied 96 S.Ct. 3200.

Radio station manager had no qualified First Amendment privilege to refuse to comply with federal grand jury subpoena for production of original of "communique," together with envelope, wrapping, or container, received from underground group claiming responsibility for bombing, although manager had been previously called upon to produce similar material received from another group, where it did not appear that any other reporter had received similar material twice or that present demand was harassment and discriminatory treatment. Lewis v. U. S. (C.A.1975) 517 F.2d 236.

Contempt

Where there was understandable uncertainty as to scope of newsmen's privilege, and where it appeared that newsmen had refused to answer certain questions in good faith, fairness required that, after they had been held in contempt for not answering certain questions and after certain of those findings of contempt had been affirmed on appeal, the cause be remanded to the superior court for the purpose of affording the newsmen an opportunity to purge the contempts before sentence was executed. Rosato v. Superior Court of Fresno County (1975) 124 Cal.Rptr. 427, 51 C.A.3d 190, certiorari denied 96 S.Ct. 3200.

Limitation placed on newsman's privilege under "shield law" by court's inherent power to control its own proceedings is applicable only when the questions asked of the newsman may tend to identify who, if anyone, among those who were subject to the court's order, might have violated it; shield law protected newsman against revelation of sources other than those subject to the order. Id.

Burden of proof

As in the case of the privilege against self-incrimination, burden is upon newsman claiming privilege under the "shield law" to show that the testimony may tend to lead to his source. Rosato v. Superior Court of Fresno County (1975) 124 Cal.Rptr. 427, 51 C.A.3d 190, certiorari denied 96 S.Ct. 3200.

Division 9

EVIDENCE AFFECTED OR EXCLUDED BY EXTRINSIC POLICIES

§ 1100. Manner of proof of character

Except as otherwise provided by statute, any otherwise admissible evidence (including evidence in the form of an opinion, evidence of reputation, and evidence of specific instances of such person's conduct) is admissible to prove a person's character or a trait of his character.
(Stats.1965, c. 299, § 1100.)

§ 1101. Evidence of character to prove conduct

(a) Except as provided in this section and in Sections 1102 and 1103, evidence of a person's character or a trait of his character (whether in the form of an opinion, evidence of reputation, or evidence of specific instances of his conduct) is inadmissible when offered to prove his conduct on a specified occasion.

(b) Nothing in this section prohibits the admission of evidence that a person committed a crime, civil wrong, or other act when relevant to prove some fact (such as motive, opportunity, intent, preparation, plan, knowledge, identity, or absence of mistake or accident) other than his disposition to commit such acts.

(c) Nothing in this section affects the admissibility of evidence offered to support or attack the credibility of a witness.
(Stats.1965, c. 299, § 1101.)

§ 1102. Opinion and reputation evidence of character of criminal defendant to prove conduct

In a criminal action, evidence of the defendant's character or a trait of his character in the form of an opinion or evidence of his reputation is not made inadmissible by Section 1101 if such evidence is:

(a) Offered by the defendant to prove his conduct in conformity with such character or trait of character.

(b) Offered by the prosecution to rebut evidence adduced by the defendant under subdivision (a).
(Stats.1965, c. 299, § 1102.)

§ 1103. Evidence of character of victim of crime to prove conduct; evidence of complaining witness' sexual conduct in rape prosecution

(1) In a criminal action, evidence of the character or a trait of character (in the form of an opinion, evidence of reputation, or evidence of specific instances of conduct) of the victim of the crime for which the defendant is being prosecuted is not made inadmissible by Section 1101 if such evidence is:

(a) Offered by the defendant to prove conduct of the victim in conformity with such character or trait of character.

(b) Offered by the prosecution to rebut evidence adduced by the defendant under subdivision (a).

(2)(a) Notwithstanding any other provision of this code to the contrary, and except as provided in this subdivision, in any prosecution under Section 261, or 264.1 of the Penal Code, or for assault with intent to commit, attempt to commit, or conspiracy to commit a crime defined in any such section, opinion evidence, reputation evidence, and evidence of specific instances of the complaining witness' sexual conduct, or any of such evidence, is not admissible by the defendant in order to prove consent by the complaining witness.

(b) Paragraph (a) of this subdivision shall not be applicable to evidence of the complaining witness' sexual conduct with the defendant.

(c) If the prosecutor introduces evidence, including testimony of a witness, or the complaining witness as a witness gives testimony, and such evidence or testimony relates to the complaining witness' sexual conduct, the defendant may cross-examine the witness who gives such testimony and offer relevant evidence limited specifically to the rebuttal of such evidence introduced by the prosecutor or given by the complaining witness.

(d) Nothing in this subdivision shall be construed to make inadmissible any evidence offered to attack the credibility of the complaining witness as provided in Section 782.

(e) As used in this section, "complaining witness" means the alleged victim of the crime charged, the prosecution of which is subject to this subdivision.
(Amended by Stats.1974, c. 569, p. 1388, § 2.)

§ 1104. Character trait for care or skill

Except as provided in Sections 1102 and 1103, evidence of a trait of a person's character with respect to care or skill is inadmissible to prove the quality of his conduct on a specified occasion.
(Stats.1965, c. 299, § 1104.)

§ 1105. Habit or custom to prove specific behavior

Any otherwise admissible evidence of habit or custom is admissible to prove conduct on a specified occasion in conformity with the habit or custom.
(Stats.1965, c. 299, § 1105.)

§ 1150. Evidence to test a verdict

(a) Upon an inquiry as to the validity of a verdict, any otherwise admissible evidence may be received as to statements made, or conduct, conditions, or events occurring, either within or without the jury room, of such a character as is likely to have influenced the verdict improperly. No evidence is admissible to show the effect of such statement, conduct, condition, or event upon a juror either in influencing him to assent to or dissent from the verdict or concerning the mental processes by which it was determined.

(b) Nothing in this code affects the law relating to the competence of a juror to give evidence to impeach or support a verdict.
(Stats.1965, c. 299, § 1150.)

§ 1153. Offer to plead guilty or withdrawn plea of guilty by criminal defendant

Evidence of a plea of guilty, later withdrawn, or of an offer to plead guilty to the crime charged or to any other crime, made by the defendant in a criminal action is inadmissible in any action or in any proceeding of any nature, including proceedings before agencies, commissions, boards, and tribunals.
(Stats.1965, c. 299, § 1153.)

Division 10

HEARSAY EVIDENCE

§ 1200. The hearsay rule

(a) "Hearsay evidence" is evidence of a statement that was made other than by a witness while testifying at the hearing and that is offered to prove the truth of the matter stated.

(b) Except as provided by law, hearsay evidence is inadmissible.

(c) This section shall be known and may be cited as the hearsay rule.
(Stats.1965, c. 299, § 1200.)

§ 1201. Multiple hearsay

A statement within the scope of an exception to the hearsay rule is not inadmissible on the ground that the evidence of such statement is hearsay evidence if such hearsay evidence consists of one or more statements each of which meets the requirements of an exception to the hearsay rule.
(As amended Stats.1967, c. 650, p. 2007, § 8.)

§ 1202. Credibility of hearsay declarant

Evidence of a statement or other conduct by a declarant that is inconsistent with a statement by such declarant received in evidence as hearsay evidence is not inadmissible for the purpose of attacking the credibility of the declarant though he is not given and has not had an opportunity to explain or to deny such inconsistent statement or other conduct. Any other evidence offered to attack or support the credibility of the declarant is admissible if it would have been admissible had the declarant been a witness at the hearing. For the purposes of this section, the deponent of a deposition taken in the action in which it is offered shall be deemed to be a hearsay declarant.
(Stats.1965, c. 299, § 1202.)

§ 1203. Cross-examination of hearsay declarant

(a) The declarant of a statement that is admitted as hearsay evidence may be called and examined by any adverse party as if under cross-examination concerning the statement.

(b) This section is not applicable if the declarant is (1) a party, (2) a person identified with a party within the meaning of subdivision (d) of Section 776, or (3) a witness who has testified in the action concerning the subject matter of the statement.

(c) This section is not applicable if the statement is one described in Article 1 (commencing with Section 1220), Article 3 (commencing with Section 1235), or Article 10 (commencing with Section 1300) of Chapter 2 of this division.

(d) A statement that is otherwise admissible as hearsay evidence is not made inadmissible by this section because the declarant who made the statement is unavailable for examination pursuant to this section.
(Stats.1965, c. 299, § 1203.)

§ 1204. Hearsay statement offered against criminal defendant

A statement that is otherwise admissible as hearsay evidence is inadmissible against the defendant in a criminal action if the statement was made, either by the defendant or by another, under such circumstances that it is inadmissible against the defendant under the Constitution of the United States or the State of California.
(Stats.1965, c. 299, § 1204.)

Editors' Note
Read Miranda v. Arizona in table of cases included in this text.

Comment—Assembly Committee on Judiciary

Section 1204 is a statutory recognition that hearsay evidence that fits within an exception to the hearsay rule may nonetheless be inadmissible under the Constitution of the United States or the Constitution of California. Thus, Section 1220, which creates an exception for the statements of a party, is subject to the constitutional rule excluding evidence of involuntary confessions against a criminal defendant.

In People v. Underwood, 61 Cal.2d 113, 37 Cal.Rptr. 313, 389 P.2d 937 (1964), the California Supreme Court held that a prior inconsistent statement of a witness could not be introduced to impeach him in a criminal action when the statement would have been inadmissible as an involuntary confession if the witness had been the defendant. To the extent that the Underwood decision is based on constitutional principles, its effect is continued by Section 1204 and its principle is made applicable to all hearsay statements.

Insofar as the Constitution of the United States is concerned, Section 1204 refers only to those rules required to be observed in state proceedings. It is not intended to make applicable in proceedings in California courts those rules the United States Constitution requires to be observed only in federal proceedings.

§ 1205. No implied repeal

Nothing in this division shall be construed to repeal by implication any other statute relating to hearsay evidence.
(Stats.1965, c. 299, § 1205.)

§ 1220. Admission of party

Evidence of a statement is not made inadmissible by the hearsay rule when offered against the declarant in an action to which he is a party in either his individual or representative capacity, regardless of whether the statement was made in his individual or representative capacity.
(Stats.1965, c. 299, § 1220.)

Notes of Decisions

In general

In view of overwhelming evidence of defendant's guilt, including admissions of guilt made to a fellow inmate, defendant was not prejudiced by erroneous admission of evidence of fellow conspirators' admissions made after the conspiracy had terminated, even though acquittal of a third defendant may have indicated that the jury placed less than total credence on the admissions of defendant since those were the admissions which provided the foundation for the case against the acquitted codefendant. People v. Leach (1975) 124 Cal.Rptr. 752, 541 P.2d 296, 15 C.3d 419.

"Admission" is an extrajudicial statement by the defendant and is an acknowledgment of some fact or circumstance which in itself is insufficient to authorize conviction and which only tends toward ultimate proof of guilt. People v. Wheelwright (1968) 68 Cal.Rptr. 356, 262 C.A.2d 63.

Admissions by accused, in general

In view of fact that charged assault with deadly weapon included exhibiting a firearm in a threatening manner, testimony that defendant, after offense charged, told deputy sheriffs that if they did not prevent people from blocking road in front of his house, he would shoot someone was properly admitted to prove that defendant had threatened victims. People v. Marceaux (1970) 83 Cal.Rptr. 798, 3 C.A.3d 613.

When motive of crime is sought to be established before jury, whole conduct, life and character of parties as affecting question is open to inquiry. People v. Helfend (1969) 82 Cal.Rptr. 295, 1 C.A.3d 873, certiorari denied 90 S.Ct. 2182, 398 U.S. 967, 26 L.Ed.2d 551.

The rationale of this section is that the party's right to cross-examine declarant is not violated since the party himself made the statement. People v. Alvarez (1968) 73 Cal.Rptr. 753, 268 C.A.2d 297.

Admissions of guilt by a defendant to third parties not acting for the police are admissible and, in addition, evidence of a prior inconsistent statement of defendant would be admissible to impeach defendant's credibility. People v. Stokley (1968) 72 Cal.Rptr. 513, 266 C.A.2d 930, certiorari denied 89 S.Ct. 1761, 395 U.S. 914, 23 L.Ed.2d 227.

Admissibility of an admission by a party is an exception to the hearsay rule. People v. Wheelwright (1968) 68 Cal.Rptr. 356, 262 C.A.2d 63.

§ 1220 EVIDENCE CODE

Admissions against interest
Regardless of whether it fell within hearsay rule, testimony of witness in murder prosecution that, previous to homicide, defendant had stated that he had had victim beat up and that witness had better keep his wife away from victim's wife because something might happen was admissible as a statement against interest. People v. Helfend (1969) 82 Cal.Rptr. 295, 1 C.A.3d 873, certiorari denied 90 S.Ct. 2182, 398 U.S. 967, 26 L.Ed.2d 551.

A plea of guilty in a criminal prosecution is admissible in civil action growing out of same offense as an admission of a party against interest. Arenstein v. California State Bd. of Pharmacy (1968) 71 Cal.Rptr. 357, 265 C.A.2d 179.

Confessions in general
People v. Erb, 45 Cal.Rptr. 503, 235 C.A.2d 650, [main volume] vacated 87 S.Ct. 1034, 386 U.S. 273, 18 L.Ed.2d 41, opinion supplemented 66 Cal.Rptr. 274.

Contentions of defendant charged with robbery that his confessions were involuntary because he was undergoing withdrawal from heroin and because improper promises were made to him were not meritorious where all evidence, except that of defendant himself, was that defendant's discomfiture from withdrawal was mild and he appeared to be able to understand questions put to him and responded rationally thereto, and that defendant was merely told by police officer that he could get medical treatment if he started having severe withdrawal symptoms. People v. Lyons (1971) 96 Cal.Rptr. 76, 18 C.A.3d 760.

Where interrogating officer's advice to defendant that his confederate had confessed was unaccompanied by any threat or promise, advice did not constitute an improper inducement to defendant's subsequent confession and it was not improper for officers to inform defendant that confederate had confessed. People v. Long (1970) 86 Cal.Rptr. 227, 6 C.A.3d 741.

In view of testimony of officer having considerable experience in narcotics matters that defendant while being interrogated started to shake but declined offer to see physician and did not yet appear to be starting on withdrawals contention that defendant was suffering from narcotic withdrawal symptoms making his confession involuntary was not supported by evidence. People v. Williams (1970) 86 Cal.Rptr. 821, 8 C.A.3d 44.

A policeman's advice or exhortation to an accused to tell the truth, or advice that it would be better to tell the truth, where accompanied by neither threat nor promise, does not render involuntary a subsequent confession. People v. Robinson (1969) 79 Cal.Rptr. 213, 274 C.A.2d 514.

When prosecution proposes to introduce defendant's extrajudicial statements implicating codefendant, trial court may permit joint trial if all parts implicating codefendant can be and are effectively deleted without prejudice to defendant, may grant severance if prosecution insists that it must use the extrajudicial statements and effective deletions cannot be made, or must exclude extrajudicial statements implicating codefendant if prosecution has successfully resisted motion for severance. People v. Boggs (1967) 63 Cal.Rptr. 430, 255 C.A. 693, certiorari denied 89 S.Ct. 160, 393 U.S. 871, 21 L.Ed.2d 140.

Extrajudicial statement by defendant consisting of acknowledgement of his participation in, and commission of, charged offenses was declaration by defendant that he was guilty as charged and represented confession. People v. Hildabrandt (1966) 53 Cal.Rptr. 99, 244 C.A.2d 423.

Evidence of improper confession before magistrate is inadmissible in any later proceeding. In re Johnson (1966) 53 Cal.Rptr. 1, 244 C.A.2d 274.

Previous testimony, judicial admissions
Accused's prior inconsistent statement relative to offense charged constitutes an "admission", within principles regarding admissibility of involuntary statements, where used to impeach accused's credibility. People v. Canard (1967) 65 Cal.Rptr. 15, 257 C.A.2d 444, certiorari denied 89 S.Ct. 231, 393 U.S. 912, 21 L.Ed.2d 198.

Drawings
Drawing of figure having a belt around its neck and a dagger protruding from its torso, posted by juvenile on bulletin board at juvenile hall, was admissible in jurisdictional proceeding as evidence of a statement proffered against the declarant in action to which he was a party. In re D. L. (1975), 120 Cal.Rptr. 276, 46 C.A.3d 65.

Admissibility in general
Statements of both defendant and codefendant overheard by a witness for prosecution and participated in by another witness were admissible under admissions exception to hearsay rule. People v. Mardian (1975) 121 Cal.Rptr. 269, 47 C.A.3d 16.

Though transcripts of telephonic conversations involving accused constituted hearsay, transcripts were admissible under admission exception to hearsay rule. People v. Fujita (1974) 117 Cal.Rptr. 757, 43 C.A.3d 454, certiorari denied 95 S.Ct. 1952, 421 U.S. 964, 44 L.Ed.2d 451.

Where defendant after being advised of his right to remain silent stated that he understood right and then confessed and thereafter withdrew his waiver and reasserted his right, statements defendant thereafter made on urgings of officers were harmlessly admitted in light of earlier confession. People v. Ross (1969) 81 Cal.Rptr. 296, 276 C.A.2d 729.

Confession will be found by reviewing court to be inadmissible if it is admitted into evidence at trial in violation of rule requiring a preliminary finding of voluntariness by trial court. People v. West (1967) 61 Cal.Rptr. 216, 253 C.A.2d 349, vacated 88 S.Ct. 2297, 392 U.S. 663, 20 L.Ed.2d 1354.

Confessions, admissibility
Record established that confession obtained from defendant, who was 21 years old and of relatively normal intelligence, who had been arrested for similar offenses and advised of his constitutional rights on previous occasions, who was not shown to have been threatened with physical violence or to have been subjected to undue psychological pressure, and who confessed approximately one-half hour into interview, was voluntarily given, notwithstanding that defendant suffered from emotional problems involving homosexuality. People v. Hutchings (1973) 106 Cal.Rptr. 905, 31 C.A.3d 16.

Improper admission into evidence of an extrajudicial statement of a codefendant does not automatically require reversal of conviction of defendant. People v. Williams (1970) 85 Cal.Rptr. 675, 6 C.A.3d 274.

Trial judge was not required again to rule on voluntariness of defendant's statement, to which officer had testified earlier, when officer was later called in connection with cross-examination of defense witness and questioned concerning his report, which contained a more detailed statement than that to which officer had testified on his first appearance. People v. Arauz (App.1970) 85 Cal.Rptr. 266.

Under evidence that dosage of drugs which was given to defendant to ease pain caused by injuries suffered in automobile collision which occurred while he was being apprehended was mild and that, after administration of the drugs defendant did not appear sedated, confession given to police officers in hospital after administration of the drugs was admissible. People v. Dacy (1970) 85 Cal.Rptr. 57, 5 C.A.3d 216.

Where prisoner or suspect initiates interview after having once asserted constitutional rights, evidencing change of mind not affected by official action, there may be an admissible confession or admission. People v. Brockman (1969) 83 Cal.Rptr. 70, 2 C.A.3d 1002.

Where a defendant, subjected to threats, violence or other improper influences, makes a confession or other incriminating statement in such a coercive atmosphere and shortly thereafter again incriminates himself under circumstances not manifestly coercive there is a presumption that influence of prior improper treatment continues to operate on mind of defendant and that subsequent confession is result of same influence which rendered prior confession inadmissible and burden is upon prosecution to clearly establish the contrary. People v. Sanchez (1969) 75 Cal.Rptr. 642, 451 P.2d 74, 70 C.2d 562.

Confession allegedly made by defendant to private citizen who had effected a citizen's arrest was not barred by failure of the citizen to advise defendant of his constitutional rights since citizen was not a policeman. People v. Cheatham (1968) 69 Cal.Rptr. 679, 263 C.A.2d 458.

Although trial counsel indicated early in proceedings that he would object to admission of statements made by defendant to police, where defense agreed to receive such evidence subject to motion to strike and motion to strike was never made, no proper objection to admission of statements was made and admission of them was not ground for reversal. People v. Elias (1968) 69 Cal.Rptr. 197, 263 C.A.2d 93.

A defendant's confession is not admissible if (1) the investigation was no longer a general inquiry into an unsolved crime but had begun to focus on a particular subject, (2) the subject was in custody, (3) the authorities had carried out a process of interrogations that lent itself to eliciting incriminating statements, (4) the authorities had not effectively informed defendant of his right to counsel or of his absolute right to remain silent, and no evidence establishes that he had waived those rights. People v. Wright (1968) 66 Cal.Rptr. 95, 258 A.C.A. 871, certiorari denied 89 S.Ct. 154, 393 U.S. 896, 21 L.Ed.2d 177.

Where police officer who had been called to investigate disturbance noticed defendant and two other injured parties and asked defendant to tell him what happened whereupon defendant stated that he had come to former wife's house to try to get $300 and had kicked door in, drawn a gun and then just started shooting, the statement was admissible even if defendant was not advised of all of his constitutional rights since statement was made prior to accusatory stage, defendant was not in custody and statement was not made in response to a process of interrogations. Id.

Principles enunciated in United States Supreme Court decision regarding admission of confessions and prospective application thereof are controlling in the federal courts, but they are not necessarily definitive as to state courts. People v. Perrin (1967) 55 Cal.Rptr. 847, 247 C.A.2d 838.

Where second defendant made an invalid and inadmissible confession of robbery, and thereafter in conversation with marshal second defendant made a voluntary and unsolicited second confession, second confession was tainted by invalidity of first confession and was inadmissible in robbery prosecution. People v. Falk (1966) 54 Cal.Rptr. 488, 244 A.C.A. 777.

Evidence that in first discussion at jail officer asked first defendant if he had attorney, that he said that he had but was unable to reach attorney, and that later he asked an officer if he could have his attorney get a writ to take him to dentist, and that he was allowed to use telephone, and that he had been in custody of federal agents who customarily advise suspects of their rights was insufficient to establish that he was aware of his right to an attorney and to remain silent and knowingly waived those rights. Id.

Double hearsay

Testimony of witnesses in murder prosecution that deceased had told them that defendant had threatened to kill her should have been excluded from evidence as "double hearsay," where such testimony referred solely to alleged past conduct on part of defendant, and there was no evidence that statements made by deceased were probably trustworthy and credible. People v. Lew (1968) 69 Cal. Rptr. 102, 441 P.2d 942, 68 C.2d 774.

Objections

Objection to admission of evidence upon ground that it is derivative evidence with a causative nexus to statements obtained illegally from defendant must be made in the trial court; it may not be raised for first time on appeal. People v. Carlin (1968) 67 Cal.Rptr. 557, 261 C.A.2d 30, certiorari denied 89 S.Ct. 658, 393 U.S. 1037, 21 L.Ed.2d 583.

Implied admissions

Apparently exculpatory statements, given to arresting officer, which were untruthful, in direct conflict with evidence, and completely contrary to testimony given by both defendant and his codefendant at trial became implied admissions showing consciousness of guilt. People v. Cooper (1970) 86 Cal.Rptr. 499, 7 C.A.3d 200.

Harmless or prejudicial error, in general

Assuming trial court erroneously permitted introduction of defendant's exculpatory statements to officers at time of his arrest, such error was harmless beyond reasonable doubt where defendant's statements did not constitute a confession, but were exculpatory statements, designed to establish innocence, incriminating only because later shown to be untruthful, and defendant made identical statements on day following his arrest after being given full and complete constitutional warnings. People v. Cooper (1970) 86 Cal.Rptr. 499, 7 C.A.3d 200.

Where defendant contended in murder prosecution that shooting of deceased was accidental, improper admission of hearsay evidence that deceased had told witnesses that defendant had threatened to kill her in the past was prejudicial error. People v. Lew (1968) 69 Cal.Rptr. 102, 441 P.2d 942, 68 C.2d 774.

Instructions

Failure to instruct that evidence of oral admissions of parties should be viewed with caution constituted harmless error where defense counsel objected to giving of cautionary instruction in unreported conference held in trial judge's chambers. People v. Jones (1967) 62 Cal.Rptr. 304, 254 C.A.2d 200, certiorari denied 88 S.Ct. 1101, 390 U.S. 980, 19 L.Ed.2d 1278.

§ 1221. Adoptive admission

Evidence of a statement offered against a party is not made inadmissible by the hearsay rule if the statement is one of which the party, with knowledge of the content thereof, has by words or other conduct manifested his adoption or his belief in its truth. (Stats.1965, c. 299, § 1221.)

Notes of Decisions

Admissibility in general

Admission of district attorney's out-of-court statement against defendant was proper for purpose of demonstrating defendant's adoption of the statement, and thus did not violate defendant's Sixth

§ 1221

**Amendment right to confront adverse witnesses (U.S.C.A.Const. Amend. 6), where prosecutor especially declared, after defendant's objection, that evidence was offered only to show response of defendant to district attorney's accusation and defendant failed to request a limiting instruction. People v. Richards (1976) 131 Cal.Rptr. 537, 552 P.2d 97, 17 C.3d 614.

Circumstances calling for answer, in general

Statements regarding details of crime made by defendants during conversations with defendants' friends or confederates were admissible against both, as had one disagreed with what other said, it would be reasonable to assume that he would have said so. People v. Osuna (1969) 76 Cal.Rptr. 462, 452 P.2d 678, 70 C.2d 759.

Response, nature of—In general

Testimony concerning statements of district attorney was properly admitted to show defendant's response to them. People v. Richards (1976) 131 Cal.Rptr. 537, 552 P.2d 97, 17 C.3d 614.

If one is accused of having committed a crime, under circumstances which fairly afford him an opportunity to hear, understand, and to reply, and which do not lend themselves to inference that he was relying on the Fifth Amendment right of silence, and he fails to speak, or he makes evasive or equivocal reply, both the accusatory statement and the fact of silence or equivocation on the part of defendant may be offered as an implied or adoptive admission of guilt. People v. Preston (1973) 107 Cal.Rptr. 300, 508 P.2d 300, 9 C.3d 308.

Silence or acquiescence of accused as response

Trial court was not required to find that defendant had not manifested his belief in truth of companion's statement implicating both of them in robbery and homicide merely because defendant remained silent or laughed when companion made such statement to a third party or on ground that in ghetto culture in which defendant lived the natural reaction of an innocent man would be to remain silent, to laugh or even claim falsely that he participated in the crime. People v. Browning (1975) 119 Cal.Rptr. 420, 45 C.A.3d 125.

In prosecution for burglary in the first degree, where evidence, including fingerprint on broken window of burglarized premises and testimony that defendant was seen trying to open cash register during burglary, of defendant's guilt was overwhelming, error in admitting evidence of defendant's silence in response to accusatory statements during interrogation was harmless. People v. Savala (1970) 89 Cal.Rptr. 475, 10 C.A.3d 958.

Co-defendants or accomplices, accusation of crimes against one of several

Trial court properly admitted in evidence as adoptive admissions extrajudicial out-of-custody statements made by codefendant which incriminated himself and defendant, and the words or conduct of defendant in response thereto. People v. Preston (1973) 107 Cal. Rptr. 300, 508 P.2d 300, 9 C.3d 308.

Fact questions

In prosecution for theft, whether defendant's response to pretrial statements of district attorney actually constituted an adoptive admission was question for jury. People v. Richards (1976) 131 Cal.Rptr. 537, 552 P.2d 97, 17 C.3d 614.

Determination whether defendant heard his companion's statements that the two of them had committed offenses at issue, whether companion's statement was such as to call for an answer from defendant, whether defendant was free to object or deny the statement and whether his conduct, i. e., laughter and failure to protest, was intended as a response and, hence, whether the people had laid a proper foundation for use of companion's statements against defendant, were factual matters to be decided by the trial court. People v. Browning (1975) 119 Cal.Rptr. 420, 45 C.A.3d 125.

Instructions

Where trial court specifically ruled that it was not admitting codefendant's statements as statements of coconspirator and that they were admitted under the adoptive admission exception to the hearsay rule to show defendant's response thereto, trial court was not required to further instruct, on its own motion or otherwise, that such evidence should be viewed with distrust because it related to statements made by an accomplice. People v. Preston (1973) 107 Cal.Rptr. 300, 508 P.2d 300, 9 C.3d 308.

§ 1222. Authorized admission

Evidence of a statement offered against a party is not made inadmissible by the hearsay rule if:

(a) The statement was made by a person authorized by the party to make a statement or statements for him concerning the subject matter of the statement; and

(b) The evidence is offered either after admission of evidence sufficient to sustain a finding of such authority or, in the court's discretion as to the order of proof, subject to the admission of such evidence.
(Stats.1965, c. 299, § 1222.)

Comment—Law Revision Commission

Section 1222 provides a hearsay exception for authorized admissions. Under this exception, if a party authorized an agent to make statements on his behalf, such statements may be introduced against the party under the same conditions as if they had been made by the party himself. The authority of the declarant to make the statement need not be express; it may be implied. It is to be determined in each case under the substantive law of agency.

§ 1223. Admission of co-conspirator

Evidence of a statement offered against a party is not made inadmissible by the hearsay rule if:

(a) The statement was made by the declarant while participating in a conspiracy to commit a crime or civil wrong and in furtherance of the objective of that conspiracy;

(b) The statement was made prior to or during the time that the party was participating in that conspiracy; and

(c) The evidence is offered either after admission of evidence sufficient to sustain a finding of the facts specified in subdivisions (a) and (b) or, in the court's discretion as to the order of proof, subject to the admission of such evidence.
(Stats.1965, c. 299, § 1223.)

Comment—Law Revision Commission

Section 1223 is a specific example of a kind of authorized admission that is admissible under Section 1222. The statement is admitted because it is an act of the conspiracy for which the party, as a co-conspirator, is legally responsible.

§ 1230. Declarations against interest

Evidence of a statement by a declarant having sufficient knowledge of the subject is not made inadmissible by the hearsay rule if the declarant is unavailable as a witness and the statement, when made, was so far contrary to the declarant's pecuniary or proprietary interest, or so far subjected him to the risk of civil or criminal liability, or so far tended to render invalid a claim by him against another, or created such a risk of making him an object of hatred, ridicule, or social disgrace in the community, that a reasonable man in his position would not have made the statement unless he believed it to be true. (Stats.1965, c. 299, § 1230.)

§ 1235. Inconsistent statement

Evidence of a statement made by a witness is not made inadmissible by the hearsay rule if the statement is inconsistent with his testimony at the hearing and is offered in compliance with Section 770. (Stats.1965, c. 299, § 1235.)

Comment—Law Revision Commission

Under existing law, a prior statement of a witness that is consistent with his testimony at the trial is admissible under certain conditions when the credibility of the witness has been attacked. The statement is admitted, however, only to rehabilitate the witness—to support his credibility—and not as evidence of the truth of the matter stated.

Notes of Decisions

Decisions under prior law

Police report, which was compiled immediately after robbery, which contained accounts of two eyewitnesses and several alibi witnesses, not just officers' conclusions, and which was prepared by officers in course of their official duties, was admissible in probation revocation hearing, notwithstanding contention that interviews with witnesses were hearsay which was not properly introduced as past recollection recorded or as prior inconsistent statements. People v. Turner (App.1975) 118 Cal.Rptr. 924.

Tape recorded conversation between police and witness was admissible in criminal prosecution as prior inconsistent statement where it appeared that witness lied in testifying in effect that she could not remember. People v. Wheeler (1972) 100 Cal.Rptr. 198, 23 C.A.3d 290.

Prior statements of a second codefendant concerning events at scene of crime were admissible for purposes of impeaching witness' testimony on direct examination by prosecution that he and defendant were elsewhere and were not involved in crime, as well as for purpose of establishing its own truth as substantive evidence, since witness' testimony on direct, if believed, constituted an alibi which would have exonerated defendant, and prosecution was within its rights in attempting to secure jury's disbelief of story. People v. Woodberry (1970) 89 Cal.Rptr. 330, 10 C.A.3d 695.

This section with respect to witness' prior inconsistent statement is designed to allow evidence of such statement not only to impeach the witness but also, in civil cases, for the truth of the contents of the statement. LeGrand v. Yellow Cab Co. of San Gabriel Valley (1970) 87 Cal.Rptr. 292, 8 C.A.3d 123.

Constitutional question whether defendant's Sixth Amendment (U.S.C.A.Const. Amend. 6) right of confrontation had been violated by allowing prosecutor to read into record the extrajudicial statements of witnesses who testified during trial could be raised for first time on appeal, where trial had been completed prior to decision used by defendant as basis for claiming denial of such right. People v. Dilworth (1969) 78 Cal.Rptr. 817, 274 C.A.2d 27, certiorari denied 90 S.Ct. 1148, 397 U.S. 1001, 25 L.Ed.2d 411.

Where witness testified that he did not remember alleged fight in which accused had kicked him because he was too drunk at time it supposedly occurred and that he also did not remember signing a police report about fight, officer's testimony that he had interviewed witness in back of an ambulance, that witness had been drinking but did not appear to him to be drunk, and that witness signed a police report which indicated that accused and several others had knocked witness down and kicked him was inadmissible both for impeachment purposes and as substantive evidence. People v. Sam (1969) 77 Cal.Rptr. 804, 454 P.2d 700, 71 C.2d 194.

In general

Where individual implicated in the robbery testified only at preliminary hearing when he denied ever making statements as to defendant's involvement in robbery and did not testify at trial, detective's testimony regarding prior inconsistent statement made by such individual was not admissible under this section authorizing admission of prior inconsistent statement of a witness to prove truth of matter asserted therein; overruling People v. Bynum, 4 Cal.3d 589, 94 Cal.Rptr. 241, 483 P.2d 1193, and People v. Browning, 45 Cal.App.3d 125, 119 Cal.Rptr. 420. People v. Williams (1976) 128 Cal.Rptr. 888, 547 P.2d 1000.

While evidence of telephone call allegedly made to mother of decedent by wife of defendant driver three days after head-on collision, wherein wife allegedly said, inter alia, that her husband had fallen asleep at the wheel, was not admissible as a prior inconsistent statement when wife first testified at trial that she had no recollection of the period of time following dinner on evening of accident until approximately ten days later, evidence of the telephone call became admissible when, subsequently, the jury was read wife's testimony, previously given out of jury's presence, that her husband had not told her he was tired, that she had not told him to stop and rest, and that he had not fallen asleep. Clifton v. Ulis (1976) 130 Cal.Rptr. 155, 549 P.2d 1251, 17 C.3d 99.

Prior inconsistent statement exception to the hearsay rule applies to inconsistent hearsay statements of a witness and not to hearsay statements of a hearsay declarant which are inconsistent with the declarant's other hearsay statements which have been admitted in evidence under some exception to the hearsay rule. Van Oosting v. Duber Indus. Sec., Inc. (1976) 129 Cal.Rptr. 173, 57 C.A.3d 376.

Witness' testimony at prior trial was not admissible at later trial, under this section providing that evidence of statement made by witness is not inadmissible hearsay if statement is inconsistent with his testimony at hearing, where witness refused to testify at all in later hearing at which question of inadmissibility of testimony arose. People v. Rojas (1975) 125 Cal.Rptr. 357, 542 P.2d 229, 15 C.3d 540.

Prior inconsistent statement of prosecution witness, who on night of offense gave statement implicating defendant but who at trial testified that because he was intoxicated at the time he could not recall whether defendant had a knife in his hand or whether he

§ 1235

stabbed victim and who testified that he couldn't recall having made a statement to the police, was admissible to prove the truth of the matters asserted therein as well as to impeach witness' credibility. People v. Romo (1975) 121 Cal.Rptr. 111, 534 P.2d 1015, 14 C.3d 189.

Out-of-court statement made by one juvenile implicating another cannot be admitted in a joint jurisdictional hearing unless the references implicating the nondeclarant have been effectively deleted; if the inculpatory references cannot be effectively deleted, the hearing must be severed if the statement is to be admitted against the declarant. In re D. L. (1975) 120 Cal.Rptr. 276, 46 C.A.3d 65.

Prior inconsistent statements which had been given by witnesses in robbery prosecution to another witness and to police and which implicated defendant in bank robbery were admissible as substantive evidence of the facts detailed in the statements following the witnesses' testimonial denial of the statements, notwithstanding that they may have been hearsay where the makers of the statements were in court and available for cross examination. People v. Collins (1975) 118 Cal.Rptr. 864, 44 C.A.3d 617.

Where witness had testified that she was not testifying under any threat or fear with respect to her testimony and thereafter refused to answer any further questions concerning incident on grounds of self-incrimination, witness' mother's testimony that witness had expressed fear for her own safety and that of her family if she testified at trial was admissible for purposes of impeachment, and its admission did not deprive defendant of his right to confrontation, in case in which witness was available for cross-examination on matters of her fears for herself and her family. People v. Allen (1974) 115 Cal.Rptr. 839, 41 C.A.3d 196.

Refusal to admit tape recording of conversation between defendant and officer, which recording had been offered to show whether defendant had been properly advised of his rights to remain silent and to have counsel and whether officer had made inconsistent statements and to ascertain defendant's physical condition and state of mind at time of the conversation, was within trial court's discretion where testimony concerning waiver of right to remain silent and to have counsel was uncontradicted, defendant was unable to demonstrate inconsistencies in officer's testimony and the recording machine produced distortion in sound quality. People v. Johnson (1974) 114 Cal.Rptr. 545, 39 C.A.3d 749.

Where evidence of defendants' guilt of homicide was overwhelming and the testimony that the prosecution found necessary to impeach clearly connected both defendants with the crime, the error in admitting prior inconsistent hearsay statements to impeach the prosecution witnesses' preliminary examination testimony, admitted at trial because of unavailability of witnesses, was harmless beyond reasonable doubt. People v. Beyea (1974) 113 Cal.Rptr. 254, 38 C.A.3d 176.

Where two women denied having stated that defendant had admitted to them his involvement in murder-robbery, and where all requirements for admissibility were followed, police officers who had taken statements were properly allowed to testify concerning them. People v. Marcus (1974) 111 Cal.Rptr. 772, 36 C.A.3d 676.

Where codefendant took stand during defendants' trial and denied making prior out-of-court statement to police officers implicating defendants in crimes charged, and was available for cross-examination during trial, defendants were not denied right to confront witnesses by admission of testimony by police officers as to contents of codefendant's out-of-court statements for purpose of proving truth of contents thereof, despite contention that defendants were deprived of right to cross-examine codefendant as to statements since he denied making them. People v. Jenkins (1973) 110 Cal.Rptr. 465, 34 C.A.3d 893.

EVIDENCE CODE

Prior inconsistent statement by defendant motorist on deposition that he was "pretty sure" that third person's car had not been moved after accident before police officer arrived constituted substantive evidence authorizing hypothetical question in personal injury case based on assumption that such car was not moved after impact; however, reversal was not required by exclusion of answer where lack of impeaching negative answer did not prevent plaintiff's counsel from arguing claimed nonmovement of car at length. Arellano v. Moreno (1973) 109 Cal.Rptr. 421, 33 C.A.3d 877.

Where various witnesses who had testified concerning their pretrial identifications of defendant by means of photographs were in court and available for cross-examination when subsequent testimony of officer, varying from testimony of such witnesses, was given, officer's testimony was admissible for truth of its contents. People v. Williams (1973) 106 Cal.Rptr. 622, 506 P.2d 998, 9 C.3d 24.

In prosecution for murder of defendants' 11-month old child by torture, wherein defendant on direct examination testified that on day of child's death defendant had been playing with child and child had accidentally slipped from his hands and had fallen to floor, and on cross-examination defendant repeated such testimony on rebuttal, deputy prosecuting attorney was properly permitted to testify that on day of child's death he had heard defendant say that "the baby had fallen off the counter," where during cross-examination defendant professed no discussion with deputy, so that it would have been fruitless for prosecution to interrogate defendant as to specific statements testified to by deputy. People v. Aeschlimann (1972) 104 Cal.Rptr. 689, 28 C.A.3d 460.

Where prior inconsistent statement of a person is admissible pursuant to statute governing admissibility of a prior inconsistent statement, defendant is not denied right of confrontation guaranteed him by the Sixth Amendment (U.S.C.A.Const. Amend. 6), and is not denied due process under the Fourteenth Amendment (U.S.CA. Const. Amend. 14), if declarant testifies at trial and is thus available for cross-examination, unless the declarant shows such apparent lapse of memory at trial as to affect defendant's cross-examination opportunities to point that his Sixth Amendment right of confrontation is violated by admission of the prior inconsistent statement. People v. Petersen (1972) 100 Cal.Rptr. 590, 23 C.A.3d 883.

This section providing that evidence of statement made by witness is not made inadmissible by hearsay rule if statement is inconsistent with his testimony at hearing and is offered in compliance with § 770 requiring that declarant be provided opportunity to explain or deny statement or he be kept available for further testimony is designed to permit evidentiary use of witness' inconsistent statement either to impeach him or as substantive evidence of truth of matters asserted. People v. Freeman (1971) 97 Cal.Rptr. 717, 20 C.A.3d 488.

Where witness when called as prosecution witness reneged on promise to testify consistent with earlier statements to deputy sheriff by categorically denying that he took defendant to robbery and shooting victim's neighborhood, that defendant ever got out of his automobile or that he ever heard a shot, defense counsel asked only whether he recalled events of night before or day of shooting to which witness gave negative answer, and made no attempt to explore inconsistency thus laid bare, and such witness on several occasions had lapses of memory permitting evasions of questions, admission for impeachment purposes of witness' prior statements did not constitute denial of defendant's right to protection from impeaching testimony when prior statements are not truly inconsistent. People v. Barranday (1971) 97 Cal.Rptr. 345, 20 C.A.3d 16.

When prosecuting witness testified that she could not recall what defendant had said the day he fired revolver, the prosecuting attorney should not have been permitted to refresh her memory by reading aloud before jury from recorded report of her account to police of the incident the next day; however, the error was harmless where the majority of the comments could have been introduced if proper procedure had been followed, the statements the witness remembered plus defendant's conduct constituted substantial evidence from which jury could infer an intent to commit a battery, and it was not probable that a result more favorable to defendant would have been reached if those declarations had been excluded. People v. Parks (1971) 95 Cal.Rptr. 193, 485 P.2d 257, 4 C.3d 955.

Confrontation clause is not violated by permitting admission of witness' prior inconsistent statement to prove truth of matter asserted therein where statement was given under circumstances closely approximating those that surround typical trial. People v. Bynum (1971) 94 Cal.Rptr. 241, 483 P.2d 1193, 4 C.3d 589.

Statements made to police officer by prosecution witness, who had originally been charged with being a participant in robbery with which defendant was charged, but who was not a codefendant in second trial, were admissible under this section providing in effect that a prior inconsistent statement of a witness is admissible not only to impeach his credibility but also to prove the truth of the matters asserted therein. People v. Bisogni (1971) 94 Cal.Rptr. 164, 483 P.2d 780, 4 C.3d 582.

Where at preliminary hearing witness related that he had secured marijuana for sale from defendant's father's house and in extrajudicial statement to police officer stated that defendant had brought marijuana to witness' house in shopping bag, but at trial witness deliberately evaded question as to how marijuana came into his possession, trial testimony was materially inconsistent with preliminary hearing testimony and extrajudicial declaration and, thus, such prior statements were properly admitted, in prosecution for furnishing marijuana to a minor, for purpose of impeachment. People v. Green (1971) 92 Cal.Rptr. 494, 479 P.2d 998, 3 C.3d 981, petition dismissed 92 S.Ct. 20, 404 U.S. 801, 30 L.Ed.2d 34.

In determining whether defendant's conversation with his wife corroborated defendant's 12-year-old stepdaughter's testimony that she and defendant had regularly engaged in various sexual practices for a period of about a year, the Court of Appeal could properly take into account not only what defendant's wife, as a witness, conceded but also what she told police but denied at trial, where at a retrial wife's entire statement to police would be admissible. People v. Brown (1971) 92 Cal.Rptr. 370, 14 C.A.3d 334.

Defendant was not deemed to have waived his constitutional right to confront witnesses by his counsel's failure to request instruction limiting testimony as to witness' prior inconsistent statement to impeachment where case was tried prior to decision [People v. Johnson (1968) 68 Cal.Rptr. 599, 441 P.2d 111, 68 C.A.2d 646] that this section allowing prior inconsistent statements of a witness to be used as substantive evidence was unconstitutional so that counsel's request for limiting instruction appeared to be fruitless act. People v. Robinson (1970) 86 Cal.Rptr. 56, 6 C.A.3d 448, certiorari denied 91 S.Ct. 149, 400 U.S. 907, 27 L.Ed.2d 145.

Answers to interrogatories need not be under oath to be admissible as prior inconsistent or consistent statements. LeGrand v. Yellow Cab Co. of San Gabriel Valley (1970) 87 Cal.Rptr. 292, 8 C.A.3d 125.

Where trial of defendant charged with murder was completed before opinion requiring that testimony as to prior inconsistent statements be limited to impeachment purposes was filed, error in allowing evidence as to witness' prior inconsistent statement as substantive evidence was not waived by defendant's failure to request limiting instruction or admonition. People v. Clark (1970) 86 Cal.Rptr. 106, 6 C.A.3d 658.

Condemnees were not precluded by § 822 from cross-examining expert witness for condemnor, for purpose of impeachment, with respect to earlier condemnation trial wherein he had testified to bare land value per square foot of other property in the neighborhood in amount twice that given in direct examination with respect to the subject property. State By and Through State Public Works Bd. v. Stevenson (1970) 84 Cal.Rptr. 742, 5 C.A.3d 60.

Statutory provision of this section that prior inconsistent statements are admissible as substantive evidence applies only when person whose statement is to be used is a witness and has opportunity to explain or deny statement. City of Pleasant Hill v. First Baptist Church of Pleasant Hill (1969) 82 Cal.Rptr. 1, 1 C.A.3d 384.

Fact that defendant did not object to admission of codefendant's extrajudicial statement at separate trial without instruction limiting its effect solely to impeachment of codefendant's inconsistent testimony would not prevent his challenging its admissibility on appeal where at time of trial statement was admissible but subsequently California Supreme Court decision held such statements inadmissible. People v. Middleton (1969) 81 Cal.Rptr. 32, 276 C.A.2d 566.

Hearsay statement which, according to testimony of police officer, was made to officer by inmate in same jail as defendant concerning defendant's request of inmate to secure signature of alleged coconspirator on a piece of paper so that defendant could fabricate a sales slip for murder weapon was not admissible, since its probative value to impeach inmate's testimony that he had never seen defendant was substantially outweighed by the probability that its admission would create substantial danger of undue prejudice. People v. Coleman (1969) 80 Cal.Rptr. 920, 459 P.2d 248, 71 C.2d 1159.

Where defense witness on direct examination corroborated defendant's pretrial statement indicating acts of aggression by victim against defendant who asserted self-defense, substantive use of testimony of victim's sister, that witness prior to trial had said that defendant had broken beer bottle and gone toward victim, was prejudicial error, especially where defense witness was only person who gave testimony as to events immediately preceding killing and gave strong evidence that victim had been the aggressor. People v. Spencer (1969) 80 Cal.Rptr. 99, 458 P.2d 43, 71 C.2d 933.

Prior inconsistent statements of witness, while admissible for impeachment purposes, cannot be given substantive use in criminal trial because to do so would deprive defendant of his constitutional right of confrontation guaranteed by Sixth Amendment. Id.

Failure of defense counsel to request a limiting instruction with respect to admission of prior inconsistent statements of witness did not constitute waiver of error on appeal where law at time of trial was that prior statements were admissible for truth of matters asserted therein and counsel would not have been entitled to such instruction. People v. Odom (1969) 78 Cal.Rptr. 873, 456 P.2d 145, 71 C.2d 709.

Admission, without limiting instruction, on codefendant's cross-examination of witness, of witness's prior inconsistent statement which exonerated codefendant but implicated defendant, deprived defendant of his constitutional right to confrontation, where statement was offered and received as substantive evidence. People v. Graham (1969) 78 Cal.Rptr. 217, 455 P.2d 153, 71 C.2d 303.

That prior inconsistent statements of witnesses were admitted for all purposes and not merely for limited purpose of impeachment did not automatically deprive accused of fair trial and conviction would be reversed only if prejudice actually ensued. People v. Neese (1969) 77 Cal.Rptr. 314, 272 C.A.2d 235.

To prove truth of matter stated, introduction of testimony given by witness at preliminary hearing contradicting witness' trial statements indicating that he could not identify which of two robbers had said that he had killed victim was error, but where

§ 1235   EVIDENCE CODE

identification was subject to cross-examination at time when jury observed witness' demeanor, error was not prejudicial. People v. McGautha (1969) 76 Cal.Rptr. 434, 452 P.2d 650, 70 C.2d 770, affirmed 91 S.Ct. 1454, 402 U.S. 183, 28 L.Ed.2d 711, rehearing denied 92 S.Ct. 2407, 406 U.S. 978, 32 L.Ed.2d 677.

Prior extrajudicial statements of defendant's relatives to investigating officers were admissible, in prosecution of defendant for Penal Code § 288 violation, for narrow purpose of impeachment but not as substantive evidence of guilt. People v. Pierce (1969) 75 Cal.Rptr. 257, 269 C.A.2d 193, appeal after remand 89 Cal.Rptr. 751, 11 C.A.3d 313.

In criminal trials, use of prior inconsistent statement of witness to prove truth of statement's content deprives accused of his Sixth Amendment (U.S.C.A.Const. Amend. 6) right to confront and cross-examine witness. People v. Hopper (1969) 75 Cal.Rptr. 253, 268 C.A.2d 774.

Although court erred in reinstructing jury that it could consider testimony of investigator, who asserted that witness, contrary to his testimony at trial that he could not recall having seen an acid drum in his sister's garage, stated in an earlier interview that he did see such a drum in his sister's backyard, as substantive evidence tending to show that the witness had in fact seen an acid drum, the error was harmless beyond a reasonable doubt, since storage of the acid in the sister's garage was strictly neutral in sense that it was consistent with both the defense and prosecution theory of events that led to the murder. People v. Bradford (1969) 74 Cal.Rptr. 726, 450 P.2d 46, 70 C.2d 333, certiorari denied 90 S.Ct. 2204, 399 U.S. 911, 26 L.Ed.2d 566.

After complaining witness had testified on direct examination, admitting, pursuant to this section which provides that prior inconsistent statements are admissible as substantive evidence, excerpts from witness' testimony at preliminary hearing at which defendant had been represented by counsel who had opportunity to cross-examine witness, without limiting admission to purposes of impeachment violated defendant's constitutional right to confront witness. People v. Vinson (1969) 74 Cal.Rptr. 340, 268 C.A.2d 672.

In light of fact that except for complaining witness' prior testimony there was little, if any, substantive evidence to justify conviction on one count and that evidence against defendant on other count was highly circumstantial and lacked the convincing quality generally required in a criminal action, error in admitting, pursuant to this section which provided that prior inconsistent statements are admissible as substantive evidence, excerpts of witness' testimony at preliminary hearing without limiting admission to purposes of impeachment was prejudicial. Id.

Even before enactment of the Evidence Code a witness' prior inconsistent statement could be used to discredit his testimony given at trial. People v. Alvarez (1968) 73 Cal.Rptr. 753, 268 C.A.2d 297.

Transcript of witness' testimony taken at previous trial which had resulted in mistrial and transcript of witness' testimony taken at preliminary examination positively identifying defendant were admissible at defendant's trial as independent evidence and did not violate any right of confrontation by defendant who was represented by counsel at preliminary hearing and whose counsel at previous trial had cross-examined witness. People v. Davis (1968) 71 Cal.Rptr. 656, 265 A.C.A. 889.

Where people's witness gave testimony which, if true, completely exculpated both of defendants on trial, attack upon witness' credibility was proper, and his prior inconsistent statement, in which witness had confessed his participation in driving the two defendants to and from scene of murder, with which the two defendants were charged, and one defendant's statement that he had shot a man were admissible in the murder prosecution for purpose of attacking witness' credibility. People v. Woodberry (1968) 71 Cal.Rptr. 165, 265 C.A.2d 351.

Under this section making prior inconsistent statements of a witness admissible for truth of matters therein asserted, it was error in violation of Sixth Amendment's guarantee of right of confrontation of witnesses by accused to admit in incest prosecution testimony of daughter and wife of defendant before grand jury that defendant had sexual intercourse with daughter after wife and daughter testified in incest prosecution that defendant did not have sexual intercourse with daughter. People v. Johnson (1968) 68 Cal.Rptr. 599, 441 P.2d 111, 68 C.2d 646, certiorari denied 89 S.Ct. 679, 393 U.S. 1051, 21 L.Ed.2d 693.

Where officer, after showing group of photographs drew a beard on photograph which witness picked as most nearly resembling bearded man witness saw, identification procedure was unfair but not denial of due process resulting in reversible error since procedure did not produce identification in first instance, however, since beard was already drawn on defendant's picture when officer showed it to next witness the identification by next witness was procured by unfair means, but error was harmless since her pretrial identification had been weakened by her trial testimony. People v. Slutts (1968) 66 Cal.Rptr. 862, 259 C.A.2d 886.

Failure to object

Defendant's failure to object to detective's testimony regarding inconsistent statement made by individual who testified only at preliminary hearing on the ground that detective's testimony was inadmissible under this section governing admission of prior inconsistent statement by witness was excusable since this section had previously been held applicable in similar circumstances and thus did not prevent appellate court from determining admissibility of detective's testimony under such section. People v. Williams (1976) 128 Cal.Rptr. 888, 547 P.2d 1000.

Prior actions

Where complaint in prior action in which allegation that accident was proximately caused by the intoxication of the driver of the vehicle was not verified by passenger, there was no showing that the passenger had seen the pleading or furnished the information on which it was based and manufacturer referred to no testimony of passenger at the second trial of passenger's action against manufacturer with which the allegation in the superseded complaint was inconsistent, manufacturer of vehicle was not entitled to examine the passenger on the basis of the superseded complaint. Ault v. International Harvester Co. (1974) 117 Cal.Rptr. 812, 528 P.2d 1148, 13 C.3d 113.

Witness

This section governing admission of prior inconsistent statement of a witness applies only to prior inconsistent statements of a trial witness. People v. Williams (1976) 128 Cal.Rptr. 888, 547 P.2d 1000.

Review

Failure of defense counsel to object to evidence of prior inconsistent statement of witness or to request limiting instruction did not preclude assertion of error on appeal where case was tried before decision establishing rule that failure to limit consideration of prior inconsistent statements to impeachment purposes denies defendant right of confrontation. People v. Todd (1969) 81 Cal.Rptr. 866, 1 C.A.3d 547.

The fact that at trial defendant failed to object to admissibility of prior inconsistent statements as substantive evidence or request an instruction that jury consider them for impeachment purposes only did not preclude him from raising the issue on appeal where in light of § 770 and this section there was no reason to object and defendant had no burden of anticipating unforeseen changes in application of this section. People v. Neese (1969) 77 Cal.Rptr. 314, 272 C.A.2d 235.

It could not be assumed that trial judge limited evidence to narrow purpose of weighing credibility, in attempted robbery prosecution occurring prior to reinstatement of common-law rule prohibiting use of witness' prior inconsistent statement to be considered as substantive evidence by trier of facts, and it would be assumed that trial judge treated prior inconsistent statements of witness as substantive as well as impeaching evidence. People v. Miles (1969) 77 Cal.Rptr. 89, 272 C.A.2d 212.

§ 1236. Prior consistent statement

Evidence of a statement previously made by a witness is not made inadmissible by the hearsay rule if the statement is consistent with his testimony at the hearing and is offered in compliance with Section 791.
(Stats.1965, c. 299, § 1236.)

§ 1237. Past recollection recorded

(a) Evidence of a statement previously made by a witness is not made inadmissible by the hearsay rule if the statement would have been admissible if made by him while testifying, the statement concerns a matter as to which the witness has insufficient present recollection to enable him to testify fully and accurately, and the statement is contained in a writing which:

(1) Was made at a time when the fact recorded in the writing actually occurred or was fresh in the witness' memory;

(2) Was made (i) by the witness himself or under his direction or (ii) by some other person for the purpose of recording the witness' statement at the time it was made;

(3) Is offered after the witness testifies that the statement he made was a true statement of such fact; and

(4) Is offered after the writing is authenticated as an accurate record of the statement.

(b) The writing may be read into evidence, but the writing itself may not be received in evidence unless offered by an adverse party.
(Stats.1965, c. 299, § 1237.)

Comment—Assembly Committee on Judiciary

Section 1237 provides a hearsay exception for what is usually referred to as "past recollection recorded." Although the provisions of Section 1237 are taken largely from the provisions of Section 2047 of the Code of Civil Procedure, there are some substantive differences between Section 1237 and existing law.

The existing law requires that a foundation be laid for the admission of such evidence by showing (1) that the writing recording the statement was made by the witness or under his direction, (2) that the writing was made at the time when the fact recorded in the writing actually occurred or at another time when the fact was fresh in the witness' memory, and (3) that the witness "knew that the same was correctly stated in the writing." Under Section 1237, however, the writing may be made not only by the witness himself or under his direction but also by some other person for the purpose of recording the witness' statement at the time it was made. In addition, Section 1237 permits testimony of the person who recorded the statement to be used to establish that the writing is a correct record of the statement. Sufficient assurance of the trustworthiness of the statement is provided if the declarant is available to testify that he made a true statement and if the person who recorded the statement is available to testify that he accurately recorded the statement.

§ 1238. Prior identification

Evidence of a statement previously made by a witness is not made inadmissible by the hearsay rule if the statement would have been admissible if made by him while testifying and:

(a) The statement is an identification of a party or another as a person who participated in a crime or other occurrence;

(b) The statement was made at a time when the crime or other occurrence was fresh in the witness' memory; and

(c) The evidence of the statement is offered after the witness testifies that he made the identification and that it was a true reflection of his opinion at that time.
(Stats.1965, c. 299, § 1238.)

§ 1240. Spontaneous statement

Evidence of a statement is not made inadmissible by the hearsay rule if the statement:

(a) Purports to narrate, describe, or explain an act, condition, or event perceived by the declarant; and

(b) Was made spontaneously while the declarant was under the stress of excitement caused by such perception.
(Stats.1965, c. 299, § 1240.)

§ 1241. Contemporaneous statement

Evidence of a statement is not made inadmissible by the hearsay rule if the statement:

(a) Is offered to explain, qualify, or make understandable conduct of the declarant; and

(b) Was made while the declarant was engaged in such conduct.
(Stats.1965, c. 299, § 1241.)

§ 1242. Dying declaration

Evidence of a statement made by a dying person respecting the cause and circumstances of his death is not made inadmissible by the hearsay rule if the statement was made upon his personal knowledge and under a sense of immediately impending death.
(Stats.1965, c. 299, § 1242.)

§ 1250. Statement of declarant's then existing mental or physical state

(a) Subject to Section 1252, evidence of a statement of the declarant's then existing state of mind, emotion, or physical sensation (including a statement of intent, plan, motive, design, mental feeling, pain, or bodily health) is not made inadmissible by the hearsay rule when:

(1) The evidence is offered to prove the declarant's state of mind, emotion, or physical sensation at that time or at any other time when it is itself an issue in the action; or

(2) The evidence is offered to prove or explain acts or conduct of the declarant.

(b) This section does not make admissible evidence of a statement of memory or belief to prove the fact remembered or believed.
(Stats.1965, c. 299, § 1250.)

§ 1251. Statement of declarant's previously existing mental or physical state

Subject to Section 1252, evidence of a statement of the declarant's state of mind, emotion, or physical sensation (including a statement of intent, plan, motive, design, mental feeling, pain, or bodily health) at a time prior to the statement is not made inadmissible by the hearsay rule if:

(a) The declarant is unavailable as a witness; and

(b) The evidence is offered to prove such prior state of mind, emotion, or physical sensation when it is itself an issue in the action and the evidence is not offered to prove any fact other than such state of mind, emotion, or physical sensation.
(Stats.1965, c. 299, § 1251.)

§ 1252. Limitation on admissibility of statement of mental or physical state

Evidence of a statement is inadmissible under this article if the statement was made under circumstances such as to indicate its lack of trustworthiness.
(Stats.1965, c. 299, § 1252.)

§ 1270. "A business"

As used in this article, "a business" includes every kind of business, governmental activity, profession, occupation, calling, or operation of institutions, whether carried on for profit or not.
(Stats.1965, c. 299, § 1270.)

§ 1271. Business record

Evidence of a writing made as a record of an act, condition, or event is not made inadmissible by the hearsay rule when offered to prove the act, condition, or event if:

(a) The writing was made in the regular course of a business;

(b) The writing was made at or near the time of the act, condition, or event;

(c) The custodian or other qualified witness testifies to its identity and the mode of its preparation; and

(d) The sources of information and method and time of preparation were such as to indicate its trustworthiness.
(Stats.1965, c. 299, § 1271.)

§ 1272. Absence of entry in business records

Evidence of the absence from the records of a business of a record of an asserted act, condition, or event is not made inadmissible by the hearsay rule when offered to prove the nonoccurrence of the act or event, or the nonexistence of the condition, if:

(a) It was the regular course of that business to make records of all such acts, conditions, or events at or near the time of the act, condition, or event and to preserve them; and

(b) The sources of information and method and time of preparation of the records of that business were such that the absence of a record of an act, condition, or event is a trustworthy indication that the act or event did not occur or the condition did not exist.
(Stats.1965, c. 299, § 1272.)

§ 1280. Record by public employee

Evidence of a writing made as a record of an act, condition, or event is not made inadmissible by the hearsay rule when offered to prove the act, condition, or event if:

(a) The writing was made by and within the scope of duty of a public employee;

(b) The writing was made at or near the time of the act, condition, or event; and

(c) The sources of information and method and time of preparation were such as to indicate its trustworthiness.
(Stats.1965, c. 299, § 1280.)

§ 1281. Record of vital statistics

Evidence of a writing made as a record of a birth, fetal death, death, or marriage is not made inadmissible by the hearsay rule if the maker was required by law to file the writing in a designated public office and the writing was made and filed as required by law.
(Stats.1965, c. 299, § 1281.)

§ 1290. "Former testimony"

As used in this article, "former testimony" means testimony given under oath in:

(a) Another action or in a former hearing or trial of the same action;

(b) A proceeding to determine a controversy conducted by or under the supervision of an agency that has the power to determine such a controversy and is an agency of the United States or a public entity in the United States;

(c) A deposition taken in compliance with law in another action; or

(d) An arbitration proceeding if the evidence of such former testimony is a verbatim transcript thereof.
(Stats.1965, c. 299, § 1290.)

§ 1291. Former testimony offered against party to former proceeding

(a) Evidence of former testimony is not made inadmissible by the hearsay rule if the declarant is unavailable as a witness and:

(1) The former testimony is offered against a person who offered it in evidence in his own behalf on the former occasion or against the successor in interest of such person; or

(2) The party against whom the former testimony is offered was a party to the action or proceeding in which the testimony was given and had the right and opportunity to cross-examine the declarant with an interest and motive similar to that which he has at the hearing.

(b) The admissibility of former testimony under this section is subject to the same limitations and objections as though the declarant were testifying at the hearing, except that former testimony offered under this section is not subject to:

(1) Objections to the form of the question which were not made at the time the former testimony was given.

(2) Objections based on competency or privilege which did not exist at the time the former testimony was given.
(Stats.1965, c. 299, § 1291.)

§ 1310. Statement concerning declarant's own family history

(a) Subject to subdivision (b), evidence of a statement by a declarant who is unavailable as a witness concerning his own birth, marriage, divorce, a parent and child relationship, relationship by blood or marriage, race, ancestry, or other similar fact of his family history is not made inadmissible by the hearsay rule, even though the declarant had no means of acquiring personal knowledge of the matter declared.

(b) Evidence of a statement is inadmissible under this section if the statement was made under circumstances such as to indicate its lack of trustworthiness.
(Amended by Stats.1975, c. 1244, p. ——, § 15.)

§ 1311. Statement concerning family history of another

(a) Subject to subdivision (b), evidence of a statement concerning the birth, marriage, divorce, death, parent and child relationship, race, ancestry, relationship by blood or marriage, or other similar fact of the family history of a person other than the declarant is not made inadmissible by the hearsay rule if the declarant is unavailable as a witness and:

(1) The declarant was related to the other by blood or marriage; or

(2) The declarant was otherwise so intimately associated with the other's family as to be likely to have had accurate information, concerning the matter declared and made the statement (i) upon information received from the other or from a person related by blood or marriage to the other or (ii) upon repute in the other's family.

(b) Evidence of a statement is inadmissible under this section if the statement was made under circumstances such as to indicate its lack of trustworthiness.
(Amended by Stats.1975, c. 1244, p. ——, § 16.)

§ 1312. Entries in family records and the like

Evidence of entries in family Bibles or other family books or charts, engravings on rings, family portraits, engravings on urns, crypts, or tombstones, and the like, is not made inadmissible by the hearsay rule when offered to prove the birth, marriage, divorce, death, parent and child relationship, race, ancestry, relationship by blood or marriage, or other similar fact of the family history of a member of the family by blood or marriage.
(Amended by Stats.1975, c. 1244, p. —, § 17.)

§ 1313. Reputation in family concerning family history

Evidence of reputation among members of a family is not made inadmissible by the hearsay rule if the reputation concerns the birth, marriage, divorce, death, parent and child relationship, race, ancestry, relationship by blood or marriage, or other similar fact of the family history of a member of the family by blood or marriage.
(Amended by Stats.1975, c. 1244, p. —, § 18.)

§ 1315. Church records concerning family history

Evidence of a statement concerning a person's birth, marriage, divorce, death, parent and child relationship, race, ancestry, relationship by blood or marriage, or other similar fact of family history which is contained in a writing made as a record of a church, religious denomination, or religious society is not made inadmissible by the hearsay rule if:

(a) The statement is contained in a writing made as a record of an act, condition, or event that would be admissible as evidence of such act, condition, or event under Section 1271; and

(b) The statement is of a kind customarily recorded in connection with the act, condition, or event recorded in the writing.
(Amended by Stats.1975, c. 1244, p. —, § 19.)

§ 1316. Marriage, baptismal and similar certificates

Evidence of a statement concerning a person's birth, marriage, divorce, death, parent and child relationship, race, ancestry, relationship by blood or marriage, or other similar fact of family history is not made inadmissible by the hearsay rule if the statement is contained in a certificate that the maker thereof performed a marriage or other ceremony or administered a sacrament and:

(a) The maker was a clergyman, civil officer, or other person authorized to perform the acts reported in the certificate by law or by the rules, regulations, or requirements of a church, religious denomination, or religious society; and

(b) The certificate was issued by the maker at the time and place of the ceremony or sacrament or within a reasonable time thereafter.
(Amended by Stats.1975, c. 1244, p. —, § 20.)

§ 1324. Reputation concerning character

Evidence of a person's general reputation with reference to his character or a trait of his character at a relevant time in the community in which he then resided or in a group with which he then habitually associated is not made inadmissible by the hearsay rule.
(Stats.1965, c. 299, § 1324.)

Division 11
WRITINGS

§ 1400. Authentication defined

Authentication of a writing means (a) the introduction of evidence sufficient to sustain a finding that it is the writing that the proponent of the evidence claims it is or (b) the establishment of such facts by any other means provided by law.
(Stats.1965, c. 299, § 1400.)

§ 1401. Authentication required

(a) Authentication of a writing is required before it may be received in evidence.

(b) Authentication of a writing is required before secondary evidence of its content may be received in evidence.
(Stats.1965, c. 299, § 1401.)

§ 1402. Authentication of altered writing

The party producing a writing as genuine which has been altered, or appears to have been altered, after its execution, in a part material to the question in dispute, must account for the alteration or appearance thereof. He may show that the alteration was made by another, without his concurrence, or was made with the consent of the parties affected by it, or otherwise properly or innocently made, or that the alteration did not change the meaning or language of the instrument. If he does that, he may give the writing in evidence, but not otherwise.
(Stats.1965, c. 299, § 1402.)

§ 1410. Article not exclusive

Nothing in this article shall be construed to limit the means by which a writing may be authenticated or proved.
(Stats.1965, c. 299, § 1410.)

§ 1411. Subscribing witness' testimony unnecessary

Except as provided by statute, the testimony of a subscribing witness is not required to authenticate a writing.
(Stats.1965, c. 299, § 1411.)

§ 1412. Use of other evidence when subscribing witness' testimony required

If the testimony of a subscribing witness is required by statute to authenticate a writing and the subscribing witness denies or does not recollect the execution of the writing, the writing may be authenticated by other evidence.
(Stats.1965, c. 299, § 1412.)

§ 1413. Witness to the execution of a writing

A writing may be authenticated by anyone who saw the writing made or executed, including a subscribing witness.
(Stats.1965, c. 299, § 1413.)

§ 1414. Authentication by admission

A writing may be authenticated by evidence that:

(a) The party against whom it is offered has at any time admitted its authenticity; or

(b) The writing has been acted upon as authentic by the party against whom it is offered.
(Stats.1965, c. 299, § 1414.)

§ 1415. Authentication by handwriting evidence

A writing may be authenticated by evidence of the genuineness of the handwriting of the maker.
(Stats.1965, c. 299, § 1415.)

§ 1416. Proof of handwriting by person familiar therewith

A witness who is not otherwise qualified to testify as an expert may state his opinion whether a writing is in the handwriting of a supposed writer if the court finds that he has personal knowledge of the handwriting of the supposed writer. Such personal knowledge may be acquired from:

(a) Having seen the supposed writer write;

(b) Having seen a writing purporting to be in the handwriting of the supposed writer and upon which the supposed writer has acted or been charged;

(c) Having received letters in the due course of mail purporting to be from the supposed writer in response to letters duly addressed and mailed by him to the supposed writer; or

(d) Any other means of obtaining personal knowledge of the handwriting of the supposed writer.
(Stats.1965, c. 299, § 1416.)

§ 1417. Comparison of handwriting by trier of fact

The genuineness of handwriting, or the lack thereof, may be proved by a comparison made by the trier of fact with handwriting (a) which the court finds was admitted or treated as genuine by the party against whom the evidence is offered or (b) otherwise proved to be genuine to the satisfaction of the court.
(Stats.1965, c. 299, § 1417.)

§ 1418. Comparison of writing by expert witness

The genuineness of writing, or the lack thereof, may be proved by a comparison made by an expert witness with writing (a) which the court finds was admitted or treated as genuine by the party against whom the evidence is offered or (b) otherwise proved to be genuine to the satisfaction of the court.
(Stats.1965, c. 299, § 1418.)

§ 1419. Exemplars when writing is 30 years old

Where a writing whose genuineness is sought to be proved is more than 30 years old, the comparison under Section 1417 or 1418 may be made with writing purporting to be genuine, and generally respected and acted upon as such, by persons having an interest in knowing whether it is genuine.
(Stats.1965, c. 299, § 1419.)

§ 1420. Authentication by evidence of reply

A writing may be authenticated by evidence that the writing was received in response to a communication sent to the person who is claimed by the proponent of the evidence to be the author of the writing.
(Stats.1965, c. 299, § 1420.)

§ 1500. The best evidence rule

Except as otherwise provided by statute, no evidence other than the original of a writing is admissible to prove the content of a writing. This section shall be known and may be cited as the best evidence rule.
(Amended by Stats.1977, c. 708, p. ——, § 3.)

§ 1501. Copy of lost or destroyed writing

A copy of a writing is not made inadmissible by the best evidence rule if the writing is lost or has been destroyed without fraudulent intent on the part of the proponent of the evidence.
(Stats.1965, c. 299, § 1501.)

§ 1502. Copy of unavailable writing

A copy of a writing is not made inadmissible by the best evidence rule if the writing was not reasonably procurable by the proponent by use of the court's process or by other available means.
(Stats.1965, c. 299, § 1502.)

§ 1503. Copy of writing under control of opponent

(a) A copy of a writing is not made inadmissible by the best evidence rule if, at a time when the writing was under the control of the opponent, the opponent was expressly or impliedly notified, by the pleadings or otherwise, that the writing would be needed at the hearing, and on request at the hearing the opponent has failed to produce the writing. In a criminal action, the request at the hearing to produce the writing may not be made in the presence of the jury.

(b) Though a writing requested by one party is produced by another, and is thereupon inspected by the party calling for it, the party calling for the writing is not obliged to introduce it as evidence in the action.
(Stats.1965, c. 299, § 1503.)

§ 1504. Copy of collateral writing

A copy of a writing is not made inadmissible by the best evidence rule if the writing is not closely related to the controlling issues and it would be inexpedient to require its production.
(Stats.1965, c. 299, § 1504.)

§ 1505. Other secondary evidence of writings described in Sections 1501–1504

If the proponent does not have in his possession or under his control a copy of a writing described in Section 1501, 1502, 1503, or 1504, other secondary evidence of the content of the writing is not made inadmissible by the best evidence rule. This section does not apply to a writing that is also described in Section 1506 or 1507.
(Stats.1965, c. 299, § 1505.)

§ 1506. Copy of public writing

A copy of a writing is not made inadmissible by the best evidence rule if the writing is a record or other writing that is in the custody of a public entity.
(Stats.1965, c. 299, § 1506.)

§ 1507. Copy of recorded writing

A copy of a writing is not made inadmissible by the best evidence rule if the writing has been recorded in the public records and the record or an attested or a certified copy thereof is made evidence of the writing by statute.
(Stats.1965, c. 299, § 1507.)

§ 1508. Other secondary evidence of writings described in Sections 1506 and 1507

If the proponent does not have in his possession a copy of a writing described in Section 1506 or 1507 and could not in the exercise of reasonable diligence have obtained a copy, other secondary evidence of the content of the writing is not made inadmissible by the best evidence rule.
(Stats.1965, c. 299, § 1508.)

§ 1509. Voluminous writings

Secondary evidence, whether written or oral, of the content of a writing is not made inadmissible by the best evidence rule if the writing consists of numerous accounts or other writings that cannot be examined in court without great loss of time, and the evidence sought from them is only the general result of the whole; but the court in its discretion may require that such accounts or other writings be produced for inspection by the adverse party.
(Stats.1965, c. 299, § 1509.)

§ 1510. Copy of writing produced at the hearing

A copy of a writing is not made inadmissible by the best evidence rule if the writing has been produced at the hearing and made available for inspection by the adverse party.
(Stats.1965, c. 299, § 1510.)

§ 1550. Photographic copies made as business records

A photostatic, microfilm, microcard, miniature photographic or other photographic copy or reproduction, or an enlargement thereof, of a writing is as admissible as the writing itself if such copy or reproduction was made and preserved as a part of the records of a business (as defined by Section 1270) in the regular

course of such business. The introduction of such copy, reproduction, or enlargement does not preclude admission of the original writing if it is still in existence.
(Stats.1965, c. 299, § 1550.)

§ 1551. Photographic copies where original destroyed or lost

A print, whether enlarged or not, from a photographic film (including a photographic plate, microphotographic film, photostatic negative, or similar reproduction) of an original writing destroyed or lost after such film was taken or a reproduction from an electronic recording of video images on magnetic surfaces is admissible as the original writing itself if, at the time of the taking of such film or electronic recording, the person under whose direction and control it was taken attached thereto, or to the sealed container in which it was placed and has been kept, or incorporated in the film or electronic recording, a certification complying with the provisions of Section 1531 and stating the date on which, and the fact that, it was so taken under his direction and control.
(Amended by Stats.1969, c. 646, p. 1298, § 1.)

§ 1560. Compliance with subpoena duces tecum for business records

(a) As used in this article:

(1) "Business" includes every kind of business described in Section 1270.

(2) "Record" includes every kind of record maintained by such a business.

(b) Except as provided in Section 1564, when a subpoena duces tecum is served upon the custodian of records or other qualified witness of a business in an action in which the business is neither a party nor the place where any cause of action is alleged to have arisen, and such subpoena requires the production of all or any part of the records of the business, it is sufficient compliance therewith if the custodian or other qualified witness, within five days after the receipt of such subpoena, delivers by mail or otherwise a true, legible, and durable copy of all the records described in such subpoena to the clerk of court or to the judge if there be no clerk or to such other person as described in subdivision (a) of Section 2018 of the Code of Civil Procedure, together with the affidavit described in Section 1561.

(c) The copy of the records shall be separately enclosed in an inner envelope or wrapper, sealed, with the title and number of the action, name of witness, and date of subpoena clearly inscribed thereon; the sealed envelope or wrapper shall then be enclosed in an outer envelope or wrapper, sealed, directed as follows:

(1) If the subpoena directs attendance in court, to the clerk of such court, or to the judge thereof if there be no clerk.

(2) If the subpoena directs attendance at a deposition, to the officer before whom the deposition is to be taken, at the place designated in the subpoena for the taking of the deposition or at his place of business.

(3) In other cases, to the officer, body, or tribunal conducting the hearing, at a like address.

(d) Unless the parties to the proceeding otherwise agree, or unless the sealed envelope or wrapper is returned to a witness who is to appear personally, the copy of the records shall remain sealed and shall be opened only at the time of trial, deposition, or other hearing, upon the direction of the judge, officer, body, or tribunal conducting the proceeding, in the presence of all parties who have appeared in person or by counsel at such trial, deposition, or hearing. Records which are not introduced in evidence or required as part of the record shall be returned to the person or entity from whom received.
(Amended by Stats.1969, c. 199, p. 484, § 2.)

§ 1561. Affidavit accompanying records

(a) The records shall be accompanied by the affidavit of the custodian or other qualified witness, stating in substance each of the following:

(1) The affiant is the duly authorized custodian of the records or other qualified witness and has authority to certify the records.

(2) The copy is a true copy of all the records described in the subpoena.

(3) The records were prepared by the personnel of the business in the ordinary course of business at or near the time of the act, condition, or event.

(b) If the business has none of the records described, or only part thereof, the custodian or other qualified witness shall so state in the affidavit, and deliver the affidavit and such records as are available in the manner provided in Section 1560.
(Amended by Stats.1969, c. 199, p. 484, § 3.)

§ 1562. Admissibility of affidavit and copy of records

The copy of the records is admissible in evidence to the same extent as though the original thereof were offered and the custodian had been present and testified to the matters stated in the affidavit. The affidavit is admissible as evidence of the matters stated therein pursuant to Section 1561 and the matters so stated are presumed true. When more than one person has knowledge of the facts, more than one affidavit may be made. The presumption established by this section is a presumption affecting the burden of producing evidence.
(Stats.1965, c. 299, § 1562.)

§ 1563. One witness and mileage fee

(a) This article shall not be interpreted to require tender or payment of more than one witness fee and one mileage fee or other charge unless there is an agreement to the contrary.

(b) Where the business records described in a subpoena issued pursuant to Section 1560 are patient records of a public or licensed hospital or of a physician and surgeon, osteopath, or dentist licensed to practice in this state, or a group of such practitioners, and the personal attendance of the custodian of such records or other qualified witness is not required, the sole fee for complying with such subpoena is twelve dollars ($12).

(c) When the personal attendance of the custodian of a record or other qualified witness is required pursuant to Section 1564, he shall be entitled to 20 cents ($0.20) a mile for mileage actually traveled, one way only, and to twelve dollars ($12) for each day of actual attendance.
(Amended by Stats.1972, c. 396, p. 719, § 1.)

§ 1564. Personal attendance of custodian and production of original records

The personal attendance of the custodian or other qualified witness and the production of the original records is required if the subpoena duces tecum contains a clause which reads:

"The personal attendance of the custodian or other qualified witness and the production of the original records is required by this subpoena. The procedure authorized pursuant to subdivision (b) of Section 1560, and Sections 1561 and 1562, of the Evidence Code will not be deemed sufficient compliance with this subpoena."
(Stats.1965, c. 299, § 1564.)

§ 1565. Service of more than one subpoena duces tecum

If more than one subpoena duces tecum is served upon the custodian of records or other qualified witness and the personal attendance of the custodian or other qualified witness is required pursuant to Section 1564, the witness shall be deemed to be the witness of the party serving the first such subpoena duces tecum.
(Amended by Stats.1969, c. 199, p. 485, § 4.)

§ 1566. Applicability of article

This article applies in any proceeding in which testimony can be compelled.
(Stats.1965, c. 299, § 1566.)

ANNOTATED TABLE OF CASES

Each case may be found on the page set out in parenthesis.

Aguilar v. Texas, 378 U.S. 108, 84 S.Ct. 1509, 12 L.Ed.2d 723 (1964) (p. 534)

Aguilar deals with the use of hearsay evidence to support an affidavit for the issuance of a search warrant. In this case the United States Supreme Court formulated the so called "two prong test" to determine if the hearsay information was (1) based upon personal knowledge and (2) received from a source with reasonable credibility.

Chimel v. California, 395 U.S. 752, 89 S.Ct. 2034, 23 L.Ed.2d 685 (1969) (p. 536)

Chimel raises basic questions concerning the permissible scope of a search which is incident to an arrest.

Kaplan v. Superior Court, 6 Cal.3d 150, 98 Cal.Rptr. 649, 491 P.2d 1 (1971) (p. 540)

In *Kaplan* evidence obtained in a "pat down" search was suppressed due to the officers belief that the object patted was not a weapon.

Miranda v. Arizona, 384 U.S. 436, 86 S.Ct. 1602, 16 L.Ed.2d 694 (1966) (p. 542)

Miranda is the landmark case interpreting the application of Fifth Amendment rights to the criminal investigation process. All police officers are required to follow the *Miranda* guidelines before questioning a criminal suspect who is in custody or deprived of freedom in a significant way.

Mozzetti v. Superior Court, 4 Cal.3d 699, 94 Cal.Rptr. 412, 484 P.2d 84 (1971) (p. 560)

Mozzetti deals with the validity and scope of an inventory search designed to reduce police and vehicle tow operator liability from claims of lost or stolen personal property in disabled vehicles. What if the police find contraband during this inventory search?

People v. Amos, 70 Cal.App.3d 562, 139 Cal.Rptr. 30 (1977) (p. 566)

Amos considers what constitutes probable cause, and what notice procedures must be followed when serving an arrest warrant in a private premises.

People v. Beagle II, 6 Cal.3d 441, 99 Cal. Rptr. 313, 492 P.2d 1 (1972) (p. 568)

Beagle deals with an arson case in which the prosecution attempted to impeach the testimony of the defendant by the introduction of evidence of a prior felony conviction. The impeachment attempt was challenged as being an improper restriction upon the defendant's right to choose to testify on his own behalf.

People v. Dumas, 9 Cal.3d 871, 109 Cal.Rptr. 304, 512 P.2d 1208 (1974) (p. 571)

This is a search and seizure case which presents a good discussion of what is needed to establish the reliability of a confidential informant, and under what circumstances the knock and notice requirement may be partially complied with. This case also examines and discusses search and seizure law and its special application to automobiles.

People v. Hamilton, 71 Cal.2d 176, 77 Cal. Rptr. 785, 454 P.2d 681 (1969) (p. 576)

Hamilton is a California case which follows and further explains Aguilar v. Texas. The objective of the court was to distinguish hearsay evidence from compounded hearsay evidence. The student may wish to formulate a decision after reading only the facts of this case. Afterward, this decision should be compared to the reasoning advanced by the court.

ANNOTATED TABLE OF CASES

People v. Knutson, 60 Cal.App.3d 856, 131 Cal.Rptr. 846 (1976) (p. 579)

This case considers what amount of cause must be present to justify a lawful detention and a lawful arrest.

People v. Kraft, 3 Cal.App.3d 890, 84 Cal. Rptr. 280 (1970) (p. 582)

Kraft provides a look at the issue of reasonable force applied to the taking of a blood sample in a drunk driving case. The case provides some insight into the distinction between reasonable police procedures and actions which are excessive.

People v. Laursen, 8 Cal.3d 192, 104 Cal. Rptr. 425, 501 P.2d 1145 (1972) (p. 585)

Laursen is a kidnap/robbery case which presents a vehicle search and seizure problem. The case reviews related case decisions and offers an answer to the question of whether a vehicle may be moved by the police prior to search.

People v. McGaughran, 149 Cal.Rptr. 584, 585 P.2d 206 (1978) (p. 591)

McGaughran is a case decision by the California Supreme Court filed in October of 1978. The case involves the right of a police officer to detain a person and conduct a warrant check when the person has merely been stopped for a traffic violation.

People v. Moreno, 67 Cal.App.3d 962, 134 Cal.Rptr. 322 (1977) (p. 603)

The issue raised and considered in this case is the constitutional propriety of the police officer's detention of Moreno.

People v. Mosher, 1 Cal.3d 379, 82 Cal.Rptr. 379, 461 P.2d 659 (1969) (p. 607)

Mosher challenges his conviction on the grounds that a past search for weapons was an impermissible search, and then considers whether the right to counsel attaches at a pre-trial lineup.

People v. Ramey, 16 Cal.3d 263, 127 Cal. Rptr. 629, 545 P.2d 1333 (1976) (p. 611)

Ramey is the landmark case which requires that arrests, made in private premises, be made by authority of an arrest warrant when there are no exigent circumstances. This case also discusses the requirements which must be established to render confidential informants reliable.

People v. Scoma, 71 Cal.2d 332, 78 Cal.Rptr. 491, 455 P.2d 419 (1969) (p. 616)

Scoma is a search warrant affidavit case following the line of reasoning established in Aguilar.

People v. Superior Court of Kern County (Hawkins), 6 Cal.3d 757, 100 Cal.Rptr. 281, 493 P.2d 1145 (1972) (p. 639)

Hawkins treats the issues of search and seizure in the taking of a blood sample for alcohol testing. It presents a challenge to the decision in the Schmerber case. The case is important because of the high incidence of driving under the influence of alcohol cases.

People v. Superior Court (Keifer), 3 Cal.3d 807, 91 Cal.Rptr. 729, 478 P.2d 449 (1970) (p. 629)

Although *Keifer* is known as a "furtive gesture" case it in the main considers what cause is sufficient to justify arrest and a search. This case presents a good discussion of the laws of arrest and search and seizure as they are applicable to automobile stops.

People v. Superior Court (Simon), 7 Cal.3d 186, 101 Cal.Rptr. 837, 496 P.2d 1205 (1972) (p. 619)

This case contains a good discussion of lawful searches which are conducted incident to an arrest for minor vehicle code violations. *Simon* also presents a good discussion of probable cause to arrest where the underlying cause is based on a minor code violation.

Rockwell v. Ventura County, 18 Cal.3d 420, 134 Cal.Rptr. 650, 556 P.2d 1101 (1976) (p. 643)

In *Rockwell*, the California Supreme Court invalidated the pre-1977 death penalty statute. The court found that the statute enacted in 1972 did not allow the trier of fact to consider mitigating evidence when deciding whether the penalty should be life imprisonment or death in the gas chamber.

ANNOTATED TABLE OF CASES

Schmerber v. California, 384 U.S. 757, 86 S.Ct. 1826, 16 L.Ed.2d 908 (1966) (p. 652)

Schmerber was the first major case dealing with the constitutionality of blood sample search procedures. The case reviews issues related to Constitutional rights contained in the Fourth and Fifth Amendments.

Wimberly v. Superior Court, 16 Cal.3d 557, 128 Cal.Rptr. 641, 547 P.2d 417 (1976) (p. 657)

Wimberly deals with the relationship of probable cause to the scope of a vehicle search. Do minor quantities of contraband in the passenger area justify searching the locked trunk?

MAJOR CASE LAW OPINIONS

AGUILAR v. STATE OF TEXAS *
Supreme Court of the United States, 1964.
378 U.S. 108, 84 S.Ct. 1509, 12 L.Ed.2d 723.

• • •

Mr. Justice GOLDBERG delivered the opinion of the Court.

This case presents questions concerning the constitutional requirements for obtaining a state search warrant.

Two Houston police officers applied to a local Justice of the Peace for a warrant to search for narcotics in petitioner's home. In support of their application, the officers submitted an affidavit which, in relevant part, recited that:

"Affiants have received reliable information from a credible person and do believe that heroin, marijuana, barbiturates and other narcotics and narcotic paraphernalia are being kept at the above described premises for the purpose of sale and use contrary to the provisions of the law."

The search warrant was issued.

In executing the warrant the local police, along with federal officers, announced at petitioner's door that they were police with a warrant. Upon hearing a commotion within the house, the officers forced their way into the house and seized petitioner in the act of attempting to dispose of a packet of narcotics.

At his trial in the state court, petitioner, through his attorney, objected to the introduction of evidence obtained as a result of the execution of the warrant. The objections were overruled and the evidence admitted. Petitioner was convicted of illegal possession of heroin and sentenced to serve 20 years in the state penitentiary. On appeal to the Texas Court of Criminal Appeals, the conviction was affirmed, 172 Tex. Cr.R. 629, 362 S.W.2d 111, affirmance upheld on rehearing, 172 Tex.Cr.R. 631, 362 S.W.2d 112. We granted a writ of certiorari to consider the important constitutional questions involved. 375 U.S. 812, 84 S.Ct. 86, 11 L.Ed.2d 48.

In Ker v. California, 374 U.S. 23, 83 S.Ct. 1623, 10 L.Ed.2d 726, we held that the Fourth "Amendment's proscriptions are enforced against the States through the Fourteenth Amendment," and that "the standard of reasonableness is the same under the Fourth and Fourteenth Amendments." Id., 374 U.S. at 33, 83 S.Ct. at 1630. Although Ker involved a search without a warrant, that case must certainly be read as holding that the standard for obtaining a search warrant is likewise "the same under the Fourth and Fourteenth Amendments."

An evaluation of the constitutionality of a search warrant should begin with the rule that "the informed and deliberate determinations of magistrates empowered to issue warrants . . . are to be preferred over the hurried action of officers . . . who may happen to make arrests." United States v. Lefkowitz, 285 U.S. 452, 464, 52 S.Ct. 420, 423, 76 L.Ed. 877: The reasons for this rule go to the foundations of the Fourth Amendment. A contrary rule "that evidence sufficient to support a magistrate's disinterested determination to issue a search warrant will justify the officers in making a search without a warrant would reduce the Amendment to a nullity and leave the people's homes secure only in the discretion of police officers." Johnson v. United States, 333 U.S. 10, 14, 68 S.Ct. 367, 369, 92 L.Ed.

---

* Prior to reading this, it is recommended that the reader review the following statutes: Penal Code §§ 1523–1542. Also see the cases of Hamilton and Scoma included in this text.

436. Under such a rule "resort to [warrants] would ultimately be discouraged." Jones v. United States, 362 U.S. 257, 270, 80 S.Ct. 725, 736, 4 L.Ed.2d 697. Thus, when a search is based upon a magistrate's, rather than a police officer's, determination of probable cause, the reviewing courts will accept evidence of a less "judicially competent or persuasive character than would have justified an officer in acting on his own without a warrant," ibid., and will sustain the judicial determination so long as "there was substantial basis for [the magistrate] to conclude that narcotics were probably present . . . ." Id., 362 U.S. at 271, 80 S.Ct. at 736. As so well stated by Mr. Justice Jackson:

> "The point of the Fourth Amendment, which often is not grasped by zealous officers, is not that it denies law enforcement the support of the usual inferences which reasonable men draw from evidence. Its protection consists in requiring that those inferences be drawn by a neutral and detached magistrate instead of being judged by the officer engaged in the often competitive enterprise of ferreting out crime." Johnson v. United States, supra, 333 U.S. at 13–14, 68 S.Ct. at 369.

Although the reviewing court will pay substantial deference to judicial determinations of probable cause, the court must still insist that the magistrate perform his "neutral and detached" function and not serve merely as a rubber stamp for the police.

In Nathanson v. United States, 290 U.S. 41, 54 S.Ct. 11, 78 L.Ed. 159, a warrant was issued upon the sworn allegation that the affiant "has cause to suspect and does believe" that certain merchandise was in a specified location. Id., 290 U.S. at 44, 54 S.Ct. at 12. The Court, noting that the affidavit "went upon a mere affirmation of suspicion and belief *without any statement of adequate supporting facts*," id., 290 U.S. at 46, 54 S.Ct. at 13 (emphasis added), announced the following rule:

> "Under the Fourth Amendment, an officer may not properly issue a warrant to search a private dwelling unless he can find probable cause therefor from *facts or circumstances* presented to him under oath or affirmation. Mere affirmance of belief or suspicion is not enough." Id., 290 U.S. at 47, 54 S.Ct. at 13. (Emphasis added.)

The Court in Giordenello v. United States, 357 U.S. 480, 78 S.Ct. 1245, 2 L.Ed.2d 1508 applied this rule to an affidavit similar to that relied upon here. Affiant in that case swore that petitioner "did receive, conceal, etc., narcotic drugs . . . with knowledge of unlawful importation . . . ." Id., 357 U.S. at 481, 78 S.Ct. at 1247. The Court announced the guiding principles to be:

> "that the inferences from the facts which lead to the complaint '[must] be drawn by a neutral and detached magistrate instead of being judged by the officer engaged in the often competitive enterprise of ferreting out crime.' Johnson v. United States, 333 U.S. 10, 14, 68 S.Ct. 367, 369, 92 L.Ed. 436. The purpose of the complaint, then, is to enable the appropriate magistrate . . . to determine whether the 'probable cause' required to support a warrant exists. The Commissioner must judge for himself the persuasiveness of the facts relied on by a complaining officer to show probable cause. He should not accept without question the complainant's mere conclusion . . . ." 357 U.S., at 486, 78 S.Ct., at 1250.

The Court, applying these principles to the complaint in that case, stated that:

> "it is clear that it does not pass muster because it does not provide any basis for the Commissioner's determination . . . that probable cause existed. The complaint contains no affirmative allegation that the affiant spoke with personal knowledge of the matters contained therein; it does not indicate any sources for the complainant's belief; and it does not set forth any other sufficient basis upon which a finding of probable cause could be made." Ibid.

The vice in the present affidavit is at least as great as in Nathanson and Giordenello. Here the "mere conclusion" that petitioner possessed narcotics was not even that of the affiant himself; it was that of an unidentified informant. The affidavit here not only "contains no affirmative allegation that the affiant spoke with personal knowledge of the matters contained therein," it does not even contain an "affirmative allegation" that the affiant's unidentified source "spoke with personal knowledge." For all that appears, the source here merely suspected, believed or concluded that there were narcotics in petitioner's possession. The magistrate here certainly could not "judge for himself the persuasiveness of the facts relied on . . . to show probable cause." He necessarily accepted "without question" the informant's "suspicion," "belief" or "mere conclusion."

Although an affidavit may be based on hearsay information and need not reflect the direct personal observations of the affiant, Jones v. United States, 362 U.S. 257, 80 S.Ct. 725, 4 L.Ed.2d 697, the magistrate must be informed of some of the underlying circumstances from which the informant concluded that the narcotics were where he claimed they were, and some of the underlying circumstances from which the officer concluded that the informant, whose identity need not be disclosed, see Rugendorf v. United States, 376 U.S. 528, 84 S.Ct. 825, was "credible" or his information "reliable."

• • •

We conclude, therefore, that the search warrant should not have been issued because the affidavit did not provide a sufficient basis for a finding of probable cause and that the evidence obtained as a result of the search warrant was inadmissible in petitioner's trial.

The judgment of the Texas Court of Criminal Appeals is reversed and the case remanded for proceedings not inconsistent with this opinion.

Reversed and remanded.

Mr. Justice HARLAN, concurring.

But for Ker v. California, 374 U.S. 23, 83 S.Ct. 1623, 10 L.Ed.2d 726, I would have voted to affirm the judgment of the Texas court. Given Ker, I cannot escape the conclusion that to do so would tend to "relax Fourth Amendment standards . . . in derogation of law enforcement standards in the *federal* system . . ." (my concurring opinion in Ker, supra, 374 U.S. at 45–46, 83 S.Ct. at 1646). Contrary to what is suggested in the dissenting opinion of my Brother CLARK in the present case . . , the standards laid down in Giordenello v. United States, 357 U.S. 480, 78 S.Ct. 1245, 2 L.Ed.2d 1503, did in my view reflect constitutional requirements. Being unwilling to relax those standards for federal prosecutions, I concur in the opinion of the Court.

Mr. Justice CLARK, whom Mr. Justice BLACK and Mr. Justice STEWART, join, dissenting.

• • •

Believing that the Court has substituted a rigid, academic formula for the unrigid standards of reasonableness and "probable cause" laid down by the Fourth Amendment itself—a substitution of technicality for practicality—and believing that the Court's holding will tend to obstruct the administration of criminal justice throughout the country, I respectfully dissent.

CHIMEL v. CALIFORNIA *

Supreme Court of the United States, 1969.
395 U.S. 752, 89 S.Ct. 2034, 23 L.Ed.2d 685.

Mr. Justice STEWART delivered the opinion of the Court.

This case raises basic questions concerning the permissible scope under the Fourth

---

* Prior to reading this case it is recommended that the reader review the following statute: Penal Code § 1523.

Amendment of a search incident to a lawful arrest.

The relevant facts are essentially undisputed. Late in the afternoon of September 13, 1965, three police officers arrived at the Santa Ana, California, home of the petitioner with a warrant authorizing his arrest for the burglary of a coin shop. The officers knocked on the door, identified themselves to the petitioner's wife, and asked if they might come inside. She ushered them into the house, where they waited 10 or 15 minutes until the petitioner returned home from work. When the petitioner entered the house, one of the officers handed him the arrest warrant and asked for permission to "look around." The petition objected, but was advised that "on the basis of the lawful arrest," the officers would nonetheless conduct a search. No search warrant had been issued.

Accompanied by the petitioner's wife, the officers then looked through the entire three-bedroom house, including the attic, the garage, and a small workshop. In some rooms the search was relatively cursory. In the master bedroom and sewing room, however, the officers directed the petitioner's wife to open drawers and "to physically move contents of the drawers from side to side so that [they] might view any items that would have come from [the] burglary." After completing the search, they seized numerous items—primarily coins, but also several medals, tokens, and a few other objects. The entire search took between 45 minutes and an hour.

At the petitioner's subsequent state trial on two charges of burglary, the items taken from his house were admitted into evidence against him, over his objection that they had been unconstitutionally seized. . . .

[W]e proceed on the hypothesis . . . that the arrest of the petitioner was valid under the Constitution. This brings us directly to the question whether the warrantless search of the petitioner's entire house can be constitutionally justified as incident to that arrest. The decisions of this Court bearing upon that question have been far from consistent, as even the most cursory review makes evident.

Approval of a warrantless search incident to a lawful arrest seems first to have been articulated by the Court in 1914 as dictum in Weeks v. United States, 232 U.S. 383, 34 S.Ct. 341, 58 L.Ed. 652, in which the Court stated:

"What then is the present case? Before answering that inquiry specifically, it may be well by a process of exclusion to state what it is not. It is not an assertion of the right on the part of the Government, always recognized under English and American law, to search the person of the accused when legally arrested to discover and seize the fruits or evidences of crime." Id., at 392, 34 S.Ct., at 344.

That statement made no reference to any right to search the *place* where an arrest occurs, but was limited to a right to search the "person." Eleven years later the case of Carroll v. United States, 267 U.S. 132, 45 S.Ct. 280, 69 L.Ed. 543, brought the following embellishment of the *Weeks* statement:

"When a man is legally arrested for an offense, whatever is found upon his person *or in his control* which it is unlawful for him to have and which may be used to prove the offense may be seized and held as evidence in the prosecution." Id., at 158, 45 S.Ct., at 287. (Emphasis added.)

Still, that assertion too was far from a claim that the "place" where one is arrested may be searched so long as the arrest is valid. Without explanation, however, the principle emerged in expanded form a few months later in Agnello v. United States, 269 U.S. 20, 46 S.Ct. 4, 70 L.Ed. 145—although still by way of dictum:

"The right without a search warrant contemporaneously to search persons lawfully arrested while committing crime and to search the place where the arrest is made in order to find and seize things connected with the crime as its fruits or as the means by which it was committed, as well as weapons and other things to effect an escape from custody, is not to be doubted. See Carroll v. United States, 267 U.S. 132, 158, 45 S.Ct. 280, 69 L.Ed. 543; Weeks v. United States, 232 U.S. 383, 392, 34 S.Ct. 341, 58 L.Ed. 652." 269 U.S., at 30, 46 S.Ct., at 5.

• • •

[I]n Harris v. United States, 331 U.S. 145, 67 S.Ct. 1098, 91 L.Ed. 1399, decided in 1947. . . . officers had obtained a warrant for Harris' arrest on the basis of his alleged involvement with the cashing and interstate transportation of a forged check. He was arrested in the living room of his four-room apartment, and in an attempt to recover two canceled checks thought to have been used in effecting the forgery, the officers undertook a thorough search of the entire apartment. Inside a desk drawer they found a sealed envelope marked "George Harris, personal papers." The envelope, which was then torn open, was found to contain altered Selective Service documents, and those documents were used to secure Harris' conviction for violating the Selective Training and Service Act of 1940. The Court rejected Harris' Fourth Amendment claim, sustaining the search as "incident to arrest." Id., at 151, 67 S.Ct., at 1101.

Only a year after *Harris*, however, the pendulum swung again. In Trupiano v. United States, 334 U.S. 699, 68 S.Ct. 1229, 92 L.Ed. 1663, agents raided the site of an illicit distillery, saw one of several conspirators operating the still, and arrested him, contemporaneously "seiz[ing] the illicit distillery." Id., at 702, 68 S.Ct. at 1231. The Court held that the arrest and others made subsequently had been valid, but that the unexplained failure of the agents to procure a search warrant—in spite of the fact that they had had more than enough time before the raid to do so—rendered the search unlawful. The opinion stated:

"It is a cardinal rule that, in seizing goods and articles, law enforcement agents must secure and use search warrants wherever reasonably practicable. . . .

"A search or seizure without a warrant as an incident to a lawful arrest has always been considered to be a strictly limited right. It grows out of the inherent necessities of the situation at the time of the arrest. But there must be something more in the way of necessity than merely a lawful arrest." Id., at 705, 708, 68 S.Ct., at 1232, 1234.

In 1950, two years after *Trupiano*, came United States v. Rabinowitz, 339 U.S. 56, 70 S.Ct. 430, 94 L.Ed. 653, the decision upon which California primarily relies in the case now before us. . . .

Rabinowitz has come to stand for the proposition, *inter alia*, that a warrantless search "incident to a lawful arrest" may generally extend to the area that is considered to be in the "possession" or under the "control" of the person arrested. And it was on the basis of that proposition that the California courts upheld the search of the petitioner's entire house in this case. That doctrine, however, at least in the broad sense in which it was applied by the California courts in this case, can withstand neither historical nor rational analysis.

• • •

Only last Term in Terry v. Ohio, 392 U.S. 1, 88 S.Ct. 1868, 20 L.Ed.2d 889, we emphasized that "the police must, whenever practicable, obtain advance judicial approval of searches and seizures through the warrant procedure," id., at 20, ...

A similar analysis underlies the "search incident to arrest" principle, and marks its proper extent. When an arrest is made, it is reasonable for the arresting officer to search the person arrested in order to remove any weapons that the latter might seek to use in order to resist arrest or effect his escape. Otherwise, the officer's safety might well be endangered, and the arrest itself frustrated. In addition, it is entirely reasonable for the arresting officer to search for and seize any evidence on the arrestee's person in order to prevent its concealment or destruction. And the area into which an arrestee might reach in order to grab a weapon or evidentiary items must, of course, be governed by a like rule. A gun on a table or in a drawer in front of one who is arrested can be as dangerous to the arresting officer as one concealed in the clothing of the person arrested. There is ample justification, therefore, for a search of the arrestee's person and the area "within his immediate control"—construing that phrase to mean the area from within which he might gain possession of a weapon or destructible evidence.

There is no comparable justification, however, for routinely searching any room other than that in which an arrest occurs—or, for that matter, for searching through all the desk drawers or other closed or concealed areas in that room itself. Such searches, in the absence of well-recognized exceptions, may be made only under the authority of a search warrant. The "adherence to judicial processes" mandated by the Fourth Amendment requires no less.

. . .

It is argued in the present case that it is "reasonable" to search a man's house when he is arrested in it. But that argument is founded on little more than a subjective view regarding the acceptability of certain sorts of police conduct, and not on considerations relevant to Fourth Amendment interests. Under such an unconfined analysis, Fourth Amendment protection in this area would approach the evaporation point. It is not easy to explain why, for instance, it is less subjectively "reasonable" to search a man's house when he is arrested on his front lawn—or just down the street—than it is when he happens to be in the house at the time of arrest. . . .

It would be possible, of course, to draw a line between *Rabinowitz* and *Harris* on the one hand, and this case on the other. For *Rabinowitz* involved a single room, and *Harris* a four-room apartment, while in the case before us an entire house was searched. But such a distinction would be highly artificial. The rationale that allowed the searches and seizures in *Rabinowitz* and *Harris* would allow the searches and seizures in this case. No consideration relevant to the Fourth Amendment suggests any point of rational limitation, once the search is allowed to go beyond the area from which the person arrested might obtain weapons or evidentiary items. The only reasoned distinction is one between a search of the person arrested and the area within his reach on the one hand, and more extensive searches on the other.

The petitioner correctly points out that one result of decisions such as *Rabinowitz* and *Harris* is to give law enforcement officials the opportunity to engage in searches not justified by probable cause, by the simple expedient of arranging to arrest suspects at home rather than elsewhere. We do not suggest that the petitioner is necessarily correct in his assertion that such a strategy was utilized here, but the fact remains that he had been arrested earlier in the day, at his place of employment rather than at home, no search of his house could have been made without a search warrant. . . .

Application of sound Fourth Amendment principles to the facts of this case produces a clear result. The search here went far beyond the petitioner's person and the area from within which he might have obtained either a weapon or something that could have been used as evidence against him. There was no constitutional justification, in the absence of a search warrant, for extending the search beyond that area. The scope of the search was, therefore, "unreasonable" under the Fourth and Fourteenth Amendments and the petitioner's conviction cannot stand.

Reversed.

. . .

MAJOR CASE LAW OPINIONS

KAPLAN v. SUPERIOR COURT *

Supreme Court of California, In Bank, 1971.
6 Cal.3d 150, 98 Cal.Rptr. 649, 491 P.2d 1.

MOSK, Justice.

The dispositive question in this proceeding for writ of prohibition is whether the enactment of section 351 of the Evidence Code, declaring generally that "Except as otherwise provided by statute, all relevant evidence is admissible," operated as a legislative repeal of the "vicarious exclusionary rule" adopted by this court in People v. Martin (1955) 45 Cal.2d 755, 290 P.2d 855, which permits a criminal defendant to object to the introduction of evidence illegally seized from a third person. We conclude the Legislature did not intend to repeal the *Martin* rule, and defendant is therefore entitled to the relief for which he prays.

The facts of the case are essentially undisputed. On June 20, 1970, during daylight hours, Police Officer Briscoe observed a small sports car traveling at 45 miles per hour in a 25-mile-per-hour zone. The vehicle contained three persons: defendant occupied the passenger seat on the extreme right, and seated between defendant and the driver was a 16-year-old juvenile named Patterson. According to Officer Briscoe's testimony at the preliminary examination, when he turned on his red light to signal the driver to stop he saw Patterson look back, reach under the front seat, and put his hand inside his coat.

Officer Briscoe observed no other suspicious circumstances or unusual conduct by the occupants of the car. Nevertheless, on the theory that Patterson's "furtive movements" suggested he might be hiding a weapon, Officer Briscoe immediately ordered him to get out of the car and submit to a pat-down search. In the course of that search the officer felt a lump in Patterson's shirt pocket; although he was "pretty sure . . . it was not a weapon," he "had an idea it was pills." He thereupon placed Patterson under arrest for "suspicion of dangerous drugs," and reached into the pocket. It was found to contain a quantity of LSD tablets in a plastic bag. On cross-examination Officer Briscoe acknowledged that he had no warrant for Patterson's arrest or search; that he neither questioned the youth about possession of a weapon nor asked his consent to conduct the search; and that Patterson himself said nothing either before or after that search.

Patterson was called as a witness for the People, and declared that 10 minutes before the arrest he had purchased the LSD tablets in question from defendant. On cross-examination he testified it was the first time defendant had sold him narcotics, and conceded he gave the police a deliberately false description of defendant because he "didn't want him to get involved at first." Patterson then admitted he had agreed to be a witness for the prosecution in exchange for a promise of immunity by the district attorney; he reiterated, moreover, that but for the promise of immunity he would not have testified against defendant.

On this showing defendant was held to answer to a felony charge of selling a restricted dangerous drug. (Health & Saf. Code, § 11912). His motion to suppress the evidence on the ground of unlawful search and seizure (Pen.Code, § 1538.5) was denied. His motion to set aside the information for lack of probable cause (Pen.Code, § 995) was likewise denied, and he seeks review of that ruling by statutory writ of prohibition (Pen. Code, § 999a).

To begin with, it is not disputed that the warrantless arrest and search of Patterson and the seizure of the contraband on his person were illegal. The trial court assumed this to be so, and the People do not contend otherwise. Thus the "furtive gesture" observed by Officer Briscoe did not, without more, give him reasonable grounds to be-

---

* Prior to reading this case it is recommended that the reader review the following statutes: Penal Code §§ 836, 1525.

lieve Patterson was in possession of a weapon. (Gallik v. Superior Court (1971) 5 Cal.3d 855, 861–862, 97 Cal.Rptr. 693, 489 P.2d 573; People v. Superior Court (1970) 3 Cal.3d 807, 828–831, 91 Cal.Rptr. 729, 478 P.2d 449.) The discovery of the unidentified lump in Patterson's shirt pocket during the pat-down search did not justify further intrusion into that pocket for the purpose of self-protection, as Officer Briscoe knew the soft object was not in fact a weapon. (People v. Collins (1970) 1 Cal.3d 658, 662–663, 83 S.Ct. 179, 463 P.2d 403; People v. Mosher (1969) 1 Cal.3d 379, 394, 82 Cal.Rptr. 379, 461 P.2d 659.) Nor could that rule be evaded by the device of arresting Patterson because the officer "had an idea" the object was contraband, and then searching the pocket as an incident to that arrest. The record is devoid of reasonable grounds to believe in the factual accuracy of the officer's "idea" or hunch, and it is settled that "An arrest may not be used as a pretext to search for evidence." (United States v. Lefkowitz (1932) 285 U.S. 452, 467, 52 S.Ct. 420, 424, 76 L.Ed. 877; People v. Haven (1963) 59 Cal.2d 713, 719, 31 Cal.Rptr. 47, 381 P.2d 927.) Finally, we cannot uphold the search on the novel theory adopted by the magistrate herein, i. e., that by testifying at the preliminary examination on behalf of the People, Patterson impliedly gave "retroactive consent" to the search or "retroactively waived" his objection thereto. His agreement to testify was admittedly the product of his arrest and search and of the district attorney's promise of immunity from the ensuing criminal charges, and it is established that "consent" induced by an illegal arrest or search is not voluntary. (People v. Johnson (1968) 68 Cal.2d 629, 632, 68 Cal.Rptr. 441, 440 P.2d 921; People v. Haven (1963) 59 Cal.2d 713, 718, 31 Cal.Rptr. 47, 381 P.2d 927.)

• • •

In 1955 this court decided the landmark case of People v. Cahan, 44 Cal.2d 434, 282 P.2d 905, adopting for California the rule that evidence obtained in violation of federal or state constitutional guarantees against unreasonable search and seizure is inadmissible in a criminal trial. The two-fold purpose of that rule, we explained, was to deter law enforcement officers from engaging in unconstitutional searches and seizures by removing their incentive to do so, and to relieve the courts from being compelled to participate in such illegal conduct.

Among the numerous decisions which thereafter implemented various aspects of the *Cahan* rule, one of the most important was People v. Martin (1955) supra, 45 Cal.2d 755, 290 P.2d 855. In that case the police searched certain offices on two occasions and found the defendant among bookmaking paraphernalia. The defendant's story was that he was a stranger who had merely been hired to watch the premises. He moved to set aside charges of bookmaking on the ground of unlawful search and seizure; relying on the federal rule on the question, the People contended that as the defendant disclaimed any interest in the premises or property he had no "standing" to challenge the legality of the searches and seizures. In a unanimous opinion (at pp. 759–760, 290 P.2d at p. 857) we squarely rejected this reasoning: "the rule of the lower federal courts is based on the theory that the evidence is excluded to provide a remedy for a wrong done to the defendant, and that accordingly, if the defendant has not been wronged he is entitled to no remedy. [Citation.] In adopting the exclusionary rule, however, this court recognized that it could not be justified on that theory, People v. Cahan, 44 Cal.2d 434, 443, 282 P.2d 905, and based its decision on the ground that 'other remedies have completely failed to secure compliance with the constitutional provisions on the part of police officers with the attendant result that the courts under the old rule have been constantly required to participate in, and in effect condone, the lawless activities of law enforcement officers.' 44 Cal.2d at page 445, 282 P.2d at page 911."

• • •

We conclude that defendant has standing under the *Martin* rule to complain of the admittedly illegal search and seizure of Patterson. There being no competent evidence to support the information, defendant is therefore entitled to a writ of prohibition to restrain further proceedings against him on this charge. (Badillo v. Superior Court (1956) 46 Cal.2d 269, 271, 294 P.2d 23.)

Let a peremptory writ of prohibition issue as prayed.

PETERS, TOBRINER and SULLIVAN, JJ., concur.

• • •

MIRANDA v. STATE OF ARIZONA *

Supreme Court of the United States, 1966.
384 U.S. 436, 86 S.Ct. 1602, 16 L.Ed.2d 694.

Mr. Chief Justice WARREN delivered the opinion of the Court.

The cases before us raise questions which go to the roots of our concepts of American criminal jurisprudence: the restraints society must observe consistent with the Federal Constitution in prosecuting individuals for crime. More specifically, we deal with the admissibility of statements obtained from an individual who is subjected to custodial police interrogation and the necessity for procedures which assure that the individual is accorded his privilege under the Fifth Amendment to the Constitution not to be compelled to incriminate himself.

We dealt with certain phases of this problem recently in Escobedo v. State of Illinois, 378 U.S. 478, 84 S.Ct. 1758, 12 L.Ed.2d 977 (1964). There, as in the four cases before us, law enforcement officials took the defendant into custody and interrogated him in a police station for the purpose of obtaining a confession. The police did not effectively advise him of his right to remain silent or of his right to consult with his attorney. Rather, they confronted him with an alleged accomplice who accused him of having perpetrated a murder. When the defendant denied the accusation and said "I didn't shoot Manuel, you did it," they handcuffed him and took him to an interrogation room. There, while handcuffed and standing, he was questioned for four hours until he confessed. During this interrogation, the police denied his request to speak to his attorney, and they prevented his retained attorney, who had come to the police station, from consulting with him. At his trial, the State, over his objection, introduced the confession against him. We held that the statements thus made were constitutionally inadmissible.

This case has been the subject of judicial interpretation and spirited legal debate since it was decided two years ago. Both state and federal courts, in assessing its implications, have arrived at varying conclusions. A wealth of scholarly material has been written tracing its ramifications and underpinnings. Police and prosecutor have speculated on its range and desirability. We granted certiorari in these cases, 382 U.S. 924, 925, 937, 86 S.Ct. 318, 320, 395, 15 L.Ed.2d 338, 339, 348, in order further to explore some facets of the problems, thus exposed, of applying the privilege against self-incrimination to in-custody interrogation, and to give concrete constitutional guidelines for law enforcement agencies and courts to follow.

• • •

Our holding will be spelled out with some specificity in the pages which follow but briefly stated it is this: the prosecution may not use statements, whether exculpatory or inculpatory, stemming from custodial interrogation of the defendant unless it demonstrates the use of procedural safeguards effective to secure the privilege against self-incrimination. By custodial interrogation, we mean questioning initiated by law enforcement officers after a person has been

---

* Prior to reading this, it is recommended that the reader review the following statutes: Evidence Code §§ 930, 940, 1204.

taken into custody or otherwise deprived of his freedom of action in any significant way. As for the procedural safeguards to be employed, unless other fully effective means are devised to inform accused persons of their right of silence and to assure a continuous opportunity to exercise it, the following measures are required. Prior to any questioning, the person must be warned that he has a right to remain silent, that any statement he does make may be used as evidence against him, and that he has a right to the presence of an attorney, either retained or appointed. The defendant may waive effectuation of these rights, provided the waiver is made voluntarily, knowingly and intelligently. If, however, he indicates in any manner and at any stage of the process that he wishes to consult with an attorney before speaking there can be no questioning. Likewise, if the individual is alone and indicates in any manner that he does not wish to be interrogated, the police may not question him. The mere fact that he may have answered some questions or volunteered some statements on his own does not deprive him of the right to refrain from answering any further inquiries until he has consulted with an attorney and thereafter consents to be questioned.

The constitutional issue we decide in each of these cases is the admissibility of statements obtained from a defendant questioned while in custody or otherwise deprived of his freedom of action in any significant way. In each, the defendant was questioned by police officers, detectives, or a prosecuting attorney in a room in which he was cut off from the outside world. In none of these cases was the defendant given a full and effective warning of his rights at the outset of the interrogation process. In all the cases, the questioning elicited oral admissions, and in three of them, signed statements as well which were admitted at their trials. They all thus share salient features—incommunicado interrogation of individuals in a police-dominated atmosphere, resulting in self-incriminating statements without full warnings of constitutional rights.

An understanding of the nature and setting of this in-custody interrogation is essential to our decisions today. The difficulty in depicting what transpires at such interrogations stems from the fact that in this country they have largely taken place incommunicado. From extensive factual studies undertaken in the early 1930's, including the famous Wickersham Report to Congress by a Presidential Commission, it is clear that police violence and the "third degree" flourished at that time. In a series of cases decided by this Court long after these studies, the police resorted to physical brutality —beatings, hanging, whipping—and to sustained and protracted questioning incommunicado in order to extort confessions. The Commission on Civil Rights in 1961 found much evidence to indicate that "some policemen still resort to physical force to obtain confessions," 1961 Comm'n on Civil Rights Rep., Justice, pt. 5, 17. The use of physical brutality and violence is not, unfortunately, relegated to the past or to any part of the country. Only recently in Kings County, New York, the police brutally beat, kicked and placed lighted cigarette butts on the back of a potential witness under interrogation for the purpose of securing a statement incriminating a third party. People v. Portelli, 15 N.Y.2d 235, 257 N.Y.S.2d 931, 205 N.E.2d 857 (1965).

The examples given above are undoubtedly the exception now, but they are sufficiently widespread to be the object of concern. Unless a proper limitation upon custodial interrogation is achieved—such as these decisions will advance—there can be no assurance that practices of this nature will be eradicated in the foreseeable future. . . .

Again we stress that the modern practice of in-custody interrogation is psychologically rather than physically oriented. As we have stated before, "Since Chambers v. State of Florida, 309 U.S. 227, 60 S.Ct. 472, 84 L.Ed. 716, this Court has recognized that coercion can be mental as well as physical, and that the blood of the accused is not the only hallmark of an unconstitutional inquisition." Blackburn v. State of Alabama, 361 U.S. 199, 206, 80 S.Ct. 274, 279, 4 L.Ed.2d 242 (1960). Interrogation still takes place in privacy. Privacy results in secrecy and this in turn results in a gap in our knowledge as to what in fact goes on in the interrogation rooms. A valuable source of information about present police practices, however, may be found in various police manuals and texts which document procedures employed with success in the past, and which recommend various other effective tactics. These texts are used by law enforcement agencies themselves as guides. It should be noted that these texts professedly present the most enlightened and effective means presently used to obtain statements through custodial interrogation. By considering these texts and other data, it is possible to describe procedures observed and noted around the country.

The officers are told by the manuals that the "principal psychological factor contributing to a successful interrogation is privacy—being alone with the person under interrogation." The efficacy of this tactic has been explained as follows:

"If at all practicable, the interrogation should take place in the investigator's office or at least in a room of his own choice. The subject should be deprived of every psychological advantage. In his own home he may be confident, indignant, or recalcitrant. He is more keenly aware of his rights and more reluctant to tell of his indiscretions or criminal behavior within the walls of his home. Moreover his family and other friends are nearby, their presence lending moral support. In his office, the investigator possesses all the advantages. The atmosphere suggests the invincibility of the forces of the law."

To highlight the isolation and unfamiliar surroundings, the manuals instruct the police to display an air of confidence in the suspect's guilt and from outward appearance to maintain only an interest in confirming certain details. The guilt of the subject is to be posited as a fact. The interrogator should direct his comments toward the reasons why the subject committed the act, rather than court failure by asking the subject whether he did it. Like other men, perhaps the subject has had a bad family life, had an unhappy childhood, had too much to drink, had an unrequited desire for women. The officers are instructed to minimize the moral seriousness of the offense, to cast blame on the victim or on society. These tactics are designed to put the subject in a psychological state where his story is but an elaboration of what the police purport to know already—that he is guilty. Explanations to the contrary are dismissed and discouraged.

The texts thus stress that the major qualities an interrogator should possess are patience and perserverance. One writer describes the efficacy of these characteristics in this manner:

"In the preceding paragraphs emphasis has been placed on kindness and stratagems. The investigator will, however, encounter many situations where the sheer weight of his personality will be the deciding factor. Where emotional appeals and tricks are employed to no avail, he must rely on an oppressive atmosphere of dogged persistence. He must interrogate steadily and without relent, leaving the subject no prospect of surcease. He must dominate his subject and overwhelm him with his inexorable will to obtain the truth. He should interrogate for a spell of several hours pausing only for the subject's necessities in acknowledgement of the need to avoid a charge of duress that can be technically substantiated. In a serious case, the interrogation may continue for days, with the required intervals for food and sleep, but with no respite from the atmosphere of domination. It is possible in this way to induce the subject to talk without resorting to duress or coercion. The method should be used only when the guilt of the subject appears highly probable."

The manuals suggest that the suspect be offered legal excuses for his actions in order to obtain an initial admission of guilt. Where there is a suspected revenge-killing, for example, the interrogator may say:

"Joe, you probably didn't go out looking for this fellow with the purpose of shooting him. My guess is, however, that you expected something from him and that's why you carried a gun—for your own protection. You knew him for what he was, no good. Then when you met him he probably started using foul, abusive language and he gave some indication that he was about to pull a gun on you, and that's when you had to act to save your own life. That's about it, isn't it, Joe?"

Having then obtained the admission of shooting, the interrogator is advised to refer to circumstantial evidence which negates the self-defense explanation. This should enable him to secure the entire story. One text notes that "Even if he fails to do so, the inconsistency between the subject's original denial of the shooting and his present admission of at least doing the shooting will serve to deprive him of a self-defense 'out' at the time of trial."

When the techniques described above prove unavailing, the texts recommend they be alternated with a show of some hostility. One ploy often used has been termed the "friendly-unfriendly" or the "Mutt and Jeff" act:

". . . In this technique, two agents are employed. Mutt, the relentless investigator, who knows the subject is guilty and is not going to waste any time. He's sent a dozen men away for this crime and he's going to send the subject away for the full term. Jeff, on the other hand, is obviously a kindhearted man. He has a family himself. He has a brother who was involved in a little scrape like this. He disapproves of Mutt and his tactics and will arrange to get him off the case if the subject will cooperate. He can't hold Mutt off for very long. The subject would be wise to make a quick decision. The technique is applied by having both investigators present while Mutt acts out his role. Jeff may stand by quietly and demur at some of Mutt's tactics. When Jeff makes his plea for cooperation, Mutt is not present in the room."

The interrogators sometimes are instructed to induce a confession out of trickery. The technique here is quite effective in crimes which require identification or which run in series. In the identification situation, the interrogator may take a break in his questioning to place the subject among a group of men in a line-up. "The witness or complainant (previously coached, if necessary) studies the line-up and confidently points out the subject as the guilty party." Then the questioning resumes "as though there were now no doubt about the guilt of the subject." A variation on this technique is called the "reverse line-up":

"The accused is placed in a line-up, but this time he is identified by several fictitious witnesses or victims who associated him with different offenses. It is expected that the subject will become desperate and confess to the offense under investigation in order to escape from the false accusations."

The manuals also contain instructions for police on how to handle the individual who refuses to discuss the matter entirely, or who asks for an attorney or relatives. The examiner is to concede him the right to remain silent. "This usually has a very undermining effect. First of all, he is disappointed in his expectation of an unfavorable reaction on the part of the interrogator. Secondly, a concession of this right to remain silent impresses the subject with the apparent fairness of his interrogator." After this psychological conditioning, however, the officer is told to point out the incriminating significance of the suspect's refusal to talk:

"Joe, you have a right to remain silent. That's your privilege and I'm the last person in the world who'll try to take it away from you. If that's the way you want to leave this, O. K. But let me ask you this. Suppose you were in my shoes and I were in yours and you called me in to ask me about this and I told you, 'I don't want to answer any of your questions.' You'd think I had something to hide, and you'd probably be right in thinking that. That's exactly what I'll have to think about you, and so will everybody else. So let's sit here and talk this whole thing over."

Few will persist in their initial refusal to talk, it is said, if this monologue is employed correctly.

In the event that the subject wishes to speak to a relative or an attorney, the following advice is tendered:

"[T]he interrogator should respond by suggesting that the subject first tell the truth to the interrogator himself rather than get anyone else involved in the matter. If the request is for an attorney, the interrogator may suggest that the subject save himself or his family the expense of any such professional service, particularly if he is innocent of the offense under investigation. The interrogator may also add, 'Joe, I'm only looking for the truth, and if you're telling the truth, that's it. You can handle this by yourself.'"

From these representative samples of interrogation techniques, the setting prescribed by the manuals and observed in practice becomes clear. In essence, it is this: To be alone with the subject is essential to prevent distraction and to deprive him of any outside support. The aura of confidence in his guilt undermines his will to resist. He merely confirms the preconceived story the police seek to have him describe. Patience and persistence, at times relentless questioning, are employed. To obtain a confession, the interrogator must "patiently maneuver himself or his quarry into a position from which the desired objective may be attained." When normal procedures fail to produce the needed result, the police may resort to deceptive stratagems such as giving false legal advice. It is important to keep the subject off balance, for example, by trading on his insecurity about himself or his surroundings. The police then persuade, trick, or cajole him out of exercising his constitutional rights.

Even without employing brutality, the "third degree" or the specific stratagems described above, the very fact of custodial interrogation exacts a heavy toll on individual liberty and trades on the weakness of individuals. This fact may be illustrated simply by referring to three confession cases decided by this Court in the Term immediately preceding our *Escobedo* decision. In Townsend v. Sain, 372 U.S. 293, 83 S.Ct. 745, 9 L.Ed.2d 770 (1963), the defendant was a 19-year-old heroin addict, described as a "near mental defective," id., at 307–310, 83 S.Ct. at 754–755. The defendant in Lynumn v. State of Illinois, 372 U.S. 528, 83 S.Ct. 917, 9 L.Ed.2d 922 (1963), was a woman who confessed to the arresting officer after being importuned to "cooperate" in order to prevent her children from being taken by relief authorities. This Court as in those cases reversed the conviction of a defendant in Haynes v. State of Washington, 373 U.S. 503, 83 S.Ct. 1336, 10 L.Ed.2d 513 (1963), whose persistent request during his interrogation was to phone his wife or attorney. In other settings, these individuals might have exercised their constitutional rights. In the incommunicado police-dominated atmosphere, they succumbed.

In the cases before us today, given this background, we concern ourselves primarily with this interrogation atmosphere and the evils it can bring. In No. 759, Miranda v. Arizona, the police arrested the defendant and took him to a special interrogation room where they secured a confession. In No. 760, Vignera v. New York, the defendant made oral admissions to the police after interrogation in the afternoon, and then signed an inculpatory statement upon being questioned by an assistant district attorney later the same evening. In No. 761, Westover v. United States, the defendant was handed over to the Federal Bureau of Investigation by local authorities after they had detained and interrogated him for a lengthy period, both at night and the following morning. After some two hours of questioning, the federal officers had obtained signed statements from the defendant. Lastly, in No. 584, California v. Stewart, the local police held the defendant five days in the station and interrogated him on nine separate occasions before they secured his inculpatory statement.

In these cases, we might not find the defendants' statements to have been involuntary in traditional terms. Our concern for adequate safeguards to protect precious Fifth Amendment rights is, of course, not lessened in the slightest. In each of the cases, the defendant was thrust into an unfamiliar atmosphere and run through menacing police interrogation procedures. The potentiality for compulsion is forcefully apparent, for example, in *Miranda*, where the indigent Mexican defendant was a seriously disturbed individual with pronounced sexual fantasies, and in *Stewart*, in which the defendant was an indigent Los Angeles Negro who had dropped out of school in the sixth grade. To be sure, the records do not evince overt physical coercion or patent psychological ploys. The fact remains that in none of these cases did the officers undertake to afford appropriate safeguards at the outset of the interrogation to insure that the statements were truly the product of free choice.

It is obvious that such an interrogation environment is created for no purpose other than to subjugate the individual to the will of his examiner. This atmosphere carries its own badge of intimidation. To be sure, this is not physical intimidation, but it is equally destructive of human dignity. The current practice of incommunicado interrogation is at odds with one of our Nation's most cherished principles—that the individual may not be compelled to incriminate himself. Unless adequate protective devices are employed to dispel the compulsion inherent in custodial surroundings, no statement obtained from the defendant can truly be the product of his free choice.

• • •

Today, then, there can be no doubt that the Fifth Amendment privilege is available outside of criminal court proceedings and serves to protect persons in all settings in which their freedom of action is curtailed in any significant way from being compelled to incriminate themselves. We have concluded that without proper safeguards the process of in-custody interrogation of persons suspected or accused of crime contains inherently compelling pressures which work to undermine the individual's will to resist and to compel him to speak where he would not otherwise do so freely. In order to combat these pressures and to permit a full opportunity to exercise the privilege against self-incrimination, the accused must be adequately and effectively apprised of his rights and the exercise of those rights must be fully honored.

It is impossible for us to foresee the potential alternatives for protecting the privilege which might be devised by Congress or the States in the exercise of their creative rule-making capacities. Therefore we cannot say that the Constitution necessarily requires adherence to any particular solution for the inherent compulsions of the interrogation process as it is presently conducted. Our decision in no way creates a constitutional straitjacket which will handicap sound efforts at reform, nor is it intended to have this effect. We encourage Congress and the States to continue their laudable search for increasingly effective ways of protecting the rights of the individual while promoting efficient enforcement of our criminal laws. However, unless we are shown other procedures which are at least as effective in apprising accused persons of their right of silence and in assuring a continuous opportunity to exercise it, the following safeguards must be observed.

At the outset, if a person in custody is to be subjected to interrogation, he must first be informed in clear and unequivocal terms that he has the right to remain silent. For those unaware of the privilege, the warning is needed simply to make them aware of it—the threshold requirement for an intelligent decision as to its exercise. More important, such a warning is an absolute prerequisite in overcoming the inherent pressures of the interrogation atmosphere. It is not just the subnormal or woefully ignorant who succumb to an interrogator's imprecations, whether implied or expressly stated, that the interrogation will continue until a confession is obtained or that silence in the face of accusation is itself damning and will bode ill when presented to a jury. Further, the warning will show the individual that his interrogators are prepared to recognize his privilege should he choose to exercise it.

The Fifth Amendment privilege is so fundamental to our system of constitutional rule and the expedient of giving an adequate warning as to the availability of the privilege so simple, we will not pause to inquire in individual cases whether the defendant was aware of his rights without a warning being given. Assessments of the knowledge the defendant possessed, based on information as to his age, education, intelligence, or prior contact with authorities, can never be more than speculation; a warning is a clearcut fact. More important, whatever the background of the person interrogated, a warning at the time of the interrogation is indispensable to overcome its pressures and to insure that the individual knows he is free to exercise the privilege at that point in time.

The warning of the right to remain silent must be accompanied by the explanation that anything said can and will be used against the individual in court. This warning is needed in order to make him aware not only of the privilege, but also of the consequences of forgoing it. It is only through an awareness of these consequences that there can be any assurance of real understanding and intelligent exercise of the privilege. Moreover, this warning may serve to make the individual more acutely aware that he is faced with a phase of the adversary system—that he is not in the presence of persons acting solely in his interest.

The circumstances surrounding in-custody interrogation can operate very quickly to overbear the will of one merely made aware of his privilege by his interrogators. Therefore, the right to have counsel present at the interrogation is indispensable to the protection of the Fifth Amendment privilege under the system we delineate today. Our aim is to assure that the individual's right to choose between silence and speech remains unfettered throughout the interrogation process. A once-stated warning, delivered by those who will conduct the interrogation, cannot itself suffice to that end among those who most require knowledge of their rights. A mere warning given by the interrogators is not alone sufficient to accomplish that end. Prosecutors themselves claim that the admonishment of the right to remain silent without more "will benefit only the recidivist and the professional." Brief for the National District Attorneys Association as *amicus curiae*, p. 14. Even preliminary advice given to the accused by his own attorney can be swiftly overcome by the secret interrogation process. Cf. Escobedo v. State of Illinois, 378 U.S. 478, 485, n. 5, 84 S.Ct. 1758, 1762. Thus, the need for counsel to protect the Fifth Amendment privilege comprehends not merely a right to consult with counsel prior to questioning, but also to have counsel present during any questioning if the defendant so desires.

The presence of counsel at the interrogation may serve several significant subsidiary functions as well. If the accused decides to talk to his interrogators, the assistance of counsel can mitigate the dangers of untrustworthiness. With a lawyer present the likelihood that the police will practice coercion is reduced, and if coercion is nevertheless exercised the lawyer can testify to it in court. The presence of a lawyer can also help to guarantee that the accused gives a fully accurate statement to the police and that the statement is rightly reported by the prosecution at trial. See Crooker v. State of California, 357 U.S. 433, 443–448, 78 S.Ct. 1287, 1293–1296, 2 L.Ed.2d 1448 (1958) (Douglas, J., dissenting).

An individual need not make a pre-interrogation request for a lawyer. While such request affirmatively secures his right to have one, his failure to ask for a lawyer does not constitute a waiver. No effective waiver of the right to counsel during interrogation can be recognized unless specifically made after the warnings we here delineate have been given. The accused who does not know his rights and therefore does not make a request may be the person who most needs counsel. As the California Supreme Court has aptly put it:

"Finally, we must recognize that the imposition of the requirement for the request would discriminate against the defendant who does not know his rights. The defendant who does not ask for counsel is the very defendant who most needs counsel. We cannot penalize a defendant who, not understanding his constitutional rights, does not make the formal request and by such failure demonstrates his helplessness. To require the request would be to favor the defendant whose sophistication or status had fortuitously prompted him to make it." People v. Dorado, 62 Cal.2d 338, 351, 42 Cal.Rptr. 169, 177–178, 398 P.2d 361, 369–370 (1965) (Tobriner, J.).

In Carnley v. Cochran, 369 U.S. 506, 513, 82 S.Ct. 884, 889, 8 L.Ed.2d 70 (1962), we stated: "[I]t is settled that where the assistance of counsel is a constitutional requisite, the right to be furnished counsel does not depend on a request." This proposition applies with equal force in the context of providing counsel to protect an accused's Fifth Amendment privilege in the face of interrogation. Although the role of counsel at trial differs from the role during interrogation, the differences are not relevant to the question whether a request is a prerequisite.

Accordingly we hold that an individual held for interrogation must be clearly informed that he has the right to consult with a lawyer and to have the lawyer with him during interrogation under the system for protecting the privilege we delineate today. As with the warnings of the right to remain silent and that anything stated can be used in evidence against him, this warning is an absolute prerequisite to interrogation. No amount of circumstantial evidence that the person may have been aware of this right will suffice to stand in its stead. Only through such a warning is there ascertainable assurance that the accused was aware of this right.

If an individual indicates that he wishes the assistance of counsel before any interrogation occurs, the authorities cannot rationally ignore or deny his request on the basis that the individual does not have or cannot afford a retained attorney. The financial ability of the individual has no relationship to the scope of the rights involved here. The privilege against self-incrimination secured by the Constitution applies to all individuals. The need for counsel in order to protect the privilege exists for the indigent as well as the affluent. In fact, were we to limit these constitutional rights to those who can retain an attorney, our decisions today would be of little significance. The cases before us as well as the vast majority of confession cases with which we have dealt in the past involve those unable to retain counsel. While authorities are not required to relieve the accused of his poverty, they have the obligation not to take advantage of indigence in the administration of justice. Denial of counsel to the indigent at the time of interrogation while allowing an attorney to those who can afford one would be no more supportable by reason or logic than the similar situation at trial and on appeal struck down in Gideon v. Wainwright, 372 U.S. 335, 83 S.Ct. 792, 9 L.Ed.2d 799 (1963), and Douglas v. People of State of California, 372 U.S. 353, 83 S.Ct. 814, 9 L.Ed.2d 811 (1963).

In order fully to apprise a person interrogated of the extent of his rights under this system then, it is necessary to warn him not only that he has the right to consult with an attorney, but also that if he is indigent a lawyer will be appointed to represent him. Without this additional warning, the admonition of the right to consult with counsel would often be understood as meaning only that he can consult with a lawyer if he has one or has the funds to obtain one. The warning of a right to counsel would be hollow if not couched in terms that would convey to the indigent—the person most often subjected to interrogation—the knowledge that he too has a right to have counsel present. As with the warnings of the right to remain silent and of the general right to counsel, only by effective and express explanation to the indigent of this right can there be assurance that he was truly in a position to exercise it.

Once warnings have been given, the subsequent procedure is clear. If the individual indicates in any manner, at any time prior to or during questioning, that he wishes to remain silent, the interrogation must cease. At this point he has shown that he intends to exercise his Fifth Amendment privilege; any statement taken after the person invokes his privilege cannot be other than the product of compulsion, subtle or otherwise. Without the right to cut off questioning, the setting of in-custody interrogation operates on the individual to overcome free choice in producing a statement after the privilege has been once invoked. If the individual states that he wants an attorney, the interrogation must cease until an attorney is present. At that time, the individual must have an opportunity to confer with the attorney and to have him present during any subsequent questioning. If the individual cannot obtain an attorney and he indicates that he wants one before speaking to police, they must respect his decision to remain silent.

This does not mean, as some have suggested, that each police station must have a "station house lawyer" present at all times to advise prisoners. It does mean, however, that if police propose to interrogate a person they must make known to him that he is entitled to a lawyer and that if he cannot afford one, a lawyer will be provided for him prior to any interrogation. If authorities conclude that they will not provide counsel during a reasonable period of time in which investigation in the field is carried out, they may refrain from doing so without violating the person's Fifth Amendment privilege so long as they do not question him during that time.

If the interrogation continues without the presence of an attorney and a statement is taken, a heavy burden rests on the government to demonstrate that the defendant knowingly and intelligently waived his privilege against self-incrimination and his right to retained or appointed counsel. Escobedo v. State of Illinois, 378 U.S. 478, 490, n. 14, 84 S.Ct. 1758, 1764, 12 L.Ed.2d 977. This Court has always set high standards of proof for the waiver of constitutional rights, Johnson v. Zerbst, 304 U.S. 458, 58 S.Ct. 1019, 82 L.Ed. 1461 (1938), and we reassert these standards as applied to in-custody interrogation. Since the State is responsible for establishing the isolated circumstances under which the interrogation takes place and has the only means of making available corroborated evidence of warnings given during incommunicado interrogation, the burden is rightly on its shoulders.

An express statement that the individual is willing to make a statement and does not want an attorney followed closely by a statement could constitute a waiver. But a valid waiver will not be presumed simply from the silence of the accused after warnings are given or simply from the fact that a confession was in fact eventually obtained. A statement we made in Carnley v. Cochran, 369 U.S. 506, 516, 82 S.Ct. 884, 890, 8 L.Ed.2d 70 (1962), is applicable here:

"Presuming waiver from a silent record is impermissible. The record must show, or there must be an allegation and evidence which show, that an accused was offered counsel but intelligently and understandingly rejected the offer. Anything less is not waiver."

See also Glasser v. United States, 315 U.S. 60, 62 S.Ct. 457, 86 L.Ed. 680 (1942). Moreover, where in-custody interrogation is involved, there is no room for the contention that the privilege is waived if the individual answers some questions or gives some information on his own prior to invoking his right to remain silent when interrogated.

Whatever the testimony of the authorities as to waiver of rights by an accused, the fact of lengthy interrogation or incommunicado incarceration before a statement is made is strong evidence that the accused did not validly waive his rights. In these circumstances the fact that the individual eventually made a statement is consistent with the conclusion that the compelling influence of the interrogation finally forced him to do so. It is inconsistent with any notion of a voluntary relinquishment of the privilege. Moreover, any evidence that the accused was threatened, tricked, or cajoled into a waiver will, of course, show that the defendant did not voluntarily waive his privilege. The requirement of warnings and waiver of rights is a fundamental with respect to the Fifth Amendment privilege and not simply a preliminary ritual to existing methods of interrogation.

The warnings required and the waiver necessary in accordance with our opinion today are, in the absence of a fully effective equivalent, prerequisites to the admissibility of any statement made by a defendant. No distinction can be drawn between statements which are direct confessions and statements which amount to "admissions" of part or all of an offense. The privilege against self-incrimination protects the individual from being compelled to incriminate himself in any manner; it does not distinguish degrees of incrimination. Similarly, for precisely the same reason, no distinction may be drawn between inculpatory statements and statements alleged to be merely "exculpatory." If a statement made were in fact truly exculpatory it would, of course, never be used by the prosecution. In fact, statements merely intended to be exculpatory by the defendant are often used to impeach his testimony at trial or to demonstrate untruths in the statement given under interrogation and thus to prove guilt by implication. These statements are incriminating in any meaningful sense of the word and may not be used without the full warnings and effective waiver required for any other statement. In *Escobedo* itself, the defendant fully intended his accusation of another as the slayer to be exculpatory as to himself.

The principles announced today deal with the protection which must be given to the privilege against self-incrimination when the individual is first subjected to police interrogation while in custody at the station or otherwise deprived of his freedom of action in any significant way. It is at this point that our adversary system of criminal proceedings commences, distinguishing itself at the outset from the inquisitorial system recognized in some countries. Under the system of warnings we delineate today or under any other system which may be devised and found effective, the safeguards to be erected about the privilege must come into play at this point.

Our decision is not intended to hamper the traditional function of police officers in investigating crime. See Escobedo v. State of Illinois, 378 U.S. 478, 492, 84 S.Ct. 1758, 1765. When an individual is in custody on probable cause, the police may, of course, seek out evidence in the field to be used at trial against him. Such investigation may include inquiry of persons not under restraint. General on-the-scene questioning as to facts surrounding a crime or other general questioning of citizens in the fact-finding process is not affected by our holding. It is an act of responsible citizenship for individuals to give whatever information they may have to aid in law enforcement. In such situations the compelling atmosphere inherent in the process of in-custody interrogation is not necessarily present.

In dealing with statements obtained through interrogation, we do not purport to find all confessions inadmissible. Confessions remain a proper element in law enforcement. Any statement given freely and voluntarily without any compelling influences is, of course, admissible in evidence. The fundamental import of the privilege while an individual is in custody is not whether he is allowed to talk to the police without the benefit of warnings and counsel, but whether he can be interrogated. There is no requirement that police stop a person who enters a police station and states that he wishes to confess to a crime, or a person who calls the police to offer a confession or any other statement he desires to make. Volunteered statements of any kind are not barred by the Fifth Amendment and their admissibility is not affected by our holding today.

To summarize, we hold that when an individual is taken into custody or otherwise deprived of his freedom by the authorities in any significant way and is subjected to questioning, the privilege against self-incrimination is jeopardized. Procedural safeguards must be employed to protect the privilege and unless other fully effective means are adopted to notify the person of his right of silence and to assure that the exercise of the right will be scrupulously honored, the following measures are required. He must be warned prior to any questioning that he has the right to remain silent, that anything he says can be used against him in a court of law, that he has the right to the presence of an attorney, and that if he cannot afford an attorney one will be appointed for him prior to any questioning if he so desires. Opportunity to exercise these rights must be afforded to him throughout the interrogation. After such warnings have been given, and such opportunity afforded him, the individual may knowingly and intelligently waive these rights and agree to answer questions or make a statement. But unless and until such warnings and waiver are demonstrated by the prosecution at trial, no evidence obtained as a result of interrogation can be used against him.

A recurrent argument made in these cases is that society's need for interrogation outweighs the privilege. This argument is not unfamiliar to this Court. See, e. g., Chambers v. State of Florida, 309 U.S. 227, 240–241, 60 S.Ct. 472, 478–479, 84 L.Ed. 716 (1940). The whole thrust of our foregoing discussion demonstrates that the Constitution has prescribed the rights of the individual when confronted with the power of government when it provided in the Fifth Amendment that an individual cannot be compelled to be a witness against himself. That right cannot be abridged. As Mr. Justice Brandeis once observed:

"Decency, security, and liberty alike demand that government officials shall be subjected to the same rules of conduct that are commands to the citizen. In a government of laws, existence of the government will be imperilled if it fails to observe the law scrupulously. Our government is the potent, the omnipresent teacher. For good or for ill, it teaches the whole people by its example. Crime is contagious. If the government becomes a lawbreaker, it breeds contempt for law; it invites every man to become a law unto himself; it invites anarchy. To declare that in the administration of the criminal law the end justifies the means . . . would bring terrible retribution. Against that pernicious doctrine this court should resolutely set its face." Olmstead v. United States, 277 U.S. 438, 485, 48 S.Ct. 564, 575, 72 L.Ed. 944 (1928) (dissenting opinion).

In this connection, one of our country's distinguished jurists has pointed out:

"The quality of a nation's civilization can be largely measured by the methods it uses in the enforcement of its criminal law."

If the individual desires to exercise his privilege, he has the right to do so. This is not for the authorities to decide. An attorney may advise his client not to talk to police until he has had an opportunity to investigate the case, or he may wish to be present with his client during any police questioning. In doing so an attorney is merely exercising the good professional judgment he has been taught. This is not cause for considering the attorney a menace to law enforcement. He is merely carrying out what he is sworn to do under his oath—to protect to the extent of his ability the rights of his client. In fulfilling this responsibility the attorney plays a vital role in the administration of criminal justice under our Constitution.

In announcing these principles, we are not unmindful of the burdens which law enforcement officials must bear, often under trying circumstances. We also fully recognize the obligation of all citizens to aid in enforcing the criminal laws. This Court, while protecting individual rights, has always given ample latitude to law enforcement agencies in the legitimate exercise of their duties. The limits we have placed on the interrogation process should not constitute an undue interference with a proper system of law enforcement. As we have noted, our decision does not in any way preclude police from carrying out their traditional investigatory functions. Although confessions may play an important role in some convictions, the cases before us present graphic examples of the overstatement of the "need" for confessions. In each case authorities conducted interrogations ranging up to five days in duration despite the presence, through standard investigating practices, of considerable evidence against each defendant. . . .

It is also urged that an unfettered right to detention for interrogation should be allowed because it will often redound to the benefit of the person questioned. When police inquiry determines that there is no reason to believe that the person has committed any crime, it is said, he will be released without need for further formal procedures. The person who has committed no offense, however, will be better able to clear himself after warnings with counsel present than without. It can be assumed that in such circumstances a lawyer would advise his client to talk freely to police in order to clear himself.

Custodial interrogation, by contrast, does not necessarily afford the innocent an opportunity to clear themselves. A serious consequence of the present practice of the interrogation alleged to be beneficial for the innocent is that many arrests "for investigation" subject large numbers of innocent persons to detention and interrogation. In one of the cases before us, No. 584, California v. Stewart, police held four persons, who were in the defendant's house at the time of the arrest, in jail for five days until defendant confessed. At that time they were finally released. Police stated that there was "no evidence to connect them with any crime." Available statistics on the extent of this practice where it is condoned indicate that these four are far from alone in being subjected to arrest, prolonged detention, and interrogation without the requisite probable cause.

Over the years the Federal Bureau of Investigation has compiled an exemplary record of effective law enforcement while advising any suspect or arrested person, at the outset of an interview, that he is not required to make a statement, that any statement may be used against him in court, that the individual may obtain the services of an attorney of his own choice and, more recently, that he has a right to free counsel if he is unable to pay. A letter received from the Solicitor General in response to a question from the Bench makes it clear that the present pattern of warnings and respect for the rights of the individual followed as a practice by the FBI is consistent with the procedure which we delineate today. It states:

"At the oral argument of the above cause, Mr. Justice Fortas asked whether I could provide certain information as to the practices followed by the Federal Bureau of Investigation. I have directed these questions to the attention of the Director of the Federal Bureau of Investigation and am submitting herewith a statement of the questions and of the answers which we have received.

" '(1) When an individual is interviewed by agents of the Bureau, what warning is given to him?

" 'The standard warning long given by Special Agents of the FBI to both suspects and persons under arrest is that the person has a right to say nothing and a right to counsel, and that any statement he does make may be used against him in court. Examples of this warning are to be found in the *Westover* case at 342 F.2d 684 (1965), and Jackson v. U. S., [119 U.S.App. D.C. 100] 337 F.2d 136 (1964), cert. den. 380 U.S. 935, 85 S.Ct. 1353,

" 'After passage of the Criminal Justice Act of 1964, which provides free counsel for Federal defendants unable to pay, we added to our instructions to Special Agents the requirement that any person who is under arrest for an offense under FBI jurisdiction, or whose arrest is contemplated following the interview, must also be advised of his right to free counsel if he is unable to pay, and the fact that such counsel will be assigned by the Judge. At the same time, we broadened the right to counsel warning to read counsel of his own choice, or anyone else with whom he might wish to speak.

" '(2) When is the warning given?

" 'The FBI warning is given to a suspect at the very outset of the interview, as shown in the *Westover* case, cited above. The warning may be given to a person arrested as soon as practicable after the arrest, as shown in the *Jackson* case, also cited above, and in U. S. v. Konigsberg, 336 F.2d 844 (1964), cert. den. [Celso v. United States] 379 U.S. 933 [85 S.Ct. 327, 13 L.Ed.2d 342] but in any event it must precede the interview with the person for a confession or admission of his own guilt.

" '(3) What is the Bureau's practice in the event that (a) the individual requests counsel and (b) counsel appears?

" 'When the person who has been warned of his right to counsel decides that he wishes to consult with counsel before making a statement, the interview is terminated at that point, Shultz v. U. S., 351 F.2d 287 ([10 Cir.] 1965). It may be continued, however, as to all matters *other* than the person's own guilt or innocence. If he is indecisive in his request for counsel, there may be some question on whether he did or did not waive counsel. Situations of this kind must necessarily be left to the judgment of the interviewing Agent. For example, in Hiram v. U. S., 354 F.2d 4 ([9 Cir.] 1965), the Agent's conclusion that the person arrested had waived his right to counsel was upheld by the courts.

" 'A person being interviewed and desiring to consult counsel by telephone must be permitted to do so, as shown in Caldwell v. U. S., 351 F.2d 459 ([1 Cir.] 1965). When counsel appears in person, he is permitted to confer with his client in private.

" '(4) What is the Bureau's practice if the individual requests counsel, but cannot afford to retain an attorney?

" 'If any person being interviewed after warning of counsel decides that he wishes to consult with counsel before proceeding further the interview is terminated, as shown above. FBI Agents do not pass judgment on the ability of the person to pay for counsel. They do, however, advise those who have been arrested for an offense under FBI jurisdiction, or whose arrest is contemplated following the interview, of a right to free counsel *if* they are unable to pay, and the availability of such counsel from the Judge.' "

The practice of the FBI can readily be emulated by state and local enforcement agencies. The argument that the FBI deals with different crimes than are dealt with by state authorities does not mitigate the significance of the FBI experience.

The experience in some other countries also suggests that the danger to law enforcement in curbs on interrogation is overplayed. The English procedure since 1912 under the Judges' Rules is significant. As recently strengthened, the Rules require that a cautionary warning be given an accused by a police officer as soon as he has evidence that affords reasonable grounds for suspicion; they also require that any statement made be given by the accused without questioning by police. The right of the individual to consult with an attorney during this period is expressly recognized.

The safeguards present under Scottish law may be even greater than in England. Scottish judicial decisions bar use in evidence of most confessions obtained through police interrogation. In India, confessions made to police not in the presence of a magistrate have been excluded by rule of evidence since 1872, at a time when it operated under British law. Identical provisions appear in the Evidence Ordinance of Ceylon, enacted in 1895. Similarly, in our country the Uniform Code of Military Justice has long provided that no suspect may be interrogated without first being warned of his right not to make a statement and that any statement he makes may be used against him. Denial of the right to consult counsel during interrogation has also been proscribed by military tribunals. There appears to have been no marked detrimental effect on criminal law enforcement in these jurisdictions as a result of these rules. Conditions of law enforcement in our country are sufficiently similar to permit reference to this experience as assurance that lawlessness will not result from warning an individual of his rights or allowing him to exercise them. Moreover, it is consistent with our legal system that we give at least as much protection to these rights as is given in the jurisdictions described. We deal in our country with rights grounded in a specific requirement of the Fifth Amendment of the Constitution, whereas other jurisdictions arrived at their conclusions on the basis of principles of justice not so specifically defined.

It is also urged upon us that we withhold decision on this issue until state legislative bodies and advisory groups have had an opportunity to deal with these problems by rule making. We have already pointed out that the Constitution does not require any specific code of procedures for protecting the privilege against self-incrimination during custodial interrogation. Congress and the States are free to develop their own safeguards for the privilege, so long as they are fully as effective as those described above in informing accused persons of their right of silence and in affording a continuous opportunity to exercise it. In any event, however, the issues presented are of constitutional dimensions and must be determined by the courts. The admissibility of a statement in the face of a claim that it was obtained in violation of the defendant's constitutional rights is an issue the resolution of which has long since been undertaken by this Court. See Hopt v. People of Territory of Utah, 110 U.S. 574, 4 S.Ct. 202, 28 L.Ed. 262 (1884). Judicial solutions to problems of constitutional dimension have evolved decade by decade. As courts have been presented with the need to enforce constitutional rights, they have found means of doing so. That was our responsibility when *Escobedo* was before us and it is our responsibility today. Where rights secured by the Constitution are involved, there can be no rule making or legislation which would abrogate them.

Because of the nature of the problem and because of its recurrent significance in numerous cases, we have to this point discussed the relationship of the Fifth Amendment privilege to police interrogation without specific concentration on the facts of the cases before us. We turn now to these facts to consider the application to these cases of the constitutional principles discussed above. In each instance, we have concluded that statements were obtained from the defendant under circumstances that did not meet constitutional standards for protection of the privilege.

No. 759. Miranda v. Arizona.

On March 13, 1963, petitioner, Ernesto Miranda, was arrested at his home and taken in custody to a Phoenix police station. He was then identified by the complaining witness. The police then took him to "Interrogation Room No. 2" of the detective bureau. There he was questioned by two police officers. The officers admitted at trial that Miranda was not advised that he had a right to have an attorney present. Two hours later, the officers emerged from the interrogation room with a written confession signed by Miranda. At the top of the statement was a typed paragraph stating that the confession was made voluntarily, without threats or promises of immunity and "with full knowledge of my legal rights, understanding any statement I make may be used against me."

At his trial before a jury, the written confession was admitted into evidence over the objection of defense counsel, and the officers testified to the prior oral confession made by Miranda during the interrogation. Miranda was found guilty of kidnapping and rape. He was sentenced to 20 to 30 years' imprisonment on each count, the sentences to run concurrently. On appeal, the Supreme Court of Arizona held that Miranda's constitutional rights were not violated in obtaining the confession and affirmed the conviction. 98 Ariz. 18, 401 P.2d 721. In reaching its decision, the court emphasized heavily the fact that Miranda did not specifically request counsel.

We reverse. From the testimony of the officers and by the admission of respondent, it is clear that Miranda was not in any way apprised of his right to consult with an attorney and to have one present during the interrogation, nor was his right not to be compelled to incriminate himself effectively protected in any other manner. Without these warnings the statements were inadmissible. The mere fact that he signed a statement which contained a typed-in clause stating that he had "full knowledge" of his "legal rights" does not approach the knowing and intelligent waiver required to relinquish constitutional rights.

No. 760. Vignera v. New York.

Petitioner, Michael Vignera, was picked up by New York police on October 14, 1960, in connection with the robbery three days earlier of a Brooklyn dress shop. They took him to the 17th Detective Squad headquarters in Manhattan. Sometime thereafter he was taken to the 66th Detective Squad. There a detective questioned Vignera with respect to the robbery. Vignera orally admitted the robbery to the detective. The detective was asked on cross-examination at trial by defense counsel whether Vignera was warned of his right to counsel before being interrogated. The prosecution objected to the question and the trial judge sustained the objection. Thus, the defense was precluded from making any showing that warnings had not been given. While at the 66th Detective Squad, Vignera was identified by the store owner and a saleslady as the man who robbed the dress shop. At about 3 p.m. he was formally arrested. The police then transported him to still another station, the 70th Precinct in Brooklyn, "for detention." At 11 p.m. Vignera was questioned by an assistant district attorney in the presence of a hearing reporter who transcribed the questions and Vignera's answers. This verbatim account of these proceedings contains no statement of any warnings given by the assistant district attorney. At Vignera's trial on a charge of first degree robbery, the detective testified as to the oral confession. The transcription of the statement taken was also introduced in evidence. At the conclusion of the testimony, the trial judge charged the jury in part as follows:

> "The law doesn't say that the confession is void or invalidated because the police officer didn't advise the defendant as to his rights. Did you hear what I said? I am telling you what the law of the State of New York is."

Vignera was found guilty of first degree robbery. He was subsequently adjudged a third-felony offender and sentenced to 30 to 60 years' imprisonment. The conviction was affirmed without opinion by the Appellate Division, Second Department, 21 A.D.2d 752,

252 N.Y.S.2d 19, and by the Court of Appeals, also without opinion, 15 N.Y.2d 970, 259 N.Y.S.2d 857, 207 N.E.2d 527, remittitur amended, 16 N.Y.2d 614, 261 N.Y.S.2d 65, 209 N.E.2d 110. In argument to the Court of Appeals, the State contended that Vignera had no constitutional right to be advised of his right to counsel or his privilege against self-incrimination.

We reverse. The foregoing indicates that Vignera was not warned of any of his rights before the questioning by the detective and by the assistant district attorney. No other steps were taken to protect these rights. Thus he was not effectively apprised of his Fifth Amendment privilege or of his right to have counsel present and his statements are inadmissible.

No. 761. Westover v. United States.

At approximately 9:45 p. m. on March 20, 1963, petitioner, Carl Calvin Westover, was arrested by local police in Kansas City as a suspect in two Kansas City robberies. A report was also received from the FBI that he was wanted on a felony charge in California. The local authorities took him to a police station and placed him in a line-up on the local charges and at about 11:45 p. m. he was booked. Kansas City police interrogated Westover on the night of his arrest. He denied any knowledge of criminal activities. The next day local officers interrogated him again throughout the morning. Shortly before noon they informed the FBI that they were through interrogating Westover and that the FBI could proceed to interrogate him. There is nothing in the record to indicate that Westover was ever given any warning as to his rights by local police. At noon, three special agents of the FBI continued the interrogation in a private interview room of the Kansas City Police Department, this time with respect to the robbery of a savings and loan association and a bank in Sacramento, California. After two or two and one-half hours, Westover signed separate confessions to each of these two robberies which had been prepared by one of the agents during the interrogation. At trial one of the agents testified, and a paragraph on each of the statements states, that the agents advised Westover that he did not have to make a statement, that any statement he made could be used against him, and that he had the right to see an attorney.

Westover was tried by a jury in federal court and convicted of the California robberies. His statements were introduced at trial. He was sentenced to 15 years' imprisonment on each count, the sentences to run consecutively. On appeal, the conviction was affirmed by the Court of Appeals for the Ninth Circuit. 342 F.2d 684.

We reverse. On the facts of this case we cannot find that Westover knowingly and intelligently waived his right to remain silent and his right to consult with counsel prior to the time he made the statement. At the time the FBI agents began questioning Westover, he had been in custody for over 14 hours and had been interrogated at length during that period. The FBI interrogation began immediately upon the conclusion of the interrogation by Kansas City police and was conducted in local police headquarters. Although the two law enforcement authorities are legally distinct and the crimes for which they interrogated Westover were different, the impact on him was that of a continuous period of questioning. There is no evidence of any warning given prior to the FBI interrogation nor is there any evidence of an articulated waiver of rights after the FBI commenced its interrogation. The record simply shows that the defendant did in fact confess a short time after being turned over to the FBI following interrogation by local police. Despite the fact that the FBI agents gave warnings at the outset of their interview, from Westover's point of view the warnings came at the end of the interrogation process. In these circumstances an intelligent waiver of constitutional rights cannot be assumed.

We do not suggest that law enforcement authorities are precluded from questioning any individual who has been held for a period of time by other authorities and interrogated by them without appropriate warnings. A different case would be presented if an accused were taken into custody by the second authority, removed both in time and place from his original surroundings, and then adequately advised of his rights and given an opportunity to exercise them. But here the FBI interrogation was conducted immediately following the state interrogation in the same police station—in the same compelling surroundings. Thus, in obtaining a confession from Westover the federal authorities were the beneficiaries of the pressure applied by the local in-custody interrogation. In these circumstances the giving of warnings alone was not sufficient to protect the privilege.

No. 584. California v. Stewart.

In the course of investigating a series of purse-snatch robberies in which one of the victims had died of injuries inflicted by her assailant, respondent, Roy Allen Stewart, was pointed out to Los Angeles police as the endorser of dividend checks taken in one of the robberies. At about 7:15 p. m., January 31, 1963, police officers went to Stewart's house and arrested him. One of the officers asked Stewart if they could search the house, to which he replied, "Go ahead." The search turned up various items taken from the five robbery victims. At the time of Stewart's arrest, police also arrested Stewart's wife and three other persons who were visiting him. These four were jailed along with Stewart and were interrogated. Stewart was taken to the University Station of the Los Angeles Police Department where he was placed in a cell. During the next five days, police interrogated Stewart on nine different occasions. Except during the first interrogation session, when he was confronted with an accusing witness, Stewart was isolated with his interrogators.

During the ninth interrogation session, Stewart admitted that he had robbed the deceased and stated that he had not meant to hurt her. Police then brought Stewart before a magistrate for the first time. Since there was no evidence to connect them with any crime, the police then released the other four persons arrested with him.

Nothing in the record specifically indicates whether Stewart was or was not advised of his right to remain silent or his right to counsel. In a number of instances, however, the interrogating officers were asked to recount everything that was said during the interrogations. None indicated that Stewart was ever advised of his rights.

Stewart was charged with kidnapping to commit robbery, rape, and murder. At his trial, transcripts of the first interrogation and the confession at the last interrogation were introduced in evidence. The jury found Stewart guilty of robbery and first degree murder and fixed the penalty as death. On appeal, the Supreme Court of California reversed. 62 Cal.2d 571, 43 Cal. Rptr. 201, 400 P.2d 97. It held that under this Court's decision in *Escobedo*, Stewart should have been advised of his right to remain silent and of his right to counsel and that it would not presume in the face of a silent record that the police advised Stewart of his rights.

We affirm. In dealing with custodial interrogation, we will not presume that a defendant has been effectively apprised of his rights and that his privilege against self-incrimination has been adequately safeguarded on a record that does not show that any warnings have been given or that any effective alternative has been employed. Nor can a knowing and intelligent waiver of these rights be assumed on a silent record. Furthermore, Stewart's steadfast denial of the alleged offenses through eight of the nine interrogations over a period of five days is subject to no other construction than that he was compelled by persistent interrogation to forgo his Fifth Amendment privilege:

Therefore, in accordance with the foregoing, the judgments of the Supreme Court of Arizona in No. 759, of the New York Court of Appeals in No. 760, and of the Court of Appeals for the Ninth Circuit in No. 761 are reversed. The judgment of the Supreme

Court of California in No. 584 is affirmed. It is so ordered.

Judgments of Supreme Court of Arizona in No. 759, of New York Court of Appeals in No. 760, and of the Court of Appeals for the Ninth Circuit in No. 761 reversed.

Judgment of Supreme Court of California in No. 584 affirmed.

Mr. Justice CLARK, dissenting in Nos. 759, 760, and 761, and concurring in the result in No. 584.

It is with regret that I find it necessary to write in these cases. However, I am unable to join the majority because its opinion goes too far on too little, while my dissenting brethren do not go quite far enough. Nor can I join in the Court's criticism of the present practices of police and investigatory agencies as to custodial interrogation. The materials it refers to as "police manuals" are, as I read them, merely writings in this field by professors and some police officers. Not one is shown by the record here to be the official manual of any police department, much less in universal use in crime detection. Moreover the examples of police brutality mentioned by the Court are rare exceptions to the thousands of cases that appear every year in the law reports. The police agencies—all the way from municipal and state forces to the federal bureaus—are responsible for law enforcement and public safety in this country. I am proud of their efforts, which in my view are not fairly characterized by the Court's opinion.

The *ipse dixit* of the majority has no support in our cases. Indeed, the Court admits that "we might not find the defendants' statements [here] to have been involuntary in traditional terms." Ante, p. 1618. In short, the Court has added more to the requirements that the accused is entitled to consult with his lawyer and that he must be given the traditional warning that he may remain silent and that anything that he says may be used against him. Escobedo v. State of Illinois, 378 U.S. 478, 490–491, 84 S.Ct. 1758, 1764–1765, 12 L.Ed.2d 977 (1964). Now, the Court fashions a constitutional rule that the police may engage in no custodial interrogation without additionally advising the accused that he has a right under the Fifth Amendment to the presence of counsel during interrogation and that, if he is without funds, counsel will be furnished him. When at any point during an interrogation the accused seeks affirmatively or impliedly to invoke his rights to silence or counsel, interrogation must be forgone or postponed. The Court further holds that failure to follow the new procedures requires inexorably the exclusion of any statement by the accused, as well as the fruits thereof. Such a strict constitutional specific inserted at the nerve center of crime detection may well kill the patient. Since there is at this time a paucity of information and an almost total lack of empirical knowledge on the practical operation of requirements truly comparable to those announced by the majority, I would be more restrained lest we go too far too fast.

Custodial interrogation has long been recognized as "undoubtedly an essential tool in effective law enforcement." Haynes v. State of Washington, 373 U.S. 503, 515, 83 S.Ct. 1336, 1344, 10 L.Ed.2d 513 (1963). Recognition of this fact should put us on guard against the promulgation of doctrinaire rules. Especially is this true where the Court finds that "the Constitution has prescribed" its holding and where the light of our past cases, from Hopt v. People of Territory of Utah, 110 U.S. 574, 4 S.Ct. 202, 28 L.Ed. 262 (1884), down to Haynes v. State of Washington, supra, is to the contrary. Indeed, even in *Escobedo* the Court never hinted that an affirmative "waiver" was a prerequisite to questioning; that the burden of proof as to waiver was on the prosecution; that the presence of counsel—absent a waiver—during interrogation was required; that a waiver can be withdrawn at the will of the accused; that counsel must be furnished during an accusatory stage to those unable to pay; nor that admissions and exculpatory statements are "confessions." To require all those things at one gulp should cause the

Court to choke over more cases than Crooker v. State of California, 357 U.S. 433, 78 S.Ct. 1287, 2 L.Ed.2d 1448 (1958), and Cicenia v. La Gay, 357 U.S. 504, 78 S.Ct. 1297, 2 L.Ed.2d 1523 (1958), which it expressly overrules today.

The rule prior to today—as Mr. Justice Goldberg, the author of the Court's opinion in *Escobedo*, stated it in Haynes v. Washington—depended upon "a totality of circumstances evidencing an involuntary . . . admission of guilt." 373 U.S., at 514, 83 S.Ct. at 1343. And he concluded:

"Of course, detection and solution of crime is, at best, a difficult and arduous task requiring determination and persistence on the part of all responsible officers charged with the duty of law enforcement. And, certainly, we do not mean to suggest that all interrogation of witnesses and suspects is impermissible. Such questioning is undoubtedly an essential tool in effective law enforcement. The line between proper and permissible police conduct and techniques and methods offensive to due process is, at best, a difficult one to draw, particularly in cases such as this where it is necessary to make fine judgments as to the effect of psychologically coercive pressures and inducements on the mind and will of an accused. . .

We are here impelled to the conclusion, from all of the facts presented, that the bounds of due process have been exceeded." Id., at 514–515, 83 S.Ct. at 1344.

I would continue to follow that rule. Under the "totality of circumstances" rule of which my Brother Goldberg spoke in *Haynes*, I would consider in each case whether the police officer prior to custodial interrogation added the warning that the suspect might have counsel present at the interrogation and, further, that a court would appoint one at his request it he was too poor to employ counsel. In the absence of warnings, the burden would be on the State to prove that counsel was knowingly and intelligently waived or that in the totality of the circumstances, including the failure to give the necessary warnings, the confession was clearly voluntary.

Rather than employing the arbitrary Fifth Amendment rule which the Court lays down I would follow the more pliable dictates of the Due Process Clauses of the Fifth and Fourteenth Amendments which we are accustomed to administering and which we know from our cases are effective instruments in protecting persons in police custody. In this way we would not be acting in the dark nor in one full sweep changing the traditional rules of custodial interrogation which this Court has for so long recognized as a justifiable and proper tool in balancing individual rights against the rights of society. It will be soon enough to go further when we are able to appraise with somewhat better accuracy the effect of such a holding.

I would affirm the convictions in Miranda v. Arizona, No. 759; Vignera v. New York, No. 760; and Westover v. United States, No. 761. In each of those cases I find from the circumstances no warrant for reversal. In California v. Stewart, No. 584, I would dismiss the writ of certiorari for want of a final judgment, 28 U.S.C. § 1257(3) (1964 ed.); but if the merits are to be reached I would affirm on the ground that the State failed to fulfill its burden, in the absence of a showing that appropriate warnings were given, of proving a waiver or a totality of circumstances showing voluntariness. Should there be a retrial, I would leave the State free to attempt to prove these elements.

• • •

MOZZETTI v. SUPERIOR COURT OF SACRAMENTO COUNTY *

Supreme Court of California, In Bank, 1971.
4 Cal.3d 699, 94 Cal.Rptr. 412, 484 P.2d 84.

• • •

---

* Prior to reading this, it is recommended that the reader review the following statutes: Penal Code § 1538.5, Vehicle Code §§ 22651, 22850.

MOZZETTI v. SUPERIOR COURT, SACRAMENTO COUNTY

MOSK, Justice.

When authorized by statute to remove from the highway and store a vehicle until the owner subsequently reclaims it, police officers routinely compile a complete inventory of the contents of the vehicle prior to storage. Petitioner, charged with possession of marijuana, seeks a writ of mandate to compel the respondent superior court to suppress evidence seized when police inventoried the contents of her automobile. We consider whether his common police practice constitutes an unreasonable search and seizure in violation of the Fourth Amendment.

On August 28, 1970, petitioner, while driving in Sacramento, was involved in a two-car collision. She sustained injuries in the accident and was promptly removed to the hospital by ambulance. When police arrived at the scene, they determined that petitioner's vehicle was blocking the roadway and arrangements were made to have the car towed to police storage, pursuant to Vehicle Code, sections 22651, subdivisions (b) and (g), and 22850.

In accordance with standard procedure, Officer Nichols of the Sacramento Police Department was instructed to prepare an inventory of the contents of petitioner's automobile prior to having it towed to police storage facilities. Nichols filled out an inventory form which listed the vehicle's equipment, such as mirrors and radio, and all of its contents in the front and back seats, the glove compartment, and the trunk.

In the course of his inventory, the officer saw a small suitcase on the back seat of the car. Finding the suitcase unlocked he opened it, apparently to determine if it contained any articles of value. Inside he found a plastic bag containing a quantity of marijuana. Because petitioner's automobile was a convertible, at the conclusion of the inventory several items found in the car's interior, including the suitcase, were locked in the trunk. The car was then towed to a police storage garage and the keys were later turned over to the petitioner. The marijuana, of course, was seized.

On October 13, a preliminary hearing was held and petitioner was bound over for trial on an information charging her with one count of possession of marijuana. Petitioner moved to suppress the evidence against her, the bag of marijuana found in the suitcase; the motion under Penal Code, section 1538.5 was denied. She now seeks mandamus to compel the suppression of the evidence on the ground that the inventory made of her automobile was a search without a warrant in violation of the Fourth Amendment.

. . .

. . . Two principal theories emerge as the basis of the doctrine urged by the People in the instant case to permit police to inventory the contents of vehicles lawfully in their custody under the removal and storage sections of the Vehicle Code. First, it is said that an "inventory" of the type conducted here and in the the cited cases is not a "search" as the term is used in the constitutional sense and, therefore, the procedure need not be justified within the rubric of the Fourth Amendment. Second, it is argued in the alternative that, even if an inventory is a search, it is reasonable and thus constitutional under the Fourth Amendment. We proceed to an analysis of both of these asserted justifications for the inventory procedure employed here.

In structuring the concept that an inventory is not police activity within the scope of the Fourth Amendment, the People reason that searches in the constitutional sense are conducted for the purpose of discovering evidence of crime or contraband to be used in criminal prosecutions. The sole purpose of the inventory in this case and in all routine police inventories, we are told, is to identify the contents of the vehicle incident to the assumption of police custody. Rather than ferreting out evidence of crime, police inventories serve to protect the owner of the vehicle, the police, and the storage bailee by identifying the contents of the vehicle and ensuring their proper care by the police and the storage bailee. The inventory is an aid to the vehicle owner because it provides him with a detailed list of the items taken into custody by the police and stored at the police garage, and it protects both the police and the storage bailee from subsequent unfounded claims of loss or damage.

In distinguishing between an inventory and a search, reliance is placed on People v. Norris (1968) supra, 262 Cal.App.2d Supp. 897, 68 Cal.Rptr. 582, which explains a source of the constricted definition of a searched espoused by the People: "In the case at bar the trial court made an express finding that the officer's activity [making an inventory of the contents of an automobile involved in a collision, prior to towing the vehicle to police storage] was not a search. . . . We believe that finding is supported by the law and the evidence and affirm primarily on that ground.

"Black's Law Dictionary (4th ed. 1951) defines a search as: 'An examination of a man's house or other buildings or premises, or of his person, with a view to the discovery of contraband or illicit or stolen property, or some evidence of guilt to be used in the prosecution of a criminal action for some crime or offense with which he is charged.'

"Webster's New International Dictionary (2d ed.) gives this definition: 'To subject to a thorough inspection for an article or articles presumably concealed.'

"This requirement that a search implies a seeking for contraband or evidence of guilt which has been concealed to use it in the prosecution of a criminal action . . . appears to be the factor that distinguishes [a search from an inventory]." (Id. at pp. 898–899, 68 Cal.Rptr. at p. 583.)

It is apparent from the foregoing and other decisions that the several Courts of Appeal have adhered to a circumscribed, semantic approach in defining the scope of the Fourth Amendment's prohibition against unreasonable searches and seizures. Such a concept was expressly rejected by the United States Supreme Court in Terry v. Ohio (1968) 392 U.S. 1, 88 S.Ct. 1868, 20 L.Ed.2d 889. Responding to the government's view that police stop-and-frisk activity was not within the scope of the Fourth Amendment, the court stated: "In our view the sounder course is to recognize that the Fourth Amendment governs all intrusions by agents of the public upon personal security, and to make the scope of the particular intrusion, in light of all the exigencies of the case, a central element in the analysis of reasonableness. [Citations.] This seems preferable to an approach which attributes too much significance to an overly technical definition of "search". . . .

"The distinctions of classical 'stop-and-frisk' theory thus serve to divert attention from the central inquiry under the Fourth Amendment—the reasonableness in all the circumstances of the particular governmental invasion of a citizen's personal security. 'Search' and 'seizure' are not talismans. We therefore reject the notions that the Fourth Amendment does not come into play at all as a limitation upon police conduct if the officers stop short of something called a 'technical arrest' or a 'full-blown search.'" (Id. at p. 18 fn. 15, p. 19, 88 S.Ct. at p. 1878.)

In applying the strictures of the Fourth Amendment to administrative searches in Camara v. Municipal Court (1967) 387 U.S. 523, 87 S.Ct. 1727, 18 L.Ed.2d 930, the Supreme Court unequivocally rejected any narrowing of the scope of the Fourth Amendment to "the typical policeman's search for the fruits and instrumentalities of crime. . . . It is surely anomalous to say that the individual and his private property are fully protected by the Fourth Amendment only when the individual is suspected of criminal behavior." (Id. at p. 530, 87 S.Ct. at p. 1731.) Instead, the court suggested a broader concept of the scope of the Fourth Amendment: "The basic purpose of this Amendment, as recognized in countless decisions of this Court, is to safeguard the privacy and security of individuals against arbitrary invasions by governmental officials. . . . [E]xcept in certain carefully defined classes of cases, a search of private property without proper consent is 'unreasonable' unless it has been authorized by a valid search warrant." (Id. at pp. 528–529, 87 S.Ct. at p. 1730.)

Moreover, language employed in decisions in both the Supreme Court and this court points toward rejection of the notion that a police inventory is not a search within the scope of the Fourth Amendment. (See Harris v. United States (1968) 390 U.S. 234, 236, 237, 88 S.Ct. 992, 19 L.Ed.2d 1067; People v. Williams (1967) 67 Cal.2d 226, 230, 60 Cal. Rptr. 472, 430 P.2d 30; People v. Grubb (1965) 63 Cal.2d 614, 618, 47 Cal.Rptr. 772, 408 P.2d 100.)

It seems undeniable that a routine police inventory of the contents of an automobile involves a substantial invasion into the privacy of the vehicle owner. Regardless of professed benevolent purposes and euphemistic explication, an inventory search involves a thorough exploration by the police into the private property of an individual. In that process suitcases, briefcases, sealed packages, purses—anything left open or closed within the vehicle—is subjected without limitation to the prying eyes of authorities. Merely because the police are not searching with the express purpose of finding evidence of crime, they are not exempt from the requirements of reasonableness set down in the Fourth Amendment. Constitutional rights may not be evaded through the route of finely honed but nonsubstantive distinctions.

Purely and simply the police inventory conducted here was a police search. Therefore, we disapprove those cases which have suggested that a police inventory may be validated without reference to the requirements of the Fourth Amendment.

We proceed to consider the People's alternative contention—that the inventory of the contents of petitioner's vehicle and the seizure of the bag of marijuana constituted a valid search and seizure under the Fourth Amendment.

* * *

In the instant case, the exigent circumstances which justify the warrantless search are said to arise out of the custody and control of petitioner's automobile by the police, as authorized by Vehicle Code, sections 22651 and 22850. The People contend the inventory search into the closed case was reasonably necessary to protect petitioner's personal property from loss or damage and to protect the police and storage bailee from unfounded tort claims. When subjected to analysis, this rationale for the search and seizure is superficial and without substantial merit in an area of constitutional protection.

The interests of a vehicle owner are said to be protected by police inventory because the procedure provides the owner with a detailed list of the articles taken into custody by the police, an itemization he can use in making valid claims for loss or damage against the police and the storage bailee. Also, the inventory brings to light articles of special value or of a perishable nature which might require unusual care by the police and the storage bailee.

This contention is rebutted by recognition of the vehicle owner's countervailing interest in maintaining the privacy of his personal effects and preventing anyone, including the police, from searching suitcases, and other closed containers and areas in his automobile at the time the police lawfully remove it to storage. In weighing the necessity of the inventory search as protection of the owner's property against the owner's rights under the Fourth Amendment, we observe that items of value left in an automobile to be stored by the police may be adequately protected merely by rolling up the windows, locking the vehicle doors and returning the keys to the owner. The owner himself, if required to leave his car temporarily, could do no more to protect his property. In the instant case, because the automobile involved was a convertible, adequate protection of valuables could be achieved by raising the top or, if necessary, by moving visible items, like the small suitcase, into the trunk for safekeeping.

We have no doubt that the police, in the course of such valid protective measures, may take note of any personal property in plain sight within the automobile being taken into custody. Any objects clearly visible without probing—including the suitcase in this instance—may be listed in an inventory or other police report. (See Harris v. United States (1968) supra, 390 U.S. 234, 236, 88 S.Ct. 992, 19 L.Ed.2d 1067. What concerns us here is the reasonableness of the search *into* the closed suitcase.

It is significant that all but two of the Court of Appeal opinions relied upon by the People as authority for the inventory search of vehicles in lawful police custody involved inventories made after the driver of the vehicle was arrested. (Veh.Code, § 22651, subd. (h).) Thus, in those circumstances, unlike the instant case, the drivers of the vehicles were on the scene and the police could have readily ascertained their preference for the care of their personal property. There is little doubt that all of them would have preferred, for protection of their property, that the police simply close the windows and lock the doors, rather than search the contents of their cars. Nevertheless, in not one of those cases did the Court of Appeal suggest that the police might have inquired of the owner what he wanted done to safeguard his property. Thus we find unpersuasive the contention made by the People that the inventory of contents not within plain sight is reasonable because it is necessary to protect the property for the benefit of the vehicle owner.

The contention that the police inventory search is necessary to protect the police and the storage bailee from tort claims is even less convincing. Several of the Court of Appeal opinions cited by the People, beginning with People v. Roth (1968) supra, 261 Cal.App.2d 430, 68 Cal.Rptr. 49, have suggested that the police, as involuntary bailees of automobiles taken into custody, have the civil obligation to inventory the contents of such vehicles for the protection of the owners. This proposition is without legal foundation. While the police are involuntary bailees within the definition of Civil Code, section 1815, the statutory duty of care imposed on such bailees is limited by Civil Code, sections 1845 and 1846 which provide that an involuntary bailee has only the obligation to use "slight care for the thing deposited." Since the police are not liable for ordinary negligence in handling automobile contents it cannot be urged seriously that they fail to adequately fulfill their duty by rolling up the windows and locking the doors of vehicles taken into custody.

• • •

It is clear that mere legal custody of an automobile by the police does not create some new possessory right to justify the search of that vehicle. In Cooper v. California (1967) supra, 386 U.S. 58, 61, 87 S.Ct. 788, 17 L.Ed.2d 730, the United States Supreme Court pointed out that " 'lawful custody of an automobile does not of itself dispense with constitutional requirements of searches thereafter made of it.' " The court indicated that "the reason for and nature of the custody may constitutionally justify the search," and it held that custody of an automobile held as evidence of crime and pending forfeiture was such custody. And in Chambers v. Maroney (1970) supra, 399 U.S. 42, 90 S.Ct. 1975, 26 L.Ed.2d 419, the Supreme Court validated a search of an automobile in lawful police custody only because there was probable cause to believe it contained weapons and stolen money.

In People v. Burke (1964) supra, 61 Cal.2d 575, 39 Cal.Rptr. 531, 394 P.2d 67, the police had lawful custody of the automobile of a suspect arrested on suspicion of burglary. Nevertheless, this court invalidated a search of the vehicle at the police storage lot. We explicitly rejected the People's contention that the authority to remove and store the vehicle under Vehicle Code, sections 22651, subdivision (h), and 22850 encompassed authority to search: "The officers were authorized by these sections to remove defendant's car from the highway and impound it but the sections do not purport to authorize the making of a search." (Id. at p. 580, 39 Cal.Rptr. at p. 534, 394 P.2d at p. 70.)

MOZZETTI v. SUPERIOR COURT, SACRAMENTO COUNTY

In a final effort to justify the search in the instant case, the People refer us to the recent United States Supreme Court decision in Wyman v. James (1971) 400 U.S. 309, 91 S.Ct. 381, 27 L.Ed.2d 408. In that case, the court held that conditioning public welfare assistance on the consent of recipients to occasional home visits by social workers was constitutional and did not involve unreasonable searches under the Fourth Amendment. In the course of its opinion, the court noted that a warrant procedure might provide little protection in a welfare context. The People contend in the case at bar that a warrant requirement would be similarly inappropriate. The contention is specious.

It is undeniable that, under the facts before us, as in the inventory context generally, there could be no basis upon which a magistrate might issue a search warrant. The inventory, by its nature, involves a random search of the articles left in an automobile taken into police custody; the police are looking for nothing in particular and everything in general. But this fact does not justify the search and establish its constitutionality. To the contrary, a random police search is the precise invasion of privacy which the Fourth Amendment was intended to prohibit. We are not dealing here with a case remotely analogous to *Wyman*, which involved visits by caseworkers in a civil setting and within the peculiar context of the welfare system.

We conclude that there were no circumstances in the instant case to justify the search of the contents of petitioner's automobile without a warrant. The search was not incident to lawful arrest, based on probable cause to believe the vehicle contained contraband, or justified by the peculiar nature of the police custody involved. Nor were there exigent circumstances which made the search reasonable and necessary. The line of authority in the Courts of Appeal which purports to validate an inventory of articles not in plain sight is disapproved.

Let a peremptory writ of mandate issue as prayed.

WRIGHT, C. J., and PETERS, TOBRINER and SULLIVAN, JJ., concur.

McCOMB, Justice:

I dissent. I would deny the writ. (Cal. Const. art. VI, § 13.)

BURKE, Justice (concurring).

I concur with the result reached by the majority herein, for I agree that the opening of petitioner's suitcase and inspection of its contents constituted an unreasonable search, violating his reasonable expectation of privacy. (People v. Bradley, 1 Cal.3d 80, 84, 81 Cal.Rptr. 457, 460 P.2d 129; People v. Edwards, 71 Cal.2d 1096, 1104–1105, 80 Cal. Rptr. 633, 458 P.2d 713.) I would emphasize, however, that our decision in no way interferes with or impinges upon the customary authority of the police to inspect and inventory all items of personal property left in plain sight within an automobile or other vehicle in police custody.

As pointed out in the numerous Court of Appeal cases cited by the majority, the routine practice of making such inventory inspections is reasonably necessary to safeguard the owner's property from loss or damage, and to protect the police and storage bailee from unfounded claims. Although, as the majority point out, the foregoing considerations do not furnish the police an excuse for rummaging through closed suitcases or sealed packages, the police do have the authority, and indeed the responsibility, to inspect and inventory all items of personal property in plain sight within the vehicle and, if necessary, to lock these items in the trunk or transfer them to some other secure place for safekeeping. If, in the course of such activity, the police observe contraband or other incriminatory evidence they may seize it, for it is well established that "objects falling in the plain view of an officer who has a right to be in the position to have that view are subject to seizure and may be introduced in evidence. [Citations.]" (Harris v. United States, 390 U.S. 234, 236, 88 S.Ct. 992, 993, 19 L.Ed.2d

1067.) The "plain sight" rule recognizes that no citizen has a reasonable expectation of privacy with respect to unconcealed items within a vehicle in police custody. (See People v. Bradley, supra, 1 Cal.3d 80, 85, 81 Cal.Rptr. 457, 460 P.2d 129.)

• • •

PEOPLE v. AMOS *
Court of Appeal, Second District, Division 4, 1977.
70 Cal.App.3d 562, 139 Cal.Rptr. 30.

KINGSLEY, Associate Justice.

Appellant was charged with robbery, "use" of a firearm and it was alleged that he had suffered three prior felony convictions. He pled not guilty, denied the priors and his 1538.5 motion was denied. Appellant was found guilty of attempted robbery in the second degree. The allegation concerning use of a firearm was found not to be true. Appellant appeals from the judgment of conviction.

At about 3:45 a. m., near Hollywood Boulevard, Martin Smith flagged down two policemen to tell them he had been robbed by a man with a gun one-half hour before. He described the robber as a male Negro with black hair, brown eyes, between 25 and 30 years of age, about 5 feet 8 inches in height, and wearing a three-quarter length brown leather jacket. The robbery had taken place on the street close to the Roxy Motel. The police went to the motel and saw a man who might be the suspect, but Mr. Smith confirmed that this was not the man who robbed him.

The man told the police that he knew about the robbery, that it was committed about 45 minutes earlier. He said the robber was a man named Tony, that Tony lived in room 48 of the Roxy Motel, and Tony had committed another robbery with a gun earlier that evening. The man said Tony knew the police were there, and Tony might attempt to use the gun on the police. The man told Officer Hall, "You'd better watch out because Tony is crazy." Smith told Officer Hall that during the robbery he heard a person call, "Tony," and in his opinion the person was yelling to the robber. In Officer Hall's opinion the victim's statement and the man's statements corroborated each other because the statements agreed as to the time of robbery, the place of the robbery, and the use of the gun.

Officer Hall and his partner went to room 48, heard some voices within, kicked in the door and arrested appellant. Appellant was taken to the police vehicle where Smith saw appellant and stated, "That is the man who robbed me."

In describing the robbery Smith said he parked across from the Roxy Motel and got out of his car. He had planned to buy a book. Appellant pointed a gun at his neck and Smith tried to memorize appellant's face. Smith pretended to be deaf and dumb, and then when people started walking on the street, Smith walked along with them. Smith walked into the motel, knocked on the door of a room and explained his situation to some occupants. When he looked down the hall he saw appellant. The occupants let Smith stay in their room and he could not call the police because the motel switchboard was closed. He hid there a half hour and then went out and found the police.

Prior to the arrest the police told the man who told them about Tony to stay with Smith by the police vehicle. The police then made the arrest and when they brought appellant to the vehicle the man already was gone. Smith said the other man "walked up the street towards Hollywood." Then Smith spontaneously exited the vehicle and identified appellant.

I

Appellant argues that there is no probable cause for arrest where the informant's relia-

---

* Prior to reading this case it is recommended that the reader review the following statute: Penal Code § 813.

bility is not established. In the case at bar the police first learned the details of the crime and the description of the robber from the victim of the crime, Smith, and not from the anonymous informant. Victims of a criminal act, absent some circumstances that would cast doubt upon their information, should be considered reliable. Probable cause will not be provided by conclusionary information or anonymous informants, but neither a previous demonstration of reliability nor subsequent corroboration is ordinarily necessary when witnesses to or victims of criminal activities report their observations in detail to the authorities. (People v. Ramey (1976) 16 Cal.3d 263, 269, 127 Cal.Rptr. 629, 545 P.2d 1333.) Smith provided the police with the details of the crime, a description of defendant and also told them someone yelled the name "Tony" at the robber. This alone may have been sufficient probable cause for arrest.

However, the police also had corroborative information from an anonymous informant. When the police went to the area of the crime, the Roxy Motel, the police then interrogated a man who said Tony in room 48 had committed another crime with a gun earlier that evening. The information given by the victim, Mr. Smith, when combined with the information given by the informant, provided ample probable cause for appellant's arrest.

In People v. Balassy (1973), 30 Cal.App.3d 614, 621, 106 Cal.Rptr. 461, it was noted that an unreliable informant's statements may be corroborated by those of another, if the two informers were interviewed independently, at a different time and place. Here, the informant and the victim were interviewed separately, and the stories they had told were each corroborative of the other. Each provided information to the effect that the robber's name was "Tony" and that he had committed a robbery earlier with a gun. In the case at bar the evidence of probable cause was far stronger than in *Balassy* because here the information came from a victim and an informant and not from two anonymous informants. As we have indicated earlier the law recognizes a higher probability of credibility in the information provided by a victim than that provided by an ordinary anonymous informant.

II

Appellant argues that the officers violated Penal Code section 844 in their entry for arrest. Appellant argues that merely because the police had been informed that he had a gun without more was insufficient grounds for dispensing with the demand requirements of Penal Code section 844. (People v. Bennetto (1974) 10 Cal.3d 695, 700, 111 Cal.Rptr. 699, 517 P.2d 1163.) The announcement requirements of Penal Code section 844 are excused when there are reasonable grounds to believe that compliance would endanger the officers or frustrate arrest. (People v. Dumas (1973) 9 Cal.3d 871, 878, 879, 109 Cal.Rptr. 304, 512 P.2d 1208.) When the police made their entry in the case at bar they knew not only that the robber possessed a gun, as in *Bennetto*, but that the robber had also used a gun just 45 minutes before to commit a robbery. They had also been informed by a man that the appellant knew the police were around and that he might use the gun on the police. The man also warned the police to "watch out" because Tony was "crazy." This was more than sufficient ground for the police to believe they would be endangering themselves by complying with the demand requirements of Penal Code section 844. The police were not required to elicit the informant's curriculum vitae to determine whether the informant's credentials were sufficiently impressive so that the police properly could accept his characterization of appellant as "crazy." Compliance with 844 is excused if police have reason to believe that a weapon will be used against them and the reasoning is based on specific facts. (People v. Dumas, supra (1973) 9 Cal.3d 878, 109 Cal.Rptr. 304, 512 P.2d 1208.) Here the police had every reason to believe that the appellant might shoot them if they made the statutory announcement, and their belief was supported by specific facts.

The judgment is affirmed.

MAJOR CASE LAW OPINIONS

PEOPLE v. BEAGLE II *
Supreme Court of California, In Bank, 1972.
6 Cal.3d 441, 99 Cal.Rptr. 313, 492 P.2d 1.

WRIGHT, Chief Justice.

Defendant Harvey Lynn Beagle II was convicted by a jury of one count of attempted arson (Pen.Code, § 451a) and one count of arson (Pen.Code, § 448a). A prior conviction of having issued a check without sufficient funds (Pen.Code, § 476a) was charged and admitted but the judgment reflects no disposition of the allegation. Defendant was sentenced to the state prison for the term prescribed by law.

Although we reject all of the many contentions presented by defendant on appeal from the judgment, we nevertheless conclude, inter alia, that a trial judge must exercise his discretion to prevent impeachment of a witness by the introduction of evidence of a prior felony conviction when the probative value of such evidence is substantially outweighed by the risk of undue prejudice. (See Evidence Code, § 352.)

The charges stem from fires independently originating in buildings housing neighboring business establishments, Rudy's Keg, a bar, and north of the bar, Lewin's Furniture Store. Both buildings were located on Vineland Avenue in North Hollywood. Other commercial enterprises are also situated on Vineland south from Rudy's Keg. Behind such establishments are open areas and areas occupied by other structures, including a building in which defendant maintained an apartment.

On May 25, 1969, Rudolph Oravsky, owner of Rudy's Keg, ordered defendant to leave the premises when defendant became intoxicated and obnoxious while a patron in the bar. Defendant attempted to induce another patron to leave with him and when met with a refusal, defendant stated: "Well, come on and go with me anyway. I want to go into Los Angeles and hire a Mexican to firebomb this place for $25.00." This conversation was overheard by a third person.

During the early afternoon of July 1, Oravsky was present in a barbershop adjacent to Rudy's Keg and defendant approached and asked if he could have a drink at the bar. Oravsky replied: "Definitely not . . . this is permanent." Defendant, who was obviously disappointed, responded: "Well, Okay," and left the barbershop. About 9 p. m. of that same day while Oravsky was in the bar he heard a noise which sounded to him like the explosion of a large firecracker. He went out through the parking lot to an alley in the rear and was able to see a fire on the roof of the building housing his bar. He climbed to the roof with a water hose and succeeded in extinguishing two small fires. There he discovered and removed a Pepsi-Cola bottle containing a small amount of gasoline and a wick. During the period of time Oravsky was at the rear and on the roof of the building, he noticed nothing unusual at Lewin's but he did see defendant's car parked near his apartment.

Oravsky returned to his bar and placed a telephone call to the police. Shortly thereafter he telephoned the police a second time and during this call Mr. Duffy, who had entered the bar during the interval between the two calls, noticed the lights of a car as it appeared to turn into the alley and stop. The car, similar to defendant's vehicle, proceeded slowly down the alley and then disappeared behind Lewin's. Both men went into the parking area and Oravsky then observed for the first time that a wooden door facing the alley on the Lewin's building was aflame. He also noticed that defendant's car was no longer in the area. Oravsky called the fire department as Duffy attempted without success to extinguish the flames. Oravsky smelled gasoline at the scene of the fire at Lewin's building and Duffy testified that the fire burned as if it

---

* Prior to reading this case it is recommended that the reader review the following statutes: Penal Code §§ 448a, 451a, 476a, Evidence Code §§ 787, 788.

had been ignited by the use of gasoline. The blaze caused approximately $100,000 in damages to Lewin's before it was extinguished.

A fire department arson investigator attributed the fire at Rudy's Keg to the ignition of a flammable liquid placed on the roof of the building. He could find no natural or accidental cause for the fire at Lewin's but a full and conclusive investigation was precluded by reason of the extensive damage.

About 10 p. m. on the evening of the fires Officer Jones went to defendant's apartment. He was admitted by defendant's wife who told him that her husband had left the apartment two to three hours earlier. While there Jones saw a cap from a gasoline can. Approximately five minutes after Jones arrived at the apartment, defendant returned home. His hands smelled of gasoline as did stains on his shoes and pants. Defendant told the officer that he worked at a service station and thereafter had been to a bar for a few beers. Jones arrested defendant and found a number of books of paper matches in his pockets.

After defendant had been removed to a police vehicle, an officer in defendant's presence conducted a field test for the flammability of the liquid in the bottle recovered from the roof by Oravsky. The officer poured out a small quantity of the contents and held a match to it. The liquid ignited rapidly. At this point defendant stated: "You can't arrest me for arson because the bottle didn't break." Prior to this statement the police in defendant's presence had made no mention of the discovery of the bottle nor had they questioned defendant as to either fire.

Defendant testified that on the day of the fires he had had an "early morning" medical appointment and "had taken off work for this at 12:00 noon." Afterwards he went to the Big H, a cocktail lounge, where he consumed a few beers. He returned home about 2 p. m. and later during the afternoon he went to the barbershop to have his hair cut. About 4:30 p. m. he returned to the Big H cocktail lounge and thereafter went to a service station to work during a shift change. Around 6:30 p. m. he returned home with a can of gasoline and a ladder as he planned to do some painting. He poured some of the gasoline into a cardboard carton prior to softening his paint brushes. As the carton began to leak he emptied the gasoline contained therein into a drain and directed his wife to return the ladder and the remaining gasoline to the service station. About 8 p. m. defendant drove his car "across the street" to the Big H and there he consumed several more beers. While at the Big H he unsuccessfully attempted to telephone his home and, becoming worried, decided to return home. There were fire engines in the vicinity and Vineland was blocked off. He parked his car at a nearby market and walked to his apartment where he was placed under arrest for arson. He admitted that he had been ejected from Rudy's Keg earlier in the year and that he saw the bottle in the possession of the police officers.

Defendant's wife testified, corroborating and contradicting defendant's testimony in certain particulars. She corroborated generally the frustrated attempt at painting but gave testimony inconsistent with defendant's as to the approximate time of his departure from the apartment.

Defendant contends that neither count is supported by sufficient evidence. The evidence is virtually all circumstantial; however, the very nature of the crime of arson ordinarily dictates that the evidence will be circumstantial. (See People v. Andrews (1965) 234 Cal.App.2d 69, 75, 44 Cal.Rptr. 94.) In any event, the evidence against defendant is clearly substantial. As to the fire at Rudy's Keg, there was proof of virtually every factor the courts have relied upon in affirming arson convictions where the sufficiency of the evidence has been challenged. . . .

In addition to his clearly unmeritorious challenge of the sufficiency of the evidence on the Rudy's Keg count, defendant contends that there is no evidence of motive as to the Lewin's fire. Motive, of course, is not an element of arson but the absence thereof may make proof of the essential elements less persuasive. At least two possible motives are suggested either of which the jury could reasonably have found to be present: diversion of suspicion or the hope by defendant that Rudy's Keg because of its proximity to Lewin's would become ignited in some manner from the Lewin's blaze.

Viewing all of the evidence and considering that there are possible innocent explanations for some of the circumstances, we conclude that there is substantial evidence in support of the verdicts reached by the jury. (See, e. g., People v. Reilly (1970) 3 Cal.3d 421, 424–425, 90 Cal.Rptr. 417, 475 P.2d 649.)

Defendant also contends that he was denied due process of law because the prosecution failed to conduct a more complete investigation as to the cause of or reason for the fires. Defendant, weaving a web of conjecture, argues that the prosecution neglected to investigate the possibility that the fires were deliberately set in order to perpetrate a fraud or frauds upon insurance companies. The record does not reveal the extent of the official investigation but it does reveal that such investigation did produce overwhelming evidence of defendant's guilt. The existence of circumstances under which insurance-fraud fire or fires might be inferred is, at best, only a remote conjecture. Contrary to defendant's contentions Eleazer v. Superior Court (1970) 1 Cal.3d 847, 851–854, 83 Cal.Rptr. 586, 464 P.2d 42, does not establish a standard of judicial review of official pretrial investigations nor does it impose a general duty on prosecutorial officials to serve as defense investigators.

On cross-examination defendant was asked about, and admitted, a 1965 felony conviction for issuing a check without sufficient funds (Pen.Code, § 476a). The jury was instructed on the limited purpose for which the prior conviction was admitted. Defendant contends that since this conviction bears no necessary relationship to either the charged offenses or his veracity, impeachment by the receipt of such evidence constitutes an improper restriction on his freedom to choose whether to testify and constitutes a denial of due process. Defendant misconstrues both the law governing impeachment by prior felony convictions and the nature of his prior offense.

Two provisions of the Evidence Code control the admission of felony convictions for impeachment. Section 788 provides, with four exceptions not here relevant, that: "For the purpose of attacking the credibility of a witness, it *may* be shown by the examination of the witness or by the record of the judgment that he has been convicted of a felony. . . ." (Italics added.) Section 352 grants the trial judge discretion to exclude otherwise admissible evidence "if its probative value is substantially outweighed by the probability that its admission will . . . create substantial danger of undue prejudice. . . ."

• • •

Section 788 is an exception, indeed the only exception, to the rule that "evidence of specific instances of his conduct relevant only as tending to prove a trait of his character is inadmissible to attack or support the credibility of a witness." (Evid. Code, § 787.) In providing this exception the Legislature used the permissive word "may" rather than a mandatory word such as "shall." We conclude that the choice of language leaves the trial court with discretion to exclude proof of prior felony convictions offered in impeachment. Such interpretation is not unique. In construing a similar provision (14 D.C.Code, § 305), the United States Court of Appeals for the District of Columbia Circuit concluded: "[It] is not written in mandatory terms. [Fn. omitted.] It says, in effect, that the conviction 'may,' as opposed to 'shall,' be admitted; and we think the choice of words in this instance is significant. The trial court is not *required* to allow impeachment by prior conviction every time a defendant takes the stand in his own defense. The statute, in our view, leaves room for the operation of a sound judicial discretion to play upon the circumstances as they unfold in a particular case."

• • •

In the instant case defendant made no objection to the receipt of evidence of his prior conviction on the grounds now urged. Such omission is understandable in light of the appellate court decisions heretofore cited. (See People v. De Santiago (1969) 71 Cal.2d 18, 22–28, 76 Cal.Rptr. 809, 453 P.2d 353.) Accordingly we have examined defendant's prior felony conviction and conclude on the merits that it was properly admitted. An essential element of the crime of issuing a check without sufficient funds is intent to defraud. (Pen.Code, § 476a.) The nature of the offense is not one likely to inflame passions or present a close analogy to the current charges. The conviction was comparatively recent and represents only a single offense (cf. People v. Chacon (1968) 69 Cal.2d 765, 777–778, 73 Cal.Rptr. 10, 447 P.2d 106). In short, the probative value of this prior felony conviction was substantially high and the risk of undue prejudice was minimized. We conclude that reasonable exercise of judicial discretion by the trial court could not have justified the exclusion of such evidence.

• • •

The judgment is affirmed.

McCOMB, PETERS, TOBRINER, MOSK, BURKE and SULLIVAN, JJ., concur.

PEOPLE v. DUMAS *

Supreme Court of California, In Bank, 1974.
9 Cal.3d 871, 109 Cal.Rptr. 304, 512 P.2d 1208.

• • •

On May 11, 1970, officers of the Los Angeles Police Department obtained a warrant to search defendant's apartment, including "all trash cans, storage areas, garages and carports which are assigned to and/or used by occupants of the aforesaid apartment," for certain stolen railroad bonds and bank checks and certain narcotics and narcotics paraphernalia. The warrant issued pursuant to a police officer's affidavit which asserted that a confidential informant had reported he recently saw these articles in defendant's possession. Neither the warrant nor the affidavit made reference to defendant's automobile or to any other vehicle.

Equipped with the warrant, a group of police officers converged on the apartment described therein and forcibly entered without announcing their authority or purpose. Inside they found defendant and a young woman, and arrested defendant immediately. The subsequent search of the apartment revealed none of the articles named in the warrant. In the course of the search, however, the officers discovered an automobile registration certificate in the name of defendant and a set of automobile keys. An automobile meeting the description on the registration certificate was then found parked in the street two lots (about 100 feet) away from defendant's apartment building. The officer in charge of the operation, who testified he suspected the automobile might contain the items specified in the search warrant, ordered it searched without obtaining defendant's consent. In the trunk of the vehicle the officers found the stolen securities, a loaded revolver, and an aluminum foil packet apparently containing some narcotic substance.

Defendant first contends the search warrant in question is defective because the supporting affidavit does not clearly establish the reliability of the confidential informant. This objection is not well taken. The affidavit states that the informant had provided information to the United States Secret Service "On one separate occasion that resulted in three (3) arrests being made of three persons and the information resulted in three persons being held to answer at a

---

* Prior to reading this case it is recommended that the reader review the following statute: Penal Code § 1531.

commissioner's hearing and are now awaiting trial in the U.S. District Court." In order to establish the reliability of an informant it is not necessary to relate that his prior information led to convictions. It is sufficient that the prior information was accurate or was "of such substance as to cause a reasonable person to conclude that it is reliable." (People v. Swayze (1963) 220 Cal.App.2d 476, 490, 34 Cal.Rptr. 5, 11.) In People v. Prewitt (1959) 52 Cal.2d 330, 341 P.2d 1, we recognized that information from an informant who had twice previously provided police with tips that had led to arrests and trial was sufficiently reliable to establish probable cause for an arrest. Prior information that had proved accurate in leading to two valid arrests was also held sufficient to establish reliability in People v. Richardson (1970) 6 Cal.App.3d 70, 85 Cal. Rptr. 607. If the fact of prior valid arrests of suspects is a sufficient index of an informant's reliability, the fact of a finding of probable cause to hold suspects by a federal magistrate is even more significant. (See People v. Superior Court (1972) 6 Cal.3d 704, 714, 100 Cal.Rptr. 319, 493 P.2d 1183.)

The affidavit also set forth substantial corroboration of the information provided by the informant. The informant stated he had seen Delaware, Lackawanna and Western Railroad bonds in defendant's possession and that defendant advised him the bonds had a face value of approximately $25,000 and were stolen. Defendant also told the informant, as of May 7, 1970, that he had been in possession of the bonds for eight weeks. Independent police investigation established that 33 Delaware, Lackawanna and Western Railroad bonds had been stolen between February 27 and March 2 of that year. Thus, independent investigation corroborated an important detail in the informant's report, and added to the probability that his information was reliable.

Defendant's second contention is that the officers violated Penal Code section 1531 in failing to announce their authority or purpose before forcibly entering his apartment. Section 1531 provides: "The officer may break open any outer or inner door or window of a house, or any part of a house, or anything therein, to execute the warrant, if after notice of his authority and purpose, he is refused admittance." We have held that strict compliance with demand and notice requirements may be excused "if the specific facts known to the officer before his entry are sufficient to support his good faith belief that compliance will increase his peril, frustrate the arrest, or permit the destruction of evidence." (People v. Tribble (1971) 4 Cal.3d 826, 833, 94 Cal.Rptr. 613, 617, 484 P.2d 589, 593; People v. Gastelo (1967) 67 Cal.2d 586, 587–588, 63 Cal.Rptr. 10, 432 P.2d 706; People v. Maddox (1956) 46 Cal.2d 301, 306, 294 P.2d 6.) In the present case, the officer in charge of the search operation testified at the section 1538.5 hearing he had been informed by the confidential informant that defendant possessed several firearms in his apartment and that he invariably answered the door with a loaded gun in his hand. The informant told the officer he had personally observed defendant answer the door in this manner.

The case presents somewhat unusual facts in that the People attempt to justify noncompliance with announcement requirements on the basis of circumstances of which the officers were aware *before* approaching defendant's residence to effect entry. In the typical case the officer discovers the facts that justify immediate entry only *after* approaching the residence. In People v. Maddox (1956) supra, 46 Cal.2d 301, 294 P.2d 6, for example, an officer who had knocked on the door of defendant's home to make a narcotics arrest heard a voice say "Wait a minute" and also heard the sound of retreating footsteps. We held it was not unreasonable for the officer to believe that further delay in entry would facilitate secretion or destruction of evidence. Likewise in People v. Tribble (1971) supra, 4 Cal.3d 826, 832–833, 94 Cal.Rptr. 613, 484 P.2d 589, officers heard running footsteps inside the defendant's residence as they approached to make entry. This perception, combined with the officers' discovery of a firearm in an automobile in defendant's driveway and their knowledge of the violent character of the crimes of which defendant was accused, was sufficient to excuse compliance with section 844.

In some exceptional circumstances, however, we have upheld unannounced entry on the basis of information received by the officers prior to arrival at the scene of the entry. In People v. Smith (1966) 63 Cal.2d 779, 797, 48 Cal.Rptr. 382, 409 P.2d 222, and People v. Gilbert (1965) 63 Cal.2d 690, 707, 47 Cal.Rptr. 909, 408 P.2d 365, the officers had good cause to believe that the persons they were seeking were armed and that they had shot—and in one case killed—police officers. In People v. Hammond (1960) 54 Cal.2d 846, 854, 9 Cal.Rptr. 233, 357 P.2d 289, unannounced entry was also excused on the basis of prior information that the defendant was presently armed and was under the influence of heroin. The proposition that unannounced entry may be excused on the basis of information received before reaching the location at which entry is to be effected, when the information reasonably leads the officer to believe that compliance would increase his peril or frustrate the arrest, has been reaffirmed more recently in Duke v. Superior Court (1969) 1 Cal.3d 314, 323, 82 Cal.Rptr. 481, 462 P.2d 10. The ability of police officers to rely on such prior information in deciding to effect an unannounced entry is also clearly established by People v. De Santiago (1969) 71 Cal.2d 18, 28–29, 76 Cal.Rptr. 809, 816, 453 P.2d 353, 360, in which we stated that no announcement is required "where officers have obtained particular information which leads them to reasonably conclude that the occupants of an apartment or residence have specifically resolved to effect disposal in the event of police intrusion or have made specific preparations in that regard."

Thus, compliance with the announcement requirements may be excused where police officers, on the basis of previously obtained information, supported by facts occurring on the scene, are aware at the time they approach particular premises to effect entry that they are faced with an emergency situation as defined in our decisions.

In the present case the information provided by the confidential informant that defendant possessed several firearms is insufficient by itself to excuse compliance with section 1531. We have recognized that one of the primary purposes of section 1531, in addition to the protection of individual privacy, is to prevent possible violent responses that might be aroused in a startled and fearful householder suddenly confronted with unknown persons breaking into his home for unannounced reasons. (Duke v. Superior Court (1969) supra, 1 Cal.3d 314, 321, 82 Cal.Rptr. 481, 462 P.2d 10.) The danger that such a confrontation will result in serious injury or death to the occupant, police officers, or innocent bystanders is obviously intensified when the householder is in possession of a firearm. Thus, where the police are aware of such a weapon, the case for requiring them to give notice of their authority and purpose becomes more rather than less compelling.

• • •

In the present case, however, the police had reliable information that defendant not only possessed weapons but habitually answered the door armed with a firearm. They could reasonably infer from this activity that a substantial possibility existed he would employ deadly force in order to prevent this apprehension. As the officers approached the location to be searched, they became aware of no further circumstances that would defeat this inference. They could therefore reasonably conclude at the time of entry that they were faced with an emergency and that compliance with the announcement requirements would substantially increase their peril. On these facts we hold that the officers' failure to comply with section 1531 does not give rise to an application of the exclusionary rule.

Defendant's final contention, that the search of his automobile was not supported by the warrant and was constitutionally unjustified in the absence of a warrant, requires somewhat more extensive analysis.

* * *

The warrant obtained by the police officers in this case does not support their search of defendant's automobile. The constitutional requirement that a warrant "particularly describ[e] the place to be searched" compels the conclusion that the privilege to search created by a warrant does not extend beyond the place or places described therein. Thus in Skelton v. Superior Court (1969) supra, 1 Cal.3d 144, 155, 81 Cal.Rptr. 613, 620, 460 P.2d 485, 492, we stated that "We are mindful of the general rule that when a search is made pursuant to a warrant, the search and seizure are limited by the terms of the warrant. Thus only the premises described in the warrant may be searched and only the property described in the warrant may be seized."

* * *

We must therefore determine whether the circumstances of the case justified a warrantless search. With respect to this issue, the People carry the burden of proving the search reasonable. (Badillo v. Superior Court (1956) 46 Cal.2d 269, 272, 294 P.2d 23.)

The pattern of prior decisions suggests that one of the most crucial determinants of the validity of warrantless searches is the nature of the place subjected to search. This pattern has been created by the interweaving of constitutional concepts with fundamental human needs and expectations. The courts have implicitly recognized that man requires some sanctuary in which his freedom to escape the intrusions of society is all but absolute. Such places have been held inviolate from warrantless search except in emergencies of overriding magnitude, such as pursuit of a fleeing felon (Warden v. Hayden (1967) 387 U.S. 294, 87 S.Ct. 1642, 18 L.Ed.2d 782) or the necessity of action for the preservation of life or property (People v. Roberts (1956) 47 Cal.2d 374, 377, 303 P.2d 721; People v. Sirhan (1972) 7 Cal.3d 710, 735–741, 102 Cal.Rptr. 385, 497 P.2d 1121;

cf. Chimel v. California (1969) supra, 395 U.S. 752, 89 S.Ct. 2034, 23 L.Ed.2d 685.) Certain other places carry with them an expectation of privacy which, although considerable, is less intense and insistent. These places may be searched upon probable cause alone under circumstances of less demanding urgency. Still other sites are regarded as so public in nature that searches are justifiable without any particular showing of cause or exigency. This hierarchy of protection arises not from the application of differing constitutional standards to various locales, but rather from an application of a single standard of reasonableness to all places in accordance with a fundamental understanding that a particular intrusion into one domain of human existence seriously threatens personal security, while the same intrusion into another domain does not.

The United States Supreme Court has held that homes and offices fall into the first category, while automobiles fit into the second. In Carroll v. United States (1925) supra, 267 U.S. 132, 45 S.Ct. 280, 69 L.Ed. 543, the court ruled that where police officers, confronted with unforeseeable circumstances, have probable cause to believe an automobile contains articles entitled to be seized, and where delay would enhance the possibility the articles would be destroyed or placed beyond the reach of the officers, an immediate warrantless search of the vehicle is justified. In similar circumstances, however, the court barred the warrantless search of a home, even though an equally pervasive danger existed that the items to be seized would disappear before a warrant could be obtained. (Vale v. Louisiana (1970) supra, 399 U.S. 30, 90 S.Ct. 1969, 26 L.Ed.2d 409.)

The decisions upholding warrantless searches of automobiles evidence no distinction between the treatment of vehicles the police stop on the highway and vehicles they find parked at the curb. (See, e. g., United States v. Scott (9th Cir. 1972) 458 F.2d 12; United States v. Castaldi (7th Cir. 1971) 453

F.2d 506.) We must pause to consider, however, whether the position of defendant's automobile in the street near his apartment house requires the vehicle be afforded some special protection it would not ordinarily receive under *Carroll* were the car parked some distance from the house. The answer appears to be negative under the authority of People v. Terry (1964) 61 Cal.2d 137, 152–153, 37 Cal.Rptr. 605, 390 P.2d 381 (1969) 70 Cal.2d 410, 428, 77 Cal.Rptr. 460, 545 P.2d 36, in which we upheld the warrantless search of an automobile parked in a common garage area of the defendant's apartment when police officers had probable cause to believe the vehicle contained marijuana. If an automobile parked in such a location may be searched without a warrant, it seems to follow that an automobile parked by the curb near a residence may be so searched.

• • •

In the case at bar, accordingly, the police officers were empowered under the *Carroll* doctrine to search defendant's automobile so long as it can be demonstrated that (1) exigent circumstances rendered the obtaining of a warrant an impossible or impractical alternative, and (2) probable cause existed for the search. We conclude that both of these conditions existed at the time of the search. The United States Supreme Court has held that exigent circumstances justifying a warrantless automobile search exist where the police unforeseeably discover facts furnishing probable cause for the search under circumstances in which the evidence may be destroyed or removed from the reach of the officers if a search or seizure is not carried out immediately. (Chambers v. Maroney (1969) supra, 399 U.S. 42, 51, 90 S.Ct. 1975, 26 L.Ed.2d 419; cf. Coolidge v. New Hampshire (1971) supra, 403 U.S. 443, 459–462, 91 S.Ct. 2022, 29 L.Ed.2d 564 (Stewart, J.).) Here the officers were apparently unaware that defendant possessed an automobile at the time they obtained the warrant. They unexpectedly discovered the existence of the vehicle only after they had entered defendant's apartment. There was at least one other person in the apartment at the time of defendant's arrest who would have been in a position to move the car or destroy the evidence if the police did not conduct an immediate search or seizure. Under these circumstances, we hold it was not practicable for the police to secure a warrant under the standards set forth in *Carroll* and *Chambers*.

Probable cause for a search exists where an officer is aware of facts that would lead a man of ordinary caution or prudence to believe, and conscientiously to entertain, a strong suspicion that the object of the search is in the particular place to be searched. (People v. Superior Court (1970) 3 Cal.3d 807, 815–816, 91 Cal.Rptr. 729, 478 P.2d 449; Skelton v. Superior Court (1969) supra, 1 Cal.3d 144, 150, 81 Cal.Rptr. 613, 460 P.2d 485.) The transcript of the section 1538.5 hearing reveals that the officer directing the search of defendant's automobile believed the objects listed in the search warrant could be found in the vehicle and that he ordered the search on this basis. In the unusual circumstances of this case, we hold that his suspicion was reasonable. It could reasonably be concluded that defendant had not yet disposed of the bonds inasmuch as he had told the informant he had possessed the bonds for eight weeks without succeeding in finding a buyer. In light of this difficulty in "fencing" the bonds, it was unlikely that he disposed of them in the four days since the informant had last seen them. A thorough search of defendant's apartment, however, failed to uncover the bonds. Upon completing this search the officers "were entitled to use their reasoning faculties upon all the facts of which they had previous knowledge" (Carroll v. United States (1925) supra, 267 U.S. 132, 161, 45 S.Ct. 280, 288, 69 L.Ed. 543) and to conclude that defendant had probably hidden the easily movable stolen property in his automobile. The bonds might have been secreted elsewhere, of course, but we cannot disregard the likelihood that a person who holds stolen property he wishes to sell will attempt to conceal it in a place under his control that is nearby and apparently secure. (See United States v. Bailey (9th Cir. 1972) 458 F.2d 408, 413 (Kilkenny, J., dissenting).) When the officers were unable to discover the bonds in defendant's apartment, his automobile, parked outside on the street, quite naturally became an object of strong suspicion.

We conclude, therefore, the police officers had probable cause to search defendant's automobile under unforeseeable circumstances in which the securing of a warrant was impracticable. The search was consequently reasonable, and the trial court did not err in denying defendant's motion to suppress the evidence discovered therein.

* * *

PEOPLE v. HAMILTON *

Supreme Court of California, In Bank, 1969.
71 Cal.2d 176, 77 Cal.Rptr. 785, 454 P.2d 681.

* * *

On July 14, 1967, about 11:20 p. m., Edward Noriega, a state narcotics agent, together with several other law enforcement officers, went to a single-family residence in Upland, California, for the purpose of executing a search warrant. Apparently the front door was open and only an unlocked screen door stood between the officers and the interior of the premises. Agent Noriega and another officer went to the screen door and knocked, and a small child appeared in the doorway behind the screen door. The agent asked the child whether her mother or "Tony" was at home. The child answered "Yes," turned, and began walking down a hallway toward the rear of the house. Agent Noreiga opened the screen door and followed the child down the hallway. As he approached the door to a rear bedroom, he encountered defendant Hamilton emerging from the bedroom. Looking through the doorway the agent saw defendant Lerma sitting on one of the beds. Before him on the bed were seven bindles of heroin. A subsequent search of the premises revealed a quantity of amphetamine tablets.

Defendants contend that Agent Noriega's entry into their residence was made in violation of section 1531 of the Penal Code, that the evidence obtained as a result of that entry was therefore illegally obtained and should not have been admitted, and that the judgments must be reversed because such evidence was crucial to the convictions. . . .

It is undisputed that the officers' conduct prior to entry did not constitute compliance with the provisions of section 1531. Moreover, the record provides no basis to conclude that compliance with that section was excused because of specific factual circumstances giving rise to a reasonable belief on the part of the officers that unannounced entry was necessary to prevent destruction of evidence, discourage escape, or insure the officers' safety. It therefore appears that the entry and the subsequent seizure of evidence were illegal. Because the evidence so obtained was crucial to the convictions, the judgments must be reversed.

The conclusions stated above do not, of course, preclude the possibility of retrial and renewed efforts by the prosecution at that time to show specific facts known to the officers which justified their noncompliance with section 1531. In view of this possibility we deem it expedient to consider at this time one other issue advanced by defendants which may arise again upon retrial. That issue concerns the sufficiency of the affidavit in support of the warrant upon the authority of which the entry was undertaken.

The affidavit in support of the warrant was subscribed and sworn to by Agent Noriega, the arresting officer. It alleged in relevant part as follows: "That said affiant was informed on July 13, 1967, by confidential reliable informant that Jane Doe Nora also known as Nora Mae Hamilton and John

---

* Prior to reading this, it is recommended that the reader review the following statute: Penal Code

§ 1531. Also see the cases of Aguilar and Scoma included in this text.

Doe Tony have in their possession at a white single story, one family dwelling located at 822 W. Alpine Street, Upland, Calif. approximately three hundred (300) rolls of dangerous drugs wrapped in tin foil in groups of ten pills per roll. [Para.] That further your affiant reviewed San Bernardino County Sheriff Office report No. D.R. 112302 which indicated Nora Mae Hamilton and Raymond David Padilla were arrested at 822 W. Alpine Street, Upland, California, on April 14, 1967 for Possession of Marijuana and Possession of dangerous drugs found there. The pills found in the April 14, 1967 arrest were amphetamine, wrapped in tin foil in groups of 10. [Para.] That said confidential reliable informant has furnished information in the past which has lead [sic] to eight (8) arrest[s] and convictions for narcotic and dangerous drug offense."

In Aguilar v. Texas (1964) 378 U.S. 108, 84 S.Ct. 1509, 12 L.Ed.2d 723, the United States Supreme Court stated: "Although an affidavit may be based upon hearsay information and need not reflect the direct personal observations of the affiant, [citation], the magistrate must be informed of some of the underlying circumstances from which the informant concluded that the narcotics were where he claimed they were, and some of the underlying circumstances from which the officer concluded that the informant, whose identity need not be disclosed [citation], was 'credible' or his information 'reliable.'" (Fn. omitted.) (378 U.S. at p. 114, 84 S.Ct. at p. 1514.) The high court has since referred to this formulation as "Aguilar's two-pronged test." (Spinelli v. United States (1969) 393 U.S. 410, 413, 89 S.Ct. 584, 21 L.Ed.2d 637.)

Following *Aguilar,* California courts have held that for an affidavit based on an informant's hearsay statement to be legally sufficient to support the issuance of a search warrant, two requirements must be met: (1) the affidavit must allege the informant's statement in language that is factual rather than conclusionary and must establish that the informant spoke with personal knowledge of the matters contained in such statement; and (2) the affidavit must contain some underlying factual information from which the magistrate issuing the warrant can reasonably conclude that the informant was credible or his information reliable.

It is the first "prong" of the *Aguilar* test which strikes the affidavit now before us: that document undertakes absolutely no effort to set forth any of "the underlying circumstances from which the informant concluded that the narcotics were where he claimed they were . . . ." (Aguilar v. Texas, supra, 378 U.S. 108, 114, 84 S.Ct. 1509, 1514, 12 L.Ed.2d 723.)

An apt parallel is provided by the recent case of Spinelli v. United States, supra, 393 U.S. 410, 89 S.Ct. 584, 21 L.Ed.2d 637. In that case the affidavit stated that the F.B.I., one of whose agents had prepared the affidavit, "has been informed by a confidential reliable informant that William Spinelli is operating a handbook and accepting wagers and disseminating wagering information by means of the telephones which have been assigned the numbers WYdown 4–0029 and WYdown 4–0136.'" (393 U.S. at p. 422, 89 S.Ct. at p. 588.) The affidavit also stated that independent investigation had confirmed that the telephones in question were located in a certain apartment at which Spinelli was a frequent visitor. The court, holding that the affidavit fell short of constitutional sufficiency because it did not reveal the basis of the informant's conclusion, stated: "The tip [of the informant as reflected in the affidavit] does not contain a sufficient statement of the underlying circumstances from which the informer concluded that Spinelli was running a bookmaking operation. We are not told how the FBI's source received his information—it is not alleged that the informant personally observed Spinelli at work or that he ever placed a bet with him. Moreover, if the informant came by the information indirectly, he did not explain why his sources were reliable. Compare Jaben v. United States, 381 U.S. 214, 85 S.Ct. 1365, 14 L.Ed.2d 345 (1965). In the absence of a statement detailing the manner in which the information was gathered, it is especially important the the tip described the accused's criminal activity in sufficient detail so that the magistrate may know that he is relying on something more substantial than a casual rumor circulating in the underworld or an accusation based merely on an individual's general reputation." (393 U.S. at p. 416, 89 S.Ct. at p. 589.)

The People, emphasizing the idea expressed in the last sentence above quoted, urge that the instant case differs from *Spinelli* in that here the criminal activity was described "insufficient detail" to permit the *inference* that the informant had personal knowledge. Emphasis is placed upon the affidavit's allegation, attributed to the informant, that the contraband harbored at the premises to be searched was "approximately three hundred (300) rolls of dangerous drugs wrapped in tin foil in groups of ten pills per roll." It is urged that only one who had personal knowledge would be able to make such an exact statement as to the quantity and preparation of the contraband, and that therefore we should *infer* such knowledge in spite of the lack of direct factual allegations on the point. This contention is not without some support in the authorities. (See People v. Cain (1968) 261 A.C.A. 413, 417, 67 Cal.Rptr. 922; People v. Hernandez (1967) 255 Cal.App.2d 478, 481–482, 63 Cal.Rptr. 133; People v. Barthel (1965) 231 Cal.App.2d 827, 831–832, 42 Cal. Rptr. 290.)

While we do not reject the possibility that an informant who fails to provide factual allegations of his own experience might nevertheless provide a description of the contraband itself or its particular location so detailed as to warrant the inference of personal observation, we do not believe that the description here in question is sufficient for that purpose. In the *Spinelli* case it was urged that the facts provided by the informant, and especially the specific telephone numbers given by him, were sufficient to show "that the informer had gained his information in a reliable way." The court rejected this argument: "This meager report could easily have been obtained from an offhand remark heard at a neighborhood bar." (393 U.S. at p. 417, 89 S.Ct. at p. 589.) Similarly in the instant case the informant could have obtained his information as to the amount of dangerous drugs involved and the way in which it was packaged from an unreliable source. In order to infer in the absence of direct factual allegations that the informant had personal knowledge of the incriminating facts related by him we must insist upon more significant detail than is present in the instant affidavit.

In view of the foregoing we hold that the affidavit in support of the search warrant here involved was insufficient to meet the standards set forth in *Aguilar*.

The People further contend, however, that even if the affidavit was insufficient to support the warrant, Agent Noriega had probable cause to arrest and the search was proper as incident to arrest. Reference is made to the transcript of the motions to quash the search warrant and suppress evidence which were heard at the time of the preliminary examination (see fn. 3, ante) and to Agent Noriega's testimony therein to the effect that his informant actually had personal knowledge of the incriminating facts reflected in the affidavit, although the affidavit itself did not show personal knowledge. Reliance is placed upon the cases of People v. Chimel (1968) 68 Cal.2d 436, 440–442, 67 Cal.Rptr. 421, 439 P.2d 333, and People v. Castro (1967) 249 Cal.App.2d 168, 173–176, 57 Cal.Rptr. 108, and it is urged that here, as in those cases, we should not in effect undertake to penalize the officer for obtaining a warrant by ignoring facts known to him but not included in the affidavit through oversight.

While we hasten to reaffirm the principles stated in *Chimel* and *Castro*, it appears that in each of those cases the defendant was informed at the trial level that the prosecution did not intend to place exclusive reliance on the warrant. (See also People v.

Grubb (1967) 250 Cal.App.2d 714, 720, 58 Cal.Rptr. 670.) In the instant case, on the other hand, no specific attempt was made to show probable cause *aliunde* the warrant until the case was on appeal. (See Giordenello v. United States (1958) 357 U.S. 480, 487–488, 78 S.Ct. 1245, 2 L.Ed.2d 1503.) Although defendants' examination of Agent Noriega upon their motions to quash the warrant and suppress evidence gave them the opportunity to examine him upon the factual elements upon which a showing of probable cause *aliunde* the warrant would be based, the present posture of the case does not require that we determine whether the presence of that opportunity should allow the People to raise the issue for the first time on appeal. Upon retrial the People are free to seek to justify defendants' arrest and the incidental search without relying on the warrant.

We do not here discuss other contentions raised by defendants which are unlikely to arise upon retrial.

The judgments are reversed.

TRAYNOR, C. J., and PETERS and TOBRINER, JJ., concur.

BURKE, J., concurs in the reversal of the judgments.

MOSK, Justice (concurring and dissenting).

I concur in the judgment. The conclusion is inescapable that the officer in his eagerness to serve a warrant, neglected to comply fully with section 1531 of the Penal Code.

I do not agree, however, that the affidavit in support of the warrant was insufficient as a matter of law. Certainly it does not have the precision of a model legal document. But courts cannot be oblivious to the fact that warrant affidavits are not drafted by lawyers; they are prepared, generally hurriedly because of exigent circumstances, by laymen with limited legal background.

This affidavit indicates narcotics were in the possession of named persons at an identified site on a date certain. The quantity and the manner of packaging of the contraband are specifically described. The process is confirmed by reference to a previous arrest involving similar packaging. The reliability of the informer is verified. Thus the affidavit is not a recitation of mere rumor, and it meets the standards prescribed in Aguilar v. Texas (1964), 378 U.S. 108, 84 S.Ct. 1509, 12 L.Ed.2d 723, and Spinelli v. United States (1969) 393 U.S. 410, 89 S.Ct. 584, 21 L.Ed.2d 637. (Cf. my dissent in People v. Sesslin (1968) 68 Cal.2d 418, 431–432, 67 Cal.Rptr. 409, 439 P.2d 321).

If reviewing courts are to insist that affidavits for warrants be drafted with the finesse of a Montgomery Street contract, the result will be discouraging to law enforcement agencies that desire to employ warrant procedures. After all, it is much simpler for police officers to rely upon probable cause. I would demonstrate more tolerance of affidavits for warrants, and would begin with the one involved in this case.

McCOMB, Justice (dissenting).

I dissent. I would affirm the judgment for the reasons expressed by Mr. Presiding Justice McCabe in the opinion prepared by him for the Court of Appeal in People v. Hamilton (Cal.App.) 70 Cal.Rptr. 58.

PEOPLE v. KNUTSON *

Court of Appeal, First District, Division 1, 1976.
60 Cal.App.3d 856, 131 Cal.Rptr. 846.

ELKINGTON, Associate Justice.

A municipal court judge sitting as a magistrate, overruling defendant Knutson's contention of a constitutionally invalid detention, arrest, search, and seizure of marijuana and PCP from his person, held him to answer for trial in the superior court on charges of possession of those substances.

---

* Prior to reading this case it is recommended that the reader review the following statutes: Penal Code §§ 813 and 836.

(See Health & Saf.Code, §§ 11357, 11378.) Thereafter the superior court, on Knutson's motion under Penal Code section 995, set aside the information insofar as it related to those charges (counts I and II). The People appeal from that order.

In our consideration of the appeal two principles of criminal procedure are apposite.

• • •

The second rule places emphasis, in judicial determination of the existence of probable cause for an arrest or search, particularly in narcotic cases, on the expertise of a trained and experienced police officer. It is expressed by our Supreme Court as follows. "The rule requiring probable cause 'should not be understood as placing the ordinary man of ordinary care and prudence and the officer experienced in the detection of narcotics offenders in the same class. Circumstances and conduct which would not excite the suspicion of the man on the street might be highly significant to an officer who had had extensive training and experience in the devious and cunning devices used by narcotics offenders to conceal their crimes.'" (People v. Medina, 7 Cal.3d 30, 37, 101 Cal.Rptr. 521, 526, 496 P.2d 433, 438; People v. Superior Court (Kiefer), 3 Cal.3d 807, 827, 91 Cal.Rptr. 729, 478 P.2d 449.) " '[E]xperienced police officers naturally develop an ability to perceive the unusual and suspicious which is of enormous value in the difficult task of protecting the security and safety of law-abiding citizens. The benefit thereof should not be lost because the cold record before a reviewing court does not contain all the particularized perceptions which may have been so meaningful at the scene.'" (People v. Gale, 9 Cal.3d 788, 795–796, 108 Cal.Rptr. 852, 858, 511 P.2d 1204, 1210).

The case before us concerns Penal Code section 647, subdivision (f), which, as here relevant, states:

"Every person . . . (f) Who is found in any public place under the influence of intoxicating liquor [or] any drug . . . in such a condition that he is unable to exercise care for his own safety or the safety of others"—is "guilty of disorderly conduct, a misdemeanor." (Emphasis ours.)

From the evidence the magistrate could reasonably have found, and presumably did find, the following facts.

Use of the controlled substance PCP tends to tighten the user's muscles so that he cannot bend his knees, causing a "stiff-legged walking manner." And the pupils of the user's eyes do not have a normal reaction to light; they are "very pinpointed" even though the eyes are wide open in daylight. An experienced police officer with knowledge of these effects, and who had made about 100 arrests of persons possessing or under the influence of PCP, was cruising in a city park with a recreation department ranger, around 2 o'clock in the afternoon. The patrolled area was "known for heavy drug traffic." Three men standing on the sidewalk near the grass area observed the approaching police car, and as they did "two of them started off across the lawn area and the third started walking westbound on the sidewalk . . . ." The third person "was walking, trying to walk quickly, stiff-leggedly, walking in a very stiff-legged manner and swaying slightly." His walk was the "common type of walk . . . when they were under the influence of PCP." The officer decided to investigate further. He emerged from his car and walked over to the man for that purpose. The subject of the investigation, who was Knutson, the defendant of this case, was thus detained by the officer.

Knutson contended in the superior court, and here contends, that this detention was a Fourth Amendment infringement, under the authority of Irwin v. Superior Court, 1 Cal.3d 423, 82 Cal.Rptr. 484, 462 P.2d 12. Irwin (p. 427, 82 Cal.Rptr. p. 486, 462 P.2d p. 14) states: "Where the events are as consistent with innocent activity as with criminal activity, a detention based on those events is unlawful." Applying this rule, we opine

PEOPLE v. KNUTSON

that the experienced officer (see People v. Medina, supra, 7 Cal.3d 30, 101 Cal.Rptr. 521, 496 P.2d 433; People v. Superior Court (Kiefer), supra, 3 Cal.3d 807, 91 Cal.Rptr. 729, 478 P.2d 449; People v. Gale, supra, 9 Cal.3d 788, 108 Cal.Rptr. 852, 511 P.2d 1204), and the magistrate, could reasonably conclude that the events were nevertheless more consistent with conduct proscribed by Penal Code section 647, subdivision (f), and thus with criminal activity, than with innocent activity.

But we think that the single sentence excerpted by Knutson from *Irwin* does not state the true rule. Elsewhere *Irwin* states (1 Cal.3d p. 427, 82 Cal.Rptr. p. 486, 462 P.2d p. 14) that in order to justify detention: "[T]here must be a 'rational' suspicion by the peace officer that some activity out of the ordinary is or has taken place . . . some indication to connect the person under suspicion with the unusual activity . . . [and] some suggestion that the activity is related to crime." More recently the high court, without reliance on, or mention of, *Irwin* stated the appropriate rule as: "Where there is a rational belief of criminal activity with which the suspect is connected, a detention for reasonable investigative procedures infringes no constitutional restraint." (People v. Flores, 12 Cal.3d 85, 91, 115 Cal.Rptr. 225, 228, 524 P.2d 353, 356.) Under the "rational belief" test of *Flores* there can be no reasonable dispute that the officer's detention of Knutson was without constitutional flaw.

We continue our narration of the facts as they bear upon Knutson's arrest.

Upon Knutson's detention for investigation the officer asked him "are you all right?" There was no answer. Asked for "some identification," Knutson "fumbled slightly through his wallet and produced his driver's license." Questioned if he had been drinking, he responded that he had "had a couple of beers." Requested so to do, he then blew his breath in the officer's face; there was no odor of alcohol. Knutson "spoke very little and when he did speak the voice, or his speech, was slightly slurred and he appeared very nervous." The officer testified: "I checked his eyes, I shielded my hands around his eyes and held them there for five to ten seconds and then removed them to see if there was any reaction of light to the pupils. . . . There was no reaction. . . . [H]is eyes were very wide open with very pinpointed pupils." Knutson was then given "field sobriety" tests; the results were uncertain, but he apparently flunked one, being unable to place his finger to the tip of his nose. His response to another was "fair," but nevertheless his "left leg was shaking and seemed to be under great strain." At this point the officer "felt that the suspect was unable to care for himself and [he] placed him under arrest for 647f drugs."

The officer was permitted to arrest Knutson if he had *reasonable cause* to believe that he was under the influence of "any drug . . . in such a condition [as to be] unable to exercise care for his own safety . . . ." (See Pen.Code, §§ 647, subd. (f), 836, subd. (1).) " ' "Reasonable cause" is defined as that state of facts as would lead a man of ordinary care and prudence to believe and conscientiously entertain an honest and strong suspicion that the person is guilty of a crime. [Citation.] No exact formula exists for determining reasonable cause, and each case must be decided on the facts and circumstances presented to the officers at the time they were required to act. [Citation.' " (People v. Terry, 2 Cal.3d 362, 393, 85 Cal.Rptr. 409, 428, 466 P.2d 961, 980 [cert. dism., 406 U.S. 912, 92 S.Ct. 1619, 32 L.Ed.2d 112].)

Under this test we opine that upon the facts appearing to the magistrate, he reasonably could, and did, conclude that Knutson's arrest was founded upon probable cause, according to Fourth Amendment standards. As said in People v. Goldberg, 2 Cal.App.3d 30, 34, 82 Cal.Rptr. 314, 317, "Manifestations of drug use such as dilated pupils, slurred speech and difficulty in balancing, when observed by an experienced officer, present grounds for a valid arrest."

MAJOR CASE LAW OPINIONS

PEOPLE v. KRAFT *
Court of Appeal, Third District, 1970.
3 Cal.App.3d 890, 84 Cal.Rptr. 280.

PIERCE, Presiding Justice.

Defendant was convicted, after a nonjury trial in the municipal court of misdemeanor drunk driving (violation of Veh.Code, § 23102, subd. (a)). He appealed to the appellate division of the superior court. That court by a two to one decision affirmed the judgment 77 Cal.Rptr. 205. This court accepted certification "to secure uniformity of decision or to settle important questions of law." (Cal.Rules of Court, rule 63, subd. (a).)

After defendant had been arrested a blood sample was taken. The analysis was introduced into evidence. It showed a blood alcohol content of .24 of one percent. Defendant had refused to submit voluntarily to that or any other of the tests specified in Vehicle Code section 13353. Force was used in the taking of the sample. This court will hold that the force used was under the circumstances unlawfully excessive. Although the actual withdrawal of blood itself may not have been objectionable, it was immediately preceded by conduct such as to constitute the process as a whole not "medically acceptable" and therefore judgment must be reversed.

• • •

In the early morning hours defendant was observed by two patrolling police officers, Curtright and Spieth, driving an automobile northward along Watt Avenue. Watt Avenue is a well traveled thoroughfare in Sacramento County. Defendant was driving on the wrong side of the street. Defendant's car made a right turn onto a side street and "with some difficulty" it proceeded into, and was parked in, a driveway. One of the officers approached defendant as he alighted from the car. He noted a strong odor of liquor about defendant. Defendant was standing in front of the door of the driver's compartment. There was a pile of gravel at that point on which defendant was standing. Curtright took hold of defendant by the arm and shoved him back into the street. He did not shove very hard but it caused defendant to fall down. When he got up he was unsteady. The officer asked for his driver's license. At first he refused to surrender it but did later. A series of roadside tests were given, as the result of which the officers determined defendant was very intoxicated. He was placed under arrest for violation of Vehicle Code section 23102, subdivision (a) (misdemeanor drunk driving). He was advised of his rights under Miranda v. Arizona (1966) 384 U.S. 436, 86 S.Ct. 1602, 16 L.Ed.2d 694. He was then handcuffed and taken to the city emergency hospital. At the time of the arrest defendant's right arm was bandaged above and at the wrist and in the metacarpel area. He told the officers that it ached but when asked the cause he said "forget it." Subsequently, he told the doctor he had suffered a fracture three weeks earlier. On the ride to the hospital defendant complained continuously about pain due to the handcuffs. To the officers this was the customary behavior of a handcuffed prisoner. During the ride downtown defendant carried on a silly conversation. When the trio reached the police station, the officers started to take defendant to the hospital. At that point he became what Officer Curtright described as "resistive." He was taken into the hospital anteroom physically. The officers "used force to get him in." As Officer Curtright testified: "It wasn't very friendly persuasion." Officer Spieth testified that he struck defendant on the left side of his "cheek" with his closed fist. The testimony of the two officers differs as to why the blow was struck; also as to the circumstances surrounding the incident. Curtright said that defendant was not "aggressive"; that he was "defensive"; that he, Curtright, had grabbed defendant's

---

* Prior to reading this, it is recommended that the reader review the following statutes: Vehicle Code §§ 13353, 23102. Also see the cases of Schmerber and People v. Superior Court (Hawkins) included in this text.

right arm and had shoved him. When Officer Spieth struck defendant Curtright could recall no provocation for the blow. Officer Spieth, however, testified that defendant had threatened during the ride he would use force when his handcuffs were removed; and that when they were removed he had raised his arms (with neither of the officers touching him) as though to strike. That testimony, however, was inconsistent with the following: "[A]fter getting out of the squad car—were the handcuffs removed at that time? A. Yes, the handcuffs were removed." At some point—the record is not clear as to just when—Curtright advised defendant of the provisions of Vehicle Code section 13353. (In defendant's condition as then and thereafter established the advice must have conveyed the knowledge equivalent to an attempt to explain the rule in Shelley's case.) It did evoke defendant's refusal, however, to submit to any of the tests that section specifies. He was informed by the officers that a test would be taken whether defendant consented or not. Defendant stated, "It's not right. It's not moral." Some force was used in causing defendant to be seated in a chair.

Dr. Hockinberry, the physician on duty, entered the examination room where defendant was seated. Requests of defendant to submit to one of the three tests were repeated. Defendant still refused. He did respond to several routine questions by the doctor.

A withdrawal of blood was made. Before that was done defendant started to submit, then resisted. Both officers grabbed his arms. There is evidence that they tried to carry or lead him to a bed located in the examination room. In the process defendant fell or was pushed from a chair and he and the officers fell to the floor. Defendant fell on top of Officer Spieth. On the floor defendant was immobilized. The officers applied force sufficient to hold his left arm still. The doctor was able to and did apply a tourniquet to the upper arm, cleanse the area, inject a syringe needle and withdraw blood. We quote the material evidence on these happenings in the margin.

The municipal judge who decided that defendant was guilty on the basis of the evidence related saw the witnesses, heard their testimony and observed their demeanor on the stand.

Ordinarily that fact would be entitled to great weight. In this case, however, the municipal court judge's position was equivocal. He limited interrogation of the doctor (who was present) to questions relating to the technical medical aspects of the blood taking, indicating that if the blood taking itself had been aseptic and by a qualified medical doctor the law would have been complied with. On the other hand, on request he permitted written argument at the close of the trial on the issue of excessive force, although the record indicates nothing either pro or con to establish whether he considered the excessive force argument. We believe, however, that the testimony of the officers which we have quoted in the margin (see fn. 1) is unequivocal. Although the testimony of Officer Spieth is somewhat less emphatic than that of Officer Curtright, neither officer contradicts the other and both make it clear to us that excessive force *was* used.

. . .

We test reasonable police behavior here by giving further consideration to the sequence of events. Up to the point when defendant with the two officers reached the portals of the police station the only thing they had done which could be challenged in the handling of this quite apparently intoxicated defendant was to push him (or cause him to fall) onto a gravel pile. The officers had more than probable cause to arrest him; also to handcuff him and take him to jail, using all force reasonably appropriate to accomplish that. To that point no constitutional right was violated; no right of privacy; no illegal search or seizure; no violation of due process—there was no lack of fair play. It is when we step over the threshold of the hospital anteroom that constitutionally forbidden practices emerge. We need not paraphrase the testimony which we have quoted in the margin (see fn. 1). But a sentence added from Officer Spieth's testimony is significant. It graphically illustrates the restraints under which defendant was being held when the blood sample was taken. The officer said: "My position [on the floor] was holding on to his left arm, trying to get it in an immobile position. *Also, I believe I had a scissor lock on his legs.*" (Italics ours.)

* * *

We hold the limits of permissible police activity were exceeded.

Judgment is reversed.

REGAN, J., concurs.

DAVID, Associate Justice Pro Tem. (concurring and dissenting).

* * *

. . . I do not conclude that "The officers . . . were aggressive beyond all need," and I am not pointed to any course of conduct at the very time and place which would have more speedily and reasonably accomplished the taking of the blood sample. The test is not whether officers are aggressive or defensive; it is whether the force which they are permitted or required to use is clearly excessive. The amount of force or strength used legally to overcome resistance must always be greater than the resistance. It is not only the one whose heart is pure whose "strength is as the strength of ten" for a loaded and resistive drunk may have the same. Drunks are not always friendly boisterous parlor comics or tragic figures weeping in alcoholic despair, to be gently ushered to a quiet corner, to sleep off the poison. One should hesitate a long time before overturning the verdict of the trier of the facts, and of the appellate department, for it is impossible to apply any gauge to a printed page to measure the mercurial moods of a resistive drunk, to guess in retrospect what was the boundary between reasonable and unreasonable force in his restraint. Even in this respect, the majority have disregarded the well-settled rule that view of conflicting facts and inferences therefrom will be taken which will support the judgment of the courts below.

If it were conceded that the taking of the blood sample was an "unreasonable search and seizure," the judgment herein still should stand. The other evidence, as the majority concedes, was of itself clear and convincing. There is no occasion to negative the conviction and to let the defendant go free, despite his clear violation of the rights of the public by his drunk driving.

There is not one iota of evidence that the taking of the blood sample by the doctor was not completely in accord with the approved medical practice. When he arose from his chair, the officers started to conduct the drunk to a bed where he could be immobilized sufficiently to enable the doctor to secure the blood sample. He fell on top of one officer, with the other officer partly upon him. The opportunity to hold him there with one officer with a scissors upon his legs, and the other twisting his arm behind him while the doctor took the blood sample, was perhaps ludicrous, but certainly not clearly excessive nor illegal. (Cf. People v. Dawson, 127 Cal.App.2d 375, 273 P.2d 938.) Had the resistive drunk been placed on the bed, as intended, it seems likely his arms and legs would have to have been pinioned for the purposes of the doctor. There is no contention that the defendant was restrained upon the floor longer than necessary, and we have noted that the application of a tourniquet, the swabbing of the arm with an antiseptic, the insertion of the needle, and the withdrawal of the blood can be accomplished in from 15 to 45 seconds.

The court is not presented in this case with any parallel to Rochin v. California, 342 U.S. 165, 72 S.Ct. 205, 96 L.Ed. 183, where the concatenation of circumstances and the final force used was held to savor of the rack and the screw and to violate due process of law.

Reasonableness of the "search and seizure" is in the first instance a substantive determination to be made by the trial court from the facts and circumstances of each case. (Ker v. California, 374 U.S. 23, 33, 83 S.Ct. 1623, 10 L.Ed.2d 726.) The determination was made upon conflicting evidence. It must be considered in the light most favorable to the People to see whether it supports the determination of the trial court and the appellate department that the evidence was properly admissible over objection and that the judgment of conviction is supported by substantial evidence. (Noto v. United States, 367 U.S. 290, 296, 81 S.Ct. 1517, 6 L.Ed.2d 836, 840, cited in Blefare v. United States, 9 Cir., 362 F.2d 870; People v. Hills, 30 Cal.2d 694, 701, 185 P.2d 11; People v. Hannon, 44 Cal.App.2d 484, 112 P.2d 719.)

It would seem that the majority have disregarded such criteria. Conceding that the former declaration that blood samples could be taken "in the absence of force and violence" inaccurately states the law, the present decision reassesses the factual situation so as to reach essentially the same conclusion. In the language of Schmerber v. California, supra, the court cannot hold that the officers "responded to resistance with inappropriate force."

It is asserted that the majority opinion will advance the purposes of the testing process. The moral seems to be that if a drunk resists enough, his chances of "beating the rap" increase proportionately with his resistance, followed by his claim of the use of inappropriate force to subdue him.

It is true, of course, that the further a drunk progresses toward alcoholic oblivion, the less able he is to intelligently choose the method of testing to be employed. That he is incapable of rational choice or refusal does not withdraw the consent given as a requirement of the law. (Veh.Code, § 13353.) The tests may be given to any person covered by the statute, even if he be dead, unconscious or otherwise in a condition rendering him incapable of refusal. (State of Arizona v. Berg, 76 Ariz. 96, 259 P.2d 261, forcible taking of breath sample; cf. Blefare v. United States, supra, 362 F.2d 870, giving of emetic; consult generally cases cited in People v. Conterno, 170 Cal.App.2d Supp. 817, 827, 339 P.2d 968.)

If the majority had adopted the view that refusal to take the test at all was a fourth option under the statute, and that refusal in fact could negative the consent implied by law, support would be found in Bush v. Bright, 264 Cal.App.2d 788, 71 Cal.Rptr. 123.

The test in this instance revealed that appellant Kraft had .24 percent of alcohol by weight in his blood. This was almost double that specified to mark the borderline.

It would be a miscarriage of justice to void his conviction.

Any claim that he unjustifiably was struck in the face en route to the hospital is not germane to the blood sampling itself. The officers admitted a blow, but the circumstances were not revealed. It is not presumed that it was not justified. If the circumstances were such that it was not, the fact that it was reprehensible does not void either the arrest or the detention. For any unjustified use of excess force, Kraft has his penal (People v. Giles, 70 Cal.App.2d Supp. 872, 161 P.2d 623) and civil (Stowell v. Evans, 211 Cal. 565, 296 P. 278) redress.

Therefore, I would affirm the judgment.

Hearing denied; McCOMB, J., dissenting.

PEOPLE v. LAURSEN *

Supreme Court of California, In Bank, 1972.
8 Cal.3d 192, 104 Cal.Rptr. 425, 501 P.2d 1145.

WRIGHT, Chief Justice.

Defendant Raymond Ross Laursen appeals from a judgment entered on jury verdicts convicting him of armed robbery (Pen.Code, §§ 211, 211a) and kidnapping for the purpose of robbery (Pen.Code, § 209). The penalty for kidnaping was fixed at life imprisonment with possibility of parole.

---

* Prior to reading this, it is recommended that the reader review the following statutes: Penal Code §§ 209, 211. Also see the case of Wimberly included in this text.

MAJOR CASE LAW OPINIONS

The principal issue presented is whether a kidnaping committed while in the act of escaping from the site of a robbery falls within the meaning of "kidnaping for the purpose of robbery" as proscribed by section 209. For reasons which will appear we conclude that it does.

On the morning of October 14, 1964, shortly after 9 o'clock, defendant and Vincent Roosevelt Lowrie committed a robbery at a food market in Fresno. They drove to the scene of the robbery in a 1955 Mercury sedan which was registered to defendant's wife and which bore Alabama license plates. Defendant parked the vehicle on a side street where it could not be observed by persons from within the market. Upon entering the market, he drew a handgun and ordered the clerk at one of the check stands to empty into a paper grocery sack all the money in the cash registers. Lowrie meanwhile, located the manager at the rear of the business establishment and forced him to the front where defendant was waiting. Following an unsuccessful attempt to compel the manager to open a safe, the robbers fled.

Defendant and Lowrie rushed out the front exit of the market, rounded the corner and hastily entered the Mercury parked a few feet away. Unable to start the motor, they promptly left the stalled car in search of substitute transportation. Defendant ran to a parking lot behind a furniture store across the side street while Lowrie searched elsewhere. A bystander, who saw the gun in defendant's hand and suspected that a robbery was in progress, flagged down a passing motorcycle patrolman, Maurice Regan, and the officer immediately started to pursue the fleeing suspects. By this time defendant and Lowrie had captured Donald Teeter in the furniture store parking lot. They entered Teeter's vehicle and ordered him at gunpoint to drive them to a place of safety. As the vehicle sped toward the exit of the parking lot, Regan approached on his motorcycle. Defendant, sitting in front on the passenger side of the commandeered automobile and leaning from the window, attempted to shoot at the patrolman. Before defendant could fire his weapon, Teeter grabbed defendant's arm, the car slammed to a halt and stalled and a struggle between Teeter and defendant ensued during the course of which Teeter was shot in the hand. Regan abandoned his motorcycle and took refuge behind a parked automobile. Teeter was thereafter subdued by his captors and forced to drive the vehicle from the lot. Regan fired five or six rounds from his service revolver into the escaping automobile but without effect.

After Teeter drove a distance of about one-and-a-half miles, he was ordered by defendant to stop. Taking the grocery sack containing the money with him defendant alighted from the vehicle, walked to a nearby service station and called a taxicab. Teeter then drove Lowrie to an orchard a few blocks away where the former was bound and the latter drove off in the car.

Immediately after the unsuccessful attempt by Regan to capture defendant and Lowrie other officers arrived at the site of the robbery. They were told by eyewitnesses that the suspects had first attempted to make their escape in the Mercury automobile. The officers searched the passenger compartment of the Mercury but were unable to open the trunk. While they were involved with the search and before procuring appropriate tools to force the trunk, they received radio information that Lowrie had been taken into custody. Without completing their search they hurried to the place where Lowrie had been apprehended, hoping that they might locate and arrest defendant as well.

By midafternoon the investigating officers discontinued their immediate efforts to locate defendant and resumed their search of the Mercury for additional clues. Without obtaining a search warrant, the officers went to the impound garage to which the car had been removed and opened the rear trunk. Inside they discovered papers and documents with the names Eddie Pierce, Edwin Cash Pierce and David Lee Rose, all aliases previously used by defendant. The information thus discovered not only led to defendant's arrest in Kansas and his return following extradition proceedings, but was also received in evidence at trial as tending to prove that defendant had been at the scene of the crime on the date it was committed.

We first address ourselves to defendant's principal contention that his conduct did not constitute a violation of section 209. The argument proceeds on either one or both of two related theories: (1), that inasmuch as the *intent* to kidnap Teeter was not formulated until after the commencement of the robbery, the kidnaping was merely an afterthought and, hence, not conduct proscribed by the provisions of section 209; and (2), that the *asportation* of Teeter was unrelated to the robbery, since it occurred after that crime had been completed. As amended in 1951, section 209 makes punishable every person, inter alias, "who kidnaps or carries away any individual to commit robbery. . . ." In People v. Daniels (1969) 71 Cal.2d 1119, 80 Cal.Rptr. 897, 159 P.2d 225, we held "that the intent of the Legislature in amending Penal Code, section 209 in 1951 was to exclude from its reach not only 'standstill' robberies [citation omitted] but also those in which the movements of the victim are merely incidental to the commission of the robbery and do not substantially increase the risk of harm over and above that necessarily present in the crime of robbery itself." (Id. at p. 1139, 80 Cal.Rptr. at p. 910, 459 P.2d at p. 238.) Thus, the primary purpose of the statute is to impose harsher criminal sanctions to deter the carrying away of persons during the commission of a robbery in a manner which substantially increases the risk that someone will suffer grave bodily or psychic injury or even death.

In accordance with the foregoing purpose, we have enunciated the rule that a kidnaping in which a robbery occurs does not constitute kidnaping for the purpose of robbery unless the specific intention to rob is present at the time of the original asportation. (People v. Tribble (1971) 4 Cal.3d 826, 94 Cal.Rptr. 613, 484 P.2d 589.) In *Tribble*, it was reasoned that a defendant who kidnaped a woman at an airport, drove her to an isolated place nearby, raped her and subsequently robbed her, "was entitled to have the jury determine whether he intended to commit robbery at the time the kidnaping commenced or whether the intent to commit robbery was an afterthought to a kidnaping that was sexually motivated." (Id., at p. 832, 94 Cal.Rptr. at p. 617, 484 P.2d at p. 593.)

Contrary to defendant's contentions, we have never held that section 209 requires that the separately defined crimes of robbery and kidnaping be tied together by a coexistence of the elements of intent at the commencement of the criminal transaction; or, to state it in a different fashion, that kidnaping, as well as robbery, must be simultaneously premeditated as a part of a single course of criminal conduct. Such a conclusion does not follow from the reasoning of *Tribble*. Since a robbery committed as an afterthought to a kidnaping generally does not substantially increase the risk that someone will be injured or killed such conduct may not be proscribed by the provisions of section 209. On the other hand, the carrying away of the victim or some other individual during the commission of a robbery, even though motivated by events occurring after the commencement of a robbery still in progress, most certainly increases the risk that he will be injured or killed and is specifically the type of conduct made punishable by section 209. The soundness of such a conclusion, in the context of the instant circumstances, becomes painfully evident. Fortuitously snatched as a hostage, Teeter was, as might reasonable be expected, wounded in the gun battle which occurred during the robbery, notwithstanding the fact that the kidnaping clearly was not premeditated at the commencement of the robbery. In sum, we are of the view that where a kidnaping is in furtherance of a robbery during which the kidnaping occurs, a violation of section 209 is committed even though the intent to kidnap was formulated after the robbery commenced.

Turning now to the second theory which defendant urges in support of his contention that his conduct did not constitute a violation of section 209, we are confronted by his claim that the kidnaping and the robbery are separate, divisible crimes because the kidnaping was not committed until after the robbery, that is, the taking of the money, had been accomplished. Since an intent to kidnap for the purpose of robbery necessarily implies that the robbery is in progress when the intent to kidnap is formed, this argument must be considered.

This court has consistently recognized that "[r]obbery . . . is not confined to a fixed locus, but is frequently spread over considerable distance and varying periods of time." (People v. Boss (1930) 210 Cal. 245, 251, 290 P. 881, 883; see also People v. Salas (1972) 7 Cal.3d 812, 822, 103 Cal.Rptr. 431, 500 P.2d 7; People v. Anderson (1965) 64 Cal.2d 633, 638, 51 Cal.Rptr. 238, 414 P.2d 366; People v. Ketchel (1963) 59 Cal.2d 503, 523, 30 Cal.Rptr. 538, 381 P.2d 394; People v. Kendrick (1961) 56 Cal.2d 71, 90, 14 Cal.Rptr. 13, 363 P.2d 13; People v. Kristy (1935) 4 Cal.2d 504, 507, 50 P.2d 798; People v. Dowell (1928) 204 Cal. 109, 117–118, 266 P. 807.) The assault of the victim, the seizure of his property and the robber's escape to a location of temporary safety are all phases in the commission of the crime of robbery linked not only by a proximity of time and distance, but a single-mindedness of the culprit's purpose as well. Accordingly, we conclude that when as in the instant case the finder of fact may have reasonably inferred and accordingly have found that the kidnaping of an individual was to effect a robber's escape such kidnaping is proscribed by the provisions of section 209.

The conclusions we reach today are not contrary to our holdings in People v. Daniels, supra, 71 Cal.2d 1119, 80 Cal.Rptr. 897, 459 P.2d 225, and People v. Timmons (1971) 4 Cal.3d 411, 93 Cal.Rptr. 736, 482 P.2d 648.

Implicit in our decision is the requirement that all asportations committed during the escape phase of a robbery which may be classified as section 209 offenses necessarily involve movement that substantially increases the risk of harm to the kidnaped individual over and above that necessarily present in the crime of robbery itself.

Applying the foregoing to the facts in the instant case, we are compelled to the conclusion that the carrying away of Teeter was for the purpose of effecting defendant's escape from the scene where the robbery was perpetrated. The robbery and kidnaping are too coincidental in time, place and purpose, and the likelihood on the increased risk of harm to which Teeter was exposed too apparent to permit any other determination.

Defendant next contends that the search without a warrant of the Mercury automobile by the police at the place where it was impounded on the afternoon of the day of the robbery constituted conduct proscribed by the Fourth Amendment. The materials recovered during the search of the vehicle consisted of papers and documents bearing the various aliases often used by defendant. As previously stated, they were introduced into evidence at trial as tending to prove that defendant was the same person as the individual named in the documents and that he was at the scene of the robbery on the date it occurred. We conclude that defendant's claim with respect to the admissibility of this evidence is without merit.

The case at bench does not fall within our proscription of unreasonable routine inventory searches as enunciated in Mozzetti v. Superior Court (1971) 4 Cal.3d 699, 94 Cal. Rptr. 412, 484 P.2d 84. In that case we did not address ourselves to instances like the present in which there was probable cause to believe the searched vehicle either contained evidence of a crime or was an instrumentality of its commission. (Id., at p. 703, 94 Cal.Rptr. 412, 484 P.2d 84.) In People v. McKinnon (1972) 7 Cal.3d 899, 103 Cal.Rptr. 897, 500 P.2d 1097, we made it clear that a search without a warrant of an automobile or another readily movable item, founded upon probable cause may be justified because of its "distinguishing characteristics of mobility" even though in otherwise similar circumstances a search of a fixed structure may be unreasonable within Fourth Amendment prohibitions. (Id., at p. 907, 103 Cal. Rptr. 897, 500 P.2d 1097.) Although in *McKinnon* we dealt with readily movable objects other than a vehicle we relied on Chambers v. Maroney (1970) 399 U.S. 42, 90 S.Ct. 1975, 26 L.Ed.2d 419 involving the search without a warrant of an automobile on probable cause. *Chambers* and *McKinnon* establish the rule that when there is probable cause to believe that an automobile stopped on a highway contains contraband, evidence of a crime, or was itself an instrumentality of the commission of one, law enforcement officers need not obtain a warrant before conducting a search since there is no distinction of constitutional proportion between an immediate search on probable cause without a warrant and the automobile's immobilization until one is secured.

Having concluded that the mere immobilization of an automobile is as substantial an intrusion on the constitutional rights of the owner or possessor as is an immediate search, we must further consider whether the fact the vehicle is impounded at a police garage before it is searched is also of no greater constitutional significance.

It was not unreasonable to transport the vehicle to the garage for safekeeping and further examination. Although defendant had apparently abandoned the automobile in effecting his escape, he or others acting in his behalf could have returned to retrieve it or to remove evidence. The officers did not possess the proper tools to open the trunk and complete their search at the time and place where the vehicle was discovered and each moment of delay significantly improved defendant's chances of avoiding apprehension. We discern no inconvenience or invasion of defendant's rights which further infringed any constitutional prohibition by the fact that the vehicle was removed from the scene of the crime to an impound garage beyond that which would have resulted had a warrant authorizing the impound and search first been obtained. (See Chambers v. Maroney, supra, 399 U.S. 42, 51–52, 90 S.Ct. 1975, where the vehicle was removed from the place of apprehension to a police station before being searched.) We conclude, accordingly, that the vehicle was properly impounded and searched in accordance with *Chambers* and *McKinnon*.

A number of fingerprints were lifted from the Mercury automobile, some of which matched those of defendant. Due to the extensive length of time which had elapsed up to the beginning of the second trial, the testimony of the officers who lifted the prints was not clear with respect to the exact number which had been taken from the vehicle and the time at which comparisons had been made. By emphasizing certain inconsistencies trial counsel attempted to create an inference that the prints had been tampered with. Counsel on appeal argues that the evidence should have been excluded. We disagree and conclude that, inasmuch as defendant "did not point to any indication of actual tampering, did not show how fingerprints could have been forged, and did not establish that anyone who might have been interested in tampering with the prints knew" where they were or had access to them, it was proper to admit the evidence and permit the speculation urged by defendant to go to its weight. (People v. Riser (1956) 47 Cal.2d 566, 581, 305 P.2d 1.)

Defendant also complains of a search of the residence of Otis Graham where for a period of approximately five days prior to the robbery defendant and Lowrie occupied a room. Police officers visited the Graham residence on the morning following the robbery. When questioned, Graham acknowledged the two men had stayed there and consented to a search of his home. He showed the officers the room which defendant and Lowrie occupied and indicated that certain garments, some hanging in a closet and others piled with documents in open cardboard cartons on the floor, belonged to the two men. Graham also gave his consent for the removal of these articles. Such evidence was introduced at trial and used as tending to link defendant with the commission of the robbery. On appeal, defendant asserts that this evidence was illegally obtained and was therefore inadmissible at trial.

It is undisputed that the officers had consensual authority to enter the Graham residence. The crucial question is whether the officers were also entitled to seize the property of defendant. The People contend that defendant's belief that Graham would safeguard his clothing from governmental inspection formed too fragile a foundation for a reasonable expectation of privacy. They argue that under the Fourth Amendment a defendant may not legitimately entertain a reasonable expectation of privacy in the event his trust in an apparent colleague is misplaced. (United States v. White (1971) 401 U.S. 745, 91 S.Ct. 1122, 28 L.Ed.2d 453.) Defendant, on the other hand, contends that at most the consent extended to the officers by Graham permitted them to look about the house and could not properly bestow upon them the authority to seize any of defendant's personal effects entrusted to Graham. (People v. Cruz (1964) 61 Cal.2d 861, 866, 40 Cal.Rptr. 841, 395 P.2d 889; see also People v. Edwards (1969) 71 Cal.2d 1096, 80 Cal.Rptr. 633, 458 P.2d 713.) Whatever the merits, a resolution of this issue need not be made. In view of other competent and overwhelming evidence of defendant's participation in the robbery we are satisfied beyond a reasonable doubt that the evidence obtained at the Graham residence "did not contribute to the verdict obtained." (Chapman v. California (1967) 386 U.S. 18, 24, 87 S.Ct. 824, 828, 17 L.Ed.2d 705; see also People v. Haston (1968) 69 Cal.2d 233, 253, 70 Cal.Rptr. 419, 444 P.2d 91.) The inculpatory documents discovered in the abandoned Mercury, defendant's fingerprints found on the car, the incriminating testimony related by Graham, coupled with the testimony of numerous individuals who positively identified defendant as one of the culprits, compellingly establish defendant's guilt and offset any material effect the meager evidence seized in Graham's house might have had.

Defendant further complains that the trial court erred in refusing to grant a motion to continue the trial to allow him an opportunity to bring the accomplice Lowrie from the State of Nebraska where he was then imprisoned to testify as a witness. The motion was made near the end of defendant's case after he had called numerous other witnesses. Lowrie had been available as a witness at the first trial but had not been called by either the prosecution or defense. The nature of Lowrie's expected testimony does not appear but defendant apparently based his defense on alibi, that he was not in the State of California at the time of the commission of the offenses and presumably, Lowrie would support testimony of defendant and other defense witnesses.

It appeared on argument of the motion that Nebraska authorities would not deliver Lowrie and that there was no current statutory procedures by which his attendance could be compelled as a witness. Defense counsel stated that Lowrie might be able to appear "within a few weeks" as extradition proceedings, although resisted by Lowrie, were then pending. The trial court was thus confronted with the circumstance that to grant the motion would require a jury trial interruption of substantial and somewhat indefinite proportions for the purpose of producing an impeachable witness whose testimony was not sought at the first trial, although available, and would likely be merely cumulative of that of other defense witnesses.

The granting or denial of a motion for a continuance in the midst of a trial traditionally rests within the sound discretion of the trial judge who must consider not only the benefit which the moving party anticipates but also the likelihood that such benefit will result, the burden on other witnesses, jurors and the court and, above all, whether substantial justice will be accomplished or defeated by a granting of the motion. In the lack of a showing of an abuse of discretion or of prejudice to the defendant, a denial of his motion for a continuance cannot result in a reversal of a judgment of conviction. (People v. Ketchel, supra, 59 Cal.2d 503, 546, 30 Cal.Rptr. 538, 381 P.2d 394; People v. Dickerson (1969) 270 Cal.App.2d 352, 361, 75 Cal.Rptr. 828.) Defendant fails to demonstrate and our examination fails to disclose either an abuse of discretion or resulting prejudice in the instant case.

Defendant also complains of pretrial photographic and lineup identification procedures. We have, however, reviewed testimony developed at the second trial on these issues and have compared such record with that considered by the Court of Appeal in disposing of the issues favorably to the People on appeal from the first judgment of conviction. (People v. Laursen, supra, 264 Cal.App.2d 932, 942–945, 71 Cal.Rptr. 71.) There is no material variance between the testimony at the two trials and basic legal principles applicable have not changed. These issues already having been litigated further consideration thereof is precluded by the doctrine of the law of the case. (People v. Terry (1964) 61 Cal.2d 137, 151, 37 Cal. Rptr. 605, 390 P.2d 381.)

Defendant's remaining contentions are either not cognizable on appeal for failure to have preserved them or, after our careful examination of the record, deemed to be so lacking in merit that they are not deserving of any discussion.

The judgment of conviction is affirmed.

McCOMB, PETERS, TOBRINER, MOSK, BURKE and SULLIVAN, JJ., concur.

PEOPLE v. McGAUGHRAN*
Supreme Court of California, 1978.
149 Cal.Rptr. 584, 585 P.2d 206.

MOSK, Justice.

Defendant was convicted of burglary committed by breaking into a locked automobile with intent to steal. (Pen.Code, § 459.) On this appeal from the judgment he contends primarily that the superior court should have granted his pretrial motion to suppress the evidence on the ground of illegal search and seizure. (Pen.Code, § 1538.5.) . . .

. . . Early on a weekday afternoon Police Officer Thomas of the City of Larkspur, Marin County, was on patrol in a marked vehicle in the vicinity of Redwood High School. He observed a Plymouth automobile proceeding in the wrong direction on a one-way public street that crosses the high school parking lot. Because of the violation the officer drove up behind the vehicle and activated his red flashing light. As he did, he saw the person in the front passenger seat turn around, lean over the back of the seat, and appear to move an object on the rear floorboard. Both cars then stopped at the curb, and Thomas approached the driver of the Plymouth, defendant McGaughran. Thomas explained why he had stopped the car and asked for identification from both occupants. They produced their driver's licenses, showing San Francisco addresses. The two men told Thomas they were lost and were looking for the Marin County Juvenile Hall, a facility that the officer knew was several miles away. Thomas then returned to his vehicle and made a radio check for outstanding arrest warrants in both names. The dispatcher reported a burglary warrant for defendant from Alameda County and two traffic warrants for the passenger, Walter Acosta. The warrant check took approximately 10 minutes.

Upon learning of the pending charges against the two men, Thomas called for assistance and requested a "confirmation" of the warrants. Officer Fischer arrived within five minutes in response to the call, and the warrants were confirmed by radio some 20 to 25 minutes later. Defendant was

---

* Prior to reading this it is recommended that the reader review the following statute: Penal Code § 836. Also see the cases of People v. Superior Court (Kiefer) and People v. Superior Court (Simon) included in this text.

then arrested on the burglary warrant, pat-searched, and seated in Fischer's patrol car. He asked Fischer to return to the Plymouth to retrieve his jacket and wallet. Fischer complied, and found the wallet lying open on the dashboard, disclosing a methadone treatment card from San Francisco. On the back seat he saw an open canvas bag containing several screwdrivers, wrenches, and pliers.

Thomas questioned Acosta about his outstanding traffic warrants. The latter replied that if he were allowed to make a telephone call he could raise the necessary bail, and defendant said that in such event he would release the Plymouth to Acosta so that he could return to San Francisco. A quick inspection of the car revealed no weapons, and Acosta was permitted to drive it to the Larkspur police station, preceded by Thomas and followed by Fischer in their respective vehicles. After they arrived at the station, Fischer searched under the front seat of the Plymouth and found a citizens band radio that had been stolen earlier the same day from a car parked about a mile from the scene of the arrest. Examination of that car revealed one door had been broken open, and defendant's fingerprints were on the door.

We recently summarized the rule that "in order to justify an investigative stop or detention the circumstances known or apparent to the officer must include specific and articulable facts causing him to suspect that (1) some activity relating to crime has taken place or is occurring or about to occur, and (2) the person he intends to stop or detain is involved in that activity. Not only must he subjectively entertain such a suspicion, but it must be objectively reasonable for him to do so. The facts must be such as would cause any reasonable police officer in a like position, drawing when appropriate on his training and experience to suspect the same criminal activity and the same involvement by the person in question. The corollary to this rule, of course, is that an investigative stop or detention predicated on mere curiosity, rumor, or hunch is unlawful, even though the officer may be acting in complete good faith." (Fn. omitted.) (In re Tony C. (1978) 21 Cal.3d 888, 893, 148 Cal. Rptr. 366, 368, 582 P.2d 957, 959.)

Defendant concedes it was proper for Officer Thomas to stop him for his traffic violation of driving in the wrong direction on a one-way street. (Veh.Code, § 21657.) He contends, however, that the ensuing detention for a warrant check was impermissible under the general rule that "A detention of an individual which is reasonable at its inception may exceed constitutional bounds when extended beyond what is reasonably necessary under the circumstances." (People v. Harris (1975) 15 Cal.3d 384, 390, 124 Cal.Rptr. 536, 539, 540 P.2d 632, 635.) [2]

Officer Thomas claimed two different justifications for detaining defendant and Acosta for the warrant check. He testified that he decided to run such a check because of certain suspicious circumstances surrounding the stop, and listed those circumstances; but he simultaneously acknowledged that he "didn't have any reason to believe" there were outstanding warrants for the two men, and agreed that the warrant check he conducted in this case was a "routine" investigation he makes of "every single individual" he stops.[3] The Attorney General adopts both theories, and we examine them seriatim.

Under the general rule stated at the outset, a brief detention for a warrant check following a valid traffic stop is justifiable when the circumstances known or apparent to the officer include specific and articulable facts causing him to reasonably suspect that

---

2. Only the initial detention, of course, is before us. If it was valid, Officer Thomas became entitled to arrest defendant and Acosta on the outstanding warrants and could lawfully detain them for the additional 20 to 25 minutes necessary to "confirm" those warrants.

3. The apparent inconsistency in this testimony makes it doubtful that Officer Thomas in fact entertained the subjective suspicion required to justify a detention on the ground of apparent criminal activity. (In re Tony C., supra, 21 Cal.3d, at p. 893, fn. 2, 148 Cal.Rptr. 366, 582 P.2d 957.)

there may be an outstanding warrant for the driver's arrest. That suspicion may properly arise, for example, when the driver takes unmistakably evasive action in the course of the stop (see, e. g., Carpio v. Superior Court (1971) 19 Cal.App.3d 790, 792–793, 97 Cal.Rptr. 186);[4] when there are objective indicia that the stopped vehicle may be stolen, such as missing or deliberately obscured license plates (see cases discussed in People v. Superior Court (*Simon*) (1972) 7 Cal.3d 186, 196–197, 101 Cal.Rptr. 837, 496 P.2d 1205);[5] or when the officer has independent grounds to infer that the motorist may be involved in more serious criminal activity (cf. People v. Herrera (1975) 52 Cal.App.3d 177, 124 Cal.Rptr. 725 (burglary); People v. Wickers (1972) 24 Cal.App.3d 12, 100 Cal.Rptr. 732 (robbery)).[6]

In the case at bar Officer Thomas listed the following circumstances when asked why he ran a warrant check on defendant and Acosta: (1) the men were not local residents, but were from San Francisco; (2) they appeared to be lost; (3) they were in the vicinity of a high school but were not of high school age; (4) a substantial traffic in illegal drugs was known to exist at the high school in question; and (5) Acosta reached over the back seat when Thomas activated his flashing light. The Attorney General contends these circumstances support a suspicion that defendant and Acosta were involved in the sale of narcotics at Redwood High School.

The inference is unreasonable. To begin with, the first three circumstances noted are wholly innocent. The fact that the occupants of the car were residents of a neighboring county is not only devoid of any sinister significance, but may well explain the further fact that they seemed to be lost. Nor is it relevant that they were lost—or found—in the vicinity of a high school. They were not, for example, loitering in its restrooms, locker rooms, or similar portions of the school premises normally frequented only by students (cf. Pen.Code, § 653g); rather, they were proceeding on a public thoroughfare that crosses the school property. There is nothing suspicious in the sight of adults—whether teachers, parents, or ordinary citizens—passing through public areas adjacent to high schools, either on school business or merely en route to another destination.

The next circumstance mentioned by Officer Thomas—that an illicit drug traffic was known to exist at Redwood High School—invokes the "high crime area" rationale. But we recently observed that "the justification is so easily subject to abuse that this fact alone should not be deemed sufficient to support the intrusion." (In re Tony C., supra, 21 Cal.3d, at p. 897, 148 Cal.Rptr. at p. 371, 582 P.2d at p. 962.) Defendant asserts that at the present time some degree of drug use occurs in virtually every high school of this state; if this is so, of course, defendant is also correct in concluding that reliance on that fact would in effect make it lawful for police to detain for a warrant check every hapless driver who is stopped for a traffic infraction on a street that happens to be "in the vicinity of" a high school—wherever the officer may choose to draw that geographic line. As long as such streets remain open to

---

4. In *Carpio*, "a Highway Patrol officer observed petitioner driving south on Highway 101 at a speed of approximately 75 miles per hour. The officer gave chase. When petitioner was aware of the officer he pulled onto the shoulder and then, when the officer was pulling in behind him, petitioner drove back onto the highway, causing the officer to pursue him further. Eventually, petitioner stopped and the officer interrogated him." (Id. 19 Cal. App.3d at p. 792, 97 Cal.Rptr. at p. 187.) Similar conduct may not be adequate, however, to support a warrantless search of the driver or his property. (See People v. Norman (1975) 14 Cal.3d 929, 932–934, 132 Cal.Rptr. 109, 538 P.2d 237.)

5. However, for the reasons stated in *Simon* (id. 7 Cal.3d at pp. 193–195, 101 Cal.Rptr. 837, 496 P.2d 1205) the motorist's inability to produce his driver's license or the registration card for the vehicle, without more, does not reasonably support a suspicion of automobile theft.

6. In neither *Herrera* nor *Wickers* was the driver first stopped for a traffic violation. The cases were therefore governed by the general rule permitting an investigative detention upon a reasonable suspicion of criminal involvement.

the public their mere use cannot be deemed a suspicious event, whatever the reputation of the local high school.

The final circumstance relied on by Officer Thomas—the observed motion of the passenger in turning and reaching over the back of the seat—invokes the "furtive gesture" rationale. But in People v. Superior Court (*Kiefer*) (1970) 3 Cal.3d 807, 91 Cal. Rptr. 729, 478 P.2d 449, we rejected a claim that a remarkably similar gesture furnished probable cause to search a vehicle for contraband after an ordinary traffic stop.[7] We there analyzed in detail the dangers of giving too much weight to such gestures, recognizing they are usually totally innocuous and unrelated to any criminal activity. (Id. at pp. 817–823, 91 Cal.Rptr. 729, 478 P.2d 449.)[8] We concluded that such a gesture can be deemed suspicious only when there are additional facts known to the officer that reasonably give it a guilty connotation, such as "prior reliable information or . . . the officer's personal observation of contraband or a deliberate act of concealment under otherwise suspicious circumstances." (Id. at pp. 819–820, 91 Cal.Rptr. at p. 736, 478 P.2d at p. 456.) And we criticized as largely inadequate the "additional facts" relied on for this purpose in a number of Court of Appeal decisions. (Id. at pp. 824–827, 91 Cal.Rptr. 729, 478 P.2d 449.)

Just as an unsupported "furtive gesture" cannot justify a vehicle search after a traffic stop, so also it cannot justify an investigative detention of the driver. (See, e. g., People v. Williams (1971) 20 Cal.App.3d 590, 91 Cal.Rptr. 815.) Applying the *Kiefer* analysis to the record before us, we conclude that Acosta's gesture alone was insufficient to furnish reasonable grounds to suspect there might be an outstanding warrant for defendant's arrest, and the listed additional circumstances cannot fairly be deemed to have invested the gesture with such significance.

In the alternative—indeed as his "primary contention"—the Attorney General asserts that no suspicious circumstances at all are required to justify the detention of a motorist for the purpose of conducting a warrant check. He claims that such a detention is reasonable per se, provided only that (1) it is preceded by a valid stop for a traffic offense and (2) it remains relatively brief. He distinguishes the cases relied on by defendant on the ground there was either no traffic offense committed in fact (People v. Grace (1973) 32 Cal.App.3d 447, 451–452, 108 Cal. Rptr. 66 (officer mistakenly believed vehicle's brake light was inoperative); see also People v. Bello (1975) 45 Cal.App.3d 970, 973, 119 Cal.Rptr. 838) or the detention was unduly long (Willett v. Superior Court (1969) 2 Cal.App.3d 555, 558–559, 83 Cal.Rptr. 22 (warrant check took 40 minutes)). For his authority the Attorney General relies on a series of four decisions of the Court of Appeal holding that "where an automobile is stopped for a traffic violation it is not unreasonable to detain the occupants for a short period of time for the purpose of determining whether there are outstanding traffic warrants against the driver or other information relating to him in police records." (People v. Gillian (1974) 41 Cal. App.3d 181, 188, 116 Cal.Rptr. 317, 322; accord, People v. Bremmer (1973) 30 Cal. App.3d 1058, 1061–1062, 106 Cal.Rptr. 797; People v. Brown (1969) 272 Cal.App.2d 448, 450, 77 Cal.Rptr. 438; People v. Elliott (1960) 186 Cal.App.2d 185, 189, 8 Cal.Rptr. 716.)

We are urged to adopt this rule.[9] The Attorney General bases his argument on the

---

7. After the officer in *Kiefer* switched on his red flashing light, the woman passenger in the front seat "turned and put her arm over the back of the seat, then faced forward again, bent down toward the floor, and reassumed a normal sitting position." (Id. at p. 811, 91 Cal.Rptr. at p. 730, 478 P.2d at p. 450.)

8. In the case at bar, for example, Officer Fischer asked Acosta what he had placed on the rear floor, and he replied it was his lunch. The officer subsequently found a brown paper bag in that location containing typical residue of a picnic lunch.

9. We observe at the outset that by its terms the proposed rule would permit a routine check for

principle that reasonableness in the constitutional sense is determined by balancing the government's need for the information against the nature and extent of the intrusion required to obtain it (Terry v. Ohio (1968) 392 U.S. 1, 20–21, 88 S.Ct. 1868, 20 L.Ed.2d 889; People v. Brisendine (1975) 13 Cal.3d 528, 538, 119 Cal.Rptr. 315, 531 P.2d 1099.) He begins by characterizing the latter intrusion as "the minor inconvenience of a brief wait by a motorist."

We recognize that in contrast to *Tony C.*, here the detention followed a lawful stop predicated not on mere curiosity or hunch but on a traffic offense committed in the officer's presence; and in contrast to People v. Superior Court (*Kiefer*) (1970) supra, 3 Cal.3d 807, 91 Cal.Rptr. 729, 478 P.2d 449, and People v. Superior Court (*Simon*) (1972) supra, 7 Cal.3d 186, 101 Cal.Rptr. 837, 496 P.2d 1205, here the ensuing intrusion was neither a search of the driver's person nor a search of his car, but a temporary detention while a warrant check was conducted by radio. Indeed, there was no "search" at all in the constitutional sense: the incriminating information—an outstanding arrest warrant—was not sought among records that a person reasonably expects will remain private, such as his bank statements (Burrows v. Superior Court (1974) 13 Cal.3d 238, 242–248, 118 Cal.Rptr. 166, 529 P.2d 590); rather, it was contained in the government's own files, compiled from official reports of law enforcement agencies and the Department of Motor Vehicles, and was retrieved via state and local police telecommunications systems.

Nevertheless we cannot say that in all or even a majority of instances the type of detention here challenged is only a "minor inconvenience." Given the pace of contemporary life, it may well be a significant interference with a motorist's schedule to make him sit idly by for a full 10 or more minutes while the police run a warrant check on him. And his embarrassment will be compounded when, as often occurs, the presence of one or more marked police vehicles parked adjacent to his car throughout the detention focuses the curiosity of passersby on his predicament.[10]

Against this intrusion we must weigh the interests of the police in running a warrant check after every traffic stop. As none of the decisions relied on by the Attorney General articulates those interests, he assays the task in the case before us. He proposes three different purposes said to be served by such a routine warrant check. First he contends the inquiry is necessary to verify the identity of the driver, as it would frustrate the citation process if the motorist were permitted to deceive the officer as to his true name and address. The only way in which the officer can be sure that the motorist is who he says he is, the argument runs, is by retrieving from the records of the Department of Motor Vehicles (hereinafter DMV) the information he disclosed when applying for his driving permit, i. e., his name, age, sex, address, and a brief identifying description. (Veh.Code, § 12800, subds. (a) and (b).[11] But the license that the driver is compelled by law to carry when operating a vehicle and present to the officer on demand (§ 12951) bears on its face exactly the same information as that contained in the DMV records (§ 12811), together with his photograph (§ 12800.5) and his signature (§ 12950). The reason for requiring such descriptive information on the license, of course, is primarily to allow the officer to compare it with the appearance of the individual before him. It is true that such a

---

outstanding warrants only "against the driver," such as defendant herein. The Attorney General wisely does not attempt to justify on any grounds Officer Thomas' act of running the same check on the *passenger* in this case.

10. In the case at bar, for example, Officer Fischer testified that he decided to move the investigation from the scene of the stop to the Larkspur police station because "High school was in the process of breaking for the day and with two patrol cars there, one subject in handcuffs and another subject detained, we were starting to draw a crowd."

11. All statutory references hereinafter are to the Vehicle Code.

license could conceivably have been altered to show a fictitious name and address;[12] but the Attorney General furnishes us with no evidence of how often a motorist stopped for a traffic infraction presents a fraudulently altered license to the arresting officer, and in view of the patent illegality of such conduct we cannot presume it to be a frequent occurrence.[13] In the vast majority of cases, rather, the officer may reasonably rely on the descriptive information on the face of the license in verifying that the motorist has correctly identified himself. Indeed, for the purpose of facilitating identification the DMV issues cards, similar to a driver's license, to nondrivers. (§ 13000.)

Next the Attorney General contends that a routine warrant check is necessary to verify the current validity of the license. The DMV or the courts may suspend or revoke a driver's license on various grounds. The Attorney General avers there is "a significant number" of such cases each year, and cites DMV statistics assertedly showing 295,006 revocations and suspensions during the 12-month period ending November 1977.[14] From this figure he concludes that without conducting a radio check the officer "has no idea whether the license handed to him by the driver is or is not valid."

The argument is not persuasive for several reasons. First, the relevant statistic is not the total number of licenses suspended or revoked during the year but the average number in that status at any one time—necessarily a lower figure.[15] In addition, the law requires that when the DMV suspends or revokes a license, it "shall be surrendered to the department" (§ 13551, subd. (a)); the surrender, of course, fully eliminates the risk that the license might thereafter be presented to an officer as valid. The Attorney General responds that the DMV "has no enforcement section," implying the statute is largely disregarded. But he cites no evidence in support, and again we cannot presume widespread disobedience of a clear statutory command that carries multiple penal consequences.[16] Moreover, many suspensions and revocations are the result not of departmental action but of court orders, and in all such cases it is the court that requires the surrender of the license in question. (§ 13550; see also §§ 13206, 13207.) For obvious reasons the Attorney General does not contend the court lacks enforcement powers.

In any event, even if we were to assume that the 295,006 annual suspensions and revocations cited by the Attorney General

12. It is highly unlikely that the license as originally issued would bear a fictitious name and address: the DMV is empowered to require every applicant for a license "to produce such identification as it determines is necessary in order to insure that the name of the applicant stated in the application is his true name and that his residence address as set forth in the application is his true residence address." (§ 12800.7.)

13. It is unlawful (1) to alter a driver's license in any unauthorized manner, (2) to display or even possess a reproduction or duplicate of the license or any fictitious or fraudulently altered license, and (3) to permit any unlawful use of a license. (§ 14610, subds. (a), (e), (g), (h).) Violation of any of the foregoing prohibitions is not merely an infraction but a misdemeanor punishable by a fine of up to $500 or imprisonment in county jail for up to six months, or by both such fine and imprisonment. (§§ 40000.11, 42002.)

14. Defendant contends these and other statistics cited by the Attorney General are not proper subjects of judicial notice (Evid.Code, § 452, subd. (h)) because no showing has been made of their reliability or significance. We need not resolve the issue: as will appear, even assuming arguendo the statistics are accurate and have the meaning attributed to them by the Attorney General, they do not support his position on the law.

15. This is so because license suspensions by definition are not permanent: they may be as brief as 30 days (§ 13200), and ordinarily do not exceed six months (§ 13556, subd. (a)). It follows that suspended licenses are continuously being reinstated, and on any given day the number of licenses in a state of suspension must be considerably lower than the total number ordered suspended in the course of the year.

16. It is a misdemeanor to fail to surrender on demand to the DMV any suspended or revoked license. (§§ 14610, subd. (d), 40000.11.) It is a misdemeanor to display or even possess a suspended or revoked license. (§§ 14610, subd. (a), 40000.-11.) And it is a still more serious misdemeanor—punishable on a second conviction within seven years by a $1,000 fine or imprisonment in the county jail of up to one year—to knowingly drive with a suspended or revoked license. (§§ 14601, 14601.1.)

represented the daily average number of motorists in that status and that none had surrendered his license as required by law, such motorists would still constitute merely 2 percent of the California driving population.[17] In People v. Superior Court (*Kiefer*) (1970) supra, 3 Cal.3d 807, 91 Cal.Rptr. 729, 478 P.2d 449, we held that it would be an intolerable and unreasonable intrusion into the lives of the motoring public "if the police were authorized to search for contraband, without probable cause, every vehicle involved in a routine traffic violation. Millions of such vehicles are stopped every year, and all but a small proportion are doubtless proceeding at the time on lawful business or innocent pleasure." (Fn. omitted; id. at p. 815, 91 Cal.Rptr. at p. 733, 478 P.2d at p. 453.) We reiterated that rationale in further holding (at p. 829, 91 Cal.Rptr. at p. 744, 478 P.2d at p. 464) that "To allow the police to routinely search for weapons in all such instances would likewise constitute an 'intolerable and unreasonable' intrusion into the privacy of the vast majority of peaceable citizens who travel by automobile." And two years later, in People v. Superior Court (*Simon*) (1972) supra, 7 Cal.3d 186, 101 Cal.Rptr. 837, 496 P.2d 1205, we held the same reasoning "equally applicable to the search of the driver," agreeing with the New York Court of Appeals that "the ordinary motorist who transgresses against a traffic regulation 'does not thereby indicate a propensity for violence or iniquity'" (id. at p. 206, 101 Cal.Rptr. at p. 851, 496 P.2d at p. 1219).

Kiefer and *Simon* are controlling here. To allow the police to detain for a routine warrant check every motorist stopped for a traffic violation simply because 2 percent of California drivers—at the very most—may be operating with suspended or revoked licenses, would also constitute an "intolerable and unreasonable" intrusion into the lives of "the vast majority of peaceable citizens who travel by automobile." (3 Cal.3d at p. 829, 91 Cal.Rptr. at p. 744, 478 P.2d at p. 464.)

The third and last justification offered by the Attorney General for a routine warrant check is that the inquiry is necessary to verify that the driver has no outstanding unpaid traffic fines. In most instances a person arrested for a traffic violation is promptly released upon giving his written promise to appear. (§§ 40500, 40504.) Thereafter he may choose to deposit the prescribed bail by mail (§ 40510) and forfeit that amount in lieu of making an appearance (§ 40512); if he neither appears nor posts bail, a complaint is filed against him (§ 40513, subd. (a)) and a warrant for his arrest is issued (§ 40515, subd. (a)). In addition, when a driver is convicted of an infraction the judgment may provide for his fine to be paid within a specified time or in specified installments, contingent on his written promise to pay or to appear on the due date; if he neither pays nor appears as promised, he is guilty of a new offense. (§ 42003.)

The Attorney General cites DMV statistics assertedly showing that it received a total of 732,520 notices of "failure to appear" or "failure to pay" during the 12-month period ending December 1977. From these figures he concludes that "a significant number" of drivers are scofflaws who deliberately ignore any traffic citations they receive, and hence that a routine warrant check after every traffic stop is justified as the "least intrusive" method of enforcing the motor vehicle laws.

The argument is no more persuasive than its predecessors. First, it appears from other figures cited by the Attorney General that during the same 12-month period the DMV also received a total of 474,082 "clearances" of notices of failure to appear or to pay. Subtracting these clearances from the

---

17. The Attorney General cites DMV sources for the proposition that as of June 1977 there were an estimated 14,355,000 valid licenses outstanding. Adding thereto the 295,006 motorists assumed for present purposes to be driving with suspended or revoked licenses gives a total of 14,650,006; and 295,006 is 2 percent of that total.

figure quoted above leaves a remainder of 258,438 unresolved notices. But even that sum does not represent an equal number of individual motorists with outstanding traffic warrants. This is so because court records reveal that persons who scoff at the motor vehicle laws tend to be recidivists and often accumulate numerous unpaid tickets before they are caught. If follows that the actual number of drivers with outstanding traffic warrants at any given time is substantially less than the foregoing net figure of 258,438 notices of failure to appear or to pay.

In any event, even if we were to assume that every one of those notices represented an individual motorist with an outstanding warrant against him, such individuals would still constitute less than 2 percent of the licensed California drivers. (See fn. 17, ante.) For the reasons given above, to permit routine police detentions of all persons stopped for a traffic violation in the hope of apprehending the relatively few scofflaws among them would be an unreasonable imposition on the motoring public. After *Kiefer* and *Simon* we cannot indulge in the assumption that the majority of California drivers are wanted criminals. (People v. Grace (1973) supra, 32 Cal.App.3d 447, 453, fn. 3, 108 Cal.Rptr. 66.)

We conclude that the intrusion resulting from routine detentions of all traffic offenders for warrant checks—without regard to the presence or absence of suspicious circumstances—is not outweighed by the government's asserted interests in conducting the checks, and hence that such detentions are constitutionally unreasonable. We therefore disapprove the Court of Appeal decisions to the contrary, and hold in the case at bar that the initial detention of defendant and Acosta for a warrant check was unjustifiable on either ground claimed by the Attorney General.

This is not to say, of course, that no detention whatever of a motorist lawfully stopped for a traffic violation is proper in the absence of suspicious circumstances.

Rather, the guiding principle is that such an intrusion is permissible when it is "'. . . reasonably related in scope to the circumstances which justified the interference in the first place.'" (People v. Brisendine (1975) supra, 13 Cal.3d 528, 538, 119 Cal. Rptr. 315, 321, 531 P.2d 1099, 1105, quoting from Terry v. Ohio (1968) supra, 392 U.S. 1, 20, 88 S.Ct. 1868, 20 L.Ed.2d 889.) Under that principle, the officer may properly detain the driver for the short period of time necessary to perform his duties arising from the traffic violation itself. For example, a brief detention is permissible while the officer explains the violation to the motorist, examines his driver's license (§ 12951, subd. (b)) and the registration card of the vehicle (§ 4462, subd. (a)), conducts appropriate equipment checks if he reasonably believes the vehicle is in an unsafe condition (§§ 2804, 2806), and either warns the driver against future violations or writes out a citation and obtains the driver's signature thereon (§§ 40500, 40504). (See, e. g., People v. Mack (1977) 66 Cal.App.3d 839, 848, 136 Cal.Rptr. 283; People v. Grace (1973) supra, 32 Cal.App.3d 447, 452, 108 Cal.Rptr. 66; People v. Lingo (1970) 3 Cal.App.3d 661, 663–664, 83 Cal.Rptr. 755.)

Performance of these duties, however, must not be used as a subterfuge to give the officer time and opportunity to run a "routine warrant check." We agree with the *Grace* court that "It is no answer to assert the procedure involves no added inconvenience to the citizen because it is carried out while the officer makes an investigation of the offense and writes out the citation. The inevitable result is that the length of the detention will be governed, not by the time reasonably required by the officer to perform his proper duty, but instead by how long it takes him to receive an 'all clear' from the source or sources to which he made inquiry." (32 Cal.App.3d at p. 453, fn. 3, 108 Cal.Rptr. at p. 70.) Nor is it an answer to say that the courts can intervene in instances of such abuse by declaring illegal any detention longer than the period that "would have been" necessary to investigate the violation and issue a citation. That period will obviously be different in every case, varying according to such factors as the time and place of the stop, the seriousness of the violation, the complexity of the equipment check in safety cases, the thoroughness of the officer, and even the argumentativeness of the driver. For a court to decree at a later date precisely how much time "would have been" necessary to perform the officer's duties in any given case would be at best hindsight and at worst sheer speculation. (footnote omitted).

The record of the case at bar amply illustrates the dangers of such abuse. Officer Thomas did not in fact issue a citation to defendant for driving in the wrong direction on the one-way street, and indeed he never intended to do so. The street in question is a two-way thoroughfare on either side of the Redwood High School parking lot, but while it crosses that lot it becomes one way only. Thomas admitted at the hearing that although he had seen a number of other drivers make the same "mistake" as defendant, he had never cited any of them, and that it was his "personal policy" in this situation to give the errant drivers "the benefit of the doubt" and "let them off with a warning." When Thomas signalled to him defendant promptly stopped his car, and just as promptly produced his driver's license and identified himself; in the circumstances a brief explanation of the unusual traffic pattern and a warning against repeating the mistake would have completed Thomas' duties as he conceived them, and would have consumed only a fraction of the time that defendant and his companion were actually compelled to wait while the officer conducted his "routine warrant check." The excessive detention was thus unnecessary to the performance of Thomas' functions arising from the traffic stop, and hence was impermissible under the rule stated above. (Willett v. Superior Court (1969) supra, 2 Cal. App.3d 555, 559, 83 Cal.Rptr. 22; cf. People v. Lingo (1970) supra, 3 Cal.App.3d 661, 664–665, 83 Cal.Rptr. 755.)

The evidence here challenged was the direct product of exploitation of that unlawful detention, and should have been suppressed. It was essential to the case against defendant, and the ensuing conviction therefore cannot stand. Accordingly, we need not reach defendant's additional contention that Officer Fischer had no probable cause to search his car at the police station.

The judgment is reversed.

BIRD, C. J., and MANUEL, and NEWMAN, JJ., concur.

CLARK, Justice, dissenting.

This case questions the validity of detention of a motorist, legally stopped for a traffic violation, for the purpose of conducting a warrant or record check. The majority conclude that police may not routinely continue a detention for such purposes and that no special circumstances exist in this case justifying any detention. I agree with the courts below that it was not unreasonable to detain defendant briefly to determine whether there existed outstanding warrants against him, or related information in police records.

Warrant checking presents one of the most effective and least intrusive methods of law enforcement, as this case illustrates. Here, a peaceful ten-minute detention resulted in a burglary suspect being apprehended, stolen property recovered, and possible future criminal activity prevented. No force was used nor was defendant placed in an embarrassing "predicament" until after the radio transmissions had been completed.[1]

The majority concede a police radio inquiry, seeking information contained in

---

1. The majority note the investigation was moved from the scene of the stop because a crowd was beginning to form. (Ante, p. 589 of 149 Cal.Rptr., p. —— of —— P.2d, fn. 10.) The testimony quoted in the footnote indicates onlookers were attracted not by the ten-minute warrant check, but by the sight of a suspect in handcuffs following arrest. Thus, the majority offer no basis for their claim a motorist's embarrassment will be "compounded" by a warrant check.

government files is not a "search" in the constitutional sense. They correctly distinguish People v. Superior Court (*Kiefer*) (1970) 3 Cal.3d 807, 91 Cal.Rptr. 729, 478 P.2d 449, and People v. Superior Court (*Simon*) (1972) 7 Cal.3d 186, 101 Cal.Rptr. 837, 496 P.2d 1205, as cases involving *searches* of a traffic violator's person or car; yet, these same cases are later relied on as "controlling here." The majority thus implicitly and incorrectly hold a ten-minute detention to be a "significant interference" of the same magnitude as a search of the motorist's person or car.

Obviously the vast majority of California drivers are not wanted criminals; they should not be and are not treated as such. "An officer may not, routinely and without any cause whatsoever, detain every citizen he encounters—even if he has violated some traffic rule—in order to interrogate him . . . about any other possible offense, and then use the reply to such questioning as an excuse for a search otherwise unlawful." (People v. Grace (1973) 32 Cal.App.3d 447, 453, 108 Cal.Rptr. 66, 70.)

On the other hand, violation of traffic laws constitutes a serious matter, involving an obvious threat to public safety.[2] Ten minutes is not an unreasonable length of time to detain a violator, check license and registration, discuss the driver's error, and issue either a warning or citation.

Nor is it improper to conduct a routine warrant inquiry during this brief period. Unlike *Grace,* the driver was not "interrogated." He was required only to present a driver's license to the arresting officer as evidence of identity. (Veh.Code, §§ 2800, 40302, subd. (a).) No further inquiry was made of the motorists regarding information unrelated to the traffic violation. As the majority note, most persons arrested for traffic violations are cited and released upon a written promise to appear. (Veh.Code, §§ 40500, 40504.) Police should be permitted to briefly detain a motorist and conduct a warrant or record inquiry as a matter of routine to determine whether the offender has a record of dishonoring such promises. The only alternative—an impractical one at best—is to release the motorist and follow him until there is a response to the inquiry. Such a procedure would constitute as great an intrusion as that in the instant case.

Because the detention was initially lawful and thereafter did not become unlawful, the evidence derived from it was properly received at trial.[3]

The judgment should be affirmed.

RICHARDSON, J., concurs.

TOBRINER, Justice, dissenting.

I dissent.

The instant case presents the issue whether a police officer who validly detains a motorist for a traffic violation may extend the detention for 10 minutes for the purpose of conducting a warrant check. On the basis of the record before us, I have concluded that specific and articulable facts known or apparent to the police officer in question caused him reasonably to suspect that some activity relating to crime had taken place and that defendant was involved in that activity and hence constitutionally justified his brief extended detention of defendant.

---

2. In the present case, defendant's automobile was observed proceeding in the wrong direction on a one-way public street crossing a high school parking lot.

3. The majority's holding is destined to be misunderstood by both law enforcement personnel and motorists. The assumption that "none of us needs to be reminded that a system of criminal justice exists not just for the protection of the innocent but for the punishment of the guilty . . ." (Witkin, *The Second Noble Experiment of the Twentieth Century* (Sept.–Nov. 1977) Prosecutor's Brief, pp. 42–45), may be incorrect. However, the author reminds us in the next sentence "that only by consistent apprehension and conviction of the murderer, the burglar, the arsonist, the rapist, the drug-peddler . . . can the system justify itself in the eyes of our people. We are therefore in deep trouble if, as these critics would have us believe, the judges of our state and federal courts are frustrating law enforcement by placing burdensome restrictions on arrest, production of evidence and trials." Certainly we should not contribute to such "deep trouble."

"[W]e have consistently held that circumstances short of probable cause to make an arrest may still justify an officer's stopping pedestrians or motorists on the streets for questioning." (People v. Mickelson (1963) 59 Cal.2d 448, 450, 30 Cal.Rptr. 18, 20, 380 P.2d 658, 660. See also People v. Martin (1956) 46 Cal.2d 106, 108, 293 P.2d 52; People v. Blodgett (1956) 46 Cal.2d 114, 117, 293 P.2d 57; People v. Simon (1955) 45 Cal.2d 645, 650, 290 P.2d 531.) The federal rules governing police investigations and arrests are in accord, for as the United States Supreme Court recognized in Terry v. Ohio (1968) 392 U.S. 1, 22, 88 S.Ct. 1868, 1880, 20 L.Ed.2d 889, "a police officer may in appropriate circumstances and in an appropriate manner approach a person for purposes of investigating possible criminal behavior even though there is no probable cause to make an arrest."

We have recently elaborated on the grounds necessary to justify such an investigative stop or detention. In In re Tony C. (1978) 21 Cal.3d 888, 893, 148 Cal.Rptr. 366, 368, 582 P.2d 957, 959, we held that "in order to justify an investigative stop or detention the circumstances known or apparent to the officer must include specific and articulable facts causing him to suspect that (1) some activity relating to crime has taken place or is occurring or about to occur, and (2) the person he intends to stop or detain is involved in that activity. Not only must he subjectively entertain such a suspicion, but it must be objectively reasonable for him to do so: the facts must be such as would cause any reasonable police officer in a like position, drawing when appropriate on his training and experience . . . , to suspect the same criminal activity and the same involvement by the person in question. The corollary to this rule, of course, is that an investigative stop or detention predicated on mere curiosity, rumor, or hunch is unlawful, even though the officer may be acting in complete good faith. . . ." (Fn. omitted.)

To summarize the circumstances involved in the case before us: Officer Thomas witnessed defendant commit the traffic violation of driving in the wrong direction on a one-way street. As Officer Thomas drove up behind defendant, he saw defendant's passenger lean over the back of the seat, apparently moving something on the rear floorboard. When Officer Thomas approached to question defendant, he noted that although defendant had been driving on the one-way street which crosses the Redwood High School parking lot, defendant was not of high school age. On Thomas' request for identification, defendant produced a driver's license showing a San Francisco address, and, appearing somewhat confused, explained that he was looking for the Marin County Juvenile Hall, a facility which Thomas knew was several miles away. At that point Thomas initiated the radio check for outstanding arrest warrants which the majority here rule "constitutionally unreasonable."

On the basis of the above-mentioned facts the trial court held Officer Thomas' action lawful and admitted subsequently discovered contraband. As the trial court explained, "obviously the facts of this case are like any . . . questions of search and seizure, and the magistrate must consider the *totality of the circumstances* which is, as they testified, number one, . . . whether they are acting honestly and in good faith in the manner in which they proceeded, and taking the *totality of the circumstances*, I believe they did act reasonably . . . ." (Emphasis added.) I would affirm the trial court.

In People v. Gale (1973) 9 Cal.3d 788, 795–799, 108 Cal.Rptr. 852, 511 P.2d 1204, we held that the reasonableness of the duration of a detention must be governed by an examination of the "totality of the circumstances." Our decision in *Tony C.*, supra, does not purport to change this standard. (See 21 Cal.3d at pp. 888, 892, 148 Cal.Rptr. 366, 582 P.2d 957.) Nevertheless the majority in the instant case, after examining each circumstance *in isolation,* dismiss the conditions surrounding defendant's detention as "wholly innocent" or otherwise "insufficient to support the intrusion." Contrary to the majority's approach, we must uphold a detention when an analysis of the *entire factual setting* in which the detention occurred reveals that "specific and articulable facts" supported the detention.

In the present case, Officer Thomas himself articulated the *combination* of specific factors upon which he based his decision to detain defendant: "The fact that they were confused, were from San Francisco, were in an area of the high school and which has high drug traffic, and were not of high school age." Officer Thomas had witnessed defendant's traffic violation, and justifiably mistrusted defendant's claim to be looking for the distant Marin County Juvenile Hall. Furthermore, Thomas understandably felt "some trepidation or concern or suspicion" at observing defendant's passenger "actually lean over the seat": as Officer Thomas testified, "It is not uncommon to glance back, but it is very uncommon for someone to actually lean over the seat." While a "furtive gesture" or a San Francisco address *alone* may not suffice to sustain a detention, nevertheless the *combination* of factors apparent to Officer Thomas in the present case reasonably deepened Thomas' suspicion; because Officer Thomas "fairly entertained growing doubts as to the veracity of defendant and his companion" (People v. Harris (1975) 15 Cal.3d 384, 389, 124 Cal.Rptr. 536, 540 P.2d 632, cert. den. (1976) 425 U.S. 934, 96 S.Ct. 1664, 48 L.Ed.2d 175), Officer Thomas properly extended his investigation.

In light of the totality of these suspicious circumstances, Officer Thomas reasonably detained defendant for a short period for purposes of investigation. In People v. One 1960 Cadillac Coupe (1964) 62 Cal.2d 92, 95–96, 41 Cal.Rptr. 290, 292, 396 P.2d 706, 708, we recognized that "a police officer in the discharge of his duties may detain and question a person when the circumstances are such as would indicate to a reasonable man in a like position that such a course is *necessary to the proper discharge of those duties.*" (Emphasis added.) As Officer Thomas testified in the present case, his original intention on witnessing defendant's traffic violation was to detain defendant "for purposes of investigation." Clearly Thomas did not exceed reasonable bounds in interpreting his duty to include a few minutes' detention to conduct a warrant check, particularly in light of his well-grounded suspicions as to defendant's bona fides. The warrant check itself constituted no invasion of defendant's privacy, as defendant himself concedes. Contrary to the majority's suggestion, the 10-minute period at issue did not expose defendant to more than minor inconvenience or embarrassment:[1] certainly defendant's detention did not involve the personally offensive and stigmatizing treatment of an arrest or search.[2]

The detention in the case before us involves a minor and unintrusive law enforcement procedure. Although I do not agree with Justice Clark that police should be permitted to detain a motorist and conduct a warrant or record inquiry as a matter of routine, I believe that the detention in the

---

1. According to testimony at trial, Officer Thomas remained in his patrol car during the warrant check, and defendant and his passenger "were in their vehicle talking." As Justice Clark notes in dissent, the curiosity of passersby focused on defendant's predicament only *after* defendant had been arrested and handcuffed.

2. The majority's reliance on People v. Superior Court (*Simon*) (1972) 7 Cal.3d 186, 101 Cal.Rptr. 837, 496 P.2d 1205 and People v. Superior Court (*Kiefer*) (1970) 3 Cal.3d 807, 91 Cal.Rptr. 729, 478 P.2d 449 is misplaced. In those cases we held that probable cause to arrest a traffic offender, "no matter how persuasive, is neither a necessary nor a sufficient condition" for a warrantless search of his vehicle or person for contraband. (3 Cal.3d 807, 815, 91 Cal.Rptr. 729, 733, 478 P.2d 449, 453, 7 Cal.3d 186, 191, 101 Cal.Rptr. 837, 841, 496 P.2d 1205, 1209.) To justify such a search, we concluded, there must be independent probable cause to believe that contraband is present.

By contrast in the instant case we are concerned with neither a search of the driver's person nor a search of his vehicle and, as we have explained, circumstances short of probable cause may suffice to justify defendant's extended detention. Thus, the majority err in applying the constitutional standard of *Kiefer* and *Simon* to the minimal intrusion which the present defendant may have experienced.

instant case falls within constitutional bounds. In weighing the competing interests here—a function inherent in all judgment—we cannot believe that a fleeting moment of delay to a motorist, provided that it is indeed of very limited duration, is so massive an intrusion as to foreclose the quite legitimate procedure of law enforcement which the warrant check constitutes.

• • •

PEOPLE v. MORENO *

Court of Appeal, First District, Division 1, 1977.
67 Cal.App.3d 962, 134 Cal.Rptr. 322.

ELKINGTON, Associate Justice.

A police officer, during the course of an investigative detention of defendant Moreno and his automobile, observed in plain sight a "billy," the possession of which is proscribed by Penal Code section 12020. The weapon was seized and Moreno was arrested. In the municipal court, where he was charged as a misdemeanant, he unsuccessfully moved under Penal Code section 1538.5 to suppress the use of the weapon as evidence. He, as permitted by Penal Code section 1538.5, subdivision (j), appealed from the order denying his motion to the appellate department of the superior court.

The issue raised on the appeal was the constitutional propriety of the police officer's detention of Moreno. The lower reviewing court thereafter, under rule 63, California Rules of Court, made the following certification:

"The Appellate Department of the Superior Court of the State of California for the County of Alameda, hereby grants the People's application and certifies that transfer of this case to the Court of Appeal of the State of California for the First Appellate District is necessary to secure uniformity of decision regarding the continuing vitality of the standard found in Irwin v. Superior Court, 1 Cal.3d 423 at 427, 82 Cal.Rptr. 484, 462 P.2d 12: 'Where the events are as consistent with innocent activity as with criminal activity, a detention based on these events is unlawful.' Cf. People v. Superior Court (*Acosta*), 20 Cal.App.3d 1085, 1091, 98 Cal.Rptr. 161 (1971); People v. Higbee, 37 Cal.App.3d 944, 950, 112 Cal.Rptr. 690 (1974); People v. Rios, 51 Cal.App.3d 1008, 1011, 124 Cal.Rptr. 737 (1975) and People v. Larkin, 52 Cal.App.3d 346, 349, 125 Cal.Rptr. 137 (1975), with People v. Lathan, 38 Cal. App.3d 911, 914, 113 Cal.Rptr. 648 (1974) and People v. Wheeler, 43 Cal.App.3d 898, 902–903, 118 Cal.Rptr. 205 (1974)."

We ordered the appeal transferred to this court.

Irwin v. Superior Court (1969) 1 Cal.3d 423, 82 Cal.Rptr. 484, 462 P.2d 12, dealt with the constitutional limitations on the right of a police officer to temporarily detain a person for the purpose of questioning, or other criminal investigation. The court applied the widely known applicable rule, as follows:

"[A] detention based on a 'mere hunch' is unlawful . . . even though the officer may have acted in good faith . . . . There must be a 'rational suspicion by the peace officer that some activity out of the ordinary is or has taken place . . . some indication to connect the person under suspicion with the unusual activity . . . [and] some suggestion that the activity is related to crime.'" 1 Cal.3d, p. 427, 82 Cal.Rptr., p. 486, 462 P.2d, p. 14.

But the court then used the language here presented for our consideration: "Where the events are as consistent with innocent activity as with criminal activity, a detention based on those events is unlawful." 1 Cal.3d, p. 427, 82 Cal.Rptr., p. 486, 462 P.2d, p. 14.

At this point we briefly consider the constitutional requirements of *probable*

---

* Prior to reading this case it is recommended that the reader review the following statute: Penal Code § 836.

cause for the warrantless arrest of a person suspected of criminal activity. Such probable cause exists when the facts apparent to the officer " 'would lead a man of ordinary care and prudence to believe and conscientiously entertain an honest and strong suspicion that the person is guilty of a crime.' " (People v. Harris, supra, 15 Cal.3d 384, 389, 540 P.2d 632, 635, 124 Cal.Rptr. 536, 539; People v. Terry (1970) 2 Cal.3d 362, 393, 85 Cal.Rptr. 409 [cert. den., 406 U.S. 912, 92 S.Ct. 1619, 32 L.Ed.2d 112]; People v. Ingle (1960) 53 Cal.2d 407, 412, 2 Cal.Rptr. 14, 348 P.2d 577 [cert. den., 364 U.S. 841, 81 S.Ct. 79, 5 L.Ed.2d 65].) And probable cause for a warrantless arrest "has also been defined as having more evidence for than against; . . ." (People v. Ingle, supra, p. 413, 2 Cal.Rptr., p. 17, 348 P.2d, p. 580; People v. Moore (1975) 51 Cal.App.3d 610, 616, 124 Cal.Rptr. 290 [hearing by S.Ct. den.; cert. den., 425 U.S. 977, 96 S.Ct. 2179, 48 L.Ed.2d 801]; Wilson v. County of Los Angeles (1971) 21 Cal.App.3d 308, 316, 98 Cal.Rptr. 525; People v. Superior Court (*Thomas*) (1970) 9 Cal.App.3d 203, 208, 88 Cal.Rptr. 21.)

Analysis of Irwin v. Superior Court's two concepts reveals opposing principles. The first permits otherwise reasonable investigative detention, upon a *rational suspicion of criminal activity,* while the second demands as a requisite for a police officer's detention that there be a *preponderant appearance of criminal activity.*

It will be seen that the additional requirement of Irwin v. Superior Court authorizes temporary police investigative detention of a person only under circumstances that would create probable cause for the person's arrest. For by any test of law or logic, if the facts apparent to the policeman amount to a preponderant appearance of criminal activity, then surely probable cause for arrest must exist. Indeed, People v. Ingle's above-quoted definition of probable cause for an arrest, i. e., "having more evidence for than against" 53 Cal.2d, p. 413, 2 Cal.Rptr., p. 17, 348 P.2d, p. 580 is a strikingly accurate paraphrasing of Irwin v. Superior Court's added investigative detention requirement of "preponderant appearance of criminal activity."

Yet it is a truism of our criminal law practice "that circumstances short of probable cause to make an arrest may still justify an officer's stopping pedestrians or motorists on the street for questioning." (People v. Mickelson, supra, 59 Cal.2d 448, 450, 30 Cal.Rptr. 18, 20, 380 P.2d 658, 660.) And the justification "which warrants an officer's detention of a person for investigative reasons is necessarily of a lesser standard than that required to effect an arrest." (People v. Flores, supra, 12 Cal.3d 85, 91, 115 Cal. Rptr. 225, 228, 524 P.2d 353, 356; and to the same effect see Terry v. Ohio, supra, 392 U.S. 1, 22, 88 S.Ct. 1868, 20 L.Ed.2d 889; People v. Harris, supra, 15 Cal.3d 384, 389, 540 P.2d 632, 124 Cal.Rptr. 536; People v. Junious, supra, 30 Cal.App.3d 432, 436, 106 Cal.Rptr. 344; People v. Griffith (1971) 19 Cal.App.3d 948, 950, 97 Cal.Rptr. 367.)

We are of the opinion that Irwin v. Superior Court did not intend a drastic change in the law such as would deny a police officer's right to temporarily detain a person for investigation, unless he had information sufficient to authorize the person's arrest. Had such been the intent we may be sure that the court would in some manner have expressed its disapproval of what then, as it appears to us, was unanimous state and federal authority to the contrary.

Further, we opine that the "preponderant appearance of criminal activity" criterion of Irwin v. Superior Court is a dictum. The court had expressly concluded that the police officer's detention of that case rested upon a "mere hunch" without "rational suspicion" and was thus, under the prevailing rule, unlawful. The case's newly announced "preponderant appearance of criminal activity" test was not necessary to the decision. The state's high court has consistently advised lower tribunals that its "Incidental statements of conclusions not necessary to the decision are not to be regarded as authority" (Simmons v. Superior Court (1959) 52 Cal.2d 373, 378, 341 P.2d 13, 17), and that the "discussion or determination of a point not necessary to the disposition of a question that is decisive of the appeal is generally regarded as obiter dictum" (Stockton Theatres, Inc. v. Palermo (1956) 47 Cal.2d 469, 474, 304 P.2d 7, 9; see also Kastigar v. United States (1972) 406 U.S. 441, 454–455, 92 S.Ct. 1653, 32 L.Ed.2d 212; People v. Clark (1941) 18 Cal.2d 449, 461, 116 P.2d 56; County of San Diego v. Hammond (1936) 6 Cal.2d 709, 724, 59 P.2d 478; Hills v. Superior Court (1929) 207 Cal. 666, 670, 279 P. 805).

Moreover, we observe that the state's Supreme Court has several times recently restated the law applicable to investigative police detention. Without approval, or even mention, of Irwin v. Superior Court's added concept of "preponderant appearance of criminal activity," it has reiterated the long-accepted first rule of that case in this manner.

People v. Gale, supra, 9 Cal.3d 788, 797–798, 108 Cal.Rptr. 852, 859, 511 P.2d 1204, 1211. " 'While a detention of a citizen by a police officer based on a "mere hunch" is unlawful, if there is a rational *suspicion* that some activity out of the ordinary is taking place, and some *suggestion* that the activity is related to crime, a detention is permissible.' "

People v. Flores, supra, 12 Cal.3d 85, 91, 115 Cal.Rptr. 225, 228, 524 P.2d 353, 356. "Where there is a rational belief of criminal activity with which the suspect is connected, a detention for reasonable investigative procedures infringes no constitutional restraint."

People v. Harris, supra, 15 Cal.3d 384, 388–389, 540 P.2d 632, 634, 124 Cal.Rptr. 536, 538. " ' "A police officer may stop and question persons on public streets . . . when the circumstances indicate to a reasonable man in a like position that such a course of action is called for in the proper discharge of the officer's duties. . . . The good faith suspicion which warrants an officer's detention of a person for investigative reasons is necessarily of a lesser standard than that required to effect an arrest. . . . Where there is a rational belief of criminal activity with which the suspect is connected, a detention for reasonable investigative procedures infringes no constitutional restraint. . . .' . . . . [¶] The foregoing standard for *detention* is of lesser degree than that applicable to an *arrest*. . . . [The court then found that the detention of that case had met] the requisite but lesser detention standards of 'good faith suspicion,' and 'rational belief of criminal activity' expressed by us in *Flores* [12 Cal.3d p. 91, 115 Cal.Rptr. 225, 524 P.2d 353]."

The latter language of People v. Harris is significant. We deem the high court's reiteration of "the requisite but lesser detention standards [for investigative police detention] of 'good faith suspicion,' and 'rational belief of criminal activity' ", unqualified by Irwin v. Superior Court's inconsistent earlier dictum of "preponderant appearance of criminal activity," to be the law of this state.

"It is an established rule of law that a later decision overrules prior decisions which conflict with it, whether such prior decisions are mentioned and commented upon or not." (In re Lane (1962) 58 Cal.2d 99, 105, 22 Cal.Rptr. 857, 860, 372 P.2d 897, 900; People v. Escarcega (1974) 43 Cal.App.3d 391, 400, 117 Cal.Rptr. 595; and see 6 Witkin, Cal. Procedure (2d ed. 1971) Appeal, § 692(2), p. 4609, and the authority there collected.)

We observe also that decisions of the state's Court of Appeal have several times *expressly* held that Irwin v. Superior Court's test of preponderant appearance of criminal activity, as justification for temporary police investigative detention, is not the law of this state. (See People v. Knutson, supra, 60 Cal.App.3d 856, 862, 131 Cal.Rptr. 846; People v. Larkin, supra, 52 Cal.App.3d 346, 349, 125 Cal.Rptr. 137; People v. Rios, supra, 51 Cal.App.3d 1008, 1011, 124 Cal.Rptr. 737; People v. Higbee, supra, 37 Cal.App.3d 944, 950, 112 Cal.Rptr. 690; People v. Superior Court (*Acosta*), supra, 20 Cal.App.3d 1085, 1088–1091, 98 Cal.Rptr. 161.)

MAJOR CASE LAW OPINIONS

Answering the question posed by the appellate department of the superior court, we hold that the language of Irwin v. Superior Court—"Where the events are as consistent with innocent activity as with criminal activity, a detention based on those events is unlawful"—has no "continuing vitality."

We consider now the "engrossed statement" of the facts on the instant appeal.

"Officer Olson, while on a routine patrol in a marked police car in Newark on Sunday, January 11, 1976, at about 7:05 PM, observed defendant's vehicle, a 1964 Chevrolet Station Wagon, traveling northbound on Willow Street at the intersection of Enterprise Drive. One and one half blocks south on Willow Street the city street ends. Beyond is a privately maintained dirt road which leads to the Newark Sportman's Club about one mile away. Surrounding the Sportman's Club are undeveloped salt flats owned by the Leslie Salt Company. The area of Enterprise Drive and Willow is commercial with no retail businesses. On January 11, 1976, at 7:00 PM none of the businesses were open. Officer Olson has patrolled this part of Newark for four and one half years and is familiar with the prevalent criminal activity, which is theft and burglary.

"On January 11, 1976, Officer Olson was aware of one theft at a nearby business within the preceding year, as well as five separate instances of burglary at the Sportman's Club within the preceding year.

"Officer Olson testified that the only moving or inhabited vehicle he observed in the area was the one defendant was driving. Defendant was the only occupant of the vehicle. Officer Olson testified he intended to stop the defendant because it was unusual for a moving car to be in that area at that time of night. Because of the burglaries in the area, Officer Olson wanted to find out why defendant was there. Upon pulling in behind defendant's vehicle, Officer Olson observed that defendant's vehicle had no outside rear-view mirror. After stopping defendant's vehicle, the defendant voluntarily exited and walked back toward Officer Olson's location. Officer Olson immediately requested defendant's drivers license and vehicle registration at this time and returned to his car in order to obtain the vehicle registration.

"Officer Olson accompanied defendant and when the defendant opened the driver's door Officer Olson observed a two foot long wooden billy club in plain view on the floorboard in front of the drivers seat. Officer Olson retrieved the billy club and arrested defendant for section 12020 of the Penal Code of California.

"At the conclusion of the hearing the [Municipal] Court made a finding that a car being in that particular area on a dead-end street having past burglaries and no open businesses was such a suspicious circumstance as justified the police officer in investigating."

We opine, as apparently did the municipal court, that the facts apparent to the officer did not meet Irwin v. Superior Court's test 1 Cal.3d, p. 427, 82 Cal.Rptr. p. 486, 462 P.2d p. 14 of "preponderant appearance of criminal activity," but that they nevertheless engendered a " 'rational belief [or suspicion] of criminal activity' " according to People v. Harris, supra, 15 Cal.3d 384, 389, 540 P.2d 632, 124 Cal.Rptr. 536, People v. Flores, supra, 12 Cal.3d 85, 91, 115 Cal.Rptr. 225, 524 P.2d 353, and People v. Gale, supra, 9 Cal.3d 788, 797–798, 108 Cal.Rptr. 852, 511 P.2d 1204. For the reasons we have pointed out, Moreno's detention was without constitutional fault, and his motion to suppress evidence, which depended upon the invalidity of that detention, was properly denied.

The order of the municipal court is affirmed.

PEOPLE v. MOSHER *

Supreme Court of California, In Bank, 1969.
1 Cal.3d 379, 82 Cal.Rptr. 379, 461 P.2d 659.

TOBRINER, Justice.

On September 28, 1966, the Grand Jury of Alameda County indicted the defendant Merle Mark Mosher for the murder of Edith Christie (Pen.Code, § 187) and charged defendant with a prior conviction of statutory rape in 1960 (Pen.Code, § 261, subd. 1). Defendant admitted the prior conviction and pleaded not guilty and not guilty by reason of insanity to the murder charge.

In a separate proceeding the trial court found the defendant mentally competent to stand trial. The jury found the defendant guilty of murder in the first degree, held the defendant sane at the time of the offense, and fixed the penalty at death. The appeal to this court is automatic. (Pen.Code, § 1239, subd. (b).)

• • •

1. *The Facts*

The homicide occurred during the early morning hours of August 2, 1966, in an apartment in Oakland where the decedent, Mrs. Edith Christie, lived alone. The evidence against defendant is exclusively circumstantial.

On August 1, 1966, Mrs. Christie and her niece, Mrs. Brooker, had lunched and then shopped in Oakland. About 4:30 p. m. Mrs. Brooker returned Mrs. Christie to her apartment. At 3:45 a. m. on August 2, 1966, a taxi driver received a call to pick up Mrs. Christie at her apartment. Mrs. Christie walked unsteadily toward the taxi and the driver assisted her to the vehicle and drove her to Peralta Hospital. Dr. Willard Peterson, Mrs. Christie's personal physician for seven years, arrived at Peralta Hospital sometime between 4 and 4:30 a. m. He observed a large hematoma about her face; she was gagging. He had never previously treated her for such physical injuries. She died in surgery that morning at 9 a. m.

A pathologist examined the deceased at the coroner's office at 2:30 p. m., August 2, 1966. He noted abrasions and cuts about the head, and injuries to the body. Numerous ribs had been fractured. The injuries were consistent with a beating by fists and feet and had not been caused by a fall. The pathologist concluded that the cause of death was a subdural hemorrhage of the brain due to trauma.

At the time of the death defendant was 30 years old. He had the equivalent of three years of college education. He had worked his way through the first few years of college at part-time night jobs. Then he had fallen behind in his studies, his grades had suffered, he had changed his major from music to education, and he had dropped out of school. He was involved in two serious automobile accidents in August and December 1960. After each accident he had remained unconscious for several hours. As a result of two barroom brawls defendant, in November 1961, had been committed for psychiatric care to Mendocino State Hospital where he remained until April 1962. Thereafter he continued on home-leave status until December 1963.

After his release from the hospital defendant held several jobs selling encyclopedias and kitchenware. In July 1966 the encyclopedia company suspended defendant for two or three weeks. Defendant's supervisor followed the customary practice in such cases, lending defendant his salesman's identification card so that defendant could continue to work during the period of suspension. According to the testimony of the supervisor and his wife, in addition to defendant's setback at work defendant was in the process of breaking up his relationship with his fiancee, Miss Marlene Norman. Defendant began to appear morose and depressed, particularly as a result of the

---

* Prior to reading this case it is recommended that the reader review the following statute: Penal Code § 833.

collapse of the engagement. On August 1 the supervisor gave defendant some $50 as commission for sales defendant had theretofore transacted. The supervisor went to pick up defendant at 5 p. m. to start work, but defendant appeared to be disoriented and did not want to work that day.

Defendant ate dinner at his apartment about 9 p. m. and at about 11:30 p. m. walked to a neighborhood bar. Defendant visited several bars that evening and consumed about five or six drinks of whiskey before closing time at 2 a. m.; after the automobile accidents in 1960 defendant had become a heavy drinker. When subsequently interrogated he could not remember anything of the night's events except that he had started walking home and while on the street two Oakland police officers had questioned him.

Mrs. Darnall lived in an apartment building about three blocks from Mrs. Christie's apartment. About 3:30 a. m., August 2, 1966, she awoke as a result of a pounding on the back door of her apartment. She heard footsteps going down the stairs and she saw defendant at the foot of the stairs. She asked him what he was doing there and he replied that he was looking for "Marlene." Mrs. Darnall informed him that there was no one by that name in the building. After some dispute with defendant concerning his wanting to use a telephone, Mrs. Darnall slammed her door shut; she got her only lighted view of defendant as he walked down the front walk, some 25 feet away. Mrs. Darnall's daughter phoned the police, asking them to investigate the prowler. Defendant visited four other persons in the area in a similar fashion during those same early morning hours.

In response to the phone call from Mrs. Darnall's daughter, Oakland Police Officers Gardner and Price arrived about 3:40 a. m. to investigate the prowler report. Mrs. Darnall described the man she had seen as white, heavy set, broad-shouldered, and of an average height of about 5 feet 9 or 10 inches. She said he was wearing a dark suit and a white shirt and had taken off his coat. She saw no bloodstains on his shirt and she could not remember whether he had worn a tie. The officers commenced a systematic search on foot, checking backyards, stairways, and areas behind the buildings. At 4 a. m., and a few blocks away, they observed a man matching Mrs. Darnall's description of the visitor, except that he was wearing a suit coat. Sergeant Price ordered the man, who was defendant, to halt. When asked what he was doing, defendant replied that he was going home to Fairmont Street. Fairmont Street lay quite far from where the officers found defendant.

The officers commenced a pat-down search for weapons. Sergeant Price felt in the suspect's lower left coat pocket "a sharp object like a knife blade." The officer pulled a gold watch with bracelet from defendant's pocket and asked defendant where he got it. Defendant indicated that he did not own the watch, but refused to say where he had obtained it. The officers also found a large ring of keys and a wallet with identification for Mark Mosher and for Mr. Tiner, defendant's supervisor. There was a bloodstain on the center panel of defendant's shirt, his hands were cut, and his breath had an odor of alcohol. The officers placed defendant under arrest for suspicion of burglary, handcuffed him, and took him to Mrs. Darnall's apartment for identification. Mrs. Darnall viewed the defendant from the same vantage point from which she had first seen him, and identified him as the prowler.

The watch found in defendant's pocket was later identified as the watch which Mrs. Christie was wearing the day before she died. The keys found in defendant's pockets belonged to the owner of several apartment houses in the area who had left his keys in the glove compartment of his car. He noted that they were missing, and discovered that someone had entered the laundry room of one of his apartment buildings without permission. The stain on defendant's shirt contained type A blood. Mrs. Christie's blood was type B. Defendant's blood type was not tested; the prosecution presented no explanation for this omission. Mrs. Christie's nightgown contained stains of type B blood; her purse and defendant's coat pocket had been stained by both type A and type B blood. No identifiable fingerprints of defendant were found in the deceased's apartment.

For the limited purpose of showing defendant's state of mind as it might bear on purpose or motive, or on plan, design, or characteristic behavior pattern the prosecution introduced the testimony of a victim of rape allegedly committed by the defendant on January 27, 1966. The defense introduced the testimony of Dr. Clarence S. Miller that defendant was unable to form the necessary specific intent to commit any of the offenses charged because of his diminished capacity. The doctor examined defendant, his family, and his fiancee; he further reviewed defendant's prior psychiatric records and all other available material. Dr. Miller concluded that defendant had suffered a "black-out" or an acute "episodic state of mind" on the morning of August 2, 1966, and that defendant had a "schizophrenic reaction, paranoid type."

In rebuttal, Dr. Walter Rapaport testified that he had examined defendant on the afternoon of August 2, 1966, at the request of the district attorney. The doctor had first introduced himself and had then warned defendant that he could remain silent, that he could talk to counsel before deciding whether to proceed with the examination, and that the doctor would testify as to his findings if requested to do so. Defendant did not object and the doctor concluded that defendant understood the warnings. After examination the doctor concluded that defendant could formulate an intent to commit robbery and was not insane.

The jury returned a verdict of guilty of first degree murder, and in the subsequent proceedings found defendant to be legally sane at the time of the commission of the crime; at the penalty phase the jury returned a verdict of death.

• • •

3. *Defendant's contention as to illegal search and seizure*

The police officers had received a misdemeanor complaint concerning a person matching the description of the defendant in the early morning hours of August 2, 1966. In making a superficial pat-down search for weapons one of the police officers "felt a sharp object like a knife blade." The police removed the object from the defendant's pocket and found that the object was not a knife but the wristwatch of the deceased. Defendant contends that the watch constituted the product of an illegal search and seizure and hence was inadmissible at trial.

On occasion, the police have used the excuse that an object in a person's pocket felt like a weapon to perform an exploratory search of the person's clothing and empty the citizen's pockets of everything. (Compare, e. g., People v. Britton (1968) 264 Cal.App.2d 711, 717, 70 Cal.Rptr. 586; People v. Martines (1964) 228 Cal.App.2d 245, 247–248, 39 Cal.Rptr. 526; with People v. Armenta (1968) 268 A.C.A. 264, 267, 73 Cal.Rptr. 819.) Terry v. Ohio (1968) 392 U.S. 1, 27, 88 S.Ct. 1868, 1883, 20 L.Ed.2d 889, explained the rationale and limits of pat-down searches for weapons: "[T]here must be a narrowly drawn authority to permit a reasonable search for weapons for the protection of the police officer, where he has reason to believe that he is dealing with an armed and dangerous individual, regardless of whether he has probable cause to arrest the individual for a crime. The officer need not be absolutely certain that the individual is armed; the issue is whether a reasonably prudent man in the circumstances would be warranted in the belief that his safety or that of others was in danger." Sibron v. New York (1968) 392 U.S. 40, 65, 88 S.Ct. 1889, 20 L.Ed.2d 917, further explained: "The search for weapons approved in *Terry* consisted solely of a limited patting of the outer clothing of the suspect for concealed objects which might be used as instruments of assault."

Hence, *Terry* and *Sibron* indicate that if an officer does not have probable cause for arrest but entertains a prudent reason to fear for his safety, he may perform a superficial pat-down search for weapons, but he may not reach inside the clothing of the suspect unless he has reason to believe a weapon is concealed there. Unless the officer feels an object which a prudent man could believe was an object usable as an instrument of assault, the officer may not remove the object from the inside of the suspect's clothing, require the suspect to take the object out of his pocket, or demand that the suspect empty his pockets. If the officer obtains contraband from the suspect's clothing, the trial court, in order to justify the search and the introduction of the fruits of the search into evidence, must find that the object could have felt like an object usable as an instrument of assault. (See Sibron v. New York, supra, 392 U.S. 40, 64–66, 88 S.Ct. 1889; People v. Britton, supra, 264 Cal.App.2d 711, 717, 70 Cal.Rptr. 586.) A box of matches, a plastic pouch, a pack of cigarettes, a wrapped sandwich, a container of pills, a wallet, coins, folded papers, and many other small items usually carried in an individual's pockets do not ordinarily feel like weapons. A more intensive or broad search "violates the guarantee of the Fourth Amendment, which protects the sanctity of the person against unreasonable intrusions on the part of all government agents." (Sibron v. New York, supra, 392 U.S. 40, 65–66, 88 S.Ct. 1889, 1904.)

In this case, however, the officer could, and did, reasonably believe that the object in the defendant's pocket was a knife. Indeed, for several years prior to *Terry* and *Sibron* we repeatedly held that "circumstances short of probable cause to make an arrest may still justify an officer's stopping pedestrians . . . on the streets for questioning. If the circumstances warrant it, he may in self-protection request a suspect . . . to submit to a superficial search for concealed weapons. Should the investigations then reveal probable cause to make an arrest, the officer may arrest the suspect and conduct a reasonable incidental search." (People v. Mickelson (1963) 59 Cal.2d 448, 450–451, 30 Cal.Rptr. 18, 20, 380 P.2d 658, 660.)

• • •

5. *Right to counsel at pretrial identification and psychiatric interview*

Defendant contends that he was denied the right to counsel at lineup under United States v. Wade (1967) 388 U.S. 218, 87 S.Ct. 1926, 18 L.Ed.2d 1149, and Gilbert v. California (1967) 388 U.S. 263, 87 S.Ct. 1951, 18 L.Ed.2d 1178. Yet the right to counsel at lineup only applies to lineups which occurred after June 12, 1967; it does not operate retroactively. Hence, a lineup conducted in August 1966 need not follow the rules established in *Wade* and *Gilbert* as to right to counsel.

The defendant might still contend that the lineup "conducted in [his] case was so unnecessarily suggestive and conducive to irreparable mistaken identification that he was denied due process of law." (Stovall v. Denno (1967) 388 U.S. 293, 301–302, 87 S.Ct. 1967, 1972, 18 L.Ed.2d 1199.) The record here fails to show any substantial unfairness in the identification of the defendant by the various neighbors of the deceased in a five-man lineup when the defendant had no attorney present. The five men were of substantially equivalent race, height, and weight, although the defendant was by two inches the shortest and by five pounds the heaviest. Mrs. Darnall identified defendant immediately after his apprehension when the police officers brought defendant back to Mrs. Darnall's apartment house. This first identification of defendant without a lineup but alone might have affected Mrs. Darnall's second identification of defendant at a properly constituted lineup. In *Stovall* the police also asked a witness-victim to identify the defendant, singly, in the witness's hospital room; in the instant case, however, unlike *Stovall*, no imperative of the witness's possible death compelled the implicative procedure of showing the defendant alone.

Nevertheless, the several minutes during which Mrs. Darnall observed the defendant, the precision of her verbal description of the defendant to the police, her vantage point in the well-lighted area of her viewing of the defendant, all indicate in this pre-*Wade* case that the witness had an independent basis for identifying the defendant. (Compare People v. Caruso (1968) 68 Cal.2d 183, 189–190, 65 Cal.Rptr. 336, 436 P.2d 336.) Furthermore, unlike in *Caruso*, we encounter no uncertainty here as to defendant's identification or his whereabouts at the time of the crime. We advocate no post-*Wade* practice of showing suspects to witnesses singly rather than as part of a lineup, although we recognize the exceptional circumstances of the particular situation in *Stovall*. In the instant case, however, in view of the surrounding circumstances, the other indicia of guilt, and the reliability of the identification, we find no denial of due process.

Defendant also contends that he suffered the deprivation of a constitutional right to the presence of counsel during the examination by a psychiatrist employed by the prosecution. Dr. Rapaport examined the defendant on the afternoon of August 2, 1966, the day of the murder. Dr. Rapaport testified that he first introduced himself as a psychiatrist, explained that the district attorney had requested him to interview the defendant, warned the defendant that he could remain silent, told him he could talk to counsel retained by himself or provided to him before deciding to proceed with the examination, and that the doctor would testify as to his findings if requested. The defendant did not object; the doctor concluded that the defendant understood the warnings. In In re Spencer (1965) 63 Cal.2d 400, 410–411, 46 Cal.Rptr. 753, 406 P.2d 33, we required that these warnings be given defendant and that he knowingly and intelligently waive his right to the presence of counsel during the interview; otherwise, the psychiatrist might disguise himself in the cloak of professionalism and yet interrogate the defendant on behalf of the prosecution.

Dr. Rapaport testified at the guilt phase after the date of the decision of *Spencer* (Miranda v. Arizona (1966) 384 U.S. 436, 86 S.Ct. 1602, 16 L.Ed.2d 694; People v. Dorado (1965) 62 Cal.2d 338, 42 Cal.Rptr. 169, 398 P.2d 361) but, in the absence of a request from the defendant or his counsel, the trial court did not rule upon the voluntariness of defendant's waiver of his right to counsel upon examination by a psychiatrist. The court should have determined, outside the hearing of the jury, whether the waiver was voluntary, particularly in view of the expressed doubts as to the defendant's mental competency, the absence of a signed waiver, and defendant's apparent lack of counsel with whom to consult so soon after his arrest. (Jackson v. Denno (1964) 378 U.S. 368, 84 S.Ct. 1774, 12 L.Ed.2d 908.) We expect that the trial court will follow the correct procedure on retrial.

• • •

Because defendant's conviction for murder must be reversed for errors discussed above, we need not reach his further contentions of error; such errors will probably not arise on retrial.

The conviction of murder of the first degree entered against defendant is reversed. The case is remanded to the Alameda County Superior Court for further proceedings consistent with this opinion.

TRAYNOR, C. J., and PETERS, BURKE and SULLIVAN, JJ., concur.

PEOPLE v. RAMEY*

Supreme Court of California, In Bank, 1976.
16 Cal.3d 263, 127 Cal.Rptr. 629, 545 P.2d 1333.

On July 30, 1973, the residence of one James Turner of Sacramento was burglarized. Among the items taken were several

---

* Prior to reading this case it is recommended that the reader review the following statute: Penal Code § 813.

firearms, one of which was a distinctive weapon, a .38 caliber Smith & Wesson Airweight. Turner immediately reported the burglary to the Sacramento police.

Turner, who was a licensed private investigator and former security guard, also decided to investigate his own case. His inquiries led him to two individuals, Reed and Weaver. Reed informed Turner that defendant Ramey had purchased the stolen weapon from Weaver. Turner was slightly acquainted with defendant, and decided to confront him about the stolen weapon.

On the afternoon of August 17, 1973, Turner went to defendant's home. Defendant first told Turner he had been offered the stolen weapon but had not purchased it. Turner insisted he had heard that defendant had bought the Airweight. Defendant responded, "oh, that one," and said he had not known it was Turner's. Defendant then admitted he had owned it briefly but said he had sold it to "some white guy." When pressed for details, defendant could not supply any further information concerning the purchaser. Turner considered defendant's manner and responses evasive and believed he was still in possession of the stolen weapon.

Turner again contacted the Sacramento police and spoke to Detective Joel Garcia. He related to Garcia the chain of events leading him to defendant's residence and his suspicion aroused by his conversation with defendant. Garcia concluded from Turner's information that there was probable cause to arrest defendant for the offense of receiving stolen property.

After a delay of some three hours, Garcia and six other officers proceeded to defendant's residence to effect the arrest of defendant and his roommate. As is the standard departmental practice, Garcia did not secure an arrest warrant prior to the prospective arrest.

Upon arriving at the apartment the officers drew their service revolvers and knocked. Defendant opened the door, and the officers identified themselves and displayed their badges. Defendant backed away towards a portable bar in the living room. The police followed him in, and when defendant was seen to reach behind the bar one of the officers grasped his arm and placed him under arrest. Detective Garcia looked behind the bar and found a .45 caliber pistol, three "lids" of marijuana in cellophane baggies, and a baggie containing tablets appearing to be benzedrine. The officers then seized other marijuana in plain view.

After placing defendant and his roommate under arrest the police searched the entire premises, discovering additional contraband. None of the items found, however, related to the Turner burglary. At the section 1538.5 hearing only those items of evidence seized in the living room were ruled admissible; the remainder was ordered suppressed under the rule of Chimel v. California (1969) 395 U.S. 752, 89 S.Ct. 2034, 23 L.Ed.2d 685.

Defendant attacks the validity of the seizure on the ground that the arrest itself was unlawful, thereby vitiating any claim that the search was conducted incident to a valid arrest. He charges illegality on two alternate theories. First, it is urged that Turner was an untested informant whose credibility had not been established and whose information thus could not furnish probable cause to arrest. Secondly, it is contended that even if there was probable cause the arrest was nevertheless invalid because article I, section 13, of the California Constitution and the Fourth Amendment to the federal Constitution require that in the absence of exigent circumstances a warrant must be obtained prior to an intrusion into the home for the purpose of effecting an arrest.

I

The issue of probable cause turns on the facts known to Detective Garcia prior to the arrest. Here the sole source of that knowledge was the information related to Garcia by Turner. The question is whether it was reasonable for Garcia to rely on that information.

The courts have recognized a distinction between informers who are virtual agents of the police and "citizen informants" who are chance witnesses to or victims of crime. The former are often criminally disposed or implicated, and supply their "tips" to the authorities on a recurring basis, in secret, and for pecuniary or other personal gain. The latter are innocent of criminal involvement, and volunteer their information fortuitously, openly, and through motives of good citizenship. (See generally People v. Schulle (1975) 51 Cal.App.3d 809, 814–815, 124 Cal.Rptr. 585 and cases cited.) Because of these characteristics, the requisite showing of reliability in the case of a citizen informant is significantly less than that demanded of a police informer. (People v. Duren (1973) 9 Cal.3d 218, 240, 107 Cal.Rptr. 157, 507 P.2d 1365; Krauss v. Superior Court (1971) 5 Cal.3d 418, 421–422, 96 Cal.Rptr. 455, 487 P.2d 1023, and cases cited.)

It may therefore be stated as a general proposition that private citizens who are witnesses to or victims of a criminal act, absent some circumstance that would cast doubt upon their information, should be considered reliable. This does not, of course, dispense with the requirement that the informant—whether citizen or otherwise—furnish underlying facts sufficiently detailed to cause a reasonable person to believe that a crime had been committed and the named suspect was the perpetrator; and the rule also presupposes that the police be aware of the identity of the person providing the information and of his status as a true citizen informant. (People v. Abbott (1970) 3 Cal.App.3d 966, 970–971, 84 Cal. Rptr. 40.) In short, probable cause will not be provided by conclusionary information or anonymous informants, but neither a previous demonstration of reliability nor subsequent corroboration is ordinarily necessary when witnesses to or victims of criminal activities report their observations in detail to the authorities.

In the present case Detective Garcia could reasonably believe that Turner was a citizen informant as herein defined. Moreover, an additional demonstration of reliability was presented in Turner's ongoing relationship with the Sacramento police: while his occupation would not of itself cloak him with any presumption of credence, there was evidence that he had dealt with the Sacramento police on other occasions without raising doubts as to his trustworthiness. For all these reasons, Detective Garcia could accept as true Turner's representations as to the circumstances which led him to defendant's residence, and the statements which defendant there made.

Having established that Turner was a reliable informant, we consider the remaining question whether the information he supplied was sufficient to constitute probable cause to believe defendant guilty of the crime of receiving stolen property.

Defendant contends the information given to Garcia consisted mainly of Turner's mere speculation that defendant was still in possession of the stolen Airweight. However, Garcia testified that he believed there was probable cause to arrest defendant for the offense of *receiving* stolen property, a crime which does not necessitate continuing possession of the goods.

With regard to this offense there was ample showing to support a conclusion of probable cause. The key evidence, of course, was defendant's own admission to Turner that he had purchased the weapon and had actually "received" it. After this admission the only element of the offense still open to question was defendant's subjective knowledge that the weapon was stolen. This is an element which must be inferred from the circumstances. As we recently stated in People v. Martin (1973) 9 Cal.3d 687, 696, 108 Cal.Rptr. 809, 814, 511 P.2d 1161, 1166, "Possession of a stolen item in and of itself is a factor which could assist a reasonable person in formulating a strong suspicion that the recipient knew the item was stolen." In addition, defendant apparently came into possession of the gun shortly after the burglary; he did not disclose to Turner the identity of the person from whom he had purchased it; and he conceded that he quickly "got rid of" the gun by selling it to an apparent stranger. Taken together, these circumstances supported an inference of guilty knowledge. Detective Garcia therefore had probable cause to arrest defendant for the crime of receiving stolen property.

II

But this determination does not end our inquiry. Defendant further contends that even if there was probable cause, the arrest was invalid because of the failure of the police to secure an arrest warrant prior to intruding into the privacy of his home. It is urged that just as warrantless searches of a private dwelling are unreasonable per se in the absence of one of a small number of carefully circumscribed exceptions (Vale v. Louisiana (1970) 399 U.S. 30, 34–35, 90 S.Ct. 1969, 26 L.Ed.2d 409, and cases cited), so too are warrantless arrests within the home unreasonable unless there are exigent circumstances sufficient to justify dispensing with the warrant requirement. The People respond that in California an arrest without a warrant may be made whenever the police have reasonable cause to believe the suspect has committed a felony (Pen.Code, § 836), and that the only condition precedent to an arrest within the home is that the police comply with the statutory "knock and notice" provision (Pen.Code, § 844). Defendant recognizes that no statute imposes the requirement he now asks us to adopt, but asserts that the legislative silence on the matter is overridden by the demands of the Constitution.

Our analysis proceeds from the premise that the proscriptions of unreasonable searches and seizures contained in article I, section 13, of the California Constitution and the Fourth Amendment to the United States Constitution embrace seizures of the person as well as seizures of property. The authority for this proposition appears first in the language of the Constitution itself. In pertinent part article I, section 13, of the California Constitution forbids any violation of "The right of the people to be secure in their persons, [and] houses, . . . against unreasonable seizures," and declares that no warrant shall issue except on probable cause particularly describing "the persons . . . to be seized." The Fourth Amendment uses similar wording.

The United States Supreme Court has not yet resolved the issue of whether the Fourth Amendment requires a warrant for arrests within the home. However, in Coolidge v. New Hampshire (1971) 403 U.S. 443, 91 S.Ct. 2022, 29 L.Ed.2d 564, five members of the court expressed agreement with the proposition that "It is clear, then, that the notion that the warrantless entry of a man's house in order to arrest him on probable cause is *per se* legitimate is in fundamental conflict with the basic principle of Fourth Amendment law that searches and seizures inside a man's house without warrant are *per se* unreasonable in the absence of some one of a number of well defined 'exigent circumstances.'" (Id. at pp. 477–478, 91 S.Ct. at p. 2044.)

As additional authority the majority pointed to the case of Warden v. Hayden (1967) 387 U.S. 294, 87 S.Ct. 1642, 18 L.Ed.2d 782: that decision, "where the Court elaborated a 'hot pursuit' justification for the police entry into the defendant's house without a warrant for his arrest, certainly stands by negative implication for the proposition that an arrest warrant is required in the absence of exigent circumstances. See also Davis v. Mississippi, 394 U.S. 721, 728, 89 S.Ct. 1394, 1398, 22 L.Ed.2d 676; Wong Sun v. United States, 371 U.S., at 481–482, 83 S.Ct. [407], at 413–415, 9 L.Ed.2d 441." (Id. 403 U.S. at pp. 480–481, 91 S.Ct. at p. 2045.) Citing Dorman v. United States (1970), 140 U.S.App.D.C. 313, 435 F.2d 385, the majority also noted (403 U.S. at p. 481, 91 S.Ct. at p. 2045) that "The Court of Appeals for the District of Columbia Circuit, sitting *en banc*, has unanimously reached the same conclusion."

Our own cases, although frequently referring to the statutory formula for making warrantless arrests (see, e. g., People v. Fein (1971) 4 Cal.3d 747, 752, 94 Cal.Rptr. 607, 484 P.2d 583), have never truly confronted the issue of the constitutionality of warrantless arrests in the home. Defendant relies heavily on language in People v. Privett (1961) 55 Cal.2d 698, 703, 12 Cal.Rptr. 874, 877, 361 P.2d 602, 605, where we stated: "The sanctity of a private home is not only guaranteed by the Constitutions of the United States and of our own state, but it is traditional in our Anglo-Saxon heritage. 'A man's home is his castle' is, and should be, more than an empty phrase. The Constitutions themselves point to the proper procedure to be followed in invading this precious sanctity. . . . There was no emergency in this case which would have prevented the officers from seeking a warrant from a magistrate to enter this home. . . . Although a private home may be broken into without a warrant, even in the nighttime, if probable cause exists, in doubtful cases the householder should be entitled to have the protection of the independent judgment of a magistrate before the constitutionally guaranteed sanctity of his home is invaded." But this language, like that in *Coolidge*, was dictum; and while persuasive, it does not definitively resolve the constitutional question.

Nevertheless, a number of federal and state appellate courts have been squarely presented with the issue and have rendered decisions in conformity with the sentiments expressed in *Coolidge* and *Privett*. First, as the Supreme Court noted in its *Coolidge* opinion, the Court of Appeals for the District of Columbia Circuit, sitting en banc, unanimously held that in the absence of a true emergency a warrantless entry into a home to arrest a suspect violates the Fourth Amendment. (Dorman v. United States (1970) supra, 140 U.S.App.D.C. 313, 435 F.2d 385.) The court reasoned that "The Fourth Amendment protects a right of privacy. This is a right that is increasingly recognized in decisions involving this and other provisions of the Constitution as a core protection safeguarding all citizens against unwarranted intrusions by police and other government officials.

Identical views have been expressed by other federal appellate courts. In Vance v. North Carolina (1970) 432 F.2d 984, the Court of Appeals for the Fourth Circuit impliedly adopted the position in *Dorman* that "an arrest inside a dwelling without a warrant, or pursuant to an invalid warrant, is *per se* unreasonable under the fourth amendment unless there are 'exigent circumstances' justifying the police in bypassing a magistrate . . . ." (Id. at p. 990.) Similarly, in United States v. Shye (1974) 492 F.2d 886, the Court of Appeals for the Sixth Circuit applied as the rule of *Dorman* the principle that "the warrantless entry of a dwelling to arrest [is] put on the same constitutional footing as warrantless entry of a dwelling for a search. See: Coolidge v. New Hampshire, 403 U.S. 443, at 454–455, 91 S.Ct. 2022, 29 L.Ed.2d 564 (1971). Entry in both instances is *per se* unreasonable unless 'exigent circumstances' justify the failure to obtain the warrant." (Id. at p. 891.) Again, in United States v. Phillips (1974) 497 F.2d 1131, 1135, the Court of Appeals for the Ninth Circuit cited *Dorman* for the proposition that "The constitutional safeguard that assures citizens the privacy and security of their homes unless a judicial officer determines that it must be overridden, is applicable not only in case of entry to search for property, but also in cases of entry to arrest a suspect." (See also Salvadore v. United States (8th Cir. 1974) 505 F.2d 1348, 1351–1352.)

Our own view of the matter comports with the *Coolidge* dictum and the opinions in the above-cited state and federal cases. An intrusion by the state into the privacy of the home for any purpose is one of the most awesome incursions of police power into the life of the individual. Unrestricted authority in this area is anathema to the system of checks envisaged by the Constitution. It is essential that the dispassionate judgment of a magistrate, an official dissociated from the "competitive enterprise of ferreting out crime" (Johnson v. United States (1947) 333 U.S. 10, 14, 68 S.Ct. 367, 369, 92 L.Ed. 436), be interposed between the state and the citizen at this critical juncture. The frightening experience of certain foreign nations with the unexpected invasion of private homes by uniformed authority to seize individuals therein, often in the dead of night, is too fresh in memory to permit this portentous power to be left to the uninhibited discretion of the police alone.

Moreover, it is incongruous to pay homage to the considerable body of law that has developed to protect an individual's belongings from unreasonable search and seizure in his home, and at the same time assert that identical considerations do not operate to safeguard the individual himself in the same setting. Where genuine exigencies exist, broad constitutional mandates often give way to the necessity for immediate action, and an arrest is no exception to this rule. But in the absence of a bona fide emergency, or consent to enter, police action in seizing the individual in the home must be preceded by the judicial authorization of an arrest warrant.

For the foregoing reasons we hold that the protection of article I, section 13, of the California Constitution and the Fourth Amendment of the federal Constitution against violation of the right of the people to be secure in their persons and houses against unreasonable seizures applies to arrests within the home, and that warrantless arrests within the home are per se unreasonable in the absence of exigent circumstances.

The remaining issue is whether there were exigent circumstances justifying the warrantless arrest in the present case. In this context, "exigent circumstances" means an emergency situation requiring swift action to prevent imminent danger to life or serious damage to property, or to forestall the imminent escape of a suspect or destruction of evidence. There is no ready litmus test for determining whether such circumstances exist, and in each case the claim of an extraordinary situation must be measured by the facts known to the officers.

In the case at bar it is clear there was no imminent danger to life or property, and no likelihood of flight or destruction of evidence. Defendant was arrested for the offense of receiving stolen property, a non-violent crime evidencing no propensity for endangering life. While it is true the stolen article was a firearm, there was no reason for Detective Garcia to assume the weapon was available for immediate use; on the contrary, according to Garcia's information the weapon had been sold and was no longer in defendant's possession. The other firearms said to be in defendant's apartment had been freely shown to Turner. Detective Garcia had no ground for inferring they were illegally possessed or presented an imminent danger to life.

PEOPLE v. SCOMA*

Supreme Court of California, In Bank, 1969.
71 Cal.2d 332, 78 Cal.Rptr. 491, 455 P.2d 419.

SULLIVAN, Justice.

Defendant Gwendolyn Lee Scoma was charged by information with possession of marijuana in violation of section 11530 of the Health and Safety Code. Following arraignment she moved that the information be set aside because she had been held to answer without reasonable and probable cause (Pen.Code, § 995) in that the only evidence against her was obtained through execution of a search warrant based upon an affidavit insufficient on its face. The motion was granted, and the People appeal from the order setting aside the information. (Pen.Code, § 1238, subd. 1.)

The affidavit whose sufficiency is here in question stated that the affiant, a detective

---

* Prior to reading this, it is recommended that the reader review the following statutes: Penal Code §§ 995, 1238. Also see the cases of Aguilar and Hamilton included in this text.

sergeant engaged in the investigation of illicit narcotics traffic, had been informed by a certain named juvenile that one "Dewey" had furnished marijuana and restricted dangerous drugs to said juvenile within the immediately preceding three weeks; that "Dewey" was presently dealing in narcotics at a certain address in the San Jose area; and that "Dewey" had previously dealt in narcotics at other premises described by the juvenile. The affidavit also alleged that affiant had been informed by the juvenile that the latter had been reported to the county sheriff's office by his father when a shoebox containing marijuana and restricted dangerous drugs was found in his possession; that affiant "was also told by the aforesaid [juvenile] that lists of telephone numbers and names contained in his wallet, which are in the possession of your affiant, contain the name of 'Dewey' among others, and contains a telephone number, 259-7962, which has been verified by your affiant to be a number listed to Mary Ann Wilkins" at the premises alleged to be "Dewey's" present address; and that affiant "also has in his possession notes from [the juvenile's] wallet which said [juvenile] has identified as being a price list for 'stuff,' which has been identified by said [juvenile] as marijuana and a price list for 'spoons' which has been identified to your affiant as being the prices for methamphetamine. [The juvenile] has told your affiant that said price list was furnished to him by 'Dewey.'" Finally, the affidavit stated that the landlady at the premises alleged by the juvenile to be "Dewey's" present address had told affiant that said premises were occupied by Mary Ann Wilkins and a man matching the physical description of "Dewey" provided by the juvenile; it was also alleged that the landlady had found "papers in the rubbish which tie Mary Ann Wilkins" to another address in San Jose which, according to the juvenile, had been "Dewey's" previous address and the scene of past narcotics transactions.

On the basis of this affidavit a warrant was issued authorizing a search of the premises alleged to be "Dewey's" present address. On March 17, 1967, police executed the warrant and observed marijuana protruding from the purse of defendant, who was in the apartment.

• • •

The basic criteria for determining the constitutional sufficiency of an affidavit supporting a search warrant were set forth by the United States Supreme Court in Aguilar v. Texas, supra, 378 U.S. 108, 84 S.Ct. 1509, 12 L.Ed.2d 723: "Although an affidavit may be based on hearsay information and need not reflect the direct personal observations of the affiant [citation], the magistrate must be informed of some of the underlying circumstances from which the informant concluded that the narcotics were where he claimed they were, and some of the underlying circumstances from which the officer concluded that the informant, whose identity need not be disclosed [citation] was 'credible' or his information 'reliable.'" . .

In the recent case of People v. Hamilton (1969) 71 A.C. 189, 77 Cal.Rptr. 785, 454 P.2d 681, we concluded that the affidavit there in question was struck by the first "prong" of the *Aguilar* test in that it failed to adequately reflect "the underlying circumstances from which the informant concluded that the narcotics were where he claimed they were . . . ." (Aguilar v. Texas, supra, 378 U.S. 108, 114, 84 S.Ct. 1509, 1514, 12 L.Ed.2d 723.) The affidavit now before us presents no such problem, for the hearsay statements by which the report of illegal activity is reflected therein are factual in nature and clearly indicate that the informant had personal knowledge of such illegal activity. It is the second "prong" of the *Aguilar* test to which this affidavit is vulnerable.

• • •

. . . In the instant case, it is clear that no facts are stated relative to the informant's *identity* which indicate the reliability of information given by him. Further, the affidavit states no facts indicating *past police experience* with the informant.

Thus, the only significant facts in the affidavit upon which the magistrate could have concluded that the informant's report of illegal activity was reliable are (1) that certain substances found in the informant's possession were identified by laboratory analysis as narcotics; (2) that the landlady at "Dewey's" alleged residence both confirmed that a man matching "Dewey's" description lived at that address, and stated that certain papers discovered by her indicated that a woman living with the suspect had lived with him at "Dewey's" alleged previous address; (3) that certain lists of names and telephone numbers obtained from the informant's wallet contained the name and telephone number of "Dewey" *among others*; and (4) that certain notes found in the informant's wallet were identified by him as narcotics price lists which had been furnished to him by "Dewey."

The foregoing facts provide absolutely no basis upon which the magistrate could reasonably conclude that the informant's report of illegal activity *on the part of "Dewey"* was reliable information. Surely the fact that the informant was found to possess narcotics gives no credence to his assertion that he obtained such narcotics from a named person; he obviously obtained them from someone, but mere possession cannot constitute support for his claim that he obtained them from one person rather than another. Of no greater assistance is the fact that "Dewey's" past and present addresses were those provided by the informant; again, no inference of criminal activity on "Dewey's" part may be drawn.

Equally without value in assessing the reliability of the incriminating information provided by the juvenile are the notes and lists obtained from his wallet. Granting that the lists and notes might have been written before the informant was apprehended or knew that he was going to be interviewed by police, this would show *at most* only that the informant possessed a narcotics price list and that the name and telephone number of the person he accused of illegal activity appeared "among others" on a list in his wallet. It cannot reasonably be maintained that the list of names and telephone numbers supported the informant's accusation of "Dewey" any more than it would have supported his accusation of any other person on that list.

Thus it appears that none of the facts in the affidavit provide corroborative support for the informant's accusation of illegal activity on the part of "Dewey." This is so because they amount to merely a reiteration of the accusation *by the informant*; the affidavit contains absolutely nothing to indicate that additional facts independently known or discovered by the police supported the accusation thereby imparting credit to the informant. As the court said in Ovalle v. Superior Court, supra, 202 Cal.App.2d 760, at page 763, 21 Cal.Rptr. 385, at page 387: "The vice of the police action lies not in the kind of information procured but in the unreliability of the source. The quantification of the information does not necessarily improve its quality; the information does not rise above its doubtful source because there is more of it."

In view of the foregoing we conclude that the affidavit in this case sets forth no facts from which the magistrate could reasonably conclude that the informant's report of illegal activity on the part of "Dewey" was reliable; that the affidavit fails to conform to constitutional requirements; and that the warrant based upon it was therefore issued in violation of the Fourth and Fourteenth Amendments. . . .

The order is affirmed.

TRAYNOR, C. J., and PETERS and TOBRINER, JJ., concur.

MOSK, Justice (dissenting).

I dissent.

• • •

There is an additional reason for finding the affidavit for issuance of a warrant adequate here. The 17-year-old juvenile involved was not an informant in the classic sense; he was essentially a victim. While not entirely blameless for his predicament, the minor had been furnished marijuana, methamphetamine and LSD by persons dealing in narcotics from described premises. The boy's father discovered the narcotics and turned him over to juvenile authorities, to whom the boy revealed his source of supply.

* * *

I believe we should adhere to the expression of this court in People v. Keener (1961) 55 Cal.2d 714, 723, 12 Cal.Rptr. 859, 863, 361 P.2d 587, 591: "One of the purposes of the adoption of the exclusionary rule was to further the use of warrants, and it obviously is not desirable to place unnecessary burdens upon their use."

McCOMB and BURKE, JJ., concur.

Rehearing denied; McCOMB, MOSK and BURKE, JJ., dissenting.

PEOPLE v. SUPERIOR COURT (SIMON) *

Superior Court of California, In Bank, 1972.
7 Cal.3d 186, 101 Cal.Rptr. 837, 496 P.2d 1205.

* * *

Police Officer Erickson, the sole witness for the People, testified he was on routine vehicular patrol with his partner Officer Amic at 7:30 p. m. on March 9, 1970, when he saw a car "driving without headlights or taillights." He stopped the vehicle and defendant, its driver and sole occupant, "got out of the car voluntarily" and "started to play around under the dash." The officer asked defendant for his identification, and "He stated he had no identification, no registration for the car. I placed him under arrest for his traffic violation under authority of [section] 40302(a) of the Vehicle Code." The officer then searched defendant's person and found in his right front pants pocket a soft plastic bag containing 7.6 grams of marijuana.

On cross-examination counsel asked Officer Erickson, "Did you at any time fear for your life, thinking that [defendant] had a weapon on him?" The officer replied he did not, and further acknowledged that in his pat-down search of defendant he found no evidence of any weapon whatever.

* * *

The trial court found that the officers did stop defendant's vehicle and had "just cause" to do so inasmuch as "the officers told the truth when they asked the defendant for his identification and registration and that he stated that he had no registration or identification, and that it was a lawful arrest under 40302(a) of the Vehicle Code."

Nevertheless the court granted the motion to suppress, finding that "the search, if one was conducted by the officers at that time was not incident to the arrest because it didn't pertain to the arrest. It would appear that there is no relationship between a search under those circumstances and an arrest. What were they looking for? The cases all hold that the search has to be related to the arrest."

* * *

It is first contended that Officer Erickson had probable cause to arrest defendant on a charge of automobile theft (Veh.Code, § 10851), and hence that the search of defendant's person was justified as an incident to such an arrest. The facts which the People assert gave Officer Erickson probable cause to believe the car was stolen are, as found by the trial court, (1) that defendant was unable to produce a vehicle registration card or other proof of ownership, and (2) that defendant was unable to produce a driver's license or other personal identification.

Upon registering a vehicle in this state the Department of Motor Vehicles issues a "registration card" to the owner thereof, containing such information as the name and

---

* Prior to reading this case it is recommended that the reader review the following statute: Penal Code § 813.

address of the owner, the assigned registration number, and a description of the vehicle. (Veh.Code, §§ 4450, 4453.) Section 4454, subdivision (a), requires that the owner maintain this card or its facsimile "with the vehicle." Our first question is whether a violation of section 4454 gives an officer probable cause to believe the vehicle he has stopped is stolen.

It would not be unreasonable for a thief to remove or destroy the registration card of an automobile he has taken; his purpose in so doing might be to prevent the true owner from being traced, to eliminate the discrepancy between the owner's name and his own, or to facilitate substitution of a forged card. Since the 1967 amendment to section 4454 (fn. 5, *ante*), it is also true that being a stranger to the vehicle he might not be able to present the card to an officer simply because he did not know where to find it.

On the other hand, a motorist's failure to have or produce the registration card for his vehicle could equally well be entirely innocent. A common instance is contemplated by the statute itself: subdivision (b) of section 4454 declares the statute inapplicable "when a registration card is necessarily removed from the vehicle for the purpose of application for renewal or transfer of registration." Renewal, of course is an annual event (Veh.Code, § 4601), and in contemporary American society automobiles are bought and sold—and titles thereto transferred—with considerable frequency. Moreover, it is not only a thief who may not immediately be able to find the registration card for presentation to an officer; the same difficulty could be experienced by a friend or relative to whom the car had been lent, or even a teenage child or spouse of the owner.

Finally, it bears remembering that section 4454 is essentially a regulatory measure and does not protect the public from either dangerous driving or unsafe equipment. A violation of its terms is treated by the Legislature as the most minor of offenses: neither a felony nor a misdemeanor, it is a simple "infraction" (Veh.Code, § 40000) punishable upon a first conviction by a fine not exceeding $50 (§ 42001, subd. (a)). It would grossly distort this legislative plan to permit a police officer to magnify such an infraction into grounds to arrest the driver on the serious charge of grand theft of an automobile. We conclude that a motorist's failure to have or produce the registration card for his vehicle, without more, cannot reasonably give rise to the belief that the vehicle is stolen.

A series of Court of Appeal decisions has found such probable cause, however, when a violation of section 4454 was coupled with certain other "suspicious circumstances." First, the opinions emphasize the circumstance—also relied on here by the People—that defendant was unable to produce a driver's license upon the officer's demand (*Galceran, Myles, Odegard, Jones, Ceccone, James, Mermuys*). Vehicle Code section 12500 requires that all drivers be licensed, and section 12951 requires that every driver have his license "in his immediate possession" while operating a vehicle on the highway (subd. (a)) and present it for examination upon demand of a peace officer enforcing the provisions of the code (subd. (b)). Thus our second question is whether a violation of section 12951, in conjunction with a violation of section 4454 (discussed *ante*), gives the officer probable cause to believe the motorist guilty of automobile theft.

On its face, of course, the presence or absence of a driver's license has no bearing whatever on the matter of title to the vehicle. The only explanation thus far offered in the California cases of the relevance of this circumstance appears in *Galceran*: "To a certain extent, the fact that the driver of a car not registered in his name was also unlicensed might be additional evidence that he did not own the car in question, since few automobile owners are not licensed as operators." (People v. Galceran (1960) supra, 178 Cal.App.2d 312, 316, 2 Cal.Rptr. 901, 903.) But this reasoning assumes that the driver is actually unlicensed (Veh.Code, § 12500) rather than simply not in physical possession of his license (§ 12951, subd. (a)). The latter alternative however, appears to be the fact in almost all the cited cases. Nor is this surprising, for unless the driver confesses outright that he is unlicensed the most the officer knows from personal observation is that he does not have a license "in his immediate possession." Admittedly, even a thief who does own a driver's license might pretend not to have it with him or deliberately fail to carry it, in order to conceal his identity and age in the event he is stopped by the police.

Nevertheless, it is equally likely that the true explanation for a motorist's failure to have his license with him is the most obvious, i. e., that he inadvertently left it in a different suit of clothing—or, in the case of a lady driver, in a different handbag. Such occasional forgetfulness is a fact of human nature, no doubt reinforced by the pressures and demands of modern life. Indeed, we daresay that at one time or another virtually every motorist has suffered the minor embarrassment of leaving his license at home. The Legislature, moreover, recognized this fact when it drastically but wisely tempered the punitive consequences of a violation of section 12951, subdivision (a): not only is such a violation a simple infraction, but even that charge must be dismissed under the statute if the defendant thereafter "produces in court a driver's license duly issued to [him] and valid at the time of his arrest. . . ." In other words, the defendant even though culpable is permitted to purge himself of his offense by a belated presentation of this document.

We conclude that the mere failure of a motorist to have his driver's license in his immediate possession is a circumstance of such generally innocent connotation that it cannot reasonably transform the coincident lack of a registration card into grounds to believe the motorist guilty of grand theft. "The mere absence of registration did not give the officer probable cause to think that the car was stolen. . . . The absence of license and identification makes it no more probable that the car was stolen." (United States v. Day (E.D.Pa.1971) 331 F.Supp. 254, 256.)

This does not mean, however, that police officers are wholly barred from making warrantless arrests for automobile theft on the basis of personal observation; it means only that something more is needed to justify such an arrest than the motorist's inability to produce a registration card or driver's license. The cited decisions of the Courts of Appeal demonstrate there usually have been additional suspicious circumstances which, taken with the considerations just discussed, combine to furnish the necessary probable cause.

To begin with, in several of the cases the officer observed that one or both of the vehicle's license plates were missing or improperly attached (*Galceran, Nebbitt, Odegard, Farley*). Such conditions are not only violations of the code (§§ 5200–5201) and hence grounds for stopping the vehicle and issuing a citation to the driver, they are also relevant to the probable cause question before us.

The lack of a license plate does not alone constitute probable cause to believe the car stolen: the plate may have fallen off, been damaged in an accident or removed by a third party; and in the case of a vehicle recently purchased, the temporary "paper plate" may have become obscured or dislodged. But this circumstance is also highly suspicious: as the court noted in *Galceran*, "It is a matter of common knowledge that automobile thieves often switch license plates from one car to another in order to conceal the identity of the stolen vehicle" (178 Cal.App.2d at p. 316, 2 Cal.Rptr. at p. 903). A thief's first step towards that concealment is to remove both original plates from the vehicle; if he possesses a stolen plate, he will then ordinarily attach it in the rear position; but if he has no such substitute, he may well prefer to drive without any plates rather than risk quick identification from a police "hot sheet." We conclude that when an officer stops a vehicle with missing or improperly attached license plates and in addition learns the motorist is unable to produce the registration card, he may reasonably entertain the belief that the vehicle is stolen.

Other observable circumstances relied on in the cases to invest the lack of a registration card with guilty significance are, for example, the motorist's evasive driving and failure to stop promptly when the officer signals him to do so (*Myles*), and reports of criminal activity in progress in the neighborhood (*Jones*). In both *Myles* and *Jones* the situation presented to the officer fully warranted that reliance (cf. also People v. Brown (1971) 14 Cal.App.3d 507, 511, fn. 1, 92 Cal.Rptr. 473); but as we admonished with respect to similar circumstances claimed to import culpable meaning to the allegedly "furtive gesture" of bending over inside a vehicle (People v. Superior Court (1970) supra, 3 Cal.3d 807, 825-826, 91 Cal. Rptr. 729, 478 P.2d 449), the police must remain alert to the danger of abusing these justifications by invoking them on the basis of inadequate facts (see, e. g., People v. Griffith (1971) 19 Cal.App.3d 948, 951, 97 Cal.Rptr. 367 [broken wing-window, insufficient grounds to stop motorist on suspicion of automobile theft]).

Secondly, even though the lack of a registration card does not alone furnish the necessary probable cause, it does give the officer reasonable grounds to inquire further into the matter, i. e., to ask the motorist for an explanation of its absence; and a number of the cases have emphasized the significance of answers by the motorist which are inconsistent, conflicting, or palpably false (*Galceran, Nebbitt, Upton, Ceccone, Clark*). Thus in *Galceran* the motorist first said he had bought the vehicle from a used car lot, then that he had bought it from a friend; in *Nebbitt* the motorist said he had borrowed the vehicle from a used car dealer, but a windshield sticker showed the dealer had previously sold it to a third person unknown to the occupants; and in *Upton* the motorist named the alleged owner of the vehicle, but the officer learned by radio that the last registered owner bore a different name. Such answers have no discernible innocent meaning, and may reasonably be taken to indicate consciousness of guilt. They constitute, accordingly, a further suspicious circumstance sufficient to support a belief that the vehicle is stolen.

• • •

The People's second contention is that the search was justified as an incident to Officer Erickson's arrest of defendant for traffic violations "under authority of [section] 40302(a) of the Vehicle Code."

At the outset, a brief explanation of the statutory reference will be helpful. The exclusive procedure to be followed after a warrantless arrest for a Vehicle Code violation is that prescribed in division 17, chapter 2 (§§ 40300–40604) of the Vehicle Code. (People v. Wohlleben (1968) 261 Cal.App.2d 461, 463, 67 Cal.Rptr. 826.) If that violation is declared to be a felony, the arrestee is to be dealt with according to the general provisions of the Penal Code on felony arrests. (Veh.Code, § 40301.) For all other cases, however, the Legislature has created a special tripartite scheme which reflects the lesser degree of criminality attached to the act of transgressing against ordinary traffic rules and regulations.

First, the scheme in effect presumes that in the vast majority of cases the violator will not be taken into custody: with the exception of the instances next discussed, the officer must prepare a written notice to appear (i. e., a citation or "ticket") and must release the violator "forthwith" when the latter in turn gives his written promise that he will appear as directed (§§ 40500, 40504). Indeed, such a violator may entirely avoid the necessity for appearing in court: he may choose to deposit the prescribed bail by mail (§ 40510) and, by failing thereafter to appear, forfeit that amount in lieu of fine (§ 40512).

Second, in certain cases section 40303 gives the officer the option either to follow the foregoing procedure or to take the violator "without unnecessary delay" before the "nearest or most accessible" magistrate having jurisdiction over the offense. The section lists a number of more serious violations as grounds for invoking this option, such as reckless driving, failure to stop after an accident, participating in speed contests, driving with an invalid license, attempt to evade arrest, and refusal to submit to safety inspections.

Third, section 40302 makes it mandatory for the officer to follow the latter branch of the section 40303 option—i. e., to take the violator before a magistrate without unnecessary delay—in four specific instances: i. e., when the violator (a) fails to present his driver's license or other satisfactory evidence of his identity, (b) refuses to give his written promise to appear, or (c) demands an immediate appearance before a magistrate, or (d) when the violator is charged with the very serious traffic offenses of misdemeanor drunk driving or driving under the influence of toxic glue or nonnarcotic drugs.

The second preliminary matter we must consider is the precise point in time at which a traffic violator is "arrested." A police officer may legally stop a motorist to conduct a brief investigation when he entertains a rational suspicion, based on specific facts, that a violation of the Vehicle Code or other law may have taken place (see People v. Griffith (1971) supra, 19 Cal.App.3d 948, 950–951, 97 Cal.Rptr. 367, and cases cited), and the temporary restraint of the suspect's movements incident to that investigation will not ordinarily be deemed an arrest. But when the officer determines there is probable cause to believe that an offense has been committed and begins the process of citing the violator to appear in court (Veh.Code, §§ 40500–40504), an "arrest" takes place at least in the technical sense: "The detention which results [during the citation process] is ordinarily brief, and the conditions of restraint are minimal. Nevertheless the violator is, during the period immediately preceding his execution of the promise to appear under arrest. [Citations.] Some courts have been reluctant to use the term 'arrest' to describe the status of the traffic violator on the public street waiting for the officer to write out the citation [citations]. The Vehicle Code, however, refers to the person awaiting citation as 'the arrested person.' Viewing the situation functionally, the violator is being detained against his will by a police officer, for the purpose of obtaining his appearance in connection with a forthcoming prosecution. The violator is not free to depart until he has satisfactorily identified himself and has signed the written promise to appear." (Fns. omitted.) (People v. Hubbard (1970) 9 Cal.App.3d 827, 833, 88 Cal.Rptr. 411, 415.)

There is no doubt, of course, that a motorist who is actually taken into police custody for transportation before a magistrate pursuant to section 40302 (or 40303) is "under arrest" in the traditional sense of the term. (Pen.Code, §§ 834, 835; People v. Hatcher (1969) 2 Cal.App.3d 71, 75, 82 Cal.Rptr. 323.) This explains why Officer Erickson and the trial judge in the case at bar both stated that defendant was arrested "under 40302(a) of the Vehicle Code." But such language is at best a kind of verbal shorthand. Upon analysis it will be seen that one cannot be arrested on the sole authority of section 40302: "such section [§ 736, predecessor to § 40302] is not penal in nature and cannot form a basis for a lawful arrest." (People v. Randolph (1957) 147 Cal.App.2d Supp. 836, 841, 306 P.2d 98, 101.) The section by its terms applies only when a person "is arrested for any [nonfelony] violation of this code" and one of the four specified conditions is met. It thus assumes the violator has already been arrested under a substantive provision of the code, and simply declares the procedure which is then to be followed.

Thus viewed, a principal purpose of the statute becomes apparent. The citation procedure of section 40500 (discussed *ante*) is essentially an honor system, requiring the good faith and cooperation of the person cited. At the very least, he must be able to convince the officer—either by exhibiting his driver's license or by "other satisfactory evidence"—that the name he is signing on the written promise to appear corresponds to his true identity (see also § 40504, subd. (b) [signing such a promise with a false name is a misdemeanor]). When he cannot do so the officer has no assurance the promise will be honored, and under those circumstances subdivision (a) prohibits the use of the citation procedure. (People v. Mercurio (1970) 10 Cal.App.3d 426, 430, 88 Cal.Rptr. 750.)

Proceeding to the merits, we inquire into the constitutionally permissible scope of a search of the person as an incident to an ordinary traffic arrest.

We take as the point of departure our *Kiefer* decision (People v. Superior Court (1970) supra, 3 Cal.3d 807, 91 Cal.Rptr. 729, 478 P.2d 449), in which we reiterated certain basic principles also bearing on the case at hand. Thus, "It is now settled that as an incident to a lawful arrest, a warrantless search limited both as to time [citation] and place [citation] may be made (1) for instrumentalities used to commit the crime, the fruits of that crime, and other evidence thereof which will aid in the apprehension or conviction of the criminal; (2) for articles the possession of which is itself unlawful, such as contraband or goods known to be stolen; and (3) for weapons which can be used to assault the arresting officer or to effect an escape." (Id. at pp. 812–813, 91 Cal.Rptr. at p. 731, 478 P.2d at p. 451.) A search may be incident to a lawful arrest, however, and yet be unlawful because it was "unreasonable in scope": that scope must be "strictly tied to and justified by" the particular circumstances which initially permitted the search. (Id. at pp. 813–814, 91 Cal.Rptr. at p. 732, 478 P.2d at p. 452.)

In applying these rules, the first two categories listed above present little difficulty. In the case of an ordinary traffic offense there are neither "instrumentalities" used to commit the crime nor "fruits" or "evidence" thereof, so that a search for such items as an incident to the driver's arrest is unreasonable per se, whether conducted in his vehicle (id. at p. 813, 91 Cal.Rptr. 729, 478 P.2d 449) or on his person.

With respect to contraband, we said in *Kiefer* that "in the typical traffic violation case . . . the 'circumstances justifying the arrest'—e. g., speeding, failing to stop, illegal turn, or defective lights—do *not* also furnish probable cause to search the interior of the car." (Id. at p. 814, 91 Cal.Rptr. at p. 732, 478 P.2d at p. 452.) If the arresting officer "cannot reasonably expect to discover either instrumentalities or fruits or seizable evidence of the offense; still less does the arrest give him reasonable grounds to believe, without more, that the vehicle contains contraband. . . . To justify that search, there must be independent probable cause to believe the vehicle does in fact contain contraband." (Id. at pp. 814–815, 91 Cal.Rptr. at p. 732, 478 P.2d at p. 452.) This reasoning applies with equal force to a search of the driver, and to justify such a search there must likewise be independent probable cause to believe that contraband is in fact secreted on his person.

The scope of a search for weapons after a routine traffic arrest however, is a more complex problem which has evoked differing responses from the courts. A leading case in point is People v. Marsh (1967) 20 N.Y.2d 98, 281 N.Y.S.2d 789, 228 N.E.2d 783. There the defendant was arrested on a traffic warrant issued for a speeding violation committed two years earlier; in a search of the defendant's person conducted incident to that arrest, a paper was found in a book of matches and was thereafter used to convict him on a gambling charge. The New York Court of Appeals reversed the judgment and directed the suppression of the evidence and dismissal of the information. On the point in issue the court reasoned (at p. 101, 281 N.Y.S.2d at p. 792, 228 N.E.2d at p. 785): "The search for weapons is a special exception to the proscription against warrantless searches, and it should not be extended beyond its purpose of securing the safety of the officer and preventing an escape. A motorist who exceeds the speed limit does not thereby indicate any propensity for violence or iniquity, and the officer who stops the speeder has not even the slightest cause for thinking that he is in danger of being assaulted. We can only conclude that, even though the 'rules of criminal law are generally applicable' to traffic violations [citation], the Legislature never intended to authorize a search of a traffic offender unless, when the vehicle is stopped, there are reasonable grounds for suspecting that the officer is in danger or there is probable cause for believing that the offender is guilty of a crime rather than merely a simple traffic infraction."

Nor did the Legislature intend a different result, said the New York high court, simply because the arrest is based on an outstanding traffic warrant: "the statutory scheme does not contemplate treating him as a common criminal to be booked, photographed, fingerprinted and jailed. It is equally degrading—and most assuredly not the Legislature's intention—to subject him to the affront of a search when one is not necessary for the proper execution of the warrant. In short, no search for a weapon is authorized as incident to an arrest for a traffic infraction, regardless of whether the arrest is made on the scene or pursuant to a warrant, unless the officer has reason to fear an assault or probable cause for believing that his prisoner has committed a crime [other than a traffic offense]." (Id. at p. 102, 281 N.Y.S.2d at p. 793, 228 N.E.2d at p. 786). And the New York court concluded by holding that this limitation on a weapons search was also compelled by the Fourth Amendment to the United States Constitution.

One year later the United States Supreme Court decided Terry v. Ohio (1968) 392 U.S. 1, 88 S.Ct. 1868, 20 L.Ed.2d 889 and Sibron v. New York (1968) 392 U.S. 40, 88 S.Ct. 1889, 20 L.Ed.2d 917, holding that "where a police officer observes unusual conduct which leads him reasonably to conclude in light of his experience that criminal activity may be afoot and that the persons with whom he is dealing may be armed and presently dangerous, . . . he is entitled for the protection of himself and others in the area to conduct a carefully limited search of the outer clothing of such persons in an attempt to discover weapons which might be used to assault him." (392 U.S. at p. 30, 88 S.Ct. at p. 1884.) The high court explained (at p. 27, 88 S.Ct. at p. 1883) that "the issue is whether a reasonably prudent man in the circumstances would be warranted in the belief that his safety or that of others was in danger. [Citations and fn. omitted.] And in determining whether the officer acted reasonably in such circumstances, due weight must be given, not to his inchoate and unparticularized suspicion or 'hunch,' but to the specific reasonable inferences which he is entitled to draw from the facts in light of his experience." The importance of these decisions to our inquiry will soon become apparent.

The first California case to construe the Terry language in the context of a traffic arrest was People v. Graves (1968) 263 Cal. App.2d 719, 70 Cal.Rptr. 509. There the defendant, a robbery suspect, was arrested on outstanding traffic warrants; a thorough search of his person was conducted, turning up a packet of marijuana cigarettes. In reviewing the legality of that search and seizure, the Court of Appeal declared as follows (at pp. 733–734, 70 Cal.Rptr. at p. 519): "A valid arrest for a traffic offense permits a search by the arresting officer of the arrestee's person for weapons, but does not justify a complete search of his person for evidence of other unrelated crimes unless the officer has probable cause for believing that the traffic offender is guilty of a crime other than the traffic offense for which he is being arrested."

To justify its rule allowing a routine weapons search in every traffic arrest situation, the Court of Appeal reasoned (at p. 734, 70 Cal.Rptr. at p. 519): "The rationale of Marsh, supra, that traffic offenders are usually noncriminals and therefore should not be subjected to the indignity of even a search for weapons must yield to the principle espoused in Terry and Sibron, supra, that a police officer may make a reasonable self-protective search for weapons if he has a constitutionally adequate reasonable ground for doing so, subject to the limitation that the scope of the search must be reasonably related to and justified by the circumstances which rendered its initiation permissible. In the case of a valid arrest the constitutional adequacy is supplied by the arrest itself. . . ."

We do not so read *Terry* and *Sibron*. It is true, as the *Graves* court emphasized (ibid.), that "the danger to the officer and the possibility of an escape are present if the arrestee possesses a weapon regardless of whether the weapon is in any way related to the crime for which he has been arrested." This is self-evident. Conversely, however, those dangers are also present when the officer has detained and is interrogating an armed suspect in circumstances which may still fall short of probable cause to effectuate the arrest. The participants are often unsure of the precise moment at which such a detention becomes an "arrest" in the legal sense (see Part II A, ante), and the suspect does not have significantly less incentive or temptation to use his weapon before than after that elusive moment. In short, the physical risk to the officer is created by the circumstances of the confrontation taken as a whole, not by the technical niceties of the law of arrest. The critical question remains, is this the kind of confrontation in which the officer can reasonable believe in the possibility that a weapon may be used against him?

The actual holding of *Graves* illustrates the point: in addition to the outstanding traffic warrants, the officer in that case had independent probable cause to arrest the defendant for five recent armed robberies, the last committed only three hours before he stopped the defendant for irregular driving. Fully aware of these facts, he approached the car with a drawn gun and immediately placed the defendant in handcuffs. Manifestly in such circumstances it was reasonable for the officer to believe that the arrestee was armed and dangerous, and to take appropriate precautionary measures. Nor is it necessary, to support such a belief, that the crime for which the suspect is arrested ordinarily be committed by means of offensive weapons: in Peters v. New York, reported sub nom. Sibron v. New York (1968) supra, 392 U.S. 40, 88 S.Ct. 1889, a companion case to *Terry*, the officer had reasonable cause to arrest the defendant on a charge of attempted burglary. Upon apprehending him the officer conducted a pat-down search for weapons and felt a hard object which might have been a knife; he removed it and found it to be a small package of burglar's tools. The United States Supreme Court upheld the search as incident to the arrest for attempted burglary, and reasonably limited in scope. (Id. at p. 67, 88 S.Ct. 1889.)

Our analysis here, however, deals with an arrest not for robbery or burglary or possession of narcotics, but for a simple traffic violation. In extending the authority for a weapons search to that class of arrests, the *Graves* court was apparently motivated by its judicial "knowledge" that "police officers have been killed or assaulted while making arrests for traffic offenses" and such arrests "frequently disclose that the arrestee is wanted by the authorities for the alleged commission of another crime or crimes or that he is a fugitive from justice." (263 Cal.App.2d at p. 735, 70 Cal.Rptr. at p. 520.) This concern for the safety of traffic officers is commendable, and we fully shared it in *Kiefer*: "We are not unmindful of the dangers daily faced by the men who bear the burden of policing our streets and highways, and of the fact that even a minor traffic citation incident can occasionally erupt into violence. We agree with the United States Supreme Court that 'Certainly it would be unreasonable to require that police officers take unnecessary risks in the performance of their duties. . . .' The courts should do all in their constitutional powers to minimize these risks." (3 Cal.3d at p. 829, 91 Cal.Rptr. at p. 743, 478 P.2d at p. 463, quoting from Terry v. Ohio, at p. 23 of 392 U.S., at p. 1881 of 88 S.Ct.)

PEOPLE v. SUPERIOR COURT (SIMON)

The question, nevertheless, is whether these risks eventuate "frequently," as the *Graves* court believed, or "occasionally," as we asserted in *Kiefer*. While statistical certainty is impossible, we adhere to *Kiefer's* commonsense appraisal of the situation: "Millions of such vehicles [involved in routine traffic violations] are stopped every year, and all but a small proportion are doubtless proceeding at the time on lawful business or innocent pleasure." (Fn. omitted; 3 Cal.3d at p. 815, 91 Cal.Rptr. at p. 733, 478 P.2d at p. 453.) We concluded in *Kiefer* (at p. 829, 91 Cal.Rptr. at p. 744, 478 P.2d at p. 464) that "Just as the arresting officer in an ordinary traffic violation case cannot reasonably expect to find contraband in the offender's vehicle, so also he cannot expect to find weapons. To allow the police to routinely search for weapons in all such instances would likewise constitute an 'intolerable and unreasonable' intrusion into the privacy of the vast majority of peaceable citizens who travel by automobile. It follows that a warrantless search for weapons, like a search for contraband, must be predicated in traffic violation cases on specific facts or circumstances giving the officer reasonable grounds to believe that such weapons are present in the vehicle he has stopped."

This reasoning is equally applicable to a search of the driver. We agree with the above-quoted observation of the New York Court of Appeals in *Marsh* (20 N.Y.2d at p. 101, 281 N.Y.S.2d at p. 792, 228 N.E.2d at p. 786) that the ordinary motorist who transgresses against a traffic regulation "does not thereby indicate any propensity for violence or iniquity," and the officer who stops him generally "has not even the slightest cause for thinking that he is in danger of being assaulted." Moreover, a search of the driver's person is obviously no less an invasion of privacy than a search of his vehicle, even when it is limited to a patdown: as the United States Supreme Court said in *Terry*, "it is simply fantastic to urge that such a procedure performed in public by a policeman while the citizen stands helpless, perhaps facing a wall with his hands raised, is a 'petty indignity.' It is a serious intrusion upon the sanctity of the person, which may inflict great indignity and arouse strong resentment, and it is not to be undertaken lightly." (Fns. omitted; 392 U.S. at pp. 16–17, 88 S.Ct. at p. 1877.) We therefore conclude that when a police officer observes a traffic violation and stops the motorist for the purpose of issuing a citation, a patdown search for weapons as an incident to that arrest must be predicated on specific facts or circumstances giving the officer reasonable grounds to believe that a weapon is secreted on the motorist's person. Language to the contrary in *Graves* (263 Cal.App.2d at p. 733, 70 Cal.Rptr. 509) is disapproved.

* * *

Turning to the facts before us, we observe that defendant was initially stopped for driving during darkness (Veh.Code, § 280) without lighted headlamps or taillamps (§§ 24250, 24400, 24600). These are simple infractions (§ 40000), punishable upon a first conviction by a fine not exceeding $50 (§ 42001, subd. (a)). As noted earlier (Part I, ante), the same is true of defendant's inability to present his driver's license and registration card; and if he had produced any other "satisfactory evidence of his identity," he would have been entitled as a matter of right to be released immediately upon signing a promise to appear. Beyond these traffic violations, however, there were no other facts or circumstances from which Officer Erickson, as a reasonably prudent man, could have inferred that defendant was carrying a concealed weapon. Indeed, we have already pointed out that when asked on cross-examination, "Did you at any time fear for your life, thinking that [defendant] had a weapon on him?" Officer Erickson replied in the negative. The patdown search of defendant cannot be justified as an incident to Officer Erickson's decision to cite him for the foregoing traffic offenses.

Pressing the analysis further, the People emphasize that Officer Erickson not only had probable cause to issue the traffic citations to defendant but was required by Vehicle Code section 40302 to take him into custody for transportation before a magistrate in order to make bail; this fact, it is urged, justified the search of defendant. We therefore address ourselves to an issue which has recently caused much uncertainty and conflict among the Courts of Appeal, namely, the constitutionally permissible scope of a search of a traffic violator who is required to be transported before a magistrate pursuant to Vehicle Code section 40302.

When a suspect has been lawfully arrested on a criminal charge and undergoes the process of "booking" at a police station prior to being held in jail (Pen.Code, § 7, subd. (21)), it is ordinarily reasonable to conduct a search of his person for the purpose of preventing the introduction of weapons or contraband into the jail facility. (People v. Ross (1967) 67 Cal.2d 64, 70, 60 Cal.Rptr. 254, 429 P.2d 606, reversed on other grounds sub nom. Ross v. California (1968) 391 U.S. 470, 88 S.Ct. 1850, 20 L.Ed.2d 750; People v. Munsey (1971) 18 Cal.App.3d 440, 448, 95 Cal.Rptr. 811, and cases cited.) From this premise the argument has been drawn that for the sake of safety a search of this kind need not be postponed until the actual booking but may reasonably be conducted "in the field," i. e., at the time of the arrest, whenever the suspect will be charged with a "jailable" offense.

Whatever the merits of this argument in generality, it is inapplicable to the case at hand. As noted above (Part II A, ante) sections 40300–40604 of the Vehicle Code provide the *exclusive* procedure to be followed after making a warrantless arrest for a traffic violation not amounting to a felony, and those provisions must be read together to effectuate the deliberate legislative scheme they embody. Section 40302 requires that a person coming within its terms be taken "without unnecessary delay" before the "nearest or most accessible" magistrate having jurisdiction, and sections 40306 and 40307 prescribe the next step in the procedure: if a magistrate is available, section 40306 provides (a) the arresting officer shall file a complaint, (b) the arrestee shall be given at least five days' continuance to prepare his case and (c) "shall thereupon be released from custody" on his own recognizance or on bail; if on the other hand a magistrate is not available, section 40307 provides that the officer shall take the arrestee before (a) the clerk of the magistrate "who shall admit him to bail" or (b) the officer in charge of the most accessible jail "who shall admit him to bail" or release him upon a simple written promise to appear.

The clear and unmistakable import of these provisions, when read together, is that a person taken into custody pursuant to section 40302 must be transported *directly* to a magistrate or to one of the officials listed in section 40307, and must *immediately* be released on bail or written promise to appear. Accordingly, he cannot lawfully be subjected to the routine booking process used in the case of a nontraffic misdemeanant; nor can he be searched as an incident of that process, either in the field or at a police station. We conclude that the search of defendant in the case at bar cannot be justified as an incident to Officer Erickson's decision to take him into custody for transportation before a magistrate pursuant to section 40302.

• • •

A divergent line of cases, however, has developed from the decision in Morel v. Superior Court (1970) 10 Cal.App.3d 913, 89 Cal.Rptr. 297. (E. g., Pugh v. Superior Court (1970) 12 Cal.App.3d 1184, 1188, 91 Cal.Rptr. 168; People v. Brown (1971) 14 Cal.App.3d 507, 511, 92 Cal.Rptr. 473.) Departing from the prior cases in point, the court there stated it was not necessary to decide whether the charged violation was a "jailable" offense. Instead, the court devised a new rationale which if valid would justify a full "body search" of each and every traffic offender whom the police propose to transport before a magistrate pursuant to section 40302 or 40303. Other Courts of Appeal, nevertheless, have scrupulously resisted adoption of the *Morel* rationale. (People v. Millard (1971) 15 Cal.App.3d 759, 762, 93 Cal.Rptr. 402; People v. Smith (1971) 17 Cal.App.3d 604, 607, 95 Cal.Rptr. 229, 231.) Indeed, *Smith* particularly circumscribed the *Morel* rule by insisting it cannot "hold that, as a matter of law, every person who is to be transported in a police vehicle, for any reason, may be subjected to a search. . . . Such a routine invasion of privacy, unsupported by some special necessity, is constitutionally unwarranted." For the reasons discussed herein, we disapprove of *Morel* and its progeny.

As Officer Erickson's search of defendant was unlawful, the evidence discovered as a result of that search was inadmissible. It follows under the substantial evidence test that the record fully supports the trial court's order granting defendant's motion to suppress.

• • •

PEOPLE v. SUPERIOR COURT (KIEFER) *

Superior Court of California, In Bank, 1970.
3 Cal.3d 807, 91 Cal.Rptr. 729, 478 P.2d 449.

MOSK, Justice.

Defendants (real parties in interest herein) were charged by information with unlawful possession and transportation of marijuana. (Health & Saf.Code, §§ 11530, 11531.) Their motion to suppress the evidence on the ground of illegal search and seizure was granted, and the People seek review by statutory writ of mandate. (Pen. Code, § 1538.5, subd. (*o*).)

The sole witness testifying to the events in question was the arresting officer, Sergeant Cameron of the California Highway Patrol. Approximately 8 a. m. on a Sunday morning Officer Cameron was on duty in his marked patrol car on Interstate Highway 5 in Yolo County, when he observed a 1960 Pontiac automobile being driven southbound at a high rate of speed. He gave chase, and switched on his red emergency light for the purpose of bringing the car to a halt. The driver immediately began to pull over to the side of the road. At this point Officer Cameron saw a woman's head rise from the passenger portion of the front seat; she turned and put her arm over the back of the seat, then faced forward again, bent down toward the floor, and reassumed a normal sitting position. The driver of the Pontiac, defendant Martell Kiefer, alighted first and walked toward Officer Cameron. The officer told Mr. Kiefer why he had stopped him, and the latter readily acknowledged he had been speeding and produced his driver's license.

Officer Cameron then approached the passenger side of the Pontiac. The female occupant, defendant Patricia Kiefer, remained sitting in the front seat with the window rolled up. Officer Cameron made no attempt to communicate with Mrs. Kiefer but immediately opened the car door next to her and looked inside. As he later testified, "My purpose was . . . several. One was to talk to the passenger and see what had been hidden and I was also concerned about my own safety."

Upon opening the door, Officer Cameron saw "some green-looking stems" lying on the floor mat between the seat and the door, and "several round seeds" in the crack of the seat cushion. Believing the latter to be marijuana, he ordered Mrs. Kiefer to step out and undertook a thorough search of defendants' car. Additional small quantities of marijuana were found in the glove compartment and in Mrs. Kiefer's purse.

The controlling issue in this proceeding is whether in the circumstances shown Officer Cameron's act of opening the door of defendants' car and looking inside was an unreasonable search within the meaning of

---

* Prior to reading this case it is recommended that the reader review the following statutes: Penal Code §§ 813, 836, 1525.

the Fourth Amendment to the United States Constitution. We conclude that the question must be answered in the affirmative, and that the trial court correctly granted defendants' motion to suppress.

I

It was stipulated at the suppression hearing that Officer Cameron did not have a warrant to search defendants' car; the burden to show proper justification for the search, accordingly, rested on the prosecution. (Badillo v. Superior Court (1956) 46 Cal.2d 269, 272, 294 P.2d 23.)

Having determined that defendants' car was being driven in excess of the posted speed limit, Officer Cameron had probable cause to stop the vehicle and arrest its driver for committing a misdemeanor in his presence. (Pen.Code, § 836, subd. 1.) That fact alone, however, would not have justified a search of the vehicle as an "incident" to the traffic arrest. (People v. Blodgett (1956) 46 Cal.2d 114, 116, 293 P.2d 57; cf. People v. Weitzer (1969) supra, 269 Cal.App.2d 274, 290, 75 Cal.Rptr. 318, and cases cited.) The latter rule has been more often stated than explained, and an analysis of its origin may prove instructive.

It is now settled that as an incident to a lawful arrest, a warrantless search limited both as to time (Preston v. United States (1964) 376 U.S. 364, 367–368, 84 S.Ct. 881, 11 L.Ed.2d 777) and place (Chimel v. California (1969) 395 U.S. 752, 762–763, 89 S.Ct. 2034, 23 L.Ed.2d 685) may be made (1) for instrumentalities used to commit the crime, the fruits of that crime, and other evidence thereof which will aid in the apprehension or conviction of the criminal; (2) for articles the possession of which is itself unlawful, such as contraband or goods known to be stolen; and (3) for weapons which can be used to assault the arresting officer or to effect an escape. (See generally Warden, Maryland Penitentiary v. Hayden (1967) 387 U.S. 294, 300–310, 87 S.Ct. 1642, 18 L.Ed.2d 782.)

In the case at bar we may quickly exclude the first of these three categories. Inasmuch as the "instrumentality" used to commit the offense of speeding is, if anything, the automobile itself, a search of any portion of its *interior* cannot be justified on this ground. (Grundstrom v. Beto (N.D.Tex. 1967) 273 F.Supp. 912, 916.) Moreover, there are no "fruits" of such an offense, and the "evidence" thereof is not subject to search and seizure as it consists essentially of the arresting officer's own observations and records. (United States v. Tate (D.Del. 1962) 209 F.Supp. 762, 765.)

II

Turning to the second of the above categories, we confront initially a more difficult question: If a police officer is ordinarily entitled to conduct a search for contraband as an incident to a lawful arrest, why has this rule been held inapplicable to routine traffic violations? When the officer, as here, has probable cause to arrest a driver for committing a traffic offense in his presence, why may he not search the offender's vehicle for contraband as an incident to that arrest? The answer deducible from the cases is that even when limited as required by *Preston* and *Chimel,* a search incident to an arrest must nevertheless remain "reasonable in scope." (People v. Cruz (1964) 61 Cal.2d 861, 866, 40 Cal.Rptr. 841, 395 P.2d 889.) As Justice White remarked in his dissent in *Chimel,* "The [Fourth] Amendment does not proscribe 'warrantless searches' but instead it proscribes 'unreasonable searches'" (395 U.S. at pp. 772–773, 89 S.Ct. at p. 2045). A search, therefore, "may be unreasonable and hence unlawful although incident to a lawful arrest." (People v. Brown (1955) 45 Cal.2d 640, 643, 290 P.2d 528, 530, and cases cited.) "What is the test of reason which makes a search reasonable? The test is the reason underlying and expressed by the Fourth Amendment: the history and the experience which it embodies and the safeguards afforded by it against the evils to which it was a response." (Chimel v. California (1969) supra, 395 U.S. 752,

765, 89 S.Ct. 2034, 2041, 23 L.Ed.2d 685, quoting from United States v. Rabinowitz (1950) 339 U.S. 56, 83, 70 S.Ct. 430, 94 L.Ed. 653 (dissenting opinion of Frankfurter, J.).) The principal evil sought to be forestalled, of course, is the invasion of individual privacy by wholesale exploratory searches conducted under color of governmental authority. (Warden, Maryland Penitentiary v. Hayden (1967) supra, 387 U.S. 294, 301, 87 S.Ct. 1642, 18 L.Ed.2d 782, and cases cited.) For this reason, "The scope of the search must be 'strictly tied to and justified by' the circumstances which rendered its initiation permissible." (Terry v. Ohio (1968) 392 U.S. 1, 19, 88 S.Ct. 1868, 1878, 20 L.Ed.2d 889; accord, People v. Collins (1970) 1 Cal.3d 658, 661, 83 Cal.Rptr. 179, 463 P.2d 403.)

These rules govern the search of automobiles. In Preston v. United States (1964) supra, 376 U.S. 364, 368, 84 S.Ct. 881, 11 L.Ed.2d 777, the defendants were arrested in their car on a charge of vagrancy, and a warrantless search thereof at a different time and place was held to be unreasonable. For the purposes of that opinion, the high court "assumed" there could be fruits or implements of the crime of vagrancy. In Chambers v. Maroney (1970) 399 U.S. 42, 47, 90 S.Ct. 1975, 1979, 26 L.Ed.2d 419, however, the court acknowledged that in *Preston* "the arrest was for vagrancy; it was apparent that the officers had no cause to believe that evidence of crime was concealed in the auto." By contrast, in *Chambers* the police received a report of an armed robbery of a service station; eyewitnesses furnished detailed descriptions of the articles stolen, the garb and weapons of the robbers, and the appearance of the getaway car; and shortly thereafter the defendants were arrested in a vehicle precisely matching that description. Upholding on grounds of probable cause a delayed search of the automobile at the police station, the court noted that although the officers had probable cause for their warrantless search of the defendant, "the validity of an arrest is not necessarily determinative of the right to search a car if there is probable cause to make the search. Here, as will be true in many cases, the circumstances justifying the arrest are also those furnishing probable cause for the search." (399 U.S. at p. 47, fn. 6, 90 S.Ct. at p. 1779.)

The contrary situation is presented, however, in the typical traffic violation case: there, the "circumstances justifying the arrest"—e. g., speeding, failing to stop, illegal turn, or defective lights—do *not* also furnish probable cause to search the interior of the car. In *Chambers* the arresting officers could reasonably expect to find weapons, clothing, loot, or other evidence of the robbery in the specifically identified vehicle in which the defendants were arrested; it was not unreasonable, therefore, to conduct a search for such items, and if contraband had been uncovered in the course of that search it could have been lawfully seized. But the arresting officer in a routine traffic case, as noted above, cannot reasonably expect to discover either instrumentalities or fruits or seizable evidence of the offense; still less does the arrest give him reasonable grounds to believe, without more, that the vehicle contains contraband. (Cf. People v. Baca (1967) 254 Cal.App.2d 428, 62 Cal.Rptr. 182 [probable cause to arrest defendant on charge of being a fugitive does not justify a search of the premises, as there is no "evidence" of that crime other than the defendant himself].) It follows that probable cause to arrest a traffic offender, no matter how persuasive, is neither a necessary nor a sufficient condition for a warrantless search of his vehicle for contraband. To justify that search, there must be independent probable cause to believe the vehicle does in fact contain contraband.

Such a requirement fulfills the purpose of the Fourth Amendment, adverted to earlier, to protect individual privacy against indiscriminate governmental intrusions. In the leading case of Carroll v. United States (1925) 267 U.S. 132, 153–154, 45 S.Ct. 280, 285, 69 L.Ed. 543, the United States Supreme Court explained that "It would be intolerable and unreasonable if a prohibition agent were authorized to stop every automobile on the chance of finding liquor and thus subject all persons lawfully using the highways to the inconvenience and indignity of such a search. . . . [T]hose lawfully within the country, entitled to use the public highways, have a right to free passage without interruption or search unless there is known to a competent official authorized to search, probable cause for believing that their vehicles are carrying contraband or illegal merchandise." (Accord, People v. Gale (1956) 46 Cal.2d 253, 256, 294 P.2d 13.) It would not be significantly less "intolerable and unreasonable" if the police were authorized to search for contraband, without probable cause, every vehicle involved in a routine traffic violation. Millions of such vehicles are stopped every year, and all but a small proportion are doubtless proceeding at the time on lawful business or innocent pleasure.

Carroll "merely relaxed the requirements for a warrant on the grounds of practicability. It did not dispense with the need for probable cause." (Henry v. United States (1959) 361 U.S. 98, 104, 80 S.Ct. 168, 172, 4 L.Ed.2d 134.) The constitutional necessity for probable cause to search an automobile has not diminished in the years since *Carroll*, as the Supreme Court makes clear in its latest expression on the subject (Chambers v. Maroney (1970) supra, 399 U.S. 42, 48–50, 90 S.Ct. 1975, 26 L.Ed.2d 419.) And while the meaning of the phrase is defined in many intervening opinions, it has perhaps nowhere been better stated than in *Carroll* itself: there the high court held that the officers acted on probable cause because "the facts and circumstances within their knowledge and of which they had reasonably trustworthy information were sufficient in themselves to warrant a man of reasonable caution in the belief that [contraband] was being transported in the automobile which they stopped and searched." (267 U.S. at p. 162, 45 S.Ct. at p. 288.) Our task is to apply this test to the facts before us.

In the United States Supreme Court decisions finding probable cause to search an automobile, the basis for the officers' conduct has primarily been "reasonably trustworthy information" that the vehicle contained contraband. Thus in *Carroll* the officers knew from past experience that the defendants were in the bootlegging business at Grand Rapids; the defendants were observed returning to that city from the direction of Detroit, known to be a major source of illegally imported liquor; and the defendants were traveling "in the same automobile they had been in the night when they tried to furnish the whisky to the officers which was thus identified as part of the firm equipment." (267 U.S. at p. 160, 45 S.Ct. at p. 288, see also Husty v. United States (1931) 282 U.S. 694, 700–701, 51 S.Ct. 240, 75 L.Ed. 629; Scher v. United States (1938) 305 U.S. 251, 253, 59 S.Ct. 174, 83 L.Ed. 151; Brinegar v. United States (1949) 338 U.S. 160, 162–163, 69 S.Ct. 1302, 93 L.Ed. 1879.) And in Chambers v. Maroney, as noted above, the officers acted on eyewitness descriptions of the robbers, their weapons and loot, and their getaway car.

In the case at bar Officer Cameron had no prior reliable information that defendants' car contained contraband. In fact he had neither seen nor heard of them until he stopped them for speeding. We add that such information would be rare in any routine traffic case, for the officer ordinarily issues the citation not because of the motorist's identity but because of the manner in which he was driving or the condition of his equipment. Indeed, even if the officer were looking for the specific driver because he knew of an outstanding warrant for his arrest on prior traffic charges, he would still lack—for the reasons analyzed above—probable cause to search the vehicle for contraband.

The second source of probable cause is facts or circumstances personally observed by the officer at the scene of the arrest: "A search for contraband is reasonable when conducted incident to a traffic violation only when the arresting officer observes *some occurrence other than the traffic offense itself* which reasonably leads the officer to believe that the motorist possesses contraband. . . . In the absence of *some fact* from which the officer can reasonably draw the belief that the motorist possesses contraband, a search for such articles is unreasonable." (Italics added.) (Grundstrom v. Beto (N.D.Tex.1967) supra, 273 F.Supp. 912, 917.)

Most reliable of these circumstances is an observation, from outside the vehicle or other lawful vantage point, of contraband or suspicious objects in plain view inside the vehicle. That observation is not itself a "search" in the constitutional sense (Harris v. United States (1968) 390 U.S. 234, 236, 88 S.Ct. 992, 19 L.Ed.2d 1067, and cases cited), but it may furnish probable cause to believe that additional contraband is secreted in the vehicle and to justify a search therefor. The rule has been applied to uphold warrantless searches of vehicles that were parked or otherwise immobilized . . .

• • •

The next group of relevant cases are those in which probable cause to search has been predicated on "furtive gestures" or "furtive movements" of an occupant of the vehicle. The theory, of course, is that although the officer does not actually *see* any contraband from outside the vehicle, he may reasonably *infer* from the timing and direction of the occupant's movements that the latter is in fact in possession of contraband which he is endeavoring to hide. From the viewpoint of the actor, the theory rests on a sound psychological basis: "It is a natural impulse on confrontation to hide immediately any contraband" (People v. Jiminez (1956) 143 Cal. App.2d 671, 674, 300 P.2d 68, 70). We can posit that sudden efforts at concealment, like flight from the scene of a crime, may well be expressions of consciousness of guilt. On the other hand, the same motion may in fact have an entirely innocuous purpose: "It is recognized that a person's reasons for concealment may run the whole spectrum from the most legitimate motives to the most heinous" (People v. Weitzer (1969) supra, 269 Cal.App.2d 274, 292, 75 Cal.Rptr. 318, 330).

The difficulty is that from the viewpoint of the *observer,* an innocent gesture can often be mistaken for a guilty movement. He must not only perceive the gesture accurately, he must also interpret it in accordance with the actor's true intent. But if words are not infrequently ambiguous, gestures are even more so. Many are wholly nonspecific, and can be assigned a meaning only in their context. Yet the observer may view that context quite otherwise from the actor: not only is his vantage point different, he may even have approached the scene with a preconceived notion—consciously or subconsciously—of what gestures he expected to see and what he expected them to mean. The potential for misunderstanding in such a situation is obvious.

It is because of this danger that the law requires more than a mere "furtive gesture" to constitute probable cause to search or to arrest. The United States Supreme Court recently reaffirmed this rule in the case of Sibron v. New York (1968) 392 U.S. 40, 66–67, 88 S.Ct. 1889, 1904, 20 L.Ed.2d 917: "deliberately furtive actions and flight at the approach of strangers or law officers are strong indicia of *mens rea,* and *when coupled with specific knowledge on the part of the officer relating the suspect to the evidence of crime,* they are proper factors to be considered in the decision to make an arrest." (Italics added.) That knowledge, of course, may be derived from the usual twin sources of information and observation; stating the rule for California, the court in People v. Tyler (1961) 193 Cal.App.2d 728, 732, 14 Cal.Rptr. 610, 612, declared: "As it is the information known to the police officers or the suspicious circumstances which turn an ordinary gesture into a furtive one, it is equally clear in this state that in the absence of information or other suspicious circumstances, a furtive gesture alone is not sufficient . . . ." (Accord, People v. One 1958 Chevrolet Impala (1963) 219 Cal.App.2d 18, 20, 33 Cal.Rptr. 64.)

• • •

A few distinguishable examples will serve to set the scene. A furtive gesture coupled with prior reliable information may constitute probable cause. (People v. Jiminez (1956) supra, 143 Cal.App.2d 671, 673, 300 P.2d 68 [downward motion of a juvenile sitting with others in a car parked in an area where officers had been told to expect a gang fight].) Probable cause may also be predicated on a furtive gesture coupled with an actual observation of contraband in the portion of the vehicle to which the gesture was directed. (People v. Mosco (1963) 214 Cal.App.2d 581, 585–586, 29 Cal.Rptr. 644 [downward motion of an occupant of a parked car, followed by the officer's observation of a marijuana cigarette under the seat]). And the officer need not even see recognizable contraband so long as he observed the suspect in the act of deliberately hiding a package or box which, in the circumstances, it is reasonable to believe contains contraband. (People v. Doherty (1967) 67 Cal.2d 9, 21–22, 59 Cal.Rptr. 857, 429 P.2d 177 [defendant and others refused to leave a service station at 3 a. m.; when officers arrived and asked for identification, defendant was seen to take a small white package from his pocket and drop it into the open motor of a parked car]; People v. Superior Court (1969) 272 Cal.App.2d 383, 387, 77 Cal.Rptr. 646 [car stopped for driving without lights at 2 or 3 a. m.; defendant bent forward and officers saw him push a small white box under the front seat].)

In each of the foregoing cases the gesture of the suspect could reasonably be given a guilty connotation from prior reliable information or from the officer's personal observation of contraband or a deliberate act of concealment under otherwise suspicious circumstances. It is true that to reach a conclusion of probable cause in each instance the officer was required to draw certain inferences from the known facts; but the inferences were eminently reasonable, and the chain of his deductions was correspondingly strong and compelling. A far different picture emerges, however, from a series of Court of Appeal decisions on facts similar to those now before us: in a number of such cases the evidence assertedly giving sinister meaning to the "furtive gesture" has been so thin as to stretch that chain almost to the breaking point.

The first of the series—and typical of many—was People v. Sanson (1957) 156 Cal.App.2d 250, 319 P.2d 422. There the officer observed an automobile being driven "very slowly" on a street in Venice, California, at 3 a. m.; he also noted there was no license plate illumination, and the taillight was blue instead of red. After following the car for five minutes he turned on his red emergency light in order to bring it to a stop. When he did so he saw, as he later testified, that the two passengers "appeared to be hiding something under the front seat." The officer went to the door on the passenger side and opened it; the passengers exited, and the officer "looked under the seat to see what they had placed there." Finding a dirty paper bag, he proceeded to open it and look inside. The bag contained marijuana. The two passengers were subsequently charged with possession of that substance; they moved to set aside the information on the ground the officer had no probable cause to search the car, and hence that the evidence was illegally obtained. The trial court granted the motion, and the People appealed.

The Court of Appeal reversed, holding the evidence admissible. The opinion begins (at p. 252, 319 P.2d 422) by characterizing the facts as "strikingly similar" to those of *Blodgett*; as noted above (ante, fn. 5), the analogy is untenable. The court then stated (at p. 253, 319 P.2d at p. 424) that the defective lights on the defendants' car gave the police cause to cite the driver for equipment violations but not to search the vehicle; that the police were justified in turning on their red light for the purpose of stopping the defendants' car; and "This signal revealed to the defendants that police officers were at hand and desired to question them."

At this point in the opinion, however, the reasoning of the Court of Appeal suddenly

PEOPLE v. SUPERIOR COURT (KIEFER)

shifts from a proper analysis of the facts observed by the officers to an improper speculation on the defendants' motives: "*Conscious of* the presence of the narcotic and *fearing* they would be apprehended for its possession, defendants immediately made movements, as did the defendant in the *Blodgett* case, which led the police to believe that they were hiding something under the front seat. . . . The significance of the movements of the defendants is that they were made immediately upon *realizing* they were to be confronted by the police. The defendants were simply exercising 'a natural impulse' [citing People v. Jiminez, supra]." (Italics added.) (Id., at p. 253, 319 P.2d at p. 424.)

The fatal defect in this reasoning is that neither the Court of Appeal nor, indeed, the arresting officer had any knowledge of what the defendants "realized," were "conscious of" or "feared," or what "impulse" they felt. To be sure, with the advantage of hindsight such speculation is not implausible. But a search cannot be justified by what it turns up (People v. Brown (1955) supra, 45 Cal.2d 640, 643–644, 290 P.2d 528, and cases cited), and probable cause cannot be based on a belated interpretation of the suspect's conduct which appears reasonable only in the light of evidence uncovered in that very search.

The *Sanson* approach also violates the broader rule that probable cause to arrest or to search must be tested by "facts which the record shows were known to the officers at the time the arrest [or search] was made." (People v. Talley (1967) 65 Cal.2d 830, 835, 56 Cal.Rptr. 492, 496, 423 P.2d 564, 568.) In the typical case, an officer on patrol observes a motorist commit a routine traffic violation, and turns on his siren or red light to stop the violator's car and issue a citation; upon giving such a signal, the officer sees the driver or other occupant of the car suddenly "lean forward" or "bend down" or otherwise reach toward the dashboard or floor. Assuming these are the only "facts known to the officer" at that moment, do they give him probable cause to believe that the person he observed moving in the car is in possession of contraband? Careful analysis reveals there are too many weak links in the officer's chain of deductions to support that conclusion. The flaws may be conveniently grouped around two assumptions.

First, the argument assumes that the movements in question were purposeful responses to the officer's appearance on the scene. But the person observed might not in fact have seen the police car, in which event any movements he made would be irrelevant. If he did see a vehicle following, he might not have recognized it to be a police car; many of the "furtive gesture" cases have arisen in the dark of night, with the officer's car some distance behind. If he recognized it as such, he might not have understood that the police were attempting to bring his own car to a halt. If he correctly inferred the intent of the police, his movements might not have been made in *response* to that awareness; they might simply have been movements he was on the point of making in any event. And if his movements were responsive to the situation, they still might not have been *purposeful*: i. e., when suddenly facing an imminent confrontation with the police for some unknown misdeed, many citizens with nothing to hide will nevertheless manifest an understandable nervousness by means of random, undirected gestures or movements.

Secondly, the argument assumes that only the guilty will react in the described manner to a policeman's signal to stop their car. The reported opinions make much of the "fact" that the claimed furtive gestures were not seen to occur *until* the officers turned on their red light or siren. (See, e. g., People v. Sanson (1957) supra, 156 Cal. App.2d 250, 253, 319 P.2d 422, 424, ["No such movements appear to have been made by any of [the defendants] during the previous period the police had their car under surveillance"].) As explained above, this sequence could be entirely fortuitous; indeed, in certain cases the movements could have preceded the officer's pursuit but not been visible until he drew closer for the purpose of stopping the car. But even assuming that this chronology also evidences a causal nexus—post hoc, ergo propter hoc—the analysis does not end there. Reflection will suggest many more innocent than guilty explanations for a motorist's act or "leaning forward" or "bending down" in the circumstances at hand.

To begin with, every motorist knows that the approaching police officer will in all likelihood ask to see his driver's license, and probably also the registration card of the car. The observed movement, therefore, might well be nothing more than the driver's act of reaching for his wallet so as to have his license ready for inspection, or reaching for the steering post or glove compartment to obtain the registration card. And as many women drivers keep their handbag—containing their license and other identification—next to them on the floor or between the seats, a reaching motion in that direction would be no less natural for them.

Furthermore, every motorist knows that the officer will wish to speak with him, however briefly; simple preparations for that conversation are therefore to be expected. It may be necessary, for example, for the driver to roll down his window. If the radio is playing at the time, the driver or a passenger might lean forward to reduce the volume or turn off the set. If the driver was smoking, he might well reach down to extinguish or store his cigarette in the car's ashtray. And if an occupant of the vehicle was consuming food or beverages, similar movements would probably follow.

• • •

Each of the foregoing gestures in some degree resembles—and could reasonably be mistaken for—the movements of a person engaged in secreting contraband inside a car. Yet each is wholly innocent, and has been made at one time or another by virtually every driver or passenger on the roads today. Accordingly, in the language of *Carroll,* such gestures are not "sufficient in themselves to warrant a man of reasonable caution in the belief that [contraband] was being transported" in the vehicle under observation.

The leading decision so holding is People v. Moray (1963) 222 Cal.App.2d 743, 35 Cal.Rptr. 432. There the defendant driver failed to stop his car at a posted sign and made a left turn from the wrong lane; the officer turned on his red light and signalled the defendant to pull over; and as the latter did so the officer saw him "raise his right shoulder as if he were reaching in his pocket, and then lean towards the right hand seat." The officer asked the defendant "what he had hidden underneath the seat," and the defendant answered "nothing." The officer nevertheless ordered the defendant out of the car, searched it, and found a small package of marijuana under the front seat. Reversing a conviction of possession of that substance, the Court of Appeal reasoned (at p. 746, 35 Cal.Rptr. at p. 434): "There is nothing in the record here to indicate that defendant was attempting to hide anything—he was not a narcotics addict, nor was he suspected of being such—the officer had never seen the defendant, nor his car, before. The defendant's automobile was not listed on any 'hot sheet.' The officer did not see the defendant's hands. In effect all that the officer saw was an arm motion. The defendant might have been scratching himself, he might have been reaching for his wallet with his identification and documents therein or he might have been simply changing his physical position, none of which activities would seem to be a reasonable cause to suspect him of committing a felony."

• • •

Moray and *Cruz* aside, however, every Court of Appeal decision on this topic beginning with *Sanson* has found sufficient other "facts" in the record to impart a guilty connotation to the furtive gesture now engaging our attention. Of the various circumstances stressed in the cited cases, perhaps the most persuasive is a driver's failure to stop his car promptly when a police officer signals him to do so. Even this fact, however, is subject to interpretation. Little difficulty is experienced when the motorist in this situation continues to drive for a substantial distance and makes sharp turns or other unusual maneuvers (*Gil, Chevrolet Impala*); such conduct can fairly be deemed evasive action, implying consciousness of guilt. Yet in other instances a delay in stopping may well be reasonable. It is a motorist's duty to use due care at all times, and when requested to pull over by a police officer he should do so at the first *safe* opportunity. But road conditions, speed, or other traffic may sometimes compel him to proceed a short way before bringing his car to a halt. (See e. g., People v. Moray (1963) supra, 222 Cal.App.2d 743, 744

• • •

Other circumstances mentioned with varying emphasis in the cited cases as bearing on the question whether the "furtive gesture" had a criminal connotation include the remoteness of the area where the confrontation took place (Brown), a report of a recent crime of violence in the neighborhood, with a description of the suspect (*Cantley*), a damaged condition of the car giving ground for belief it might be stolen (*Wigginton*), the motorist's lack of a driver's license and other identification (*Goodrick*), erratic or dangerous driving by the operator of the suspected car (*Williams, Shapiro, Sirak, Goodrick*), and "nervousness" of the motorist while under police investigation (*Gil*).

• • •

Our list of various elements which have contributed to the finding of probable cause in "furtive gesture" cases is intended to be illustrative rather than exhaustive. In analyzing these elements separately, moreover, we do not mean to depart from the settled rule that "There is no exact formula for the determination of reasonableness. Each case must be decided on its own facts and circumstances [citations]—and on the total atmosphere of the case. [Citations.]" (People v. Ingle (1960) 53 Cal.2d 407, 412, 2 Cal.Rptr. 14, 17, 348 P.2d 577, 580.) We also agree

that "The rule should not be understood as placing the ordinary man of ordinary care and prudence and the officer experienced in the detection of narcotics offenders in the same class. Circumstances and conduct which would not excite the suspicion of the man on the street might be highly significant to an officer who had had extensive training and experience in the devious and cunning devices used by narcotics offenders to conceal their crimes." (People v. Williams (1961) supra, 196 Cal.App.2d 726, 728, 16 Cal.Rptr. 836, 837; accord, People v. Cowman (1963) 223 Cal.App.2d 109, 117–118, 35 Cal.Rptr. 528.)

Even so, we will not countenance abuses of that experience. The near-insufficiency of the evidence of probable cause upheld in certain of the cited Court of Appeal decisions suggests that police reliance on so-called "furtive movements" has on occasion been little short of a subterfuge, and that in order to conduct a search on the basis of mere suspicion or intuition, guilty significance has been claimed for gestures or surrounding circumstances that were equally or more likely to be wholly innocent. A recent study indicates that our concern in this regard may be well-founded. The solution, as it has always been, is simply to insist upon good-faith compliance with the Constitution: the police officer should remember there is no substitute for patient and thorough investigation, and should avoid drawing a hasty or preconceived conclusion that the movements he observes are prompted by guilty motives; the trial court ruling on the issue of probable cause should make an independent and dispassionate judgment on the basis of common sense and in the light of all the circumstances presented as of the time of the event; and the appellate court, while giving due deference to the trier of fact's determination of the weight and credibility of the testimony, and affirming the ruling if there is substantial evidence to support it, should keep firmly in mind the high purpose of the Fourth Amendment and remain ever vigilant to forestall any encroachment on its fundamental guarantees.

Turning to the facts of the case before us, we find only that (1) Mrs. Kiefer made a "furtive gesture" toward the seat or the floor of defendants' automobile, and (2) Mr. Kiefer walked back to Officer Cameron's car rather than wait for the officer to come to him. For the reasons stated above, Mrs. Kiefer's gesture alone is insufficient to constitute probable cause to search, and Mr. Kiefer's walk toward the police car cannot reasonably be deemed to invest her gesture with guilty significance. It follows that Officer Cameron could not lawfully search defendants' vehicle for contraband.

III

The third category of articles which may be the object of a search incident to a lawful arrest is weapons: "When an arrest is made, it is reasonable for the arresting officer to search the person arrested in order to remove any weapons that the latter might seek to use in order to resist arrest or effect his escape. Otherwise, the officer's safety might well be endangered, and the arrest itself frustrated." (Chimel v. California (1969) supra, 395 U.S. 752, 762–763, 89 S.Ct. 2034, 2040, 23 L.Ed.2d 685.)

We are not unmindful of the dangers daily faced by the men who bear the burden of policing our streets and highways, and of the fact that even a minor traffic citation incident can occasionally erupt into violence. We agree with the United States Supreme Court that "Certainly it would be unreasonable to require that police officers take unnecessary risks in the performance of their duties. American criminals have a long tradition of armed violence, and every year in this country many law enforcement officers are killed in the line of duty, and thousands more are wounded. Virtually all of these deaths and a substantial portion of the injuries are inflicted with guns and knives." (Terry v. Ohio (1968) supra, 392 U.S. 1, 23–24, 88 S.Ct. 1868, 1881, 20 L.Ed.2d 889.) The courts should do all in their constitutional powers to minimize these risks.

. . .

Yet in *Terry* the high court held that when an officer observes suspicious behavior short of probable cause to arrest, he may conduct a "pat-down" search for weapons only if he has reasonable grounds to believe the suspect is "armed and presently dangerous." (Id. at pp. 24, 27, 30, 88 S.Ct. 1868.) The requirements for a weapons search are not as strict if the officer has probable cause to arrest (id. at p. 25, 88 S.Ct. 1868); but for the reasons explained in Part II of this opinion, even a search incident to such an arrest must remain "reasonable in scope."

That scope, moreover, is dictated by similar considerations. Just as the arresting officer in an ordinary traffic violation case cannot reasonably expect to find contraband in the offender's vehicle, so also he cannot expect to find weapons. To allow the police to routinely search for weapons in all such instances would likewise constitute an "intolerable and unreasonable" intrusion into the privacy of the vast majority of peaceable citizens who travel by automobile. It follows that a warrantless search for weapons, like a search for contraband, must be predicated in traffic violation cases on specific facts or circumstances giving the officer reasonable grounds to believe that such weapons are present in the vehicle he has stopped.

No such facts or circumstances appear in the record of the case at bar. Mrs. Kiefer's act of bending down and Mr. Kiefer's walk toward the officer's car are clearly insufficient for this purpose: if, as we conclude in Part II, those observations did not give Officer Cameron reasonable grounds to believe there was contraband in the car, by the same token they could not reasonably justify a belief that the same persons were in possession not of contraband but of weapons.

As Officer Cameron's initial entry into defendants' car was unlawful, all the evidence discovered as a consequence of that entry was inadmissible. It follows that the trial court's order of suppression is supported by substantial evidence.

The alternative writ of mandamus is discharged and the peremptory writ is denied.

WRIGHT, C. J., and PETERS, TOBRINER, BURKE and SULLIVAN, JJ., concur.

McCOMB, Justice.

I dissent. I would grant the writ.

PEOPLE v. SUPERIOR COURT OF KERN COUNTY (HAWKINS) *

Supreme Court of California, In Bank, 1972.
6 Cal.3d 757, 100 Cal.Rptr. 281, 493 P.2d 1145.

SULLIVAN, Justice.

Defendant (real party in interest) Allan Foster Hawkins was charged by information with one count of vehicle manslaughter (Pen.Code, § 192, subd. (3) (a)) and one count of felony drunk driving (Veh.Code, § 23101). He moved pursuant to section 1538.5 of the Penal Code to suppress as evidence the results of a blood-alcohol test on the ground that they were the product of an illegal search and seizure. Defendant's motion was granted and the People seek review by writ of mandate. (Pen.Code, § 1538.5, subd. (*o*).)

The pertinent facts giving rise to the motion to suppress are as follows: On the evening of June 21, 1970, defendant, accompanied by his sister, was driving a pickup truck along Allen Road in Kern County. At the same time Robert Craig accompanied by his wife and children was driving his station wagon along Rosedale Highway, a through highway. (See Veh.Code, § 600.) Without stopping or slowing down at the stop sign, defendant drove his truck into the intersection and collided with the Craig vehicle. Defendant's sister was killed and Mrs. Craig was seriously injured.

Officers of the California Highway Patrol arrived upon the scene within 10 minutes. They found defendant standing near the station wagon in a dazed condition, eyes bloodshot, shirt off, back and head bloody from injuries. Officer Hernandez testified that defendant's breath smelled of alcoholic beverages and that there were three beer cans in defendant's truck, two full and one empty. Due to defendant's physical condition, he was not given a field sobriety test, but placed in an ambulance along with Mrs. Craig and sent to the Kern General Hospital for medical attention.

At the hospital defendant and Mrs. Craig were transferred to the emergency room. After completing their investigation at the scene of the accident, the two officers also proceeded to the hospital. While defendant was lying in the emergency room awaiting treatment, Officer Apsit approached defendant and asked that he consent to a blood-alcohol test for intoxication. Defendant apparently agreed and signed a written consent. A blood sample was thereupon taken in a medically approved manner. Several hours later defendant was released from the hospital. At no time was defendant placed under arrest.

The result of the blood-alcohol test showed that defendant's blood contained 203 milligrams percent alcohol. Several weeks after the accident a complaint was filed in the Bakersfield Municipal Court charging defendant with the above-mentioned felonies. Defendant voluntarily surrendered to the authorities. At the preliminary hearing, the magistrate, found that defendant had consented to the blood-alcohol test, denied his motion to suppress the results of the test and held him to answer.

Defendant renewed his motion to suppress in the superior court. (§ 1538.5, subd. (i).) At the special hearing his motion was submitted on the transcript of the preliminary hearing, supplemented by defendant's testimony. The People conceded that the only ground upon which they sought to justify the seizure of defendant's blood was his written consent. The trial judge found that defendant's written consent was not free

---

* Prior to reading this, it is recommended that the reader review the following statutes: Penal Code §§ 192, 1538.5, Vehicle Code §§ 13353, 23101. Also see the cases of Schmerber and Kraft included in this text.

and voluntary and granted the motion to suppress. The People thereupon filed the instant petition for a writ of mandate. (§ 1538.5, subd. (*o*).)

The People concede, as indeed they must, that there is substantial evidence in the record to support the trial court's finding that defendant's written consent to the blood-alcohol test was not freely and voluntarily given. They contend, however, that the taking of a blood sample in a medically approved manner but without the consent of the subject is not violative of his right to be secure against unreasonable searches and seizures under the Fourth and Fourteenth Amendments to the United States Constitution where there is probable cause to arrest at the time the sample is taken, even though the taking of the sample is not pursuant to a search warrant or incident to an arrest. We disagree. Accordingly we deny the People's petition for the writ.

It is clear that the Fourth Amendment does not bar a compulsory seizure, without a warrant, of a person's blood for the purposes of a blood alcohol test to determine intoxication, provided that the taking of the sample is done in a medically approved manner, is incident to a lawful arrest, and, is based upon the reasonable belief that the person is intoxicated. (Schmerber v. California (1966) 384 U.S. 757, 766–772, 86 S.Ct. 1826, 16 L.Ed.2d 908; People v. Duroncelay (1957) 48 Cal.2d 766, 771–772, 312 P.2d 690.) As previously indicated, the People claim, without any citation of authority, that such a seizure of a person's blood is lawful even when it is *not* incident to a lawful arrest. They argue that the real thrust of *Schmerber* and *Duroncelay* is that intrusion into the privacy of a person's body depends upon a clear indication of his intoxication and that his arrest is a mere formality. They point to the following language in *Schmerber*: "The interests in human dignity and privacy which the Fourth Amendment protects forbids any such intrusions on the mere chance that desired evidence might be obtained. In the absence of a clear indication that in fact such evidence will be found, these fundamental human interests require law officers to suffer the risk that such evidence may disappear unless there is an immediate search." (Schmerber v. California, supra, 384 U.S. 757, 769–770, 86 S.Ct. 1826, 1835.)

Contrary to the People's claim, *Schmerber's* approval of the compulsory seizure of blood is clearly grounded on the premise that it is incidental to a lawful arrest. "In this case, as will often be true when charges of driving under the influence of alcohol are pressed, these questions arise in the context of an arrest made by an officer without a warrant." (Id. at 768, 86 S.Ct. at 1834.) "While early cases suggest that there is an unrestricted 'right on the part of the government, always recognized under English and American law, to search the person of the accused when legally arrested to discover and seize the fruits or evidences of crime,' [citations] the mere fact of a lawful arrest does not end our inquiry." (Id. at p. 769, 86 S.Ct. at p. 1835.) "Given these special facts, we conclude that the attempt to secure evidence of blood-alcohol content in this case was an *appropriate incident to petitioner's arrest*." (Id. at p. 771, 86 S.Ct. at p. 1836, italics added.) Similarly in *Duroncelay*, we made it perfectly clear that the seizure of the blood sample could only be justified as "incident to the lawful arrest of one who is reasonably believed to have violated section 501 of the Vehicle Code." (People v. Duroncelay, supra, 48 Cal.2d 766, 772, 312 P.2d 690, 699.)

The People favor us with no authority supportive of their startling proposition that in this context a lawful arrest is but a mere formality. Indeed this proposition runs directly counter to the law on search and seizure developed by the United States Supreme Court. "[T]his Court has never sustained a search upon the sole ground that officers reasonably expected to find evidence of a particular crime and voluntarily confined their activities to the least intrusive means consistent with that end. Searches conducted without warrants have been held unlawful 'notwithstanding facts unquestionably showing probable cause,'

. . .

★ ★ ★

. . . Although it is clear under *Schmerber* that a person who has been lawfully arrested may have a blood sample forcibly removed without his consent, provided it is done in a reasonable, medically approved manner and provided further that the arresting officer had probable cause to believe the arrestee was intoxicated, nevertheless such an episode remains an unpleasant, undignified and undesirable one.

However, the shocking number of injuries and deaths on the highways caused by drunk drivers has compelled society to adopt extreme measures in response. By its enactment in 1966 of section 13353, the Legislature devised an additional or alternative method of compelling a person arrested for drunk driver to submit to a test for intoxication, by providing that such person will lose his automobile driver's license for a period of six months if he refuses to submit to a test for intoxication. The effect of this legislation is to equip peace officers with an instrument of enforcement not involving physical compulsion. It is noteworthy that in so doing, the Legislature took pains to condition its use upon a lawful arrest for driving under the influence of intoxicating liquor and upon the reasonable belief of the peace officer that the arrestee was in fact so driving.

The People have not even attempted to justify the taking of a blood sample from defendant under any of the "few specifically established and well-delineated exceptions" to the "basic constitutional rule in this area . . . that 'searches conducted outside the judicial process, without prior approval by judge or magistrate, are *per se* unreasonable under the Fourth Amendment" (Coolidge v. New Hampshire, supra, 403 U.S. 443, 454–455, 91 S.Ct. 2022, 2032, quoting Katz v. United States, supra, 389 U.S. 347, 357, 88 S.Ct. 507), . . .

Since in the light of the foregoing authorities the People have failed to meet their burden of justifying the taking of a blood sample from defendant and since there is substantial evidence in the record to support the trial court's finding that defendant did not freely and voluntarily consent to the taking of his blood, it follows that the trial court quite correctly suppressed the results of the blood-alcohol test as having been obtained by an unlawful search and seizure.

The order to show cause is discharged and the petition for a peremptory writ of mandate is denied.

WRIGHT, C. J., and PETERS, TOBRINER, and MOSK, JJ., concur.

BURKE, Justice (concurring and dissenting).

With extreme reluctance I concur in the judgment. In my opinion, contrary to that of the majority, the People's theory for sustaining the taking of the blood sample would have been valid had it been timely presented and the trial court determined the circumstances to be those asserted by the People.

The People's theory is that in the absence of a warrant, consent, or an arrest the taking of Allan Hawkins' blood sample did not violate his right to be secure against unreasonable searches and seizures. The police officers had witnessed a clear indication of his intoxication at the scene of the accident, and there was probable cause for Hawkins' arrest. Time had already elapsed in taking him to the hospital and there was ample justification for the police to have a blood sample taken by a doctor in a hospital.

The majority, in rejecting the theory, fail to give adequate recognition to the fact that an emergency was presented in that the delay necessary to obtain a warrant threatened the destruction of evidence since alcohol soon disappears from the blood. The theory, however, unfortunately was not presented in the municipal or superior court and for the reasons hereinafter stated may not be presented for the first time here. The record contains evidence that would have supported determinations that the recited circumstances existed, and had the theory been urged below and the trial court made such determinations the taking of the blood sample was permissible under California and other state court decisions and clear implications in United States Supreme Court decisions since the evidence was in the process of destruction.

• • •

Support for upholding the taking of a blood sample under the circumstances heretofore recited is found by analogy to cases involving searches of movable vehicles stopped on the highway where there is probable cause to believe that they contain contraband. The rationale for sustaining such searches is that it is not practicable to secure a warrant because the vehicle can be quickly moved out of the locality in which the warrant must be sought. (Coolidge v. New Hampshire, 403 U.S. 443, 459–460, 91 S.Ct. 2022, 29 L.Ed.2d 364; Chambers v. Maroney, 399 U.S. 42, 48–51, 90 S.Ct. 1975, 26 L.Ed.2d 419; Carroll v. United States, 267 U.S. 132, 153–154, 45 S.Ct. 280, 69 L.Ed. 543.) A similar rationale applies to blood samples under the recited circumstances for alcohol soon disappears from the blood (see, e. g., Schmerber v. California, supra, 384 U.S. 757, 770–771, 86 S.Ct. 1826; In re Martin, 58 Cal.2d 509, 512, 24 Cal.Rptr. 833, 374 P.2d 801; People v. Huber, supra, 232 Cal.App.2d 663, 670, 43 Cal.Rptr. 65). Indeed, blood sampling under such circumstances may present a stronger case for dispensing with a warrant, since movable vehicles are at most only *very likely* to be unavailable for inspection at a later date, while the alcohol in a suspect's blood is *certain* to disappear. (See 79 Harv.L.Rev. 677, 678.)

Furthermore, the United States Supreme Court has repeatedly recognized that where evidence is in the process of destruction a warrantless search in the absence of an arrest may be justified. (See, e. g., Vale v. Louisiana, 399 U.S. 30, 34–35, 90 S.Ct. 1969, 26 L.Ed.2d 409; Chapman v. United States, 365 U.S. 610, 615, 81 S.Ct. 776, 5 L.Ed.2d 828; McDonald v. United States, 335 U.S. 451, 455, 69 S.Ct. 191, 93 L.Ed. 153; Johnson v. United States, 333 U.S. 10, 15, 68 S.Ct. 367, 92 L.Ed. 436.)

The implied consent law (Veh.Code, § 13353) by its terms is inapplicable in the absence of an arrest. However, in enacting this law the Legislature did not intend to preempt the field of chemical sobriety tests by complete statutory regulation, and the admissibility of blood alcohol tests under established case law is not affected by the cited section. (See People v. Wren, 271 Cal.App.2d 788, 791–792, 76 Cal.Rptr. 673; People v. Fite, 267 Cal.App.2d 685, 687–691, 73 Cal.Rptr. 666.)

Regrettably, however, the People failed in the lower courts to present the theory now urged. In the superior court the People conceded that the only ground upon which they sought to justify the search and seizure was consent. (See fn. 3 in majority opinion.) In the municipal court the People likewise relied upon such consent and also on other grounds not asserted here presumably because of their patent lack of merit.

The People cannot for the first time assert their present theory in the instant mandamus proceeding since Hawkins, being entitled to assume that the theories advanced by the prosecutor constituted the only purported justification for the search and seizure had no reason to cross-examine prosecution witnesses and adduce evidence of his own to rebut the theory now advanced by the People. (See Giordenello v. United States, 357 U.S. 480, 488, 78 S.Ct. 1245, 2 L.Ed.2d 1503; Reinert v. Superior Court, 2 Cal.App.3d 36, 42, 82 Cal.Rptr. 263; People v. Adam, 1 Cal.App.3d 486, 489, 81 Cal.Rptr. 738.)

Gross miscarriages of justice may occur in cases such as the instant one where a motion to suppress evidence is granted at a special hearing in the superior court and the theory upon which the search and seizure might be upheld is not presented until the People seek mandamus. In such cases under Penal Code section 1538.5, as it now reads, the People do not have an opportunity to have the legality of the search and seizure relitigated in the light of their new theory. The section currently reads, ". . . If defendant's motion is granted at a special hearing in the superior court, the people, if they have additional evidence relating to the motion and not presented at the special hearing, shall have the right to show good cause at the trial why such evidence was not presented at the special hearing and why the prior ruling at the special hearing should not be binding, *or the people may seek appellate review. . . . If the people prosecute review by appeal or writ to decision, or any review thereof, in a felony or misdemeanor case, it shall be binding upon them.*" (Pen. Code, § 1538.5, subd. (j).)

It is for these reasons that I join in the judgment.

McCOMB, J., concurs.

ROCKWELL v. SUPERIOR COURT OF VENTURA COUNTY *

Supreme Court of California, In Bank, 1976.
18 Cal.3d 420, 134 Cal.Rptr. 650, 556 P.2d 1101.

WRIGHT, Chief Justice.

Petitioner was charged by information with the murder of Linda Beth Coverly. The charging allegations asserted that the homicide was committed with malice; was wilful, deliberate, and premeditated; and occurred in the perpetration or attempted perpetration of rape. It was further alleged that "special circumstances" enumerated in section 190.2, subdivisions (b)(2), (b)(3)(ii), and (b)(3)(iii) were present. A jury found petitioner guilty of first degree murder. The jury was dismissed and a mistrial declared as to the special circumstances phase of the trial, however, when the jury was unable to agree on the special circumstances allegations. Petitioner contends that he should not be required to undergo a retrial of the special circumstances charges inasmuch as the United States Supreme Court has held that death penalty statutes which do not provide for consideration of mitigating circumstances in the decision to impose capital punishment violate the Eighth and Fourteenth Amendments.

The People recognize that under the United States Supreme Court's decisions in Gregg v. Georgia, supra, 428 U.S. 153, 96 S.Ct. 2909 and the companion cases decided the same day, statutes providing for imposition of the death penalty may neither make that penalty mandatory nor give the jury or judge charged with determining the penalty absolute discretion in the choice of life or death, but must provide standards so that the sentencing authority will "focus on the particularized circumstances of the crime and the defendant." (Gregg v. Georgia, supra, 428 U.S. 153, 96 S.Ct. 2909.) A statute which enumerates aggravating circumstances, one or more of which must be found as a prerequisite to imposition of the death penalty but which does not provide for "meaningful opportunity for consideration of mitigating factors presented by the circumstances of the particular crime or by the attributes of the individual offender" (Roberts v. Louisiana, supra, 428 U.S. 325, 96 S.Ct. 3001, 3006) permits the imposition of capital punishment in violation of the Eighth Amendment's proscription of cruel and unusual punishment, as does a statute which makes death a mandatory punishment for specified categories of murder. (Woodson v. North Carolina, supra, 428 U.S. 280, 96 S.Ct. 2978) "[I]n capital cases the fundamental respect for humanity underlying the Eighth Amendment . . . requires consideration of the character and record of the individual offender and the circumstances of the particular offense as a constitutionally indispensable part of the process of inflicting the penalty of death." (Id., at p. ——, 96 S.Ct. at p. 2991.)

Section 190 specifies that "[e]very person guilty of murder in the first degree *shall*

---

* Prior to reading this case it is recommended that the reader review the following statute: Penal Code § 192.

suffer death if any one or more of the special circumstances enumerated in Section 190.2 have been charged and found to be true in the manner provided in Section 190.1." (Emphasis added.) Section 190.1 specifies that "[i]f the trier of fact finds . . . that any one or more of the special circumstances enumerated in Section 190.2 as charged is true, *the defendant shall suffer the penalty of death* . . . ." (Emphasis added.) And section 190.2 further specifies that "[t]he penalty for a person found guilty of first-degree murder *shall be death* in any case in which the trier of fact" makes a finding that one or more charged special circumstances exist. (Emphasis added.)

The People do not claim that the "special circumstances" enumerated in section 190.2 are other than aggravating factors creating categories of first degree murder for which death is the prescribed penalty. It is urged, however, that notwithstanding the Legislature's repeated stipulation that death "shall" be the penalty for murders thus categorized, capital punishment is not, in fact, mandatory because both the trial judge and the appellate court have power to reduce the penalty from death to life imprisonment. This power, it is argued, makes possible consideration of mitigating factors in the circumstances of the offense and in the character and record of the individual defendant as required by the Eighth Amendment.

The People find this power in sections 1181, subdivision 7 and 1385. The former had been held to allow a trial court to reduce to life imprisonment a death penalty decreed by a jury under capital punishment provisions in effect prior to the enactment of sections 190.1 and 190.2 in 1973. (People v. Moore (1960) 53 Cal.2d 451, 454, 2 Cal.Rptr. 6, 348 P.2d 584, cert. den. 364 U.S. 895, 81 S.Ct. 226, 5 L.Ed.2d 189.) The latter, it is suggested, permits a trial court to strike special circumstances allegations "in the interest of justice," and thus to exercise mercy based on mitigating circumstances.

Gregg v. Georgia, supra, 428 U.S. 153, 96 S.Ct. 2909, is the leading case in which the court set forth its views both as to the constitutionality of capital punishment in general, and the features of the Georgia statutory procedures which offered assurance that the decision to inflict the death penalty in particular cases would be made and affirmed on the basis of criteria adequate to avoid arbitrary, capricious or discriminatory (and thus unconstitutional) decisions. Only two members of the court, Justices Brennan and Marshall, were of the view that the death penalty is excessive and thus unconstitutional *per se* under the Eighth Amendment. The remaining members, Justices Stewart, Powell, and Stevens, in the lead opinion, concurred in by Justice White with whom the Chief Justice and Justice Rehnquist joined in a separate opinion and Justice Blackmun who separately concurred in the judgment, all agreed that the Georgia procedures met the test set forth earlier in Furman v. Georgia (1972) 408 U.S. 238, 92 S.Ct. 2726, 33 L.Ed.2d 346, that the death penalty "not be imposed under sentencing procedures that created a substantial risk that it would be inflicted in an arbitrary and capricious manner," (428 U.S. at p. 188, 96 S.Ct. 2909 at p. 2932) and that "the decision to impose it . . . be guided by standards so that the sentencing authority would focus on the particularized circumstances of the crime and the defendant." (Id., at p. ——, 96 S.Ct. at p. 2937.)

Several features of the Georgia legislation enacted in response to *Furman* were particularly noted by Justice Stewart in his opinion upholding that death penalty scheme as contributing assurance that the *Furman* defects had been eliminated. First among these was "narrow[ing] the class of murderers subject to capital punishment by specifying 10 statutory aggravating circumstances, one of which must be found by the jury to exist beyond a reasonable doubt before a death sentence can ever be imposed." (—— U.S. at p. ——, 96 S.Ct. 2909 at p. 2936.) Next was the fact that "the jury is authorized to consider any other appropriate aggravating or mitigating circumstances." (Id.) Thus, Justice Stewart noted, the jury's attention was directed both to the particular circumstances of the crime and to relevant personal characteristics of the defendant such as his past record, youth, cooperation with the police, and his emotional state at the time of the offense. It is noteworthy in this regard that the Georgia procedure permits the judge or jury to hear argument on and "additional evidence in extenuation, mitigation, and aggravation of punishment . . . [p]rovided, however, that only such evidence in aggravation as the State has made known to the defendant prior to his trial shall be admissible." (Ga.Code Ann. § 27–2503 (Supp.1975).) Under this provision "the defendant is accorded substantial latitude as to the types of evidence that he may introduce." (—— U.S. at p. ——, 96 S.Ct. at p. 2920.)

Finally, Justice Stewart found a further safeguard against arbitrariness and discrimination in the application of the death penalty in the Georgia procedure for expedited appeal and oversight of capital punishment by the Georgia Supreme Court which is charged by statute with responsibility to determine not only whether the evidence supports the jury's determination as to special circumstances, but also whether the death penalty "was imposed under the influence of passion, prejudice, or any other arbitrary factor," and to consider whether that penalty is excessive in comparison with penalties "imposed in similar cases, considering both the crime and the defendant." (Ga.Code Ann. § 27–2537 (Supp.1975).) Provision is also made for compilation of the data necessary to the last decision, and for preparation by the trial judge of a report regarding factors relevant to possible influence of passion or prejudice in the jury's decisions, and to any disproportionality in the sentence. This review, Justice Stewart wrote, "serves as a check against the random or arbitrary imposition of the death penalty. In particular, the proportionality review substantially eliminates the possibility that a person will be sentenced to die by the action of an aberrant jury." (—— U.S. at p. ——, 96 S.Ct. at p. 2940.)

Concurring in the judgment, Justice White, joined by the Chief Justice and Justice Rehnquist, described the appellate review procedure as "an important aspect" of the Georgia scheme, but implied it might not be necessary to meet the requirements of *Furman* (428 U.S. at p. 153, 96 S.Ct. 2909.) The aspects of the Georgia scheme which a majority of the court considered essential to its constitutionality therefore appear to be the narrowly defined aggravating factors or categories of murder for which capital punishment is authorized and the opportunity for the defendant to present evidence and argument on and to have the jury consider mitigating circumstances with respect to both the commission of the offense and his personal characteristics which militate against imposition of the extreme penalty.

This analysis finds support in the court's reasoning in Proffitt v. Florida, supra, 428 U.S. 242, 96 S.Ct. 2960 and Jurek v. Texas, supra, 428 U.S. 262, 96 S.Ct. 2950 in which death penalty legislation of Florida and Texas was also upheld. Patterned after the Model Penal Code, the Florida law provides for a separate penalty hearing after conviction of a capital offense. At this hearing evidence may be introduced of any matters relevant to statutory aggravating and/or mitigating circumstances, and counsel may argue whether, in light of this evidence, death is an appropriate punishment. The jury must consider whether sufficient mitigating circumstances exist to outweigh those aggravating circumstances and whether the defendant should be sentenced to life imprisonment or death. This jury verdict is advisory only, however, and the sentencing judge must independently weigh the aggravating and mitigating circumstances. If the judge imposes death, he must set out the facts upon which he has determined the existence of aggravating circumstances and that the mitigating circumstances do not outweigh them. Although the appellate review is not as comprehensive as that in

Georgia, the lead opinion in *Proffitt*, of Justices Stewart, Powell, and Stevens, noted that the requirement that the sentencing judge justify the death penalty with written findings assured meaningful appellate review. These justices concluded that these procedures, too, met the constitutional deficiencies of the *Furman* statute because: "The sentencing authority in Florida, the trial judge, is directed to weigh eight aggravating factors against seven mitigating factors to determine whether the death penalty shall be imposed. This determination requires the trial judge to focus on the circumstances of the crime and the character of the individual defendant. . . . [¶] Under Florida's capital-sentencing procedures, in sum, trial judges are given specific and detailed guidance to assist them in deciding whether to impose a death penalty or imprisonment for life. Moreover, their decisions are reviewed to ensure that they are consistent with other sentences imposed in similar circumstances. . . . On its face the Florida system thus satisfies the constitutional deficiencies identified in *Furman*." (—— U.S. at p. ——, 96 S.Ct. at p. 2966.) Again Justice White, joined by the Chief Justice and Justice Rehnquist, concurred in the judgment, this time noting that he agreed "with the plurality . . . that although the statutory aggravating and mitigating circumstances are not susceptible to mechanical application . . . they are by no means so vague and overbroad as to leave the discretion of the sentencing authority unfettered." (—— U.S. at p. ——, 96 S.Ct. at p. 2970.)

Of crucial importance to constitutional validity of the Florida procedure was the fact that the "sentencing authority"—that it was the judge rather than the jury was not considered significant—was charged with responsibility to hear evidence on both aggravating and mitigating factors, and to decide with the assistance of "specific and detailed guidance" whether to impose the death penalty. (—— U.S. at p. ——, 96 S.Ct. 2960.)

The Texas law permits imposition of the death penalty for a limited category of murders. The court found that this limitation, by encompassing conduct similar to that for which death was a permissible punishment in Georgia and Florida, serves the same purpose as does the itemization of aggravating circumstances in the statutes of those states. Texas also makes provision for a separate penalty trial after guilt has been adjudicated. At that hearing any evidence and/or argument relevant to the appropriate penalty is admissible. If after that hearing upon consideration of the evidence, the jury unanimously answers "yes" to each of three questions, the death penalty is to be imposed. Those questions are:

"(1) whether the conduct of the defendant that caused the death of the deceased was committed deliberately and with the reasonable expectation that the death of the deceased or another would result;

"(2) whether there is a probability that the defendant would commit criminal acts of violence that would constitute a continuing threat to society; and

"(3) if raised by the evidence, whether the conduct of the defendant in killing the deceased was unreasonable in response to the provocation, if any, by the deceased." (Tex.Code Crim.Proc., Art. 37.071(b).)

The court found that in directing the focus of the sentencing authority to specific aggravating factors, the Texas statute differs from those of Florida and Georgia only in permitting capital punishment for a smaller class of murderers. The statute does not, however, on its face require consideration of mitigating factors, prompting, Justices Stewart, Powell and Stevens to warn that "a sentencing system that allowed the jury to consider only aggravating circumstances would almost certainly fall short of providing the individualized sentencing determination . . . required by the Eighth and Fourteenth Amendments. . . A jury must be allowed to consider on the basis of all relevant evidence not only why a death sentence should be imposed, but also why it should not be imposed. [¶] Thus, in order to meet the requirement of the Eighth and Fourteenth Amendments, a capital-sentencing system must allow the sentencing authority to consider mitigating circumstances." (Jurek v. Texas, supra, —— U.S. at p. ——, 96 S.Ct. at p. 2956.) The court then found that as construed by the Texas Court of Criminal Appeals to permit a defendant to introduce and the jury to consider evidence of mitigating circumstances relevant to the second question, the Texas procedure did focus the attention of the jury on an "objective consideration of the particularized circumstances of the individual offense and the individual offender before it can impose a sentence of death." (Id., at p. ——, 96 S.Ct. at p. 2957.)

By contrast, the court found the capital punishment laws of North Carolina and Louisiana constitutionally lacking. (Woodson v. North Carolina, supra, 428 U.S. 280, 96 S.Ct. 2978; Roberts v. Louisiana, supra, 428 U.S. 325, 96 S.Ct. 3001.) The North Carolina law, which made death a mandatory punishment for all first degree murder and thereby sought to remove all discretion as to penalty from the jury was found defective on grounds that a statute imposing death as a penalty for every person convicted of a specified offense departs too far from the "evolving standards of decency that mark the progress of a maturing society" by which a plurality of the court had suggested in Trop v. Dulles (1958) 356 U.S. 86, 101, 78 S.Ct. 590, 598, 2 L.Ed.2d 630, punishment be tested under the Eighth Amendment. The plurality also found the North Carolina statute defective in its failure to base the decision to inflict the death penalty on a "particularized consideration of relevant aspects of the character and record of each convicted defendant." (Woodson v. North Carolina, supra, —— U.S. at p. ——, 96 S.Ct. at p. 2991.)

Of more significance, however, is the Louisiana law which the court also found constitutionally wanting. Louisiana then defined first degree murder, for which death was the prescribed punishment, in terms which encompass several of the special circumstances included in section 190.2. No separate penalty trial was provided and the death penalty was ostensibly mandatory. The jury was to be instructed on and provided with verdict forms not only for first degree murder, but also for lesser offenses of second degree murder and manslaughter, as well as not guilty, whether or not there was evidence from which it could be inferred that the offense was less than first degree murder. This procedure was characterized by the court as an invitation to the jury to convict the defendant of a lesser offense whenever they believed the death penalty to be inappropriate, thus introducing an "element of capriciousness in making the jurors' power to avoid the death penalty dependent on their willingness to accept this invitation to disregard the trial judge's instructions. The Louisiana procedure neither provides standards to channel jury judgments nor permits review to check the arbitrary exercise of the capital jury's *de facto* sentencing discretion. [¶] . . . As in North Carolina, there are no standards provided to guide the jury in the exercise of its power to select those first-degree murderers who will receive death sentences, and there is no meaningful appellate review of the jury's decision." (Roberts v. Louisiana, supra, —— U.S. at p. ——, 96 S.Ct. at p. 3007.)

We turn now to consideration of the People's contention that the powers granted to trial courts by sections 1181, subdivision 7, and 1385, and that granted appellate courts by section 1181, subdivision 7, are adequate to meet the criteria established by the United States Supreme Court. To do so it must appear that the death penalty will be imposed on defendants subject to sections 190 through 190.3 only after the "sentencing authority" has considered evidence of both aggravating and mitigating circumstances, in light of specific and detailed standards offering such sufficient guidance in deciding when the death penalty should be imposed as to offer assurance that capital punishment will not be decreed in an arbitrary, capricious, or discriminatory manner.

No argument is made that the "special circumstances" delineated in section 190.2 fail to meet the court's criterion that those aggravating circumstances which warrant capital punishment be specifically set forth. Our inquiry is therefore directed to whether the "sentencing authority" is given the opportunity to consider mitigating as well as aggravating factors and whether it has sufficient guidance as to what mitigating factors should be considered, in deciding whether to impose the death penalty. It follows that we must also determine whether the defendant is afforded adequate opportunity to present to the sentencing authority evidence on and argument regarding these mitigating factors and their relevance to the appropriate penalty. If our inquiry is limited to the express provisions of sections 190 through 190.3, the answer to these questions necessarily must be "no," since those sections include no provision either for presentation of evidence regarding mitigating circumstances or for consideration of such circumstances, at the hearing on special circumstances.

The People argue that mitigating factors other than those relevant to determination of the defendant's guilt or innocence are considered at the special circumstances phase of the trial in that the defendant may present evidence to show that he did not personally commit the act that caused death (§§ 190.2, subd. (b), 190.3, subd. (b)), or to establish that the killing was not wilful, deliberate, and premeditated (§ 190.2, subd. (b)(3)), and thereby avoid imposition of the death penalty. Evidence which merely refutes the existence of an alleged special circumstance goes only to aggravating factors, however, and does not afford a basis for the "particularized consideration of the character and record of each convicted defendant" that the Supreme Court found lacking in the North Carolina statutory scheme. It does not serve to focus the attention of the jury or court on both the "particularized circumstances of the individual offense *and the* individual offender" as did the constitutionally adequate Texas procedure (Jurek v. Texas, supra, 428 U.S. 262, ——, 96 S.Ct. 2950), and does not afford the "sentencing authority" the opportunity to weigh the aggravating and mitigating factors in reaching a decision to impose the death penalty. Similarly the exclusion of an entire category of youthful murderers from potential application of the death penalty (§ 190.3) fails to afford individualized consideration of the circumstances of the offender or the offense.

Thus sections 190 through 190.3, like the laws of North Carolina and Louisiana, by their terms make death a mandatory penalty for those categories of murder described in section 190.2, without provision for consideration of mitigating factors.

The People suggest, however, that sections 1181, subdivision 7, and 1385 permit the trial held on the special circumstances allegations pursuant to section 190.1 to be conducted as a bifurcated hearing during which the jury first determines the truth of these allegations, and the court then decides whether to reduce the otherwise applicable death penalty to life imprisonment. The People thus equate the judge to the "sentencing authority" whether or not the special circumstances are tried by a jury, and argue that the judge has power to base his decision as to penalty on mitigating circumstances and in the interest of mercy. This power, the People urge, is not the constitutionally impermissible unbridled discretion which undermined pre-*Furman* law, because, before the death penalty can be imposed, the trier of fact must examine the particular circumstances of the individual offense.

Two flaws in this argument are immediately apparent. First, no provision is made under section 190.1, section 1181, subdivision 7, section 1385, or otherwise for the introduction of evidence of mitigating factors, and no guidance is given as to what factors should be considered "mitigating." Second, the procedures approved by the United States Supreme Court require that the sentencing authority, be it judge or jury, weigh the aggravating and mitigating factors in light of specific and detailed guidelines. None of the approved procedures permits the trier of fact to find the aggravating factors of the offense and then permits reduction of an otherwise mandatory death penalty only if the sentencing authority independently finds mitigating circumstances sufficient to warrant mercy.

Even if we assume that such a procedure is sanctioned by the Eighth and Fourteenth Amendments, however, neither section 1181, subdivision 7, nor section 1385, permits a trial judge to act in the manner suggested by the People. Section 1181 empowers the trial court to grant *a new trial* upon application of the defendant "when a verdict has been rendered or a finding made against the defendant." Subdivision 7 provides that the court may, in lieu of granting a new trial, reduce the punishment when the "verdict or finding is contrary to law or evidence," but the statute expressly provides that this power is to be exercised "in any case wherein authority is vested by statute in the trial court or jury to recommend or determine as part of its verdict or finding the punishment to be imposed . . . ."

By its terms, subdivision 7 of section 1181 is presently inapplicable to the death penalty. Section 190.2 states that death shall be imposed when the trier of fact makes a finding that one or more special circumstances existed in the commission of first degree murder. Under section 190.2, therefore, the trier of fact has no authority to "recommend or determine as a part of its verdict or finding the punishment to be imposed." Further, any motion for a new trial under this subdivision on grounds that "the verdict or finding is contrary to law or evidence" is necessarily directed exclusively to the finding of special circumstances, the only finding which the trier of fact is called upon, or permitted, to make.

The People suggest that we may interpret subdivision 7 in such a way that, on a motion for new trial made on grounds that the finding of special circumstances is contrary to the law or the evidence, the court may conduct an evidentiary hearing on the existence of mitigating circumstances, and, if mitigation is found, impose a sentence of life imprisonment rather than death. The express purpose of the hearing provided by section 190.1, however, is to determine whether "any one or more of the special circumstances enumerated in Section 190.2 as charged is true." The possible existence of mitigating factors is outside that purpose.

The procedure suggested by the People would not only expand the function of the motion for new trial beyond that of reviewing a verdict or finding already made by the trier of fact to an evidentiary hearing on an issue never considered by the trier of fact, but, contrary to every indication of legislative intent, would also impose responsibility for determining which defendants should be sentenced to death on the trial judge. At no time since the penalty of death was made discretionary in 1874 (Code Am. 1873–74, c. 508, p. 457, § 1) has the Legislature placed this awesome burden exclusively on the trial judge.

We conclude that section 1181, subdivision 7, presently does not, and cannot reasonably be interpreted to, permit a trial court to conduct an evidentiary hearing on the existence of mitigating circumstances, and does not authorize a trial judge to reduce to life imprisonment the penalty of death which section 190.1 provides a defendant shall suffer if the trier of fact finds any one or more special circumstances as charged to be true.

A fortiori, the power granted this court by section 1181, subdivision 7, to modify a verdict by imposing a lesser punishment, if applicable to a sentence of death imposed pursuant to section 190.2, cannot assure the requisite individualized consideration which the United States Supreme Court held necessary to satisfy the Eighth and Fourteenth Amendments. The automatic appeal from a judgment imposing death (§ 1239) does offer the prompt review by a court of statewide jurisdiction which the court found to be an additional "check against the random or arbitrary imposition of the death penalty" in Gregg v. Georgia, supra, 428 U.S. 153, 205, 96 S.Ct. 2909, 2940, but the California procedures leading to the decision to impose the death penalty do not permit the same "meaningful review" of that decision as do those of Georgia. Inasmuch as neither section 190.1 nor subdivision 7 of section 1181 provides an opportunity for a defendant to present evidence of mitigating circumstances, and no guidelines have been provided by the Legislature upon which to weigh mitigating circumstances against the aggravating factors which permit imposition of the death penalty, the record affords no basis upon which a reviewing court can assess whether, in a particular case, death is an excessive punishment, is disproportionate to penalties imposed in similar cases, or is the product of "passion, prejudice, or any other arbitrary factor." (Gregg v. Georgia, supra, 428 U.S. 153, 212, 96 S.Ct. 2909, 2943.)

The People also suggest that since the trial court's power to dismiss an action under section 1385 includes the power to dismiss a part but not all of the allegations of an accusatory pleading in the interest of justice, even after a jury verdict of guilt (People v. Superior Court (Howard) (1968) 69 Cal.2d 491, 501, 72 Cal.Rptr. 330, 446 P.2d 138), it may dismiss an allegation of special circumstances in the interest of justice if mitigating circumstances suggest that the death penalty is not an appropriate punishment. Although section 1385 provides that a dismissal "in furtherance of justice" may be ordered either on the motion of the district attorney, or on the court's motion, a defendant may invite the court to exercise its power by an application to strike a count or allegation of an accusatory pleading, and the court must consider evidence offered by the defendant in support of his assertion that the dismissal would be in furtherance of justice. (In re Cortez (1971) 6 Cal.3d 78, 98 Cal.Rptr. 307, 490 P.2d 819; People v. Tenorio (1970) 3 Cal.3d 89, 89 Cal.Rptr. 249, 473 P.2d 993.) Thus, unlike subdivision 7, of section 1181, section 1385 does provide a procedure which would permit the trial court to consider striking special circumstances allegations and findings if section 1385 is applicable to allegations made pursuant to section 190.2.

We have not heretofore had occasion to consider whether this power to strike allegations in an accusatory pleading extends to the integrated statutory scheme for imposition of the death penalty established by sections 190 through 190.3. The language of those sections, the omission therefrom of any provision for a hearing on mitigating circumstances, and the history of their adoption leads us to conclude that this would be contrary to the legislative purpose. The Legislature did not intend the jury verdict on special circumstances to be merely advisory, but contemplated death as a mandatory penalty whenever special circumstances were found unless precluded by section 190.-3.

Our conclusion is based first on the clear language of the statute which we are obliged to interpret according to its usual and ordinary import. (People ex rel. Younger v. Superior Court (1976) 16 Cal.3d 30, 43, 127 Cal.Rptr. 122, 544 P.2d 1322; People v. Knowles (1950) 35 Cal.2d 175, 182–183, 217 P.2d 1.) The Legislature has directed in mandatory language, in sections 190, 190.1, and 190.2 that a person found guilty of first degree murder "shall suffer death" (§ 190), "shall suffer the penalty of death" (§ 190.1), and "the penalty . . . shall be death" (§ 190.2), in any case in which a special circumstances allegation is found to be true. This direction is supplemented in section 190.1 with detailed procedures by which such special circumstances are to be charged, how the question is to be tried, including specific rules regarding representation by counsel, burden of proof, how findings are to be made, and when retrial of the question shall be had. Also included is a direction that if two juries have been unable to reach a unanimous verdict that one or more of the special circumstances are true, "the court shall dismiss the jury and impose the punishment of confinement in the state prison for life." The Legislature gave the court the power to impose a sentence of life imprisonment only in this instance. Section 190.1 permits the defendant to waive a jury and have the special circumstances allegations tried to the court. In this case too, the section specifies that if the trier of fact finds an allegation true, the penalty shall be death. No part of section 190.1 suggests that the court which has made such a finding may then strike the allegation it has found true and avoid the command that the death penalty be imposed. These detailed provisions governing the manner by which special circumstances are to be charged and found lead to the conclusion that sections 190 through 190.3 are special legislation and that the court presently has no power under the general grant of authority of section 1385 to strike special circumstances allegations in the interest of justice as an exercise of mercy. (Code Civ.Proc., § 1859; Agricultural Labor Relations Bd. v. Superior Court (1976) 16 Cal.3d 392, 420, 128 Cal.Rptr. 183, 546 P.2d 687; People v. Gilbert (1969) 1 Cal.3d 475, 479, 82 Cal.Rptr. 724, 462 P.2d 580.)

The People argue finally that the defects in the California statutory scheme for imposition of capital punishment can be overcome by judicially mandated procedures, which this court should pronounce because the Legislature intended to write a constitutional death penalty law. They urge that we find the mandatory "shall" to be permissive in those cases in which the Legislature has directed that the penalty "shall" be death, and suggest that since the form of the hearing at which judgment is pronounced is not set out in these statutes this court may prescribe procedures that will satisfy the requirements of the Eighth and Fourteenth Amendments. We decline the People's invitation. They ask us not to interpret but to rewrite the law in a manner which we have shown would be contrary to the manifest legislative intent in enacting sections 190 through 190.3. Decisions as to which criminal defendants shall suffer the death penalty, whether these decisions shall be made by judge or jury, whether and to what extent a jury determination is reviewable by the trial court and/or the reviewing court, and the scope of responsibility to be given this court to safeguard against arbitrary imposition of the death penalty are matters of legislative concern. Were this court to attempt to devise the necessary procedures and criteria we would not only invade the legislative province, but would also be in the position of having to pass objectively on the constitutionality of procedures of our own design. (Cf. Reynolds v. Superior Court (1974) 12 Cal.3d 834, 845–846, 117 Cal.Rptr. 437, 528 P.2d 45.)

We conclude therefore that because sections 190 through 190.3 make death a mandatory punishment for those categories of first degree murder encompassed by the special circumstances enumerated in section 190.2, without provision for consideration of evidence of mitigating circumstances as to the offense or in the personal characteristics of the defendant, and afford no specific detailed guidelines as to the relevance of such evidence in determining whether death is an appropriate punishment, they permit arbitrary imposition of the death penalty in violation of the Eighth and Fourteenth Amendments to the United States Constitution. Those provisions which establish procedures for imposition of the death penalty are therefore invalid and petitioner may not be required to stand trial thereunder. The death penalty provisions are, however, clearly severable from the remaining penalty provisions of section 190 decreeing that the penalty for murder in the first degree in cases in which death is not imposed shall be "confinement in the state prison for life." The Legislature has expressed its intent that if any provision of these sections is invalid, the invalidity shall not affect those remaining provisions which can be given effect. (Stats.1973, ch. 719, p. 1302, § 15.) Petitioner may therefore be sentenced to a term of life imprisonment if no other bar to imposition of judgment on the jury verdict of first degree murder is shown.

Let the peremptory writ of prohibition issue as prayed.

SCHMERBER v. STATE OF CALIFORNIA *

Supreme Court of United States, 1966.
384 U.S. 757, 86 S.Ct. 1826, 16 L.Ed.2d 908.

Mr. Justice BRENNAN delivered the opinion of the Court.

Petitioner was convicted in Los Angeles Municipal Court of the criminal offense of driving an automobile while under the influence of intoxicating liquor. He had been arrested at a hospital while receiving treatment for injuries suffered in an accident involving the automobile that he had apparently been driving. At the direction of a police officer, a blood sample was then withdrawn from petitioner's body by a physician at the hospital. The chemical analysis of this sample revealed a percent by weight of alcohol in his blood at the time of the offense which indicated intoxication, and the report of this analysis was admitted in evidence at the trial. Petitioner objected to receipt of this evidence of the analysis on the ground that the blood had been withdrawn despite his refusal, on the advice of his counsel, to consent to the test. He contended that in that circumstance the withdrawal of the blood and the admission of the analysis in evidence denied him due process of law under the Fourteenth Amendment, as well as specific guarantees of the Bill of Rights secured against the States by that Amendment: his privilege against self-incrimination under the Fifth Amendment; his right to counsel under the Sixth Amendment; and his right not to be subjected to unreasonable searches and seizures in violation of the Fourth Amendment. The Appellate Department of the California Superior Court rejected these contentions and affirmed the conviction. . . .

• • •

. . . We therefore must now decide whether the withdrawal of the blood and admission in evidence of the analysis involved in this case violated petitioner's privilege. We hold that the privilege protects an accused only from being compelled to testify against himself, or otherwise provide the State with evidence of a testimonial or communicative nature, and that the withdrawal of blood and use of the analysis in question in this case did not involve compulsion to these ends.

It could not be denied that in requiring petitioner to submit to the withdrawal and chemical analysis of his blood the State compelled him to submit to an attempt to discover evidence that might be used to prosecute him for a criminal offense. He submitted only after the police officer rejected his objection and directed the physician to proceed. The officer's direction to the physician to administer the test over petitioner's objection constituted compulsion for the purposes of the privilege. The critical question, then, is whether petitioner was thus compelled "to be a witness against himself."

If the scope of the privilege coincided with the complex of values it helps to protect, we might be obliged to conclude that the privilege was violated. In Miranda v. Arizona, 384 U.S. 436, at 460, 86 S.Ct. 1602, at 1620, 16 L.Ed.2d 694, at 715, the Court said of the interests protected by the privilege: "All these policies point to one overriding thought: the constitutional foundation underlying the privilege is the respect a government—state or federal—must accord to the dignity and integrity of its citizens. To maintain a 'fair state-individual balance,' to require the government 'to shoulder the entire load,' . . . to respect the inviolability of the human personality, our accusatory system of criminal justice demands that the government seeking to punish an individual produce the evidence against him by

---

* Prior to reading this, it is recommended that the reader review the following statute: Vehicle Code § 23102. Also see the cases of People v. Superior Court (Hawkins) and Kraft included in this text.

its own independent labors, rather than by the cruel, simple expedient of compelling it from his own mouth." The withdrawal of blood necessarily involves puncturing the skin for extraction, and the percent by weight of alcohol in that blood, as established by chemical analysis, is evidence of criminal guilt. Compelled submission fails on one view to respect the "inviolability of the human personality." Moreover, since it enables the State to rely on evidence forced from the accused, the compulsion violates at least one meaning of the requirement that the State procure the evidence against an accused "by its own independent labors."

As the passage in *Miranda* implicitly recognizes, however, the privilege has never been given the full scope which the values it helps to protect suggest. History and a long line of authorities in lower courts have consistently limited its protection to situations in which the State seeks to submerge those values by obtaining the evidence against an accused through "the cruel, simple expedient of compelling it from his own mouth. . . . In sum, the privilege is fulfilled only when the person is guaranteed the right 'to remain silent unless he chooses to speak in the unfettered exercise of his own will.'" Ibid. The leading case in this Court is Holt v. United States, 218 U.S. 245, 31 S.Ct. 2, 54 L.Ed. 1021. There the question was whether evidence was admissible that the accused, prior to trial and over his protest, put on a blouse that fitted him. It was contended that compelling the accused to submit to the demand that he model the blouse violated the privilege. Mr. Justice Holmes, speaking for the Court, rejected the argument as "based upon an extravagant extension of the 5th Amendment," and went on to say: "[T]he prohibition of compelling a man in a criminal court to be witness against himself is a prohibition of the use of physical or moral compulsion to extort communications from him, not an exclusion of his body as evidence when it may be material. The objection in principle would forbid a jury to look at a prisoner and compare his features with a photograph in proof." 218 U.S., at 252–253, 31 S.Ct., at 6.

It is clear that the protection of the privilege reaches an accused's communications, whatever form they might take, and the compulsion of responses which are also communications, for example, compliance with a subpoena to produce one's papers. Boyd v. United States, 116 U.S. 616, 6 S.Ct. 524, 29 L.Ed. 746. On the other hand, both federal and state courts have usually held that it offers no protection against compulsion to submit to fingerprinting, photographing, or measurements, to write or speak for identification, to appear in court, to stand, to assume a stance, to walk, or to make a particular gesture. The distinction which has emerged, often expressed in different ways, is that the privilege is a bar against compelling "communications" or "testimony," but that compulsion which makes a suspect or accused the source of "real or physical evidence" does not violate it.

Although we agree that this distinction is a helpful framework for analysis, we are not to be understood to agree with past applications in all instances. There will be many cases in which such a distinction is not readily drawn. Some tests seemingly directed to obtain "physical evidence," for example, lie detector tests measuring changes in body function during interrogation, may actually be directed to eliciting responses which are essentially testimonial. To compel a person to submit to testing in which an effort will be made to determine his guilt or innocence on the basis of physiological responses, whether willed or not, is to evoke the spirit and history of the Fifth Amendment. Such situations call to mind the principle that the protection of the privilege "is as broad as the mischief against which it seeks to guard." Counselman v. Hitchcock, 142 U.S. 547, 562, 12 S.Ct. 195, 198.

In the present case, however, no such problem of application is presented. Not even a shadow of testimonial compulsion upon or enforced communication by the accused was involved either in the extraction or in the chemical analysis. Petitioner's testimonial capacities were in no way implicated; indeed, his participation, except as a donor, was irrelevant to the results of the test, which depend on chemical analysis and on that alone. Since the blood test evidence, although an incriminating product of compulsion, was neither petitioner's testimony nor evidence relating to some communicative act or writing by the petitioner, it was not inadmissible on privilege grounds.

THE RIGHT TO COUNSEL CLAIM.

This conclusion also answers petitioner's claim that, in compelling him to submit to the test in face of the fact that his objection was made on the advice of counsel, he was denied his Sixth Amendment right to the assistance of counsel. Since petitioner was not entitled to assert the privilege, he has no greater right because counsel erroneously advised him that he could assert it. His claim is strictly limited to the failure of the police to respect his wish, reinforced by counsel's advice, to be left inviolate. No issue of counsel's ability to assist petitioner in respect of any rights he did possess is presented. The limited claim thus made must be rejected.

THE SEARCH AND SEIZURE CLAIM.

In *Breithaupt,* as here, it was also contended that the chemical analysis should be excluded from evidence as the product of an unlawful search and seizure in violation of the Fourth and Fourteenth Amendments. The Court did not decide whether the extraction of blood in that case was unlawful, but rejected the claim on the basis of Wolf v. People of State of Colorado, 338 U.S. 25, 69 S.Ct. 1359, 93 L.Ed. 1782. That case had held that the Constitution did not require, in state prosecutions for state crimes, the exclusion of evidence obtained in violation of the Fourth Amendment's provisions. We have since overruled *Wolf* in that respect, holding in Mapp v. Ohio, 367 U.S. 643, 81 S.Ct. 1684, 6 L.Ed.2d 1081, that the exclusionary rule adopted for federal prosecutions in Weeks v. United States, 232 U.S. 383, 34 S.Ct. 341, 58 L.Ed. 652, must also be applied in criminal prosecutions in state courts. The question is squarely presented therefore, whether the chemical analysis introduced in evidence in this case should have been excluded as the product of an unconstitutional search and seizure.

The overriding function of the Fourth Amendment is to protect personal privacy and dignity against unwarranted intrusion by the State. In *Wolf* we recognized "[t]he security of one's privacy against arbitrary intrusion by the police" as being "at the core of the Fourth Amendment" and "basic to a free society." 338 U.S., at 27, 69 S.Ct. at 1361. We reaffirmed that broad view of the Amendment's purpose in applying the federal exclusionary rule to the States in *Mapp*.

The values protected by the Fourth Amendment thus substantially overlap those of the Fifth Amendment helps to protect. History and precedent have required that we today reject the claim that the Self-Incrimination Clause of the Fifth Amendment requires the human body in all circumstances to be held inviolate against state expeditions seeking evidence of crime. But if compulsory administration of a blood test does not implicate the Fifth Amendment, it plainly involves the broadly conceived reach of a search and seizure under the Fourth Amendment. That Amendment expressly provides that "[t]he right of the people to be secure in their *persons,* houses, papers, and effects, against unreasonable searches and seizures, shall not be violated . . . .." (Emphasis added.) It could not reasonably be argued, and indeed respondent does not argue, that the administration of the blood test in this case was free of the constraints of the Fourth Amendment. Such testing procedures plainly constitute searches of "persons," and depend antecedently upon seizures of "persons," within the meaning of that Amendment.

Because we are dealing with intrusions into the human body rather than with state interferences with property relationships or private papers—"houses, papers, and effects"—we write on a clean slate. Limitations on the kinds of property which may be seized under warrant, as distinct from the procedures for search and the permissible scope of search, are not instructive in this context. We begin with the assumption that once the privilege against self-incrimination has been found not to bar compelled intrusions into the body for blood to be analyzed for alcohol content, the Fourth Amendment's proper function is to constrain, not against all intrusions as such, but against intrusions which are not justified in the circumstances, or which are made in an improper manner. In other words, the questions we must decide in this case are whether the police were justified in requiring petitioner to submit to the blood test, and whether the means and procedures employed in taking his blood respected relevant Fourth Amendment standards of reasonableness.

In this case, as will often be true when charges of driving under the influence of alcohol are pressed, these questions arise in the context of an arrest made by an officer without a warrant. Here, there was plainly probable cause for the officer to arrest petitioner and charge him with driving an automobile while under the influence of intoxicating liquor. The police officer who arrived at the scene shortly after the accident smelled liquor on petitioner's breath, and testified that petitioner's eyes were "bloodshot, watery, sort of a glassy appearance." The officer saw petitioner again at the hospital, within two hours of the accident. There he noticed similar symptoms of drunkenness. He thereupon informed petitioner "that he was under arrest and that he was entitled to the services of an attorney, and that he could remain silent, and that anything that he told me would be used against him in evidence."

* * *

Although the facts which established probable cause to arrest in this case also suggested the required relevance and likely success of a test of petitioner's blood for alcohol, the question remains whether the arresting officer was permitted to draw these inferences himself, or was required instead to procure a warrant before proceeding with the test. Search warrants are ordinarily required for searches of dwellings, and absent an emergency, no less could be required where intrusions into the human body are concerned. The requirement that a warrant be obtained is a requirement that inferences to support the search "be drawn by a neutral and detached magistrate instead of being judged by the officer engaged in the often competitive enterprise of ferreting out crime." . . .

The officer in the present case, however, might reasonably have believed that he was confronted with an emergency, in which the delay necessary to obtain a warrant, under the circumstances, threatened "the destruction of evidence," Preston v. United States, 376 U.S. 364, 367, 84 S.Ct. 881, 883, 11 L.Ed.2d 777. We are told that the percentage of alcohol in the blood begins to diminish shortly after drinking stops, as the body functions to eliminate it from the system. Particularly in a case such as this, where time had to be taken to bring the accused to a hospital and to investigate the scene of the accident, there was no time to seek out a magistrate and secure a warrant. Given these special facts, we conclude that the attempt to secure evidence of blood-alcohol content in this case was an appropriate incident to petitioner's arrest.

Similarly, we are satisfied that the test chosen to measure petitioner's blood-alcohol level was a reasonable one. Extraction of blood samples for testing is a highly effective means of determining the degree to which a person is under the influence of alcohol. See Breithaupt v. Abram, 352 U.S., at 436, n. 3, 77 S.Ct. at 410, 1 L.Ed.2d 448. Such tests are a commonplace in these days of periodic physical examinations and experience with them teaches that the quantity of blood extracted is minimal, and that for most people the procedure involves virtually no risk, trauma, or pain. Petitioner is not one of the few who on grounds of fear, concern for health, or religious scruple might prefer some other means of testing, such as the "breathalyzer" test petitioner refused, see n. 9, supra. We need not decide whether such wishes would have to be respected.

Finally, the record shows that the test was performed in a reasonable manner. Petitioner's blood was taken by a physician in a hospital environment according to accepted medical practices. We are thus not presented with the serious questions which would arise if a search involving use of a medical technique, even of the most rudimentary sort, were made by other than medical personnel or in other than a medical environment—for example, if it were administered by police in the privacy of the stationhouse. To tolerate searches under these conditions might be to invite an unjustified element of personal risk of infection and pain.

We thus conclude that the present record shows no violation of petitioner's right under the Fourth and Fourteenth Amendments to be free of unreasonable searches and seizures. It bears repeating, however, that we reach this judgment only on the facts of the present record. The integrity of an individual's person is a cherished value of our society. That we today hold that the Constitution does not forbid the States minor intrusions into an individual's body under stringently limited conditions in no way indicates that it permits more substantial intrusions, or intrusions under other conditions.

Affirmed.

Mr. Justice HARLAN, whom Mr. Justice STEWART joins, concurring.

In joining the Court's opinion I desire to add the following comment. While agreeing with the Court that the taking of this blood test involved no testimonial compulsion, I would go further and hold that apart from this consideration the case in no way implicates the Fifth Amendment. Cf. my dissenting opinion and that of Mr. Justice White in Miranda v. Arizona, 384 U.S. 504, 526, 86 S.Ct. 1643, 1655, 16 L.Ed.2d 740, 753.

Mr. Chief Justice WARREN, dissenting.

While there are other important constitutional issues in this case, I believe it is sufficient for me to reiterate my dissenting opinion in Breithaupt v. Abram, 352 U.S. 432, 440, 77 S.Ct. 408, 412, as the basis on which to reverse this conviction.

Mr. Justice BLACK with whom Mr. Justice DOUGLAS joins, dissenting.

I would reverse petitioner's conviction. I agree with the Court that the Fourteenth Amendment made applicable to the States the Fifth Amendment's provision that "No person . . . shall be compelled in any criminal case to be a witness against himself . . . ." But I disagree with the Court's holding that California did not violate petitioner's constitutional right against self-incrimination when it compelled him, against his will, to allow a doctor to puncture his blood vessels in order to extract a sample of blood and analyze it for alcoholic content, and then used that analysis as evidence to convict petitioner of a crime.

The Court admits that "the State compelled [petitioner] to submit to an attempt to discover evidence [in his blood] that might be [and was] used to prosecute him for a criminal offense." To reach the conclusion that compelling a person to give his blood to help the State convict him is not equivalent to compelling him to be a witness against himself strikes me as quite an extraordinary feat. The Court, however, overcomes what had seemed to me to be an insuperable obstacle to its conclusion by holding that " . . . the privilege protects an accused only from being compelled to testify against himself, or otherwise provide the State with evidence of a testimonial or communicative nature, and that the withdrawal of blood and use of the analysis in question in this case did not involve compulsion to these ends." (Footnote omitted.)

I cannot agree that this distinction and reasoning of the Court justify denying petitioner his Bill of Rights' guarantee that he must not be compelled to be a witness against himself.

In the first place it seems to me that the compulsory extraction of petitioner's blood for analysis so that the person who analyzed it could give evidence to convict him had both a "testimonial" and a "communicative nature." The sole purpose of this project which proved to be successful was to obtain "testimony" from some person to prove that petitioner had alcohol in his blood at the time he was arrested. And the purpose of the project was certainly "communicative" in that the analysis of the blood was to supply information to enable a witness to communicate to the court and jury that petitioner was more or less drunk.

* * *

How can it reasonably be doubted that the blood test evidence was not in all respects the actual equivalent of "testimony" taken from petitioner when the result of the test was offered as testimony, was considered by the jury as testimony, and the jury's verdict of guilt rests in part on that testimony? The refined, subtle reasoning and balancing process used here to narrow the scope of the Bill of Rights' safeguard against self-incrimination provides a handy instrument for further narrowing of that constitutional protection, as well as others, in the future. Believing with the Framers that these constitutional safeguards broadly construed by independent tribunals of justice provide our best hope for keeping our people free from governmental oppression, I deeply regret the Court's holding. For the foregoing reasons as well as those set out in concurring opinions of Black and Douglas, JJ., in Rochin v. People of California, 342 U.S. 165, 174, 177, 72 S.Ct. 205, 210, 212, 96 L.Ed. 183, and my concurring opinion in Mapp v. Ohio, 367 U.S. 643, 661, 81 S.Ct. 1684, 1694, 6 L.Ed.2d 1081, and the dissenting opinions in Breithaupt v. Abram, 352 U.S. 432, 440, 442, 77 S.Ct. 408, 412, 413, 1 L.Ed.2d 448, I dissent from the Court's holding and opinion in this case.

Mr. Justice DOUGLAS, dissenting.

I adhere to the views of The Chief Justice in his dissent in Breithaupt v. Abram, 352 U.S. 432, 440, 77 S.Ct. 408, 412, 1 L.Ed.2d 448, and to the views I stated in my dissent in that case (id., 442, 77 S.Ct. 413) and add only a word.

We are dealing with the right of privacy which, since the *Breithaupt* case, we have held to be within the penumbra of some specific guarantees of the Bill of Rights. Griswold v. State of Connecticut, 381 U.S. 479, 85 S.Ct. 1678, 14 L.Ed.2d 510. Thus, the Fifth Amendment marks "a zone of privacy" which the Government may not force a person to surrender. Id., 484, 85 S.Ct. 1681. Likewise the Fourth Amendment recognizes that right when it guarantees the right of the people to be secure "in their persons." Ibid. No clearer invasion of this right of privacy can be imagined than forcible bloodletting of the kind involved here.

Mr. Justice FORTAS, dissenting.

I would reverse. In my view, petitioner's privilege against self-incrimination applies. I would add that, under the Due Process Clause, the State, in its role as prosecutor, has no right to extract blood from an accused or anyone else, over his protest. As prosecutor, the State has no right to commit any kind of violence upon the person, or to utilize the results of such a tort, and the extraction of blood, over protest, is an act of violence. Cf. Chief Justice Warren's dissenting opinion in Breithaupt v. Abram, 352 U.S. 432, 440, 77 S.Ct. 408, 412, 1 L.Ed.2d 448.

WIMBERLY v. SUPERIOR COURT OF SAN BERNARDINO COUNTY *

Supreme Court of California, In Bank, 1976.
16 Cal.3d 557, 128 Cal.Rptr. 641, 547 P.2d 417.

* * *

---

* Prior to reading this, it is recommended that the reader review the following statute: Vehicle Code § 22350. Also see the case of Laursen included in this text.

MAJOR CASE LAW OPINIONS

At approximately 2:30 a. m., California Highway Patrol Officers Moffett and Najera observed a car as it swerved a couple of feet into an adjoining lane on a state highway. The officers followed the vehicle for about three-quarters of a mile, clocking it at speeds ranging as high as 14 m. p. h. above the lawful speed. The car continued weaving, moving several times over the dividing line between the two lanes.

It appeared to Moffett that the driver of the automobile was having some sort of problem, possibly drowsiness or intoxication. The officer activated his emergency lights and the car was stopped. Najera approached the driver's side of the vehicle and discussed the reason for the stop with the driver, petitioner Steven Brian Wimberly. Moffett approached the passenger's side where petitioner, Richard Michael Harrison, was seated. With the aid of his flashlight he peered into the vehicle and saw a jacket, a paper bag, a water jug, and a smoking pipe on the floor near Harrison's feet.

As Moffett continued to look into the car, Harrison aided Wimberly in retrieving some vehicle registration papers from the glove compartment. Moffett then observed about 12 round, dark seeds next to the pipe on the floor. The general characteristics of the seeds, coupled with their proximity to the pipe, led Moffett to believe them to be marijuana seeds. Moffett requested Harrison to hand him the pipe and Harrison complied. Moffett smelled the pipe and detected the odor of burnt marijuana. He also noticed a burnt residue which included some seeds and stems in the pipe.

Both petitioners responded to an order to leave the car. Both officers then detected a slight odor of burnt marijuana from inside the car. Moffett searched the interior of the car. Secreted in a pocket of the jacket he found a plastic bag containing a small quantity of marijuana. He placed the marijuana seeds which he had removed from the floor of the vehicle into that bag. No other contraband was found inside the passenger compartment. However, the officers used the car keys to open the trunk compartment of the car where they found several pounds of marijuana, in both vegetable and hashish form, in a suitcase.

WARRANTLESS SEARCH OF THE INTERIOR OF THE CAR

Petitioners first challenge the validity of the warrantless search of the passenger compartment of their car. . . .

The Fourth Amendment to the United States Constitution and the essentially identical but independent guarantee of personal privacy of article I, section 13 of the California Constitution (see People v. Brisendine (1975) 13 Cal.3d 528, 548–550, 119 Cal.Rptr. 315, 531 P.2d 1099; People v. Dumas (1973) 9 Cal.3d 871, 879, 109 Cal.Rptr. 304, 512 P.2d 1208) have long been interpreted to require the impartial approval of a judicial officer before the undertaking of most searches. The warrant requirement of these provisions "may be dispensed with in only 'a few specifically established and well-delineated' circumstances. (Katz v. United States (1967) 389 U.S. 347, 357, 88 S.Ct. 507, 514, 19 L.Ed.2d 576.)" (People v. Dumas, supra, 9 Cal.3d 871, 880, 109 Cal.Rptr. 304, 310, 512 P.2d 1208, 1214.)

"In People v. Dumas (1973) 9 Cal.3d 871, 109 Cal.Rptr. 304, 512 P.2d 1208, we stated that officers are empowered under the *Carroll* [Carroll v. United States (1925) 267 U.S. 132, 45 S.Ct. 280, 69 L.Ed. 543] doctrine to search an automobile as 'long as it can be demonstrated that (1) exigent circumstances rendered the obtaining of a warrant an impossible or impractical alternative, and (2) probable cause existed for the search.' . . .

We must, therefore, decide whether Officer Moffett had probable cause to seize the pipe and subsequently search the interior of the car for contraband. We have often stated that probable cause for a search exists where an officer is aware of facts that would lead a man of ordinary caution or prudence to believe, and conscientiously to entertain, a strong suspicion that the object of the search is in the particular place to be searched. (See, e. g., People v. Hill, supra, 12 Cal.3d 731, 747–748, 117 Cal.Rptr. 393, 528 P.2d 1; People v. Dumas, supra, 9 Cal.3d 871, 885, 109 Cal.Rptr. 304, 512 P.2d 1208; People v. Superior Court (*Kiefer*), supra, 3 Cal.3d 807, 815–816, 91 Cal.Rptr. 729, 478 P.2d 449.) On review, the appellate court must uphold probable cause findings if supported by substantial evidence. (People v. Gale (1973) 9 Cal.3d 788, 792–793, 108 Cal.Rptr. 852, 511 P.2d 1204; People v. Lawler (1973) 9 Cal.3d 156, 160, 107 Cal.Rptr. 13, 507 P.2d 621.)

Here there is substantial evidence in support of the finding below that Moffett had probable cause. The observation of the seeds alone was sufficient to justify the search and seizure. In People v. Superior Court (*Kiefer*), supra, 3 Cal.3d 807, 816–817, 91 Cal.Rptr. 729, 478 P.2d 449, we held that the observation from outside the vehicle of contraband in plain view inside the vehicle may furnish probable cause to believe that additional contraband is secreted therein and to justify a search therefor. (See fn. 2, ante). Thus, the observation of even an unusable quantity of marijuana has been deemed sufficient to justify the search of a vehicle for additional contraband. (People v. Evans (1969) 275 Cal.App.2d 78, 82–83, 79 Cal.Rptr. 714 (seeds and debris observed on seat of vehicle); People v. Schultz (1968) 263 Cal.App.2d 110, 114, 69 Cal.Rptr. 293, approved in People v. Fein (1971) 4 Cal.3d 747, 754–755, 94 Cal.Rptr. 607, 484 P.2d 583 (a single seed, plus a few strands of debris observed on left rear floor of vehicle); see also People v. Terry, supra, 70 Cal.2d 410, 428, 77 Cal.Rptr. 460, 454 P.2d 36 (one marijuana cigarette on an open ashtray); People v. Spelio (1970) 6 Cal.App.3d 685, 688, 86 Cal.Rptr. 113 (seeds along door runner); but see Thomas v. Superior Court, supra, 22 Cal.App.3d 972, 976–977, 99 Cal.Rptr. 647 (plain view of hand-rolled cigarettes does not furnish probable cause).) Additionally, the observation of the seeds adjacent to the smoking pipe on the floor of the vehicle which had been operated in an erratic manner further supported the reasonableness of Moffett's conclusion that the seeds were marijuana.

Petitioners cite People v. Fein, supra, 4 Cal.3d 747, 94 Cal.Rptr. 607, 484 P.2d 583 for the proposition that the observation of a few burnt marijuana seeds and the subsequent observation of a residue of burnt marijuana in the pipe bowl did not support the inference that a search would uncover larger, usable quantities of marijuana. In *Fein* we held that the observation of a few burnt marijuana seeds "would not give rise to a reasonable inference or strong suspicion that the occupants of the apartment in which the seeds were found were presently guilty of a crime." (Id., at p. 754, 94 Cal.Rptr. at p. 612, 484 P.2d at p. 588.) But *Fein* involved probable cause to arrest and concluded that the evidence of useless traces would not justify an arrest for present use, possession, or sale. (Id., at p. 754, 94 Cal.Rptr. 607, 484 P.2d 583.) *Fein* specifically did not decide the issue of probable cause to believe that additional contraband might be found in the passenger compartment of a vehicle. (Id., at pp. 754–755, 94 Cal.Rptr. 607, 484 P.2d 583 (approving People v. Schultz, supra, 263 Cal.App.2d 110, 69 Cal.Rptr. 293).)

Petitioners argue that Officer Moffett was not an expert in the identification of marijuana, that he could not have reasonably believed the seeds were contraband, and that a mere hunch that the seeds were marijuana could not have justified the search and seizure. It is fundamental that an officer's observations can give rise to probable cause only if that officer had sufficient training and experience from which to draw the conclusions necessary to create a reasonable belief in the presence of contraband. (See People v. McKinnon (1972) 7 Cal.3d 899, 917, 103 Cal.Rptr. 897, 500 P.2d 1097.) It is also true that a search cannot be justified by only a mere hunch. (Kaplan v. Superior Court (1971) 6 Cal.3d 150, 154, 98

MAJOR CASE LAW OPINIONS

Cal.Rptr. 649, 491 P.2d 1.) It is not necessary, however, that the officer qualify as an expert to be able to form the reasonable belief necessary to justify his actions.

There is here substantial evidence to support the conclusion that Officer Moffett had sufficient experience to reasonably believe the seeds were marijuana. He testified at the suppression hearing that his experience and training in observing and detecting marijuana included "quite a few arrests for marijuana" as well as various law enforcement training classes. Although the court expressly stated that Moffett would not be accepted as an expert at identifying marijuana, the court differentiated between expert identification and probable cause and found that Moffett had enough experience to formulate a reasonable suspicion.

Finally, petitioners cite People v. Williams (1971) 5 Cal.3d 211, 95 Cal.Rptr. 530, 45 P.2d 1146 for the proposition that there was no probable cause to believe additional marijuana was secreted in the vehicle because Moffett had no evidence to show that either of the petitioners was aware of the nature of the seeds on the floor. Petitioners' reliance on *Williams* is misplaced. That case did not involve probable cause to search. Rather, it dealt with the sufficiency of evidence to convict. Williams was charged with the unlawful possession of a restricted dangerous drug. We reversed the judgment of conviction because there was no substantial evidence to show that he had the requisite knowledge of the character of the pills found in the vehicle in which he had been arrested.

We conclude that Moffett had probable cause to believe the vehicle contained contraband, that he acted reasonably in seizing and examining the pipe to confirm his suspicions (see Guidi v. Superior Court, supra, 10 Cal.3d 1, 10–12 and fns. 9–10, 109 Cal.Rptr. 684, 513 P.2d 908), and that the subsequent search of the passenger compartment was constitutionally permissible.

WARRANTLESS SEARCH OF TRUNK COMPARTMENT

Petitioners further challenge the validity of the warrantless search of the trunk on the ground that even if *Carroll* and its progeny justify the initial warrantless search of the passenger compartment, there was no probable cause to justify the intrusion into the trunk.

We proceed first to an analysis of whether independent justification is required for the trunk search. The People maintain that the police have a right to conduct a warrantless search of the entire vehicle where there is probable cause to believe any part of it contains evidence of a crime or contraband. The resolution of the issue must turn on the question whether the trunk of a vehicle is a distinct part of the car in which there is a reasonably greater expectation of privacy than in the passenger compartment. (People v. Superior Court (*Courie*), supra, 44 Cal.App.3d 207, 211, fn. 5, 118 Cal.Rptr. 586.) Our cases have recognized this expectation of privacy in concealed areas as opposed to those portions of the vehicle subject to plain view observations. (Mestas v. Superior Court, supra, 7 Cal.3d 537, 540, 102 Cal.Rptr. 729, 498 P.2d 977; Mozzetti v. Superior Court (1971) 4 Cal.3d 699, 707, 94 Cal.Rptr. 412, 484 P.2d 84.)

In *Mozzetti* the petitioner was involved in a two-car collision and was removed to a hospital. Because her car blocked the roadway, police took custody of the vehicle and towed it to police storage. A routine inventory search uncovered marijuana in a closed suitcase on the back seat. We held that the vehicle owner's interests in maintaining the privacy of his personal effects in closed containers and concealed areas outweighed the police interest in protecting the owner from loss or damage while the vehicle was in storage. We concluded that "because the automobile involved was a convertible, adequate protection of valuables could be achieved by raising the top or, if necessary, by moving visible items, like the small suitcase, into the trunk for safekeeping." (Mozzetti v. Superior Court, supra, 4 Cal.3d 699, 707, 94 Cal.Rptr. 412, 417, 484 P.2d 84, 89.)

In *Mestas* we were also concerned with an impound search of a vehicle during the course of which the trunk was opened and incriminating evidence was found. Relying on *Mozzetti* we concluded that "while the police may observe and inventory items in plain sight, they may not, in the absence of probable cause, open and search closed areas of the vehicle or closed containers within the car." (Mestas v. Superior Court, supra, 7 Cal.3d 537, 540, 102 Cal.Rptr. 729, 730, 498 P.2d 977, 978.)

In People v. Superior Court (*Courie*), supra, 44 Cal.App.3d 207, 211, footnote 5, 118 Cal.Rptr. 586, 588, the court recognized that "a separate and distinct intrusion of defendant's privacy occurred when the trunk was unlocked and opened—an intrusion, moreover, into the area of the car in which defendant probably had the greatest reasonable expectation of privacy."

It is also true that "a search which is reasonable at its inception may violate the Fourth Amendment by virtue of its intolerable intensity and scope." (Terry v. Ohio (1968) 392 U.S. 1, 18, 88 S.Ct. 1868, 1878, 20 L.Ed.2d 889; see also People v. Brisendine, supra, 13 Cal.3d 528, 538, 119 Cal.Rptr. 315, 531 P.2d 1099.) Consequently, "the scope of an automobile search, like any other search, must be strictly tied to and justified by the circumstances occasioning it." (People v. Superior Court (*Courie*), supra, 44 Cal. App.3d 207, 213, 118 Cal.Rptr. 586, 590; cf. Cooper v. California (1967) 386 U.S. 58, 61, 87 S.Ct. 788, 17 L.Ed.2d 730.)

In light of the foregoing principles we can only conclude that the existence of probable cause to search the interior of a car is not necessarily sufficient to justify the search of the car's trunk. A search based on probable cause which reasonably only tends to support the inference that contraband or evidence will be found in the passenger compartment will be of intolerable intensity and scope if expended to include a closed trunk. In such a situation there must be some specific articulable facts which give reasonable cause to believe that seizable items are, in fact, concealed in the trunk. (People v. Cook, supra, 13 Cal.3d 663, 670, 119 Cal.Rptr. 500, 532 P.2d 148; People v. Superior Court (*Courie*), supra, 44 Cal.App.3d 207, 211, fn. 5, 118 Cal.Rptr. 586; People v. Gregg (1974) 43 Cal.App.3d 137, 141–142, 117 Cal.Rptr. 496; see generally People v. Jochen (1975) 46 Cal.App.3d 243, 119 Cal.Rptr. 914 (holding that the search of a car was too extensive where the officers searched the glove and trunk compartments without probable cause or urgency).)

In support of their contention that there are no spatial limitations on the scope of automobile search based upon probable cause, the People argue that a long line of both federal and California cases supports the proposition that because of the mobile nature of automobiles, the police have a right to conduct a warrantless search of the entire vehicle when there is probable cause to believe any part of the vehicle contains evidence of a crime or contraband. For reasons which follow we do not agree with the People's analysis of the cited cases.

We turn first to the federal cases. The People correctly note that Carroll v. United States, supra, 267 U.S. 132, 45 S.Ct. 280, 69 L.Ed. 543 and Chambers v. Maroney, supra, 399 U.S. 42, 90 S.Ct. 1975, 26 L.Ed.2d 419 did not distinguish between the different compartments of an automobile, but merely upheld warrantless searches based upon probable cause where exigent circumstances existed. We note, however, that in both cases the probable cause upon which the search was based applied to the vehicles *as a whole* and was not focused solely upon the passenger compartments thereof. Thus in *Carroll* the law enforcement officers had probable cause to believe that "the Carroll boys, as they called them, were so-called 'bootleggers' " (Carroll v. United States, supra, 267 U.S. 132, 160, 45 S.Ct. 280, 287, 69 L.Ed. 543) who generally transported contraband in their vehicle. It was proper to search the entire car for hidden contraband.

MAJOR CASE LAW OPINIONS

And in *Chambers,* where officers stopped the vehicle and arrested its occupants for robbery, the police had probable cause to believe the entire car contained weapons and the fruits of recent crime. (Chambers v. Maroney, supra, 399 U.S. 42, 47, 90 S.Ct. 1975, 26 L.Ed.2d 419.)

In Cady v. Dombrowski (1973) 413 U.S. 433, 93 S.Ct. 2523, 37 L.Ed.2d 706 the United States Supreme Court specifically upheld the search of a trunk where police officers were looking for a revolver as part of an inventory search of the vehicle. Dombrowski was an out-of-state police officer involved in a one-car accident. He was arrested for drunken driving and his car was towed to a garage for safekeeping. The high court upheld the caretaking search for the gun because of the police "concern for the safety of the general public who might be endangered if an intruder removed a revolver from the trunk of the vehicle." (Id. at p. 447, 93 S.Ct. at p. 2531.) The court approved of the intrusion into the trunk because the officers reasonably believed it contained the gun. (Id., at p. 448, 93 S.Ct. 2523.)

Nor do the California cases support the People's contention. In People v. Laursen, supra, 8 Cal.3d 192, 104 Cal.Rptr. 425, 501 P.2d 1145, police searched an automobile which eyewitnesses identified as the vehicle used by the robbers in an aborted attempt to escape. We upheld the search, including a search of the trunk even though there was no specific information that the trunk contained any evidence relating to the crime. It is important to note, however, that the probable cause upon which we upheld that search pertained to the vehicle as a whole. Thus, we said: "Having connected the robbery with the Mercury on the basis of these reports the officers had reason to suspect that some evidence helpful in the apprehension of the culprits and investigation of the crime would be contained within." (Id., at p. 201, fn. 8, 104 Cal.Rptr. at p. 431, 501 P.2d at p. 1151.)

People v. Dumas, supra, 9 Cal.3d 871, 109 Cal.Rptr. 304, 512 P.2d 1208, also upheld the warrantless search of a car and its trunk. Again, the search was justified on reasonable belief that some part of the vehicle contained stolen bonds.

Finally, in People v. Hill, supra, 12 Cal.3d 731, 117 Cal.Rptr. 393, 528 P.2d 1, we upheld both the roadside search and the later, exhaustive post-impound search of defendants' car because the officers had probable cause to believe it contained contraband. When the police attempted to halt defendants for failing to make a required traffic stop, defendants accelerated to high speeds and took evasive actions. They were eventually stopped and a search was conducted after a pat-down of one of the defendants uncovered a large roll of money and a box of .32 caliber bullets, and what was believed to be marijuana was observed in plain view in the car (a "kilo" on the rear seat and three "joints" on the front floorboards). The vehicle was then impounded and an exhaustive search disclosed evidence ultimately helping to link defendants to the murder for which they were convicted. As before, the probable cause which justified the searches applied to the vehicle as a whole. We specifically held that because of the plain view observations *and the desperate attempts to avoid apprehension,* "it was reasonable to conclude that the defendants were transporting contraband in their automobile." (Id. at p. 748, 117 Cal.Rptr. at p. 407, 528 P.2d at p. 15; for additional cases, see People v. Balassy (1973) 30 Cal.App.3d 614, 622, 106 Cal.Rptr. 461 (specific knowledge that counterfeit checks were kept in trunk); People v. Stafford (1973) 29 Cal. App.3d 940, 946–948, 106 Cal.Rptr. 72 (probable cause to search trunk for stolen items); People v. Medina (1972) 26 Cal.App.3d 809, 817, 103 Cal.Rptr. 337 (probable cause to search trunk for fruits of robbery).)

The People also raise various policy considerations in support of their contention that there are, and should be, no spatial limitations on the scope of an automobile search based upon probable cause. They first argue that once an officer has the right to search a portion of the vehicle, it is absurd to recognize any right of privacy as to the remaining portions thereof. In conjunction therewith, the People also claim that it is inappropriate to compartmentalize a car into various divisions in light of the overall size of the car and proximity of each area to the other areas.

"However, we must keep in mind that if the officers have the right to engage in a warrantless search of the entire car they may do so by any means reasonably available; thus, if the trunk key cannot be located they may break open the trunk. Carried to its logical end, if the officers have the right to search the entire car and it is necessary to accomplish their purpose, they may rip apart any part of the car in which they should suspect that additional contraband may be found." (People v. Gregg, supra, 43 Cal. App.3d 137, 141–142, 117 Cal.Rptr. 496, 498; see also People v. Cook, supra, 13 Cal.3d 663, 668, 119 Cal.Rptr. 500, 532 P.2d 148 (the trunk lid was pried open).) Therefore, the People's arguments must be rejected. As noted, there is a recognized and protectible privacy interest in concealed areas of a car, and the search of a car like all other searches must be properly circumscribed to be "reasonable" within the meaning of the Fourth Amendment and article I, section 13, of the California Constitution.

As their final policy argument, the People contend that the rule we announce today will put an extreme burden on the courts, attorneys, and law enforcement officials in determining what circumstances serve as justification for a full search of a vehicle. We are fully cognizant of how convenient it would be (save for citizens subjected to searches) if we adopted the rule proffered by the People, but appellate courts are constitutionally bound to analyse each warrantless search on a case-by-case basis as to "whether the extent of the search exceeded the attainment of the objectives which justified its inception." (People v. Brisendine, supra, 13 Cal.3d 528, 541, 119 Cal.Rptr. 315, 323, 531 P.2d 1099, 1107; see also Cooper v. California, supra, 386 U.S. 58, 59, 87 S.Ct. 788, 77 L.Ed.2d 730; People v. Lawler, supra, 9 Cal.3d 156, 160, 107 Cal.Rptr. 13, 507 P.2d 621 (appellate courts have the ultimate responsibility to measure the facts, as found by the trier of facts, against the constitutional standard of reasonableness).)

We now reach the issue whether there was probable cause to justify the particular warrantless search of the trunk of petitioners' car. We have seen that probable cause for a search exists when an officer is aware of facts that would lead a man of ordinary caution or prudence to believe, and conscientiously to entertain, a strong suspicion that the object of the search is in the particular place to be searched.

People v. Gregg, supra, 43 Cal.App.3d 137, 117 Cal.Rptr. 496, presented a factual situation almost identical to the instant case. After a traffic stop for speeding law enforcement officers observed approximately 10 marijuana seeds on the seat of the car and detected a strong odor of burning marijuana. The occupants were placed under arrest and the car was searched. Marijuana debris was found in a jacket pocket which was located on the rear seat. Although no other contraband was found in the passenger compartment, the officers opened the trunk and found approximately six pounds of marijuana. (Id. at pp. 139–140, 117 Cal. Rptr. 496.) The court, concluding that "these facts logically do not aid in the determination of whether marijuana might be concealed in the trunk" (id. at p. 143, 117 Cal.Rptr. at p. 500), reasoned: "[t]he lawful observation of marijuana debris on a seat or the floor of the interior of the car, or in the clothing of the occupants, or the smell of burned marijuana emanating from the interior of the car would give probable cause to believe that marijuana might be found in the areas *adjacent and immediately accessible to the occupants,* such as ashtrays, a passenger console, a glove compartment and underneath and between the seats . . . . [¶] Similarly, if a substantial quantity of marijuana is found inside the automobile or on the person of an occupant, it reasonably may be inferred that additional contraband may be concealed in areas of the car not immediately accessible and adjacent to the occupants, such as the trunk or under the hood. A substantial quantity of marijuana in the interior of the car would give rise to a logical inference that the car was being used to transport marijuana." (Id. at p. 142, 117 Cal.Rptr. at p. 499.)

The result reached in *Gregg* is eminently sound. Just as the statutes differentiate between the casual user and the dealer of narcotics (compare Health & Saf.Code, §§ 11350, 11357 with Health & Saf.Code, §§ 11351, 11352, 11359, 11360), logic compels that we also differentiate between the two and recognize that all casual users are not dealers. Here, the erratic driving, the plain view observation of the marijuana seeds adjacent to the pipe, the odor of burnt marijuana, the burnt residue in the pipe, and the small quantity of marijuana secreted in the jacket indicate only that petitioners were casual users of marijuana. It was thus proper to search adjacent areas of the vehicle (see generally People v. Superior Court (*Silver*) (1970) 8 Cal.App.3d 398, 402–403, 87 Cal.Rptr. 283), but it was not reasonable to infer that petitioners had additional contraband hidden in the trunk.

We do not conclude, however, that trunk searches are never justified when the quantity of contraband found is indicative only of personal use. Rather, we recognize that additional circumstances may generate the reasonable suspicion necessary to justify the further intrusion. Thus, for example, in People v. Hill, supra, 12 Cal.3d 731, 748, 117 Cal.Rptr. 393, 528 P.2d 1, it was reasonable to assume the defendants were transporting marijuana where a desperate attempt to avoid apprehension was followed by the plain view discovery of contraband in the car. (See also People v. Martin (1956) 46 Cal.2d 106, 108, 293 P.2d 52.) And, in People v. Cook, supra, 13 Cal.3d 663, 670, 119 Cal.Rptr. 500, 532 P.2d 148, we held that the officers had probable cause to search the trunk where the odor of fresh marijuana was much stronger than that which could be attributed to the items found in the passenger compartment.

COMMINGLING OF THE MARIJUANA SEEDS

Finally, petitioners contend that they were denied due process of law and a fair hearing on their motion to suppress because of the commingling of the marijuana seeds with the marijuana found in the plastic bag. Petitioners argue that the commingling of the seeds deprived them of the opportunity to test their nature and existence for purposes of challenging probable cause. To the extent petitioners claim the commingling of the seeds deprived them of the opportunity to test the nature of the seeds, their contention must fail. They do not claim, nor have they shown, that laboratory tests cannot be performed on all the seeds in the plastic bag, revealing which seeds, if any, are not marijuana or do not resemble marijuana seeds. Therefore, petitioners have suffered only minimal prejudice by the added burden of having to examine all the seeds.

To the extent petitioners claim that they have been deprived of the opportunity to prove that no seeds ever existed, the essence of their claim is not the destruction of evidence, but rather the officers' lack of credibility. They thus urge not that Moffett destroyed evidence but that his claim to have seen the seeds and Najera's confirmation that he also saw the seeds were fabrications. Again, petitioners were not denied any material evidence.

Let a peremptory writ of mandate issue compelling the respondent court to suppress evidence found in the trunk of petitioner's vehicle.

TOBRINER, MOSK, and SULLIVAN, JJ., concur.

RICHARDSON, Justice (concurring).

I concur in the judgment. Under the particular facts of this case, the officers lacked probable cause to believe that the trunk of petitioners' vehicle contained contraband. However, in those cases in which the circumstances tend to support a strong suspicion that the trunk of an automobile may contain contraband, I would permit a reasonable search of the trunk and its contents.

CLARK, Justice (dissenting).

The majority conclude generally that probable cause to search part of a car does not necessarily justify searching the entire car. They conclude specifically that discovery of a quantity of marijuana "indicative only of personal use" in the interior of a car does not provide probable cause to believe that more marijuana will be found in the trunk. Neither conclusion is supported by reason or authority.

For their general conclusion, the majority rely on Mozzetti v. Superior Court (1971) 4 Cal.3d 699, 94 Cal.Rptr. 412, 484 P.2d 84; Mestas v. Superior Court (1972) 7 Cal.3d 537, 102 Cal.Rptr. 729, 498 P.2d 977; People v. Gregg (1974) 43 Cal.App.3d 137, 117 Cal. Rptr. 496; and People v. Superior Court (*Courie*) (1974) 44 Cal.App.3d 207, 118 Cal. Rptr. 586.

Mozzetti and *Mestas* are inapposite. *Mozzetti* held that police may observe and inventory items in plain view in an impounded car, but may not, in the absence of probable cause, open and search a suitcase found in the passenger compartment. *Mestas* followed *Mozzetti*, suppressing evidence discovered in a routine inventory search of the trunk of an impounded automobile. Had the police discovered evidence or contraband in plain view during their routine inventories of the impounded vehicles, *Mozzetti* and *Mestas* would have presented the question whether such a discovery provides probable cause to search closed areas of a vehicle or closed containers within it for additional evidence or contraband. However, as the police made no such discovery in either case, neither *Mozzetti* nor *Mestas* casts light on the question presented here.

In reaching the novel conclusion that the discovery of a small amount of marijuana in the passenger compartment of an automobile provides probable cause to search the remainder of the passenger compartment, but not the trunk, *Gregg* relied entirely on the following cases: People v. Superior Court (*Silver*) (1970) 8 Cal.App.3d 398, 87 Cal.Rptr. 283; People v. Spelio (1970) 6 Cal.App.3d 685, 86 Cal.Rptr. 113; Fraher v. Superior Court (1969) 272 Cal.App.2d 155, 77 Cal.Rptr. 366; and People v. Schultz (1968) 263 Cal.App.2d 110, 69 Cal.Rptr. 293.

Fraher did not involve an automobile search. An officer looking through the window of a house observed what he believed to be a marijuana pipe. He knocked on the door, entered with permission, observed marijuana debris in the bowl of the pipe, arrested the occupants and searched the house, finding additional narcotics. Upholding the search, the court stated, "The observation of marijuana debris which is insufficient to sustain a conviction is sufficient to constitute reasonable cause to make an arrest and to believe that a larger amount of marijuana may be present in close proximity to the debris." (272 Cal. App.2d at p. 163, 77 Cal.Rptr. at p. 372.) Perhaps because *Fraher* was decided prior to Chinel v. California (1969) 395 U.S. 752, 89 S.Ct. 2034, 23 L.Ed.2d 685, the court did not bother to specify exactly how close the remaining contraband was to either the pipe or the occupants. However, *Fraher* clearly provides no support for the novel position taken in *Gregg*.

In *Silver*, an officer looking through the window of a Volkswagen van observed a hashish pipe in plain view on the back shelf of the vehicle. A search of the van then revealed a bag of hashish within a few feet of the pipe, a bag of marijuana behind the driver's seat, and narcotic paraphernalia "throughout the vehicle." Citing *Fraher*, the court upheld the search, observing, "From the presence of a homemade instrument designed to smoke a contraband narcotic it is logical to infer that the contraband itself may be hidden in close proximity to the smoking device." (8 Cal.App.3d at p. 402, 87 Cal.Rptr. at p. 285.) As Volkswagen vans do not have trunks, the court obviously had no occasion to consider whether a trunk search would have been justified under the circumstances.

In *Schultz* and *Spelio,* officers observed marijuana seeds in plain view in the passenger compartments of the defendants' automobiles. Searches of the automobiles then revealed more marijuana. In *Schultz,* the court held "the officer, upon observing a marijuana seed in the automobile in which defendants were riding, had reason to believe other marijuana might be located in the automobile." (263 Cal.App.2d at p. 114, 69 Cal.Rptr. at p. 295.) In *Spelio,* the court held "[h]aving seen the marijuana seeds, Officer Clements certainly had probable cause to believe the car contained further contraband." (6 Cal.App.3d at p. 688, 86 Cal.Rptr. at p. 114.) There is no indication in either case that the search was limited to the passenger compartment, or that the court was of the opinion that it should have been so limited.

Its reliance on prior authority being misplaced, *Gregg* should be overruled, not followed. *Courie* adds nothing to *Gregg*; it merely accepts *Gregg* without analysis, distinguishing *Gregg* on its facts. (44 Cal. App.3d at pp. 211–214, 118 Cal.Rptr. 586.) The majority's vain attempt to distinguish all of the other cases bearing on this question underscores the fact that the rule announced today is unprecedented in the decisions of this court or the United States Supreme Court.

The majority's specific conclusion is based on their assumption that a "casual user" of marijuana transporting the contraband by car will keep his entire supply in the passenger compartment. Granted, a court may take judicial notice of facts and propositions that are matters of such common knowledge that they cannot reasonably be the subject of dispute. (Evid.Code, § 452, subd. (g); Daar v. Yellow Cab Co. (1967) 67 Cal.2d 695, 716, 63 Cal.Rptr. 724, 433 P.2d 732; People v. Torres (1961) 56 Cal.2d 864, 866, 17 Cal.Rptr. 495, 366 P.2d 823.) And, true, some propositions concerning the drug culture have become matters of such common knowledge that judicial notice may be taken of them. (See, e. g., People v. Torres, supra, 56 Cal.2d 864 at pp. 866–867, 17 Cal.Rptr. 495, 366 P.2d 823 (capsules and milk sugar are used in processing narcotics); People v. Hubbard (1970) 9 Cal.App.3d 827, 831, 88 Cal.Rptr. 411 ("reds" is a slang term for Seconal capsules).)

However the assumption made by the majority is not such a proposition. Rather than it being a matter of common knowledge that a marijuana user keeps his entire supply in the passenger compartment, this assumption is plainly inconsistent with what we know of the behavior patterns of persons transporting contraband. As the majority themselves point out, marijuana being contraband, neither a user nor a dealer transporting it by car will likely leave it in plain view. As the majority further point out, there is a greater expectation of privacy toward the trunk than the passenger compartment. Therefore, would a person transporting marijuana by car not more likely keep it in the trunk rather than in the passenger compartment? And if he kept some in the passenger compartment to use during the trip, where would he likely stash the remainder? The answers being obvious, I would deny the writ.

McCOMB, J., concurs.

HOW TO DO LEGAL RESEARCH

It is axiomatic that in order for a person to function as a professional peace officer, one must know the law. In order to know and understand the application of the law to various circumstances, one must know how to find and interpret the law. This chapter will briefly explain the more common methods of legal research and explain where the law may be found.

Law in California is derived from a variety of sources, federal, state, and local; and is further divided into statutory, case decision, and administrative law.

Federal law is contained in the U.S. Constitution, in the federal codes (e. g., Federal Criminal Code), in the administrative regulations promulgated by administrative agencies (e. g., the Law Enforcement Assistance Administration), and by the case law of the United States Supreme Court and the other federal courts. Federal law is binding on the states if specifically made applicable to them, or if it is grounded in the Constitution and affords citizens a greater level of protection than the applicable state law.

California law is contained in the California Constitution, in the statutory codes (e. g., the Penal Code), in administrative regulations, and in the published opinions of the California Supreme Court, the Courts of Appeals and the appellate department of the Superior Courts. The provisions of the California Constitution and statutory law are binding on all political subdivisions of the state. Interpretations given these laws by the appellate courts are also binding throughout the state.*

Local law is that which is contained in the city or county charter, county ordinances, and city municipal codes. This law is binding only within the jurisdictional boundaries of the political subdivision. Local ordinances and codes are, in many respects, the easiest to locate since they are made, interpreted, and enforced at the same location. The bulk of the ensuing discussion on legal research will concern itself with state law.

As earlier stated, the three different primary sources of law are statutory, case decisions, and administrative regulations. The following chart depicts where the various types of federal and state law may be found:

FEDERAL LAW

STATUTORY

The U.S. Constitution, the U.S. Codes, consisting of twenty Titles, (crimes and criminal procedure are contained in Title 18), and the Federal Rules of Criminal Procedure.

DECISIONAL

Case decisions by the U.S. Supreme Court, the Circuit Courts of Appeals, and the U.S. District Courts—Decisions of these courts may be located in the following series of books: (The official abbreviations for each series is noted in parenthesis.)

---

* California statutes and interpretations given the California Constitution may impose greater limitations on the actions of California's peace officers than federal statutes or interpretation of federal Constitutional law by federal courts. It is not unusual for the California Supreme Court to decide an issue based on the California Constitution and set a stricter standard of conduct for peace officers than the United States Supreme Court has set. Thus, new decisional law by the United States Supreme Court, which is based on the federal

LEGAL RESEARCH

United States Supreme Court—*United States Reports* (—— U.S. ——), *United States Reports, Lawyers Edition* (—— L.Ed. ——) or (—— L.Ed.2d ——), *Supreme Court Reporter* (—— S.Ct. ——)

Circuit Court of Appeals—*The Federal Reporter* (—— F. ——) or (—— F.2d ——)

District Courts—*Federal Supplement* (—— F.Supp. ——), *Federal Rules Decisions* (—— F.R.D. ——)

ADMINISTRATIVE

Regulations promulgated by federal agencies.

Federal Register—

Since March 14, 1936, all federal regulations promulgated by federal agencies, before becoming effective, must be published in the *Federal Register*.

The *Code of Federal Regulations* organizes by general subject matter regulations which have been published in the *Federal Register*, and, additionally, examines these regulations.

STATE LAW

STATUTORY

The California Constitution, the California statutory codes, e. g., Penal, Health & Safety, Vehicle, etc.

DECISIONAL

Case decisions of the California Supreme Court, and the published opinions of the Courts of Appeal and the appellate department of the superior courts. This law may be located in the following series of books: (The official abbreviations for each series is noted in parenthesis.)

California Supreme Court—*California Reports*

—— Cal. —— or

—— Cal.2d —— or

—— Cal.3d ——

California Courts of Appeal—*California Appellate Reports*

—— Cal.App. —— or

—— Cal.App.2d —— or

—— Cal.App.3d ——

Appellate Department of Superior Courts—*California Appellate Reports, Supplement*

—— Cal.App.2d Supp. —— or

—— Cal.App.3d Supp. ——

The *California Reporter* series of West Publishing contains both decisions by the Courts of Appeal and the Supreme Court. This series is cited as —— Cal.Rptr. ——.

ADMINISTRATIVE

Regulations promulgated by state agencies. Regulations may be found in the *California Administrative Code* (there is no index, check Table of Titles in front of vol. 1.)

Constitution must be viewed cautiously by California law enforcement departments. One can readily see the conflict and confusion that results from this dichotomy of opinion, and realize the need to research the law.

LEGAL RESEARCH

LOCAL LAW

City and County Codes, ordinances, and charters are available in the City Attorney's or County Counsel's office and also from the official Clerk of the local government body.

RESEARCHING THE LAW

Now that we know where the law may be found, we need to know how to use the codes and reference books.

Research Tools

The reference most frequently used by you will probably be the statutory codes. The codes are divided into general subject matters, c. f. this text, with the code sections placed in ascending numerical order.

The language contained in the codes is as it was drafted by the legislature. If you are seeking an explanation or clarification of the statutory language, then reference should be made to the annotated codes. The annotated codes include references to case decisions which have interpreted that section, as well as law review commentaries and cross references, all of which may assist in the interpretation of the section.

Penal Code Section 148.5, from *West's Annotated Penal Code* illustrates the format of the annotated codes.

§ 148.5. False report of criminal offense; misdemeanor

Every person who reports to any police officer, sheriff, district attorney, deputy sheriff, deputy district attorney, or member of the California Highway Patrol that a felony or misdemeanor has been committed, knowing such report to be false, is guilty of a misdemeanor.

(Added by Stats.1957, c. 813, p. 2028, § 1.)

Cross References

False report of theft of undocumented vessel, see Harbors and Navigation Code § 751.

Punishment for misdemeanor, see § 19. [The section numbers refer to sections of the same code, i. e., the Penal Code, unless otherwise noted.]

Law Review Commentaries

Background and general effect of 1957 edition. (1957) 32 S.Bar.J. 616.

Library References

Obstructing Justice (☞) 7. C.J.S. Obstructing Justice § 5.

Notes of Decisions

1. Conspiracy

Testimony of alleged friend, who claimed to have overheard arrangement of defendant and co-defendant to have defendant's wife arrested and prosecuted for possessing marijuana, and testimony of wife and co-defendant were sufficient to show that co-defendant had testified falsely against wife and to thus support conviction of defendant for conspiracy to commit perjury. *People v. Rainey* (1964) 36 Cal.Rptr. 291, 224 C.A.2d 93.

In many instances, the case decisions following a section will fill multiple pages.

LEGAL RESEARCH

Pocket Parts

In researching any material, care must be taken to make certain that you are referring to the most recent version of the statute, and that the annotations are current. Therefore, after you have located the code section in the main volume, consult the pocket part to the code you are using to determine whether or not the section has recently been amended or interpreted differently by a new case decision.

Annotated Codes

The annotated codes enable one to go from the statutes to the decisional law and other reference sources. You will note that under the general topic, Library References, the words "Obstructing Justice" appear along with (☞) 7. This is a reference to *West's California Digest*. If you refer to *West's California Digest*, "Obstructing Justice," Keynote 7 you will find a reference to Penal Code Section 148.5.

Often the material in the annotated code following the section will also include notes on the legislative history of the section. These notes will detail the evolution of the law including all amendments and changes to the original section. The legislative history will also, on occasion, contain notes relating to the legislative intent behind the enactment of that section. The case decision reported in the *California Reporter,* or other case books, is another reference source. The reported decision of the case is printed in full. The *California Reporter* series also contains helpful cross references to *West's California Digest*.

Digests

If there is no statute concerning your particular research problem, then you will need to examine appellate court cases to determine the state of the law. One method of locating cases is by using *West's California Digest*. There are three primary methods for locating your topic area in the *Digest*: by topic, by index, and by case name.

The *Digest* is basically a collection of appellate court case summaries organized by topic, and the topics are covered in alphabetical order. If your research problem concerns some aspect of arrest, you would first look to the front of the first volume of the *Digest* where the digest topics are listed. There you will note a separate topic heading for arrest.

Now, locate the *Digest* volume containing the topic "arrest." At the beginning of the topic, there is an outline of the sub-topics covered. To the right of each sub-topic is a key-number. When you have found the applicable sub-topic, turn to the page with that key-number.

Under each key-number, there are a number of short paragraphs preceded by initials indicating the deciding court *, and the date of the decision. Each paragraph contains a capsulized summary of the case, the name and citation of the case, and the statute construed.

Another way to locate cases in the *Digest* is by index. *West's California Digest* has two indices—a Descriptive Word Index and a Words and Phrases Index. The Descriptive

---

* The deciding court abbreviations are as follows:
U.S.—United States Supreme Court
U.S.C.C.A.—United States Circuit Court of Appeals
U.S.D.C.—United States District Court
Cal.—California Supreme Court
App. or Cal.App.—California District Court of Appeal

LEGAL RESEARCH

Word Index is not unlike a normal index. The main word or topic (e. g., arrest) is in bold face print and is followed by several descriptive subheadings. To the right of each subheading are topic headings and key-numbers. The Words and Phrases Index, on the other hand, is keyed toward legal definitions. Thus, if you wanted to know the legal definition of "arrest," the Words and Phrases Index would direct you to cases defining that term.

A final method of locating cases in the *Digest* is the Table of Cases. If you know the name of a case in a topic area and wish to find other related cases, then turn to the Table of Cases in the *Digest* and locate that case name. Following the case name is the deciding court, the case citation, and digest topic headings with key-numbers directing you to that case in the *Digest*.

Treatises

Another valuable tool for research is Witkin's Treatises on *California Criminal Law* and *Criminal Procedure*. These two sets of volumes summarize both statutory and case law. To find a discussion of your particular research problem, *Witkin's* has an index, a table of code sections, and a table of cases. Once you have located the topic in the hardbound volume, however, be sure to check the paperback supplements for subsequent cases, or amendments to a particular code section.

Journals

If your research concerns a relatively new code section, it is very likely that there are no court decisions construing its terms. The January issue of the *Pacific Law Journal* contains a Review of Selected California Legislation which summarizes, explains, and comments upon the significant legislation recently enacted into law. The review of legislation is broken down into several major topic areas, with subheadings for each law analyzed. At the back of the review is a table of summarized code sections.

Citators

Once you have located a case concerning your problem area, you will probably want to know if there have been any subsequent court decisions expanding or limiting that case. To do this, you will use the *Sheppard's Citator*. First, however, you need to know the citation of your case, and the headnote number(s) of the portion of your case that is relevant to your research. At the beginning of the case, you will notice several short paragraphs preceded by a number and a heading in bold face print. These are known as headnotes and they identify the particular legal issues discussed in the case. Find the headnote that identifies the issue relevant to your research and note its number.

Now you are ready to locate your case in *Sheppard's California Citations*. You will notice that there are several volumes, each of which is divided into two parts: cases and statutes—we are only concerned with the part entitled cases. You should find a small paperback supplement, usually dated a month previous, a cumulative paperback supplement for 1974–76, a hard bound volume for 1970 (one for California Supreme Court Cases and another for decisions by the California District Courts of Appeal), and a hard bound volume for cases prior to 1970.*

Starting with the most recent volume, locate the reporter (i. e., Cal.App.3d), volume, and page number of your case. If you cannot find your case cited in a particular volume of *Sheppard's,* it means that case was not cited in any decisions reported during the period of time covered by that volume. Once you have located your particular case citation in *Sheppard's,* you will see a list of citations beneath it in lighter print, such as:

---

* You need not be concerned with volumes that are dated prior to the time your case was decided.

LEGAL RESEARCH

60 A.3d 276, or 22 C.3d 582. The first citation tells you that your case is cited at 60 Cal.App.3d, (*California Appellate Court Reports,* 3d Series) page 276. The superior number, 5, tells you that this particular citation concerns the issue identified in headnote 5 of your case. The second citation refers you to page 582 of 22 Cal.3d (*California Reports,* 3d series), where your case has been cited in reference to a discussion of the issue identified in headnote 7 of your case.

You should now have a basic understanding of the research tools available to you. A basic understanding, however, is all that can be conveyed by a mere reading of this chapter. Therefore, this author has provided you with a sample research problem in the hope that you will take it to a law library and look up the sources mentioned. Completion of this exercise should serve to better your understanding of the research process.

SAMPLE RESEARCH PROBLEM

FACTS: A legal search of an "adult" book store has turned up several magazines depicting apparently pre-teenage males and females engaging in a variety of sex acts. What crimes have been committed, and who may be charged?

RESEARCH PROCESS: Unless you are familiar with a particular code section that is directly on point, your starting point should be with the general index to the codes. Prior to picking up the index, however, you should try to list as many different index topic headings as possible (e. g., child, pornography, obscene, etc.). Often you will find that the indexers have used a different index heading than you would have used. Another point to remember is to check the main volume prior to consulting the updated pocket part.

If you had checked the index for "obscene" or "obscenity," you would have found the topics under this heading were instead listed under "Lewdness and Obscenity". Under the latter heading a reference to Penal Code Section 311.2 is found for the topic "Distribution, obscene matter." Before going to that section, however, the pocket part should be consulted for any recent changes in the law. In the pocket part you will note that there are code sections dealing specifically with children and minors. There is a general reference to Penal Code Sections 311.2 and 311.4 and a heading entitled "Identity of suppliers" with a reference to Labor Code Sections 1309.5 and 1309.6. Since the relevant code sections were found in the pocket part of the index, the code sections themselves will most likely be found in the pocket part of the relevant volume of *West's Annotated Codes* (volume 48 of the Penal Code for Sections 311.2 and 311.4, volume 44 for Labor Code Sections 1309.5 and 1309.6).

Once you have located and read these code sections, you will probably wish to locate an interpretation of the new law either by case decision or Law Review Commentary. First check the annotations, if there are any, listed beneath the text of the code. Since these are new code sections, there are no annotations to cases interpreting them. Next, check the listing of "Library References" also located beneath the text of the code. In this case under the text of Penal Code Section 311.4 and Labor Code Section 1309.5 there is a digest reference to the topic of "Infants" with the key-number 13. If you were to go to the *West's California Digest* and look up the topic "Infants" at key-number 13, you would find that there are no cases interpreting this code section.

When using the *Digest,* first check the main volume in which the topic appears, then consult the pocket part for decisions reported since the printing of the main volume. There are also paperback supplements containing all of the digest topics for very recent cases. Another source to check is Witkin's Treatise on *California Crimes.* Again, however, you will find that the code sections may be too recent for their inclusion in the most recent supplement. If this is the case, then check the *Pacific Law Journal's* Review of Selected California Legislation. Since these sections were enacted in 1977, they would be analyzed in the issue of the *Journal* dated January 1978. To find the article analyzing this new law, flip to the back of the green pages to the table of code sections. Reference to either Penal Code Sections 311.2 or 311.4 or Labor Code Sections 1309.5 or 1309.6, would lead you to the same article.

Now that you have read the code sections and the article in the *Pacific Law Journal*, you know that Labor Code Section 1309.5 requires the proprietor of an "adult" store to maintain a record containing the names and addresses of the suppliers of this type of material. Failure to maintain the records or failure to present them to law enforcement officials upon demand, is a misdemeanor. Further, the publisher who employed or used the minors is guilty of a felony under Penal Code Section 311.4, and the parents of the minors, if they consented to the use of the children, are also guilty of a felony under that section.

But what about Penal Code Section 311.2? To charge the book store proprietor with felony distribution, you must first know what constitutes "obscene matter." To determine the definitions of a particular word or phrase, go to *West's California Digest*, the final volumes of the *Digest* are entitled "Words and Phrases." In this case, looking up the terms "obscene" or "obscenity" you would locate two United States Supreme Court cases, *Hamling v. United States* and *Miller v. California*, defining obscenity within the context of the federal Constitution. California, however, often employs different standards. If California does have a different standard, and it is by case law, it would be found in the same listing of words and phrases where the United State Supreme Court Cases were found. There are, however, no California Supreme Court cases listed. Thus, we will need to return to the codes to see if there is a statutory definition.

Again, in the general index under the topic heading "Lewdness and Obscenity," there is a reference to Penal Code Section 311 *et seq.* That section defines the term "obscene matter" as it is used in the following code sections. Whether or not a particular work is obscene depends upon whether, applying contemporary community standards, the average adult would find not only that the work appeals to the prurient interest, but also, that the depiction goes beyond the customary limits of candor. Further, it must be shown that the work is utterly without redeeming social value. Penal Code Section 311, also defines "utterly without redeeming social value." Therefore, if the depictions in the magazines fit this definition, then the proprietor of the "adult" store would be charged with felony distribution under Penal Code Section 311.2 as recently amended.

As you have seen, research is a several step process that can be broken down into two main sections. First you need to find the law, and second, you need to find an interpretation of the law. There are several tools at your disposal to locate statutory law and case interpretations, but the use of these tools requires patience and knowledge of the alternatives available. You will find that your research skills will grow with experience.

GLOSSARY

A

ABATEMENT. A reduction or decrease. Removal of a nuisance.

ABET. To encourage, incite, or set another on to commit a crime.

ABROGATION. The repealing of a former law by legislative act or by usage.

ACCESSORY. See Penal Code § 32.

ACTION. A suit or judicial proceeding. See Evidence Code § 105.

ACTUS. An act or action.

ACTUS REUS. The criminal act; the act of a person committing a crime.

ADJUDICATE. To determine finally; to adjudge.

ADJUDICATION. The giving or pronouncing a judgment or decree in a cause; also the judgment given. The equivalent of "determination."

ADVANCE SHEETS. Are current pamphlets containing the most recently reported opinions of a court or the courts of several jurisdictions. The volume and page numbers usually are the same as in the subsequently bound volumes of the series, which cover several numbers of the advance sheets.

ADVERSARY. An opponent. The opposite party in a writ or action.

ADVERSARY PROCEEDING. One having opposing parties, as distinguished from an *ex parte* proceeding.

ADVERSARY SYSTEM. The practice of conducting legal proceedings as a battle between opposing parties under the judge as an impartial umpire with the outcome determined by the pleadings and evidence introduced into court; an Anglo-American jurisprudence includes the presumption of innocence of the accused. To be distinguished from the accusatory system used in continental law where the accusation is taken as evidence of guilt which must be disproved by the accused.

ADVOCATE. One who assists, defends, or pleads for another.

AFFIANT. The person who prepares and swears to an affidavit.

AFFIDAVIT. A written or printed declaration or statement of facts, taken before an officer having authority to administer oaths.

ALIUNDE. From another source; from elsewhere; from outside.

ALLEGATION. The assertion declaration or statement by a party to an action setting out what he expects to prove.

AMICUS CURIAE. A friend of the court. Also a person who has no right to appear in a suit but is allowed to introduce argument, authority or evidence to protect his interests.

GLOSSARY

ANNOTATIONS. Are: (1) Statutory: brief summaries of the law and facts of cases interpreting statutes passed by Congress or state legislatures which are included in codes, or (2) Textual: expository essays of varying length on significant legal topics chosen from selected cases published with the essays.

ANTE. A notation used to refer the reader to a previous part of a case or book.

APPEAL. The removal of a cause from a court of inferior to one of superior jurisdiction for the purpose of obtaining a review and retrial.

APPELLANT. The party who takes an appeal from one court of justice to another. In criminal law usually the defendant in the lower court.

APPELLATE JURISDICTION. The right of a court to review the decision of a lower court; the power to hear cases appealed from a lower court.

APPEARANCE. The coming into court as party to a suit.

ARRAIGN. To bring a prisoner before the court to answer the indictment or information. In practice, used to refer to any appearance of the accused before a magistrate, or before the trial court to enter his plea.

ARRAIGNMENT. The step at which the accused is read the charges against him and is asked how he pleads. In addition, the accused is advised of his rights. Possible pleas are guilty, not guilty, nolo contendere, and not guilty by reason of insanity.

ARREST. The taking of a person into the custody of the law, the legal purpose of which is to restrain the accused until he can be held accountable for the offense at court proceedings. The legal requirement for an arrest is probable cause. Arrests for investigation, suspicion, or harassment are improper and of doubtful legality. The police have the responsibility to use only reasonable physical force necessary to make an arrest. The summons has been used as a substitute to arrest. See Penal Code § 834.

ARREST WARRANT. A written court order issued by a magistrate authorizing and directing that an individual be taken into custody to answer criminal charges.

ASPORTATION. The removal of things from one place to another, such as is in some states required in the offense of larceny.

ATTORNEY GENERAL OPINIONS. Are issued by the government's chief counsel at the request of some governmental body and interpret the law for the requesting agency in the same manner as a private attorney would for his client. The opinions are not binding on the courts but are usually accorded some degree of persuasive authority.

AUTHORITY. Refers to the precedential value to be accorded an opinion of a judicial or administrative body. A court's opinion is binding authority on other courts directly below it in the judicial hierarchy. Opinions of lower courts or of courts outside the hierarchy are governed by the degree to which it adheres to the doctrine of stare decisis. See: Stare decisis.

B

BAIL. To procure the release of a person from legal custody, by undertaking that he shall appear at the time and place designated, and submit himself to the jurisdiction and judgment of the court. In New York, cash bail or a bail bond.

BAILMENT. A delivery of good or personal property by one person to another to carry out a special purpose and redeliver the goods to the bailor.

GLOSSARY

BAILEE. One to whom goods are delivered under a contract or agreement of bailment.

BAILOR. One who delivers goods under a contract or agreement of bailment.

BENCH WARRANT. Process issued by the court itself, or "from the bench," for the attachment or arrest of a person; either in case of contempt, or whether an indictment has been found, or to bring in a witness who does not obey a subpoena. So called to distinguish it from a warrant issued by a justice of the peace or magistrate. In New York, a bench warrant means a process of a criminal court in which a criminal action is pending, directing a police officer to take into custody a defendant in such action who has previously been arraigned upon the accusatory instrument by which the action was commenced, and to bring him before such court. The function of a bench warrant is to achieve the court appearance of a defendant in a pending criminal action for some purpose other than his initial arraignment in the action. See Penal Code § 979 et al.

BEYOND A REASONABLE DOUBT. It is proof to a moral certainty, such proof as satisfies the judgment and consciences of the jury, as reasonable men, that the crime charged has been committed by the defendant.

BOOKING. The clerical process involving the entry on the police "blotter" or arrest book of the suspect's name, the time of the arrest, the offense charged and the name of the arresting officer. Used in practice to refer to the police station-house procedures that take place from arrest to the initial appearance of the accused before the magistrate.

BURDEN OF PRODUCING EVIDENCE. See Evidence Code § 110.

BURDEN OF PROOF. See Evidence Code § 115.

C

CAPIAS. Lat. "That you take." The general name for several species of writs, the common characteristic of which is that they require the officer to take the body of the defendant into custody.

CASE LAW. Law derived from the decisions of previous court decisions, as opposed to *statutory law* which is passed by legislatures.

CERTIORARI. To be informed of, to be made certain in regard to. The name of a writ of review or inquiry; a writ directed by a superior court to an inferior court asking that the record of a case be sent up for review; a method of obtaining a review of a case by the United States Supreme Court.

CHANGE OF VENUE. The removal of an action begun in one county or district to another county or district for trial.

CHARGE. To impose a burden, duty, or obligation; to claim, demand; to accuse; to instruct a jury on matters of law.

CIRCUMSTANTIAL EVIDENCE. All evidence of an indirect nature; the existence of a principle fact is inferred from circumstances.

COMPETENCY. The presence of those characteristics, or the absence of those disabilities, which render a witness legally fit and qualified to give testimony. See Evidence Code § 700 et al.

COMPLAINT. A sworn allegation made in writing to a court or judge that an individual is guilty of some designated (complained of) offense. This is often the first legal document filed regarding a criminal offense, the complaint can be "taken out" by the

GLOSSARY

victim, the police officer, the District Attorney, or other interested party. Although the complaint "charges" an offense, an indictment or information may be the formal charging document.

CONCURRENT. Running together; contemporaneous. Concurrent sentences run at the same time and each day served by the prisoner is credited on each of the concurrent sentences.

CONCURRING OPINION. Is an opinion of a judge which agrees with the decision of the majority but disagrees with the reasoning.

CONSECUTIVE SENTENCES. Sentences which are served one after the other.

CONTEMPT. A willful disregard or disobedience of a public authority.

CONTEMPT OF COURT. Any act which is calculated to embarrass, hinder, or obstruct the court in the administration of justice, or which is calculated to lessen its authority or dignity.

CORPUS DELICTI. The body of the crime; the essential elements of the crime; the substantial fact that a crime has been committed. The actual commission by someone of the offense charged.

CORROBORATE. To add weight or credibility to an issue by additional and confirming evidence. To offer evidence of a different nature to prove the same point.

CREDIBILITY. Worthy of belief.

CRIME. See Penal Code § 15.

CUMULATIVE. Evidence of the same nature used to prove an issue at trial.

CURTILAGE. The enclosed space of ground and buildings immediately surrounding the dwelling house.

D

DE JURE. By right and just title.

DE NOVO. Anew, fresh, a second time.

DECLARANT. See Evidence Code § 135.

DEFENDANT. The person defending or denying; the party against whom relief or recovery is sought in an action or suit. In criminal law, the party charged with a crime.

DEMURRER. The process of disputing the sufficiency in the law argued by the opposing party.

DEPOSITION. A written declaration made under oath.

DETAINER. A kind of "hold order" filed against an incarcerated man by another state or jurisdiction which seeks to take him into custody to answer to another criminal charge whenever he is released from the current imprisonment.

DICTUM. See: Obiter Dictum.

DIGEST. Is an index to reported cases, providing brief, unconnected statements of court holdings or facts of cases, which is arranged by subject and subdivided by jurisdiction and courts.

DISSENTING OPINION. Expresses disagreement of one or more judges of a court with a decision in a case rendered by the majority.

GLOSSARY

DUCES TECUM. From the Latin "bring with you." A subpoena duces tecum requires a party to appear in court and bring with him certain documents, pieces of evidence, or other matters to be inspected by the court.

E

EN BANC. Refers to a session where the entire bench of the court will participate in the decision rather than the regular quorum.

ENHANCEMENT. An additional term or length of imprisonment imposed upon conviction of certain crimes where there are extenuating conditions related to the commission of the crime.

ET AL. An abbreviation meaning, "and others".

EVIDENCE. See Evidence Code § 140.

EX REL. By or on the information of. Used in case title to designate the person at whose instance the government or public official is acting.

EX PARTE. On one side only; by or for one party; done for, in behalf of, or on the application, of one party only.

EXCULPATORY. Clearing or tending to clear from alleged fault or guilt.

EXCLUSIONARY RULE. The principle which prohibits the use of evidence which was illegally obtained in a trial. Based on the Fourth Amendment "right of the people to be secure in their persons, houses, papers, and effects, against unreasonable searches and seizures," the rule excludes the fruits of those searches as evidence. However, the rule is not a bar to prosecution, as legally obtained evidence may be available which may be used in a trial.

EXIGENT. Emergency. Circumstances calling for immediate action.

EXTRADITION. The surrender by one state to another of an individual accused or convicted of an offense outside of its own territory.

EXTRAJUDICIAL. Action taken or statements made out of court.

EXTRINSIC. From outside sources.

F

FACSIMILE. An exact copy.

FELONY. A serious crime. See Penal Code § 17.

FRUITS OF A CRIME. Material objects acquired by means of and in consequence of the commission of a crime, and sometimes constituting the subject matter of the crime.

G

GRAND JURY. A group (usually comprised of 23 citizens) chosen to hear testimony in secret and to issue formal criminal accusations (indictments). It also serves an investigatory function concerning possible violations of law.

H

HABEAS CORPUS. Literally, "you have the body." See Writ of Habeas Corpus.

GLOSSARY

HEADNOTE. Is a brief summary of a legal rule or significant facts in a case, which, among other headnotes applicable to the case, precedes the printed opinion in reports.

HEARSAY. See Evidence Code § 1200.

HOLDING. Is the declaration of the conclusion of law reached by the court as to the legal effect of the facts of the case.

I

IBID. An abbreviated notation meaning, "in the same place".

ID. An abbreviated notation meaning, "the same in substance".

IMPEACHMENT. An attack on the credibility of a witness. See Evidence Code § 780 et al.

IN FORMA PAUPERIS. In the form of a pauper; as a poor person or indigent. Permission to bring legal action without the payment of required fees for counsel, writs, transcripts, and the like.

INFERENCE. See Evidence Code § 600.

INJUNCTION. A writ prohibiting an individual or organization from performing some specified action.

IN BANK. See en banc.

IN CAMERA. In chambers; in private. Certain parties and the jury may be excluded from in camera hearings.

IN LIEU. In place of.

IN RE. In the affair; in the matter of; concerning. This is the usual method of entitling a judicial proceeding in which there are no adversary parties. For this reason, used in the title of cases in a juvenile court.

INCARCERATION. The sentencing of a convicted offender to imprisonment in jail, or prison.

INCULPATORY. Tending to establish guilt.

INDICTMENT. A written accusation returned by a grand jury charging an individual with a specified crime after determination of probable cause; the prosecutor presents enough evidence (prima facie case) to establish probable cause. See Penal Code § 889.

INDIRECT EVIDENCE. See Circumstantial Evidence.

INFAMOUS. Shameful or disgraceful. See Infamous Crimes.

INFORMATION. Like the indictment, a formal charging document. The prosecuting attorney makes out the information and files it in court. Probable cause is determined at the preliminary which, unlike grand jury proceedings, is public and attended by the accused and his attorney.

INFRACTION. The name given to minor offenses. See Penal Code § 19a.

INSTRUMENTALITIES OF A CRIME. Tools or implements used to commit a crime.

INTENT. The state of mind of a person when committing an act.

INTER ALIA. Among other things.

GLOSSARY

INTRINSIC. Self explanatory.

IPSE DIXIT. An assertion resting solely on the authority of the person making it.

ISSUE. A single, certain, and material point, deduced from the pleadings of the parties, which is affirmed by the one side and denied on the other; a fact put in controversy by the pleadings; in criminal law a fact which must be proved to convict the accused, or which is in controversy.

J

JUDGMENT. In general, the official and authentic decision of a court of justice upon the respective rights and claims of the parties to the action or suit therein litigated and submitted to its determination. In New York, a judgment is comprised of a conviction and the sentence imposed thereon and is completed by imposition and entry of the sentence.

JUDICIAL PROCESS. The sequence of steps taken by the courts in deciding cases or disposing of legal controversies.

JURISDICTION. The power conferred upon a court to hear certain cases; the power of the police or judicial officer to act. The extent of the power of a public official to act by virtue of his authority. See also Original Jurisdiction, Trial Jurisdiction, Appellate Jurisdiction, and Preliminary Jurisdiction.

L

LOCUS. The place where a thing is done.

M

MALA IN SE. Wrong in themselves; acts immoral or wrong in themselves.

MALA PROHIBITA. Crimes *mala prohibita* embrace things prohibited by statute as infringing on other's rights, though no moral turpitude may be attached, and constituting crimes only because they are prohibited.

MANDAMUS. An order from a higher court to a lower one directing the performance of a specified act.

MISDEMEANOR. See Penal Code § 17.

MISTRIAL. An invalid trial resulting from a legal error or mistake.

MITIGATION. Reducing or lessening. Applied to civil damages or criminal penalties.

MOOT. Points are no longer subjects of contention and are raised only for purposes of discussion or hypothesis. Many law schools have moot courts where students gain practice by arguing hypothetical or moot cases.

MOTIVE. The reason or cause for committing an act.

N

NISI PRIUS. Generally refers to a court where a case is first tried, as distinguished from an appellate court.

GLOSSARY

O

OBITER DICTUM. Is an official, incidental comment, not necessary to the formulation of the decision, made by the judge in his opinion which is not binding as precedent.

ORDINANCE. Is the equivalent of a municipal statute, passed by the city council and governing matters not already covered by federal or state law.

P

PARALLEL CITATION. Is a citation reference to the same case printed in two or more different reports.

PARDON. An act of grace, proceeding from the power entrusted with the execution of the laws, which exempts the individual on whom it is bestowed from the punishment the law inflicts for the crime he has committed.

PARENS PATRIAE. Literally, "father of his country." The doctrine that the juvenile court treats the child as "a kind and loving father."

PEACE OFFICER. See Penal Code § 830 et al.

PER CURIAM OPINION. Is an opinion of the whole court as distinguished from an opinion written by a specific judge.

PERCEIVE. See Evidence Code § 170.

PEREMPTORY CHALLENGE. Self determined, arbitrary, requiring no cause to be shown. As applied to selection of jurors, challenges allowed by law to both the state and defense to remove a prospective juror without cause from the panel of jurors.

PETITIONER. One who presents a petition for relief by the court.

PLAINTIFF. The person who initiates an action.

PLEA OF NOLO CONTENDERE. One which has the same effect in a criminal action as a plea of guilty, but does not bind the defendant in a civil suit for the same wrong. Literally, "No contest."

POCKET SUPPLEMENT. Is a paper-back supplement to a book, inserted in the book through a slit in its back cover. Depending on the type of publication, it may have textual, case or statutory references keyed to the original publication.

PRECEDENT. An adjudged case or decision of a court of justice considered as furnishing an example or authority for an identical or similar case afterwards arising on a similar question of law. See *Stare Decisis.*

PRELIMINARY HEARING. The step at which criminal charges initiated by an "information" are tested for *probable cause*; the prosecution presents enough evidence to establish probable cause, i. e., a *prima facie* case. The Hearing is public and may be attended by the accused and his attorney.

PREPONDERANCE. The larger part of; the most, in quality or quantity.

PREPONDERANCE OF THE EVIDENCE. Greater weight of evidence: the preponderance of the evidence rests with the evidence which produces the stronger impression and is more convincing as to its truth when weight against the evidence in opposition.

PRESENTENCE REPORT. An investigation performed by a probation officer attached to a trial court after the conviction of a defendant. The report contains information

GLOSSARY

about the defendant's background, education, previous employment, family, his own statement concerning the offense, prior criminal record, interviews with neighbors or acquaintances, his mental and physical condition (i. e., information which would not be made record in the case of a guilty plea or which would be inadmissible as evidence at a trial but could be influential and important at the sentencing stage).

PRESUMPTION. See Evidence Code § 600.

PRIMA FACIE CASE. A case developed with evidence such as will suffice until contradicted and overcome by other evidence.

PRIMA FACIE EVIDENCE. Evidence good and sufficient on its face; such evidence as in the judgment of the law, is sufficient to establish a given fact, or the group or chain of facts constituting the party's claim or defense, and which if not rebutted or contradicted, will remain sufficient.

PROBABLE CAUSE. Reasonable cause. Having more evidence for than against. An apparent state of facts which would induce a reasonably intelligent and prudent man to believe, in a criminal case, that the accused person had committed the crime charged. More than suspicion, less than certainty.

PROBATION. The release of a convicted defendant by a court under conditions imposed by the court for a specified period during which the imposition of sentence is suspended. Probation is in lieu of incarceration and is a judicial act.

PROBATIVE. Tending to prove.

PROXIMATE CAUSE. That which, in a natural and continuous sequence, unbroken by any efficient intervening cause, produces the injury, and without which the result would not have occurred.

PURSUANT. In accordance with.

R

RATIO DECIDENDI. Is the point in a case which determines the result—the basis of the decision.

RELEVANT. Applying to the matter in question. A fact is relevant to another fact when, according to common course of events, existence of one taken alone or in connection with the other fact renders existence of the other certain or more probable.

REMAND. To send back.

REPORTS. Are (1) (court reports) published judicial cases arranged according to some grouping, such as jurisdiction, court, period of time, subject matter or case significance, (2) (administrative reports or decisions) published decisions of an administrative agency, (3) annual statements of progress, activities or policy issued by an administrative agency or an association.

RES GESTAE. Things done. The whole of the transaction under investigation and every part of it. *Res gestae* is considered an exception to the hearsay rule, and is extended to include not only declarations by the parties to the suit, but includes statements made by bystanders and strangers under certain circumstances.

RELEASE ON OWN RECOGNIZANCE. Nonmonetary condition for the pretrial release of an accused individual; an alternative to monetary bail which is granted after a determination that the individual has ties in the community, has no prior record of default, and is likely to appear at subsequent proceedings.

GLOSSARY

RESPONDENT. The defendant on appeal; the party who contends against an appeal.

REUS. A person judicially accused of a crime; a person criminally proceeded against.

RULES OF COURT. Regulate practice and procedure before the various courts. In most jurisdictions, these rules are issued by the court itself, or by the highest court in that jurisdiction.

S

SEARCH WARRANT. A court order authorizing and directing a police officer to search designated premises for articles and property stated in the order. See Penal Code § 1523.

SECONDARY AUTHORITY. Are sources of the law which have only persuasive and no mandatory authority, e. g., encyclopedia.

SENTENCE. The criminal sanction imposed by the court upon a convicted defendant, usually in the form of a fine, incarceration, or probation. Sentencing may be carried out by a judge, jury, or sentencing council (panel of judges), depending on the statutes of the jurisdiction.

SESSION LAWS. Are published laws of a state enacted by each assembly and separately bound for the session and for extra sessions. The session laws are published in bound or pamphlet volumes after adjournment of the legislatures for the regular or special sessions.

STARE DECISIS. (Literally, "let the decision stand"); the practice by which courts apply legal precedence to cases involving similar circumstances. For example, the court decisions Weeks v. United States (1914) and Wolf v. Colorado (1949) were at one time the precedents for use of "tainted" evidence by the prosecution in state courts. From 1949 until 1961, the Supreme Court let that practice stand. The practice was overruled by Mapp v. Ohio (1961), which applied the Exclusionary Rule to the states.

STATUTES. Are acts of a legislature. Depending upon its context in usage, a statute may mean a single act of a legislature or a body of acts which are collected and arranged according to a scheme or for a session of a legislature.

STIPULATE. To agree and/or settle definitely.

SUBSTANTIVE LAW. Statutes which define criminal offenses and establish punishments.

SUBPOENA. A process issued by a court to cause a witness to appear and give testimony for the party named.

SUMMONS. An alternative to arrest usually used for petty or traffic offenses; a written order notifying an individual that he has been charged with an offense. A *summons* directs him to appear in court to answer that charge. It is used primarily in instances of low risk where the person will not be required to appear at later date. The summons is advantageous to the police officer in that he is freed from the time normally spent for arrest and booking procedures; it is advantageous to the accused in that he is spared time in jail.

SUPRA. A notation referring the reader to a previous part of the reading.

SUPREME COURT. The only federal court established by the constitution (Article III). The Court has original jurisdiction—i. e., the power to try a case, to determine the facts and law concerning a particular dispute or offense—in cases involving ambassadors, public ministers, and consuls; cases in which the United States is involved; and controversies between the states. The Court has appellate jurisdiction (i. e., the right to review lower court decisions) over cases from state courts of last resort which raise substantial federal questions and over federal lower court decisions.

SUSTAIN. To uphold.

T

TABLE OF CASES. Is a list of cases, arranged alphabetically by case names, with citations and references to the body of the publication where the cases are treated.

TORT. A private or civil wrong or injury; a legal wrong committed upon the person or property independent of contract which is redressed in a civil court. A personal tort involves or consists in an injury to the person or to the reputation or feelings as distinguished from an injury or damage to real or personal property, called a "property tort."

TRANSCRIPT OF RECORD. Refers to the printed record as made up in each case of the proceedings and pleadings necessary for the appellate court to review the history of the case.

TREATISE. Is an exposition, which may be critical, evaluative, interpretative, or informative, on case law or legislation. Usually it is more exhaustive than an encyclopedia but less detailed or critical than a periodical article.

TRIAL. The examination of an issue before an appropriate court; in a criminal case, the issue is guilt or innocence and the criterion of proof is *beyond a reasonable doubt*; in civil proceedings the issue is liability and extent of damages and the criterion of proof is *preponderance* (greater weight or amount) of *evidence*. A trial may take place before a judge (bench trial) or before judge and jury (trial by jury).

TRIER OF FACT. See Evidence Code § 235.

V

VENIRE. (From the Lat. to come, to appear). The name given to the writ for summoning the jury, and also to the body of jurors summoned.

VENUE. A neighborhood; the neighborhood, place, or county in which an injury is declared to have been done, or fact declared to have happened. "Jurisdiction" of the court means the inherent power to decide a case, whereas "venue" designates the particular county or city in which a court with jurisdiction may hear and determine the case.

VERDICT. The formal and unanimous (or one concurred in by the majority of jurors required by law) decision or finding made by a jury, impaneled and sworn for the trial of a cause, and reported to the court (and accepted by it) upon the matters or questions duly submitted to them upon the trial. From the Latin "veredictum," a true declaration.

VOIR DIRE. Literally "To speak the truth." The preliminary examination of a witness or juror as to his competency, interest, etc.

W

WAIVER. The act of voluntarily relinquishing a right or advantage; often used in the context of waiving one's right to counsel) (e. g., Miranda Warning) or waiving certain steps in the criminal justice process.

GLOSSARY

WARRANT. A written order issued by a competent magistrate authorizing a police officer or other official to perform duties relating to the administration of justice.

WRIT. Of which there are many types, is a written order, issued by a court and directed to an official or party, commanding the performance of some act.

WRIT OF *CERTIORARI*. See *Certiorari*.

WRIT OF *HABEAS CORPUS*. A writ directed to a person detaining another and commanding him to produce the body of the prisoner or person detained.

WRITING. See Evidence Code § 250.

*

INDEX

	Page
Penal Code	688
Vehicle Code	776
Health and Safety Code	784
Business and Professions Code	786
Welfare and Institutions Code	787
Evidence Code	791

Index To
PENAL CODE

ABANDONED OR UNCLAIMED PROPERTY
Bicycles, sale, § 1411.
Documentary exhibits, disposition, § 1418.5.
Embezzlement, disposal, § 1411.
Exhibits, disposition, § 1417 et seq.
Firearms, destruction or sale, § 12028.
Fraud, insured property, § 548.
Insured property, intent to defraud insurer, § 548.
Money, disposition, § 1420 et seq.
Sale, lease or other disposition, weapons, § 12028.
Theft, disposal, § 1411.
Time, claims, stolen property unclaimed, disposal, § 1411.
Weapons, destruction or sale, § 12028.

ABANDONMENT
Children and minors,
  Under fourteen, § 271.

ABATEMENT
Destructive devices, possession, § 12307.
Machine guns, possession, § 12251.
Weapons,
  Destruction, §§ 12028, 12029.
  Machine guns, § 12251.

ABDUCTION
  See, also, Kidnapping, generally, this index.
  Generally, § 207 et seq.
Children and minors, §§ 278, 278.5.
Evidence,
  Wiretap evidence, § 633.5.
Illicit relationship, § 266b.
Jurisdiction, § 784.
Prostitution, abduction of persons, §§ 266a, 267.
Wiretap evidence, § 633.5.

ABETTORS
Accomplices and Accessories, generally, this index.

ABORTION
Aiding and abetting,
  Death of fetus, murder, § 187.
Death of fetus, murder, § 187.
Homicide, murder of fetus, § 187.
Physicians and surgeons, murder of fetus, § 187.
Solicitation, death of fetus, murder, § 187.

ABSCONDERS
Defrauding innkeepers, § 537.

ABSENCE AND ABSENTEES
Arraignment, presence of accused, waiver, § 977.
Bigamy, spouse for five years, § 282.
County jail prisoners, work furlough program, §§ 1208, 1208.5.
Defendant at trial, § 1043.
Five years, spouse, bigamy, § 282.
Limitation of prosecutions, computation of time, § 802.
Trial, absence of defendant, § 1043.

ABSTRACTS
Arrest warrants, sending by telegraph or teletype, §§ 850, 851.

ACCESSORIES
Accomplices and Accessories, generally, this index.

ACCIDENTS
Commission of crime by act or omission, § 26.
False emergency reports, § 148.3.
Homicide, excusable, § 195.

ACCOMMODATIONS
False pretenses to obtain, § 537.

ACCOMPLICES AND ACCESSORIES
  Generally, § 30.
Abduction of persons, § 784.
Abrogation, distinction between accessories and principals, § 971.
Acts prior to offense, § 31.
Acts subsequent to offense, § 31.
Arrest, aiding felon to avoid arrest, § 32.
Arson, §§ 448a, 450a.
Causing others to commit crime, § 31.
Children,
  Advising or encouraging to commit crime, § 31.
  Stealing child, § 784.
Classification, parties to crime, § 30.
Concealment of felons, § 32.
Concealment of principal, accessory status, § 32.
Conviction on testimony of accomplice, § 1111.
Correctional institutions,
  Intoxicating liquors or narcotics, bringing into prison, § 4573.
  Weapons, bringing into prison, § 4574.
Corroboration of testimony, § 1111.
Cruel and unusual punishment, infliction, § 673.
Definitions, §§ 31, 32, 1111.
Degrees, principals in first and second degree, distinction abrogated, § 971.
Distinction between accessories and principals abrogated, § 971.

ACCOMPLICES AND ACCESSORIES —Cont'd
Dogs, fighting, fines and penalties, § 597.5.
Eavesdropping,
  Aiding escape, police radio service communications, § 636.5.
  Wiretapping, invasion of privacy, § 631.
Escape, § 4533 et seq.
Evidence,
  Conviction on testimony of accomplice, § 1111.
False imprisonment, § 784.
Fetus, murder, § 187.
Fines and penalties, § 33.
Foreign states, aiding crime in state, § 27.
Harboring fugitives, § 32.
Homicide, murder of fetus, § 187.
Indictment and information, § 971.
Invasion of privacy, wiretapping and electronic eavesdropping, § 631.
Jurisdiction, § 791.
  Principal not present at commission of offense, § 792.
  Principal or aider and abettor without state subsequently found in state, § 778b.
Kidnapping, §§ 209, 210, 784.
Mentally deficient and mentally ill persons, advising to commit crime, § 31.
Personal property in custody of officer, damaging, etc., § 102.
Police radio service communications, eavesdropping and aiding escape, § 636.5.
Process, resistance to execution, §§ 723, 724.
Prosecution without regard to principal, § 972.
Prostitution, this index.
Rape, force or violence in committing, § 264.1.
Rescue, prisoners, § 4550.
Resistance to process, §§ 723, 724.
Seduction, § 266.
Sentence and punishment, §§ 33, 972.
Soliciting commission of certain offenses, § 653f.
Theft,
  Child stealing, § 784.
Trial,
  Concealment of felony to avoid or escape trial, § 32.
  Conviction on testimony of accomplice, § 1111.
  Distinction between accessories and principals abrogated, § 971.

688

Penal Code

ACCOMPLICES AND ACCESSORIES —Cont'd
Trial—Cont'd
Prosecution without regard to trial of principal, § 972.
Wiretapping, § 631.

ACCOUNTS AND ACCOUNTING
Counterfeiting, § 470.
Extradition, expenses of returning fugitives, § 1557.
Falsification by public officers, § 424.
Forgery, § 470.
Fraudulent accounts, presentation to state, etc., board or officer, § 72.
Probationers, earnings to support dependents, § 1203.1.

ACCUSATORY PLEADINGS
Complaints, generally, this index.
Defined, § 691.
Indictment and Information, generally, this index.

ACCUSED
Allocution, § 1200.
Arraignment, generally, this index.
Counsel for Accused, generally, this index.
Presence,
Trial, § 1043.
Telephone call permitted, misdemeanor for preventing, § 851.5.
Waiver, presence at trial, § 1043.

ACETORPHINE
See, also, Drugs and Medicine, generally, this index.

ACETYLENE TORCHES
Burglary with explosives, § 464.

ACETYLMETHADOL
See, also, Drugs and Medicine, generally, this index.

ACIDS
Assault, § 244.

ACQUITTAL
Generally, § 1118 et seq.
Accusatory pleading, one or more counts, § 954.
Appeal, judgment of acquittal, § 1118.2.
Arrest records, sealing, § 851.8.
Authority of court to order, § 1118.1.
Bar to subsequent prosecution, § 1023.
Detention record, sealing, § 851.8.
Former Jeopardy, this index.
Indigent accused, return to place of arrest upon acquittal, § 686.5.
Judgments of acquittal, § 1118 et seq.
Appealability, § 1118.2.
Jurisdiction,
Concurrent, acquittal in another state or county, former jeopardy, § 793.
Two or more courts, jeopardy in another court having jurisdiction upon, § 794.
Minors, sealing court records, § 851.7.
Motion to seal records, § 851.8.
Not guilty finding, trial without jury, § 1118.

ACQUITTAL—Cont'd
One or more of several defendants, single indictment, § 970.
Plea of autrefois acquit, § 1016 et seq.
Principal, prosecution of accessory without regard to, § 972.
Reasonable doubt, § 1096.
Several defendants, one or more acquitted, single indictment, § 970.

ACQUITTANCE
Forging or counterfeiting instrument, § 470.

ACTIONS AND PROCEEDINGS
Appeals in Criminal Prosecutions, generally, this index.
Arrest by public officers or employees, civil liability, § 836.5.
Conspiracy to maintain false action, etc., § 182.
Correctional Institutions, this index.
Counterfeiting or forging instruments relating to, § 470.
Dismissal and Nonsuit, generally, this index.
Forging or counterfeiting instruments, § 470.
Habeas Corpus, generally, this index.
Injunction, generally, this index.
Judgments and Decrees, generally, this index.
Libel and Slander, generally, this index.
New Trial, generally, this index.
Parties, generally, this index.
Process, generally, this index.
Production of Books and Papers, generally, this index.
Public officers and employees effecting arrest, civil liability, § 836.5.
Slander. Libel and Slander, generally, this index.
Special Proceedings, generally, this index.
Subpoenas, generally, this index.
Supersedeas or Stay, generally, this index.
Venue, generally, this index.

ACTORS AND ACTRESSES
Buttocks or breasts, ordinances prohibiting exposure, §§ 318.5, 318.6.

ACTS
Overt Acts, generally, this index.
Unity of act or intent to constitute crime, necessity, § 20.

ADDICTS
Drug Addicts, generally, this index.
Drunkards and Drunkenness, generally, this index.

ADDING MACHINES
Serial number or identification mark removed, sale, § 537e.

ADDITIONAL PUNISHMENT
Fines and Penalties, this index.

ADDRESS
Firearms, sale of concealable firearms, falsification, § 12076.

ADVERTISEMENTS

ADDRESS—Cont'd
Peace officers, residence address, disclosure maliciously with intent to obstruct justice, § 146e.
Sex offenders, notice of change, § 290.
Weapons, falsification, sale of concealable firearms, § 12076.

ADMINISTRATIVE LAW AND PROCEDURE
Adjudication, records, criminal identification and investigation bureau, correction of errors, § 11126.
Evidence, withdrawn guilty and nolo contendere pleas specifying punishment, § 1192.5.
Guilty plea, withdrawn pleas specifying punishment, evidence, § 1192.5.
Nolo contendere pleas, withdrawn pleas specifying punishment, evidence § 1192.5.

ADMISSIBILITY OF EVIDENCE
Evidence, generally, this index.

ADMISSION TO BAIL
Bail, this index.

ADMISSIONS
Nolo contendere pleading, exclusionary protection, § 1016.

ADOPTION OF CHILDREN
Concealment of child, § 280.

ADULT AUTHORITY
Community Release Boards, generally, this index.

ADULT DETENTION FACILITIES
Maximum term of confinement, § 19a.

ADULT SCHOOLS AND CLASSES
Annoying or molesting persons in attendance, § 647b.
Disruptive persons, denial of access to campus or facilities, etc., § 626.8.
Loitering, schools in which classes held, § 647b.
Molesting persons in attendance, § 647b.

ADULTERY
Incest, § 285.

ADULTS
Probation officers, generally. Parole and Probation, this index.

ADVANCES AND ADVANCEMENTS
Extradition, expenses of returning fugitive, § 1557.

ADVERSE OR PECUNIARY INTEREST
Limitation of prosecutions, § 800.

ADVERTISEMENTS
Billboards. Outdoor Advertising, generally, this index.
Concealed weapons, § 12020.5.
Eavesdropping equipment, § 635.
Nongovernmental organization with terms peace officer, etc., incorporated in name, publication issued by, § 146c.

689

ADVERTISEMENTS

ADVERTISEMENTS—Cont'd
Obscene matter, § 311.5.
Outdoor Advertising, generally, this index.
Weapons, possession, § 12020.5.
Wiretapping equipment, § 635.

AERONAUTICS
Aircraft, generally, this index.

AERSOL SPRAYS
Tear gas and tear gas weapons, § 12403.7.

AFFIDAVITS
Aggravation or mitigation of punishment, § 1204.
Bail, this index.
Complaint charging felony, supporting, § 806.
Contempt, subpoena, failure to appear, agreement to appear at different time, § 1331.5.
Expense accounts, persons designated to return fugitives from justice, § 1557.
Extradition,
    Application for requisition, § 1554.2.
    Expenses of returning fugitives, § 1557.
False affidavits, § 118a.
Pardons, reprieves and commutations,
    Examination, § 4812.
    Proof of service, notice of intention to apply, § 4804.
Perjury, this index.
Subpoenas, agreement to appear at different time, § 1331.5.

AGE
Homicide conviction, capital punishment, § 190.5.

AGED PERSONS
Crimes against, § 1203.09.
Social Services, generally, this index.

AGENTS AND AGENCIES
Attorney in fact. Power of Attorney, generally, this index.
Embezzlement, § 508.
Power of Attorney, generally, this index.
State Agencies, generally, this index.

AGGRAVATING CIRCUMSTANCES
Evidence, § 1204.

AGREEMENTS
Contracts, generally, this index.

AGRICULTURAL PRODUCTS
Burning, § 449a.
    Malicious mischief, §§ 449b, 449c.
Fruits, generally, this index.
Hay, generally, this index.
Malicious mischief,
    Burning, §§ 449b, 449c.
Poultry and Poultry Products, generally, this index.
Vegetables, generally, this index.

AIDERS AND ABETTORS
Accomplices and Accessories, generally, this index.

AIR GUNS
Sale to minors, §§ 12551, 12552.

AIR POLLUTION
Arrest, ordinance of air pollution control district, § 836.5.
Definitions, ordinance, arrest, § 836.5.
Ordinance, air pollution control district, arrest, § 836.5.
Rules and regulations, arrest, § 836.5.

AIRCRAFT
Bombs and explosives,
    False reports of planting, § 148.1.
Burglary, § 459.
    Possession of burglary tools, § 466.
Discharging weapons, § 247.
Hijacking, reward, § 1547.
Jurisdiction, offenses committed on aircraft, § 783.
Reward,
    Hijacking, § 1547.
    Robbery, § 1547.
Robbery, reward, § 1547.
Shooting at plane, § 247.
Weapons, shooting at plane, § 247.

AIRPLANES
Aircraft, generally, this index.

AIRPORTS AND LANDING FIELDS
Bombs and explosives, false reports of planting, § 148.1.
Course of instruction, security officers, training, peace officers, § 832.1.
Peace officers,
    Training course, § 832.1.
Security officers,
    Training course, § 832.1.
Training, special security officers, § 832.1.

ALCOHOLIC BEVERAGES
Administering intoxicating agent with felonious intent, § 222.
Begging or soliciting patron or customer to purchase for one, § 303a.
Correctional Institutions, this index.
Drunkards, sale to drunks, § 397.
Incompetent persons, sales, § 397.
Industrial farms and road camps,
    Bringing into camp, § 4573.
Jails,
    Bringing into jail, § 4573.
Mentally deficient and mentally ill persons, sale to, § 397.
Municipal jails,
    Bringing into jail, § 4573.
Parole and Probation, this index.
Rape, resistance prevented, § 261.
Sales, § 397.
    Between hours of 2 and 6 a. m., § 398.
    Drunkards, § 397.
    Incompetent persons, § 397.
    Insane persons, § 397.
Sex offenses involving alcohol, probation, § 1203.02.
Soliciting patron to purchase for one, § 303a.

ALCOHOLICS
Drunkards and Drunkenness, generally, this index.

ALLEYS
Streets and Alleys, generally, this index.

ALLIGATORS
See, also, Fish and Game, generally, this index.

ALLOCUTION
Generally, § 1200.

ALLYLPRODINE
See, also, Drugs and Medicine, generally, this index.

ALMS
Soliciting alms, disorderly conduct, § 647.

ALPHACETYLMETHODOL
See, also, Drugs and Medicine, generally, this index.

ALTERATION OF INSTRUMENTS
Credit cards, § 484d et seq.
Evidence, altered instrument, § 132.
Forgery, generally, this index.
Utterance of altered instrument, § 470.

AMMUNITION
Blowgun ammunition,
    Defined, manufacture, sale, etc., § 12581.
    Manufacture, sale, etc., §§ 12581, 12582.

AMPHETAMINE
See, also, Drugs and Medicine, generally, this index.

AMUSEMENTS
Burglary tools, coin-operated machines, § 466.3.

ANESTHETICS
Administering to assist in commission of a felony, § 222.
Rape, resistance overcome by, § 261.

ANILERIDINE
See, also, Drugs and Medicine, generally, this index.

ANIMAL POUNDS
Officers,
    Killing unfit animals, § 599e.
Unfit animals, killing, § 599e.

ANIMALS
Assaulting sexually, § 286.5.
Carcasses. Dead animals, generally, post.
Cruelty, § 597.
    Acts constituting, § 597.
Dead animals,
    Theft, § 487a.
Dogs, generally, this index.
Fish and Game, generally, this index.
Game. Fish and Game, generally, this index.
Hogs, generally, this index.
Horses, generally, this index.
Impounding. Animal Pounds, generally, this index.

Penal Code   **ARREST**

ANIMALS—Cont'd
Killing or injuring,
    Unfit animals, § 599e.
Malicious Mischief, this index.
Mules, generally, this index.
Notice to kill unfit animals, § 599e.
Pounds. Animal Pounds, generally, this index.
Refusal to kill unfit animals, § 599e.
Regulation officers, public agencies,
    Killing unfit animals, § 599e.
Sexually assaulting, § 286.5.
Substances likely to injure animals, throwing on highways, § 588a.
Theft, §§ 487, 487a.
Throwing substances likely to injure animals on highway, § 588a.
Unfit animals, killing, § 599e.

ANSWER
Indictment and information, answer on denial of motion to set aside, § 997.
Witnesses, generally, this index.

ANTEDATED INSTRUMENTS
Evidence, offering evidence, § 132.

ANTI–OBSCENITY ACT
Generally, § 311 et seq.

ANTIQUE FIREARMS
Defined, weapons, possession, manufacture or sale, § 12020.

ANTIQUE WEAPONS
Manufacture, sale or possession, exemption, § 12020.
Possession, § 12027.

APARTMENT HOUSES
Assignation or prostitution, letting, § 316.
Burglary, § 459.
Employees remaining in apartment without permission, § 602.5.
Fraud upon proprietor, § 537.
Gambling, use for gambling purposes, § 337a.
Malicious mischief,
    Forcible entry, vandalism, § 603.
    Unauthorized entry, § 602.5.
Person remaining without permission, § 602.5.
Prostitution, letting apartment for, § 316.
Unauthorized entry, § 602.5.

APOMORPHINE
See, also, Drugs and Medicine, generally, this index.

APPAREL
Wearing Apparel, generally, this index.

APPEAL AND REVIEW
Capital punishment, application for modification of verdict, ruling on application, § 190.4.
State, supersedeas or stay, § 1242.

APPEALS IN CRIMINAL PROSECUTIONS
Acquittal judgments, § 1118.2.

APPEALS IN CRIMINAL PROSECUTIONS—Cont'd
Custody of defendant pending appeal, § 1244.
    Stay pending appeal, suspension of further execution, § 1245.
Judgment of acquittal, § 1118.2.
Parole and Probation, this index.
Searches and seizures, motion to suppress evidence, § 1538.5.
    Capital offenses, stay pending appeal, § 1243.
    Custody of defendant pending appeal, § 1244.
    Execution of judgment, stay, § 1245.
    Motion to suppress evidence, unreasonable search and seizure, § 1538.5.
    Supersedeas or stay, § 1242.
Supersedeas or Stay, this index.
Unreasonable search or seizure motion, § 1538.5.

APPEARANCE
Accused, personal presence, § 977.
    Trial, § 1043.
Arraignment, this index.
Arrested person released on own recognizance, signature, § 853.6.
Bail, forfeiture, nonappearance of defendant for sentence, § 1195.
Citations for misdemeanors, § 853.6 et seq.
Commitment of defendant on bail, § 1129.
Corporations, this index.
Defendant, personal presence, § 977.
    Trial, § 1043.
Delay, appearance before magistrate, arrest without warrant, § 849.
Deposits in court, forfeiture, nonappearance of defendant for sentence, § 1195.
Magistrates, appearance before, time limit, § 825.
Misdemeanor, direction to appear, § 822.
Probation modification, waiver of appearance, right to counsel, § 1203.2.
Promise to appear, arrested person, release on own recognizance, § 853.6.
Sentencing, nonappearance for, § 1195.
Time,
    Defendant before magistrate, § 825.
Written promises to appear in court, violation, § 853.7.

APPROPRIATIONS
Criminal identification and investigation bureau, fees appropriated for department of justice, § 11123.

ARBITRATION AND AWARD
Intimidation, § 95.

ARGUMENT AND CONDUCT OF COUNSEL
Generally, §§ 1044, 1093.
Capital offenses,
    Number of counsel, § 1095.
Closing trial, § 1093.
Mentally deficient and mentally ill persons, trial of sanity issue, § 1369.
Opening and closing trial, § 1093.

ARMED FORCES
Military Forces, generally, this index.

ARMORED VEHICLES
Guards, firearms, § 12031.

ARMS
Weapons, generally, this index.

ARRAIGNMENT
Appearance,
    Counsel for defendant, § 977.
    Nonappearance, defendant discharged on bail or deposit, § 979.
Attorneys. Counsel for accused, generally, post.
Bench warrants, § 979 et seq.
    Service, § 983.
Citations, misdemeanor offenses, § 853.6.
Counsel for accused,
    Appearance, § 977.
Custody of defendant, nonbailable offense, § 982.
Degree of offense, specification in guilty plea, § 1192.2.
Deposit of money or property, forfeiture, nonappearance of accused, § 979.
Forfeitures, nonappearance of defendant discharged on bail or deposit, § 979.
Forms, waiver of accused's personal presence, § 977.
Guilty plea, specifying degree, § 1192.2.
Habeas corpus, bail, § 982.
Judgment, § 1200.
Municipal courts, counties of first or third class, § 936.
Nonbailable offense, custody of defendant, § 982.
Presence of defendant, necessity, § 977.
Service, bench warrants, § 983.
Waiver, presence of accused, § 977.

ARREST
Generally, § 830.1 et seq.
Abstracts, warrants, sending by telegraph or teletype, § 850.
    Filing certified copy in telegraph office, return of original, § 851.
Accomplices, harboring felons to avoid arrest, § 32.
Accused,
    Right to visit from attorney, § 825.
    Telephone calls, right to make, § 851.5.
Aid, authority to summon, § 839.
Air pollution ordinances, § 836.5.
Appearance before magistrate, § 825.
Attorneys, right to visit prisoner, § 825.
Authority, § 834.
    Magistrates, § 807.
    Summoning aid to make arrest, § 839.
Bail, generally, this index.
Bench warrants, § 979 et seq.
    Absence of defendant at trial, § 1043.
    Accused not in custody upon finding indictment, § 945.
    Arraignment, forms, § 982.
    Authority to issue, § 980.
    Bringing defendant before court for sentence, § 1195 et seq.
    Defendant on bail, § 1195 et seq.
    Delivery of defendant to court, § 1199.
    Felony case, forms, § 981.

ARREST

ARREST—Cont'd
Bench warrants—Cont'd
  Forms, § 1197.
  Increased bail on felony charge, § 986.
  Issuance, § 1196.
  Judgments, nonappearance of defendant on bail or deposit, § 1195 et seq.
  Nonappearance of defendant for judgment, § 1195 et seq.
  Service, §§ 983, 1198.
Breaking open door or window to effect arrest, §§ 844, 845.
Bringing defendant on bail before court for sentencing, § 1195 et seq.
Certificate of detention, § 851.6.
Children and Minors, this index.
Citations for misdemeanors under state law, § 853.6 et seq.
Citizen's arrest. Private persons, generally, post.
Close Pursuit Law, § 852 et seq.
College and university police department personnel, § 830.2.
Complaint, arrest without warrant, § 849.
Compliance with warrant, § 848.
Concealment, felons avoiding arrest, accomplices, § 32.
Conspiracy, causing arrest of third persons, § 182.
Coroners, power, § 830.10.
Courses of instruction, peace officers, § 832.
Cruel treatment of arrested persons, § 147.
Custody pursuant to another arrest, time of day, misdemeanor or infraction, § 840.
Daytime, § 840.
Defendant released on bail, surrender of defendant, § 1301.
Defined, § 834.
Delay in taking before magistrate, § 145.
Demand for admittance, breaking open door or window, § 844.
Detention,
  Arrest without warrant, § 849.
  Distinguished, § 849.5.
Detention certificate, release of arrested person without formal charge, § 851.6.
Disarming person arrested, § 846.
Disclosure, indictment or information for felony before arrest, §§ 168, 924.
Display of warrant on request, § 842.
Doors, breaking, §§ 844, 845.
Drugs, persons, under influence, release from custody, § 849.
Drunkards and Drunkenness, this index.
Duty to take prisoner before magistrate, §§ 847, 849.
Electronic devices and equipment, copies or abstracts of warrants, § 850.
Escape, this index.
Exhibition of warrant on request, § 842.
Extradition, this index.
False Imprisonment, generally, this index.
False personation, arresting officer, § 146a.

ARREST—Cont'd
Fines and penalties,
  Default in payment, § 1205.
Force and Violence, this index.
Foreign peace officers, arrest pursuant to Fresh Pursuit Law, § 852.2.
Formalities in making arrest, § 841.
  Detention certificate, release from custody without formal charge, § 851.6.
Forms,
  Notice to appear, reasons for nonrelease, § 853.6.
  Warrants, post.
Fresh pursuit, § 852 et seq.
  Formalities, § 841.
Fugitives from Justice, this index.
Habeas Corpus, generally, this index.
Homicide, justifiable, § 196.
Hot Pursuit Law, §§ 841, 852 et seq.
Inferior courts, warrant, form, etc., § 1427.
Infractions,
  Release procedures, § 853.5.
  Time, § 840.
Insufficient grounds for complaint, release, § 849.
Justifiable homicide committed during arrest, § 196.
Kidnapping, § 207.
Liability of arresting officer, § 146.
Magistrates,
  Powers, § 807.
  Taking defendant before, §§ 821, 822.
  On-call magistrate when court not in session, § 810.
Malicious procuring warrant for arrest, § 170.
Marihuana, possession, release on own recognizance, § 853.6.
Method, § 835.
Money or property taken from defendant, receipts, § 1412.
National guard, § 830.2.
Nighttime, § 840.
Notice,
  Appearance, persons arrested for misdemeanors, § 853.6.
  Sex offenses, schoolteachers, § 291.
  Telephone call rights, § 851.5.
Obstructing justice, § 69.
Offense triable in another county, § 827 et seq.
Oppressive treatment, arrested persons, § 147.
Orders of magistrates, oral, § 838.
Parole and Probation, this index.
Persons resisting process, § 723.
Possession of dangerous weapons, § 833.
Pretrial diversion programs, § 1001.9.
Private persons,
  Authority to make, §§ 834, 837.
  Breaking open door or window to effect arrest, § 844.
  Duty to take prisoner before magistrate or deliver him to peace officer, § 847.
  Without warrant, filing complaint, § 849.
  Order of magistrate, oral, § 838.

ARREST—Cont'd
Probable cause,
  Private persons, § 837.
  Refusal to allow inspection of loaded weapon, § 12031.
Process, persons resisting execution, § 723.
Process servers, eligibility to execute warrants, public officers and employees, § 816.
Public officers and employees, arrest in presence without warrant, § 836.5.
Public place, time of day, misdemeanors or infractions, § 840.
Reasonable force to effect arrest, § 835a.
Records,
  Acquittal, sealing, § 851.8.
  Correction of errors, § 11126.
  Detention,
    Certificate, release without formal charge, § 851.6.
    Use of drugs, etc., § 849.
  Examination, § 11120 et seq.
  Information from records, unauthorized furnishing, § 11140 et seq.
  Local summary criminal history information, § 13300 et seq.
  Release, §§ 849, 849.5.
  Restrictions on judge reading arrest reports, § 1204.5.
Release, § 849.
  Certificate, § 851.6.
  Detention,
    Certificate, release without formal charge, § 851.6.
    Recording in arrest records, § 849.
  Insufficient grounds for complaint, etc., § 849.
  Persons arrested for misdemeanors, § 853.6.
  Recording in arrest records, § 849.
  Without pleading, record of release, § 849.5.
Resisting arrest, §§ 69, 148, 834a.
  Contempt, § 166.
  Force permissible, § 843.
  Justifiable homicide, § 196.
  Overcoming resistance, § 835a.
Resisting execution of process, § 723.
Restraint, amount, § 835.
Return of indigent accused to place of arrest upon release, § 686.5.
Rewards, § 1547.
Riotous assemblies,
  Failure of persons to disperse, § 727.
  Neglect or refusal, magistrate or officer, § 410.
Searches and Seizures, generally, this index.
Self defense, § 835a.
  Public officers and employees, § 836.5.
Service, bench warrants, § 983.
Sex Offenders, this index.
Shoplifting, probable cause, § 490.5.
State police authority, § 830.2.
Summoning aid, authority, § 839.
Telegraphic warrant, §§ 850, 851.
Telephone calls, § 851.5.
  On-call magistrate, release on bail, § 810.

Penal Code ASSAULT

ARREST—Cont'd
Time, § 840.
  Appearance before magistrate, § 825.
  Felony or misdemeanor, § 840.
  Making arrests, § 840.
  Telephone rights of arrested persons, § 851.5.
Traffic rules and regulations, release on promise to appear, § 818.
Training, courses of instruction for peace officers, § 832.
Treatment of arrested persons, § 147.
Uniform Act on Fresh Pursuit, § 852 et seq.
University of California police department personnel, § 830.2.
Unlawful or riotous assemblies,
  Failure of persons to disperse, § 727.
  Offenders neglect or refusal, magistrate or officer, § 410.
Unnecessary restraint of persons charged with public offenses, § 688.
Verbal order by magistrate to officer or private person, § 838.
Warrants, § 813 et seq.
  Absence of accused at trial, § 1043.
  Abstracts, sending by telegraph or teletype, §§ 850, 851.
  Accompanied by complaint of offense, triable in another county, § 827.
  Accused not in custody at time of indictment, § 945.
  Bench warrants, generally, ante.
  Citations for offenses, § 853.6.
  Contents, § 815.
  County of issuance, arrest for felony, § 821.
  Delivery of warrant and undertaking, § 823.
  Detention, arrest without warrant, release for treatment, § 849.
  Direction, § 816.
  Appearance before magistrate, § 822.
  Discharge of defendant, § 823.
  Display of warrant on request, § 842.
  Electronic devices, transmission, § 850.
  Endorsement of admission to, bail, § 815a.
  Execution, § 816.
  Exhibition on request, § 842.
  Extradition, this index.
  Fixing amount of bail at time of issuance, §§ 815a, 1269b.
  Force permissible, § 843.
  Forms,
    Abstracts, sending by telegraph or teletype, § 850.
    Bench warrants, felony cases, § 981.
    Inferior courts, § 1427.
  Fugitive, § 847.5.
  Grounds, without warrant, § 836.
  Inferior courts, § 1427.
  Informing defendant of right to be taken before magistrate, § 821.
  Issuance, §§ 813 et seq., 1427.
  Magistrates, issuance, § 813.
  Malicious procuring, § 170.
  Nighttime arrests, warrant endorsement, § 840.
  Notice to appear, nonrelease of persons with outstanding warrants, § 853.6.

ARREST—Cont'd
Warrants—Cont'd
  Number, telegraphic abstract, § 850.
  Offense committed in presence of officer, § 836.
  Offense triable in another county,
    Delivery of complaint and warrant, § 828.
    Inferior court, procedure, § 829.
    Requisites, complaint to accompany, § 827.
  Persons to whom directed, § 816.
  Probationer, re-arrest, § 1203.2.
  Proceedings on taking bail, certification, § 823.
  Return, telegraphic warrant, § 851.
  Search of person arrested, § 833.
  Telegraphic warrants, §§ 850, 851.
  Teletype, §§ 850, 851.
  Transmittal, offense, triable in inferior court of another county, § 829.
Weapons,
  Carrying dangerous weapons, search and seizure, § 833.
  Delivery to magistrate, § 846.
  Disarming person arrested, § 846.
  Loaded weapons while making lawful arrest, carrying, § 12031.
  Resisting arrest, purpose, § 834a.
  Search and seizure, carrying dangerous weapons, §§ 833, 12031.
Windows, breaking, §§ 844, 845.
Without warrant,
  Detention certificate, issuance, release from custody without formal charge, § 851.6.
  Escapees, § 836.3.
  Public officers or employees, § 836.5.
  Release, certificate of detention, § 851.6.
  Time, § 840.

ARREST OF JUDGMENT
Cause against pronouncement or judgment, § 1201.
Extension of time to pronounce judgment in order to hear motion, § 1191.
Mentally deficient and mentally ill persons, § 1201.

ARREST ON CIVIL PROCESS
Confinement, § 4000 et seq.

ARSON
Generally, § 447a et seq.
Accomplices and accessories, § 447a et seq.
Soliciting aid, § 653f.
Campers, § 447a.
Defined, § 447a.
  Unauthorized fire, prisoners in local detention facilities, § 451b.
Detention facilities, § 451b.
Dwelling house and appurtenances, § 447a.
Fire bombs, § 452.
  Reward, § 1547.
Homicide resulting, degree of offense, § 189.
House cars, § 447a.
Insurance, intent to defraud insurers, §§ 450a, 548.

ARSON—Cont'd
Local detention facilities, prisoners, § 451b.
Malicious mischief, § 449b.
Mentally incompetent defendant, commitment or outpatient treatment, § 1370.
Murder resulting, degree, § 189.
Possession of explosives or combustible materials with intent to set fire, § 452.
Probation, § 1203.
Public property, reward, § 1547.
Reward, person burning public property, § 1547.
Soliciting commission, § 653f.
Stores, § 448a.
Trailer coaches, § 447a.

ART AND ARTISTS
Correctional institution inmates, civil rights, § 2601.
Exhibitions, indecent exposure, § 314.
Lewdness and Obscenity, generally, this index.
Prisoners, civil rights, § 2601.

ASSAULT AND BATTERY
Generally, §§ 216 et seq., 240 et seq.
Acids, § 244.
Aircraft, shooting at aircraft, § 247.
Bodily injury, force likely to produce, § 245.
Buildings, occupied buildings, firearms, discharge, § 246.
Caustic chemicals, § 244.
Children and minors, reports, §§ 11110, 11161.5.
Correctional institutions, assault by prisoners, § 4500 et seq.
Corrosive acids, § 244.
Crime against nature, assault with intent to commit, § 220.
Cruelty to children, §§ 11110, 11161.5.
Custodial officers, local detention facilities, § 243.1.
Deadly weapons. Weapons, generally, post.
Defined, §§ 240, 242.
Disfigurement, caustic chemicals, § 244.
Dwellings, firearms, discharge, § 246.
Federal employees, United States property,
  Deadly weapon, § 245.4.
Felony, assault with intent to commit, § 220 et seq.
Fines and penalties, § 241 et seq.
  Assault with intent to commit felony, § 220 et seq.
  Assault with intent to murder, § 217.
  Force likely to produce great bodily injury, § 245.
  Intent to commit felony, §§ 220, 221.
Firearms. Weapons, generally, post.
Firemen, §§ 241, 243.
  Deadly weapons, §§ 245, 245.2.
Governor, § 217.1.
Grand larceny, assault with intent to commit, § 220.
Industrial farms and road camps, against noninmates, § 4131.5.

693

ASSAULT

ASSAULT AND BATTERY—Cont'd
Inmates, jails or industrial farms and road camps, against noninmates, § 4131.5.
Jails, against noninmates, § 4131.5.
Judges, § 217.1.
Larceny, assault with intent to commit, § 220.
Life-term prisoners, § 4500.
Mayhem, assault with intent to commit, § 220.
Occupied buildings, firearms, discharge, § 246.
Parole and probation, § 1203.
  Assault with deadly weapon by prisoner, § 4500.
  Eligibility, § 1203.06.
  Second and subsequent offenses, eligibility, § 1203.08.
Peace Officers, this index.
President of the United States, § 217.1.
Prisoners, jails or industrial farms and road camps, against noninmates, § 4131.5.
Probation. Parole and probation, generally, ante.
Reward, apprehension of person assaulting police officer, § 1547.
Robbery, assault with intent to commit, § 220.
Shooting at aircraft, § 247.
Sodomy, assault with intent to commit, § 220.
Soliciting commission, assault with deadly weapon or instrument, § 653f.
State college police, § 245.
United States department secretary, § 217.1.
Vice-president of United States, § 217.1.
Vitriol, § 244.
Weapons, § 245.
  Accusatory pleading, nature of firearm used, § 969d.
  Discharge at inhabited dwelling house or occupied building, § 246.
  Possession with intent to assault, § 467.
  Prisoner under life sentence, § 4500.

ASSEMBLY
Disturbance, §§ 403, 416.
Refusal to disperse, unlawful assembly, § 416.
Unlawful assembly,
  Arrest for failure to disperse, § 727.
  Command to disperse, §§ 726, 727.
  Defined, § 407.
  Magistrate or officer, neglect or refusal to disperse, § 410.
  Participation, punishment, § 408.
  Refusal to disperse, § 416.
  Remaining present after warning to disperse, § 409.

ASSIGNMENTS
Counterfeiting, § 470.
Forgery, § 470.

ASSOCIATIONS AND SOCIETIES
Nongovernmental organization, term peace officer, etc., incorporated in name, § 146c.

ASSOCIATIONS AND SOCIETIES —Cont'd
Religious Organizations and Societies, generally, this index.
Sale of membership card, inference of less rigid law enforcement against displayer, § 146d.
Weapons,
  Carrying loaded firearms, § 12031.
  Exemptions, § 12027.

ASSUMED OR FICTITIOUS NAMES
Credit cards, § 484d et seq.
Indictment and information, accused charged by fictitious or erroneous name, insertion of true name, § 953.
Leases, theft by fraud, § 484.
Sales,
  Concealable firearms, § 12076.
Theft by fraud, leases, § 484.
Weapons, purchases, § 12076.

ATHLETICS
Boxing and Wrestling, generally, this index.
Bribery, § 337b et seq.
Fines and penalties, bribery, § 337b et seq.
Referees, bribery, §§ 337d, 337e.

ATTACHMENT
Jail prisoners, work furlough earnings, § 1208.

ATTEMPTS
Generally, § 663 et seq.
Arbitrators, corrupt influencing, § 95.
Assault, § 240.
Coin operated vending machines, use of slugs, § 640a.
Coin-box telephones, use of slugs, § 640b.
Commercial paper, fictitious paper, uttering, passing or publishing, § 476.
Conviction though offense perpetrated, § 663.
Corrupt influencing of arbitrators, etc., § 95.
County jail, imprisonment, § 664.
Deadly weapons, armed offenses, additional punishment, §§ 12022, 12022.5.
Death penalty, § 664.
Eavesdropping, wiretapping, invasion of privacy, § 631.
Escape, this index.
Extortion, § 524.
Felonies while armed, additional punishment, §§ 12022, 12022.5.
Fictitious commercial paper, uttering, passing or publishing, § 476.
Fines and penalties, § 663 et seq.
Former jeopardy, subsequent prosecutions, § 1023.
Governor, attempt to kill or commission of assault upon, § 217.1.
Homicide, § 216 et seq.
Imprisonment, county jail, § 664.
Indictment and information, prior conviction, allegation, § 969.
Invasion of privacy, wiretapping and electronic eavesdropping, § 631.
Judges, attempt to kill or commission of assault upon, § 217.1.

ATTEMPTS—Cont'd
Jurors, corrupt influencing, § 95.
Life imprisonment, crime punishable by, § 664.
Murder, § 216 et seq.
Officers, obstructing or resisting officer, § 69.
Personal property in custody of officers, taking, injuring or destroying, § 102.
Poison, administering, § 216.
President of the United States, attempt to kill or assault, § 217.1.
Punishment, § 663 et seq.
  Weapons, enhancement, § 1170.1.
Registration of sex offenders, § 290.
Retaking goods from custody of officer, etc., § 102.
Robbery, § 213.
  Reward for arrest of fugitive, § 1547.
Sentence and punishment, § 663 et seq.
  Weapons, enhancement, § 1170.1.
Sex offenders, registration, § 290.
Slot machines, use of slugs, § 640a.
Telephones, coin box, use of slugs, § 640b.
Train wrecking, § 218.
Umpires, corrupt influencing, § 95.
United States officers, attempt to kill or assault, § 217.1.
Vending machines, use of slugs, § 640a.
Vice-president of United States, attempt to kill or assault, § 217.1.
Weapons, armed offenses, additional punishment, §§ 12022, 12022.5.
Wiretapping, § 631.

ATTENDANCE
Witnesses, compelling attendance, § 1326 et seq.

ATTORNEY GENERAL
Arrest, magistrates issuing warrant, concurrence, § 813.
Detention certificate, prescribing form, release of arrested person without formal charge, § 851.6.
Eavesdropping, wiretap or electronic, § 633.
Grand jury,
  Convening for investigation, § 923.
  Employment of special counsel and special investigators, § 936.
Indictments, authority to prepare, § 923.
Invasion of privacy, wiretap or electronic eavesdropping, § 633.
Investigations,
  Witnesses immunity, § 1324.
Magistrates, complaints before, concurrence, warrants of arrest, § 813.
Preliminary examination, presence, § 868.
Recording private communications, wiretapping or electronic eavesdropping, § 633.
Special agents and investigators,
  Wiretapping and electronic eavesdropping, § 633.
Subpoenas, grand jury proceedings, issuance, § 923.
Wiretapping, § 633.

ATTORNEY IN FACT
Power of Attorney, generally, this index.

ATTORNEYS
Argument and Conduct of Counsel, generally, this index.
Attorney General, generally, this index.
Bail, notice of surrender of defendant, § 1300.
Corporations, appearance by counsel, § 1396.
Correctional Institutions, this index.
Counsel for Accused, generally, this index.
County counsel, advice to grand jury, § 934.
Criminal history information, local summary criminal history information, furnishing, § 13300 et seq.
District Attorneys, generally, this index.
Juvenile Delinquents and Dependents, this index.
Municipal Attorneys, generally, this index.
Parole and probation, representation, § 1203.
Public Defenders, generally, this index.
Right to counsel, probation modification, § 1203.2.
Subpoenas, counsel for accused, signing, § 1326.

AUCTIONS AND AUCTIONEERS
Firearms, § 12028.

AUDITORIUMS
Arson, § 448a.

AUDITS AND AUDITORS
Extradition, expenses of returning fugitives, § 1557.

AUTHORITIES
Youth Authority, generally, this index.

AUTOMOBILES
Motor Vehicles, generally, this index.

AUTREFOIS ACQUIT
Indictment, information or complaint, § 1016 et seq.

AUTREFOIS ATTAINT
Indictment, information or complaint, § 1016 et seq.

AWARDS
Arbitration and Award, generally, this index.

BABIES
Children and Minors, generally, this index.

BADGES, EMBLEMS AND INSIGNIA
Peace officers, impersonating, § 538d.
Sale with inference of less rigid law enforcement against displayer, § 146d.

BAGGAGE
Destructive devices, carrying or placing, passenger vehicles for hire, § 12303.1.

BAGS
Containers, generally, this index.

BAIL
Generally, § 1268 et seq.
Acceptance and approval, § 1269b.
Acknowledgment,
  Surrender, certificate, § 1300.
Admission to bail,
  Defined, § 1268.
  Offense triable in inferior court of another county, § 829.
  Persons having authority, § 1277.
Affidavits,
  Exoneration or release, time elapsed, § 1269.
After conviction, § 1272.
  Conditions, § 1273.
After hours, on-call magistrates when court not in session to expedite release, § 810.
After indictment, § 1273.
Amount,
  Arrest warrant, § 1269b.
  Entry in register of actions, § 1269.
  Increase or decrease,
    Arrest for felony without warrant, § 1269c.
  Schedule, § 1295.
Appeals,
  Pending appeal, §§ 1272, 1273.
Application for release on bail lower than provided in bail schedule, § 1269c.
Approval, § 1269a.
Arrest without warrant,
  Increase or reduction, bail schedule, § 1269c.
Attorney for defendant, notice of surrender, § 1300.
Authority,
  Acceptance, § 1269b.
Before conviction, §§ 1271, 1273.
Before indictment, § 1273.
Bench warrant, direction on bench warrant, bailable offense, § 982.
  Nonappearance of defendant for sentence, § 1195 et seq.
Bonds or recognizances, § 1298.
  Application for release on own recognizance, § 1269c.
  Executed by certified, admitted surety insurers, § 1269b.
  Exoneration, narcotics and drug abuse cases, § 1000.2.
  In lieu of bail, forfeitures, sales, § 1298.
  Telephone call, arrested person to bondsman, § 851.5.
Bondsmen, arrest of fugitive without order, § 847.5.
Capital Offenses, this index.
Certificates and certification,
  Acknowledgment of surrender, § 1300.
  Deposit, § 1295.
  Warrant, § 823.
Citations for misdemeanors, § 853.6.
Commitment,
  Appearance, § 1129.
  Increase,
    Arraignment, § 986.
    Felony charge, §§ 985, 986.
Committing authority, admission, § 1277.

BAIL—Cont'd
Conditions, § 1273.
Custody until increased bail given on felony charge, § 985.
Date of bond, entry in register of actions, § 1269.
Declaration of belief, bail schedule use sufficient to assure felon's appearance, § 1269c.
Decrease in amount,
  Arrest for felony without warrant, § 1269c.
Delivery, order admitting to bail, § 1269a.
Deposits,
  Bonds in lieu of money, § 1298.
  In lieu of bail, § 1295 et seq.
  Magistrate, § 823.
  Money in lieu of bail, § 1295 et seq.
  Surrender of defendant, § 1302.
Destruction of bond, § 1269.
Discharge of bail, grant of motion to set aside indictment or information, § 997.
Discretion, §§ 1272, 1274.
Domicile and residence, qualifications, § 1279.
Endorsement,
  Amount on arrest warrant, § 815a.
Enlarging amount, § 1273.
Equity in real property, § 1279.
Escaping bail, bondsman's arrest of fugitive without order, § 847.5.
Exoneration,
  Facts constituting offense, want of, § 1117.
  Grant of motion to set aside indictment or information, § 997.
  Judgment announced, probation granted defendant, § 1195.
  Narcotics and drug abuse cases, § 1000.2.
  Surrender of defendant, § 1300 et seq.
Extradition, this index.
Failure to surrender defendant, § 1301.
Felonies, § 821.
  Uniform countywide bail schedule, § 1269b.
Fire hazards,
  Littering, § 853.6.
Foreign counties, arrests, misdemeanors, §§ 822, 823.
Foreign states, arrests, § 1301.
Forfeitures, § 1269b et seq.
  Absence of accused at trial, § 1043.
  Arrested person released on own recognizance, § 853.6.
  Defendant absent from trial, § 1043.
  Littering, § 853.6.
  Nonappearance,
    Arraignment, § 979.
    Sentence, § 1195.
  Sale of security, § 1298.
Freeholders, qualifications, § 1279.
Fugitives from Justice, this index.
Habeas Corpus, this index.
Hearings, real property equity, determination of value, § 1279.
Highways and roads, littering, § 853.6.
Imprisonment, misdemeanor cases, § 1272.

BAIL

BAIL—Cont'd
Improper surrender of defendant, § 1300.
In lieu of deposit of money, § 1298.
Increase of amount,
  Felony charge, § 985.
Infractions,
  Schedule, § 1269b.
  Uniform countywide bail schedule, § 1269b.
Issuance of order, authority, § 1269b.
Jumping bail, extradition, § 1548 et seq.
Littering, § 853.6.
Magistrates, on-call status when court not in session to expedite release, § 810.
Matter of right, §§ 1271, 1272.
Mentally Deficient and Mentally Ill Persons, this index.
Misdemeanors, uniform countywide bail schedule, § 1269b.
Money in lieu of bail. Deposits, ante.
Municipal Courts, this index.
Names of surety, entry in register of actions, § 1269.
Nature and conditions, § 1273.
New trial, § 1273.
Nonappearance, release on own recognizance, arrest for, § 1318.8.
Nonbailable offenses, § 1270.
  Custody of defendant, § 982.
Notice,
  Application,
    Discretionary bail, § 1274.
    District attorney, § 1274.
  Return of deposit on surrender, § 1302.
  Surrender, § 1302.
    Attorney for defendant, § 1300.
    Time and place to appear, § 1295.
On-call magistrates when court not in session to expedite release, § 810.
Orders of court,
  Discharge, § 1269a.
Parks,
  Littering state parks, § 853.6.
Pending appeal, § 1272.
Place for appearance, authority to set, § 1269b.
Power to arrest defendant, § 1301.
Pretrial diversion programs, § 1001.6.
Prima facie evidence, register of action, § 1269.
Proceedings on taking bail, § 823.
Qualifications, § 1279.
Real estate,
  Equity, § 1279.
  Deposit as security, § 1298.
  Security, § 1298.
Receipt for, deposit,
  Issuance to defendant, § 823.
Recognizance. Bonds or recognizances, generally, ante.
Refunds,
  Discharge of defendant, § 1117.
  Improper surrender of defendant, § 1300.
  Surrender of defendant, § 1302.
Release of defendant, § 1269a.
Release on own recognizance,
  Agreement, filing, § 1318.4.
  Arrest order following release, grounds, § 1318.8.

BAIL—Cont'd
Release on own recognizance—Cont'd
  Bail or other security, § 1318.6.
  Clerk, power to authorize, § 1319.2.
  Discretion of court, § 1318.2.
  Extradition, waiver, § 1318.4.
  Felonies, failure to appear, § 1319.4.
  Misdemeanors, failure to appear, § 1319.6.
  Nonappearance after, § 1319.4.
  Revocation, § 1318.4.
  Subsequent arrest, § 1318.8.
Residence, qualifications, § 1279.
Resubmission of case, § 998.
Return of deposit on surrender, § 1302.
Sale of bonds made in deposit, § 1298.
Saturday or Sunday, delivery, defendant to court or magistrate, § 1301.
Schedule of bail, § 1269b.
Searches and seizures, motion to suppress evidence, appeals, § 1538.5.
Second and subsequent offenses, littering and water pollution convictions, § 853.6.
Signatures,
  Order admitting to bail, § 1269a.
  Order for release, authority, § 1269b.
State bonds, deposit, § 1298.
State parks, littering, § 853.6.
Surrender of defendant, § 1300 et seq.
Taking of bail, defined, § 1269.
Telephone calls, persons arrested, § 851.5.
Time,
  Appearance, authority to set, § 1269b.
  Delivery of defendant to court or magistrate, § 1301.
  Surrender of defendant, § 1300.
Transmittal of bond or cash taken for bail, §§ 823, 1295.
Unauthorized release on bail, § 1269a.
Uniform countywide bail schedule, § 1269b.
United States bonds, deposit, § 1298.
Unreasonable search or seizure motion, § 1538.5.
Value,
  Equity, bonds, § 1298.
  Property, § 1279.
Waiver,
  Surrender of defendant, § 1301.
Warrants,
  Amount of bail, § 1269b.
  Endorsement of admission to bail, § 815a.
  Fixing amount at time of issuance, §§ 815a, 1269b.
  Taking bail, certification, on warrant, § 823.
Water pollution,
  Littering, § 853.6.
Wealth, qualifications, § 1279.
Witnesses, this index.
Written order of discharge, § 1269a.

BAILIFFS
Preliminary examination, presence, § 868.

BAILMENT
Fraud, § 484.
Larceny by fraud, bailed property, § 484.

BANKS AND BANKING
Messengers, carrying firearms, § 1203.1.

BANKS AND BANKING—Cont'd
Weapons,
  Carrying loaded firearms, § 12031.
  Exemptions, § 12027.

BARBITAL
See, also, Drugs and Medicine, generally, this index.

BARBITURATES
See, also, Drugs and Medicine, generally, this index.

BARGAINING
Plea bargaining, § 1192.5.

BARNS
Arson, §§ 447a, 448a.
Burglary, § 459.

BARRACKS
Arson, § 449a.

BARROOMS
Taverns and Saloons, generally, this index.

BASTARDS AND BASTARDY PROCEEDINGS
Illegitimate Children, generally, this index.

BATTERED CHILDREN
Generally, §§ 273a, 273d.
Reports, §§ 11110, 11161.5.

BATTERY
Assault and Battery, generally, this index.

BAY AREA RAPID TRANSIT DISTRICT
Police, powers and duties, § 830.2.

BAYS
Jurisdictions, offense upon vessels navigating, § 783.

BEDS AND BEDDING
Arson, prisoners in local detention facilities, § 451b.
Fires, prisoners in local detention facilities, § 451b.

BEGGING
Disorderly conduct, § 647.

BENCH WARRANTS
Arrest, this index.

BENZEDRINE
See, also, Drugs and Medicine, generally, this index.

BEQUESTS
Gifts, Devises and Bequests, generally, this index.

BESTIALITY
Generally, § 286.5.

BETACETYLMETHADOL
See, also, Drugs and Medicine, generally, this index.

Penal Code

BETA-EUCAINE
See, also, Drugs and Medicine, generally, this index.

BETTING
Gambling, generally, this index.

BEVERAGES
Alcoholic Beverages, generally, this index.

BEZITRAMIDE
See, also, Drugs and Medicine, generally, this index.

BIAS AND PREJUDICE
Insurance, acts to prejudice insurer, § 548.

BICYCLES
Abandoned or unclaimed property, theft, disposal, § 1411.
Joy Riding Law, § 499b.
Lost or stolen bicycles, records, criminal justice information system, § 11111.
Records and recordation, lost or stolen bicycles, criminal justice information system, § 11111.
Sale of unclaimed stolen bicycles, § 1411.
Serial number or identification mark removed, sale, § 537e.
Stolen bicycles,
  Records, criminal justice information system, § 11111.
  Unclaimed property, disposal, § 1411.
Theft, § 499b.
  Disposal of unclaimed property, § 1411.
  Record of stolen bicycles, criminal justice information system, § 11111.
  Taking for temporary use, § 499b.

BIDS AND BIDDING
Auctions and Auctioneers, generally, this index.

BIGAMY
Absence of spouse for five years, § 282.
Annulment of marriage, § 282.
Defined, § 281.
Divorce, § 282.
Exceptions, § 282.
Fines and penalties, § 283.
Void marriage, § 282.

BILLBOARDS
Outdoor Advertising, generally, this index.

BILLIES
Weapons, generally, this index.

BILLS AND NOTES
Commercial Paper, generally, this index.

BILLS OF EXCHANGE
Commercial Paper, generally, this index.

BINGO
Generally, § 326.5.

BIRDS
Fish and Game, generally, this index.

BIRTH CONTROL
Family Planning Services, generally, this index.

BLACKJACKS
Weapons, generally, this index.

BLACKMAIL
Extortion, generally, this index.

BLANKS
Checks, possession with intent to defraud, § 475.
Money orders, possession with intent to defraud, § 475.
Traveler's checks, possession with intent to defraud, §§ 475, 475a.

BLIND PERSONS
Social Services, generally, this index.

BLOWGUN AMMUNITION
Defined, manufacture, sale, etc., § 12581.

BLOWGUNS
Defined, manufacture, sale, etc., § 12580.

BOARD AND ROOM
Extradition, payment of expenses, § 1557.

BOARDING AND LODGING HOUSES
See, also, Hotels, generally, this index.
Disorderly conduct, unpermitted lodging, public or private premises, § 647.
Fraud upon proprietor, § 537.

BOARDS AND COMMISSIONS
Community Release Boards, generally, this index.
Corrections, Board of, generally, this index.
Crime prevention councils, probation officers, cooperation, § 1203.13.
Criminal Identification and Investigation, Bureau of, generally, this index.
False emergency reports, § 148.3.
Fraudulent claims, presentation, § 72.
Limitation of prosecution, § 800.
Limitation of prosecution, fraudulent claims, § 800.
Peace Officers, this index.

BOATS AND BOATING
Arson, § 449a.
Borrowing without permission, § 499b.
Burning, malicious mischief, § 449b.
Destructive devices, carrying or placing on vehicles transporting passengers for hire, § 12303.1.
Explosives, carrying or placing on vehicles transporting passengers for hire, § 12303.1.
Gambling, § 337a.
Jurisdiction, offenses committed on vessels, § 783.
Malicious mischief,
  Burning, § 449b.
Passengers, transporting for hire, carrying or placing explosive or destructive device, § 12303.1.

BOXING

BOATS AND BOATING—Cont'd
Theft, taking for temporary use, § 499b.
Use of boats for gambling purposes, § 337a.

BOMBS
See, also, Explosives, generally, this index.
Carrying or placing on passenger vehicles for hire, § 12303.1.
False report of planting, § 148.1.
Fire bombs, possessing, manufacturing or disposing, § 452.
Making, unlicensed possession of materials or substances, § 12312.
Passenger vehicles for hire, carrying or placing device or explosives, § 12303.1.
Possession, § 12301 et seq.
Reward, person bombing public property, § 1547.
Unlicensed persons, possession of substances or materials with intent to make, § 12312.

BONDS
See, also, Securities, generally, this index.
Counterfeiting, § 470.
False or facsimile bonds, mail or mailing, § 148.1.
Forgery, § 470.
Guards, weapons, §§ 12027, 12031.
Mail and mailing, false or facsimile bonds, § 148.1.

BONDS (OFFICERS AND FIDUCIARIES)
Parole and probation, § 1203.1.

BONE FRACTURE
Assault and battery, fines and penalties, § 243.

BOOKMAKING
Generally, § 337a.

BOOKS AND PAPERS
Alteration of Instruments, generally, this index.
Defined, § 7.
Evidence, preparation, falsification, § 134.
Exhibits, disposition, § 1418.5.
Forgery, generally, this index.
Lewdness and Obscenity, generally, this index.
Lost or Destroyed Documents, generally, this index.
Subpoena duces tecum. Production of Books and Papers, generally, this index.
Written Instruments, generally, this index.

BOXES
Containers, generally, this index.

BOXING AND WRESTLING
Bribery, § 337b et seq.
Officials,
  Offer or attempt to bribe, § 337d.

BOXING

BOXING AND WRESTLING—Cont'd
Officials—Cont'd
  Receiving or attempting to receive bribe, § 337e.

BRANDS, MARKS AND LABELS
Identification marks, removed from radios, etc., purchase, sale, etc., § 537e.
Mace, § 12403.7.
Peace officers, impersonating by wearing, insignia, § 538d.
Tear gas and tear gas weapons, § 12403.7.

BRASS
Junk and secondhand dealers, purchases, determination of seller's title, § 496a.

BRASS KNUCKLES
Weapons, generally, this index.

BRIBERY AND CORRUPTION
Generally, § 67 et seq.
Accomplices and accessories, soliciting aid, § 653f.
Athletics, § 337b et seq.
Compounding or concealing crimes, § 153.
Corruptly, defined, § 7.
Defined, § 7.
Evidence, wiretap evidence, admissibility, § 633.5.
Forfeiture of office, asking or receiving, § 68.
Jurors, § 95.
Limitation of prosecutions, public employee or official, § 800.
Ministerial officers, §§ 67½, 68.
Officers and employees, § 67 et seq.
Parole and probation, eligibility, § 1203.
Solicitation, § 653f.
Wiretap evidence, admissibility, § 633.5.
Witnesses, § 136½ et seq.

BRIDGES
Highways and Roads, this index.

BRUTALITY
Cruel, corporal or unusual punishment, § 673.
Prisoners, inhuman or oppressive treatment of, § 147.

BUFOTENINE
See, also, Drugs and Medicine, generally, this index.

BUILDINGS
See, also, Public Buildings and Works, generally, this index.
Apartment Houses, generally, this index.
Barns, generally, this index.
Bombs and other explosives, false reports, § 148.1.
Burglary, generally, this index.
Construction loan funds, false vouchers, submission, § 484c.
Construction of buildings, diversion of funds, § 484b.
Contractors, generally, this index.
Disorderly conduct, lodging without permission, § 647.

BUILDINGS—Cont'd
Dwellings, generally, this index.
Explosives and bombs, false reports, § 148.1.
Firearms, discharge at occupied building, § 246.
Gambling,
  Use for gambling purposes, § 337a.
Garages, generally, this index.
Keys, unauthorized duplication, § 469.
Malicious mischief,
  Refusal to leave private property upon request, § 602.
Planting of bombs and explosives, false reports, § 148.1.
School Buildings and Grounds, generally, this index.
Squatters, disorderly conduct, § 647.
Trespass, private property, § 602.

BURDEN OF PROOF
Evidence, this index.

BUREAUS
Criminal Identification and Investigation, Bureau of, generally, this index.
Federal Bureau of Investigation, generally, this index.

BURGLAR ALARM COMPANIES
Employees or agents, carrying loaded weapons, § 12031.
Ordinances, § 12031.

BURGLARY
Generally, § 459 et seq.
Accomplices and accessories, soliciting aid, § 653f.
Aircraft, possession of burglary tools, § 466.
Burning bar, use, § 464.
Campers, § 459.
Crow, possession with intent to break or enter, § 466.
Deadly weapons. Weapons, generally, post.
Defined, § 459.
Degrees, § 460.
Dwelling house, degree, § 460.
Fines and penalties, § 461.
Firearms. Weapons, generally, post.
Homicide,
  Degree of offense, § 189.
  Special circumstance, punishment, § 190.2.
House car, § 459.
Instruments, possession with intent to use to break or enter, § 466.
Jurisdiction, property taken transported between jurisdictional territories, § 786.
Keys, alteration or making for use in committing offense, § 466.
Motor vehicles, possession of burglary tools, § 466.
Murder resulting, degree, § 189.
Nighttime,
  Defined, § 463.
  Degree, § 460.
Oxygen lance, § 464.
Parole and probation, § 1203.
  Eligibility, § 1203.06.

BURGLARY—Cont'd
Parole and probation—Cont'd
  Second and subsequent offenses, eligibility, § 1203.08.
Railroads, possession of burglary tools, § 466.
Ships and shipping, possession of burglary tools, § 466.
Soliciting commission, § 653f.
Thermal lance, § 464.
Tools,
  Possession, § 466.
Trailer coach, degree, § 460.
Weapons,
  Accusatory pleading, nature of firearm used, § 969d.
  Enhancement, § 1170.1.

BUSES
See, also, Motor Carriers, generally, this index.
Bombs and explosives, false reports, § 148.1.
Destructive devices, carrying or placing, passenger vehicles for hire, § 12303.1.
Explosives, carrying or placing explosives or destructive devices, passenger vehicles for hire, § 12303.1.
Hijacking reward, § 1547.
Reward,
  Hijacking, reward, § 1547.
  Robbery, § 1547.
Robbery,
  Drivers, § 211a.
  Reward for arrest, § 1547.

BUSINESS AND COMMERCE
Lewdness and obscenity, exploiting obscene matter, evidence, § 311.

BUSINESS CORPORATIONS
Corporations, generally, this index.

BUTYN
See, also, Drugs and Medicine, generally, this index.

CALENDARS
Trial calendars, § 1048.

CAMPERS
Arson, § 447a.
Burglary, § 459.
Weapons, discharge, § 246.

CAMPS
Correctional Institutions, this index.
Defrauding, § 537.
Industrial Farms and Road Camps, generally, this index.
Weapons, carrying loaded firearms, temporary residences, § 12031.

CAMPUS DISORDERS
Generally, § 626 et seq.

CANALBOATS
Defined, § 7.

CANALS
Jurisdiction of offenses upon vessels navigating, § 783.

Penal Code

CANDY AND CONFECTIONS
See, also, Food, generally, this index.
Children and minors,
  Parents liability to provide, §§ 270 et seq.

CANE GUNS
Defined, § 12020.
Weapons, generally, this index.

CANS
Containers, generally, this index.

CAPACITY TO COMMIT CRIME
Elements of offenses, § 26.

CAPITAL OFFENSES
Arguments and conduct of counsel, § 1095.
Bail, § 1270.
  Extradition, § 1552.1.
Destructive devices, § 189.
Determinate Sentence Law, § 1170.
Determination of sentence, trier of fact, § 190.3.
Explosive devices, § 189.
Extradition, bail, § 1552.1.
First degree murder, § 190.
  Trial, separate phases, special circumstances charged, § 190.1.
Fugitives, arrest without warrant, § 1551.1.
Hearings, separate penalty hearings, § 190.4.
Homicide, first degree murder, § 190.
Jury,
  Determination of sentence, § 190.3.
Perjury, procuring execution of innocent person, § 128.
Reward for apprehension of person charged with capital offense, § 1547.
Separate penalty hearings, § 190.4.
Trial,
  Arguments of counsel, § 1095.
  First degree murder, separate phases, special circumstances charged, § 190.1.

CAPITAL PUNISHMENT
Generally, § 1105 et seq.
Appeals,
  State, stay of execution, § 1243.
  Stay of execution, § 1243.
  Time requirement, decision of state supreme court, § 190.6.
Application for modification of verdict, ruling on application, § 190.4.
Assault with deadly weapon by life prisoner, § 4500.
Attempts, crime punishable by death penalty, § 664.
Children and minors, § 190.5.
Classification of offenses, § 17.
Delivery for execution,
  Judgment, § 1202a.
Determination by trier of fact, § 190.3.
Discretion of court or jury, § 190.
Documentary exhibits, disposition, § 1418.5.
Enhancement of prison terms, prior offenses, § 667.5.
Exhibits, disposition, § 1417 et seq.

CAPITAL PUNISHMENT—Cont'd
First degree murder, § 190.
  Special circumstances, §§ 190.2, 190.3.
Homicide, first degree murder, § 190.
  Special circumstances charged, § 190.2.
Jury,
  Determination, § 190.3.
Life-term prisoner committing assault, § 4500.
Minors, § 190.5.
Murder in first degree, § 190.
  Circumstances requisite, § 190.2.
Pardons, reprieves and commutations,
  Applicability of provisions, § 4852.01.
Perjury, procuring execution of innocent person, § 128.
Persons under 18, § 190.5.
Presence of principal during commission of crime, § 190.5.
Principal, presence during commission of crime, § 190.5.
Rescue, prisoner under death penalty, § 4550.
Time,
  State supreme court decision, § 190.6.
Verdict,
  Application for modification, ruling on application, § 190.4.

CARD ISSUER
Defined, credit cards, § 484d.

CARD MACHINES
Slot Machines, generally, this index.

CARDHOLDER
Defined, credit cards, § 484d.

CARDS
Credit Cards, generally, this index.
Gambling, generally, this index.
Peace officers, impersonating by exhibiting, § 538d.

CAREER CRIMINAL PROSECUTION PROGRAM
Generally, § 999b et seq.

CARNAL KNOWLEDGE
Generally, §§ 261.5, 264.
Incest, § 285.
Rape, generally, this index.

CARRIERS
Destructive devices, carrying or placing, passenger vehicles for hire, § 12303.1.
Explosives, carrying or placing explosives or destructive devices, passenger vehicles for hire, § 12303.1.
Hijacking, reward, § 1547.
Jurisdiction of offenses committed, § 783.
Motor Carriers, generally, this index.
Railroads, generally, this index.
Reward,
  Hijacking, § 1547.
  Robbery, § 1547.
Robbery, reward, § 1547.
Ships and Shipping, generally, this index.
Street Railways, generally, this index.

CERTIFIED

CARRIERS—Cont'd
Weapons,
  Carrying loaded firearms, § 12031.
  Exemption, § 12027.

CARRYING DANGEROUS WEAPONS
Weapons, generally, this index.

CARS
Motor Vehicles, generally, this index.
Railroads, generally, this index.

CARTONS
Containers, generally, this index.

CATS
See, also, Animals, generally, this index.

CATTLE
Animals, generally, this index.

CAUSTIC CHEMICALS
Assault, § 244.

CEMETERIES AND DEAD BODIES
Coroners, generally, this index.

CENSORSHIP
Correctional institutions, mail and packages, § 2601.

CENTRAL NERVOUS SYSTEM DEPRESSANTS
See, also, Drugs and Medicine, generally, this index.

CEREBRAL PALSY
Competency to stand trial, § 1370.1.

CERTIFICATES AND CERTIFICATION
Arrest and firearm training, security guards, § 12033.
Bail, this index.
Detention certificates, release of arrested person without formal charge, § 851.6.
Firearms and arrest training, security guards, § 12033.
Guards, firearm and arrest training, § 12033.
Mentally deficient and mentally ill persons, restoration of sanity, § 1372.
Peace officer standards and training commission certificates, peace officers, requirement, § 832.4.
Peace officers, impersonating by exhibiting, § 538d.
Rehabilitation and pardon, § 4852.01 et seq.
Security guards, firearm and arrest training, § 12033.
Telegraphs and telephones, subpoenas, telegraphic copies, § 1328b.

CERTIFICATES OF REHABILITATION
Petitions, filing time, § 4852.06.

CERTIFIED COPIES
Fugitives from justice, sworn charge or complaint in affidavit attached to warrant for arrest, § 1551.

CERTIFIED

CERTIFIED COPIES—Cont'd
Statement of views of judge and district attorney respecting person convicted, § 1203.01.

CERTIFIED OR REGISTERED MAIL
Mail and Mailing, this index.

CHARACTER AND REPUTATION
Disorderly houses, common repute, evidence, § 315.
Mercantile character, false reports, procurement, theft, § 484.
Prostitution, disorderly houses, common repute, evidence, § 315.

CHARGE TO JURY
Instructions to jury, generally. Trial, this index.

CHARITIES
Bingo, § 326.5.
Solicitation, public places, § 647.

CHARTERS
Counterfeiting or forgery, § 470.

CHEATS AND CHEATING
False Pretenses, generally, this index.
Fraud, generally, this index.

CHECKS
Commercial Paper, this index.

CHEMICALS, CHEMISTRY AND CHEMISTS
Assault with chemicals, § 244.

CHICKENS
Poultry and Poultry Products, generally, this index.

CHIEF ADMINISTRATIVE OFFICER
Defined, campus disorders, § 626.

CHIEF OF POLICE
Police, this index.

CHILD CARE CENTERS
Battered and sexually molested children, administrator's report, § 11161.5.

CHILD COUNSELORS
Privileges and immunities, battered or sexually molested children, reports, § 11161.5.

CHILD MOLESTATION LAW
Generally, § 647a.

CHILD PORNOGRAPHY
Generally, §§ 311.2, 311.4.

CHILD STEALING
See, also, Kidnapping, generally, this index.
Defined, § 278.

CHILDBIRTH
Murder of fetus, § 187.

CHILDREN AND MINORS
Abandonment. Desertion, generally, this index.

CHILDREN AND MINORS—Cont'd
Abduction, § 278.
 Persons under 18 for purposes of prostitution, § 267.
Abortion, death of fetus, murder, § 187.
Abuse. Cruelty to child, generally, post.
Acquittal, sealing court records, § 851.7.
Adoption proceedings, removal of child from county, § 280.
Adult prisoners, confinement with children, § 273b.
Advising children to commit crime, § 31.
Annoyance or molestation of children under 18, vagrancy, § 647a.
Arrest,
 Cruelty to children, records, § 11110.
Artificial insemination, husband as father of child, § 270.
Bastardy proceedings. Illegitimate Children, generally, this index.
Battered children. Cruelty to child, generally, post.
Bingo, § 326.5.
Capacity to commit crime, § 26.
Capital punishment, § 190.5.
Child beating, § 273d.
Child stealing, defined, § 278.
Cigarettes and cigars,
 Sale or furnishing to minor under eighteen, § 308.
Concealment, decoying or enticing to detain and conceal, § 784.
Confinement of minors with adults, § 273b.
Contributing to Delinquency of a Minor, generally, this index.
Corporal injury, infliction upon child, § 273d.
Cruelty to child, §§ 273a, 273d.
 Probation officers, reports, § 11161.6.
 Reports, § 11161.5.
  Physician or surgeon, §§ 11110, 11161.5.
Custody, abduction of child, § 278.
Damages, shoplifting, liability of parents, § 490.5.
Death,
 Cruelty to children, § 273a.
 Fetus, murder, § 187.
Death penalty, § 190.5.
Decoying or enticing to detain and conceal, § 784.
Defense,
 Justifiable homicide, § 197.
Defined, harmful matter, § 313.
Dependent children. Juvenile Delinquents and Dependents, generally, this index.
Descent and Distribution, generally, this index.
Desertion, generally, this index.
Disorderly houses,
 Admitting or keeping minors, § 309.
Employment,
 Perform obscene act, §§ 311.4, 311.9.
Encouraging children to commit crime, principals, § 31.
Enticement, § 784.
 Females under 18 for prostitution, § 266.

CHILDREN AND MINORS—Cont'd
Evidence,
 Libel and slander proceedings, opening of sealed records, § 851.7.
Expenses, abduction, return of child, § 278.
False representation that child is orphan, § 271a.
Females, unlawful sexual intercourse, §§ 261.5, 264.
Fetus, murder, § 187.
Fines and penalties, abduction of child, § 278.
Firearms. Weapons, generally, post.
Food, furnishing, parent's liability, § 270 et seq.
Fraud, child represented to be orphan, § 271a.
Gifts, support, ability to contribute, § 270.
Guardian and Ward, generally, this index.
Harmful matter, distribution or exhibition, § 313 et seq.
Health, endangering, § 273a.
Homicide,
 Accident and misfortune while correcting, excusable, § 195.
 Acts upon body of child under 14, special circumstance, punishment, § 190.2.
 Fetus, murder, § 187.
 Justifiable, defense, § 197.
Houses of ill fame,
 Admitting or keeping minors, § 309.
Illegitimate Children, generally, this index.
Indecent liberties, probation, second and subsequent offenses, eligibility, § 1203.08.
Jurisdiction, § 784.
 Enticing, etc., minor child away from parent, § 784.
Justifiable homicide, defense, § 197.
Juvenile Delinquents and Dependents, generally, this index.
Kidnapping, § 278.
Lewdness and Obscenity, this index.
Life, endangering, § 273a.
Machine guns, permit, § 12230 et seq.
Medical attendance and treatment, § 270 et seq.
Miscreant child. Juvenile Delinquents and Dependents, generally, this index.
Misrepresentation as parent or guardian, exhibition of harmful matter, § 313.1.
Mistreatment. Cruelty to child, generally, ante.
Molesting or annoying children under eighteen, vagrancy, § 647a.
Murder, death of fetus, § 187.
Neglected child. Juvenile Delinquents and Dependents, generally, this index.
Nude pictures, distribution or exhibition, § 313 et seq.
Oral copulation, § 288a.
Pain and suffering, cruelty to children, § 273a.
Physical pain, punishing child, § 273a.

Penal Code

CHILDREN AND MINORS—Cont'd
Priorities, trial calendar, § 1048.
Prisoners, confinement of minors with adults, § 273b.
Probation officers, child abuse, reports, § 11161.6.
Prostitution, this index.
Punishment,
  Cruel punishment, reports, §§ 11110, 11161.5.
  Inhuman corporal punishment, § 273d.
  Unjustifiable, § 273a.
Records, sealing court records, § 851.7.
Reports,
  Abused, battered or sexually molested children, § 11161.5.
    Probation officers, § 11161.6.
  Cruelty to children, §§ 11110, 11161.5.
    Form, § 11161.7.
Sales, tear gas and tear gas weapons, § 12403.7.
Sealing records of offenses, § 851.7.
Services, shoplifting, working off fine, § 490.5.
Sex materials,
  Distribution or exhibition, § 313 et seq.
Shelter, § 270 et seq.
Shoplifting, liability of parents, § 490.5.
Sodomy, § 286.
Stealing of children, § 278.
Support, generally, this index.
Tear gas and tear gas weapons, sale, § 12403.7.
Tobacco, sale or furnishing to minor under 18, § 308.
Torts,
  Battered children, reports, immunity, § 11161.5.
  Shoplifting, liability of parents, § 490.5.
Trial, precedence where minor is victim or detained as material witness, § 1048.
Unlawful sexual intercourse, §§ 261.5, 264.
Victim, a minor, speedy trial, § 1048.
Weapons,
  Machine guns, § 12230 et seq.
  Sale, § 12072.
Wearing apparel, § 270 et seq.
Youth Authority, generally, this index.

CHIROPRACTORS
Battered children, reports, § 11161.5.
  Form, § 11161.7.
Cruelty to children, reports, §§ 11110, 11161.5.

CHLORAL BETAINE
See, also, Drugs and Medicine, generally, this index.

CHLOROFORM
Commission of felony, administering to effectuate, § 222.

CHOSES IN ACTION
Defined, § 7.

CHURCHES
Religious Organizations and Societies, generally, this index.

CIGARETTES AND CIGARS
Children and minors,
  Sales, etc., § 308.
Delivery of unsolicited products to dwellings, §§ 308, 308b.
Fire hazards, littering, bail, § 853.6.
Littering, § 374.
  Bail, § 853.6.
Sale or furnishing to minors,
  Under 18, § 308.

CINEMA
Motion Pictures, generally, this index.

CITATION
Process, generally, this index.

CITIES
Municipalities, generally, this index.

CITIES AND COUNTIES
Criminal history information,
  Local summary criminal history information, furnishing, § 13300 et seq.
Probation officers, generally. Parole and Probation, this index.

CITIZENS AND CITIZENSHIP
Adult probation officers, § 1203.6.
Fully pardoned convicts, § 4852.17.

CIVIL DEFENSE
War and Civil Defense, generally, this index.

CIVIL PROTECTIVE CUSTODY
Inebriates, § 647.

CIVIL RIGHTS
Correctional Institutions, this index.
Pardons and reprieves, restoration, § 4852.01 et seq.
Parole and probation, restoration, § 1203.4.
Prisoners, §§ 2600, 2601.

CIVIL RULES
Competency of witnesses, application in criminal actions, § 1321.

CIVIL SERVICE
Community release board,
  Appointing authority, § 5075.

CLASSIFICATION OF OFFENSES
Generally, § 17.

CLEANING, DYEING AND PRESSING
Burglar tools, coin laundry machines, § 466.3.
Machinery and equipment, burglar tools, coin-operated machines, § 466.3.

CLERGYMEN
Children and minors, battered children, reports, §§ 11110, 11161.5.
Reports,
  Battered children, § 11110.
  Cruelty to children, § 11161.5.

CLERKS
Embezzlement, § 508.

COLLEGES

CLERKS OF COURT
Bench warrant, issuance, § 980 et seq.
Blank subpoenas, issuance, § 1326.
Release of prisoner on own recognizance, authority, § 1319.2.
Statement of views of judge and district attorney respecting defendant and crime committed, filing, § 1203.01.
Subpoenas issued, § 1326.
Warrant of arrest, complaint and undertaking,
  Delivery to on proceedings on taking bail, § 823.
  Offense triable in inferior court of another county, § 829.

CLONITAZENE
See, also, Drugs and Medicine, generally, this index.

CLOSE PURSUIT
Fresh Pursuit, generally, this index.

CLOTHING
Wearing Apparel, generally, this index.

COAL AND COAL MINES
Arson, § 449a.

COBEY WORK FURLOUGH LAW
Generally, § 1208.

COCA LEAVES
See, also, Drugs and Medicine, generally, this index.

COCAINE
See, also, Drugs and Medicine, generally, this index.

COCKFIGHTING
Clipping comb, prima facie evidence of intent, § 597j.

CODEINE
See, also, Drugs and Medicine, generally, this index.

CODICIL
Wills, § 7.

COERCION
Duress or Coercion, generally, this index.

COHABITATION
Corporal injury, inflicting, crimes and offenses, § 273.5.
Receiving money for placing in custody for purposes, § 266d.

COIN OPERATED DEVICES
Slot Machines, generally, this index.
Vending Machines, generally, this index.

COINS
Vending machines, coin operated, use of slugs or counterfeited coins, § 640a.

COLLEGES AND UNIVERSITIES
Buildings and grounds, possession of firearms, § 626.9.
Campus disorders, § 626.
Chief administrative officer, defined, campus disorders, § 626.

COLLEGES

COLLEGES AND UNIVERSITIES
—Cont'd
Community colleges,
  Buildings and grounds, disruptive persons, denial of access to campus facilities, § 626 et seq.
  Defined, disturbance of the peace, § 415.5.
  Demonstrations, § 415.5.
    Denial of access to campus or facilities, § 626 et seq.
  Disorderly conduct, § 415.5.
  Disturbing the peace, § 415.5.
  Dormitories, searches and seizures, § 626.11.
  Keys to public buildings, unauthorized duplication, § 469.
  Obstructing teachers or students, § 602.10.
  Officers and employees, disruptive persons, denial of access to campus facilities, § 626 et seq.
  Searches and seizures, § 626.11.
  Students, obstructing, § 602.10.
  Teachers, obstructing, § 602.10.
  Trespass, disruptive presence of employees or students, § 626 et seq.
Defined,
  Denial of access to disruptive person, § 626.
Disciplinary proceedings, unlawful searches and seizures, § 626.11.
Disorderly conduct, § 415.5.
Disruptive persons, denial of access to campus or facility, § 626 et seq.
Disturbances, § 415.5.
Dormitories,
  Disruptive persons, denial of access to campus or facilities, § 626 et seq.
  Searches and seizures, § 626.11.
Evidence, administrative proceedings, unlawful searches and seizures, § 626.11.
Fines and penalties,
  Disruptive persons, denial of access to campus or facilities, § 626 et seq.
Firearms, possession, § 626.9.
Guns, possession of firearms on grounds, § 626.9.
Jail prisoners, work furloughs, § 1208.
Junior colleges. Community colleges, generally, ante.
Keys to public buildings, unauthorized duplication, § 469.
Leases, dormitory, unlawful searches and seizures, § 626.11.
Malicious mischief, obstructing teachers or students, § 602.10.
Obstructing, teachers or students, § 602.10.
Peace officers,
  Assault, § 245.
  Possession of firearms, § 626.9.
  Status, § 830.2.
Prisoners, work furloughs, participation, § 1208.
Privacy, right to privacy, student dormitories, § 626.11.
Public policy, searches and seizures, student dormitories, § 626.11.
Right of privacy, student dormitories, § 626.11.

COLLEGES AND UNIVERSITIES
—Cont'd
Searches and seizures, teachers, unlawful searches and seizures, § 626.11.
Second and subsequent offenses, disturbances, § 415.5.
Students and employees,
  Disruptive persons, denial of access to campus or facility, § 626 et seq.
  Obstruction, § 602.10.
Teachers,
  Obstruction, § 602.10.
  Searches and seizures, unlawful searches and seizures, § 626.11.
Trespass, § 626 et seq.
University of California,
  Buildings and grounds, possession of firearms, § 626.9.
  Disorderly conduct, disturbances, § 415.5.
  Disruptive person, denial of access to campus or facilities, § 626 et seq.
  Disturbances, § 415.5.
  Firearms, possession, § 626.9.
  Obstructing teachers or students, § 602.10.
  Police,
    Peace officer status, § 830.2.
  State university, defined, campus disorders, § 626.
  Students, obstructing, § 602.10.
  Students and employees, disruptive persons, exclusion from campus, § 626 et seq.
  Teachers, obstructing, § 602.10.
  Trespass, § 626 et seq.
  Weapons, possession of firearms, § 626.9.
Waiver, searches and seizures, student dormitories, § 626.11.
Weapons, possession, § 626.9.
Work furlough programs, jail prisoners, § 1208.

COMBUSTIBLES
Explosives, generally, this index.
Possession with intent to burn property, § 452.

COMMENTS OF JUDGES
Generally, § 1093.

COMMERCE
Business and Commerce, generally, this index.

COMMERCIAL PAPER
Bad checks, § 476a.
Checks,
  Blanks, possession with intent to defraud, § 475.
  Counterfeiting, § 470.
  Credit, defined, § 476a.
  Fictitious, making, possessing, uttering, with intent to defraud, § 476.
  Forgery, § 470.
  Insufficient funds, § 476a.
  Making fictitious checks with intent to defraud, § 476.
  Penalties, issuance without sufficient funds or credit, § 476a.
  Possessing fictitious checks with intent to defraud, § 476.

COMMERCIAL PAPER—Cont'd
Checks—Cont'd
  Protest, insufficient funds, presumption of knowledge, § 476a.
  Uttering fictitious checks with intent to defraud, § 476.
Counterfeiting or forgery, § 470 et seq.
Drafts,
  Counterfeiting, § 470.
  Credit, defined, § 476a.
  Forgery, § 470.
Embezzlement, description of property, evidence, § 1131.
Fictitious, making, possessing, uttering, etc., with intent to defraud, § 476.
Forgery. Counterfeiting or forgery, generally, ante.
Indictment and information,
  Larceny or embezzlement, § 1131.
Passing fictitious instruments with intent to defraud, § 476.
Possession or receipt of forged instrument with intent to pass to defraud, § 475.
Protest, insufficiency of funds or credit, presumptive evidence of knowledge, § 476a.
Theft,
  Description, of property, evidence, § 1131.
  Sufficiency of evidence to sustain allegations of description, § 1131.
  Weight and sufficiency of evidence, theft or embezzlement, § 1131.

COMMISSIONS
Boards and Commissions, generally, this index.

COMMITMENT
Bail, this index.
Juvenile Delinquents and Dependents, this index.
Mentally Deficient and Mentally Ill Persons, this index.

COMMON CARRIERS
Carriers, generally, this index.
Motor Carriers, generally, this index.

COMMON SCHOOL DISTRICTS
Schools and School Districts, generally, this index.

COMMUNICATIONS
Police radio service communications, interception, § 636.5.
Prison inmates, unauthorized communications with, § 4570 et seq.
Simulating official inquiries, § 146b.

COMMUNITY COLLEGES
Colleges and Universities, this index.

COMMUNITY PROGRAMS
Work furlough programs, jail prisoners, § 1208.

COMMUNITY RELEASE BOARDS
Administrative head, § 5075.
Appointment by governor, § 5075.
Chairman, § 5075.

Penal Code

COMMUNITY RELEASE BOARDS
—Cont'd
Civil service,
  Appointing authority, § 5075.
Correctional Institutions, generally, this index.
Cross section of population, § 5075.
Determinate sentences, § 1170 et seq.
Parole and Probation, generally, this index.
Parole date, setting, § 1170.2.
Prior members of adult authority or women's board of terms and parole, § 5075.
Reappointment, § 5075.
Sentence and punishment, powers and duties, § 1170.
Term of office, § 5075.
Vacancy in office, § 5075.

COMPENSATION AND SALARIES
Adult probation officers, board, § 1203.6.
Correctional Institutions, this index.
Industrial Farms and Road Camps, this index.
Jails, this index.
Officers and employees, asking or receiving, § 70.
Pardons and reprieves,
  Person procuring or assisting, § 4807.2.
Work Furlough Law, disposition, § 1208.

COMPETENCY
Witnesses, this index.

COMPETENT COURT
Defined, jurisdiction, § 691.

COMPLAINTS
Abrogation, distinction between accessories and principals, § 971.
Accusatory pleading, § 691.
Affidavit, supporting complaint charging felony, § 806.
Arrest without warrant, duty to file, § 849.
Autrefois acquit, § 1016 et seq.
Autrefois attaint, § 1016 et seq.
Autrefois convict, § 1016 et seq.
Change of plea, § 1016 et seq.
Citation for misdemeanor violations, filing complaints, § 853.9.
Consolidation accusatory pleading, § 954.
Dangerous weapons, commission of felonies, § 969c.
Degrees, principals in first and second degree, distinction abrogated, § 971.
Different statements of same offense, § 954.
Distinction between accessories and principals abrogated, § 971.
Election between counts, § 954.
Entry of plea, § 1017.
Filing after citation for misdemeanor, § 853.9.
Former acquittal, plea, § 1016 et seq.
Former conviction, plea, § 1016 et seq.
Former jeopardy, § 1016 et seq.
Forms,
  Complaints before magistrates, § 806.
  Pleas, § 1017.
Guilty Plea, generally, this index.

COMPLAINTS—Cont'd
Inferior courts,
  Offenses triable, § 740.
Insanity plea, § 1016 et seq.
Joinder of counts, § 954.
Joinder of offenses, § 954.
Judicial notice,
  Pleading matters judicially noticed, § 961.
Justice Courts, this index.
Magistrates, proceedings, § 806 et seq.
Misdemeanors, limitation of time for filing, § 801.
Multiple defendants, conviction or acquittal of one or more, § 970.
Multiple offenses, § 954.
Multiple pleas, § 1016 et seq.
Nolo Contendere, generally, this index.
Not Guilty Plea, generally, this index.
Offense triable in another county,
  Delivery of complaint, § 828.
  Inferior court of, transmittal, § 829.
  Warrant of arrest, requisites, § 827.
Open court, entry of plea, § 1017.
Parties, naming, § 950.
Police, citizens' complaints against personnel of departments, procedure, § 832.5.
Presumptions, § 961.
Sanity, § 1016.
Principals, distinction between accessories and principals, abrogated, § 971.
Probable cause, felony charge, affidavit establishing, § 806.
Statement of offense charged, §§ 950, 952.
Sufficiency, § 959.
Time, pleas, § 1017.
Time offense committed, pleading, § 955.
Title of action, § 950.
Weapons, commission of felonies, § 969c.

COMPOUNDING CRIMES
Generally, § 153.

COMPTOMETER
Serial number or identification mark removed, sale, etc., § 537e.

CONCEALED WEAPONS
Weapons, this index.

CONCEALMENT
Accomplices and accessories, aiding felons, § 32.
Adoption of children, concealment or removal of child, § 280.
Aiding felons, § 32.
Bomb or other explosive, false report of placing or concealing, § 148.1.
Compounding or concealing crimes, § 153.
Documentary evidence, § 135.
Fugitives from justice, § 32.
Insured property, defrauding insurer, § 548.
Minor child, parent or guardian, § 784.
Public officers' accounts, § 424.
Receiving stolen goods, § 496.
Secondhand dealers, stolen goods, § 496.
Sniperscope, § 468.

CONFLICT

CONCURRENT SENTENCES
Uniform sentence, § 1170.3.

CONCUSSION
Assault and battery, fines and penalties, § 243.

CONDEMNATION
See, also, Confiscation, generally, this index.
Fighting animals or birds seized, § 599aa.
Fish and game, paraphernalia, fighting animals or birds, seizure, § 599aa.
Obscene material, § 312.
Weapons, machine guns, § 12251.

CONDUCT OF COUNSEL
Argument and Conduct of Counsel, generally, this index.

CONFESSIONS
Previous conviction, reading to jury, § 1093.

CONFIDENTIAL OR PRIVILEGED INFORMATION
Access, records and reports, § 13200 et seq.
Children and minors, criminal records, sealing, § 851.7.
Corrections department director, diagnostic reports, § 1203.03.
Definitions, invasion of privacy, § 632.
Diagnostic report, convicted defendant, § 1203.03.
Grand jury,
  Indictment or information for felony before defendant's arrest, § 924.
  Proceedings, §§ 915, 924 et seq.
Indictment or information for felony, disclosure before defendant's arrest, § 924.
Juvenile delinquents and dependents,
  Libel and slander proceedings, opening of sealed records, §§ 851.7, 1203.45.
Libel and slander,
  Juvenile delinquents and dependents, opening of sealed records, § 851.7.
Right of access, records and reports, § 13200 et seq.
Sealed records, libel and slander proceedings, juvenile delinquents and dependents, opening of records, § 851.7.
Sex offenders, registration forms, § 290.

CONFISCATION
See, also, Condemnation, generally, this index.
Destructive devices, § 12307.
Firearms, disposition, § 12028.
Machine guns, § 12251.
Obscene material, § 312.
Weapons, disposition, § 12028.

CONFLICT OF INTEREST
Adverse or Pecuniary Interest, generally, this index.

CONFLICT

CONFLICT OF LAWS
Generally, § 778 et seq.

CONSCIOUSNESS
Capacity to commit crime, § 26.

CONSECUTIVE SENTENCES
Uniform sentences, § 1170.3.

CONSERVATORS AND CONSERVATORSHIP
Public conservators, limitation of prosecutions, § 800.

CONSERVATORS OF THE PEACE
Peace Officers, generally, this index.

CONSOLIDATION
Accusatory pleadings, § 954.

CONSPIRACY
Generally, § 182 et seq.
Defined, § 182.
Eavesdropping, wiretapping, invasion of privacy, § 631.
Evidence, §§ 184, 1104.
Fines and penalties, § 182.
Indictment and information,
   Allegation of overt acts, § 1104.
   Conspiracy to indict another for a crime, § 182.
Invasion of privacy, wiretapping and electronic eavesdropping, § 631.
Overt acts,
   Alleging and proving, § 1104.
   Necessity within state, §§ 184, 1104.
Probation, § 1203.
Telegraph or telephone messages, forging, § 474.
Venue, §§ 182, 184.
Wiretapping, invasion of privacy, § 631.

CONSTABLES
See also,
   Peace Officers, generally, this index.
   Sheriffs, generally, this index.
Generally, §§ 830, 830.1.
Arrest, generally, this index.
Authority, §§ 830, 830.1.
Concealed Weapons Law, applicability, § 12027.
Courses of instruction,
   Arrests, § 832.
   Weapons, use of firearms, § 832.
Criminal history information, local summary criminal history information, furnishing, § 13300 et seq.
Dangerous Weapons Law, exemption, § 12002.
Delay in taking arrested persons before magistrate, § 145.
Escapes, aiding, § 4533.
Jurisdiction, § 830.1.
Powers and duties, §§ 830, 830.1.
Refusal to aid in arrest, etc., § 142.
Riotous assemblies, command to disperse, §§ 726, 727.
Training,
   Arrests, training for making arrests, § 832.
   Weapons, use of firearms, § 832.

CONSTABLES—Cont'd
Unlawful or riotous assembly, command to disburse, §§ 726, 727.

CONTAINERS
Defrauding innkeepers, § 537.
Depositing containers on highways, etc., § 588a.

CONTEMPT
Generally, §§ 166, 1324, 1331.
Affidavits, subpoena, failure to appear, agreement to appear at different time, § 1331.5.
Appearance, subpoena, failure to appear, agreement to appear at different time, § 1331.5.
Conduct constituting in presence of jury, § 166.
Criminal contempt, § 166.
Jail prisoners, work release, § 1208.
Jails,
   Confinement of persons, § 4000 et seq.
   Good time allowance, § 4019.
Maximum period of confinement, § 19a.
Process, § 166.
   Resistance, § 724.
Resistance to process, § 724.
Self incrimination, privilege,
   Compelling testimony, § 1324.
Subpoena, witness disobeying, etc., § 1331.

CONTESTS
Sporting events, bribery, § 337b et seq.

CONTINUANCE
Parole and probation, hearing, § 1203.
Trial, this index.

CONTRABAND
Correctional institutions, inspection, § 2601.
Exhibits in criminal prosecutions, release, § 1418.6.
Weapons, generally, this index.

CONTRACTORS
Construction loan funds, false vouchers, § 484c.
Diversion of funds or property, § 484b.

CONTRACTS
Adverse or Pecuniary Interest, generally, this index.
Conflict of interest. Adverse or Pecuniary Interest, generally, this index.
Construction funds, diversion, § 484b.
Fraud, theft by fraud, § 484.
Jail prisoners, work release, § 1208.
Larceny by fraud, § 484.
Personal interest. Adverse or Pecuniary Interest, generally, this index.
Probation modification, waiver of court appearance, right to counsel, § 1203.2.
Theft by fraud, § 484.
Work furlough administrator, facilities and services, § 1208.

CONTRIBUTING TO DELINQUENCY OF A MINOR
Generally, § 272.
Registration of offenders, § 290.

CONTRIBUTIONS
Gifts, Devises and Bequests, generally, this index.

CONTROLLED SUBSTANCES
Drugs and Medicine, this index.

CONVERSION
Embezzlement, generally, this index.
Real property into personal property, theft, §§ 487b, 487c.

CONVEYANCES
Deeds and Conveyances, generally, this index.

CONVICTION OF CRIME
Accomplice, testimony, § 1111.
Attempt to commit crime even though offense perpetrated, § 663.
Autrefois convict. Prior convictions, generally, post.
Bar to subsequent prosecution, former conviction, § 1023.
Felonies, prior conviction, punishment, § 666.
Finding of court, condition precedent, § 689.
Jurisdiction,
   Concurrent, conviction in another state or country, § 793.
   Two or more courts, jeopardy in another court, § 794.
Multiple offenses, § 954.
   Direction for concurrent or consecutive terms, § 669.
One or more of several defendants, § 970.
Petit theft, prior conviction of, punishment, § 666.
Prior convictions,
   Bar to subsequent prosecution, § 1023.
   Felony, punishment for petty theft, § 666.
   Foreign conviction, punishment for subsequent offense, § 668.
   Indictment, information or complaint, § 1016 et seq.
   Petit theft, punishment, § 666.
   Plea of guilty, condition precedent, § 689.
   Proceeding on discovery of after sentence for subsequent offense, § 669.
Probation, grant of probation without imposition of sentence, § 17.
Proceeding on discovery of prior conviction after sentence for subsequent offense, § 669.
Records,
   Restriction on judge reading conviction reports, § 1204.5.
Second and Subsequent Offenses, generally, this index.
Several defendants, one or more of convicted, § 970.
Testimony of accomplices, § 1111.

Penal Code   **CORRECTIONAL**

CONVICTION OF CRIME—Cont'd
Verdict of jury, condition, precedent, § 689.
Verdict to state offense for which convicted, § 954.
Weapons, possession, § 12021.

CONVICTS
Correctional Institutions, generally, this index.

COPPER
Purchasing, determination of seller's right, § 496a.

CORONERS
Deputy, peace officers, § 830.10.
Peace officers, § 830.10.

CORPORAL PUNISHMENT
Generally, § 673.

CORPORATIONS
Agents, service of process, § 1392.
Appearance, § 1396.
  Guilty plea, §§ 1396, 1427.
Attorneys, criminal charges, representation, § 1396.
Banks and Banking, generally, this index.
Burglar alarm companies, employees or agents, carrying loaded weapons, § 12031.
Cashier, service of summons, § 1392.
Counsel, § 1396.
Fines and penalties, collection, § 1397.
Guilty plea,
  Appearance, §§ 1396, 1427.
Managing agent, service of summons, § 1392.
Not guilty plea, § 1396.
  Inferior courts, § 1427.
Officers and employees,
  Burglar alarm companies, carrying loaded weapons, § 12031.
  Service of summons, § 1392.
Personal property, execution, § 1397.
Pleas, § 1396.
  Not guilty, § 1396.
  Inferior courts, § 1427.
President, service of summons, § 1392.
Process. Summons, generally, post.
Real property, execution, § 1397.
Religious Organizations and Societies, generally, this index.
Secretary, service of summons, § 1392.
Service of summons, § 1392.
Shares and shareholders,
  Counterfeiting or forgery, certificates for shares, § 470.
  Theft or embezzlement, sufficiency of evidence to sustain allegations of description, § 1131.
Stock and stockholders. Shares and shareholders, generally, ante.
Summons,
  Agent for service of process, § 1392.
  Inferior courts, § 1427.
  Method of service, § 1392.
    Traffic violations, § 1427.
Time, service of summons, § 1392.
Traffic violations, service of process, § 1427.
Water Companies, generally, this index.

CORRECTIONAL INSTITUTIONS
Abstract of judgment, delivery to warden, § 1216.

CORRECTIONAL INSTITUTIONS —Cont'd
Actions and proceedings,
  Prison custodian, failure to allow attorney visitation, § 825.
Alcoholic beverages,
  Bringing into or within grounds, § 4573.
Assault and battery, § 4500 et seq.
  Against noninmates, § 4131.5.
Attorneys,
  Correspondence, of civil rights of prisoners, § 2601.
  Right to visit prisoner, § 825.
Black-jacks, possession, § 4502.
Bringing defendant before court for judgment, procedure, § 1194.
Camps,
  Fraudulent entry, § 4570.5.
Censorship of mail and packages, § 2601.
Certificates of rehabilitation and pardon, § 4852.01 et seq.
Children and minors, confinement with adult prisoners, § 273b.
Civil rights, § 2600 et seq.
Classification of offenses, § 17.
Communications with prisoners, § 4570 et seq.
Community Release Boards, generally, this index.
Compensation and salaries,
  Probationers, public works, § 1203.1.
Containers sent to inmates, inspection, § 2601.
Controlled substances. Drugs and medicine, generally, post.
County jails. Jails, generally, this index.
Credit on term of imprisonment,
  Determinate sentences, §§ 1170, 2930 et seq.
  Diagnostic facility, § 1203.03.
  Imprisonment for nonpayment of fine, § 1205.
  Jails, industrial farms, road camps, § 4019.
Crimes and offenses by prisoners, § 4500 et seq.
Cruel and inhuman punishment, §§ 147, 673.
Delivery of prisoner, § 1216.
Designation of institution for imprisonment, § 1202a.
  Work furlough prisoners, § 1208.
Destruction of buildings, § 4600.
Diagnostic facilities, observation and treatment, § 1203.03.
Discharge of prisoners,
  Order of court, § 1203.3.
Drugs and medicine,
  Bringing into prison, § 4573.5.
  Paraphernalia for consuming narcotics or other drugs,
    Bringing into prison, §§ 4573, 4573.5.
Education, inmates,
  Work furlough program, county jails, §§ 1208, 1208.5.
Employees. Officers and employees, generally, post.
Employment. Labor and employment, generally, post.
Escape, generally, this index.

CORRECTIONAL INSTITUTIONS —Cont'd
Ex-convicts coming upon or near grounds, unauthorized communications, § 4571.
Explosives,
  Books describing manufacture, censorship, § 2601.
  Possession, §§ 4502, 4574.
Facility for confinement of prisoners under work furlough law, § 1208.
False personation, fraudulent entry, § 4570.5.
Forfeitures,
  Officer refusing to allow attorney to visit prisoner, § 825.
Fraudulent entry, § 4570.5.
Grand jury,
  Free access, § 921.
  Inquiry into condition and management, § 919.
Guards,
  Peace officer status, § 830.5.
Hostages, holding person, § 4503.
Imprisonment without indictment, grand jury inquiry, § 919.
Inhuman treatment of prisoners, §§ 147, 673.
Inspection,
  Packages, inmates, § 2601.
Intermittent service of sentences, probationers, § 1203.1.
Intoxicating liquors. Alcoholic beverages, generally, ante.
Jails, generally, this index.
Knives, possession, § 4502.
Letters, unauthorized communications, § 4570.
Life imprisonment, assault and battery, § 4500.
Literature, unauthorized communications, § 4570.
Mail and mailing,
  Censorship, § 2601.
  Unauthorized communications, § 4570.
Malicious mischief, injury or destruction of facilities, § 606.
Medicine. Drugs and medicine, generally, ante.
Narcotics. Drugs and medicine, generally, ante.
Nevada state prison officers and employees, peace officers, § 830.5.
Notice,
  Discharge of prisoner, § 1203.3.
Officers and employees,
  Inhumane or oppressive treatment of prisoners, § 147.
Paraphernalia for consuming drugs, § 4573 et seq.
Pardon, certificate of rehabilitation and pardon, § 4852.01 et seq.
Peace officers, authority of wardens, superintendents, etc., § 830.5.
Photographs, reports,
  Visitation of prisoners, § 825.5.
Physicians and surgeons,
  Visitation of prisoners, § 825.5.
Place of commitment, sentence and punishment, § 1202a.
Possession of deadly weapon, § 4502.

CORRECTIONAL

CORRECTIONAL INSTITUTIONS
—Cont'd
Proceedings. Actions and proceedings, generally, ante.
Psychiatrists, visitation of prisoners, § 825.5.
Public officers and employees, prisoners, correspondence, civil rights, § 2601.
Public training schools, cruel and unusual punishment, § 673.
Punishment not specifically prescribed, felony, § 18.
Reading material, unauthorized communications, § 4570.
Receipts,
  Delivery of prisoner and abstract to warden, § 1216.
Records and recordation,
  Criminal identification and investigation bureau, examination while imprisoned, § 11125.
  Examination, § 11125.
Recreational facilities, § 6030.
Rehabilitation,
  Services, standards, § 6030.
Reparations, condition of probation, § 1203.1.
Reports,
  Diagnosis and recommendation, retention by supervising probation officer, § 1203.03.
  Personnel, training and standards, § 6031.2.
Rescues, § 4550.
Restoration of rights after discharge, § 1203.4.
Road camps,
  Fraudulent entry, § 4570.5.
Salaries. Compensation and salaries, generally, ante.
Sales,
  Civil rights, § 2601.
San Quentin state prison. Correctional Institution, San Quentin, generally, this index.
Sex offenders, discharge or parole, notice of duty to register, § 290.
Standards, local detention facilities, § 6030.
Statement of views of judges and district attorneys regarding convicts, § 1203.01.
Surgeons. Physicians and surgeons, generally, ante.
Telephones, eavesdropping, invasion of privacy, §§ 631, 632.
Time,
  Resentencing, recall of commitment and sentence, § 1170.
Transcript, sentencing proceedings, copy provided, § 1203.01.
Transfer of prisoners,
  Work furlough confinement, § 1208.
Unauthorized communications, § 4570 et seq.
United States,
  Safe keeping of prisoners, § 4006.
Visitation of prisoners,
  Attorney, right of prisoner, § 825.
  Civil rights, § 2601.
  Physicians and surgeons, § 825.5.

CORRECTIONAL INSTITUTIONS
—Cont'd
Wardens,
  Aiding escape, § 4533.
  Peace officers, powers, § 830.5.
  Receipt for prisoners, § 1216.
  State prisons, peace officers, § 830.5.
Weapons,
  Assault with deadly weapon, § 4500 et seq.
  Books describing manufacturer, censorship, § 2601.
  Convicts, possessing, §§ 4502, 12021.
  Possession, §§ 4502, 4574.
  Wiretapping, invasion of privacy, §§ 631, 632.
Work release programs, failure to return to place of confinement, § 4530.
Workers' compensation,
  Civil rights of prisoners, § 2601.

CORRECTIONS, BOARD OF
Apprehension of criminals, study, § 6027.
Chairman, § 6025.
Crime study, § 6027.
Detection of crime, study of methods, § 6027.
Membership, § 6025.
Penology, study of, § 6027.
Powers and duties, study and recommendations, § 6027.
Prevention of crime, study of methods, § 6027.
Quorum, § 6025.
Removal, members, § 6025.
Term of office, § 6025.

CORRECTIONS, STATE DEPARTMENT OF
Diagnostic reports, designation of place for test, § 1203.03.
Emergency powers, peace officers, § 830.5.
Group insurance, peace officers, § 830.5.
Insurance, group insurance, § 830.5.
Law enforcement liaison unit, peace officer status, § 830.5a.
Mutual aid powers, § 830.5.
Officers and employees,
  Mutual aid powers, § 830.5.
  Peace officers, § 830.5.
Peace officers, law enforcement liaison unit, peace officer status, § 830.5a.
Statement of views of judge and district attorney respecting person convicted, copy, § 1203.01.
Superintendents, peace officers, § 830.5.
Women's board of terms and parole,
  Community Release Boards, generally, this index.

CORRESPONDENCE
Letters and Other Correspondence, generally, this index.

CORROBORATION
Evidence, this index.

CORRUPTION
Bribery and Corruption, generally, this index.

COUNCIL
Judicial Council, generally, this index.

COUNSEL
Attorneys, generally, this index.

COUNSEL FOR ACCUSED
Appearance,
  Arraignment, § 977.
Arraignment, this index.
Extradition, § 1550.1.
Preliminary Examination, this index.
Probation modification, § 1203.2.
Public Defenders, generally, this index.
Refusal or neglect to allow visit to prisoner, § 825.
Statement respecting defendant and crime committed, filing, § 1203.01.
Telephone call of arrested person, preventing, § 851.5.
Visitation of prisoner, time, § 825.

COUNTERFEITING
See, also, Forgery, generally, this index.
Acceptance, § 470.
Altering or passing counterfeit instruments, § 470.
Bonds, § 470.
Charters, § 470.
Checks, drafts, bills of exchange, etc., § 470.
Codicils, § 470.
Coins, use in coin operated vending machines, etc., § 640a.
Commercial Paper, this index.
Credit cards, § 484d et seq.
Definitions, § 470.
Drafts, § 470.
Due bills, § 470.
Instruments, § 470.
Passage tickets, § 470.
Patents, § 470.
Receipts, § 470.
Records, § 470.
Shares of stock, § 470.
Trading stamps, § 470.
  Possession, § 475.
Vending machines, use of counterfeit coins, § 640a.
Warrants for payment of money, § 470.
Wills, § 470.

COUNTIES
Buildings, keys, unauthorized duplication, § 469.
Charges, criminal cases, § 1329.
Cities and Counties, generally, this index.
Conduct of persons, public places, regulating, § 647c.
Counties over 4,000,000, grand jury,
  Required number of jurors, § 888.2.
County institutions, cruel and unusual punishments, § 673.
Criminal history information,
  Local summary criminal history information, furnishing, § 13300 et seq.
Defined, § 7.
Employees. County Officers and Employees, generally, this index.
False emergency reports, § 148.3.

Penal Code

CREDIT

COUNTIES—Cont'd
Fraudulent claims, presentation to board or officer, § 72.
  Limitation of prosecution, § 800.
Industrial Farms and Road Camps, generally, this index.
Joint agreements, jail prisoners, work release, § 1208.5.
Junk dealers, metals, purchases, § 496a.
Juvenile Probation Officers, generally, this index.
Limitation of prosecution, fraudulent claims, § 800.
Mentally deficient and mentally ill persons, trial of sanity issue, transportation expenses, § 1373.
Metals, purchases by junk or secondhand dealers, § 496a.
Officers. County Officers and Employees, generally, this index.
Reports, battered and sexually molested children, county welfare departments, § 11161.5.
Secondhand dealers, metals, purchases, § 496a.
Sheriffs, generally, this index.
Simulating official inquiries, § 146b.
Supervisorial districts, grand jury, selection, § 899.
Witnesses, this index.

COUNTS
Indictment and Information, this index.

COUNTY COUNSEL
Grand jury, advising, § 934.

COUNTY HEALTH DEPARTMENT
Reports, battered and sexually molested children, § 11161.5.

COUNTY INDUSTRIAL FARM OR ROAD CAMP
Fraudulent entry, § 4570.5.

COUNTY JAIL
Jails, generally, this index.

COUNTY OFFICERS AND EMPLOYEES
Accounts,
  Falsification, § 424.
Application of law, illegal acts, § 77.
Bribery, §§ 67½, 68.
County counsel, advice to grand jury, § 934.
Cruel treatment of prisoners, § 147.
Disqualification from office, embezzlement and falsification of accounts, § 424.
District Attorneys, generally, this index.
Embezzlement, § 424.
Emoluments, asking or receiving, § 70.
False impersonation, § 146a.
Falsification of accounts, § 424.
Fugitives from justice, persons designated to return, expenses, payment, § 1557.
Grand jury,
  Removal proceedings, § 922.
Gratuity or reward,
  Asking or receiving, § 70.

COUNTY OFFICERS AND EMPLOYEES—Cont'd
Inhuman or oppressive treatment of prisoners, § 147.
Misappropriation, public moneys, § 424.
Obstructing or resisting in performance of duties, § 69.
Oppressive treatment of prisoners, § 147.
Personal property, injury, destruction or taking from custody, § 102.
Probation officers, generally. Parole and Probation, this index.
Public moneys,
  Defined, embezzlement or other misuse, § 424.
Removal,
  Grand jury proceedings, § 922.
Rewards, asking or receiving, § 70.
Sentence and punishment, embezzlement, falsification of accounts, misappropriation, etc., § 424.
Sheriffs, generally, this index.
Threatening, § 71.

COUNTY WARRANTS
Counterfeiting, § 470.
Forgery, § 470.

COUNTY WELFARE DEPARTMENTS
Reports, cruelty to dependent child, § 11161.5.

COURT REPORTERS
Presence, preliminary examination, § 868.

COURTHOUSES
Arson, § 448a.

COURTROOMS
Juvenile delinquents, presence of adult prisoners, § 273b.

COURTS
Appellate courts. Courts of Appeal, generally, this index.
Clerks of Court, generally, this index.
Conspiracy to pervert or obstruct justice, § 182.
Contempt, generally, this index.
Courts of Appeal, generally, this index.
Criminal history information,
  Local summary criminal history information, § 13300 et seq.
Deposits in Court, generally, this index.
Inferior Courts and Tribunals, generally, this index.
Interruption of court proceedings, § 166.
Judges, generally, this index.
Justice Courts, generally, this index.
Juvenile Courts, generally, this index.
Magistrates, generally, this index.
Marshals, generally, this index.
Municipal Courts, generally, this index.
Orders of Court, generally, this index.
Publication of false reports of court proceedings, § 166.
Records,
  Counterfeiting, § 470.
  Forgery, § 470.
  Inspection, search warrants, § 1534.

COURTS—Cont'd
Records—Cont'd
  Petition to seal, minor arrested for misdemeanor, § 851.7.
  Search warrants, public inspection, § 1534.
Reporters. Court Reporters, generally, this index.
Reports,
  Diagnostic treatment of prisoner, § 1203.03.
  False reports, publication, § 166.
Sex offenders, duty regarding registration, § 290.
Superior Courts, generally, this index.
Supreme Court, generally, this index.

COURTS OF APPEAL
Judges,
  Magistrates, designation, § 808.
Magistrates, judges designated, § 808.

COVENANTS
Counterfeiting or forgery, § 470.

COVERTURE
Husband and Wife, generally, this index.

COWS
Carcasses, theft, § 487a.

CRATES
Containers, generally, this index.

CREDIBILITY
Witnesses, this index.

CREDIT
Apartment houses, obtaining credit by false pretenses, § 537.
Boarding houses, obtaining credit by false pretenses, § 537.
Bungalow courts, obtaining credit by false pretenses, § 537.
Defined, bad checks, § 476a.
False credit reports, theft by fraud, § 484.
False pretenses, § 537.
  Hotels, § 537.
Hotels, obtaining credit by false pretenses, § 537.
Innkeepers, defrauding, obtaining credit by false pretenses, § 537.
Lodging houses, obtaining credit by false pretenses, § 537.
Motels, obtaining credit by false pretenses, § 537.
Restaurants, obtaining credit by false pretenses, § 537.

CREDIT CARDS
Generally, § 484d et seq.
Alteration, § 484f.
Avoiding payment of lawful charge, § 484j.
Cancellation, use after cancellation, etc., § 484d et seq.
Defined, § 484d.
Drafts, credit card transaction, forgery, § 484f.
Expired credit cards, use after expiration, § 484g.

CREDIT

CREDIT CARDS—Cont'd
False representations, card holder identity, § 484g.
Forgery, theft, etc., § 484d et seq.
Holder, false representation, § 484g.
Incomplete card, possession with intent to defraud, § 484i.
Larceny, § 484e.
Machinery or plates, reproduction of credit cards, possession, § 484i.
Misdemeanors, avoiding payment of lawful charge, § 484j.
Preparation or reproduction with fraudulent intent, § 484i.
Retailers, theft, credit card transactions, § 484h.
Revoked credit cards, use after revocation, § 484g.
Theft, forgery, etc., § 484d et seq.
Uttering forged credit cards, § 484f.

CREDIT ON SENTENCES
Determinate sentencing, § 2930 et seq.

CREDIT UNIONS
See, also, Banks and Banking, generally, this index.

CRESCENT CITY, CITY OF
See, also, Municipalities, generally, this index.

CRIBS
Arson, § 449a.

CRIME AGAINST NATURE
Sodomy, generally, this index.

CRIME PREVENTION COUNCILS
Probation officers, establishment and cooperation, § 1203.13.

CRIMINAL ATTEMPT ACT
Generally, § 663 et seq.

CRIMINAL IDENTIFICATION AND INVESTIGATION, BUREAU OF
Investigators, § 11050 et seq.
  Assignment, § 11050.
Records,
  Examination, § 11120 et seq.
Reports,
  Lost, stolen, found, pledged or pawned property, § 11108.
  Sex crimes and felonies, § 11107.
Weapons, records, § 11106.

CRIMINAL NEGLIGENCE
Necessity to constitute crime, § 20.

CRIMINAL TRESPASS ACT
Generally, § 602.

CRIPPLED PERSONS
Handicapped Persons, generally, this index.

CROCODILES
See, also, Fish and Game, generally, this index.

CROPS
Agricultural Products, generally, this index.

CRUEL OR UNUSUAL PUNISHMENT
Generally, § 673.
Prisoners, § 147.

CULVER CITY, CITY OF
See, also, Municipalities, generally, this index.

CULVERTS
Train robbery, interference, § 214.

CUNNILINGUS
Oral Copulation, generally, this index.

CURRENCY
Money, generally, this index.

CURSING
Profanity and Offensive Language, generally, this index.

CUSTODIAL OFFICER
Assault and battery, local detention facilities, § 243.1.
Defined, cities, local detention facilities, § 831.
Los Angeles, city of, battery against, § 243.1.
Preliminary examination, presence, § 868.

CUTOVER LAND
Malicious mischief, burning, § 449c.

CYPREMORPHINE
See, also, Drugs and Medicine, generally, this index.

DAGGERS
Weapons, generally, this index.

DAMAGES
Extortion, property damage, threat to inflict, § 519.
Habeas corpus, disobedience, § 1505.
Insured property, intent to defraud insurer, § 548.
Personal property in custody of officer, damaging, etc., § 102.

DANGEROUS WEAPONS
Weapons, generally, this index.

DARTS
Blowguns, § 12580 et seq.

DAVIS, CITY OF
See, also, Municipalities, generally, this index.

DAY CARE NURSERY SCHOOLS
Battered and sexually molested children, reports, summer day camps, § 11161.5.

DAYTIME
Arrests, felony or misdemeanor offenses, § 840.
Defined, § 7.

DEAD ANIMALS
Animals, this index.

DEADLY WEAPONS
Weapons, generally, this index.

DEATH
Capital Punishment, generally, this index.
Coroners, generally, this index.
Drugs, mislabeling or misbranding causing, § 380.
Emergencies, false reports, § 148.3.
Fetus, murder, § 187.
Fire alarms, false reports, § 148.4.
Pardons and reprieves, imminent danger, § 4806.
Prescription for drugs or medicines, deviation from causing, § 380.
Sentence. Capital Punishment, generally, this index.
Wrecking trains resulting in death, punishment, § 219.

DEATH PENALTY
Capital Punishment, generally, this index.

DEBENTURES
Bonds, generally, this index.

DEBTS
Indebtedness, generally, this index.

DECEDENTS' ESTATES
Descent and Distribution, generally, this index.

DECEIT
Fraud, generally, this index.

DECOYING
Minor child with intent to detain and conceal, § 784.

DECREES
Judgments and Decrees, generally, this index.

DEEDS AND CONVEYANCES
Correctional institution,
  Civil rights, § 2601.
Counterfeiting, § 470.
Forgery, § 470.
Prisoners, civil rights, § 2601.

DEFACING
Generally, § 594.5.
Serial number or identification mark on machines, sale, § 537e.

DEFAMATION
Libel and Slander, generally, this index.

DEFILE
Rape, generally, this index.

DEFINITIONS
See Words and Phrases, generally, this index.

DEFORMITIES
Extortion, threat to expose, § 519.

DEGREES OF OFFENSE
Burglary, § 460.
Determination before passing sentence, § 1192.

Penal Code

DEGREES OF OFFENSE—Cont'd
Guilty plea, specifying degree, § 1192.1 et seq.
Reasonable doubt, conviction of lowest degree of offense, § 1097.
Theft, § 486.
  Grand theft, defined, § 487.

DEL MAR, CITY OF
See, also, Municipalities, generally, this index.

DEL NORTE COUNTY
See, also, Counties, generally, this index.

DELANO, CITY OF
See, also, Municipalities, generally, this index.

DELINQUENT CHILDREN
Juvenile Delinquents and Dependents, generally, this index.

DENTISTS
Battered or sexually molested children, reports, §§ 11110, 11161.5, 11161.7.
Jail prisoners, work release, § 1208.
Witnesses, production of books and papers, attendance outside county of residence, § 1330.

DEPARTMENTS
State Departments, generally, this index.

DEPENDENT CHILDREN
Juvenile Delinquents and Dependents, generally, this index.

DEPENDENTS
Jail prisoners, work furlough earnings, support, § 1208.
Probationers, support, § 1203.1.

DEPOSE
Defined, § 7.

DEPOSITIONS
Grand jury,
  Names of deponent, insertion or indorsement on indictment, § 943.

DEPOSITS
Bail, this index.

DEPOSITS IN COURT
Bench warrants, nonappearance of defendant for sentence, § 1195 et seq.
Forfeiture, nonappearance,
  Arraignment, § 979.
  Sentence, § 1195.
Nonappearance of defendant discharged on bail or deposit, § 979.
Return to defendant, § 1195.

DESCENT AND DISTRIBUTION
Correctional institutions,
  Civil rights of inmates, § 2601.
Mentally deficient and mentally ill persons, transportation expenses, state hospital, § 1373.
Prisoners, civil rights, § 2601.
Probate Proceedings, generally, this index.

DESERTION
Generally, § 270 et seq.
Evidence, § 270.
False representation that child is orphan, § 271a.
Intent to abandon child under 14, §§ 271, 271a.
Juvenile Delinquents and Dependents, generally, this index.
Support, generally, this index.

DESOMORPHINE
See, also, Drugs and Medicine, generally, this index.

DESTRUCTION OF EVIDENCE
Documentary evidence, § 135.

DESTRUCTIVE DEVICES
Capital offense, § 189.
Carrying or placing on passenger vehicles for hire, § 12303.1.
Confiscation, § 12307.
Fees, licenses and permits, § 12305.
Homicide, use of destructive devices, degree of offense, § 189.
Injunction, nuisance, § 12307.
Making, unlicensed possession of materials, or substances, § 12312.
Nuisance, § 12307.
Passenger vehicles for hire, carrying or placing device or explosives, § 12303.1.
Possession,
  Substances or materials with intent to make, unlicensed persons, § 12312.
Transporting, § 12303.6.

DETENTION
False Imprisonment, generally, this index.
Kidnapping, child stealing, etc., § 784.

DETENTION FACILITIES
Arson, prisoners in local detention facilities, § 451b.
Assault and battery, custodial officers, § 243.1.
Custodial officers, assault and battery, § 243.1.
Fires, prisoners in local detention facilities, § 451b.
Maximum term of confinement, § 19a.
Minimum standards, local detention facilities, § 6030.
Probationers, temporary removal or release for purposes preparatory to return to community, § 1203.1a.
Rehabilitative services, standards, § 6030.
Reports, inspection of local detention facilities, § 6031.2.
Standards, local detention facilities, § 6030.

DEVELOPMENTALLY DISABLED PERSONS
Competency to stand trial, §§ 1369, 1370.1.

DEVICE OR TRICK
Theft by fraud, § 484.

DIPHENYLAMINE

DEVICES
Drugs and Medicine, generally, this index.

DEVISES AND DEVISEES
Gifts, Devises and Bequests, generally, this index.
Probate Proceedings, generally, this index.
Wills, generally, this index.

DEXTROMORAMIDE
See, also, Drugs and Medicine, generally, this index.

DEXTRORPHAN
See, also, Drugs and Medicine, this index.

DIAMPROMIDE
See, also, Drugs and Medicine, generally, this index.

DICTAPHONES
Serial number or identification mark removed, sale, etc., § 537e.

DIETHYL MALONATE
See, also, Drugs and Medicine, generally, this index.

DIETHYLTHIAMBUTENE
See, also, Drugs and Medicine, generally, this index.

DIHYDROCODEINE
See, also, Drugs and Medicine, generally, this index.

DIHYDROCODEINONE
See, also, Drugs and Medicine, generally, this index.

DIHYDROMORPHINE
See, also, Drugs and Medicine, generally, this index.

DIMENOXADOL
See, also, Drugs and Medicine, generally, this index.

DIMEPHEPTANOL
See, also, Drugs and Medicine, generally, this index.

DIMETHYLTHIAMBUTENE
See, also, Drugs and Medicine, generally, this index.

DIMETHYLTRYPTAMINE
See, also, Drugs and Medicine, generally, this index.

DIOXAPHETYL BUTYRATE
See, also, Drugs and Medicine, generally, this index.

DIPHENOXYLATE
See, also, Drugs and Medicine, generally, this index.

DIPHENYLAMINE
See, also, Drugs and Medicine, generally, this index.

DIPIPANONE
See, also, Drugs and Medicine, generally, this index.

DIRKS
Weapons, generally, this index.

DISABLED PERSONS
Handicapped Persons, generally, this index.

DISASTERS
War and Civil Defense, generally, this index.

DISCHARGE
Forgery or counterfeiting, § 470.
Grand jury, § 915.
Homicide, justifiable or excusable, § 199.
Jury, this index.
Weapons, this index.

DISCLOSURE
Grand Jury, this index.
Indictment or information for felony, disclosure before arrest of defendant, § 924.
Private communications, invasion of privacy, § 637.

DISFIGUREMENT
Generally, § 203.
Assault,
Caustic chemicals, § 244.
Fines and penalties, § 243.

DISGRACE
Extortion, threat to expose, § 519.

DISMISSAL AND NONSUIT
Bar to subsequent prosecution, § 1387.
Certificates of rehabilitation and pardon, §§ 1203.4, 4852.01 et seq.
Court's own motion, § 1385.
Criminal prosecution,
Newly discovered evidence, § 1387.
Former Jeopardy, this index.
Mentally incompetent persons, dismissal of misdemeanor charge, § 1370.2.
Reasons, entry upon minutes, § 1385.
Rehabilitation and pardon, certificates, §§ 1203.4, 4852.01 et seq.
Searches and seizures, motion to suppress evidence, § 1538.5.

DISORDERLY CONDUCT
Generally, §§ 403, 415, 647.
Adult classes, annoying or molesting persons in attendance, § 647b.
Assembly for purpose of disturbing the peace,
Refusal to disperse, § 416.
Begging, § 647.
Civil protective custody, inebriates, § 647.
Colleges and universities,
Disruptive persons, denial of access to campus or facility, § 626.2.
Disturbances, § 415.5.
Comfort stations, loitering in or about, § 647.

DISORDERLY CONDUCT—Cont'd
Community colleges and districts, § 415.5.
Disruptive persons, denial of campus facilities, § 626 et seq.
Contempt, § 166.
Defined, § 647.
Disruptive persons, denial of access to college or school campus or facility, § 626 et seq.
Drugs, under influence of in public places, § 647.
Drunkenness, § 647.
Fires, interference with extinguishment, § 148.2.
Glue sniffing, § 647.
Hindering or preventing public meetings, § 403.
Judicial proceedings, § 166.
Lodging in public or private buildings without permission, § 647.
Loitering on streets or private property, § 647.
Neighborhood, keeping disorderly houses, § 316.
Peeping Tom, § 647.
Prostitution, defined, § 647.
Prowling upon private property, § 647.
Public meetings, hindering or preventing, § 403.
Public toilets, loitering in or about, § 647.
Rest rooms, loitering in or about, § 647.
Schools, disruptive persons, § 626 et seq.
Second and subsequent offenses, disturbances in colleges and universities, § 415.5.
Sex offenses, § 647.
Sit-ins, § 647.
Solicitation, § 647.
Squatters, § 647.
State colleges and universities,
Disruptive persons, denial to facilities, § 626 et seq.
Disturbances, § 415.5.
Toluene, under influence of drug, § 647.
University of California,
Disruptive persons, denial of access to facilities, § 626.2.
Disturbances, § 415.5.
Window peeping, § 647.

DISORDERLY HOUSES
See, also, Prostitution, generally, this index.
Females under 18 unmarried, inveiglement or enticement, § 266.
Keeping or residing in house, § 315.
Pandering, § 266i.
Wives, placing or permitting placement, § 266g.

DISPOSES
Defined, fire bombs, § 452.

DISRUPTIVE PERSONS
Colleges and universities, denial of access to campus or facility, § 626 et seq.
Defendants, felony trials, removal from courtroom, § 1043.

DISSOLUTION OF MARRIAGE
Marriage, this index.

DISTRIBUTE
Defined,
Harmful matter, § 313.
Obscene matter, § 311.

DISTRICT ATTORNEYS
Bench warrant, application for issuance, § 980 et seq.
Blank subpoenas, issuance, § 1326.
Bombs and explosives, false reports of planting, § 148.1.
Career criminal prosecution program, § 999b et seq.
Charges, investigation, § 935.
Criminal history information,
Local summary criminal history information, furnishing, § 13300 et seq.
Defined, § 691.
Eavesdropping, wiretap or electronic, § 633.
Explosives or bombs, false reports of planting, § 148.1.
False crime reports, § 148.5.
Fugitive escaping bail, hearing on bondsmen's application for return, § 847.5.
Grand Jury, this index.
Habeas corpus, service of writ, § 1475.
Inspectors, designation as peace officers, § 830.1.
Invasion of privacy, wiretap or electronic eavesdropping, § 633.
Investigation and investigators,
Assignment, bureau of criminal identification and investigation, § 11050.
Designation as peace officers, § 830.1.
Petitioners for certificates of rehabilitation, § 4852.12.
Magistrates, complaints, concurrence, § 813.
Pardons, reprieves and commutations,
Notice of intention to apply, service, § 4804.
Summarized statement of facts, § 4803.
Peace officers, inspectors or investigators employed by office, designation as, § 830.1.
Preliminary Examination, generally, this index.
Recording private communications, wiretapping or electronic eavesdropping, § 633.
Statement of views respecting person convicted or sentenced, § 1203.01.
Subpoenas,
Grand jury investigations, § 939.2.
Signing and issuance, § 1326.
Tapping wires, § 633.
Telegraphs and telephones, wiretapping, § 633.
Wiretapping, § 633.

DISTRICT COURTS OF APPEAL
Courts of Appeal, generally, this index.

DISTRICTS
Claims against districts, fraud, § 72.
Criminal history information,
Local summary criminal history information, furnishing, § 13300 et seq.

DRUGS

DISTRICTS—Cont'd
Fraudulent claims, presentation to board or officer, § 72.
Grand jury, removal of officers and employees from office, § 922.
Officers and employees,
  Embezzlement and falsification of accounts, § 424.
  Public funds,
    Offenses involving, § 424.
  Removal, grand jury, § 922.

DISTURBANCE OF PEACE
Disorderly Conduct, generally, this index.

DIVERSION PROGRAMS
Pretrial diversion, § 1001 et seq.

DIVIDENDS
Offering after motion for judgment of acquittal denied, §§ 1118, 1118.1.

DIVORCE
Dissolution of marriage, generally. Marriage, this index.

D–LYSERGIC ACID
See, also, Drugs and Medicine, generally, this index.

DOCTORS
Physicians and Surgeons, generally, this index.

DOGS
See, also, Animals, generally, this index.
Arrest, possession of animal, § 599aa.
Fighting,
  Arrest, possession of animal, § 599aa.
Fines and penalties, fighting, § 597.5.
Medical research, theft, § 487g.
Theft of dogs, § 487e et seq.

DOMESTIC ANIMALS
Animals, generally, this index.

DOMICILE AND RESIDENCE
Bail, qualifications, § 1279.
Battered children, reports, § 11110.
Certificates of rehabilitation and pardon, crimes, § 4852.01 et seq.
Peace officers, disclosing officer's address or telephone number maliciously with intent to obstruct justice, § 146e.
Probationer, transfer of jurisdiction, § 1203.9.
Weapons, this index.
Witnesses, this index.

DONATIONS
Gifts, Devises and Bequests, generally, this index.

DOORS
Arrest, breaking open to arrest, §§ 844, 845.
Escapes or rescues, authority to break to retake prisoners, § 855.
Search warrants,
  Breaking down door to execute warrant, § 1531.

DOORS—Cont'd
Search warrants—Cont'd
  Breaking to liberate person aiding in execution of warrant, § 1532.

DORMITORIES
Colleges and Universities, this index.

DOUBLE JEOPARDY
Former Jeopardy, generally, this index.

DOUBLE PUNISHMENT
Generally, § 654.

DRAFTS
Commercial Paper, this index.
Counterfeiting or forgery, § 470.

DRAWINGS
Vending machines, burglar tools, § 466.3.

DRIVERS LICENSES
Motor Vehicles, this index.

DRIVING WHILE INTOXICATED
Traffic Rules and Regulations, this index.

DRUG ABUSE PROGRAMS
Jails, work furlough programs, counseling of prisoners, § 1208.

DRUG ADDICTS
Arrest, release, persons arrested without warrant, delivery to hospital or facility for treatment, § 849.
Concealed weapons, § 12021.
Criminal defendant, diversion from prosecution for education, treatment or rehabilitation, § 1000 et seq.
Delivery to hospital or facility for treatment, arrest without warrant, release, § 849.
Educational programs,
  Criminal defendant, diversion from prosecution, § 1000 et seq.
  Work furlough program, § 1208.
Jails, work furlough programs, counseling of prisoners, § 1208.
Parole and probation, qualifications, § 1203.07.
Records and recordation, detention, recording in arrest records, § 849.
Rehabilitation,
  Criminal defendant, diversion from prosecution, § 1000 et seq.
Tear gas and tear gas weapons, purchase, possession or use, § 12403.7.
Treatment,
  Criminal defendant, diversion from prosecution, § 1000 et seq.
Weapons,
  Possession, § 12021.
  Purchase of concealable firearm, § 12076.
Work furlough program, § 1208.

DRUGGISTS
Pharmacists, generally, this index.

DRUGS AND MEDICINE
Addicts. Drug Addicts, generally, this index.

DRUGS AND MEDICINE—Cont'd
Administering,
  Assisting in commission of felony, § 222.
Anesthetics, generally, this index.
Arrest without warrant,
  Detention certificate, § 851.6.
  Release of persons delivered to facility or hospital for treatment, § 849.
Controlled substances,
  Sales, Health & S 11379.
    Heroin,
      Conviction, probation or suspended sentence, § 1203.07.
Correctional Institutions, this index.
Dangerous drugs,
  Arrest without warrant, release of persons delivered to hospital or facility for treatment, § 849.
  Restricted dangerous drugs, criminal defendant, diversion for education, treatment or rehabilitation, § 1000 et seq.
Delivery to hospital or facility for treatment, arrest without warrant, release, § 849.
Destruction of exhibits, § 1419.
Deviation from prescription causing death, § 380.
Disorderly conduct, § 647.
Disposition, § 1419.
Diversion from criminal prosecution, § 1000 et seq.
Educational programs,
  Criminal defendant, diversion from prosecution, § 1000 et seq.
Exhibits in criminal prosecutions, release, § 1418.6.
False representation as physician to obtain, § 377.
Fines and penalties. Offenses and penalties, generally, post.
Fraud,
  Personating physician to obtain, § 377.
Heroin, probation or suspended sentence upon conviction, § 1203.07.
Industrial farms and road camps,
  Bringing drugs into camp, §§ 4573, 4573.5.
Inspection,
  Firearms, carrying loaded firearms, § 12031.
Marijuana, Health & S 11000 et seq., 11357 et seq.
  Arrest for possession, release on own recognizance, § 853.6.
Medical treatment, criminal defendant, diversion from prosecution, § 1000 et seq.
Misbranding, § 380.
Offenses and penalties, Health & S 11350 et seq., 11372, 11374.
  Administering to assist in commission of felony, § 222.
  Bail, bond, exoneration, diversion program, § 1000.2.
  Paraphernalia for controlled substances injecting or smoking, possession, Health & S 11364.
    Correctional institutions, § 4573 et seq.

711

DRUGS

DRUGS AND MEDICINE—Cont'd
Parole and probation, qualifications, § 1203.07.
Poisons, generally, this index.
Prescriptions,
 Deviation from causing death, § 380.
 False representation as physician to obtain, § 377.
 Misbranding causing death, § 380.
Pretrial diversion program, § 1000 et seq.
Probation, violations dealing with heroin, § 1203.07.
Rape, resistance prevented, § 261.
Rehabilitation, criminal defendant, diversion from prosecution, § 1000 et seq.
Restricted dangerous drugs, criminal defendant, diversion for education, treatment or rehabilitation, § 1000 et seq.
Sales. Controlled substances, ante.
Suspended sentence, violations dealing with heroin, § 1203.07.
Telephonic communication to obtain, false representation, § 377.
Treatment,
 Criminal defendant, diversion from prosecution, § 1000 et seq.
Uniform controlled substances. Controlled substances, generally, ante.

DRUNKARDS AND DRUNKENNESS
Accomplices or accessories, causing drunk person to commit crime, § 31.
Arrest,
 Release, § 849.
 Notice to appear, persons not released, § 853.6.
Civil protective custody, § 647.
Defenses, voluntary intoxication, § 22.
Disorderly conduct, § 647.
Exceptions, civil protective custody, § 647.
Inducing intoxication for purposes of committing crime, § 31.
Jails, work furlough programs, counseling of prisoners, § 1208.
Juvenile court proceedings, persons placed in treatment facility for inebriates, § 647.
Motive, purpose or intent, commission of crime, voluntary intoxication, consideration, § 22.
Parole and probation, conditions, § 1203.02.
Protective custody, treatment and evaluation of inebriates, § 647.
Sales of alcoholic beverages to habitual drunkards, § 397.
Sex offenses, probation, § 1203.02.
Treatment, civil protective custody, § 647.
Voluntary intoxication, defenses, criminal prosecutions, § 22.

DUCKS
Poultry and Poultry Products, generally, this index.

DUE–BILL
Counterfeiting or forgery, § 470.

DURESS OR COERCION
See, also, Threats, generally, this index.
Abduction of person to live in illicit relationship, § 266b.
Accomplices and accessories, causing others to commit crime, § 31.
Arbitrators, § 95.
Capacity to commit crime, person under menace, § 26.
Causing others to commit crime, § 31.
Defrauding innkeepers, § 537.
Extortion, element of offense, §§ 518, 519.
Jurors, § 95.
Justifiable homicide, § 198.
Obscene matter, acceptance as condition of sale of other merchandise, §§ 311.7, 311.9.
Oppressive treatment of prisoners, § 147.
Oral copulation, § 288a.
Pandering, § 266i.
Perjury, inducing false testimony, § 137.
Principals in crime, § 31.
Subornation of perjury, § 137.
Umpires, § 95.
Witnesses, inducing false testimony, § 137.

DWELLINGS
Apartment Houses, generally, this index.
Arson, § 447a.
Breaking and entering, search warrants, § 1531.
Burglary, §§ 459, 460.
Firearms, discharge at inhabited dwellings, § 246.
Malicious mischief,
 Unauthorized entry, § 602.5.
 Vandalism, § 603.
Mobilehomes and Mobilehome Parks, generally, this index.
Person remaining in dwelling without permission, § 602.5.
Remaining in dwelling without permission, § 602.5.
Search warrants, breaking and entering, § 1531.
 Person aiding in execution of warrant, liberating, § 1532.
Squatters, disorderly conduct, § 647.
Vandalism, § 603.
Weapons,
 Carrying loaded firearms, § 12031.

DYNAMITE
Explosives, generally, this index.

EARS
Slitting, mayhem, §§ 203, 204.

EATING PLACES
Restaurants, generally, this index.

EAVESDROPPING
Arrested persons, telephone calls, § 851.5.
Police radio service communications, aiding escape, § 636.5.

ECGONINE
See, also, Drugs and Medicine, generally, this index.

EDUCATION
Adult Schools and Classes, generally, this index.
Colleges and Universities, generally, this index.
Correctional Institutions, this index.
County prisoners,
 Work furlough program, § 1208.
 Defined, Cobey Work Furlough Law, § 1208.
Drug abuse control plans, criminal defendant, diversion from prosecution, § 1000 et seq.
Furloughs, jail inmates, facility for confinement, designation, § 1208.
Honor camps, release for educational purposes, § 1208.
Industrial farm and road camps, inmates, Facility for confinement, designation, § 1208.
Jails, work furlough programs, § 1208.
Narcotics offenders, diversion from prosecution for education, treatment or rehabilitation, § 1000 et seq.
Obscene materials, use, § 311.8.
Schools and School Districts, generally, this index.
Sniperscope, use, § 468.
Work furloughs, § 1208.

EDUCATIONAL PROGRAMS
Drug Addicts, this index.

ELECTIONS
Registrars of voters, compensation for performing official acts, § 70.

ELECTRIC ARC
Burglary, use of electric arc, § 464.

ELECTRICITY
See, also, Public Utilities, generally, this index.
Junk and secondhand dealers, purchasing metals used for, diligence to determine seller's right, § 496a.

ELECTRONIC DEVICES AND EQUIPMENT
Arrest warrants, transmission, § 850.
Recordings, harmful matter, children and minors, distribution or exhibition, § 313 et seq.

ELEMENTARY SCHOOLS
Schools and School Districts, generally, this index.

EMBEZZLEMENT
See, also, Theft, generally, this index.
Generally, § 503 et seq.
Abandoned or unclaimed property, disposal, § 1411.
Agents, § 508.
Bringing embezzled property into state, §§ 27, 497.
Claim of title as defense, § 511.
Clerks, § 508.
Commission of crime in foreign state, bringing embezzled property into state, § 27.
Construction loans funds, § 484c.

Penal Code

EMBEZZLEMENT—Cont'd
County officers and employees, § 424.
Defalcation of public funds, § 514.
Defenses,
  Claim of title, § 511.
  Intent to restore property, § 512.
  Restoration of property or tender before indictment or information, § 513.
Defined, § 503.
Description of property, evidence, § 1131.
Distinct act of taking, § 509.
District officers and employees, § 424.
Evidence,
  Debt,
    Value, determination, § 514.
  Description of property, § 1131.
  Disposition of property, § 1411.
  Property retained as evidence, disposition, § 1413.
Falsification of officer's accounts, etc., § 424.
Fines and penalties, § 514.
  Offense occurring in foreign state, bringing embezzled goods into state, § 27.
Indictment and information,
  Description of property, § 1131.
  Intent to restore property, §§ 512, 513.
Insured property, intent to defraud insurer, § 548.
Intent to restore property, § 512.
Jurisdiction,
  Offense committed out of state and property brought into state, § 789.
  Property taken transported between jurisdictional territories, § 786.
Limitation of prosecutions, § 799.
Mitigation of punishment, §§ 512, 513.
Municipal officers and employees, § 424.
Notice, property used as evidence, disposition, § 1411.
Parole and probation, eligibility, § 1203.
Property used as evidence, disposition, § 1413.
  Notice to owner, § 1411.
Public moneys, § 514.
  Defined, § 424.
Public office, disqualification to hold, § 514.
Recording description of property embezzled, § 1413.
Restoration of property, §§ 512, 513.
Retention of property to offset or pay demands, § 511.
Search warrants, issuance, § 1524.
Sentence and punishment,
  Bringing embezzled property into state, § 497.
  Mitigation, §§ 512, 513.
Servants, § 508.
Setoff, retention of property, § 511.
State officers and employees, § 424.
Town officers and employees, § 424.
Trial, § 1131.
Unmarked property, disposal as embezzled property, § 537e.
Value, determination, § 514.
Weight and sufficiency of evidence, description of property, § 1131.

EMBLEMS
Badges, Emblems and Insignia, generally, this index.

EMERGENCIES
Calls, false reports, § 148.3.
False alarms, fire, § 148.4.
False reports, § 148.3.
Honor camps, release, family emergencies, § 1208.
Industrial farm and road camps, release, family emergencies, § 1208.
Jail prisoners,
  Hospitalization, § 4011.5.
  Release, family emergencies, § 1208.
Prisoners, release, family emergencies, § 1208.
Reports, false, § 148.3.
Work furloughs, release, family emergencies, § 1208.

EMERGENCY RESCUE PERSONNEL
Fire departments, interference, § 148.2.

EMOLUMENTS
Officers, asking or receiving, misdemeanor, § 70.

EMPLOYEES
Labor and Employment, generally, this index.

EMPLOYERS
Labor and Employment, generally, this index.

EMPLOYMENT
Labor and Employment, generally, this index.

ENDORSEMENT
Forgery or counterfeiting, § 470.
Indictment and Information, this index.

ENEMY ATTACK
War and Civil Defense, generally, this index.

ENTERTAINMENT
Exposure of body parts, waiters, waitresses or entertainers, restaurants, §§ 318.5, 318.6.
Theaters and Shows, generally, this index.

ENTICEMENT
Kidnapping, § 207.
Person for concubinage or prostitution, § 784.

ENTRY ON PROPERTY
Correctional institutions, free access by grand jury, § 921.
Disorderly conduct, § 647.
Grand jury, public prisons, § 921.
Malicious Mischief, this index.
Public prisons, free access by grand jury, § 921.
Squatters, disorderly conduct, § 647.
Unauthorized entry, § 602.5.
Vandalism, § 603.

ESCHEAT

EPILEPSY
Competency to stand trial, § 1370.1.

EQUIPMENT
Machinery and Equipment, generally, this index.

ESCAPE
Generally, § 4530 et seq.
Accomplices or accessories, §§ 32, 4533 et seq.
Arrest, § 836.3.
  Force to prevent, § 835a.
  Formalities, § 841.
  Industrial farms and road camps, § 836.3.
  Jail prisoners, § 836.3.
  Public officers and employees effecting arrest, force to prevent escape, § 836.5.
Article sent into prison, facilitating, § 4535.
Attempts, § 4530 et seq.
Accomplices and accessories, § 4533 et seq.
Articles sent into prison to facilitate escape, § 4535.
Instructions to jury, § 1127c.
Authority to pursue and retake prisoner, §§ 854, 855.
Breaking doors or windows to retake prisoner if admittance refused, § 855.
Doors, authority to break to retake prisoner, § 855.
Facilitating by sending things into prison, § 4535.
Fines and penalties,
  Guards or jail keepers, § 4533.
Force and violence, § 4530 et seq.
  Prevention, § 835a.
  Public officers and employees effecting arrest, § 836.5.
Fraudulent aid of keeper, sheriff, etc., § 4533.
Fugitives from justice, § 1547 et seq.
Guards aiding escape, § 4533.
Instructions to jury, evidence of flight, § 1127c.
Justifiable homicide, retaking felons, § 196.
Parole and Probation, this index.
Police radio service communications, intercepting and aiding escape, § 636.5.
Retaking prisoner, §§ 854, 855.
Reward for apprehension, § 1547.
Sentence and punishment,
  Reimprisonment, § 1170.1.
Voluntary permission of jail keeper, § 4533.
Windows, authority to break to retake prisoner, § 855.
Work furlough, § 1208.
Work release programs, failure of prisoner to return to place of confinement, § 4530.

ESCHEAT
See, also, Abandoned or Unclaimed Property, generally, this index.
Exhibits, § 1418.

ESCHEAT

ESCHEAT—Cont'd
Money, unclaimed money, § 1420 et seq.
Stolen or embezzled property, § 1411.

ESTATES
Counterfeiting or forging instruments relating to tenements, § 470.
Real property coextensive with tenements, § 7.

ETHCHLORVYNOL
See, also, Drugs and Medicine, generally, this index.

ETHER
Administering to assist in commission of felony, § 222.

ETHINAMATE
See, also, Drugs and Medicine, generally, this index.

ETHYL–4–PHENYLPIPERIDINE–4–CARBOXYLATE
See, also, Drugs and Medicine, generally, this index.

ETHYLMETHYLTHIOMBUTENE
See, also, Drugs and Medicine, generally, this index.

ETHYLMORPHINE
See, also, Drugs and Medicine, generally, this index.

ETONITAZENE
See, also, Drugs and Medicine, generally, this index.

ETORPHINE
See, also, Drugs and Medicine, generally, this index.

ETOXERIDINE
See, also, Drugs and Medicine, generally, this index.

EVACUATION
False emergency reports, § 148.3.

EVIDENCE
Accomplice, corroboration of testimony, § 1111.
Aggravation of punishment, method of presentment, § 1204.
Altered instruments, offering, § 132.
Ante-dated instruments, offering, § 132.
Argument and conduct of counsel, § 1093.
Burden of proof,
  Capital offenses,
    Minors, age, § 190.5.
    Special circumstances, § 190.4.
  Children and minors, capital punishment, age, § 190.5.
  Homicide, justification or excuse, exception, § 1105.
  Infractions, § 19d.
  Murder, mitigating circumstances, § 1105.
  Perjury prosecution, § 1103a.
  Receiving stolen goods, § 496.
Capital offenses, determination of sentence and punishment, § 190.3.

EVIDENCE—Cont'd
Capital punishment,
  Burden of proof, minors, age, § 190.5.
Child support, liability of parent, § 270.
Claims against state, persons erroneously convicted of crime, § 4903.
Cockfighting, clipping mature cock's comb, intent, § 597j.
Comments of court, § 1093.
Commercial exploitation, lewdness and obscenity, § 311.
Concealment of documentary evidence, § 135.
Confidential or privileged communications, wiretap evidence, admissibility, § 631 et seq.
Conspiracy, overt acts, §§ 184, 1104.
Corroboration,
  Accomplices, § 1111.
  Perjury, § 1103a.
  Solicitation of commission of certain crimes, § 653f.
Criminal intent, § 21.
Defrauding innkeepers, prima facie evidence, § 537.
Depositions, generally, this index.
Desertion, § 270.
Destruction of documentary evidence, § 135.
Disposition, § 1417 et seq.
  Dangerous or deadly weapons, § 1419.
  Destruction of unlawful property, § 1419.
  Exhibits, § 1418.
  Explosives, § 1419.
  Narcotic drugs, § 1419.
  Notice, § 1418.
  Orders, § 1418.
  Poisonous drugs, § 1419.
  Time, disposal of exhibits, § 1418.
  Unlawful property, destruction, § 1419.
  Weapons, § 1419.
Disturbing the peace, state college or university, § 415.5.
Documentary evidence, falsification, preparation, § 134.
Eavesdropping, wiretap evidence, admissibility, § 631 et seq.
Electronic eavesdropping, wiretap evidence, admissibility, § 631 et seq.
Embezzlement, this index.
Exhibits, generally, this index.
Falsification, §§ 132 et seq., 470.
Fighting cocks, possession with intent to use, § 597j.
First degree murder, special circumstances, determination of sentence and punishment, § 190.3.
Forgery,
  Offering forged evidence, § 132.
Grand Jury, this index.
Guilty pleas, withdrawn pleas specifying punishment, § 1192.5.
Habeas corpus, false evidence, inquiry, § 1473.
Homicide, special circumstances, determination of sentence and punishment, § 190.3.
Houses of ill-fame, common repute as evidence, § 315.
Indictment and Information, this index.
Innocence, presumptions, § 1096.
Intent,
  Fraud, § 8.
  Manifestations of criminal intent, § 21.

EVIDENCE—Cont'd
Invasion of privacy, wiretap evidence, admissibility, § 631 et seq.
Judicial notice, pleading matters judicially noticed, § 961.
Juvenile Delinquents and Dependents, this index.
Larceny, description of property, § 1131.
Lewdness and obscenity,
  Commercial exploitation, § 311.
Libel and Slander, this index.
Limitation to relevant and material matters, § 1044.
Material matters, § 1044.
Mentally deficient and mentally ill persons, trial of sanity issue, § 1369.
Mitigation of punishment, method of presentment, § 1204.
Murder, shifting of burden of proof, § 1105.
Nolo contendere pleas, withdrawn pleas specifying punishment, § 1192.5.
Offering false evidence, § 132.
Perjury,
  Weight and sufficiency, § 1103a.
Post conviction hearing, aggravation or mitigation of punishment, § 1204.
Preparing false documentary evidence, § 134.
Presumptions,
  Accusatory pleadings, pleading presumptions, § 961.
  Innocence of defendant, § 1096.
  Instructions to jury, § 1096a.
  Insufficiency of funds, knowledge from notice of protest, of check, draft or order, § 476a.
  Receiving stolen property, § 496.
  Sanity, pleas, §§ 1016, 1026.
  Theft by fraud, rented property, § 484.
  Weapons, this index.
Private communications, wiretap evidence, admissibility, § 631 et seq.
Proceedings to determine penalty, capital offenses, trier of fact, determination, § 190.3.
Property retained as evidence, disposition, § 1413.
Rape, this index.
Reasonable doubt, defined, § 1096.
Relevant matters, restriction, § 1044.
Soliciting commission of offenses, degree of proof, § 653f.
State college or university, disturbance of peace, § 415.5.
Subsequent testimony contrary to affidavit, § 118a.
Support, evidence of nonsupport, § 270.
Suppression of evidence,
  Unreasonable search or seizure, § 1538.5.
Theft, this index.
Unreasonable searches or seizures, suppression of evidence, § 1538.5.
Weapons, this index.
Weight and sufficiency of evidence, acquittal, § 1118.1.
Wiretap evidence, private communications, admissibility, § 631 et seq.
Witnesses, generally, this index.

Penal Code

EVIDENCE—Cont'd
Written instruments,
  Destruction or concealment, § 135.
  Falsification, preparation, § 134.

EVIDENCES OF INDEBTEDNESS
Counterfeiting, § 470.
Defined, § 7.
Embezzlement,
  Value, determination, § 514.
Forgery, § 470.

EXCRETION
Children and minors, harmful matter depicting, distribution or exhibition, § 313 et seq.

EXCUSABLE HOMICIDE
Homicide, this index.

EXECUTION
Capital Punishment, generally, this index.

EXECUTIONS
Corporations, fines and penalties, enforcement, § 1397.
Fines and penalties, § 1214.
Imprisonment or fine and imprisonment until paid, § 1215.
Officer making levy without process or legal authority, § 146.
Penalties, § 1214.
Prisoners, work furlough earnings, § 1208.
Support order, § 270.

EXEMPTIONS
Dogs, fighting, fines and penalties, § 597.5.
Drunkards and drunkenness, civil protective custody, § 647.
Extradition, service of process in civil action, § 1555.
Obscenity, motion picture machine operators, § 311.2.
Weapons, this index.

EXHIBITIONS
Fairs and Expositions, generally, this index.
Indecent exposure, § 314.
Lewdness and obscenity, § 311.2 et seq.
Obscene live conduct, managing, producing, exhibiting, etc., § 311.6.
Sporting events, bribery, § 337b et seq.

EXHIBITS
Defined,
  Harmful matter, § 313.
  Obscene matter, § 311.
Destruction of exhibits, § 1418.
Disposition, § 1417 et seq.
Documentary exhibits, disposition, § 1418.5.
Explosives, disposition, § 1419.
Narcotics, disposition, § 1419.
Notice to owner, disposition of property used in evidence, § 1418.
Release, § 1418.6.
Weapons, disposal, § 1419.

EXONERATION
Bail, this index.

EXPIRED CREDIT CARDS
Defined, § 484d.

EXPLOSIVES
Baggage, carrying or placing explosives or destructive devices, passenger vehicles for hire, § 12303.1.
Bombs, generally, this index.
Burglary with explosives,
  Defined, § 464.
  Probation, § 1203.
Buses, carrying or placing explosives or destructive devices, passenger vehicles for hire, § 12303.1.
Capital offenses, § 189.
Carriers, carrying or placing explosives or destructive devices, passenger vehicles for hire, § 12303.1.
Concealed explosives, § 12020 et seq.
Correctional Institutions, this index.
Defined, homicide, § 189.
Evidence, disposition, § 1419.
Exhibits in criminal prosecutions, release, § 1418.6.
False or facsimile explosives, mail and mailing, § 148.1.
False report of placing or secreting, § 148.1.
Fire departments, false reports of planting, § 148.1.
First degree murder, special circumstance, punishment, § 190.2.
Gunpowder, burglary, § 464.
Homicide, § 189.
  First degree murder, special circumstance, punishment, § 190.2.
Industrial farms and road camps, possession, § 4574.
Intent to commit murder by means of, § 12308.
Intent to destroy buildings, etc., § 452.
Jails, possession, § 4574.
Licenses and permits, unlicensed possession with intent to make explosive or destructive device, § 12312.
Mail or mailing, false or facsimile bonds, § 148.1.
Making explosive or device, unlicensed possession of substances or materials, § 12312.
Mentally incompetent defendant, commitment or outpatient treatment, § 1370.
Motor vehicles, carrying or placing explosives or destructive devices, passenger vehicles for hire, § 12303.1.
Municipal prisoners, possession, § 4574.
Nitroglycerine, burglary, use on vault, safe, etc., § 464.
Possession,
  Unlicensed possession, intent to make explosive or destructive device, § 12312.
Railroads, this index.
Robbery, trains, § 214.
Trains,
  Robbery, use for, § 214.
  Wrecking, §§ 218, 219.

EXTRADITION

EXPLOSIVES—Cont'd
Transporting passengers for hire, carrying or placing explosives or destructive devices, § 12303.1.
Vending machines, burglar tools, § 466.3.

EXPORTS AND IMPORTS
Destructive devices, permit, § 12305.
Eavesdropping equipment, § 635.
Sawed-off shotgun, § 12001.5.
Weapons, § 12020.
Wiretapping equipment, § 635.

EXPOSITIONS
Fairs and Expositions, generally, this index.

EXPOSURE
Extortion, threat to expose deformity, disgrace or crime, § 519.

EXPRESS MALICE
Defined, homicide, § 188.

EXTORTION
Accomplices and accessories, soliciting aid, § 653f.
Accusation of crime, § 519.
Attempts, § 524.
Color of official right, element of offense, §§ 518, 521.
Crime, threat to expose, § 519.
Defined, § 518.
Deformity, threat to expose, § 519.
Disgrace, threat to expose, § 519.
Evidence, wiretap evidence, admissibility, § 633.5.
Fear,
  Element of offense, § 518.
  Sufficiency to constitute, § 519.
Force, element of offense, § 518.
Injury to person or property, threat, § 519.
Kidnapping, §§ 209, 210.
Letters, threatening, § 523.
Personal injuries, threat to injure, § 519.
Probation, § 1203.
Property damage, threat to damage, § 519.
Secret, threat to expose, § 519.
Sentence and punishment, § 520 et seq.
Signature, obtaining by threats, § 522.
Soliciting commission of extortion, § 653f.
Third person, threat of injury, § 519.
Wiretap evidence, admissibility, § 633.5.

EXTRADITION
Generally, § 1547 et seq.
Accounts and accounting, expenses of returning fugitives, § 1557.
Act committed in state intentionally resulting in crime in other state, § 1549.1.
Actions and proceedings, civil process, exemptions, § 1555.
Advances, expenses of returning fugitive, § 1557.
Affidavits,
  Demand, § 1548.2.
  Magistrate's warrant, § 1551 et seq.
Appearance of fugitive, bail jumping, § 1553.

EXTRADITION

EXTRADITION—Cont'd
Arrest, § 1548.1.
  Aid and assistance from other persons, § 1551.
  Authority, § 1549.3.
  Hearing, § 1550.1.
  Jumping bail, § 1553.
  Magistrate's warrant, § 1551 et seq.
    Commitment pending governor's warrant, § 1552.
  Notice, § 1551.3.
  Testing legality, § 1550.1.
  Warrants, § 1549.2.
    Disobedience, § 1550.2.
    Issuance to agent to receive person demanded from foreign state, § 1554.1.
    Recall, § 1554.
    Seal, § 1549.2.
    Without warrant, § 1551.1.
Arresting officer, authority, § 1550.
Audit and payment of expenses, § 1557.
Bail,
  Arrest of fugitive pending governor's warrant, § 1552.
  Capital offenses, § 1552.1.
  Fugitive from bail, bondsman's application for return, § 847.5.
  Jumping bail, § 1548 et seq.
Capital offenses,
  Arrest without warrant, § 1551.1.
  Bail, § 1552.1.
Certification of indictment and information, etc., by executive authority making demand, § 1548.2.
City officers designated to return fugitives, expenses, payment, § 1557.
Civil actions, service of process, § 1555.
Commitment, person arrested on magistrate's warrant, § 1551.2.
Confinement of prisoner on executing warrant of arrest, § 1550.3.
Consent to return, written instrument, § 1555.1.
Construction of law, § 1556.1.
Counsel for accused, § 1550.1.
Crimes other than specified in requisition, trial, § 1556.
Custody, prisoner passing through state, § 1550.3.
Definitions, § 1548.
Delivery of fugitive, § 1548.1.
  Arrest warrant, § 1549.3.
Demand, § 1548.2.
  Application, § 1554.2.
  Fugitive from foreign state, § 1554.1.
  Investigation, § 1548.3.
District attorney, application for requisition, § 1554.2.
Evidence, commitment of person arrested on magistrate's warrant, § 1551.2.
Exemptions, service of process in civil actions, § 1555.
Expenses,
  Keeping prisoner en route to demanding state, § 1550.3.
  Returning fugitives, § 1557.
Fines and penalties, disobedience to warrant, § 1550.2.
Form, demand, § 1548.2.
Fugitive from bail, bondsman's application for return, § 847.5.

EXTRADITION—Cont'd
Guilt or innocence of accused, inquiry, § 1553.2.
Habeas corpus, right to apply for writ, § 1550.1.
Hearings, § 1550.1.
  Inquiry into guilt or innocence, § 1553.2.
Identification of party, inquiry, § 1553.2.
Indictment or information, copy to accompany demand, § 1548.2.
Innocence of accused, inquiry, § 1553.2.
Investigation, § 1548.3.
Issuance of warrant of arrest to agent to receive person demanded, § 1554.1.
Jails, confinement of prisoners en route to demanding state, § 1550.3.
Judgment of conviction, copy to accompany demand, § 1548.2.
Jumping bail, arrest, § 1553.
Legality of arrest, right to test, § 1550.1.
Magistrate's warrant, § 1551 et seq.
Oaths and affirmations, application for requisition, § 1554.2.
Other crimes, trial, § 1556.
Parole and probation, escaped parolee, § 1548 et seq.
Peace officers, authority, § 1550.
Pending prosecutions, surrender of fugitive, § 1553.1.
Presence in demanding state at time of commission of crime, § 1549.1.
Privileges and immunities, civil process, § 1555.
Procedure, waiver, § 1555.1.
Recall, warrant of arrest, § 1554.
Receipts for expenses, § 1557.
Recognition of demand, § 1548.2.
Recommitment, fugitive arrested on magistrate's warrant, § 1552.2.
Reimbursement to counties, § 1557.
Reissuance of warrant of arrest, § 1554.
Release on own recognizance, waiver, § 1318.4.
Reports, investigation, § 1548.3.
Return, excess advances, § 1557.
Right to counsel, § 1550.1.
Seal,
  Warrant,
    Arrest, § 1549.2.
    Demand from foreign state, § 1554.1.
Service of process in civil actions, exemption, § 1555.
Specified crimes in requisition, trial of other crimes, § 1556.
Speedy trial, arrest without warrant, § 1551.1.
State's rights, waiver, § 1555.2.
Statutory fees, § 1557.
Subsistence of fugitive, fees and costs, § 1557.
Surrender of person committing act resulting in crime in demanding state, § 1549.1.
Testing legality of arrest, § 1550.1.
Time, magistrate's warrant, period for arrest, § 1552.2.
Trial for other crimes, § 1556.
Waiver,
  Issuance and service of warrant, § 1555.1.

EXTRADITION—Cont'd
Waiver—Cont'd
  Passing through state, § 1550.3.
  State rights, § 1555.2.
Witnesses, expenses of producing, payment by state seeking fugitive, § 1557.
Written application for requisition, § 1554.2.
Written demand, § 1548.2.

EYES AND EYESIGHT
Putting out, mayhem, §§ 203, 204.

FACTORIES
Manufacturers and Manufacturing, generally, this index.

FAIRS AND EXPOSITIONS
See, also, Exhibitions, generally, this index.
Dogs, fighting, fines and penalties, § 597.5.

FAITH HEALING
Battered or sexually molested children, reports, § 11161.5.

FALSE ARREST
False Imprisonment, generally, this index.

FALSE EVIDENCE
Perjury, generally, this index.

FALSE IMPRISONMENT
Generally, §§ 236, 237.
Civil liability of peace officer, § 847.
Conspiracy, § 182.
Defined, § 236.
Fines and penalties, § 237.
Jurisdiction, § 784.
Liability of peace officer,
  Civil liability, § 847.
  Criminal liability, § 146.
Public officers or employees, civil liability, § 836.5.
Shoplifting, defenses, § 490.5.

FALSE OR FRAUDULENT REPORTS
Instruments for record, § 115.

FALSE PERSONATION
Concealable firearms, sales, § 12076.
Correctional institutions, fraudulent entry, § 4570.5.
Credit cards, theft for use, sale or transfer, §§ 484e, 484g et seq.
Drugs, impersonating physician to obtain, § 377.
Firearms, sales, § 12076.
Jails, fraudulent entry, § 4570.5.
Officers, § 146a.
Peace officers, § 538d.
Physicians and surgeons, representing to obtain prescription drugs, § 377.
Police officers, § 538d.
Public officers, making arrest, etc., without process or authority, § 146.
State investigators, § 146a.

FALSE PRETENSES
Generally, § 484.
Apartment houses, obtaining credit, § 537.
Auto camps, obtaining credit, § 537.
Boarding houses, obtaining credit, § 537.
Bungalow courts, obtaining credit, § 537.
Campgrounds, obtaining credit, § 537.
Conspiracy to obtain money or property, § 182.
Credit, this index.
Females, procurement by for illicit intercourse, § 266.
Hotels, obtaining credit, § 537.
Innkeepers, defrauding, § 537.
Inns, obtaining credit, § 537.
Lodging houses, obtaining credit, § 537.
Money, obtaining, §§ 484, 490a.
Motels, obtaining credit, § 537.
Obtaining money by false pretenses, § 484.
  Statutory reference, larceny, embezzlement or stealing meaning theft, § 490a.
Official inquiries, simulating, § 146b.
Parole and probation, eligibility, § 1203.
Property, obtaining, § 484.
Restaurants, obtaining credit, § 537.
Statutory reference, larceny, embezzlement or stealing meaning theft, § 490a.
Theft, § 484.

FALSE REPORTS
Emergency reports, § 148.3.
Police officers, § 148.5.

FALSE REPRESENTATIONS
Fraud, generally, this index.

FALSE SWEARING
Perjury, generally, this index.

FAMILY
Relatives, generally, this index.

FAMILY COUNSELORS
Privileges and immunities, battered or sexually molested children, reports, § 11161.5.

FAMILY PLANNING SERVICES
Jails, female prisoners, § 4023.5.

FARM PRODUCE
Agricultural Products, generally, this index.

FEAR
Defined, robbery, § 212.
Duress or Coercion, generally, this index.

FEDERAL BUREAU OF INVESTIGATION
Reports,
  Certificates of rehabilitation or pardons granted, § 4852.17.

FEDERAL CRIMES
Concealed weapons, conviction, § 12021.
Jurisdiction, § 777.

FEDERAL GOVERNMENT
United States, generally, this index.

FEEBLE-MINDED PERSONS
Mentally Deficient and Mentally Ill Persons, generally, this index.

FELLATION
Generally, § 288a.
Oral Copulation, generally, this index.
Sodomy, generally, this index.

FELONY MURDER ACT
Generally, § 189.

FEMALES
Women, generally, this index.

FENCES
Malicious mischief, § 602.
  Burning, § 449b.
Trespasses, § 602.

FENTANYL
See, also, Drugs and Medicine, generally, this index.

FERAL HORSES
See, also, Fish and Game, generally, this index.

FETAL DEATH
Homicide, § 187.

FICTITIOUS NAMES
Assumed or Fictitious Names, generally, this index.

FIDELITY BONDS
Bonds (Officers and Fiduciaries), generally, this index.

FIDUCIARIES
Bonds (Officers and Fiduciaries), generally, this index.
Embezzlement, generally, this index.
Guardian and Ward, generally, this index.

FIGHTING
Boxing and Wrestling, generally, this index.
Disorderly Conduct, generally, this index.
Firearm or deadly weapon, drawing, exhibiting or using, § 417.

FIGHTING ANIMALS
Animals, this index.

FINANCIAL INSTITUTIONS
Guards or messengers, carrying firearms, § 12031.

FINANCIAL INTEREST
Adverse or Pecuniary Interest, generally, this index.

FINANCIAL STATEMENTS AND REPORTS
False reports,
  Credit reports, theft by fraud, § 484.
  Theft by fraud, § 484.

FINDING LOST PROPERTY
Theft, § 485.

FINES AND PENALTIES
Generally, §§ 1 et seq., 1168.
Abandonment, insured property, defrauding insurer, § 548.
Abduction,
  Children, § 278.
Absence,
  Jail work furlough program, counties, § 1208.
Accomplices and accessories, § 33.
  Outside state subsequently found in California, § 778b.
Additional punishment,
  Discretion of court, § 1170.1.
  Firearms used, § 12022.5.
  Principals, § 12022.
Administering drugs, etc., to assist in commission of felony, § 222.
Administration of poisons, attempt to kill, § 216.
Adoption,
  Proceeding pending, concealment or removal of child, § 280.
Adult classes, annoying or molesting persons in attendance, § 647b.
Aggravation, § 1170.
  Evidence, § 1204.
Aiding and abetting escape, § 4533.
Allocution, § 1200.
Alternate punishment to county jails, felonies, § 18.
Annoying or molesting persons attending adult classes, § 647b.
Arson, § 447a et seq.
  Insured property, § 548.
  Personal property, § 449a.
  Soliciting commission, § 653f.
Assault and battery, § 241 et seq.
  Intent to commit felony, §§ 220, 221.
  Intent to murder, § 217.
Assault with deadly weapon,
  Life prisoner, § 4500.
  Prison inmate, § 4501.
  Soliciting assault with deadly weapon or instrument, § 653f.
Attempts, § 663 et seq.
  County jail, § 664.
  Extortion, § 524.
  Kill, § 216 et seq.
  Rescue prison inmate, § 4550.
Authority to impose fines and penalties, § 13.
  Fines in addition to imprisonment, § 672.
Authority to sentence,
  Fines in addition to imprisonment, § 672.
Bad checks, passing, etc., § 476a.
Bail,
  Release on own recognizance, failure to appear, § 1319.4.
Battered children, § 273d.
Battery, § 241 et seq.
Bicycles, using without permission, § 499b.
Bigamy, § 283.
Bingo, § 326.5.

FINES

FINES AND PENALTIES—Cont'd
Boats and boating,
  Unpermitted taking for temporary use, § 499b.
Bomb or other explosive placed or secreted,
  False report, § 148.1.
  Passenger vehicles for hire, carrying or placing, § 12303.1.
  Unlicensed possession of materials for purpose of making, § 12312.
Bribery,
  Public officers, etc., § 67 et seq.
  Soliciting commission, § 653f.
    Public officers, etc., § 67 et seq.
Bringing defendant before court for judgment, § 1194.
Bringing stolen property into state, § 27.
Brutality, cruel, corporal or unusual punishment, § 673.
Burglary, § 461.
  Explosives, § 464.
  Soliciting commission, § 653f.
Burglary tools, possession, § 466.
Burning property not subject to arson, malicious mischief, §§ 449b, 449c.
Campus disorders, colleges and universities, § 626.2 et seq.
Capital Punishment, generally, this index.
Checks,
  Fictitious, making, uttering, etc., with intent to defraud, § 476.
  Issuance without sufficient funds or credit, § 476a.
  Possession, completed check with intent to defraud, § 475a.
Children and minors,
  Abduction, § 278.
  Sodomy, § 286.
  Stealing, § 278.
  Under eighteen, annoying or molesting, § 647a.
  Unjustifiable punishment of child, § 273a.
Cigarettes, sale or furnishing to minor under 18, § 308.
Civil rights, restoration, discharged probationer, § 1203.4.
Claims against state and other public bodies, fraud, § 72.
Classification of offenses, discretion of court, § 17.
Clerks of court, payment, § 1205.
Colleges and universities,
  Campus disorders, junior colleges, § 626.2 et seq.
  Disruptive persons, denial of access to campus or facilities, § 626 et seq.
  Disturbing the peace, state institutions, § 415.5.
  Teachers or students, obstructing, § 602.10.
Combustible material, possession with intent to set fire to property, § 452.
Commercial paper, fictitious paper, making, possessing, etc., with intent to defraud, § 476.
Commitment, diagnostic facility for examination, § 1203.03.
Communications, simulating official inquiries, § 146b.

FINES AND PENALTIES—Cont'd
Compounding crimes, § 153.
Concealment of crimes, § 153.
Concealment of property,
  Insured property, defrauding insurer, § 548.
Concurrent terms,
  Multiple offenses, § 669.
  Rehabilitation period, pardons, § 4852.03.
Conflict of laws, § 778 et seq.
Consecutive sentences,
  Armed with deadly weapon, §§ 12022, 12022.5.
  Assault with deadly weapon by inmate, § 4501.
  Assault with deadly weapon by life prisoner, § 4500.
  Battery by inmate, § 4501.5.
  Escape, § 4530.
  Firearms used, § 12022.5.
  Hostages held by inmates, § 4503.
  Multiple offenses, §§ 669, 1170.1.
  Rehabilitation period, pardons, § 4852.03.
  Weapons carried by inmates, § 4502.
Conspiracy, § 182.
Construction funds, diversion, § 484b.
Continuance, probation hearing, § 1203.
Contributing to delinquency of a minor, § 272.
Conversion of real property to personal property, severance, § 487b.
Conviction of crimes,
  Committed before and after July 1, 1977, § 1170.2.
Corporal injury, infliction upon child, § 273d.
Corporal punishment, § 673.
Corporations, enforcement, § 1397.
Correctional institutions,
  Intentional destruction, § 4600.
Counties, fraudulent claims against, presentation, § 72.
County jail,
  Attempts, § 664.
  Work furlough program, unauthorized absence, § 1208.
Credit for time served,
  Determinate sentences, § 1170.2.
  Diagnostic facilities, § 1203.03.
  Reports to corrections officers, § 1170.
Criminal syndicalism, § 11401.
Cruel or unusual punishment, § 673.
Cruel treatment of prisoners, § 147.
Cruelty to children, § 273a.
Custody,
  Defendant in custody, bringing before court for judgment, § 1194.
Deadly weapons,
  Assault with, prison inmates, §§ 4500, 4501.
  Possession by prison inmate, § 4502.
Death,
  Imminent danger, pardon or reprieve, § 4806.
Death penalty. Capital Punishment, generally, this index.
Declaration of offenses as misdemeanors, § 17.
Defacing property of another, § 594.5.
Defalcation, public funds, § 514.
Default in payment of fine,
  Discretion of court, § 1205.

FINES AND PENALTIES—Cont'd
Default in payment of fine—Cont'd
  Imprisonment at discretion of court, § 1205.
  Maximum period of confinement, § 19a.
Definitions, § 7.
Degrees of offense, determination before passing sentence, § 1192.
Delay in taking arrested person before magistrate, § 145.
Delaying officer in discharge of duty, § 148.
Delivery of prisoner into custody after judgment, § 1202a.
Desertion of child under fourteen, § 271.
Destruction, insured property, defrauding insurer, § 548.
Destructive devices,
  Passenger vehicles for hire, carrying or placing, § 12303.1.
  Purchase, sale or possession, §§ 12303, 12304.
Determinate sentences, § 1170 et seq.
  Additional sentence, § 1170.
  Annual sentencing institutes for trial court judges, § 1170.5.
  Armed with deadly weapon, prior conviction, § 1170.2.
  Attorneys to represent accused, prior conviction, § 1170.2.
  Credit for time served, § 1170.2.
    Term of imprisonment, § 2930 et seq.
  Effective date of law, prior sentencing, § 1170.2.
  Enhancing sentence, § 1170.
  Expiration of sentence, parole, § 3000.
  Good behavior, reduction of sentence, § 2930 et seq.
  Information relating to sentencing practices, § 1170.4.
  Lower term, § 1170.
  Middle of three possible terms, § 1170.
  Parole at expiration of term, § 3000.
  Prior sentencing, § 1170.2.
  Recall of sentence and commitment, § 1170.
  Reports, review, § 1170.6.
  Rules of judicial council, § 1170.4.
  Uniformity in sentences, §§ 1170, 1170.3.
  Weapons, prior conviction, § 1170.2.
Diagnosis and recommendation, diagnostic facility report, § 1203.03.
Diagnostic facilities, credit for time spent, § 1203.03.
Disclosure of private communications, invasion of privacy, § 637.
Discretion of court, imprisonment for default in payment of fine, § 1205.
Disorderly conduct, § 415.
  State college or university, § 415.5.
Disruptive presence in schools, § 626.8.
Dissuading witness from attending trial, §§ 136, 136½.
Districts, fraudulent claims against, presentation, § 72.
Disturbing the peace, § 415.
  State college or university, § 415.5.
Diversion, construction funds, § 484b.

Penal Code   **FINES**

FINES AND PENALTIES—Cont'd
Documentary evidence, destroying or concealing, § 135.
Dogs,
    Fighting, § 597.5.
Double punishment, § 654.
Drugs, administering to assist in commission of felony, § 222.
Duration of imprisonment, § 1168.
Embezzlement, § 514.
    Bringing embezzled property into state, § 27.
    Mitigation of punishment, §§ 512, 513.
Emergencies,
    False reports, § 148.3.
Emoluments, public officers, asking or receiving, § 70.
Enhancement,
    Multiple felonies, § 1170.1.
    Prison term for new offenses, § 667.5.
    Single offenses, § 1170.1.
Escape,
    Aiding and abetting, § 4533.
    Facilitating by sending things to prison, § 4535.
Evidence, aggravation or mitigation of punishment, § 1204.
Execution of judgment, § 1214.
Execution of sentence,
    Change of order, § 1203.3.
Executive officers, attempts to kill or assault, § 217.1.
Explosive or bomb placed or secreted, False report, § 148.1.
Extortion, § 520 et seq.
    Soliciting commission, § 653f.
Extradition, deliverance of arrested person to agent of demanding state without hearing, § 1550.2.
False arrest, § 146.
False emergency reports, § 148.3.
False fire alarm, § 148.4.
False imprisonment, § 237.
False reports,
    Emergencies, § 148.3.
    Explosive or bomb placed or secreted, § 148.1.
False representation,
    Child as orphan, § 271a.
Falsifying evidence, § 132 et seq.
Federal offenses, § 777.
Felons, firearms possession, § 12560.
Felony, prior conviction, punishment for petty theft, § 666.
Fictitious instruments, making, passing or uttering with intent to defraud, § 476.
Fire alarms,
    False alarms, § 148.4.
    Tampering, § 148.4.
Fire bombs, possessing, manufacturing or disposing, § 452.
Firearms,
    Prior prison term, additional punishment, § 667.5.
First degree murder, §§ 190, 190.1.
Flammable material, possession with intent to set fire to property, § 452.
Foreign states,
    Accomplice or accessory out of state subsequently found in California, § 778b.

FINES AND PENALTIES—Cont'd
Foreign states—Cont'd
    Offenses commenced in foreign state and consummated within state, § 778.
    Offenses consummated in foreign state but commenced in California, § 778a.
Forgery, § 473.
    Bills and notes, possession, § 475.
    Soliciting commission, § 653f.
    Telegraph or telephone messages, § 474.
Fraud,
    Insurers, intent to defraud, § 548.
Fraudulent claims, public funds, § 72.
Gags, use for punishment, § 673.
Grand juror failing to attend, § 907.
Grand larceny, assault with intent to commit, § 220.
Grand theft, § 489.
    Assault with intent to commit, § 220.
    Conversion of real property to personal property by severance, §§ 487b, 487c.
    Soliciting commission, § 653f.
Guards, jail keepers, etc., aiding escape, § 4533.
Habeas corpus,
    Disobedience, § 1505.
    Refusal to obey writ, § 1479.
Harmful matter, distribution or exhibition of minor, § 313.1.
Hearings, mitigation of punishment, § 1204.
Homicide,
    Assault with intent to murder, § 217.
    Poison, administering with intent to kill, § 216.
    Soliciting commission, § 653f.
Hostages, prison inmates holding, § 4503.
Husband, failure to support spouse, § 270a.
Impersonation of officer, § 146a.
Importation,
    Eavesdropping equipment, § 635.
Imposition, § 1205.
Imprisonment,
    County jail, attempts, § 664.
    Default of payment of fine, § 1205.
Incest, § 285.
Indecent exposure, § 314.
Infractions, classification of offenses, § 17.
Inhuman treatment of prisoners, § 147.
Initial sentencing, § 1170 et seq.
Installment payment of fine, § 1205.
Insured property, intent to defraud insurer, § 548.
Intent to commit felony, assault, §§ 220, 221.
Intent to murder, assault, § 217.
Intermittent periods, commitment, condition of probation, § 1203.1.
Involuntary manslaughter, § 193.
Jail prisoners, work release, § 1208.
Jail work furlough program, counties, unauthorized absence, § 1208.
Jails, demolishing, § 4600.

FINES AND PENALTIES—Cont'd
Judgments,
    Execution, § 1215.
    Issuance, § 1214.
    Imposition, § 1205.
Judicial council, rules, §§ 1170, 1170.6.
Judicial officers, attempts to kill or assault upon, § 217.1.
Junk dealers, purchasing metals used in transportation or public utility service, § 496a.
Keys to public buildings, unauthorized duplication, § 469.
Kidnapping, § 208 et seq.
    Prior prison term, additional punishment, § 667.5.
    Soliciting commission, § 653f.
Larceny, bringing stolen property into state, § 27.
Lesser included offenses, § 654.
Lewdness and obscenity, § 311.9.
    Children, prior prison term, additional punishment, § 667.5.
Lieu of imprisonment, § 1205.
Loitering about schools or public places, Adult classes in attendance, § 647b.
Lotteries, § 319 et seq.
Machine guns, unlawful sale, possession or transportation, § 12220.
Making fictitious instruments with intent to defraud, § 476.
Malicious mischief,
    Burning property not subject to arson, §§ 449b, 449c.
Manslaughter, § 193.
    Prior prison term, additional punishment, § 667.5.
Maximum term, misdemeanors, § 19a.
Mayhem, § 204.
    Assault with intent to commit, § 220.
    Prior prison term, additional punishment, § 667.5.
Misdemeanors, § 17.
    Fines in addition to imprisonment, § 672.
    Punishment not otherwise prescribed, § 19.
Mitigation, § 1170.
    Embezzlement, §§ 512, 513.
    Evidence, § 1204.
    Hearing, § 1204.
    Presentment of circumstances, method, § 1204.
    Probation, § 1203 et seq.
Molesting persons attending adult classes, § 647b.
Molotov cocktails, possession, manufacturing, possessing or disposing of, § 452.
Money order, possessing with intent to defraud, § 475a.
Motor vehicles, unpermitted taking for temporary use, § 499b.
Motorboats, unpermitted taking for temporary use, § 499b.
Motorcycles, using without permission, § 499b.
Multiple offenses, § 1170.1.
    Concurrent or consecutive terms, direction, § 669.
    Single act, § 654.

FINES

FINES AND PENALTIES—Cont'd
Murder,
  Prior prison term, additional punishment, § 667.5.
  Soliciting commission, § 653f.
Newspapers, peace officer's residence address or telephone number, disclosing maliciously with intent to obstruct justice, § 146e.
Obscene matter, publication, distribution, etc., § 311.9.
Obstructing or resisting officers in performance of duties, §§ 69, 148.
Obstruction of college or university students or teachers by physical force, § 602.10.
Offenses commenced in foreign state and consummated within state, § 778.
Offenses consummated in foreign state but commenced in California, § 778a.
Officer unnecessarily assaulting or beating person, § 149.
Oppressive treatment of prisoners, § 147.
Oral copulation, § 288a.
  Prior prison term, additional punishment, § 667.5.
Pandering, § 266i.
Parole and Probation, this index.
Payment, § 1205.
  Default, imprisonment, discretion of court, § 1205.
Peace officers, disclosing officer's residence address or telephone number, maliciously with intent to obstruct justice, § 146e.
Penalty not specifically prescribed,
  Felonies, § 18.
  Misdemeanors, § 19.
Perjury, § 126.
  Procuring execution of innocent persons, § 128.
  Soliciting commission, § 653f.
  Subornation of perjury, §§ 127, 128.
Personal property,
  Arson, § 449a.
  Custody of officer, damaging, etc., § 102.
Persons liable to punishment, § 27.
Petty theft, § 490.
  Prior conviction, § 666.
Physical force, obstructing college or university teachers or students, § 602.10.
Pimping, § 266h.
Poisons, administering, attempts to kill, § 216.
Possession,
  Blank bills and notes, § 475.
  Completed check, money order or traveler's check with intent to defraud, § 475a.
  Fictitious instruments with intent to defraud, § 476.
  Forged bills and notes, § 475.
Post conviction hearing, aggravation or mitigation of punishment, § 1204.
Preparing false documentary evidence, § 134.
Presence of defendant,
  Commitments, § 1203.2a.
Pre-sentence investigation, § 1203 et seq.

FINES AND PENALTIES—Cont'd
Preventing witness from attending trial, § 136.
Prior convictions,
  Burglary, § 666.
  Determinate sentences, § 1170.2.
  Foreign states, subsequent offenses, punishment, § 668.
  Grand theft, § 666.
  Petit theft, § 666.
  Robbery, § 666.
Prior prison term, additional punishment, § 667.5.
Prior sentence, determinate sentences, § 1170.2.
Prison inmate,
  Assault with deadly weapon, § 4501.
  Hostages, holding, § 4503.
Probation, § 1203.1.
Probationer, release from penalties, § 1203.4.
Proceeding on discovery of prior conviction after sentence for subsequent offense, § 669.
Pronouncement of sentence, §§ 1191 et seq., 1202 et seq.
  After suspension of sentence, § 1203.2.
  Probationer committed for another offense, § 1203.2a.
Public funds,
  Defalcation, § 514.
  Fraudulent claims, § 72.
Public officials, assaulting or beating persons, § 149.
Rape, § 264.
  Acting in concert by force or violence, § 264.1.
  Assault with intent to commit, § 220.
  Force and violence, soliciting commission, § 653f.
  Soliciting commission, § 653f.
Recall of sentence and commitment, resentence, § 1170.
Receiving stolen goods, § 496.
  Outside state, § 27.
  Soliciting commission, § 653f.
Recommendation and diagnosis, diagnostic facility report, § 1203.03.
Records, master criminal record sheet or information from unauthorized furnishing, § 11140 et seq.
Refusal of peace officers, etc., to receive or arrest person charged with offense, § 142.
Release of prisoner,
  Own recognizance,
    Discretion of court, § 1318.2.
    Failure to appear, § 1319.4.
Reports, false emergency reports, § 148.3.
Rescue of prisoners, § 4550.
Resentence, recall of sentence and commitment, § 1170.
Resisting officers in performance of duties, §§ 69, 148.
Robbery, § 213.
  Assault with intent to commit, § 220.
  Bringing stolen property into state, § 27.
  Soliciting commission, § 653f.

FINES AND PENALTIES—Cont'd
Sales,
  Destructive devices, § 12303.6.
  Eavesdropping equipment, § 635.
  Machine guns, § 12220.
School buildings and grounds,
  Disrupting, § 626.8.
Schools,
  Disrupting, § 626.8.
Secondhand dealers,
  Purchasing metals used in transportation and public utilities service, § 496a.
Self-incrimination, witnesses, § 1324.
Sequence of sentences, commitment of probationer after sentence for another offense, § 1203.2a.
Severance, conversion of real property, § 487b.
Sex materials, distribution or exhibition to children and minors, § 313.4.
Ships and shipping,
  Unpermitted taking for temporary use, § 499b.
Shoplifting, § 490.5.
Shower bath, use for punishment, § 673.
Silencers, firearms, possession, § 12520.
Simulating official inquiries, § 146b.
Single act, multiple offenses, § 654.
Sit-ins,
  Colleges and universities, § 626.2 et seq.
  Schools and school districts, § 626.8.
Sniperscopes, possession and use, § 468.
Sodomy, § 286.
  Assault with intent to commit, § 220.
  Children and minors, § 286.
Solicitation,
  Commission of certain offenses, degree of proof, § 653f.
Sporting events, bribery, § 337b et seq.
State college or university,
  Campus disorders, § 626.2 et seq.
  Disturbing the peace, § 415.5.
Straight jackets, use for punishment, § 673.
Studies, reports, § 1170.6.
Subornation of perjury, §§ 127, 128.
  Soliciting commission, § 653f.
Subsequent offenses, additional punishment, § 667.5.
Suspension of sentence,
  Change of order, § 1203.3.
  Determinate Sentence Law, § 1170.
  Heroin, violations dealing with heroin, § 1203.07.
  Misdemeanor cases, § 1203a.
  Probation officer, supervision, § 1215.
  Pronouncement of judgment after revocation of probation, § 1203.2.
Tampering with fire alarms, § 148.4.
Tear gas weapons, §§ 12420, 12422.
  Purchase, possession or use, § 12403.7.
Telegraphs and telephones,
  Forgery, § 474.
Temporary confinement, diagnostic facility, § 1203.03.
Term of imprisonment,
  Fixing, § 1168.
Theft,
  Grand theft, § 489.
  Assault with intent to commit, § 220.

Penal Code   **FORCE**

FINES AND PENALTIES—Cont'd
Theft—Cont'd
  Grand theft—Cont'd
    Conversion of real property to personal property by severance, § 487b.
    Soliciting commission, § 653f.
  Petty theft, § 490.
    Conversion of real property to personal property by severance, § 487c.
    Prior conviction, § 666.
  Vehicle or vessel, taking for temporary use, § 499b.
Threatening witnesses to prevent trial attendance, § 136.
Threats to public or school officials, § 71.
Thumbscrew, use for punishment, § 673.
Time,
  Period specified, § 1170.
  Pronouncing judgment, § 1191.
    Effect of placing in diagnostic facility, § 1191.
Tobacco, sale or furnishing to minor under 18, § 308.
Torture, punishment, § 673.
Trains, wrecking, §§ 218, 219.
Traveler's check, possessing completed check with intent to defraud, § 475a.
Trespass,
  Invasion of privacy, § 634.
Trial, sanity hearings, § 1367 et seq.
Tricing up, use for punishment, § 673.
Two or more felonies, § 1170.1.
Uniformity in sentences, §§ 1170, 1170.3.
  Studies, § 1170.6.
University of California,
  Campus disorders, § 626.2 et seq.
  Teachers or students, obstructing, § 602.10.
Unlawful sexual intercourse, §§ 261.5, 264.
Unusual punishment, § 673.
Uttering fictitious instruments with intent to defraud, § 476.
Vagrancy,
  Annoying or molesting child under eighteen, § 647a.
Vessels,
  Unpermitted taking for temporary use, § 499b.
Violent felonies, additional punishment, § 667.5.
Voluntary manslaughter, § 193.
Weapons,
  Deadly weapons, sale or transporting, § 12303.6.
  Possession,
    Prison inmate, § 4502.
  Uniform sentencing, § 1170.3.
Wife beating, § 273d.
Withholding evidence of criminal offenses, § 153.
Witnesses,
  Contempt, § 1331.
  Self-incrimination, § 1324.
Work furlough program, county jails, authorized absence, § 1208.
Work release programs, failure to return to place of confinement, § 4530.
Worthless checks, passing, etc., § 476a.

FINGERPRINTS AND FINGERPRINTING
Criminal history information,
  Local summary furnishing, § 13300 et seq.
Probationer, § 1203.1.
Records, § 11106.
  Application for examination, § 11122.
Sex offenders, registration, § 290.
Weapons, concealed, licenses to carry, § 12052.

FIRE BOMBS
Defined, § 452.
Possession or use, § 452.

FIREARMS
Weapons, generally, this index.

FIREBAUGH, CITY OF
See, also, Municipalities, generally, this index.

FIREMEN AND FIRE DEPARTMENTS
Assault, § 241.
  Deadly weapon or force likely to produce great bodily injury, §§ 245, 245.2.
Battery, § 243.
Bombs and explosives, false reports of planting, § 148.1.
Disorderly conduct interfering with official duties, § 148.2.
Emergencies, false reports of, § 148.3.
Emergency rescue personnel, defined, interference with personnel, § 148.2.
Explosives or bombs, false reports of planting, § 148.1.
False emergency reports, § 148.3.
False fire alarms, § 148.4.
Fire bombs, possession or use, § 452.
Interference with discharge of official duty, § 148.2.
Orders, disobedience of lawful orders, § 148.2.
Tampering with fire alarms, § 148.4.
Training program, courses on powers to arrest and use of firearms, § 832.

FIRES AND FIRE PROTECTION
Alarms,
  False alarms, § 148.4.
  Tampering with fire alarm system, § 148.4.
Arson, generally, this index.
Bail,
  Littering, § 853.6.
Cigarettes and cigars, littering, bail, § 853.6.
Disorderly conduct preventing extinguishment, § 148.2.
Emergencies, false reports of, § 148.3.
False alarms, § 148.4.
False fire reports, § 148.3.
Fire bombs, § 452.
Interference with extinguishment, § 148.2.
Littering,
  Bail, § 853.6.
Malicious mischief, building fires, § 602.

FIRES AND FIRE PROTECTION—Cont'd
Railroads,
  Robbery, acts with intention of committing, § 214.
  Wrecking, §§ 218, 219.
Sidewalks, throwing cigars and cigarettes on sidewalks, § 853.6.
Tampering with fire alarms system, § 148.4.
Trespass, § 602.

FIRST DEGREE MURDER
Generally, § 189.
Homicide, this index.

FISH AND GAME
Assault and battery, state peace officers, § 241 et seq.
Firearms, licenses and permits, § 12027.
Posted lands, trespass, § 602.
Trespass § 602.
Weapons, § 12027.

5–METHOXY–3, 4–METHYLENEDIOXY AMPHETAMINE
See, also, Drugs and Medicine, generally, this index.

FLECHETTE DARTS
Defined, weapons, possession, manufacture or sale, § 12020.
Weapons, generally, this index.

FLIGHT
Instructions to jury, form, § 1127c.

FONTANA, CITY OF
See, also, Municipalities, generally, this index.

FOOD
Candy and Confections, generally, this index.
Extradited prisoner, expenses, payment, § 1557.
False pretenses, obtaining food by, § 537.
Fruits, generally, this index.
Parent's liability to feed minors, § 270 et seq.
Vegetables, generally, this index.

FOOTBALL
Bribery,
  Officials, §§ 337d, 337e.
  Players, § 337b et seq.

FORCE AND VIOLENCE
Arrest, permissible force, §§ 835, 835a, 843.
  Overcoming resistance to arrest, § 835a.
  Resisting arrest, §§ 834a, 843.
Correctional institutions, holding hostages, § 4503.
Escape, this index.
Extortion, element of offense, § 518.
False imprisonment, § 237.
Malicious mischief, forcible entry, § 603.
Officers, obstructing or resisting in performance of duties, § 69.

FORCE

FORCE AND VIOLENCE—Cont'd
Oral copulation, § 288a.
Pandering, § 266i.
Physical force, defined, obstructing college teachers or students, § 602.10.
Prostitution house, placing or permitting placement of wife, § 266g.
Rape, this index.
Resistance to commission of offense, § 692 et seq.
Resisting arrest, force to overcome resistance, § 835a.
Riot, defined, § 404.
Search warrants, execution, §§ 1531, 1532.
Self defense, § 692 et seq.
Subornation of perjury, § 137.
Vandalism, forcible entry, § 603.
Wiretap evidence, admissibility, § 633.5.
Witnesses, inducing false testimony, § 137.

FORCIBLE ENTRY AND DETAINER
Officer dispossessing person without process or authority, § 146.

FOREIGN COUNTRIES
Accomplices and accessories, § 27.
Bringing stolen property into state, § 27.
Conviction or acquittal in, current jurisdiction, former jeopardy, § 793.
Extradition, payment of expenses, § 1557.
Former jeopardy, conviction or acquittal in foreign country, concurrent jurisdiction, § 793.
Peace officers, criminal history information, furnishing, §§ 11105, 13300 et seq.
Prior convictions, punishment for subsequent offenses, § 668.
Stolen goods,
  Bringing into state, § 497.
  Receiving stolen goods from, § 27.

FOREIGN STATES
Accomplices and accessories, § 27.
  Subsequently found in California, § 778b.
Adoption proceedings, removal of child, § 280.
Bail, arrest of defendant, § 1301.
Bringing obscene materials into state, § 311.2.
Bringing stolen property into state, § 27.
Commencement of offense within state, consummation outside state, jurisdiction, § 778a.
Commencement of offense without state, consummation within state, jurisdiction, § 778.
Conviction or acquittal in, current jurisdiction, former jeopardy, § 793.
Former jeopardy, conviction or acquittal in foreign state, concurrent jurisdiction, § 793.
Nevada state prison officers and employees, peace officer status, § 830.5.
Obscene materials, sending or bringing into state, § 311.2.
Police, carrying weapons, § 12031.

FOREIGN STATES—Cont'd
Prior convictions, punishment for subsequent offenses, § 668.
Receiving stolen goods from, § 27.
Sending obscene materials into state, § 311.2.
Stolen goods, bringing into state from another state, § 497.

FORESTS AND FORESTRY
Burning, malicious mischief, § 449c.
Malicious mischief, burning, § 449c.

FORFEITURES
Bail, this index.
Correctional institution officer, refusal to allow attorney to visit prisoner, § 825.
Correctional Institutions, this index.
County officers, employees or appointees, bribes, § 68.
Fighting animals or birds, § 599aa.
Habeas corpus, disobedience, § 1505.
Jail officer, refusal to allow attorney to visit prisoner, § 825.
Municipalities, officers, employees or appointees, bribes, § 68.
Office,
  Refusal to allow attorney to visit prisoner, § 825.
Paraphernalia, fighting animals or birds, § 599aa.

FORGERY
  See, also, Counterfeiting, generally, this index.
  Generally, § 470 et seq.
Acceptance, § 470.
Accomplices and accessories, soliciting aid, § 653f.
Acts constituting, § 470.
Blank bills and notes, possession with intent to defraud, § 475.
Credit cards, § 484d et seq.
Defined, § 470.
Due bills, § 470.
Evidence,
  Offering forged evidence, § 132.
False entries in records or returns, § 471.
Fines and penalties, § 473.
Indictment and information, misdescription of instrument, § 965.
Limitation of prosecution, § 800.
Patents, § 470.
Possession or receipt of forged bills and notes with intent to pass, § 475.
Procuring or offering false instruments for record, § 115.
Records,
  False entries, § 471.
  Procuring or offering false or forged instrument for record, § 115.
Returns, false entries, § 471.
Shares of stock, § 470.
Soliciting commission, § 653f.
Stock shares, § 470.
Telegraph or telephone messages, § 474.
Trading stamps, § 470.
Uttering forged instrument, § 470.
  Credit cards, § 484f.

FORMER JEOPARDY
Generally, § 654.
Acquittal, § 1118.2.
Bar to subsequent prosecution, § 1023.
Concurrent jurisdiction, conviction or acquittal in another state or country, § 793.
Dismissal and nonsuit,
  Want of prosecution, § 1387.
Habeas corpus, § 1496.
Indictment or information, order setting aside, application of law, § 999.
Jurisdiction,
  Concurrent, conviction or acquittal in another state or country, § 793.
  Jeopardy in another court having jurisdiction, § 794.
Lesser included offenses, § 654.
Multiple offenses, single act, § 654.
Plea, § 1016 et seq.
  Bar to subsequent prosecution, § 1023.
Single act, multiple offenses, § 654.
Speedy trial, dismissal of action for delay, § 1387.

FORMS
Arraignment, waiver of accused's personal presence, § 977.
Arrest, this index.
Children and minors, abuse, reports, § 11161.7.
Complaints, this index.
Detention certificate, release of arrested person without formal charge, § 851.6.
Indictment and Information, this index.
Machine guns, license application, § 12231.
Pleas, indictment, information or complaint, § 1017.
Search warrants, § 1529.
Subpoena, § 1327.
Uniform misdemeanor and traffic citation, §§ 853.6, 853.7, 853.9.
Waiver of accused's personal presence, arraignment, § 977.
Warrants. Arrest, this index.
Weapons, this index.

FORNICATION
Generally, §§ 261.5, 264.
Incest, § 285.

4–CYANO–1–METHYL–4–PHENYL-PIPERIDINE
See, also, Drugs and Medicine, generally, this index.

4–CYANO–2–DEMETHYLAMINO–4, 4–DIPHENYL BUTANE
See, also, Drugs and Medicine, generally, this index.

4–METHYL–2, 5–DIMETHOXYLAM-PHETAMINE
See, also, Drugs and Medicine, generally, this index.

FOWL
Poultry and Poultry Products, generally, this index.

Penal Code   **GAMBLING**

FOWLER, CITY OF
See, also, Municipalities, generally, this index.

FRANCHISES
Obscene materials, merchandising establishments accepting as condition of continuing franchise, §§ 311.7, 311.9.

FRAUD
Absconders, defrauding innkeepers, § 537.
Accounts by public officers, § 424.
Apartment house, defrauding, § 537.
Baggage, defrauding innkeepers, § 537.
Blank checks, money orders, etc., possession with intent to defraud, § 475.
Boarding and lodging houses, § 537.
Bombs and explosives, false reports of planting, § 148.1.
Causing others to commit crime by fraud, contrivance or force, § 31.
Child represented to be orphan, § 271a.
Claims, presentation to state, etc., board or officer, § 72.
Conspiracy, § 182.
Construction funds,
  Larceny, § 484b.
Counterfeiting or forgery with intent to defraud, § 470.
Credit cards, § 484d et seq.
Drugs and Medicine, this index.
Emergency reports, false statements, § 148.3.
Explosives or bombs, false reports of planting, § 148.1.
False imprisonment, § 237.
False vouchers, construction loan funds, embezzlement, § 484c.
Falsification, public records, limitation of prosecutions, § 799.
Fictitious instruments, making, possessing or uttering with intent to defraud, § 476.
Hotels,
  Defrauding, § 537.
Instruments for record, false or forged instruments, § 115.
Insurance, this index.
Intent to defraud, sufficiency, § 8.
Kidnapping, § 207.
Leases,
  Theft, § 484.
Motels and motor courts, § 537.
Orphans, children represented to be orphans, § 271a.
Pandering, § 266i.
Prostitution, procurement of persons, § 266a.
Public funds, § 72.
Public officers and employees, accounts, § 424.
Public records, falsification, limitation of prosecutions, § 799.
Reports,
  False crime reports, § 148.5.
Restaurants, defrauding, § 537.
Retailers, credit card transactions, § 484h.
Serial number or identification mark removed from radio, etc., sale, etc., § 537e.

FRAUD—Cont'd
Telegraphs and Telephones, this index.
Theft by fraud, § 484.
Trick, theft by fraud, § 484.
Uttering false instruments, § 470.
Water meters, alteration, § 499.
Women, procuring for illicit intercourse, § 266.

FREE ROAMING FERAL HORSE
See, also, Fish and Game, generally, this index.

FREEDOM OF PRESS
Searches and seizures, motion to suppress evidence, § 1538.5.

FREEDOM OF SPEECH
Searches and seizures, motion to suppress evidence, § 1538.5.

FRESH PURSUIT
Generally, § 852 et seq.
Arrest, formalities, necessity, § 841.
Justifiable homicide, retaking felons, § 196.
Uniform Act on Fresh Pursuit, § 852 et seq.

FRIENDS
Jail prisoners, hospitalization, support, § 4011.

FRUITS
Burning, malicious mischief, § 449b.
Malicious mischief,
  Burning, § 449b.
Theft, § 487.

FUEL
Arson, § 449a.
Gas, theft, § 498.

FUGITIVES FROM JUSTICE
See, also, Escape, generally, this index.
Generally, § 1547 et seq.
Arrest,
  Application of bail bondsmen, procedure, § 847.5.
  Reward, § 1547.
  Without warrant, § 1551.1.
Bail,
  Amount, § 1552.1.
  Arrest pending governor's warrant, § 1552 et seq.
  Bond or undertaking, § 1552.1.
  Jumping, § 1553.
  New bail, § 1552.2.
Capital offenses, arrest without warrant, § 1551.1.
Close pursuit. Fresh Pursuit, generally, this index.
Commitment to county jail after arrest without warrant, § 1552.
Complaint, § 1551.
Discharge at expiration of time specified in warrant, bonds or undertaking, § 1552.2.
Discretion to surrender or hold on application of other state, § 1553.1.
Exemplified copy of indictment found, evidence, § 1551.2.

FUGITIVES FROM JUSTICE—Cont'd
Expenses for returning fugitives, § 1557.
Extradition, generally, this index.
Forfeitures, bail bond, § 1553.
Fresh Pursuit, generally, this index.
Hot pursuit. Fresh Pursuit, generally, this index.
Information, evidence, § 1551.2.
Judicial proceedings, evidence, § 1551.2.
Justifiable homicide, § 196.
Magistrates, warrant, § 1551 et seq.
New bail, § 1552.2.
Notice of arrest, § 1551.3.
Parole,
  Extradition, § 1548 et seq.
Proceedings for commitment, § 1551.2.
Recommitment for further period, § 1552.2.
Return, expenses, § 1557.
Return with bail bondsmen, procedure, § 847.5.
Reward for apprehension, § 1547.
Time limit on commitment, § 1552.2.
Uniform Act on Fresh Pursuit, § 852 et seq.
Verified complaint, evidence, § 1551.2.

FUNDS
Career criminal prosecution program, § 999c.

FURETHIDINE
See, also, Drugs and Medicine, generally, this index.

FURLOUGHS
Prisoners, county jails, work furlough program, §§ 1208, 1208.5.

FURNITURE
Beds and Bedding, generally, this index.

GAGS
Punishment by use, § 673.

GAMBLING
Acceptance or making wagers, § 337a.
Bingo, § 326.5.
Boats, use for gambling purposes, § 337a.
Book making or pool-selling, § 337a.
Booths, use for gambling purposes, § 337a.
Buildings,
  Use for gambling purposes, § 337a.
Horse Racing, generally, this index.
Keeping or occupying place with paraphernalia for recording wagers, etc., § 337a.
Lotteries, generally, this index.
Pool-selling, § 337a.
Recording wagers, § 337a.
Rooms, use for gambling, § 337a.
Sheds, use for gambling purposes, § 337a.
Ships,
  Use for gambling purposes, § 337a.
Single acts, § 337a.
Slot Machines, generally, this index.
Stake holding, § 337a.
Tenements, use for gambling purposes, § 337a.

GAMBLING

GAMBLING—Cont'd
Tents, use for gambling purposes, § 337a.
Use of room, etc., for gambling, § 337a.

GAME
Fish and Game, generally, this index.

GAMING
Gambling, generally, this index.

GARAGES
Arson, § 448a.

GARBAGE AND REFUSE
Bail, littering conviction, § 853.6.
Parks, littering, bail, § 853.6.
  Second and subsequent offenses, § 853.6.
State parks, littering, bail, § 853.6.
Water pollution,
  Bail, § 853.6.

GARMENTS
Wearing Apparel, generally, this index.

GAS
Oil and Gas, generally, this index.

GAS–OPERATED GUNS
Sale to minors, §§ 12551, 12552.

GATES
Trespasses, acts constituting, § 602.

GELDINGS
Theft, § 487.

GENERAL LAWS
Statutes, generally, this index.

GIFT ENTERPRISES
Defined, lotteries, § 319.

GIFTS, DEVISES AND BEQUESTS
Compounding or concealing crimes, § 153.
County officers or employees, asking or receiving, § 70.
Municipal officers and employees, asking or receiving, § 70.
Nongovernmental organization with term peace officer, incorporated in name, solicitation, § 146c.
Officers, etc., asking or receiving gifts, § 70.
Pardons and reprieves,
  Person procuring, report, § 4807.3.
Sawed-off shotguns, § 12001.5.
State officers and employees, asking or receiving, § 70.

GLASS
Deposit or throwing upon highways, § 588a.

GLUTETHIMIDE
See, also, Drugs and Medicine, generally, this index.

GOATS
Theft, § 487.
  Carcasses, § 487a.

GOLD
Guards, weapons, gold bullion, §§ 12027, 12031.

GOOD TIME ALLOWANCE
Jails, this index.

GOODS, WARES AND MERCHANDISE
Arson, intent to defraud insurers, § 450a.
Counterfeiting instruments, § 470.
Forgery of instruments, § 470.
Secondhand Goods and Dealers, generally, this index.

GOODS AND SERVICES
Definitions, § 7.

GOVERNOR
Appointments,
  Community release board, § 5075.
Attempt to kill or commission of assault upon, § 217.1.
Conspiracy to commit crime against, § 182.
Pardons and Reprieves, generally, this index.

GRAIN
Agricultural Products, generally, this index.

GRAND JURY
Generally, § 888 et seq.
Advice of court, § 934.
Appearance, district attorney, § 935.
Assistants, § 934 et seq.
Attorney General, this index.
Compelling attendance, § 907.
Compelling self-incriminating testimony, § 1324.
Composition, § 888.
Correctional Institutions, this index.
County Officers and Employees, this index.
Declarations, failure to return indictment, request of person charged, § 939.91.
Defined, § 888.
Discharge, § 915.
Disclosure,
  Evidence, post.
  Manner of voting, § 924.1.
District attorneys,
  Advice, §§ 934, 935.
  Appearance, § 935.
  Issuing process for witnesses, § 939.7.
  Subpoena requiring attendance of witness, §§ 939.2, 939.7.
District officers, removal proceedings, § 922.
Duties, § 888.
  Defendant's evidence, consideration, § 939.7.
Disclosure, § 924.1.
  Authorized disclosure of evidence or manner of voting, § 924.
  Request of court, § 924.2.
Self-incrimination, witness refusing to answer, § 939.3.
Weighing, §§ 939.7, 939.8.
Examination, public records, § 921.
Fine, failing to attend, § 907.

GRAND JURY—Cont'd
Foreman,
  Indorsement of indictment, signing, § 940.
  Free access to prisons, § 921.
Impaneling,
  Compelling attendance, § 907.
Indictment and Information, generally, this index.
Inquiries,
  Public offenses committed or triable within county, § 917.
  Scope, §§ 915, 919.
Investigations,
  Charges against district attorney, etc., § 935.
  Employment of special investigators, § 936.
  Failure to return indictment, report or declaration, request of person charged, § 939.91.
  Offenses within knowledge of jurors, § 918.
  Refusal to answer on ground of self-incrimination, procedure, § 939.3.
Judge,
  Advice from, § 934.
  Presence during sessions, § 934.
Knowledge of offense, duty to inform other jurors, § 918.
Legal assistants, § 934 et seq.
Listening or observing without consent, § 891.
Listing and selection, § 895 et seq.
  Persons selected, placing in possession of county clerk, § 896.
Management of public prisons, inquiry, § 919.
Misconduct in office, inquiry, § 919.
Misdemeanor, recording proceedings without consent, § 891.
Municipal officers, removal proceedings, § 922.
Notes, taking permitted, § 891.
Number constituting, § 888.2.
Orders,
  Designating estimated number required, § 895.
  Estimate, § 895.
Perjury,
  Disclosure of testimony, court compelling, § 924.2.
  Grand juror, § 924.3.
Personal interview, qualifications, § 896.
Presence during sessions, § 934.
Private sessions, § 915.
Proceedings for removal of district, county or city officers, § 922.
Process, witnesses, § 939.7.
Public records, examination, § 921.
Qualifications,
  Statement, possessing necessary qualification, § 896.
  Questioning for things said or vote cast, § 924.3.
Records and recordation,
  Access to public records, § 921.
  Proceedings, recording without consent, § 891.
Removal of district, county or city officers, proceedings, § 922.

Penal Code   **HABEAS**

GRAND JURY—Cont'd
Reports,
  Failure to return indictment, request of person charged, § 939.91.
Secrecy, § 924.2.
  Disclosure of making out information or indictment without authority, § 924.
Selection, § 895 et seq.
Self-incrimination, § 1324.
  Witness, refusal to answer, procedure, § 939.3.
Signature, foreman, endorsement as true bill, § 940.
Special counsel, employment by attorney general, § 936.
Statements, qualifications to be member, possessing, § 896.
Subpoenas, §§ 939.2, 939.7.
  Attendance of witnesses, §§ 939.2, 939.7.
  Attorney general's power to issue, § 923.
  Witnesses, § 939.7.
Superior court,
  Designating estimated number of grand jurors, § 895.
  Listing grand jurors required, § 896.
  Subpoena requiring attendance of witness, § 939.2.
Supervisorial districts, selection, § 899.
Voting,
  Concurrence of jurors, number required, § 940.
  Disclosing manner of voting, § 924.1.
  Secrecy, § 924.2.
Witnesses,
  District attorney as witness, § 935.
  Fees, § 1329.
  Interrogation by district attorney, § 935.
  Issuance of process, § 939.7.
  Refusal to answer on ground of self-incrimination, procedure, § 939.3.
  Report or declaration, request of person called, § 939.91.
  Subpoenas, § 939.7.
    Signed by district attorney or by judge, §§ 939.2, 939.7.

GRAND THEFT
Theft, this index.

GRANTS
Deeds and Conveyances, generally, this index.

GRASS AND GRASSLANDS
Malicious mischief, burning, § 449c.

GRATUITIES
Gifts, Devises and Bequests, generally, this index.

GUARDIAN AND WARD
Abduction, person under 18 for purpose of prostitution, from, § 267.
Battered children, §§ 273a, 273d.
Child stealing, defined, § 278.
Corporal injury, infliction upon children, § 273d.
Cruelty or unjustifiable punishment of children, § 273a.

GUARDIAN AND WARD—Cont'd
Fines and penalties, desertion, child under 14 with intent to abandon, § 271.
Jurisdiction, enticing minor child away from guardian, § 784.
Prostitution, house of, admitting or keeping minors, in, § 309.
Public guardians, limitation of prosecutions, § 800.
Shoplifting, liability for actions of ward, § 490.5.
Unjustifiable punishment of children, § 273a.

GUARDS
Armored vehicles, firearms, § 12031.
Certificate of firearm and arrest training, § 12033.
Jails, this index.
Peace officers, powers, § 830.5.
Security Guards, generally, this index.
Weapons,
  Armored vehicles, § 12031.
  Carrying loaded firearms, § 12031.
  Exemption, § 12027.
  Possession, § 12027.
  Wooden clubs or batons, § 12002.

GUILTY PLEA
Generally, § 1016 et seq.
Bargaining, plea bargaining, § 1192.5.
Conviction,
  Necessity of plea, § 689.
Corporations, § 1396.
Degree of offense, § 1192 et seq.
Evidence, withdrawn plea specifying punishment, § 1192.5.
Necessity of indictment or information, § 682.
Probationer, withdrawal of plea, § 1203.4.
Specifying degree of offense, § 1192.1.
Withdrawal, § 1192.4.
  After fulfilling conditions of probation, § 1203.4.
  Certificate of rehabilitation and pardon, § 1203.4.
  Plea specifying punishment, § 1192.5.

GUN CONTROL LAW
Generally, § 11106.

GUNS
Weapons, generally, this index.

HABEAS CORPUS
Generally, § 1473 et seq.
Affidavits, examination, § 1488.
Application for writ, § 1474.
Bail, §§ 1269, 1476, 1490 et seq.
  Amount, § 1491.
  Arraignment, § 982.
  Bench warrants, § 982.
  Crime of violence, § 1491.
  Deadly weapon offenses, § 1491.
  Destruction of property, § 1491.
  Forcible taking of property, § 1491.
  Nonviolent crimes, § 1491.
  Pending hearing, § 1476.
  Purpose of giving, § 1490 et seq.
Commitment to legal from illegal custody, § 1493.

HABEAS CORPUS—Cont'd
Contents of writ, § 1477.
Damages, disobedience, § 1505.
Deadly weapon offenses, bail, § 1491.
Defects,
  Form of warrant of commitment, § 1488.
  Process, discharge, § 1487.
Destruction of property, bail, § 1491.
Direction of writ, § 1477.
Discharge from custody, after remand, § 1475.
Disobedience of writ, § 1479.
  Defect of form, § 1495.
Disposition of party pending proceedings on return, § 1494.
Endorsements upon petition, § 1476.
Evidence, false evidence, inquiry, § 1473.
Exceptions, production of body, § 1481.
Extradition, § 1550.1.
Forcible taking or destruction of property, bail, § 1491.
Forfeitures, failure to obey writ, § 1505.
Form of writ, defects, disobedience, § 1495.
Former jeopardy, § 1496.
Granting of writ, endorsement of hour and date, § 1476.
Handicapped persons, production of body, § 1482.
Hearing,
  Return, § 1480.
  Without grounds, § 1482.
Hour and date of petition's presentation, endorsement, § 1476.
Illegal restraint or custody, § 1493.
Illness, production of body, § 1482.
Imprisonment after discharge, § 1496.
Infirmity of person, hearing without production of body, § 1482.
Irreparable injury, § 1497.
Jurisdiction, grounds of discharge, § 1487.
Keeping in custody after discharge, § 1496.
Method of granting, § 1475.
Oath or affirmation to petition, § 1474.
Petition, § 1474.
Prior writs, issuance of subsequent writs, § 1475.
Production of body, § 1481.
Reasonable or probable cause for commitment, grounds of discharge, § 1487.
Refusal to obey writ, § 1479.
Reimprisonment, § 1496.
Remand, party into custody, §§ 1486, 1492.
Return, §§ 1475, 1478, 1480.
Robbery, bail, § 1491.
Service of writ, §§ 1475, 1478.
Sickness, hearing without production of body, § 1482.
Signature, petition, § 1474.
Subsequent applications, § 1475.
Unlawful imprisonment, grounds of discharge, § 1487.
Verification, application, § 1475.
Violent crimes, bail, § 1491.
Want of bail, § 1490.
Warrant in lieu of writ, § 1497 et seq.

HABEAS

HABEAS CORPUS—Cont'd
Warrant of arrest, defects, discharge from custody, § 1488.
Weapons, crimes involving deadly weapons, bail, § 1491.

HABIT FORMING DRUGS
Drug Addicts, generally, this index.

HABITUAL CRIMINALS
Generally, § 666 et seq.
Second and Subsequent Offenses, generally, this index.

HABITUAL DRUNKARDS
Drunkards and Drunkenness, generally, this index.

HALLUCINOGENIC SUBSTANCES
See, also, Drugs and Medicine, generally, this index.

HANDICAPPED PERSONS
Crimes against, § 1203.09.
Habeas corpus, production of body, § 1482.
Social Services, generally, this index.

HANDWRITING
Counterfeiting or forgery, § 470.

HARBORING FUGITIVES
Generally, § 32.

HARBORS AND PORTS
Bays, generally, this index.

HARMFUL MATTER
Lewdness and Obscenity, generally, this index.

HAY
Arson, § 449a.
Malicious mischief, burning, § 449b.

HEALTH AND SANITATION
Battered children, reports, § 11110.
Children and minors, endangering health, willful cruelty or unjustifiable punishment, § 273a.
Comfort Stations and Rest Rooms, generally, this index.
Conspiracy to commit act injurious, § 182.
Drugs and Medicine, generally, this index.
Hospitals, generally, this index.
Institutions, treatment, § 673.
Jails,
   Women, personal hygiene, § 4023.5.
Probation officers, improvement of facilities for prevention of crime, § 1203.13.

HEALTH CARE FACILITIES
Abuse of patients, reports, § 11161.8.
Neglect of patients, reports, § 11161.8.

HEARING AIDS
Invasion of Privacy Law, application, § 632.

HERMOSA BEACH, CITY OF
See, also, Municipalities, generally, this index.

HEROIN
See, also, Drugs and Medicine, generally, this index.

HIDING
Concealment, generally, this index.

HIGH SCHOOLS OR SECONDARY SCHOOLS
Disruption of schools, § 626 et seq.
Disruptive persons, denial of access to campus or facilities, etc., § 626.8.

HIGHWAY PATROL
Arrest, courses of training, § 832.
Authority, § 830.2.
Bombs and explosives, false reports of planting, § 148.1.
Courses of instruction,
   Arrest, § 832.
   Weapons, use of firearms, § 832.
Eavesdropping, wiretap or electronic, § 633.
Electronic eavesdropping, § 633.
Explosives or bombs, false reports of planting, § 148.1.
False crime reports, § 148.5.
Firearms, courses of training, § 832.
Invasion of privacy, wiretap or electronic eavesdropping, § 633.
Jurisdiction, § 830.2.
Powers, duties, jurisdiction and responsibility, § 830.2.
Recording private communications, wiretapping or electronic eavesdropping, § 633.
Tapping wires, § 633.
Telegraphs and telephones, wiretapping, § 633.
Traffic control, primary duty, enforcement, § 830.2.
Training,
   Arrests, courses of instruction for making arrests, § 832.
   Weapons, use of firearms, § 832.
Weapon,
   Carrying loaded firearms, § 12031.
   Courses of instruction, use of firearms, § 832.
Wiretapping, § 633.

HIGHWAYS AND ROADS
See, also, Streets and Alleys, generally, this index.
Bail, littering convictions, § 853.6.
Bridges,
   Arson, § 448a.
   Burning, malicious mischief, § 449b.
   Viaducts, train robbery, interference, § 214.
Cigarettes and cigars, littering, bail, § 853.6.
Deposit of glass, nails, etc., § 588a.
Industrial Farms and Road Camps, generally, this index.
Littering,
   Bail, § 853.6.
   Malicious mischief, highway signs, § 602.

HIGHWAYS AND ROADS—Cont'd
Obstructions,
   Nuisance, § 647c.
Oil or grease deposits, penalty, § 588a.
Signs,
   Malicious mischief, § 602.
Throwing substances on highways,
   Likely to injure persons, animals, or vehicles, § 588a.
Traffic Rules and Regulations, generally, this index.
Trespass, § 602.
Signs, malicious mischief, § 602.

HIJACKING
Reward, § 1547.

HISTORICAL WEAPONS
Possession, § 12027.

HOGS
See, also, Animals, generally, this index.
Carcasses, theft, § 487a.
Theft, § 487.

HOLIDAYS
Bail, delivery of defendant to court or magistrate, § 1301.
Sunday, generally, this index.

HOMES
Dwellings, generally, this index.

HOMICIDE
Generally, § 187 et seq.
Abortion, death of fetus, § 187.
Accidental, excusable, § 195.
Accomplices and accessories, soliciting aid, § 653f.
Acquittal, justifiable and excusable homicide, § 199.
Additional punishment,
   Prior prison term, prior sentencing, § 1170.2.
Aggravating circumstances, alternative death or life imprisonment determination, § 190.3.
Agreement to commit, principal not present during commission of offense, capital punishment, § 190.5.
Aiding and abetting, death of fetus, § 187.
Apprehension of person for felony, justifiable, § 197.
Arrest, committed during, justifiable, § 196.
Assault with intent to commit murder, § 217.
   Mentally incompetent defendant, commitment or outpatient treatment, § 1370.
   Probation, § 1203.
Attempts, § 216 et seq.
Bodily injury, resisting justifiable, § 197.
Bomb, use of, degree of offense, § 189.
Burden of proving mitigating circumstances, § 1105.
Burglary, special circumstance, punishment, § 190.2.
Capital Punishment, generally, this index.
Children and Minors, this index.

Penal Code   **HORSE**

HOMICIDE—Cont'd
Combat, § 195.
Consecutive sentence, prior prison term, § 667.5.
Consent, death of fetus, § 187.
Correcting children, § 195.
Deadly weapons. Weapons, generally, post.
Death of fetus, § 187.
Death within three years and day, necessity, § 194.
Defense of children, § 197.
Definitions, § 187.
   Malice, § 188.
Degree of offense, § 189.
Evidence, shifting of burden of proof, § 1105.
Excusable homicide, § 195.
   Burden of proving, § 1105.
   Discharge of defendant, § 199.
   Sentence and punishment, § 199.
Explosives,
   Degree of offense, § 189.
   Special circumstance, punishment, § 190.2.
Express malice, defined, § 188.
Fear justifying, § 198.
Felons, retaking, justifiable, § 196.
Felony, prevention, justifiable, § 197.
Fetus, § 187.
Firearms. Weapons, generally, post.
First degree murder, § 189.
   Punishment, §§ 190, 190.1.
   Sentence and punishment, § 190.2.
   Special circumstances,
      Determination by trier of fact, § 190.4.
      Punishment, determination by trier of fact, § 190.3.
      Separate penalty hearing, § 190.4.
      Special finding, trier of fact, § 190.4.
   Trial, separate phases, § 190.1.
Habitation, etc., defense, justifiable, § 197.
Hearings, first degree murder, special circumstances, § 190.4.
Heat of passion, § 195.
Hired murder,
   Principal not present during commission of offense, capital punishment, § 190.5.
   Special circumstance charged, punishment, § 190.2.
Husband and wife,
   Defense of, justifiable homicide, § 197.
Implied malice, defined, § 188.
Insanity plea, trial, separate phases, special circumstances charged, § 190.1.
Intent,
   Assault with intent to murder, § 217.
   Poison, administering, intent to kill, § 216.
Involuntary manslaughter, § 192 et seq.
   Death within three years and day, necessity, § 194.
   Defined, § 192.
   Limitation of prosecutions, § 800.
   Penalty, § 193.
Judgments, obedience, § 196.
Justifiable homicide, § 196 et seq.
   Burden of proof, § 1105.

HOMICIDE—Cont'd
Justifiable homicide—Cont'd
   Defense of children, § 197.
   Discharge of defendant, § 199.
   Fear, § 198.
   Persons other than officers, § 197.
   Public officers, § 196.
Kidnapping, special circumstance, punishment, § 190.2.
Labor and employment,
   Accident and misfortune while correcting employee, excusable, § 195.
   Defense of, justifiable, § 197.
Limitation of prosecutions, § 799.
   Manslaughter, § 800.
Malice, defined, § 188.
Manslaughter, § 192 et seq.
   Additional punishment,
      Prior prison term, § 667.5.
      Prior sentencing, § 1170.2.
   Death within three years and day, necessity, § 194.
   Defined, § 192.
   Driving a vehicle, defined, § 192.
   Limitation of prosecutions, § 800.
   Motor vehicles, use, § 192 et seq.
      Death within three years and a day, § 194.
   Penalties, § 193.
   Subsequent offenses, additional punishment, § 667.5.
   Voluntary, defined, § 192.
Mentally incompetent defendant, commitment or outpatient treatment, § 1370.
Misfortune, § 195.
Mitigating circumstances,
   Alternative death or life imprisonment determination, § 190.3.
   Evidence, § 1105.
Motor vehicles, § 192 et seq.
Multiple offenses, special circumstance, punishment, § 190.2.
Parent, defense, justifiable, § 197.
Parole and probation, § 1203.
   Eligibility, § 1203.06.
   First degree murder, § 190.
      Special circumstances charged, § 190.2.
   Second and subsequent offenses, eligibility, § 1203.08.
Peace, justifiable, keeping and preserving, § 197.
Penalty hearing, first degree murder, special circumstances, § 190.4.
Physicians and surgeons, fetus, § 187.
Poisons, administering,
   Degree of offense, § 189.
   Intent to kill, § 216.
Police,
   Advocating, § 151.
   Apprehension of person, reward, § 1547.
   Killing, special circumstance, § 190.2.
   Penalty, § 190.2.
Premeditated killing, § 189.
Principal, presence during commission of crime, capital punishment, § 190.5.
Prior prison term, additional punishment, § 667.5.
   Prior sentencing, § 1170.2.

HOMICIDE—Cont'd
Process, justifiable in overcoming actual resistance to execution, § 196.
Property, defense, justifiable, § 197.
Provocation, excusable, § 195.
Public officers, justifiable, § 196.
Rape, special circumstance, punishment, § 190.2.
Resisting attempt to commit crime, justifiable, § 197.
Riots, suppression, justifiable, § 197.
Robbery, first degree murder, special circumstance, § 190.2.
Sanity, determination, first degree murder, charging special circumstances, § 190.1.
Second degree murder, §§ 189, 190.
Shifting burden of proof, § 1105.
Soliciting commission, § 653f.
   Fetus, § 187.
Special circumstances, determination, first degree murder, § 190.1.
   Determination by trier of fact, §§ 190.3, 190.4.
   Sentence and punishment, § 190.2.
Subsequent offenses, additional punishment, § 667.5.
Therapeutic Abortion Act, murder of fetus, § 187.
Time, death within three years and a day, § 194.
Torture, special circumstance, punishment, § 190.2.
Trial,
   Burden of proving mitigating circumstances, § 1105.
   Separate phases, first degree murder, § 190.1.
Voluntary manslaughter,
   Defined, § 192.
   Manslaughter, generally, ante.
Weapons,
   Accusatory pleading, nature of firearm used, § 969d.
   Explosives, degree of offense, § 189.
Wife,
   Defense, justifiable homicide, § 197.
Witnesses, killing to prevent testimony, special circumstance, § 190.2.

HOMOSEXUALITY
Sex Offenders, generally, this index.

HOOPS
Deposit or throwing upon highways, § 588a.

HORSE RACING
Betting odds, transmitting information, § 337i.
Book making, § 337a.
Bribery,
   Acceptance or attempting to accept bribe by participant, § 337c.
   Offer or attempt to bribe official, § 337d.
   Offer or attempt to bribe participant, § 337b et seq.
   Official receiving or attempting to receive bribe, § 337e.
Information concerning races, transmitting, § 337i.

HORSE

HORSE RACING—Cont'd
Officials,
  Offer or attempt to bribe, § 337d.
  Receiving or attempting to receive bribes, § 337e.
Participants,
  Accepting or attempting to accept bribes, § 337c.
  Offering or attempting to bribe, § 337b et seq.
Progress of races, transmitting information, § 337i.
Results of races, transmitting information, § 337i.
Transmitting information, § 337i.

HORSES
See, also, Animals, generally, this index.
Carcasses, theft, § 487a.
Cruelty, § 597.

HOSPITALS
Mentally Deficient and Mentally Ill Persons, generally, this index.
Patients received from another health facility, injuries caused by neglect or abuse, reports, § 11161.8.
Personal injuries,
  Abuse in nursing home, reports, § 11161.8.
Production of books and records, attendance of witnesses outside county of residence, § 1330.
Records, witnesses, attendance outside county of residence, § 1330.
Reports, abuse of persons by other health facilities, § 11161.8.
Tort liability, reports of physical abuse from patients received from other health facilities, § 11161.8.
Witnesses, production of hospital records, attendance outside county of residence, § 1330.

HOSTAGES
Prisoners, holding persons, § 4503.

HOT PURSUIT
Fresh Pursuit, generally, this index.

HOTELS
Baggage, removal without paying for food or accommodations, § 537.
Evidence, intent to defraud proprietor, § 537.
Fraud,
  Evidence, § 537.
  Intent, prima facie evidence, § 537.
Prima facie evidence, intent to defraud, § 537.

HOUSE BREAKING
Generally, § 459 et seq.

HOUSE CARS
Campers, generally, this index.

HOUSE TRAILERS
Mobilehomes and Mobilehome Parks, generally, this index.

HOUSES
Dwellings, generally, this index.

HOUSES OF ILL FAME
Disorderly Houses, generally, this index.

HOUSING
Jail prisoners, work furloughs, § 1208.
Prisoners, work furloughs, participation, § 1208.
Work furlough programs, jail prisoners, § 1208.

HUMANE TREATMENT
Prisoners, § 147.

HUNTERS AND HUNTING
Fish and Game, generally, this index.

HUSBAND AND WIFE
Abandonment. Desertion, generally, this index.
Artificial insemination, husband consenting in writing, father of child for support and maintenance purposes, § 270.
Bigamy, generally, this index.
Clothing, failure to provide for spouse, § 270a et seq.
Corporal injury,
  Inflicting upon spouse, crimes and offenses, § 273.5.
Desertion, generally, this index.
Food, failure to provide for spouse, § 270a et seq.
Homicide,
  Justifiable, defense, § 197.
Inflicting corporal injury, crimes and offenses, § 273.5.
Jails, separation, § 4002.
Justifiable homicide, defense, § 197.
Marriage, generally, this index.
Medical attendance, failure to provide for spouse, § 270a et seq.
Prostitution, placing or permitting placement of wife in house, § 266g.
Rape, impersonation of husband, § 261.
Shelter, failure to provide for spouse, § 270a et seq.
Spouse beating, crimes and offenses, § 273.5.
Support, generally, this index.
Witnesses,
  Competency,
    Prosecution for placing or permitting placement in house of prostitution, § 266g.

HYDROCODONE
See, also, Drugs and Medicine, generally, this index.

HYDROMORPHINOL
See, also, Drugs and Medicine, generally, this index.

HYDROMORPHONE
See, also, Drugs and Medicine, generally, this index.

HYDROXYPETHIDINE
See, also, Drugs and Medicine, generally, this index.

HYGIENE
Health and Sanitation, generally, this index.

HYPNOTIC DRUGS
Drugs and Medicine, generally, this index.

IBOGAINE
See, also, Drugs and Medicine, generally, this index.

IDENTIFICATION CARD
Motor Vehicles, this index.

IDENTIFICATION NUMBERS
Alteration, destruction, etc., purchase, sale or possession of items, § 537e.

IDENTITY AND IDENTIFICATION
Arrest, release under notice to appear, § 853.6.
Credit card holders, false representation, § 484g.
Criminal Identification and Investigation, Bureau of, generally, this index.
Extradition, fugitive, inquiry, § 1553.2.
Fingerprints and Fingerprinting, generally, this index.
Junk dealers, metal sellers, § 496a.
Leases, theft by fraud, § 484.
Metal sellers, junk dealers and secondhand dealers purchasing metals, § 496a.
Numbers. Identification Numbers, generally, this index.
Secondhand dealers, identification of metal sellers, § 496a.
Tear gas weapon, § 12422.
Weapons, this index.

IDIOTS
Mentally Deficient and Mentally Ill Persons, generally, this index.

IGNORANCE
Commission of crime, § 26.

ILLEGITIMATE CHILDREN
Generally, § 270 et seq.
Disposition of fines for failure to support children, § 270d.
Evidence,
  Child supportability, § 270.
Gifts, supportability, determination, § 270.
Income, supportability determination, § 270.
Support, § 270 et seq.

ILLNESS
Habeas corpus proceedings, production of body, exceptions, § 1482.
Witnesses,
  Post conviction hearing, deposition, § 1204.

IMBECILES
Mentally Deficient and Mentally Ill Persons, generally, this index.

Penal Code

INDICTMENT

IMMUNITIES
Privileges and Immunities, generally, this index.

IMPERSONATIONS
False Personation, generally, this index.

IMPLIED MALICE
Defined, homicide, § 188.

IMPORTS
Exports and Imports, generally, this index.

IMPOUNDING
Animal Pounds, generally, this index.

IMPRISONMENT
Correctional Institutions, generally, this index.
False Imprisonment, generally, this index.

IMPROVEMENTS
See, also, Public Buildings and Works, generally, this index.
Embezzlement, construction funds, § 484c.
Funds, theft, § 484b.
Sidewalks, generally, this index.
Theft,
  Construction funds, § 484b.

INCEST
Generally, § 285.

INCOME
Child supportability of parent determination, § 270.

INCOMPETENT PERSONS
Mentally Deficient and Mentally Ill Persons, generally, this index.

INCOMPLETE CREDIT CARD
Defined, § 484d.

INCORRIGIBLE CHILDREN
Juvenile Delinquents and Dependents, generally, this index.

INCRIMINATION
Self Incrimination, generally, this index.

INDEBTEDNESS
Counterfeiting or forgery, instruments relating to, § 470.
Evidences of Indebtedness, generally, this index.
Jail prisoners, work furlough earnings, payment, § 1208.

INDECENCY
Lewdness and Obscenity, generally, this index.

INDECENT EXPOSURE
Generally, § 314.
Restaurants and taverns, entertainers or food servers, §§ 318.5, 318.6.

INDEMNITY
Persons erroneously convicted of crime, § 4900 et seq.

INDENTURES
Counterfeiting, § 470.
Forgery, § 470.

INDICTMENT AND INFORMATION
Abrogation, distinction between principals in first and second degree, § 971.
Absence of defendant from state, § 802.
Acquittal, one or more of several defendants, single indictment, § 970.
Answer on denial of motion to set aside, § 997.
Arrest of defendant, disclosure before arrest, § 924.
Assumed or fictitious name, defendant charged, § 953.
Attempts,
  Former jeopardy, prior to subsequent prosecution, § 1023.
  Prior conviction, form of allegation, § 970.
Autrefois acquit, § 1016 et seq.
Autrefois attaint, § 1016 et seq.
Autrefois convict, § 1016 et seq.
Bribery, acceptance by public official or employee, time, filing, § 800.
Change of plea, § 1016 et seq.
Charge of two or more different offenses, § 954.
Charging defendant by fictitious or erroneous name, § 953.
Commitment, setting aside for improper commitment of defendant, § 995.
Concealed deadly weapon, defendant, § 969c.
Concurrence of grand jurors, § 940.
Consolidation, two or more accusatory pleadings of same class of crimes or offenses, § 954.
Conspiracy, this index.
Counts,
  Acquittal of one or more, § 954.
  Defendant armed with dangerous weapon, allegation in each count, § 969c.
  Election between, § 954.
  Joinder, § 954.
  Statement of offense, § 952.
  Two or more different offenses under separate counts, § 954.
Dangerous weapons, defendant armed, § 969c.
Defendant not in custody, procedure upon finding indictment, § 945.
Defined, § 889.
  Accusatory pleading, § 691.
Demurrer,
  Answering, § 997.
Different statements of same offense, § 954.
Disclosure before arrest of defendant, § 924.
Dismissal,
  Fulfilling conditions of probation, § 1203.4.
  Probationer, discharged, § 1203.4.
Election between different offenses or counts, § 954.
Embezzlement, restoration of property or tender before, §§ 512, 513.

INDICTMENT AND INFORMATION —Cont'd
Endorsement,
  Names of witnesses, § 943.
  Setting aside for improper endorsement, § 995.
  True bill, § 940.
Entry of plea, § 1017.
Erroneous name, defendant charged by, insertion of true name, § 953.
Evidence,
  Judicial notice, § 961.
  Presumptions, pleading presumptions or matters judicially noticed, § 961.
  Warranting conviction, grounds for issuing indictment, § 939.8.
Failure to return, reports, request of person charged, § 939.91.
Fictitious name, defendant charged by, insertion of true name, § 953.
Filing,
  District attorney, § 739.
    Absence of defendant from state, § 802.
    Acceptance of bribe by public official or employee, § 800.
    District attorney, § 739.
    Felony offenses, § 800.
    Misdemeanor offenses, § 801.
Finding and presentment of indictment, § 940 et seq.
  Setting aside for improper finding, § 995.
Firearms, defendant armed, allegations, § 969c.
Forgery, instrument destroyed or withheld by defendant, misdescription, § 965.
Former jeopardy, § 1016 et seq.
Forms, §§ 739, 950, 951.
  Bench warrant, felony case, § 981.
  Pleas, § 1017.
  Prior conviction allegations, §§ 969, 970.
Grounds for setting aside, § 995.
Guilty Plea, generally, this index.
Hearing, motion to set aside, § 997.
Indorsement. Endorsement, generally, ante.
Inquiry into imprisonment without indictment, § 919.
Insertion or indorsement, names of witnesses on indictment, § 943.
Issuance of indictments, § 939.8.
Joinder of counts, § 954.
Judicial notice,
  Allegations, § 961.
Jurisdiction,
  Misdemeanors, sitting as juvenile court, necessity, § 682.
Justices' courts, offenses tried, § 682.
Juvenile courts, superior court sitting, § 682.
Language,
  Statutory language, § 952.
Limitation of prosecution, indictment found when presented and filed, § 803.
Lost or destroyed documents,
  Forged instrument, misdescription, § 965.

729

INDICTMENT

INDICTMENT AND INFORMATION
—Cont'd
Mentally deficient and mentally ill persons,
  Plea, § 1016 et seq.
Militia, offenses, § 682.
Multiple defendants, conviction or acquittal of one or more, § 970.
Multiple offenses,
  Charge, § 954.
Multiple pleas, § 1016 et seq.
Municipal courts,
  Offenses tried, necessity, § 682.
Names,
  Court and parties, § 950.
  Defendant charged by fictitious or erroneous name, amendment, § 953.
  Witnesses,
    Insertion or indorsement on indictment, § 943.
Nature of weapon with which defendant armed, allegations, § 969c.
Nolo Contendere, generally, this index.
Not Guilty Plea, generally, this index.
Objections, waiver,
  Move to set aside, § 996.
Open court, entry of plea, § 1017.
Orders,
  Setting aside, bar to subsequent prosecution, § 999.
Parole and probation, eligibility, § 1203.06.
Parties, names, § 950.
Preliminary examination, § 738.
Preparing, § 923.
Presentment, § 917.
  Setting aside for improper presentment, § 995.
Presumptions, § 961.
Sanity, § 1016.
Principals,
  Distinction between accessories and principals abrogated, § 971.
  Prosecution of accessory without regard to prosecution of principal, § 972.
Probable cause, setting aside for commitment of defendant, § 995.
Probationer, dismissal, § 1203.4.
Reading, jury, § 1093.
Reasonable cause, setting aside, commitment of defendant, § 995.
Receiving stolen goods, § 496.
Removal of state civil officers, necessity, § 682.
Requisites, §§ 827, 959.
Resubmission of case,
  Custody or bail of defendant, § 998.
  Failure to find new indictment or file new information, § 998.
  Want of facts constituting offense, § 1117.
Separate trial, different offenses or counts, § 954.
Setting aside, § 995 et seq.
  Motion, § 997.
  Objections, waiver by failure to move, § 996.
  Order, bar to subsequent prosecution, § 999.
Several defendants, conviction or acquittal of one or more, single indictment, § 970.

INDICTMENT AND INFORMATION
—Cont'd
Several offenses, § 954.
State civil officers, removal, necessity, § 682.
Statement of offense, §§ 950, 952, 954.
Statutes,
  Charging offense in words of enactment, § 952.
  Theft substituted for larceny, embezzlement or stealing, § 490a.
Subsequent prosecution, order setting aside, bar, § 999.
Sufficiency, § 959.
Superior court, mode of prosecution, § 737 et seq.
Technical averments, § 952.
Theft, this index.
Time,
  Commission of offense, § 955.
  Filing, ante.
  Indictment found when presented and filed, § 803.
  Offense, time of commission, § 955.
  Pleas, § 1017.
Title of action, § 950.
True bill, indorsement, § 940.
Waiver,
  Objections,
    Failure to move to set aside, § 996.
War, offenses arising in land and naval forces, § 682.
Weapons, defendant armed, § 969c.
Witnesses,
  Names, insertion or indorsement on indictment, § 943.
  Reports, request of person called, § 939.91.

INDIGENT PERSONS
Arrest, return to place of arrest upon release, § 686.5.
Counsel for Accused, generally, this index.
Jails,
  Medical care and treatment, § 4011.
Probation modification, right to counsel, § 1203.2.
Release of arrested indigent, return to place of arrest, § 686.5.
Social Services, generally, this index.

INDORSEMENT
Endorsement, generally, this index.

INDUSTRIAL FARMS AND ROAD CAMPS
Alcoholic beverages,
  Bringing into prison, § 4573.
Arrests, escapees, § 836.3.
Assault and battery, against noninmates, § 4131.5.
Compensation and salaries,
  Public works, § 1203.1.
Conduct of prisoners, good time credits, § 4019.
Drugs,
  Bringing into prison, § 4573.5.
Escape, generally, this index.
Ex-convict, unauthorized communications, § 4571.

INDUSTRIAL FARMS AND ROAD CAMPS—Cont'd
Explosives, possession, § 4574.
Family emergencies, temporary release, § 4018.6.
Fraudulent entry, § 4570.5.
Good time allowance, § 4019.
Maximum term of confinement, § 19a.
Narcotics,
  Bringing into prison, § 4573.
Probation, § 1203.1.
  Temporary removal or release for purposes preparatory to return to community, § 1203.1a.
Release or removal for purposes preparatory to return to community, probationers, § 1203.1a.
Rescues, § 4550.
Salaries. Compensation and salaries, generally, ante.
Temporary release, § 4018.6.
  Preparation to return to community, probationers, § 1203.1a.
Weapons, possession, § 4574.
Work Furlough Law, § 1208.
Work performance of prisoners, time credits, § 4019.

INDUSTRIAL PLANTS
Manufacturers and Manufacturing, generally, this index.

INEBRIATES
Drunkards and Drunkenness, generally, this index.

INFANTS
Children and Minors, generally, this index.

INFERIOR COURTS AND TRIBUNALS
Arraignment,
  Informing defendant of right to trial in district, § 1462.2.
Arrest warrant, § 1427.
Corporations, summons for traffic violations, etc., § 1427.
Defined, jurisdiction, § 691.
Forms, warrant of arrest, § 1427.
Misdemeanors, venue, determination, § 1462.2.
Offenses triable, prosecution by written complaint, § 740.
Pleas,
  Enumeration, § 1016 et seq.
  Misdemeanors,
    Insanity plea, § 1430.
Warrant of arrest, § 1427.

INFLAMMABLES
Possession with intent to burn property, § 452.

INFORMATION
Indictment and Information, generally, this index.

INFRACTIONS
Generally, §§ 16, 17.
Application of law, § 19d.
Arrest, time of day, § 840.

Penal Code — JAILS

INFRACTIONS—Cont'd
Bail, this index.
Burden of proof, § 19d.
Defined, § 17.
Jurisdiction, § 19d.
Limitation of prosecution, § 19d.
Motor Vehicles, this index.
Practice and procedure, § 19d.
Probation, summary grant of, § 1203b.
Release procedures, § 853.5.
Schedule, bail, § 1269b.
Time, arrest, § 840.
Traffic Rules and Regulations, this index.
Trial, § 19d.

INHABITED
Defined,
  Arson, § 447a.
  Burglary, § 459.
  Weapons discharge, § 246.

INHALATION
Toluene or other poison, disorderly conduct, § 647.

INHERITANCE
Descent and Distribution, generally, this index.

INITIAL SENTENCING
Generally, § 1170 et seq.

INJUNCTION
Bingo, operation without license, § 326.5.
Destructive devices, possession, § 12307.
Machine guns, possession, § 12251.
Weapons, machine gun, § 12251.

INJURIES
Personal Injuries, generally, this index.

INMATE
Correctional Institutions, generally, this index.

INNKEEPERS
Hotels, generally, this index.

INNOCENCE
Presumptions, innocence of defendant, § 1096.
Instructions to jury, § 1096a.

INSANE PERSONS
Mentally Deficient and Mentally Ill Persons, generally, this index.

INSIGNIA
Badges, Emblems and Insignia, generally, this index.

INSOLENT BEHAVIOR
Criminal contempt, § 166.

INSPECTION AND INSPECTORS
Correctional Institutions, generally, this index.
Court records on search warrants, § 1534.
Machine guns,
  Sales record, § 12250.
Person carrying loaded weapon, § 12031.
Records and Recordation, this index.

INSPECTION AND INSPECTORS —Cont'd
Search warrants, court records and documents, § 1534.
Sex offenders, records, § 290.
State inspectors, false personation, § 146a.
Weapons, this index.

INSTALLMENTS
Fines, payment, § 1205.

INSTRUCTIONS TO JURY
Trial, this index.

INSTRUMENTS
Books and Papers, generally, this index.

INSURANCE
Abandonment, insured property, defrauding insurer, § 548.
Acts to defraud or prejudice insurer, § 548.
Annuities,
  Counterfeiting or forgery of instruments relating to, § 470.
Arson, personal property, intent to defraud insurers, § 450a.
Burning insured property, defrauding insurer, §§ 450a, 548.
Concealment, insured property, defrauding insurer, § 548.
Destruction, insured property, defrauding insurer, § 548.
Fraud, § 548.
  Arson, personal property, intent to defraud, insurers, § 450a.
  Claims for medical care, social services, § 72.
Group insurance, peace officers, § 830.5.
  Corrections department, law enforcement liaison unit, § 830.5a.

INTENT
Assault with deadly weapons, § 467.
Defrauding,
  Innkeepers, § 537.
  Sufficiency, § 8.
Fraud,
  Innkeepers, § 537.
  Sufficiency, § 8.
Intoxication, voluntary, consideration when necessary element, § 22.
Manifestations, § 21.
Unity of act or intent to constitute crime, necessity, § 20.

INTERCEPTION
Police radio service communications, § 636.5.

INTERNS
Battered children, reports, §§ 11110, 11161.5.
Form, § 11161.7.

INTERRUPTING JUDICIAL PROCEEDINGS
Criminal contempt, § 166.

INTOXICATING LIQUORS
Alcoholic Beverages, generally, this index.

INTOXICATION
Drunkards and Drunkenness, generally, this index.

INVALIDS
Handicapped Persons, generally, this index.

INVOICES
Fraudulent bills, presentation to state, board, or officer, § 72.

INVOLUNTARY MANSLAUGHTER
Homicide, this index.

INVOLUNTARY SERVITUDE
Jurisdiction, § 784.
Kidnapping, § 207.

IRON
Purchasing, determination of seller's right, § 496a.

ISOMETHADONE
See, also, Drugs and Medicine, generally, this index.

ISOQUINOLINE ALKALOID OF OPIUM
See, also, Drugs and Medicine, generally, this index.

ISSUES, PROOF AND VARIANCE
Not guilty plea, § 1019.

JACKS OR JENNYS
See, also, Animals, generally, this index.
Theft, § 487.
  Carcasses, § 487a.

JAGUARS
See, also, Fish and Game, generally, this index.

JAILS
Generally, § 4000 et seq.
Absence of prisoner, authorization, § 4011.5.
Alcoholic beverages,
  Bringing into prison, § 4573.
Alternate sentence to county jail, felonies, § 18.
Arrest, escapees charged with or convicted of misdemeanor, § 836.3.
Arson, § 448a.
  Local detention facilities, § 451b.
Assault and battery, against noninmates, § 4131.5.
Attachment, work furlough earnings, § 1208.
Attorney general, prisoner removed to state prison, report, § 4007.
Birth control measures, continuation, § 4023.5.
Bringing alcoholic beverages or narcotics into, § 4573.
Bringing defendant before court for judgment, § 1194.
Burning, prisoners in local detention facilities starting fires, § 451b.
Care. Medical attendance and treatment, generally, post.

JAILS Index

JAILS—Cont'd
Children and minors, confinement with adult prisoners, § 273b.
City facilities for prisoners, § 4004.5.
City jail,
  Medical treatment, expenses, payment, § 4011.
Civil process, persons committed, separation, § 4002.
Classes of prisoners, separation, §§ 4001, 4002.
Classification of offenses according to imprisonment in, § 17.
Clerks, execution of arrest warrant, person in custody, § 816.
Communication with prisoners, § 4570 et seq.
Compensation and salaries,
  Attachment, § 1208.
  Execution, § 1208.
  Prisoners for work, § 4019.3.
  Work furloughs, § 1208.
Conduct of prisoners, good time credits, § 4019.
Contempt, confinement of persons, § 4000 et seq.
Contiguous county,
  Removal for safe treatment, § 4007 et seq.
Convicted persons, separation, § 4002.
Conviction of crime, confinement of persons, § 4000 et seq.
Credit on time, work furlough, § 1208.
Criminal process, detention for trial, classes of prisoners, separation, § 4002.
Cruel treatment of prisoners, §§ 147, 673.
Custodial officers, § 831.
Custodian, forfeiture for failure to allow attorney visitation, § 825.
Custody of persons in city facilities, § 4004.5.
Damage or injury, malicious mischief, § 606.
Definitions, unauthorized fire, local detention facility, § 451b.
Demolishing, punishment, § 4600.
Dependents, support, work furlough earnings, § 1208.
Designation, contiguous county jail, § 4008.
Destruction, § 4600.
Detention of persons, § 4000 et seq.
Drugs,
  Bringing into prison, § 4573.5.
  Paraphernalia for consuming narcotics or other drugs,
    Bringing into prison, §§ 4573, 4573.5.
  Work furlough programs, counseling of prisoners, § 1208.
Drunkards and drunkenness,
  Work furlough programs, counseling of prisoners, § 1208.
Education,
  Programs, § 1208.
Emergencies, removal of prisoners to hospital, § 4011.5.
Escape, generally, this index.
Ex-convict coming upon grounds or adjacent lands, § 4571.

JAILS—Cont'd
Execution of judgment, work furlough earnings, § 1208.
Expenses and expenditures,
  Detention of state parolees, reimbursement of county, § 4016.5.
  Removal of inmates to other facilities, § 4007.
  Transportation of mentally deficient criminals, § 1373.
Explosives, possession, § 4574.
Extradition, confinement of prisoner under warrant of arrest, § 1550.3.
Facilities, municipalities furnishing to counties, § 4004.5.
False personation, fraudulent entry, § 4570.5.
Family emergencies, release, §§ 1208, 4018.6.
Family planning services, women, § 4023.5.
Females. Women, generally, post.
Financial ability of prisoner to pay for care, support and maintenance, § 4011.
Fires,
  Local detention facilities, prisoners starting fires, § 451b.
Forfeitures, jail officer refusing to allow attorney to visit prisoner, § 825.
Fraudulent entry, § 4570.5.
Fugitives from justice, arrest without warrant, commitment, § 1552.
Good time allowance, § 4019.
  Work release, § 1208.
Grand jury, inquiry into condition and management, § 919.
Guards,
  Matrons, generally, post.
  Removal, hospitalization of prisoners, §§ 4011, 4011.9.
Hospitalization of prisoners, §§ 4007, 4011 et seq.
  Removal of guard, § 4011.9.
Husband and wife, separation, § 4002.
Indigent persons,
  Medical care, § 4011 et seq.
Industrial Farms and Road Camps, generally, this index.
Inhuman treatment of prisoners, § 147.
Injury during employment or education, release for medical treatment, § 1208.
Intercounty work furlough agreements, § 1208.5.
Intoxicating liquors,
  Bringing into prison, § 4573.
Keepers, § 4000 et seq.
Labor and employment,
  Work furloughs, generally, post.
Labor disputes, work furloughs, § 1208.
Malicious mischief, injury or destruction, § 606.
Matrons,
  Presence during entry of cell by male officer, § 4021.
Maximum term of confinement, § 19a.
Medical attendance and treatment, § 4007.
  Emergencies, removal of inmate without court order, § 4011.5.

JAILS—Cont'd
Medical attendance and treatment—Cont'd
  Expenses, § 4011 et seq.
  Hospitalization of prisoners, generally, ante.
  Removal for treatment, § 4011 et seq.
  Surgical treatment of prisoners, § 4011 et seq.
  Work furlough, release for medical treatment, § 1208.
Medicine. Drugs, generally, ante.
Multicounty work furlough agreements, § 1208.5.
Municipal corporations, § 4004.5.
Narcotics. Drugs, generally, ante.
Oppressive treatment of prisoners, § 147.
Paraphernalia for consuming narcotics or other drugs,
  Bringing into prison, §§ 4573, 4573.5.
Parolees, detention of state parolees, reimbursement of county, § 4016.5.
Pay. Compensation and salaries, generally, ante.
Personal hygiene, women, § 4023.5.
Personal property, receipts, § 4003.
Physicians and surgeons, § 4023.
  Medical attendance and treatment, generally, ante.
Preexisting debts, work furlough earnings, payment, § 1208.
Priorities and preferences, work furlough earnings, collection by work furlough administrator, § 1208.
Privacy, female prisoners, § 4021.
Private security guards, hospitalization of prisoners, § 4011.
Probationers,
  Commitment, § 1203.1.
  Temporary removal or release for purposes preparatory to return to community, § 1203.1a.
Punishment not specifically prescribed, misdemeanors, § 19.
Purposes, § 4000 et seq.
Receipt,
  Property taken from prisoner, § 4003.
Record and recordation,
  Criminal identification and investigation bureau, examination of records while imprisoned, § 11125.
  Examination, § 11125.
Refusal of officials to receive person charged with offense, § 142.
Rehabilitation, work furlough programs, counseling of prisoners, § 1208.
Release,
  Bail, call to on-call magistrate when court not in session, assistance, § 810.
  Family emergencies, §§ 1208, 4018.6.
  Medical treatment, § 1208.
  Preparatory to return to community, probationers, § 1203.1a.
  Temporary release, § 4018.6.
Release time, education and employment, §§ 1208, 1208.5.
Removal of prisoners,
  Medical or surgical treatment, § 4011 et seq.
  Probationers, temporary release or removal for purposes preparatory to return to community, § 1203.1a.

Penal Code — JUNK

JAILS—Cont'd
Rescue, § 4550.
Revocation of order of confinement in contiguous county jail, §§ 4009, 4010.
Rooms, separation of prisoners, § 4001.
Safekeeping prisoners, transferring, § 4007.
Salaries. Compensation and salaries, generally, ante.
Search,
  Presence of deputy sheriff of same sex, § 4021.
Separate facilities, male and female prisoners, § 4001.
Sex offenders, discharge or parole, notice of duty to register, § 290.
Sexes, separation, §§ 4001, 4002.
Sheriffs, § 4000 et seq.
Special agreement with inmate for care, support, maintenance and hospital expenses, § 4011.
State parolees, detention, reimbursement of counties, § 4016.5.
Support,
  Federal prisoners, § 4005.
  Hospitalized inmates, § 4011.
  Work furlough earnings, § 1208.
Telephones,
  Call to on-call magistrate to seek release, assistance, § 810.
  Eavesdropping, invasion of privacy, §§ 631, 632.
Temporary release, § 4018.6.
Temporary removal from custody,
  Powers and duties, § 4018.6.
  Purposes preparatory to return to community, probationers, § 1203.1a.
Transfer of prisoners,
  Work furlough facility, § 1208.
  Work furlough programs, §§ 1208, 1208.5.
Treatment. Medical attendance and treatment, generally, ante.
Unauthorized fire, defined, prisoners in local detention facilities, § 451b.
Unfit for confinement, § 4007.
United States prisoners, receiving and safekeeping, §§ 4005, 4006.
Unsafe jails, removal of prisoners to contiguous county, § 4007 et seq.
Visitation by attorney, right of prisoner, § 825.
Vocational training and rehabilitation of prisoners,
  Facility for confinement, designation, § 1208.
  Family emergencies, release, § 1208.
  Medical treatment, release, § 1208.
Wages. Compensation and salaries, generally, ante.
Warrants for arrest, clerks, execution, city or county jails, § 816.
Weapons,
  Possession, § 4574.
  Receipts, § 4003.
Wiretapping, invasion of privacy, §§ 631, 632.
Witnesses, detention to secure attendance, § 4000 et seq.

JAILS—Cont'd
Women,
  Birth control measures, continuation, § 4023.5.
  Entering cell of female without female deputy sheriff, § 4021.
  Family planning services, § 4023.5.
  Male officer entering cell, presence of matron, § 4021.
  Personal hygiene, § 4023.5.
  Privacy, § 4021.
  Separation, §§ 4001, 4002.
Work furlough administrators,
  Agreement to transfer prisoners, delegation of authority, § 1208.5.
  Joint persons performing functions, § 1208.
Work furloughs, §§ 1208, 1208.5.
  Facilities for confinement of prisoners, designation, § 1208.
  Family emergencies, § 1208.
  Medical treatment, § 1208.
  Transfer of prisoners to county of employment, § 1208.5.
Work performance of prisoners, time credits, § 4019.

JEOPARDY
Former Jeopardy, generally, this index.

JOINDER OF COUNTS
Accusatory pleading, § 954.

JOINT AUTHORITY
Defined, public officers, § 7.

JOINT COUNTY JAILS
Jails, generally, this index.

JOY RIDING
Generally, § 499b.

JUDGES
Argument and conduct of counsel, control of proceedings, § 1044.
Attempt to kill or assault, § 217.1.
Bench warrant, issuance, § 980 et seq.
Conspiracy to commit crime, § 182.
Courts of Appeal, this index.
Criminal history information, local summary criminal history information, furnishing, § 13300 et seq.
Institutes and seminars, sentencing procedure, § 1170.5.
Justice Courts, this index.
Magistrates, generally, this index.
Pardons, reprieves and commutations, summarized statement of facts, § 4803.
Reading other reports on accused, § 1204.5.
Records, conviction record on accused, restrictions on reading, § 1204.5.
Reports, arrest reports on accused, reading, § 1204.5.
Sentencing institutes, determinate sentences, § 1170.5.
Statement of views respecting person convicted or sentenced, § 1203.01.
Superior Court Judges, generally, this index.
Supreme Court Justices, generally, this index.

JUDGMENTS AND DECREES
Generally, § 1191 et seq.
Abstracts of judgment,
  Delivery of prisoner to correctional institution, § 1216.
Acquittal judgments, § 1118 et seq.
Allocution, § 1200.
Appeals in Criminal Prosecutions, generally, this index.
Arrest of Judgment, generally, this index.
Bringing defendant before court for judgment, § 1194.
Counterfeiting or forgery, § 470.
Custody, defendant in custody, bringing before court for judgment, § 1194.
Deferring judgment, causes, § 1201.
Delivery of prisoner for custody, § 1202a.
Diagnostic facilities, placement of persons, §§ 1191, 1203.03.
Entry of judgment,
  Acquittal judgments, § 1118 et seq.
Executions, generally, this index.
Forgery or counterfeiting, § 470.
Homicide, justifiable homicide in obedience to, judgment, public officers, § 196.
Justifiable homicide, obedience to judgment, public officers, § 196.
Municipal Courts, this index.
Pronouncement of judgment, §§ 1191, 1202.
  Causes against pronouncement, § 1201.
  Extension of time, § 1191.
  Inquiry as to cause why judgment should not be pronounced, § 1200.
Rendition of judgment, § 1191 et seq.
Reports, probation officer, pronouncing judgment, § 1191.
Specification of imprisonment, nonpayment of fine, § 1205.

JUDICIAL COUNCIL
Sentence and punishment,
  Reports, publication, § 1170.4.
  Rules, § 1170.

JUDICIAL DISTRICTS
Constables and deputies, carrying loaded firearms, § 12031.

JUDICIAL NOTICE
Pleading matter judicially noticed, § 961.

JUDICIAL REVIEW
Appeals in Criminal Prosecutions, generally, this index.

JUKE–BOX
Burglar tools, § 466.3.
Coin operated, use of slugs, etc., § 640a.

JUNK AND JUNK DEALERS
Fines and penalties, metals, purchasing without using diligence to determine seller's right, § 496a.
Identification of metal sellers, obtaining, § 496a.
Purchasing metals used in transportation or public utility service, § 496a.
Receiving stolen goods, § 496a.
Records, metal purchases, § 496a.

JURISDICTIONAL

JURISDICTIONAL TERRITORY
Defined, § 691.

JURY
See, also, Trial, generally, this index.
Advice to enter judgment of acquittal, § 1118.1.
Capital offenses,
  Consideration of insanity defense and special circumstances, § 190.4.
  Determination of sentence, § 190.3.
Capital Punishment, this index.
Corrupt influencing, § 95.
Criminal acts, voluntary intoxication of accused, consideration as defense, § 22.
Discharge,
  Facts constituting offense, want of, § 1117.
    Discharge of defendant and exoneration of bail, § 1117.
Dismissal, first degree murder prosecution, unable to reach verdict on issue of penalty, § 190.4.
Drunkenness of accused, voluntary intoxication, consideration, § 22.
Facts constituting offense, want of, discharge, § 1117.
First degree murder, special circumstances, determination of sentence, § 190.3.
Grand Jury, generally, this index.
Impaneling, new jury, alternative death or life imprisonment determination, § 190.4.
Intimidation, § 95.
Intoxication, criminal accused, voluntary nature, consideration, § 22.
Mentally deficient and mentally ill persons, determination, § 1368 et seq.
Proceedings to determine penalty,
  Capital offenses, determination of penalty, § 190.3.
  First degree murder, special circumstances, § 190.4.
Rape, recommendation of punishment, § 264.
Sanity issue on plea of not guilty, § 1026.
Sentence and punishment, capital offenses, determination, § 190.3.
Special findings, first degree murder, special circumstances charged, § 190.4.
Verdict, generally, Trial, this index.
Voluntary intoxication of criminal accused, consideration, § 22.
Waiver,
  Alternative death or life imprisonment determination, § 190.4.
  Judgment on not guilty finding, § 1118.

JUSTICE, STATE DEPARTMENT OF
Investigation functions, § 11050 et seq.
Officers and employees, master criminal record sheets or information from, unauthorized furnishing, § 11140 et seq.
Records,
  Master criminal record sheets or information from, unauthorized furnishing, § 11140 et seq.

JUSTICE, STATE DEPARTMENT OF—Cont'd
Sex offenders,
  Duty to register with, § 290.
  State department of, § 288a.

JUSTICE COURTS
Arraignment, determination of venue, § 1462.2.
Arrest,
  Issuance of warrants, judge as magistrate, § 813.
  Warrants, § 1427.
Complaints,
  Filing time, § 1426a.
  Warrant for arrest, § 1427.
Concurrent jurisdiction, § 1462.1.
Corporations, crimes and offenses, summons, § 1427.
Form,
  Warrant of arrest, § 1427.
Indictment and information, offenses tried in, necessity, § 682.
Inferior court includes, § 691.
Judges,
  Magistrates, designation as, § 808.
  Warrants of arrest, issuance, § 813.
  Unlawful or riotous assemblies, command to disperse, §§ 726, 727.
Jurisdiction,
  Concurrent jurisdiction, § 1462.1.
Limitation of prosecutions, § 1426a.
Magistrates. Judges, ante.
Orders, transfer of cases, venue in misdemeanor cases, § 1462.2.
Time,
  Filing misdemeanor complaints, § 1426a.
  Transfer of cases, determination of venue, § 1462.2.
Venue,
  Misdemeanors, § 1462.2.
Warrant for arrest, issuance, § 1427.

JUSTICES OF THE PEACE
Justice Courts, generally, this index.

JUSTIFIABLE FORCE
Resistance to commission of offense, § 692 et seq.

JUSTIFIABLE HOMICIDE
Generally, § 196 et seq.
Homicide, this index.

JUVENILE COURTS
Indictment or information, application of law, § 682.
Records and recordation,
  Libel and slander proceedings, opening of sealed records, §§ 851.7, 1203.45.

JUVENILE DELINQUENTS AND DEPENDENTS
Generally, § 270 et seq.
Attorneys,
  Probation modification, § 1203.2.
Classification of crimes, discharge, commitment to youth authority, § 17.
Commitment,
  Adult convicts, minors under sixteen confined with, § 273b.

JUVENILE DELINQUENTS AND DEPENDENTS—Cont'd
Commitment—Cont'd
  Youth authority. Commitment to youth authority, generally, post.
Commitment to youth authority,
  Classification of crimes, discharge, § 17.
  Discharge, Welf & I 1765.
    Classification of crime, § 17.
  Termination of probation, § 1203.2.
Contributing to delinquency, § 272.
Offenders, registration, § 290.
County welfare department, reports of cruelty to child, § 11161.5.
Court rooms, presence of adult prisoners, § 273b.
Discharge,
  Commitment to youth authority, ante.
Evidence,
  Libel and slander proceedings, opening of sealed records, § 851.7.
Indigent persons,
  Probation modification, § 1203.2.
Juvenile Courts, generally, this index.
Libel and slander proceedings, opening of sealed record, § 851.7.
Material witness, speedy trial, § 1048.
Materiality of witness' testimony, endorsement on subpoena, § 1330.
Misdemeanors,
  Conviction, libel and slander proceedings, opening of sealed records, § 851.7.
  Sealing records, § 851.7.
Parole and probation,
  Commitment to youth authority, revocation and termination of probation, § 1203.2.
  Modification, right to counsel, waiver of court appearance, § 1203.2.
Persons under 16, confinement with adult convicts, restriction, § 273b.
Probation officers. Juvenile Probation Officers, generally, this index.
Records and recordation,
  Court records,
  Sealing, § 851.7.
  Libel and slander proceedings, opening of records, § 851.7.
Waiver, court appearance, probation modification, § 1203.2.
Witnesses,
  Attendance outside county, § 1330.
Youth Authority, generally, this index.

JUVENILE PROBATION OFFICERS
Battered children, reports, § 11161.5.
Group insurance, § 830.5.
Insurance, group insurance, § 830.5.
Juvenile courts, officers appointed under as ex officio adult probation officers, § 1203.5.
Mutual aid powers, § 830.5.

KETOBEMIDONE
See, also, Drugs and Medicine, generally, this index.

KEYBIT
Burglars, possession with intent to break or enter, § 466.

KEYS
Burglars, alteration or making with intent to break or enter, § 466.
Motor Vehicles, this index.
Public buildings, unauthorized duplication, § 469.
Vending machines, burglar tools, § 466.3.

KIDNAPPING
See, also, Abduction, generally, this index.
Generally, § 207 et seq.
Accomplices and accessories, §§ 209, 210.
Soliciting aid, § 653f.
Acts comprising, §§ 207, 209.
Additional punishment, prior prison term, prior sentencing, § 1170.2.
Bodily harm, § 209.
Children and minors, § 278.
Definitions, § 207.
Evidence, wiretap evidence, § 633.5.
First degree murder, special circumstance, punishment, § 190.2.
Homicide, special circumstance, punishment, § 190.2.
Jurisdiction, § 784.
Life imprisonment, § 209.
Limitation of prosecution, §§ 799, 800.
Mentally incompetent defendant, commitment or outpatient treatment, § 1370.
Murder resulting, penalty, § 190.2.
Parole and probation, §§ 209, 1203.
Eligibility, § 1203.06.
Second and subsequent offenses, eligibility, § 1203.08.
Penalties, § 208 et seq.
Posing as kidnapper, § 210.
Soliciting commission, § 653f.
Stealing of children, § 278.
Subsequent offenses, additional punishment, § 667.5.
Weapons,
Accusatory pleading, nature of firearm used, § 969d.
Wiretap evidence, § 633.5.

KILLING
Homicide, generally, this index.
Unfit animals, § 599e.

KNIVES
Weapons, generally, this index.

KNOWINGLY
Defined, § 7.
Harmful matter, § 313.
Obscene matter, § 311.

KNUCKLES
Metallic knuckles. Weapons, generally, this index.

LABELS
Brands, Marks and Labels, generally, this index.

LABOR AND EMPLOYMENT
Children and minors,
Obscene matter, employment to assist in distribution, etc., §§ 311.4, 311.9.

LABOR AND EMPLOYMENT—Cont'd
Construction of buildings, willful diversion of funds, §§ 484b, 484c.
Correctional Institutions, this index.
Criminal history information,
Local summary criminal history information, furnishing, § 13300 et seq.
Defense of employer or employee, justifiable homicide, § 197.
Defined, Cobey Work Furlough Law, § 1208.
Embezzlement, generally, this index.
Hiring without notice of unpaid claims, larceny by fraud, § 484.
Homicide, this index.
Justifiable homicide, defense of employer or employee, § 197.
Theft, § 487.
Hiring employees without notice of unpaid claims, § 484.
Work furloughs, generally. Jails, this index.

LABOR DISPUTES
Jails, work furloughs, § 1208.
Peace officers, picketing, uniforms, weapons, § 12590.
Picketing,
Carrying deadly weapons or wearing peace officers uniforms, § 12590.

LAKES AND PONDS
Fish and Game, generally, this index.
Jurisdiction, offenses upon vessels navigating, § 783.

LAMBS
Theft, § 487.

LAND
Real Estate, generally, this index.

LANDING FIELDS
Airports and Landing Fields, generally, this index.

LANDLORD AND TENANT
See, also, Leases, generally, this index.
Apartments, letting for purposes of prostitution, § 316.
Tenements, letting for purposes of prostitution, § 316.
Theft by fraud, rental agreements, § 484.

LANGUAGE
Offensive language,
Disturbance of the peace, § 415.
State college or university, disturbance of the peace, § 415.5.

LARCENY
Theft, generally, this index.

LAUDANUM
See, also, Drugs and Medicine, generally, this index.
Administering to assist in commission of felony, § 222.

LAW OF THE ROAD
Traffic Rules and Regulations, generally, this index.

LAWFUL BUSINESS
Defined, disruption of schools, § 626.8.

LAWS
Ordinances, generally, this index.
Popular Name Laws, generally, this index.
Statutes, generally, this index.
Uniform Laws, generally, this index.

LAWYERS
Attorneys, generally, this index.

LEAD
Purchasing by junk or secondhand dealers, determination of seller's right, § 496a.

LEASES
See, also, Landlord and Tenant, generally, this index.
Assumed names, theft by fraud, § 484.
Bingo, place of holding games, § 326.5.
Counterfeiting or forgery, § 470.
Evidence, theft by fraud, § 484.
False identification, theft, § 484.
Fictitious names, theft by fraud, § 484.
Forgery, § 470.
Fraud,
Theft, § 484.
Mail, certified or registered mail, written demands for return of property, § 484.
Notice, written demands for return of property, certified or registered mail, § 484.
Theft by fraud, § 484.
Tools, theft by fraud, § 484.
Weapons, register, § 12073 et seq.

LEGACIES AND LEGATEES
Probate Proceedings, generally, this index.

LEGISLATURE
Reports,
Career criminal prosecution program, § 999c.
Pretrial diversion programs, § 1001.10.
Senate, advice and consent, community release board members, § 5075.

LEOPARDS
See, also, Fish and Game, generally, this index.

LETTERS AND OTHER CORRESPONDENCE
Correctional institutions, unauthorized communications with inmates, § 4570.
Extortion, threatening letters, § 523.
Prisoners, civil rights, § 2601.
Simulating official inquiries, § 146b.

LETTERS OF ATTORNEY
Power of Attorney, generally, this index.

LETTERS PATENT
Counterfeiting, § 470.
Forgery, § 470.

LEVOMETHORPHON

LEVOMETHORPHON
See, also, Drugs and Medicine, generally, this index.

LEVOMORAMIDE
See, also, Drugs and Medicine, generally, this index.

LEVOPHENACYLMORPHAN
See, also, Drugs and Medicine, generally, this index.

LEVORPHANOL
See, also, Drugs and Medicine, generally, this index.

LEWDNESS AND OBSCENITY
Generally, §§ 311.2, 313 et seq.
Advertising, § 311.5.
Children and minors,
  Acts upon body of child under fourteen,
    First degree murder, special circumstance, punishment, § 190.2.
  Additional punishment, prior prison term, prior sentencing, § 1170.2.
  Distribution or exhibition to minor, § 313 et seq.
  Employment to do obscene acts, §§ 311.4, 311.9.
  Homicide resulting in lewd acts on body of child under fourteen, § 189.
  Misrepresentation as parent or guardian, exhibiting harmful matters, § 313.1.
  Pornography, §§ 311.2, 311.4.
  Prior prison term, additional punishment, § 667.5.
  Vending machines, near schools or playgrounds, § 313.1.
Coercion, acceptance of obscene matter as condition of sale of other merchandise, §§ 311.7, 311.9.
Commercial exploitation, evidence, § 311.
Defenses, § 311.8.
Definitions, § 311.
Disorderly conduct, § 647.
Distribute, defined, § 311.
Distribution,
  Children and minors, § 313 et seq.
  Obscene material, § 311.2.
Evidence, § 312.1.
  Commercial exploitation, § 311.
Exemption, motion picture machine operators, § 311.2.
Exhibitions, this index.
Exposure of body in public place, § 314.
Fines and penalties, § 311.9.
Harmful matter, § 313 et seq.
Homicide, acts upon body of child under 14, special circumstance, punishment, § 190.2.
House of ill-fame, keeping for purposes, § 315.
Knowingly, defined, § 311.
Machine operators, motion pictures, application of law, § 311.2.
Matter, defined, § 311.
Obscene live conduct,
  Defined, § 311.
  Managing, producing, sponsoring, etc., § 311.6.

LEWDNESS AND OBSCENITY
—Cont'd
Obscene matter, defined, § 311.
Person, defined, § 311.
Possession, obscene material, § 311.2.
Publication, § 311.2.
Registration of offenders with sheriff or police chief, § 290.
Reports, § 11107.
Sale or distribution, § 311.2.
Sentence and punishment, § 311.9.
Soliciting, § 647.
Telephones,
  Wiretap evidence, admissibility, § 633.5.
Threats, acceptance of obscene matter as condition of sale of other merchandise, §§ 311.7, 311.9.
Tie-in sales, §§ 311.7, 311.9.
Vending machines near schools or playgrounds, § 313.1.

LIBEL AND SLANDER
Evidence,
  Juvenile delinquents and dependents, opening of sealed records, § 851.7.
Shoplifting, false imprisonment, defenses, § 490.5.

LICENSES AND PERMITS
Bingo, fees, § 326.5.
Carrying concealed weapons, fines and penalties, § 12025.
Destructive devices, possession, sale, transportation or use, § 12305.
Machine guns, § 12230 et seq.
  Sales, § 12250.
Tear gas weapons. Weapons, this index.
Weapons, this index.

LIFE IMPRISONMENT
Assault with deadly weapon, life prisoner, § 4500.
Attempts, crime punishable by life imprisonment, § 664.
Determinate Sentence Law, § 1170.
Determination of sentence by trier of fact, § 190.3.
Enhancement of prison terms, prior offenses, § 667.5.
First degree murder, special circumstances charged, § 190.2.
Homicide, § 190.
  First degree murder, special circumstances charged, § 190.2.
Jury, determination, § 190.3.
Kidnapping, § 209.
Merger, multiple offenses, § 669.
Murder in first degree, § 190.
Rehabilitation period, § 4852.03.
Train wrecking, § 219.

LIGHT AND POWER COMPANIES
Electricity, generally, this index.

LIMITATION OF PROSECUTIONS
Generally, § 799 et seq.
Absence of defendant from state, exclusion of period, § 802.
Bribery, acceptance by public employee or officer, § 800.
Computation of time, exclusion of period of defendant's absence from state, § 802.

LIMITATION OF PROSECUTIONS
—Cont'd
Embezzlement, public moneys, § 799.
Erroneous convictions, claims against state, § 4901.
Evidence, false documentary evidence, § 800.
Falsification, public records, §§ 799, 800.
Felonies, § 800.
Forgery, § 800.
Fraudulent claims against state boards, counties, municipalities, etc., § 800.
Grand theft, § 800.
Homicide, § 799.
Indictment, found when presented and filed, § 803.
Infractions, § 19d.
Involuntary manslaughter, § 800.
Justice courts, time for filing misdemeanor complaint, § 1426a.
Kidnapping, §§ 799, 800.
Manslaughter, § 800.
Misdemeanors, § 801.
Murder, § 799.
One year limitation, § 801.
Perjury, § 800.
Probate proceedings, public administrators, § 800.
Public officers and employees, § 800.
Public records, falsification, §§ 799, 800.
Six year limitation, § 800.
Three year limitation, § 800.

LIPS
Slitting, mayhem, §§ 203, 204.

LIQUOR
Alcoholic Beverages, generally, this index.

LIQUOR ADDICTS
Drunkards and Drunkenness, generally, this index.

LITERATURE
Prisoners, unauthorized communications, § 4570.

LITTERING
Highways and Roads, this index.
Water Quality, this index.

LITTLE LINDBERGH ACT
Generally, § 209.

LIVESTOCK
Animals, generally, this index.

LOANS
Construction fund loans,
  Diversion of funds, § 484b.
  Embezzlement, § 484c.
Diversion of funds, construction of loans, § 484b.
Evidences of Indebtedness, generally, this index.
Public officers, unauthorized loans of public money, § 424.
Sawed-off shotgun, § 12001.5.

LOCAL AGENCIES
Criminal history information, local summary criminal history information, furnishing, § 13300 et seq.

Penal Code

MANTECA

LOCKS
Malicious mischief, posted lands, tampering, § 602.
Tampering, gate locks, posted lands, § 602.

LODGING HOUSES
Boarding and Lodging Houses, generally, this index.

LOGS AND LOGGING
Timber and Lumber, generally, this index.

LOITERING
Adult classes in attendance, annoying or molesting persons, § 647b.
Disorderly conduct, § 647.

LOST OR DESTROYED DOCUMENTS
Credit cards, § 484e.
Documentary evidence, § 135.
Indictment and information,
 Forged instrument, misdescription, § 965.

LOST OR DESTROYED PROPERTY
Credit cards, § 484e.
Finding lost property, theft, § 485.
Reports, §§ 11106, 11108.
Theft by appropriation, § 485.

LOTTERIES
Generally, § 319 et seq.
Defined, § 319.
Fines and penalties, § 319 et seq.
Penalties, § 319 et seq.
Schemes comprising, § 319.

LUMBER
Timber and Lumber, generally, this index.

LYING IN WAIT
Murder perpetrated, degree, § 189.

LYNX
See, also, Fish and Game, generally, this index.

LYSERGIC ACID
See, also, Drugs and Medicine, generally, this index.

LYSERGIC ACID AMIDE
See, also, Drugs and Medicine, generally, this index.

LYSERGIC ACID DIETHYLAMIDE
See, also, Drugs and Medicine, generally, this index.

MACE
Purchase, possession or use, § 12403.7.

MACHINE GUNS
Weapons, this index.

MACHINERY AND EQUIPMENT
Construction equipment,
 Diversion of funds, § 484b.
Credit card reproduction equipment, possession, § 484i.

MACHINERY AND EQUIPMENT
—Cont'd
Electronic eavesdropping, § 635.
Leases, theft by fraud, § 484.
Presumptions, theft by fraud, § 484.
Serial number or identification mark removed, sale, etc., § 537e.
Slot Machines, generally, this index.
Theft by fraud, § 484.
Wiretap equipment, § 635.

MAGAZINES
Advertisements, generally, this index.
Correctional institution inmates, civil rights, § 2601.
Lewdness and Obscenity, generally, this index.
Prisoners, civil rights, § 2601.

MAGISTRATES
Appearance before, time, § 825.
Arrest, this index.
Complaints, § 806 et seq.
Custody, release on bail when court not in session, § 810.
Defined, §§ 807, 808.
Delay in bringing accused before magistrate, §§ 145, 825, 849.
Fugitive escaping bail, hearing, bondsmen's application for return, § 847.5.
Judges, designation, § 808.
Misdemeanor offenses, citations under state law, § 853.6 et seq.
On-call status when court is not in session, § 810.
Oral orders to make arrests, § 838.
Persons designated as, § 808.
Riots, neglect or refusal to disperse, § 410.
Search warrants, issuance when court not in session, § 810.
Speedy trial, extension of term, appearances by arrested persons, § 825.
Term of court, extension, appearances by arrested persons, § 825.
Time, appearance before, § 825.
Unlawful assembly, neglect or refusal to disperse, § 410.
Warrant, arrest, issuance, § 813.

MAIL AND MAILING
Certified or registered mail,
 Correctional institutions, delivery of prisoner, notice to judges, § 1202a.
 Written demand, return of leased or rented personal property, § 484.
Corporations, traffic violations, summons, § 1427.
Summons, traffic violation, corporation, § 1427.
Weapons, this index.

MALICE
Child abuse, reports, personal liability, § 11161.5.
 Probation officers, § 11161.6.
Defined, §§ 7, 188.
Homicide, § 188.
Peace officers, residence address or telephone number, disclosing with intent to obstruct justice, § 146e.

MALICIOUS MISCHIEF
Generally, § 594 et seq.
Animals,
 Cruelty, § 597.
Apartment houses,
 Forcible entry, vandalism, § 603.
 Unauthorized entry, § 602.5.
Burning, property not subject to arson, §§ 449b, 449c.
Cabins, forcible entry, § 603.
Classification of offense, § 594.
Cruelty to animals, § 597.
Defined, § 594.
Dwellings,
 Forcible entry, vandalism, § 603.
 Unauthorized entry, § 602.5.
Entry on property,
 Forcible, § 603.
 Oyster lands, § 602.
 Posted lands, § 602.
 Unauthorized, § 602.5.
Fences, destroying, § 602.
Fighting cocks, possession, § 597j.
Fires,
 Building without permission, § 602.
 Burning property not subject to arson, §§ 449b, 449c.
Forcible entry, vandalism, § 603.
Gates, opening, § 602.
Jails, injury or destruction, § 606.
Motor vehicles,
 Trespass, § 602.
Oyster lands, entering without permission, § 602.
Places of confinement, injury or destruction, § 606.
Posted lands, entering without permission, § 602.
Private property, refusal to leave upon request, § 602.
Public buildings and works, refusal to leave at closing time, § 602.
Signs and signals,
 Tearing down, damaging, § 602.
Soil, removal without permission, § 602.
Telegraphs and Telephones, this index.
Timber, cutting, destroying, or carrying away without permission, § 602.
Trespasses, § 602.
Unauthorized entry on property, § 602.5.
University of California, trespass, § 626 et seq.

MALICIOUSLY
Defined, § 7.

MANAGERS AND MANAGEMENT
Obscene live conduct, § 311.6.

MANDAMUS
Searches and seizures, motion to suppress evidence, review, § 1538.5.

MANIFESTATIONS
Intent, § 21.

MANSLAUGHTER
Generally, § 192 et seq.
Homicide, this index.

MANTECA, CITY OF
See, also, Municipalities, generally, this index.

MANUFACTURERS

MANUFACTURERS AND MANU-FACTURING
Arson, § 448a.
Bombs, unlicensed possession of materials or substances, § 12312.
Destructive devices,
  Permits, § 12305.
  Unlicensed possession of materials or substances, § 12312.
Eavesdropping equipment, § 635.
Explosives, unlicensed possession, § 12312.
Fire bombs, § 452.
Nunchakus, § 12020.
Sawed-off shotgun, § 12001.5.
Slugs,
  Coin-box telephones, § 640b.
  Coin-operated vending machines, manufacture and distribution, § 640a.
Weapons,
  Metal plates used as weapons, § 12020.
  Nunchakus, § 12020.
Wiretap equipment, § 635.

MARIJUANA
Drugs and Medicine, this index.

MARKS
Brands, Marks and Labels, generally, this index.

MARRIAGE
Bigamy, generally, this index.
Correctional institutions inmates, civil rights, § 2601.
Dissolution of marriage,
  Bigamy, § 282.
Support, failure to provide, § 270.
Prisoners, civil rights, § 2601.

MARRIAGE COUNSELORS
Privileges and immunities, battered or sexually molested children, reports, § 11161.5.

MARRIED WOMEN
Husband and Wife, generally, this index.

MARSHALS
Generally, §§ 830, 830.1.
Concealed Weapons Law, applicability, § 12027.
Municipal courts, firearms, § 12031.
Powers and duties, §§ 830, 830.1.
Training, § 832.

MASCULINE GENDER
Construction of statute, § 7.

MASTER AND SERVANT
Labor and Employment, generally, this index.

MASTER KEYS
Motor vehicles, sale or possession, § 466.5.

MATERIAL WITNESSES
Witnesses, this index.

MATERIALS
Construction funds, diversion, §§ 484b, 484c.

MATRONS
Jails, this index.

MATTER
Defined,
  Harmful matter, § 313.
  Obscenity, § 311.

MATTRESSES
Fires, prisoners in local detention facilities, § 451b.

MAYHEM
Generally, §§ 203, 204.
Additional punishment, prior prison term, prior sentencing, § 1170.2.
Assault with intent to commit, § 220.
Defined, § 203.
Mentally incompetent defendant, commitment or outpatient treatment, § 1370.
Murder resulting, degree, § 189.
Second and subsequent offense,
  Additional punishment, § 667.5.
  Probation, eligibility, § 1203.08.

MEDICAL ATTENDANCE AND TREATMENT
Arrest, release on notice to appear, failure to release persons requiring medical examination or care, § 853.6.
Drug offenders, diversion from prosecution, § 1000 et seq.
Governmental institutions, treatment impairing health, § 673.
Jails, this index.
Social Services, generally, this index.

MEDICAL RECORDS
Altering or modifying, fraudulent intent, § 471.5.

MEDICAL RESEARCH
Dogs, theft, § 487g.

MEDICAL SCHOOLS
Disruptive persons, § 626.8.

MEDICINE
Drugs and Medicine, generally, this index.

MEETING HOUSE
Arson, § 448a.

MEN
Cohabitation, receiving money from placing in custody, § 266d.
Purchase for placing for immoral purposes, § 266e.
Sale for immoral purposes, § 266f.
Support, generally, this index.

MENACE
Principals in crime, § 31.

MENS REA ACT
Generally, § 20.

MENSES
Correctional institutions and jails, § 4023.5.

MENTAL CAPACITY
Mentally Deficient and Mentally Ill Persons, generally, this index.

MENTAL SUFFERING
Children and minors, causing, § 273a.

MENTALLY DEFICIENT AND MENTALLY ILL PERSONS
Advising mentally ill persons to commit crime, principals, § 31.
Alcoholic beverages, sales to, § 397.
Argument to jury, § 1369.
Arsonists,
  Commitment or outpatient treatment, § 1370.
Assault with intent to commit crime, commitment or outpatient treatment, § 1370.
Bail, § 1370.
  Mental competence regained after commitment, § 1372.
Burden of proof, sanity hearings, § 1369.
Burglary, commitment or outpatient treatment, § 1370.
Capacity to commit crimes, § 26.
Capital Punishment, this index.
Care and treatment, § 1370.
Cause against pronouncement of judgment, § 1201.
Certificates and certification,
  Mental competence regained after conservatorship established, § 1372.
  Restoration of sanity, § 1372.
Commitment, § 1026.
  Criminal defendant,
    Credit on term of imprisonment, § 1375.5.
    Mentally incompetent during trial or hearing, § 1370.
  Developmentally disabled persons, criminal defendants, § 1370.1.
  Sex offenders, commitment as prior prison term, subsequent offenses, § 667.5.
  State hospitals, §§ 1026, 1370.
Competency to stand trial, § 1370.1.
Confinement, developmentally disabled persons charged with crimes, § 1370.1.
Conservators and conservatorship,
  Committed during trial by hearing on offense, § 1370.
  Mental competence regained after conservatorship established, certification, § 1372.
Cruel, corporal or unusual punishment or treatment, § 673.
Descent and distribution, payment of transportation expenses, § 1373.
Detention in state hospital, restoration to sanity, § 1372.
Developmentally disabled persons, competency to stand trial, §§ 1369, 1370.1.
Dismissal,
  Charges before becoming sane, Lanterman-Petris-Short Act, § 1370.

Penal Code

MENTALLY DEFICIENT AND MENTALLY ILL PERSONS—Cont'd
Dismissal—Cont'd
  Misdemeanor charge, person judged mentally incompetent during trial or hearing, § 1370.2.
Encouraging mentally ill persons to commit crime, accessories, § 31.
Evaluation, outpatient treatment, §§ 1026, 1026.1, 1370.3.
Evidence, sanity hearings, § 1369.
Examination, regional center for mentally retarded persons, criminal defendant, § 1370.1.
Exceptions, capacity to commit crimes, § 26.
Expense, transportation to state hospital and back, § 1373.
Explosives, commitment or outpatient treatment, § 1370.
Fines and penalties, § 1367 et seq.
Guardian and Ward, generally, this index.
Hearings,
  Developmentally disabled persons, competency to stand trial, § 1370.1.
  Extension of time for pronouncing sentence, § 1191.
  Instructions to jury, § 1369.
  Jury, sanity hearing, § 1368 et seq.
  Mental competence regained after commitment, § 1372.
  Outpatient treatment, § 1026.1.
    Committed defendant, § 1374.
Homicide, commitment or outpatient treatment, § 1370.
Hospitalization,
  Commitment pending insanity of defendant, § 1370 et seq.
Intoxicating liquors, sale to, § 397.
Judgments, cause against pronouncement, § 1201.
Jury trial,
  Developmentally disabled persons, competency to stand trial, § 1369.
  Mental competence, question of, application of law, § 1367.
Kidnapping, commitment or outpatient treatment, § 1370.
Leave of absence, persons committed on criminal commitments, state hospitals, § 1374.
Mayhem, commitment or outpatient treatment, § 1370.
Murder, commitment or outpatient treatment, § 1370.
Not guilty plea. Plea of insanity, generally, post.
Order of trial, § 1369.
Outpatient treatment, § 1026 et seq.
  Committed criminal defendant, § 1374.
    Credit on term of imprisonment, § 1375.5.
  Nondangerous defendants, §§ 1370, 1370.3.
Own recognizance, release, § 1370.
Pendency of action, § 1368.
Plea of insanity, §§ 1016 et seq., 1026 et seq.
  Commitment on finding of insanity, § 1026.

MENTALLY DEFICIENT AND MENTALLY ILL PERSONS—Cont'd
Plea of insanity—Cont'd
  Jury trial, issue of mental illness, § 1026.
  Outpatient treatment, § 1026 et seq.
  Proceedings, § 1026 et seq.
  Restoration of sanity, § 1026.
  Separate trial of other pleas, § 1026.
  Trial of sanity before jury, § 1026.
Presumption of sanity, §§ 1016, 1026.
Psychiatric examination,
  Developmentally disabled persons, competency to stand trial, § 1369.
  Trial of question of mental competence, § 1369.
Rape, § 261.
  Commitment or outpatient treatment, § 1370.
Regional centers, criminal defendants, examination and recommendation, § 1370.1.
Relatives, transportation expenses, § 1373.
Reports,
  Criminal defendant committed, progress toward recovery, § 1370.
Restoration of sanity, § 1372.
Robbery, commitment or outpatient treatment, § 1370.
Sanity finding, § 1369.
Sex offenders,
  Commitment as prior prison term, subsequent offenses, § 667.5.
Sound mind, defined, § 21.
State hospitals, commitment, §§ 1026, 1370.
Supersedeas or stay, trial pending sanity hearing, §§ 1368, 1370.
Suspension of proceedings pending sanity hearing, § 1368.
Transportation,
  State hospital, to and from, § 1373.
Trial, § 1367 et seq.
  After restoration of sanity, § 1372.
  Developmentally disabled persons, § 1370.1.
    Competency to stand trial, § 1369.
  Issue of insanity, §§ 1021, 1026, 1367 et seq.
  Mental competence, question of, §§ 1368, 1369.
  Suspension, examination by regional center for mentally retarded, § 1370.1.
  Transportation expenses to state hospital, § 1373.
  Violent felonies, developmentally disabled persons, commitment during evaluation, § 1370.1.
Weapons, concealable firearms, purchase, § 12076.

MENTALLY DISORDERED SEX OFFENDERS
Defined, registration of sex offenders, § 290.

MENTALLY INCOMPETENT
Defined, trial or punishment for crime, § 1367.

MEPROBAMATE
See, also, Drugs and Medicine, generally, this index.

MERCHANDISE
Goods, Wares and Merchandise, generally, this index.

MERCHANT
Stores and Storekeepers, generally, this index.

MERCURY
Purchasing, determination of sellers right, § 496a.

MESCALINE
See, also, Drugs and Medicine, generally, this index.

MESSENGERS
Weapons,
  Carrying loaded firearms, § 12031.
  Exemption, § 12027.

METAL KNUCKLES
Weapons, generally, this index.

METAL PIPES
Weapons, generally, this index.

METAL PLATE WEAPONS
Weapons, generally, this index.

METALS AND METAL PRODUCTS
Purchasing,
  Determination of seller's right, § 496a.
  Secondhand dealers, purchasing, determining seller's right, § 496a.

METAZOCINE
See, also, Drugs and Medicine, generally, this index.

METERS
Gas meters, malicious interference, etc., § 498.
Theft, this index.
Water, alteration, fraud, § 499.

METHADONE
See, also, Drugs and Medicine, generally, this index.

METHADONE–INTERMEDIATE
See, also, Drugs and Medicine, generally, this index.

METHAMPHETAMINE
See, also, Drugs and Medicine, generally, this index.

METHAQUALONE
See, also, Drugs and Medicine, generally, this index.

METHOHEXITAL
See, also, Drugs and Medicine, generally, this index.

METHYL–4–PHENYL–PIPERIDINE–4–CARBOXYLIC ACID
See, also, Drugs and Medicine, generally, this index.

METHYLAMINE

METHYLAMINE
See, also, Drugs and Medicine, generally, this index.

METHYLDESORPHINE
See, also, Drugs and Medicine, generally, this index.

METHYLDIHYDROMORPHINE
See, also, Drugs and Medicine, generally, this index.

METHYLPHENIDATE
See, also, Drugs and Medicine, generally, this index.

METHYLPHENOBARBITAL
See, also, Drugs and Medicine, generally, this index.

METHYPRYLON
See, also, Drugs and Medicine, generally, this index.

METOPON
See, also, Drugs and Medicine, generally, this index.

MILEAGE
Traveling Expenses, generally, this index.

MILITARY FORCES
Colleges and universities, possession of firearms on grounds, § 626.9.
Courses of instruction, national guard, arrests, § 832.
Fire bombs, possession or use, § 452.
National guard,
  Arrest powers, § 830.2.
  Arrests, courses of instruction for making arrests, § 832.
  Training,
    Arrests, § 832.
    Weapons, use of firearms, § 832.
  Weapons,
    Courses of instruction, use of firearms, § 832.
School buildings and grounds, possession of firearms, § 626.9.
Sniperscopes, use or possession, § 468.
Tear gas weapons, possession, § 12403.1.
Weapons,
  Carrying loaded firearms, § 12031.
  Courses of instruction, § 832.
  Exemption, § 12027.
  Possession, § 12027.

MILITARY ORGANIZATIONS
Weapons, exemption, § 12027.

MINERALS
Mines and Minerals, generally, this index.

MINES AND MINERALS
Burglary, § 459.
Gold, generally, this index.

MINISTERS
Clergymen, generally, this index.

MINORS
Children and Minors, generally, this index.

MISBRANDING
Brands, Marks and Labels, generally, this index.

MISCARRIAGE
Abortion, generally, this index.

MISCHIEF
Malicious Mischief, generally, this index.

MISCREANT CHILDREN
Juvenile Delinquents and Dependents, generally, this index.

MISDEMEANORS
Absence, defendant from trial, § 1043.
Appearance, citations for misdemeanors, § 853.6 et seq.
Arrest, time for making, § 840.
Bail, arrest in another county, § 822.
Citations for, § 853.6 et seq.
  Delivery to arrested persons, § 853.6.
Defined, § 17.
Fines and penalties,
  Maximum term of confinement, § 19a.
  Not otherwise prescribed, § 19.
Forms,
  Uniform misdemeanor and traffic citation, fol. §§ 853.6, 853.7, 853.9.
  Uniform misdemeanor citation, fol. §§ 853.6, 853.7, 853.9.
Maximum confinement, § 19a.
Parole and probation, § 1203.
  Declaration of offense as misdemeanor on grant, § 17.
  Maximum term, § 1203a.
Presence of defendant,
  Trial, § 1043.
  When required, § 977.
Priorities, trial calendar, § 1048.
Punishment not specifically prescribed, § 19.
Time, arrest, § 841.
Trial, priorities, § 1048.
Venue, justice or municipal courts, § 1462.2.
Youth authority, § 17.

MISREPRESENTATION
Fraud, generally, this index.

MISTRIAL
Absence of accused, felony case, § 1043.

MITIGATING CIRCUMSTANCES
Murder, burden of proof, § 1105.

MITIGATION OF PUNISHMENT
Evidence, mitigation of punishment, § 1204.
Probation, when granted, § 1203.

MOBILEHOMES AND MOBILE-HOME PARKS
Arson, §§ 447a, 449a.
Burglary, §§ 459, 460.

MOBS
Riots and Mobs, generally, this index.

MODELS
Artist exhibitions, indecent exposures, § 314.

MOLDS
Vending machines, burglary, possession of molds of keys, tools, etc., § 466.3.

MOLOTOV COCKTAILS
Possessing, manufacturing or disposing of, § 452.

MONEY
Arrest, money taken from defendant, receipts, § 1412.
Bail, deposit in lieu of bail, § 1295 et seq.
Conspiracy to obtain by false pretenses, § 182.
Construction funds,
  Wrongful diversion, §§ 484b, 484c.
Counterfeiting, generally, this index.
Credit cards, § 484d et seq.
Defined, § 7.
Embezzlement, generally, this index.
Exhibits, disposition of evidence, § 1418.
False pretenses, obtaining by. False Pretenses, generally, this index.
Forgery, possession or receipt of forged bills for payment, § 475.
Guards,
  Carrying loaded weapon, § 12031.
  Weapons, exemption, § 12027.
Indictment and information, larceny or embezzlement, § 1131.
Larceny, description of property, evidence, § 1131.
Larceny by fraud, § 484.
Money Orders, generally, this index.
Public Money, generally, this index.
Theft, generally, this index.
Unclaimed money, disposition, §§ 1418, 1420 et seq.

MONEY CHANGERS
Burglar tools, § 466.3.

MONEY ORDERS
Blanks, possession,
  Fraudulently completing, § 475.
  Intent to defraud, § 475.
Completed money order, possession with intent to defraud, § 475a.

MONTH
Defined, § 7.

MORAL SUPPORT
Prosecution witnesses, § 868.

MORALS
Conspiracy to commit act injurious to public morals, § 182.
Pardons, reprieves and commutations, conduct during rehabilitation period, § 4852.05.

MORAMIDE–INTERMEDIATE
See, also, Drugs and Medicine, generally, this index.

MORONS
Mentally Deficient and Mentally Ill Persons, generally, this index.

MORPHERIDINE
See, also, Drugs and Medicine, generally, this index.

MORPHINE
See, also, Drugs and Medicine, generally, this index.

MORPHINE METHYLBROMIDE
See, also, Drugs and Medicine, generally, this index.

MORPHINE METHYLSULFONATE
See, also, Drugs and Medicine, generally, this index.

MORPHINE–N–OXIDE
See, also, Drugs and Medicine, generally, this index.

MOTELS AND MOTOR COURTS
Fraud upon proprietor, § 537.

MOTION PICTURES
Destructive devices, use by studio, permit, § 12305.
Lewdness and Obscenity, generally, this index.
Licenses and permits, sawed-off shotguns, props with blank cartridges, § 12095 et seq.
Sawed-off shotguns, props with blank cartridges, permits, § 12095 et seq.

MOTIONS
Acquittal, sealing record of arrest or detention, § 851.8.
Acquittal judgments, §§ 1118, 1118.1.
Exhibits, disposition of evidence, § 1418.
Indictment and information, setting aside, § 995 et seq.
Return of property, unreasonable search or seizure, § 1538.5.
Searches and seizures, return of property or suppression of evidence, § 1538.5.
Suppression of evidence, unreasonable searches and seizures, § 1538.5.

MOTOR CARRIERS
Armored vehicles, guards, firearms, § 12031.
Destructive devices, carrying or placing, passenger vehicles for hire, § 12303.1.
Explosives, carrying or placing explosives or destructive devices, passenger vehicles for hire, § 12303.1.
Hijacking, reward, § 1547.
Jurisdiction, offenses committed on carriers, § 783.
Reward,
　Hijacking, § 1547.
　Robbery, § 1547.
Robbery, reward, § 1547.

MOTOR COURTS
Motels and Motor Courts, generally, this index.

MOTOR VEHICLES
Alteration,
　Drivers licenses, §§ 470a, 470b.
　Identification cards, §§ 470a, 470b.
Arson, § 449a.

MOTOR VEHICLES—Cont'd
Burglary, § 459.
　Possession of burglary tools, § 466.
Campers, generally, this index.
Corporations,
　Guilty plea, §§ 1396, 1427.
　Traffic violations, process, § 1427.
Counterfeiting,
　Driver's licenses, §§ 470a, 470b.
　Identification cards, §§ 470a, 470b.
Destructive devices, carrying or placing, passenger vehicles for hire, § 12303.1.
Drivers licenses,
　Alteration, §§ 470a, 470b.
　Counterfeiting, §§ 470a, 470b.
　Forgery, §§ 470a, 470b.
Duplicates, identification cards, §§ 470a, 470b.
Keys, records, crimes and offenses, § 466.6.
Explosives, carrying or placing explosives or destructive devices, passenger vehicles for hire, § 12303.1.
Fines and penalties,
　Manslaughter, § 193.
　Using without permission, § 499b.
Firearms, carrying or discharging,
　Peace officers, § 12031.
Forgery,
　Driver's licenses, §§ 470a, 470b.
　Identification cards, §§ 470a, 470b.
Identification cards,
　Alteration, §§ 470a, 470b.
　Counterfeiting, §§ 470a, 470b.
　Forgery, §§ 470a, 470b.
Infractions, § 17.
　Application of law, § 19d.
　Arrest, time of day, § 840.
　Burden of proof, § 19d.
　Jurisdiction, § 19d.
　Limitation of criminal prosecutions, § 19d.
　Schedule, bail, § 1269b.
　Time, arrest, § 840.
　Trial, § 19d.
Joy Riding Law, § 499b.
Jurisdiction, offense, § 783.
Keys,
　Duplication, records, crimes and offenses, § 466.6.
　Master keys, sale or possession, § 466.5.
Leases,
　Theft by fraud, § 484.
Licenses and permits,
　Drivers licenses, generally, ante.
Malicious mischief to vehicle,
　Trespass with vehicle, § 602.
Master keys, sale or possession, § 466.5.
Motor Carriers, generally, this index.
Notice, issuance in lieu of taking person before magistrate, § 818.
Presumptions, theft by fraud, § 484.
Process, corporations, traffic violations, § 1427.
Records and recordation, keys, duplication, crimes and offenses, § 466.6.
Rules of the road. Traffic Rules and Regulations, generally, this index.
Sales, master key, § 466.5.

MOTOR VEHICLES—Cont'd
Signatures,
　Keys, duplication, records, crimes and offenses, § 466.6.
Theft, §§ 487, 499b.
　Fraud, leased vehicles, § 484.
　Temporary use, § 499b.
Traffic Rules and Regulations, generally, this index.
Trespass with vehicle, § 602.
Weapons, § 12025.
　Concealment, § 12027.
　Shooting, § 246.
Wheel lock master keys, sale or possession, § 466.5.

MOTORBOATS
Boats and Boating, generally, this index.

MOTORCYCLES
Borrowing without permission, § 499b.
Temporary use, theft, § 499b.
Theft, § 499b.
Traffic Rules and Regulations, generally, this index.

MULES
See, also, Animals, generally, this index.
Carcasses, theft, § 487a.
Theft, § 487.

MULTIPLE OFFENSES
Generally, § 666 et seq.
Second and Subsequent Offenses, generally, this index.

MUNICIPAL ATTORNEYS
Habeas corpus, service of writ, § 1475.
Prosecuting attorney, § 691.

MUNICIPAL BUILDINGS AND GROUNDS
Keys, unauthorized duplication, § 469.

MUNICIPAL CORPORATIONS
Municipalities, generally, this index.

MUNICIPAL COURTS
Arraignment,
　Determination of venue, § 1462.2.
　Informing defendant of right to trial in district, § 1462.2.
Bail,
　Acceptance, § 1269b.
Concurrent jurisdiction, § 1462.1.
Indictment and information,
　Necessity, § 682.
Inferior court, § 691.
Judges, designation as magistrates, § 808.
Judgments and decrees,
　Transfer of cases, § 1462.2.
Jurisdiction, § 1462 et seq.
　Concurrent jurisdiction, § 1462.1.
Magistrates, municipal judges as magistrates, § 808.
Marshals,
　Firearms, carrying loaded firearms, § 12031.
Misdemeanors,
　Venue, § 1462.2.

MUNICIPAL

MUNICIPAL COURTS—Cont'd
Orders. Judgments and decrees, generally, ante.
Transfer of cases, § 1462.2.

MUNICIPAL OFFICERS AND EMPLOYEES
Accounts, falsification, § 424.
Application of law, illegal acts, § 77.
Bribery, §§ 67½, 68.
Cruel treatment of prisoners, § 147.
Disqualification from office, embezzlement and falsification of accounts, § 424.
Embezzlement, § 424.
Emoluments, asking or receiving, § 70.
False personation, § 146a.
Falsification of accounts, § 424.
Fugitives from justice, persons designated to return, expenses, payment, § 1557.
Grand jury proceedings, removal from office, § 922.
Gratuities,
  Asking or receiving, § 70.
Inhuman or oppressive treatment of prisoners, § 147.
Misappropriation of public moneys, § 424.
Obstructing or resisting in performance of duties, § 69.
Oppressive treatment of prisoners, § 147.
Personal property in custody of officer, taking, injuring or destroying, § 102.
Probation officers, generally. Parole and Probation, this index.
Public moneys,
  Defined, embezzlement or other misuse, § 424.
Removal from office,
  Grand jury proceedings, § 922.
Rewards,
  Asking or receiving, § 70.
Sentence and punishment, embezzlement, falsification of accounts, misappropriation, etc., § 424.
Threatening, § 71.

MUNICIPALITIES
Alleys. Streets and Alleys, generally, this index.
Attorneys. Municipal Attorneys, generally, this index.
Cities and Counties, generally, this index.
Claims against municipalities, fraud, § 72.
Conduct of persons, public places, regulating, § 647c.
Courts. Municipal Courts, generally, this index.
Criminal history information, furnishing, § 11105.
  Local summary criminal history information, § 13300 et seq.
Custodial officers, local detention facilities, § 831.
False emergency reports, § 148.3.
Firearms, mail order purchases, records, filing fees, § 12079.
Firemen and Fire Departments, generally, this index.

MUNICIPALITIES—Cont'd
Fraudulent claims, presentation to board or officer, § 72.
  Limitation of prosecution, § 800.
Fugitives from justice, payment of expenses of returning fugitives, § 1557.
Institutions, cruel and unusual punishments, § 673.
Junk dealers, metals, purchases, § 496a.
Limitation of prosecution, fraudulent claims, § 800.
Metals, purchases by junk or secondhand dealers, § 496a.
Officers and employees. Municipal Officers and Employees, generally, this index.
Ordinances, generally, this index.
Parks, generally, this index.
Police, generally, this index.
Riotous assemblies, arrest of persons failing to disperse, § 727.
Schools and School Districts, generally, this index.
Seals, custodial officers, § 831.
Secondhand dealers, metals, purchases, § 496a.
Sidewalks, generally, this index.
Simulating official inquiries, § 146b.
Streets and Alleys, generally, this index.
Unlawful or riotous assemblies,
  Arrest of persons failing to disperse, § 727.
  Command to disburse, § 726.
Weapons, carrying loaded firearms, § 12031.

MURDER
Defined, § 187.
Homicide, generally, this index.

MURDER BY POISONS ACT
Generally, § 189.

MUSIC AND MUSICIANS
Coin operated machines, use of slugs or counterfeited coins, etc., § 640a.
Jukeboxes, burglar tools, § 466.3.

MUTILATION
Animals, malicious mischief, § 597.

MYROPHINE
See, also, Drugs and Medicine, generally, this index.

NAILS
Deposit or throwing upon highways, § 588a.

NALORPHINE
See, also, Drugs and Medicine, generally, this index.

NALOXONE HYDROCHLORIDE (N–ALLYL–14–HYDROXY–NORDIHYDROMORPHINONE HYDROCHLORIDE)
See, also, Drugs and Medicine, generally, this index.

NAMEPLATES
Alteration, destruction, etc., purchase, sale or possession of items, § 537e.

NAMES
Assumed or Fictitious Names, generally, this index.
Counterfeiting or forgery, § 470.
Fictitious names. Assumed or Fictitious Names, generally, this index.
Forgery or counterfeiting, § 470.
Indictment and Information, this index.
Peace officer, etc., nongovernmental organization, incorporating term in name, § 146c.
Weapons, sale of concealable firearms, § 12076.

NARCOTIC ADDICTS
Drug Addicts, generally, this index.

NARCOTICS
Drug Addicts, generally, this index.
Drugs and Medicine, generally, this index.

NATIONAL CITY, CITY OF
See, also, Municipalities, generally, this index.

NATIONAL DEFENSE
War and Civil Defense, generally, this index.

NATIONAL GUARD
Military Forces, this index.

NATURAL GAS
Oil and Gas, generally, this index.

NAVY
Military Forces, generally, this index.

NEBRASKA
See, also, Foreign States, generally, this index.

NEEDY PERSONS
Indigent Persons, generally, this index.

NEGLECTED CHILDREN
Juvenile Delinquents and Dependents, generally, this index.

NEGLIGENCE
Defined, § 7.
Elements of criminal negligence, § 20.

NEGOTIABLE INSTRUMENTS
Commercial Paper, generally, this index.

NERVOUS SYSTEM DEPRESSANTS
See, also, Drugs and Medicine, generally, this index.

N–ETHYL–3–PIPERIDL BENZILATE
See, also, Drugs and Medicine, generally, this index.

NEUTER GENDER
Construction of statutes, § 7.

NEVADA
See, also, Foreign States, generally, this index.
State prison officers and employees, peace officer status, § 830.5.

Penal Code

NEVADA CITY, CITY OF
See, also, Municipalities, generally, this index.

NEVADA COUNTY
See, also, Counties, generally, this index.

NEW MEXICO
See, also, Foreign States, generally, this index.

NEW TRIAL
Bail, § 1273.
Cause against pronouncement of judgment, § 1201.
Time of application,
  Pronouncing judgment, hearing and motion, § 1191.

NEWSPAPERS
Advertisements, generally, this index.
Bombs and explosives, false reports of planting, § 148.1.
Correctional institutions,
  Inmates, civil rights, § 2601.
Explosives or bombs, false reports of planting, § 148.1.
Horse races, publishing results and betting odds, § 337i.
Lewdness and Obscenity, generally, this index.
Libel and Slander, generally, this index.
Peace officers, residence address or telephone number of, disclosure maliciously with intent to obstruct justice, § 146e.
Prisoners, civil rights, § 2601.
Reporters, bombs and explosives, false reports of planting, § 148.1.

NICKELODEON
Coin operated, use of slugs, § 640a.

NICOCODEINE
See, also, Drugs and Medicine, generally, this index.

NICOMORPHINE
See, also, Drugs and Medicine, generally, this index.

NIGHT WATCHMEN
Weapons, carrying loaded firearms, § 12031.

NIGHTTIME
Arrests, felony offenses, § 840.
Burglary, degree of offense, § 460.
Defined, burglary, § 463.
Loitering or prowling on private property, § 647.
Search warrants, service, § 1533.

N–METHYL–3–PIPERIDYL BENZILATE
See, also, Drugs and Medicine, generally, this index.

NOISE
Court proceedings, interrupting, § 166.

NOISE—Cont'd
Disturbance of the peace, § 415.
State colleges and universities, § 415.5.

NOLO CONTENDERE
Generally, § 1016 et seq.
Admissions, exclusionary protection, § 1016.
Certificate of rehabilitation and pardon, withdrawal of plea, § 1203.4.
Citation for misdemeanors, complaints, § 853.9.
Evidence, withdrawn plea specifying punishment, § 1192.5.
Plea bargaining, § 1192.5.
Privileges and immunities, civil actions, § 1016.
Specification of punishment in plea, § 1192.5.
Withdrawal of plea,
  After fulfilling conditions of probation, § 1203.4.
  Persons fulfilling probation conditions, § 1203.4.
  Punishment specified in plea, § 1192.5.

NONBAILABLE OFFENSES
Bail, this index.

NONPROFIT CORPORATIONS
Bingo, place of holding games, § 326.5.
Jail prisoners, work release, contracts, § 1208.

NONSUIT
Dismissal and Nonsuit, generally, this index.

NONSUPPORT
Support, generally, this index.

NORACYMETHADOL
See, also, Drugs and Medicine, generally, this index.

NORLEVORPHANOL
See, also, Drugs and Medicine, generally, this index.

NORMETHADONE
See, also, Drugs and Medicine, generally, this index.

NORMORPHINE
See, also, Drugs and Medicine, generally, this index.

NORPIPANONE
See, also, Drugs and Medicine, generally, this index.

NORTH SACRAMENTO, CITY OF
See, also, Municipalities, generally, this index.

NOSES
Slitting, mayhem, §§ 203, 204.

NOT GUILTY PLEA
Generally, § 1016 et seq.
Corporations, § 1396.
Dangerous weapons, defendant armed with, trial by court or jury, § 969c.

NURSES

NOT GUILTY PLEA—Cont'd
Insanity as defense, § 1016 et seq.
Issues, § 1019.

NOTES
Commercial Paper, generally, this index.

NOTICE
Abandoned or unclaimed money, disposition, § 1420 et seq.
Animals, killing of unfit animals, § 599e.
Arraignment, time and place of appearance, bail, § 1295.
Arrest, this index.
Bail, this index.
Citations for misdemeanors, § 853.6 et seq.
Correctional Institutions, this index.
Destruction or disposal of exhibits, § 1418.5.
Documentary exhibits, destruction, § 1418.5.
Indictment or information, sufficiency to give notice of offense, § 952.
Lease or rental agreements, demand for return of property, § 484.
Pardons and Reprieves, this index.
Parole and Probation, this index.
Perjury, materiality and effect of testimony, § 123.
Petition for certificate of rehabilitation, notice of filing, § 4852.07.
Posting, generally, this index.
Receiving stolen goods, § 496.
Sex offenders, duty to register, § 290.
Written demands for return of leased or rented property, § 484.

NUDITY
Lewdness and Obscenity, generally, this index.
Restaurants or taverns, entertainers or food servers, §§ 318.5, 318.6.

NUISANCES
Concealed weapons, destruction, §§ 12028, 12029.
Destructive devices, possession, § 12307.
Firearms used in commission of crime, § 12028.
Injunction,
  Destructive devices, possession, public nuisances, § 12307.
  Machine guns, enjoining possession, § 12251.
Machine guns, possession, § 12251.
Nunchakus, § 12029.
Weapons,
  Machine gun, § 12251.
  Sale or destruction, §§ 12028, 12029.

NUMBERS AND NUMBERING
Identification Numbers, generally, this index.
Serial number removed from radios, etc., purchase, sale, etc., § 537e.

NUNCHAKU
Weapons, generally, this index.

NURSES
Abused children, reports, §§ 11110, 11161.5, 11161.7.

NURSING

NURSING HOMES
Abuse of patients, reports, § 11161.8.
Neglect of patients, reports, § 11161.8.

NUTS
Theft, § 487.

OATHS AND AFFIRMATIONS
Complainant, examination before issuance of search warrant, § 1526.
Complaint,
  Offenses triable in inferior courts, § 740.
  Proceeding for examination before magistrate, § 806.
Defined, § 7.
Perjury, § 119.
Extradition, application for requisition, § 1554.2.
Habeas corpus petition, § 1474.
  Verification of return, § 1480.
Pardons, reprieves and commutations, authority to administer, § 4812.
Perjury, generally, this index.

OATS
Arson, § 449a.

OBSCENITY
Lewdness and Obscenity, generally, this index.

OBSTRUCTING FIREMEN
Generally, § 148.2.

OBSTRUCTION OF JUSTICE
Conspiracy, § 182.
Peace officers, residence address or telephone number, disclosure maliciously, § 146e.

OBSTRUCTION OF OFFICERS
Generally, §§ 69, 148.

OBSTRUCTIONS
College and university teachers or students, obstructing, malicious mischief, § 602.10.
Persons in public places, § 647c.
Public streets, influence of liquor, drugs, toluene or other poisons, § 647.
Railroad to cause wreck, §§ 218, 219.

OBTAINING PROPERTY BY FALSE PRETENSES
False Pretenses, generally, this index.

OCELOTS
  See, also, Fish and Game, generally, this index.

OFFENSIVE LANGUAGE
Profanity and Offensive Language, generally, this index.

OFFICIAL ADVERTISEMENTS
Advertisements, generally, this index.

OFFICIAL BONDS
Bonds (Officers and Fiduciaries), generally, this index.

OFFICIAL COURT REPORTERS
Court Reporters, generally, this index.

OIL AND GAS
Highways, depositing oil upon, § 588a.
Theft, § 498.

OIL AND GAS PIPELINES
Theft of gas, § 498.

OLIVES
Theft, § 487.

ONE YEAR LIMITATION OF PROSECUTIONS
Misdemeanors, § 801.

ONTARIO, CITY OF
  See, also, Municipalities, generally, this index.

OPIATES
  See, also, Drugs and Medicine, generally, this index.

OPIUM
  See, also, Drugs and Medicine, generally, this index.

OPIUM EXTRACTS
  See, also, Drugs and Medicine, generally, this index.

OPIUM POPPY
  See, also, Drugs and Medicine, generally, this index.

ORAL COPULATION
  See, also, Sodomy, generally, this index.
Generally, § 288a.
Additional punishment, prior prison term, prior sentencing, § 1170.2.
Subsequent offense, additional punishment, § 667.5.

ORDERS
Grand Jury, this index.

ORDERS OF COURT
Bail, this index.
Discharge from custody on bail, § 1269a.
Joint or separate trials, defendants jointly charged, § 1098.
Witnesses, this index.

ORDINANCES
Air pollution, arrest, § 836.5.
Burglar alarm companies, § 12031.
Counties,
  Educational and work programs for prisoners, § 1208.
  Entertainment, exposure of private parts in public places, §§ 318.5, 318.6.
  Jails, work furloughs, transfer of prisoners, § 1208.5.
  Work furlough program, county jails, § 1208.

OREGON
  See, also, Foreign States, generally, this index.

Index

ORPHANS AND ORPHANAGES
False representation that child is an orphan, § 271a.

OSTEOPATHS
Production of books and papers, attendance of witnesses outside county of residence, § 1330.

OUTDOOR ADVERTISING
Malicious mischief, § 602.
Mutilating or destroying, § 602.
Weapons, possession prohibited, advertising ban, § 12020.5.

OUTHOUSES
Comfort Stations and Rest Rooms, generally, this index.

OUTPATIENT TREATMENT
Mentally Deficient and Mentally Ill Persons, this index.

OVERT ACTS
Conspiracy, § 184.
Evidence, § 1104.

OXYCODONE
  See, also, Drugs and Medicine, generally, this index.

OXYGEN LANCE
Burglary, § 464.

OXYMORPHONE
  See, also, Drugs and Medicine, generally, this index.

OYSTERS
Trespass, oyster lands, § 602.

PACKAGES
Containers, generally, this index.

PAINT
Defacing property of another, § 594.5.

PANDERING
Sale of persons for immoral purposes, § 266f.

PAPERS
Books and Papers, generally, this index.
Newspapers, generally, this index.

PARADES
Weapons, exemption, § 12027.

PARALDEHYDE
  See, also, Drugs and Medicine, generally, this index.

PARDONS AND REPRIEVES
Affidavits,
  Examination, § 4812.
  Service, notice of intention to apply, § 4804.
Applications,
  Investigations and reports, § 4812.
Authority to grant, § 4800.
Certificate of rehabilitation, §§ 1203.4, 4852.01 et seq.
Civil rights, restoration, § 4852.01 et seq.

Penal Code

PAROLE

PARDONS AND REPRIEVES—Cont'd
Claims, persons erroneously convicted and pardoned, § 4900 et seq.
Compensation, paid person for procuring or assisting, § 4807.2.
　Report, § 4807.3.
Concurrent sentences, rehabilitation period, computation, § 4852.03.
Conditions, § 4852.01 et seq.
Consecutive sentences, rehabilitation period, computation, § 4852.03.
Constitutional authority, § 4800.
Damages, persons erroneously convicted, § 4900 et seq.
Death, imminent danger, § 4806.
District attorney by whom action prosecuted, summarized statement of facts, § 4803.
Effect of full pardon, §§ 4853, 4854.
Examination of applications, § 4812.
Franchises, full pardon, § 4853.
Full pardon, §§ 4853, 4854.
General authority, § 4800.
Gifts, person procuring or assisting in procuring pardon, report, § 4807.3.
Good conduct, § 4801.
Indemnity for persons erroneously convicted and pardoned, § 4900 et seq.
Innocence, indemnity, § 4900 et seq.
Investigation,
　Applications, § 4812.
　Petitioners for certificates of rehabilitation, § 4852.12.
Judge before which conviction had, summarized statement of facts, § 4803.
Life imprisonment, rehabilitation period, computation, § 4852.03.
Mandatory life parole, pardons, reprieves and commutations, § 4852.01.
Medical Practice Act, effect of provisions, § 4853.
Multiple crimes, rehabilitation period, computation, § 4852.03.
Notice,
　Intention to apply served upon district attorney, § 4804.
　Petitions for certificate of rehabilitation, notice of filing, § 4852.07.
Pecuniary injury, claims, § 4900 et seq.
Petitions for certificate of rehabilitation, filing, § 4852.06.
Privileges, full pardon, § 4853.
Procedure, § 4852.01 et seq.
Procurement, compensation, § 4807.2.
Recommendations, § 4812.
　Supreme court, § 4850 et seq.
Rehabilitation,
　Certificate, § 4852.01 et seq.
Reports,
　Applications, § 4812.
　Certificate of rehabilitation, § 4852.17.
　Legislature, § 4807.
　Names of deserving prisoners, § 4801.
　Person receiving compensation or gift for procuring, § 4807.3.
Rights, full pardon, § 4853.
Second and subsequent offenses, § 4802.
　Recommendations, § 4813.
Summarized statement, facts proved at trial, § 4803.
Supreme court, § 4850 et seq.

PARDONS AND REPRIEVES—Cont'd
Term of imprisonment near expiration, § 4806.
Time, rehabilitation period, commencement, § 4852.03.
Transcripts of judicial proceedings, examination, § 4812.
Weapons, possession, § 4854.
Witnesses, applications, § 4812.

PARENT AND CHILD
Children and Minors, generally, this index.

PARKING METERS
Burglar tools, § 466.3.

PARKS
Bail, littering state parks, § 853.6.
State parks,
　Littering,
　　Bail, § 853.6.

PAROCHIAL SCHOOLS
Private Schools, generally, this index.

PAROLE AND PROBATION
Generally, § 1203 et seq.
Adult probation officers. Probation officers, generally, post.
Agriculture, placing probationers on farms, § 1203.1.
Alcoholic beverages,
　Abstinence as condition, § 1203.02.
　Inquiry into intoxication or addiction to use, § 1203.02.
　Sex offenses in which alcohol involved, § 1203.02.
Annual report, § 1203.08.
Another offense, commitment, jurisdiction, § 1203.2a.
Appeals,
　Bail, defendant applying for probation, § 1272.
　Stay, § 1243.
Appeals in criminal prosecutions, stay, § 1243.
Appearance, waiver, modification of probation, right to counsel, § 1203.2.
Armed with deadly weapon, § 1170.2.
Arrest,
　Rearrest of probationer,
　　Request for sentence by court granting probation, § 1203.2a.
　　Violation of conditions, § 1203.2.
　Violation of conditions, § 1203.2.
Arson, § 1203.
Assault and Battery, this index.
Attorneys,
　Modification proceedings, § 1203.2.
Bail, applicant for probation, § 1272.
Bodily injury inflicted upon victim, § 1170.2.
Bonds, probationer, § 1203.1.
Burglary, this index.
Campus disorders, § 626.2 et seq.
Certificate of rehabilitation and pardon, §§ 1203.4, 4852.03 et seq.
Civil rights, restoration, discharged probationer, § 1203.4.
Commission of a crime while on parole or probation, eligibility, § 1203.08.

PAROLE AND PROBATION—Cont'd
Commitment of probationer for another offense, § 1203.2a.
Compensation,
　Probation officers, § 1203.6.
　Public works, § 1203.1.
Conditions,
　Fines, payment as condition, § 1205.
　Imposition, § 1203.1.
　Intoxicating liquors, abstinence, sex offense involved, § 1203.02.
　Reconsideration, § 3000.
　Statement furnished to probationer, § 1203.12.
　Violation, re-arrest, § 1203.2.
Confidential information, diagnostic report, retention for supervision, § 1203.03.
Conspiracy, § 1203.
Copy of order, § 1203.04.
Councils for crime prevention, establishment and cooperation, § 1203.13.
County supervisors, authority to provide public work, § 1203.1.
Crime prevention councils, establishment, § 1203.13.
Date not set at prior sentencing, § 1170.2.
Deadly weapons,
　Carrying at time of perpetration of crime, § 1203.
　Commission of crime, § 1170.2.
Declaration of offenses as misdemeanor, § 17.
Defacing property of another, conditions, § 594.5.
Determinate sentences, § 1170 et seq.
Diagnostic reports, presentence investigation, access, § 1203.03.
Discharge of probationer,
　Notice, § 1203.3.
　Release from penalties and disabilities, § 1203.4.
　Restoration of rights, § 1203.4.
　Temporary removal or release preparatory to return to community, § 1203.1a.
Dismissal of charge, discharged probationer, § 1203.4.
Disruptive persons, campuses, § 626.2 et seq.
Documentary exhibits, disposition, § 1418.5.
Domicile and residence, probationer, transfer of jurisdiction, § 1203.9.
Drug violations, heroin, § 1203.07.
Eligibility,
　Determinate sentences, § 1170.2.
Escape, § 1203.
　Eligibility, §§ 1203, 1203.06.
　Reports, § 4530.
Exhibits, disposition, § 1417 et seq.
Expiration, release, § 3000.
Explosives,
　Burglary with explosives, § 1203.
Extortion, § 1203.
Extradition, escaped parolee, § 1548 et seq.
Farms, placing probationer, § 1203.1.
Felonies, reference, § 1203.

PAROLE

PAROLE AND PROBATION—Cont'd
Fines and penalties,
  Payment as condition of probation, § 1205.
  Recommendation, probation officers, § 1203.
  Release of probationer from penalties, §§ 1203.1, 1203.4.
Fingerprinting, § 1203.1.
Firearms, use during crime, § 1203.06.
First degree murder, § 190.
  Special circumstances charged, § 190.2.
Foreign states, release, § 1203.
Fugitives from justice,
  Extradition, § 1548 et seq.
Granting, § 17.
  Summary grant, misdemeanor and infraction cases, § 1203b.
  Without imposition of sentence on conviction, § 17.
Group insurance, parole and probation officers, § 830.5.
Guilty plea, withdrawal of court approval, § 1192.5.
Habitual criminals, § 1203.
Hearing, § 1203.
Heroin, violations dealing with heroin, § 1203.07.
Homicide, this index.
Indigent persons, right to counsel, § 1203.2.
Infraction cases, summary grant, § 1203b.
Inspection,
  Probation officer's report, § 1203.05.
Insurance, group insurance, parole and probation officers, § 830.5.
Investigations,
  Defendant ineligible, § 1203.
  Transfer of probationer, residence, receiving court's investigation, § 1203.9.
Jails, detention of state parolees, reimbursement of county, § 4016.5.
Jurisdiction,
  Cases transferred, § 1203.9.
  Rearrest, terminating by issuing order of commitment, § 1203.2a.
  Sentence after commission of subsequent offense, § 1203.2a.
Juvenile Delinquents and Dependents, this index.
Juvenile Probation Officers, generally, this index.
Kidnapping, this index.
Limitation, § 3000.
Maximum term, misdemeanor cases, § 1203a.
Misdemeanors, this index.
Mitigating circumstances, § 1203.
Modification, § 1203.3.
  Waiver of court appearance, right to counsel, § 1203.2.
Motion of court, modify, revoke or terminate, § 1203.2.
Mutual aid powers, parole and probation officers, § 830.5.
Narcotic violations, heroin, § 1203.07.
Nolo contendere plea, withdrawal by persons having completed probation conditions, § 1203.4.

PAROLE AND PROBATION—Cont'd
Notice,
  Modify, revoke or terminate probation, §§ 1203.2, 1203.3.
Number of crimes committed, § 1170.2.
Objectives, § 1203.1.
Offenses for which probation cannot be granted, § 1203.
Option of court, § 1203.
Pardon, certificates of rehabilitation and pardon, §§ 1203.4, 4852.03 et seq.
Parole officers,
  Criminal history information, furnishing, § 11105.
    Local summary, § 13300 et seq.
  Powers and duties, § 830.5.
Period of confinement, time on parole, consideration, § 19a.
Perjury, procuring execution of innocent persons, life sentence without parole, § 128.
Petition, probation report, inspecting or receiving copies, § 1203.05.
Police department, copy of probation order, § 1203.04.
Power to grant, § 1203.
Powers and duties, emergency powers, § 830.5.
Presence of defendant, commitments, § 1203.2a.
Pre-sentence investigation, § 1203.
Prevention of crime,
  Cooperation, § 1203.13.
Prior convictions, determination, § 1170.2.
Priorities and preferences, transfer of probationer, investigation by receiving court, § 1203.9.
Probation officers, §§ 1203.5, 1203.6.
  Annual report, § 1203.08.
  Authority, § 1203.1.
  Child abuse, reports, § 11161.6.
  Civil service, § 1203.6.
  Compensation, § 1203.6.
  Cooperation with public crime prevention councils, § 1203.13.
  Creation of office, § 1203.5.
  Criminal history information, furnishing, § 11105.
    Local summary criminal history information, § 13300 et seq.
  Deputies, § 1203.5.
  Diagnostic reports, access, § 1203.03.
  Emergency powers, § 830.5.
  Employees, § 1203.6.
  Ex officio, officers appointed under juvenile law, exception, § 1203.5.
  Fines and penalties, recommendations to pay, § 1203.
  Group insurance, § 830.5.
  Insurance, group insurance, § 830.5.
  Juvenile Court Law, officers appointed under as ex officio officers, exception, § 1203.5.
  Mutual aid powers, § 830.5.
  Peace officers, powers, § 830.5.
  Presentence reports, discussion with defendant, § 1203.
  Re-arrest of probationer without warrant, § 1203.2.

PAROLE AND PROBATION—Cont'd
Probation officers—Cont'd
  Recommendations,
    Restitution, § 1203.
  Removal, § 1203.6.
  Reports, §§ 1203, 1203c.
    Annual report, § 1203.08.
    Child abuse, § 11161.6.
    Commitment of probationer for another offense, § 1203.2a.
    Inspection, § 1203.05.
    Person convicted or sentenced, § 1203.01.
  Violations, §§ 1203.2, 1203.12.
  Restitution, recommendations, § 1203.
  Time, annual report, § 1203.08.
  Transfer of cases, jurisdiction, § 1203.9.
  Work furlough program administrator, county jail prisoners, § 1208.
Probationer committed for another offense, sentence, § 1203.2a.
Procedure for entry into in another state, § 1203.
Pronouncement of sentence, after probationer committed for another offense, § 1203.2a.
Prostitution, prior offenses, § 647.
Public works, § 1203.1.
Rape, § 1203.
Rearrest of probationer,
  Request for sentence by court granting probation, § 1203.2a.
  Violation of conditions, § 1203.2.
Recommendations, § 1203.
Reference of case, report, § 1191.
Rehabilitation and pardon, certificates, §§ 1203.4, 4852.03 et seq.
Release from penalties and disabilities, discharged probationer, § 1203.4.
Release or removal preparatory to return to community, § 1203.1a.
Reparations, conditions, § 1203.1.
Reports, § 1203.
  Annual report, § 1203.08.
  Arrest of prisoner for another offense, § 1203.2a.
  Defendant ineligible, § 1203.
  Diagnosis and recommendation, retention for supervision, § 1203.03.
  Probation officers, ante.
  Probationer to court in misdemeanor cases, § 1203b.
  Release to work, § 1203.1.
  Summary probation, misdemeanor cases, § 1203b.
Request for sentence of probationer by releasing court, § 1203.2a.
Residence, transfer of probationer, investigation, § 1203.9.
Restitution, condition of probation, § 1203.1.
Restoration of rights, discharged probationer, § 1203.4.
Revocation, §§ 1203.2, 1203.3.
  Commitment for another offense, § 1203.2a.
  Commitment upon revocation, § 1215.
  Discussed in court, § 1203.3.
  Motion by court, § 1203.2.
  Police department furnished copy, § 1203.2.

Penal Code   PEACE

PAROLE AND PROBATION—Cont'd
Revocation—Cont'd
  Setting aside judgment and order revoking probation, § 1203.2.
  Youth authority, department of, commitment, § 1203.2.
Road camps, probationer, placing, § 1203.1.
Robbery, § 1203.
Schools, disruptive persons, § 626.8.
Second and subsequent offenses, §§ 1203, 1203.08.
  Eligibility, § 1203.06.
  Jurisdiction to commit for offense for which probation was given, § 1203.2a.
Sequence of sentences, commitment of probationer after sentence for another offense, § 1203.2a.
Service of sentence at intermittent periods, § 1203.1.
Setting aside judgment and order revoking probation, § 1203.2.
Sex offenders,
  Drunkenness, § 1203.02.
  Registration, § 290.
State parolees, detention in jails, reimbursement of county, § 4016.5.
Statement,
  Terms and conditions furnished to probationer, § 1203.12.
Summary denial, § 1203.
Summary probation,
  Infraction cases, § 1203b.
  Misdemeanor cases, responsibility, § 1203b.
Supervision,
  Suspension of sentence or execution, § 1215.
Suspension, § 1203.2.
Suspension of sentence, § 1203.1.
Temporary removal or release for purposes preparatory to return to community, § 1203.1a.
Termination, probation, § 1203.1 et seq.
  Commitment, § 1215.
  Temporary removal or release preparatory to return to community, § 1203.1a.
Time,
  Annual report, § 1203.08.
  Part of period of confinement, § 19a.
Torture of persons, § 1203.
Train wreckers, §§ 218, 1203.
Transfer of cases, jurisdiction, § 1203.9.
Transmittal of report on denial, § 1203.
Uniform sentences, § 1170.3.
Unusual cases, § 1203.
Violations, § 1203.1.
  Reports, § 1203.12.
Waiver,
  Court appearance, modification of probation, § 1203.2.
  Expiration of determinate sentence, § 3000.
  Probation reports, § 1203.
Weapons, crime committed with deadly weapon, §§ 1170.2, 1203.
Work furlough rehabilitation, § 1208.
Work to support dependents or pay fine, § 1203.1.

PAROLE AND PROBATION—Cont'd
Written request by defendant to court which granted probation, § 1203.2a.
Youth Authority, this index.

PARTIES
Absence and absentees, defendants, § 1043.
Classification, parties to crime, § 30 et seq.
Depositions, generally, this index.
Disruptive behavior of defendant, removal from court, § 1043.
Indictment and information, naming, § 950.
Persons liable to punishment for crime, § 27.
Principals, defined, § 31.
Resistance to commission of offense, § 692 et seq.
Self-defense, § 692 et seq.

PASSENGERS
Explosives, carrying or placing explosives or destructive devices, passenger vehicles for hire, § 12303.1.

PASTORS
Clergymen, generally, this index.

PATENTS
Counterfeiting, § 470.
Forgery, § 470.

PATERNITY
Illegitimate Children, generally, this index.

PAUPERS
Indigent Persons, generally, this index.

PAWNBROKERS
Reports, § 11106.
  Pawned property, law enforcement officers, § 11108.
  Weapons, sale, § 12073.

PAYMENT
Counterfeiting, instruments, § 470.
Forgery,
  Instruments, § 470.
  Possession or receipt of forged bills, § 475.

PEACE
Justifiable homicide, keeping and preserving, § 197.
Security to keep the peace,
  Method of prevention of public offenses, § 697.

PEACE OFFICERS
See, also, Police, generally, this index.
Generally, § 830 et seq.
Address,
  Residence, disclosure maliciously with intent to obstruct justice, § 146e.
  Testimony, § 1328.5.
Advocating injuring or killing, § 151.
Aid to peace officers, § 698.
Arrest, courses of training, § 832.

PEACE OFFICERS—Cont'd
Assault and battery, §§ 241, 243.
  Deadly weapons, § 245.
  Line of duty, § 243.2.
    Deadly weapons, § 245.2.
  Reward for apprehension, § 1547.
  Unnecessarily assaulting or beating person, § 149.
Authority of peace officers, § 830 et seq.
Boards and commissions, peace officers standards and training commission,
  Approval, § 832.3.
    Persons carrying loaded firearms in prohibited area, § 12031.
  Certificates, peace officers, requirements, § 832.4.
Certificate, peace officer standards and training commission, requirement, § 832.4.
Colleges and Universities, this index.
Constables, generally, this index.
Coroners, § 830.10.
Correctional institutions, § 830.5.
Corrections, department of law enforcement liaison unit,
  Parole officers, § 830.5.
  Peace officers status, § 830.5a.
Courses of instruction, peace officers training, arrest, § 832.
Criminal history information, furnishing, § 11105.
  Local summary criminal history information, § 13300 et seq.
Dangerous Weapons Law, exemptions, § 12002.
Defined, § 7.
  Assault upon officer, § 241.
    Deadly weapon or force likely to produce great bodily injury, § 245.
  Authority, etc., § 830 et seq.
  Battery upon officer, § 243.
  Firearms, exhibiting, § 417.
  Fresh pursuit, § 852.1.
  Incorporation of term into name of nongovernmental organization, § 146c.
  Powers and duties, § 830.
Delay in taking arrested person before magistrate, § 145.
Deputy coroners, § 830.10.
Designation, § 830 et seq.
Drunkards and drunkenness, civil protective custody, force, § 647.
Emergencies, false reports, § 148.3.
Extradition, generally, this index.
False arrest, civil liability, § 847.
False emergency reports, § 148.3.
False imprisonment, civil liability, § 847.
False personation, § 538d.
Fines and penalties, assault, line of duty, § 243.2.
Fingerprints and weapons transactions, furnishing information, § 11106.
Fire bombs, possession or use, § 452.
Firearms, carrying loaded firearms, § 12031.
First degree murder, special circumstance, punishment, § 190.2.
Force, civil protective custody of inebriates, § 647.
Foreign peace officers, arrest pursuant to Fresh Pursuit Law, proceedings, § 852.2.

PEACE

PEACE OFFICERS—Cont'd
Fresh Pursuit Law, § 852 et seq.
Fugitives from justice, arrest without warrant, § 1551.1.
Group insurance, § 830.5.
   Corrections department, law enforcement liaison unit, § 830.5a.
Guards, department of corrections, § 830.5.
Homicide, special circumstance, punishment, § 190.2.
Impersonation, § 538d.
Inspectors, district attorneys inspectors, powers and duties, § 830.1.
Insurance, group insurance, § 830.5.
   Corrections department, law enforcement liaison unit, § 830.5a.
Investigators,
   District attorneys investigators, powers and duties, § 830.1.
Jurisdiction, § 830.1 et seq.
Labor disputes, picketing, wearing peace officers uniform, § 12590.
Marshals, generally, this index.
Motor vehicles,
   Crimes and offenses, highway patrol powers and duties, § 830.2.
Name or term incorporated into nongovernmental organization name, § 146c.
National guard, active duty, § 830.2.
Nevada state prison officers and employees, § 830.5.
Parole and probation,
   Re-arrest without warrant, § 1203.2.
Parole officers, state department of, corrections or youth authority, § 830.5.
Personal injuries, advocating injuries, fines and penalties, § 151.
Picketing, labor disputes, wearing peace officers uniform, § 12590.
Powers and duties, § 830 et seq.
Prison officers and employees, powers, § 830.5.
Probation officers and deputies, power, § 830.5.
Public officers, restricting function affecting retirement status, § 830.
Publication, residence address or telephone number of officers, disclosure maliciously with intent to obstruct justice, § 146e.
Refusal to arrest or receive person charged with offense, § 142.
Reports,
   False emergency reports, § 148.3.
Residence address or telephone number, disclosure maliciously with intent to obstruct justice, § 146e.
Resistance to process, power to overcome, § 723.
Retirement,
   Restriction of functions, retirement status, § 830.
   Weapons, privileged to carry, §§ 12027, 12031.
San Francisco port authority,
   Assault upon officer with deadly weapon or force likely to produce great bodily injury, § 245.
San Francisco port commission policemen, assault with deadly weapon or instrument, § 245.

PEACE OFFICERS—Cont'd
School buildings and grounds, possession of firearms, § 626.9.
Schools,
   Weapons, possession, § 626.10.
Search for dangerous weapons, § 833.
Sex offenders, records, inspection, § 290.
Sheriffs, generally, this index.
Sniperscopes, use and possession, § 468.
State police, § 830.4.
   Authority, § 830.2.
Subpoenas, service, § 1328.
Superintendents and supervisors, department of corrections, § 830.5.
Telegraphic or teletype copy, subpoena of witnesses, § 1328a et seq.
Telephone number, residence, disclosing maliciously with intent to obstruct justice, § 146e.
Training,
   Airport security officers, § 832.1.
   Arrest, courses of instruction, § 832.
   Peace officer standards and training commission approval, § 832.3.
Uniform Act on Fresh Pursuit, § 852 et seq.
Uniforms,
   Picketing, wearing peace officers uniform, § 12590.
Wardens, department of corrections, powers, § 830.5.
Weapons,
   Carrying loaded firearms, § 12031.
   Dangerous Weapon Law, exemptions, § 12002.
   Exhibiting before, § 417.
   Retired officers, §§ 12027, 12031.
   Tear gas weapons, purchasing, possessing or transporting, § 12403.
   Transactions, furnishing information, § 11106.
Witnesses,
   Address, testimony as to, § 1328.5.
   Subpoena, service on officer, § 1328.
Youth authority, institutions for delinquents, etc., § 830.5.

PEATGROUND
Malicious mischief, burning, § 449b.

PECUNIARY INTEREST
Adverse or Pecuniary Interest, generally, this index.

PEEPING TOMS
Disorderly conduct, § 647.

PENAL INSTITUTIONS
Correctional Institutions, generally, this index.

PENALTIES
Fines and Penalties, generally, this index.

PENSIONS
Retirement and Pensions, generally, this index.

PER DIEM
See, also, Compensation and Salaries, generally, this index.

PERIODICALS
Lewdness and Obscenity, generally, this index.

PERJURY
   Generally, § 118 et seq.
Accomplices and accessories, soliciting aid, § 653f.
Affidavits,
   False affidavit as to testimony, § 118a.
   Limitation of prosecutions, § 800.
Bribery, influencing testimony, § 137.
Compliance with order requiring answer to questions or production of evidence, witnesses, § 1324.
Conviction of perjury, proof, § 1103a.
Corroborating, circumstances to prove, § 1103a.
Death, procuring execution of innocent person, § 128.
Defined, § 118.
   Oath, § 119.
   Subornation, § 127.
False return required to be under oath, § 129.
Fines and penalties, § 126.
Force or threat inducing false testimony, § 137.
Grand juror, § 924.3.
   Disclosure, court compelling, § 924.2.
Knowledge of materiality and effect of testimony, § 123.
Limitation of prosecutions, § 800.
Prima facie evidence, subsequent testimony contrary to affidavit, § 118a.
Report, false report under oath, § 129.
Self incrimination, privilege, § 1324.1.
   Compelling testimony, § 1324.
Sentence and punishment, § 126.
   Subornation of perjury, §§ 127, 128.
Soliciting commission, § 653f.
Statement, false statement required to be under oath, § 129.
Subornation of perjury, §§ 127, 128.
   Defined, § 127.
   Execution of innocent person, § 128.
   Force or threat, § 137.
   Penalties, §§ 127, 128.
   Punishment, §§ 127, 128.
   Soliciting commission, § 653f.
Subsequent testimony contrary to affidavit, § 118a.
Unqualified statement not known to be true, § 125.

PERMITS
Licenses and Permits, generally, this index.

PERSON
Defined, § 7.
   Harmful matter, lewdness, § 313.
   Obscene matter, § 311.

PERSONAL INJURIES
Arrest by public officers and employees, civil liability, § 836.5.
Assault and battery, fines and penalties, § 243.
Children, reports, §§ 11110, 11161.5.
Cruelty to children, records, § 11110.
Emergencies, false reports, § 148.3.

Penal Code / PHYSICIANS

PERSONAL INJURIES—Cont'd
Extortion, threat to inflict, § 519.
False emergency reports, § 148.3.
Highways, throwing substances likely to injure persons, § 588a.
Peace officers, advocating, § 151.
Police,
  Advocating, § 151.
  Assaulting or beating person unnecessarily, § 149.
Probation, inflicting personal injuries during perpetration of crime, § 1203.
Protection, carrying loaded weapons, § 12031.
Public officers and employees effecting arrest, civil liability, § 836.5.

PERSONAL PROPERTY
Arrest, property taken from defendant, receipts, § 1412.
Arson,
  Intent to defraud insurers, § 450a.
Auctions and Auctioneers, generally, this index.
Bailment, generally, this index.
Conspiracy to obtain by fraud, § 182.
Conversion of real property, theft, §§ 487b, 487c.
Corporations, fines and penalties, execution, § 1397.
Correctional institutions,
  Civil rights, § 2601.
Counterfeiting or forging instruments, § 470.
Defined, § 7.
Forgery or counterfeiting of instruments, § 470.
Goods, Wares and Merchandise, generally, this index.
Injury, destruction or taking from custody of officer, § 102.
Larceny by fraud, § 484.
Lost or Destroyed Property, generally, this index.
Prisoners,
  Civil rights, § 2601.
Shoplifting, fines and penalties, § 490.5.
Theft, § 487.
  Fraud, § 484.

PERSONAL SERVICES
Credit cards, § 484d et seq.

PERSONALITY
Mitigation of punishment, hearing, § 1204.

PERSONATION
False Personation, generally, this index.

PERSONS OF SOUND MIND
Defined, § 21.

PERVERSION OF JUSTICE
Conspiracy, § 182.

PETHIDINE
See, also, Drugs and Medicine, generally, this index.

PETHIDINE–INTERMEDIATE–A
See, also, Drugs and Medicine, generally, this index.

PETHIDINE–INTERMEDIATE–B
See, also, Drugs and Medicine, generally, this index.

PETHIDINE–INTERMEDIATE–C
See, also, Drugs and Medicine, generally, this index.

PETIT JURY
Jury, generally, this index.

PETIT LARCENY
Theft, generally, this index.

PETRICHLORAL
See, also, Drugs and Medicine, generally, this index.

PETROLEUM PRODUCTS
Oil and Gas, generally, this index.

PETTY THEFT ACT
Generally, § 488.

PEYOTE
See, also, Drugs and Medicine, generally, this index.

PHARMACISTS
Drugs and Medicine, generally, this index.
Prescriptions,
  Deviation causing death, § 380.
Telephonic communication, false representation as physician, § 377.

PHENADOXONE
See, also, Drugs and Medicine, generally, this index.

PHENAMPROMIDE
See, also, Drugs and Medicine, generally, this index.

PHENAZOCINE
See, also, Drugs and Medicine, generally, this index.

PHENCYCLIDINE
See, also, Drugs and Medicine, generally, this index.

PHENMETRAZINE
See, also, Drugs and Medicine, generally, this index.

PHENOBARBITAL
See, also, Drugs and Medicine, generally, this index.

PHENOMORPHAN
See, also, Drugs and Medicine, generally, this index.

PHENOPERIDINE
See, also, Drugs and Medicine, generally, this index.

PHENYL–2–PROPANONE
See, also, Drugs and Medicine, generally, this index.

PHOCLODINE
See, also, Drugs and Medicine, generally, this index.

PHONOGRAPHS
Coin operated, use of slugs, or counterfeit coins, etc., § 640a.
Lewdness and Obscenity, generally, this index.
Serial number or identification mark removed, sale, § 537e.

PHOTOGRAPHY AND PICTURES
Exhibits in criminal prosecutions, release, § 1418.6.
Lewdness and Obscenity, generally, this index.
Motion Pictures, generally, this index.
Pornography, vending machines near schools or playgrounds, § 313.1.

PHYSICAL FORCE
Defined, obstructing college and university teachers or students, § 602.10.

PHYSICALLY HANDICAPPED PERSONS
Handicapped Persons, generally, this index.

PHYSICIANS AND SURGEONS
See, also, Medical Attendance and Treatment, generally, this index.
Abortions,
  Murder, § 187.
Battered or sexually molested children,
  Reports, §§ 11110, 11161.5.
  Form, § 11161.7.
Children, cruelty, reports, § 11161.5.
Correctional Institutions, this index.
Cruelty to children, reports, § 11161.5.
False representation as physician to obtain drugs, § 377.
Female prisoners, family planning services, § 4023.5.
Fraud, prescription drugs, obtaining, § 377.
Homicide, fetus, § 187.
Privileges of physician-patient,
  Battered or sexually molested children, reports, § 11161.5.
Production of books and papers, attendance of witnesses outside county of residence, § 1330.
Psychiatrists and Psychiatry, generally, this index.
Records and recordation,
  Production of books and records, attendance of witnesses outside county of residence, § 1330.
Reports,
  Cruelty or unusual punishment inflicted on minor, § 11161.5.
  Form, § 11161.7.
  Personal injuries caused by abuse, patients received from another health facility, § 11161.8.
Tort liability, report of physical injuries due to abuse on patients received from another health facility, § 11161.8.
Witnesses, production of books and papers, attendance outside county of residence, § 1330.

PIANOS

PIANOS
Serial number or identification mark removed, sale, etc., § 537e.

PICKETING
Labor Disputes, this index.

PICKLOCK
Burglars, possession with intent to break or enter, § 466.

PICTURES
Photography and Pictures, generally, this index.

PIEDMONT, CITY OF
See, also, Municipalities, generally, this index.

PIGS
Hogs, generally, this index.

PIMINODINE
See, also, Drugs and Medicine, generally, this index.

PIMPS AND PIMPING
Generally, §§ 266h, 266i.
Sale of persons for immoral purposes, § 266f.

PIPERIDINE
See, also, Drugs and Medicine, generally, this index.

PIPES AND PIPELINES
Oil and Gas Pipelines, generally, this index.

PIRITRAMIDE
See, also, Drugs and Medicine, generally, this index.

PISTOLS
Weapons, generally, this index.

PLACERVILLE, CITY OF
See, also, Municipalities, generally, this index.

PLANES
Aircraft, generally, this index.

PLATES
Credit card reproduction plates, possession, § 484i.

PLAYGROUNDS AND RECREATION CENTERS
Pornography, vending machines, § 313.1.

PLEA BARGAINING
Generally, § 1192.5.

PLEADINGS
Habeas Corpus, generally, this index.

PLEAS
Arraignment, this index.
Change of plea,
  Discharged probationer, § 1203.4.
Corporations, this index.
Entry of plea, § 1017.
Form, § 1017.
Guilty Plea, generally, this index.
Inferior Courts and Tribunals, this index.
Nolo Contendere, generally, this index.

PLEAS—Cont'd
Not Guilty Plea, generally, this index.
Once in jeopardy, § 1016 et seq.
Open court, entry of plea, § 1017.
Presumption of sanity, § 1016.
Waiver, defendants' personal presence, § 977.

PLEDGES
Pawnbrokers, generally, this index.
Reports, law enforcement officers, § 11108.

PODIATRISTS (CHIROPODY)
Child abuse or sexual molestation, reports, § 11161.5.
Form, § 11161.7.

POISONS
Administering, intent to kill, § 216.
Correctional institution inmates, books describing manufacture, censorship, § 2601.
Evidence, disposition, § 1419.
Fines and penalties, administering, attempt to kill, § 216.
Homicide, § 189.
Murder by Poison Act, § 189.

POLAR BEARS
See, also, Fish and Game, generally, this index.

POLES AND WIRES
Deposit or throwing wire upon highways, § 588a.
Purchasing, determination of seller's right, § 496a.

POLICE
See, also, Peace Officers, generally, this index.
Generally, §§ 830, 830.1.
Advocating killing or wounding police officer, § 151.
Assault,
  Beating person unnecessarily, § 149.
  Officer, assailant apprehension reward, § 1547.
Authority, §§ 830, 830.1.
Bay area rapid transit district, powers and duties, § 830.2.
Bombs and explosives, false reports of planting, § 148.1.
Certificates and certification, peace officer standards and training commission certificate, requirement, § 832.4.
Chief of police,
  Arrest of teachers for sex offense, notice, § 291.
  Investigators, assignment, bureau of criminal identification and investigation, § 11050.
  Notice, teachers arrested for sex offense, § 291.
  Registration of sex offenders, § 290.
Citizens' complaints against personnel of departments, procedure, § 832.5.
Communications, interception, police radio, § 636.5.
Complaints against personnel of departments, procedure, § 832.5.

POLICE—Cont'd
Courses of instruction,
  Arrest, § 832.
  Weapons, use of firearms, § 832.
Cruel treatment of prisoners, § 147.
Dangerous Weapons Law, exemption, § 12002.
Defined, authority, etc., § 830 et seq.
Delay in taking arrested persons before magistrate, § 145.
Drunkards and drunkenness, civil protective custody, force, § 647.
Eavesdropping, wiretap or electronic, § 633.
  Arrested persons, telephone calls, § 851.5.
Emergencies, false reports, § 148.3.
Explosives or bombs, false reports of planting, § 148.1.
False crime reports, § 148.5.
False emergency reports, § 148.3.
False personation, § 538d.
Fire bombs, possession or use, § 452.
Firearms, carrying loaded firearms, § 12031.
Force, inebriates, civil protective custody, § 647.
Foreign states, carrying loaded weapons, § 12031.
Formation of police force, prevention of public offenses, § 697.
  Justification of persons aiding officers, § 698.
Group insurance, § 830.5.
Highway Patrol, generally, this index.
Homicide, this index.
Impersonating police officer, § 538d.
Inhuman treatment of prisoners, § 147.
Insurance, group insurance, § 830.5.
Invasion of privacy, wiretap or electronic eavesdropping, § 633.
Investigations,
  Assignment to aid police, bureau of criminal identification and investigation, § 11050.
  Citizens' complaints against personnel of departments, procedure, § 832.5.
Jurisdiction, § 830.1.
Killing police officer,
  Advocating, § 151.
  Reward for apprehension, § 1547.
Membership cards, badges, etc., sale, inference of less rigid law enforcement against displayer by police, § 146d.
Money or property taken from defendant on arrest, receipts, § 1412.
Notice, arrested persons, telephone calls, posted notice of rights, § 851.5.
Oppressive treatment of prisoners, § 147.
Personal injuries,
  Advocating injuries, fines and penalties, § 151.
Persons aiding police officers, justification, § 698.
Powers and duties, §§ 830, 830.1.
Prevention of offenses by forming police force, § 697.
  Justification of persons aiding officers, § 698.
Radio, interception, § 636.5.
Recording private communications, wiretapping or electronic eavesdropping, § 633.

750

Penal Code / POWER

POLICE—Cont'd
Refusal to arrest or receive person charged with offense, § 142.
Reports,
  False emergency reports, § 148.3.
  Restrictions on judge reading police reports, § 1204.5.
San Francisco bay area rapid transit district, § 830.2.
Searches and Seizures, generally, this index.
Sniperscopes, use or possession, § 468.
State police,
  Powers and duties, § 830.2.
Subpoena, service on officer, witness in criminal prosecution, § 1328.
Tapping wires, § 633.
Telegraphs and telephones, wiretapping, § 633.
Term police incorporated in name of nongovernmental organization, § 146c.
Training,
  Arrests, § 832.
  Peace officer standards and training commission approval, § 832.3.
  Weapons, use of firearms, § 832.
Weapons,
  Carrying loaded firearms, § 12031.
  Exemption, § 12027.
Wiretapping, § 633.
Witnesses, subpoena, service on officer, § 1328.

POLITICAL SUBDIVISIONS
Bribery, officers, employees or appointees, §§ 67½, 68.
Counties, generally, this index.
Emoluments, asking or receiving by officer, etc., § 70.
Gratuities, asking or receiving by officer, etc., § 70.
Junk dealers, metals, purchases, § 496a.
Metals, purchases by junk or secondhand dealers, § 496a.
Municipalities, generally, this index.
Officers and employees,
  Bribery, §§ 67½, 68.
  Gratuities, asking or receiving, § 70.
Rewards, asking or receiving by officer, etc., § 70.
Secondhand dealers, metals, purchases, § 496a.

POLLUTION
Water Quality, generally, this index.

PONDS
Lakes and Ponds, generally, this index.

POOL—SELLING
Generally, § 337a.

POOR PERSONS
Indigent Persons, generally, this index.

POPPY STRAW
See, also, Drugs and Medicine, generally, this index.

POPULAR NAME LAWS
Anti-Obscenity Act, § 311 et seq.

POPULAR NAME LAWS—Cont'd
Arrest Law, § 813 et seq.
Bad Check Law, § 476a.
Bookmaking Act, § 337a.
Burglary Act, § 459 et seq.
Child Molestation Law, § 647a.
Close Pursuit, Uniform Act on Fresh Pursuit, § 852 et seq.
Cobey Work Furlough Law, § 1208.
County Jail Act, § 4000 et seq.
Criminal Extradition Act, § 1548 et seq.
Criminal Trespass Act, § 602.
Drunkenness Act, § 647.
Embezzlement Act, § 503 et seq.
Escape Act, § 4530 et seq.
Extradition, Uniform Criminal Extradition Act, § 1548 et seq.
False Pretenses Act, § 484.
Felony Murder Act, § 189.
Fresh Pursuit Act, § 852 et seq.
Grand Theft Law, § 487 et seq.
Indecent Exposure Act, § 314.
Joy-Ride Law, Vehicles and Vessels, § 499b.
Lantermann-Petris-Short Act, Mentally Deficient and Mentally Ill Persons, application of law, § 1370.
Little Lindbergh Act, § 209.
Lottery Law, § 319 et seq.
Mens Rea Act, § 20.
Multiple Offenders Act, § 666 et seq.
Murder by Poison Act, § 189.
Obscenity Act, § 311 et seq.
Pardon Law, § 4800 et seq.
Petty Theft Act, § 488.
Probation, § 1203 et seq.
Public Drunkenness Act, § 647.
Quimby-Walsh Act, exposure of body parts, restaurants, waiters or waitresses, § 318.5.
Recidivist Act, § 666 et seq.
Reprieves, Pardons and Commutations Law, § 4800 et seq.
Rubber Check Law, § 476a.
Sex Offenders' Registration Law, § 290.
Sex Perversion Act, § 288a.
Telephone Call Act, right of accused, § 851.5.
Theft,
  Grand Theft Law, § 487 et seq.
  Petty Theft Act, § 488.
Trespass, Criminal Trespass Act, § 602.
Two Trial Act (Capital Offenses), § 190.1.
Uniform Act on Fresh Pursuit, § 852 et seq.
Uniform Criminal Extradition Act, § 1548 et seq.
Walsh-Quimby Act, exposure of body parts, restaurants, waiters or waitresses, § 318.5.
Worthless Check Law, § 476a.

PORNOGRAPHY
Lewdness and Obscenity, generally, this index.

POSSESSION
Articles with serial number or identification mark removed, etc., § 537e.
Burglars' tools, § 466.

POSSESSION—Cont'd
Check, completed check with intent to defraud, § 475a.
Completed check, money order or travelers check with intent to defraud, § 475a.
Credit cards, § 484d et seq.
  Reproduction plates or machinery, § 484i.
Eavesdropping equipment, offenses, § 635.
Fictitious commercial paper or instruments with intent to defraud, § 476.
Keys,
  Motor vehicle master keys, unauthorized persons, § 466.5.
  Public buildings, unauthorized duplicate keys, § 469.
Lewd or obscene material, § 311.2.
Master keys, motor vehicles, § 466.5.
Money order, completed money order with intent to defraud, § 475a.
Motor vehicles,
  Master keys, § 466.5.
Tear gas and tear gas weapons, § 12403.7.
Trading stamps, forged, § 475.
Traveler's check, completed check with intent to defraud, § 475a.
Vending machines, burglary, possession of keys, tools, etc., § 466.3.
Weapons, this index.
Wiretapping equipment, § 635.

POST CONVICTION HEARING
Evidence, aggravation or mitigation of punishment, § 1204.

POST OFFICE
Mail and Mailing, generally, this index.

POSTING
Police facility or place of detention, telephone call rights, arrested persons, § 851.5.
Tobacco, copy of act by dealers regarding sales to minors, § 308.

POSTS
Arson, § 449a.

POTATOES
Malicious mischief, burning, § 449b.

POULTRY AND POULTRY PRODUCTS
Cockfighting, generally, this index.
Theft, § 487.

POUNDS AND POUND MASTERS
Animal Pounds, generally, this index.

POWER COMPANIES
Electricity, generally, this index.

POWER OF APPOINTMENT
Correctional institution, inmates, civil rights, § 2601.

POWER OF ATTORNEY
Counterfeiting or forgery, § 470.
Forgery or counterfeiting, § 470.

751

POWER

POWER OF ATTORNEY—Cont'd
Prisons and prisoners, civil rights, § 2600 et seq.

PRAYER HEALING
Parents medical care obligation, prayer healing exception, § 270.

PREACHERS
Clergymen, generally, this index.

PREFERENCES
Priorities and Preferences, generally, this index.

PREJUDICE
Bias and Prejudice, generally, this index.

PRELIMINARY EXAMINATION
Arrested person, delay in appearance before magistrate, § 145.
Attorney general, presence, § 868.
Attorneys. Counsel for accused, generally, post.
Bailiff, presence, § 868.
Complaint,
   Arrest without warrant, duty to file, § 849.
   Citation for misdemeanor offense, filing, § 853.9.
   Commencement, § 738.
   Offenses triable in another county,
     Delivery of complaint, § 828.
     Inferior courts, transmittal, § 829.
     Requisites, § 827.
Counsel for accused,
   Presence, § 868.
   Right to counsel, § 825.
Court reporter,
   Presence, § 868.
Custodial officer of prisoner, presence, § 868.
Delays, § 825.
   Taking arrested person before magistrate, §§ 145, 849.
Exclusion of witnesses, § 868.
Guilty plea,
   Specifying degrees of offense, § 1192.2.
Indictment and information, resubmission of case, denial of motion to set aside, § 997.
Investigating officer, presence, § 868.
Lawyers. Counsel for accused, generally, ante.
Magistrates, proceeding, § 806 et seq.
Officer having custody of prisoner, presence, § 868.
Presence,
   Defendant, felony prosecution, § 977.
   District attorney, § 868.
Prosecutor and counsel, presence, § 868.
Public, exclusion at defendant's request, § 868.
Superior court, § 738.
Time, § 825.
Waiver,
   Defendants' personal presence, § 977.
Witnesses,
   Exclusion, § 868.

PRELIMINARY INJUNCTION
Injunction, generally, this index.

PRESCRIPTIONS
Drugs and Medicine, this index.

PRE-SENTENCE INVESTIGATIONS
Generally, § 1203 et seq.

PRESIDENT OF THE UNITED STATES
Attempt to kill or commission of assault, § 217.1.
Conspiracy to commit crime, § 182.

PRESS
Newspapers, generally, this index.

PRESUMPTIONS
Evidence, this index.

PRETENSES
False Pretenses, generally, this index.

PRETRIAL DIVERSION
Generally, § 1001 et seq.

PREVENTION OF CRIME
Justification of persons aiding officers, § 698.
Officers of justice, intervention, methods, § 697.
Self-defense, § 692 et seq.

PRIMA FACIE EVIDENCE
Evidence, generally, this index.

PRINCIPAL
Defined, § 31.

PRINCIPAL AND ACCESSORY
Accomplices and Accessories, generally, this index.

PRINCIPAL AND AGENT
Agents and Agencies, generally, this index.

PRINTING
Defined, § 7.
Lewdness and Obscenity, generally, this index.

PRINTS
Vending machines, burglary, § 466.3.

PRIOR CONVICTION
Conviction of Crime, this index.

PRIORITIES AND PREFERENCES
Court calendar, cases for trial, § 1048.
Jail prisoners, work furlough earnings, collection by work furlough administrator, § 1208.
Speedy trial, § 1048.
Trial calendar, § 1048.

PRISONS AND PRISONERS
Correctional Institutions, generally, this index.

PRIVACY
Colleges and universities, right of privacy, student dormitories, § 626.11.

PRIVATE CORPORATIONS
Corporations, generally, this index.

PRIVATE INVESTIGATORS AND ADJUSTORS
Weapons,
   Carrying loaded firearms, employees, § 12031.

PRIVATE SCHOOLS
Battered children, reports, §§ 11110, 11161.5.
Self-defense schools, nunchakus, possession, § 12020.

PRIVIES
Comfort Stations and Rest Rooms, generally, this index.

PRIVILEGE TAXES
Licenses and Permits, generally, this index.

PRIVILEGED INFORMATION
Confidential or Privileged Information, generally, this index.

PRIVILEGES AND IMMUNITIES
Actions and proceedings, nolo contendere plea, § 1016.
Arrest, public officers effecting arrest, civil liability, § 836.5.
Battered children, reports, § 11161.5.
Child abuse or sexual molestation, reports, § 11161.5.
Civil suit, nolo contendere plea, § 1016.
Extradition, civil process, § 1555.
Grand jury,
   Statements made and vote cast, § 924.3.
Public officers and employees effecting arrest, civil liability, § 836.5.
Self-incrimination, § 1324.

PRIZE FIGHTS
Boxing and Wrestling, generally, this index.

PROBABLE CAUSE
Arrest, § 836.
   Private persons, § 837.
Complaint charging felony, affidavit, § 806.
Search warrants, issuance, §§ 1525, 1527.
Searches and seizures, restoration of property, § 1540.

PROBATE PROCEEDINGS
Limitation of prosecutions, public administrators, § 800.
Public administrators, limitation of prosecutions, § 800.

PROBATION
Parole and Probation, generally, this index.

PROBATION OFFICERS
Parole and Probation, this index.

PROCEEDINGS
Actions and Proceedings, generally, this index.

Penal Code   PUBLIC

PROCESS
Arrest, warrants, process servers, eligibility to execute, public officers and employees, § 816.
Bench warrants, defendant on bail or deposit, § 1198.
Certification, persons resisting or aiding or abetting, § 724.
Counterfeiting or forgery, § 470.
Definitions, § 7.
Extradition proceedings, civil actions, § 1555.
Forgery or counterfeiting, § 470.
Habeas Corpus, generally, this index.
Homicide, justifiable, overcoming actual resistance to execution, § 196.
Justifiable homicide in overcoming actual resistance to execution, § 196.
Making dispositions without process, criminal liability of officer, § 146.
Misdemeanor citations, § 853.6 et seq.
Resistance,
  Certification to court of resisters, § 724.
  Power of sheriff or other officer to overcome, § 723.
Return of service,
  Corporations, summons by inferior courts, § 1427.
  Counterfeiting, § 470.
  False entries, forgery, § 471.
  Forgery, §§ 470, 471.
Service of process,
  Return of service, generally, ante.
  Search warrants, time, §§ 1530, 1533.
  Subpoena, manner of making, § 1328.
  Telegraphic subpoenas, § 1328a et seq.

PRODUCERS
Obscene live conduct, managing, producing, sponsoring, etc., § 311.6.

PRODUCTION OF BOOKS AND PAPERS
Generally, § 1327.
General records, attendance of witnesses outside county of residence, § 1330.
Hospital records, attendance of witnesses outside county of residence, § 1330.
Medical records, witnesses, attendance outside county of residence, § 1330.
Witnesses, medical records, attendance of witness outside county of residence, § 1330.

PROFANITY AND OFFENSIVE LANGUAGE
Disturbance of the peace, § 415.
  State colleges and universities, § 415.5.

PROFESSIONS AND OCCUPATIONS
Dentists, generally, this index.
Pawnbrokers, generally, this index.
Physicians and Surgeons, generally, this index.
Podiatrists (Chiropody), generally, this index.
Psychiatrists and Psychiatry, generally, this index.
Psychologists and Psychology, generally, this index.

PROFITS
Public funds, use or loans by officers, § 424.

PROHEPTAZINE
See, also, Drugs and Medicine, generally, this index.

PROHIBITION
Searches and seizures, motion to suppress evidence, review, § 1538.5.

PROMISES
Appearance in court, violations, § 853.7.

PROMISSORY NOTES
Commercial Paper, generally, this index.

PRONOUNCEMENT OF JUDGMENT
Judgments and Decrees, this index.

PROOF
Evidence, generally, this index.
Issues, Proof and Variance, generally, this index.

PROPERIDINE
See, also, Drugs and Medicine, generally, this index.

PROPERTY
Counterfeiting or forgery of instruments, § 470.
Credit cards, offenses, § 484d et seq.
Defined, § 7.
Description, search warrants, § 1525.
Forgery of instruments, § 470.
  Possession or receipt of forged bills for payment, § 475.
Justifiable homicide, defense, § 197.
Personal Property, generally, this index.
Protection, carrying loaded weapon, § 12031.
Real Estate, generally, this index.
Retained as evidence, disposition, § 1413.

PROPIRAN
See, also, Drugs and Medicine, generally, this index.

PROSECUTING ATTORNEYS
Defined, § 691.
District Attorneys, generally, this index.

PROSTITUTION
Abduction,
  Fraudulent inducement, § 266a.
  Person under 18, § 267.
Accomplices and accessories,
  Enticing persons, § 784.
  Inveigelment or enticement of unmarried female under 18, § 266.
Apartment or tenement, letting, § 316.
Children and minors,
  Abduction of persons under 18, § 267.
  Admitting or keeping in houses of ill fame, § 309.
  Unmarried females under 18, enticement, § 266.
Defined, disorderly conduct, § 647.
Disorderly Houses, generally, this index.
Enticement of unmarried female under 18, § 266.

PROSTITUTION—Cont'd
Evidence,
  Common repute as to keeping or resorting, § 315.
Inveigelment of unmarried female under 18, § 266.
Jurisdiction, enticing person, § 784.
Keeping or residing in house, § 315.
Letting apartment or tenement, § 316.
Pimping, §§ 266h, 266i.
Procurement by fraudulent inducement, § 266a.
Purchase of persons for placement, § 266e.
Second and subsequent offenses, § 647.
Soliciting, § 647.

PROVOCATION
Homicide, § 195.

PROWLERS
Disorderly conduct, § 647.

PSILOCYBIN
See, also, Drugs and Medicine, generally, this index.

PSILOCYN
See, also, Drugs and Medicine, generally, this index.

PSYCHIATRISTS AND PSYCHIATRY
Correctional institutions, visitation of prisoners, § 825.5.
Mentally Deficient and Mentally Ill Persons, generally, this index.

PSYCHOLOGISTS AND PSYCHOLOGY
Jails, work furlough programs, counseling of prisoners, § 1208.
Privileges and immunities, battered or sexually molested children, reports, § 11161.5.

PSYCHOPATHS
Mentally Deficient and Mentally Ill Persons, generally, this index.

PUBLIC AGENCIES
See, also, State Agencies, generally, this index.
Animal regulation department officers, duties,
  Unfit animals, killing, § 599e.
Security guards, carrying concealed weapons, § 12031.

PUBLIC ASSISTANCE
Social Services, generally, this index.

PUBLIC AUCTIONS
Auctions and Auctioneers, generally, this index.

PUBLIC BUILDINGS AND WORKS
See, also,
  Buildings, generally, this index.
  Improvements, generally, this index.
Arson, § 448a.
Disorderly conduct, lodging without permission, § 647.

PUBLIC

PUBLIC BUILDINGS AND WORKS—Cont'd
Keys, unauthorized duplication, § 469.
Probationer, working, § 1203.1.
Refusal to leave building at closing time, § 602.
Sit-ins, refusal to leave at closing time, § 602.
Squatters, disorderly conduct, § 647.
Trespass, refusal to leave at closing time, § 602.

PUBLIC CONSERVATORS
Limitation of prosecutions, § 800.

PUBLIC DEFENDERS
Criminal history information,
  Local summary criminal history information, § 13300 et seq.

PUBLIC DRUNKENNESS ACT
Generally, § 647.
Drunkards and Drunkenness, generally, this index.

PUBLIC EATING PLACES
Restaurants, generally, this index.

PUBLIC GUARDIANS
Limitation of prosecutions, § 800.

PUBLIC HEALTH
Health and Sanitation, generally, this index.

PUBLIC HIGHWAYS AND ROADS
Highways and Roads, generally, this index.

PUBLIC HOSPITALS
Hospitals, generally, this index.

PUBLIC IMPROVEMENTS
Improvements, generally, this index.

PUBLIC INSTRUCTION
Schools and School Districts, generally, this index.

PUBLIC LANDS
Arson, reward, persons burning public property, § 1547.
Bombs, reward, arrest person bombing public property, § 1547.
Reward,
  Arson, § 1547.
  Bombing public property, § 1547.

PUBLIC MEETINGS
Disturbance, § 403.

PUBLIC MONEY
Defined, embezzlement, § 424.
Embezzlement, § 424.
Limitation of prosecutions for embezzlement, § 799.

PUBLIC NOTICE
Advertisements, generally, this index.
Notice, generally, this index.

PUBLIC NUISANCES
Nuisances, generally, this index.

PUBLIC OFFICERS AND EMPLOYEES
Acceptance of bribe by public officer or employee, limitation of prosecutions, § 800.
Assaulting or beating person, § 149.
Corporations, generally, this index.
Correctional Institutions, this index.
County Officers and Employees, generally, this index.
Depriving arrested person of telephone call rights, offenses, § 851.5.
Disqualification for office or employment, Embezzlement and falsification of accounts, § 424.
District officers, removal, grand jury proceedings, § 922.
Embezzlement, public funds, §§ 424, 514.
Forfeitures,
  Attorneys, refusal to allow visit with prisoner, forfeiture, § 825.
Fraud, accounts, § 424.
Grand jury, inquiry into misconduct in office, § 919.
Interference with, § 71.
Misappropriation of public moneys, § 424.
Municipal Officers and Employees, generally, this index.
Profits, unauthorized loan or use of public moneys, § 424.
Public Defenders, generally, this index.
Public moneys,
  Defined, embezzlement or other misuse, § 424.
Riot or unlawful assembly, neglect or refusal to disperse, § 410.
Transfer or payment over of public moneys, failure, § 424.
Unlawful assembly, neglect or refusal to disperse, § 410.

PUBLIC POLICY
Colleges and universities, searches and seizures, student dormitories, § 626.11.
Probation, § 1203.
Tear gas and tear gas weapons, purchase, possession or use, § 12403.7.

PUBLIC PROPERTY
Public Lands, generally, this index.

PUBLIC RECORDS
Records and Recordation, generally, this index.

PUBLIC SCHOOLS
Schools and School Districts, generally, this index.

PUBLIC SERVICE CORPORATIONS
Public Utilities, generally, this index.

PUBLIC UTILITIES
Criminal history information,
  Local summary criminal history information, § 13300 et seq.
Junk and secondhand dealers, purchase of metals used for service, diligence to determine seller's right, § 496a.
Railroads, generally, this index.
Street Railways, generally, this index.

PUBLIC WATER SUPPLY
Water Supply, generally, this index.

PUBLIC WORKS
Public Buildings and Works, generally, this index.

PUBLICATION
Counterfeited matters, § 470.
Fictitious instruments with intent to defraud, § 476.
Forged matters, § 470.
Lewd or obscene material, §§ 311.2, 311.5.
Nongovernmental organization with term peace officer incorporated in name, soliciting subscriptions, § 146c.
Peace officers, residence address or telephone number, disclosure maliciously with intent to obstruct justice, § 146e.

PUBLICITY
Extortion, threat to expose or impute deformity, disgrace or crime, § 519.

PUBLISHES
Defined, credit cards, § 484j.

PUNISHMENT
Fines and Penalties, generally, this index.

PUPILS
Schools and School Districts, generally, this index.

PURCHASE
Tear gas and tear gas weapons, § 12403.7.

PURSUIT
Uniform Act on Fresh Pursuit, § 852 et seq.

QUESTIONS OF LAW AND FACT
Trial, generally, this index.

QUICKSILVER
See, also, Mines and Minerals, generally, this index.

QUIMBY–WALSH ACT
Waiters and waitresses exposure of breasts or buttocks, ordinances, § 318.5.

RABBIS
Clergymen, generally, this index.

RACEMETHORPHAN
See, also, Drugs and Medicine, generally, this index.

RACEMORAMIDE
See, also, Drugs and Medicine, generally, this index.

RACEMORPHAN
See, also, Drugs and Medicine, generally, this index.

RADIO
Television and Radio, generally, this index.

Penal Code

RAFFLES
Defined, lotteries, § 319.
Lotteries, generally, this index.

RAILROADS
See, also,
  Carriers, generally, this index.
  Public Utilities, generally, this index.
Arson, § 449a.
Attempt to wreck train, § 218.
Bombs. Explosives, generally, post.
Burglary, § 459.
  Possession of burglary tools, § 466.
Derailing or obstructing train, §§ 218, 219.
Explosives,
  False reports, § 148.1.
  Intention of blowing up or derailing trains, § 219.
Hijacking, reward, § 1547.
Junk and secondhand dealers, purchasing metals used by, diligence to determine seller's right, § 496a.
Jurisdiction of offenses, § 783.
Lights and lighting,
  Train robbery, acts with intention of committing, § 214.
Malicious mischief, burning railroad cars or ties, § 449b.
Obstruction to cause wreck, §§ 218, 219.
Rails, removal to cause wreck, §§ 218, 219.
Reward,
  Hijacking, § 1547.
  Robbery, § 1547.
Robbery, § 214.
  Reward for arrest, § 1547.
Signs and signals,
  Robbery, acts with intention of committing, § 214.
Switches,
  Train robbery, interference, § 214.
  Train wrecking, §§ 218, 219.
Wrecking trains, §§ 218, 219.
  Acts with intention of committing train robbery, § 214.
  Probation, § 1203.

RANSOM
Kidnapping, §§ 209, 210.

RAP SHEET
Examination of criminal records, § 11120 et seq.

RAPE
Accomplices and accessories, § 264.1.
  Soliciting aid, § 653f.
Additional punishment, prior prison term, prior sentencing, § 1170.2.
Alcoholic beverages, resistance prevented, § 261.
Anesthetics, resistance overcome, § 261.
Assault with intent to commit, § 220.
Consecutive term, prior prison term, § 667.5.
Deadly weapons. Weapons, generally, post.
Defined, § 261.
Drugs, resistance prevented, § 261.
Enhancement of prison terms, prior prison terms, § 667.5.

RAPE—Cont'd
Evidence,
  Penetration, § 263.
Fines and penalties, § 264.
  Assault with intent to commit rape, § 220.
  Force or violence in committing, additional punishment, § 1170.2.
  Great bodily injury resulting, § 264.
  Prior prison term, additional punishment, § 667.5.
Firearms. Weapons, generally, post.
First degree murder, special circumstance, punishment, § 190.2.
Force and violence, §§ 261, 264.1.
  Additional punishment, prior prison sentence, § 1170.2.
  Prior prison term, additional punishment, § 667.5.
Homicide, result,
  Degree, § 189.
  Penalty, § 190.2.
  Special circumstance, punishment, § 190.2.
Husband, impersonation, § 261.
Impersonation of husband, § 261.
Jury, recommendation of punishment, § 264.
Mentally deficient and mentally ill persons, § 261.
  Defendant, commitment or outpatient treatment, § 1370.
Narcotics, resistance prevention, § 261.
Parole and probation, eligibility, § 1203.06.
Penetration, sufficiency, § 263.
Prior prison sentence, additional punishment, § 667.5.
  Prior sentencing, § 1170.2.
Probation, § 1203.
Registration of offenders, § 290.
Second and subsequent offenses, probation, eligibility, § 1203.08.
Sentence and punishment, weapons, enhancement, § 1170.1.
Soliciting commission, § 653f.
Subsequent offense, additional punishment, § 667.5.
Sufficiency of penetration, § 263.
Threats, § 261.
Unconsciousness, § 261.
Violence, §§ 261, 264.1.
Violent felony, enhancement of prison terms, § 667.5.
Weapons,
  Accusatory pleading, nature of firearm used, § 969d.
  Enhancement of punishment, § 1170.1.

RATES AND CHARGES
Counterfeiting or forgery, § 470.

RAW OPIUM
See, also, Drugs and Medicine, generally, this index.

RAZORS
Weapons, generally, this index.

REAL ESTATE
Bail, this index.
Conspiracy to obtain by fraud, § 182.

RECEIVING

REAL ESTATE—Cont'd
Construction funds, diversion, §§ 484b, 484c.
Corporations, fines and penalties, execution, § 1397.
Correctional institutions,
  Inmates, civil rights, § 2601.
Counterfeiting or forging instruments relating to, § 470.
Deeds and Conveyances, generally, this index.
Defined, § 7.
Forgery or counterfeiting of instrument relating to, § 470.
Funds received for improving real estate, illegal disposition, §§ 484b, 484c.
Improvements, generally, this index.
Landlord and Tenant, generally, this index.
Larceny by fraud, § 484.
Leases, generally, this index.
Malicious mischief, acts constituting trespass, § 602.
Prisoners, civil rights, § 2601.
Public Lands, generally, this index.
State lands. Public Lands, generally, this index.
Theft, § 487.
  Conversion of real property into personal property, § 487b.
  Severance from realty of another, § 487c.
  Fraud, § 484.
Title to Property, generally, this index.
Trespass, generally, this index.

REAL PROPERTY
Real Estate, generally, this index.

REASONABLE DOUBT
Defined, § 1096.
Degree of offense, conviction of lowest degree, § 1097.
Instructions to jury, § 1096a.

RECEIPTS
Bail, deposits, § 823.
Counterfeiting or forgery, § 470.
Forgery or counterfeiting, § 470.
Fugitives from justice, expenses of officers returning fugitives, § 1557.
Jails, property taken from prisoner, § 4003.
Money or property taken from defendant on arrest, § 1412.
Search warrants, property, § 1535.

RECEIVING STOLEN GOODS
Generally, § 496 et seq.
Accomplices and accessories, soliciting aid, § 653f.
Bringing into state property stolen or embezzled in another state, §§ 27, 497.
Concealment, § 496.
Elements of offense, § 27.
Indictment or information, § 496.
Junk dealers, § 496a.
Jurisdiction, § 789.
Knowledge, § 496.
Presumptions, § 496.
Probation, § 1203.

755

RECEIVING Index

RECEIVING STOLEN GOODS
—Cont'd
Secondhand dealers, § 496 et seq.
Soliciting commission, § 653f.

RECIDIVISTS
Second and Subsequent Offenses, generally, this index.

RECOMMENDATIONS
Parole and Probation, this index.

RECORDS AND RECORDATION
Battered children, § 11110.
Bets, § 337a.
Bicycles, lost or stolen bicycles, criminal justice information system, § 11111.
Coin operated, use of slugs, etc., § 640a.
Confidential or Privileged Information, generally, this index.
Correction of errors, criminal identification and investigation bureau, records, § 11126.
Correctional Institutions, this index.
Counterfeiting or forgery, § 470.
Criminal identification and investigation, bureau of,
  Examination of records, § 11120 et seq.
Criminal records sheet, criminal identification and investigation bureau,
  Correction of errors, § 11126.
  Examination of records, § 11120 et seq.
Dealers' records, sales of deadly weapons, § 11106.
Destruction, evidence, § 135.
Embezzled property, § 1413.
Errors, correction, criminal identification and investigation bureau records, § 11126.
Evidence, forged, altered or ante-dated, offering, § 132.
Examination,
  Arrest records, § 11120 et seq.
  Criminal identification and investigation bureau, records, § 11120 et seq.
False entries,
  Forgery, § 471.
  Public records, limitation of prosecutions, § 799.
False instruments, procuring or offering for record, § 115.
Falsification of records, limitation of prosecution, §§ 799, 800.
Fees, criminal identification and investigation bureau, examination of records, § 11123.
Fingerprints, § 11106.
Gambling, recording wagers or bets, § 337a.
Grand Jury, this index.
Inspection and inspectors,
  Criminal identification and investigation bureau record, § 11120 et seq.
  Search warrants, court documents and records, § 1534.
Junk dealers, metal purchases, § 496a.

RECORDS AND RECORDATION
—Cont'd
Justice, state department of, § 13010 et seq.
  Examination, § 11120 et seq.
Juvenile Delinquents and Dependents, this index.
Lewdness and Obscenity, generally, this index.
Libel and slander proceedings, juvenile delinquents and dependents, opening of sealed records, § 851.7.
Licenses to carry concealed weapons, § 11106.
Limitation of prosecutions for falsification, §§ 799, 800.
Local summary criminal history information, § 13300 et seq.
Medical records, subpoena duces tecum, attendance of witness outside county, § 1330.
Metal purchases, junk and secondhand dealers, § 496a.
Rap sheet, criminal identification and investigation bureau,
  Correction of errors, § 11126.
  Examination of records, § 11120 et seq.
Releases from arrest, recording in arrest records, § 849.
Reproduction process, records of criminal identification and investigation bureau, inspection, § 11124.
Revenues, inspection,
  Deadly weapons, § 11106.
Right of access, § 13200.
Search warrants, inspection, § 1534.
Secondhand dealers, metal purchases, § 496a.
Stolen property, § 1413.
Transcript of Record, generally, this index.
Unauthorized furnishing, § 11140 et seq.
Wagers, § 337a.
Weapons, this index.

RECREATION AND RECREATIONAL FACILITIES
Boats and Boating, generally, this index.
Correctional institutions,
  Standards, § 6030.
Jail, standards, § 6030.
Pornography, vending machines, § 313.1.
Probation officers, prevention of crime, § 1203.13.
Skiing, generally, this index.

RECREATIONAL VEHICLES
Campers, generally, this index.

RED WOLVES
Fish and Game, generally, this index.

REFERENCE AND REFEREES
Contempt, § 166.
Corrupt influencing, § 95.
Intimidation, § 95.
Sporting events, bribery, §§ 337d, 337e.

REFUNDS
Bail, this index.

REFUSE
Garbage and Refuse, generally, this index.

REGIONAL CENTERS
Developmentally disabled persons, criminal defendants, § 1370.1.

REGIONAL OCCUPATIONAL CENTERS
Disruptive persons, § 626.8.

REGISTRARS OF VOTERS
Compensation, registration of voters, allowable emoluments, § 70.

REGISTRATION
Contributors to delinquency of minors, § 290.
False or forged instruments, § 115.
Sex offenders, § 290.
Weapons, this index.

REHABILITATION
Certificates of rehabilitation and pardon, crimes, §§ 1203.4, 4852.01 et seq.
Correctional Institutions, this index.
Drug abuse control plans, criminal defendant, diversion from prosecution, § 1000.
Jails, work furlough programs, counseling of prisoners, § 1208.
Mitigation of punishment, hearing, § 1204.

REHABILITATION CENTER
Criminal defendants confined in center, credit for time spent on sentence, § 1203.03.

RELATIVES
Adultery, incest, § 285.
Fornication, incest, § 285.
Incest, § 285.
Jail prisoners, hospitalization, support, § 4011.
Telephone call by arrested person, § 851.5.

RELEASE
Arrest, this index.
Bail, this index.
Counterfeiting or forgery, § 470.
Custodial officers, local detention facilities, § 831.
Documentary evidence, § 1418.5.
Exhibits, §§ 1417 et seq., 1418.6.
Forgery or counterfeiting, § 470.
Indigent accused, return to place of arrest upon release, § 686.5.
Infractions, release procedures, § 853.5.
Jails, this index.
Probationers, temporary removal or release preparatory to return to community, § 1203.1a.
Sex offenders, notice of duty to register, § 290.

RELIGIOUS ORGANIZATIONS AND SOCIETIES
Arson, churches, § 448a.
Clergymen, generally, this index.

Penal Code **RIGHT**

RELIGIOUS ORGANIZATIONS AND SOCIETIES—Cont'd
Healing by prayer, substitute, parents medical care obligation, § 270.

REMOVAL OR TRANSFER OF CAUSES
Municipal courts, § 1462.2.
Probationer, transfer within state, § 1203.9.

REPORTERS
Court Reporters, generally, this index.

REPORTS
Battered children, § 11110.
Bombs or other explosives, false reports of placing or secreting, § 148.1.
Certificates of rehabilitation and pardon, petitions, hearings, §§ 4852.1, 4852.17.
Children and Minors, this index.
Claims against state, persons erroneously convicted of crime, hearing findings, § 4904.
Contempt, publication of false reports of court proceedings, § 166.
Correctional Institutions, this index.
Correctional personnel, standards and training, § 6031.2.
Corrections, Board of, this index.
Court Reporters, generally, this index.
Courts, this index.
Credit reports, falsification, theft by fraud, § 484.
Criminal Identification and Investigation, Bureau of, this index.
Criminal records and reports, right of access, § 13200 et seq.
Detention facilities, inspection of local facilities, § 6031.2.
Diagnosis and recommendation, retention by supervising probation officer, § 1203.03.
Diagnostic and treatment centers, § 1203.03.
Emergencies, false reports, § 148.3.
Explosives or bombs, false report of placing or secreting, § 148.1.
Extradition, investigations, § 1548.3.
False or Fraudulent Reports, generally, this index.
Financial Statements and Reports, generally, this index.
Grand Jury, this index.
Lewdness and obscenity, § 11107.
Lost property, §§ 11106, 11108.
Pardons and Reprieves, this index.
Parole and Probation, this index.
Pawned property, §§ 11106, 11108.
Peace Officers, this index.
Perjury, false report under oath, § 129.
Physicians and Surgeons, this index.
Pledged property, §§ 11106, 11108.
Police, this index.
Probation. Parole and Probation, this index.
Right of access, criminal records and reports, § 13200 et seq.
Sentence and punishment, studies, § 1170.6.

REPORTS—Cont'd
Stolen property, §§ 11106, 11108.
Theft, this index.

REPRIEVES
Pardons and Reprieves, generally, this index.

REPUTATION
Character and Reputation, generally, this index.

RESCUE
Generally, § 4550.
Accomplices and accessories, § 4550.
Authority to pursue and retake prisoner, §§ 854, 855.
Breaking doors or windows to retake prisoner if admittance refused, § 855.
Doors, authority to break to retake prisoner, § 855.
Jails, § 4550.
Justifiable homicide in retaking felons, § 196.
Retaking prisoner, §§ 854, 855.
Windows, authority to break to retake prisoner, § 855.

RESEARCH
Criminal history information,
  Local summary criminal history information, furnishing, § 13300 et seq.
Dogs, theft, § 487g.
Fire bombs, use, § 452.

RESIDENCE
Domicile and Residence, generally, this index.

RESISTANCE
Firemen, interference with extinguishment of fires, § 148.2.
Officers, § 148.
  Obstructing or resisting in performance of duties, § 69.
Prevention of public offenses, parties authorized, § 692 et seq.
Process,
  Certification to court of resisters, § 724.
  Power of sheriffs or other officers to overcome, § 723.

RESISTING ARREST
Generally, § 834a.
Arrest, this index.

REST ROOMS
Comfort Stations and Rest Rooms, generally, this index.

RESTAURANTS
Evidence, intent to defraud proprietor, § 537.
Fraud upon proprietor, § 537.
Prima facie evidence, intent to defraud proprietor, § 537.
Waiters and waitresses, nudity, §§ 318.5, 318.6.

RESTITUTION
Defacing property of another, § 594.5.

RESTITUTION—Cont'd
Parole and probation,
  Condition of probation, § 1203.1.
  Probation officers, recommendations, § 1203.

RESTRAINING ORDERS
Injunction, generally, this index.

RESTRAINT
Arrest, amount, § 835.
Unnecessary restraint of person charged with public offense, § 688.

RESUBMISSION OF CASE
Indictment and Information, this index.

RETAIL SALES
Sales, generally, this index.

RETAIL STORES
Stores and Storekeepers, generally, this index.

RETAILER
Defined, credit cards, § 484d.

RETIREMENT AND PENSIONS
Housing authorities, Los Angeles city housing authority retirement system, housing authority patrol officers, § 832.4.

REVENUE BONDS
Bonds, generally, this index.

REVIEW
Appeal and Review, generally, this index.
Appeals In Criminal Prosecutions, generally, this index.

REVOKED CREDIT CARD
Defined, § 484d.

REVOLVERS
Weapons, generally, this index.

REWARDS
Apprehension of criminals, § 1547.
Bombing public property, § 1547.
Capital offenses, apprehension of person charged with capital offense, § 1547.
Compounding or concealing crimes, § 153.
County officers or employees, asking or receiving, § 70.
Escape, apprehension of escapee, § 1547.
Fugitives from justice, arrest, § 1547.
Hijacking, § 1547.
Kidnapping, §§ 209, 210.
Municipal officers and employees, asking or receiving, § 70.
Officers asking or receiving, § 70.
State officers and employees, asking or receiving, § 70.

RIFLES
Weapons, generally, this index.

RIGHT TO COUNSEL
Counsel for Accused, generally, this index.

RIOTS

RIOTS AND MOBS
Arrest for failure to disperse, § 727.
Command to disperse, §§ 726, 727.
Definitions, § 404.
    Unlawful assembly, § 407.
Homicide, justifiable, suppression, § 197.
Justifiable homicide, suppression, § 197.
Magistrate or officer, neglect or refusal to disperse, § 410.
Prevention of offenses by suppressing, § 697.
Remaining present after warning to disperse, § 409.
Suppression, §§ 697, 726, 727.
Unlawful assembly, defined, § 407.

RIPARIAN RIGHTS
Water Rights, generally, this index.

RIVERS AND STREAMS
Canals, generally, this index.
Jurisdiction, offenses upon vessels navigating, § 783.

RIVERSIDE COUNTY
See, also, Counties, generally, this index.

ROAD CAMPS
Industrial Farms and Road Camps, generally, this index.

ROADS
Highways and Roads, generally, this index.

ROBBERY
Generally, § 211 et seq.
Accomplices and accessories, soliciting aid, § 653f.
Air carriers, reward, § 1547.
Assault with intent to commit, § 220.
Attempted robbery, § 213.
    Reward for arrest of fugitive, § 1547.
Bringing stolen property into state, § 27.
Buses, reward for arrest, § 1547.
Cab drivers, § 211a.
Carriers, reward, § 1547.
Defined, § 211.
Fear, defined, § 212.
Fines and penalties, § 213.
    Assault with intent to commit robbery, § 220.
    Bringing stolen property into state, § 27.
Firearms. Weapons, generally, post.
First degree murder, special circumstance, punishment, § 190.2.
Habeas corpus, bail, § 1491.
Homicide, special circumstance, punishment, § 190.2.
Jurisdiction, property taken transported between jurisdictional territories, § 786.
Kidnapping, § 209.
Mentally incompetent defendant, commitment or outpatient treatment, § 1370.
Motor carriers, reward, § 1547.
Murder resulting,
    Degree, § 189.
    Penalty, § 190.2.

ROBBERY—Cont'd
Probation, § 1203.
    Eligibility, § 1203.06.
Punishment, § 213.
Railroads, § 214.
    Reward for arrest, § 1547.
Second and subsequent offenses, probation, eligibility, § 1203.08.
Sentence and punishment, weapons, enhancement, § 1170.1.
Ships, reward, § 1547.
Soliciting commission, § 653f.
Street car operators, § 211a.
Taxicab drivers, § 211a.
Trackless trolley operators, § 211a.
Weapons,
    Accusatory pleading, nature of firearm used, § 969d.
    Deadly weapons, nature of firearm used, § 969d.

ROOMING HOUSES
Boarding and Lodging Houses, generally, this index.

ROUT
Participation, punishment, § 408.
Remaining present after warning to disperse, § 409.

RUBBISH
Garbage and Refuse, generally, this index.

RULES OF THE ROAD
Traffic Rules and Regulations, generally, this index.

SABBATH
Sunday, generally, this index.

SACKS
Containers, generally, this index.

SAFES
Burglary with explosives, § 464.
Serial number or identification mark removed, sale, etc., § 537e.

SAINT HELENA, CITY OF
See, also, Municipalities, generally, this index.

SALARIES
Compensation and Salaries, generally, this index.

SALES
Alcoholic Beverages, this index.
Articles with serial number or identification mark removed, etc., § 537e.
Auctions and Auctioneers, generally, this index.
Bicycles, unclaimed stolen bicycles, § 1411.
Children and minors, tear gas and tear gas weapons, § 12403.7.
Coin-operated vending machines, use of slugs or foreign coins, § 640a.
Concealable firearms, § 12076.
Controlled substances. Drugs and Medicine, this index.

SALES—Cont'd
Correctional Institutions, this index.
Credit Cards, generally, this index.
Dogs,
    Theft for purposes of sale, § 487g.
Eavesdropping equipment, § 635.
Evidence, unclaimed property, § 1418.
Exhibits, unclaimed property, § 1418.
Fire bombs, § 452.
Identification mark removed from articles sold, § 537e.
Lewd or obscene material, § 311.2.
Membership cards, badges, etc., inference, less rigid law enforcement, § 146d.
Obscene matter, § 311.5.
Peace officer badges, emblems or insignias, § 538d.
Persons,
    Immoral purposes, § 266f.
Serial number removed from articles sold, § 537e.
Sniperscope, offense, § 468.
Tear gas weapons. Weapons, this index.
Tie-in sales, obscene matter, §§ 311.7, 311.9.
Tobacco to minors, § 308.
Weapons, this index.
Wiretapping equipment, offenses, § 635.

SALESMEN
Weapons, signature, register of sale, § 12076.

SALOONS
Taverns and Saloons, generally, this index.

SAN FRANCISCO, CITY AND COUNTY
See, also,
    Cities and Counties, generally, this index.
    Counties, generally, this index.
    Municipalities, generally, this index.
Port authority,
Peace officers,
    Assault and battery, §§ 241, 243, 245.

SAN FRANCISCO BAY AREA RAPID TRANSIT DISTRICT
Police, § 830.2.

SAN FRANCISCO HARBOR
Port commission, peace officers,
    Assault against, §§ 241, 243, 245.

SAN FRANCISCO PORT COMMISSION
Police, peace officers,
    Assault against, §§ 241, 243, 245.

SANDBAGS
Weapons, generally, this index.

SANDCLUBS
Weapons, generally, this index.

SANITATION
Health and Sanitation, generally, this index.

Penal Code

SATURDAY
Bail, delivery of defendant to court or magistrate, § 1301.

SAWED–OFF SHOTGUNS
Definition, concealed weapons, § 12020.
Weapons, this index.

SCABS
Jails, Work Furlough Law, § 1208.

SCHOOL BUILDINGS AND GROUNDS
Annoying or molesting persons in attendance at adult classes, § 647b.
Disruption of schools, § 626 et seq.
Firearms, possession on grounds, § 626.9.
Keys to buildings, unauthorized duplication, § 469.
Security patrols, assault on member, § 245.
Trespass, disruptive persons, denial of access, § 626.8.
Weapons, possession on grounds, § 626.9.

SCHOOL FUNDS
Shoplifting fines, allocation of funds, § 490.5.

SCHOOL OFFICERS AND EMPLOYEES
Arrest,
 Sex offenses, notice, § 291.
Battered babies, reports, §§ 11110, 11161.5.
Cruelty or sexual molestation of children, reports, § 11161.5.
Disruption of schools, § 626 et seq.
Interference, § 71.
Reports, cruelty or sexual molestation of children, §§ 11110, 11161.5.
Sex offenses, arrest, § 291.

SCHOOL PRINCIPALS
Battered children, reports, §§ 11110, 11161.5.
Defined, disruption of schools, § 626.

SCHOOLS AND SCHOOL DISTRICTS
Adult Schools and Classes, generally, this index.
Arson, § 448a.
Assault and battery, security patrol, § 245.
Battered children, reports, §§ 11110, 11161.5.
Buildings and grounds. School Buildings and Grounds, generally, this index.
Corporal injury upon children, § 273d.
County superintendent of schools, battered babies, reports, §§ 11110, 11161.5.
Cruel treatment of children, § 273a.
Definitions,
 Disruption of schools, § 626.
 Disruptive persons, § 626.8.
Disruption of schools, § 626 et seq.
Disruptive persons,
 Denial of access to campus or facilities, § 626.8.

SCHOOLS AND SCHOOL DISTRICTS—Cont'd
Employees. School Officers and Employees, generally, this index.
Entry upon school after written notice of suspension or dismissal without permission, § 626.2.
Fines and penalties,
 Disruption of schools, § 626 et seq.
High Schools or Secondary Schools, generally, this index.
Jail inmates,
 Work furloughs, § 1208.
Lawful business, defined, disruptive presence in schools, § 626.8.
Military forces, possession of weapons, § 626.10.
Nonstudents, denial of access, disruption of schools, § 626.6.
Notices, arrest of employees, sex offenses, § 291.
Officers and employees. School Officers and Employees, generally, this index.
Peace officers, weapons, possession, § 626.10.
Pornography, vending machines near schools and playgrounds, § 313.1.
Prisoners, work furloughs, participation, § 1208.
Private Schools, generally, this index.
Reports, disruption on campus or in programs, withdrawal of consent to remain on school facilities, § 626.4.
Searches and seizures, weapons, § 626.10.
Second and subsequent offenses, disruption of schools, § 626 et seq.
Suspension or expulsion of pupils, disruption of schools, § 626 et seq.
Teachers. Schoolteachers, generally, this index.
Trespass, disruptive persons, § 626.8.
Unjustifiable punishment of pupils, § 273a.
Vending machines, pornography, near schools and playgrounds, § 313.1.
Vocational Education, generally, this index.
Weapons, possession, § 626.10.
Work furlough programs, jail prisoners, § 1208.

SCHOOLTEACHERS
Arrest,
 Sex offenses, notice, § 291.
Reports, battered or sexually molested children, § 11161.5.

SCIENCE
Fire bombs, possession or use for scientific purposes, § 452.
Obscene materials, use in aid of scientific purposes, § 311.8.
Sniperscope, use in research, § 468.

SEALS
Counterfeiting or forgery, § 470.
Defined, § 7.
Extradition, arrest warrants, § 1549.2.
Forgery or counterfeiting, § 470.
Juvenile delinquents and dependents, libel and slander proceedings, opening, sealed records, § 851.7.

SEARCHES

SEARCHES AND SEIZURES
Appeal, motion to suppress evidence, § 1538.5.
Certified transcribed statement, warrant, § 1526.
College dormitories, unlawful searches and seizures, § 626.11.
Dangerous weapons, arrest, § 833.
Disposition of property, unreasonable searches and seizures, § 1538.5.
Doors, breaking to liberate person aiding in execution, § 1532.
Evidence, motion to suppress, § 1538.5.
 Warrants, issuance, § 1524.
False impersonation of officer, § 146a.
Fighting animals or birds, § 599aa.
Implements, fighting animals or birds, § 599aa.
Inventory. Warrants, post.
Making without process or authority, § 146.
Malicious procuring, search warrant, § 170.
Mandate, motion to suppress evidence, § 1538.5.
Officer making without process or authority, criminal liability, § 146.
Oral statement in lieu of affidavit for warrants, § 1526.
Paraphernalia, fighting animals or birds, § 599aa.
Persons resisting execution of process, § 723.
Probable cause,
 Restoration of property, § 1540.
Process, making without, criminal liability of officer, § 146.
Prohibition to review motion to suppress evidence, § 1538.5.
Restoration of property, probable cause, § 1540.
Return of property, unreasonable search or seizure, § 1538.5.
Schools and school districts, weapons, § 626.10.
Suppression of evidence, unreasonable search or seizure, § 1538.5.
Unreasonable searches and seizures, return of property or suppression of evidence, § 1538.5.
Warrants, § 1523 et seq.
 Affidavits, § 1525.
 Contents, 1527.
 Filing warrant in return, § 1541.
 Inventory, § 1537.
 Issuance, § 1525.
 Oral statement under oath in lieu of, § 1526.
 Petitioner, § 1526.
 Probable cause, § 1527.
 Appeal and review, motion to suppress evidence, § 1538.5.
 Bail, motion to suppress evidence, pending appeal, § 1538.5.
 Breaking and entering, §§ 1531, 1532.
 Constitutional law, motion to suppress evidence, § 1538.5.
 Contents, time of service, § 1533.
 Continuance, special hearing on motion to suppress evidence, § 1538.5.
 Court's own motion, dismissal, § 1538.5.

SEARCHES

SEARCHES AND SEIZURES—Cont'd
Warrants—Cont'd
  Custody of property, § 1536.
  Defined, § 1523.
  Description of property, § 1525.
  Dismissal of prosecution, motion to suppress evidence, § 1538.5.
  Disposition of property, § 1536.
  Doors, breaking open to execute warrant, § 1531.
  Duplicate original,
    Signature, § 1528.
    Time of execution, § 1534.
  Dwellings,
    Breaking in,
      Executing warrant, § 1531.
      Liberating person aiding in execution of warrant, § 1532.
  Embezzled property, § 1524.
  Evidence, § 1524.
    Motion to suppress, § 1538.5.
  Execution and return, time, § 1534.
  Force and violence, §§ 1531, 1532.
  Form, § 1529.
  Freedom of press, motion to suppress evidence, § 1538.5.
  Freedom of speech, motion to suppress evidence, § 1538.5.
  Hearings, motion to suppress evidence, § 1538.5.
  Inspection of records, § 1534.
  Inventory, § 1537 et seq.
    Delivery of copies, § 1538.
    Filing, § 1541.
  Issuance, § 1524 et seq.
    Court not in session, issuance by magistrate, § 810.
  Liberating person aiding execution, § 1532.
  Malicious procuring, § 170.
  Mandate, motion to suppress evidence, appeals, § 1538.5.
  Motion to suppress evidence, § 1538.5.
  Nighttime, service, § 1533.
  Oaths and affirmations, issuance, § 1526.
  Person appearing before magistrate, §§ 833, 1542.
  Preliminary hearing, motion to suppress evidence, § 1538.5.
  Probable cause, § 1525.
    Affidavits, § 1527.
  Prohibition, motion to suppress evidence, review, § 1538.5.
  Public inspection, court records and documents pertaining to, § 1534.
  Receipts, § 1535.
  Records of court, § 1534.
  Release of defendant pending hearing on motion to suppress evidence, § 1538.5.
  Renewal, motion to suppress evidence, § 1538.5.
  Restoration of property, § 1540.
  Return,
    Filing, § 1541.
    Inventory, § 1537.
    Magistrate, issuing, § 1534.
    Time, § 1534.
  Return of property, unreasonable search and seizure, § 1538.5.

SEARCHES AND SEIZURES—Cont'd
Warrants—Cont'd
  Service, § 1530 et seq.
  Signature, § 1528.
  Speedy trial on motion to suppress evidence, § 1538.5.
  State, appeals on motion to suppress evidence, § 1538.5.
  Stay of proceedings pending motion to suppress evidence, § 1538.5.
  Stolen property, § 1524.
  Suppression of evidence, § 1538.5.
  Time for execution and return, § 1534.
  Time of service, § 1533.
  Transcribed statement, certifying, § 1526.
  Trial, motion to suppress evidence, § 1538.5.
  Weapons on person before magistrate, § 1542.
  Windows, breaking,
    Executing warrant, § 1531.
    Liberating person aiding in execution of warrant, § 1532.
  Witnesses, § 1526.
  Without process or legal authority, § 146.

SEBASTOPOL, CITY OF
See, also, Municipalities, generally, this index.

SECOND AND SUBSEQUENT OFFENSES
Generally, § 666 et seq.
Aggravation or mitigation of punishment, hearing, § 1204.
Annoying or molesting child under eighteen, § 647a.
Campus disorders, § 626.2 et seq.
Certificates of rehabilitation and pardon, §§ 1203.4, 4852.01 et seq.
Children and minors, molesting child, § 647a.
Colleges and universities, campus disorders, § 626.2 et seq.
Concurrent or consecutive terms, multiple offenses, § 669.
Consecutive terms, violent felonies, § 667.5.
Deadly weapons, felony commission or attempt while armed, §§ 12022, 12022.5.
Destructive devices, possession, purchase or sale, § 12304.
Disorderly conduct, state colleges and universities, § 415.5.
Eavesdropping, invasion of privacy, § 631 et seq.
Felonies while armed, §§ 12022, 12022.5.
Forgery, § 476a.
Indecent exposure, § 314.
Invasion of privacy, wiretapping and electronic eavesdropping, § 631 et seq.
Molesting or annoying child under eighteen, § 647a.
Multiple offenses, concurrent or consecutive terms, § 669.
Pardons and reprieves, § 4802.
  Recommendations, § 4813.
Parole and Probation, this index.
Petty theft, § 666.
  Conviction after prior conviction of felony, § 666.
Pleading, § 954.

SECOND AND SUBSEQUENT OFFENSES—Cont'd
Prior conviction,
  Foreign states, § 668.
  Petit theft, punishment, § 666.
Prostitution, § 647.
Restoration of rights after completing sentence, § 1203.4.
Schools, disruptive persons, § 626.8.
Sexual materials, distribution to minors, § 313.4.
Shoplifting, fines and penalties, § 490.5.
State colleges and universities, disturbing the peace, § 415.5.
Suspension of sentence, § 1203.08.
Theft, petty theft, § 666.
Threatening public officers and school officers, § 71.
Trespass to commit invasion of privacy, § 634.
Vagrancy, annoying or molesting child under eighteen, § 647a.
Violent felonies, additional punishment, § 667.5.
Weapons, felonies while armed, §§ 12022, 12022.5.
Wiretapping, invasion of privacy, § 631 et seq.

SECOND DEGREE MURDER
Generally, §§ 189, 190.

SECONDHAND GOODS AND DEALERS
Buying stolen goods, § 496.
Concealing stolen goods, § 496.
Identification of metal sellers, obtaining, § 496a.
Junk and Junk Dealers, generally, this index.
Metals, purchasing without using diligence to determine seller's right, § 496a.
Public utilities, purchase of metals used for service by, diligence to determine seller's right, § 496a.
Receiving stolen goods, §§ 496, 496a.
Records, § 496a.

SECRETS AND SECRECY
Confidential or Privileged Information, generally, this index.
Extortion, threat to expose, § 519.
Grand jury proceedings, §§ 915, 924 et seq.

SECURITIES
Description of property, theft or embezzlement, § 1131.
Indictment and information, § 1131.
Weight and sufficiency of evidence, theft or embezzlement, § 1131.

SECURITY GUARDS
Weapons,
  Loaded firearms, carrying, § 12031.
  Training, certificate, § 12033.

SEDUCTION
Aiding and abetting, § 266.
Kidnapping, § 207.
Prostitution, § 266.

Penal Code

SEIZURES
Searches and Seizures, generally, this index.

SELF DEFENSE
Generally, § 692 et seq.
Arrest, public officers and employees effecting arrest, § 836.5.
Justifiable homicide, § 197.
Peace officers effecting an arrest, § 835a.
Public officers and employees effecting arrest, § 836.5.
Weapons,
   Drawing, exhibiting, or using, § 417.
   Nunchakus, possession by schools of self-defense, § 12020.

SELF INCRIMINATION
Generally, § 1324.
Compelling testimony, exemption from prosecution, § 1324.
Grand jury, § 1324.
   Witnesses, refusal to answer questions, § 939.3.
Order to answer questions or produce evidence, § 1324.
Privileges and immunities, § 1324.
Production of evidence, orders, § 1324.

SENTENCE AND PUNISHMENT
Fines and Penalties, generally, this index.

SERIAL NUMBERS
Alteration, destruction, etc., purchase, sale or possession of items, § 537e.

SERVICE OF PROCESS
Process, this index.

SERVICES
Credit cards, § 484d et seq.

SET-OFF AND COUNTERCLAIM
Embezzlement, retention of property, § 511.

SETTING ASIDE
Indictment and Information, this index.

SEWING MACHINES
Serial number or identification mark removed, sale, etc., § 537e.

SEX
Jails, separation of persons, §§ 4001, 4002.
Materials, distribution or exhibition to minors, § 313.1.

SEX OFFENDERS
Arrest,
   School employees, notice, § 291.
   Teachers, notice, § 291.
Children and minors,
   Battered or sexually molested children, report, § 11161.5.
   Reports, probation officers, § 11161.6.
Commitment as prior prison term, subsequent offenses, § 667.5.
Disorderly conduct, § 647.
Enhancement of prison terms, commitment deemed to be prior offense, § 667.5.

SEX OFFENDERS—Cont'd
Force or violence in committing, § 264.1.
Forms, registration, § 290.
Harmful matter, § 313.
Notice,
   Duty to register, § 290.
   Teachers arrested, § 291.
Oral copulation, § 288a.
Parole and probation,
   Drunkenness, § 1203.02.
   Registration, § 290.
Registration, § 290.
Reports, § 11107.
Sodomy, generally, this index.

SEX OFFENDERS REGISTRATION LAW
Generally, § 290.

SEX PERVERSION ACT
Generally, § 288a.

SEXUAL CONDUCT
Defined, child pornography, § 311.4.

SEXUAL PSYCHOPATHS
Sex Offenders, generally, this index.

SEXUAL RELATIONS
Generally, §§ 261.5, 264.
Incest, § 285.
Oral Copulation, generally, this index.
Prostitution, generally, this index.
Rape, generally, this index.
Sex Offenders, generally, this index.
Unlawful sexual intercourse, §§ 261.5, 264.

SEXUALLY ASSAULTING ANIMALS
Generally, § 286.5.

SHARES AND SHAREHOLDERS
Forgery or counterfeiting of shares, certificates for shares, § 470.

SHEEP
See, also, Animals, generally, this index.
Theft, § 487.
   Carcasses, § 487a.

SHELLFISH
Trespass, oyster lands, § 602.

SHERIFFS
Generally, §§ 830, 830.1.
Assistants. Deputies and assistants, generally, post.
Authority, §§ 830, 830.1.
Bombs and explosives, false reports of planting, § 148.1.
Citizens complaints against personnel of departments, procedure, § 832.5.
Courses of instruction,
   Arrests, § 832.
   Firearms, § 832.
Criminal history information, local summary criminal history information, furnishing, § 13300 et seq.
Custody of defendant, nonbailable offense, § 982.
Dangerous Weapons Law, exemption, § 12002.

SHIPS

SHERIFFS—Cont'd
Delay in taking arrested persons before magistrates, § 145.
Deputies and assistants,
   Certificates, peace officer standards and training commission, requirement, § 832.4.
   Firearms, carrying loaded firearms, § 12031.
   Training, peace officer standards and training commission approval, § 832.3.
Eavesdropping, wiretap or electronic, § 633.
Explosives or bombs, false reports of planting, § 148.1.
False crime reports to, § 148.5.
Fire bombs, possession or use, § 452.
Invasion of privacy, wiretap or electronic eavesdropping, § 633.
Investigators, assignment, bureau of criminal identification and investigation, § 11050.
Jurisdiction, § 830.1.
Mailing copy of dealer's record of sale of revolver, § 12076.
Powers and duties, §§ 830, 830.1.
Recording, private communications, wiretapping or electronic eavesdropping, § 633.
Refusal to arrest person charged with offense, § 142.
Resistance to process,
   Certification to court of resisters, § 724.
   Power to overcome, § 723.
Riotous assemblies, command to disburse, §§ 726, 727.
Schoolteachers arrested for sex offense, notice, § 291.
Sex Offenders, generally, this index.
Sniperscopes, use and possession, § 468.
Tapping wires, § 633.
Telegraphs and telephones, wiretapping, § 633.
Training,
   Arrests, § 832.
   Peace officer standards and training commission approval, § 832.3.
   Weapons, use of firearms, § 832.
Undersheriffs, certificates, peace officer standards and training commission, requirement, § 832.4.
Unlawful assembly, command to disburse, §§ 726, 727.
Weapons,
   Carrying loaded firearms, § 12031.
Wiretapping, § 633.
Work furlough administrator, function as, § 1208.

SHIPS AND SHIPPING
See, also,
   Boats and Boating, generally, this index.
   Carriers, generally, this index.
Arson, § 449a.
Borrowing without permission, § 499b.
Burglary, § 459.
   Possession of burglary tools, § 466.
Burning, malicious mischief, § 449b.

SHIPS

SHIPS AND SHIPPING—Cont'd
Commission of offense upon ship, jurisdiction, § 783.
Gambling ships, § 337a.
Hijacking, reward, § 1547.
Jurisdiction, offenses committed on vessels, § 783.
Malicious mischief,
    Burning, § 449b.
Reward,
    Hijacking, § 1547.
    Robbery, § 1547.
Robbery, reward, § 1547.
Theft,
    Temporary use, § 499b.
Use,
    Gambling purposes, § 337a.
    Without permission, § 499b.
Vessel, defined, § 7.

SHOOTING CLUBS
Weapons, exemption, § 12027.

SHOPLIFTING
Fines and penalties, § 490.5.

SHORT TITLE
Popular Name Laws, generally, this index.

SHORTHAND REPORTERS
Court Reporters, generally, this index.

SHOWER BATHS
Correctional institutions, cruel or unusual punishment, § 673.

SHOWS
Theaters and Shows, generally, this index.

SICKNESS
Illness, generally, this index.

SIDEWALKS
Littering, cigarettes, fire hazard, bail, § 853.6.
Obstructing free movement, § 647c.
Parking near access ramps,
    Persons under influence of drugs or liquor, disorderly conduct, § 647.
Pornography, vending machines, near schools or playgrounds, § 313.1.

SIGNATURES
Arrest, release on own recognizance, promise to appear, § 853.6.
Bail, orders for discharge from custody, § 1269a.
Extortion, obtaining by threats, § 522.
Forgery, generally, this index.
Habeas corpus,
    Petition, § 1474.
    Return, § 1480.
Search warrants, § 1528.
Weapons, this index.

SIGNS AND SIGNALS
Malicious Mischief, this index.
Outdoor Advertising, generally, this index.
Police facility or place of detention, telephone call rights, arrested persons, § 851.5.

SIGNS AND SIGNALS—Cont'd
Railroads, this index.
Trespasses, § 602.

SISTER STATES
Foreign States, generally, this index.

SIT-INS
Colleges and universities, § 626 et seq.
Disorderly conduct, § 647.
Public buildings and works, § 602.
Schools and school districts, § 626.8.

SIX YEAR LIMITATION OF PROSECUTIONS
Generally, § 800.
Bribery, public official or employee, § 800.

SKIING
Areas, trespass, § 602.

SLANDER
Libel and Slander, generally, this index.

SLASHING
Malicious mischief, burning, § 449c.

SLAVERY
Cohabitation, receiving money for placing persons in custody for purposes of, § 266d.
Jurisdiction, seizure for, § 784.
Kidnapping, § 207.

SLOT MACHINES
Counterfeited coins, etc., misdemeanor, § 640a.
Slugs, counterfeited coins, etc., use, § 640a.
Use of slugs, § 640a.

SLOUGHS
Jurisdiction of offenses upon vessels navigating, § 783.

SLUGS
Coin-box telephones, use, § 640b.
Manufacturers and Manufacturing, this index.

SLUNGSHOT
Weapons, generally, this index.

SNIPERSCOPES
Concealing or possessing, etc., § 468.

SNOWSHEDS
Malicious mischief, burning, § 449b.

SOCIAL SERVICES
Battered children, reports, § 11110.
Fraud,
    Claims, § 72.
Nonsupport proceedings, fines, payment to county department, § 270d.
Reports, cruelty or sexual molestation of dependent child, § 11161.5.
Supportability, child, determination, § 270.

SOCIETIES
Associations and Societies, generally, this index.

SODOMY
See, also,
    Oral Copulation, generally, this index.
    Sex Offenders, generally, this index.
Generally, § 286 et seq.
Animals, sexually assaulting, § 286.5.
Assault with intent to commit, § 220.
Children and minors, § 286.
    Harmful matter, distribution or exhibition, § 313 et seq.
Fines and penalties, § 286.
    Assault with intent to commit sodomy, § 220.
    Prior prison term, additional punishment, § 667.5.
Prior prison term, additional punishment, § 1170.2.
Registration of offenders, § 290.
Unconscious persons, oral copulation, § 288a.

SOIL
Removal of soil without permission, § 602.

SOLDER
Junk and secondhand dealers, purchasing, determination of sellers' rights, § 496a.

SOLICITATION
Abortions, § 187.
Alcoholic beverages, begging or soliciting patron or customer to purchase, § 303a.
Alms, public places, § 647.
Evidence, degree of proof, § 653f.
Fetus, murder, § 187.
Lewd or unlawful act, § 647.
Membership in nongovernmental organization with term peace officer, etc., incorporated in name, § 146c.
Obscene materials, publication of advertising, § 311.5.
Prostitution, § 647.

SPANISH LYNX
See, also, Fish and Game, generally, this index.

SPARRING CONTESTS
Boxing and Wrestling, generally, this index.

SPECIAL PROCEEDINGS
Guilty plea, withdrawn plea specifying punishment, evidence, § 1192.5.
Nolo contendere pleas, withdrawn pleas specifying punishment, evidence, § 1192.5.

SPECTATORS
Dogs, fighting, fines and penalties, § 597.5.

SPEEDY TRIAL
Trial, this index.

SPONSORS
Obscene live conduct, managing, producing, sponsoring, etc., § 311.6.

Penal Code — STREETS

SPORTS
Athletics, generally, this index.

SPOUSE
Husband and Wife, generally, this index.
Support, generally, this index.

SQUATTERS
Disorderly conduct, § 647.

STABLES
Arson, §§ 447a, 448a.
Burglary, § 459.

STALLIONS AND JACKS
Theft, § 487.
    Carcasses, § 487a.

STATE
Agencies. State Agencies, generally, this index.
Appeals In Criminal Prosecutions, this index.
Bonds, bail security, § 1298.
Claims against state,
    Fraud, § 72.
    Persons erroneously convicted of crime, § 4900 et seq.
Defined, § 7.
    Fresh pursuit, § 852.1.
Departments. State Departments, generally, this index.
Employees. State Officers and Employees, generally, this index.
Legislature, generally, this index.
Officers. State Officers and Employees, generally, this index.
Public Lands, generally, this index.
Simulating official inquiries, § 146b.

STATE AGENCIES
See, also, Public Agencies, generally, this index.
Criminal history information,
    Local summary criminal history information, § 13300 et seq.
Keys to buildings, unauthorized duplication, § 469.

STATE BONDS
Bail, deposit as security, § 1298.

STATE COLLEGES
Colleges and Universities, generally, this index.
Defined,
    Campus disorders, § 626.
    Disturbance of the peace, § 415.5.

STATE DEPARTMENTS
Corrections, State Department of, generally, this index.
False emergency reports, § 148.3.
Justice, State Department of, generally, this index.
Treasury. State Treasury, generally, this index.

STATE HOSPITALS
Hospitals, generally, this index.
Mental hospitals. Mentally Deficient and Mentally Ill Persons, generally, this index.

STATE LANDS
Public Lands, generally, this index.

STATE OFFICERS AND EMPLOYEES
Accounts and accounting, falsification by officers, § 424.
Application of law, illegal acts, § 77.
Bribery, § 67 et seq.
Civil Service, generally, this index.
Compensation and salaries, asking and receiving emoluments, § 70.
Cruel treatment of prisoners, § 147.
Disqualification from office, embezzlement and falsification of accounts, § 424.
Embezzlement,
    Public moneys, § 424.
Emoluments, asking or receiving, § 70.
Executive officers,
    Bribes, §§ 67, 68.
    Obstructing or resisting in performance of duties, § 69.
False impersonation, § 146a.
Fines and penalties,
    Bribery, §§ 67, 67½, 68.
    Embezzlement, falsification of accounts, misappropriation, etc., § 424.
Fraudulent claims, presentation to, § 72.
Fugitives from justice, persons designated to return, expenses, payment, § 1557.
Governor, generally, this index.
Gratuities,
    Asking or receiving, § 70.
Indictment or information, removal, necessity, § 682.
Inhuman or oppressive treatment of prisoners, § 147.
Misappropriation of public moneys, § 424.
Obstructing or resisting in performance of duties, § 69.
Oppressive treatment of prisoners, § 147.
Personal property, injury, destruction or taking from custody, § 102.
Profits, unauthorized loan or use of public moneys for, § 424.
Public moneys,
    Defined, embezzlement or other misuse, § 424.
Rewards,
    Asking or receiving, § 70.

STATE PATROL
Highway Patrol, generally, this index.

STATE POLICE
Peace Officers, this index.

STATE PRISONS
Correctional Institutions, generally, this index.

STATE TREASURY
Payments, expenses, persons designated to return fugitives from justice, § 1557.

STATE UNIVERSITIES
Defined,
    Campus disorders, § 626.
    Disturbance of the peace, § 415.5.

STATEMENTS
Financial Statements and Reports, generally, this index.
Indictment and information,
    Offense charged, contents, § 950.
    Statement of offense, § 952.
Pretrial diversion programs, § 1001.5.

STATISTICS
Criminal history information,
    Local summary criminal history information, furnishing, § 13300 et seq.

STATUTES
Indictment and Information, this index.
Tobacco, posting copy by dealers regarding sales to minors, § 308.
Uniform Laws, generally, this index.

STAY OF PROCEEDINGS
Supersedeas or Stay, generally, this index.

STEALING
Theft, generally, this index.

STEALING CHILDREN
Generally, § 278.

STEAMBOATS AND STEAMSHIPS
Defined, § 7.

STICKUPS
Robbery, generally, this index.

STIPULATIONS
Exhibits, release, § 1418.6.

STOLEN PROPERTY
Theft, generally, this index.

STORAGE
Stolen or embezzled property, restoration to owner, expenses, § 1408 et seq.

STORES AND STOREKEEPERS
Arson, § 448a.
Burglary, § 459.
Credit cards, offenses, § 484d et seq.
Shoplifting, fines and penalties, § 490.5.
Weapons, exemption, § 12027.

STRAITJACKETS
Prisoners, cruel, corporal or unusual punishment, § 673.

STRAW
Malicious mischief, burning, § 449b.

STREAMS
Rivers and Streams, generally, this index.

STREET RAILWAYS
See, also,
    Carriers, generally, this index.
    Public Utilities, generally, this index.
Arson, § 449a.
Operators, robbery, § 211a.
Robbery, operators, § 211a.

STREETS AND ALLEYS
See, also, Highways and Roads, generally, this index.

STREETS

STREETS AND ALLEYS—Cont'd
Drunkenness on public streets, § 647.
Loitering, § 647.
Nuisance, obstruction of free passage or use, § 647c.
Obstructions,
    Free passage or use, nuisance, § 647c.
    Persons under influence of drugs or liquor, § 647.
Sidewalks, generally, this index.
Traffic Rules and Regulations, generally, this index.
Weapons, carrying loaded firearms, § 12031.

STRIKES
Labor Disputes, generally, this index.

SUBORNATION OF PERJURY
Perjury, this index.

SUBPOENA DUCES TECUM
    Generally, § 1327.
    Production of Books and Papers, generally, this index.

SUBPOENAS
    Generally, § 1326 et seq.
Appearance at different time, agreement, § 1331.5.
Attendance of witnesses,
    Outside county of residence, § 1330.
Blank subpoenas, § 1326.
Contempt, § 1331.5.
Form, § 1327.
Grand Jury, this index.
Issuance, § 1326.
Outside county of residence, attendance of witnesses, § 1330.
Police officers, service, criminal prosecution, § 1328.
Return of service,
    Criminal prosecutions, § 1328.
    Telegraphic or teletype copy, § 1328c.
Service, § 1328.
    Telegraphic or teletype copy, § 1328a et seq.
Signatures, § 1326.
Telegraphic or teletype copy, § 1328a et seq.

SUBSCRIPTIONS
Publication of nongovernmental organization with term peace officer, etc., incorporated in name, solicitation, § 146c.

SUBSEQUENT OFFENSES
Second and Subsequent Offenses, generally, this index.

SUITS
Actions and Proceedings, generally, this index.

SULFONDIETHYLMETHANE
    See, also, Drugs and Medicine, generally, this index.

SULFONETHYLMETHANE
    See, also, Drugs and Medicine, generally, this index.

SULFONMETHANE
    See, also, Drugs and Medicine, generally, this index.

SUMMARY PROBATION
Misdemeanor cases, § 1203b.

SUMMER DAY CAMPS
Battered and sexually molested children reports, § 11161.5.

SUMMONS
Process, generally, this index.

SUNDAY
Bail, delivery of defendant to court or magistrate, § 1301.

SUPERIOR COURT JUDGES
Designation as magistrates, § 808.
Magistrates, designation as, § 808.

SUPERIOR COURTS
Judges. Superior Court Judges, generally, this index.
Offenses triable, § 737 et seq.
Preliminary examinations, § 738.

SUPERSEDEAS OR STAY
Appeals in criminal prosecutions, § 1242 et seq.
    Custody of defendant, § 1244.
    Suspension of execution of judgment, § 1245.
    Unreasonable search or seizure motion, § 1538.5.
Mentally deficient and mentally ill persons, suspension of trial pending insanity of defendant, § 1370.
Orders granting probation, § 1243.
Sanity hearing, § 1368 et seq.
Searches and seizures, motion to suppress evidence, § 1538.5.

SUPPORT
    Generally, § 270a.
Disposition of proceeds from fines for failure to support spouse or children, § 270d.
Evidence,
    Child supportability of parent, § 270.
Failure to maintain child under fourteen, § 271a.
Gifts, parents child supportability, determination, § 270.
Illegitimate children, § 270 et seq.
Income, parents child supportability determination, § 270.
Jails, this index.
Medical care and attendance, § 270a.
    Obligation, parents, religious exception, § 270.
Mentally deficient and mentally ill persons, transportation expenses, state hospital, § 1373.
Mutual obligation of spouses, § 270a.
Shelter, § 270a.
Unborn children, § 270.
Witnesses, moral support, § 868.
Work furlough earnings, support of prisoners' dependents, § 1208.

SUPPRESSION OF EVIDENCE
Evidence, this index.

SUPREME COURT
Capital punishment, appeals, time requirement for decision, § 190.6.
Justices. Supreme Court Justices, generally, this index.
Pardons and Reprieves, this index.

SUPREME COURT JUSTICES
Designation as magistrates, § 808.
Magistrates, designation as, § 808.

SURETY BONDS
Bonds (Officers and Fiduciaries), generally, this index.

SURETYSHIP AND GUARANTY
    See, also, Bonds (Officers and Fiduciaries), generally, this index.

SURGEONS
Physicians and Surgeons, generally, this index.

SURRENDER
Bail, surrender of defendant, § 1300 et seq.

SUSPENSION OF SENTENCE
Probation, § 1203.1.

SWEARING
Profanity and Offensive Language, generally, this index.

SWINE
Hogs, generally, this index.

SWITCHBLADE KNIVES
Weapons, generally, this index.

SWITCHES
Railroads, this index.

TACKS
Deposit or throwing upon highways, § 588a.

TAMPERING
Fire alarm system, § 148.4.
Gate locks, § 602.

TAPE RECORDINGS
Lewdness and Obscenity, generally, this index.

TAVERNS AND SALOONS
Exposure of body parts, entertainers or waitresses, §§ 318.5, 318.6.

TAXICABS
Robbery of driver, § 211a.

TEACHER PREPARATION, COMMISSION FOR
Arrest, teachers for sex offenses, notice, § 291.

TEACHERS
Schoolteachers, generally, this index.

Penal Code   **THEFT**

TEAR GAS WEAPONS
Weapons, this index.

TELEGRAPHS AND TELEPHONES
Arrested persons, calls permitted, § 851.5.
Bombs and explosives, false reports of planting, § 148.1.
Burglar tools, coin telephones, § 466.3.
Burning telephone poles, malicious mischief, § 449b.
Calls with intent to threaten or annoy, wiretap evidence, admissibility, § 633.5.
Coin-box telephones,
   Burglar tools, § 466.3.
   Use of slugs, § 640b.
Drugs and poisons, false representation, obtaining by telephonic communication, § 377.
Explosives, false reports of planting, § 148.1.
Forgery of messages, § 474.
Fraud,
   Messages, § 474.
Horse racing information, transmitting, gambling, § 337i.
Junk and secondhand dealers, purchasing metals, etc., used for, diligence to determine seller's right, § 496a.
Lewd language,
   Wiretap evidence, admissibility, § 633.5.
Malicious mischief,
   Burning poles, § 449b.
Obscene language,
   Wiretap evidence, admissibility, § 633.5.
Peace officers, telephone number, disclosure maliciously with intent to obstruct justice, § 146e.
Subpoena of witnesses by telegraphic copy, § 1328a et seq.
Telephone call permitted by accused, depriving of right, § 851.5.
   On-call magistrate when court not in session, assistance, § 810.
Threats,
   Wiretap evidence, admissibility, § 633.5.
Transmission of horse racing information, gambling, § 337i.
Warrant of arrest,
   Authorization, effect, proceedings under, §§ 850, 851.
   Filing certified copy in telegraph office and return of original, § 851.
Witnesses, telegraphic copy of subpoena, § 1328a et seq.

TELEPHONE CALL ACT
Right of accused, § 851.5.

TELEPHONES
Telegraphs and Telephones, generally, this index.

TELETYPE
Subpoenas, § 1328a et seq.
Warrants for arrest, §§ 850, 851.
Witnesses, teletype copy of subpoena, § 1328a et seq.

TELEVISION AND RADIO
Advertisements, generally, this index.
Betting odds on horse races, broadcasting, § 337i.
Bombs and explosives, false reports of planting, § 148.1.
Destructive devices, use, permit, § 12305.
Explosives or bombs, false reports of planting, § 148.1.
Horse races, broadcasting information concerning results, betting odds, § 337i.
Information concerning horse races, broadcasting, § 337i.
Libel and Slander, generally, this index.
Police radio service communications, interception, § 636.5.
Props, sawed-off shotguns, permits, § 12095 et seq.
Results of horse races, broadcasting, § 337i.
Sawed-off shotgun, props with blank cartridges, permits, § 12095 et seq.
Serial number or identification mark removed, sale, etc., § 537e.

TENANT
Landlord and Tenant, generally, this index.

TENEMENTS
Apartment Houses, generally, this index.

TENTS
Burglary, § 459.
Gambling, use for gambling purposes, § 337a.
Malicious mischief, burning, § 449b.
Use for gambling purposes, § 337a.

TERRITORIES
Defined, § 7.

TERRORISM
Threats, § 422.

TESTAMENTS
Wills, generally, this index.

TESTIFY
Defined, § 7.

TESTIMONY
Evidence, generally, this index.
Witnesses, generally, this index.

TETRAHYDROCANNABINOLS
See, also, Drugs and Medicine, generally, this index.

THEATERS AND SHOWS
Children and minors,
   Harmful matter exhibited to minors, § 313 et seq.
Dogs, fighting, fines and penalties, § 597.5.
Motion Pictures, generally, this index.

THEBACON
See, also, Drugs and Medicine, generally, this index.

THEBAINE
See, also, Drugs and Medicine, generally, this index.

THEFT
Generally, § 487.
Abandoned or unclaimed property, disposal, § 1411.
Accomplices and accessories, soliciting aid, § 653f.
Amusement machines, coin-operated, burglar tools, § 466.3.
Appropriation of lost property, § 485.
Artichokes, § 487.
Assault with intent to commit, § 220.
Avocados, § 487.
Barrows, § 487.
Bicycles, this index.
Boars, § 487.
Boats,
   Taking for temporary use, § 499b.
Bringing stolen property into state, §§ 27, 497.
Carcasses of animals, etc., § 487a.
Carriers, hijacking, reward, § 1547.
Child stealing, § 784.
Citrus fruits, § 487.
Cleaning, dyeing and pressing, coin-operated machines, § 466.3.
Coin-operated machines, burglar tools, § 466.3.
Construction funds, § 484b.
Credit, obtaining falsely, § 484.
Credit cards, § 484d et seq.
Defaced property, disposal of unmarked property as stolen property, § 537e.
Defined, §§ 484, 488.
Degrees, § 486.
Description of property, evidence, § 1131.
Determination of value. Value determination, generally, post.
Disposal of property stolen or embezzled,
   Delivery to owner, §§ 1408, 1409.
   Description of articles, entry in book, § 1413.
   Duplicate receipts, § 1412.
   Expenses incurred in preservation, payment, § 1408.
   Police officers in incorporated cities or towns, duties, § 1413.
   Proof of title, §§ 1409, 1410.
   Receipts, taken from defendant, § 1412.
   Restoration to owner, order, § 1410.
   Sale, § 1411.
   Satisfactory proof of ownership, § 1408.
   Unclaimed property, § 1411.
Dogs, § 487e et seq.
Domestic fowl, § 487.
Embezzlement, generally, this index.
Evidence,
   Description of property, § 1131.
   Disposition of property, § 1411.
   Property retained as evidence, disposition, § 1413.
   Sufficiency, to sustain allegations of description of money, § 1131.
False representations, § 484.
Finder of lost property, appropriation, § 485.

765

THEFT

THEFT—Cont'd
Fines and penalties,
  Petty theft, § 490.
  Prior conviction of felony, § 666.
  Vending machines, burglar tools, § 466.3.
Firearms, § 487.
Fraud, § 484.
Fruits, § 487.
Fuel gas, § 498.
Gas, § 498.
Geldings, § 487.
Gilts, § 487.
Goats, § 487.
Grand theft, § 487 et seq.
  Assault with intent to commit, § 220.
  Carcasses of animals, etc., § 487a.
  Defined, § 487.
  Dogs, §§ 487e, 487g.
  Entry with intent to commit as burglary, § 459.
  Limitation of prosecutions, § 800.
  Punishment, § 489.
  Soliciting commission, § 653f.
Hijacking, reward, § 1547.
Hogs, § 487.
Illuminating gas, § 498.
Indictment and information, § 952.
  Contents, larceny by fraud, § 484.
  Description of property, § 1131.
  Statement of offenses, § 952.
Insured property, intent to defraud insurer, § 548.
Intent, theft by fraud, rented property, § 484.
Jacks, § 487.
Jenny, §§ 487, 487a.
Jukeboxes, burglar tools, § 466.3.
Jurisdiction,
  Offense committed out of state and property brought into state, § 789.
  Property taken transported between jurisdictional territories, § 786.
Labor of another, § 487.
  Hiring without notice of unpaid claims, § 484.
Lambs, § 487.
Lost property, appropriation, § 485.
Mares, § 487.
Meters,
  Gas, § 498.
  Water, § 499.
Money changers, burglar tools, § 466.3.
Motor Vehicles, this index.
Motorboats, temporary use, § 499b.
Motorcycles, taking for temporary use, § 499b.
Notice, property used as evidence, disposition, § 1411.
Nuts, § 487.
Olives, § 487.
Parking meters, burglar tools, § 466.3.
Penalties. Fines and penalties, generally, ante.
Person of another, property taken, § 487.
Pigs, § 487.
Poultry, § 487.
Prior convictions,
  Petit theft, § 666.
Property retained as evidence, disposition, §§ 1411, 1413.

THEFT—Cont'd
Real Estate, this index.
Receiving Stolen Goods, generally, this index.
Records,
  Description of property, § 1413.
  Stolen and lost bicycles, criminal justice information system, § 11111.
Reports, §§ 11106, 11108.
Retailer, credit card transactions, § 484h.
Search warrants, grounds for issuance, § 1524.
Sheep, § 487.
Shoplifting, fines and penalties, § 490.5.
Statutory reference, larceny, embezzlement or stealing meaning theft, § 490a.
Telephones, coin-operated, burglar tools, § 466.3.
Trial, § 1131.
Unmarked property, disposal as stolen property, § 537e.
Value determination, § 484.
Vehicle, taking for temporary use, § 499b.
Vending machines, burglar tools, § 466.3.
Vessels, temporary use, § 499b.
Water, § 499.
Weapons, § 487.
  Burglar tools, vending machines, § 466.3.
  Return of stolen weapons to owner, § 12028.
Weight and sufficiency of evidence, description of property, § 1131.

THERAPEUTIC ABORTION ACT
Generally, § 187.

THERMAL LANCE
Burglary, § 464.

THINGS IN ACTION
Personal property includes, § 7.

THREATS
See, also, Duress or Coercion, generally, this index.
Accomplices and accessories, causing others to commit crime, § 31.
Arbitrators, § 95.
Blackmail. Extortion, generally, this index.
Capacity to commit crime, § 26.
Causing others to commit crime, accessories, § 31.
Defrauding innkeepers, § 537.
Extortion, generally, this index.
False imprisonment, § 237.
Jurors, § 95.
Obscene matter, acceptance as condition of sale of other merchandise, §§ 311.7, 311.9.
Officers, obstructing or resisting officers in performance of duties, § 69.
Oral copulation, § 288a.
Pandering, § 266i.
Perjury, subornation by threat of force, § 137.
Prisoners,
  Holding persons as hostages, § 4503.
Prostitution, placing or permitting placement of wife in house of prostitution, § 266g.

THREATS—Cont'd
Public officers or employees, § 71.
Rape, § 261.
School officials, § 71.
Telephone calls,
  Wiretap evidence, admissibility, § 633.5.
Terrorist threats, § 422.
Umpires, § 95.
Witnesses,
  Inducing false testimony, § 137.
  Preventing trial attendance, § 136.

3, 4—METHYLENEDIOXY AMPHETAMINE
See, also, Drugs and Medicine, generally, this index.

3, 4, 5—TRIMETHOXY AMPHETAMINE
See, also, Drugs and Medicine, generally, this index.

THREE YEAR LIMITATION OF PROSECUTIONS
Generally, § 800.

THUMB–SCREWS
Punishment by use, § 673.

TICKETS
Counterfeiting,
  Passage tickets, §§ 470, 481.
Passage, forgery or counterfeiting, § 470.

TIE–IN SALES
Obscene matter, §§ 311.7, 311.9.

TIGERS
See, also, Fish and Game, generally, this index.

TIMBER AND LUMBER
Arson, § 449a.
Malicious mischief,
  Burning, §§ 449b, 449c.
  Trespass, § 602.
Trespass, § 602.

TIMBER WOLVES
Fish and Game, generally, this index.

TIME
Alcoholic beverages, sales between 2 and 6 a. m., § 398.
Appearance, this index.
Arrest, this index.
Bail, this index.
Capital Punishment, this index.
Commission of offense, pleading, § 955.
Corporations, service of summons, § 1392.
Delay, appearance before magistrate, § 825.
Destruction of exhibits, § 1418.5.
Exhibits, release from custody of court, § 1418.
Homicide, death within three years and day, necessity, § 194.
Indictment and Information, this index.
Justice Courts, this index.
Lease agreements, written demand for return of property, § 484.

Penal Code   **TRANSCRIPT**

TIME—Cont'd
Limitation of Prosecutions, generally, this index.
Misdemeanors, filing complaint in justice court, § 1426a.
Murder, death within three years and day, necessity, § 194.
Nighttime, generally, this index.
Parole and Probation, this index.
Petitions for certificates of rehabilitation, filing, § 4852.06.
Preliminary Examination, this index.
Probation officers,
  Annual report, § 1203.08.
Registration of sex offenders, § 290.
Rental agreements, written demand for return of property, § 484.
Resentencing, recall of commitment and sentence, § 1170.
Search warrant,
  Execution and return, § 1534.
  Service, § 1533.
Sex offenders, registration, § 290.
Telephoning rights, arrested persons, exercise, § 851.5.

TIPPLING HOUSES
Taverns and Saloons, generally, this index.

TITLE OF ACTION
Accusatory pleading to contain, § 950.

TITLE TO PROPERTY
Claim of title, defense in embezzlement, § 511.
Correctional institution inmates, civil rights, § 2601.
Defenses, claim of title, embezzlement, § 511.
Prisoners, civil rights, § 2601.

TOBACCO AND TOBACCO PRODUCTS
Cigarettes and Cigars, generally, this index.
Sale or furnishing to minors under 18, § 308.

TOILETS
Comfort Stations and Rest Rooms, generally, this index.

TOLUENE
Disorderly conduct, person under influence, § 647.

TONGUE
Cutting or disabling, mayhem, §§ 203, 204.

TOOLS
Burglars, possession with intent to break or enter, § 466.
Leases, theft by fraud, § 484.
Presumptions, theft by fraud, § 484.
Vending machines, theft, § 466.3.

TORTS
Battered children, reports, immunity, § 11161.5.
Hospitals, reports of physical abuse of patients received from health facilities, § 11161.8.

TORTS—Cont'd
Parents, shoplifting by minor child, § 490.5.
Physicians and surgeons, reports, abuse of patients by another health facility, § 11161.8.
Public officers and employees effecting arrest, civil liability, § 836.5.

TORTURE
Animals, malicious mischief, § 597.
First degree murder, special circumstance, punishment, § 190.2.
Murder, degree, § 189.
Probation, inflicting torture during perpetration of crime, § 1203.
Punishment, § 673.

TOWN OFFICERS AND EMPLOYEES
Accounts, falsification, § 424.
Disqualification from office, embezzlement and falsification of accounts, § 424.
Embezzlement, falsification of accounts, etc., § 424.
Misappropriation, public moneys, § 424.
Public moneys,
  Defined, embezzlement or other misuse, § 424.
Sentence and punishment, embezzlement, falsification of accounts, misappropriation, etc., § 424.

TOWNS
Employees. Town Officers and Employees, generally, this index.
Officers. Town Officers and Employees, generally, this index.
Police force, forming, prevention of public offenses, § 697.
Riotous assemblies,
  Arrest of persons failing to disperse, § 727.
  Command to disperse by officials, §§ 726, 727.
Unlawful or riotous assemblies,
  Arrest of persons failing to disperse, § 727.
  Command to disperse by officials, §§ 726, 727.

TRACKS
Railroads, generally, this index.

TRADE AND BUSINESS
Business and Commerce, generally, this index.

TRADING STAMPS
Counterfeiting, § 470.
Possession, § 475.

TRAFFIC RULES AND REGULATIONS
Appearance, corporations, guilty pleas, §§ 1396, 1427.
Arrest,
  Notice to appear, issuance in lieu of arrest, § 818.
  Release on promise to appear, nonrelease of certain persons, § 853.6.

TRAFFIC RULES AND REGULATIONS—Cont'd
Corporations, appearance, guilty pleas, §§ 1396, 1427.
Driving under influence of drugs, Veh 23101 et seq.
  Arrest, release under notice to appear, persons not released, § 853.6.
Driving while intoxicated,
  Arrest, release under notice to appear, persons not released, § 853.6.
Drugs. Driving under influence of drugs, generally, ante.
Drunken driving. Driving while intoxicated, generally, ante.
Infractions, § 17.
  Arrest, time of day, § 840.
  Bail schedule, § 1269b.
  Burden of proof, § 19d.
  Corporations, guilty plea, §§ 1396, 1427.
  Jurisdiction, § 19d.
  Limitation of criminal prosecutions, § 19d.
  Schedule, bail, § 1269b.
  Time, arrest, § 840.
  Trial, § 19d.
Notices,
  Appearance, issuance in lieu of taking vehicle code violator before magistrate, § 818.

TRAILER CAMPS
Mobilehomes and Mobilehome Parks, generally, this index.

TRAILER COACH
Arson, § 447a.

TRAILERS
Theft by fraud, § 484.

TRAINING
Airport security officers, peace officers, § 832.1.
Armored vehicle guards, firearms possession, § 12031.
Custodial officers, maintaining custody of prisoners and operating local detention facilities, § 831.
Guards or messengers for banks or financial institutions, firearms possession, § 12031.
Peace Officers, this index.
Police, this index.
Sheriffs, this index.
Tear gas and tear gas weapons, § 12403.7.

TRAINS
Railroads, generally, this index.

TRANSCRIPT OF RECORD
Correctional institutions, copies, sentencing proceedings, § 1203.01.
Pardons, reprieves and commutations, examination, § 4812.
Search warrants, sworn oral statement, certifying and filing, § 1526.
Sentencing proceedings, copies, correctional institutions, § 1203.01.

TRANSFER

TRANSFER OF CAUSES
Removal or Transfer of Causes, generally, this index.

TRANSIENTS
Vagrants and Vagrancy, generally, this index.

TRANSIT DISTRICTS
San Francisco Bay Area Rapid Transit District, generally, this index.

TRANSPORTATION
Animal carcasses, theft, § 487a.
Eavesdropping equipment, offenses, § 635.
Junk and secondhand dealers, purchasing metals used in, diligence to determine seller's right, § 496a.
Machine guns, § 12220.
Mentally deficient and mentally ill persons, state hospital, payment of expenses, § 1373.
Motor Carriers, generally, this index.
Wiretapping equipment, offenses, § 635.

TRASH
Garbage and Refuse, generally, this index.

TRAVELERS CHECKS
Blanks, possession with intent to defraud, § 475.
Completed check, possession with intent to defraud, § 475a.

TRAVELING EXPENSES
Witnesses, § 1329.

TREATMENT
Drug Addicts, this index.
Medical Attendance and Treatment, generally, this index.

TREES
Burning, malicious mischief, § 449c.
Malicious mischief,
    Burning, § 449c.

TRESPASS
    Generally, § 602.
Apartment, unauthorized entry, § 602.5.
Colleges and universities, § 626 et seq.
Community colleges, § 626 et seq.
Dwelling house, unauthorized entry, § 602.5.
Eavesdropping, invasion of privacy, § 634.
Fires, hazardous fire area, § 602.
Invasion of privacy, wiretapping, § 634.
Motor vehicles, § 602.
Public buildings and works, refusal to leave at closing time, § 602.
Refusal to leave upon request, § 602.
Schools, disruptive persons, § 626.8.
Second and subsequent offenses, invasion of privacy, wiretapping, § 634.
Ski areas or trails, § 602.
State colleges, disruptive presence of employees or students, § 626 et seq.
University of California,
    Disruptive presence of employees or students, § 626 et seq.

TRIAL
Absence,
    Defendant, § 1043.
Accomplices and Accessories, this index.
Acquittal judgments, § 1118 et seq.
Argument and Conduct of Counsel, generally, this index.
Arrest reports, restrictions on judge reading, § 1204.5.
Calendars, priorities and preferences, § 1048.
Change of order of procedure, §§ 1093, 1094.
Charge to jury. Instructions to jury, generally, post.
Citations for misdemeanors, § 853.6 et seq.
Closing argument, order, § 1093.
Comments by judge, § 1093.
Commitment of defendant on bail, § 1129.
Concealment of felon to avoid or escape trial, accomplices, § 32.
Confession, previous conviction, reading to jury, § 1093.
Conspiracy, § 1104.
Continuance,
    Absence of accused, § 1043.
    Children and minors as victims or detained as material witnesses, § 1048.
    Minor involved in case, § 1048.
    Searches and seizures, motion to suppress evidence, § 1538.5.
    Unreasonable search or seizure motion, § 1538.5.
Control of proceedings, § 1044.
Conviction records, restriction on judge reading, § 1204.5.
Degrees of offense, reasonable doubt, conviction of lowest degree, § 1097.
Disruptive behavior by defendant, removal from courtroom, § 1043.
Embezzlement, § 1131.
Evidence, restrictions, § 1044.
Extradition, other crimes, § 1556.
Harboring felon to avoid or escape trial, accomplices, § 32.
Innocence of defendant, presumption, § 1096.
Insanity issue, § 1201.
Instructions to jury, § 1093.
    Escape, attempt, § 1127c.
    Flight, form, § 1127c.
    Form,
        Flight, § 1127c.
    Mentally deficient and mentally ill persons, trial of sanity issue, § 1369.
    Presumption of innocence, § 1096a.
    Reasonable doubt, § 1096a.
Jointly charged defendants,
    Joint or separate trials, § 1098.
Judgment, acquittal judgment, § 1118 et seq.
Larceny, § 1131.
Mentally Deficient and Mentally Ill Persons, this index.
Minor involved in prosecution, § 1048.
Mistrial, absence of defendant, felony case, § 1043.
New Trial, generally, this index.

TRIAL—Cont'd
Not guilty finding, judgment, § 1118.
Number of counsel, argument, death penalty, § 1095.
Opening argument, order, § 1093.
Order of proceedings, §§ 1048, 1093.
    Change of order, § 1094.
Orders of court, separate trials, § 1098.
Plea, reading to jury, § 1093.
Presence of accused, § 1043.
Presentencing information, § 1203.
Presumption of innocence, § 1096.
    Instructions to jury, § 1096a.
Previous conviction, reading to jury, § 1093.
Principals, distinction between principal and accessory abrogated, § 971.
Priorities and preferences, trial calendar, § 1048.
Reading of indictment or information to jury, § 1093.
Reasonable doubt,
    Defined, § 1096.
    Degree, conviction of lowest degree, § 1097.
    Instructions to jury, § 1096a.
Rebuttal testimony, discretion of court, § 1093.
Sanity hearings, § 1367 et seq.
Searches and seizures, motion for suppression of evidence, § 1538.5.
Separate trials,
    Defendants jointly charged, § 1098.
    Different offenses or counts set forth in indictment or information, § 954.
Speedy trial,
    Extradition, arrest without warrant, § 1551.1.
    Narcotics and drug abuse cases, waiver, education, treatment or rehabilitation, § 1000 et seq.
    Priorities and preferences, § 1048.
    Searches and seizures, motion to suppress evidence, § 1538.5.
Statement of plea to jury, § 1093.
Theft, § 1131.
Unreasonable search or seizure motion, return of property or suppression of evidence, § 1538.5.
Verdicts,
    Death penalty,
        Application for modification of verdict, ruling, § 190.4.
    First degree murder, special circumstances, special finding, § 190.4.
    Mental capacity, § 1026.
Probationer, setting aside verdict of guilty, § 1203.4.
Setting aside,
    Certificate of rehabilitation and pardon, § 1203.4.
    Statement, offense for which convicted, § 954.
    Vacation, discharged probationer, § 1203.4.
Waiver,
    Defendants' personal presence, § 977.
Without jury, judgment, § 1118.

Penal Code

TRICING UP
Cruel or inhuman punishment, § 673.

TRIMEPERIDINE
Drugs and Medicine, generally, this index.

TRUCKS
Motor carriers, generally, this index.

TURKEYS
Poultry and Poultry Products, generally, this index.

TWO TRIAL ACT (CAPITAL OFFENSES)
Generally, § 190.1.

2–METHLY–3 MORPHOLINO–1, 1–DIPHENYL–PROPANE–CARBOXYLIC ACID
Drugs and Medicine, generally, this index.

TYPEWRITERS
Serial number or identification mark removed, sale, etc., § 537e.

UMPIRES
Bribery, §§ 337d, 337e.
Corrupt influencing, § 95.
Intimidation, § 95.

UNAUTHORIZED FIRE
Defined, prisoners in local detention facility, § 451b.

UNCLAIMED PROPERTY
Abandoned or Unclaimed Property, generally, this index.

UNCONSCIOUS PERSONS
Capacity to commit crime, § 26.

UNDERTAKINGS
Bail, generally, this index.

UNIFORM LAWS
Extradition, § 1548 et seq.
Fresh pursuit, § 852 et seq.
Hot pursuit, Uniform Act on Fresh Pursuit, § 852 et seq.

UNIFORM MISDEMEANOR AND TRAFFIC CITATIONS
Form, fol. §§ 853.6, 853.7, 853.9.

UNIFORMS
Labor disputes, picketing, wearing peace officers uniform, § 12590.

UNITED STATES
Bail, bonds, § 1298.
Conspiracy to commit crime against officials, § 182.
Correctional Institutions, this index.
Defined, § 7.
Employees. Officers and employees, generally, post.
Extradition, payment of expenses, § 1557.
Federal Bureau of Investigation, generally, this index.

UNITED STATES—Cont'd
Immigration officers, local summary criminal history information, furnishing, § 13300 et seq.
Jails, receiving prisoners, § 4005.
Law enforcement officers, tear gas weapons, purchasing, possessing or transporting, § 12403.1.
Officers and employees,
  Assault and battery, United States property, § 243.4.
  Deadly weapon, § 245.4.
  Attempt to kill or assault, § 217.1.
  Conspiracy to commit crime against, § 182.
  Law enforcement officers, tear gas weapons, purchasing, possessing or transporting, § 12403.1.
Peace officers, criminal history information, furnishing, § 11105.
  Local summary, § 13300 et seq.
Punishment of federal crimes by state, § 777.
Real estate,
  Assault and battery, federal employees, § 243.4.
  Deadly weapon, § 245.4.
Weapons, concealed weapons, conviction of federal crimes, § 12021.

UNITED STATES COURTS
Criminal history information, furnishing, § 11105.
  Local summary criminal history information, § 13300 et seq.

UNIVERSITIES
Colleges and Universities, generally, this index.

UNIVERSITY OF CALIFORNIA
Colleges and Universities, this index.

UNLAWFUL ASSEMBLY
Assembly, this index.

UNLAWFUL SEXUAL INTERCOURSE
Generally, §§ 261.5, 264.

UNUSUAL PUNISHMENT
Generally, § 673.

USED PROPERTY
Junk and Junk Dealers, generally, this index.

UTILITIES
Public Utilities, generally, this index.

UTTERING
Fictitious instruments with intent to defraud, § 476.
Forged or counterfeited matter, § 470.

VAGRANTS AND VAGRANCY
Annoying or molesting child under 18, § 647a.
Defined, annoying or molesting child under eighteen, § 647a.
Second and subsequent offenses, annoying or molesting child under eighteen, § 647a.

VALUE
Embezzlement, determination, § 514.
Theft, this index.

VANDALISM
Malicious Mischief, generally, this index.

VARIANCES
Issues, Proof and Variance, generally, this index.

VAULTS
Burglary with explosives, § 464.

VEGETABLES
Malicious injury or destruction,
  Burning, § 449b.
Theft, § 487.

VEHICLES
Motor Vehicles, generally, this index.

VENDING MACHINES
Burglar tools, § 466.3.
Fines and penalties, burglar tools, § 466.3.
Pornography, near schools or playgrounds, § 313.1.
Slugs, use, § 640a.
Telephones, coin box phones, use of slugs, § 640b.

VENUE
Arraignments,
  Determination of venue, inferior courts, § 1462.2.
Conspiracy prosecution, §§ 182, 184.
Misdemeanors, § 1462.2.

VERDICTS
Trial, this index.

VESSELS
Ships and Shipping, generally, this index.

VETERANS ORGANIZATIONS
Weapons, exemption, § 12027.

VICE–PRESIDENT OF THE UNITED STATES
Attempt to kill or commission of assault, § 217.1.
Conspiracy to commit crime against, § 182.

VICUNA
See, also, Fish and Game, generally, this index.

VILLAGES
See, also, Municipalities, generally, this index.

VIOLENCE
Force and Violence, generally, this index.

VISITATION
Accused in custody, attorney, communication with, § 825.
Correctional Institutions, this index.
Prisoners, civil rights, § 2601.

VISTA

VISTA, CITY OF
See, also, Municipalities, generally, this index.

VITRIOL
Assault and battery, § 244.

VOCATIONAL EDUCATION
County prisoners,
    Work furloughs, § 1208.
Disruptive persons, denial of access to campus or facilities, etc., § 626.8.
Drug addicts, work furloughs, § 1208.
Industrial farms, road camps or honor camps, release of inmates,
    Educational purposes, § 1208.
Jail inmates, § 1208.

VOUCHERS
Construction loan funds, false vouchers, embezzlement, § 484c.
Embezzlement, construction loan funds, false vouchers, § 484c.
Fraudulent vouchers, presentation to state, etc., board or officer, § 72.

WAGERS AND WAGERING
Gambling, generally, this index.

WAGES
Compensation and Salaries, generally, this index.

WAITERS AND WAITRESSES
Nudity, §§ 318.5, 318.6.

WALLET GUNS
Defined, weapons, possession, manufacture or sale, § 12020.
Weapons, generally, this index.

WAR AND CIVIL DEFENSE
Indictment and information, offenses arising in land and naval forces, necessity, § 682.

WARD
Guardian and Ward, generally, this index.

WARDENS
Correctional Institutions, this index.
Jails, prisoners delivered to prison for safekeeping, § 4007.

WAREHOUSES AND WAREHOUSEMEN
Arson, § 448a.
Burglary, § 459.

WARES
Goods, Wares and Merchandise, generally, this index.

WARNINGS
Tear gas and tear gas weapons, containers, § 12403.7.

WARRANTS
Arrest, this index.
Bail, this index.
Searches and Seizures, this index.
Service, time, § 1533.

WARRANTS FOR PAYMENT OF MONEY
See, also, Vouchers, generally, this index.
Forgery or counterfeiting, § 470.

WASHING MACHINES
Serial number or identification mark removed, sale, etc., § 537e.

WASHROOMS
Comfort Stations and Rest Rooms, generally, this index.

WATCHES
Serial number or identification mark removed, sale, etc., § 537e.

WATCHMEN
Weapons, carrying loaded firearms, § 12031.

WATER COMPANIES
See, also, Water Supply, generally, this index.
Theft of water, § 499.

WATER CONDUITS
Theft of water, § 499.

WATER FLUMES
Theft of water, § 499.

WATER POLLUTION
Water Quality, generally, this index.

WATER QUALITY
Bail,
    Littering, § 853.6.
Littering,
    Bail, § 853.6.

WATER RIGHTS
Flumes. Water Flumes, generally, this index.
Theft of water, § 499.

WATER SUPPLY
Fraud, meters, alteration, § 499.
Meters, alteration, fraud, § 499.
Theft, § 499.

WATERCRAFT
Boats and Boating, generally, this index.
Ships and Shipping, generally, this index.

WATERS AND WATERCOURSES
Canals, generally, this index.
Lakes and Ponds, generally, this index.
Pollution of water. Water Quality, generally, this index.

WEALTH
Bail, qualifications, § 1279.

WEAPONS
Generally, § 467.
Abandoned or unclaimed property, destruction or sale, § 12028.
Abatement as nuisances, §§ 12028, 12029.
Accusatory pleading, nature of firearm used, §§ 969c, 969d.

WEAPONS—Cont'd
Advertising, prohibited weapons, § 12020.5.
Aircraft, shooting at, § 247.
Alteration of number of identifying marks, § 12090 et seq.
Ammunition, generally, this index.
Antique weapons,
    Manufacture, sale or possession, § 12020.
    Possession, § 12027.
Armed offenses,
    Additional punishment, §§ 12022, 12022.5.
    Prior conviction, § 1170.2.
Armored vehicles, guards, § 12031.
Arrest, this index.
Assault and Battery, this index.
Assignment of identification mark, § 12092.
Associations and societies,
    Carrying loaded weapons, § 12031.
    Possession, § 12027.
Assumed names, purchases, § 12076.
Attempted felony, while armed, additional punishment, §§ 12022, 12022.5.
Bank guards, carrying loaded weapons, § 12031.
Banks, possession, § 12027.
Batons or clubs, guards or security officers, § 12002.
Birth date, purchases, § 12076.
Bonds, guards, possession, § 12027.
Building, discharge at occupied building, § 246.
Burglar alarm company employees or agents, § 12031.
Burglary, this index.
Camp sites, carrying loaded weapons, § 12031.
Campers, shooting, § 246.
Carriers, possession, § 12027.
Carrying concealed weapons, § 12031.
    Licenses and permits, post.
Children and Minors, this index.
Civil organizations, possession, § 12027.
Clubs or batons, guards or security officers, § 12002.
Colleges and universities, possession, § 626.9.
Commission of felony while armed,
    Additional punishment, §§ 12022, 12022.5.
    Prior conviction, § 1170.2.
Committing crime with deadly weapon, probation, § 1203.
Complaints, commission of felonies, § 969c.
Concealed weapons, § 12000 et seq.
    Federal crimes, conviction, § 12021.
    Labor disputes, picketing, § 12590.
    Mail order purchases, § 12079.
    Nuisance, sale or destruction, § 12028.
Confiscation and destruction, § 12028 et seq.
    Machine guns, § 12251.
Consecutive sentences, additional punishment for armed offenses, §§ 12022, 12022.5.
Correctional Institutions, this index.
Courses of instruction, peace officers, use of firearms, § 832.

Penal Code   WEAPONS

WEAPONS—Cont'd
Dealers,
  Licenses and permits, § 12070 et seq.
  Mail orders, § 12079.
Defined,
  Blowgun, manufacture, sale, etc., § 12580.
Delivery,
  Dealers, time, § 12071.
Destruction,
  Abandoned property or exhibits in criminal actions, §§ 1419, 12028.
  Confiscation, §§ 12028, 12029.
  Machine guns, § 12251.
  Nuisances, §§ 12028, 12029.
Detectives, carrying loaded weapons, § 12031.
Discharge,
  At inhabited dwelling house, occupied building or motor vehicle, § 246.
  Campers, § 246.
  House cars, § 246.
  On private land, misdemeanor, § 602.
Display of licenses, dealers, § 12071.
Domicile and residence,
  Carrying loaded firearms, § 12031.
  Mail orders, § 12079.
  Sale of concealable firearms, § 12076.
Drawing weapons, § 417.
Drug addicts,
  Possession, § 12021.
  Purchase of concealable firearm, § 12076.
Dwellings,
  Carrying loaded weapons, § 12031.
Evidence,
  Disposition, § 1419.
  Possession,
    Tear gas weapon without serial number, § 12422.
  Presumptions,
    Tear gas weapon, possession without serial number, § 12422.
Ex-convict,
  Concealable firearm, purchase, § 12076.
  Possession, § 12021.
Exemptions, §§ 12027, 12031.
  Armored vehicle, guards, § 12031.
  Labor disputes, picketing, peace officers, § 12590.
  Law enforcement officers, Dangerous Weapons Law, § 12002.
  Sawed-off shotguns, motion picture or television use with blank cartridges, § 12095 et seq.
  Tear gas weapons, § 12403 et seq.
Exhibition, threatening manner, § 417.
Exhibits in criminal actions,
  Destruction or sale, § 1419.
  Release, § 1418.6.
Exports and imports, § 12020 et seq.
Federal crimes, conviction of, concealed weapons, § 12021.
Fees,
  License to carry concealed firearms, §§ 12052, 12054.
  Mail orders, record, § 12079.
  Security guards, training certificate, § 12033.
Felons, possession, §§ 12021, 12560.

WEAPONS—Cont'd
Felony,
  Commission while armed, additional punishment, §§ 12022, 12022.5.
Fictitious names, sale, § 12076.
Fines and penalties,
  Additional punishments, felonies while armed, §§ 12022, 12022.5.
  Armed with deadly weapon, prior conviction, § 1170.2.
  Concealed weapons, licenses and permits, § 12025.
  Discharge at inhabited dwelling house or occupied building, § 246.
  Drug addicts, possession, § 12021.
  Felons, possession, § 12560.
  Machine guns, sale or possession, § 12220.
  Mail order purchases, records, § 12079.
  Silencers, § 12520.
  Tear gas weapons, §§ 12420, 12422.
  Uniform sentences, § 1170.3.
Fingerprints, license to carry concealed weapon, § 12052.
Firearms offenses, prior prison terms, additional punishment, § 667.5.
Foreign states,
  Police, carrying loaded weapon, § 12031.
Former convicts,
  Concealable firearms, purchase, § 12076.
  Possession, § 12021.
Forms,
  Mail orders, § 12079.
Gifts, § 12020 et seq.
Gold bullion, guards, possession, § 12027.
Guards, this index.
Gun Control Law, § 11106.
Habeas corpus, crimes involving deadly weapons, bail, § 1491.
Historical weapons, possession, § 12027.
Holsters, carrying concealed weapon, § 12025.
Homicide, this index.
House cars, shooting, § 246.
Identity and identification,
  Marks,
    Alteration, § 12090 et seq.
    Assignment, § 12092.
    Tear gas weapons, identification number, § 12422.
    Unassigned mark, affixing, § 12093.
  Purchaser,
    Dealer's records, § 12071.
    Delivery of weapon, § 12072.
Imports, § 12020 et seq.
Indictment and information, defendant armed with, § 969c.
Industrial farms and road camps, possession, § 4574.
Injunction,
  Possession of machine guns, § 12251.
Inspection and inspectors,
  Person carrying loaded weapons, § 12031.
Jails,
  Possession, § 4574.
  Receipt for property taken from prisoner, § 4003.

WEAPONS—Cont'd
Kidnapping,
  Accusatory pleading, nature of firearm used, § 969d.
Labor disputes, picketing, carrying deadly weapons, § 12590.
Leases, register, § 12073 et seq.
Licenses and permits,
  Carrying concealed weapons, §§ 12025, 12031.
  Application fee, §§ 12052, 12054.
  Records, § 11106.
  Fingerprints, carrying concealed weapon, § 12052.
  Machine guns, post.
  Sales, § 12070 et seq.
  Sawed-off shotguns, motion picture or television props with blank cartridges, § 12095 et seq.
  Tear gas weapons, post.
Loaded firearms, persons allowed to carry in prohibited area, § 12031.
Loans, § 12020 et seq.
Machine guns, § 12200 et seq.
  Children and minors, permit, § 12230 et seq.
  Display of license, sale, § 12250.
  Licenses and permits, § 12230 et seq.
    Application, § 12231.
    Sales, § 12250.
  Nuisance, § 12251.
  Possession, § 12220.
    Permit, § 12230 et seq.
  Public nuisance, abatement, § 12251.
  Record, sale, § 12250.
  Sale, § 12220.
  Transportation, permit, § 12230 et seq.
Mail and mailing,
  Purchases, records, fees and filing, § 12079.
  Records, fees and filing, § 12079.
  Sale, § 12073.
Malicious mischief, discharge, private lands, § 602.
Manufacturers and manufacturing, §§ 12020 et seq., 12582.
  Number, alteration, § 12090 et seq.
Marks. Identity and identification, ante.
Mental institution patient, purchase of concealable firearm, § 12076.
Merchants, possession, § 12027.
Messengers,
  Carrying loaded weapons, § 12031.
  Possession, § 12027.
Military Forces, this index.
Misdemeanors, destruction of firearms used, § 12028.
Model number, alteration, § 12090 et seq.
Money, guards, possession, § 12027.
Motor Vehicles, this index.
Municipal corporation, carrying loaded weapon, § 12031.
Municipal prisoners, possession, § 4574.
Murder, accusatory pleading, nature of firearm used, § 969d.
Names, alteration, § 12090 et seq.
National Guard, possession, § 12027.
National institutions, possession, § 12027.
Night watchman, carrying loaded weapons, § 12031.

WEAPONS

WEAPONS—Cont'd
Notice,
   Sale or destruction, § 12028.
Nuisances,
   Destruction, §§ 12028, 12029.
   Firearms used in commission of crime, § 12028.
Pardons, possession, § 4854.
Parole and probation,
   Deadly weapons, carrying at time of perpetration of crime, § 1203.
   Eligibility, § 1203.06.
Patrol operators, carrying loaded weapons, § 12031.
Pawnbrokers, sales, register, § 12073 et seq.
Peace Officers, this index.
Penalties. Fines and penalties, generally, ante.
Permits. Licenses and permits, generally, ante.
Personal protection, carrying loaded weapons, § 12031.
Picketing, carrying deadly weapons, § 12590.
Pleading, accusatory pleadings, nature of firearm used, §§ 969c, 969d.
Police, this index.
Possession, § 12020 et seq.
   Armored vehicle, guards, § 12031.
   Evidence, ante.
   Felons, § 12560.
   Fire bombs, § 452.
   Identification mark, § 12094.
   Intent to assault, § 467.
   Machine guns, ante.
   Schools and colleges, § 626.9.
   Silencers, § 12520.
   Sniperscope, § 468.
   Tear gas weapons, post.
Presumptions. Evidence, ante.
Private detectives, carrying loaded weapons, § 12031.
Property protection, carrying loaded weapons, § 12031.
Purchases. Sales, generally, post.
Rape, this index.
Records and recordation,
   License to carry concealed weapons, § 12053.
   Mail order purchases, filing and fees, § 12079.
   Registration of sales, § 12073 et seq.
   Signature purchaser, § 12076.
   State printer,
      Issuance, § 12075.
Reports, license to carry concealed weapons, § 12052.
Residence. Domicile and residence, generally, ante.
Resisting arrest, § 834a.
Robbery, this index.
Sales, §§ 12020 et seq., 12303.6.
   Abandoned property or exhibits in criminal actions, etc., § 12028.
   Birth date, purchasers, § 12076.
   Business regulations, § 12071.
   Concealable firearms, violations, § 12076.
   Gas-operated guns, minors, §§ 12551, 12552.
   Identification marks, § 12094.
   Identity of purchaser,
      Dealer's records, § 12071.
      Delivery of weapon, § 12072.

WEAPONS—Cont'd
Sales—Cont'd
   Licenses, §§ 12070 et seq., 12250.
   Mail order, § 12079.
   Records, § 11106.
   Reports, § 11106.
   Sniperscope, § 468.
Salesmen, signature, § 12076.
Sawed-off shotguns,
   Manufacturing, importing or selling, penalty, § 12020.
   Nuisance, § 12029.
Schools, possession, §§ 626.9, 626.10.
Searches and seizures,
   Person appearing before magistrate, §§ 833, 1542.
Second and subsequent offenses, additional punishment, §§ 12022, 12022.5.
Security officers, § 12002.
   Training, certificates, § 12033.
Self defense, drawing, exhibiting or using, § 417.
Serial number or identification mark removed, sale, § 537e.
Sheaths, carrying concealed weapon, § 12025.
Shooting,
   Vehicles on public roads, §§ 246, 247.
Shooting clubs,
   Carrying loaded weapons, § 12031.
   Possession, § 12027.
Signatures,
   Machine guns,
      License application, § 12231.
      Sales, record, § 12250.
   Register of sales, purchaser, § 12076.
Signs, dealers, display, § 12071.
Sniperscope, buying, selling, receiving, concealment, possessing, § 468.
Stolen weapons, return to owner, § 12028.
Streets and alleys, carrying loaded weapon, § 12031.
Target ranges, carrying loaded weapon, § 12031.
Theft, this index.
Third persons, sales, § 12072.
Training,
   Loaded firearms, carrying in prohibited area, § 12031.
   Security guard, certificate, § 12033.
Transporting deadly weapons or destructive devices, § 12303.6.
Unclaimed property, sale or destruction, § 12028.
United States, conviction of federal crimes, concealed weapons, § 12021.
University of California, possession, § 626.9.
Use in commission of misdemeanor or felony, nuisance, § 12028.
Use in fight or quarrel, § 417.
Use to resist arrest, § 834a.
Wallet guns, advertising, § 12020.5.
Watchman, carrying loaded weapons, § 12031.
Wholesale dealers,
   Mail orders, § 12079.
   Register of sale, § 12073 et seq.
Witnesses, sale, § 12076.

WEARING APPAREL
Children and minors, parents liability, § 270 et seq.
Husband and wife, failure to provide for spouse, § 270a et seq.

WELFARE
Social Services, generally, this index.

WHEAT
Arson, § 449a.

WIFE
Husband and Wife, generally, this index.

WILD ANIMALS AND BIRDS
Fish and Game, generally, this index.

WILFULLY
Defined, § 7.

WILLS
Codicils, counterfeiting or forgery, § 470.
Correctional institutions,
   Civil rights, § 2601.
Counterfeiting or forgery, § 470.
Defined, § 7.
Forgery or counterfeiting, § 470.
Prisoners, civil rights, § 2601.
Probate Proceedings, generally, this index.

WINDOW PEEPERS
Disorderly conduct, § 647.

WINDOWS
Arrest, breaking open to effect arrest, §§ 844, 845.
Escapes or rescues, authority to break to retake prisoners upon, § 855.
Search warrants, breaking to,
   Execute warrant, § 1531.
   Liberate person aiding in execution of warrant, § 1532.

WIRES
Poles and Wires, generally, this index.

WIRETAPPING
Arrested persons, telephone calls, § 851.5.

WITNESSES
Generally, § 1321 et seq.
Address, peace officers, testimony, § 1328.5.
Allowances, discretion of court, § 1329.
Asking for bribes, § 138.
Bail,
   Exoneration or release, time elapsed, § 1269.
   Real property equity, determination of value, § 1279.
   Valuation of equity, § 1298.
Bribery, § 136½ et seq.
Children and minors, material witnesses, priority of trial, § 1048.
Civil rules, application in criminal actions, § 1321.
Compelling attendance, § 1326 et seq.
Compensation, § 1329.
Competency, § 1321 et seq.

Penal Code

WITNESSES—Cont'd
Contempt, generally, this index.
Corroboration of testimony, solicitation of commission of certain crime, § 653f.
Counties,
 Court or magistrate out of county, § 1330.
 Fees and expenses, § 1329.
 Jails, detention to secure attendance, § 4000 et seq.
Credibility,
 Comments by judge, § 1093.
Depositions, generally, this index.
Dissuading witness from attending trial, §§ 136, 136½.
Domicile and residence,
 Medical records, production of books and records, appearance outside county of residence, § 1330.
 Prosecution, § 1330.
Expenses, extradition proceedings, payments, state seeking fugitive, § 1557.
Extradition proceedings, expenses of producing witnesses, payment, § 1557.
Fees,
 Amount of fees for day's actual attendance, § 1329.
 Gross salary in lieu of fees, court authorizing payment, § 1329.
Fines and penalties,
 Evidence produced on order, § 1324.
 Refusal to be sworn or to testify, § 1331.
First degree murder, killing to prevent testimony, special circumstance, § 190.2.
Forfeiture,
 Evidence produced on order, § 1324.
Fugitives from justice, return, expenses of producing witnesses, payment, § 1557.
Good cause for non-attendance, § 1331.
Grand Jury, this index.
Gross salary in lieu of witness fees, court authorizing payment, § 1329.
Homicide, prevention of testimony, penalty, § 190.2.
Hospital records, appearance of witness outside county of residence, § 1330.
Husband and Wife, this index.
Indictment and Information, this index.
Influencing testimony, bribery, § 137.
Insane persons, issue, § 1369.
Judge, comments on credibility, § 1093.
Juvenile Delinquents and Dependents, this index.
Material witnesses,
 Attendance outside, County, § 1330.
 Jails, confinement, § 4000 et seq.
 Minors, priority of trial, § 1048.
 Medical records, appearance of witness outside county of residence, § 1330.
Mileage, § 1329.
Moral support, prosecution witnesses, § 868.
Murder, prevention of testimony, penalty, § 190.2.
Necessity, attendance, out of county, § 1330.

WITNESSES—Cont'd
Orders of court,
 Answering of questions or production of evidence, § 1324.
Osteopath's records, appearance of witness outside county of residence, § 1330.
Out of county, attendance, § 1330.
Payments,
 County charges, § 1329.
 Gross salary in lieu of witness fees, court authorizing, § 1329.
Peace officers, address, testimony, § 1328.5.
Penalties,
 Evidence produced on order, § 1324.
 Refusal to be sworn or to testify, § 1331.
Perjury, generally, this index.
Physicians' records, appearance of witness outside county of residence, § 1330.
Post conviction hearing, aggravation or mitigation of punishment, § 1204.
Preliminary Examination, this index.
Preventing witness from attending, §§ 136, 136½.
Privileges and immunities, prosecution, orders compelling testimony, § 1324.
Prosecution, evidence produced on order, § 1324.
Receiving bribes, § 138.
Refusal to be sworn, § 1331.
Search warrants, examination before issuance, § 1526.
Soliciting commission of certain offenses, degree of proof by, § 653f.
Subpoenas, generally, this index.
Traveling expenses, § 1329.

WOLVES
 See, also, Fish and Game, generally, this index.

WOMEN
Abduction, generally, this index.
Abortion, generally, this index.
Cohabitation, receiving money for placing in custody, § 266d.
Family Planning Services, generally, this index.
Jails, this index.
Masculine gender includes, § 7.
Purchase for placing for immoral purposes, § 266e.
Sale, immoral purposes, § 266f.
Seduction, generally, this index.
Support, generally, this index.

WOMEN'S BOARD OF TERMS AND PAROLE
Community Release Boards, generally, this index.

WOOD
Timber and Lumber, generally, this index.

WORDS AND PHRASES
Accessories, § 32.
Accomplice, § 1111.
Accusatory pleading, § 691.

WORDS AND PHRASES—Cont'd
Admission to bail, § 1268.
Aircraft, shooting at aircraft, § 247.
Antique firearms, possession, manufacture or sale of weapons, § 12020.
Armed with a firearm, probation, § 1203.06.
Arrest, § 834.
Arson, § 447a.
Assault, § 240.
Battery, § 242.
Bigamy, § 281.
Bingo, § 326.5.
Blowgun, manufacture, sale, etc., § 12580.
Blowgun ammunition, § 12581.
Book, § 7.
Bribe, § 7.
Burglary, § 459.
Cane gun, possession, manufacture or sale of weapons, § 12020.
Card issuer, credit cards, § 484d.
Cardholder, credit card offenses, § 484d.
Chief administrative officer, campus disorders, § 626.
Child stealing, § 278.
Coin-operated machines, burglar tools, § 466.3.
Community college, disturbance of the peace, § 415.5.
Competent court, jurisdiction, § 691.
Confidential communications, invasion of privacy, § 632.
Conspiracy, § 182.
Corruptly, § 7.
Counterfeiting, § 470.
County, § 7.
 Jurisdiction, § 691.
Credit, bad checks, § 476a.
Credit cards, § 484d.
Custodial officers, cities, local detention facilities, § 831.
Daytime, § 7.
Depose, § 7.
Destructive device, homicide, degree, § 189.
Developmental disability, competency, criminal defendants, § 1370.1.
Directly communicated, interference with school officials or public officers, § 71.
Disorderly conduct, § 647.
Disposes of, fire bombs, § 452.
Distribute,
 Harmful matter, § 313.
 Obscene matter, § 311.
Driving of vehicle, manslaughter, § 192.
Education, Cobey Work Furlough Law, § 1208.
Educator, Cobey Work Furlough Law, § 1208.
Embezzlement, § 503.
Emergency,
 False reports, § 148.3.
Employment, Cobey Work Furlough Law, § 1208.
Exhibit,
 Harmful matter, § 313.
 Obscene matter, § 311.
Expired credit card, § 484d.
Explosives, degree of murder, § 189.

WORDS

WORDS AND PHRASES—Cont'd
Express malice, homicide, § 188.
Extortion, § 518.
Extradition, § 1548.
False imprisonment, § 236.
Fear, robbery, § 212.
Felonies, § 17.
Fire bombs, § 452.
Flechette dart, possession, manufacture or sale of weapons, § 12020.
Forgery, § 470.
Fresh pursuit, § 852.1.
Gift enterprises, lotteries, § 319.
Grand jury, § 888.
Grand theft, § 487.
Harmful matter, § 313.
Implied malice, homicide, § 188.
Incomplete card, credit card offenses, § 484d.
Indictment, grand jury, § 889.
Inferior court, jurisdiction, § 691.
Infractions, § 17.
Inhabited,
  Arson, § 447a.
  Burglary, § 459.
  Weapons discharge, § 246.
Involuntary manslaughter, § 192.
Joint authority, § 7.
Jurisdictional territory, § 691.
Kidnapping, § 207.
Knowingly, § 7.
  Harmful matter, § 313.
  Obscene matter, § 311.
Lawful business, schools, disruption, § 626.8.
Local detention facility,
  Women, personal hygiene and birth control measures, § 4023.5.
Lottery, § 319.
Magistrate, §§ 7, 807, 808.
Malice, §§ 7, 188.
  Homicide, § 188.
Malicious mischief, § 594.
Maliciously, § 7.
Manslaughter, § 192.
Matter,
  Harmful matter, § 313.
  Obscenity, § 311.
Mayhem, § 203.
Mentally disordered sex offenders, registration of offenders, § 290.
Mentally incompetent, trial or punishment for crime, § 1367.
Minor, harmful matter, § 313.
Misdemeanors, § 17.
Month, § 7.
Motor vehicle master key, § 466.5.
Motor vehicle wheel lock master key, § 466.5.
Murder, § 187.
Neglect, § 7.
Negligence, § 7.
Negligently, § 7.
Nighttime, burglary, § 463.
Nunchaku, weapons, § 12020.
Oaths, § 7.
  Perjury, § 119.
Obscene live conduct, § 311.
Obscene matter, § 311.
Ordinance, air pollution, arrest, § 836.5.
Other remedial care, parents medical care obligation, § 270.
Pandering, § 266i.

WORDS AND PHRASES—Cont'd
Peace officer, § 7.
  Assault and battery, §§ 241, 243, 243.2.
    Deadly weapon or force likely to produce great bodily injury, §§ 245, 245.2.
  Authority, etc., § 830 et seq.
  Firearms, exhibiting, § 417.
  Fresh pursuit, § 852.1.
  Incorporation of term into name of nongovernmental organization, § 146c.
Perjury, § 118.
Person, § 7.
  Harmful matter, § 313.
  Invasion of privacy, § 632.
  Obscene matter, § 311.
Person authorized by law to receive a record, criminal records, § 11140.
Personal property, § 7.
Persons of sound mind, § 21.
Petty theft, § 488.
Physical force, obstructing college and university teachers or students, § 602.10.
Pimping, § 266h.
Police radio service communications, § 636.5.
Principal of schools, chief administrative officer, disruption of schools, § 626.
Principals, § 31.
Printing, § 7.
Prior separate prison terms, additional punishment for new offenses, § 667.5.
Process, § 7.
Property, § 7.
Prosecuting attorney, § 691.
Prostitution, disorderly conduct, § 647.
Public moneys, embezzlement or falsification of accounts, § 424.
Publishes, credit cards, § 484j.
Raffle, lotteries, § 319.
Rape, § 261.
Real property, § 7.
Reasonable doubt, § 1096.
Record, criminal records, unlawful furnishing, § 11140.
Remedial care, parents medical care obligation, § 270.
Required number, grand jury, § 888.2.
Retailer, credit cards, § 484d.
Revoked credit card, § 484d.
Riot, § 404.
Robbery, § 211.
Sawed-off shotgun, concealed weapons, § 12020.
School, disruption of schools, § 626.
Seal, § 7.
Search warrant, § 1523.
Section, § 7.
Sniperscopes, § 468.
State, § 7.
  Fresh pursuit, § 852.1.
State college,
  Campus disorders, § 626.
  Disturbance of the peace, § 415.5.
State university,
  Campus disorders, § 626.
  Disturbance of the peace, § 415.5.
Subornation of perjury, § 127.

WORDS AND PHRASES—Cont'd
Subpoena, § 1326.
Taking of bail, § 1269.
Territories, defined, § 7.
Testify, § 7.
Theft, § 484.
Threat of force, witnesses, § 137.
Time spent in a hospital or other facility, commitment of mentally incompetent defendant, § 1375.5.
Unauthorized fire, prisoners in local detention facilities, § 451b.
United States, § 7.
Unlawful assembly, § 407.
Used a firearm, probation, § 1203.06.
Vagrant, annoying or molesting child under eighteen, § 647a.
Vessel, § 7.
Violent felony, additional punishment for new offenses, § 667.5.
Voluntary manslaughter, § 192.
Wallet gun, possession, manufacture or sale of weapons, § 12020.
Wilfully, § 7.
Will, § 7.
Writ, § 7.
Writing, § 7.

WORK FURLOUGHS
Education, this index.
Escape, failure of prisoner to return to place of confinement, § 4530.
Jails, this index.

WORK RELEASE PROGRAMS
Work Furloughs, generally, this index.

WORKERS' COMPENSATION
Correctional Institutions, this index.
Jails, work furlough, medical treatment, § 1208.

WRESTLING
Boxing and Wrestling, generally, this index.

WRITS
Defined, § 7.

WRITTEN INSTRUMENTS
Defined, § 7.

WRONGFUL DEATH
Death, generally, this index.

YOUTH AUTHORITY
Assistant superintendents, institutions, peace officers, § 830.5.
Commitment,
  See, also, Juvenile Delinquents and Dependents, this index.
Declaration of offenses as misdemeanors, § 17.
Misdemeanors, commitment to authority for crime deemed for misdemeanor, § 17.
Mutual aid powers, § 830.5.
Officers and employees,
  Custody of wards, peace officers, § 830.5.
  Powers and duties, § 830.5.

Penal Code

YOUTH AUTHORITY—Cont'd
Parole and probation,
  Revocation or termination, § 1203.2.
Parole officers, peace officer designation, § 830.5.
Peace officers, § 830.5.
Powers and duties,
  Officers and employees, § 830.5.

YOUTH AUTHORITY—Cont'd
Superintendents, institutions, peace officers, § 830.5.
Supervisors, custody of wards and institutions, peace officer, § 830.5.
Transportation officer,
  Peace officer, § 830.5.
  Powers and duties, § 830.5.

YUBA

YREKA, CITY OF
  See, also, Municipalities, generally, this index.
YUBA CITY, CITY OF
  See, also, Municipalities, generally, this index.
YUBA COUNTY
  See, also, Counties, generally, this index.

Index To
VEHICLE CODE

ABANDONMENT OF VEHICLES
Generally, § 22700 et seq.
Colleges and universities, removal, § 22702.
Cost of removal, liability, § 22701.
County or city employees, removal, § 22702.
Foreign registered vehicles, parking violation, impounding, § 22651.
Local ordinances, removal procedures, § 22660 et seq.
Ordinances, removal of abandoned vehicles, etc., § 22660.
Parks, regional park districts, § 22702.
Police, removal, § 22651 et seq.
Presumption of registered owner's liability for abandoning vehicle, § 22701.
Property owner, consent to abandonment on property, § 22700.
Public or private property, vehicles on, consent, § 22700.
Removal of parked or standing vehicles, § 22650 et seq.
Unlicensed vehicles, parking violations, impounding, § 22651.

ACCIDENTS
Arrest,
  Driving under influence of intoxicating liquor and drugs, arrest without warrant, § 40300.5.
  Failure to stop, § 40303.
Assistance to person injured, duty, § 20003.
Costs, removal of debris, § 17300.
Crimes and offenses, failure to stop, § 20001.
Debris, tow car equipment, § 27700.
Driver, identification of accident, § 20006.
Driverless vehicle, § 20002.
Driving hours, limitation, § 21702.
Duty of driver to stop, § 20001.
Financial responsibility, § 16000 et seq.
Grease, covering with dirt, § 27700.
Identification of driver, § 20006.
Information, striking unattended vehicle, § 20002.
Information and aid by driver, duty, § 20003.
Investigations, § 2412.
Notice,
  Property damage, written notice posted on property, § 20002.
  Traffic violations, § 40600 et seq.
Option of officer to take arrested person before magistrate, § 40303.
Property damage,
  Duty of driver, § 20002.
  Option of officer to take arrested person before magistrate, § 40303.

ACCIDENTS—Cont'd
Public agencies, civil liability, § 17004 et seq.
Records, engineering and traffic survey, § 627.
Reports, §§ 16000 et seq., 20002.
  Attorneys, disclosure, § 20012.
  Certificate of making, § 20013.
  Common carrier, § 20009.
  Confidential or privileged information, § 20012.
  Death or personal injuries, §§ 20001, 20004.
  Department of motor vehicles, confidential use, § 20012.
  Disclosure of contents, § 20012.
  Driverless vehicles, § 20002.
  Evidence, § 20013.
  Financial responsibility, § 16000 et seq.
  Physical inability to make, § 20010.
  Property damage, § 20002.
  Runaway vehicles, § 20002.
  Supplemental reports, § 20009.
  Use of, § 16005.
  Witnesses, § 20009.
    Disclosure, § 20012.
Runaway vehicle, § 20002.
Tow car drivers, duties, § 27700.
Traffic Rules and Regulations, this index.
Unattended vehicle, § 20002.

ACCOMPLICES AND ACCESSORIES
Speed contest or exhibition on highway, § 23109.
  Arrest, procedure, § 40303.

ALCOHOLIC BEVERAGES
Bus passengers, § 23125.
Campers, §§ 23123, 23125.
Drinking in motor vehicles, § 23121 et seq.
Driving while intoxicated,
  Drivers' Licenses, this index.
  Traffic Rules and Regulations, this index.
Open bottles, § 23122 et seq.
Personal possession of vehicle occupant, § 23122.
  Minor, 23123.5.
Possession by persons under 21 years, § 22123.5.
Presence in vehicle, § 23123.
  Clergymen, § 23125.
  Medicinal purposes, § 23125.
Storage of open container in motor vehicle, § 23123.
Taxicab passengers, § 23125.
Traffic Rules and Regulations, this index.

AMBER LIGHTS
See Lights and Lighting, generally, this index.

APPROVED LIGHTING EQUIPMENT
Lights and Lighting, generally, this index.

AREA REFLECTORIZING MATERIAL
Generally, § 25500.

ARM SIGNALS
Regulations, §§ 22110, 22111.

ARRAIGNMENT
Traffic Rules and Regulations, this index.

ARREST
Driver's Licenses, this index.
Juvenile Delinquents and Dependents, this index.
Quota, § 41602.
  Peace officers, § 41600.
Traffic Rules and Regulations, this index.

ATTORNEYS
Accident reports, disclosure, § 20012.
Appearance under written promise, sufficiency, § 40507.
Traffic Rules and Regulations, this index.

AUTOMOBILE INSURANCE
Motor Vehicle Insurance, generally, this index.

BACKING VEHICLE
Traffic rules and regulations, § 22106.

BACK–UP LAMPS
Generally, § 24606.

BAIL
Written notice, § 40309.5.

BEAM INDICATOR
Equipment, requirement, § 24408.

BELTS
Safety Belts, generally, this index.

BICYCLES
Generally, § 21200 et seq.

BLOOD TESTS
Generally, §§ 13353, 13354, 23126.

BRAKES
Generally, § 26450 et seq.

BREATH TESTS
Drunken driving, §§ 13353, 13354, 23126.

BRIDLE PATHS AND TRAILS
Traffic rules and regulations, right-of-way, § 21805.

Vehicle Code

BUMPERS
Damage control, § 34715.

CAMPERS
Exit requirements, § 23129.
Signalling device, § 28080 et seq.

CHILDREN AND MINORS
Alcoholic beverages, possession by person under 21 years, § 23123.5.
Arrested persons, place of appearance, § 40502.
Driver's Licenses, this index.

CITATION
Defined, § 41061.
Peace officer arrest quota, § 41603.
Traffic Rules and Regulations, this index.

CLEARANCE AND SIDE MARKER LAMPS
Vehicles 80 inches or more in width, § 25100.

COASTING
Traffic control, coasting down grade in neutral, § 21710.

COMPLAINT
Arrest for misdemeanor or infraction, filing with magistrate, § 40306.
Traffic Rules and Regulations, this index.

CRIMES AND OFFENSES
Generally, §§ 23101 et seq., 40000.1 et seq., 42000 et seq.
Accidents, Duties, §§ 20001, 20002.
Acquittal, defense in criminal prosecution, § 41400.
Altered or defaced identity numbers, §§ 10750, 10751.
Arrest, generally. Traffic Rules and Regulations, this index.
Climbing into vehicle with intent to commit, § 10853.
Conviction of crime, § 42000 et seq.
  Intoxicating liquor, driving under the influence, §§ 23101, 23102.
  Jurisdiction, speed traps, § 40805.
  Reckless driving, §§ 23103, 23104.
  Striking unattended vehicle, failure to stop, etc., § 20002.
Counsel for accused, chemical tests for alcohol in blood, breath or urine, § 13353.
Defaced or altered identification numbers, §§ 10750, 10751.
Defenses,
  Entitled use of drugs, § 23107.
  Prosecutions for code violations, § 41400 et seq.
Discharge of firearms at vehicle or occupant, § 23110.
Disobedience to officer, § 2800.
Disregard for siren and flashing light, § 2800.
Drivers' Licenses, this index.
Emergency Services Act, violation required by governor's order or directive, § 41402.
Employer's responsibility, § 40001 et seq.
  Arrest of driver, misdemeanor, § 40005.

CRIMES AND OFFENSES—Cont'd
Exhaust systems violating noise regulations or standards, business of selling or installing, § 27150.1.
Failure to pay fine, § 40508.
Failure to stop at accident involving property damage, § 20002.
False information, giving, § 31.
False information to peace officer, § 40000.5.
False or fictitious name, signing written promise to appear after arrest, § 40504.
Firearms, discharge at vehicle or occupant, § 23110.
Firemen, failure to obey orders, § 40000.7.
Guilty plea, evidence, reports of witnesses or police, § 40806.
Hiking trails, operation of unauthorized motor vehicles, § 23127.
Identification cards, § 40000.7.
  Alteration, § 13004.
Identification numbers, altered or defaced, §§ 10750, 10751.
Infractions, generally, this index.
Injuring or tampering with vehicle, §§ 10852, 10853, 40000.9.
Inspection, failure to submit, §§ 2800, 40000.7.
Lamp and brake testing stations, § 40000.11.
Malicious mischief, § 40000.9.
Notice to appear,
  Equipment violations, § 40150.
  Owner's and employer's responsibility, § 40002.
Numbers, altering or defacing identification numbers, § 40000.9.
Odometers, § 28050 et seq.
Orders, failure to obey lawful order, § 40000.7.
Owner's responsibilities, § 40000.25.
Refusal to display license, § 12951.
Registration, this index.
Release on promise to appear, violation of promise, § 40508.
Scrap metal processing facilities, purchasing vehicles subject to registration, § 40000.5.
Second and subsequent offenses,
  Driving when operating privileges suspended or revoked, § 14601.
  Garbage and refuse, littering, § 42001.7.
  Infractions, § 42001.
  Peace officers' training penalty assessments, § 42050 et seq.
Signatures, false signatures, § 40000.25.
Snowmobiles, operation, § 23128.
Speed contest or exhibition on highway, § 23109.
Stored vehicles, unlawful use, § 40000.9.
Suspended drivers, §§ 14601, 14601.1.
  Violations, § 40000.11.
Tampering with or injuring vehicle, §§ 10852, 10853, 40000.9.
Theft, generally, this index.
Throwing substance at vehicle or occupant, § 23110.
Traffic Rules and Regulations, this index.

DRIVER

CRIMES AND OFFENSES—Cont'd
Traffic Signs and Signals, this index.
Unlicensed driver, § 12500.
Venue, change, traffic violations, § 40517.

DEFACING
Identification mark or number, §§ 10750, 10751.

DON'T WALK SIGNALS
Pedestrian traffic control, § 21456.1.

DOOR HANDLES
Notice of parking or standing violation, attachment to handle, § 41103.

DOORS
Opening, restrictions, § 22517.
Reflectorizing devices or materials, § 25105.

DOUBLE JEOPARDY
Crimes and offenses, defenses to prosecution, § 41400.

DOUBLE LINES
Driving restrictions, § 21460.

DRIVER'S LICENSES
Generally, § 12500 et seq.
Accompanying licensed driver, instruction permits, § 12509.
Age, § 12502 et seq.
  Children and minors, issuance of license, § 12512.
  Instruction permits, § 12509.
  Limitation, § 12512.
  Minors' licenses, § 12507.
  Nonresidents, § 12502 et seq.
  Persons accompanying minor driver, § 12509.
  Persons under age of 18, § 12512.
Alteration, fraud, display or possession, § 14610.
Arrest,
  Failure to exhibit, optional appearance before magistrate, § 40302.
  Procedure, § 40303.
  Production in court, § 12951.
Crimes and offenses, § 40001.
  Alteration of license, § 14610.
Domicile and residence,
  Generally, § 12505.
  Children and minors, § 12504.
  Establishing residence in state, § 12505.
  Exemptions, § 12502.
  Foreign jurisdiction license, § 12502.
  Foreign vehicles, unlicensed persons, § 12503.
Driver training, completion of course, § 12509.
Driving on highway without license, § 12500.
Driving when license suspended, etc., § 14601.
  Arrest, procedure, § 4303.
Duplicate licenses, lost, destroyed or mutilated license, § 12815.
Examination, termination of suspension, mental or physical condition, § 13102.
Failure to display, § 40000.11.

777

DRIVER

DRIVER'S LICENSES—Cont'd
False or fraudulent license, use of minor, § 15501.
Instruction permits, § 12509.
Juveniles committed to youth authority, revocation or suspension, § 41500.
Labor and employment, medical certificate, § 14606.
Limited term, § 12508.
Machinery and equipment, agricultural machinery and equipment, exemption, § 12501.
Minors, § 15500.
More than one license, possession, § 12511.
Motorized bicycles, § 12509.
Nolo contendere, conviction under plea, suspension or revocation, § 13103.
Operation without license, §§ 12500, 40000.11.
Paroled convict, revocation or suspension, § 41500.
Period of operating in state without license, § 12505.
Permitting unlicensed minor to drive, § 14607.
Residence, § 12505.
Revocation, § 13101.
Temporary license, § 12506.
Possession, § 12951.
Violation of restrictions, § 14603.

DRIVING WHILE INTOXICATED
Traffic Rules and Regulations, this index.

EARPLUGS
Wearing while operating motor vehicle, § 27400.

EMERGENCY VEHICLES
Civil liability, exemptions, § 17004.
Defined, code, § 165.
Duty to drive with due regard for safety, § 21807.

ENGINEERING AND TRAFFIC SURVEY
Defined, code, § 627.
Speed limits, changing, § 22358.3 et seq.

EQUESTRIAN CROSSINGS
Signs and signals, § 21805.

EQUIPMENT
Air pollution control devices, § 27156.
Clearance and side-marker lamps, vehicles 80 inches or more in length, § 25100.
Color, lamps, § 25106.
Cowl or fender lamps, § 25106.
Horns, § 27000.
Lights and Lighting, generally, this index.
Mirrors, § 26709.
  Obstructed view, application of law, § 26708.
Noise limits, § 23130.
Nonconforming equipment, sale, replacement, etc., § 24005.
Notice, vehicle not equipped as required, § 24004.
Pollution control devices, § 27156.

EQUIPMENT—Cont'd
Rear trunk lid handle, windows, obstruction of view, § 26708.
Reflectors,
  Generally, §§ 24608, 24609.
  Front and side, § 24608.
  Red, rear mounting, § 24607.
Sirens, § 27002.
Tinted glass, § 26708.5.
Tires, generally, this index.
Unsafe or not equipped, generally, § 24002.
Windshields, generally, this index.

EVASION OF ARREST
Option of officer to take arrested person before magistrate, § 40303.

EVIDENCE
Generally, § 40800 et seq.
Abandonment of vehicle, prima facie evidence, § 22701.
Accident reports, § 20013.
Blood tests, driving while intoxicated, §§ 13353, 13354, 23126.
Breath tests, driving while intoxicated, §§ 13353, 13354, 23126.
Defenses, prosecution, § 41400 et seq.
Department action, § 40807.
Driving while intoxicated, blood tests, etc., § 23126.
Illegal evidence, § 40800 et seq.
Incompetency, obtained by maintenance or use of speed traps or failure to wear uniform, etc., § 40804.
Presumptions, § 41100 et seq.
  Abandonment, liability, § 22701.
Urine tests, driving while intoxicated, §§ 13353, 13354, 23126.
Written notice, motor vehicle violation causing accident, probable cause, § 40600.

EXHAUST SYSTEM
Noise standards, § 27150.1 et seq.

EYEGLASSES
Lateral vision, glasses interfering with, temple width, § 23120.

FEDERAL LAW
Generally, § 41401.

FELONY
Crimes and Offenses, generally, this index.
Procedure, § 40301.

FICTITIOUS DOCUMENTS
Limitation of prosecutions, § 40004.

FIRE EXTINGUISHERS
Tow truck equipment, § 27700.

FOOTRESTS
Motorcycles, equipment, § 27800.

FORGERY
Arrested person, release on promise to appear, § 40504.
Certificate of ownership, etc., § 4463.
Drivers' licenses, fraudulent alteration, § 14610.
Limitation of prosecutions, filing of forged documents, § 40004.

Index

FREEWAYS
Accidents, reporting, standing, stopping or parking vehicle, § 22520.
Disabled vehicles, removal, § 22654.
Pedestrians, arrest, refusal to leave freeway, § 40303.
Tow trucks, stopping on freeways, § 22520.

FUSEES
Red light required, § 25305.

GLASS
Tinted glass, § 26708.5.

HEADSETS
Wearing while operating vehicle, § 27400.

HEARINGS
Abatement and removal, abandoned, etc., local ordinances, § 22660 et seq.

HIGHWAY PATROL
Abandoned vehicles, powers and duties, § 22702.
Emergency vehicles, § 165.
False personation, § 40000.5.
Notice, written notice, motor vehicle violations as cause of accident, § 40600.
Removal of vehicles,
  Hit-and-run accidents, § 22655.
  Railroad right-of-way, § 22656.

HIGHWAY PATROL, DEPARTMENT OF
Inspection of loads to prevent theft, § 2810.
Organization, § 2100.
Traffic direction, § 2100.

HIGHWAYS AND ROADS
Parks, speed limit, local authorities, § 22358.3.
Snowmobile operation, § 23128.

HITCHHIKING
Arrest, refusal to leave freeway, overpass or bridge, § 40303.

HORNS
Generally, § 27000.
Warning, mountain driving, § 21662.

HOURS
Driving, limitation, § 21702.

IDENTIFICATION CARDS
Aged persons, § 13000.
Alteration, § 13004.
Crimes and offenses, §§ 13004, 40000.11.
Documentary evidence of age and identity of applicant, § 13000.

IDENTITY AND IDENTIFICATION
Alteration of vehicle marks, § 40000.9.
Arrest, traffic violator, detention to determine identity, § 40307.
Destruction of vehicle marks, § 40000.9.

INFRACTIONS
See, also, Crimes and Offenses, generally, this index.

Vehicle Code

INFRACTIONS—Cont'd
Abandoning vehicle, § 42001.5.
Arrest, procedure, § 40306.
Complaint, § 40306.
Contempt, violation of court order impounding license on failure to pay fine, § 40508.
Defined, § 40000.1.
Fines and penalties, § 42001.
Release on own recognizance, § 40306.
Second and subsequent offenses, § 42001.
Traffic Rules and Regulations, this index.

INJURING VEHICLE
Generally, §§ 10852, 10853, 40000.9.

INSPECTION AND INSPECTORS
Failure to submit, violations, § 40000.7.

INSTALLATION
Exhaust systems violating noise regulations and standards, crimes and offenses, § 27150.1.

JUSTICE, STATE DEPARTMENT OF
Stolen vehicles, reports, § 10500 et seq.

JUVENILE DELINQUENTS AND DEPENDENTS
Traffic offenses, suspension or revocation, § 13100 et seq.

LICENSE PLATES
Alteration, destruction, etc., §§ 4463, 10750.
Altered plate, display, § 4464.
Certification, request by political subdivisions for issuance, attorney general, § 5001.
Duplicates, § 4457.
Loan or use, § 4461.
Lost or stolen plates, § 4457 et seq.
Notice, § 4458.
Reports, § 10500 et seq.
Police seizing, § 4460.
Vehicle other than one for which issued, § 4457.

LIGHTS AND LIGHTING
Generally, §§ 24250 et seq., 24400, 40151.
Arrest, refusal to stop and submit to inspection or test, § 40303.
Authorized equipment, § 24003.
Back up lamps, § 24606.
Beam distance, requisites, § 25951.
Boat trailers, clearance lamps, § 25100.
Candle power, spot lamps, § 24404.
Color, § 25950.
Cornering lamps, § 25107.
Courtesy lamp, § 25105.
Cowl lamps, § 25106.
Display, red flag or cloth on wide vehicles, § 25104.
Dome lights, § 24003.
Door mounted courtesy lamps, § 25105.
Equipment, generally, this index.
Fusees, generally, this index.
Height, mounted, lamps and reflectors, § 25952.

LIGHTS AND LIGHTING—Cont'd
Parking lamps, § 24800.
Pilot indicators, § 25108.
Red flag or cloth, display on wide vehicles, § 25104.
Running lamps, § 25950.
Turn signal system, § 24950.

LIMIT LINE
Defined, code, § 377.

MALICIOUS MISCHIEF
Generally, § 40000.9.

MISDEMEANORS
Crimes and Offenses, generally, this index.
General, vehicle code, § 42002.

MOTOR VEHICLE, DEPARTMENT OF
Business and transportation agency, department part of agency, § 1500.

MOTOR VEHICLE INSURANCE
Accident reports, § 16000 et seq.
Confidential information, § 16005.

MOTORCYCLES
Crimes and offenses, exhaust systems violating noise regulations and standards, business of selling or installing, § 27150.1.
Footrests and handgrips for passengers, § 27800.
Handlebars, height, § 27801.
Helmets, safety, regulations establishing specifications and standards, § 27802.
Instruction permits, § 12509.
Lights and lighting,
  Headlamps, § 25650.5.
  Taillamps, energy storing system, § 24253.
Mirrors, § 26709.
Mufflers, § 27150.
Multiple-beam headlamp, § 25651.
Noise limits, § 23130.
Traffic Rules and Regulations, generally, this index.
Turn signals, § 24951.

MUD GUARDS
Generally, § 27600.

MUFFLERS
Generally, § 27150 et seq.
Construction and maintenance in gastight condition, § 27154.
Cutout or bypass, § 27150.
Gases, exhaust gases, directing from vehicle, § 27152.
Installation, etc., non-conforming mufflers, § 24005.
Modification to amplify or increase noise, § 27151.
Noise limits, § 23130.

NOLO CONTENDERE
Notice, accidents, § 40603.

NOTICE TO APPEAR
Copy, § 40505.
Filing, § 40506.
Time to appear, § 40501.

NUISANCE
Removal of parked or standing vehicles, local ordinances, § 22660 et seq.

NUMBERS AND NUMBERING
Altering or defacing identifying numbers, § 40000.9.

OCCUPANTS OF VEHICLES
Lighted cigarette, etc., throwing upon highway, § 23111.
Throwing substance, etc., at, punishment, § 23110.

ODOMETERS
Advertisements, device for resetting, § 28051.5.
Disconnection, § 28050.5.

OFF-HIGHWAY VEHICLES
Generally, § 38280 et seq.

OFFICIAL TRAFFIC CONTROL DEVICE
Defined, traffic signs and signals, § 440.

OFFICIAL TRAFFIC CONTROL SIGNAL
Defined, traffic signs and signals, § 445.

OIL AND GAS
Operation to prevent excessive escape of residue, § 27153.

OWNERS AND OWNERSHIP
Consent, take or drive vehicle, subsequent taking effect, § 10851.
Crimes and offenses, § 40000.25.
Defined, incidents, § 460.
Non-ownership affidavit, parking violations, notice, § 41103.

PEACE OFFICERS
Arrest, generally. Traffic Rules and Regulations, this index.
Arrest quotas, § 41600 et seq.
Compliance with orders, etc., of on vehicular crossings, § 23253.
Crimes and offenses, disobedience of lawful order, § 2800.
Defined, motor vehicle violations, written notice, § 40600.
Demotion, arrest quotas, use in determining, § 41603.
Emergency vehicles, vehicles operated by state park system or school district security patrol peace officer personnel, § 165.
False information, obstructing justice, § 31.
Members of highway patrol, § 2409.
Notice, vehicle in unsafe condition, § 24004.
Orders, disobedience, § 2800.
Promotion, use of arrest quota in determining, § 41603.
School districts, security patrols, § 165.

PEACE

PEACE OFFICERS—Cont'd
State park system, emergency vehicles, § 165.
Written notice, motor vehicle violation as cause of accident, probable cause, § 40600.

PEACE OFFICERS TRAINING PENALTY ASSESSMENTS
Generally, § 42050 et seq.

PEDESTRIANS
Arrest, pedestrians zone, freeways, overpasses or bridges, § 40303.
Fines and penalties, infractions, § 42001.
Traffic Rules and Regulations, this index.
Traffic Signs and Signals, this index.

POLICE
Traffic Rules and Regulations, generally, this index.

POSSESSION
Alcoholic beverages, persons under 21 years, § 23123.5.

PRIMA FACIE SPEED LIMITS
Traffic Rules and Regulations, this index.

PRIVATE PROPERTY
Removal of vehicles, damages, § 22658.

PROBABLE CAUSE
Written notice of motor vehicle violations, § 40600.

QUOTA
Arrest quotas, peace officers, § 41600 et seq.

RADIAL TIRES
Inner tubes, § 27455.

RAILROADS
Right-of-way, motor vehicles, removal, § 22656.

REAR WINDOWS
Defects, § 26710.
Obstruction of view, § 26708.

REARVIEW MIRRORS
Generally, § 26709.
Obstruction of view, § 26708.

RECKLESS DRIVING
Traffic Rules and Regulations, this index.

RECUT OR REGROOVED TIRES
Defined, sales and use, §§ 27460.5, 27461.

RED FLAGS
Generally, § 25104.
Loads, projecting, § 25104.

REFLECTORS
Generally, §§ 24608, 24609.
Front and sides, § 24608.
Red, rear mounting, § 24607.

REGISTRATION
Generally, § 4000 et seq.

REGISTRATION—Cont'd
Certificate, stolen, lost, damaged, § 4459.
Commercial vehicles, § 4454.
Display, vehicle other than one for which issued, § 4462.
Duplicates, § 4457.
Examination, presentation to peace officer, § 4462.
Facsimile copy, display in vehicle, § 4454.
Forgery, alteration, etc., § 4463.
Loan or use prohibited, § 4461.
Seizure by department or highway patrol, § 4460.
Signature and visibility, § 4454.
Stolen, lost, mutilated or illegible, § 4457.

RELEASE ON PROMISE TO APPEAR
Traffic Rules and Regulations, this index.

REMOVAL
Abandonment of Vehicles, this index.
Nuisance, prohibited sign, signal, etc., § 21467.

REMOVAL OF PARTS
Lighting equipment or device on direction of officer making inspection, § 40151.

REMOVAL OF VEHICLES
Procedure, § 22650 et seq.
State police, § 22659.

RIGHT OF WAY
Traffic Rules and Regulations, this index.
Traffic Signs and Signals, this index.

RUBBISH VEHICLES
Generally, § 23115.

RULES OF THE ROAD
Generally, § 21001.
Traffic Rules and Regulations, generally, this index.

RUNNING LAMPS
Front of vehicle, § 25109.

SAFETY
Unsafe condition, defined, modification of vehicle, § 24008.5.

SAFETY BELTS
Driver training schools and driver education, § 27304.

SAFETY CHAINS
Towing vehicles, § 29004.

SCHOOL BUSES
Tires, tread depths, application of law, § 27465.

SEARCHES AND SEIZURES
Documents and plates, § 4460.

SHOVELS
Tow cars, duty to carry, § 27700.

SKIING
Motor vehicles pulling skiers, § 21712.

SNOW TIRES
Generally, §§ 27459, 27460.

SNOWMOBILES
Unlawful operation, § 23128.

SPEED
Traffic Rules and Regulations, this index.
Traffic Signs and Signals, this index.

SPEED TRAPS
Generally, § 40801 et seq.
Defined, evidence, § 40802.
Jurisdiction, § 40805.

TELEVISION AND RADIO
Television receivers in vehicles, § 27602.

TEMPORARY REGISTRATION
Registration, this index.

TESTS
Brakes, stopping distance requirements, § 26456.
Mechanical condition and equipment, § 2814.
Stopping distance, brakes, § 26456.

THEFT
Generally, § 10851 et seq.
False report, § 10501.

TIRE CHAINS
Generally, §§ 27454, 27459.

TIRES
Inner tubes, radial tires, § 27455.
Standards, § 27500.

TOW TRUCKS
Freeway, stopping on freeways, § 22520.
Lights and lighting, utility flood or loading lamps, § 25110.
Reflectors, additional reflectors, § 24607.
Stoplamps, additional stoplamps, § 24603.
Taillamps, additional taillamps, § 24600.

TOYS
Riders, motor vehicles towing toy vehicles carrying riders, § 21712.

TRAFFIC RULES AND REGULATIONS
Generally, § 21000 et seq.
Accidents,
  Arrest, failure to stop, § 40303.
  Crimes and offenses, § 20002.
  Notice of violations, § 40600 et seq.
Alleys, right-of-way, entering or crossing highway from, § 21804.
Animals, application of traffic laws to persons riding or driving, § 21050.
Appearances,
  Failure to appear, § 40000.25.
  Failure to pay fine, § 40000.25.
Approaching riders, duties, § 21759.
Approaching vehicles,
  Emergency vehicles, § 21806.
  Lights, adjustment, § 24409.
  Mountain driving, § 21662.
  Narrow roadways, § 21661.
  Right of way, § 21800 et seq.
  Right side, passing, § 21660.
Arraignment,
  Failure to appear,
    Forfeiture of bail, § 40512.
    Warrant for arrest, § 40514.
  Scheduling, § 40519.

Vehicle Code

TRAFFIC

**TRAFFIC RULES AND REGULA-
TIONS**—Cont'd
Arrest, § 40300 et seq.
  Felony, § 40301.
  Detention, delay to determine identity, § 40307.
  Misdemeanors, § 40306.
  Notice to appear, form, § 40500.
  Offenses not specified in code, highway patrol members, § 40304.
  Pedestrians, refusal to leave freeway, overpass or highway, § 40303.
  Quotas, peace officers, § 41600 et seq.
  Release,
    Misdemeanors and infractions, custody, § 40306.
    Nonresident from custody, § 40305.
  Release on promise to appear,
    Refusal to give promise, § 40302.
    Violation of promise, § 40508.
  Violation of promise to appear, § 40508.
    Notice to department, § 40509.
    Prisoners, nonprosecution, § 41500.
  Warrants,
    Other violations, § 40311.
    Service,
      Highway patrol authority, § 2411.
    Without warrant, § 40300.
      Driving under influence of liquor or drugs, § 40300.5.
Attorneys,
  Appearance, sufficiency under written promise, § 40507.
  Chemical tests for alcoholic content of blood, § 13353.
Backing vehicle on highway, safety, § 22106.
Bail,
  Amount fixed by magistrate, § 40511.
  Appearance,
    Deposit prior to date, § 40510.
    Filing complaint on failure, § 40513.
    Forfeiture for failure, §§ 40512, 40512.5.
    Persons authorized to receive, § 40502.
  Assessments, special penalties,
    Driver training penalty assessments, § 42050 et seq.
    Peace officer training penalty assessment, § 42050 et seq.
  Check, § 40521.
  Deposits, § 40519.
  Forfeiture,
    Forwarding by mail, § 40521.
  Mail and mailing, § 40309.
  Payment, form, § 40521.
Bicycles, § 21200 et seq.
  Rights and duties of persons riding, application of law, § 21050.
Blood tests, drunken driving, evidence, § 23126.
Brakes, setting, § 22515.
Breath tests, drunken driving, evidence, § 23126.
Bridle path designation, § 21805.
Business or residence districts,
  Commercial vehicles, parking, standing or stopping, § 22502.

**TRAFFIC RULES AND REGULA-
TIONS**—Cont'd
Business or residence districts—Cont'd
Defined,
  Business district, § 235.
  Determination, § 240.
  Overtaking and passing, § 21754.
  Turning, § 22102.
Caravans or motorcades, spacing, § 21705.
Clearance and side-marker lamps, vehicles 80 inches or more in width, § 25100.
Coasters, towing coasters carrying riders, § 21712.
Coasting down grade in neutral, prohibited, § 21710.
Crimes and offenses, § 40000.15.
  Crossing, school crossing guard, disobedience, § 40000.7.
  Exhibitions of speed, highways, § 40000.15.
  Exhaust system sales, § 40000.15.
  Explosives, § 40000.19.
  Flammable liquids, § 40000.19.
  Hazardous materials, § 40000.21.
  Height of vehicle or load, § 40000.7.
  Length of vehicle or load, § 40000.7.
  Loads and loading, § 40000.7.
  Off-highway vehicles, § 40000.24.
  Parking, handicapped persons, facilities, placards, § 22507.8.
  School crossing guard, disobedience, § 40000.7.
  Throwing, substances at vehicles, § 40000.15.
  Traffic school, failure to attend, § 40000.25.
  Trespassing, § 40000.15.
  Width of vehicle or load, § 40000.7.
Crosswalks, right of way, § 21950.
Deposit or throwing of glass, etc., on highway likely to injure animal, § 23112.
Divided highways, § 21651.
Drawbars,
  Length, § 29005.
  Towing vehicles, § 29003 et seq.
Driving while intoxicated, §§ 13353 et seq., 23101.
  Arrest, without warrant, § 40300.5.
  Blood tests, etc., administration, §§ 13354, 23126.
  Combined influence of liquor and drugs, § 23102.
  Counsel, right to, chemical tests, tests of blood, breath or urine, § 13353.
  Driver improvement or treatment program, reduction in fine upon completion, § 23102.
  Driving upon other than highway, § 23102.
  Felony, § 23101.
  Fines and penalties, reduction upon completion of driver improvement or treatment program, § 23102.
  Misdemeanor driving, § 40000.15.
  Tests to determine alcohol content of blood, breath or urine, §§ 13354, 23126.

**TRAFFIC RULES AND REGULA-
TIONS**—Cont'd
Driving while under influence of drugs, §§ 23101 et seq., 23105, 23106.
  Arrest, § 40302.
  Bodily injury, § 23106.
  Conviction, absolution or striking, § 23105.
  Driver improvement or treatment program, reduction in fine upon successful completion, § 23105.
  Drivers' licenses, driving after revocation or suspension of license, § 14601.
  Driving upon other than highway, §§ 23102, 23105, 23106.
  Fines and penalties, §§ 14601, 23105.
    Bodily injuries, § 23106.
    First offense, §§ 14601, 23105.
  Misdemeanor driving, § 40000.15.
Earplugs, wearing while operating motor vehicle, § 27400.
Emergency vehicles, exemption from traffic law, conditions, § 21055.
Engineering and traffic survey,
  Defined, § 627.
  Speed limits, § 22354 et seq.
Entering public highway via service road, § 21652.
Equipment,
  Clearance and side-marker lamps, vehicles 80 inches or more in width, § 25100.
  Reflectors,
    Front and sides, § 24608.
    Red, rear mounting, § 24607.
Equipment unsafe, § 24002.
Evidence, § 40800 et seq.
  Presumptions, § 41100 et seq.
    Parking violations, owner's responsibility, §§ 41102, 41103.
Explosives, crimes and offenses, § 40000.19.
Fines and penalties, § 40000.15.
  Deposit applied, § 40519.
  Failure to appear or pay, § 40000.25.
  Pedestrians, § 42001.
Fire hoses, driving over, § 21708.
Flags, wide vehicles, § 25104.
Flammable liquids, crimes and offenses, § 40000.19.
Following too closely, § 21703.
Following vehicles,
  Caravan or motorcade, § 21705.
  Dimming lights, § 24409.
  Distance, reasonable and prudent, § 21703.
  Overtaking and passing, § 21750 et seq.
  Two-lane highways, slow-moving vehicles, § 21656.
Fusees, stalled vehicle or traffic hazard, § 25305.
Garbage and refuse, § 23112.
Grade,
  Crest, driving on left side of roadway, § 21752.
  Descending, truck-tractor, etc., speed, determination, § 22407.
  Parking, blocking wheels, § 22509.
  Passing, speed of vehicles, § 21758.

TRAFFIC

TRAFFIC RULES AND REGULATIONS—Cont'd

Handicapped persons,
  Local parking or standing regulations, § 22507.5.
  Parking spaces, exclusive use, designation, § 21458.
Hazardous materials, transportation, crimes and offenses, § 40000.21.
Hazards, red fusees, § 25305.
Headsets, wearing while operating motor vehicle, § 27400.
Height, § 35250.
  Crimes and offenses, § 40000.7.
Highway patrol,
  Railroad right-of-way, § 22656.
  Removal of vehicles,
    Hit-and-run accidents, § 22655.
Hitchhiking, § 21957.
Horns, use of, § 27001.
Horse drawn vehicles, drivers approaching, duties, § 21759.
Horseback rider, yielding right-of-way to, § 21805.
Infractions, § 42000 et seq.
Inspection and inspectors, stickers, § 2814.
Interference with driver, § 21701.
Intersections,
  Approaching,
    Driving on left side, § 21752.
    Entrance, stopping vehicle, § 22450.
  Left turns,
    Right hand lane, exception, § 21654.
    Yielding right-of-way, § 21801.
  Permitting pedestrian to cross roadway, § 21951.
  Prima facie speed limit, traversing, § 22352.
  School bus, passing, § 22454.
  Stopping, standing or parking vehicle within, § 22500.
  Yielding right of way, § 21451.
    Driver on left on entering, § 21800.
    Emergency vehicles, §§ 21806, 21807.
    Turning left at intersection, § 21801.
Lanes,
  Explosives, § 21655.
  Heavy vehicles designation, § 21655.
  Left-turn lanes, two-way lanes, § 21460.5.
  Roadway divided into three lanes, § 21659.
  Speed limits, § 22364.
  Travel at reduced speeds, § 21655.
Lawyers. Attorneys, generally, ante.
Leaving public highway via service road, § 21652.
Leaving scene of accident, § 20001.
  Arrest, procedure, § 40303.
Left turns, § 21650.
Length, vehicles or combinations, § 25400 et seq.
Lights and lighting,
  Color fusees, § 25305.
  Display, etc., blinding or dazzling light, § 21466.
  Emergency vehicles,
    Lighted red lamp, § 21055.
    Right-of-Way, §§ 21806, 21807.
  Taillamps remaining operative, § 24253.

TRAFFIC RULES AND REGULATIONS—Cont'd

Lights and lighting—Cont'd
  Towing vehicles, clearance and side-marker lamp, § 25100.
  Vision impairing lights, § 21466.5.
Limit line, defined, § 377.
Limitation on driving hours, § 21702.
Local authorities, parking exemptions, § 22507.
Locked vehicle, duty, § 22516.
Misdemeanors, § 20002.
Motorcycles, parking, § 22502.
Mountain highways, § 21662.
Multiple-lane highways, traffic moving in one direction, § 21658.
Notice to appear, violations involving accidents, written notice, § 40604.
Obstructing traffic,
  Minimum speed limits, § 22400.
  Removal of vehicles, § 22650 et seq.
  Stopping, standing or parking vehicles, § 22500 et seq.
Obstruction of driver's view or control over driving mechanism, § 21700.
  Loads and loading, § 26709.
  Windshields and rear windows, defective condition, § 26710.
One-way roadways, § 21650.
  Designation of lanes or part of roadway, § 21657.
  Driving on right half of roadway, exemption, § 21650.
  Overtaking and passing, § 21754.
  Parking, § 22502.
On-ramp exit, § 21664.
Overtaking and passing, § 21750 et seq.
  One-way street, § 21754.
  Right side of roadway, §§ 21650, 21654.
  Conditions, § 21755.
  Two lane highway, § 21751.
  Vehicles proceeding in opposite directions, § 21660.
    Grade, yielding right-of-way, § 21661.
  Vehicles proceeding in same direction, §§ 21750, 21751.
  Speed, overtaken vehicle, § 21753.
  View obstruction, § 21752.
Parking, § 22500 et seq.
  Fire hydrants, § 22514.
  Meter zones, § 22508.
  One-way roadway, § 22502.
  Railroad track, § 22521.
  School bus stops, § 22405.
  Tow cars, § 22513.
  Two or three-wheeled vehicles, § 22503.5.
Pedestrians,
  Crossing between signals, § 21955.
  On roadway, § 21956.
  Outside crosswalks, § 21954.
Permits, handicapped persons or residents of high-density multiple-family dwelling areas, § 22507.5.
Private property, removal of vehicles, § 22653 et seq.
Projecting loads,
  Lights, § 25103.
    Red lights or red flag, § 24604.
Public nuisance, prohibited signs, signals, etc. removal, § 21467.

TRAFFIC RULES AND REGULATIONS—Cont'd

Radiator ornaments, § 27601.
Railroad crossings, removal of vehicles, § 22656.
Reckless driving, § 23103.
  Arrest procedure, § 40303.
  Bodily injuries, punishment, § 23104.
  Punishment, § 40000.15.
  Snowmobiles, § 23128.
Red flags, wide vehicles, § 25104.
Red lights,
  Emergency vehicles, § 21055.
  School buses, § 22112.
Reflectors, §§ 24607, 24608.
Registration renewal, failure to pay parking offense bail, § 4760 et seq.
Riders, towing bicycles, sleds, etc., carrying riders, § 21712.
Riding on vehicles, restrictions, § 21712.
Right of way, § 21800 et seq.
Right side of roadway, § 21654.
Right turns, flashing lights, § 21454.
Roller skates, towing skaters, § 21712.
Safety zones, driving over, § 21709.
Sidewalk,
  Driving on, § 21663.
  Right of way, § 21952.
Size of vehicles, etc., § 35100 et seq.
Snowmobiles, unlawful operation, § 23128.
Speed, §§ 22348, 22349 et seq.
  Alleys, § 22352.
  Bridges and structures.
    Limit revision, § 22404.
    Local, § 22403.
    Violations, § 22405.
  Charged, § 40503.
  Contests and exhibitions, highways, § 40000.15.
  Freeway increase of limit, § 22355.
  Local authorities, setting speed limit, § 22358.3.
  Prima facie speed limits,
    Narrow streets, public parks, § 22358.3.
    Public parks, narrow streets, § 22358.3.
  Schools, decrease of local limits near, § 22358.4.
  Snow or ice, restrictions because of, § 22363.
  Variable limits, § 22355.
  Violation of speed law, § 22351.
  Visibility, due regard for, § 22350.
  Weather, due regard for, § 22350.
  Width of highway, due regard for, § 22350.
Speed traps, § 40801 et seq.
Spilling loads, § 23114.
Stopping,
  Signal required, § 22109.
  Train crossing, § 22451.
Television, § 27602.
Tires, fastened in front of vehicle, length limitations, § 35413.
Towing vehicles, unsafe, § 21711.
Tunnel, right of way, § 21953.
U-turns, two-way left-turn lanes, § 21460.5.
Violations, handicapped persons, facilities, § 22507.8.

Vehicle Code   **YOUTH**

TRAFFIC RULES AND REGULATIONS—Cont'd
Warrants, violations involving accidents, § 40600.
Yielding right of way,
   Descending grade, § 21661.
   Through highways, § 21802.

TRAFFIC SIGNS AND SIGNALS
Arrow, green, § 21454.
Crossings,
   Equestrian crossings, designation, § 21805.
   Pedestrians, § 21456.1.
Definitions,
   Official traffic control devices, § 440.
   Official traffic control signals, § 445.
Evidence,
   Presumptions,
      Speed restriction signs, corrections, § 41100.
      Validity, § 41101.
Failure of driver to obey unlawful, § 21461.
Fines and penalties, § 21461.
Flashing signals, green arrow replaced by flashing red or yellow signals, § 21454.
Green arrow, § 21454.
Illegal operation, § 21463.
Left turn, flashing signal, § 21454.

TRAFFIC SIGNS AND SIGNALS—Cont'd
Lights and lighting,
   Flashing signals,
      Obedience, § 21457.
      Red lamps, school bus, § 22112.
         Stopping, § 22454.
      Impairing driver's vision, § 21466.5.
Limit line, defined, § 377.
Pedestrians, walk signals, § 21456.1.
Red lights, § 21453.
Reflectorizing material, use, § 25500.
Right turns,
   Arm and hand signals, § 22111.
   Duration of signal, § 22108.
Signals,
   Timing of, § 22401.
   Train, § 22451.
Stop light, § 21453.
Turning movements, § 22107.
Unauthorized devices, § 21465.
Yellow flashing lights, replacement of green arrow, § 21454.
Yellow light, § 21452.

TRAFFIC SURVEY
Engineering and traffic survey, defined, § 627.

TURN SIGNALS
Flashing lights, § 24953.
Motorcycles, § 24951.

VEHICLE CODE
Synopsis, § 1656.
Uniformity, § 21.

WINDSHIELDS
Generally, § 26700.
Windshield wipers, § 26707.

WORDS AND PHRASES
Bumpers, motor vehicles, § 28071.
Citation, peace officers arrest quota, § 41601.
Driver, § 305.
Infractions, §§ 40000.1, 40000.3.
May, defined, § 15.
Peace officer, motor vehicle violations, written notice, § 40600.
Right of way, § 525.
Roadway, § 530.
Shall, defined, § 15.
Sidewalk, § 555.
Stop or stopping, § 587.
Street, § 590.
Vehicle, § 670.

WORN TIRES
Sale or use, § 27465.

YOUTH AUTHORITY
Driver's licenses, suspension or revocation, juveniles committed to youth authority, § 41500.

Index To

HEALTH AND SAFETY CODE

CONTROLLED SUBSTANCES
  Generally, § 11000 et seq.
  Drugs and Medicine, this index.

DRUG ADDICTS
  Control of controlled substances users, § 11550 et seq.
  Controlled Substances Act, § 11000 et seq.
  Controlled substances offenders registration, § 11590 et seq.
  Methadone maintenance program, arrested persons, program continuance, § 11222.
  Registration, controlled substances offenders, § 11590 et seq.
  Uniform Controlled Substances Act, § 11000 et seq.

DRUGS & MEDICINE
  Abatement, nuisances, controlled substances, § 11570 et seq.
  Abuse of controlled substances educational programs, § 11600 et seq.
  Actions and proceedings,
    Abatement of nuisance, controlled substances, § 11570 et seq.
    Forfeiture proceedings, controlled substances violations, § 11491 et seq.
  Addicts. Drug Addicts, generally, this index.
  Aircraft, controlled substances violations, seizure and disposition, §§ 11470 et seq., 11490 et seq.
  Boats, controlled substances violations, seizure and disposition, §§ 11470 et seq., 11490 et seq.
  Certificates and certification, reports accuracy, perjury, § 11105.
  Children and minors,
    Adult using minor as agent, § 11380.
    Furnishing controlled substances to minor, § 11380.
    Inducing controlled substances violations, §§ 11354, 11371, 11371.1.
  Contempt, controlled substances, nuisances, § 11580.
  Control of controlled substances users, § 11550 et seq.
  Controlled substances,
    Abatement of nuisances, § 11570 et seq.
    Adults using minor as agent, § 11380.
    Alteration of prescriptions, § 11368.
    Children and minors,
      Inducing violations, § 11371.1.
      Phencyclidine, fines and penalties, § 11380.5.
    Control of users, § 11550 et seq.
    Counterfeit, controlled substances, sale or furnishing, § 11382.

DRUGS & MEDICINE—Cont'd
Controlled substances—Cont'd
  Definitions, § 11101 et seq.
  Enforcement, peace officers, immunity from prosecution, § 11367.
  Forfeitures, § 11470 et seq.
  Forgery of prescriptions, § 11368.
  Fraud, § 11371.1.
    Obtaining by fraud, § 11371.1.
    Obtaining or attempting to obtain, § 11173.
    Prescriptions, § 11130.
    False names or addresses, §§ 11157, 11174.
  Furnishing to minors, § 11380.
  Imports phencyclidine, § 11379.5.
  Injecting or smoking, paraphernalia, possession, § 11364.
  Manufactures, § 11379.
    Identification, § 11382.5.
    Phencyclidine, § 11379.5.
    Sales, recipients, known unlawful use, § 11104.
  Nuisances, abatement, § 11570 et seq.
  Offenses and penalties, § 11350 et seq.
  Perjury, reports, certifying accuracy, § 11105.
  Pharmacists, phencyclidine, prescriptions to minors, § 11380.5.
  Pharmacy records, § 11205 et seq.
  Phencyclidine, fines and penalties, § 11378.5 et seq.
  Possession,
    Designated controlled substances, §§ 11350, 11351.
    Injecting or smoking paraphernalia, § 11364.
    Methylamine and phenyl-2-propanone, intent to manufacture methamphetamine, § 11383.
    Piperidine and cyclohexanone, possession with intent to manufacture phencyclidine, § 11383.
  Sale, § 11378.
  Unauthorized possession, § 11377.
  Prescriptions, § 11150 et seq.
    Alteration or forgery, § 11368.
    Copies of prescriptions, § 11195.
    Official blanks, § 11161 et seq.
    Pharmacy records, § 11205 et seq.
    Prescriber's records, § 11190 et seq.
    Violations, § 11371.
  Refilling prescriptions, § 11200.
  Registration of offenders, § 11590 et seq.
  Reports,
    Certifying accuracy, perjury, § 11105.
    Theft, logs and discrepancy reports, § 11103.
    Transferor reports, manufacturers, wholesalers, retailers, etc., § 11100 et seq.
  Sales, § 11379.

DRUGS & MEDICINE—Cont'd
Controlled substances—Cont'd
  Sales—Cont'd
    Counterfeit controlled substances, § 11382.
    Designated controlled substances, fines and penalties, § 11352.
    Employment or use of minors, controlled substances violations, fines and penalties, § 11353.
    Fines and penalties, § 11379.
    Furnishing substances falsely represented to be controlled substances, § 11355.
    Heroin,
      Fines and penalties, § 11352.5.
    Marijuana, § 11360.
      Possession for sale, § 11359.
    Phencyclidine, § 11379.5.
      Possession, § 11378.5.
      Possession for sale, § 11378.
    Recipients, unlawful use, § 11104.
    Searches and seizures, § 11470 et seq.
    Seized and forfeited property, § 11355.
    Substances falsely represented to be controlled substances, § 11355.
    Without prescription, § 11250 et seq.
  Schedule I substances, § 11054.
  Schedule II substances, § 11054.
  Schedule III substances, § 11056.
  Schedule IV substances, § 11057.
  Schedule V substances, § 11058.
  Schedules, § 11053 et seq.
  Search and seizures, §§ 11470 et seq., 11490 et seq.
  Standards and schedules, § 11053 et seq.
  Surrender of prescription privilege, § 11155.
  Tests, use of controlled substances, §§ 11551, 11552.
  Transfer reports, manufacturers, wholesalers, retailers, etc., § 11100 et seq.
  Transportation, § 11379.
  Use of substances,
    Sales to recipient, known unlawful use, § 11104.
Controlled Substances Act, § 11000 et seq.
Dangerous drugs,
  Defined,
    Controlled substances, § 11001 et seq.
Discrepancies, controlled substances, reports, § 11103.
Education, controlled substances violation, probation condition, §§ 11373, 11376.

Health and Safety Code — DRUGS

DRUGS & MEDICINE—Cont'd
Forfeitures, controlled substances, § 11470 et seq.
Fraud, false or fictitious prescription, § 11157.
Gifts, designated controlled substances, fines and penalties, § 11352.
Injecting paraphernalia, controlled substances, possession, § 11364.
Lists, controlled substances, standards of schedule, § 11053 et seq.
Losses, controlled substances, reports, § 11103.
Manufacturers and manufacturing,
  Fines and penalties, § 11379.
  Identification, controlled substances, § 11382.5.
  Transferor reports, § 11100 et seq.
Marijuana, §§ 11000 et seq., 11357 et seq.
  Destruction, possession, arrest, and conviction records, §§ 11361.5, 11361.7.
Methadone maintenance program, arrested persons, program continuance, § 11222.
Motor vehicles, controlled substances violations, seizure and disposition, §§ 11470 et seq., 11490 et seq.
Nuisance, controlled substances, § 11570 et seq.
Offenses and penalties, §§ 11350 et seq., 11372, 11374.
  Adult inducing controlled substances violations by minors, § 11353.
  Adult using minor as agent, § 11380.
  Aliens, arrest, notice to federal agency, § 11369.
  Counterfeit controlled substances, sale or furnishing, § 11382.
  Fraud, § 11371.1.
  Furnishing controlled substances to minor, § 11380.
  Inducing controlled substances violations by minors, § 11371.
  Maintaining places for furnishing or using drugs, § 11366.
  Marijuana, § 11357 et seq.
  Methylamine and phenyl-2-propanone, possession with intent to manufacture methamphetamine, §§ 11383, 11384.
  Opening places for furnishing or using drugs, § 11366.

DRUGS & MEDICINE—Cont'd
Offenses and penalties—Cont'd
  Paraphernalia for controlled substances injecting or smoking, possession, § 11364.
  Phencyclidine, §§ 11378.5, 11379.5.
    Children and minors, § 11380.5.
  Possession of designated controlled substances, § 11350.
  Sale, § 11351.
  Prescriptions,
    Alteration or forgery, § 11368.
    Violations, § 11371.
  Probation,
    Condition, education or treatment, § 11376.
    Controlled substances violations, § 11370.
  Recipients, sales to, known unlawful use, § 11104.
  Registration of controlled substances offenders, § 11590 et seq.
  Reports, certifying accuracy, perjury, § 11105.
  Substances falsely represented to be controlled substances, sale or furnishing, § 11355.
  Suspension of sentence, controlled substances violations, § 11370.
  Transportation, sale, giving away, etc. of designated, controlled substances, §§ 11352, 11379.
  Unauthorized possession controlled substances, § 11377.
  Visitation, places for smoking or using drugs, § 11365.
Opium pipes, possession, fines and penalties, § 11364.
Order of court, continuation of orders and regulations under prior law, § 11651.
Perjury, reports, certifying accuracy, § 11105.
Pharmacy records, substances, § 11205 et seq.
Phencyclidine,
  Offenses and penalties, § 11378.5 et seq.
  Schedule II controlled substances, § 11055.
Records and recordation,
  Pharmacy records, controlled substances, § 11205 et seq.
  Prescriber's records, controlled substances prescription, § 11190 et seq.

DRUGS & MEDICINE—Cont'd
Registration of controlled substances, offenders, § 11590 et seq.
Research, use of controlled substances, detection, § 11554.
Research advisory panel, § 11478 et seq.
Retailers, sales, known unlawful use by recipient, § 11104.
Sales,
  Nuisance abatement, removal and sale of property, § 11581 et seq.
  Substances falsely represented to be controlled substances, fines and penalties, § 11355.
  Without prescriptions, § 11250 et seq.
Schedule I controlled substances, § 11054.
Schedule II controlled substances, § 11055.
Schedule III controlled substances, § 11056.
Schedule IV controlled substances, § 11057.
Schedule V controlled substances, § 11058.
Schedules, controlled substances, listings, §§ 11053 et seq., 11490 et seq.
Searches and seizures, controlled substances, §§ 11470 et seq., 11490 et seq.
Smoking paraphernalia, controlled substances, possession, § 11364.
Standards, controlled substances, lists, § 11053 et seq.
Theft, controlled substances, reports, § 11103.
Transportation, designated controlled substances, fines and penalties, § 11352.
Treatment, controlled substances violations, probation condition, §§ 11373, 11376.
Treatment control units, controlled substances, § 11560 et seq.
Uniform Controlled Substances Act, § 11000 et seq.
Users of controlled substances, control, § 11550 et seq.
Wholesalers, sales, known unlawful use by recipient, § 11104.

Index To
BUSINESS AND PROFESSIONS CODE

ALCOHOLIC BEVERAGES
Bringing into prison, jail or reformatory, § 25603.
False evidence of age and identity, selling or furnishing, § 25660.5.
Use and possession, § 25661.
Minors,
    Entering and remaining on premises, § 25665.
    Possession by, § 25662.
    Selling or furnishing to, § 25658.
Sales to intoxicated person, § 25602.

CONSUMER AFFAIRS, STATE DEPARTMENT OF
Authorization for department, § 100.

CONSUMER AFFAIRS, STATE DEPARTMENT OF—Cont'd
Boards, function of, § 108.
Investigators, peace officers, § 160.
Licenses,
    Disqualifying acts, § 480 et seq.
    Fraudulent use of, § 119.

DANGEROUS DRUGS
Defined, § 4211.
Possession without prescription, § 4230.

DRUGS
See Dangerous Drugs, this index.

FALSE ADVERTISING
See Weights and Measures, this index.

HYPODERMIC SYRINGES AND NEEDLES
Unlawful possession, § 4143.

LICENSES
Authority for regulation, § 16000.

PRESCRIPTION
See Dangerous Drugs, this index.

WEIGHTS AND MEASURES
False advertising, § 12024.6.
Misrepresentation, § 12024.1.
Short quantity, § 12024.
Untrue value, § 12024.2.

Index To
WELFARE AND INSTITUTIONS CODE

ALCOHOLISM
Admission, detoxification treatment facility, § 5172.1.
Application, treatment and evaluation of inebriates, § 5170.
Apprehension officers, wearing apparel and vehicle markings, § 5153.
Arrest, detention for evaluation and treatment, § 5170 et seq.
Civil protective custody, § 5170 et seq.
Commitment, § 5001 et seq.
Detention for treatment, § 5170 et seq.
Detoxification facilities, § 5170 et seq.
Evaluation and treatment services, § 5001.
Intensive treatment, chronic alcoholics, § 5172.
Mental Health Act, legislative intent, § 5001.
Priorities and preferences, voluntary patients in evaluation facilities, § 5171.
Temporary conservatorship, chronic alcoholics, appointment for, § 5172.

APPEAL AND REVIEW
See, also, Social Services, this index.
Conservatorship for gravely disabled persons, § 800.
Juvenile court judgments, decrees or orders, § 800.

ARREST
Alcoholism, evaluation and treatment, § 5170 et seq.

ATTORNEYS
Juvenile Delinquents and Dependents, this index.

CONFIDENTIAL OR PRIVILEGED INFORMATION
Juvenile delinquents and dependents, §§ 827, 828.
Libel or slander suits, opening sealed records, § 781.
Libel and slander proceedings, juvenile delinquents and dependents, opening of sealed records, § 389.

CONFISCATION
Mentally deficient and mentally ill persons, firearms in possession, § 8102.

CORRECTIONS, DEPARTMENT OF
Narcotic detention, treatment and rehabilitation facility, § 3001.

COUNTERFEITING
Food stamps, § 18910.

CRIMES AND OFFENSES
Arrest, generally, this index.
Counsel for accused, juvenile delinquents, § 625.

CRIMES AND OFFENSES—Cont'd
Final disposition, victims of crime, notification, § 742.
Firearms, certificate of competency to possess, § 8103.

DETENTION
Juvenile Delinquents and Dependents, this index.

DETENTION HEARING
Juvenile courts, § 630.

DISCRIMINATION
Youth authority, members, sex, § 1711.

DOUBLE JEOPARDY
Juvenile court, certification of proceedings, § 604.

DRUG ABUSE
Narcotic addict, defined, § 3009.
Public policy, § 3000.

DRUG ADDICTS
Children and minors,
  Care and treatment, § 350.
  Evaluation and treatment, § 359.

EVIDENCE
Juvenile delinquents and dependents, detention hearing, § 635.
Libel and slander proceedings, juvenile delinquents and dependents, opening of sealed records, § 781.

FORMER JEOPARDY
Juvenile court, certification of proceedings, § 604.

FRAUD
Food stamps, § 18910.
Medi-Cal beneficiary, false personation, § 14026.
Mentally deficient and mentally ill persons, involuntary treatment, false statements, § 5150.

HOME SUPERVISION
Establishment of program, § 840.

JEOPARDY
Juvenile court, certification of proceedings, § 604.

JUVENILE COURTS
Generally, § 245 et seq.
Appearance citation, § 338.
Attorney representing minor, continuing representation, § 318.
Calendar,
  Detention hearing calendar, §§ 311, 630.
  Priorities of hearings, §§ 245, 675.
Citation, issuance and service, § 661.

JUVENILE COURTS—Cont'd
Continuance, § 638.
Criminal prosecution prohibition, § 606.
Declaration of unfitness of minor, § 707.1.
Detention hearing calendar, § 311.
Dismissal, petition for treatment or rehabilitation, § 390.
Handicapped persons, jurisdiction, § 300.
Hearings, continuance, §§ 352, 354.
Informal atmosphere, § 680.
Jurisdiction, § 607.
Libel and slander proceedings, opening of sealed records, § 389.
Limitation of prosecutions, suspension, § 605.
Mentally deficient and mentally ill persons, minors, jurisdiction, § 300.
Order,
  Detention criteria, § 636.
  Home supervision criteria, § 636.
  Removal of minor on public assistance, copy to social service official to cause reduction, § 363.
  Retention of minor by parent and subsequent finding of unfit home, § 364.
Petition, dismissal, § 782.
Petition for treatment or rehabilitation dismissal, § 390.
Proceedings, details, § 653.
Sessions, § 345.
Superior court, § 245.
Termination of jurisdiction, destruction of records, § 826.5.
Venue, § 327.

JUVENILE DELINQUENTS AND DEPENDENTS
Admissibility of evidence, § 355.
  Social study, § 358.
Admission of public or interested persons to hearings, §§ 346, 676.
Adult, treatment as, fitness hearing, § 707.
Adult institutions, detention or sentence of juvenile, § 208.
Adverse or pecuniary interest, parent or guardian and child, appointment of counsel, § 317.
Advisory arbitration, grievance procedure, state wards, § 1766.5.
Affidavits, commencement or proceedings, § 329.
Age,
  Jurisdiction of juvenile court, §§ 360, 361.
  Misrepresentation, § 631.1.
  Release from custody, §§ 313, 314.
  Temporary custody, § 305.

JUVENILE

JUVENILE DELINQUENTS AND DEPENDENTS—Cont'd

Age limits,
  Misrepresentation, release from custody, §§ 631, 631.1.
  Temporary custody, § 625.
Alternative proceedings, temporary custody, § 626.
Appeal and review, §§ 395, 800.
  Commitment orders, delay in execution, § 737.
  Failure to file petition by probation officers, §§ 331, 655.
  Grievance procedure, state wards, § 1766.5.
Appearance, § 626.
  Calendar, continuing hearing, dependent child, § 366.
  Citations, § 338.
  District attorney, purpose, §§ 351, 681.
  Probation officer, appearance before, written promise, § 629.
  Promise, § 307.
    Custody, release condition, § 310.
    Failure to perform promise, § 214.
  Reappearance order, § 323.
Arbitration, grievance procedure, state wards, § 1766.5.
Arrest, § 340.
  Information, disclosure, § 828.
  Parent or guardian, § 339.
  Record of detention as record of arrest, § 206.
  Warrant of arrest,
    Minor, § 663.
    Parent or guardian, § 662.
Attorney general, grievance procedure, report, § 1766.5.
Attorneys, §§ 349, 625, 679.
  Advising of rights, § 353.
  Appointment, § 679.
    Advising minor rights, §§ 625, 627.5.
    Compulsory appointment, § 634.
    Detention hearings, § 634.
  Appointment by court, §§ 318, 349, 353.
  Dependent child, hearing continuance, § 366.
  Detention hearings, §§ 316, 317, 633, 634.
  District attorney, § 351.
  Inspection of petition and reports, § 827.
  Notice of hearing, §§ 312, 630.1.
    Commencement of proceedings, §§ 335, 658.
    Information supplied, §§ 336, 659.
  Petition, copy to attorney, §§ 335, 658.
  Probation officers, advising of constitutional rights, § 627.5.
  Prosecuting attorney, duties, § 681.
  Representation of minor, district attorney, § 351.
  Service of notice and copy of petition on, §§ 337, 660.
  Telephone communication, §§ 308, 627.
  Waiver, intelligent waiver of right, § 634.
Calendar, appearance, continued hearing, dependent children, § 366.
Certification to juvenile court, § 604.

JUVENILE DELINQUENTS AND DEPENDENTS—Cont'd

Certified mail, notice of hearing and copy of petition, § 337.
Change of circumstance, modification of order, § 388.
Changes of circumstance, modification of order, § 778.
Citations, appearance, § 338.
Commencement of proceedings, § 325 et seq.
Commitment,
  Custody and care, § 362.
  Delays, execution of order, periodic review, § 367.
  Modification of order, § 387.
  Shelter-care facility, § 731.
Commitment papers, § 735.
Commitments to youth authority, § 731.
  Acceptance, § 1731.5.
  Age determination, §§ 1731, 1731.5.
  Conditions, § 734.
  Criminal court, evaluation and report prior to sentence, § 707.2.
  Delay in execution of order, periodical review of case, § 737.
  Determination of age, §§ 1731, 1731.5.
  Discharge of persons, § 1769.
  Grievance procedure, § 1766.5.
  Incorrigible persons, § 1737.1.
  Juvenile court, return of person to committing court, § 1737.1.
  Modification of order, §§ 367, 387, 730, 777, 779.
  Probation, revocation and termination, § 1731.5.
  Resentencing, § 1737.
  Return of person to committing court, § 1737.1.
  Review pending execution of order of commitment, delayed execution of order, § 737.
  Suspension, § 1737.
  Term of confinement, § 731.
  Termination of probation, § 1731.5.
  Terms of confinement, designated offenses, § 1769.
Conduct of proceedings, § 680.
Confession, denial, § 355.
Confidential information, §§ 827, 828.
Confrontation of witnesses, §§ 311, 630, 702.5.
Constitutional rights, advising minor, §§ 625, 627.5.
Contents of petition, § 656.
Continuance, § 682.
  Further evidence, § 702.
  Social study, § 702.
Control of minor by parent, limiting, §§ 361, 726.
Control proceedings, § 680.
Counseling centers, § 654.
Counseling programs, § 362 et seq.
Court orders, effect, § 203.
Criminal complaints, misrepresentation of age preventing timely filing, release from custody, §§ 631, 631.1.
Criminal court, commitments to youth authority, § 707.2.
Crisis resolution homes, § 654.
Cross-examination of witnesses, §§ 311, 630, 702.5.

JUVENILE DELINQUENTS AND DEPENDENTS—Cont'd

Custody, §§ 356, 626, 627, 726.
  Order of court, § 362.
  Parent or guardian,
    Modification of order, § 387.
    Notice, § 308.
    Removal, § 361.
  Period of detention, § 320.
Definitions,
  Department of probation, § 215.
  Physical confinement, § 726.
  Probation officer, § 215.
Delay, release from custody, reports, §§ 313, 631.
Delivery of minor to custody by officer taking custody, § 626.
Destruction of records, § 826.
Detention, §§ 207, 320.
  Adult institutions, § 208.
  Circumstances and gravity of alleged offense, §§ 635, 636.
  Dismissal of petition, §§ 702, 707.
  Pending adjudication of petition to change previous order of detention, § 777.
Detention facilities,
  Nonsecure criteria, § 636.2.
  Segregation, § 206.
  Separation from adults, § 208.
Detention hearing, §§ 311, 632.
  Absence of parent and guardian, § 637.
  Continuance, §§ 638, 682.
  Control and conduct of proceedings, § 680.
  District attorney, participation, §§ 351, 681.
  Evidence, § 635.
  Examination, § 635.
  Examination of minor before release, § 319.
  Home supervision, § 628.1.
  Indigent minors, appointment of counsel, § 634.
  Information supplied minor and parent, § 316.
  Nature of proceedings, informing minor and parents, § 633.
  Notice, § 630.
  Period of detention, § 320.
  Presence of minor and interested parties, § 659.
  Reappearance order, §§ 323, 639.
  Reasons for custody, informing minor and parents, § 633.
  Rehearing, § 637.
  Self-incrimination, privilege against, §§ 311, 630.
  Service of petition and notice, §§ 311, 630.
  Speedy detention hearing, § 315.
  Time, §§ 315, 657.
  Witnesses, right of confrontation and cross-examination, §§ 311, 630.
Detention hearing calendar, § 311.
Dismissal, unverified petition to commence proceedings, § 656.5.
Disposition of case, custody information, disclosure, § 828.
Disposition order, § 706.
  Evidence, § 358.

Welfare and Institutions Code   **JUVENILE**

JUVENILE DELINQUENTS AND DEPENDENTS—Cont'd
District attorney,
  Copy of petition, § 658.
    Notice of hearing, § 658.
    Participation in proceedings, § 681.
  Representation of minor, § 681.
Documents, inspection, § 827.
Drug addicts, care and treatment, § 330.
Due process, grievance procedure, state wards, § 1766.5.
Educational centers, § 654.
Escape, § 871.
  Custody of minor after, advising of constitutional rights, § 625.
  Detention, §§ 635, 636.
Evidence,
  Admissibility of evidence, § 355.
  Disposition of minor, § 358.
  Libel and slander proceedings, opening of sealed records, § 389.
  New evidence, modification of order, § 388.
  Objections to evidence, § 355.
  Prima facie case, request for evidence, § 637.
  Reports, behavioral patterns and social history, fitness hearing, § 707.
  Social study, admissibility, § 358.
  Weight, insufficiency, § 355.
Examination, conditions of release, § 319.
Explaining petition, § 353.
Federal law violators, § 602.
Filing of petition, § 650.
Findings, §§ 356, 702.
  Order for detention, § 636.
Fitness hearings, considerations, § 707.
Forms,
  Notice of hearing, §§ 366, 659.
  Petition,
    Commence proceedings, § 656.
    Modification of order, § 778.
Grievance procedure, state wards, § 1766.5.
Habitual truant, § 601.
  Segregated facilities, § 206.
Handicapped persons, custody by juvenile probation office, § 309.
Hearings, § 345 et seq.
  Admission of public and persons having interest, § 346.
  Attorneys, appointment by court, § 318.
  Commitment or placement change, § 387.
  Conduct of proceedings, § 350.
  Continuance, §§ 352, 354, 682.
    Further evidence, § 356.
    Notice, § 366.
    Social study, § 356.
  Control and conduct of proceedings, § 680.
  District attorney, attendance, §§ 351, 681.
  Evidence, § 355.
    Prima facie case, request by attorney, § 637.
  Findings, § 702.
  Fitness hearings, considerations, § 707.
  Grievance procedure, state wards, § 1766.5.

JUVENILE DELINQUENTS AND DEPENDENTS—Cont'd
Hearings—Cont'd
  Inspection of records, § 827.
  Modification of order, § 388.
  Presence of minor and interested parties, §§ 349, 679.
  Reading petition, § 353.
  Sessions, § 345.
  Time, § 657.
Illness, temporary custody by peace officer, § 305.
Indigent juveniles,
  Attorneys,
    Appointment, §§ 625, 679.
    Detention hearings, § 634.
Inspection, sealed records, § 781.
Interrogation of minor, advising of right to presence of counsel, §§ 625, 627.5.
Investigations,
  Child needing court's protection, § 652.
  Temporary custody of minor, § 628.
Investigations and investigators, commencement of proceedings, § 329.
Judgments, §§ 360 et seq., 725 et seq.
  Modification, §§ 385 et seq., 775 et seq.
Jurisdiction, §§ 300, 301.
  Termination, petition and hearing, § 388.
Jurisdictional hearing, § 657.
Mail,
  Dependent child hearing continuance, notice, § 366.
  Notice of hearing and copy of petition, § 337.
Medical, surgical or dental care, § 309.
Mentally Deficient and Mentally Ill Persons, this index.
Misrepresentation of age, release from custody, §§ 313, 314.
Modification, judgments and orders, § 775 et seq.
Notice,
  Appearance in juvenile court, § 626.
  Attorney representing minor, hearings, § 312.
  Certification of proceedings to juvenile court, § 604.
  Continuance, hearings, § 366.
  Custody, § 308.
  Custody of minor, § 627.
  Detention hearing, §§ 311, 630.
    Absence of notice to parent or guardian, § 637.
  Filing of supplemental petitions, § 777.
  Form, § 366.
  Hearing, § 335.
  Modification of order, §§ 386, 388.
  Objections to evidence, § 355.
Order of court,
  Detention,
    Pending adjudication of petition to change prior detention order, § 387.
    Periodic review, § 367.
  Effect, § 203.
Parent or guardian, custody, § 308.
Parental control limitations, § 361.
Pending adjudication of petition to change previous order of detention, § 387.

JUVENILE DELINQUENTS AND DEPENDENTS—Cont'd
Personal service, notice and copy of petitions, § 337.
Petitions,
  Commencement of proceedings, filing, §§ 325, 337.
    Failure to file, § 331.
    Supervision program, failure to participate, § 654.
    Time, custody of child, § 311.
  Custody change, § 387.
  Dismissal, § 390.
    Unverified petition to commence proceedings, § 656.5.
  Felonies, specifying, § 656.1.
  Jurisdiction, termination, § 388.
  Misdemeanors, specifying, § 656.1.
  Misrepresentation of age preventing timely filing, § 314.
  Modification of order, § 388.
  Records, sealing, § 389.
Place of detention, § 207.
  Notice, § 627.
Placement with relative, § 281.5.
Presence of persons at sessions, § 345.
Records, § 825 et seq.
  Arrest, detention record as record of arrest, § 206.
  Delay in release, § 313.
  Destruction, § 826.
  Detention order, § 320.
  Inspection, § 827.
  Sealing, §§ 389, 781.
Representation of ward or dependent, § 280.
School attendance review board, failure of parents to respond, § 601.2.
Segregated facilities, § 206.
Self-incrimination, §§ 630, 702.5.
  Privilege against, detention hearings, § 311.
Sheltered-care facilities,
  Commitments, § 731.
  Placement, § 654.
Social study, §§ 280, 358.
Stay of proceedings, § 395.
Subpoenas, §§ 341, 664.
Supervision orders, § 362.
Telephone calls, right of minor taken into custody, § 308.
Temporary custody, §§ 305 et seq., 625 et seq.
  Release by probation officer, § 628.
Temporary custody to parents, guardian or relative, § 307.
Time,
  Detention hearing, § 315.
  Hearing, § 334.
Truants,
  Habitual, referral to school attendance review board, § 601.1.
  Segregated facilities, § 206.
Venue, §§ 327, 651.
Warrant of arrest,
  Minor, § 663.
  Parent or guardian, § 662.
Warrants,
  Arrest of minors, § 340.
  Parent or guardian, § 339.
Weight and sufficiency of evidence, § 355.

JUVENILE

JUVENILE DELINQUENTS AND DEPENDENTS—Cont'd
Witnesses, confrontation and cross-examination, § 311.
Work programs, § 731.

JUVENILE HALLS
Generally, § 850 et seq.

JUVENILE INSTITUTIONS AND SCHOOLS
Homes, ranches, camps,
    Establishment, § 881.
    Maximum population, § 886.
Juvenile halls, § 850 et seq.
    Conduct, § 851.
    School facilities, § 856 et seq.
Juvenile homes, ranches and camps, terms of confinement, §§ 726, 731.

JUVENILE PROBATION OFFICERS
Deputies and assistants, powers of peace officers, § 283.
Home supervision, duties, § 841.
Investigations, § 281.
    Court protection, § 328.
    Temporary custody of minor, § 309.
Peace officer, powers, § 283.
Presence in court, § 280.
Program of supervision, § 330.
Protection of minor, retaining temporary custody, § 309.
Recommendations, § 280.
    Dependent child hearing, continuance, § 366.
    Disposition of case, § 281.
Records, sealing, § 389.
Release of minor,
    Forty-eight hours limitation, § 313.
    Promise to appear, § 310.
    Temporary custody, § 309.
Reports,
    Bureau of criminal statistics, § 285.
    Delay in release of minor, § 313.
    Dependent child hearing, continuance, § 366.
    Disposition of case, § 281.
Sealing records, § 389.
Social studies, juvenile before court, § 280.

MENTALLY DEFICIENT OR MENTALLY ILL PERSONS
Accomplices and accessories, escape, § 7326.
Actions and proceedings, involuntary treatment, false statements, § 5150.

MENTALLY DEFICIENT OR MENTALLY ILL PERSONS—Cont'd
Appeal and review, safeguard of rights, § 5001.
Counties, 72 hour treatment for inebriates, § 5176.
Detention, §§ 5157, 5171.
Emergency treatment, exemption from liability, §§ 5154, 5173.
Equal protection, § 5004.
Evaluation, treatment, care under 72 hour facility, § 5152.
Notice, escape, § 7325.
Poor and indigent, treatment by peace officers, § 6800.
Probable cause, involuntary treatment, § 5150.
Records, concealable weapons, § 8104.
Time, detention period for evaluation and treatment, § 5151 et seq.
Weapons, providing, § 8101.

OFFENSES
Crimes and Offenses, generally, this index.

PEACE OFFICERS
Juvenile offenders, temporary custody, § 625 et seq.
Juvenile probation officers, power, § 283.
Treatment of poor and indigent committed persons, § 6800.

PRELIMINARY EXAMINATION
Requirement to hold juvenile court hearing, § 603.

PROBATION
Home supervision program, § 840.

RECORDS AND RECORDATION
Juvenile courts, § 825 et seq.
    Destruction, § 826.5.
Libel and slander proceedings, juvenile delinquents and dependents, opening of sealed records, § 389.

REPORTS
Youth authority, § 284.

SCHOOLS AND SCHOOL DISTRICTS
Attendance review boards, § 601.1 et seq.

SERVICES
Child convicted of shoplifting, working off fine, § 731.5.

SEX OFFENDERS
Generally, § 6300 et seq.
Defined, sex offenses, § 6302.

SOCIAL SERVICES
Court order, priority, aid to families with dependent children, § 11476.
Crimes and offenses,
    Food stamp violations, § 18910.
    Medi-Cal beneficiaries, § 14026.
Public assistance,
    False representation, § 11482.
    Perjury, § 12850.
    Unlawful receipt or use, § 11480.

SOCIAL STUDIES
Juvenile Delinquents and Dependents, this index.

STATE PUBLIC DEFENDER
Reports, grievance procedure, state wards, § 1766.5.

SUBPOENA
Juvenile delinquents and dependents, § 341.

VENUE
See, also, Juvenile Courts, this index.
Juvenile courts, § 651.

VICTIMS
Crimes and offenses, final disposition, notice, § 742.

WARRANTS
Juvenile Delinquents and Dependents, this index.

WELFARE AND INSTITUTIONS
Code,
    Construction, § 201 et seq.
    Purpose, § 19.
    Title, § 1.

YOUTH AUTHORITY
Board, appeal of decision of case hearing representative, § 1711.5.
Construction of law, § 1700.
Delegation powers and duties, § 1711.3.
Director, powers and duties, § 1711.3.
Reports, § 284.

Index To
EVIDENCE CODE

ACCOMPLICES AND ACCESSORIES
Hearsay rule, § 1238.

ACCUSED
Consent, examinations, § 772.
Self-incrimination, privilege, §§ 404, 930, 940.

ACT
Admissibility of part, inquiry, adverse party on whole, § 356.

ADMINISTRATION
Presumptions, property of others, § 605.

ADMINISTRATIVE CODE
Judicial notice, rules and regulations, § 451.

ADMINISTRATIVE LAW AND PROCEDURE
Evidence code applicability, § 300.
Identity of informer, confidential information, § 1041.
Judicial notice, rules and regulations, § 451.
Newspaper editors, etc., contempt, information source, § 1070.
Privileges, § 911 et seq.
Rules and regulations, judicial notice, § 451.

ADMISSIBILITY OF EVIDENCE
Generally, § 350 et seq.
Absence of accident or mistake, § 1101.
Adverse party, part of act, etc., inquiry on whole, § 356.
Affidavit, hospital records, § 1562.
Attack on credibility of witness, § 1101.
Best evidence rule, § 1500 et seq.
Character and reputation, § 1100.
Conditionally, subsequent evidence of preliminary fact, § 403.
Confession, § 402.
Copies, best evidence rule, § 1500 et seq.
Credibility of witnesses, § 785 et seq.
  Support or attack, § 1101.
Crime, commission, § 1101.
Custom, § 1105.
Declaration, part, inquiry by adverse party on whole, § 356.
Defined, § 400.
Determination,
  Existence or nonexistence of preliminary fact, § 402.
  Question out of presence or hearing of jury, § 402.
  Questions of law by court, § 310.
Documentary evidence, best evidence rule, § 1500 et seq.
Exceptions to hearsay rule, § 1220 et seq.

ADMISSIBILITY OF EVIDENCE
—Cont'd
Existence of preliminary facts, § 400 et seq.
Extrinsic policies affecting, § 1100 et seq.
Facts, preliminary facts, § 400 et seq.
Finding of fact, prerequisite, § 402 et seq.
Former testimony, § 1290 et seq.
Foundation, § 400 et seq.
Habit, § 1105.
Hearing existence of preliminary facts, §§ 402, 403.
Hearing out of presence of jury, § 402.
Hearsay rule, exceptions, § 1220 et seq.
Hospital records, § 1562.
Identity of informer, § 1042.
Jury determination of preliminary fact out of presence, § 402.
Limitations, former testimony, § 1291.
Limited admissibility, § 355.
Mistake, § 353.
Nonexistence of preliminary facts, § 400 et seq.
Objections, former testimony, § 1291.
Official information, § 1042.
Opinion and Expert Testimony, generally this index.
Personal knowledge by witness, § 702.
Photographic copies, §§ 1550, 1551.
Preliminary facts, defined, § 400.
Presence of jury, determination of preliminary facts out of, § 402.
Privileged information, § 914.
Proffered evidence, § 401 et seq.
  Defined, § 401.
Purpose, § 355.
Questions of law, determination by court, § 310.
Relevant evidence, §§ 350, 351.
Reputation, § 1100.
Ruling on, § 402.
Self-incrimination, § 404.
Verdict, inquiry, validity, § 1150.
Writing used to refresh memory of witness, § 771.

ADMISSIONS
Generally, § 1220 et seq.
Authentication of writing, § 1414.
Criminal action, defendant, determination, § 402.
Hearsay rule, exceptions, § 1220 et seq.
Identity of declarant, § 403.

ADULTERY
Privilege,
  Confidential marital communications, § 985.
  Testimony against spouse, § 972.

ADVERSE OR PECUNIARY INTEREST
Hearsay rule, declarations against interest, § 1230.
Witness, § 780.

ADVERSE PARTY
Admissibility of part of act, etc., inquiry on whole, § 356.
Expert witness, compensation, inquiry by, § 722.
Hearsay evidence, examination of declarant, § 1203.
Husband and wife, calling spouse as witness, § 971.
Inspection of writing, § 771.
Notice, request to take judicial notice, § 453.
Production, accounts or writings for inspection, §§ 1509, 1510.

ADVICE
Court,
  Appointment of experts to advise, § 460.
  Information not received in open court, §§ 454, 455.
Judicial Notice, this index.

AFFIDAVIT
Copies, §§ 1560, 1561.
Hospital records, admissibility in evidence, § 1562.

AFFIRMATIONS
Oaths and Affirmations, generally, this index.

AGED PERSONS
Witnesses, capacity, § 780.

AIDERS AND ABETTORS
Hearsay rule, § 1238.

ALMANAC
Judicial notice, accuracy of sources, § 452.

ALTERATION
Authentication, altered writing, § 1402.

ANCESTRY
Generally, § 1310 et seq.
Certificate of clergyman, etc., § 1316.
Church certificate or record, §§ 1315, 1316.
Entries in family Bible, etc., § 1312.
Hearsay rule, exception, § 1310 et seq.
Religious society, written record, § 1315.
Reputation among family members, § 1313.

791

ANSWER

ANSWER
Letter, evidence, § 356.
Witnesses, responsive to questions, § 766.

APPEAL AND REVIEW
Admission of evidence, §§ 353, 354.

APPEARANCE
Witnesses, credibility, § 780.

APPELLATE COURT
Judicial notice, reviewing court, § 459.
Remand for dismissal, inability to determine foreign law, § 311.

APPOINTMENTS
Expert witnesses by court, §§ 722, 730 et seq.
Judicial notice, persons for advice on subject matter, § 460.
Psychotherapist by court, § 1017.
Witnesses, expert witnesses, §§ 722, 730, et seq.

ARREST
Mentally Deficient and Mentally Ill Persons, this index.
Presumption, lawfulness, § 664.
Reasonable cause, informer evidence, admissibility, § 1042.

ASSUMPTION
Presumption, existence of presumed fact, § 604.

ATTACK
Collateral attack, presumption, act of court or judge, § 666.
Witnesses, credibility, §§ 785 et seq. 1101.

ATTITUDE
Witnesses, § 780.

ATTORNEYS
Breach of duty, § 985.
Burden of proof, confidential communication, § 917.
Claim of privilege, § 911 et seq.
Communications, privileged communications, §§ 911 et seq., 950 et seq.
Judicial notice, rules of professional conduct, § 451.
Mentally Deficient and Mentally Ill Persons, this index.
Presumption, confidential communication, § 917.
Privilege of lawyer-client,
  Aiding commission of crime, § 956.
  Attorney, defined, § 950.
  Authority to claim, § 954.
  Burden of proof, confidential communications, § 917.
  Claim,
    Lawyer, §§ 954, 955.
    Waiver, § 912.
  Comment on exercises, § 913.
  Conduct of holder, consent to disclosure, § 912.
  Confidential communication between client and lawyer, defined, § 952.

ATTORNEYS—Cont'd
Privilege of lawyer-client—Cont'd
  Consent, disclosure by holder, waiver, § 912.
  Contempt, failure to disclose, § 914.
  Crime, plan to commit, § 956.
  Disclosure,
    Confidential communication, refusal, § 954.
    Holder, waiver, § 912.
  Exceptions, § 956 et seq.
  Failure to claim, consent to disclosure, § 912.
  Fraud, plan to commit, § 956.
  Holder of privilege,
    Claim, § 954.
    Defined, § 953.
    Disclosure, § 954.
  Instruction, permit disclosure, § 954.
  Joint holders, waiver, § 912.
  Law corporation, § 954.
  Lawyer, defined, § 950.
  Presumption, confidential communication, § 917.
  Prevention, disclosure of confidential communication, § 954.
  Statement of holder, consent to disclosure, § 912.
  Waiver, claim, § 912.
Privileged communications, §§ 911 et seq., 950 et seq.
Rules of professional conduct, judicial notice, § 451.

AUTHENTICATION
Generally, § 1400 et seq.
Acting upon writing by party, § 1414.
Admission of authenticity, § 1414.
Ancient document or writing, § 1419.
Author of writing, § 1420.
Communication, writing in response, § 1420.
Comparison of handwriting, § 1417 et seq.
Construction of law, § 1410.
Defined, § 1400.
Execution of writing, § 1410 et seq.
Finding, necessity, § 1400.
Foundational fact determination, § 403.
Genuineness of handwriting of maker, § 1415 et seq.
Means, § 1410 et seq.
Nature of evidence, § 1414.
Necessity, § 1400 et seq.
Opinion evidence of handwriting, § 1416.
Persons who may authenticate writing, § 1413.
Preliminary fact dispute, § 403.
Production of altered writing, § 1402.
Proof of handwriting, §§ 1417, 1418.
Requirement, § 1400 et seq.
Secondary evidence, contents of writing, § 1401.
Statute, testimony of subscribing witness, § 1412.
Subscribing witnesses, § 1411 et seq.
Testimony of subscribing witness, §§ 1411, 1412.
Witnesses, subscribing witnesses, § 1411 et seq.

BEST EVIDENCE
Generally, § 1500 et seq.
Examination of witnesses, § 768.

BIAS AND PREJUDICE
Exclusion of evidence, § 352.
Judge, calling and interrogating witnesses, § 775.
Witnesses, credibility, §§ 780, 791.

BURDEN OF PRODUCING EVIDENCE
Affidavit, contents of hospital records, § 1562.
Defined, § 110.
Existence of preliminary facts, § 403.
Incrimination, proffered evidence, § 404.
Judicial notice of facts presented, § 452.
Particular facts, § 550.
Parties, § 550.
Presumptions, this index.
Proponent of proffered evidence, § 403.
Rebuttable presumption, §§ 601, 630.

BURDEN OF PROOF
Generally, §§ 115, 500 et seq.
Assignment in criminal action, § 501.
Attorneys, confidential communications, § 917.
Care, failure to exercise, § 521.
Claim for relief or defense, § 500.
Confidential and privileged communications, § 917.
Crime, § 520.
Criminal action, assignment, § 501.
Defined, § 115.
Degree of care, failure to exercise, § 521.
Guilty plea of crime, § 520.
Husband and wife, confidential communications, § 917.
Incrimination, proffered evidence, § 404.
Insanity, § 522.
Instruction to jury, party bearing, § 502.
Judicial notice matter, § 452.
Mentally deficient or mentally ill persons, § 522.
Nonexistence of fact, § 502.
  Presumed fact, § 606.
Particular facts, § 550.
Parties, § 500.
Penal code, statute assigning in criminal action subject to, § 501.
Physicians and surgeons, confidential communications, § 917.
Presumptions, this index.
Psychotherapist, confidential communications, § 917.
Reasonable doubt, §§ 115, 502.
  Presumption, § 607.
Rebuttable presumption, § 601.
Specific issues, § 520.
Statute, assignment in criminal action, § 501.
Wrongdoing, § 520.

BUSINESS RECORDS
Hearsay rule, exceptions, § 1270 et seq.
Photographic copies of writings, § 1550.

CALLING WITNESSES
Juror, § 704.
Presiding judge, § 703.

Evidence Code   **CRIMINAL**

CAPACITY
Statement by party in individual or representative capacity, § 1220.

CERTIFIED COPIES
Best evidence rule, § 1507.
Hospital records, § 1560 et seq.

CHARACTER AND REPUTATION
Generally, § 1100 et seq.
Conduct on specified occasion, § 1100 et seq.
Criminal action, defendant, §§ 1102, 1103.
Family history, § 1313.
Hearsay rule, exception, § 1313.
Rebuttable evidence, criminal prosecution, §§ 1102, 1103.
Witnesses, credibility, § 780.

CHILDREN AND MINORS
Competency, witnesses, § 704.
Crime against,
   Confidential and privileged communications, § 985.
   Testimony against spouse, § 972.
Presumption of due care, statute violation etc., § 669.
Witnesses, competency, § 701.

CIRCUMSTANTIAL EVIDENCE
Generally, § 351.

CIVIL ACTION
Defined, § 105.

CLAIMS
Burden of proof, claim for relief or defense, § 500.

CLERGYMEN
Burden of proof, confidential communication, § 917.
Certificates, family history, § 1316.
Claim of privilege, § 911 et seq.
Confidential communications, § 1030 et seq.
Presumption, confidential communication, § 917.
Privilege of clergymen-penitent,
   Burden of proof, confidential communications, § 917.
   Claim,
      Clergymen, § 1034.
      Penitent, § 1033.
      Waiver, § 912.
   Clergyman, defined, § 1030.
   Consent, disclosure by holder, waiver, § 912.
   Contempt, failure to disclose privileged information, § 914.
   Disclosure,
      Refusal,
         Clergyman, § 1034.
         Penitent, § 1033.
         Waiver, § 912.
   Failure to claim, consent to disclosure, § 912.
   Penitent, defined, § 1031.
   Penitential communication defined, § 1032.
   Presumptions, confidential communications, § 917.

CLERGYMEN—Cont'd
Privilege of clergymen-penitent—Cont'd
   Prevention of disclosure, § 1033.
   Statement of holder, consent to disclosure, § 912.
   Waiver, claim, § 912.

CLIENT
Defined, lawyer-client privilege, § 951.

COMMON KNOWLEDGE
Judicial Notice, generally, this index.

COMMON LAW
Judicial notice of law, § 450.

COMPETENCY
Mentally Deficient and Mentally Ill Persons, this index.
Witnesses, § 700 et seq.

CONCLUSIVE PRESUMPTIONS
Generally, §§ 601, 620 et seq.

CONDUCT
Character and reputation, § 1100 et seq.
Contemporaneous declarations, § 1241.
Hearsay Evidence, this index.
Jury room, evidence on inquiry as to validity of verdict, § 1150.
Privileges, holder, consent to disclosure, § 912.
Specified occasions, § 1100 et seq.
Witnesses, attacking or supporting credibility, §§ 787, 780.

CONFESSION
Generally, § 1220 et seq.
Admissibility, § 402.
Involuntary confession, § 1204.

CONFIDENTIAL AND PRIVILEGED COMMUNICATIONS
Generally, § 911 et seq.
Attorney and client, §§ 911 et seq., 950 et seq.
Claim of privilege, § 911 et seq.
Clergymen and penitent, §§ 911 et seq., 1030 et seq.
Husband and wife, §§ 911 et seq., 971 et seq.
Official information, disclosure, privilege, § 1040 et seq.
Physician and patient, §§ 911 et seq., 992 et seq.
Psychotherapist and patient, §§ 911 et seq., 1010 et seq.

CONFLICT OF INTEREST
Hearsay rule, declarations against interest, § 1230.
Witnesses, § 780.

CONFRONTATION
Witnesses, § 711.

CONFUSION
Issues, exclusion of evidence, § 352.

CONSENT
Husband and wife, spouse as witness, privilege, § 971.
Identity of informer, disclosure, § 1401.

CONSENT—Cont'd
Motion for mistrial,
   Juror as witnesses, § 704.
   Trial judge as witness, § 703.
Official information, disclosure, § 1040.
Privileges, consent to disclosure by holder, waiver, § 912.
Witnesses, accused in criminal action, examination, § 772.

CONSISTENT STATEMENTS
Witnesses, supporting credibility, § 791.

CONSPIRACY
Admissions, preliminary fact dispute, § 403.
Hearsay rule, statement made prior to or during, § 1223.

CONSTITUTIONAL LAW
Hearsay evidence, exclusion under, § 1204.
Judicial notice, § 450 et seq.
Law includes, § 160.
Self-incrimination privilege, §§ 930, 940.
Statute as including, § 230.

CONTEMPT
Newspaper publisher, information source, refusal to disclose, § 1070.
Privileged information, failure to disclose, § 914.

CREDIBILITY OF WITNESSES
Witnesses, this index.

CRIMINAL ACTIONS
Action includes, § 105.
Admissibility of evidence,
   Commission, § 1101.
   Confession or admission of defendant, § 402.
Attorney-client privilege, § 956.
Burden of proof, § 520.
   Assignment, § 501.
   Existence of presumed fact, § 607.
Character or reputation of defendant, §§ 1102, 1103.
Church certificate or record, §§ 1315, 1316.
Claim of privilege, § 911 et seq.
Confessions, § 1220 et seq.
   Admissibility, § 402.
   Involuntary, § 1204.
Conspiracy to commit crime, statement while participating, exception to hearsay rule, § 1223.
Conviction of crime, preliminary fact determination, § 403.
Defined, § 130.
Guilty, burden of proof, § 520.
Guilty, exclusion of evidence, subsequent action, § 1153.
Hearing, admissibility of confession or admission, § 402.
Hearsay evidence, § 1204.
   Exceptions, conspiracy to commit crime, statement while participating, § 1223.
Husband and wife, privilege, confidential communications, § 980.
Identity of informer, claim of privilege, § 1042.

CRIMINAL

CRIMINAL ACTIONS—Cont'd
Involuntary confession, § 1204.
Judicial notice of federal rules, § 451.
Opinion evidence, character of defendant, §§ 1102, 1103.
Physician-patient privilege, § 998.
Presence of jury, admissibility of confession or admission determined out of, § 402.
Presumption, § 607.
    Intent, §§ 665, 668.
Production of writing, request out of presence of jury, § 1503.
Psychotherapist-patient privilege,
    Defense, § 1017.
    Services to plan or commit crime, § 1018.
Reasonable doubt, presumption affecting burden of proof, § 607.
Record, § 1281.
Self-incrimination, privilege against, §§ 930, 940.
Witnesses,
    Consent to examination, § 772.
    Unavailable as witness meaning, § 240.

CROSS–EXAMINATION
Defined, § 761.

CUSTODIAN
Hospital records,
    Affidavit, § 1561.
    Subpoena, §§ 1560, 1564, 1565.

DEATH
Generally, § 1311 et seq.
Bibles, entry in family bible, etc., § 1312.
Certificate of clergyman, etc., § 1316.
Hearsay evidence, exception, §§ 1281, 1311 et seq.
Presumption, absent seven years, § 667.
Psychotherapist-patient privilege, § 1016.
Religious society, certificate of record, §§ 1315, 1316.
Seven years absence, presumption, § 667.

DECISIONS
Judgments and Decrees, generally, this index.

DECLARANT
Defined, § 135.

DECLARATION
Admissibility of part, inquiry by adverse party on whole, § 356.
Oath as including, § 165.
Presumptions, conclusiveness, § 620.
Witnesses, § 710.

DECLARATION AGAINST INTEREST
Hearsay rule, exception, § 1230.

DEFENSE
Burden of proof, claim, § 500.

DEFINITIONS
Words and Phrases, generally this index.

DEGREE OF CARE
Burden of proof, failure to exercise, § 521.

DEMEANOR
Witnesses, credibility, § 780.

DEPOSITIONS
Hearsay evidence,
    Deponent as hearsay declarant, § 1202.
    Former testimony, § 1290.
Hospital records, § 1560.

DIRECT EVIDENCE
Defined, weight of evidence, § 410.

DIRECT EXAMINATION
Defined, § 760.

DISCLOSURE
Confidential and privileged communications, § 911 et seq.
Elections, political vote, § 1050.
Identity of informer, §§ 1041, 1042.
Information, official information, § 1040.
Information source, newspaper reporters, etc., contempt, § 1070.
Judge, information concerning case, § 703.
Juror as witness, § 704.
Political vote, § 1050.
Privileged communications, § 911 et seq.
Writing on examining witness, necessity, § 768.

DISCRETION OF COURT
Exclusion of evidence, § 352.
Hearsay evidence, exceptions, §§ 1222, 1223.
Order of proof, § 320.
Production of accounts or writings, inspection by adverse party, § 1509.

DISMISSAL
Criminal accusatory pleading against witness, credibility, § 788.

DISTRICT COURTS OF APPEAL
Code, applicability, § 300.

DOCUMENTARY EVIDENCE
Generally, § 1400 et seq.
Accounting for altered writing, § 1402.
Admissibility in evidence, best evidence rule, § 1500 et seq.
Authentication, generally, this index.
Best evidence rule, § 1500 et seq.
Business records, § 1270 et seq.
Construction of law, proof of writing, § 1410.
Contents of writing, best evidence, § 1500.
Custody of public entity, best evidence rule, § 1506.
Failure to produce, copy admissible, § 1503.
Hearsay evidence, prior statements of witnesses, § 1237.
Hospital records, § 1560 et seq.
Lost or destroyed writing, copy, § 1501.
Official writings, § 1280 et seq.
Partial admissibility, inquiry by adverse party on whole, § 356.
Photographic copies of writings, §§ 1550, 1551.
Possession of writing, secondary evidence, § 1508.

DOCUMENTARY EVIDENCE—Cont'd
Process, writing not procurable by, § 1502.
Proof of writings, § 1410 et seq.
Request for writing at hearing, § 1503.
Secondary evidence, § 1500 et seq.

DOMICILE AND RESIDENCE
Hearsay rule, character and reputation of community resident, § 1324.
Presumptions, letter correctly addressed, § 641.

DUE CARE
Burden of proof, § 521.
Presumption, violation of statute, etc., § 669.

DYING DECLARATIONS
Generally, § 1242.

EAVESDROPPERS
Attorney-client privilege, § 954.
Clergymen-penitent privilege, § 1033.
Confidential marital communication privilege, § 980.

ELECTRONIC EAVESDROPPERS
Attorney-client privilege, § 954.
Clergymen-penitent privileges, § 1033.
Confidential marital communication privilege, § 980.

EMOTIONS
Hearsay evidence, statement of declarant, exception, § 1250.
Psychotherapist-patient privilege, §§ 1016, 1024.

ENGLISH LANGUAGE
Judicial notice, true signification, § 451.

EXCEPTIONS
Attorney-client privilege, § 956 et seq.
Hearsay rule, § 1220 et seq.
Husband and wife, privilege, §§ 970 et seq., 980 et seq.
Psychotherapist-patient privilege, § 1016 et seq.

EXCLUSION
Witnesses from courtroom, § 777.

EXCLUSION OF EVIDENCE
Generally, § 352.
Affected or excluded by extrinsic policies, § 1100 et seq.
Hearsay evidence, § 1200 et seq.
Mistake, § 354.
Opinion, § 803.
Preliminary determinations, § 400 et seq.
Privilege, burden of showing, § 404.
Proffered evidence, § 401 et seq.
Self-incrimination, § 404.

EXEMPTIONS
Witnesses, unavailable as witnesses, § 240.

EXISTENCE
Preliminary facts admissibility of evidence, § 400 et seq.

Evidence Code

EXPERT TESTIMONY
Opinion and Expert Testimony, generally this index.

FALSE ARREST
Presumptions, official duty regularly performed, § 664.

FAMILY HISTORY
Hearsay rule, exception, § 1310 et seq.

FELONY
Witnesses, record of conviction, attacking credibility, § 788.

FINDING OF FACT
Admissibility of evidence, prerequisite, § 402 et seq.
Authentication of writing, § 1400.
Burden of producing evidence, particular fact, § 500.
Hearsay rule,
   Authority to make statements for party, § 1222.
   Statement of conspiracy to commit crime or civil wrong, § 1223.
Identity of informer, claim of privilege, § 1042.
Official information, claim of privilege, § 1042.
Ruling on admissibility of evidence, § 402.
Setting aside, erroneous admission or exclusion, §§ 353, 354.

FINES AND PENALTIES
Oath includes affirmation or declaration under penalty of perjury, § 165.
Witnesses, conviction of felony, credibility, § 788.

FORMER TESTIMONY
Defined, § 1290.
Hearsay rule, exceptions, § 1290.

GRAND JURY
Claim of privilege, § 911 et seq.
Code, applicability, proceedings before, § 300.
Husband-wife privilege, § 971.

HANDWRITING
Ancient writings, comparison, § 1419.
Authentication, § 1415 et seq.
Comparison, § 1417 et seq.
Genuineness, § 1415 et seq.
Knowledge, personal knowledge of witness, § 1416.
Letters of writer, proof, § 1416.
Opinion or expert testimony, §§ 1416, 1418.
Witnesses, § 1416 et seq.
Writing as meaning, § 250.

HARASSMENT
Witnesses, protection by court, § 765.

HEARINGS
Admissibility of evidence, determination of preliminary fact, §§ 402, 403.
Criminal action, confession or admission of defendant, § 402.

HEARINGS—Cont'd
Defined, § 145.
Hospital records, § 1560.
Industrial accident commission, contempt, § 914.
Witnesses,
   Presence of parties, § 711.
   Testimony of other witnesses, exclusion from courtroom, § 777.

HEARSAY EVIDENCE
Generally, § 1200 et seq.
Admissibility of evidence, § 1200 et seq.
Admissions,
   Application of law, § 1203.
   Exceptions to hearsay rule, § 1220 et seq.
Adverse party, examination of declarant, § 1203.
Ancestry, establishment, § 1310 et seq.
Application of law, § 1203.
Arbitration proceeding, transcript of former testimony, § 1290.
Authorized statements by party on subject matter, § 1222.
Bibles, entries in family bibles, § 1312.
Birth, establishment, § 1310 et seq.
Birth record, § 1281.
Blood relationship, establishment, etc., § 1310 et seq.
Books, entries in family books, § 1312.
Business records, § 1270 et seq.
Capacity, statement by party, individual or representative capacity, § 1220.
Certificate, family history, § 1316.
Charts, entries on family charts, § 1312.
Church records, birth, etc., § 1315.
Conduct or statement by declarant, § 1202.
   Contemporaneous declarations, § 1241.
   Party adopting statement as true, § 1221.
Confessions, application of law, § 1203.
Consistent statements, prior statements, prior statements of witnesses, § 1236.
Conspiracy, statement, participating, § 1223.
Constitution, exclusion under, § 1204.
Construction of law, § 1205.
Contemporaneous declarations, § 1241.
Content of statement, knowledge of party, adoption, § 1221.
Credibility of declarant, § 1202.
Criminal Actions, this index.
Cross-examination of declarant, § 1203.
Declarations against interest, § 1230.
Defined, §§ 150, 1200.
Depositions,
   Deponent as hearsay declarant, § 1202.
   Former testimony, § 1290.
Discretion of court, order of proof, §§ 1222, 1223.
Documentary evidence, official writings, § 1280 et seq.
Dying declarations, § 1242.
Emotions, statement of declarant, § 1250 et seq.
Examination of declarant, § 1203.
Exceptions to hearsay rule, § 1220 et seq.

HUSBAND

HEARSAY EVIDENCE—Cont'd
Exclusion, § 1200 et seq.
Family history, § 1310 et seq.
Former testimony, § 1290.
Identity of declarant, § 403.
Inconsistent conduct or statement,
   Declarant, § 1202.
   Prior statements of witnesses, exception, § 1235.
Mental state of declarant, § 1250 et seq.
Motive, statement of declarant, § 1250 et seq.
Oaths and affirmations, former testimony, § 1290.
Official records, § 1280 et seq.
Official writings, § 1280 et seq.
Order of proof, court's discretion, §§ 1222, 1223.
Parties, exceptions, § 1220 et seq.
Preliminary fact determination, § 403.
Prior statements of witnesses, § 1235 et seq.
   Application of law, § 1203.
   Exceptions, § 1235 et seq.
Records,
   Business records, § 1270 et seq.
   Official records, § 1280 et seq.
Relevant evidence, § 210.
Resident of community, character and reputation, § 1324.
Rings, engravings on, § 1312.
Spontaneous declarations, § 1240.
State of mind, § 1250 et seq.
Statements, § 1200 et seq.
Subject matter authorized by party, § 1222.
Unavailable as witness, former testimony, § 1291.

HOLDER OF THE PRIVILEGE
Defined,
   Lawyer-client privilege, § 953.
   Psychotherapist-patient privilege, § 1013.

HONESTY
Witnesses,
   Credibility, § 780.
   Attacking or supporting, § 786.

HUSBAND AND WIFE
Actions and proceedings,
   Privilege,
      Confidential communications, § 980 et seq.
      Testimony against spouse, § 970 et seq.
Attorney-client privilege, presence, § 952.
Burden of proof, confidential communication, § 917.
Commitment of spouse,
   Privilege,
      Testimony against spouse, § 972.
Crimes and offenses, privilege,
   Confidential communications, § 985.
   Testimony against spouse, § 972.
Criminal proceeding, privileged communications, offer in evidence, § 987.
Juvenile court proceeding, privilege, testimony against spouse, § 972.
Presumption, confidential communications, § 917.

HUSBAND

HUSBAND AND WIFE—Cont'd
Privilege, confidential communications or testimony against spouse,
   Aid to commit crime or fraud, § 981.

HYPOTHETICAL QUESTIONS
Expert witness, § 720 et seq.

IDENTITY
Admissibility of evidence, § 1101.
Informer, privilege to refuse, §§ 1041, 1042.

IMPEACHMENT
Verdict, competence of juror to give evidence, § 1150.
Witnesses, § 785 et seq.

IN CAMERA
Ruling on claim of privilege, § 915.

INADMISSIBILITY OF EVIDENCE
Defined, § 400.

INCONSISTENT STATEMENTS
Hearsay evidence, §§ 1202, 1235.
Preliminary fact dispute, § 403.

INFERENCES
Generally, § 600 et seq.
Defined, § 600.
Direct evidence, proof of fact without inference, § 410.
Drawing, §§ 413, 604.
Privileges, drawing from exercise, § 913.

INFORMATION
Identity of informer, privilege to refuse, §§ 1041, 1042.
Judicial notice,
  Source,
    Propriety of taking, §§ 454, 455.
    Reviewing court, § 459.
Newspaper reporters, etc., refusal to disclose source, contempt, § 1070.
Official information,
  Chambers of court, ruling on claim of privilege, § 915.
  Defined, privileges, § 1040.
Privileged information,
  Disclosure, order of court, §§ 914, 915.
  Official information, § 1040 et seq.
Psychotherapist-patient privilege, § 1026.
Radio or television, refusal to disclose source, contempt, § 1070.
Witnesses,
  Juror as witness, § 704.
  Trial judge as witness, § 703.

INFORMER
Identity, privilege to refuse, §§ 1041, 1042.

INTENT
Admissibility of evidence to prove, § 1101.
Crimes and offenses, presumption, §§ 665, 668.
Hearsay evidence, statement of declarant, § 1250 et seq.
Presumptions, this index.

INVOLUNTARY CONFESSION
Generally, § 1204.

JUDGMENTS AND DECREES
Erroneous admission or exclusion of evidence, reversal, §§ 353, 354.
Judicial notice, §§ 451, 452 et seq.
Law defined, § 160.
Reversal, erroneous admission or exclusion of evidence, §§ 353, 354.
Witnesses, record of conviction, attacking credibility, § 788.

JUDICIAL COUNCIL
Judicial notice, rules of practice and procedure, § 451.

JUDICIAL NOTICE
  Generally, § 450 et seq.
Authority, § 450.
Constitutional law, §§ 451, 452.
Court records, § 451 et seq.
Criminal procedure, federal rules, § 451.
Decisional law, §§ 451, 452.
English words and phrases, true signification, § 451.
Exclusionary rules of evidence, inapplicable, § 454.
Failure or refusal of trial court to take, § 458.
Federal rules of criminal procedure, § 451.
Foreign states, official acts, § 452.
Information, source,
  Propriety of taking, §§ 454, 455.
  Reviewing court, § 459.
Instruction of jury, §§ 457, 458.
Knowledge, facts and propositions of generalized knowledge, § 451.
Law, decisional, constitutional and statutory, §§ 451, 452.
Legal expressions, true signification, § 451.
Legislative enactments, § 452.
Official acts, § 452.
Pleading rules, § 451.
Practice and procedure rules, § 451.
Private acts, § 452.
Public entity, regulations and legislative enactments, § 452.
Resolutions, § 452.
Reviewing court, § 459.
Rules and regulations, §§ 451, 452.
Rules of court, § 451 et seq.
State law, §§ 451, 452.
Statutory law, §§ 451, 452.
United States law, §§ 451, 452.
United States supreme court, rules of pleading, practice and procedure, § 451.
Universally known facts and propositions of generalized knowledge, § 451.

JURISDICTION
Presumptions, lawful exercise, § 666.

JURY
Admissibility of evidence, determination of preliminary fact out of presence or hearing of, § 402.
Appointment of expert witnesses, reviewing, § 722.

JURY—Cont'd
Credibility of witnesses, § 780 et seq.
  Determination, § 312.
Drawing inferences from evidence, § 413.
Effect of evidence, determination, § 312.
Grand jury, applicability of Code, proceedings before, § 300.
Hearsay evidence, determination of effect and value, § 312.
Impeachment of verdict, competence to give evidence, § 1150.
Inquiry on validity of verdict, § 1150.
Instructions,
  Accept judicially noticed matter, § 457.
  Burden of proof, party bearing, § 502.
  Determination of preliminary facts, admissibility of proffered evidence, § 403.
  Inference, drawing from exercise of privilege, § 913.
  Judicial notice, §§ 457, 458.
  Presumptions, exercise of privilege, § 913.
  Scope of evidence, § 355.
Judicial notice, instruction to jury, §§ 457, 458.
Misleading by evidence, exclusion, § 352.
Oaths and affirmations, compelling jurors sworn to testify as witness, § 704.
Privileges, drawing inference from exercise, § 913.
Province of jury, § 310 et seq.
Questions of fact, determination by, § 312.
Support of verdict, competence to give evidence, § 1150.
Trier of fact as including, § 235.
Value of evidence, determination, § 312.
Witnesses, this index.

JUSTICE COURTS
Code, applicability, § 300.

JUVENILE COURT
Claim of privilege, § 911 et seq.
Husband and wife, privilege, testimony against spouse, § 972.

JUVENILE OFFENDERS
Due care, presumption, § 669.

KNOWLEDGE
Admissibility of evidence to prove, § 669.
Expert witnesses, opinion based on special knowledge, §§ 801, 802.
Handwriting, personal knowledge of witness, § 1416.
Hearsay rule, party, content of statement, adoption, § 1221.
Judicial notice, common knowledge, §§ 451, 452.
Witnesses,
  Personal knowledge, §§ 403, 702.
  Special knowledge of expert witness, § 720.

LAW
Defined, § 160.
Judicial notice, decisional, constitutional and statutory law, §§ 451, 452.

Evidence Code

LAW ENFORCEMENT OFFICERS
Identity of informer, confidential information to, privilege, § 1041.
Peace officers, generally, this index.

LAW REVIEW
Judicial notice of law, § 450.

LAWYERS
Attorneys, generally, this index.

LEADING QUESTION
Defined, witnesses, § 764.

MENTALLY DEFICIENT OR MENTALLY ILL PERSONS
Burden of proof, § 522.
Competency, witnesses, § 701.
Opinion of witness, § 870.
Psychotherapist-patient privilege,
  Criminal action, § 1017.
    Mental condition of patient, §§ 1016, 1024.
Witnesses, § 240.
  Disqualification, § 701.

MICROFILM
Copies of writings, §§ 1550, 1551.

MINORS
Children and Minors, generally, this index.

MISCARRIAGE OF JUSTICE
Erroneous admission or exclusion of evidence, §§ 353, 354.

MISTRIAL
Witnesses,
  Objection to juror as witness, § 704.
  Trial judge as witness, § 703.

MOTIONS
Exclude or strike erroneous evidence, § 353.
Mistrial,
  Juror as witness, § 704.
  Trial judge as witness, § 703.
Privilege, exclude information subject to claim of, § 916.
Strike answers not responsive to questions, § 766.
Witnesses, this index.

MOTIVES
Admissibility of evidence, § 1101.
Hearsay evidence, statement of declarant, § 1250 et seq.
Witnesses, credibility, §§ 780, 791.

MUNICIPAL COURTS
Code, applicability, § 300.

OATHS AND AFFIRMATIONS
Defined, § 165.
Hearsay evidence, former testimony under oath, § 1290.
Jurors, compelling jurors sworn to testify as witness, § 704.
Witness, this index.

OBJECTIONS
Admission of evidence, §§ 353, 354.

OBJECTIONS—Cont'd
Expert witness, §§ 720, 805.
  Exclusion of opinion, § 803.
Former testimony, § 1291.
Witnesses, this index.

OFFICIAL ACTS
Judicial notice, § 452.

OFFICIAL DUTY
Presumptions, regular performance, § 664.

OFFICIAL INFORMATION
Chambers, court ruling on claim of privilege, § 915.
Defined, privileges, § 1040.

ONE WITNESS
Sufficiency of evidence, § 411.

OPEN COURT
Judicial notice, source of information, §§ 454, 455.
  Reviewing court, § 459.

OPINION AND EXPERT TESTIMONY
Generally, §§ 720 et seq., 800 et seq.
Adverse party, inquiry, compensation of expert witness, § 722.
Appointment of expert, §§ 722, 730 et seq.
Character and reputation, § 1100 et seq.
Compensation of expert, §§ 722, 730 et seq.
  Adverse party, inquiry by, § 722.
Appointed by courts, § 730.
Court's own motion, appointment of experts, § 730.
Credibility of witnesses, § 780 et seq.
  Inquiry into compensation and expenses, § 722.
Criminal action, character of defendant, §§ 1102, 1103.
Cross-examination, § 721.
  Opinion of expert, § 721.
  Qualifications of expert, § 721.
  Reasons for opinion, § 721.
  Subjects of expertise, § 721.
Direct examination, statement, reasons for opinion, § 802.
Discretion of court, examination, basis of opinion, § 802.
Education of expert, § 720.
  Opinion based on, §§ 801, 802.
Exclusion, § 803.
Expenses of expert, § 722.
Experience of expert, § 720.
  Opinion based on, §§ 801, 802.
Knowledge of expert,
  Opinion based on, §§ 801, 802.
  Special knowledge, § 720.
Mentally deficient and mentally ill persons, §§ 240, 870.
Non-expert testimony, § 800.
Objections, §§ 720, 805.
  Exclusion of opinions, § 803.
Particular subjects, § 870.
Qualifications of expert, §§ 720, 721.
  Cross-examination, § 721.
Reasons for opinion, § 802.
Reports of expert, § 730.
Skill of expert, § 720.
  Opinion based on, §§ 801, 802.

PHRASES

OPINION AND EXPERT TESTIMONY—Cont'd
Special knowledge,
  Opinion based on, §§ 801, 802.
  Qualification, § 720.
Subjects, experts, §§ 720, 721.
Subscribing witness, §§ 870, 1411 et seq.
Training of expert, § 720.
  Opinion based on, §§ 801, 802.
Weight of testimony, § 722.

ORDINANCES
Judicial notice, § 452.
Presumption, failure to exercise due care violations, § 669.

PARDON
Witnesses, conviction of crime, § 788.

PARTIES
Adverse Party, generally, this index.
Burden of producing evidence, § 550.
Burden of proof, § 500.
Exclusion from courtroom, § 777.
Hearsay rule, exceptions, § 1220 et seq.
Husband and wife, calling spouse as witness, privilege, § 971.
Obligation to introduce evidence, § 110.
Witnesses, generally, this index.

PAST RECOLLECTION RECORDED
Refreshing memory by witness, §§ 771, 1237.

PATIENT
Defined psychotherapist-patient privilege, § 1011.
Psychotherapist, generally, this index.

PEDIGREE
Hearsay rule, § 1310 et seq.

PENAL CODE
Burden of proof, statute assigning subject to, § 501.

PENITENT
Defined, clergyman-penitent privileges, § 1031.

PENITENTIAL COMMUNICATION
Privileges of clergyman-penitent, §§ 911 et seq., 1030 et seq.

PERCEIVE
Defined, § 170.

PERJURY
Admission of untruthfulness, § 780.
Oath includes affirmation or declaration under penalty of perjury, § 165.

PERSON
Defined, § 175.

PERSONAL KNOWLEDGE
Knowledge, generally, this index.

PHOTOGRAPHS
Copies of writings, §§ 1550, 1551.

PHRASES
Words and Phrases, generally, this index.

PLEADINGS

PLEADINGS
Judicial notice,
  Notice to adverse party of request to take, § 453.
  Rules, § 451.
Motions, generally, this index.

POLICE
Identity of informer, confidential information, privilege, § 1041.

POSSESSION
Copy of writing, secondary evidence, § 1508.
Presumptions, this index.

PREJUDICE
Bias and Prejudice, generally, this index.

PRELIMINARY EXAMINATION
Generally, § 1042.

PRELIMINARY FACT
Admissibility of evidence, § 400 et seq.
Defined, admissibility of evidence, § 400.

PRELIMINARY HEARING
Hearing, defined, § 145.

PREPONDERANCE OF EVIDENCE
Weight of Evidence, generally, this index.

PRESENCE
Criminal action, admissibility of confession out of jury's presence, § 402.
Opening sealed copies of hospital records, § 1560.
Witnesses,
  Examination, officer or employee designated by attorney, § 777.
  Hearing only in presence of parties, § 711.

PRESIDING JUDGE
Witness, § 703.

PRESUMPTIONS
Generally, § 600 et seq.
Absent seven years, death, § 667.
Addressed letter, received in ordinary course of mail, § 641.
Affidavit, contents of hospital records, § 1562.
Arrest, lawfulness, § 664.
Assumption, existence of presumed fact, § 604.
Attorneys, confidential communication, § 917.
Burden of producing evidence, § 603.
  Affidavit, contents of hospital records, § 1562.
  Effect, § 604.
  Established to facilitate determination of action, § 603.
  Presumptions affecting, § 630 et seq.
  Rebuttable presumption, § 601.
Burden of proof,
  Presumptions affecting, § 660 et seq.
  Criminal action, § 607.
  Rebuttable presumption, § 601.
Classification, § 601.
Clergymen, confidential communications, § 917.

PRESUMPTIONS—Cont'd
Collateral attack, act of court of judge, § 666.
Conclusive presumptions, §§ 601, 620 et seq.
Confidential and privileged communications, § 917.
Conflicting presumptions, § 600.
Courts, lawful exercise of jurisdiction, § 666.
Criminal Actions, this index.
Date of writing, § 640.
Death, absence seven years, § 667.
Declared by law, conclusiveness, § 620.
Defined, § 600.
Delivery, money to another, § 631.
Direct evidence, proof of fact without presumption, § 410.
Due care exercise, violation of statute, etc., § 669.
Establishment to implement public policy, § 605.
Guilty, affecting burden of proof, § 607.
Husband and Wife, this index.
Instruction to jury, exercise of privilege, § 913.
Intent,
  Crimes and offenses, §§ 665, 668.
  Ordinary consequences of voluntary act, § 665.
Judges, lawful exercise of jurisdiction, § 666.
Jurisdiction, lawful exercise, § 666.
Letter, received in ordinary course of mail, § 641.
Marriage, validity, § 605.
Money due, § 631.
Negligence, violation of statute, etc., § 669.
Official duty, performance, § 664.
Performance, official duty regularly, § 664.
Physicians and surgeons, confidential communications, § 917.
Possession, things, ownership, § 637.
Privileges, confidential communications, § 917.
Psychotherapist, confidential communications, § 917.
Public policy, presumption established to implement, § 605.
Rebuttable presumptions, § 601.
  Burden of producing evidence, § 630.
  Burden of proof, affecting, § 660.
  Statutes, fact or group of facts as prima facie evidence, § 602.
Receiving letter in ordinary course of mail, § 641.
Seven years absence, death, § 667.
Specific intent of crime charged, §§ 665, 668.
State courts, lawful exercise of jurisdiction, § 666.
Statute, ordinance or regulation violation, § 669.
Thing, possession, ownership, § 637.
Unlawful intent, unlawful act, § 668.
Validity of marriage, § 605.
Warrant, arrest without, lawfulness, § 664.
Writings, truly dated, § 640.

PRIOR CONVICTION
Witness, attaching credibility, § 788.

PRIVILEGED COMMUNICATIONS
Generally, § 911 et seq.
Attorney and client, §§ 911 et seq., 950 et seq.
Clergymen and penitent, §§ 911 et seq., 1030 et seq.
Husband and wife, §§ 911 et seq., 980 et seq.
Official information, § 1040 et seq.
Psychotherapist and patient, §§ 911 et seq., 1010 et seq.

PRIVILEGES AND IMMUNITIES
Admissibility of evidence, § 914.
Burden of proof, § 917.
Claim, § 912 et seq.
  Disallowance of claim, § 918.
  Identity of informer, §§ 1041, 1042.
  Official information, § 1040.
  Political vote, § 1050.
  Trade secret, §§ 915, 1060.
  Waiver, § 912.
Communications, § 911 et seq.
Conduct of holder, consent of disclosure, § 912.
Consent, disclosure, waiver, § 912.
Contempt,
  Failure to disclose information, § 914.
  Newspaper employees, information source, § 1070.
Credibility of witness, inference drawn from exercise, § 913.
Criminal actions, privilege against self-incrimination, §§ 404, 930, 940.
Disclosure, § 911 et seq.
Error, disallowance, § 918.
Exemption of witnesses on ground of, § 240.
Exercise of privilege not to testify, § 913.
Existence, § 400.
Failure to claim, consent to disclosure, § 912.
Holder of privilege, disallowance, error on ruling, § 918.
Identity of informer, court ruling on claim, § 915.
Inferences, drawn from exercise, § 913.
Joint holders, waivers, § 912.
Jury, drawing of inference from exercise, § 913.
Motion, exclude information subject to claim, § 916.
Newsmen, citation for contempt, § 1070.
Nonexistence, inadmissibility of evidence as including, § 400.
Official information and identity of informer, § 915.
Political vote, disclosure, § 1050.
Presumption,
  Arising from exercise, § 913.
  Confidential communication, § 917.
Production of writing, object or thing, refusal, § 911.
Proffered evidence, § 404.
Refusal to be witness, § 911.
Reporters, etc., of newspapers, information source, § 1070.
Self-incrimination, privilege against, §§ 404, 930, 940.

Evidence Code

PRIVILEGES AND IMMUNITIES—Cont'd
Statement of holder, consent to disclosure, § 912.
Trade secret, § 1060.
Waiver, claim of privilege, § 912.

PROBATIVE VALUE
Exclusion, § 352.

PROCESS
Best evidence rule, writing not procurable by, § 1502.
Witnesses,
  Compelling attendance by, § 240.
  Writing not procurable by, §§ 771, 1502.

PRODUCTION OF BOOKS, DOCUMENTS AND THINGS
Adverse party, accounts or writings, inspection, § 1509.
Authentication, production of altered writing, § 1402.
Best evidence rule, copy of writing, § 1504.
Criminal actions, request of writing out of presence of jury, § 1503.
Discretion of court, inspection by adverse party, § 1509.
Failure to produce writing, copy admissible, § 1503.
Hospital records, § 1560 et seq.
Inexpedient admissibility of copy, § 1504.
Inspection, adverse party, §§ 1509, 1510.
Privileges, refusal, § 911.
Records, hospital records, § 1560 et seq.
Witnesses, production of writing used to refresh memory, § 771.

PROFFERED EVIDENCE
Generally, § 401 et seq.
Defined, § 401.

PROOF
Defined, § 190.

PROPERTY
Defined, § 185.

PROTECTION
Witnesses, undue harassment or embarrassment, § 765.

PSYCHIATRISTS
Psychotherapist-patient privilege, § 1010 et seq.

PSYCHOLOGISTS
Psychotherapist-patient privilege, § 1010 et seq.

PSYCHOTHERAPIST
Burden of proof, confidential communication, § 917.
Communications, privileged communications, § 911 et seq.
Confidential communications, § 911 et seq.
Inspection, report or record, public inspection, § 1026.
Joint holders, waiver, § 912.

PSYCHOTHERAPIST—Cont'd
Mental or emotional condition of patient, §§ 1016, 1024.
  Defense in criminal action, § 1017.
Officers and employees, report to public employee, § 1026.
Orders of court, appointment, § 1017.
Patient, defined, § 1011.
Presumption, confidential communications, § 917.
Prevention, disclosure of confidential communication, § 1014.
Privilege, psychotherapist-patient,
  Aid in committing crime or tort, § 1018.
  Appointment by court, § 1017.
  Apprehension after crime, service to escape, § 1018.
  Attorney, examination of defendant to enter plea, § 1017.
  Authority to claim, § 1014.
  Burden of proof, confidential communication, § 917.
  Claim,
    Psychotherapist, §§ 1014, 1015.
    Waiver, § 912.
  Competence of patient, proceedings to establish, § 1025.
  Condition of patient, § 1016.
  Conduct of holder, consent to disclosure, § 912.
  Confidential communication between patient and psychotherapist, defined, § 1012.
  Consent, disclosure by holder, waiver, § 912.
  Contempt, failure to disclose, § 914.
  Contract, beneficiary of patient, § 1016.
  Crime, plan to commit, § 1018.
  Criminal action, defense, § 1017.
  Detection, crime or tort, services, to escape, § 1018.
  Disclosure,
    Confidential communications, § 1014.
    Holder, waiver, § 912.
  Escape after commission of crime, § 1018.
  Examination of patient, court order, § 1017.
  Exceptions, § 1016 et seq.
  Holder of privilege,
    Claims, § 1014.
    Defined, § 1013.
    Disclosure, waiver, § 912.
  Privileged communications, §§ 911 et seq., 1010 et seq.
  Psychotherapist defined, § 1010.
  Reasonable cause, patient dangerous to himself or others, § 1024.
  Records and recordation,
    Information in public office, § 1026.
    Open to public inspection, § 1026.
  Waiver, claim, § 912.

PUBLIC EMPLOYEE
Defined, § 195.

PUBLIC INTEREST
Informer, disclosure of identity, § 1041.

RECROSS–EXAMINATION

PUBLIC POLICY
Presumption established to implement, § 605.
Prima facie evidence, one fact of another fact, § 602.

PUBLIC RECORDS
Records and Recordation, generally, this index.

QUALIFICATIONS
Witnesses, this index.

QUESTIONS OF LAW AND FACT
Admissibility of evidence, determination by court, § 310.
Court determination, § 310.
Foreign law, application and determination, §§ 310, 311.
Judicial notice, §§ 451, 452.
Jury, determination of fact questions, § 312.

REASONABLE CAUSE
Psychotherapist-patient privilege, patient dangerous to himself or others, § 1024.

REASONABLE DOUBT
Burden of proof, § 115.
  Criminal action, § 501.
  Existence or nonexistence of fact, § 502.
  Presumption, § 607.

REBUTTABLE PRESUMPTIONS
Presumptions, this index.

RECOLLECTION
Refreshing memory by witness, §§ 771, 1237.

RECORDS AND RECORDATION
Best evidence, § 1506.
Business records, § 1270 et seq.
Business records, photographic copies of writings, § 1550.
Copy of writing, best evidence, § 1507.
Court records, judicial notice, § 452.
Documentary Evidence, generally, this index.
Erroneous admission or exclusion, §§ 353, 354.
Hearsay rule, exception, business records, § 1270 et seq.
Hospital records, § 1560 et seq.
Judicial notice,
  Court records, § 452.
  Denial of request to take, § 456.
  Source of information, § 455.
Official records, § 1280 et seq.
Refreshing memory of witnesses, §§ 771, 1237.
Religious societies, birth, etc., § 1315.
Witnesses, conviction record, attacking credibility, § 788.
Writing as meaning, Evidence Code, § 250.

RECROSS–EXAMINATION
Defined, § 763.

REDIRECT

REDIRECT EXAMINATION
Defined, § 762.

REEXAMINATION
Witnesses, § 774.

REFRESHING MEMORY
Witnesses, §§ 771, 1237.

REHABILITATION
Witnesses, certificate, conviction of felony, credibility, § 788.

RELEVANT EVIDENCE
Admissibility, §§ 350, 351.
Defined, § 210.
Proffered evidence, existence of preliminary fact, § 403.

RELIEF
Burden of proof, claim for relief or defense, § 500.

RELIGIOUS BELIEF
Witnesses, credibility, § 789.

REMAND
Trial court for dismissal, inability to determine foreign law, § 311.

REPORTERS
Information source, refusal to disclose, § 1070.

REPORTS
Documentary Evidence, generally, this index.
Expert witnesses, § 730.

REPRODUCTION
Copies of writings, §§ 1550, 1551.
Hospital records, § 1560.

REPUTATION
Character and Reputation, generally, this index.

REQUEST
Restriction of evidence to proper scope, § 355.

RES GESTAE
Generally, §§ 1240, 1241.

REVERSAL
Judgments or decrees, erroneous admission or exclusion of evidence, §§ 353, 354.

REVIEWING COURT
Appellate Court, generally, this index.

RULES OF COURT
Judicial notice, § 451 et seq.

RULES OF EVIDENCE
Judicial notice, inapplicable, § 454.
Questions of law, determination by court, § 310.

SCIENTIFIC EVIDENCE
Generally, § 800 et seq.

SCOPE OF EVIDENCE
Instructing jury, § 355.

SEARCHES AND SEIZURES
Identity of informer, § 1042.

SECONDARY EVIDENCE
Writings, §§ 1401, 1500 et seq.

SECRET BALLOT
Privilege against disclosure of vote, § 1050.

SELF–INCRIMINATION
Witnesses, privilege against, §§ 404, 930, 940.

SENSES
Acquisition of knowledge through, § 170.
Evidence as meaning things presented to, § 140.

SETTING ASIDE
Findings or verdict, erroneous admission or exclusion of evidence, §§ 353, 354.

SEVEN YEAR ABSENCE
Presumption of death, § 667.

SHERIFFS
Identity of informer, confidential information privilege, § 1041.

SPECIAL KNOWLEDGE
Expert witnesses, opinion based on, §§ 801, 802.

SPECIFIC INTENT
Presumptions, crime charged, element, §§ 665, 668.

SPONTANEOUS DECLARATIONS
Hearsay rule, exceptions, § 1240.

SPOUSES
Husband and Wife, generally, this index.

STATE
Defined, § 220.
Identity of informer, claim of privilege, § 1042.
Judicial notice, state law, §§ 451, 452.
Official act, judicial notice, § 452.

STATE OF MIND
Hearsay evidence, § 1250 et seq.

STATEMENTS
Defined, § 225.
Hearsay evidence, § 1200 et seq.
Exceptions, § 1220 et seq.
Privileges, statement of holder, consent to disclosure, § 912.

STATUTES
Application of state law, § 311.
Attested or certified copy of recorded writing, § 1507.
Authentication of writing, testimony of subscribing witness, § 1412.
Burden of proof, assignment in criminal action, § 501.
Construction, determination by court, § 310.

STATUTES—Cont'd
Defined, § 230.
Facts, prima facie evidence, rebuttable presumption, § 602.
Identity of informer disclosure forbidden, §§ 1041, 1042.
Judicial notice, §§ 451, 452.
Law includes, § 160.
Official information, disclosure forbidden, § 1040.
Presumption, failure to exercise due care, violation, § 669.
Prima facie evidence, facts, rebuttable presumption, § 602.
Questions of law, construction, determination by court, § 310.

STOOL PIGEON
Generally, § 1040 et seq.

SUBMISSION OF EVIDENCE
Generally, § 1220 et seq.

SUBPOENA
Hospital records, §§ 1560, 1564, 1565.

SUBPOENA DUCES TECUM
Production of Books, Documents and Things, generally, this index.

SUBSCRIBING WITNESSES
Authentication of writing, § 1411 et seq.
Opinion evidence, § 870.

SUCCESSOR
Lawyer-client privilege, § 953.

SUFFICIENCY OF EVIDENCE
Weight of Evidence, generally, this index.

SUMMONS
Process, generally, this index.

SUPERIOR COURTS
Code, applicability, § 300.

SUPPRESSION OF EVIDENCE
Willful suppression, § 413.

SUPREME COURTS
Code, applicability, § 300.

SYRINGES AND NEEDLES
See Hypodermic Syringes and Needles, this index.

TESTIMONY
Code, applicability, § 300.
Evidence, generally, this index.
Witnesses, generally, this index.

TEXTS
Cross-examination, expert witness forming opinion from, § 721.

THIRD PERSONS
Attorney-client privilege, presence, § 952.
Husband and wife, against,
Privilege not to testify against spouse, § 972.
Privileged and confidential communications, § 985.

Evidence Code   **WITNESSES**

TRADE SECRET
Privilege, § 1060.
   Court ruling on claim, § 915.

TREATISE
Cross-examination, expert witness forming opinion from, § 721.
Judicial notice,
   Accuracy of sources, § 452.
   Law, § 450.

TRIAL
Assignment before another jury, juror as witness, § 704.
Mistrial,
   Juror as witness, § 704.
   Trial judge as witness, § 703.
Opening, sealed copies, hospital records, § 1560.
Order of proof, § 320.

TRIER OF FACT
Defined, § 235.

TRUTH
Witness, admission of untruthfulness, § 780.
   Understanding of duty to tell, § 701.

UNAVAILABLE AS A WITNESS
Defined, § 240.

UNDUE PREJUDICE
Discretion of court to exclude evidence, § 352.

UNITED NATIONS
Application and determination of law, §§ 310, 311.
Judicial notice of law, §§ 452, 454.

UNITED STATES
Identity of informer forbidden by laws, §§ 1041, 1042.
Judicial notice,
   Decisional, constitutional and statutory law, §§ 451, 452.
   Regulations, etc., § 452.

UNITED STATES AGENCIES
Hearsay evidence, former testimony to determine controversy, § 1290.
Judicial notice, rules and regulations, § 451.

UNITED STATES CODE
Judicial notice, § 451.

UNITED STATES CONSTITUTION
Hearsay evidence, exclusion under, § 1204.
Privilege against self-incrimination, §§ 930, 940.

UNITED STATES COURTS
Judicial notice, records and rules, § 452.
Presumptions, lawful exercise of jurisdiction, § 666.

UNITED STATES SUPREME COURT
Judicial notice, rules of pleading, practice and procedure, § 451.

VERACITY
Witnesses, credibility, §§ 780, 786.

VERDICT
Impeachment, competence of juror to give evidence, § 1150.
Inquiry on validity, § 1150.
Setting aside, erroneous admission or exclusion of evidence, §§ 353, 354.
Support, competence of juror to give evidence, § 1150.

VOICE
Evidence, defined, § 140.

VOTES AND VOTING
Privilege against disclosure of vote, § 1050.

WAIVER
Evidence, erroneous admission, § 353.
Privileged communications, claim, § 912.

WARRANTS
Presumption, arrest without warrant, § 664.

WEIGHT OF EVIDENCE
Generally, § 410 et seq.
Burden of proof, § 115.
Direct evidence, §§ 410, 411.
Distrust, weaker and less satisfactory evidence, § 412.
Drawing of inferences from, § 413.
Expert testimony, § 722.
Proof of fact, § 411.
Right of party to introduce evidence relevant to, § 406.

WITNESSES
Generally, § 700 et seq.
Absence and absentees,
   Objection,
      Juror as witness, § 704.
      Trial judge as witness, § 703.
   Unavailable as witness, § 240.
Accused,
   Consent to examination, § 772.
   Privilege against self-incrimination, §§ 404, 930, 940.
Adverse party, inspection of writing, § 771.
Answers, responsive to questions, § 766.
Appointment, experts by court, §§ 722, 730 et seq.
Attacking credibility, § 785 et seq.
   Admissibility of evidence, § 1101.
Authentication of writing, subscribing witnesses, § 1411 et seq.
Bias or prejudice, credibility, § 780.
   Attacking or supporting, § 791.
Calling,
   Juror as witness, § 704.
   Presiding judge as witness, § 703.
Certificate, rehabilitation and pardon, credibility, § 788.
Character or reputation, credibility, § 780.
Character or reputation, credibility, attacking or supporting, §§ 786, 787, 790.
Choice of parties to examine, § 711.

WITNESSES—Cont'd
Claim of privilege, § 911 et seq.
Compelling juror to testify, § 704.
Compensation, expert witnesses, §§ 722, 730 et seq.
Competency, § 700 et seq.
Concealment, § 240.
Conduct, specific instances, attacking or supporting credibility, § 787.
Confrontation, § 711.
Consent,
   Motion for mistrial,
      Juror as witness, § 704.
      Trial judge as witness, § 703.
Consistent statements, supporting credibility, § 791.
Control of interrogation, § 765.
Conviction of felony, attacking credibility, § 788.
Courtroom, exclusion, § 788.
Court's own motion, call and interrogation, § 775.
Credibility, § 780 et seq.
   Admissibility of evidence, support or attack, § 1101.
   Conviction of crime, § 403.
   Determination by jury, § 312.
   Expert witness, § 722.
   Hearsay evidence, § 1202.
   Inference drawn from exercise of privilege, § 913.
   Relevant evidence, § 210.
Criminal action, consent, accused, examination, § 772.
Cross-examination,
   Call by court, § 775.
   Defined, § 761.
   Former testimony, § 1291.
   Hearsay declarant, § 1203.
   Interruption, § 772.
   Leading questions, § 767.
   Matter within scope of direct examination, § 773.
   Phase of examination, § 772.
   Prior inconsistent statements, §§ 769, 770.
   Reasons for expert opinion, § 721.
   Redirect examination, defined, § 762.
   Writing, use to refresh memory, § 771.
Death, unavailable as witnesses meaning, § 240.
Declaration, § 710.
Demeanor, credibility, § 780.
Direct evidence, sufficiency, proof of fact, § 411.
Direct examination,
   Cross-examination upon matter within scope, § 773.
   Leading question, restriction, § 767.
   Phase of examination, § 772.
   Reasons for opinion, statement, § 802.
Disabilities, credibility, § 788.
Disclosure, writing on examining, § 768.
Discretion of court,
   Interruption, examination, § 772.
   Recall, excused witness, § 778.
   Reexamination, § 774.
Dismissal, accusatory pleading against, credibility, § 788.
Disqualification, § 700.
   Grounds, § 701.

WITNESSES

WITNESSES—Cont'd
Education, expert witness, § 720.
  Opinion based on, §§ 801, 802.
Examination, § 765 et seq.
  Answers to questions, § 766.
  Attacking credibility, § 788.
  Control of interrogation, § 765.
  Court, § 775.
  Hearsay declarant, § 1203.
  Inconsistent statement or conduct, §§ 769, 770.
  Interrogation by court, § 775.
  Interruption, discretion of court, § 772.
  Mode of interrogation, § 765.
  Order, § 773.
  Phases, § 772.
  Presence, officer or employee designated by attorney, § 777.
  Reexamination, § 774.
  Scope and method, § 760 et seq.
  Subject to examination of parties, § 711.
  Writing, § 768.
Exclusion from courtroom, § 777.
Excused, leave of court to recall, § 778.
Exemption, ground of privilege, § 240.
Experience of expert, § 720.
  Opinion based on, §§ 801, 802.
Fabricated testimony, attacking or supporting credibility, § 791.
Fees, mileage, hospital records, § 1563.
Felony, record of conviction, attacking credibility, § 788.
Fines and penalties, conviction of felony, credibility, § 788.
Foreign jurisdiction, conviction of felony, credibility, § 788.
Handwriting, § 1416 et seq.
Harassment, protection by court, § 765.
Hearing,
  Other witnesses, exclusion from courtroom, § 777.
  Presence of parties, § 711.
Honesty or veracity, credibility, § 780.
  Attacking or supporting credibility, § 786.
Hospital records, § 1560 et seq.
Husband and wife, privilege not to testify against spouse, § 970 et seq.
Hypothetical questions, § 720 et seq.
Impeachment, § 785 et seq.
Inability to compel attendance by process, § 240.
Inconsistent statements,
  Attacking credibility, § 791.
  Examination, § 769.
Incrimination, privilege against self-incrimination, §§ 404, 930, 940.
Information,
  Juror as witness, § 704.
  Trial judge as witness, § 703.
Informers, evidence concerning reasonable cause to make arrest, admissibility, § 1042.
Judgment, record of conviction, attacking credibility, § 788.
Judges, competency, § 703.
Juror,
  Competency, § 704.
    Evidence to impeach or support verdict, § 1150.
  Credibility, determination, § 312.
Knowledge,
  Personal knowledge, §§ 403, 702.
  Special knowledge of expert, § 720.

WITNESSES—Cont'd
Memory, refreshing, §§ 771, 1237.
Mentally deficient and mentally ill persons, §§ 240, 870.
Method of examination, § 760 et seq.
Motions,
  Appointment of expert, § 730.
  Call and interrogation, § 775.
  Mistrial, §§ 703, 704.
Motives, attacking or supporting credibility, § 791.
Number of experts, limitations, § 723.
Oaths and affirmations, § 710.
Objections,
  Exclusion of opinion, § 803.
  Expert witnesses, §§ 720, 805.
  Interrogation by court, § 775.
  Juror as witness, § 704.
  Motion for mistrial, §§ 703, 704.
  Personal knowledge, necessity to show, § 702.
  Objections, trial judge as witness, § 703.
One witness, § 411.
Pardon, conviction of felony, credibility, § 788.
Past recollection recorded, §§ 771, 1237.
Payment,
  Compensation of experts, § 722.
  Hospital records, § 1563.
Perjury, oath includes affirmation or declaration under penalty of, § 165.
Process,
  Inability to compel attendance by, § 240.
  Writing not procurable by, § 771.
Production of writing, use to refresh memory, § 771.
Protection, undue harassment or embarrassment, § 765.
Qualification, § 700 et seq.
  Admissibility of evidence, § 400.
  Experts, §§ 720, 721.
Reasons for opinion, § 802.
Reexamination, § 774.
Refreshing memory, use of writing, §§ 771, 1237.
Rehabilitation, conviction of felony, credibility, § 788.
Religious belief, attacking or supporting credibility, § 789.
Report of expert, § 730.
Scope of examination, § 760 et seq.
Self-incrimination, privilege, §§ 404, 930, 940.
Special knowledge of expert, § 720.
  Opinion based on, §§ 801, 802.
Subscribing witnesses, §§ 870, 1411 et seq.
Supporting credibility, § 785 et seq.
  Admissibility of evidence, § 1101.
Trial judge, competency, § 703.
Truth, understanding duty to tell, § 701.
Unavailable as a witness,
  Defined, Evidence Code, § 240.
  Former testimony, § 1291.
Writing,
  Examination, § 768.
  Refreshing memory, § 771.

WORDS AND PHRASES
Action, § 105.

WORDS AND PHRASES—Cont'd
Admissibility of evidence, § 400.
Authentication of writings, § 1400.
Burden of producing evidence, § 110.
Burden of proof, § 115.
Business, hearsay rule, exceptions, business records, § 1270.
Clergyman, privileges of clergyman-penitent, § 1030.
Client, lawyer-client privilege, § 951.
Confidential communication,
  Client and lawyer, § 952.
  Patient and physician, § 992.
  Patient and psychotherapist, § 1012.
Criminal action, § 130.
  Action includes, § 105.
Criminal proceedings, criminal action includes, § 130.
Cross-examination, witnesses, § 761.
Declarant, § 135.
Direct evidence, weight of evidence, § 410.
Direct examination, witnesses, § 760.
Evidence, § 140.
Former testimony, exceptions, hearsay rule, § 1290.
Hearing, § 145.
Hearsay evidence, §§ 150, 1200.
Holder of the privilege,
  Lawyer-client privilege, § 953.
  Psychotherapist-patient privilege, § 1013.
Hospital, records, secondary evidence of writing, § 1560.
Inadmissibility of evidence, § 400.
Inference, § 600.
Judicial notice, true signification of English words and phrases, § 451.
Law, § 160.
Lawyer, lawyer-client privilege, § 950.
Leading question, witnesses, § 764.
Oaths, § 165.
Officers and employees, § 195.
Patient, psychotherapist-patient privilege, § 1011.
Penitential communication, privileges of clergyman-penitent, § 1032.
Perceive, § 170.
Person, § 175.
Personal property, § 180.
Preliminary fact, admissibility of evidence, § 400.
Presumptions, § 600.
Proffered evidence, § 401.
Proof, § 190.
Property, § 185.
Psychotherapist, privilege of psychotherapist-patient, § 1010.
Public employee, § 195.
Public entity, § 200.
Real property, § 205.
Recross-examination, witnesses, § 763.
Redirect examination, witnesses, § 762.
Relevant evidence, § 210.
State, § 220.
Statement, § 225.
Statute, § 230.
The hearing, § 145.
Trier of fact, § 235.
Unavailable as a witness, § 240.
Writing, § 250.

Evidence Code

WRITINGS
Generally, § 1400 et seq.
Admissibility of part, inquiry by adverse party on whole, § 356.
Application of article, § 1566.
Best evidence rule, § 1500 et seq.
Business records, § 1270 et seq.

WRITINGS—Cont'd
Construction, questions of law, determination by court, § 310.
Defined, § 250.
Documentary Evidence, generally, this index.
Handwriting, generally, this index.
Hearsay Evidence, generally, this index.

WRITINGS—Cont'd
Meaning, § 140.
Photographs, §§ 1550, 1551.
Presumptions, this index.
Questions of law, construction, determination by court, § 310.
Refreshing memory by witness, § 1237.
Secondary evidence, § 1509.
Witnesses, this index.

WRONGDOING
Burden of proof, § 520.

†